Clinical Aspects
of Aging
THIRD EDITION

Clinical Aspects
of Aging
THIRD EDITION

William Reichel, M.D.
Editor

Clinical Professor
Department of Community and Family Medicine
Georgetown University School of Medicine
Washington, D.C.

Formerly
Chairman,
Department of Family Practice
Franklin Square Hospital Center
Baltimore, Maryland

WILLIAMS & WILKINS
Baltimore • Hong Kong • London • Sydney

Editor: Nancy Collins
Associate Editor: Carol Eckhart
Copy Editor: Shelley Potler and Susan Vaupel
Design: Alice Johnson
Illustration Planning: Ray Lowman
Production: Raymond E. Reter

Copyright ©1989
Williams & Wilkins
428 East Preston Street
Baltimore, MD 21202, USA

Accurate indications, adverse reactions, and dosage schedules for drugs are provided in this book, but it is possible that they may change. The reader is urged to review the package information data of the manufacturers of the medications mentioned.

Printed in the United States of America

First edition 1978
Second edition 1983

Library of Congress Cataloging-in-Publication Data

Clinical aspects of aging.
    Includes bibliographies and index.
    1. Geriatrics. 2. Aging. I. Reichel, William,
1937–   . [DNLM: 1. Aging. 2. Geriatrics.
WT 100 C644]
RC952.C53 1988   618.97   87-34094
ISBN 0-683-07204-8

89 90 91 92
4 5 6 7 8 9 10

The sign in the West Virginia lunch counter read:
Don't criticize the coffee.
You may be old and weak yourself someday.

Preface to the Third Edition

As we rapidly approach the end of the 20th century, the proportion of elderly continues to rise significantly. More and more of our daily clinical practice will involve the care of the elderly.

As in previous editions, it is again our purpose to place a major emphasis on the problems of the elderly patient rather than simply preparing a subspecialty treatise. As before, we do not want a collection of subspecialty chapters, but rather we hope to emphasize the older person. An attempt is made to focus on such issues as compassion and humanism, continuity of care, health maintenance and prevention, the role of the family in the care of the elderly, medical care in the nursing home, alternatives to institutional care, and principles of intelligent assessment and management. An entirely new section discusses ethical issues and dilemmas that are challenging us on a daily basis. Hopefully, this new edition represents progress in the evolution of what is special about the aged person and the care of the elderly. Hopefully, this volume will enhance the practitioner's ability to understand and integrate all aspects of the health care of the older person.

William Reichel, M.D.

Acknowledgments

The Third Edition of *Clinical Aspects of Aging* was prepared during my tenure as Chairman of the Department of Family Practice at Franklin Square Hospital Center, as were the first and second editions. I gratefully acknowledge the encouragement, support, and resources of Franklin Square Hospital Center during the period 1970–1988. Without this exceptional support, *Clinical Aspects of Aging* would not have been possible.

I am also most grateful for the assistance of the following individuals who served as editorial consultants: Stanford A. Alliker, Michael Auerbach, M.D., Thomas Crawford, M.D., Risa Davis, M.D., David Doukas, M.D., Philip Ferris, M.D., James Flynn, M.D., Gerald Goodenough, M.D., Patricia Greve, M.D., Bea Grossfeld, M.S.W., Gordon Handelsman, M.D., Norris Horwitz, M.D., Ella Kick, R.N., Joan Kramer, R.N., Julie Pierson Lees, Steven Levenson, M.D., James T. Moore, M.D., Clayton Moravec, M.D., Jane Nelson, M.D., Sue Nelson, M.D., Orris Rollie, M.D., Steven Shearer, Ph.D., Jerry Solon, Ph.D., Paul Tecklenberg, M.D., Joy Ufema, R.N., Michael Vernon, M.D., Gregg Warshaw, M.D., and Larry Wilson, M.D.

Special mention should be given to the Department of Medical Communications, Franklin Square Hospital Center, Baltimore, Maryland, under the direction of James F. Todesco, M.A., R.B.P., F.B.P.A..

Editorial Board

Contributors

Emily M. Agree, M.A.
Research Associate
Department of Demography
Center for Population Research
Georgetown University
Washington, D.C.

Lillian M. Andersen, R.N., Ed.D.
Graduate Program
Gerontologic Nursing Specialty
Georgetown University School of Nursing
Washington, D.C.

Uriel S. Barzel, M.D.
Professor of Medicine
Albert Einstein College of Medicine
Attending Physician in Endocrinology and
   Metabolism
Montefiore Medical Center
Bronx, New York

Gabrielle Bemis Batzer, M.D.
Consulting Associate
Division of Social and Community Psychiatry
Duke University Medical Center
Durham, North Carolina

Bruce E. Beacham, M.D., F.A.C.P.
Consultant in Dermatology
Franklin Square Hospital Center
Assistant Professor of Dermatology
University of Maryland School of Medicine
Baltimore, Maryland

B. Lynn Beattie, M.D.
Head, Division of Geriatric Medicine
Department of Medicine
University of British Columbia
Clinical Director, Geriatric Medicine
UBC Health Sciences Centre Hospital
Vancouver, British Columbia
Canada

Nathan Billig, M.D.
Associate Professor
Department of Psychiatry
Georgetown University School of Medicine
Director, Geriatric Psychiatry Service
Director, Center on Aging
Georgetown University Medical Center
Washington, D.C.

Louis Breschi, M.D.
Consultant in Urology
Franklin Square Hospital Center
Assistant Clinical Professor of Urology
University of Maryland School of Medicine
Baltimore, Maryland

James F. Burris, M.D.
Assistant Dean for Sponsored Research
Associate Professor of Medicine
Georgetown University Medical Center
Washington, D.C.

M. Janette Busby, M.D.
Assistant Professor of Medicine
The Johns Hopkins University
School of Medicine
Baltimore, Maryland

Stanley L. Cohan, M.D., Ph.D.
Associate Professor
Departments of Neurology and Pharmacology
Georgetown University School of Medicine
Washington, D.C.

Dorothy H. Coons
Associate Research Scientist
Director, Alzheimer's Disease Projects
Institute of Gerontology
The University of Michigan
Ann Arbor, Michigan

Ada Romaine Davis, R.N., Ph.D., C.A.N.P.
Nurse Consultant
Division of Nursing
Bureau of Health Professions
Health Resources and Services Administration
Public Health Service
Department of Health and Human Services
Rockville, Maryland

David Doukas, M.D.
Instructor, Department of Community and Family
    Medicine
Georgetown University School of Medicine
Fellow, Kennedy Institute of Ethics
Georgetown University
Washington, D.C.

Dorothy J. Duvall, R.D.H., R.N., M.S.
Lecturer, Department of Community Dentistry
Georgetown University School of Dentistry
Washington, D.C.
Coordinator, Geriatric Dentistry
Baltimore City Health Department
Baltimore, Maryland

Pierre F. Faubert, M.D.
Division of Nephrology and Hypertension
The Brookdale Hospital Medical Center
Linden Boulevard at Brookdale Plaza
State University of New York
Health Science Center at Brooklyn
Brooklyn, New York

William E. Flynn, M.D.
Assistant Professor
Department of Psychiatry
Georgetown University School of Medicine
Washington, D.C.

Vincent F. Garagusi, M.D.
Professor of Medicine and Microbiology
Georgetown University School of Medicine
Director, Division of Infectious Diseases
Director, Clinical Microbiology and Serology
    Laboratories
Georgetown University Medical Center
Washington, D.C.

Junette C. Gibbons, M.D.
Associate Clinical Professor of Medicine
George Washington University
Chief of Gastroenterology
Providence Hospital
Washington, D.C.

Gerald A. Glowacki, M.D.
Chairman, Department of Obstetrics and
    Gynecology
Franklin Square Hospital Center
Assistant Professor
Department of Gynecology and Obstetrics
The Johns Hopkins University
School of Medicine
Baltimore, Maryland

John C. Gordon, M.D.
Consultant in Orthopedic Surgery
Franklin Square Hospital Center
Baltimore, Maryland

David Grob, M.D.
Director, Departments of Medicine and Medical
    Education
Maimonides Medical Center
Professor of Medicine
State University of New York
Health Science Center at Brooklyn
Brooklyn, New York

Richard J. Ham, M.D.
State University of New York Distinguished Chair
    in Geriatric Medicine
Chairman, Program in Geriatrics
Professor of Medicine and Professor of Family
    Medicine
State University of New York
    Health Science Center at Syracuse
Syracuse, New York
Formerly
Mount Pleasant Legion Professor of Community
    Geriatrics
Department of Family Practice
University of British Columbia
Director, Short-Term Assessment and Treatment
    Centre
Vancouver, British Columbia
Canada

Raymond Harris, M.D., F.A.C.C.
Clinical Associate Professor of Medicine
Albany Medical College
President, Center for the Study of Aging, Inc.
Albany, New York

Arthur E. Helfand, D.P.M.
Professor and Chairman
Department of Community Health and Aging
Pennsylvania College of Podiatric Medicine
Philadelphia, Pennsylvania

Elizabeth M. Hughes, Ph.D.
Professor
Georgetown University School of Nursing
Washington, D.C.

Robert R. Huntley, M.D.
Professor and Chairman
Department of Community and Family Medicine
Georgetown University School of Medicine
Washington, D.C.

Judith K. Jones, M.D., Ph.D.
Clinical Associate Professor
Departments of Medicine, Community and Family
    Medicine, and Pharmacology
Director, Geriatric Special Care Unit
Associate Clinical Research Director,
Center on Aging
Georgetown University Hospital
Washington, D.C.

Alvin I. Kahn, M.D., F.A.C.P.
Vice President, Medical Affairs
Director, Medical Education
Brookdale Hospital Medical Center
Brooklyn, New York
Associate Clinical Dean
State University of New York
Health Science Center at Brooklyn
Brooklyn, New York

Harold Kallman, M.D.
Professor
Department of Family Medicine
Director, Geriatric Division
East Carolina University School of Medicine
Greenville, North Carolina

Sheila Kallman, M.A.
Geriatric Division
Department of Family Medicine
East Carolina University School of Medicine
Greenville, North Carolina

Robert L. Kasper, M.D.
Chief, Division of Ophthalmology
Franklin Square Hospital Center
Assistant Clinical Professor of Ophthalmology
University of Maryland School of Medicine
Baltimore, Maryland

David C. Kennie, M.D.
Consultant Physician
Department of Geriatric Medicine
The Royal Infirmary
Stirling
Scotland

Sheldon C. Kravitz, M.D.
Chief, Division of Hematology and Oncology
Union Memorial Hospital
Baltimore, Maryland

Steven A. Levenson, M.D.
Medical Director
Levindale Hebrew Geriatric Center and Hospital
Baltimore, Maryland

Susan M. Levy, M.D.
Chief, Section of Geriatrics
Department of Internal Medicine
Franklin Square Hospital Center
Baltimore, Maryland

Robert D. Lindeman, M.D.
Professor of Medicine
Chief, Division of Geriatric Medicine
University of New Mexico School of Medicine
Associate Chief of Staff for Extended Care
Albuquerque Veterans Administration Medical
    Center
Albuquerque, New Mexico

Steven Lipson, M.D., M.P.H.
Medical Director
Hebrew Home of Greater Washington
Rockville, Maryland
Associate Professor
Department of Community and Family Medicine
Georgetown University School of Medicine
Washington, D.C.

Victoria Y. Louie, M.Sc., R.D.N.
Nutrition Consultant
Lecturer, School of Family and Nutritional
    Sciences
University of British Columbia
Vancouver, British Columbia
Canada

John R. Marshall, M.D.
Professor and Chairman
Department of Psychiatry
University of Wisconsin
Madison, Wisconsin

Laurence B. McCullough, Ph.D.
Professor of Medicine and Community Medicine
Center for Ethics, Medicine, and Public Issues
Baylor College of Medicine
Houston, Texas
Formerly
Professor, Department of Community and Family
    Medicine
Georgetown University School of Medicine
Washington, D.C.

Jack H. Medalie, M.D.
Dorothy Jones Weatherhead Professor
Department of Family Medicine
Case Western Reserve University
Cleveland, Ohio

Paul J. Melluzzo, M.D.
Clinical Associate Professor of Surgery
Georgetown University School of Medicine
Washington, D.C.

James H. Mersey, M.D.
Chief, Endocrinology Division
Greater Baltimore Medical Center
Associate Professor of Medicine
University of Maryland School of Medicine
Baltimore, Maryland

Arthur J. Moss, M.D.
Clinical Professor of Medicine and Preventive,
    Family and Rehabilitative Medicine
University of Rochester School of Medicine and
    Dentistry
Rochester, New York

Russell J. Nauta, M.D.
Assistant Professor of Surgery
Georgetown University School of Medicine
Washington, D.C.

Catherine E. O'Connor, R.N.C., M.S.
Gerontological Clinical Specialist
Veterans Administration
Fort Howard, Maryland

James J. Pattee, M.D.
Assistant Professor
Coordinator, Geriatric Program
Department of Family Practice and Community
    Health
University of Minnesota
Minneapolis, Minnesota

Jerome G. Porush, M.D., F.A.C.P.
Chief, Division of Nephrology and Hypertension
Brookdale Hospital Medical Center
Professor of Medicine
State University of New York
Health Science Center at Brooklyn
Brooklyn, New York

David L. Rabin, M.D., M.P.H.
Professor and Associate Chairman
Department of Community and Family Medicine
Director, Division of Health Care Studies
Georgetown University School of Medicine
Washington, D.C.

Peter V. Rabins, M.D.
Associate Professor of Psychiatry and Behavioral
    Sciences
The Johns Hopkins University
School of Medicine
Baltimore, Maryland

John B. Redford, M.D.
Professor and Chairman
Department of Rehabilitation Medicine
University of Kansas College of Health Sciences
Kansas City, Kansas

Julian W. Reed, M.D.
Associate Professor, Internal Medicine, Family
    Practice, Epidemiology and Preventive Medicine
University of Maryland School of Medicine
Baltimore, Maryland

Joseph Reichel, M.D.
Professor of Internal Medicine
Albert Einstein College of Medicine
New York, New York

William Reichel, M.D.
Clinical Professor, Department of Community and
    Family Medicine
Georgetown University School of Medicine
Washington, D.C.
Formerly
Chairman, Department of Family Practice
Franklin Square Hospital Center
Baltimore, Maryland

Vincent C. Rogers, D.D.S., M.P.H.
Associate Professor and Chairman
Department of Community Dentistry
Georgetown University School of Dentistry
Washington, D.C.

Warren B. Shapiro, M.D.
Physician-in-Charge, Hemodialysis Unit
The Brookdale Hospital Medical Center
Associate Professor of Clinical Medicine
State University of New York
Health Science Center at Brooklyn
Brooklyn, New York

George G. Shashaty, M.D.
Associate Professor of Medicine
Georgetown University School of Medicine
Director, Coagulation Laboratory
Georgetown University Hospital
Washington, D.C.

Herbert Shore, Ed.D.
Executive Vice President
Dallas Home for Jewish Aged
Dallas, Texas

Norma R. Small, R.N., Ph.D.
Director, Graduate Program and Gerontologic
    Nursing
Georgetown University School of Nursing
Washington, D.C.

Frank C. Snope, M.D.
Professor of Family Medicine
University of Medicine and Dentistry of New
    Jersey
Robert Wood Johnson Medical School
New Brunswick, New Jersey

Beth J. Soldo, Ph.D.
Associate Professor
Chair, Department of Demography
Georgetown University
Washington, D.C.

Edna M. Stilwell, R.N.C., Ph.D.
Editor
Journal of Gerontological Nursing
Coordinator, Gerontological Nursing Program
Graduate Program
University of Maryland School of Nursing
Baltimore, Maryland

Gordon F. Streib, Ph.D.
Graduate Research Professor
Department of Sociology
University of Florida
Gainesville, Florida

Joel E. Streim, M.D.
Assistant Professor of Psychiatry and Assistant
    Professor of Psychiatry in Physical Medicine and
    Rehabilitation
University of Pennsylvania School of Medicine
Philadelphia, Pennsylvania

Daniel B. Walsh, M.D.
Assistant Professor of Surgery
Dartmouth Medical School
Hanover, New Hampshire

Gregg Warshaw, M.D.
Associate Professor
Department of Family Medicine
University of Cincinnati Medical Center
Cincinnati, Ohio

Milton G. Yoder, M.D., F.A.C.S.
Consultant in Otolaryngology
Franklin Square Hospital Center
Clinical Instructor in Otolaryngology and Head and
    Neck Surgery
The Johns Hopkins University
School of Medicine
Baltimore, Maryland

Contents

Section I

Care of the Elderly Patient: Evaluation, Diagnosis, and Management

CHAPTER 1

Essential Principles in the Care of the Elderly

WILLIAM REICHEL

In 1900, the average life expectancy at birth was 48.3 years for females and 46.3 years for males; 4% of the American population were over 65 years old. In 1983, life expectancy at birth was 78.3 years for females and 71.0 years for males. As of 1980, the population of the United States was 226,505,000, and 11.3% were over the age of 65. It is projected (13) that, in the year 2000, 13.1% of the total population will be 65 years of age or older. By year 2020, those over 65 years will comprise 17.3% of the population and, by year 2040, 21.6%. It is conceivable that, with increased achievements in combating the leading causes of mortality, the proportion of elderly in America will rise even higher.

With these remarkable changes in life expectancy since the turn of the century, it is important for all physicians to have a strong foundation in essential concepts in the care of the elderly.

Eleven of the most essential aspects of care of the elderly individual are considered.

ROLE OF PHYSICIAN AS INTEGRATOR OF BIOPSYCHOSOCIAL MODEL

With increasing subspecialization and high technology, and with increasing concern for cost-containment, there will be greater demands and societal pressure to have a physician at the helm, a physician who can understand, administer, integrate, and coordinate the health care of an elderly individual and his or her family. The narrower the scope of various subspecialty skills and practices, the more society will demand an integrator in the care of the elderly patient.

The elderly patient will not have the best of health care if he or she is seen from a single specialty point of view without the full appreciation of other organ systems, emotional or psychosocial factors, information based on continuity over a period of time, and knowledge of the patient's family and community.

Wasson and associates (22) demonstrated that continuity of outpatient provider care for men aged 55 years and older resulted in more patient satisfaction, shorter hospitalizations, and fewer emergent hospital admissions. The carefully controlled study by Wasson et al. backs up, by vigorous research methodology, the value of continuity of care, and its beneficial influence on medical care. In addition, one might envision improved critical care by having the same personal physician involved with the total health care team in specialized units. Communicating the substance of knowledge and understanding of the personal physicians to other specialists is an important function of the personal physician.

One might also anticipate that this role of continuity applies in general hospital care, in the home, and in the long-term care facility (16). Visitation to the home and to the nursing home are absolutely indicated if we seek excellence in patient care of the elderly. The ideal situation for the elderly patient is a warm and supportive relationship with the same personal physician serving as advisor, advocate, and friend as the patient moves throughout the labyrinth of medical care.

CONTINUITY OF CARE

It is unfortunate to see the many disruptions that take place in today's medical environment as the patient moves between office, home, hospital, specialized care units (coronary care units, intensive care units, stroke units, or oncology center) and nursing home. The failure of physicians to make visits as necessary in the home and in the long-term care facility relates to several factors in the United States, including training, physician attitudes, and reimbursement systems. Our educational systems have been imperfect in excluding the home and the nursing home as proper environments for medical education. Physician attitudes have also been a problem, in that doctors have been more interested in the acute aspects of care than in chronic and long-term care. The lack of reasonable reimbursement for visits to the home and nursing home remains a major problem.

Many of our most serious problems in health care are related to failure in the continuity of care. With the population becoming increasingly older, with increasing specialization and emphasis on technology, and with the cost of care spiraling, the greatest attention in the future must be given to the principle of continuity of care by a personal physician.

BOLSTERING FAMILY AND HOME

With over 1.2 million elderly individuals in the United States confined to long-term care facilities and the elderly population expanding rapidly, every physician should enlist those means that would keep an elderly person either in the individual's own home or in an extended family setting. It should certainly be our goal as physicians to keep elderly persons functioning independently, preserving their lifestyles and self-respect as long as possible. The physician should use the prescription for a nursing home as specifically as a prescription for an antibiotic or an antihypertensive medication.

A number of forces have resulted in patients going to institutional settings when other alternatives might have been possible. Between 1960 and 1975, a massive push toward institutionalization took place, creating hundreds of thousands of nursing home beds. What are the forces that contributed to excessive institutional care? Funding mechanisms have been directed solely toward reimbursement for institutional care rather than for other alternatives. With the increased mobility of families, there simply may not be family members available in the community to participate in the elderly person's care. Homes are architecturally based on a small, nuclear family and do not permit housing an elderly patient. Finally, the increasing movement of women into the work force has been an important factor in the lack of an available family member to remain home with the impaired or disabled elderly person.

What alternatives can the physician recommend to these caregivers? A simple list includes homemakers, home health aides, other types of home care, day care, after care, specialized housing settings, visiting nurses, friendly visitors, foster home care, chore services, home renovation and repair services, congregate and home-delivered meal programs, transportation programs, and shopping services (see Chapter 44, New Community Options for the Elderly). Personal physicians should also understand and utilize legal and protective services for the elderly whenever indicated.

Who are the caregivers in American society? An examination of data from the 1982 National Long-Term Care Survey (20) revealed that caregivers to the disabled have the following characteristics: they are predominantly female; three-quarters of them live with the person for whom they provide care. One-third of the caregivers themselves are over 65 years old, are poor or near-poor, and are in fair to poor health. Some caregivers face conflicts between their caregiving duties and the needs of other family members and their jobs. Over 90% of the caregivers carry the burden without assistance from the formal health care system.

In the study by Stone et al. (20), 71.5% of caregivers to the functionally impaired elderly were female, daughters constituting 28.9%. Husbands accounted for 12.8% and sons for 8.5% of this population. In the case of sons, it is often the son's spouse, the daughter-in-law, who actually provides the care. The burden of caregiving is felt by many women today, sandwiched between the demands of their parents and of their children and grandchildren. It has been said that the empty nest syndrome has been replaced by a crowded nest syndrome.

The belief that old people are rejected by their families has been exploded as a social myth (18). There is tremendous evidence that families are struggling to cope with the needs of parents who are frail and debilitated. The family member, friend, or neighbor is often the crucial link in guaranteeing that the dependent elder will remain in the community. In repeated studies, the characteristics of the caregiver, more than those of the elderly patient, are essential in predicting institutional placement.

Even when adult children and elderly parents are separated by distance, their quality of relationship may be unaffected, maintaining cohesion despite limited face-to-face contact. At a certain distance, the telephone becomes an important means as a substitute for visits (4). Nevertheless, for many adult children, separation by distance causes increased tension and difficulty in their efforts to carry out the caregiver role.

Cost-containment today, particularly in the prospective payment system, will require greater reliance on alternatives to institutional care. We can expect to see many new resources and support systems, including innovative experiments in housing and transportation, more home-delivered care, a cadre of respite workers, and perhaps tax credits for family-oriented care. The personal physician in his community can be a significant advocate for the development of new resources and support systems that can help keep the elderly patient in his or her own home or in the home of a family member. We can also expect to see increased educational media (television programs, brochures, books, and courses not only at local hospitals and long-term care facilities but also at the high school, community college, and university levels) that will provide information to the many families who are striving to keep an elderly member at home, either with spouse, with family, or alone.

COMMUNICATION SKILLS

Specific communication skills are critical in good management of the elderly patient. Most important in good communication is listening and allowing patients to express themselves. The physician should use an open-ended approach, interpreting what the patient is saying and reading between the lines. The physician can utilize intuition in deciding what the patient really means. Why did the patient really come to see the physician? The elderly patient complaining of headache or backache may be expressing depression or grief. We should not miss important verbal clues when the patient tells us, "Doctor, I really think these headaches started when I lost my husband."

It is helpful to leave the door open for other questions or comments by the patient, both at the conclusion of the visit and in the future. It is always helpful to say: "Are there other questions or concerns that you have at this time?" A physician anticipating a specific problem can make it easier for the patient to discuss this issue. For example, "You are doing well, but I know that you are concerned about your arthritis and whether or not you will be able to climb the stairs in your home. At some point, we may

want to discuss the various alternatives that are open to you."

Just as the physician providing care to pediatric patients must deal with the children's parents, the physician providing care to the elderly patient must be able to deal with their adult children. These children play a vital role in decision-making and providing support, and the physician must, therefore, possess skills in communicating with them and also in dealing with their emotional reactions, such as guilt or grief. The physician taking care of an elderly patient with cancer must be prepared when the adult daughter tells him: "Whatever you do, please don't tell my father that he has cancer," especially when it is apparent that the parent is totally and fully aware of all aspects of his problem.

The physician should be careful when meeting with an elderly patient who discusses his absent spouse or child, or when dealing with adult children or grandchildren who are discussing the parent or grandparent who is not present. The physician should not necessarily accept the assumptions that are stated about the absent family member. Physicians must be able to listen carefully, ask questions, and collect information; our opinion of the situation might be entirely different if we had an opportunity to hear the view of the absent family member.

Peabody (12) in 1927 said: "The good physician knows his patients through and through, and his knowledge is bought dearly. Time, sympathy and understanding must be lavishly dispensed, but the reward is to be found in that personal bond which forms the greatest satisfaction of the practice of medicine." The physician who enters the patient's universe and understands the patient's perceptions, assumptions, values and religious beliefs is a tremendous advantage. Frankl (7) in *Man's Search for Meaning,* demonstrated how physicians can help patients understand the meaning and value of their lives. It is therapeutic for the patient to feel that the physician cares enough about that individual to understand his life, particularly the meaning and purpose of his present existence. Frankl (6) stated in *The Doctor and the Soul* that human life can be fulfilled, not only in creating and enjoying, but also in suffering. He provides examples in which suffering becomes an opportunity, an achievement, a means for ennoblement. Frankl's existential psychiatry or logotherapy is a useful psychologic method that helps the elderly patient appreciate the positive attributes, meanings, and purposes of his or her life.

Yalom (23) defines existential psychotherapy as "a dynamic approach to therapy which focuses on concerns that are rooted in the individual's existence." Many individuals are tormented by a crisis of meaning. Many suffer an existential vacuum, experiencing a lack of meaning in life (6, 7, 11, 23). The patient experiencing an existential vacuum may demonstrate many symptoms that will rush in to fill it in the form of somatization, depression, alcoholism, hypochondriasis, etc. The physician recognizing an existential vacuum can help the patient find meaning. Frankl's main theme is that meaning is essential for life. Engagement or involvement in life's activities is a therapeutic answer to a lack of meaning in life. The physician can help guide the patient toward engagement with life, life's activities, other people, and other satisfactions.

Frankl (6, 7) provides advice to all physicians in utilizing hope as a therapeutic tool. The physician dealing with the elderly must focus on the significant role of hope in daily practice. As physicians, we must eventually understand the biologic basis of hope. We do not understand sufficiently the biochemical, neurophysiologic, and immunologic concomitants of different attitudes and emotions, and how they are affected by what is communicated from the physician. Physicians have an opportunity to worsen panic and fear; physicians also have an opportunity to create a state of confidence, calm, relaxation, and hope.

In this day and age of increasing technology and subspecialization, the patient's recovery may still depend on the physician's ability to reduce panic and fear, and to raise the prospect of hope. Cousins (5) describes the "quality beyond pure medical competence that patients need and look for in their physicians. They want reassurance. They want to be looked after and not just over. They want to be listened to. They want to feel that it makes a difference to the physician, a very big difference, whether they live or die. They want to feel that they are in the physician's thoughts." For example, in building the doctor-elderly patient relationship, nothing is more effective than the physician picking up the phone and calling the patient and saying: "I was thinking about your problem. How are you doing?" This expression of interest by telephone represents a potent method for cementing the relationship of doctor with patient.

Jules Pfeiffer's cartoon character, the "modern Diogenes," carries on the following discourse upon meeting an inquisitive fellow traveler through the sands of time. "What are you doing with the lantern?" asks the traveler. "I'm searching," replies Diogenes. "For an honest man?" he asks. "I gave that up long ago!" exclaims Diogenes. "For hope?" "Lots of luck." "For love?" "Forget it!" "For tranquility?" "No way."

"For happiness?" "Fat chance." "For justice?" "Are you kidding?" "Then what are you looking for?" he implores of Diogenes. "Someone to talk to."

DOCTOR-PATIENT RELATIONSHIP

WHAT THE DOCTOR AND PATIENT BRING TO EACH ENCOUNTER

The physician must understand what both he and the patient bring to each interaction, including both positive and negative feelings (3). The patient's views of old age may be negative and fearful, believing illness signifies misery, approaching death, loss of self-esteem, loneliness, and dependency. The physician's own fears about aging and death may color the interview as well. He may simply not view helping the older, impaired patient as worthwhile. He may have low expectations for success of treatment, writing off the elderly patient as "senile," "mentally ill," or "hypochondriac." The doctor may have significant conflicts in his own relationship with parent figures or may feel threatened that the patient will die.

KNOWING THE PATIENT

Several steps are recommended in building a sound doctor-patient relationship, particularly applicable to the elderly patient (3, 12). The first rule is that the physician should know the patient thoroughly; the second rule is that the physician should know the patient thoroughly; and the third rule is that the physician should know the patient thoroughly. The interested physician performs the first step in building a sound doctor-patient relationship by gathering a complete history, including the personal and social history, and doing a complete physical. Ideally, the physician should be a good listener, warm and sensitive, providing the patient ample opportunity to express multiple problems and reflect upon his or her life history and current life situation. Thus, the physician will be able to understand the meanings and purposes of the patient's present existence.

As stated above, family and friends represent the principal support system for the elderly and usually call for nursing home placement only as a last resort, after all alternatives have failed. However, the physician must be able to recognize the dysfunctional family. There are elderly who have been rejected by children. Like King Lear, these elderly may say: "How sharper than a serpent's tooth, it is to have a thankless child." There are elderly who have rejected a child for a variety of reasons. There are families with members estranged from each other for many years. The physician should understand what has happened over the years in the patient's marriage. Before the physician can hope to help families with such problems, it is important as a first step to recognize that these problems exist (see Chapter 39, The Elderly and Their Families).

CREATING A PARTNERSHIP WITH THE PATIENT

In all dealings with the patient, the physician should be frank and honest and share information truthfully (see Chapter 55, Truthtelling and Confidentiality). The patient should feel a sense of partnership with the physician. In this partnership, the doctor first reviews his perception of the patient's problems. Then, for each problem, alternative choices are considered, and decision-making is shared with the patient. Although there are situations in which frankness is counterproductive, with most patients, frankness is helpful. There are also situations in which the elderly patient does not want to share in decision-making, but simply wants to surrender his or her autonomy to a relative such as spouse or adult child, or to the physician. Again, in most cases, the physician should attempt to enter a partnership with the patient and share as much decision-making as possible.

Discussions with the patient or family members should be presented in a hopeful manner. As discussed above, it is important to offer a positive approach whenever possible. The physician's infusion of optimism and cheerfulness is therapeutic. The physician should help patients appreciate such positive attributes or purposes in their lives as religious beliefs, relationships with children and grandchildren, the enjoyment of friends, or the enjoyment of the relationship with doctors, nurses, and other health professionals in the immediate therapeutic environment.

The physician should be cautious that discussions with family members be held with the patient's consent. If the patient is sufficiently mentally impaired, then it might be appropriate to deal with the closest relative. Complex ethical questions arise in the matter of confidentiality and decision-making in regard to the elderly patient with partial mental impairment (see Chapter 52, Informed Consent, and Chapter 55, Truthtelling and Confidentiality).

NEED FOR THOROUGH EVALUATION AND ASSESSMENT

The physician must avoid prejudging the patient. We must not allow preconceived notions of common patterns of illness to preclude the most careful individualized assessment of each patient. Conscientious history and physical examination are essential. Treatment choices should be considered only following a thorough evaluation. Judicious consideration of all factors may result in a decision to treat or not to treat certain problems in certain patients. Attention to lesser problems may be postponed according to the priorities of the moment, rather than complicate an already variegated therapeutic program.

Physicians must avoid wastebasket diagnoses. The past concept of "chronic brain syndrome" or "arteriosclerotic brain disease" is one such example. Not all mental disturbance in the elderly represents dementia; not all dementias in the elderly (in fact, only a minority) are arteriosclerotic. Neuropsychiatric disturbance in the elderly might be placed into a wastebasket and casually accepted as both expectable and untreatable when, in reality, a very treatable cause may be present (see Chapter 14, The Evaluation and Management of the Confused, Disoriented, or Demented Elderly Patient). The physician must consider and seek out treatable disease.

For example, neuropsychiatric disturbance may be caused by severe depression that is a very treatable disorder. Or it may actually be a form of dementia. The most common types of dementia include senile dementia of the Alzheimer type and multi-infarct dementia. There are other forms of dementia, some very treatable, including myxedema, chronic drug intoxication, pernicious anemia, folic acid deficiency, normal pressure hydrocephalus, and chronic subdural hematoma. Neuropsychiatric disturbance may also include delirium or acute confusional state secondary to many types of medical illness or drug toxicity. Such delirious states can be helped if the primary disorder is recognized and treated.

It is often difficult to disentangle the physical from the emotional. Emotional disorder may present in the elderly as a physical problem, such as musculoskeletal tension being the principal manifestation of depression. Conversely, physical disease in the elderly might present as a mental disorder with confusion, disorientation, or delirium often being the first sign of many common medical ailments including myocardial infarction, pulmonary embolism, occult carcinomatosis, pneumonia, urinary tract infection, or dehydration.

Thus, it cannot be emphasized too many times that proper diagnosis is essential in order to make specific treatment plans, such as the treatment of urinary tract infection in the case of an acute delirious state, or the treatment of folic acid deficiency in the case of a specific dementia or in the treatment of depression. Each of these is very specific. Treatment in each case would be irrational if a specific diagnosis were not known.

It is often not sufficient to know the organic or anatomic or psychiatric diagnosis; rather we should seek a more total understanding of the elderly patient. At times, it is more important to assess the elderly patient's functional status which might have greater significance than the diagnostic or anatomic label. For example, in the case of a cerebrovascular accident, knowledge of the exact anatomic location as determined by arteriography may not help the patient as much as understanding the patient's functional state. It may be more important to know whether the patient can walk or climb stairs, can handle his or her own bathing, eating, and dressing, whether he or she can get out of bed and sit in a chair, handle a wheelchair, or require a cane or walker. All these functional concerns must be considered in evaluating an elderly patient.

Affecting our diagnostic thinking in evaluating an elderly patient should be the consideration of what is physiologic versus what is pathologic. Aging itself can be defined as the progressive deterioration or loss of functional capacity, which takes place in an organism after a period of reproductive maturity. The Longitudinal Study of the Gerontology Research Center in Baltimore for over 30 years has studied this decline in each of several specific functional capacities, such as glucose tolerance. There is a progressive deterioration of glucose tolerance with each decade of life, such that Andres (1) formulated a percentile system which ranks a subject with age-matched cohorts (Fig. 1.1). Although currently the accepted definitions allow the same diagnostic criteria to be applied at any age (see Chapter 31), it is often unclear who is truly diabetic. The physician must not be quick in treating a laboratory value that simply may represent an altered physiologic state and not a true disease or pathologic disorder.

Also affecting our diagnostic ability in the elderly is the latency of disease, which is characteristic of the aged population. Pain, white blood cell response, and fever and chills are examples of defense mechanisms that may be diminished in older persons. The aged person may have pneumonia or renal infection without chills or a rise in temperature. Myocardial infarction, ruptured abdominal aorta, perforated appendix, or mesenteric infarction may be present without pain in the elderly.

Multiple clinical, psychologic and social problems are characteristic of the elderly (15). Clinically and pathologically, an elderly patient may have 10 or 15 problems (9). Geriatric patients should benefit

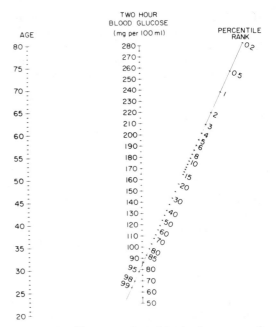

Figure 1.1. Nomogram for judging performance on the oral glucose tolerance test. (From Andres R: Relation of physiologic changing in aging to medical changes of disease in the aged. *Mayo Clin Proc* 42:674, 1967.)

from the use of a problem-oriented approach to medical records. Medical records should include not only the medical problem, but should demonstrate an understanding of functional, psychologic, social, and family problems as well. The key feature of the problem-oriented record is the problem list, which serves as a table of contents of the patient's total medical history. It behooves us to use a problem list as a minimal or core component of a problem-oriented system in caring for the elderly patient. Without a problem list, we can easily lose track over time of the elderly patient's multiple problems; for example, that the patient in 1953 was hospitalized for a psychiatric problem or that, in 1975, the patient suffered a compression fracture of the T10 vertebra secondary to slipping on ice. These problems may be lost to memory without some form or problem-oriented system. In addition, care is enhanced by maintaining a medication list that is kept current at each patient visit.

PREVENTION AND HEALTH MAINTENANCE

A tremendous revolution is taking place in the United States with emphasis on prevention, health maintenance, and wellness. Unfortunately, not all the facts are in. For example, less is known about risk factors for heart disease and stroke for the elderly patient than for younger adults. However, enough is known about prevention that we are seeing a decline in the mortality rate from heart disease and cerebrovascular disease (see Chapter 40, Characteristics of the Elderly Population), which probably relates to increased preventive measures. As a result, life expectancy at age 65 years has risen from 13.9 years in 1950 to 16.4 years in 1980 (13).

More and more physicians and nurses are emphasizing health maintenance and wellness in their practice and in their community educational programs (see Chapter 2, Health Maintenance and Health Screening in the Elderly). However, the drive for wellness is coming not only from the health professionals, but also from the public itself. The personal physician has an opportunity in his practice to encourage preventive medicine and health maintenance at every age level and at each level of functional ability or disability.

It is helpful if physicians and health professionals can institute a philosophy of wellness and health maintenance in their own lives. Otherwise, the patient looking across the desk may say: "Physician, heal thyself. Don't you know that an ounce of prevention is worth a pound of cure?"

INTELLIGENT TREATMENT

Increased adverse effects of drugs are present in the elderly who often tolerate medications poorly. Polypharmacy is a major problem in the care of the elderly patient (see Chapter 4, Drugs and the Elderly). Not only do psychotropic medications cause an altered response of the CNS resulting in confusion and delirium, but also antibiotics or digitalis may cause these problems. Altered renal and hepatic functions may affect drug elimination. In general, the elderly demonstrate greater variability and idiosyncrasy in drug response in comparison to younger individuals.

Prudence is, therefore, extremely important in prescribing drugs for the elderly individual. The physician must determine if the patient's complaint is justification for treatment. Is this medication absolutely necessary? The skill of the physician is required in weighing benefit versus risk. The benefit-risk balance is more crucial in the elderly patient than in younger individuals. The physician must attempt to keep the total number of medications down to as small a number as possible.

The doctor should resist the temptation to treat a new problem that is poorly understood with still more medications. The question should be raised whether the present symptoms, such as confusion or depression, might be related to current drug use.

Therefore, the aphorism, "First, do no harm." A similar concept was stated by Seegal (17) as the "principle of minimal interference" in the management of the elderly patient. "First, do no harm" and the "principle of minimal interference" should be remembered when one reviews the abundant examples of iatrogenic problems that the elderly experience (14, 19).

The principle of minimal interference can be applied not only to drug therapy, but to other decisions, including the use of diagnostic tests (the principle of diagnostic parsimony), surgical intervention, and decision-making in regard to hospitalization or placement in a long-term care facility. The principle of minimal interference may result in decisions that are both humanistic and cost-effective; for example, a decision that the patient should remain in his or her own home, despite limited access to medical therapy, rather than reside in a long-term care facility; or the decision not to do a gastrointestinal workup in the evaluation of anemia when the patient is preterminal as a result of malignant brain tumor.

In the care of the elderly, there are times for minimal interference and there are times for maximal intervention. Again, certainly the patient with dementia caused by myxedema deserves every effort to replace thyroid hormone carefully. The elderly patient with severe congestive heart failure secondary to rheumatic or congenital heart disease deserves full consideration for definitive treatment, including surgery, for his cardiac problems. The elderly patient with depression deserves specific treatment for this very treatable disorder.

In the future, we will be faced with more and more difficult decisions of an ethical nature (see Section 3, in the Care of the Elderly Patient: Ethical Issues). For example, an 80-year-old gentleman may present with a past history of resection of an abdominal aneurysm in 1980, multiple myocardial infarctions, and multiple strokes causing severe dementia. His main problem on the current hospitalization is pneumonia causing a worsening of his confused state. Because of periods of sinus arrest, a pacemaker is considered. Should a pacemaker be utilized in patients with significant dementia? Should pneumonia be treated in patients with severe dementia or terminal carcinoma? Difficult and ambiguous clinical problems such as these will face the personal physician with increasing frequency. The physician in the future will be called upon to make complex decisions according to the accepted traditions and values of his or her religion, nation, and society or culture. Section 3 of this text attempts to deal with the ethical dilemmas we face in daily practice in caring for the elderly.

In regard to all therapeutic decisions, a personal physician is at an advantage if his or her understanding of the patient is based on continuity of care. The physician then can consider the patient in totality including psychologic, social, family, and environmental factors. To recommend intelligently any treatment plan, it is beneficial to have the knowledge of home or institutional environment, the family constellation, the availability of friends, access to transportation, and the economic situation of the patient. Also, as the physician grapples with complex decisions of an ethical nature, specific knowledge of the patient's value systems and beliefs is critically important. Chapters 52–56 describe in detail the importance of eliciting a value history from patients not only when they are terminally ill, but during the entire doctor-elderly patient relationship.

INTERDISCIPLINARY COLLABORATION

The physician must understand when to call upon other health professionals. One must know when to call upon visiting home nurses, social workers, psychologists, or representatives of community agencies. One must know when to call for legal or financial counseling. All physicians would do well to work in closer harmony with the patient's or family's clergyman or pastor.

The physician should know when to recommend specific rehabilitative therapies. Specific use of physical, occupational, recreational, and speech therapies are vital for the proper care of certain problems (see Chapter 17, Rehabilitation and the Aged). For example, the elderly patient with diabetic neuropathy and a flapping gait might benefit from bilateral leg braces. Another patient recovering from stroke might benefit from occupational therapy that should be used as a reintroduction of the patient to the activities of normal daily living, and not simply as a recreational or diversionary therapy.

The improvement of health care of the chronically ill elderly requires that health professionals work together for the best interest of the patient. What is required is a genuine collaborative effort to act in a unified fashion to bring about a system that will best meet the needs of the frail elderly.

RESPECT FOR THE USEFULNESS AND VALUE OF THE AGED INDIVIDUAL

Much in our society works to reject or devalue the aged. We are certainly living in a youth-oriented era

and a physician must guard against viewing the elderly as useless, insignificant, or worthless.

The rejection of our elderly is not a new phenomenon as attested to by the ancient story from "The Teaching of Buddha" (2).

Once upon a time there was a country which had the very peculiar custom of abandoning its aged people in remote and inaccessible mountains.

A certain minister of the State found it too difficult to follow this custom in the case of his own aged father, and so he built a secret underground cave where he hid his father and cared for him.

One day a god appeared before the king of that country and gave him a puzzling problem, saying that if he could not solve it satisfactorily, his country would be destroyed. The problem was: "Here are two serpents; tell me the sex of each."

Neither the king nor anyone in the palace was able to solve the problem; so the king offered a great reward to anyone in his kingdom who could.

The minister went to his father's hiding place and asked him for the answer to that problem. The old man said: "It is an easy solution. Place the two snakes on a soft carpet; the one that moves about is the male, and the other that keeps quiet is the female." The minister carried the answer to the king and the problem was successfully solved.

Then the god asked other difficult questions which the king and his retainers were unable to answer, but which the minister, after consulting his aged father, could always solve.

Here are some of the questions and their answers...

"How can you weigh a large elephant?" "Load it on a boat and draw a line to mark how deep the boat sinks into the water. Then take out the elephant and load the boat with stones until it sinks to the same depth and weigh the stones."

What is the meaning of the saying, "A cupful of water is more than the water of an ocean?" This is the answer: "A cupful of water given in a pure and compassionate spirit to one's parents or to a sick person has an eternal merit, but the water of an ocean will some day come to an end"...

"Here is a plank of Candana wood; which end was the bottom of the tree?" "Float the plank in water; the end that sinks a little deeper was the end nearest the root."

"Here are two horses apparently of the same size and form; how can you tell the mother from the son?" "Feed them some hay; the mother horse will push the hay toward her son."

Every answer to these difficult questions pleased the god as well as the king. The king was grateful to find out that the answers had come from the aged father whom the son had hidden in the cave, and he withdrew the law of abandoning aged people in the mountains and ordered that they were to be treated kindly.

The next 20 years will see considerable social change with redefinition of the age for retirement and many other social and economic changes that will allow the elderly to function as a continuing resource in our society (see Chapter 41, Retirement As Seen by the Health Professional and the Social Scientist). We can expect to see reduced restrictions on older workers with particular reference to mandatory retirement. We can also expect to see more educational programs that will provide skilled training, job counseling, and placement for older men and women in order to initiate, enhance, and continue their voluntary participation in the workforce. Hopefully, we will see the breakdown of stereotypes and greater recognition of the value of the elderly as a human resource.

COMPASSIONATE CARE

In an increasingly technologic society, caring and compassion must be foremost in the practice of medicine. We must avoid the possible dehumanization that takes place when patients simply become subjects for study and treatment. Every year in the United States, we are seeing new accomplishments in medical technology and specialization. Computerized tomography, computerized nuclear medicine, magnetic resonance imaging, positron emission tomography (PET), organ transplants, achievements in cardiovascular surgery, achievements in hemodialysis, and achievements in intensive and critical care—all these are becoming part of our routine medical environment. In such a new medical world, it is imperative that compassionate care not be lost in daily encounters between health professionals and elderly patients.

In all the great religions, various forms of a Golden Rule are stated; many religions teach: "You must love your neighbor as you do yourself," and, "What you do not want done to yourself, do not do to others." Surpassing new technical achievements and new specialized knowledge is the need to express compassion (8). The physician's duty is "to cure sometimes . . . to comfort always."

Critically important is the attitude of the doctor toward the elderly patient. Is the physician willing to spend time with the patient? Is the physician willing to be involved in the chronic and long-term aspects of the patient as well as in the acute illness? Is the physician concerned with the social, psychologic and family aspects of the patient, in addition to clinical and organic aspects?

Care and compassion mean that the physician must dispense sufficient time in his encounters with elderly patients. There is actually evidence in one study (10) that physicians spend less time with eld-

erly patients than with younger ones. Fifteen to twenty minutes may be minimal time to carry out a visit in the office, home, hospital or long-term care facility. One and one-half hours, not necessarily in one sitting, may be required to complete an examination of a new patient, particularly in the presence of multiple complex problems. More time will be required in each encounter if the various functions of counseling, psychologic support, health maintenance and prevention are to be carried out, in addition to making decisions about treatment and possible rehabilitation.

Examples of failure in caring and compassion include the physician who waves at the door of the patient's room; the physician who quickly resorts to psychotropic drugs in the office, rather than taking the time to listen; and the physician on teaching rounds who never sees the patient and who limits his or her discussion to laboratory studies or some specific, interesting aspect of the case in a nearby conference room.

The physician should be a good listener and read between the lines what the patient is saying. Often, by nonverbal means, the physician can express warmth, understanding, or sympathy. Staying close to the patient and maintaining eye contact is helpful. Sitting adjacent to the patient's bed or sitting on the edge of the bed in the hospital or long-term care facility brings the doctor right into the patient's small universe. The physician might put a hand on the patient's shoulder and pat or touch the patient or hold hands at appropriate points during the visit.

As the revered physician, Eugene Stead, Jr., would say: "What this patient needs is a doctor" (21). Our elderly patients, and in fact, all of our patients are yearning for a physician who will listen and understand. Again, we remember Peabody's words (12), "The good physician knows his patients through and through, and his knowledge is bought dearly. Time, sympathy and understanding must be lavishly dispensed, but the reward is to be found in that personal bond which forms the greatest satisfaction of the practice of medicine. One of the essential qualities of the clinician is interest in humanity, where the secret of the care of the patient is in caring for the patient."

CHANGING TIMES IN HEALTH CARE

In the performance of these essential aspects of care of the elderly patient, the physician may be distraught that these are difficult times and a revolution in health care is taking place. The physician may feel discouragement during this period of increased competition, cost-containment, alternative patterns of health care delivery, the malpractice threat, the nursing shortage, and other forces in health care. The physician may be disheartened by a system that provides financial incentives for saving money and that puts the physician at risk for spending; that excessively scrutinizes and profiles the physician in the hospital; and that may often seem to emphasize the financial bottom line rather than excellence of patient care. Despite this tug of war, the physician must simply have faith that excellence of patient care—care that is compassionate and humane, care that is characterized by continuity, care that is sensitive to psychosocial and family issues, and care that is characterized by all the other essential principles—will endure. Although the organization of health care delivery will undoubtedly change, we can expect that society will ultimately demand a quality of care that we would each want for ourselves.

SUMMARY

In the care of the elderly patient, eleven essential principles should be considered: (1) the role of the physician as the integrator of the biopsychosocial model; (2) continuity of care; (3) bolstering the family and home; (4) good communication skills; (5) building a sound doctor-patient relationship; (6) the need for thorough evaluation and assessment; (7) prevention and health maintenance; (8) intelligent treatment; (9) interdisciplinary collaboration; (10) respect for the usefulness and value of the aged individual; and (11) compassionate care. The embodiment of these eleven principles represents a standard of excellence to which we should all aspire.

REFERENCES

1. Andres R: Relation of physiologic changing in aging to medical changes of disease in the aged. *Mayo Clin Proc* 42:674, 1967.
2. Bukkyo Dendo Kyokai, *The Teaching of Buddha,* Rev. Ed. 45. Tokyo, Kosaido Printing, 1978 pp. 264–270.
3. Butler R: The doctor and the aged patient. In Reichel W (ed): *The Geriatric Patient.* New York, Hospital Practice, 1978, pp. 199–206.
4. Climo J: Visits of distant living adult children and elderly parents. *J Aging Studies* 2:57, 1988.
5. Cousins N: The physician as communicator. *JAMA* 248: 587, 1982.
6. Frankl VE: *The Doctor and the Soul.* New York, AA Knopf, 1955.
7. Frankl VE: *Man's Search for Meaning.* New York, Beacon Press, 1959.
8. Glick S: Humanistic medicine in a modern age. *N Engl J Med.* 304:1036, 1981.
9. Howell TH: Causation of diagnostic errors in octogenarians. A clinicopathological study. *J Am Geriatr Soc* 14:41, 1966.
10. Keeler EB: Solomon DH, Beck JC, Mendenhall RC, Kane RL: Effect of patient age on duration of medical encounters with physicians. *Med Care* 20:1101, 1982.
11. Kushner H: *When All You've Ever Wanted Isn't Enough.* New York, Summit Books, 1986.
12. Peabody FW: The care of the patient. *JAMA* 88:877, 1927.
13. Rabin DL, Stockton P: *Long-Term Care for the Elderly: A Fact Book.* New York, Oxford University Press, 1987.
14. Reichel W: Complications in the care of 500 elderly hospitalized patients. *J Am Geriatr Soc* 13: 973, 1965.
15. Reichel W: Multiple problems in the elderly. In Reichel, W. (ed.). *The Geriatric Patient.* Hospital Practice, New York, 1978, pp. 17–22.
16. Reichel W: The continuity imperative. *JAMA* 246: 2065, 1981.
17. Seegal D: The principle of minimal interference in the management of the elderly patient. *J Chron Dis* 17: 299, 1964.
18. Shanas E: Social myth as hypothesis: The case of the family relations of old people. *Gerontologist* 19:3, 1979.
19. Steel K, Gertman PM, Crescenzi C, Anderson J: Iatrogenic illness on a general medical service at a university hospital. *N Engl J Med* 304:638, 1981.
20. Stone R, Cafferata GL, Sangl J: *Caregivers of the Frail Elderly: A National Profile.* National Center for Health Service Research and Health Care Technology Assessment, Rockville, MD, 1986.
21. Wagner GS, Cebe B, Rozear MP (eds): *E. A. Stead, Jr., What This Patient Needs is a Doctor.* Durham, NC, Carolina Academic Press, 1978.
22. Wasson JH, Sauvigne AE, Mogielnicki RP, Frey WG, Sox CH, Gaudette C, Rockwell A: Continuity of outpatient medical care in elderly men. A randomized trial. *JAMA* 252:2413, 1984.
23. Yalom ID: *Existential Psychotherapy.* New York, Basic Books, Inc., 1980.

CHAPTER 2

Health Maintenance and Health Screening in the Elderly

DAVID C. KENNIE
GREGG WARSHAW

The problems of old age pose an unprecedented challenge to the medical profession. The potential contribution of preventive health care in improving the well-being of the elderly, in procuring economic savings resulting from caring for a less disabled population, and in providing a more humane and less technologic approach to medical care, have aroused considerable interest. Nevertheless, health maintenance of the elderly remains a complex, controversial, and emotive topic (10). Fundamental to the successful application of preventive strategies for the elderly is a better understanding of the scope of prevention as it applies to the elderly (18).

The purpose of this chapter is to consider the tasks of health maintenance, to discuss the principles and guidelines by which health maintenance strategies should be applied to this older age group; to outline strategies by which the health maintenance packages could be applied to the elderly population; and to provide specific health maintenance packages.

Effective health maintenance of the elderly requires that a number of tasks be performed by many sectors of society both individually and collectively. These are summarized in Table 2.1. This chapter focusses primarily on those pertinent to the health care provider, in particular the practicing physician.

To progress toward a rational and effective preventive approach for geriatric care, physicians must continue to clarify the complexities of applying anticipatory strategies to this age group. In addition to implementing valid strategies to address the prevention of specific disease, health maintenance plans for the elderly should consider: a re-evaluation of the traditional preventive health delivery systems, personalized health maintenance measures, further reduction of iatrogenic problems, the needs of family caregivers, strategies to enhance functional status, and strategies to strengthen social supports.

PRINCIPLES OF APPLYING HEALTH MAINTENANCE STRATEGIES TO THE ELDERLY

SCIENTIFIC VALIDATION OF MANEUVERS

The first task, that of ensuring a sound scientific basis for any intervention strategy, has been addressed in recent years initially by the Canadian Task Force and, more recently, by the United States Task Force on the Periodic Health Examination. This task has been essential in order to protect the healthy population from iatrogenic insult, to prevent unnecessary costs both to the individual and to society, and to maintain the "scientific integrity" of the professionals concerned. It has led to careful study of the impact of disease, the efficacy of detection maneuvers and the quality of evidence supporting the effectiveness of intervention strategies.

Yet, the relevance of this work to the elderly is somewhat limited, for it has focussed on primary

13

Table 2.1.
Tasks of Health Maintenance

1. For the Elderly
   Continued self-development
   Adaptation to loss
   Adoption of healthy life-style
2. For families
   Provision of informal supports
   Respect for elders' autonomy
   Avoidance of overprotection
3. For health care providers
   Scientific validation of maneuvers
   Re-evaluation of traditional strategies (e.g.,
      screening)
   Personalize health maintenance measures
   Reduction of iatrogenic insult
   Recognition of the needs of family caregivers
   Adoption of wider focus
      Prevention of illness
      Promotion of functional independence
      Maintenance of an adequate support
4. For governmental administration
   Fiscal
      e.g.,
      Funding of appropriate selection of health mainte-
         nance maneuvers
      Financial disincentives for consumption of toxic
         products
   Legislative
      e.g.,
      Seat belt legislation
      Smoking controls
5. Collective tasks
   Education to dispel agism
   Minimization of costs

and secondary prevention strategies that address biomedical disorders in young populations. This is important, for old age is not a separate period of life but is part of a continuum and, for full effectiveness, preventive measures need to start in childhood and continue throughout adult life. Nevertheless it does not provide the practicing physician with the details of what he or she should do or how to do it when confronted with frail elderly patients.

STRATEGIES FOR APPLYING HEALTH MAINTENANCE MEASURES

Screening and Case Finding in the General Population

A conventional approach to applying preventive care strategies has been through annual or regular screening programs. In the elderly, this has been extended to the identification of symptomatic but un-

reported illness by case finding. A number of reports from the United Kingdom over the last 20 years have suggested the benefit of screening elderly populations but a number of more recent controlled studies and one randomized control trial by Tulloch and Moore (16) give a clearer picture of the worth of this strategy.

Screening of the community living elderly may have some slight improvement on mortality rates, but the results remain inconclusive (4, 17). There has been even less impact shown on functional status with only marginal nonstatistical improvements being observed, though in some of the studies, the reliability and validity of the scales used to measure the outcomes have not been well defined. Most investigators believe their patients benefit from a screening and surveillance program and report a perceived increase in patient morale and esteem but these subjective impressions have not been borne out when more sophisticated measurement has been employed (17). At best, screening and surveillance programs for the elderly have been demonstrated to have a marginal and transient effect on the quality of life. Lastly, although further clarification is required, it would seem that certain types of screening and health maintenance programs may reduce rates of institutionalization. Two studies have shown reduction in the number of admissions to hospital and the number of hospital bed days utilized (4, 16). Nevertheless, referrals for inpatient care and for hospital clinic attendance may increase and it seems that the degree of institutionalization depends more on the experience and biomedical orientation of the health professionals acting as gatekeeper to these resources.

Screening of the institutionalized elderly has been shown in a number of recent studies to be of dubious benefit. In one study, it was found that approximately half of the annual screening examinations produced either a new finding or revision of an old problem (6). These were then assessed independently for their degree of importance by the primary care physician concerned in the patients' care. It was estimated that 3.4% were of major importance, 26.8% were of intermediate importance, and 69.8% were of minor importance. These results provided only modest support for endorsing annual medical examinations for nursing home residents. Likewise, in another survey of an academically affiliated Veterans' Administration Nursing home, it was concluded that ongoing health care as part of an academic geriatric program might obviate the need for annual examinations.

The current evidence, therefore, suggests that

global screening or case finding of the elderly population is time-consuming, costly, and relatively ineffective. It appears that preventive programs will need to be more limited, directed to specific problems with well-defined methods and goals for the intervention strategies.

Screening and Case Finding in Selected Patient Groups

Rather than screen the whole of the elderly population, an alternative is to focus on selected patient groups. The elderly may self-select themselves. For instance, a postal questionnaire has been used to allow those fit enough and with no significant problems to exclude themselves from further study. By using this self-report technique, about one-fifth of a screening workload can be avoided.

The results of several preadmission screening programs suggest that referral for nursing home-type care is a further opportunity for the instigation of health maintenance measures as part of a multidimensional assessment. Apart from bringing to light undetected disease, the subsequent rehabilitation and provision of home supports can do much to avert or delay institutionalization and allow resettlement at a lesser level of care.

A third method is to select only those elderly patients perceived to be "at risk." This concept has at least two problems. The first is that the term has been used variously to imply risk of death, of increased morbidity, and of being institutionalized, and thus, creates stress and stigma. Also, recent attempts to validate at risk groups previously defined in the world literature failed to show any of them as being particularly effective in terms of case finding for various parameters of health and psychosocial well-being (15).

Opportunistic Case Finding

A final strategy for the application of health maintenance measures is opportunistic case finding, that is, seeking out unreported illness during normal doctor-patient relationships. This has been shown to be particularly effective where the health care delivery system has a strong primary care base with primary care providers serving a defined population and "gatekeeping" to a variety of resources. In this way, over 90% of an identified elderly patient population may make contact with the primary care base over a 1-year period (19). The concept offers both a challenge and opportunity to primary care providers particularly those operating within health maintenance organizations.

Opportunistic case finding also removes the artificial dichotomy between preventive and traditional medical care. Health maintenance measures would no longer be carried out as a separate activity being performed on a relatively fit population. Instead, health maintenance and traditional medical care become integrated and the medical process serves as a major channel for the delivery of preventive health services.

PERSONALIZE HEALTH MAINTENANCE MEASURES

The elderly are a heterogeneous population and this must be reflected by personalizing preventive maneuvers. In doing this, the following principles should be considered.

Recognize that Death May be a Legitimate End Point. A patient's right to live and benefit from the developments of medical science is incontestible but, at some point in the life cycle, a patient also has the right to die peacefully and with dignity. This is particularly true for those suffering from irremediable disease. Health maintenance of the elderly, therefore, has as its principal goal not the prolongation of life but an improvement in the quality of that life.

Minimize Unnecessary Disruption to Life-Style. A number of health maintenance measures have the potential for disrupting a patient's lifestyle. The prescription of a low-sodium or weight-reduction diet or advice to stop smoking are some common examples. All these measures have a place in the management of selected groups of patients but the physician should appreciate that, in old age when the scope for prolongation of life becomes limited, issues concerned with the quality of life become more relevant. To many patients, restriction of diet or the cessation of smoking may seriously affect what little enjoyment they have left. These emotive issues regarding life satisfaction must always be balanced against the theoretical advantages to health. If the community living elderly perceive the equation to be unequal, they can opt out by noncompliance. The institutionalized elderly are less fortunate and can be a captive audience to the zealous application of preventive strategies.

Respect Patients' Autonomy. As elderly patients age they become more frail and at risk living alone in the community. Families may become sufficiently anxious that they try to institutionalize old persons despite the latters' expressed wishes to remain in their own homes. The physician at these times must respect the patient's right to self-determination. The only exception to this is the mentally incompetent patient although even here the presence of dementia does not necessarily imply incompetence.

Time the Intervention Precisely. It should be appreciated that there is a critical intervention time or "window" regarding when the various types of preventive support should be provided. A patient's functional status may deteriorate slowly for several years until a crisis develops and then the situation will deteriorate rapidly. If support is added too late, institutionalization is often the outcome. If it is provided too early, however, it merely fosters dependency, wastes resources, is costly to society, and is considered by many patients to be an intrusion on their privacy.

MINIMIZE IATROGENIC INSULT

In the elderly, there is decline in physiologic functioning in almost every organ system resulting in impaired homeostasis. A reduction in iatrogenic insult is, therefore, an important goal of health maintenance. Drug-induced disease is perhaps the most commonly appreciated problem, but even the hospitalization process is not without risk for this age group. An increasing literature (8, 14) reveals significant iatrogenesis from the procedures used, from nosocomial infections, from falls within the institutions, and from the psychologic insult associated with the relocation (3).

Reduction of iatrogenic insult should not only be a goal of health maintenance but should be a principle by which health maintenance strategies are applied. For instance, the Hemoccult Slide Test has been recommended for the detection of colorectal carcinoma in those over 50 years yet is far from ideal as a routine test for use with the frail elderly. In this population, the majority of positive tests may not be due to carcinoma but to asymptomatic diverticular disease or duodenal ulceration (12). This is of importance because the Hemoccult is not an innocuous test. A positive result mandates an extensive workup from sigmoidoscopy to double contrast enema and colonoscopy. The morbidity in the elderly from these procedures, from the required bowel preparation, and from any accompanying hospitalization is significant. These factors must be weighed in the balance when considering the routine use of the Hemoccult Test for the frail but asymptomatic elderly population.

HEALTH MAINTENANCE PACKAGES

Effective health maintenance of the elderly requires an appreciation of problems outside the narrow biomedical focus. Health in old age is, in fact, a multidimensional matrix of three interwoven components: the absence of disease (including iatrogenic disease), an optimal functional status, and an adequate support system. The two health care packages presented include a selection of strategies in each of these areas. These are summarized in Tables 2.2 and 2.3. Selected items are discussed further in the text. These packages are a personal selection of methods of varying proven value that currently seem useful, safe, simple, and reasonably cost-effective to apply. They are intended to achieve the following goals:

1. Prevent or palliate physical, psychiatric, and iatrogenic disorders.
2. Prolong the period of effective activity and independent living.
3. Ensure a support system adequate to preserve the patient's autonomy, independence, and quality of life at all levels of care.
4. Avoid institutionalization as far as is practicable in both humanitarian and economic terms.
5. Ensure that when illness is terminal there is as little distress as possible to patient and caregivers.
6. Minimize the burden on family and other caregivers to improve their quality of life and prolong the period of time they are willing to undertake the caring role.

The emphasis within each package may need to be varied, with strategies aimed at disease prevention being stressed in early old age while functional and supportive measures are employed increasingly in advanced age with the frail elderly. In order for secondary and tertiary preventive strategies to be applied, a problem must initially be recognized yet the traditional medical model of care minimizes consideration of patients' functional status and support systems. If problems in these areas are not to be missed, the physician must learn to enter them into his frame of working reference. This may best be done by routinely measuring physical and mental status using one of the short instruments of measurement available for this purpose. Similarly, the physician should personally assess the patient's formal and informal support systems. Problems should be routinely entered into the medical record in the form of a multidimensional problem list. A taxonomy of social or support problems meaningful to medical care needs to be developed for this purpose.

Table 2.2
Health Maintenance of the Community-Living Elderly[a]

Disease Prevention	Enhancement of Functional Status	Maintenance of the Support System
Delayed presentation for care	**General deconditioning with age**	**Poverty**
Health education program targeted at the elderly and their caregivers to remove the nihilistic views about health and health care in old age	Maintain or promote exercise program into the daily routine	Ensure adequate pension
	Immobility	Eliminate major third-party reimbursement gaps in existing Medicare/Medicaid system
Regular surveillance of those too frail to attend the office or clinic	Avoid overprotection by family caregivers	**Poor housing**
Travel illness and injury	Provide intermittent home or day care therapy to maintain stroke (and other) patients after hospital discharge	Ensure an adequate supply of congregate, warden supervised, and specially adapted housing
Regular use of seat belts and head restraints by car occupants		Increase the supply of aids and adaptations in existing housing
Counsel to discontinue driving if increasing mental frailty	Ensure the provision of an appropriate walking aid	Install community-based monitoring alarm systems
Immunization procedures relating to travel abroad	Adapt the home environment as necessary with ramps and other devices	**Breakdown of family support**
Hypertension	**Falls**	Avoid patient relocation away from family and friends
Treatment of systolic-diastolic hypertension except in those with severe bilateral carotid occlusive disease	Avoid sedative medication	Provide formal and informal supports for the stressed caregiver
	Remove home hazards	Provide respite care for selected groups of stressed caregivers
	Provide better home lighting	**Loss**
Disorders of the integument	Ensure correct footwear	Provide counseling for the bereaved
Routine examination for skin cancer	Ensure the correct pattern of use with walking aid	**Relocation stress**
Foot and shoe care for those with diabetes or peripheral vascular disease	Eliminate nocturia	Avoid relocation to different housing if already demented or blind
	Install monitoring alarm system	Ensure patient has perception of choice and control with any move
Regular podiatry for those who are unable to cut their own nails or suffering from severe diabetes or peripheral vascular disease	**Poor vision**	Provide counseling to avoid social stresses when patient moves into another family member's home
	Routine ophthalmoscopic examination plus assessment of visual acuity, central vision, and visual fields	
Influenza and pneumonia	Improve home lighting	
Immunization in selected groups	Provide glasses if required	
Iatrogenic insult	Provide low vision aids (magnifying glass, large print books, eye shades, etc.)	
Investigate patients on the principle of "minimal interference"	**Deafness**	
Avoid fostering dependency by the premature prescription of community supports	Routine otoscopic examination plus subjective impression of hearing loss	
Avoid unnecessary institutionalization	Use rating scale to assess likelihood of hearing aid use prior to further investigation	
Smoking hazards	Provide hearing aid and other deaf aids	
Advice and assistance to stop smoking in these with severe cardiovascular, respiratory, or osteoporotic disease		
Advice and assistance to quit smoking in the healthy elderly only if motivated to do so		
Breast Cancer		
Routine clinical examination for all age groups		

Table 2.2. continued

Disease Prevention	Enhancement of Functional Status	Maintenance of the Support System
Additional mammography in the young old	**Incontinence**	
Cervical cancer	Health education program to promote earlier referral	
Routine Pap smear in the young old; no repeat if negative	Community screening and surveillance to identify those in need	
Pap smear in the old old only if requested, symptomatic, or a high risk patient	Improve mobility to the toilet	
Hypothyroidism	Improve stability at the toilet by supplying aids and adaptations	
Routine assessment of thyroid function avoiding, if possible, times of severe illness	Provide appropriate incontinence pads and garments	
Malnutrition	**Inability to do domestic chores**	
Weight reduction of the obese only if arthritic, hypertensive, or paralyzed	Provides choreworker or Meals on Wheels if patient cannot carry out functional tasks of cooking, cleaning, shopping	
Provide chore worker or Meals on Wheels only for those unable to cook for themselves	**Nocturia**	
Depression	Avoid diuretics	
Increase detection by incorporation of a screen into the medical examination	Eliminate daytime leg edema	
	Use anticholinergic at night	
Environmental manipulation for the lonely and isolated by voluntary visiting and social day care	**Constipation**	
	Increase fiber content of diet	
Dementia	Avoid drugs with systemic anticholinergic effect	
Increase detection by incorporation of a screen into the medical examination	**Insomnia**	
Ensure adequate workup for the confused with short, rapid, or atypical histories	Eliminate distressing symptoms and provide comfort measures at night	
Drug misuse		
Prescribe drugs less often		
Prescribe to a maximum of 3 or 4 drugs		
Prescribe in accordance with good pharmacokinetic and dynamic principles		
Counsel on the use of drugs		
Avoid the use of child-proof containers		
Review medication frequently and attempt to reduce the number of drugs by discontinuing those with no apparent benefit		
Hypo- and hyperthermia		
Ensure adequate heating in the home		
Avoid undue sun exposure especially if suffering from stroke disease or multi-infarct dementia		

Table 2.2. continued

Disease Prevention	Enhancement of Functional Status	Maintenance of the Support System
Perioperative complications		
Use anticoagulation to prevent pulmonary thromboembolic disease		
Minimize the use of strongly anti-cholinergic drugs to prevent confusional states		
Administer systemic antibiotics for selected operational procedures		

[a]Modified from Kennie DC: Health maintenance of the elderly. *Clin Geriatr Med* 2:65, 1986.

STRATEGIES AIMED AT DISEASE PREVENTION

Hypertension

In recent years, there have been several well-conducted trials of the treatment of systolic-diastolic hypertension in the elderly. Although these have shown minimal benefit in terms of overall mortality, they have consistently shown a reduction in the incidence of stroke disease. Hard evidence of this effect is still confined to those under 80 years of age for there have been insufficient numbers of the very old enrolled in the existing trials from which to draw statistical conclusions. There is, therefore, still doubt about the risk-benefit equation of treatment in the very old away from the carefully monitored conditions of a controlled trial. It is the very old population that is most at risk from excessive or rapid hypotensive therapy as well as from the side effects of the medication. Compliance with therapy in the general elderly population may not be as good as in the relatively fit, motivated elderly populations attending blood pressure clinics. This may be particularly true in the case of the very old population in whom 1 in 5 will have some degree of cognitive impairment. Effective prevention of the complications of hypertension still, therefore, requires considerable research into strategies with the very old.

The case for treating isolated systolic hypertension is not as yet proved and awaits the result of two large controlled trials.

Iatrogenic Insult

The prevention of iatrogenic insult is a priority in the health care of the elderly. Iatrogenic insult oc-

curs throughout the complete range of medical management. Considerable benefit would arise by altering clinical behavior to prescribe drugs not only more skillfully but to prescribe them less, by the adoption of a stronger case-management principle throughout the numerous consults in the acute-care hospital, by adopting the principle of minimal interference in the medical workup, and by the introduction of multidisciplinary geriatric assessment units that have been shown to improve functional outcome.

Influenza

There is good evidence of the efficacy of influenza vaccine in the community living elderly and moderately good evidence for its efficacy in the institutionalized elderly population. Influenzal vaccination reduces mortality, morbidity, and hospitalization rates. Several recent studies have also demonstrated that this could result in a saving of medical costs if widely administered to the elderly population. However, vaccination rates remain low although a number of strategies such as postal and telephone reminders have improved compliance with this procedure. There are, however, ethical constraints on the extent to which this disease should be prevented, for it often terminates suffering in many of the most physically and mentally disabled. Therefore, patients should be carefully selected for this primary disease-prevention measure.

Pneumonia

Several studies now attest to the efficacy of pneumococcal vaccination in the elderly. The appro-

Table 2.3.
Health Maintenance of the Institutionalized Elderly[a]

Disease Prevention	Enhancement of Functional Status	Maintenance of the Support System
Hypertension Treatment of systolic-diastolic hypertension except in those with severe bilateral carotid occlusive disease **Disorders of the integument** Routine examination for skin cancer Foot and shoe care for those with diabetes or peripheral vascular disease Regular podiatry for those unable to cut their own nails or who are suffering from severe diabetes or peripheral vascular disease Routinely employ prognostic rating scale for the likelihood of developing pressure sores Use of specialized cushions, underblankets, and beds to prevent pressure sores in those at risk **Influenza and pneumonia** Immunization in selected groups with severe chronic cardiorespiratory disease who are free from terminal illness or severe suffering **Iatrogenic insult** Investigate patients on the principle of minimal interference Stronger case management in the hospital setting to orchestrate and coordinate a comprehensive plan of management Keep patient's wishes central to plan of management **Smoking hazards** Advice and assistance to stop smoking only in those with accompanying cardiovascular or respiratory disease **Breast cancer** Routine clinical examination for all age groups **Hypothyroidism** Routine assessment of thyroid function avoiding, if possible, times of severe illness **Malnutrition** Weight reduction of the obese if arthritic, hypertensive, or paralyzed or if posing severe difficul-	**Immobility** Practice functionally oriented care in all institutional settings Ensure the provision of appropriate walking aid Minimize use of wheelchairs for indoor use Minimize use of formal and informal patient restraints Provide suitable beds and chairs for rising and transferring Reduce staff anxiety about reprimands from hierarchy should patients occasionally fall Permit the nursing staff to sacrifice less important tasks in order to have more time to conduct functionally oriented care **Falls** Avoid sedative medication Ensure correct footwear Ensure correct pattern of use with walking aid Ensure adequate staff/patient ratios for adequate supervision of patients at times rising from and going to bed **Poor vision** Routine ophthalmoscopic examination plus assessment of visual acuity, central vision, and visual fields Provide glasses if required Provide low vision aids (magnifying glass, large print books, eye shades, etc.) **Deafness** Routine otoscopic examination plus subjective impression of hearing loss Use rating scale to assess likelihood of hearing aid use prior to further investigation Provide hearing aid and other deaf aids **Incontinence** Improve mobility to the toilet Provide appropriate incontinence pads and garments Ensure adequate staff/patient ratios to operate effective toilet training programs	**Poverty** Amend current reimbursement rules whereby a patient must spend-down to poverty level before receiving supplementation for long-term nursing home care **Poor housing** Provide adequate housing as an outlet option for the relatively fit currently residing in intermediate-care facilities **Family stress** Alleviate guilt of families in institutionalizing their relatives by counseling and ego boosting on the caring role they have previously undertaken Provide psychologic support for families of the severely demented and the dying and for the bereaved Discuss the patient's resuscitation status with family and obtain consensus **Staff stress** Intercede if any staff/family friction Discuss patient's resuscitation status and obtain consensus Provide counseling and psychologic support for those caring for patients with severe feeding problems Provide counseling for specific problems of stress arising in the staff **Depersonalized care** Adopt a primary care system of nursing Improve communication skills of nursing personnel

Table 2.3. continued

Disease Prevention	Enhancement of Functional Status	Maintenance of the Support System
ties to nurse handling because of size	**Nocturia**	
Ensure adequate nurse/patient staff ratios to ensure adequate time to mouth-feed those with feeding difficulties	Avoid diuretics Eliminate daytime leg edema Use anticholinergic at night	
Avoid prolonged or excessive cooking of food to preserve vitamin C and folate content	**Constipation** Increase fiber content of diet Avoid drugs with systemic anticholinergic effect	
Depression	Maintain patient mobility	
Increase detection by incorporation of a screen into the medical examination	Ensure high fluid intake Ensure privacy when toileting	
Dementia	**Insomnia**	
Increase detection by incorporation of a screen into the medical examination	Eliminate distressing symptoms and provide comfort measures at night	
Drug misuse	Ensure adequate exercise and fresh air by day	
Prescribe drugs less often	Avoid patient napping in the late afternoon	
Prescribe in accordance with good pharmacokinetic and dynamic principles		
Review medication frequently and attempt to reduce the number of drugs by discontinuing those with no apparent benefit		
Avoid the regular prescription of a hypnotic		
Avoid the prescription of PRN drugs		
Perioperative complications		
Use anticoagulation to prevent pulmonary thromembolic disease		
Minimize the use of strongly anticholinergic drugs to prevent confusional states		
Administer systemic antibiotics for selected operational procedures		

[a]Modified from Kennie DC: Health maintenance of the elderly. *Clin Geriatr Med* 2:65, 1986.

priateness of widespread vaccination programs must, however, be seen in the context of the populations for which they are recommended. It is essential to consider the effect of other concomitant disease on mortality rates from pneumococcal pneumonia. When no other conditions coexist the mortality from pneumococcal pneumonia is low (9/100,000 cases), but this increased a hundred-fold for those with two or more high risk associated conditions. Therefore, two target populations may exist: (a) one fit group, mostly living in the community, who respond well to antibiotic therapy and who have a good prognosis irrespective of vaccination status; (b) the second group, many of whom will be institutionalized, are seriously debilitated from concomitant disease, have a poor prognosis, and prevention might be better than attempted cure. For a significant proportion of this latter population, pneumonia will, however, terminate suffering so that ethical considerations come into play and the decision to vaccinate must be individually determined. It should also be noted that it is in precisely this frail population that there are still doubts about the efficacy of the vaccine (13).

Smoking Habits

Although smoking rates tend to fall in old age, 17.9% of men and 16.8% of women of this age group in the United States still smoke. Although the principle of minimizing disruption to the patient's lifestyle must be seriously considered, data suggest that in addition to its correlation with coronary heart disease, peripheral vascular disease, lung cancer, and chronic obstructive lung disease, smoking in the elderly is also associated with decreased bone mineral density, loss of body weight, decreased muscle strength, and accelerated lung aging. The demented elderly who smoke also pose a fire hazard.

The benefits of stopping smoking in younger patients has been well described. Jajich et al. (9) have shown that stopping smoking late in life is associated with a rapid and sustained reduction in mortality from coronary disease. Many programs are available to assist individuals to stop smoking. Although there may be isolated successes, their success in the elderly is generally poor.

Breast Cancer

The age-specific incidence of breast cancer, that is, the number of cases per year per 100,000 females in each age group, shows a progressive rise with age. A recent carefully conducted trial from Sweden showed that prognosis was best when the age at diagnosis was between 45 and 49 years, but thereafter survival worsened with increasing age. The difference in relative survival between those older than 75 years and those 45–49 years increased from 8.6% at 2 years, to 12.2%, 20.3%, and 27.5% after 5, 10, and 15 years of follow-up, respectively.

No data are available on the screening of the very old for breast cancer, but a controlled trial from Sweden and other case-control studies from Europe indicate a definite value for mammographic screening in reducing mortality in patients up to 74 years of age. It is suggested, therefore, that physical examination of the breasts be included routinely as a procedure for women of all ages and that additional screening by mammography be included for women in their 60s.

Hypothyroidism

Hypothyroidism is present in about 1 in 500 of the community-living adult population, but the incidence increases with age so that it is a condition commonly encountered by those physicians dealing with the elderly. Bahemuka and Hodkinson (1) found it in 2.3% of consecutive admissions to a geriatric department. Because of its frequency, its impact on physical and psychiatric morbidity, the simplicity and low cost of the test for its detection, and the efficacy of its treatment, periodic evaluation of thyroid function in an aged population is a useful health maintenance strategy.

Cervical Cancer

There is general agreement that the value of regular screening for cervical cancer by use of the Pap smear recedes in old age. It is suggested that when physicians are confronted by relatively young elderly women they should perform this procedure on those who are motivated and willing to tolerate the procedure. If the test is negative, no further screening seems to be required because the age-specific incidence of conversion from negative to positive smears decreases from 0.3/1000 in women 55–59 years old to 0 for those over 80 years old.

It is well known that urban, black, and hispanic populations have a high incidence of carcinoma as do those with multiple sexual partners, prior venereal disease, and those in the lower income group. It may be that screening of these high risk groups should be more aggressive as was demonstrated in a recent survey of an elderly New York population where a prevalence rate of abnormal smears was found to be 13.5/1000 (11).

Depression

Depression and dysphoria are common in the elderly and are amenable to antidepressant therapy, environmental manipulation, and other measures. As with dementia, the greatest hindrance to its management is lack of recognition. Increased awareness of depression as a treatable entity would be improved by the inclusion of a short screening instrument into the routine clinical evaluation.

Dementia

The recognition of dementia in the elderly is important primarily to improve the behavioral and functional problems associated with the disease and to provide support to the caregivers. The identification of dementia at an early stage may assume increasing importance as research into new treatment modalities expands.

STRATEGIES TO ENHANCE FUNCTIONAL STATUS

General Deconditioning with Age

There is considerable potential for the maintenance of physical function in old age by physicial exercise programs. Physical training programs have been shown to reduce the decline in maximum oxygen consumption that accompanies aging, to increase muscle strength, to improve joint mobility, and to improve the sense of balance. Imaginative yet acceptable exercise programs need to be developed and integrated into the social life of the elderly. Guidelines and precautions for the prescription of these programs have been described. An unanswered question is whether the elderly population, particularly those that are frail, will have the motivation to carry out such exercise sufficiently, frequently, and at a level of intensity needed to achieve a conditioning response.

Immobility

Although exercise programs may be considered a primary preventive strategy, rehabilitation and functionally oriented care are the main tertiary preventive strategies aimed at minimizing disability. In the United States, rehabilitation tends to be considered a specialist topic conducted by therapists and psychiatrists often in specialized units remote from the mainstream of medical practice. It is also strongly biased toward the admission of younger age groups and has a work-oriented goal. The term functionally oriented care is used therefore in the context of the elderly, and it is the duty of nurses and physicians to conduct it as well as therapists. In many cases, it is as effective as more specialized rehabilitative programs. Functionally oriented care is of paramount importance in assisting the frail, aged patient to return home from the acute hospital setting.

Falls

Falls in the elderly are associated with significant morbidity and mortality and an increased rate of institutionalization. Isaacs' work (7) from the United Kingdom shows that it is possible to identify those at high risk of falling based on an assessment of their speed of walking, the extent of body sway, and the extent to which the person mobilizes. A high correlation has been shown between a simple clinical

score and more sophisticated biomedical measuring techniques in making these assessments.

Although theoretical frameworks have been devised for the prevention of falls and checklists exist for the elimination of home hazards, the elderly themselves may be reluctant to make the necessary lifestyle changes to reduce their chances of falling. In one program, only 10% of the environmental manipulations suggested by a health maintenance nurse were adopted by the elderly.

Poor Vision

About one-fifth of those over 65 years of age have poor vision. This may severely restrict daily activities, result in social isolation, produce depression, and aggravate paranoid and delusional states. A simple test of vision carried out by relatively untrained personnel emphasizing near rather than distance vision (for example, by the use of print charts) would uncover many problems that could then be referred to physicians for ophthalmoscopic examination. There is insufficient evidence at present to support routine screening for open angle glaucoma by tonometry.

Apart from specific treatment, such as cataract extraction or laser photocoagulation for senile macular degeneration, simple methods such as the provision of glasses or low vision aids can be of value. Much of the visual difficulty experienced by the elderly at home can also be relieved by improved illumination.

Deafness

Hearing deficits in the elderly are also common and can result in problems similar to those resulting from visual loss. The vast majority of patients are suffering from presbycusis, wax in the external auditory canal, or both. The first part of any screen for hearing deficit should consist of the physician's assessment of how well the patient hears conversational or whispered speech coupled with a self-estimate from the patient about any hearing difficulties. Thereafter, otoscopic examination should be performed to exclude wax and other abnormalities. Because many of the elderly are unable or unwilling to comply with aural rehabilitation, estimate the likelihood of a hearing aid being used before proceeding to a more sophisticated assessment.

Incontinence

For the elderly without dementia, a high cure rate should be expected for incontinence, yet there is considerable shame and reluctance about reporting this problem. A priority for the prevention of incontinence, therefore, must be to educate the older population and their caregivers that incontinence can be treatable. A simple clinical algorithm is available for the assessment of the elderly incontinent woman. This has been shown to correlate well with sophisticated urodynamic studies, and the approach may do much to remove the need for invasive procedures and, hence, reduce iatrogenic insult (5).

The prevention of incontinence may depend on a wide range of other strategies such as improving the patient's mobility, improving access to and stability at the toilet, and, in the case of institutionalized patients, ensuring an adequate nurse-to-patient ratio to permit an effective toilet-training program.

In established incontinence in demented patients, cure is less likely, but considerable benefit can result from the correct use of behavioral strategies, specialized garments, appliances, and indwelling catheters. A major contribution toward implementing these measures would be a community-based case-finding and surveillance program by nursing staff.

Inability to Perform the Domestic Activities of Daily Living

There is a subgroup of the frail elderly who, although still able to attend to their personal care by retaining mobility, continence, and the ability to dress and feed themselves, are physically or mentally too frail to attend to the domestic tasks of shopping, cooking, and cleaning. Families provide considerable assistance with these jobs, but in the situation in which this is not possible or when institutionalization threatens because of stress in providing this care by the family, then community services in the form of choreworkers, home health aides, and home-delivered meals should be provided.

Other Functional Problems

Nocturia, a problem in around 60% of the elderly female population, may be precipitated by diuretics or the return of edema fluid from the limbs at night but many have an uninhibited neuropathic bladder as the underlying pathophysiologic cause. This may be helped significantly by the use of an anticholinergic agent such as flavoxate hydrochloride at night.

Constipation, a problem more often perceived than real in the community-living elderly, nevertheless can result in psychologic distress, impaction with overflow soiling, hemorrhoids, and diverticular disease. It may be managed by the maintenance of

physical activity and an adequate fluid intake and by additional dietary fiber in the form of bread or supplements. Fiber may also protect against symptomatic diverticular disease of the colon.

Around 40% of elderly females in the United Kingdom are prescribed hypnotic drugs, but insomnia is best dealt with by counseling, by the prescription of comfort measures, and by an increase in daytime activity rather than by medication.

STRATEGIES TO STRENGTHEN THE SUPPORT SYSTEM

Poverty and Inadequate Housing

The elderly, as a group, are poor. Health maintenance strategies must allow for this by providing adequate income, not just because of the correlation between poverty, poor health, and limitation of activities, but to enable the elderly to cope with major problems within the health reimbursement structure. The latter include increasing out-of-pocket expenses for medical care, the lack of funding for hearing aids, glasses, walking aids, dental care, and so forth, and the need to spend-down almost to poverty level before receiving any supplementation for long-term nursing home care.

Substandard housing has an indirect effect on the health of many elderly and results in isolation, accidents in the home, and hypothermia. Upgrading of such accommodations, therefore, should be a part of any health maintenance program. The provision of adequate sheltered housing would also act as an outlet for many of the frail elderly currently residing in intermediate-care facilities and would prevent the back-up of relatively fit people in nursing home care.

Breakdown of Family Support

Families in most western societies provide over 80% of all home health care for the elderly. However, in undertaking this caring role, they often experience significant burdens that may result in a number of adverse outcomes including psychologic distress, physical illness, family disruption, increased institutionalization, increased consumption of community resources, and, if no help is provided to them, abuse of the elderly themselves. It is, therefore, in everyone's best interests to avoid this breakdown of family support.

A number of strategies can be employed to minimize this burden although evaluative research on them is still in its early stages. There is, however, good evidence that the provision of a caregivers' informal support system is vital to the outcome and evidence is accumulating from a number of trials and demonstration projects that the provision of formal support services such as the homemaker programs are also of benefit not only in reducing stress but in preventing institutionalization.

A further type of support is to provide respite care for selected groups of stressed caregivers. For the demented, a very valuable resource is an in-home sitting service. Day care respite may also be of value particularly for the physically frail. Traditional inpatient respite care has been widely used for many years in the United Kingdom; however, there are still only descriptive studies evaluating efficacy. This efficacy is still being estimated in terms of ultimate prevention of long-term care rather than improving the quality of life of the families concerned.

Counseling is a further valuable form of support, particularly for the relatives of patients with Alzheimer's disease. One of the important goals of counseling with family caregivers is in preventing overprotection. This can result in the premature provision of community services which merely fosters dependency. A further example of overprotection is in the imposition of unnecessary rest accompanying and following minor illness, which merely worsens balance and mobility.

Loss

Death of a spouse or loved one carries a significant risk of morbidity and mortality for the bereaved. Several studies now show the benefit of bereavement counseling for the elderly; this may be considered a useful health maintenance measure. Similar support may be required for the caregivers of the demented elderly during the latter part of their illness.

Retirement has been estimated as the tenth most stressful event occurring over the life cycle. However, studies suggest that less than one-third of persons have difficulties adjusting to it. The case for the benefit of preretirement counseling is unproved although more satisfied retirees start thinking and planning for retirement at an earlier age.

Relocation Stress

There is now a sizable literature on the mortality and morbidity associated with relocation stress. Factors that seem to reduce these negative effects are the opportunity for choice, personal preparation for the move, and a perception of control in the decision-making process. Simple measures have been outlined to effect these goals. When an elderly person relocates to another person's house, social stresses should be prevented by giving advice on such matters as privacy, daily routine, financial responsibilities, and the sharing of household tasks.

REFERENCES[1]

1. Behemuka M, Hodkinson HM: Screening for hypothyroidism in elderly patients. Br Med J 2:601, 1975.
2. Canadian Task Force on the Periodic Health Examination: The periodic health examination. CMAJ 122:1, 1979.
3. Gillick MR, Serrell NA, Gillick LS: Adverse consequences of hospitalization in the elderly. Soc Sci Med 16:1033, 1982.
4. Hendricksen C, Lund E, Strengard E: Consequences of assessment and intervention among elderly people: A 3 year randomized control trial. Br Med J 289:1522, 1984.
5. Hilton T, Stanton SL: Algorithmic method for assessing urinary incontinence in elderly women. Br Med J 292:940, 1981.
6. Irvine PW, Carlson K, Adock M, et al: The value of annual medical examinations in the nursing home. J Am Geriatr Soc 32:540, 1984.
7. Isaacs B: Clinical and laboratory studies of falls in old people. Prospects for prevention. Clin Geriatr Med 1:513, 1985.
8. Jahnigen D, Hannan C, Laxson L, et al: Iatrogenic disease in hospitalized elderly veterans. J Am Geriatr Soc 30:387, 1982.
9. Jajich CL, Ostfeld AM, Freeman DH: Smoking and coronary heart disease mortality in the elderly. JAMA 252:2831, 1984.
10. Kennie DC: Health maintenance of the elderly. Clin Geriatr Med 2:53, 1986.
11. Mandelblatt J, Gopaul I, Wistreich M: Gynecological care of elderly women. Another look at papanicolau smear testing. JAMA 256:367, 1986.
12. Mangla JC, Pereira M, Murphy J: Diagnosis of occult gastrointestinal lesions by stool guaiac testing in a geriatric hospital. J Am Geriatr Soc 29:473, 1981.
13. Simberkoff MS, Cross AP, Al-Ibrahim M, et al: Efficacy of pneumococcal vaccine in high risk patients. N Engl J Med 315:1318, 1986.
14. Steel K: Iatrogenic disease on a medical service. J Am Geriatr Soc 32:445, 1984.
15. Taylor R, Ford G, Barber H: The Elderly at Risk: A Critical Review of Problems and Progress in Screening and Case Finding. Research Perspectives on Ageing 6. Age Concern Research United Kingdom, 1983.
16. Tulloch AJ, Moore V: A randomized control trial of geriatric screening and surveillance in general practice. J Roy Coll Gen Pract 29:733, 1979.
17. Vetter NJ, Jones DA, Victor CR: Effect of health visitor working with elderly patients in general practice: a randomized control trial. Br Med J 288:369, 1984.
18. Warshaw GA: Prevention and the elderly. J Fam Pract 22:119, 1986.
19. Williams EI: Characteristics of patients aged over 75 not seen during one year in general practice. Br Med J 288:119, 1984.

[1]A complete list of references for this Chapter is available from the authors.

CHAPTER 3

Functional Assessment of the Elderly Patient

RICHARD J. HAM

FUNCTION IN GERIATRICS

The maintenance of optimal function, with the individual as independent as possible, doing as much as possible physically and socially, is one of the major objectives in good geriatric care. Dysfunction in one area inevitably leads, in a downward spiral, to dysfunction in other areas. Social disruption and dislocation affect physical mobility; illnesses that inhibit mobility lead to social isolation, withdrawal, depression, and giving up. Thus *"function," the loss of it, the maintenance of it, and the promotion of it is at the core of geriatric medicine* (8, 15).

As a *presenting symptom*, modified functioning is frequently the change that brings to the attention of physician or other health professional the patient who may be suffering from one of many individual illnesses, or manifesting the cumulative effects of several interacting physical, psychologic, social, or other factors. For example, hypothyroid or Alzheimer's patients may well become manifest because they cease to go shopping. The patient developing congestive heart failure may, instead of manifesting dyspnea with exertion, simply "take to his bed." Thus, being alert to functional change (which means knowing the pre-existing functional status as accurately as possible) is necessary in order to recognize promptly a number of specific illnesses. Such promptness is known to increase the effectiveness of intervention, and to reduce the often permanent residual functional aftereffects that many episodes of acute illness leave in elderly patients.

Each individual diagnosis and problem in the elderly patient must be assessed functionally. It is the *impact of each problem* on the individual's daily life and daily functioning (and the impact of potential therapy) that will ultimately be of most significance to the patient and family, and perhaps to whomever pays the health care bill (since the most functionally dependent are ultimately, because of institutionalization, the most expensive patients). Even investigation can have permanent functional impact: the usefulness of careful diagnostic investigation of an elusive problem producing worrying symptoms, such as headache or weight loss, in an older patient, is often negated because the galaxy of individuals involved in attempting to turn over every stone fail to take cognizance of the fact that their patient, while awaiting the diagnosis, has become immobilized, stiff, and perhaps even posturally hypotensive, whilst waiting out all those tests and opinions in a hospital setting!

A functional emphasis helps to make *diagnosis* as precise as possible, since such precision will enable more rational decisions to be made about appropriate management. Part of this precision is precise characterization of the impact of the illness on daily functioning. Thus, in a patient who has clinical evidence of cerebrovascular accident, the precise cause and site of the lesion is important, but no more so than the speed and degree of recovery of movement and skill; and the impact that any residual disability will have will depend on the individual's pre-existing psychologic makeup, energy and drive, and the degree to which support and appropriate encouragement is available in the home setting. Indeed, the actual degree of recovery of strength and coordination is probably of less relevance to the overall prognosis than psychologic, environmental, and family factors. In the even more common situation of a patient with Alzheimer's disease, whereas objective mental status testing should be utilized to characterize as precisely as possible the degree of cognitive impairment, such characterization will not give the complete picture. The impact that a given degree of dementia will have on the caregiving family members or others available will depend on the functional impairment, i.e., how much the patient can (or will) do for him- or herself; this, in turn, will depend on psychologic and other factors in the patient and caregiver and their relationship. The motivation and skill of the caregiver to respond appropriately to these functional needs are major factors in determining the impact of the disease on the patient. Whether or not the caregiver encourages passivity or activity is a crucial element in determining the prognosis for dependency and the potential for institutionalization, morbidity, and mortality. Thus, in both "physical" and "mental" illness in the elderly, the functional impact on the patient and on the caregivers needs to be known and appreciated, in order to proceed logically with management.

Conventional medical management decisions are influenced by functional impact. It may not be worthwhile to treat a quite elevated blood pressure, if the functional impact of the therapy will be to the patient's detriment, even if it might influence the overall prognosis for life. Thus, treatment will often be "limited" by accepting the importance of functional considerations. Frequently, it is functional change, not improved prognosis, nor "control" of some physiologic parameter, that will be the objective of management. For example, the extremely impaired patient with chronic obstructive pulmonary disease may appear to get only marginal improvement in pulmonary function from the addition of yet another medication, yet that small improvement may make a major functional difference—maybe the patient can now manage a stair or two, and thus, move out of the room, for example.

A functional emphasis should also be maintained in the development of the *"problem list."* The naive medical model that is still generally taught in medical school of "C/O ⟶ interview ⟶ physical examination ⟶ investigations ⟶ diagnosis ⟶ treatment ⟶ recovery" is, of course, a rare scenario in most elderly patients. For them, the problem list frequently contains no "complaints" generated by the patient at all. If the job has been done well, the problem list will usually be a curious mixture of formal diagnoses, situational observations (e.g., "lives

alone"), risk factors, necessary health maintenance and screening procedures, and (last but not least) specific functional problems. These specific functional problems may be unclassifiable in traditional diagnostic nomenclatures, but they include some of the most common presenting syndromes in geriatric practice: falling, musculoskeletal stiffness, instability, etc. Thus, the problem list, by taking a functional emphasis, will indeed reflect all of the problems,—not only those perceived by the patient, and not only those graced with a "proper diagnosis," but also those problems that the physician or other team member identifies as needing their own individual management plans.

In the patient with multiple problems, a functional emphasis helps in the often complex process of *prioritization*. In deciding which of many aspects of the multiple problem patient to invest time and energy in first, to the list of facts to consider (treatability, prognosis, degree of discomfort or distress produced, danger to the patient or society at large, etc.) should be added "functional impact."

The *degree* of functional disruption produced is an important factor in management. Also, the *speed of change* of functional impairment in response to therapy is invaluable in prognosis and management. Therefore, the accurate measurement of the most commonly impaired functions is an essential skill for all health care practitioners involved in the care and management of elderly patients. To assess change, the "baseline" must be known. Thus, even in a situation where the assessment is not being made in response to emergent problems, but as a baseline for future care, as objective a measurement as is practical for the particular circumstances should be made. This chapter will detail the functional aspects of assessment, in particular with regard to impairment of the ability to carry out the ordinary activities of daily living, mental status, and the family and caregiver impacts of illness. The need to apply functional approaches, especially in relation to assessment of elderly patients for institutional placement, rehabilitation, and for their need for in-home and other community social support services will be reviewed.

COMPREHENSIVE ASSESSMENT

Justification for the need for comprehensive assessment can be found in every chapter in this book. In every organ system, as the body ages, changes insidiously take place which, although they may appear almost "normal," not only to patients but also to professionals, nonetheless warrant professional intervention for their amelioration and for management strategies to reduce their functional impact.

Many problems in the elderly are "hidden"—they are the problems that are frequently not mentioned through embarrassment, negativity, modesty or ignorance. Many important problems are not perceived by the patient, caregiver, or even professionals. The list is long, including as it does hearing loss, falling, musculoskeletal stiffness, cognitive impairment, depression, sexual dysfunction, and incontinence. The list of hidden problems thus potentially includes those disabilities that form the core of the geriatric medical care needs of the frailest elderly patients. Thus, physicians must possess sufficient knowledge about elderly health problems, must not only be good listeners, but (probably even more important) must "ask the right questions," if geriatric assessments are to achieve their full potential of elucidating all of the problems that require attention.

A system of comprehensive geriatric assessment of all older people "at risk" might be reasonable, but the quantity of work is beyond our present capabilities (although in an era of "doctor excess" it seems illogical that so little preventive or even anticipatory work is done for most elderly). For now, the situation is that all health professionals must take every opportunity given them to be as broad and all-embracing in outlook, considering the whole person in relation to their own unique environment as they practicably can be, even when they are primarily being asked to deal with only one problem or assess a situation in order to make one judgment. Table 3.1 identifies the known "risk factors" to dependency

Table 3.1
Risk Factors for Dependency and Institutionalization

Living alone
Recently relocated
Recently discharged from hospital
Recently divorced or separated
Recently bereaved
Very elderly
Poor
Of low social class
Socially isolated
Lacking relatives nearby
Incontinent
Suffering multiple problems
Experiencing major problems with mobility
Demented or otherwise mentally impaired
Depressed
Losing daily living skills
Female

and institutionalization that should provide some direction: patients with one or several of the risk factors listed should be considered for more comprehensive assessment, such as referral to a Geriatric Assessment Unit or Clinic, where available (for objectives of such assessment, see Table 3.2).

Thus, comprehensive assessment should initially be undertaken and repeated at intervals in the majority of the more frail elderly patients. Assessment efforts should naturally be focused, depending on the particular reasons for the assessment. The *primary care physician*, facing an elderly patient new to his or her practice, will need to complete a very thorough assessment over the first few office visits (and probably should complete a home visit in selected instances). The plan will be for this assessment, including the evaluation of not only the patient, but also of the caregiver, family and home situation, to be the basis for a lifelong relationship; thus, even "inactive" aspects will be included in the problem list for future reference. For the *orthopaedic surgeon* making decisions about the suitability of an older patient for knee replacement, for example, assessment aimed at giving as reasonable an indication as possible of previous functional level and the patient's capability of returning to it after surgery would be the focus of the assessment. For the *social worker* involved in decisions about institutional placement or the provision of in-home services, the patient's prognosis will be combined with judgments of the environmental suitability of the home and the ability of the family or other caregivers to cope, for appropriate decision-making. The *physiotherapist*, rightly limiting restricted professional time to those patients who will benefit most, should focus assessment on defining the patients most responsive to physical therapy (i.e., those who would be most

Table 3.2
Objectives of Elderly Assessment

The Health Professional should:
Appreciate overall functional status
Define all factors interfering with or modifying normal function
Identify all correctable factors to optimize function
Appreciate caregivers' problems and potential
Judge appropriateness of current and future environment
Objectively test the mental status
Evaluate the rehabilitation potential
Define the existing support and services available
Implement provision of other support as necessary
Evaluate overall prognosis
Construct an anticipatory plan for the future

functionally improved). In these, and in many other instances that could be quoted, the necessity for a comprehensive baseline assessment, defining all the nonpresented problems and other important features that impinge on the patient's prognosis and function, can be easily perceived. Yet such assessment is rarely achieved. The need for a functional, available, willing, personal primary care physician in whose records such comprehensive assessment information is collected, recorded and updated, appears to this author the most practical way to improve continuity and reduce the duplication and loss of direction that characterize so much elderly patient management.

The objectives of comprehensive assessment are summarized in Table 3.2.

THE TEAM

Many physicians react negatively to "the team concept." Yet it is evident that the frail elderly patient with multiple problems may well require many different professionals and services if optimal function and independence is to be achieved and maintained. Thus, it is appropriate, whenever possible, to make the comprehensive assessment of an elderly patient a collaborative information-sharing exercise, in which the various disciplines that should properly be involved in the ongoing care of the patient take part. This team assessment should ideally be done with minimal duplication and will, hopefully, lead to the development of better recognition of each professional's scope and limitations by others on the team. Such teams can be formal or informal, but function best if they consist of a number of individuals of different disciplines working together on a regular basis. The smallest team is probably the traditional pairing of physician and nurse—the latter not necessarily working "under the direction of" the former. A good alternative "basic primary care team" would be a physician and a social worker.

Many different models of a geriatric assessment unit are in existence across the United States and Canada (30, 31). Most of them focus on the most needy, frail, and threatened elderly patients and most of them utilize a multidisciplinary team for assessment and therapy. The team at the STAT (Short Term Assessment and Treatment) Centre of the Vancouver General Hospital (39), for example, consists of the following professionals, regularly working, conferencing, and rounding together: physician, social worker, nurse, occupational therapist, physical therapist, dietician, and activity aides.

Larger assessment teams such as this require coordination, involve some duplication of activity, and are bound to involve ongoing definition and redefinition of individual professionals' roles. All team members should have input—each person uniquely and individually may have an observation from their own discipline that was not fully appreciated by another. In practice, however, one discipline will frequently dominate the activities at any given time. For example, the physician may dominate when the situation is medically unstable and new therapeutic modalities are being considered, the social worker when placement and ongoing community family-supported therapy need to be arranged, the nurse when the ongoing professional handling of the patient's behaviors and functions are an issue, the occupational therapist when daily living skills must be specifically relearned or when home safety and adaptation is an issue, the physiotherapist when reacquisition of major mobility problems dominates, the activity aide when social withdrawal and the need for its resolution by activity dominates, etc.

Similar ranges of health professionals exist in most communities, but it is rare to find their activities properly coordinated. Such a coordinated "teamlike" approach would greatly help to increase the availability and comprehensiveness of assessment and care available for elders in the community.

NEEDED SERVICES

Such a multidisciplinary approach will help in the imaginative use of existing community health care services and, as important, their active development in those many areas where such services are lacking. The community health care services that are summarized in Table 3.3 should be borne in mind whenever assessment of an older person is carried out. The emphasis in the provision of all of these services should be on the maintenance of function; some services naturally do things *for* the old person, but the optimal services encourage active social and physical functions by the elders themselves. Services that maintain social functions are as important as those that maintain physical function. The renewed emphasis on volunteers and elderly self-help typifies the best of these approaches: these are programs that have the potential to improve the physical and social functioning both of the helper and the helped (11) (Table 3.4).

ACTIVITIES OF DAILY LIVING

The "*activities of daily living*" (ADL) are basic self-care activities. As has been emphasized, knowledge of such information is essential in assessing and judging change, especially in the most frail pa-

Table 3.3
Useful Community Health Care Services

In addition to the Health Professionals of the "Geriatric Team"; physician, nurse, physician assistant, nurse practitioner, social worker, home health aide, occupational and physical therapist, etc.:

Meals on Wheels
Companions and sitting services
Laundry services
Friendly and volunteer visitation
Structural alterations and repairs
Shopping services
Transportation
House maintenance
Telephone reassurance
Readers for partially sighted
High school, etc., programs
In-home equipment
Day care
Respite care
Caregiver support groups
Senior centers
Nursing programs
Alternative housing

Table 3.4
Examples of Elderly Self-Help

Retired services volunteer/programs
Foster grandparents
Skill exchange registry
Lay health coordinators
Special interest groups
Visitation of institutionalized children

tients. Few physicians, even today, are taught to incorporate inquiries about these very basic human activities into their routine of history-taking. Yet, as the population ages, all professionals will have to become skilled at routinely and objectively defining the ability to carry out the types of functions succinctly identified by Katz et al. (19): bathing, dressing, toileting, transferring, walking, continence, and feeding. These six areas of human activity, and some variations on them, are recognized as covering the basic independence-promoting activities that are frequently progressively lost in the older person as physical or mental powers decline. The loss usually occurs in the order stated (with reacquisition, if it occurs, in the reverse order). Other basic areas of ADL that might be evaluated include: communication, grooming, being able to see, and use of the upper extremities.

The terminology "*instrumental activities of daily living*" (IADL) describes the more complex activities that are necessary to lead an independent life. These include such activities as cooking, cleaning, telephoning, reading, writing, shopping, doing the laundry, managing medications, using public transportation, walking outdoors, climbing stairs, managing money, traveling out of town, and holding down a paying job.

The *Katz Index* (19) (Table 3.5) is one of many ADL scales that have been developed to measure

and record the ability of elderly patients to function independently. More widespread inquiry regarding the functions addressed in the above instruments would greatly increase the relevance of efforts to help elders, both in the health care and social service provision areas. At present, such scales are rarely used in routine primary care practice. They are increasingly used in geriatric referral or specialty units because they provide a reasonably objective measurement that aids communication; this is especially important for individuals, since transfer from place to place, or at least between professional caregivers, is so commonplace. In terms of research and the determination of community needs, use of such instruments also allows a unit to compare its data with that of other centers. These scales are not designed to be used in isolation in order to make decisions for individual patients. However, the Katz Index is sufficiently simple (and sufficiently sensitive) to be a helpful clinical adjunct for the family physician or general internist evaluating a patient. It will give a score that will have some sensitivity to change over time, thus providing documentation of functional change in response to interventions, or functional deterioration because of illness or a lack of interventions. Of equal importance, the use of such a scale routinely would allow much better comparison of one patient's status with another when functional abilities in daily living skills are a particular concern in decision-making. With limited resources, it is an unfortunate truth that the means need to be found to prioritize patients by area of need appropriately. The use of ADL scales can be seen to be one mechanism for not only increasing the emphasis on function in all management decisions, but also in adding some objectivity and comparability to such assessments.

The other major established ADL instrument is the *Barthel Index* (Table 3.6) (26). This was designed for used in rehabilitation settings, and the content of the questions tends to be more concordant with a somewhat more dependent type of patient than the Katz scale. This scale, with its carefully weighted differences between some of the

Table 3.5
Katz Index of Independence in Activities of Daily Living[a]

The Index of Independence in Activities of Daily Living is based on an evaluation of the functional independence or dependence of patients in bathing, dressing, going to the toilet, transferring, continence and feeding. Specific definitions of functional independence and dependence are provided.

A. Independent in feeding, continence, transferring, going to the toilet, dressing and bathing.
B. Independent in all but one of these functions.
C. Independent in all but bathing and one additional function.
D. Independent in all but bathing, dressing, and one additional function.
E. Independent in all but bathing, dressing, going to the toilet and one additional function.
F. Independent in all but bathing, dressing, going to the toilet, transferring and one additional function.
G. Dependent in all six functions.
Other Dependent in at least two functions not classifiable as C, D, E or F.

Independence refers to the ability to function without supervision, direction or active personal assistance, except as specifically noted in the definitions. This is based on actual status and not ability. Patients who refuse to perform a function are considered not able to perform the function even though they are deemed able.

Bathing (sponge, shower or tub)
Independent: assistance only in bathing a single part (such as the back of a disabled extremity) or bathes self completely
Dependent: assistance in bathing more than one part of the body; assistance in getting in or out of the tub or does not bathe self

Dressing
Independent: gets clothes from closets and drawers; puts on clothes, outer garments; manages fasteners; act of tying shoes is excluded
Dependent: does not dress self or remains partly undressed

Toileting
Independent: gets to the toilet; gets on and off the toilet; arranges clothes, cleans organs of excretion (may manage own bedpan used only at night and may use mechanical supports)
Dependent: uses bedpan or commode or receives assistance in getting to the toilet and using it

Transferring
Independent: moves in and out of the bed independently; moves in and out of the chair independently (may use mechanical supports)
Dependent: assistance in moving in or out of the bed and/or chair; does not perform one or more transfers

Continence
Independent: urination and defecation entirely self-controlled
Dependent: partial or total incontinence in urination or defecation; partial or total control by enemas or catheters or regulated use of urinals and/or bedpans

Feeding
Independent: gets food from the plate or its equivalent into the mouth (precutting of meat and preparation of food, such as buttering bread, are excluded from evaluation)
Dependent: assistance needed in act of feeding; does not eat at all or uses parenteral feeding

[a]From Katz S, et al: Progress in development of the index of ADL. *Gerontologist* 10: 20, 1970.

defined aspects of function (reflected in the differential scores given for different aspects depending on their importance) has been modified into a self-care index (33). These Barthel indices are probably more sensitive in terms of showing change than is the Katz, which remains probably the most widely regarded and utilized ADL score presently in use.

These measures of ADL functioning, and many other instruments for measuring the elderly, have been critically reviewed (18). Physicians working in special units devoted to the elderly should be aware of the many other instruments that are available, particularly the Kenny Self-Care Evaluation (32), which, although it excludes continence, is quite sensitive to change (it rates 17 activities on a 4-point scale in six categories) and the widely validated

OARS: Physical Health (7). Some individual states already use ADL scores in assessing individual patient's needs (e.g., in New York State, the PRI: Patient Review Instrument). New federal nursing home regulations presently in process probably will recommend wider use of such scales; hopefully, validated instruments will be used so that comparable data will be obtained in the different states. This will help individual patient management when there is transfer between states and will encourage meaningful data collection.

Several questionnaires exist to measure the equally practical information implied by the term instrumental activities of daily living. A brief IADL measure (by Fillenbaum) that has been recently published holds promise, in view of its brevity, as a

Table 3.6
Barthel Index[a]

Activities Rated	Scoring	
	Independent	With Assistance
Feeding (if food needs to be cut-help)	10	5
Moving from wheelchair to bed (includes sitting up in bed)	15	10–5
Personal toilet (wash face, comb hair, shave, clean teeth)	5	0
Getting on and off toilet (handling clothes, wipe, flush)	10	5
Bathing self	5	0
Walking on level surface	15	10
Propel wheelchair (score only if unable to walk)	5	0
Ascend and descend stairs	10	5
Dressing (includes tying shoes, fastening fasteners)	10	5
Controlling bowels	10	5
Controlling bladder	10	5

[a]From Mahoney FI, Barthel DW: Functional evaluation: The Barthel Index. *Md State Med J* 61: 5, 1965.

useful, reproducible means of recording such aspects, especially useful for the clinician (9). This is reproduced in Table 3.7.

Several other IADL instruments are available, and the Lawton (23) and OARS IADL (7) are good examples. Choice of questionnaire and questions obviously depends again on the purpose of the assessment.

The accuracy of any such estimate by these instruments depends on the honesty of the reading; clearly, asking the patient is not enough. Asking a relative may be inaccurate, too—they may be positively or negatively biased in their opinions. Even observing an elderly person carry out a particular activity may not give much useful information if the circumstances bear little relationship to the environment to which he or she will return. One scale, the Performance ADL (PADL) (22), uniquely includes props, so that the estimate of skills is more standardized. Detailed review of the instruments is beyond the scope of this chapter, but should be done by those involved in complex geriatric assessment in special units, and by those who are regularly involved in decisions based on a patient's functional skills. Major examples of the latter are decisions to place in long-term institutional care and decisions regarding prescription of supportive home services. A recent thoughtful review by Applegate (3) wisely counsels the clinical care provider in the use of appropriate instruments to answer the questions and concerns of relevance in the particular assessment situation involved. Many ADL, IADL, and other instruments (especially those rating social function) were not designed as clinical care adjuncts or are designed for whole populations rather than individual patients.

HOME VISITS

A visit to the home is an essential step in the assessment of many elderly persons (6, 13, 14). Home visits are also required for the proper ongoing care of many less mobile, or less willing, elderly patients. The extra information that might be obtained from a visit to the patient's home, information that will not be fully or accurately obtained in an office or institutional setting, is summarized in Table 3.8.

It is in the home that the most objective assessment of the patient's functional level and the suitability of the home environment can be obtained. One of the objectives of good geriatric care—the maintenance of independent function in a familiar environment for as long as possible—could be greatly expedited by an increased emphasis on home care by physicians and other health professionals.

It is in the home that the other people in the elder's life are seen in context. The likely results of a medical emergency, and the appropriateness of modifications both in services and in the physical environment of the home, can be seen firsthand. The physical aspects of the home and its safety are within the range of the particular skills of the occupational therapist, who should be used much more often than at present to assist in appropriate environmental modifications to keep elders at home.

Important assessment information can be affirmed or refuted by the home visit. Nutritional and alcohol habits, both important considerations in many diagnostic situations (and notoriously difficult to assess), can often be quickly deduced by a perceptive look in the kitchen and the rest of the house. Medication compliance can be assessed, and sometimes previously unrecognized medical problems, such as incontinence, will be made evident.

Table 3.7
Fillenbaum: Brief IADL Measure[a]

1. Can you get to places out of walking distance?
   1 Without help (can travel alone on buses or taxis or drive your own car)
   0 With some help (need someone to help you or go with you when traveling), or are you unable to travel unless emergency arrangements are made for a specialized vehicle like an ambulance?
   – Not answered

2. Can you go shopping for groceries or clothes (assuming the patient has transportation)?
   1 Without help (take care of all shopping needs yourself, assuming you had transportation)
   0 With some help (need someone to go with you on all shopping trips), or are you completely unable to do any shopping?
   – Not answered

3. Can you prepare your own meals?
   1 Without help (plan and cook full meals yourself)
   0 With some help (can prepare some things but are unable to cook full meals yourself), or are you completely unable to prepare any meals?
   – Not answered

4. Can you do your housework?
   1 Without help (can scrub floors, etc.)
   0 With some help (can do light housework but need help with heavy work), or are you completely unable to do any housework?
   – Not answered

5. Can you handle your own money?
   1 Without help (write checks, pay bills, etc.)
   0 With some help (manage day-to-day buying but need help with managing your checkbook and paying your bills), or are you completely unable to handle money?
   – Not answered

[a]From Fillenbaum GG: Screening the elderly. A brief instrumental activities of daily living measures. *J Am Geriatr Soc* 33: 698, 1985.

Table 3.8
Extra Assessment Information from the Home Visit

Suitability and safety of home for patient's functional level
Patient's nutritional, alcoholic, and smoking habits
Attitudes and presence of other persons in the home
Proximity and helpfulness of neighbors and relatives
Emergency assistance arrangements
Actual and required daily living skills
Patient's hygiene habits
Patient's medication compliance
Presence or absence of safety and convenience modifications
Previously unrecognized medical problems

A home visit is probably indicated as part of the assessment in any patient showing one or more of the risk factors summarized in Table 3.1. The other special situations where a home visit is probably indicated are summarized in Table 3.9.

MENTAL STATUS

Global impairment of cerebral function is very common in the elderly and is important in assessing and prognosticating for the patient's future. Therefore, not only physicians but also all other health professionals (and even nonprofessionals who will be involved) should be familiar with techniques to assess mental status objectively.

Assessment of mental status involves an interviewer asking specific testing questions regarding memory, judgment, orientation, abstract thinking, etc., to "test" the patient's mental functioning. The most utilized instruments to accomplish this will be described in this chapter and their place in making such assessments clarified. They should probably be used far more widely. However, assessing the effective level of mental function of a patient is much more subtle than merely asking a set of questions from a prepared questionnaire. Patients of formerly high academic achievement may score well on screening tests; the tests are not absolute proof in and of themselves of disability or ability. Professionals caring for the elderly must develop sensitivity to the multitude of subtle ways in which deteriorating cognitive function, either acutely, implying a possible delirium, or more chronically, implying a probable dementia (which is probably going to be Alzheimer's disease), may be manifested. Patients with either of these major syndromes of diminished cognitive functioning often present because of functional change; for example, the relatives note that the patient has ceased going shopping, refuses to go out, or complains of tiredness or weakness. Often, there is an apparent personality change, perhaps with a loss of humor, or irritability, or just a vague

Table 3.9
Indications for the Home Visit

Major mobility problems
Recently began living alone
Mental impairment sufficient to interfere with daily living
Presence of several dependency risk factors
History of accidents and/or falling
Progressive dementia
Imminent institutionalization
Imminent hospital discharge with incomplete recovery
Recent hospital discharge (in most cases)

sense of "something wrong," which will often precede by weeks formal recognition of the nature of the disability (20). It is at this stage of rather nonspecific presentation that formal mental status testing has its place as an adjunct to the clinical acumen that leads to the realization that dementia or delirium (or depression) may underlie many of these sometimes psychologic, and often more physical-sounding, presenting scenarios.

COGNITIVE FUNCTION

Patients with dementia often retain social graces and skill until surprisingly late in their illness, and frequently can "rise to the occasion" when, for example, their beleaguered relatives finally persuade them to see the doctor. Ordinary history-taking, examination, and conversation may reveal no problems unless formal questions to test orientation, memory, abstract thought, and other cognitive skills are undertaken.

Many physicians, skilled and adept at asking the right questions and combining the art of "listening to the patient" with the art of asking the right questions, nonetheless feel constrained and awkward when asking "formal," test-type questions. It could certainly be inappropriate to jump clumsily into obvious test questions with a patient who has clearly demonstrated his or her mental ability in the interview and whose history, even from the relatives, gives no indication of much possibility of cognitive impairment. However, a skilled interviewer usually can smooth the transition, perhaps by frankly stating that a formal test is now going to be done, and by separating the formal test from the conversational part of the interview. It is more likely that the more widespread use of such formal questionnaires will produce increased objective and useful information than it will cause embarrassment for the physician or patient.

Because of the tendency for cognitive impairment to be missed easily, many physicians increasingly use at least parts of one or other of the major validated mental status tests that are now used virtually routinely in most formal geriatric referral centers and in geriatric research. These two mental status questionnaires are Folstein's Mini-Mental Status Examination (10) (Table 14.2) and Pfeiffer's Short Portable Mental Status Questionnaire (SPMSQ) (29) (Table 14.3).

One of the most clearcut criteria for dementia is "progressive decline" over time (27). Such decline can only be recorded and tested objectively and adequately by the use of formal mental status testing, repeated at intervals. This may, therefore, provide diagnostic clarification.

When issues arise concerning trusteeship, committeeship, or testamentary capacity, it is of great value to have such a validated instrument recorded with its results on the patient's chart.

These short mental status questionnaires then become useful screening tools to pick out those cognitively impaired patients who might otherwise go undetected and to provide objective and recordable evidence of mental status and its deterioration. These can be useful diagnostically, legally, and in making comparisons of patients or groups of patients with one another for research or clinical planning purposes. They have limitations, however, and are truly an "adjunct" to skilled clinical evaluation.

The *SPMSQ* (Table 14.3) (29) has been extensively utilized and studied; norms have been developed to aid in the interpretation of the score, from 0–10. It covers orientation and memory, including remote ("mother's maiden name") as well as essential survival skills (remembering the telephone number and street address). It also assesses mathematical ability. Pfeiffer (29) has developed norms which can be adjusted for race and education—an advantage over other short questionnaires. This test should be regarded as a useful screening test for the purposes mentioned above.

The *Mini-Mental State Examination* (Table 14.2) (10) also measures cognitive function. It has been tested with nonhealth professionals asking the questions and has been found reliable. It takes 5–10 minutes to administer and, although some of it has the feel of "psychologic testing," it generally fits well into the context of clinical history-taking and examination. It has become the most widely used mental status test.

As well as questions similar to those in SPMSQ that test orientation, the examination formally tests short-term memory and attests to language and writing abilities, drawing, and the ability to remember and act on a simple sequence of tasks ("the three-stage command") somewhat more comprehensively than the SPMSQ. Patients with visual problems or physical impairment to writing or the performance of this three-stage command may be unfairly biased against. Both instruments bias against institutionalized patients who are clearly "forgivable" for losing track of the date and day in the absence of the usual cues. However, the good clinician can reasonably take such factors into account.

This instrument does distinguish between patients with diagnoses of dementia, depression and schizophrenia. Patients who are depressed but are cognitively impaired ["pseudodementia" as Wells described it (35)] do show improvements on their mini-mental status as their depression improves.

Several other mental status tests exist (17, 24), a full description of which is beyond the scope of this review. They may be particularly indicated in cases of diagnostic doubt or in situations where the patient has some of the barriers mentioned which might have biased their score.

Once the diagnosis of the major illness producing the cognitive impairment has been made (not always Alzheimer's disease), there are some scales that are useful in objectively recording the level of deterioration (5, 16). For those working regularly with such patients, they may add objectivity to the clinical assessment of the patient and allow easier comparison between patients and centers.

AFFECTIVE FUNCTION

Whereas declining cognitive function lends itself effectively to formal questioning and scoring, it is unfortunate that the other major area of mental functioning to be assessed objectively, i.e., affective function (mainly the issue of whether or not depression is present), is not so satisfactory. Various questionnaires, including self-assessment ones, have sought to reliably demonstrate the often extraordinarily occult changes that might imply the presence of depression. Depression is, of course, an illness that is much missed in the elderly, a common illness, and one that mimics and, in particular, complicates many conditions.

Despite the work on the well-regarded Zung Self-rating Depression Scale (SDS) (41) and the Beck Depression Inventory (4), it is generally still true in practice that most clinicians prefer a clinical history-taking technique with observation of the patient as their criteria for the evaluation of the individual patient and for the assessment of whether or not depression is present. Fairly abrupt functional change, combined with some of the symptoms that characterize older patients' depressions should be particular signals (28). Further discussion of the diagnosis of depression is beyond the scope of this review.

THE CAREGIVER

If available, other family members or other caregivers provide essential information about the patient's history, symptoms, and function. Whereas the caregiver's contribution is inevitably biased, either positively or negatively, it nonetheless provides an essential, corroborative view. Whereas the wise professional will always listen to the patient, he or she will soon realize that, in providing good geriatric

care, time can be saved and objectives more quickly achieved by routinely involving the caregiver in such ways. Particularly when an elderly patient becomes institutionalized, the opportunity is frequently missed to tap the existing caregiver's wisdom about the patient, his or her likes or dislikes, particular characteristics or ways of managing certain situations. All those involved in nursing home care should be aware of this and should involve themselves with the existing caregiver when they are called on to take over.

But just as much as contributing to the assessment, so, too, is the caregiver being assessed. In many geriatric situations, an especially good example being Alzheimer's disease, the qualities, skills, and knowledge of the caregiver are essential determinants in the future fate of the patient (12). If available, a good caregiver can be the therapeutic tool to implement one of the underlying goals of geriatric care—the maintenance of optimal function, despite disability. Clinical experience shows that, in many instances, it is failure of caregiver skill in managing behavioral problems, or, as so often occurs, overburdening of the caregiver, that ultimately often leads to hospitalization or institutional care, perhaps earlier than was necessary.

The most challenging situations in the elderly are those in which the patient is irrevocably deteriorating, functionally, physically, and/or mentally. The negativity that such a month-by-month, increasing burden adds to the already-present stress on the caregiver is but one of the reasons why the caregivers's own perception of their burden or stress, is an important factor to assess objectively. The relief of caregiver burden is also one of the aims of geriatric care. Thus, it is of interest that attempts have been made, notably by Zarit (40) and Kosberg (21) to quantify such observations of caregiver stress by the use of developed instruments. As with the ADL indices, for the practicing clinician, it may not be appropriate to score such instruments numerically. Undoubtedly, though, greater attention to caregiver burden and its relief should be given, especially in those situations where either the state of the patient is particularly challenging, or where the caregiver, for whatever reason, is particularly vulnerable.

Aspects of patients that caregivers find especially *stressful* include: disturbed nights, uncontrolled aggression, wandering and falling, uncontrolled incontinence, and the inability to walk without assistance. The first of these, disturbed nights, stands out: a question about the state of sleep is essential in any "review of symptoms" in the elderly.

Aspects of caregivers that make them especially *vulnerable* to stress include: their own frailty (caregivers are frequently of a comparable age to, or older than, the "patient"), alcoholism, depression (both of these possibly interrelated to the stress itself), other "caregiving demands" (e.g., the caregiver's own spouse, or younger family), and, in this author's experience, the set of qualities, whether they be martyrdom or impatience, that lead to the type of care that actually induces dependence rather than encouraging increased or maintained function (i.e., the caring person who "does things for" rather than encouraging the patient's own efforts).

Thus, the assessment of the caregiver should particularly address these issues, look for these risk factors, and recognize the potential, and limitations, of caregivers as the therapeutic agents that they may be for the maintenance of independent function.

The involvement of the caregiver in assessment for institutionalization is of particular note, so intertwined are the feelings of guilt and burden with the decision to seek institutional care. These factors link in with the frequently observed withdrawal, once the patient is "off the hands" of the caregiver.

SOCIAL FUNCTION

Assessing the caregiver is but one aspect of the overall social functioning of the patient, and it is well-accepted that social functioning interacts with physical illness and psychologic problems, often in a "vicious circle," one problem begetting another, and another. The elder with a diminished social circle will lack the necessary backup to implement plans that involve mobility, function, health maintenance, and may lack flexibility for planning when physical frailty or mental frailty makes it necessary for help to be provided for daily activities.

Formally and succinctly measuring and scoring social functioning, in the way that a Folstein or an SPMSQ measure and score cognitive function, is not possible, although attempts have been made. Social functioning is too broad and comprehensive an aspect of life, too uniquely tied in with the person's own ethnic background and unique situation, to make it measurable in such standardized ways. The family APGAR (34) is an interesting screening instrument designed for family physicians to record family health systematically. The social dysfunction rating scale (SDRS) (25) and others all attempt to rate the combination of social interaction, in quantity and quality, to record objectively the availability of the social circle to the individual patient.

Such scales represent part of much sociologic research that has frequently revealed concrete data about social functioning that runs counter to the illness-oriented images that many health profes-sionals have of the elderly. The current impression that families do not care for, and reject, their elders, for example, or that families are not as involved as they used to be "in the old days" are common pervasive myths. Objective study of families and others and their relationships to elders has disproved these myths.

For the practicing primary care health professional, simple, subjective and nonquantitative measurements of social functioning are adequate. Table 3.10 summarizes some of the content that a minimal social assessment might include.

REHABILITATION POTENTIAL

The emphasis on function, obtaining good baseline data about ability to perform ADLs and IADLs, and realistic objective assessment of mental status, home environment, and caregiver's capabilities, (in other words, everything discussed so far in this account) all have their place in providing essential information when consideration is being given to a patient's potential for rehabilitation (38).

There is an accumulated wisdom concerning the qualities of patient, environment, and caregiver which make them "good" or "bad" candidates for rehabilitation efforts when function has abruptly deteriorated because of some major event, especially major trauma and fracture of the hip, and, of course, the completed stroke. Detailed discussion of the factors that influence the prognosis for such individual situations is beyond the scope of this chapter, but the importance not only of the patient's mental status, but also their motivation and outlook on life, and the same qualities in those around them (not only lay caregivers, but also the members of the therapeutic team) will all count for a great deal in the prognosis for degree and speed of recovery. Experience shows that the speed of recovery of function

Table 3.10
Brief Social Assessment

Content of average day for the patient
Quality and frequency of social contacts
Abilities in activities of daily living
Suitability and safety of home
Proportion of time spent outside the home
Availability, attitude and health of caregivers and neigh-
  bors
Availability of emergency help
Services received and/or needed
Transportation needs
Financial status
Occupational history and interests

(i.e., not in response to the recovery or progression of pathologic process) is of prognostic significance. Thus, the patient who is already making great strides toward coping with the residual disability of a stroke, should indeed have major rehabilitation efforts made. Alternatively, the patient who is "giving up" may well indeed have a poorer prognosis. Of course, a depression may be present in the latter group of patients, for example, and comprehensive efforts must be made to correct anything that might be inducing apathy in such a situation. It is recognized that different pre-existing personality types are important when a patient is challenged by a new disability—pleasant, affable, passive people may be "delightful" or "easy to handle," and aggressive, disgruntled, complaining, angry patients may turn off everybody on the team. However, it is the latter personality type that probably has more potential, more energy to be redirected toward the reacquisition of physical skills than the former. "Discontinuing" physical therapy is a major decision. Immobility induces apathy, as does hospitalization; reasonable efforts must be made to break into this circle. The recovery for some older patients is *very* slow (see below), even though it may be ultimately nearly complete.

In assessing speed of recovery, objective measurement of the skills of daily living will obviously provide much better evidence than any quantity of descriptive prose concerning the patient's abilities. Also, inevitably such patients must have their care divided up between different institutions, different teams of people, so that progress over time, particularly if it is very slow (as is so often seen in the very frail, who are recovering, but so slowly that the improvement can hardly be perceived on a day-to-day or even week-to-week basis) *must* have objective ADL measurements done serially so that communication of skills can be achieved between the different individuals therapeutically involved and the change can be recorded objectively. These same comments apply when the objective of the physical therapy is not improvement but maintenance of function.

NEED FOR SUPPORTIVE SERVICES

The same rationale described for assessment of the provision of rehabilitative services applies to decisions about who should receive, given the limited nature of such resources, supportive, generally community-based, services, such as those summarized in Tables 3.3 and 3.4.

Nowhere in North America have comprehensive efforts been made to ensure the "case finding" approach that has developed over the years in some parts of the United Kingdom, as described by Sir Ferguson Anderson (1, 2). The provision of services is still frequently sporadic, varying from community to community, but, even within the community, the methods by which patients gain access to such services are very variable. It should not always be that only the patients who are their own best advocates, or who happen to have caregivers or personal physicians who are good advocates, should be the ones to obtain services. The frequent unawareness that the most at risk elders of a community have of their own needs, and their own potential, mandate that those organizing such services make reasonable attempts to ensure that those receiving them are indeed those in particular need, as well as those who will respond best.

Frequently, essential support services are administered by, and decisions about their provision are made by, dedicated individuals who nonetheless have little formal training either about the elderly or about the rationale for clinical decision-making. (This may not remain so, but is still often true.) Professionals should be helping such individuals to set appropriate priorities and to understand the nature and importance of having objectives and goals for any such intervention. For example, in designing a senior citizens center, is the objective just to feed people or will there be an attempt to improve function? Will such a center be very biased to those most motivated to come, thus potentially excluding the unmotivated but needy? If home-based nutrition is to be provided, will the meals just be delivered, as with Meals on Wheels, or is there to be an attempt to educate the isolated elder in good nutritional habits?

It can be seen that, at community and local levels, the assessment of need for services in individuals is necessarily closely linked with the development of appropriate services in the community itself. Many community services and projects have been utilized very widely, and, although scientific study of their impact has, for all kinds of valid reasons, been scant, there is easily enough accumulated worldwide wisdom to support the usefulness, in selected cases, of many of the services and the activities listed in Tables 3.3 and 3.4 to improve the quality of life of elders. Some of these services will improve the elders' potential to function independently for longer than would otherwise have been possible in the home setting.

NEED FOR PREVENTIVE MEASURES

An aspect that is easily missed, especially in a patient weighed down with multiple medical problems, is an emphasis on prevention, and indeed on the promotion of health, despite concurrent disability. In reviewing every problem, and in looking at the functional impact of every problem, the professional must look to ways in which future difficulties can be prevented and function can be improved or at least maintained. Such preventive measures clearly go beyond the formal problem list because they include many aspects of which patient and caregiver may be quite unaware.

INSTITUTIONALIZATION

When institutional placement of an elderly patient is about to take place, it is absolutely essential that everyone involved, especially the personal physician, review all aspects of the case. It is ideal if this is done well in advance of placement. Unfortunately, a comprehensive, functional assessment has frequently never been properly achieved until it is clear that long-term care placement in a nursing home setting is imminent (36). It has long been believed that many elderly patients are cared for at a higher degree institutionally than would be necessary if all appropriate community support and rehabilitative services had been made comprehensively available. As many as 40–50% of older people may be located in settings inappropriate to their needs; "usually this is the case in institutional settings which provide more intensive services than the person needs" (37). So, faced with a patient for whom the caregivers, for example, are requesting urgent placement, the health professional's first duty must be to ask whether it is actually necessary for this move to be made at this time, or whether it can at least be postponed by the provision of comprehensive services in the home setting.

Once it is clear that the patient will indeed need to be placed, then the functional assessment has modified objectives. The facility to be chosen must be chosen with care. The particular behavioral and physical characteristics of the patient, their religious preferences, alcohol habits, the quality of the relationship with potentially visiting family, their need for privacy or companionship, for physical or rehabilitative therapy, and, in particular, their need for supervision and direction, are all factors that should be considered and related to the potential environment to which the person is to be moved. Very frail and forgetful older people can achieve remarkable independence in an institutional setting, provided the institution itself is not large and impersonal, and provided the staff and environment combine to produce something with which the person can become familiar and comfortable and secure.

The choice of institution also interrelates to the difficult issue of assessing the patient's real prognosis, not only in terms of morbidity and mortality, but also in terms of degree of dependency and mental frailty expected over the coming period of months or years. Institutional placement should, if possible, only have to take place once. Relocation stress is a real phenomenon, and sometimes produces a permanent reduction in the person's functional status (especially if unwise exhibition of tranquillizing medications, not discontinued as soon as possible, is undertaken). The potential management disaster of a frail and forgetful older patient having to undergo several "relocations" as their function deteriorates and their nursing and supervisory needs change, is to be avoided if at all possible by seeking institutional placement that will accommodate the patients likely (or inevitable) deterioration. Far too often, placement is achieved in a rush, without careful consideration of whether it is absolutely necessary at that time for that patient, and in particular without careful consideration of what this will mean for the patient months and years down the road.

While emphasizing the desirability of maintaining a person in the home setting, it must be recognized that institutionalization is entirely appropriate for many patients. Often the negativity of health professionals in the community toward institutional care interacts with the guilt of the family. Even though appropriate, inevitable institutionalization occurs, it is seen so negatively that the best efforts are not made to make the process work effectively. Family members, overcome with guilt, may be troublesome to nursing home staff, or may withdraw altogether rather than visit their relative in a place that makes them uncomfortable. Thus, provided the decision has been well made, institutionalization should be approached positively.

Assessment of the patient for institutional placement involves, then, the recognition that such placement is part of the continuum of care for the patient and the family. Neither physician nor family must feel that this is a terminal decision. Both should remain very active in management, encouraging as much independence and mobility as possible, and enrichment of life within the nursing home. Ongoing ways to improve nursing home lifestyle, ways that the personal physician and the family can encourage, include: getting the resident dressed and walking as much as possible, out of the bedroom; encouraging the sharing of abilities and past experiences with others; looking carefully at room sharing; encouraging volunteering within the facility; fostering appropriate weekend visitation with the family;

shopping and group trips; facilitating some privacy; considering pets; and, in particular, ensuring the "personalization" of the resident's own particular space, with photographs of the person as they were, personal mementos, objects that will encourage people to talk about the person, and, through health reminiscence, to activate their long-term memory and enrich their life experiences. Achieving these objectives involves careful working by the physician and family with the nursing home staff—the development of yet another "team" (14).

SUMMARY

There is a central need to focus on function when comprehensively assessing elderly patients, because of its significance diagnostically, because its maintenance and improvement (if possible) are of overriding importance to patients and their families, and because of its importance in practicing, prognosticating, and planning therapy, both for individual patients and for populations. Health professionals must continue to work toward a teamlike approach to seek out the needy and implement the services that will allow the maintenance of the dignity of independence, preferably in the patient's own familiar home environment, for as long as practicable. The present system, especially in its complexity of funding, is often a barrier to these altruistic but achievable aims.

REFERENCES

1. Anderson F: Geriatric medicine, a practical methodology. In Ham R (ed): Geriatric Medicine Annual 1987. Oradell NJ, Medical Economic Books, 1987.
2. Anderson F: Organization of health care services for the elderly. J Am Geriatr Soc 34:240, 1986.
3. Applegate W: Use of assessment instruments in clinical settings. J Am Geriatr Soc 35:45, 1987.
4. Beck A, Ward C, Mendelson M, et al: An inventory for measuring depression. Arch Gen Psychiatr 4:53, 1961.
5. Blessed G, Tomlinson B, Roth M: Association between quantitative measures of dementia and of senile change in the cerebral grey matter of elderly subjects. Br J Psychiatr 114:797, 1968.
6. Burton J: The house call: An important service for the frail elderly. J Am Geriatr Soc 33:291, 1985.
7. Duke University Center for the Study of Aging and Human Development: Multidimensional Functional Assessment, The OARS Methodology. Durham, Duke University, 1978.
8. Feigenbaum L: Geriatric medicine and the elderly patient. In Krupp M, Chatton M (eds): Current Medical Diagnosis and Treatment 1984. Los Altos, Lange, 1984.
9. Fillenbaum G: Screening the elderly. A brief instrumental activities of daily living measure. J Am Geriatr Soc 33:698, 1985.
10. Folstein M, Folstein S, McHugh P: Mini-mental state: A practical method for grading the cognitive state of patients for the clinician. J Psychiatr Res 12:187, 1975.
11. Ham R: Alternatives to institutionalization. Am Fam Phys 21:95, 1980.
12. Ham R: Alzheimer's and the family. In Ham R (ed): Geriatric Medicine Annual 1987. Oradell NJ, Medical Economics Books, 1987.
13. Ham R: Getting the most out of a home visit. Can Fam Phys 32:2677, 1986.
14. Ham R: Home and nursing home care of the dependent elderly patient. Am Fam Phys 31:163, 1985.
15. Ham R, Holtzman J, Marcy M, et al: Evaluation of the elderly patient. In Ham RJ, et al (eds): Primary Care Geriatrics. Boston, John Wright-PSG, 1983, pp. 58–66.
16. Hersch E, Kral V, Palmer R: Clinical value of the London Psychogeriatric Rating Scale. J Am Geriatr Soc 26:348, 1978.
17. Kahn R, Goldfarb A, Pollack M, et al: Brief objective measures for the determination of mental status in the aged. Am J Psychiatr 117:326, 1960.
18. Kane R, Kane R: Assessing the Elderly: A Practical Guide to Measurement Lexington, D.C. Heath, 1981.
19. Katz S, Ford A, Moskowitz R, et al: Studies of illness in the aged. The index of ADL: a Standardized measure of biological and psychosocial function. JAMA 185:94, 1963.
20. Katzman R: Alzheimer's disease. N Engl J Med 314:964, 1986.
21. Kosberg J (ed): Abuse and Maltreatment of the Elderly: Causes and Interventions. Boston, John Wright-PSG, 1983.
22. Kuriansky J, Gurland B: Performance test of activities of daily living. Int J Aging Hum Devel 7:343, 1976.
23. Lawton M: Assessing the competence of older people. In Kent D, Castenbaum R, Sherwood S (eds): Research Planning and Action for the Elderly. New York, Behavioral Publications, 1972.
24. Libow L: A rapidly administered, easily remembered mental status evaluation: FROMAJE. In Libow L, Sherman F (eds): The Core of Geriatric Medicine. St. Louis, CV Mosby, 1981.
25. Linn M, Sculthorpe W, Evje M, et al: A social dysfunction rating scale. J Psychiatr Res 6:299, 1969.
26. Mahoney F, Barthel D: Functional evaluation: The Barthel index. Md State Med J 14:61, 1965.
27. McKhann G, Drachman D, Folstein M, et al: Clinical diagnosis of Alzheimer's disease. Neurology 34:934, 1984.
28. Moore J: The new antidepressants. In Ham R (ed): Geriatric Medicine Annual 1986. Oradell NJ, Medical Economics Books, 1986.
29. Pfeiffer E: A short portable mental status questionnaire for the assessment of organic brain deficit in elderly patients. J Am Geriatr Soc 23:433, 1975.
30. Robertson D, Christ L, Stalder L: Geriatric assessment unit in a teaching hospital. Can Med Assoc J 126:1060, 1982.

31. Rubenstein L, Josephson K, Wieland G, et al: Effectiveness of a geriatric evaluation unit: A randomized clinical trial. *N Eng J Med* 311:1664, 1983.

32. Schoening H, Iversen I: Numerical scoring of self-care status: A study of the Kenny self-care evaluation. *Arch Phys Med Rehabil* 49:221, 1968.

33. Sherwood S, Morris J, Mor V, et al: *Compendium of Measures for Describing and Assessing Long Term Care Populations.* Boston, Hebrew Rehabilitation Center for Aged, 1977 (mimeographed).

34. Smilkstein G: The family APGAR: A proposal for a family function test and its use by physicians. *J Fam Prac* 6:123, 1978.

35. Wells C: Pseudodementia. *Am J Psychiatr* 36:895, 1979.

36. Williams T, Hill J, Fairbank M, et al: Appropriate placement of the chronically ill and aged: A successful approach by evaluation. *JAMA* 226:1332, 1973.

37. Williams T: Assessment of the geriatric patient in relation to needs for services and facilities. In Reichel W (ed): *Clinical Aspects of Aging*, 2nd ed. Baltimore, Williams & Wilkins, 1983.

38. Williams T (ed): *Rehabilitation in the Aging.* New York, Raven Press, 1984.

39. Wolochow M, Ham R: The geriatric day hospital: A Canadian experience. *Can Fam Phys* 32:2625, 1986.

40. Zarit SH, Reever KE, Bach-Petersen J: Relatives of the impaired elderly: Correlates of feelings of burden. *Gerontologist* 20:649, 1980.

41. Zung W: A self-rating depression scale. *Arch Gen Psychiatr* 12:63, 1965.

CHAPTER 4

Drugs and the Elderly

JUDITH K. JONES

The topic of drugs in the elderly is broad and a central concern in geriatrics. Drug therapy in this age group acquires a greater importance because of several factors. Most elderly are taking medicines, frequently more than one. They often get them from multiple providers and sources (including nonmedical). They are costly, they often are changed, and patients may or may not take them. Finally, drugs are likely to be significant sources of ilatrogenic disease in this group.

The elderly as a group represent a highly diverse group of individuals with changing physiology and, thus, variable kinetics and dynamics in the handling of drugs. Therefore, the use of drugs in the elderly is a therapeutic challenge that taps the knowledge and resources of what we have learned in clinical pharmacology in recent years about the pharmacokinetics and pharmacodynamics of drugs. In addition, there are a large number of disorders that are often being treated with multiple drugs. This presents a separate challenge in the actual management of a complex therapeutic regimen that will avoid drug interactions and assure optimal compliance by the patient.

This chapter will consider first, briefly, the epidemiology of drug use in the elderly. This will include consideration of the extensive use of drugs by the elderly, and of studies that describe what is known thus far about the problems with drug reactions and interactions. Second will be a consideration of the physiologic changes that occur in the aging as they relate to pharmacokinetics and pharmacodynamics, and the practicalities of adhering to a drug regimen. Third will be a general discussion of how therapy can be optimized. This will consider the need for therapeutic goals, ways of improving compliance, and avoiding adverse reactions and interactions. The chapter concludes with a brief review of some of the major therapeutic classes of drugs used

in the elderly, including cardiovascular agents, antidiabetics, and nonsteroidal anti-inflammatory agents. Since several texts and reviews on geriatric pharmacology are available (6, 28, 49, 54), there is no attempt to discuss the entire range of drugs. Instead, this section uses these therapeutic groups as examples to highlight special problem areas of drug therapy in the elderly and to demonstrate the generic considerations in geriatric therapeutics.

DRUG EPIDEMIOLOGY: CURRENT USE AND PROBLEMS WITH DRUGS IN OLDER PATIENTS

USE OF DRUGS

The Extent of Use in the Over-65 Age Group

It has long been recognized that the population over 65 years takes a high proportion of the total amount of drugs used by the entire population. In the 1982 National Disease and Therapeutic Index (NDTI), survey of drug mentions[1] in visits to office-based physicians, the over-60 population accounted for 30% of the office visits and 38% of drug mentions, even though this group represented only 16% of the population sampled (5). In an earlier NDTI survey of this population in 1981, there were 1.46 drug mentions/visit and 11.08 drug mentions/person/year (4). Since this survey methodology may underestimate total drugs in a regimen, the actual numbers of drugs/person are probably higher, as shown in other studies that provide further estimates of exposure. The National Ambulatory Medical Care Survey (NAMCS) of visits to internists and

---

[1] Drug "mentions" in this survey refer to the drugs listed by the physician on any one visit for a given patient. This may include new and/or ongoing therapy. Its completeness depends on the extent that a complete drug history was obtained.

family practitioners found that 38% of those over age 65 years were taking three or more drugs (9, 10). In a national telephone survey carried out by the American Association of Retired Persons (AARP), 24% of the over-65 population were taking three or more drugs (1). An ongoing survey of Iowa rural households by Wallace (56) reported that 40% of the more than 3000 patients surveyed were taking more than three drugs, and 10% were taking more than five drugs at any given time. Finally, a detailed survey of a geriatric ambulatory population in Florida in 1982 showed that the average number of drugs used was 3.2 medications (women: 3.5; men: 2.8), and that only 11% were taking no medications (33). An update of this study showed this has increased to an average of 3.7 medications, which reflects increases in both prescription and over-the-counter (OTC) drug use (17).

Characteristics of Use in the Elderly Population

The characteristics of use, by age group, relative to drug category and source, have been described by Baum et al. (5); their findings of the most commonly used drugs are presented in Table 4.1. These findings have been corroborated by other surveys, e.g., the NAMCS and NCUES studies (9, 26, 27, 42). In general, use appears generally to increase with age, and the use of OTC medications is significant, suggesting that the older, frailer elderly may be exposed to a large array of different drugs. Reflecting the underlying pathology, the cardiovascular/diuretic drugs comprise the largest proportion of geriatric drug use, which, in turn, accounts for up to 65% of the *total* national use of this drug category. Since the mid-1970s, there has been a considerable increase in number of different cardiovascular and antiarthritic drugs introduced. Many of these, the numerous nonsteroidal anti-inflammatory drugs and the various vasodilators such as calcium channel blockers and angiotensin converting enzyme (ACE) inhibitors, are targeted to the older age group. The appearance of the H_2 antagonists, cimetidine, ranitidine, and famotidine, have added still another therapeutic category that is among the most frequently used in this population (17).

Reasons for Increased Drug Use in the Elderly

The reasons for this increase have been described in many reviews. Most attribute it to the recognized increase both in chronic diseases and medical visits in this population, which alone are associated with increased prescribing. Mandolini (32) has reviewed this area in a broad context and described both medical and complex social reasons that may contribute to this. These include not only the increase in the number of diseases in this population, but other factors such as the need by the physician to provide a technical solution to each problem, the influence of the pharmaceutical industry, and possible age grading and practitioner bias to devote less time (substituting prescriptions) to the elderly.

In the nursing home setting, use of drugs may be increased for many reasons. Although this population represents only about 5% of the total elderly population, those residing in long-term care facilities tend to have a larger number of medical problems and also have multiple active caregivers, e.g., nurses, physicians, and physical and occupational therapists, all of whom may prompt the initiation of drug therapy. Further, given the long-term nature of the care and the use of standardized, computer rewritten orders every 30 days, there is some tendency toward continuation of therapy that may or may not be needed.

Drug use in the hospital setting is as yet not well characterized, but is known to be high, and the complex dosage regimens not easily transferred to the home setting.

CURRENTLY KNOWN PROBLEMS WITH DRUGS IN THE ELDERLY

A priori, it would be expected that the elderly would have more problems with drug reactions and interactions simply because of their intake of a larger number of different drugs (2, 30). Further, because of the nature of their underlying diseases, the drugs used in the elderly are more likely to be potent, have a narrower therapeutic index (e.g., digoxin), and be more toxic (39, 57).

Difficulties in Identifying and Quantitating Adverse Drug Effects in the Elderly

There is some difficulty in obtaining data on the frequency of these problems in the elderly. The documentation of actual drug exposure may be difficult and documentation of discrete problems that might reasonably be attributable to drugs is likewise complicated. This has been demonstrated in a previous study by Jones (23) that showed that the most frequent presenting complaints in the elderly may be very similar to the common side effects of the drugs most commonly used. Further, although rashes and liver abnormalities are commonly seen and recognized as adverse reactions, such drug-associated

Table 4.1
A Summary of Geriatric Drug Use: Prescriptions[a]/1000/Year and Rank[b,c]

USC Category	Age Group (years)				
	0–44	45–54	55–64	65–74	75+
Systemic antiarthritics	113 (8)	419 (1)	590 (2)	747 (1)	785 (2)
β-blockers	53 (20)	415 (2)	676 (1)	800 (2)	638 (6)
Thiazide and related diuretics	36 (28)	295 (3)	496 (3)	679 (3)	693 (4)
Digitalis preparations	6 (99)	56 (34)	191 (9)	521 (4)	1071 (1)
Potassium-sparing diuretics	31 (49)	281 (5)	460 (4)	628 (5)	774 (5)
Other oral diuretics e.g., furosemide	15 (78)	106 (18)	249 (8)	521 (6)	880 (3)
Other antihypertensives e.g., aldomet	18 (73)	194 (8)	371 (5)	495 (8)	501 (8)
Nitrite/nitrate vasodilators	7[d]	140 (16)	348 (7)	589 (7)	739 (7)
Benzodiazepine tranquilizers	144 (14)	491 (4)	488 (6)	494 (10)	420 (12)
Diabetes therapy oral	7 (100)	98 (17)	201 (11)	340 (9)	327 (9)
Codeine + combinations oral analgesics	199 (10)	371 (6)	411 (9)	407 (15)	368 (16)
Plain corticoids, oral	42 (15)	86 (12)	111 (13)	156 (14)	132 (15)
Xanthine broncho-dilators	60 (18)	87 (23)	170 (14)	276 (11)	231 (13)
Diabetes therapy, insulin	14 (56)	63 (19)	112 (12)	164 (12)	113 (21)
Tricyclic + other antidepressants	54 (17)	160 (7)	145 (15)	136 (20)	114 (27)

[a]Only prescriptions from retail pharmacies.
[b]Rank based on National Disease and Therapeutic Index only, cited in Baum et al: 1985.
[c]Based on data from the National Disease and Therapeutic Index and the National Prescription Audit, IMS America, LTD, 1982, cited in Baum C, Kennedy DL, Forbes MB, et al: Drug use and expenditures in 1982. *JAMA* 253:382, 1985.
[d]Not in top 100.

problems as falls (due to postural hypotension, syncope, or ataxia), confusion or delirium (due to excess sedation or paradoxic effects of sedatives or tricyclics), or excessive hyponatremia (due to diuretics) may be missed (34). This emphasizes the need to consider adverse drug reactions as part of any differential diagnosis, as will be discussed later.

In addition to the problem of recognition, the development of information that relates to this general population is always difficult because any given adverse effect is more often than not a function of several factors, including genetic factors, disease states, compliance, dose timing, and other drugs. Thus, the frequency of reactions in any given population may be a function of the dose typically given, the care of monitoring which may, in turn, compensate for genetic predispositions (e.g., fast vs. slow acetylators who will handle such drugs as hydralazine and procainamide differently), the level of compliance which is a documented problem (46), and the presence of other diseases or conditions. For example, one of the major determinants of frequency of drug adverse effects is the duration of therapy. Both Idanpaan-Heikkila (20) and O'Neill (36) have demonstrated an array of characteristic patterns for various drug effects over time, including effects seen only early (such as somnolence with benzodiazepines), or after chronic therapy (liver abnormalities), or increasing with duration of exposure (gastrointestinal bleeding with nonsteroidal antiinflammatory drugs).

Current Data on Adverse Effects in the Elderly

Despite these difficulties, studies ranging from special clinical trials of drugs in the elderly prior to marketing, which are being encouraged by the Food and Drug Administration (FDA), to special epidemiologic studies, are being carried out to clarify this. Some studies have clearly demonstrated an increased risk of adverse effects in this age group as compared with younger patients (7, 18, 53). Shaw (46) has suggested that adverse effects may account for 10–25% of hospital admissions to geriatric hospitals and about 16% of admissions to psychogeriatric units. Another 3-year study found that 3% of *all* hospital admissions could be attributed to drug effects and 40% of these admissions were in patients over age 60 years (7). A significant proportion of ilatrogenic illness in the hospitalized elderly is due to drugs, particularly anticoagulants, cardiovascular agents, and antibiotics (50).

Some of these studies suggest an increase in incidence of adverse effects with age (18, 45) and the adverse reactions appear to occur more frequently in women than in men (7, 11). This may be due partially to a greater use of drugs by women. Not surprisingly, adverse reactions are more common in patients with a history of previous adverse reactions (28), cancer, or *compromised renal function* (29). This latter factor is probably *the* most important clinical factor in predisposing to adverse effects of drug therapy. More often than not, reactions related to decreased renal function may often be prevented by correcting dose and/or timing of therapy. Some concepts regarding recognition, handling, and prevention of adverse effects of drugs are presented subsequently in this chapter.

Drug interactions have been an area of particular concern in the elderly because of the increased number of drugs used in combination (19). Earlier studies of hospitalized patients in the Boston Collaborative Drug Surveillance Program found approximately 6.5% of drug reactions were due to interactions (31). Further, studies of ambulatory patients and nursing home patients revealed that 6.2% and 22.2%, respectively, had been prescribed interacting drug combinations (52). However, with the rapidly evolving and complex drug regimens in the elderly, clear documentation of the frequency of significant interaction in this group is lacking, but the potential for significant problems clearly exists. Therefore, considering the most common drugs used, certain known clinically significant drug interactions can be anticipated and these are presented in Table 4.2

OLDER PATIENT: PHYSIOLOGY RELATIVE TO DRUG ACTION

OVERVIEW: "AVERAGE" AGING PATIENT

One of the characteristics of the aging population that has made study of drugs and understanding of their actions so difficult is the tremendous variability within this group. Nonetheless, there are some specific physiologic changes that occur with increasing age. Many of these can affect pharmacokinetics and, possibly, pharmacodynamics. In turn, they can affect the overall therapeutic outcome. These alterations are now part of the standard teachings in geriatrics and have been covered extensively in many reviews (13, 15, 28, 37, 38, 44) that can be consulted for detailed discussions. This chapter will outline the major changes currently thought to be of clinical significance in therapeutics.

The physiologic changes which can affect therapeutics in the elderly do so in at least one of three ways:

1. The physiologic changes can affect the handling of the drug in the body, i.e., the pharmacokinetics.
2. The changes can affect the ultimate effect of the drug once it reaches the receptor and acts, i.e., the "pharmacodynamics" (which is less well-defined).
3. The changes with aging can affect the adherence to a drug regimen, a complex of factors ranging from the ability to remember to take the drug to the logistics of actually ingesting or swallowing the drug.

CHANGES THAT CAN AFFECT PHARMACOKINETICS AND THE RESULTING DRUG CONCENTRATION AND THERAPEUTIC EFFECTS

Pharmacokinetics deals with the measures of a drug's absorption, metabolism, distribution in, and elimination from the body. All of these factors determine the *concentration of drug at the receptor site over defined periods of time*. Thus, the rate and degree of absorption of a drug from the stomach or intestine will determine the amount and rate of drug entering the body and the early part of the time concentration curve (time to peak concentration). A drug's metabolism, mostly in the liver, can deter-

Table 4.2
Clinically Important and Common Drug Interactions That May Occur in the Elderly

Drug/Generic Category	Interacting Drug	Result
Sympatholytics antihypertensives	OTC nasal sprays Cough-cold decongestants	Increased BP
Warfarin anticoagulants	Aspirin	↑ Risk of bleeding
	Phenytoin	↑ Drug level + ataxia + ↑ risk of bleeding
	Sulfonylureas (first generation)	↓ Blood sugar
	NSAIDS	↑ Risk of bleeding, especially GI
Digoxin	Quinidine	↑ Level of digoxin
	Diuretics	↓ K^+; digoxin toxicity
Anticholinergic drug	Other drugs with anticholinergic effects	Excess effects: urinary retention; constipation; glaucoma
Sedating drug (tranquilizer, sedative, neuroleptic)	Other drugs with sedating effects	Excessive sedation or confusion mistaken for dementia

mine how much active drug enters the circulation and/or is modified to a more water-soluble form (active or not) for excretion. Distribution of a drug in the body is dependent on the characteristics of the drug (e.g., lipid-soluble, water-soluble), and the body makeup (e.g., percent of lean body mass). Elimination of the drug from the body via the kidneys, liver, and gastrointestinal tract, and/or the lungs is the determinant of ultimate clearance of the drug from the body in a defined period of time. In the elderly, all of these factors—absorption, metabolism, distribution, and elimination—may change to alter the level of drug at the receptor site and its duration at that site. This section will provide a very brief review of pharmacokinetic concepts and methods. This is followed by a discussion of how the many possible changes that occur with aging may affect pharmacokinetics.

Basic Pharmacokinetics

The most commonly used pharmacokinetic expression in clinical medicine is the "half-life" or $T_{1/2}$ of a drug, which is defined as the period of time required for elimination of one-half of the drug from the body after distribution equilibrium is attained (that is, after the drug is distributed evenly in the body after absorption or intravenous injection).

As a simple example, if a drug that is predominantly excreted by the kidneys is given to an elderly person with compromised renal function and limited ability to excrete the drug, excretion of the drug will be delayed. This will result in an increased half-life of the drug. As a result, continued dosing at the usual level *and frequency* will result in an increase in blood levels of the drug and possible toxicity. If recognized, either the dose and/or the dosing interval can be changed to compensate for this change.

However, the half-life is not simply a function of drug elimination, but rather is related to two other pharmacokinetic measures that determine the half-life for a drug in any given person, the volume of distribution, V_d, and the clearance of a drug, which represents elimination from all sites. They are related in the following way:

$$t\frac{1}{2} = \frac{0.693 \times V_d}{\text{Clearance}}$$

Clearance, expressed in units of volume per unit of time (e.g., ml/min), represents a hypothetical volume of blood from which a drug is completely cleared in a unit of time. It represents the sum of clearances for the various clearing organs, primarily the kidney and liver. It is the best index of the ability to remove or eliminate a drug and is inversely proportional to the t½.

The volume of distribution, or V_d, is most important in the elderly because of changes in lean mass and adipose tissue described below. V_d is the hypothetical volume relating the amount of drug in the body to the plasma concentration at all times after the attainment of distribution equilibrium. It is expressed in liters/kg. For example, if a drug's distribution is limited to the intravascular space, the V_d will be similar to the plasma volume; in contrast, if a drug is highly lipid-soluble and distributed to all the lipid body compartments (fat, brain, etc.), the V_d

may be higher. For example, for the fat-soluble drug, diazepam (Valium), the V_d for young healthy men was shown to be in the 40–100 liters/kg range, but for older men, with a higher proportion of fat to lean body mass, it ranged from 75–175 liters/kg. In contrast, aminopyrine, a water-soluble drug not distributed in fat, had V_d values from 0.6–0.8 liter/kg in the younger men, falling to 0.45–0.6 in the older men with diminished lean body mass (15).

Therefore, a renally excreted, lipid-soluble drug whose half-life is prolonged in the presence of renal failure (due to decreased renal clearance) might be even more prolonged in an elderly person with a higher proportion of fat to lean body mass, since the V_d may be greater.

At present, the description of generic pharmacokinetics for specific drugs and drug groups awaits further study. Reviews of this topic have suggested that any characteristics expressed in a single study, unless carefully defined must be interpreted with caution. Schmucker's excellent review of aging and drug disposition (44) concludes that despite much data, there are "few clinical studies which have afforded a significant improvement in our present depth of knowledge concerning drug disposition in the geriatric population."

Despite these limitations and the complexity of extrapolating from one category of physiologic change to overall therapeutic outcome, the following physiologic changes may, in selected cases, contribute or cause major changes in drug handling by the elderly should be considered.

It is important to emphasize that despite the limited study data, the *absence* of data on important effects due to altered physiology does not preclude their existence. This still suggests the need for the "alerted clinician" armed with the knowledge of the altered physiology that may contribute to unexpected therapeutic outcomes.

Factors Affecting Drug Absorption

A number of changes occur in the gastrointestinal tract with advancing age, including decreased gastric acid secretion and increased stomach pH, reduced splanchnic blood flow, reduced gastrointestinal motility, and declines in the number and absorptive capacity of intestinal epithelial cells (44). In general, however, data from both clinical pharmacokinetic studies and careful animal studies have not revealed consistent changes in drug absorption clearly correlated with age (16, 44). In fact, studies of acetaminophen and aspirin specifically suggest no important alterations in older persons.

Despite limited clinical importance found thus far, some of the changes may affect the absorption of specific drugs under certain clinical conditions or in the presence of additional drugs, as illustrated below.

Gastric Acidity. Although only certain drugs are absorbed from the stomach, the possibility has been raised that certain acid-labile agents such as levodopa, erythromycins, and penicillins may be more readily absorbed at a higher pH (38).

Decreased Motility and Gastric Emptying Time. This characteristic that has been demonstrated can be potentiated by various anticholinergic drugs commonly found in an elderly person's regimen, e.g., antihistamines (e.g., diphenhydramine), and tricyclic antidepressants (e.g., amitriptyline).

Decreased Intestinal Absorptive Capacity. It has been shown that the absorption of nutrients, such as thiamine, calcium, and iron, is impaired (38).

Factors Affecting Drug Distribution

Lean Body Mass. With age, the total body water, plasma volume, and extracellular fluid decreases (37) and the proportion of the lean body mass declines in proportion to adipose tissue mass relative to the total body weight. However, differences in body composition between men and women may be almost as great as those between the elderly and the younger (15). The fraction of total body weight composed of adipose tissue may increase from 18–36% in men and from 33–48% in women. This can affect the drug distribution (V_d) of lipophilic drugs such as the benzodiazepines and lidocaine which will be more extensively distributed, particularly in older women. In the presence of an unchanged rate of drug clearance, this can result in a longer half-life for those drugs. Conversely, water-soluble drugs such as acetaminophen may decrease in their distribution and (this is the case for water-soluble alcohol) which will attain higher blood levels in the presence of unchanged clearance.

Serum Albumin Levels. Several studies have shown that albumin concentration declines with age (37); however, total plasma protein is less frequently lower. This may be more marked in the frail and ill elderly where a compromised nutritional state exists (13) and is important for those drugs which are known to be highly protein bound (phenytoin, warfarin, sulfonyureas, thyroxine, and some nonsteroidal anti-inflammatory drugs, notably phenylbutazone). Age-related decreases in the protein bound/unbound ratio for several compounds have been reported, including for phenytoin and warfarin. This can result in increased effects due to the significantly higher free drug levels.

The lower albumin levels might be most important when more than one highly protein bound drug is administered, increasing the likelihood of interactions (37).

Hepatic Blood Flow. Drugs given orally are absorbed into the portal circulation and are transported to the liver were they are metabolized before they reach the systemic circulation to exert their effects. Independent of any changes in hepatic enzymes with aging, hepatic blood flow can be a major determinant of the total clearance of several drugs commonly used in the elderly, including propranolol (16). Partially due to reduced cardiac output, up to 40–45% reduction in liver blood flow may be observed in the elderly and decreases in clearance of drugs with high hepatic clearance (e.g., propranolol and lidocaine) have been demonstrated for lidocaine (16). In another study, Swift et al. (51) found that the reduction in antipyrine clearance correlated with a diminished hepatic volume, which also occurs with increased age.

Hepatic Metabolism. Two factors are important here: (a) the volume of the liver and the number of hepatocytes, which decrease with age (49), and (b) the capacity of the metabolizing enzymes. There are two categories of hepatic metabolism of drugs. Phase 1 metabolism results in either the oxidation, reduction, or hydrolysation of drugs, producing metabolites that may have greater, similar, or little pharmacologic activity and are usually more water-soluble than the unmetabolized drug. Several studies of the biotransformation processes of a number of drugs (diazepam, quinidine, theophylline, propranolol) suggest an age-related reduction in hepatic clearance probably associated with diminished activity. However, a number of other drugs have not shown a decreased clearance (warfarin, lidocaine, ethanol) (16), suggesting a highly variable effect which requires further study (44). Phase 2 metabolism, or biotransformation, which involves conjugation to glucuronide, sulfate, or acetate to provide metabolites which are inactive and excreted in the urine, does not change with age (44).

A number of important drugs used in the elderly undergo extensive "first pass" metabolism in the liver which accounts for the discrepancy between intravenous and oral doses. These drugs include β-blockers, verapamil, hydralazine, and tricyclic antidepressants. Alterations in effects relative to dose of these drugs may be dependent on blood flow, functioning liver size, and metabolism. If there is diminished capacity to metabolize these drugs in an elderly person, the amount of drug presented to the systemic circulation may be higher. Consequently, lower initial and maintenance doses of these drugs are often required.

Factors Affecting Excretion

Renal Excretion. Renal function is probably the most important and consistent physiologic change that occurs with aging that can clinically affect drug handling, since the kidney is a major source of elimination for most drugs (44). The basal renal function of an elderly patient is usually much reduced compared to a younger person despite similar serum creatinine and blood urea nitrogen (BUN) levels. The seemingly "normal" creatinine and BUN is due to both a decreased lean body mass and a decreased production of creatinine. Creatinine clearance may decrease from age 20–29 years by 1 ml/min/1.73 m^2/year with an average reduction of 30–46% in the elderly (38). This is compounded by physiologic decreases in renal blood flow of up to 50–60% by age 70 years, partly because of a redistribution of cardiac output. Renal plasma flow has been estimated to decrease by 1–1.9%/year from age 20–90 years (8, 38). Overall, this results in a 20–50% decrease in glomerular filtration rate, which may not be reflected clinically unless a creatinine clearance is determined. Thus, a "normal" level can exist in the presence of considerably reduced function. For example, a study of males showed an average creatinine clearance in the 30–39 age group of 97 ml/min/1.73 m^2 with an average serum creatinine of 1.14. In contrast, the 80 to 89-year-old males had an average serum creatinine of 1.06, but a clearance of only 47 (48).

Another change affecting excretion is the decline of renal tubular secretion and absorption, at a rate of approximately 7% per decade. This can have an effect on the handling of several drugs such as penicillin and procainamide (44) and may account for differences in response to furosemide.

It is most important to emphasize that renal function, though naturally declining with age, is also frequently affected significantly by the common diseases of the elderly: heart failure with resulting decreased renal blood flow, diabetes, and urinary retention. All tend to confound the other changes, and make the need for careful monitoring more critical.

Some drugs not only are excreted primarily by the kidneys but also affect renal function. The aminoglycosides are cases in point. This effect on renal function can be a major contributor to drug interactions. Not only can a drug decrease renal function, but it can decrease the excretion of other drugs and cause accumulation of the other drugs as well as of itself.

Almost all therapy in the elderly requires consideration of the level of renal function, ideally based on the creatinine clearance. For drugs whose clearance is mostly by renal excretion, the total drug *clearance* will predictably decrease roughly in proportion to the reduced glomerular filtration rate (16). Although measurement of an actual creatinine clearance is preferred, particularly where its level will determine dosing of a drug with a narrow therapeutic range, its measurement is sometimes logistically difficult. The following estimation can be used for men as suggested by Ouslander (37):

$$\frac{\text{Creatinine}}{\text{Clearance}} = \frac{(140-\text{Age}) \times \text{body weight(kg)}}{\text{serum creatinine} \times 72}$$

and for women, the result is multiplied by 0.85.

Further, in the presence of considerable obesity or edema, lean body weight, rather than total body weight should be used (38):

Lean Body Weight [weight in kg; height in cm]:
$\text{LBW}_{\text{male}} = 128(1.10 \times \text{weight}) \times \text{weight}^2/\text{height}^2$
$\text{LBW}_{\text{female}} = 148 \times \text{weight}^2/\text{height}^2$

Since such a large number of drugs are primarily excreted by the kidneys and other drugs can significantly compromise renal function, a calculation of creatinine clearance should be a routine clinical data element. This calculation would be useful for periodic checks in the outpatient setting, and every few days in the more dynamic inpatient acute care setting since the creatinine clearance estimate can often affect dosing levels or timing of one or more medications. A listing of commonly used drugs which are primarily excreted by the kidneys are included in Table 4.3.

Excretion by Other Routes. Some drugs are significantly eliminated via biliary excretion. However, other than in animal studies, there are few specific data to suggest a trend with aging (44).

PHYSIOLOGIC CHANGES AND PHARMACODYNAMICS

This second group of changes is far less well defined. Pharmacodynamic response has been defined as the "change in function of an end organ (site of action) that results from drug-end organ interaction" (38). End organ sensitivity can be altered by many changes with aging, for example, autonomic function and potential responsiveness to autonomic drugs.

Physiologic changes, such as reduced peripheral venous tone, altered baroreceptor response, or depletion of cellular receptors or neurotransmitters such as dopamine and acetylcholine, can all alter responses to, for example, antihypertensive and neuroleptic drugs (38).

Further, nutritional status may alter pharmacodynamics as well as affect pharmacokinetic factors such as serum albumin levels (38).

Although it has been the belief that the elderly are more "sensitive" to drugs, data that show that lower blood levels of a drug achieve equal or greater effects with increasing age are sparse (37). This was demonstrated for the benzodiazepines, diazepam, flurazepam, chlordiazepoxide, and nitrazepam (15, 38, 41) and for warfarin (47).

Although not strictly ruling out pharmacokinetic causes, other studies have shown apparent increased

Table 4.3
Drugs Affected by Altered Renal Function

Drugs primarily excreted by the kidney
    Digoxin
    Cimetidine
    Lithium
    Procainamide
    Chlorpropamide
    Many antibiotics
        (penicillin, aminoglycosides)

Drugs with active metabolites excreted by the kidneys
    Diazepam
    Flurazepam
    Procainamide
    Meperidine
    Sulindac
    Propoxyphene
    Disopyramide
    Carbamazepine
    Allopurinol

sensitivity to analgesics in the elderly. It has been demonstrated that the amount of epidural anesthesia required to achieve an effective block per spinal segment decreased with age. Further, apparent greater pain relief with equal doses of morphine or pentazocine (corrected for decreasing patient weight with age) was shown with increasing age (5a).

These findings are in contrast to the findings of age-related decline in receptor affinities or numbers (44). For example, both biochemical and clinical studies suggest a decreasing responsiveness of the β-adrenergic receptor with age, specifically to the cardiac effects of isoproterenol and propranolol (55). However, this decreasing responsiveness may be restricted to β_1-receptors (e.g., those affecting heart rate and contractility) since β_2-responses were preserved in one study. These investigators used terbutaline and found reaction in both systolic and diastolic blood pressures in the older patients. This was interpreted as β_2 vasodilatation unopposed by β_1 cardiac effects, an effect that may be of clinical significance in elderly asthmatics.

Overall, data clearly defining pharmacodynamic changes are limited and will probably continue to be so because of the limitations on interpretations of pharmacokinetic data in the elderly. Despite the potential significance, it is likely that only when the pharmacokinetics are better delineated that clinically useful information on pharmacodynamics will be advanced.

PHYSIOLOGIC CHANGES AFFECTING OTHER ASPECT OF THERAPEUTICS

There are other physiologic changes occurring with aging which affect the achievement of therapeutic goals, independent of the pharmacokinetic and pharmacodynamic alterations. These include such factors as whether the patient remembers to take the drug, can see the drug to differentiate it from others, and can swallow it, as well as other changes that may affect the likelihood of compliance. These are briefly considered below.

Diminished Mental Function

The progression into age is typically characterized by some changes in mental function, although the range of normal in this area is still being defined. It is clear that a certain proportion of patients begin to lose short-term memory and develop various manifestations of mild to moderate dementia. These patients are still sufficiently functional to be living independently and taking their own drugs;

however, they may not understand or remember the drug regimen. The possibility of this eventuality is high, but is not always evaluated by the clinician dispensing prescriptions. This may result in a variety of problems ranging from redundant to missed therapy.

Psychiatric Conditions

Depression is a common occurrence in the elderly and may occur in as many as 10% or more (52a, 52b). Less frequently, thought disorder with paranoia may occur, particularly with some types of dementia. The concomitant use of alcohol may also compound this problem. These conditions can result in problems with taking prescribed medications, ranging from refusal or fear to take, to overdose. The possibility of this should be anticipated.

Impaired Vision

This factor can alter drug therapy due to difficulty differentiating medications of similar appearance, or, to measuring insulin. In the latter case, special aids are available for those with impaired vision.

Upper Oral Physiology and Esophageal Function

The presence of oropharyngeal and/or esophageal dysfunction in the elderly is recognized but its frequency and effect on drug intake is unknown. However, it is clinically apparent that this factor, when present, can sometimes determine whether a drug is taken as prescribed or discarded due to inability to swallow.

Musculoskeletal Conditions

In some cases, these conditions may also affect drug intake. The "childproofed" pill container problem is well appreciated. In most cases, prescriptions for the elderly can be obtained without these caps, although consideration should be given to children in the household, since many childhood poisonings are related to access to adult medications.

GENERAL GUIDELINES FOR OPTIMIZING DRUG THERAPY AND MINIMIZING PROBLEMS WITH COMPLIANCE, ADVERSE DRUG REACTIONS, AND INTERACTIONS

There are certain general therapeutic practices that will help minimize the problems with drugs in the elderly. Although seemingly simplistic and obvious, they are often practically hard to apply, given limited time in the practice setting. However, they are of particular importance in the aging patient, who, for all the reasons discussed in this chapter, poses a highly individualized and sometimes complex therapeutic challenge. These principles are discussed in detail below.

KNOW THE DRUGS PRESCRIBED

A prescriber should always be quite familiar with drugs prescribed including their pharmacology, kinetics, and common and serious adverse reactions. Although this principle is obvious, this is a problem area with both old and very new drugs. Old established drugs do not get the careful review of their labeling by their prescribers who may have learned of them in training. This is despite the fact that the information on many drugs continues to accrue, particularly adverse effects and interactions, and the manufacturer is often updating this information in conformity with FDA requirements. Familiarity with this type of information is extremely important, especially in therapy in the elderly.

With respect to new drugs, it is probable that many drugs are used before the prescriber has actually informed himself of the full range of actions and effects of a drug. It is important to recognize that new drugs are relatively unknown when they enter the market. Typically, a drug that has entered the market has been tested on only 500 to a maximum of 3000 patients. Several important facts apply here. First, the patients selected for a clinical trial are typically male, relatively healthy without serious chronic diseases, and middle aged. Until recently, clinical trials of new drugs were not carried out in the older population because of their multiple diseases and other confounding factors which, in an ideal clinical trial design, would make analysis difficult. Thus, there is often *no* information about the prototype frail elderly patient with multiple chronic diseases; even if this person represents a typical future user of the drug. The FDA has been developing guidelines for the testing of drugs in the elderly and has been encouraging this, recognizing that a large proportion of the use will be in this age group.

Second, the number of patients who have been exposed to the new drugs for any period of time is very small. Thus, there is very limited experience with adverse effects that might occur rarely (less than 1/500-1000) or that are seen only after 1 or 2 months of exposure (e.g., methyldopa hepatotoxicity, etc.). Since many of the common adverse reactions typically occur at a frequency less than 1 in 5000, it is probable that many of the usual toxicities of a drug will not be discovered until after it has reached the market.

Third, a typical clinical trial can only evaluate certain body systems, so adverse effects may be missed. For example, trials of the ophthalmic β-blockers (e.g., timolol) did not adequately anticipate the degree of pulmonary and cardiac conduction problems seen after their introduction, possibly because of a focus on effects seen in the eye.

Given these factors, how can the prescriber be optimally informed? Most physicians will review the package insert of a drug newly entering the market. However, the primary information about toxicity is not yet in the label and appears only years after marketing (after a sufficient population has been exposed and/or postmarketing studies have been done). If the drug is similar to others, for example, another histamine$_2$ antagonist, or angiotensin converting enzyme (ACE) inhibitor, it is likely to share a similar profile to its established progenitors, despite its sparse adverse reaction labeling. If it is truly new, the prescriber may wish to be particularly alert to new events, as discussed below, and if concerned, contact the manufacturer for specific information on use in the elderly.

With respect to established drugs, it should be recognized that new information (particularly on effects in special populations, adverse effects, drug interactions) is continually developing and, if significant, will ultimately appear in the official drug labeling. This will also be reflected in periodic reviews in such standard resources as The Medical Letter, AMA Drug Evaluations, and other similar sources. The drug information publication of the U.S. Pharmacopoeia, the *USP Drug Information Compendium*, specifically summarizes information on drug usage in the elderly.

The typical prescriber seldom frequently prescribes more than 25–50 different drugs/year (4), so some type of periodic review of the labeling for these drugs seems warranted. Of importance are the more toxic drugs; specifically those excreted primarily by the kidney, those which are highly protein-bound, and those drugs which have narrow therapeutic to toxic ratios, such as digoxin, lithium, anticonvulsants, and disease-modifying antirheumatic drugs. In sum, it behooves the physician to know the warnings and contraindications for a drug since often these are the most critical pieces of information relating risk to the patient. This is particularly critical in the elderly but also is important with use of drugs in all patients.

KNOW THE PATIENT WELL

*The prescribing physician should have a thorough knowledge of the patient's **risk factors** and social habits that may affect the therapeutic regimen.* Despite the often hurried setting of prescribing, it is important to know as much as possible about the patient with respect to both intrinsic risk factors such as renal disease, liver disease, and environmental exposure and social factors such as likelihood of compliance, alcohol use, etc. The prescriber should also obtain a thorough history of current and significant past drug intake, and drug allergies or intolerance. The risk factors can be assessed at the time of initiating therapy, and vary with the therapy, but almost always include determination of renal function (and estimation of creatinine clearance), liver function, serum albumin, and stool guaiac. The latter, for example, is important when initiating anticoagulant, steroid, nonsteroidal antiinflammatory, or aspirin therapy.

Assessing social factors may be more difficult and time-consuming, but for a chronic regimen can be spread out over multiple visits. Several techniques may help in dealing with these issues.

1. A social history will give a better concept of how a person may comply with a complex regimen and whether any complicating factors exist, such as alcohol. A detailed description of the previous day's activities, from waking, pill-taking, meals, and activities, will often provide useful insights for tailoring a regimen to achieve compliance.
2. An adjustment in the dosing regimen may be very helpful in improving compliance. It is not unusual for patients to be given a drug with a long half-life on a two-to-three times per day basis. Anticonvulsants and neuroleptic agents are cases in point. When stable regimens are reached with these agents, they can be given once a day, usually at night. Compliance can be improved by simply minimizing the absolute numbers of drugs and sharing this goal with the patient.
3. A schedule for daily dosing and refilling of the medications should be indicated *explicitly* in writing, rather than casually as is frequently done. Counting tablets over a given period allows some estimate of compliance, and provides a basis for discussion of any problems.
4. An understanding and *agreement* with the full treatment plan by the patient is ideal. Thus, a discussion of the overall regimen and its goals may be helpful. Factors known to interfere with compliance with drug therapy include misunderstanding the drug regimen, characteristics of the medicine itself (difficult to swallow, unpleasant side effects, and bad taste), and *cost*. Cost is a frequent cause of failure to take medications. Developing a mutually acceptable regimen that is within realistic cost limits should be a subject discussed on a

frequent basis in chronic geriatric care. In many cases, there are ways in which cost may be minimized. The physician should make himself aware of the various requirements of third party paying programs and the availability of special programs with generic or reduced price drugs, such as provided by the AARP. For example, some states provide supplemental payments for prescription drugs. For patients on Medicaid, individual state requirements may markedly affect drug costs depending on how they are prescribed. The ultimate goal is the patient's adherence to a regimen that is mutually recognized as beneficial and agreed upon by patient and physician alike.

INFORMING THE PATIENT ADEQUATELY

*The prescriber must personally make sure that the patient is at all times informed about the medications he is taking **to the patient's satisfaction.*** In the last several years, patients have become more aware of their drugs and their interest has accordingly been increased. Consistent with the previous discussion, it is important for the physician to discuss the nature of the prescriptions and have the patient recite back what he is taking. It is also important that the patient has access to all of the information he desires. At present, there are a large number of excellent resources that detail information on drug effects and reactions. The prescriber may wish to refer patients to these resources but should primarily assure that the patient has the information he or she desires, and/or a route to get that information. For example, the suggestion may be made to call if questions or concerns occur, or to write out questions for discussion at subsequent office visits. It is helpful for a patient to have a *written list* of *all* the medicines, with doses (and timing) of the drugs he should be taking. This is particularly important after hospital discharge, but could also be done at periodic visits.

SYSTEMATICALLY MONITORING THERAPY

*The physician should have a **system of monitoring therapy** for all drugs being taken by a patient, with specific **therapeutic and toxic endpoints identified.*** Drug therapy is the primary therapeutic tool of the geriatrician and many of the drugs used in the elderly are potent and require specific monitoring. The development of structured monitoring can assist to clarify and simplify a regimen and ideally improve compliance. A monitoring flow sheet could be developed that would be included in an outpatient chart to summarize both drug doses and refills and therapeutic and toxic end points. It may be helpful to set up an a priori schedule of monitoring times for specific end points. For example, digoxin, antiarrhythmic, or anticonvulsant drug blood levels can be assessed on a regular basis (e.g., bimonthly or quarterly) and shortly after addition of any new therapy that might affect levels of one or another drug. For example, if an additional highly protein-bound drug (e.g., thyroxin, a first generation sulfonylurea, or warfarin) were prescribed for a patient on phenytoin (Dilantin), which is also highly protein bound, it would be helpful to plan for specific monitoring since their coadministration may raise the free blood level of the phenytoin.

Application of this structured format for therapeutic monitoring may raise critical questions about the actual role certain drugs play in the regimen.

In some cases, the patient can act as a partner in monitoring therapy. This can be the case particularly for antihypertensive and diabetic therapy in motivated patients, but can also apply to other therapies such as anticoagulants and anticonvulsants. Sharing the task with the patient in monitoring his or her therapy can sometimes facilitate compliance and it places an onus of responsibility on that patient to reach the mutually agreed upon therapeutic goal.

Therapeutic monitoring also includes the determination of compliance, which can be done through a combination of drug blood level monitoring, detailed history, pill counts, and calls to the pharmacist to determine if refills are being obtained.

CONSIDERING NEW EVENTS AS POSSIBLY DRUG RELATED

The physician should always **consider any new event as a possible drug reaction or interaction.** It is important to realize that adverse drug reactions are so varied in their presentation that they can mimic the entire range of pathology seen in man. In a broad sense, adverse reactions can encompass even trauma such as falls and auto accidents that are due to drug effects such as hypotension or ataxia. Accordingly, it is important to think of *any new event* as a possible drug effect and/or interaction. This is important for several reasons. First, serious adverse reactions may be prevented if early manifestations are suspected to be drug effects and the drug is then discontinued. This may be true for some renal and hepatic adverse effects as well as gastrointestinal and skin reactions. Second, this perspective will promote the careful scrutiny of drug regimens for any possible drug interactions, which may also be occurring and contributing to a reaction. Third, as noted above, adverse reactions are most frequently discovered after marketing, and often by

the astute clinician. As discussed in detail in a previous part of this chapter, the elderly, by virtue of their exposure to a greater number of potent pharmaceuticals, as more likely to manifest adverse effects. The alert physician is likely to encounter many of these adverse events, and can contribute considerably to the body of knowledge of the effects of drugs.

Certain simple questions can be applied to determine whether or not a new event is, in fact, related to a drug. These questions stem from several algorithms used to determine causality of a suspected adverse effect (21, 22, 24). *First*, is there a reasonable temporal relationship between initiation of therapy and onset of the event? *Second*, is the event more likely to be a manifestation of underlying disease? *Third*, did the event subside when the drug was discontinued? *Fourth*, if the drug was reintroduced, did the event reoccur? *Finally*, is there evidence in the literature that this event is associated with this drug or its analogues? Any suspect adverse drug event can quite readily be reported to the FDA[2] and also in the literature. New, serious events, especially associated with newly introduced drugs are of special importance, since the alert clinician is the best and earliest source of information about new, undiscovered effects. Guidelines outlining the critical information needed to evaluate a drug effect have been published in several journals (12). This can contribute considerably to development of important information on new effects of drugs.

DRUGS USED FOR ANXIETY, DEPRESSION, AND THOUGHT AND BEHAVIOR DISORDERS, INCLUDING THOSE ASSOCIATED WITH DEMENTIA

This discussion will provide examples of the types of special considerations that occur repeatedly in geriatric therapeutics which are based on the principles discussed earlier in the chapter.

The elderly frequently have symptoms of anxiety, and/or depression and the older, frailer elderly may develop disorders of thinking that accompany other losses of cognitive function. All of these symptoms may be caused directly by underlying disease processes or the drug therapy used to treat them. Alternately, they may not be caused by either, but represent the relatively common neuropsychiatric disorders seen in this age group.

---

[2] Reports can be made using the FDA's 1639 form, which is regularly printed on the back of the FDA Drug Bulletin, and in the back of the *AMA Drug Evaluations* and *The Physicians Desk Reference*, or by sending the report directly to the Division of Epidemiology, FDA, 5600 Fishers Lane, Rockville, MD 20852, or calling 301-443-4580.

A number of diseases are associated with anxiety, confusion, or disordered thought in the elderly. These include hypoxia associated with acute (e.g., pneumonia or pulmonary edema) or chronic pulmonary disease, arrhythmias, head injuries (concussion, subdural hematomas), hyponatremia, renal failure, sepsis, and central nervous system lesions such as a cerebrovascular accident or tumor.

Drug therapy can be a common cause of these symptoms. Increased anxiety and/or confusion presenting as an organic brain syndrome may be seen in susceptible patients receiving benzodiazepines, nonsteroidal anti-inflammatory drugs, tricyclic antidepressants, cimetidine, corticosteroids, and L-dopa (49). The hyponatremia associated with longstanding loop diuretic use can be associated with symptoms that may be interpreted as dementia. Depression is a relatively common side effect seen with certain antihypertensives, notably reserpine, but also other sympatholytics such as methyldopa and clonidine. Further, some β-blockers, such as propranolol, and long-acting benzodiazepines, such as chlordiazepoxide, are also associated with depression. Therefore, before initiating therapy for depression, these potentially reversible causes of the symptoms should be ruled out.

ANXIETY AND INSOMNIA: DRUG THERAPY AND ALTERNATIVES

Anxiety is a common symptom in the elderly, which normally can be associated with many of the life events that are occurring, including impending or real loss of income, independence, or health, or loss of friends and loved ones. The anxiety may be manifested by daytime symptoms, by insomnia, or by both. The presence of one should suggest the other, and the full extent of the symptomatology characterized. Anxiety, with or without depression, associated with these life events should be identified and addressed first with supportive therapy, psychotherapy, and/or social service assistance when possible.

Insomnia and sleep disorders in the elderly may be manifestations of this anxiety or due to other causes, but in the absence of the latter, can often be treated without using hypnotics. Unfortunately, hypnotics are probably overprescribed in this country. They have been routinely used for nighttime sedation in hospitalized patients, and it is in this setting that physicians in training develop prescribing habits. The automatic prescribing of a hypnotic is questionable unless other therapeutic alternatives have been explored. A careful history of the nature of insomnia is important followed by trials of nonpharmacologic maneuvers such as elimination of stimulants in the evening, analgesic for any pain prior to bedtime (e.g., for arthritis), regular sleeping hours, and elimination of daytime naps (49). It is important for the patient to realize that sleep patterns tend to change with age, and that lack of sleep is not in itself a dangerous or life-threatening symptom.

If nondrug approaches to anxiety and/or insomnia are not successful, drug therapy should be focused and limited to alleviation of disabling symptoms. Ideally, this should be on a short-term basis only. If anxiety and insomnia are both present, it may be useful to avoid using two separate agents and direct one therapy to both, since they are likely associated.

Several antianxiety agents and hypnotics are currently available for treatment of anxiety and insomnia. These include the long-acting benzodiazepines, chlordiazepoxide (Librium), diazepam (Valium), flurazepam (Dalmane), and the shorter-acting, newer members of this class (triazolam, or Halcion which is approved as a hypnotic), and newer nonbenzodiazepines, such as buspirone (BuSpar). Additionally, sedating antihistamines like diphenhydramine (Benadryl) have been used in this age group. Barbiturates and meprobamate which were formerly used as sedative and/or hypnotics have receded from common use and are less desirable due to their potential for both habituation and drug interactions. Chloral hydrate has long been used as a hypnotic in the elderly. Although it is associated with drug interactions caused by displacing highly protein-bound drugs from serum proteins (e.g., warfarin) and can rarely be habituating, it remains as one possible alternative hypnotic in selected cases.

The actual selection of an agent is somewhat dependent on the therapeutic goals and desired end points, as well as on practical considerations. With respect to the benzodiazepines, two characteristics may be helpful to optimize use: (a) the rapidity of effect after an oral dose, and (b) the usual duration of action. Table 4.4 summarizes the currently available benzodiazepines and their estimated elimination half-lives. After oral ingestion, diazepam, flurazepam, chlorazepate, and triazolam are quickly absorbed and produce a prompt effect. This can be useful for producing sleep by reducing sleep "latency." These agents can be troublesome if they produce initial oversedation with daytime use. In contrast, prazepam and temazepam are not associated with a prompt effect. This may be useful in cases where rapid sedation would not be desired.

The short-acting agents such as triazolam and oxazepam are sometimes associated with a "rebound" anxiety or insomnia as their effect wears off.

Table 4.4
Currently Available Benzodiazepines for Treatment of Anxiety and Insomnia[a]

Generic Name	Trade Name	Elimination Half-Life
Longer Acting Agents		
Chlordiazepoxide	Librium	6–30[b]
Chlorazepate dipotassium	Tranxene	20–40[b]
Diazepam	Valium	20–50[b]
Flurazepam hydrochloride	Dalmane	50–100
Halazepam	Paxipam	14[b]
Prazepam	Centrax	24–200[b]
Shorter Acting Agents		
Alprazolam	Xanax	12–15[c]
Lorazepam	Ativan	10–15
Oxazepam	Serax	3–21
Temazepam	Restoril	9–12
Triazolam	Halcion	2–3

[a]Adapted with permission from Sloan RW: *Practical Geriatric Therapeutics.* Oradell, NJ, Medical Economics Books, Copyright © 1986. All rights reserved.
[b]These drugs all are metabolized to an active metabolite, N-desmethyldiazepam, which has a half-life of 50–100 hours and may account for a significant proportion of effect at steady state.
[c]Increased in elderly women to 9–23 hours; in elderly men, 9–27 hours.

If anxiety is chronic and/or early awakening is a problem, these agents may not work as well as the longer acting ones. However, the latter, when used as hypnotics may produce a morning "hangover." They may be useful for producing a sustained tranquilizing effect for those with chronic anxiety.

The use of nonbenzodiazepines may be considered as an alternative. As of yet, there is little experience in the elderly with buspirone. Diphenhydramine is often used and serves as a reasonable alternative if its anticholinergic effects do not add to those of another therapy and/or cause undesired effects.

Dosing of these agents should be individualized. Although officially recommended to be used in divided doses, the longer acting agents may be effective in alleviating low level anxiety by use only of a nighttime dose, thus also providing nighttime sedation. Given the goal of minimizing use and avoiding dependence, patients can be encouraged to use antianxiety agents only if absolutely needed. This gives patients a degree of control (versus dependence) and responsibility for dealing with their symptoms.

The adverse effects of these drugs primarily involve sedation and withdrawal. Withdrawal can occur acutely, as in the case of triazolam which may cause dysphoria. In the longer acting agents, abrupt discontinuation can result in significant withdrawal symptoms ranging from anxiety and insomnia, to seizures. In some cases, paradoxic excitement can occur, but this is not common. Taken in overdose, these agents are less lethal than the older barbiturates, but when ingested with alcohol, the toxicity is increased and deaths have been reported.

In summary, use of antianxiety agents in the elderly should be limited to those cases where there appear to be no identifiable causes for the anxiety and where nondrug therapy has not been effective. When elected, the clinician should identify, ideally in partnership with the patient, some specific goals that will allow for focussed, short duration therapy and avoid prolonged regular use. Therapy can be tailored to specific needs and can address both daytime anxiety and insomnia. The nature of these problems should be detailed to allow therapy and the discovery of alternatives to drug therapy. Since oversedation and depression associated with these drugs in the elderly is a common problem, the clinician needs to be continually alert to this potential.

THE AFFECTIVE DISORDERS: DEPRESSION AND MANIC DEPRESSIVE ILLNESS: DIFFERING APPROACHES—DRUG VS. NONDRUG THERAPY

Mood changes in the elderly population are extremely common and are associated with normal life events that produce grief, sadness, or disappointment on the one hand, and with psychotic disorders on the other. In between are *disorders* of mood, major depression, and the bipolar manic-depressive states. True depression is characterized by a wide variety of mental and physical changes, including intense sadness, loss of concentration, self-depreciation, suicidal ideation, weight loss or gain, loss of energy, and sleep disturbances. Many of these may disrupt overall life function. The bipolar disorders include the above array of symptoms alternating with periods of elation, which may include such manifestations as hyperactivity, pressured speech, and irritability (3).

In the aged, significant depression is quite common but may be more subtle and overlooked in the presence of other more defined medical conditions. Further, true endogenous depression may be compounded by the many life events that occur in the elderly: loss of a home; loss or separation from loved ones; frequent medical visits; entry into supervised care settings; loss of bowel and/or bladder function. The resulting depression can be severe, serious, and even life-threatening. This is particularly so when manifested by severe anorexia and "giving up" in the absence of other underlying medical causes.

Since the pharmacologic treatment of depression carries certain risks, particularly in the elderly patient, it is important to identify all contributing factors to this problem. These include a clear history of significant depressive illness (and drug therapy) in the past. As with other psychiatric disorders, depressive symptoms are a common manifestation of underlying medical disease (hypothyroidism, Parkinson's disease) and of drug therapy (tranquilizers, sympatholytic antihypertensives, cimetidine, even antihistamines). These possibilities must be explored and defined before drug therapy is considered.

Frequently, assistance with certain social problems, facilitation of a stable support network of friends and/or family, and identification of factors in the elderly patient's life that enhance his or her sense of usefulness in society, can assist in alleviating depression and can complement drug therapy if still required. Some aspects of this therapy can be diffused to the several caregivers interacting with a particular patient if this therapeutic goal is recognized and organized.

Frequently, drug therapy must be considered, however, and can be very helpful in improving a patient's ability to function and enjoy life. An increasing array of antidepressants is available, and these have been recommended for use in the elderly. Some surveys of use of neuropsychiatric drugs in the elderly suggest that there may be a relative underusage relative to the need for tricyclic and related antidepressant drugs (25).

The agents available for treatment of depression include tricyclic and tetracyclic antidepressants, stimulants such as Ritalin, selected benzodiazepines, such as alprazolam, and rarely, monoamine oxidase (MAO) inhibitors. The tricyclic antidepressants are the most commonly used, and there is considerable experience with them in the elderly. The choice of an agent for an elderly patient requires careful consideration of several characteristics of these drugs including their pharmacologic ability to block norepinephrine or serotonin uptake in central nerve endings, and their side effects, which vary from agent to agent. Although the ability to identify patients who will respond to either a blocker of serotonin or epinephrine uptake has not yet been refined, ongoing studies suggest that this may be feasible in the future. Therefore, selection of an initial agent will often depend on both the manifestation of depression (e.g., anxiety vs. decreased activity) and any concomitant medical conditions. Table 4.5, adapted from Sloan (49), describes several of the drugs used for treatment of depression, including nontricyclics. These are categorized by effects that relate to therapeutic goals, side effects and pharmacologic mechanisms of action. In most cases, therapy should be initiated with the smallest dose and increased every few days, with careful monitoring. Ideally, a specific clinical measure of depression should be used for baseline and follow-up assessment. This is described in detail elsewhere in this book. It is worth noting that in some cases, tricyclic antidepressants are used to treat bladder dysfunction in patients with mild to moderate incontinence. In some cases, this therapy can dually approach both the depression and incontinence. This anticholinergic therapeutic effect can also be hazardous in patients, especially males with prostatic hypertrophy, who have urinary retention or related difficulties in voiding. The effect can result in acute urinary retention in these patients and should be anticipated and monitored in such patients at risk.

In addition to the common anticholinergic effects, to which tolerance often develops, the tricyclics and related tetracyclic drugs have other cardiovascular effects in addition to postural hypotension which is variably seen (Table 4.5). Postural hypotension can be severe in those individuals on vasodilators and in those with moderately advanced arteriosclerotic disease. Additionally, these drugs can cause various effects on cardiac conduction including arrhythmias due to their prolongation of the Q-T$_c$ interval. Although the newer agents, such as trazodone, have been claimed to have fewer cardiac effects, this remains to be established. Antidepressants can interfere with sympatholytic antihypertensive therapy. These sympatholytic agents can also produce depression. This should be clarified and alternative therapy begun before initiation of an antidepressant.

The majority of these drugs can lower the seizure threshold, thus making their use in patients with pre-existing seizure disorders potentially problematic. These drugs also have other less common adverse effects, include allergic reactions, hematologic and hepatic reactions, and, particularly in the elderly, paradoxical psychoses.

In selected cases, it may be necessary to treat depression and tricyclic or related agents cannot be used. In certain cases, MAO inhibitors can provide beneficial relief of depression. However, because of their ability to produce serious reactions when interacting with tyramine containing foods or with other drugs, their use should only be initiated under the careful supervision of a clinician experienced with their use. Additionally, the patient should receive a thorough education on the use of these agents.

Lithium carbonate is reserved for the treatment of bipolar disorders, which commonly begin in earlier years. The use of lithium can be complicated in elderly patients due to declining renal function. This can decrease the excretion of lithium and elevate its blood levels. Interaction with thiazide diuretics may also increase its toxicity. This drug, and its underly-

Table 4.5
Use of Characteristics of Antidepressant Drugs to Tailor Therapy to Individual Needs in the Elderly

High	Moderate	Low
Therapeutic goals		
Sedation		
Amitriptyline	Imipramine	Desipramine
Doxepin	Maprotiline	[None: protriptyline]
	Amoxapine	
	Trazodone	
	Alprazolam	
Appetite stimulation		
Amitriptyline		Protriptyline
		[None: imipramine, desipramine]
Psychopharmacologic mechanisms		
Serotonin uptake		
Amitriptyline	Imipramine	Desipramine
Trazodone		Amoxapine
		[None: maprotiline, alprazolam]
Norepinephrine uptake		
Desipramine	Imipramine	Amitriptyline
Maprotiline		[None: trazodone, alprazolam]
Amoxapine		
Common side effects		
Anticholinergic effects		
Amitriptyline	Doxepin	Desipramine
	Imipramine	
	Protriptyline	
Orthostatic hypotension		
Amitriptyline	Doxepin	Desipramine
	Protriptyline	

ing disorder should be under the careful, ongoing monitoring of an experienced therapist and should include regular monitoring of blood levels, renal and thyroid function (since hypothyroidism may also be associated with its use).

Finally, methylphenidate (Ritalin) has been used sporadically for many years in the treatment of depression in the elderly. It can be considered as an alternative if other modalities are not successful, but requires monitoring of cardiovascular status (49).

In summary, there are many options for treatment of depression in the elderly. Because the therapy can sometimes produce troublesome side effects, nondrug therapies should be explored first and as adjuncts to the drug therapy. The variety of agents with their range of differing pharmacologic effects requires the prescriber to define rather specific therapeutic goals and monitor the patient carefully.

TREATMENT OF THOUGHT AND BEHAVIOR DISORDERS IN THE ELDERLY: NEUROLEPTICS

Acute psychoses and related behavior disorders are frequently seen as new events in the elderly and may be associated with certain diseases, including stroke, hypoxia, and electrolyte disturbances. Of importance is that these disorders may also be seen with a variety of drugs, such as tricyclic antidepressants, steroids, and nonsteroidal anti-inflammatory agents. Acute confusion, hostility, wandering, and other behavioral disorders are associated with the dementias of various causes seen in this age group. If the reversible medical or drug causes of this behavior are ruled out, the use of neuroleptic agents in low doses are often used to prevent excessive disruptive behavior and/or assist with improving function.

Neuroleptic drugs are also indicated for those patients with schizophrenia and selected patients with bipolar disorders. In these cases, the regimen of neuroleptics has usually been established at a younger age and dosages required may be higher than for the newly appearing behavior problems in the older patient. This discussion will primarily focus on the treatment of the newly appearing behavior problem in the elderly.

Behavior problems of many types appear with dementia in the elderly. The behaviors vary considerably and include confusion of various degrees, wandering and, in some cases, angry or abusive behavior. This is amenable to treatment with neuroleptics, but there has been some concern relating to the overuse of these drugs for this purpose. There has been concern about patients, particularly those in nursing homes, being overly sedated and also experi-

encing possibly unnecessary side effects, such as extrapyramidal effects and tardive dyskinesia (35, 40, 58). Accordingly, regulations for long-term care facilities now incorporate a rather strict requirement for initiation of so-called chemical restraints or neuroleptics, which require definition of the purpose of therapy and regular monitoring.

As in the case for all psychiatric symptoms, the possibility of an underlying reversible cause for the acute symptoms should be ruled out before initiation of neuroleptic therapy. In selected cases, neuroleptics may be useful for short-term management in reversible cases.

There are a large number of neuroleptic agents available that include compounds with chemically different structures. The many compounds and their diverse pharmacologic effects are described in detail in many reviews (3). They share the same therapeutic psychotropic effect and can be generally grouped into two categories: (a) the high-dose, low-potency agents, such as chlorpromazine, and (b) the high-potency, low-dose agents, such as fluphenazine, thiozanthenes, and haloperidol (49).

The selection of a particular agent relates less to the therapeutic effects, which are roughly comparable in the two categories and more to the side effects associated with these agents. These side effects can be critical in the elderly patient.

The high-dose, low-potency agents represented by chlorpromazine and thioridazine have a lower frequency of extrapyramidal effects but have significant other effects that become problematic in the older patient. Both of these drugs have considerable anticholinergic effects which can be an important problem in the elderly. These effects can add to the anticholinergic effects of any other drugs in use (e.g., antiparkinsonian, antihistaminic drugs). Further, this group of agents have significant α_1-adrenergic blocking effects, manifested by postural hypotension. This can be a cause for falls in patients already predisposed. In some cases, tolerance will develop to both the anticholinergic and α-adrenergic effects; thus, initiation of therapy with very low doses may minimize them. Thioridazine can have significant quinidine-like effects which may complicate preexisting cardiac changes and predispose to arrhythmias. In contrast to these adverse effects, the low-potency drugs have a lower frequency of extrapyramidal effects compared to the more potent agents, which can be advantageous.

Because of these side effects, the other category of neuroleptics may often be more appropriate for use in the elderly. However, the increased incidence of causing extrapyramidal side effects with this group of drugs in this age group can also be debilitating. Extrapyramidal effects can be, to a certain extent, controlled by the use of anticholinergic agents like benztropine (Cogentin) or trihexiphenidyl (Artane). Use of the anticholinergic drugs should not be routine, but initiated only with the appearance of significant extrapyramidal effects. This is to avoid both extra drugs and the additional anticholinergic effects that these agents exert.

Unfortunately, the neuroleptic agents are often initiated in the acute hospital setting and often in high doses given frequently. This can cause oversedation in the frail and can result in hypotension, decreased food intake, and associated complications. Many elderly patients will actually respond to very small doses (e.g., 0.5 mg of haloperidol, 10–25 mg of thioridazine) of these drugs given once or twice daily. This practice may minimize the other undesired effects. The old adage "start low, go slow" applies especially to the use of either category of these drugs.

An additional major concern with use of these drugs involves the development of tardive dyskinesias that can develop in a certain proportion (10–40%) of these patients. This malady is often irreversible and worsened by discontinuing the drug and the use of the anticholinergic agents (49). It appears to be minimized by using the smallest effective dose, and by using "drug-free holidays" (e.g., no drug on weekends once a steady state has been attained).

Finally, all of these drugs are associated with other adverse effects, which are less common and include dermatologic reactions, neutropenia, and jaundice. The latter two reactions may only appear after 1 or more months of therapy and may not be initially recognized as a possible adverse reactions. For example, the leukopenia may be only manifested by acute sepsis; the jaundice may initially raise the suspicion of other common causes in this age group, although the presence of eosinophilia makes its recognition easier. It has not been determined whether one or another neuroleptic has a greater or lesser likelihood of producing these effects due to their rarity, but they have been reported in association with most of the members of this drug group (3, 43).

All of these factors suggest that the decision to use a neuroleptic agent, both initially and for any prolonged period should only be made after their use is clearly indicated. Second, these agents should be used in as low a dose as is possible to produce effective control of the thought or behavior disorder. Because the development of tardive dyskinesia is a distinct possibility, long-term use should be discussed with the patient's family in an attempt to share with them the potential advantages and disadvantages of this therapy.

OVERALL SUMMARY

This chapter has addressed a wide range of topics relating to use of drugs in the elderly and this chapter could only cover some of these in a general outline.

The epidemiology of drugs in the elderly demonstrates that most elderly persons receiving medical care will take one or more prescriptions during a period of a year, and many will take more than three. Thus, this age group accounts for a very high proportion of all drug use. The drugs taken can improve or disrupt function, can determine disposition after hospitalization, and can account for a large proportion of the elderly person's health care costs. Because drugs are prescribed by multispecialty providers, a patient's drug regimen can be complex, redundant, expensive, and even hazardous. This potential underscores the need for coordination of care to develop a coherent regimen and structured therapeutic monitoring.

The elderly as a group undergo a variety of physiologic changes which can affect their handling of drugs, but these changes do not occur consistently in each patient. Each patient frequently has a complex complement of disorders and a varied therapeutic regimen. These characteristics makes the use of drugs in the elderly one of the more challenging areas in geriatrics, but also an opportunity to expand the horizons of clinical pharmacology to synthesize the complex pharmacokinetic and pharmacodynamic findings observed into useful therapeutic principles. These challenges should be welcomed since the use of drugs in an elderly individual requires the physician to practice what has been considered optimal therapeutics, i.e., to know the drug, its pharmacology, its kinetics, and to organize therapy with therapeutic goals and end points.

Although the actual practice of this type of therapeutics has yet to reach its ideal, the practitioner should strive, in the management of complex drug regimens in the elderly, to optimize efficacy and avoid toxicities. This will assist in advancing our understanding of how drugs may best be used in the entire population.

REFERENCES

1. American Association of Retired Persons: A survey on attitudes toward drug use in the over-45 population in the U.S. 1984.

2. Armstrong WA, Driever CW, Hays RL: Analysis of drug-drug interactions in a geriatric population. *Am J Hosp Pharm* 37:385, 1980.

3. Baldassarini RJ: Drugs and the treatment of psychiatric disorders. In: Goodman, Gilman, (Eds): *The Pharmacological Basis of Therapeutics.* New York, Macmillan, Chap. 19. pp. 387-445, 1986.

4. Baum C, Kennedy DL, Forbes MB, Jones JK: Drug use in the United States in 1981. *JAMA* 251:1293, 1984.

5. Baum C, Kennedy DL, Forbes MB, Jones JK: Drug use and expenditures in 1982. *JAMA* 253:382, 1985.

5a. Bellville JW, Forrest WH, Miller E, Brown BW: Influence of age on pain relief from analgesics: A study of postoperative patients. *JAMA* 217:1835, 1971.

6. Brocklehurst JC (ed): *Geriatric Pharmacology and Therapeutics.* London, Blackwell Scientific Publications, 1984.

7. Caranasos GJ, Stewart RB, Cluff LE: Drug-induced illness leading to hospitalization. *JAMA* 228:713, 1974.

8. Crooks J, Stevenson IH (eds): *Drugs and the Elderly.* London, Macmillan, 1979.

9. Cypress BK: Drug utilization in general and family practice by characteristics of physicians and office visits. National Center for Health Statistics, Advance Data from Vital and Health Statistics, No. 87, DHHS Pub. No. (PHS) 83-1250. Public Health Service, Hyattsville, MD, March 18, 1983.

10. Cypress BK: Patterns of ambulatory care in general and family practice medicine. The National Ambulatory Care Survey, U.S., Jan 1980-Dec. 1981. Vital and Health Statistics Series 13, No. 80, DHHS Pub. No. (PHS) 84-1741, Government Printing Office, 1984.

11. Domecq C, Naranjo CA, Ruiz I, Busto U: Sex-related variations in the frequency and characteristics of adverse drug reactions. *Int J Clin Pharmacol Ther Toxicol* 18:362, 1980.

12. Editorial: *Br Med J* 289:898, 1985.

13. Everitt DE, Avorn J: Drug prescribing for the elderly. *Arch Intern Med* 146:2393, 1986.

14. Greenblatt DJ, Allen MD, Shader RI: Toxicity of high-dose flurazepam in the elderly. *Clin Pharmacol Ther* 21:355, 1977.

15. Greenblatt DJ, Divoll M, Abernathy DR, et al: Antipyrine kinetics in the elderly: Prediction of age-related changes in benzodiazepine oxidizing capacity. *J Pharmacol Exp Ther* 220:120, 1982.

16. Greenblatt DJ, Sellers EM, Shader RI: Drug disposition on old age. *N Engl J Med* 306:1081, 1982.

17. Hale WE, May FE, Marks RG, Stewart RB: Drug use in an ambulatory elderly population: A five-year update. *Drug Intell Clin Pharm* 21:530, 1987.

18. Hurwitz N: Predisposing factors in adverse reactions to drugs. *Br Med J* 1:536, 1969.

19. Hussar DA: Drug Interactions in geriatric drug use. In Moore SR, Teal TW (Eds): *Clinical Drug Use-Clinical & Social Perspectives.* New York, Pergamon Press, pp. 135-143, 1985.

20. Idanpaan-Heikkila J: A review of safety information obtained from Phases I-II and Phase III clinical investigations of sixteen selected drugs. U.S. Dept. of Health and Human Statistics, FDA, 1983.

21. Irey NS: Diagnostic problems in drug-induced diseases. In Meyler L, Peck HM (eds): *Drug-Induced Diseases.* Amsterdam, *Excerpta Medica,* 4:1, 1972.

22. Jones JK: Adverse drug reactions in the community health setting: approaches to recognizing, counseling and reporting. *Drug Inform J* 16:87, 1982.

23. Jones JK: Adverse drug reaction considerations in geriatric drug research. *Drug Inform J* 19:459, 1985.

24. Karch FE, Lasagna L: Toward the operational identification of adverse drug reactions. *Clin Pharmacol Ther* 21:247, 1977.

25. Keller MB, Klerman GL, Lavori PW, Fawcett JA, Coryell W, Endicott J: Treatment received by depressed patients. *JAMA* 248:1848, 1982.

26. Koch H: (National Center for Health Statistics) Drug utilization in office practice by age and sex of the patient: National ambulatory medical care survey, 1980. Vital and Health Statistics, Series 2-No. 90 DHHS Pub. No. (PHS) 82-1364. Public Health Service, Washington, 1982.

27. Knapp DA, Knapp DA, Wiser TH, Michocki RJ, Nuessle SJ, Knapp WK: Drug prescribing for ambulatory patients 85 years of age and older. *J Am Geriatr Soc* 32:138, 1984.

28. Lamy PP: Drug prescribing for the elderly. In Reichel W (ed): *Clinical Aspects of the Aging: A Comprehensive Text,* 2nd ed. Baltimore, Williams & Williams, pp. 21-71, 1983.

29. Lawson DH, Henry DA, Lowe JM, Gray JMB, Morgan G: Severe hypokalemia in hospitalized patients. *Arch Intern Med* 139:987, 1979.

30. Levy MH, Kewitz W, Altwein W, Hillebrand J, Eliakim M: Hospital admissions due to adverse drug reactions: Comparative study from Jerusalem and Berlin. *Eur J Clin Pharmacol* 17:25, 1980.

31. Levy MH, Lipshitz M, Eliakim M: Hospital admissions due to adverse drug reactions. *Am J Med Sci* 277:49, 1979.

32. Mandolini A: The social contexts of aging and drug use: theoretical and methodological insights. *J Psychoactive Drugs* 13:135, 1981.

33. May FE, Stewart RB, Hale WE, Marks RG: Prescribed and nonprescribed drug use in an ambulatory elderly population. *South Med J* 75:522, 1982.

34. *Med Lett Drug Ther* 26:59, 1984.

35. Milleren JW: Some contingencies affecting the utilization of tranquilizers in long-term care of the elderly. *J Health Soc Behav* 18:206, 1977.

36. O'Neill RT: Statistical analyses of adverse event data from clinical trials: Special emphasis on serious events. *Drug Inform J* 21:9, 1987.

37. Ouslander JG: Drug therapy in the elderly. *Ann Intern Med* 95:711, 1981.

38. Pucino F, Beck CL, Seifert RL, Strommen GL, Sheldon PA, Silbergleit IL: Pharmacogeriatrics. *Pharmacother* 5:314, 1985.

39. Ramsey LE, Tucker GT: Clinical pharmacology: Drugs and the elderly. *Br Med J* 282:125, 1981.

40. Ray WA, Federspiel CF, Schaffner W: A study of antipsychotic drug use in nursing homes: Epidemiologic evidence suggesting misuse. *Am J Public Health* 70:485, 1980.

41. Reidenberg MM, Levy M, Warner H, et al: Relationship between diazepam dose, plasma level, age and central nervous system depression. *Clin Pharm Ther* 23:371, 1978.

42. Rossiter LF: Prescribed medicines: National medical care expenditure survey. *Am J Public Health* 73:1312, 1983.

43. Schader RI, Dimascio AD: *Psychotropic Drug Side Effects*. Baltimore, The Williams & Wilkins Co., 1970.

44. Schmucker DL: Aging and drug disposition: An update. *Pharmacol Rev* 37:133, 1985.

45. Seidl LG, Thornton GF, Smith JW, Cluff LE: Studies on the epidemiology of adverse reactions. III. Reactions in patients on a general medical service. *Bull Johns Hopkins Hosp* 119:299, 1966.

46. Shaw PG: Common pitfalls in geriatric drug prescribing. *Drugs* 23:324, 1982.

47. Shepherd AM, Hewick DS, Moreland TA, Stevenson IH: Age as a determinant of sensitivity to warfarin. *Br J Clin Pharmacol* 4:315, 1977.

48. Siersback-Nielsen J, Hansen JM, Kampmann J, Kristensen M: Appropriateness of vitamin and mineral prescription orders for residents of health related facilities. *J Am Geriat Soc* 27:245, 1979.

49. Sloan RW: *Practical Geriatric Therapeutics*. Oradell, NJ, Medical Economics Books, 1986.

50. Steel K, Gertman PM, Creanzi C, Anderson J: Iatrogenic illness in a general medical service at a university hospital. *N Engl J Med* 304:638, 1981.

51. Swift C, Homeida M, Halliwell M: Antipyrine disposition and liver size in the elderly. *Eur J Clin Pharmacol* 14:149, 1981.

52. Talley RB, Laventurier MF: The incidence of drug-drug interactions in a Medi-Cal population. *Cal Pharm* 20:18, 1972.

52a. Thompson TL II, Moran MG, Nies AS: Drug therapy. Psychotropic drug use in the elderly, Part 2. *N Engl J Med* 308:194, 1983.

52b. Thompson TL II, Moran MG, Nies AS: Psychotropic drug use in the elderly. *N Eng J Med* 308:134, 1983.

53. Vestal RE: Drug use in the elderly: A review of problems and special considerations. *Drugs* 6:358, 1978.

54. Vestal RE (ed): *Drug Treatment in the Elderly*. Sydney, Australia, ADIS Health Science Press, p. 33, 1984.

55. Vestal RE, Wood A, Shand D: Reduced beta-adrenoceptor sensitivity in the elderly. *Clin Pharmacol Ther* 26:818, 1979.

56. Wallace RB: Drug utilization in the rural elderly: Perspectives from a population study. In: Moore SR, Teal TW (eds): *Geriatric Drug Use: Clinical and Social Perspectives*. New York, Pergamon Press, pp. 78-85, 1984.

57. Williamson J, Chopin JM: Adverse reactions to prescribed drugs in the elderly: A multicentre investigation. *Age Aging* 9:73, 1980.

58. Zawadski RT, Glazer GB, Lurie E: Psychotropic drug use among institutionalized and noninstitutionalized Medicaid aged in California. *J Gerontol* 33:825, 1978.

CHAPTER 5

Common Complaints of the Elderly

ROBERT R. HUNTLEY

A principal responsibility of the primary physician to his elderly patients is to assist them in maintaining function in the face of the inevitable reduction in reserve of all organ systems with progressively advancing age. Nowhere is this more critical than in the psychologic sphere and in the functioning of the musculoskeletal system. In this chapter, several common complaints of elderly patients will be used to illustrate the principle that careful attention to the need for physical activity, good nutrition, intimacy, and social interactions are at least as important in the maintenance of well-being as is the meticulous medical management of diseases.

Proper management requires first that the complaint be elicited and taken seriously. Next, it is required that the exact nature of the complaint be characterized and a precisely focused medical assessment be completed to elucidate causative factors. Finally, the appropriate therapy must be prescribed (rarely drugs) and follow-up maintained. This is simply good medical practice but it is outlined explicitly here because of the temptation to attribute many common complaints in the elderly to "old age," especially in individuals aged 75 years and over. It is important to remember that patients also may attribute symptoms to old age and fail to mention them unless specifically asked. Another common reason for the physician's discounting symptoms in elderly patients is the belief that hypochondriasis is common in the old. In fact, the elderly are no more likely to be hypochondriacal than are younger patients (2). When they are, hypochondriasis is often a manifestation of depression.

Concern about *memory loss* is one of the most common worries of elderly people, and, even more commonly, of their children. Everyone experiences difficulty retrieving names, telephone numbers, etc.,

from time to time. Because it is commonly believed that memory loss is a concomitant of aging, an older person experiencing this difficulty will become concerned, especially because it is now common knowledge that memory loss is an early sign of the onset of dementia, which both the elderly and their families fear, quite appropriately.

The principal change in memory in normal aging is an impairment in recall (4). Thus, memory loss is especially likely to bother an elderly patient who lives alone and who has minimal opportunities for the social interactions that provide cues to memory retrieval. Lonely old people also often become withdrawn, depressed, or hostile. Such patients may be difficult to test for mental status because they may be unwilling to try to remember.

The primary care physician faced with a patient complaining of memory loss, with or without symptoms of withdrawal or hostility, must proceed promptly to careful examination and precise diagnosis. It is never appropriate to assume "benign forgetfulness," and this label, carelessly applied, will not reassure the patient, his family, or the physician.

The workup should include a search for symptoms or signs of depression and of medical problems that might affect mentation, with special attention to nutritional deficiencies and drug and alcohol intake. In all cases, it should also include a formal, brief mental status examination. Detailed advice on further workup, if significant intellectual impairment is discovered, is provided in Chapter 14.

Most patients with a complaint of memory loss will, upon evaluation, be found not to have significant intellectual impairment. Reassurance, increased social stimulation, increased physical activity, and careful attention to medication and nutrition, constitute the recommended management for these patients. Education of the patient's children or other concerned adults to the importance of attention to these matters is also an essential component of management.

Complaints about *sleep difficulties* are common in elderly patients, even in the absence of pain or other physical discomfort. Most commonly, the complaint is about difficulty getting to sleep or awakening too often during the night, and many older patients are explicit: "I just can't sleep like I used to when I was younger." Careful questioning usually reveals that the pattern is within normal limits for elderly people, who take somewhat longer to get to sleep and have frequent awakenings, with the result that total wake time is markedly increased when compared to young adults (5). This fact is not common knowledge and often a simple explanation is all that is required to "treat" this complaint.

If the complaint is compatible with true insomnia, with inability to get to sleep for over an hour after retiring and/or long periods of wakefulness during the night, the patient's 24-hour sleep and physical activity schedule should be reviewed. Inactive elderly patients who nap during the day and get little exercise can be helped by having them increase physical activity and refrain from daytime naps. In addition, they should refrain from caffeine after noon, from alcohol after dinner, and they should spend the last hour before bed in a quiet activity and in restful surroundings. They also should go to bed at a set time every night. If, in spite of these changes in life-style, the patient still cannot get to sleep within an hour of retiring, suggest that he or she get up, and read for a while, then go back to bed. After a few weeks, this regimen will usually result in the restoration of a normal sleep pattern.

In those instances where insomnia is the result of situational anxiety or grief, the use of a low dose of a short-acting benzodiazepine, such as triazolam (0.125–0.25 mg) for a few nights only is justified, to avoid excessive fatigue. This is the only circumstance in which hypnotics are indicated for the treatment of an isolated complaint of insomnia in the elderly.

Finally, insomnia is frequently the presenting complaint in depressed elderly patients (5), who often focus on their sleep symptoms to avoid facing the fact that they are depressed. Thus, depression should be suspected even in the absence of vegetative symptoms or an obviously flattened affect if the simple measures outlined above do not correct the insomnia.

"I just don't have any energy anymore." "I'm weak and tired all the time." Complaints of fatigue are very common in older patients. A careful history, physical examination, and selected laboratory studies are required to rule out depression, organic illness (especially heart disease and anemia), or medication-related fatigue. However, at the end of the workup, physician and patient are often left without an explanation for this common symptom.

At this point, it is useful to explore the patient's life-style in some detail. Is he or she lonely or bored? What does the patient eat and when? How many hours of every 24 does he or she spend in bed? How much physical exercise does the patient get?

As humans age, there is a gradual decline in physical activity, even in the absence of intercurrent illness. However, the training effects of regular exercise are the same in old age as in youth (3). Consequently, the institution of a regular (daily, if possible) regimen of walking, gardening, or swimming to increasing tolerance is an excellent treatment for the isolated complaint of fatigue. Suggest that the patient invite a friend to exercise with him or her, if possible. This will improve the likelihood that the regimen will be followed and will provide an opportunity for valuable social interaction, especially for the patient who lives alone.

Shopping malls are excellent places for the elderly to walk because they are climate controlled, well lit, flat, and safe.

Regular exercise to maintain cardiovascular, respiratory, and musculoskeletal conditioning is clearly beneficial to the elderly whether they complain of fatigue or not. This becomes increasingly important as very old age is approached and the occurrence of serious intercurrent illnesses requires temporary immobility periodically. Reconditioning after such immobility is much more effective if preillness conditioning was good. Maintaining physical conditioning will also be protective against falls and fractures.

To assure physical conditioning often requires relief of the *pain* of osteoarthritis of the hips, knees, and spine and the correction of foot problems. Advice to use a hot tub soak morning and night, combined with the prescription of nonsteroidal antiinflammatory agents, beginning with buffered aspirin if tolerated, is a reasonable approach to pain management. The prescription of proper walking shoes is frequently indicated in the overall management of physical deconditioning because painful feet are a strong deterrent.

For elderly patients, *falls* are a common problem. It is estimated that almost one of three persons over age 65 years falls each year. It is important to minimize falling to prevent fractures of the hip, vertebrae, and forearms to which Caucasian women are particularly prone because osteoporosis is most severe in this group of old people (1).

A tendency to fall may be related to a variety of neurologic, cardiovascular, visual, or musculoskeletal disorders, which must be considered in the patient's evaluation. Whether a predisposing condition is present or not, preventive measures are important to minimize falls in all elderly people, especially those at high risk: improving indoor lighting, the removal of throw rugs and electrical cords, and the addition of handrails to stairs, showers, and tubs. The use of a cane to improve stability, especially when walking outside the home, should be encouraged. The use of alcohol and sedatives should be actively discouraged.

Frail old people frequently refrain from walking much because they are "unsteady" and fear falling. These patients should be strongly encouraged to walk to tolerance daily, using a cane and accompanied if possible by a child, a friend, or an attendant.

Deterioration in *vision* and *hearing* is progressively more common with advancing age. Screening questions, such as: "can you see to read the newspaper?" and "can you hear well enough to use the phone?" should be asked routinely. Referral for precise diagnosis, and, where possible, the institution of corrective treatment, is always worthwhile when deficits are detected because deficits in these functions exacerbate isolation, loneliness, and physical deconditioning. The provision of a properly functioning hearing aid or the removal of a cataract may contribute greatly to improving health and the quality of life.

Elderly patients sometimes complain of *loss of appetite* as a presenting symptom. More commonly, the physician detects weight loss in the course of routine office visits. While cancer is the most common medical diagnosis in elderly patients with weight loss, it only accounts for about 20% of such patients (6). Poverty, inability to shop because of immobility, depression, poor dentition, and decreased enjoyment of food because of decreased taste and smell are all important factors contributing to decreased food intake and decreased intake is the most common cause of weight loss in the elderly.

Because this is true, an important component of the workup of elderly patients is a careful dietary history, from both the patient and family members if possible, looking specifically for the factors cited above. Even in patients without weight loss, a dietary history will frequently make it evident to the physician that the intakes of protein, calories, and vitamin sources are inadequate. These patients should be considered to be chronically marginally malnourished, even in the absence of weight loss.

The history should give clues as to the cause of malnutrition; poverty, immobility, dental problems, chronic depression, etc. The variety of interrelated reasons often requires the physician to mobilize family and community resources in resolving this problem.

Sometimes it is impossible to improve the appetite of frail elderly patients enough to assure adequate nutrition. A nutritional supplement (milk or soy-based) to provide extra protein and calories and a multivitamin/mineral preparation is recommended for these patients.

Constipation is a common complaint that often can be resolved by simply finding out precisely what the actual symptoms are. If stool consistency is normal, and the patient occasionally skips a day, reassurance and a simple explanation that some large bowel tone is lost with age may be all that is needed. If there is a significant change in bowel habit, further workup may be in order. (See Chapter 18 for detailed discussion.) The addition of fiber (bran) and fluid to the diet of older people is good general advice as is increasing physical activity. The periodic use of the test for occult blood in the stool as a screen for bowel disease is strongly recommended.

Sexual complaints are not commonly spontaneously voiced, but, if asked about, will often be elicited. If possible, an interview with the patient's partner to achieve an understanding of the perceptions of both, followed by a session with both, can resolve the problem. Often there is misconception as to the appropriateness of an active sex life in old age. Sexual activity is sometimes terminated because of an intercurrent illness and is not resumed after resolution. Sometimes, after recovery from myocardial infarction, sexual activity is not resumed because no one remembered to tell the patient that it is safe. Atrophic vaginitis may cause painful intercourse; the prescription of topical estrogen will usually correct the problem.

For many elderly couples, simply insisting that they have privacy in the home or nursing home where they live will allow them to resume intimate relations. Intimacy is a valuable part of life for humans of all ages. Assisting older couples to maintain intimacy through the expression of their sexuality can contribute substantially to the quality of their lives.

Nonsexual intimacy is also valuable and children, friends, caretakers, and the patient's doctor all need to share of themselves to ameliorate the loneliness and alienation that is so often an accompaniment of old age.

Common problems with memory, sleep, fatigue, vision, hearing, physical activity, appetite, nutrition, and sexuality have been especially highlighted because these are complaints that often have their origins in the physiologic, psychologic and social changes inherent in aging. The interrelatedness of these problems, and their synergistic effects in contributing to diminished function in the elderly, means that physicians who address them systematically and thoroughly can make substantial contributions to the maintenance of function and enhancement of the quality of life of their aging patients.

REFERENCES

1. Cummings SR, Kelsey JL, Nevitt MC, O'Dowd KJ: Epidemiology of osteoporosis and osteoporotic fractures. *Epidemiol Rev* 1:178, 1985.
2. Denney D, Kole DM, Matarazzo RG: The relationship between age and the number of symptoms reported by patients. *J Gerontol* 20:50, 1965.
3. Editorial: Physical activity in old age. *Lancet* 2:1431, 1986.
4. Fryer DG: Understanding the aging brain. *Postgrad Med* 80:99, 1986.
5. Kales A, Kales JD: Sleep disorders: Recent findings in the diagnosis and treatment of disturbed sleep. *N Engl J Med* 290:487, 1974.
6. Morley JE, Silver AJ, Fiatarone M, Mooradian AD: Geriatric grand rounds: Nutrition and the elderly, UCLA. *J Am Geriatr Soc* 34:823, 1986.

CHAPTER 6

Diagnosis and Management of Heart Disease in the Elderly

ARTHUR J. MOSS

Cardiovascular performance declines progressively with age and there is an increased probability of having one or more of the numerous cardiac diseases that afflict mankind. The elderly patient, in contrast to his/her younger brethren, has to contend with both an aging heart and superimposed cardiac disease—a combination that markedly increases the risk of disability and death. It is important for the physician to differentiate between the "normal" decline that ensues with age and problems resulting from specific cardiovascular diseases.

What is the potential functional state of an elderly individual without cardiac disease? The physiologic characteristics of a world champion distance runner, age 77, were reported by Webb et al. in 1977 (19). The subject held 14 recognized world records in track for competitors in the 74–76-year-old category. At age 77, the individual ran record races of 1 mile in 6:53.6 (min:sec.tenths) and 10,000 meters in 47:30.0. Physiologic studies of this subject revealed that he was slim and trim (height 5′9½″ and weight 151 lb) with resting blood pressure 120/70 mm Hg, resting heart rate 55 beats/min, maximum heart rate 160 beats/min, and maximum minute ventilation of 83 liters/min (normal range 45–80 liters/min for men of equivalent age). This single-patient study provides some insight into the optimal performance that can be achieved in a trained, elderly individual without complicating cardiopulmonary disease—an image that we should keep in mind as we care for patients in the older age croup.

CARDIOVASCULAR PATHOPHYSIOLOGY AND AGING

During the past decade, a considerable amount of valuable data has been accumulated about the cardiac aging process from in vitro metabolic studies of senescent animal hearts. In addition, investigations of intact hearts from senescent animals and evaluation of cardiovascular performance in aging human beings provide important background information for understanding the setting of cardiac disease in the elderly (7). Comprehensive reviews of this subject are provided in a monograph edited by Weisfeldt entitled *The Aging Heart* (20) and in the book *Geriatric Cardiology* by Berman (2).

BIOCHEMICAL CHANGES IN THE HEART

Energy Production

Various myocellular mitochondrial enzyme activities (fatty acid oxidation, the tricarboxylate cycle, and oxidative phosphorylation) progressively decrease with age. This diminution is explained in part by a reduction in the number of mitochondria per unit volume or weight, and also by a shift of specific enzyme activity away from active fatty acid oxidation. It is reasonable to speculate that a reduction in this enzymatic machinery in the older heart contributed to diminished work performance in the intact organ.

Electrophysiologic Properties

The various characteristics of the myocellular action potential including the level of the resting membrane potential, dV/dt, the plateau duration, the repolarization time, and the effective refractory period, are similar in hearts from adult and senescent animals. However, spontaneous automaticity of the pacemaker cells in the sinus node and in the Purkinje network of the ventricles declines with age. This effect results primarily from a reduction in the rate of phase 4 depolarization in pacemaker cells —an alteration that may contribute to enhanced arrhythmogenesis and bradycardia in the elderly and an increased susceptibility to the bradycardic effects of antiarrhythmic agents. The conduction velocity of the electrical impulse is minimally altered in Purkinje fibers of senescent animals, but conduction is slowed through nodal tissue, such as the atrioventricular node, possibly from the disordered pacemaker cells in the junctional regions.

Sarcoplasmic Reticulum

Central to the myocardial contractile process is the release and uptake of calcium ion by the sarcoplasmic reticulum. With excitation of the myocardial cell, calcium is released by the sarcoplasmic reticulum and binds with troponin C, permitting actin-myosin crossbridging and sarcomere shortening. Reuptake of calcium by the sarcoplasmic reticulum terminates contraction and promotes sarcomere relaxation. The aged heart contracts and relaxes more slowly than the younger heart and studies from the National Institute of Aging indicate that the reduction in the rate of these time-related phenomena is caused by a decrease in the rate of calcium release and removal by the sarcoplasmic reticulum. It is unclear whether these age-related effects in sarcoplasmic reticulum function are primary or secondary, and as yet structural changes in the sarcoplasmic reticulum with age have not been demonstrated. Certainly, older patients would be more susceptible to the cardiodepressant effects of the calcium antagonists such as nifedipine, verapamil, and diltiazem.

Cardiac Receptors

One of the most striking changes that occurs in the aged heart is a decline in the response to stress. Studies involving adrenergic-mediated stress in the aged heart by Lakatta (9) and Vestal et al. (18) reveal a decline in postsynaptic response to β-adrenergic stimulation suggesting a reduction in either the number or the function of the receptors. Other investigators have shown that isolated muscle from old animals has fewer adrenergic receptors than muscle from young animals. In addition, current evidence indicates that the number of cardiac receptors for digitalis declines with age. This finding may explain why digitalis is less effective as an inotropic agent in older than in younger people. These findings with regard to adrenergic and digitalis receptors may be part of a universal characteristic of aging—a reduction in the number of all hormonal receptors with age. The net result would be a diminished effectiveness to agonists (catecholamines) and an enhanced sensitivity to antagonists (β-blockers, calcium blockers) in the elderly patient.

Anatomic Changes

Age-related anatomic changes occur in the myocardial collagen and in the conduction system. Collagen becomes more plentiful and it increases the stiffness of the heart. These changes reduce ventricular diastolic compliance more than systolic contractility, and they may affect impulse transmission. Myocardial deposition of lipid substances is also common. Sclerodegenerative changes also develop in the conduction system with patchy fibrosis, a loss of myofibers, and an increase in the elastic tissue in the His-Purkinje network. The number of pacemaker cells in the sinoatrial node decreases with age. It has been estimated that after age 75 years, the sinus node contains less than 10% of the pacemaker cells present in younger patients (5). These anatomic findings explain, in part, the increased prevalence of high ventricular filling pressures, fascicular block conduction disturbances, and sinus node dysfunction in the elderly.

CARDIOVASCULAR DYSFUNCTION

Arrhythmic Disorders

Sinus node dysfunction may manifest itself in terms of sustained sinus bradycardia at rates less than 50 beats/min, intermittent sinus arrest with varying durations of asystole, or the atrial brady-tachy syndrome with alternating episodes of atrial tachycardia followed abruptly by profound sinus arrest. Patients with sinus node dysfunction may present clinically with fatigue or tiredness due to the bradycardia with reduced cardiac output, syncope from the asystolic sinus arrest, or troublesome palpitations or angina from the tachycardia. Sinus node dysfunction is quite prevalent in patients over 70 years of age and is responsible for considerable morbidity.

Atrioventricular block unrelated to acute myocardial infarction is a disorder primarily of older individuals. It may present as an abrupt syncope, the so-called Morgagni-Adams-Stokes attack, or simply with fatigue and palpitations from varying degrees of heart block. Two common causes of heart block in the geriatric patient are Lenegre's disease and Lev's disease. The former is an idiopathic sclerodegenerative process involving the Purkinje conducting system. Lenegre's disease is one of the most common causes of right bundle branch block and left anterior hemiblock in older patients, and there is usually a slow progression to complete heart block over several years. Lev's disease is a degeneration of the fibrous supporting tissues of the heart with invasion of the adjacent conducting system by fibrosis or calcification. Calcification may begin either in the aortic or mitral valve anulus and extend into the bundle of His or the proximal bundle branches to produce bundle branch block, hemiblock, or complete heart block.

Ventricular arrhythmias occur more frequently in the older than the younger age group, even in the absence of demonstrable organic heart disease. Several studies have utilized 24-hour Holter recordings to evaluate the frequency and complexity of ventricular premature beats (VPBs) in different age groups. Fleg and Kennedy (6) reported the 24-hour Holter electrocardiographic (ECG) findings in 98 elderly (age 60–85 years) healthy subjects. Although the sample size was small, 80% of the individuals had VPBs present on the recording, and 50% had complex VPBs (multiform, paired, or ventricular tachycardia). These findings argue for restraint in the treatment of asymptomatic ventricular irritability in older patients.

Left Ventricular Dysfunction

Longitudinal studies of aging and studies comparing cardiovascular function in younger and older healthy subjects have demonstrated decreases in maximum stroke volume, cardiac output, and oxygen uptake in the older individuals in response to exercise. A study by Port et al. (15) assessed the effects of age on left ventricular ejection fraction (radionuclide technique) at rest and during upright bicycle exercise. Age did not influence left ventricular function at rest, but the ejection fraction was significantly reduced during exercise in subjects over age 60 years. Furthermore, wall motion abnormalities during exercise occurred with increasing frequency in the older subjects, and these changes were not associated with abnormalities in end-diastolic volume or blood pressure.

The age-related decrease in left ventricular func-

tion with activity may be due to one of four mechanisms: a reduction in the Frank-Starling heterometric regulation, increased afterload, decreased contractility due to disease, or decreased contractility due to aging. The available evidence favors the last explanation, and this would be consistent with the impaired release and uptake of calcium by the sarcoplasmic reticulum and the diminished number of myocardial adrenergic receptors reported in senescent animals.

Disordered Regulation of Blood Pressure

Many factors influence the regulation of blood pressure, including cardiac output (determined by heart rate, blood volume, venous return, and cardiac contractility), peripheral arteriolar resistance, the status of the renin-angiotensin-aldosterone system, the functional state of the baroreceptor reflexes, and the autonomic nervous system. The mean blood pressure increases progressively with age as a result of increased peripheral resistance. Wide fluctuations in blood pressure are commonly observed in elderly subjects as a result of increased aortic rigidity, autonomic neuropathy, and decreased baroreceptor function. Hypertension and orthostatic hypotension may coexist in the same patient, and therapy for one condition often exacerbates the associated condition.

CARDIAC DISEASES IN THE ELDERLY

Various pathologic studies of hearts of aged patients reveal the usual cardiac lesions observed in younger age groups as well as less commonly recognized disorders somewhat specific to the elderly. These cardiac diseases in the geriatric patient are usually manifest by alterations in cardiac rhythm, by congestive heart failure, or with ischemic chest pain.

COMMONLY OCCURRING CARDIAC DISEASES

Coronary Heart Disease

Ischemic heart disease, both acute myocardial infarction and chronic coronary disease, is the most common pathologic finding in elderly patients with congestive heart failure, but also is frequently found in patients not in failure. With an acute myocardial infarction, elderly patients have a fourfold increased mortality rate when compared to younger patients. Advanced age is associated with disproportionately high in-hospital mortality rates, even in the so-called good risk myocardial infarction patient. The major causes of death in hospitalized patients aged

70 and older with acute myocardial infarction are shock and cardiac rupture (10). This high incidence of myocardial rupture in the elderly may be due to chronic pathologic changes that affect the aged myocardium or possibly secondary to an increased occurrence of hypertension in the elderly. The symptom presentation of coronary heart disease in the elderly may be quite atypical because classic anginal chest pain is the exception rather than the rule.

Hypertensive Heart Disease

It is now recognized that hypertension is one of the leading causes of congestive heart failure in all age groups, especially in the elderly. Hypertension may remain silent for many years, and the ravages of this disorder may not be evident until the individual passes retirement age. Concentric left ventricular hypertrophy with or without chamber dilation and ECG findings of either hypertrophy or a bundle branch block pattern are the usual findings.

Aortic Stenosis

This disorder, in which the orifice of the aortic valve is reduced, often with associated calcification, may be due to rheumatic heart disease with commissural fusion, a congenitally deformed bicuspid aortic valve or degenerative calcification of a normal valve. With the decline in acute rheumatic fever, the elderly patients are the remaining reservoir for rheumatic aortic stenosis. Within a generation rheumatic aortic stenosis will be a rare cause of this disorder. In contrast, bicuspid and degenerative aortic valve disease will make up the major proportion of elderly patients with aortic stenosis. As with younger patients with aortic stenosis, the occurrence of syncope, angina, or congestive heart failure has ominous implications.

Aortic Insufficiency

Aortic incompetence is the most common valve lesion found in the elderly. It may occur as an isolated lesion or in association with aortic stenosis or rheumatic mitral valve disease. Syphilitic aortic insufficiency is now a rare disease that is found almost exclusively in the older age groups. Dilatation of the aortic root in association with long-standing hypertension is a frequent cause of an aortic insufficiency murmur, but it rarely causes significant regurgitation. Significant aortic regurgitation with left ventricular volume overload often produces some of the largest hearts observed in clinical medicine. The patients may do surprisingly well for many years despite an enormous heart and chronic congestive

heart failure. The development of angina pectoris and atrial fibrillation are often associated with a rapidly deteriorating clinical course.

Rheumatic Mitral Valve Disease

Most patients with significant rheumatic mitral stenosis, insufficiency, or a combination of both, usually develop progressive cardiac dysfunction before entering the geriatric age group. Those who make it into the older ages have usually been spared the complication of reactive pulmonary hypertension. In the pathologic study by Pomerance (14), 8% of the elderly patients with heart failure were found to have rheumatic mitral valve disease, but less than 2% of the patients without failure had rheumatic findings.

Bacterial Endocarditis

This disorder, often presenting with protean manifestations, is occurring with increasing frequency in the elderly. Preexisting mitral or aortic valve disease is not a prerequisite. Since many of the elderly are edentulous, *Streptococcus viridans* is less frequently the offending organism in this age group than in younger patients. Because of the high frequency of urologic disorders in older patients, enterococcal infection of the valves has become more prevalent. The mitral valve is more frequently involved than the aortic, usually with vegetations on the line of valvular apposition. Fever, anemia, and a heart murmur are the triad that should raise suspicion of possible bacterial endocarditis. However, these findings coexist in many elderly hospitalized patients without endocarditis. By the same token, elderly patients with endocarditis may be afebrile. Thus, if a patient with recent clinical deterioration has an unexplained anemia and a heart murmur, then blood should be drawn for aerobic and anaerobic cultures.

Cor Pulmonale

Pulmonary hypertension secondary to hypoxic chronic lung disease with right ventricular hypertrophy and congestive heart failure is a troublesome problem in all age groups, and especially in the elderly. The hypoxia often results in secondary polycythemia. Complicating atrial arrhythmias are common and often compound the management problem. The etiology of chronic cor pulmonale is usually chronic bronchitis-emphysema, but special factors in the older age group include the late secondary effects from kyphoscoliosis and other thoracic deformities, as well as the hypoxic diffusion problems associated with diffuse pulmonary parenchymal disease, for example, pulmonary fibrosis or late stage sarcoidosis.

Cardiomyopathy

This disorder of cardiac muscle is often categorized by etiology as well as the type of functional derangement. For the vast majority of elderly patients with cardiomyopathy but without overt systemic disease, the etiology is not uncovered and the patient is categorized as having idiopathic cardiomyopathy. Alcoholic cardiomyopathy and hemochromatosis with cardiomyopathy should be considered since both disorders are treatable. Functionally, cardiomyopathy may be subdivided into congestive, restrictive, and obstructive types. The latter is of particular interest since hypertrophic obstructive cardiomyopathy (HOCM) is being diagnosed more frequently in the elderly with the increasing use of echocardiography. Patients with HOCM may present with angina or syncope, and therapy with β-blockers, diametrically opposite to that given for most other cardiomyopathies, may be associated with dramatic symptomatic improvement. The anatomic substrate for HOCM is asymmetric septal hypertrophy with narrowing of the aortic outflow tract, disordered muscle bundles in the septum with fiber disarray, and abnormalities in the mitral valve support apparatus.

Pericarditis

Acute pericarditis infrequently occurs in the elderly, but effusive pericarditis secondary to neoplasm or tuberculosis, constrictive pericarditis from prior pericardial disease, and uremic pericarditis have a higher incidence in the older population than is generally appreciated. Diagnosis has been facilitated by echocardiography, especially the presence of pericardial effusion. Pericardial tamponade with the classic diagnostic triad of pulsus paradoxus, Kussmaul's sign, and pulsating neck veins may occur in association with both benign and malignant conditions; aggressive and prompt therapy (needle aspiration and/or surgical drainage) is indicated.

CARDIAC DISORDERS SOMEWHAT SPECIFIC TO THE ELDERLY

Calcific Degenerative Diseases

Calcification of the fibrous skeleton of the heart with involvement of the mitral anulus is often associated with a murmur of mitral insufficiency and atrioventricular conduction abnormalities. This degenerative condition is more frequent in females than in males and is especially common in patients with diabetes mellitus and a history of prior hypertension. The diagnosis may be substantiated by the presence of a J-shaped calcification on lateral chest x-ray of the heart or by echocardiography with prominent reflectivity in the mitral anular region. A second degenerative condition commonly encountered in the elderly is calcification and sclerosis of the fibrosa portion of the aortic cusps with reduced cusp mobility. An aortic systolic murmur of moderate intensity is usually present. Progression from sclerosis to stenosis is infrequent since there is minimal if any fusion of the commissures. Innocuous aortic valve sclerosis must be differentiated from calcific aortic valvular stenosis, in which the orifice area of the aortic valve is significantly reduced with secondary hemodynamic effects.

Myxomatous Degeneration of the Cardiac Valves

Primary myxomatous degeneration of the cardiac valves, but principally of the mitral and aortic valves, may produce varying degrees of valvular insufficiency. The etiology of this condition is not known, but the normal aging process is a contributing factor. The histologic pattern in the myxomatous degeneration of the mitral valve is similar to that seen in patients with mitral valve prolapse. Although this disorder may occur at any age, it is generally more severe in the elderly (12). Frequently, there is disruption of the support apparatus with chordal rupture (mitral valve), enlargement of the mitral annulus, or aortic root dilatation. The echocardiogram provides precise diagnostic information.

Senile Cardiac Amyloidosis

This disorder is clinically distinct from primary systemic amyloidosis since the deposits of amyloid material are localized to the myocardium, and the condition occurs almost exclusively in individuals of advanced age. Senile cardiac amyloid has been found at autopsy in 10% of patients over 80 years, and in 50% of those over 90 years of age. The patients usually present with congestive heart failure, ventricular conduction disturbances, and cardiac arrhythmias in the absence of angina or hypertensive disease. Congestive heart failure ensues from diminished contractility and a reduction in the diastolic compliance characteristics of both ventricular chambers. Recent clinical studies indicate unique echocardiographic findings in this condition with a thickened ventricular wall, reduced wall motion, and a generalized increased reflectivity from the entire myocardium. Patients with senile cardiac amyloidosis may have an increased sensitivity to digitalis preparations.

Thrombotic Endocarditis

Nonbacterial thrombotic (marantic) endocarditis is frequently observed at autopsy in elderly, debilitated patients, especially those with underlying malignant disease. Thrombotic endocarditis is most frequently associated with adenocarcinomas of the lung, colon, and pancreas. The mitral and aortic valves are most commonly involved, frequently both valves are affected, and this type of endocarditis is not associated with significant valvular dysfunction. The disorder is usually manifested clinically by unexplained systemic emboli and negative blood cultures.

Senile Cardiomyopathy

This unexplained pathologic finding has been found at autopsy examination in patients with and without congestive heart failure. The heart is generally decreased in size and is distinctly brown in color (brown atrophy). It occurs in severe inanition and chronic wasting diseases such as pulmonary tuberculosis, cancer, and chronic sepsis. Although this disorder may be found in young adults, it primarily affects elderly persons.

DIAGNOSTIC CONSIDERATIONS

In the elderly patient, the usual clinical evaluation may be less precise than can be achieved in younger patients. The clinical history that is central to all medical workups may be incomplete because of confusion and memory deficits. Therefore, it is essential to obtain supplementary information from knowledgeable family members or health service personnel where appropriate. Even when elderly patients are mentally alert with intact cognitive function, the history may be misleading since many cardiac disorders have vague symptom presentations in the older age group. For example, in those over 70 years of age, acute myocardial infarction does not usually present with severe precordial chest pain. Dyspnea, syncope, stroke, and gastrointestinal symptoms are often the presenting complaint in elderly patients with an acute coronary event (13).

Laboratory tests and procedures in the older patients also leave something to be desired. Many times the patients may not be strong enough to complete a vigorous test, and often the standards of "normality" have not been defined for this age group. A common error is to apply the criteria of normality obtained from younger patients to this unique older population, and thus inadvertantly overdiagnose and assign disease entities to these patients when in fact none exist.

Routine aspects of the history, physical exam, and standard laboratory tests including the ECG and chest x-ray will not be covered in this chapter. Rather, the focus will be on special testing, especially as it relates to many of the noninvasive procedures that have expanded the diagnostic armamentarium available to the clinician.

HOLTER MONITORING

Twenty-four-hour Holter ECG monitoring has become a valuable diagnostic technique in the evaluation of cardiac rhythm disturbances. Many elderly patients experience transient syncope, dizziness, and palpitations, and Holter monitoring may uncover a potentially life-threatening arrhythmia for which effective therapy is available. We have used Holter monitoring in the routine evaluation of postinfarction patients prior to hospital discharge. The frequency of transient yet asymptomatic ventricular tachycardia, heart block, and sinus node dysfunction is considerably higher in the older group than in younger patients. Similarly, we have obtained 24-hour Holter recordings on all patients after pacemaker implantation to assess the sensing and pacing function of the newly implanted units. Finally, follow-up Holter monitoring has provided valuable insight into the efficacy of antiarrhythmic drug therapy, especially as it relates to the suppression of ventricular premature beats and the control of the ventricular response rate to atrial fibrillation. In this regard, recent studies have shown that for individual patients a 70-80% reduction in ventricular premature beats between baseline and posttherapy tracings is required before ascribing the effect to the administered antiarrhythmic agent.

EXERCISE TOLERANCE TEST

A variety of activity protocols exist, but common to all is the adjustment of the work load to the patient's capacity, continuous ECG monitoring, intermittent recording of blood pressures, and attention to the patient's symptomatic state during the activity test with emphasis on safety. The exercise protocol used depends on the indications for the test. The indications may include functional evaluation after myocardial infarction, evaluation of patients with chest pain, determination of the severity of underlying cardiac disease, or the determination of activity-related arrhythmias.

The treadmill is the most widely used technique for activity testing, and its major advantage is the adjustment of the grade and speed of walking to the agility of the patient. The submaximal Bruce protocol, which is targeted to 75–90% of the maximum age-predicted heart rate, may be too difficult for elderly patients. The initial walking rate begins at 1.7 miles/hour at a 10% grade, and the speed and grade are progressively increased at 3-min intervals. Most elderly patients cannot follow this protocol, and frequently the activity test is terminated prematurely because of leg and joint problems rather than cardiac symptoms or signs. Elderly patients seem to perform better when the speed is kept constant and the grade gradually increased. The modified Naughton protocol (Table 6.1) is particularly useful in the older patient; the speed is kept constant at 2.0 miles/hour, the initial grade is flat at 0°, and the grade is increased by 3.5% every 2 min. For low-level activity testing, the protocol is terminated after 8 min with peak level of activity equivalent to stage 1 of the standard Bruce protocol. For higher level testing, the protocol can be continued for additional time at steeper grades.

We have carried out the aforementioned low-level exercise test in over 500 postinfarction patients prior to hospital discharge without major problems. This predischarge activity evaluation has proved useful for recommending safe activity levels at home and in uncovering serious ischemic and arrhythmic disorders. A higher level exercise test such as the standard Bruce protocol may be used in the diagnostic and functional evaluation of ambulatory outpatients. Regardless of the test utilized, a maximum target heart rate should be chosen either on the basis of clinical judgment or by established norms according to the age of the patient, and the test should be terminated when adverse symptoms or signs appear. Elderly patients, especially elderly women, have a higher percentage of false-positive ischemic ST segment changes with activity testing, and stringent criteria of ≥2.0 mm ST segment shifts should be used for defining abnormality.

ECHOCARDIOGRAM AND DOPPLER ULTRASOUND

The echocardiogram provides dynamic visualization of cardiac structures with particular evaluation of the pericardium and pericardial space, ventricular walls, ventricular septum, valves, the atrial and ventricular chamber sizes, and the presence of mass lesions such as thrombus or myxoma. Two echocardiographic techniques are currently available: (a) the single-dimensional M-mode method, which provides an "ice pick" view of the heart, and (b) the two-dimensional cross-sectional method, which provides images in various planes through the heart. Doppler ultrasound provides diagnostic information about blood flow velocity. It is the most reliable noninvasive technique available for estimating stenotic valvular pressure gradients and the magnitude of valvular insufficiency.

Echocardiography has been particularly helpful in the diagnosis of pericardial effusion, asymmetric septal hypertrophy, mitral valve prolapse, flail mitral valve, mitral stenosis, ventricular aneurysm, ventricular thrombus, atrial myxoma, and infective endocarditis, to name but a few. In addition, echocardiography can provide qualitative information about cardiac performance, cardiac shunts, and the degree of valvular stenosis and insufficiency. Doppler ultrasound has been especially useful in evaluating the severity of aortic and mitral valve disease.

Many elderly patients have chest deformities such as senile emphysema or rib cage distortion that contribute to technical difficulties in the ultrasonic examination of the heart. The success rate for technically satisfactory echocardiograms is usually highest in younger patients, and even when echocardiograms can be done in older patients, the studies may be of limited quality and extent. Likewise, suitable Doppler signals are also more difficult to obtain in the elderly.

RADIONUCLIDE IMAGING

Radionuclide techniques are widely applied for the evaluation of cardiac function (ejection fraction) and myocardial perfusion (hot and cold spot imaging). The tests are essentially noninvasive and re-

Table 6.1
Modified Naughton Protocol for Activity Testing in the Elderly Patient

Stage	Time (min)	Grade (%) 2.0 mph	METs[a]
1	0–2	Rest	1
2	2–4	0	2
3	4–6	3.5	3
4	6–8	7.0	4
5	8–10	10.5	5
6	10–12	14.0	6
7	12–14	17.5	7

[a]Metabolic equivalents.

quire the intravenous administration of a small amount of radioactive tracer and precordial counting with a gamma scintillation camera. The function and perfusion studies can be done at rest and after exercise.

The radionuclide ejection fraction (RNEF) can be obtained either by first-pass or gated techniques. The former method involves recording the time-activity curves of the passage of a bolus of radioactive substance through the heart, usually for 5–10 heart beats. Peaks and valleys of the time-activity curve correspond to end-diastole and end-systole, and the ejection fraction is computed from these measurements. The gated equilibrium method requires that the radiopharmaceutical agent remain in the blood for several hours so that the cardiac blood pool can be imaged. End-systolic and end-diastolic volumes are determined by synchronization with the R wave of the patient's ECG, and the data from many cardiac cycles are added in phase to one another. Information on regional wall motion can be obtained with both techniques.

Recent studies on healthy volunteers indicate that the resting RNEF does not deteriorate with age. Port et al. (15) reported that the resting RNEF was above the normal value of 0.60 in most healthy subjects over age 60. However, during exercise, the RNEF declined abnormally in most elderly subjects, indicating underlying subclinical myocardial dysfunction and a reduction in reserve capacity. These RNEF techniques provide valuable quantitative information on cardiac performance in patients with coronary heart disease, congestive heart failure, ventricular aneurysm, hypertensive heart disease, and cardiomyopathy. An RNEF less than 0.35 reflects significant underlying heart disease, and an RNEF less than 0.20 is associated with an ominous prognosis. Serial RNEF measurements can be helpful in evaluating the efficacy of therapeutic interventions such as afterload reduction, digitalization, and diuresis. The RNEF technique is particularly useful in the elderly patient since precise information can be obtained with minimal effort on the part of the patient.

Myocardial perfusion imaging can detect acute myocardial necrosis with technetium pyrophosphate uptake (hot spot) or a perfusion deficit with thallium (cold spot). The former is useful in the diagnosis of acute myocardial infarction in the coronary care unit when other data are equivocal. The thallium test is usually carried out in conjunction with exercise testing to identify a perfusion deficit in patients with coronary artery disease.

HEMODYNAMIC MONITORING IN THE ICU

Critically ill patients with myocardial, circulatory, or respiratory problems require hemodynamic monitoring in order to provide appropriate and optimal therapy. The elderly patient is especially vulnerable to volume fluctuations, and measurements of the left ventricular filling pressure, cardiac output, and the calculated peripheral vascular resistance provide invaluable insight for therapeutic intervention with inotropic agents, afterload reduction, volume addition, and diuresis. In 1970, Swan, Ganz, and colleagues introduced the flow-directed, balloon-tipped pulmonary artery catheter (16). With either a venous cutdown or a percutaneous venous puncture, the catheter is advanced from a peripheral vein into the pulmonary artery without the absolute requirement for fluoroscopy, although the latter may aid in its placement. The pulmonary arterial systolic and diastolic pressures are recorded, and when the balloon is inflated, the catheter becomes "wedged" with pressure measurements reflecting left atrial pressure. The presently designed catheter also records right atrial pressure and has a thermistor probe for measurement of cardiac output by the thermodilution technique. Since a considerable discrepancy may exist between the functions of the right and left ventricles in critically ill patients with hemodynamic embarrassment, the balloon-tipped pulmonary artery catheter provides essential information for the proper management of these individuals. An intra-arterial line also should be placed to directly record systemic pressure. In patients with the low output state, a cuff blood pressure is not an accurate measure of the systemic arterial pressure.

CARDIAC CATHETERIZATION AND CORONARY ANGIOGRAPHY

These invasive diagnostic procedures are reserved for patients with significant valvular or coronary heart disease who may require surgical intervention for treatment of life-threatening or disabling symptoms. In experienced hands, these procedures are associated with only a minimally increased risk in older as compared to younger patients. Quantitation of the severity of valvular stenotic or insufficient lesions and the direct visualization of the coronary arterial tree and the left ventricular contraction pattern are essential for proper decision making in these patients. Significant aortic stenosis and left main coronary disease are eminently correctable disorders, even in patients in the 70- and 80-year age groups.

MEDICAL MANAGEMENT OF SELECTED CARDIAC DISORDERS

During the past decade there have been significant advances in the management of the entire spectrum of cardiac disorders. With better understanding of the pathophysiologic mechanisms of disease and the introduction of new pharmacologic agents, there has ensued a significant improvement in the quality and longevity of life. This section will focus on the current management of four common cardiac disorders with emphasis on the use of pharmacologic agents released during the past decade. As has been pointed out in other chapters in this book, the dynamics of drug absorption, distribution, metabolism, excretion, and organ responsiveness are different in the geriatric age group from those of younger patients. A conservative therapeutic approach together with careful monitoring of physiologic parameters and drug blood levels are essential for optimal efficacy and safety in this age group. For a comprehensive presentation of the medical management of the following selected cardiac disorders, the reader is referred to standard cardiology texts.

CONGESTIVE HEART FAILURE

Congestive heart failure (CHF) has many diverse causes, but long-standing hypertension and chronic coronary heart disease (ischemic cardiomyopathy) account for the majority of the cases. The severity of the CHF is largely dependent on the extent of myocardial involvement and the degree of global cardiac dysfunction. Significant compromise of coexisting organ system function, such as that of the kidneys and liver, exacerbate the CHF and reduce the effectiveness of therapeutic measures. Reduction in physical activity, restriction of dietary salt, digitalis, and diuretics are the mainstays of therapy. More potent diuretics, vasodilators, and new inotropic agents have expanded the therapeutic armamentarium available to the physician.

Diuretics

The available diuretics may be categorized into three groups depending on their site and mechanism of action: (a) loop diuretics, (b) distal convoluted tubule diuretics, and (c) potassium-sparing diuretics. The loop diuretics include furosemide, bumetanide, and ethacrynic acid and are the most potent agents available. Furosemide has an excellent dose-response relationship over a wide range of doses. In refractory cases of CHF and in patients with significant underlying renal disease, large oral doses of the loop diuretics may be ineffective; much smaller intravenous doses may produce a profound diuresis. When using intravenous loop diuretics in older patients, it is best to start with small doses in the range of half of the usual starting dose, and gradually increase the dose as determined by the response.

Thiazide diuretics, which act in the distal convoluted tubule, are categorized as moderately potent agents. These drugs are poorly effective in patients with reduced glomerular filtration rates (<30 ml/min) and thus are of limited potency when administered alone to older patients with severe CHF. However, these agents may induce a profound diuresis when used in combination with the more potent loop diuretics.

The potassium-sparing diuretics (spironolactone, triamterene, and amiloride) are the weakest of the diuretics and should be used with caution in elderly patients. The antikaluretic action of these agents may produce unexpected hyperkalemia with secondary cardiac conduction disturbances, especially in patients with preexisting cardiac and renal disease.

Vasodilator Therapy

Vasodilator agents, which reduce preload (venous filling pressure) and afterload (arterial resistance), have significantly improved the therapy for CHF since their introduction in the mid-1970s. The currently available agents that span the spectrum from primary arterial dilators to venous dilators are presented in Table 6.2. In acute pulmonary edema with normal or elevated blood pressure, intravenous nitroprusside provides a significant addition to the traditional therapy with oxygen, morphine, diuretics, digitalis, and rotating tourniquets. Nitroprusside acts directly to relax both arterioles and veins. Nitroprusside should be administered with

Table 6.2
Spectrum of Action of Vasodilator Agents

ARTERIAL DILATION
Hydralazine
Minoxidil
Nifedipine
Diazoxide
Phentolamine
Enalapril
Captropril
Nitroprusside
Prazosin
Nitrates
VENOUS DILATION

continuous intraarterial pressure monitoring. The starting intravenous dose of nitroprusside is 0.5 µ/kg/min, and the infusion rate should be increased in increments until the systolic blood pressure is lowered to 110 mm Hg.

In chronic CHF, therapy with oral hydralazine plus topical (nitroglycerin ointment) or oral (isosorbide dinitrate) nitrates provides excellent afterload and preload reduction (3). In elderly patients, the initial dose of these agents should be attenuated to avoid drug-induced hypotension. If the patient tolerates hydralazine, 10 mg by mouth, and isosorbide dinitrate, 5 mg by mouth, then the oral dosage should be increased in increments over 2–3 days to full therapy: hydralazine, 50 mg every 6 hours, and isosorbide dinitrate, 20 mg every 6 hours. Prazosin, a balanced vasodilator equally effective on arterioles and veins, may be used in place of the hydralazine-nitrate combination. However, prazosin is frequently associated with orthostatic hypotension with initial dosing and tachyphylaxis during chronic administration, and these effects limit the usefulness of this agent in the older age group.

Recently, angiotensin-converting enzyme (ACE) inhibitors have produced impressive hemodynamic improvement in patients with CHF. Captopril and its longer acting analog, enalapril, block the conversion of angiotensin I to angiotensin II, the latter causing vasoconstriction. Captopril and enalapril result in hemodynamic improvement at rest and with exercise with an augmentation in cardiac output and a reduction in filling pressures and systemic vascular resistance (11). Captopril, in gradually increasing doses to 6.25–50 mg three times daily, produces sustained hemodynamic improvement in most patients. The elderly may be particularly sensitive to some of the adverse side effects of the ACE inhibitors, and caution should be exercised in the use of these agents in patients with hyponatremia, reduced renal function, and low blood pressure.

Inotropic Agents

During the past decade two sympathomimetic agents have been introduced that are useful in treating the low output syndrome with secondary CHF in the acute care setting. Dopamine, the immediate precursor of norepinephrine, and dobutamine, a synthetic cardioactive sympathomimetic amine, must be given intravenously with intraarterial pressure monitoring. Simultaneous recording of cardiac filling pressures using a Swan-Ganz catheter is strongly recommended. Both agents augment cardiac contractility through their β-agonist activity.

However, dobutamine produces less tachycardia and more effective vasodilation of vascular beds than dopamine, and it is usually the preferred agent when administration is required for 24 or 48 hours. Infusion rates up to 2–5 µg/kg/min with either agent are associated with a beneficial hemodynamic response. These agents are usually reserved for patients with refractory CHF. Sustained intravenous administration of either of these agents is associated with progressive loss of hemodynamic improvement, probably as a result of "down regulation" of β-adrenergic receptors.

CARDIAC ARRHYTHMIAS

Atrial Fibrillation

This rhythm disorder commonly occurs in the elderly, frequently complicates CHF, and may develop in the absence of demonstrable heart disease. The loss of the atrial "kick" with reduction in cardiac output and the variable and erratic rate may exacerbate left ventricular dysfunction. Acute onset of temporary atrial fibrillation may be caused by fever, electrolyte imbalance, myocardial infarction, pericarditis, or a pulmonary embolus, and the arrhythmia usually resolves with treatment of the underlying condition and acute digitalization. Paroxysmal recurrent atrial fibrillation often accompanies sinus node dysfunction, and the associated brady-tachy rhythm disorders may require pacemaker therapy in addition to pharmacologic measures. Chronic atrial fibrillation is usually secondary to ischemic or hypertensive heart disease, but apathetic thyrotoxicosis, rheumatic heart disease, and the usual spectrum of cardiac disorders also occur in the elderly and may contribute to this rhythm disorder.

Management of atrial fibrillation involves: (a) rate control; (b) conversion, either pharmacologically or electrically; and (c) reduction of systemic embolization. Rate control can usually be achieved with digitalization, and the parenteral or oral route of therapy is usually dictated by the urgency of the situation and the clinical state of the patient. Digoxin is the digitalis drug of choice, and a loading dose is indicated for prompt control of a rapid ventricular response to atrial fibrillation. A loading dose of 0.75 mg or 0.5 mg of digoxin with 0.25 mg maintenance daily should produce digoxin levels within the therapeutic range (1–2 ng/ml) within 48 hours when renal function is normal. With impaired renal function or in the octogenarian age group, a reduced maintenance dose of 0.125 mg should be used. Propranolol in small doses (1.0 mg intravenously or 10 mg orally every 6 hours) is useful in combination with digoxin to slow rapid atrial fibrillation and to prevent accelerated rates during activity in patients receiving chronic digitalis therapy.

Cardioversion from atrial fibrillation to sinus rhythm should be considered in acute onset rapid atrial fibrillation that is poorly tolerated hemodynamically. Synchronized, direct current electrical cardioversion is the procedure of choice in such a situation, and quinidine conversion should be avoided. Elective cardioversion of chronic atrial fibrillation carries a significant risk in the older population because of the high frequency of underlying sinus node dysfunction. This disorder is often associated with asystolic atrial arrest or systemic embolization from mural atrial thrombi, and thus cardioversion is contraindicated in the elderly with chronic atrial fibrillation except in unusual situations. Furthermore, atrial fibrillation frequently recurs after cardioversion in these patients.

It has recently been appreciated that chronic atrial fibrillation is often associated with subclinical systemic emboli, frequently involving the brain with secondary neurologic abnormalities including progressive dementia. Anticoagulants are recommended in patients with recurrent or chronic atrial fibrillation. Oral coumarin anticoagulants are the drugs of choice, and one should aim for a prothrombin time that is twice normal. Many elderly patients cannot be safely anticoagulated with the coumarin derivatives, and in such situations antiplatelet aggregating agents such as low-dose acetylsalicylic acid or sulfinpyrazone should be utilized.

Ventricular Arrhythmias

Ventricular premature beats are common in the elderly, and standard antiarrhythmic agents like lidocaine, quinidine, procainamide, and disopyramide are poorly tolerated. Thus, the indications for treating simple or complex patterns of ventricular arrhythmias are quite stringent, and only ventricular arrhythmias of truly life-threatening potential should be treated. In the over-70 age group, repetitive ventricular premature beats complicating acute myocardial infarction should be treated with intravenous lidocaine. However, the loading and maintenance doses of lidocaine should be reduced to one-half the usually recommended values, and the duration of therapy should be attenuated to 12 hours unless a life-threatening arrhythmia persists. Lidocaine toxicity with respiratory depression, confusion, hypotension, and seizures is common in the elderly, and lidocaine administration requires careful monitoring for adverse side effects.

In the absence of acute cardiac disease, asymptomatic short runs of ventricular tachycardia at rates less than 150 beats/min or lesser degrees of ventricular irritability do not require prophylactic antiarrhythmic therapy. There is a small subset of patients with recurrent life-threatening ventricular tachyarrhythmias, often with associated symptoms of lightheadedness or near syncope. These patients should be followed by a cardiac consultant since therapy with multiple antiarrhythmic agents is required, blood levels of the drugs have to be monitored, and frequent Holter recordings are needed to evaluate drug efficacy.

ANGINA PECTORIS

Angina pectoris in the elderly may have atypical presentations, and age-related neurologic and cognitive deficits may complicate the history. The pattern of the discomfort or weakness, which comes on with physical or emotional activity or else awakens the patient at night, is more important in establishing the diagnosis than the character or location of the pain. A therapeutic trial with sublingual nitroglycerin may provide the most sensitive and specific diagnostic information. The ECG may reveal nonspecific ST and T wave changes, a left bundle branch block pattern, or Q waves of an old myocardial infarction, but these findings are not sufficient to establish an unequivocal diagnosis of angina. Exercise testing is often indicated to establish the diagnosis and to determine the relative severity of the coronary disease process. Precipitation of the patient's characteristic discomfort within the first few minutes of activity testing, usually with significant ST and T wave changes that regress after activity termination, indicates major double- or triple-vessel coronary artery disease or left main coronary artery stenosis. Coronary angiography may be utilized for more precise diagnosis depending on the age of the patient, the intractability of the angina, and the potential for intervention with coronary artery bypass surgery or angioplasty.

Although anginal pains are usually due to coronary disease, two noncoronary conditions that may present with angina in the elderly are hypertrophic obstructive cardiomyopathy and aortic valvular stenosis. The heart murmurs in both of these conditions may be minimal, and the echocardiogram should be used to diagnose or rule out these obstructive outflow tract conditions.

The more troublesome forms of angina in the elderly include decubitus angina, nocturnal angina, and postprandial angina. Common to all three patterns of angina is extensive triple-vessel coronary disease or left main coronary artery stenosis. General management, which involves normalization of blood pressure, decongestive therapy, correction of brady-tachy rhythm disturbances, and treatment of coexisting medical problems, such as thyroid abnormalities, is essential. Specific therapy with nitrates, β-blockers, and the new calcium antagonists warrants further comment.

Nitrates

These agents are the mainstay of anginal treatment. Sublingual and chewable preparations have very short durations of action, and the need for frequent dosing at 1–3-hour intervals complicates compliance. Recently it has been appreciated that large oral doses of isosorbide dinitrate have excellent efficacy in controlling angina. Isosorbide dinitrate in gradually increasing oral doses, 10–30 mg every 4–6 hours, should be tried. Nitroglycerin ointment, an old form of long-acting nitroglycerin that has recently had a resurgence in usage, has beneficial effects lasting up to 6 hours after each topical application. Doses between ½ and 2 inches every 4–6 hours are especially effective in patients with decubitus, nocturnal, and postprandial angina. Slow release, long-acting topical nitrate preparations that need be applied only once daily are also available, but they are quite expensive.

β-Adrenergic Blocking Agents

There is considerable variability in the elderly patient's tolerance of the currently available β-blocking drugs. These drugs have unquestioned efficacy, but because of variable absorption and the potential for serious adverse side effects such as bradycardia, CHF, bronchial asthma, and mental depression, caution must be exercised in patient selection and dosage. In the over-70 age group, propranolol should be started at a low dose of 10–20 mg every 6–8 hours, and the amount gradually increased at weekly intervals depending on the clinical state. Some elderly patients may require propranolol doses as high as 80 mg every 6 hours for control of angina, but this is certainly the exception. Selection of dosage of propranolol must be individualized.

Calcium Antagonists

This class of agents includes nifedipine, verapamil, and diltiazem. These drugs are useful in the treatment of variant angina (Prinzmetal type) and classical angina. These agents have both vasodilator and antispasm effects, and preliminary findings indicate significant efficacy in the treatment of intractable, recurrent angina. Diltiazem, 30–60 mg orally three to four times daily, is generally well tolerated in the elderly. However, the concurrent administration of β-blocking agents with diltiazem may produce excessive sinus bradycardia, especially in patients with underlying sinus node dysfunction.

ACUTE MYOCARDIAL INFARCTION

Thrombolytic therapy is now being utilized to open acute thrombotic coronary occlusion in patients seen within 4–6 hours of onset of acute myocardial infarction. Current data in the under-75 age group indicate that thrombolysis can be achieved in approximately 50% of patients treated with intravenous streptokinase and 75% of patients given tissue plasminogen activator (17). Very few data are available in the older patients, but surely these thrombolytic agents will be tried in the geriatric population. Caution is advised since these agents produce a systemic lytic state and may be associated with considerable bleeding. The elderly individual with poor tissue turgor, reduced vascular reactivity, and possible hypertension is especially vulnerable to life-threatening hemorrhagic complications.

INVASIVE CARDIAC INTERVENTIONS

Coronary angioplasty, pacemaker therapy, and open heart surgery are being utilized extensively in the elderly to improve the quality and quantity of life. The advance in technology has created a dilemma for society because these interventions are expensive and may cost more than the government is willing to expend in Medicare reimbursement.

PACEMAKERS

When pacemakers became available for clinical use in the early 1960s, the primary indication for pacemaker implantation was intermittent or fixed atrioventricular block with bradycardia and Stokes-Adams attacks. The majority of elderly patients with atrioventricular block do not have significant coronary heart disease. Rather, the etiology of their heart block is due to fibrosis and calcification of the skeleton of the heart with impingement on the atrioventricular conduction system. This condition, frequently called Lev's syndrome, is age related and occurs with increasing frequency as patients pass from septuagenarian to octogenarian status. A second major indication for pacemakers in the elderly is sinus node dysfunction with intermittent or sustained sinus bradycardia, sinus arrest, or episodes of atrial bradycardia alternating with atrial tachycardia. These atrial arrhythmias appear to be related to degeneration of the sinus node together with fibrosis and scarring of the atrium and its specialized conducting system. Not infrequently, patients manifest sinus bradycardia with rates in the 50/min range, then develop paroxysmal supraventricular tachycardia with rates of 150 or 160/min terminating in periods of asystole lasting 3–5 sec with accompanying syncope. A third indication for pacemakers in the elderly relates to a special subgroup of patients with troublesome recurrent paroxysmal tachycardia, either of the atrial or ventricular type. Rapid tachycardias in the elderly are not well tolerated and antiarrhythmic drugs are frequently ineffective. Episodes of tachycardia often occur in the setting of relative bradycardia. By the selection of an appropriate atrial demand pacing rate, the atrial bradycardia is prevented and episodic atrial tachycardia is usually inhibited.

Numerous types of pacemakers are currently available for the treatment of a wide spectrum of cardiac arrhythmias. The pacing site may be located in the atrium or the ventricle, or in both chambers for specialized types of dual-chamber sequential pacing. Unipolar and bipolar electrodes are available and are used with equal advantage. Electrodes may be positioned pervenously to stimulate the endocardium or placed in the epicardium by surgical techniques utilizing subxyphoid or transthoracic approaches. Epicardial placement of electrodes is usually reserved for patients in whom the transvenous endocardial approach is not technically feasible.

The current generation of pacemaker pulse generators are programmable, meaning that certain electrical characteristics of the generator can be programmed externally after implantation. Pacing rate, output strength, sensitivity, pulse width, duration of refractoriness after discharge of the impulse, and a variety of other parameters may be programmed noninvasively. At the present time, almost all the implanted pacemaker generators for atrial or ventricular pacing are of the demand type. The pacemaker senses the intrinsic electrical signals of the heart and impulses are discharged only when the intrinsic heartbeat is slower than the preset pacing rate of the generator. Also, isolated premature beats are sensed by the demand pacemaker and the generator is inhibited so that the heart will not be stimulated during the vulnerable period of the ectopic beat.

Presently, 70% of the pacemakers implanted in the United States are of the ventricular demand type, and 20% are atrial demand units. The remaining 10% are the dual-chamber pacemakers, either sequential atrioventricular (bifocal) pacemakers or atrial-synchronized ventricular pacemakers. The latter two types maintain proper synchrony in the atrial-ventricular contraction sequence, and thus, global cardiac performance is optimized during pacemaker therapy.

As with any surgical procedure, pacemaker implantation is associated with certain complications, and these complications occur more frequently in the elderly than in the younger age group. Despite meticulous attention to surgical technique, bleeding into and around the pacemaker battery pocket site is often quite striking. The elderly patient has poor tissue turgor with impaired vessel contraction, and extensive postoperative hematomas sometimes occur. Also, many elderly patients have the pacemakers implanted as a semiemergency, and such drugs as aspirin, which are frequently used in the elderly, impair platelet function and hemostasis. A large hematoma may be a factor in the production of battery pocket breakdown—a condition that is definitely more frequent in the geriatric population than in the younger patients. Battery pocket breakdown with disruption of the incision may be due to removal of the cutaneous stitches too early in a pocket with a hematoma, which puts the incision under considerable stress. Also, low-grade infection with a skin organism, *Staphylococcus epidermidis,* has been associated with battery-pocket erosion in the subacute and chronic postimplantation phase.

The geriatric patient who has a ventricular demand pacemaker implanted for sinus node dysfunction (sinus bradycardia or sinus arrest) may develop hypotension and/or low output during the periods of ventricular pacing. This problem, frequently referred to as the pacemaker syndrome, results from a loss of the synchronized atrial contraction (1). In elderly patients with impaired myocardial contractile performance, the atrial "kick" is an important factor in optimizing the contractile efficiency of the heart. Direct pacing of the ventricular chamber eliminates the normal synchrony between atrial and ventricular contraction. In the patient with preexisting reduced cardiac reserve, this ventricular pacing may cause significant cardiac dysfunction despite pacing at a physiologic rate. The problem can be avoided by using an atrial pacemaker if atrioventricular conduction is intact, or else a dual-chamber sequential atrioventricular pacemaker. It is important to choose the correct type of pacemaker at the time of the implantation procedure, and this requires simple physiologic testing with blood pressure measurements during brief trials with atrial and ventricular pacing.

The induction of pacemaker malfunction by the electric fields from microwave ovens, electric blankets, and electric beds is vastly overrated, and these problems are essentially nonexistent with the current generation of pacemakers. Follow-up of patients with implanted pacemakers is imperative since the pacemaker generators have a limited life expectancy (variable from 2–8 years depending on the characteristics of the generator), and the generators must be replaced prior to battery failure. Regular transtelephone monitoring of pacemaker function (rate, pulse width, sensing, magnet characteristics) at monthly intervals is essential if one is to identify potential pacemaker problems before they assume life-threatening consequences. Most pacemaker manufacturers provide this telephone pacemaker monitoring service. In addition, there are numerous commercial monitoring systems available, as well as programs run by major pacemaker clinics. The cost for such monitoring is covered by Medicare, provided the guidelines outlined by the federal government are followed. Periodic monitoring is extremely useful in picking up sensing and pacing problems whether related to the generator or the electrode.

In addition to regular telephone monitoring, each pacemaker patient should be followed at less frequent intervals by a cardiologist who is knowledgeable in the field of pacemakers. Generally, the cardiologist should see the patient 1 month after pacemaker implantation to check the function of the implanted unit and to reprogram the parameters of the generator (rate, output, sensitivity, hysteresis) if so indicated. Thereafter, the frequency of cardiologic follow-up may be reduced to 9- to 12-month intervals providing a monthly or every other month monitoring schedule has been established.

The current generation of lithium-powered pacemakers has had a remarkably stable function for many years. A gradual change in the functional characteristics of the lithium unit occurs as the power supply declines near the end of life of the battery. This feature permits adequate time for the identification of a diminishing power source to allow for prophylactic replacement of the generator. Abrupt failure of the electronic as opposed to the battery components cannot be anticipated unless the manufacturer identifies an intrinsic defect in the unit and a recall is issued.

CORONARY ANGIOPLASTY AND VALVULOPLASTY

Since its introduction by Gruentzig et al. in 1978, percutaneous transluminal coronary angioplasty (PTCA) has been performed in an ever-increasing number of patients of all ages with stenotic and occluded coronary vessels (8). Although originally applied to patients under age 65 with single-vessel disease, PTCA is now being performed in older patients with multivessel coronary disease and early after myocardial infarction to open occluded or residually stenotic coronary vessels. Under local anesthesia and heparin anticoagulation, a guiding catheter system is introduced through a major peripheral artery and advanced to the orifice of the coronary artery containing the narrowed or obstructed coronary lesion. A balloon catheter is then advanced through the guide system to the site of obstruction using a steerable guide wire. Dilation of the stenosis is achieved by balloon inflations of 5–10 atm for 30–60 sec. Balloon sizes ranging from 2.0 mm to 4.0 mm are utilized depending on the size of the intrinsic coronary artery to be dilated.

Proper patient selection is critical to obtain favorable outcomes, and this is especially true in elderly patients where the risk of complications are significantly increased. In general elderly patients should be selected for PTCA if they are having recurrent life-inhibiting or life-threatening angina and are candidates for coronary bypass surgery. PTCA is a preferable alternative to surgery if the stenotic lesion does not involve the left main coronary artery, a major bifurcation such as the origin of the left anterior descending and left circumflex vessels, or a 2-cm or greater length of vessel. Coronary angioplasty is a specialty unto itself, and consultation with such a specialist with review of the diagnostic angiogram is essential before proceeding with PTCA.

PTCA may produce acute coronary occlusion in approximately 5% of elderly patients, and emergency standby coronary surgery should be available should such a complication develop. Other potential problems include bleeding at the peripheral artery entrance site, occlusion of the peripheral artery, sepsis, and myocardial perforation from a temporary pacemaker catheter, which is usually introduced into the right ventricle at the time of angioplasty procedure.

In elderly patients the stenotic lesion may be more difficult to reach with the balloon catheter than in younger patients because of the more tortuous coronary vessels. Once the lesion is reached, older patients have more calcified plaques with greater resistance to dilation and a greater potential for coronary dissection. Overall, the success rate is 70–80% for obtaining an effective dilation (defined as a 50% or greater improvement in luminal diameter), and a recurrence of the stenosis may occur in 15–20% of the successful cases within 6 months of the initial PTCA. The stenotic lesion may not be reached or adequately dilated in 15–20% of the cases, and acute occlusion occurs in about 5% of the patients with a mortality rate of 1% or less.

In contrast to these risks, one must consider the fact that PTCA can often provide prompt functional and symptomatic improvement, a relatively short hospital stay of 2–3 days, and a quick return to normal activity with minimal convalescent delay. The risks and benefits of the procedure should be fully discussed with the patient and a family member, and an informed consent should always be obtained.

More recently, a percutaneous balloon technique has become available for the dilation of aortic valvular stenosis in the elderly (4). Although still experimental, this procedure has produced some impressive early results with marked reductions in large pressure gradients across the severely stenotic aortic valve and dramatic functional improvement. To date, there have been few major complications, although systemic embolization from the calcified valve and secondary aortic valvular insufficiency are potential concerns. If aortic valvuloplasty becomes a safe and effective therapy for aortic stenosis, it will represent a significant advance for the treatment of aortic stenosis in the elderly. The existing therapeutic approach, valvular replacement surgery, requires a prolonged postoperative convalescence that severely taxes the older patient. Thus, valvuloplasty is a desirable alternative.

CORONARY ARTERY BYPASS GRAFT SURGERY

Coronary artery bypass graft surgery (CABG) is now being performed in patients in the 70- and 80-year age groups. The indications for bypass surgery in the elderly are more stringent than for younger patients, and the usual requirements are: (a) life-inhibiting and life-threatening angina unresponsive or poorly responsive to maximal medical or angioplasty treatment; (b) angiographically demonstrated left main or severe double- or triple-vessel proximal coronary artery stenosis; (c) preservation of left ventricular function with an ejection fraction of 0.30 or more; (d) the absence of major morbidity

involving other organ systems; and (e) patient understanding and motivation regarding the reason and need for the surgery. The total operative mortality and morbidity are between 5% and 15%. It should be recognized that graft patency is significantly lower in the older age group because of the frequent presence of venous varicosities in the graft vessel and sclerosis of coronary arteries, which complicates vein-artery anastamoses. Internal mammary arteries are being preferentially utilized on all age groups, and this appears to increase the likelihood of graft patency.

PROSTHETIC VALVE REPLACEMENT

Although all types of significant valvular disease may occur in the elderly, the most common hemodynamically significant lesions requiring operative intervention are aortic stenosis (rheumatic or congenital bicuspid valvular stenosis) and mitral insufficiency (rheumatic, myxomatous valvular degeneration, or ruptured chordae or papillary muscles). In addition to hemodynamic evaluation of the severity of the valvular disease by echocardiography, Doppler ultrasound, and cardiac catheterization, the status of the coronary arteries also must be investigated. Critical factors that profoundly influence operative mortality include: (a) the extent of valvular and aortic calcification; (b) the degree of myocardial and cardiac dysfunction; (c) the severity of coexisting pulmonary hypertension from active or passive pulmonary vascular disease; (d) the location and extent of coexisting coronary disease; and (e) the type and extent of diseases of other organ systems. Valvular replacement surgery produces a greater insult to the circulatory system than CABG surgery, and the net result is a more complicated perioperative course and a delayed functional recovery. If the porcine bioprothesis is utilized in the aortic position, long-term anticoagulation is not required. Otherwise, coumarin anticoagulation is indicated despite the increased hemorrhagic risk. Once again, risk-benefit considerations dictate an operative recommendation only for those patients with a life-threatening valvular lesion as manifest by progressive cardiac-related symptomatology.

CARDIAC REHABILITATION

The goal of cardiac rehabilitation is the restoration of the individual patient to an optimal state of mental and physical health. An essential ingredient in this process is a positive yet realistic attitude on the part of the primary physician involved in caring for the patient. This physician's attitude is transmitted to the patient directly and indirectly by intangible cues. The atmosphere generated by the physician regarding prognosis and outcome can profoundly influence the spirit and motivation of the elderly patient, and it is an essential ingredient in achieving a successful overall result. The way the physician utilizes (a) physical therapy for muscle strengthening and functional rehabilitation; (b) dietary measures for nutritional support; (c) social services for family and patient counseling; and (d) home care programs, including visiting nursing services, for enhancing the transfer from hospital to home influences the patient's desire to recover and to comply with the prescribed therapy. Numerous institutional services are available in every hospital. The primary physician should make contact personally with the individuals heading up the aforementioned services to impress upon them the importance of the specific rehabilitation activity and also to individualize the medical-cardiac needs of the patient to these support personnel. Finally, the physician's personal interaction with the patient to discuss future preventive cardiac considerations (e.g., antibiotic and anticoagulant therapy in patients with prosthetic valves, dietary salt restriction to prevent CHF, the importance of follow-up drug adjustment in managing hypertension) is an important factor in the patient's perception of a favorable outcome.

REFERENCES

1. Ausubel K, Furman S: The pacemaker syndrome. *Ann Intern Med* 103:420, 1985.
2. Berman ND: *Geriatric Cardiology.* Lexington, The Collamore Press, 1982, pp 11–20.
3. Cohn JN, Archibald DG, Ziesche S, et al: Effect of vasodilator therapy on mortality in chronic congestive heart failure. *N Engl J Med* 314:1547, 1986.
4. Cribier A, Savin T, Saoudi N, et al: Percutaneous transluminal valvuloplasty of acquired aortic stenosis in elderly patients. An alternative to valve replacement? *Lancet* 1:63, 1986.
5. Davies MJ: Pathology of the conduction system. In Caird FI, Dall JLC, Kennedy RD (eds): *Cardiology in Old Age.* New York, Plenum Press, 1976, p. 57.
6. Fleg J, Kennedy HL: Cardiac arrhythmias in a healthy elderly population. *Chest* 81:302, 1982.
7. Higginbothan MB, Morris KG, Williams RS, et al: Physiologic basis for the age-related decline in aerobic work capacity. *Am J Cardiol* 57:1374, 1986.
8. Holmes DR Jr, Vlietstra RE: Percutaneous transluminal coronary angioplasty: current status and future trends. *Mayo Clin Proc* 61:865, 1986.
9. Lakatta EG: Age-related alternations in cardiovascular response to adrenergic mediated stress. *Fed Proc* 39:3173, 1980.
10. Latting CA, Silverman ME: Acute myocardial infarction in hospitalized patients over age 70. *Am Heart J* 100:311, 1980.
11. McCall D, O'Rourke RA: Congestive heart failure: II. Therapeutic options, old and new. *Mod Concepts Cardiovasc Dis* 54:61, 1985.
12. Naggar CZ, Pearson WN, Seljan MP: Frequency of complications of mitral valve prolapse in subjects aged 60 years and older. *Am J Cardiol* 58:1209, 1986.
13. Pathy MS: Clinical presentation of myocardial infarction in the elderly. *Br Heart J* 29:190, 1967.
14. Pomerance A: Pathology of the heart with and without failure in the aged. *Br Heart J* 27:697, 1965.
15. Port S, Cobb FR, Coleman RE, et al: Effect of age on the response of the left ventricular ejection fraction to exercise. *N Engl J Med* 303:1133, 1980.
16. Swan HJC, Ganz W, Forresteer J, et al: Catheterization of the heart in man with the use of flow-directed balloon-tipped catheters. *N Engl J Med* 283:447, 1970.
17. TIMI Study Group: The Thrombolysis in Myocardial Infarction trial. Phase I findings. *N Engl J Med* 312:932, 1985.
18. Vestal RE, Wood AJJ, Shand DG: Reduced beta-adrenoreceptors sensitivity in the elderly. *Clin Pharmacol Ther* 26:181, 1979.
19. Webb JL, Urner SC, McDaniels J: Physiologic characteristics of a champion runner age 77. *J Gerontol* 32:286, 1977.
20. Weisfeldt ML (ed): *The Aging Heart. Its Function and Response to Stress.* New York, Raven Press, 1980, vol. 12.

CHAPTER 7

Hypertension in the Elderly

JAMES F. BURRIS

IMPORTANCE OF HYPERTENSION IN THE ELDERLY

Hypertension is a common and dangerous condition in the elderly. The prevalence of elevated systolic blood pressure tends to rise progressively with age, while diastolic blood pressure rises with age until tending to level off after approximately age 55 years, so that the overall prevalence of hypertension (including isolated systolic hypertension) is highest in the elderly (15). The prevalence of hypertension is estimated at 50% or more in those 55 years and older, 64% in persons aged 65–74 years, and as much as 76% in blacks over age 65 years (14).

Hypertension is one of the most important risk factors for cardiovascular disease. Elderly individuals with hypertension not only have a higher risk of cardiovascular disease than normotensive individuals their own age, but also have a higher absolute risk for every cardiovascular complication than younger individuals with the same degree of hypertension; they also have a higher mortality rate after myocardial infarction or cerebrovascular accident than do younger individuals (20). Because of the increased prevalence and risk of hypertension in the elderly, almost 60% of the excess mortality attributable to hypertension occurs in older persons with mild hypertension, although individuals over the age of 60 years constitute only about 11% of the population (10). Since the over-70 age group is the fastest growing segment of the population and it is estimated that almost 20% of Americans will be over age 60 years by 1995, hypertension in the elderly will be an increasingly important medical problem in the future (4).

IMPACT OF DRUG THERAPY IN THE ELDERLY

Several large randomized, prospective multicenter trials have demonstrated that treatment of diastolic hypertension is beneficial in the elderly. In the Veterans Administration Cooperative Study, patients between the ages of 60 and 69 years with moderate to severe hypertension had a mortality rate, after several years of treatment, of 63% if treated with placebo, but only 29% if treated with active medication (18). Results of this study suggested that the benefits of treatment actually increased with age (15). The Hypertension Detection and Follow-Up Program (HDFP) study showed that 5-year mortality from all causes was reduced by more than 16% in patients aged 60–69 years with mild to moderate hypertension who received aggressive antihypertensive therapy using a stepped-care approach compared to patients referred to usual sources of care in the community (8). Fatal and nonfatal strokes were reduced by more than 45% in these older HDFP participants (9). In the Australian Therapeutic Trial, fatal and nonfatal end points were reduced 26% in actively treated patients 60–69 years old with entry diastolic blood pressures of 95–109 mm Hg compared with placebo-treated controls (13). The European Working Party on High Blood Pressure in the Elderly (EWPHE) study enrolled patients over age 60 years with diastolic pressures 90–119 mm Hg and is the only completed trial that was designed to include patients age 70 years and older (average age of the participants was approximately 72 years). There was a 36% reduction in terminating plus nonterminating cardiovascular events in actively treated patients compared to placebo-treated controls (1). Thus, all the major trials completed to date suggest that older individuals benefit at least as much from antihypertensive therapy for diastolic hypertension as younger patients do. Data in very elderly patients are quite scanty, however, and it is not certain that results in the 60–70 year age group can be extrapolated to the "old old" as well.

No definitive studies on the benefits of drug

treatment for isolated systolic hypertension in the elderly have yet been completed. It is well established that systolic blood pressure elevations correlate at least as well as diastolic elevations with cardiovascular risk and many clinicians recommend treatment for patients whose systolic pressure exceeds 160 mm Hg (5). The Systolic Hypertension in the Elderly Program (SHEP), now in progress, is specifically designed to study this problem. Results of a preliminary feasibility study for the SHEP trial demonstrated that chlorthalidone is effective in lowering systolic blood pressure in this group of patients and that elderly patients comply well with therapy (7). Older patients also had better compliance rates than younger ones in the HDFP study (8). These results belie the popular notion that noncompliance is particularly common in the elderly.

SPECIAL CONSIDERATIONS IN MANAGEMENT OF THE ELDERLY

Hypertension exacerbates the cardiovascular changes associated with aging (3). Left ventricular function, vascular compliance, baroreceptor sensitivity, total body volume, plasma renin activity, and regional blood flow all tend to decline with age (3, 12). These changes have a number of consequences for the elderly hypertensive. For example, patients may be especially susceptible to orthostatic hypotension and it is important to measure the blood pressure in the standing as well as seated position before initiating therapy or changing doses and when assessing the patient's complaints of side effects or the effectiveness of therapy. Drugs that potentiate orthostatic changes, such as guanethidine or prazocin, should be avoided in this population. Inelastic brachial arteries may cause falsely elevated readings, so-called "pseudohypertension," when blood pressure is measured by the cuff technique (16). This is most likely to be a problem in patients who have palpably inelastic peripheral arteries, vascular calcifications on x-ray, or a failure to respond to reasonable doses of antihypertensive drugs (12). Markedly lower direct intra-arterial blood pressure readings confirm this diagnosis, but are not appropriate for routine clinical care. Impaired renal and hepatic blood flow and organ function may influence drug metabolism and excretion and impair fluid and electrolyte homeostasis, potentially enhancing the risks of drug therapy for hypertension. Initiating therapy with small drug doses, titrating doses slowly, and monitoring for adverse drug reactions will minimize such problems. In fact, although the elderly are generally considered more susceptible to adverse drug reactions, elderly patients in the HDFP, Australian, and EWPHE studies tolerated antihypertensive drugs well.

The vast majority of older individuals with high blood pressure have essential hypertension and an extensive search for an underlying cause for secondary hypertension is rarely indicated (15). Atherosclerotic renal artery stenosis, however, should be suspected in an older patient who experiences sudden de novo onset or acceleration of hypertension. In addition, thyrotoxicosis, aortic insufficiency, and other high-output states can cause isolated systolic hypertension in the elderly. Failure of the blood pressure to respond to usual antihypertensive regimens can be a clue that an underlying cause of the hypertension is present.

Older patients often have concomitant diseases such as diabetes mellitus, arthritis, and coronary artery disease in addition to their hypertension. These concomitant conditions significantly affect management of hypertension in the elderly. β-adrenergic antagonist antihypertensive agents, for example, should be avoided in insulin-dependent diabetics because they may prolong hypoglycemia, mask hypoglycemic symptoms, and exacerbate symptoms of peripheral vascular disease. These drugs are especially useful, however, in patients with coronary artery disease where they can be used to treat both hypertension and angina. Nonsteroidal antiinflammatory agents used to treat arthritis may promote fluid retention and partially antagonize the action of antihypertensive medications. Since elderly individuals with multiple medical problems may be taking several different medications, the risk of adverse drug reactions and drug-drug interactions is enhanced in this population.

Compliance with therapy is currently a major problem in the management of high blood pressure (6). Factors that contribute to noncompliance include the asymptomatic nature of the disease and lack of perceived benefit from therapy, inconvenience and cost of office visits and medications, and the side effects of drugs. Noncompliance is often assumed to be even more of a problem in elderly than in younger individuals (10, 15) but, as already noted, this was not the case among the relatively healthy older participants in the HDFP and SHEP studies. Older patients who are taking multiple medications, who are confused or forgetful, or who have difficulty opening pill bottles because of arthritis or weakness are at special risk for noncompliance.

CHOICE OF THERAPY IN THE ELDERLY

Nonpharmacologic means for lowering blood pressure offer the possibility of avoiding the problems associated with drug therapy in the elderly. Weight reduction in the obese, salt restriction, and avoidance of excessive alcohol consumption are effective antihypertensive measures; smoking cessation to reduce cardiac risk should also be encouraged (10, 12). Elderly patients may have particular difficulty adhering to a low-salt diet because of diminished taste sensation.

Thiazide diuretics are very effective and generally well tolerated in elderly hypertensives (Table 7.1). Though some concerns have been raised recently about the metabolic side effects of thiazide diuretics (3), it must remembered that they were the basic drugs used in all of the major clinical trials that have demonstrated the efficacy of antihypertensive therapy in reducing cardiovascular morbidity and mortality caused by hypertension. They appear to be the drugs of choice for isolated systolic hypertension in particular. Patients with concomitant cardiac or renal disease should be closely monitored for potassium and other electrolyte disturbances when thiazides are used.

β-Adrenergic antagonists are somewhat less effective than diuretics in elderly patients and are contraindicated in those with congestive heart failure, diabetes mellitus, chronic obstructive pulmonary disease, and peripheral vascular disease (3, 12). Nevertheless, they are often effective in older individuals and may be specifically indicated in those with arrhythmias or angina pectoris and for prophylaxis against recurrent myocardial infarction (3). β-Blockers that are relatively cardioselective or which have intrinsic sympathomimetic activity may be better tolerated than those which lack these properties (12).

Centrally acting sympathetic inhibitors such as clonidine and methyldopa are effective antihypertensive agents in the elderly. They have the advantage of not reducing blood flow to the brain, heart, or kidneys despite their hypotensive effect (3). As with many other antihypertensive agents, diuretics potentiate their action. Methyldopa can induce hepatitis and is more prone to cause orthostatic hypotension, so is probably less desir-

Table 7.1
Antihypertensive Therapy in the Elderly

Medications	Advantages	Precautions
Drugs of choice		
Thiazide diuretics	Demonstrated efficacy and safety in the elderly	Monitor for adverse metabolic effects (e.g., hypokalemia)
Calcium channel antagonists	Efficacy increases with age; generally well tolerated	Potential adverse effects on cardiac conduction with some of these agents.
Useful drugs		
β-Adrenergic antagonists	Especially useful for concomitant therapy of angina or prophylaxis against recurrent myocardial infarction	Avoid in patients with bradyarrhythmias, congestive heart failure, COPD, diabetes mellitus, peripheral vascular disease
Clonidine	Transdermal formulation reduces side effects and permits once weekly administration of therapy	Sedation can be a limiting side effect
Hydralazine	Better tolerated as step 2 agent in elderly than in young patients	Requires concomitant diuretic therapy to prevent fluid retention
Angiotensin converting enzyme (ACE) inhibitors	Generally considered relatively free of symptomatic side effects	May be less effective in elderly than in younger patients; cost and side effect of impaired taste sensation may reduce compliance
Drugs to avoid		
Prazocin		Causes postural hypotension
Guanethidine, Guanadrel		Causes postural hypotension, sedation, impotence
Methyldopa		Causes postural hypotension, sedation, impotence, hepatic dysfunction, hemolytic anemia

able than other drugs in its class for elderly patients (12, 15). Clonidine is often effective in a single evening dose in older patients, which may convert a mild sedating side effect of the drug into an advantage. In higher doses, however, all of these drugs may cause mental depression, confusion, or excessive sedation, particularly in the elderly. The recently released transdermal formulation of clonidine reduces the incidence of symptomatic side effects with this drug and may enhance compliance since it need be administered only once a week (2).

Vasodilation is an attractive therapeutic mechanism in the elderly, who characteristically have increased peripheral resistance as the primary hemodynamic component of their hypertension (15). Hydralazine, a direct peripheral vasodilator, has traditionally been used as a third agent to be added to a diuretic and sympathetic inhibitor. It can sometimes be used as a second agent (with a diuretic to prevent sodium and fluid retention) in elderly individuals because the reflex increases in sympathetic activity that cause disturbing tachycardia are often blunted in this population. Calcium channel antagonists are an even more attractive group of vasodilators for use in elderly patients. They are less likely to provoke reflex tachycardia than other vasodilators and do not reduce coronary, renal or cerebral blood flow (3, 12). Calcium channel blockers are more effective in older patients and those with low plasma renin activity than in younger patients and those with high plasma renins (11) and so may be especially useful in patients who do not respond to β-blockers. Side effects frequently associated with calcium antagonists include headache, flushing, dizziness, fatigue, and ankle swelling. In higher doses particularly, some of these agents can have negative inotropic effects and impair electrical conduction, so they must be used judiciously in patients with compromised cardiac function.

Angiotensin converting enzyme inhibitors are most effective in high-renin hypertensive states and, thus, are thought to be somewhat less effective in the elderly as a group. However, these drugs probably have more than one mechanism of action and they are effective in many elderly patients. They are especially effective when combined with a low dose of a thiazide diuretic (19). They are usually relatively free of symptomatic side effects, but loss of taste is a relatively common side effect that can be particularly detrimental in older persons who may already have impaired taste sensation. The high cost of these agents and calcium antagonists in comparison to older drugs may be a disincentive for poorer elderly patients to comply with their use. Leuko-

penia and proteinuria, which were serious side effects initially reported with captopril, appear related to use of unnecessarily large doses of the drug, especially in patients with an underlying impairment of renal function.

The goal of therapy is normalization of blood pressure. Achieving this goal in elderly patients may cause marked side effects and interfere with the patient's quality of life more severely than can be justified by the potential benefits of therapy. Since even partial lowering of blood pressure conveys some benefit in reducing cardiovascular risk (17), it is reasonable to accept a less than optimal blood pressure result if the patient's comfort and compliance are enhanced.

REFERENCES

1. Amery A, Brilo P, Clement D, et al: Mortality and morbidity results from the European Working Party on High Blood Pressure in the Elderly Trial. *Lancet* 1:1349, 1985.
2. Burris JF, Mroczek WJ: Transdermal clonidine administration—a new approach to antihypertensive therapy. *Pharmacotherapy* 6:30, 1986.
3. Chobanian AV: Treatment of the elderly hypertensive patient. *Am J Med* 77(2B):22, 1984.
4. Coodley EL: Hypertension in the elderly. *Angiology* 36:45, 1985.
5. Gifford RW: Isolated systolic hypertension in the elderly: Some controversial issues. *JAMA* 247:781, 1982.
6. Haynes RB, Sackett DL, Taylor DW: Practical management of low compliance with antihypertensive therapy: A guide for the busy practitioner. *Clin Invest Med* 1:175, 1979.
7. Hulley SB, Furberg CD, Gurland B, et al: Systolic Hypertension in the Elderly Program (SHEP): Antihypertensive efficacy of chlorthalidone. *Am J Cardiol* 56:913, 1985.
8. Hypertension Detection and Followup Program Cooperative Group: Five year findings of the Hypertension Detection and Followup Program. II. Mortality by race, sex, and age. *JAMA* 242:2572, 1979.
9. Hypertension Detection and Followup Program Cooperative Group: Five-year findings of the Hypertension Detection and Followup Program. III. Reduction in stroke incidence among persons with high blood pressure. *JAMA* 247:633, 1982.
10. Kannel WB: Treating hypertension in the elderly. *Cardiovasc Med* November:41, 1985.
11. Kiowski W, Buhler FR, Fadayomi MO, et al: Age, race, blood pressure, and renin: Predictors for antihypertensive treatment with calcium antagonists. *Am J Cardiol* 56:81H, 1985.
12. Kirkendall WM: Treatment of hypertension in the elderly. *Am J Cardiol* 57:63C, 1986.
13. National Heart Foundation of Australia: Treatment of mild hypertension in the elderly: Report by the Management Committee. *Med J Austral* 2:398, 1981.
14. National High Blood Pressure Working Group on Hy-

pertension in the Elderly: Statement on hypertension in the elderly. U.S. Public Health Service, September 20, 1985.

15. Onrot J, Wood AJJ: Hypertension in the elderly—the benefits of therapy. *Postgrad Med* 76:46, 1984.

16. Spence JD, Sibbald WJ, Cape RD: Pseudo-hypertension in the elderly. *Clin Sci Molec Med* 55:3995, 1978.

17. Taguchi J, Freis ED: Partial reduction of blood pressure and prevention of complications in hypertension. *N Engl J Med* 291:329, 1974.

18. Veterans Administration Cooperative Study Group on Antihypertensive Agents: Effects of treatment on morbidity in hypertension. III. Influence of age, diastolic pressure, and prior cardiovascular disease. Further analysis of side effects. *Circulation* 45:991, 1972.

19. Veterans Administration Cooperative Study Group on Antihypertensive Agents: Low-dose captopril for the treatment of mild to moderate hypertension. *Hypertension* 5 (Suppl III):139, 1983.

20. Weinberger MH: Natural history, consequences, and therapeutic philosophy of hypertension in the elderly. *Geriatr Med Today* 4:81, 1985.

CHAPTER 8

Exercise and Physical Fitness for the Elderly

RAYMOND HARRIS

BENEFITS OF PHYSICAL EXERCISE

Exercise training plays an important role in the maintenance of high level wellness, health, and functional capacity in middle and old age. The work of Herbert deVries (8–10), Lawrence Frankel (11), Hans Kraus (21, 22), Ernst Jokl (20) and others (17, 32–34) confirm that vigorous physical conditioning of the healthy older organism can improve the cardiovascular system, the respiratory system, the musculature, and body composition significantly. In general, physical conditioning produces a more vigorous individual capable of better relaxation. The work of these investigators demonstrates that training programs for the aged have practical importance and produce physiologic gains, even if these gains may be relatively smaller in older than in younger people (32). Regular physical exercise programs for the elderly can produce beneficial physiologic, biologic, and biochemical effects that reduce the rate of physiologic decline with age, increase physical fitness and longevity, compensate for the decline in maximum oxygen uptake capacity, and counter the increase in body fat content with aging. Older men and women who exercise can maintain max VO_2 levels 20% or higher and be physiologically 10–15 years younger than more sedentary people of the same chronologic age.

Older individuals who benefit most from regular physical exercise are those without serious illness and who are physically unfit as a result of under-exercising, overeating, overdrinking, or smoking (21). Regular exercise enables older people to look

younger, feel better, and reduce detrimental stress responses. It also improves mobility, self-independence, happiness, sexual libido and function, and other factors that control the quality of life in later years (14, 35, 36). Exercise also exerts beneficial effects on depression in the elderly.

In addition, epidemiologic studies demonstrate that regularly performed exercise reduces the risk of developing ischemic heart disease by about 50%. Recent pathophysiologic studies provide evidence that prolonged, vigorous exercise training can improve the oxygenation and function of ischemic areas of the myocardium in patients with ischemic heart disease, protect against the deterioration of glucose tolerance with aging, reduce insulin resistance, and improve glucose tolerance in older individuals with impaired glucose tolerance. Vigorous exercise improves serum lipid patterns, aging metabolic processes, heart enzymes, and oxygen transport. It also effectively improves overweight, high blood sugar, and high blood pressure conditions (18).

Aging people often suffer from a decrease in the number of muscle cells and a significant decline in muscular strength by the time they reach 65 years of age. They show pronounced limitations of mobility and coordination as flexion movements become dominant and rotation components decrease. Faulty feedback between movement and body image further narrow the range and versatility of their motor responses (16).

A majority of late-developing postural deviations in the elderly are due to muscular imbalances and/or weakened musculature. These and many other physical changes in older people, mistakenly attributed solely to the aging process, are often due to hypokinetic disorders arising from poor physical fitness and disuse and muscular imbalance and weakness involving the antigravity, postural musculature. For example, shortened flexor muscles, weak antigravity muscles supporting the head and body joints, and deteriorated back and joint muscles may produce poor posture and functional kyphosis in the sedentary elderly. These changes restrict expansion of the chest and diaphragm, curtail ventilation, and reduce the volume of oxygen that can be inhaled, further limiting physical activity and mobility. As a result, inactive elderly people become more physically unfit and appear older than their chronologic age. With specific exercises, disuse postural deviation can be prevented. Successful treatment includes relief of pain, adoption of an appropriate exercise program that incorporates both stretching and strengthening, and a conditioning program that prevents recurrence and identifies proper mechanics (3).

A sedentary life-style and lack of physical fitness may also be responsible for many functional physical problems and medical complaints in aging patients, such as headaches, insomnia, constipation, joint pain, back trouble, aching and throbbing muscles, high blood pressure, overweight, and fatigue.

Many elderly patients with sedentary life-styles often complain of weakness and stiffness of back and hip muscles and difficulty in standing up from a sitting position, in going up and down stairs, and in performing the sexual act. Stretching and strengthening of the involved muscles can improve these problems and restore enjoyment in movement and sex.

Osteoporosis due to loss of bone mass, increased bone porosity, and decreased bone thickness is another major health problem for the elderly. It is a worldwide syndrome that affects 15–20 million individuals in the United States alone, that can be decelerated, delayed, and even halted and repaired by the use of hormones, physical activity, and adequate nutrition. Exercise can produce a positive effect by building up vertebral and skeletal tissues in both men and women. Preventive measures such as exercise and nutrition would result in untold savings of money, pain, and disability that affect aging men and women, and particularly elderly ones who fall and suffer fractures as a result of weakened bones.

The loss of bone with age is a gradual and apparently universal process that can be affected by many factors, including hormonal changes, physical activity, nutrition, and the responsiveness of bone cells to

stimuli. The rate at which bone is lost with age is independent of the initial bone mass. Persons with more than average bone mass earlier in life will maintain a higher level as they age. Osteoporotic fractures occur when the bone mass of an individual falls below a "fracture threshold" defined by one or more of several bone measurement techniques. Measures that maintain bone mass above this threshold can prevent the development of osteoporosis. While the exact mechanism by which exercise programs exert a positive effect on building vertebral skeletal tissue in both men and women is unknown, factors such as increased blood flow to the bone, supra-normal mechanical stress, or elevations in certain hormone levels known to affect bone (e.g., growth hormones and sex hormones) may be responsible. Aerobic and anaerobic regimens have distinct effects upon both trabecular and cortical bone in the spine—as assessed by quantitative computed tomography. Cross-sectional data show that athletes, in general, have an elevated level of trabecular and cortical spine bone mineral as compared with age-matched controls, although longitudinal data are not yet available to determine if exercise has an effect on retarding the rate of bone loss in this population. A differential skeletal response to exercise, depending on the type of regimen, may be found in different age populations. However, an optimal fitness program may increase bone mass in the young population. The increased bone mass may be carried along as this population ages and protect against the early development of osteoporosis in later life.

Vigorous physical exercise is the only nonpharmacologic means of building up bone after normal bone growth is completed. Studies by Professor Everett L. Smith of the University of Wisconsin have demonstrated that elderly women can increase bone mass if they start exercising. New bone is formed when bones are subjected to compression stresses during exercise. Postmenopausal hypoestrogenism, low calcium intake, and lack of physical stress contribute to bone atrophy in middle-aged women. Since the damage caused by osteoporosis in vertebral collapse is irreversible, prevention is the key. Longitudinal studies have shown that exercise can stimulate bone hypertrophy and prevent the involution of bone tissue. Excessive exercise, however, may be contraindicated in women, as the hypoestrogenism connected with athletic amenorrhea may lead to bone loss. There is adequate evidence that regular physical exercise improves body bone mass and, together with a daily intake of 1,000 mg of calcium, is helpful in preventing or treating osteoporosis (27). Estrogenic replacement therapy is also helpful after menopause to slow the loss of bone with age.

Regular, moderate physical exercise programs also improve longevity (4, 14, 15, 25). Dr. R. S. Paffenbarger's 16-year-old ongoing study of the 16,920 Harvard male alumni who graduated between 1916 and 1950 showed that habitual contemporary exercise predicts a low risk of death from all causes between the ages of 34-85 years (26). Active men who participated in activities such as walking, stair climbing, and sports and burned up 2000 or more kcal/week had a death rate one-quarter to one-third lower than those who were least active. Men expending less than 2000 kcal/week had a 64% higher risk of death than their less active exclassmates. For an average-sized man, 2000 kcal of exercise per week is the equivalent of 20 miles of walking or running per week. In calculating ordinary activity, one can estimate that walking seven city blocks consumes 56 kcal; climbing 70 stairs, 28 kcal; light exercise, 5 kcal min; and vigorous exercise, 10 kcal/min. By the age of 80 years, the amount of additional life attributed to exercise as compared with sedentary activities was 1-2 years or more. Men who walked 9 or more miles per week had a 21% lower risk of death than men who walked less than 3 miles. The increased survival with moderate exercise appeared independent of adverse personal characteristics and life-styles, such as hypertension, cigarette smoking, overweight, weight changes, and early parental mortality. Vigorous exercise did not appear to offer any greater protection from coronary heart disease than did moderate activity (26).

Moderate physical exercise, together with proper nutrition, provides the physiologic basis for a much healthier aging process and an improvement in the physical capacities, health, and skills of older people. Additional social and psychologic benefits of exercise and fitness include more personal enjoyment and life satisfaction, greater self-confidence, better social relationships, more self-awareness, and improved sexual libido. Active old people can expect to remain in good health longer and experience a shorter period of illness and disability before they die. To obtain these benefits, one should become actively engaged in a regular exercise program as early in life as possible in order to develop better lifetime fitness, performance skills, wellness, life-style, relaxation, and health. However, since the body's ability to benefit from exercise and its adaptability to exercise remain unimpaired with age, one is never too old to exercise (20).

Physical training can compensate for the effects of genetically programmed trends toward reduction of the body's adjustability to physiologic stresses, at times, even in the presence of pathologic processes. Moderately vigorous physical training regimens can (a) counterbalance the age-related changes in work capacity and physical performance; (b) develop, maintain, and improve range of motion, muscular strength, flexibility, balance, and endurance; and (c) reduce the damage and disability of associated cardiovascular, musculoskeletal, and other organ systems in the elderly. They provide the ambulatory well aged and the ambulatory or institutionalized sick aged with the opportunity to function at a more optimal level and to do another cost-effective therapeutic modality to prevent illness and improve medical care (17).

Geriatric patients in nursing homes and psychiatric hospitals should not be overlooked. They are as vulnerable as other members of the general geriatric population to fractures and musculoskeletal deformities. Many older psychiatric patients have a greater tendency to contractures of extremities due to immobility caused by lack of motivation, disinterest, and inactivity. The psychogeriatric population should be involved in exercise programs that are individualized according to their psychiatric and behavioral status and ability to participate in physical exercises (23).

CLINICAL ASSESSMENT FOR EXERCISE

Before exercise is prescribed, a thorough history and physical examination should be performed to assess the patient's fitness, the extent and seriousness of his or her aging and hypokinetic changes, and significant cardiac, vascular, muscular, orthopaedic or other disorders that may affect his ability to exercise. (Consult other chapters in this book for further information).

Clinical assessment of the cardiovascular system is an important part of the pre-exercise medical examination because of the high incidence of cardiac disease in the elderly. A thorough cardiovascular evaluation is necessary to obtain baseline data on heart size, blood pressure, and the cardiovascular responses during rest and exertion. This should include a careful health history and a cardiovascular evaluation with an electrocardiogram and an exercise test. Solid initial baseline data for the geriatric patient's physiologic condition (cardiopulmonary, musculoskeletal, endocrinologic, ophthalmologic, and other organ systems) and a clear understanding of common pathophysiologic changes are prerequisites for an accurate exercise prescription.

Clinical markers of poor physical fitness include a resting pulse rate greater than 80 beats per minute and the development of undue shortness of breath, dizziness, or irregular heart beat after mild exercise. Pre-exercise fasting blood sugar and lipid profiles are medically useful to diagnose lipid or diabetic disorders. Patients over 40 years of age who plan vigorous exercise should first have a treadmill stress test to determine their cardiovascular fitness and physical condition and how much exercise they can perform safely. Elderly patients with a history of chest pain and a normal electrocardiogram at rest may show an abnormal electrocardiographic response (ST depressions greater than 1 mm, T wave changes, and/or cardiac arrhythmias) under the stress of exercise (12). In patients with heart disease or with a positive stress test, the amount of exercise prescribed must be correlated with what the patient can do on the treadmill. The patient should be advised to exercise only to the degree that significant clinical pain, dyspnea, or undue symptoms such as fatigue or excessive blood pressure changes are not produced. His or her heart rate should be maintained at or below the rate at which such symptoms or electrocardiographic abnormalities occurred during exercise stress testing. On the other hand, persons with a normal electrocardiographic response during such exercise stress tests have a substantially lower probability of significant coronary artery obstruction and may safely follow the exercise prescription detailed in the next section.

A new generation of rate responsive pacemakers that can detect the patient's activity and respond with an appropriate heart rate is now available for the active elderly cardiac patient who needs a pacemaker and wishes to remain active. These new pacemakers increase the cardiac output to meet the physiologic demands of everyday activities and greatly improve the patient's ability to lead a more normal active life-style (13, 19, 29, 30).

Clinical assessment of the musculoskeletal system, using the Kraus-Weber muscle tests, which are easily performed in the doctor's office or gymnasium without elaborate equipment, is essential to appraise the muscular fitness and to prescribe remedial exercises that strengthen the musculoskeletal system of the elderly (22). The treadmill stress test, which challenges the older person's ability to walk or run at different rates of speed, can also be used to check walking ability and to detect disturbances in coordination, gait, and movement that may be camouflaged by the customarily slower pace of the elderly person. Many untrained middle-aged and older people cannot walk long on a treadmill because of weak back and leg muscles or painful feet.

PHYSICAL ACTIVITY PROGRAMMING FOR THE ELDERLY

Every older individual should have an activity prescription adjusted for sex, fitness level, and health. The fitness levels of the elderly range from 2.5 metabolic equivalents (METs) for institutionalized elderly to as high as 12–14 METs for competitive elderly athletes. A MET is equal to 3.5 ml $\times$ kg^{-1} $\times$ min^{-1} of oxygen consumption and represents the person's metabolic rate at rest (31). Most exercise regimens for the elderly include flexibility calisthenics and exercising supported by a chair. They usually do not exceed the 2-to 4-MET level. Occupational and recreational exercise activities for the healthy 80-year-old differ substantially from those for the arthritic, diabetic, or hypertensive 70-year-old. However, some form of physical activity is appropriate for all geriatric individuals.

The prescription should include the type, intensity, frequency, and duration of the exercise training. Periodic training reviews are necessary in order to identify problem areas and modify training goals (5). The exercise experience may be improved by providing program variety that meets the needs and interests of the participants, adequate rewards and social support, and a sound educational base to promote understanding of the principles and benefits of the exercise program (7).

Medical approval to engage in a vigorous aerobics fitness program specifically designed to meet the patient's condition and safety requirements should be secured prior to exercise. Prospective exercisers should be advised that as little as 20–30 minutes of exercise spent in aerobic and stretching exercises 3 days per week is the best investment of their time and energy. A program of good physical conditioning will improve strength, flexibility, endurance, foot work, coordination, and strength.

The recommendations outlined in this chapter are more applicable to most healthy senior citizens without serious incapacitating disease. Those with physical and medical problems require more clinical supervision and instruction. Individuals aged 60 years and older unaccustomed to vigorous exercise who wish to exercise and become fit should arrange for proper medical screening by physicians, obtain individual assessment of exercise responses, and be carefully supervised during exercise by well-qualified physical educators and trainers in order to prevent injuries and problems. They should be advised to wear loose-fitting, attractive athletic clothing, suitable for the weather, sport, and activity. Thick woolen socks and good supportive foot wear will protect walkers and other participants in sports against serious foot injuries.

All elderly people, regardless of age or condition, should be encouraged to perform stretching and static exercises to improve their flexibility, joint motion, balance, muscular coordination, and mobility (1, 2, 8, 11). Much of the loss of flexibility in the elderly is usually due to muscle joint stiffness. The stiffness in a joint is largely associated with changes in the soft tissue of the muscle, tendons, ligaments, and joint capsule as a result of age-related changes, disuse, and sometimes, disease. Since more than 80% of the elderly have some stigmata of osteoarthritis, this condition must also be considered in evaluating loss of flexibility in the elderly patient. Pain and swelling associated with the osteoarthritic joint may contribute to the elderly patient's decreased range of joint motion, reduced muscle strength and loss of function (24).

Exercises for the mobile and independent elderly should emphasize the movements that improve the flexibility essential for safety and ease of locomotion. For example, neck flexibility exercises increase the safety and comfort of senior citizens while driving or crossing streets.

Hospitals and institutions for the aged and disabled should provide a variety of individual and group participation exercises and recreational activities under the supervision of qualified leaders. Occupational therapy, reality orientation, games, sports, and other activity programs tailored to the needs of chronically ill and disabled patients can suitably improve their mental and physical condition (6, 28). Range of motion and stretching exercises improve the ability of elderly patients to progress from bed, to chair, and then to walking.

EXAMPLES OF EXERCISE FOR THE ELDERLY

Walking is the best beginning exercise for the elderly. It can be used as part of a relaxing warm-up and for more vigorous conditioning exercises. A daily brisk 30-minute walk at a rate of 3¾ miles per hour burns up 150 calories a day and, in ½ year's time, can produce a 15-pound weight loss.

Most ambulatory, physically unfit elderly patients may safely begin an exercise program to improve their fitness by walking their usual distance

and then gradually increasing it to 2–3 miles daily over a period of several weeks. When the longer distance can be completed without undue complaint, the rate of walking should be increased by alternately walking 50 feet slowly and then moving rapidly at a rate of 120 steps per minute according to the patient's tolerance. After several weeks, this regimen can be advanced to a brisk walk or walk-jog program according to the patient's ability. However, brisk walking remains the safest exercise for the elderly.

Vigorous aerobic exercises that use major groups of muscles are necessary to reach the age-related target training heart rate required for cardiovascular endurance. An effective exercise program should include a carefully planned and supervised regimen of brisk walking or walk/jogging for 2–3 miles daily. Swimming, bicycling, calisthenics (Fig. 8.1), or a combination of all may be incorporated into the program, depending on the preference of the exerciser. Calisthenics performed in water are excellent initial conditioning exercises for the heart, lung, and blood vessels, especially for patients with arthritis or other musculoskeletal problems that limit normal ambulation on land. The resistance and buoyancy of water allow the elderly with musculoskeletal and other orthopaedic problems to move more freely and to exercise in a much less taxing way than they could on land. Aquatic exercises help many elderly and handicapped individuals to increase their range of joint motion and muscular strength and to relax. Such exercise in water at a comfortable temperature relieves muscle pain and spasm and induces greater relaxation. The water exercises can be easily graded and

Figure 8.1 Calisthenics class taking place at Bykota Senior Center in Towson, MD. The "holding" position of the half sit-up is shown here. It is not necessary for the individual to touch her toes during this exercise, which is also performed with bent knees. Benefits to be derived are strengthened abdominal and back muscles.

progressively increased to meet the cardiovascular fitness needs of the elderly (16).

To reach maximum cardiovascular fitness and endurance, one should exercise vigorously and aerobically for at least 20–30 minutes three or more times weekly at one's optimal target training heart rate. This rate can be calculated by first subtracting one's chronologic age from 220 to get the age-adjusted maximum heart rate, and then multiplying the result by 60–70% to get the optimal target training heart rate. The heart rate and rhythm of the carotid pulse during exercise should be checked frequently to make sure the rate is not higher than the optimal target training heart rate and that no heart irregularities are present.

CONCLUSION

Commitment to an active style of life sets the tone, health, and quality of life for one's later years. It plays an important role in the maintenance of high level wellness, better health, and good functional capacity in the elderly. Vigorous physical conditioning of the healthy older person significantly improves the cardiovascular system, respiratory system, musculature, body composition, and bone mass. Physical conditioning produces a more vigorous elderly individual capable of enjoying a better quality and length of life.

REFERENCES

Additional information on exercise programs for the elderly may be obtained from: The President's Council on Physical Fitness and Sports, Washington, D.C., 20201 and the Center for the Study of Aging, 706 Madison Avenue, Albany, NY 12208.

1. Adrian MJ: FLexibility in the aging adult. In Smith EL, Serfass RC (eds): *Exercise and Aging: The Scientific Basis.* Hillside, NJ, Enslow Publishers, 1981.

2. Anderson B: *Stretching.* Bolinas, CA, Shelter Publications, 1980.

3. Benson J: Postural deviation in the elderly. In Harris R, Harris S (eds): *Physical Activity, Aging and Sports. Volume I, Scientific and Medical Aspects.* Albany NY, Center for the Study of Aging, in press.

4. Berdyshev GD, Asadov SA: On the maximal chronological age of man. *Z Alternforsch* 40:289, 1985.

5. Birrer RB, Stein R, Brecker D: Comprehensive prescription of exercise for the elderly patient. In Harris R, Harris S (eds): *Physical Activity, Aging and Sports. Volume I, Scientific and Medical Aspects.* Albany, NY, Center for the Study of Aging, in press.

6. Caplow-Lindner E, Harpaz L, Samberg S: *Therapeutic Dance/Movement.* New York, Human Sciences Press, 1979.

7. Clark BA: Principles of physical activity programming for the older adult. *Topic Geriatr Rehabil* 1:68, 1985.

8. deVries HA: Physiological effects of an exercise training regimen upon men aged 52 to 88. *J Gerontol* 25:325, 1970.

9. deVries HA: Physiology of physical conditioning for the elderly. In Harris, R. Frankel LJ (eds): *Guide to Fitness After 50.* New York, Plenum Press, 1977, p. 47.

10. deVries HA: *Vigor Regained.* Englewood Cliffs, NJ, Prentice Hall, 1974.

11. Frankel LJ, Richard BB: *Be Alive as Long as You Live.* New York, Lippincott & Crowell, 1980.

12. Glasser SP, Clark PI: *The Clinical Approach to Exercise Testing.* New York, Harper & Row, 1980.

13. Gillette P: Critical analysis of sensors for physiological pacing. *PACE* 7:1263, 1984.

14. Harris R: Exercise and sex in the aging patient. *Med Aspects Hum Sexual* 22:148, 1988.

15. Harris R: Aging, exercise and longevity. Report on International Round Table panel, XIIIth International Congress of Gerontology, New York City, July 15, 1985. In *International Review of Sport Science.* Köln, Bundesrepublik Deutschland, International Council of Sport Science and Physical Education, 1986, pp. 56–59.

16. Harris R: Fitness and the aging process. In Harris R, Frankel LJ (eds): *Guide to Fitness After 50.* New York, Plenum Press, 1977.

17. Harris R, Frankel LJ (eds): *Guide to Fitness After 50.* New York, Plenum Press, 1977.

18. Holloszy JO: Exercise, aging and health (abstract). Second International Conference on Physical Activity, Aging and Sports, West Point, NY, July 8–12, 1985.

19. Humen D, Kostuk W, Klein G: Activity-sensing, rate-responsive pacing: Improvement in myocardial performance with exercise. *PACE* 8:52, 1985.

20. Jokl E: Abstract, XII International Congress of Gerontology, Hamburg, July 12–17 1981, p. 35.

21. Kraus H: Preservation of physical fitness. In Harris R, Frankel LJ (eds): *Guide to Fitness After 50.* New York, Plenum Press, 1977, p. 35.

22. Kraus H: Principles of exercise for musculoskeletal reconditioning and fitness. In Harris R, Frankel LJ (eds): *Guide to Fitness After 50.* New York, Plenum Press, 1977.

23. Krementsov YG: Physical exercise among geriatric patients in a psychiatric hospital. In Harris R, Harris S (eds): *Physical Activity, Aging and Sports. Volume I, Scientific and Medical Aspects.* Albany, NY, Center for the Study of Aging, in press.

24. Laird T: Developing exercise protocols for geriatric functional effectiveness in primary care. Interim Report 1983–84, National Council on Aging, Inc.

25. Manton KG: Past and future life expectancy increase at later ages: Their implication for the linkage of chronic morbidity, disability and mortality. *J Gerontol* 41:672, 1986.

26. Paffenbarger RS, Wing AL, Hsieh C: Physical activity, all-cause mortality and longevity of college alumni. *N Engl J Med* 314:605, 1986.

27. Raab DM, Smith EL: Exercise and aging effects on bone. *Topic Geriatr Rehabil* 1:31, 1985.

28. Rodstein M: Changing habits and thought patterns of

the aged to promote better health through activity programs. In Harris R, Frankel LJ (eds): *Guide to Fitness After 50.* New York, Plenum Press, 1977, p. 215.

29. Ryden L, Kristensson BE: Rate responsive pacing: Effects on hemodynamics, exercise tolerance, and subjective feeling of well-being. In Zipes DP, Jalife J (eds): *Cardiac Electrophysiology and Arrhythmias.* Orlando, Grune & Stratton, 1985, pp. 513–522.

30. Ryden L, Smedgard P, Kruse J, et al: Rate responsive pacing by means of activity sensing. *Stimucoeur* 12:181, 1984.

31. Serfass RC, Agre JC, Smith EL: Exercise testing for the elderly. *Topic Geriatr Rehabil* 1:58, 1985.

32. Shephard RJ: *Physical Activity and Aging.* Chicago, Croom Helm/Year Book Medical Publishers, Inc., 1978, p. 273.

33. Sidney KN: Cardiovascular benefits of physical activity in the exercising aged. In Smith EL, Serfass RC (eds): *Exercise and Aging: The Scientific Basis.* Hillside, NJ, Enslow Publishers, 1981.

34. Smith EL, Serfass RC (eds): *Exercise and Aging: The Scientific Basis.* Hillside, NJ, Enslow Publishers, 1981.

35. Stanford D: Sexuality and aging. In Hall BA (ed): *Mental Health and the Elderly.* Orlando, Grune & Stratton, Inc., 1984.

36. Wasow M: Sexuality and aging: It does exist. *Aging Network News* 3:October, 1986.

CHAPTER 9

Thrombo-embolism in the Elderly

GEORGE G. SHASHATY

Thromboembolic disease is a major proximate cause of death in people with a wide range of medical and surgical disease. Although it is difficult to state an incidence with validity, estimates of annual deaths in the United States due to pulmonary embolism (PE) range from 50,000–100,000. Although about half of these individuals suffer from other fatal diseases, the remainder succumb primarily to sudden cardiorespiratory failure from obstruction of the pulmonary vasculature. In addition, deep venous thrombosis (DVT) frequently inflicts damage on the veins of the lower extremity, leading to recurrent thrombosis, poor venous return, leg edema, pain, and skin ulceration.

Although there is no clear evidence that age itself predisposes to the development of thromboembolism, a convergence of risk factors in the elderly produces significant mortality and morbidity related to this disease. In one series of patients, 75% of deaths from PE occurred in patients over the age of 50 years.

Table 9.1 lists risk factors for thrombosis common in the elderly. Table 9.2 shows other, more unusual factors that may contribute to this propensity. Immobility related to stroke, fractures, debilitation, and surgery, as well as the frequency of cancer in this age group, should be emphasized.

It is usually stated that phlebothrombosis may be initiated by (a) changes in constituents of the blood; (b) changes in the vessel wall; (c) stasis. It is probable that the last is the most important cause of clotting. The reason for this is not entirely clear, but may be related to the local accumulation of activated clotting factors that is an ongoing intravascular process.

Potentially lethal pulmonary emboli almost always arise in the femoral, iliac, or pelvic veins and it is to these sites that diagnostic and therapeutic attention should be directed. Embolization from upper extremity veins is rare.

Table 9.1
Common Risk Factors for Thrombosis in the Elderly

Immobilization
    Stroke
    Mycardial infarction
    Postsurgical
    Vertebral collapse
Hip surgery
Cancer
Heart failure
Varicose veins
Previous thrombophlebitis

Table 9.2
Uncommon Risk Factors for Thrombosis in the Elderly

Septic states
Immune complex disease
Obesity
Estrogen use
Polycythemia vera
Thrombocytosis

DIAGNOSIS

It is established that neither the patient's history nor the physician's physical examination is adequate to make or exclude a diagnosis of DVT of the lower extremities. For example, a number of studies in high risk patients, mostly postoperative, using the technique of localization of I-125 labeled fibrinogen as an indicator of thrombosis, have shown that as many as 30–50% of such persons have clots in the legs, most often in the calf veins. Only a small percentage of these individuals had either symptoms or signs usually ascribed to thrombosis. Similarly, in one study of almost 500 patients with clinical features of venous thrombosis, only 45% had thrombosis demonstrable by venography. The presence of calf and leg pain and tenderness, leg swelling, and Homans' sign are neither sensitive nor specific for this diagnosis. Therefore, the main functions of the physician are to consider the diagnosis repetitively in those with risk factors and to perform appropriate investigations to make the diagnosis.

Because of the lack of validity of patient symptoms or the physician's examination, the diagnosis of DVT relies upon laboratory evaluation. (See Fig. 9.1). Most studies made to evaluate the efficiency of a particular diagnostic procedure have attempted to correlate the test in question with the results of venography, the latter being the final arbiter of the presence or absence of thrombosis. Venography, although presumably sensitive and specific, is cumbersome. Venography is costly; it requires special personnel and equipment, it may be associated with reactions to radiocontrast dyes, and it may cause venous irritation and subsequent chemical phlebitis. For all these reasons, venography cannot practically be performed repetitively to assess therapeutic efficacy. Therefore, other less invasive methods for diagnosis have been devised.

Two procedures have been studied extensively as alternatives to venography. Of these, the most useful has been impedance plethysmography. This is a safe, noninvasive, low-cost test which can, if necessary, be done repetitively. It possesses a high degree of specificity and sensitivity when compared to venography, although false-positive and false-negative results may occur. Although plethysmography is a very useful tool in assessing proximal thrombosis (femoral or iliac), it is not capable of detecting clots in the calf and popliteal veins. However, PE from these distal venous sites rarely occurs and spontaneous resolution is the rule, so their main danger resides in proximal propagation to the femoral and iliac vessels. This proximal extension can be detected by performing follow-up plethysmographic tests. If extension does not occur, specific antithrombotic treatment is probably not indicated.

The other technique for detecting DVT is I-125 fibrinogen. This method has been most useful in epidemiologic studies to demonstrate the incidence and natural history of DVT. From a clinical viewpoint, there are a number of reasons why it cannot be recommended as a procedure for diagnosing DVT in a single individual. In fact, it is generally only performed in those institutions with a research interest in DVT and PE.

Other procedures that have been either less well evaluated or that do not show good sensitivity and/or specificity include Doppler flow studies, radionuclide venography, and measures of various products of fibrinogen/fibrin metabolism. None of these presently can be recommended for the clinical evaluation of patients suspected of having DVT.

The diagnosis of PE is more difficult. It should be thought of in any person who develops a cardiorespiratory complaint, particularly when risk factors for DVT are present. Although physical examination, chest x-ray, and the electrocardiogram may reveal various abnormalities, none is specific. Radionuclide ventilation-perfusion scans are helpful mostly in a negative sense. If the scan is normal, embolism is very unlikely. Unfortunately, the sensitivity and specificity of an abnormal scan are not great. If the scan is abnormal, a very reasonable algorithm would suggest that impedance plethysmography be performed on the legs. If plethysmography shows a thrombus in the proximal leg veins, standard antithrombotic therapy would be employed and would be the same whether or not PE were present. If the plethysmography is not diagnostic for DVT, the next approach before therapy would have to be the more invasive pulmonary arteriogram.

ANTICOAGULANT THERAPY

Initial therapy for DVT with or without PE is anticoagulation with heparin. Heparin is a potentiator of the serine protease inhibitor, antithrombin III. This heparin antithrombin III complex inactivates all of the clotting factors which are converted in the coagulation cascade from a zymogen to an active enzyme. The effect is immediate, potent, and quickly reversible with protamine or within several hours of discontinuation of the drug by normal hepatic and renal catabolic processes. Although no acceptable randomized control studies of its efficacy have ever been performed, it is widely believed that heparin reduces the morbidity and mortality of venous thrombosis and PE.

Figure 9.1. Algorithm for suspected thromboembolism (does not apply to suspected pelvic or upper extremity thrombosis).

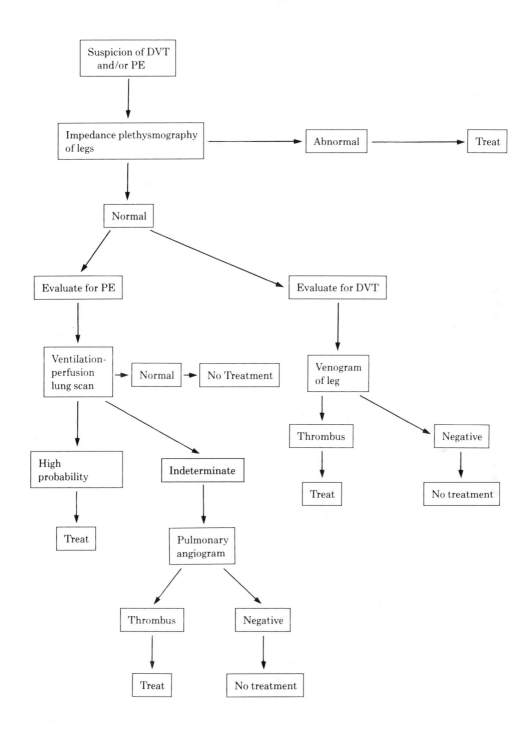

An activated partial thromboplastin time (aPTT) should be performed, and a bolus of 5000 units of heparin should be given intravenously. Thereafter, a continuous intravenous infusion of heparin should be administered to keep the aPTT between 1½–2 times the baseline value. Studies have shown that when the aPTT is kept in this range, recurrent thrombosis and PE rarely occur. Intermittent heparin administration is no more effective than continuous administration and may be associated with a higher incidence of side effects. Subcutaneous heparin is probably effective, but is rarely used unless venous access is a problem.

The major side effect of heparin therapy is hemorrhage and its use may be absolutely or relatively contraindicated in a number of situations (recent cerebral hemorrhage, central nervous system surgery, gastrointestinal bleeding, etc.). A fairly common complication of the drug is the development of a peripheral destructive thrombocytopenia. As a rule, if this does occur, the platelet count does not fall to a critically low level and the drug can be continued. A number of other uncommon reactions may occur, the most important of which is paradoxical widespread thrombosis.

Standard practice suggests that heparin should be administered for 7–10 days. For the last 2–3 days of heparin administration, oral anticoagulant (i.e., coumadin) therapy is also given so that at no time is the patient unprotected. Oral anticoagulants are vitamin K antagonists, require several days to achieve their effects, and are reversible with vitamin K administration. The dosage of coumadin varies widely, but is usually started at a dose of 10–15 mg for 3 days and then guided by keeping the prothrombin time from 1½–2 times control levels. Recent data suggest that anticoagulant effectiveness is provided even when the prothrombin time is in a lower range, but this is not yet widely accepted. Studies suggest that persons taking oral anticoagulants require approximately 3 months of maintenance therapy and that treating beyond that length of time confers no advantage. In fact, the frequency of significant hemorrhage from oral anticoagulants appears to increase in direct relation to the length of use of these agents. During their use, no other drugs, particularly aspirin, should be taken without the advice of the physician, since many drugs alter coumadin metabolism leading to a greater or lesser degree of anticoagulation. If there is some contraindication to the use of oral anticoagulants, it has been demonstrated that twice daily subcutaneous heparin is as effective, provided that sufficient heparin is given to prolong the aPTT to 1½ times the control values 6 hours after injection.

FIBRINOLYTIC THERAPY

Fibrinolytic agents act directly on the fibrin of the clot by activating plasminogen, a plasma zymogen, to plasmin, a potent fibrinolytic enzyme. Unfortunately, when given intravenously, the lytic state is widespread rather than being confined to the area of the clot. Hemorrhage, therefore, is the most important side effect.

Most studies involving fibrinolytic agents have employed streptokinase rather than urokinase because of cost and availability. A new fibrinolytic agent, tissue plasminogen activator, is available, but has been used primarily for coronary and peripheral arterial thrombosis. In comparison to heparin, streptokinase has been shown to produce more rapid dissolution of venous clots, preservation of venous and valvular architecture, more rapid improvement in pulmonary abnormalities after embolism, and perhaps less postphlebitic syndrome. However, there has been no documentation of improvement in survival, and because of the cost and greater likelihood of hemorrhage with lytic agents than with anticoagulants, lytic drugs have not gained favor with most physicians.

If fibrinolytic therapy is elected, streptokinase is administered intravenously at a dose of 250,000 units over 30 min, followed by approximately 100,000 units per hour. The presence of a fibrinolytic state demonstrated by a prolonged thrombin time, fibrin degradation products, or hypofibrinogenemia indicates an adequate therapeutic effect. The duration of treatment is 12–24 hours for PE and 48–72 hours for DVT. During therapy, extreme care must be used when performing either venous or arterial puncture, since these are often sites of severe hemorrhage.

INTERRUPTION OF THE INFERIOR VENA CAVA

The major indication for interruption of the interior vena cava is the presence of a contraindication to anticoagulant/antifibrinolytic therapy in a patient with DVT and/or PE. Patients with thrombocytopenia, recent surgery in critical body areas, and irreversible risk factors such as metastatic cancer are obvious candidates. The procedure should also be considered when, despite adequate antithrombotic therapy, clot extension or recurrent pulmonary emboli are detected. The most common method of interruption is the transvenous placement of a Greenfield filter. This device has a low failure rate and is relatively simple to insert. However, it is irreversible and may be associated with persistent lower extremity edema. There is some controversy as to whether or not anticoagulants should be given after its insertion.

SEQUELAE OF DEEP VENOUS THROMBOSIS

Recurrence of DVT after cessation of maintenance anticoagulation occurs in about 10% of patients. Most of these develop in individuals with persistent risk factors. Therapy is the same as for the initial episode, but more prolonged periods of maintenance are probably advisable. Postphlebitic syndrome is seen primarily after proximal DVT. Its frequency is uncertain, but probably around 10%. Leg swelling, venous dilatation, pigmentation and ulceration of the skin, and pain or aching of the leg may be seen. Individually fitted compression stockings (Jobst) are often helpful in relieving symptoms, but their long-term benefits are not clearly known.

DEEP VENOUS THROMBOSIS OF THE UPPER EXTREMITY

More than 95% of DVT involves veins of the legs or pelvis. DVT of the upper extremities in the elderly is due primarily to obstruction of flow as the result of an invasive tumor, particularly cancers of the lung and breast. The axillary vein is the usual site of clot formation. Effort thrombosis (Paget-Schrotter syndrome) has occasionally been described in the elderly and is thought to be caused by unusual exertion of the arm. Pain, swelling of the arm and venous dilatation are usually present. If necessary, the diagnosis can be confirmed with venography. Embolization of clinical importance does not usually occur. The main clinical sequela of axillary vein thrombosis is chronic venous insufficiency. For this reason, fibrinolytic therapy may be preferable to anticoagulent therapy, in order to salvage venous function.

PREVENTION OF DEEP VENOUS THROMBOSIS

The incidence of both asymptomatic and symptomatic DVT in certain situations (postoperatively, in congestive heart failure, immobility following stroke, fracture, or myocardial infarction) in the elderly has led to the introduction of prophylactic therapy to prevent DVT. Extensive studies with small doses of heparin have shown that there is a reduction in DVT from as much as 25–45% to approxi-

mately 5% when sensitive diagnostic tests such as I-125 labeled fibrinogen are employed. In addition, one large study showed a significantly reduced death rate from PE in postoperative patients prophylactically treated with heparin given subcutaneously at a dose of 5000 units 12 hours before surgery, then every 12 hours until mobilization is complete. Using these doses, the aPTT remains normal or is only minimally raised. Bleeding manifestations are unusual and frequently lead to no important clinical consequences for the patient.

The efficacy of antiplatelets agents (aspirin), oral anticoagulants, and dextran in the prevention of DVT has never been proven clearly in large randomized studies and may be associated with a greater frequency of hemorrhage in postsurgical patients.

Devices that produce intermittent calf compression have been shown to decrease the rate of DVT in immobilized patients. However, they are cumbersome to employ and have not gained wide favor. Nonetheless, they may play a role in persons who have a contraindication to the use of prophylactic anticoagulant therapy.

SUGGESTED READINGS

1. Bell WR, Simon TL, DeMets DL: The clinical features of submassive and massive pulmonary emboli. *Am J Med* 62:355, 1977.
2. Goldhaber S, Buring JE, Lipnick RJ, et al: Interruption of the inferior vena cava by clip or filter. *Am J Med* 76:512, 1984.
3. Goldhaber S, Buring JE, Lipnick RJ, et al: Pooled analysis of randomized trials of streptokinase and heparin in phlebographically documented acute deep venous thrombosis. *Am J Med* 76:393, 1984.
4. Hirsh J, Genton E, Hull R: *Venous Thromboembolism.* New York, Grune & Stratton, 1981.
5. Hull R, Delmore T, Carter C, et al: Adjusted subcutaneous heparin vs. warfarin sodium in the long term treatment of venous thrombosis. *N Engl J Med* 306:189, 1982.
6. Hull R, Hirsh J: Effectiveness of intermittent pulsatile elastic stockings in the prevention of deep venous thrombosis after knee surgery. *Thromb Res* 16:37, 1979.
7. Hull R, Hirsh J: Long term anticoagulant therapy in patients with venous thrombosis. *Arch Intern Med* 143:2061, 1983.
8. Hull R, Hirsh J, Carter CJ, et al: Diagnostic efficacy of impedance plethysmography for clinically suspected deep vein thrombosis. *Ann Intern Med* 102:21, 1985.
9. Hull R, Hirsh J, Jay R, et al: Different intensities of oral anticoagulant therapy in the treatment of proximal vein thrombosis. *N Engl J Med* 307:1676, 1982.
10. Hull R, Hirsh J, Sackett DL, et al: Cost-effectiveness of clinical diagnosis, venography and non-invasive

testing in patients with symptomatic deep venous thrombosis. *N Engl J Med* 304:1561, 1981.

11. International Study Group: Prevention of fatal post-operative pulmonary embolism with low dose heparin. *Lancet* 2:45, 1975.

12. Kakkar V: Prophylaxis for post-operative deep venous thrombosis. *JAMA* 241:39, 1979.

13. Leyvraz P, Richard J, Bachmann F, et al: Adjusted vs. fixed dose subcutaneous heparin in the prevention of deep vein thrombosis after total hip replacement. *N Engl J Med* 309:954, 1983.

14. Petitti DB, Strom BL, Melmon KL: Duration of warfarin anticoagulation therapy and the probabilities of recurrent thromboembolism and hemorrhage. *Am J Med* 81:255, 1986.

CHAPTER 10

Pulmonary Problems in the Elderly

JOSEPH REICHEL

The most common and important pulmonary problems in the elderly include pneumonia, chronic obstructive pulmonary disease (COPD), adult onset asthma, tuberculosis, carcinoma of the lung, and pulmonary thromboembolism. Pulmonary thromboembolism is covered in Chapter 9.

PNEUMONIA

Pneumonia occurs in the geriatric population sporadically or as a complication of a chronic disease process. Pulmonary infections in the aged are frequently difficult to treat and hence carry a higher mortality than in younger age groups (14). Not uncommonly, the onset of pneumonia in an aged person is signaled by general deterioration, tachycardia, and increase of respiratory rate. There may be confusion or a full-blown organic brain syndrome. The classic symptoms of cough, chest pain, sputum, and fever are often absent. A generalized, nonspecific deterioration of the patient's previous condition can mark the onset of a pulmonary infection.

Physical findings may be less clear cut in aged patients. The absence of findings may be due to inability of the patient to cooperate fully during the physical examination (sitting up, taking a deep breath). Also, the presence of some signs, particularly rales, may be misleading. For example, rales may be of no clinical significance (perhaps due to microatelectasis that occurs with aging) or may be due to chronic congestive heart failure, often present in elderly patients. For these reasons, a chest x-ray must be obtained in all cases where the diagnosis of pneumonia is suspected.

If the chest x-ray does show an acute pulmonary

infiltrate, it is important to determine whether one is dealing with a bacterial, mycoplasmal, or viral infection. The presence of leukocytosis or of underlying lung disease, such as bronchiectasis, usually points to a bacterial etiology. Particular situations, such as an influenza virus or *Mycoplasma* outbreak, may lead to the suspicion of viral or mycoplasmal pneumonia. However, *Mycoplasma pneumoniae* is significantly less common in a geriatric population than in a population of younger adults. When pneumonia is suspected, it is crucial to draw blood cultures and to perform a Gram stain and culture of the sputum. The Gram stain of fresh sputum will assist in selecting the most appropriate antibiotic therapy. However, in many instances, obtunded, aged individuals are unable to produce sputum. Nasotracheal suctioning may produce a satisfactory sputum specimen. If this fails, then it may be useful to request consultation to obtain bronchial brushings for Gram stain and culture using the fiberoptic bronchoscope and special sterile bacteriologic brushes. During fiberoptic bronchoscopy, it is important to take every precaution to maintain ventilation and prevent hypoxia. Hypoxic deaths have been noted in individuals with coronary artery disease during fiberoptic bronchoscopy.

Classic lobar pneumonia is rather unusual in elderly patients. It is more common to find bronchopneumonia when the pneumococcus is the causative organism. In the absence of allergy, penicillin is the drug of choice for a patient with patchy bronchopneumonia or lobar pneumonia and Gram-positive diplococci in the sputum smear. If there is a concomitant urinary tract infection, ampicillin and an aminoglycoside may be tried first. If one suspects *Haemophilus influenzae* because the sputum smear shows small pleomorphic Gram-negative rods, ticarcillin-clavulanate, cefamandole, cefuroxime, or another third-generation cephalosporin or intravenous trimethoprim-sulfamethoxazole may be given until ampicillin sensitivity is established (4). Erythromycin, 1 g every 6 hours intravenously, should be given in epidemic situations that suggest the presence of *Mycoplasma* infection or if the clinical picture suggests *Legionella*. *Legionella* is seen most commonly in elderly males who present with sudden prostration, high fever, dry cough, change in mental status, and rapidly progressing infiltrates. If Gram-negative organisms are seen on sputum smears, or if the pneumonia is hospital acquired, a third-generation cephalosporin and an aminoglycoside should be administered. Peak and trough aminoglycide levels should be measured whenever aminoglycosides are used (10). If the patient presents with any of the following—cyanosis, hypotension, tachycardia, tachypnea, and diaphoresis —he/she should be hospitalized for treatment. It may be appropriate in such a case, after all cultures are obtained, to institute broad spectrum coverage. One such regimen would be a combination of a third-generation cephalosporin, an aminoglycoside, and oxacillin, pending blood and sputum culture results. Alternatively, cefamandole may be given. Although prophylactic antibiotics are not advised, one must have a low threshold for antibiotic treatment and hospitalization in the aged. If the diagnosis of bacterial infection is suspect, an antibiotic should be administered.

Supportive therapy is important as part of the treatment of pneumonia in the aged. Adequate hydration must be maintained, preferably by intravenous fluids in the first several days unless one is assured of adequate oral intake. The frequent presence of concomitant cardiovascular disease makes it important to avoid precipitating pulmonary congestion. Auscultation for basal rales, daily measurement of weight, inspection for neck vein distention and examination of the chest x-ray for evidence of Kerley lines, interstitial edema or pulmonary venous congestion will help the physician maintain appropriate fluid balance. In certain circumstances, a central venous pressure or a Swan-Ganz catheter may have to be used to monitor for fluid overload. If congestive cardiac failure is present or strongly suspected or if atrial fibrillation occurs, the patient should be digitalized. Diuretics may be indicated for heart failure or fluid overload. Arterial blood gas samples should be drawn and examined for pH, $PaCO_2$, PaO_2, and oxygen saturation. Hypoxemia in

pneumonia is caused by areas of low ventilation-perfusion ratios. Oxygen should be administered by nasal cannula or mask to maintain the percent saturation above 85%. In individuals with hypercapnea (who may have coexisting COPD), it is wise to begin oxygen therapy with measured concentrations of oxygen, beginning with 24% oxygen administered by Venturi mask. The patient should be observed for progressive obtundation associated with worsening of hypercapnea and respiratory acidosis, which may result from suppression of hypoxic drive. It is of primary importance to treat hypoxemia with oxygen and other modalities as described below. Progressive hypoventilation with respiratory acidosis and obtundation will require intubation with ventilatory assistance.

It is very important to perform adequate physical therapy. Apart from antibiotics, deep breathing, good coughing, and sputum production are the most important aspects of therapy. The patient's position must be changed frequently. The patient should be assisted out of bed and into a chair whenever possible and a physical therapist should be asked to perform postural drainage and vibratory percussion. Most aged patients cannot tolerate the classic positioning used by physical therapists. Instead, a modification in which the patient is placed over pillows in bed is very useful. If bronchoconstriction is present, manifest by wheezes or rhonchi, bronchodilators should be administered.

It is well known that the aged are extremely sensitive to sedatives and hypnotics. One must beware of the excessive use of sedation when treating a geriatric patient for pneumonia. Depressant drugs can lead to confusion, obtundation, inability to cough, and respiratory depression.

The importance of vaccinating individuals over the age of 50 years, nursing home patients, debilitated persons, or those with cardiopulmonary diseases against pneumococcal and influenzal viral infection cannot be overemphasized. Polyvalent pneumococcal vaccine (0.5 cc) injected either subcutaneously or intramuscularly prevents about 75% of pneumococcal pneumonias in susceptible patients. Revaccination of adults is not recommended. Similarly, yearly doses of 0.5 ml of influenza vaccine intramuscularly will usually protect against influenza virus infection. Amantadine hydrochloride (Symmeterel), 100 mg twice daily, may be given to susceptible elderly individuals at risk during periods of influenza A prevalence. When used early, it may shorten the period of infection or prevent the spread of influenza A within a nursing home. Side effects, more prevalent in the elderly, include lethargy and alterations of coordination and judgment.

CHRONIC OBSTRUCTIVE PULMONARY DISEASE

COPD often presents during the middle years of life. However, the incidence of COPD increases with age. This diagnosis (COPD) encompasses the entities chronic bronchitis, emphysema, asthma, bronchiectasis, bronchiolitis, and small airways disease, which may coexist singly or in varying combinations. COPD is characterized by airways obstruction, small airways disease, or the clinical presence of a chronic productive cough which is not otherwise specifically explained.

The term chronic bronchitis describes a clinical entity in which an individual has chronic productive cough for more than 3 months yearly for 2 successive years, unexplained by another specific disease entity.

Emphysema, by contrast, is an anatomic diagnosis in which there is destruction of terminal alveolar septa and loss of terminal air units. Clinically, patients with emphysema have shortness of breath, airways obstruction, hyperlucent lung fields on chest x-ray, decrease of carbon monoxide diffusion, and increase of the total lung capacity. Small airways disease is obstructive disease of airways less than 2 mm in diameter.

Bronchial asthma is characterized by bronchial reactivity. There is generalized reversible airways obstruction. This can be documented by demonstrating more than 15% improvement of the FEV-1 by spirometry after administration of an inhaled bronchodilator. Although it is useful to think of patients with chronic bronchitis (so-called Blue Bloaters) as squat, ruddy, plethoric individuals with cough, wheeze, airways obstruction, and abnormalities of arterial blood gases and of patients with emphysema (so-called Pink Puffers) as thin, lanky individuals with relatively little disturbance of arterial blood gas measurement, in most instances, emphysema and bronchitis coexist in the same patient. These disease entities are caused by cigarette smoking, environmental pollution, recurrent infection and bronchial irritation.

It is normal for the vital capacity and the FEV-1 to decrease with age. Concurrently, there is an increase of the residual volume. The latter change is related to loss of elastic recoil with age (6). In consequence, there is increase of the closing volume and premature closure of terminal air units (1). The resulting areas of decreased ventilation-perfusion ra-

tios result in decrease of the arterial partial pressure of oxygen. [For a convenient table of normal values for pulmonary function tests, see Bates et al., (3)]. COPD adds the physiologic consequence of airways obstruction (in bronchitis) and excessive loss of elastic recoil (in emphysema) to the aforementioned abnormalities. As a result, there are changes in ventilation-perfusion ratios throughout the lungs with resultant abnormalities of arterial blood gas measurements (hypoxia and hypercapnea).

A basic principle in the management of COPD is the early and aggressive treatment of pulmonary infection. Accordingly, patients should be instructed that, when there is increase of sputum, febrile bronchitis, change in color or characteristics of sputum, or increase of chronic cough, an antibiotic should be administered. Tetracycline, ampicillin, amoxicillin, or trimethoprim-sulfamethoxazole are commonly given for 10–14 days to treat infection during these periods of time.

The physician should stress the maintenance of bronchial hygiene to individuals with chronic obstructive pulmonary disease. Smoking should be discontinued and bronchodilators administered. Metaproterenol, isoetharine or albuterol by inhalation using the metered dose inhaler may be effective and should be given in dosage of two inhalations, 10 min apart every 3–4 hours to promote bronchodilatation. Elderly individuals frequently have difficulty synchronizing their respiratory effort with the metered dose inhaler. Commercially available spacers, such as InspirEase, greatly facilitate the use of hand nebulizers by the older patient. Morning and evening, the bronchitis patient should be encouraged to take bronchodilators, inhale steam, and perform simple postural drainage maneuvers (9, 12). As noted, individuals in the geriatric population cannot perform classic postural drainage; however, simple exercises over pillows in bed may be done with the assistance of a family member. Many individuals with COPD use their accessory muscles of respiration and spontaneously relax the abdomen during inspiration and contract the abdominal muscles during expiration. Individuals who have not learned to do this on their own should be taught to breathe slowly using the abdominal muscles to facilitate lung emptying during expiration. General physical conditioning exercises that improve muscle tone are extremely useful for individuals with COPD. Both because exercise tolerance may be increased and for the favorable psychologic effect that these exercises have on patients, individuals with COPD should be encouraged to learn general conditioning exercises in a rehabilitation center and to continue these exercises at home.

Recently, simple, commercially available devices to increase respiratory muscle strength have become available and may be clinically useful.

Corticosteroid therapy is of very limited value in individuals with COPD. In some persons with recent onset of airways obstruction who have intercurrent bronchitis or bronchiolitis, a course of steroids over 10 days to 2 weeks may help to control this intercurrent episode. In general, there is no beneficial effect of steroids on the overall course of COPD. The side effects of chronic oral steroid therapy, including cataract formation, osteoporisis, diabetes, electrolyte imbalance, and impaired resistance to infection, outweigh the benefits.

Geriatric patients, like other individuals with COPD, frequently, despite optimum management, suffer extreme breathlessness and disability. The presence of secondary polycythemia should suggest chronic arterial hypoxemia. If the patient's oxygen tension is below 55 mm Hg on room air and if all other modalities of management have been tried, then one should administer continuous oxygen therapy at home (11). Oxygen may be administered by nasal cannula at 1–4 liters/min to keep the PaO_2 at 60–80 mm Hg. Oxygen can be supplied from large oxygen tanks, from large or small liquid oxygen reservoirs, or from an oxygen concentrator, which utilizes the molecular sieve principle. Continuous oxygen therapy has the effect of reducing pulmonary hypertension, promoting arterial oxygenation, preventing secondary polycythemia, relieving congestive heart failure, preventing salt and water retention, and reducing mortality.

Individuals with COPD frequently have exacerbations of airways obstruction and ventilatory failure. The exact triggering cause of these episodes is rarely known. It is postulated that viral infection produces bronchoconstriction, mucus plugging and edema and that this leads to alveolar hypoventilation. In these circumstances, an individual may become hypoxic with hypercapnea and respiratory acidosis. It must be stressed that the diagnosis of ventilatory failure cannot be made clinically. The most experienced clinician cannot estimate accurately the presence of ventilatory insufficiency or of hypoxemia. Arterial blood gases must be measured. If the patient's $PaCO_2$ is above 50 or if the PaO_2 is below 50, or if both situations exist and these changes have developed acutely, then it must be assumed that the patient is in acute respiratory failure, for which hospital treatment is indicated. In-hospital treatment will include oxygenation, hydration, humidity, antibiotics, and bronchodilators.

A brief course of intravenous steroids may be useful during an acute exacerbation of ventilatory failure.

Oxygen is administered serially in concentrations of 24, 28, 35, and 40% with close observation of the patient's clinical condition and arterial blood gases. The lowest inspired oxygen concentration, which produces adequate arterial oxygenation (arterial oxygen saturation greater than 85%) without seriously increasing hypercapnea, is given. A minority of individuals with COPD have a disturbance of ventilatory control such that the administration of oxygen removes the hypoxic drive to breathe and the patient's hypoventilation (measured by $PaCO_2$) is, therefore, aggravated. In these instances, it may be necessary to intubate the patient and to provide ventilatory assistance with a mechanical ventilator. However, determining when this is indicated should depend both on the clinical picture and the blood gases, not on either one alone. Of particular importance is the patient's mental status. Drowsiness or obtundation with a rising $PaCO_2$ and increasing acidosis are main reasons for intubation, since such patients can no longer exert the necessary effort to lower their $PaCO_2$. Sedatives or hypnotics must never be given to individuals with chronic obstructive lung disease or ventilatory failure. Obtundation can be aggravated and ventilatory failure precipitated by even small doses of depressant medication.

In those instances when ventilatory failure is precipitated by bacterial pneumonia, antibiotic treatment, as outlined previously, should be begun. In many cases, the offending pathogen will not be obvious when the patient first presents. The sputum smear may be unrevealing and the sputum and blood cultures may not yet be available. Under these circumstances, it is wise to begin an intravenous broad-spectrum antibiotic such as ampicillin or cefamandole. Even if an infiltrate is not seen from the chest x-ray, it is often wise to treat for bronchitis with a broad-spectrum antibiotic, pending cultures.

All patients should be well-hydrated because inspissation of secretions frequently complicates ventilatory failure. Because, in aged persons, one often encounters left ventricular dysfunction, one should be alert for pulmonary congestion. In this setting, a Swan-Ganz catheter may be useful to monitor the pulmonary capillary wedge pressure.

Bronchodilators should be administered by aerosol and intravenous routes. We usually prescribe

Alupent 0.3 ml in 2 ml of saline every 3–4 hours by face mask nebulizer. If the patient has not been on a theophylline compound, a loading dose of 5 mg/kilogram of intravenous aminophylline is given by soluset over 20-30 minutes. A maintenance dosage of 0.3-0.5 mg/kilo/hr is given, the lower dosage in patients with cardiac or hepatic dysfunction, because of delayed clearance of theophylline in these individuals. Insofar as possible, the patient should be treated in the upright position and his position changed frequently. Physical therapy including coughing, deep breathing, and chest percussion should be administered four times daily. If the patient fails to respond to these measures, steroids may be tried for several days. Our practice is to give 100 mg of hydrocortisone every 6 hours intravenously.

ASTHMA

Infrequently, asthma may occur de novo in an aged indiviudal. Under these circumstances, management should be similar to that of the management of asthma in the younger individual (8). A bronchodilator can be given both orally and by inhalation (metaproterenol isoetharine or albuiterol hand nebulizer, 1–2 puffs every 3–4 hours). Usually, either a short- or long-acting thyophylline compound is administered and the dose is adjusted to maintain the plasma theophylline level at 10–20 µg/ml.

If the patient does not respond to regular inhalation of a β-agonist bronchodilator and oral ingestion of a theophylline compound, inhalation steroids should be tried.

Beclomethasone inhalation, 2–4 puffs four times daily may be administered 10 min after inhalation of the β-agonist aerosol. The β-agonist permits the inhaled steroid to penetrate into smaller airways. Often, after a week of inhalation steroid therapy, asthmatic episodes and need for inhaled bronchodilators and steroids are reduced. The patient should gargle or rinse his throat with water after steroid inhalation to prevent pharyngeal candidiasis. Corticosteroids may be useful during acute exacerbations of asthma, in initial dosage of 40 mg of prednisone daily which is rapidly tapered during a 2-week period. Individuals who require more than one course of prednisone per month may have to be maintained on chronic corticosteroid therapy.

Determination of the peak expiratory flow is useful for monitoring an acute attack of asthma from moment to moment. Peak expiratory flow is measured easily by having the patient blow into a Wright peak flow meter as forcefully as possible. A peak expiratory flow of less than 100 liters/min suggests danger. If the peak expiratory flow rate is less than 60 liters/min, hospitalization is indicated. Other danger signals are a "normal" or elevated $PaCO_2$ during an acute asthmatic attack, an FEV-1 below 1 liter, and poor air entry on physical examination.

An acute attack of asthma may be managed, as in a younger patient, by administering small doses of nebulized isoproterenol. In the absence of heart disease, for example, one inhalation may be given every 5 min by hand nebulizer so long as there is an increase of the peak expiratory flow rate. After this, isoproterenol inhalations may be given every 3 hours. If heart disease is present, judgment must be exercised, and the patient must be monitored; however, isoproterenol, metaproterenol, isoetharine, or albuterol can usually be given and frequently results in improvement of the asthmatic paroxysm with decrease of tachycardia. In addition, it is usually safe, in the absence of severe heart disease or ventricular ectopy, to administer epinephrine, 0.2-0.3 ml of 1:1000 solution, intramuscularly. If the patient's peak flow improves, this can be repeated every 20–30 min. Hydrocortisone, 100 mg, may be given intravenously immediately and every 8 hours thereafter. An initial loading dose of 5 mg/kg of aminophylline can be given intravenously, slowly. Thereafter, 0.3–0.6 mg/kg/hour may be given by continuous intravenous drip. As noted, in both ambulatory and acutely ill patients, theophylline blood levels should be monitored. Seizures due to aminophylline toxicity are particularly dangerous in aged persons. Infection should be treated and hydration maintained. The peak expiratory flow rate should be measured frequently and oxygenation maintained as determined by arterial blood gas measurements. It is frequently sufficient to administer 24% oxygen with humidity by face mask. After the acute episode is over, steroids may usually be tapered rapidly and the patient switched to oral medications, inhaled β-agonists and other agents, such as inhalation steroids, as needed. Treatment and observation must be intensified if the $PaCO_2$ increases, if the peak expiratory flow rate does not increase, if there is persistent tachycardia and respiratory distress, or if the breath sounds become inaudible, which suggests worsening of obstruction.

As in COPD, the decision whether or not to intubate the patient and initiate mechanical ventilation should be made on the basis of the patient's worsening clinical condition, judged by worsening fatigue and obtundation and worsening of the arterial blood gases, not by worsening of the arterial blood gases alone.

TUBERCULOSIS

Tuberculosis is a disease that has occurred increasingly in the geriatric population during recent years. A high index of suspicion must be maintained for this diagnosis when an elderly individual develops a pulmonary infiltrate, the nature of which is not obvious. The diagnosis is frequently suggested by chest x-ray findings that may include upper lobe infiltration, cavitation, bilaterality, calcification, and apical pleural thickening. The diagnosis must be confirmed by sputum smear for acid-fast bacilli and culture of the sputum for the tubercle bacillus. In recent years, tuberculosis has been treated in the hospital less frequently. Indications for hospitalization include hemoptysis, extreme toxicity, fever, need for education of the patient and for obtaining adequate material for culture (by gastric culture, bronchoscopy, or sputum induction). Individuals who do not cough, have been on antituberculosis chemotherapy for a short period of time, and who understand the need for control of sputum, may be considered relatively noncontagious and may be managed out-of-hospital if their clinical condition otherwise permits.

The principles of therapy of active tuberculosis include the use of isoniazid (INH) whenever possible, the use of at least two drugs (one of which is INH), and the use of an adequate dosage of drugs for an adequate period of time.

The first line drugs in contemporary tuberculosis treatment are isoniazid (isonicotinic acid hydrazide), ethambutol, and rifampin. INH is given in a single dose of 300 mg orally daily. The chief side effects of INH include hepatotoxicity, which is more dangerous in the older population, and neurotoxicity (peripheral neuritis). Ethambutol is initially given in dosages of 25 mg/kg/day for 90 days and then 15 mg/kg/day. The main toxic effect of ethambutol is on the optic nerve. The patient may note loss of visual acuity. Loss of two lines of visual acuity on the Snellen chart, loss of color discrimination, or constriction of the visual fields should alert the physician to ethambutol ophthalmic toxicity, which is reversible when the drug is discontinued. Rifampin is given in dosage of 600 mg daily, either 1 hour before or 2 hours after a meal. The main toxic effect of rifampin is hepatoxicity manifest by an increase of the SGOT or SGPT. PAS (p-aminosalicylic acid) is not currently employed because of the high incidence of gastrointestinal toxicity, allergic reactions, and hepatotoxicity accompanied with its use. If streptomycin is used for initial treatment, or for retreatment, the daily dose must be reduced to 0.5 g/day in aged individuals. It must be remembered that streptomycin has eighth nerve toxicity and is excreted by the renal route. In addition, streptomycin is nephrotoxic.

During the initial months of therapy, patients receiving antituberculosis drugs should be screened monthly for signs of drug toxicity—for example, monthly questioning for nausea and anorexia (INH and rifampin) and ophthalmic examination and visual acuity testing (ethambutol). It is advisable to administer 25 mg of pyridoxine daily to elderly patients receiving INH to help prevent neurotoxicity.

The so-called second-line drugs include injectable drugs, such as kanamycin or viomycin which may be nephrotoxic and ototoxic, and pyrazinamide and ethionamide which may be hepatotoxic. Cycloserine is a second-line drug of limited usefulness that can cause neurologic symptoms including convulsions and psychosis. In an initial treatment case, when combined therapy is given, the chest x-ray may begin to show improvement after 2 months of treatment. In most individuals, the sputum culture converts to negative during the initial 4 months of treatment. It has been conventional to treat individuals with initial treatment pulmonary tuberculosis with at least two drugs for 2 years; however, Stead and Dutt (13) have suggested that INH, 300 mg, and rifampin, 600 mg, given daily for 1 month followed by INH, 900 mg, and rifampin, 600 mg, given twice weekly for 8 months is as satisfactory as other treatment regimens of longer duration. Surgery is rarely necessary in the treatment of tuberculosis today.

Miliary tuberculosis is seen in the aged, occasionally manifest as a protracted febrile illness of an obscure nature. The presence of a miliary picture on x-ray may be a late or final event. Under these circumstances, the liver biopsy, transbronchial biopsy, bone marrow biopsy, lumbar puncture, or urine culture may give a clue to the correct diagnosis.

CARCINOMA OF THE LUNG

Carcinoma of the lung occurs commonly in middle years but is not unusual in the aged. Of all individuals who present with lung cancer, some 40% will come to surgery. About 25–30% of the initial population will have an attempt at curative resectional surgery. Of this latter group, about 25% will be cured. The overall 5-year cure rate is, therefore, in the range of 5–8%. Hence, because of poor cure rates and because of the high mortality and morbidity of thoracic surgery in individuals over the age of 70 years, every attempt should be made to rule out the presence of metastatic disease after the initial diagnosis is made (2). In addition to these considerations, the presence of coronary artery disease or pulmonary insufficiency will mitigate against surgery in aged individuals with lung cancer. In considering the question of pulmonary insufficiency, individuals who have poor exercise tolerance, or in whom the 1-sec forced expiratory volume might be less than 1 liter postoperatively, are at increased risk from pneumonectomy. [The reader should consult Block and Olsen, (5) for references outlining the specific method of predicting the postoperative FEV-1] The operative mortality rate of pneumonectomy in individuals over the age of 70 years is about 30% and the mortality of lobectomy in individuals over the age of 70 years is about 15%. The recent availability of fiberoptic bronchoscopy and needle aspiration biopsy of the lung has made it possible to obtain a tissue diagnosis of both central and peripheral lesions in aging individuals who are poor operative risks without resorting to thoracotomy.

An occasional individual may be found with fairly good pulmonary function and no contraindication to surgery because of cardiac or systemic disease. In the absence of metastatic disease, such an individual should have an attempt at curative resection. Radiotherapy is of very limited benefit in the treatment of lung cancer insofar as cure is concerned. This modality is of some value for treatment of bony metastatic disease, bronchial obstruction, superior vena cava obstruction, and local metastatic disease, such as brain and skin implants. Chemotherapy is of little value in the treatment of lung cancer and may be counterproductive because of systemic toxicities. The specific exception to this is small cell anaplastic (oat cell) carcinoma of the lung, where significant prolongation of survival has been achieved using multiple-agent chemotherapeutic regimens that include combinations of cyclophosphamide, methotrexate, methyl-CCNU, and vincristine (7).

REFERENCES

1. Anthonisen JR, Danson J, Robertson PC, Ross WRD: Airway closure as a function of age. *Respir Physiol* 8:58, 1969.

2. Bates D: Results of surgery for bronchial carcinoma in patients aged 70 and over. *Thorax* 25:77, 1970.

3. Bates DV, Macklem PT, Christie RV: *Respiration Function in Disease*, Ed. 2. WB Saunders, p. 93, Philadelphia 1971.

4. Berk SL, Holtslaw SA, Weiner SL, Smith JK: Nontypable *H. influenzae* in the elderly. *Arch Intern Med* 143:537, 1982.

5. Block AJ, Olsen GN: Preoperative pulmonary function testing. *JAMA* 235:257, 1976.

6. Burrows B, Nider AD, Barclay WR, Kaplik JE: Chronic obstructive lung disease. Clinical and physiological findings in 175 patients and their relationship to age and sex. *Am Rev Respir Dis* 91:521, 1965.

7. Greco FA, Oldham RK: Current concepts in cancer: Small-cell lung cancer. *N Engl J Med* 301:355, 1979.

8. Lee HY, Stretton TB: Asthma in the elderly. *Br Med J*, 2:93, 1972.

9. Miller WF: Physical therapeutic measures in the treatment of chronic bronchopulmonary disorders. *Am J Med* 24:929, 1958.

10. Moore RD, Smith CR, Lietman PS: Association of aminoglycoside plasma levels with therapeutic outcome in Gram-negative pneumonia. *Am J Med* 77:657, 1984.

11. Nocturnal Oxygen Therapy Group, 1980. Continuous or nocturnal oxygen therapy in hypoxic chronic obstructive lung disease, a clinical trial. *Ann Intern Med* 93:391.

12. Petty TL, Nett LM: *For Those Who Live and Breathe with Emphysema and Chronic Bronchitis*. Springfield, IL, Charles C. Thomas, 1967.

13. Stead W, Dutt AK: An advance in treatment of tuberculosis. *Ann Intern Med* 93:364, 1980.

14. Woodford-Williams E: Diagnosis and management of pneumonia in the aged. *Br Med J* 1:467, 1966.

CHAPTER 11

Peripheral Vascular Disease in the Geriatric Patient

DANIEL B. WALSH
RUSSELL J. NAUTA

Atherosclerosis represents, by far, the greatest threat to life in geriatric patients (31). Atherosclerosis is responsible for most cases of coronary artery disease, aneurysms, and lower extremity arterial disease, particularly among patients in older age groups. In 1980, atherosclerosis was responsible for twice the number of deaths as cancer.

At Georgetown University Hospital, nearly 2000 major vascular procedures have been performed since 1981. Of these, 593 (30%) have been performed in patients over 69 years old. Surprisingly, peripheral vascular reconstructions were more common both in percentage and absolute number among patients 70 years of age and older than were coronary artery revascularizations. In great part this is due to effective nonsurgical measures for treatment of coronary artery disease and the paucity of useful nonsurgical techniques for treatment of peripheral vascular disease. Certainly, peripheral vascular disease represents a great threat to the geriatric population.

PERIPHERAL VASCULAR DISEASE: THE THEORY

Atherosclerosis, the thickening, hardening, and roughening the walls of the larger arteries is primarily a disease of arterial intima, the innermost layer of the arterial wall. At microscopic examination, atherosclerotic lesions are characterized by (a)

smooth muscle cell proliferation within the intimal layer, (b) invasion of damaged intima by macrophages derived from blood-borne monocytes, and (c) intimal accumulation of lipid and connective tissue matrix. The activity within the intimal layer is thought to be a repair response to endothelial injury (39).

Any injury to the endothelial cell layer can cause release of growth factors. These stimulate platelet aggregation and smooth muscle cell proliferation. Such direct injury may be the means by which known risk factors for atherosclerosis act. Changes in physiochemical composition of arterial walls with age also may contribute to atherogenesis. Deterioration in elastic media and consequent loss of flexibility of collagen occur with age. The resulting loss of resiliency changes hemodynamics within blood vessels. Variations in shear stress associated with pulsatile flow become more abrupt due to loss of arterial wall flexibility. These changes cause significant injury to endothelial cells and subendothelial constituents triggering repair responses that lead to atherosclerosis (54).

RISK FACTORS AND PREVENTION

ASSOCIATED DISEASES

The most important cause of death and complications among patients with peripheral vascular occlusive disease is coexisting cardiovascular and cerebrovascular disease. Significant correctable coronary artery disease is present in 15–30% of patients with peripheral vascular disease (16). Among patients with intermittent claudication, only 5% progress to amputation over a 5-year span, whereas 23% develop symptoms of coronary artery disease, 13% suffered cerebrovascular accidents, and 20% die (35). Any diagnostic or therapeutic manipulations must take these facts into account.

The Framingham study has demonstrated that the incidence of peripheral vascular disease is directly related to hypertension. Even mild elevations impose substantial risk. High blood pressure is particularly prevalent among the elderly. In the United States, high salt intake is one causative factor leading to hypertension (34). Although little evidence exists concerning hypertension control specifically related to peripheral vascular disease, effective blood pressure control has been found to reduce patient morbidity and prolong life (26).

HYPERCHOLESTEROLEMIA

Evidence continues to accumulate indicating a strong relationship between blood lipids, lipoproteins, and atherosclerosis (25). No doubt remains that serum cholesterol levels are related to clinical manifestations of atherosclerosis. This association is independent of other risk factors and occurs in both sexes. This relationship has been demonstrated consistently in diverse populations. Cholesterol predominates among lipid constituents in atherosclerotic plaque. Manipulation of serum cholesterol induces or diminishes atherosclerotic lesions in experimental models (3, 4).

The cornerstone of prevention and treatment of atherosclerosis is diet modification. Low density lipoprotein (LDL)-cholesterol must be reduced to and maintained at normal levels. (180–200 mg/dl). If diet is unsuccessful, Hoeg et al. (19) recommend niacin. Niacin effectively reduces plasma LDL-cholesterol levels, cardiovascular morbidity, and mortality. Niacin, however, can cause adverse cutaneous and gastrointestinal side effects. Fasting blood glucose levels, liver function tests, and uric acid levels should be determined at regular intervals during niacin therapy. If niacin fails to lower LDL levels to normal, other agents such as gemfibrozil and probucol, should be considered.

DIABETES MELLITUS

Diabetes mellitus, whether insulin-dependent or not, places patients at significantly increased risk for limb loss. Diabetics are 17 times more likely to develop foot gangrene than nondiabetics (28). The yearly amputation risk among diabetics is 6.5% per year. This is five to six times greater than among nondiabetics. Among diabetic amputees, 30–40% will require contralateral amputation within 3 years.

Three components of diabetic extremity disease threaten limb survival. First, at least 35% of all diabetics have demonstrable neuropathy. This causes anhydrosis with consequent cracking and flaking of skin. Skin changes often progress to fissures and excoriation, allowing entrance of bacteria beneath the skin. Lower extremity neuropathy also changes pressure distribution in the foot due to extension of the metacarpal-phalangeal joints and flexion of the interphalangeal joints. This "clawing" of the foot redistributes pressure to metatarsal heads leading to pressure sores, the so-called "neurotrophic" ulcers, commonly seen among diabetics (15). This situation is further complicated by distal arteriolar disease common among diabetics in their retinal, renal, and peripheral microcirculation. Finally, 50% of all diabetics with lower extremity vascular disease have large vessel occlusive atherosclerosis (22).

Prevention of limb loss among diabetics requires control of blood sugar, arterial hypertension, and weight. Meticulous daily inspections of each lower extremity must be made by the patient or some visually unimpaired individual. Great care must be taken to obtain well fitting shoes. New shoes should be broken in slowly (1 to 2 hours/day) over an extended period of time. Nail care must include attentive cuticle care and aggressive treatment in case of fungal infections. Nail removal should be considered only after vascular surgical consultation. Finally, primary care physicians should examine lower extremities of diabetics at regular intervals to ensure that this regimen is implemented successfully.

SMOKING

Since the Surgeon General's report in 1964, sizable reductions in cigarette smoking have occurred; yet, almost 60 million Americans smoke. This is associated with consistently elevated risk for peripheral vascular occlusive disease (24). Cigarette smoking increases platelet adhesiveness, raises blood pressure, and accelerates heart rate. Simultaneously, carboxyhemoglobin buildup reduces oxygen carrying capacity while myoglobin oxygen utilization is impaired (33). Cigarette smoking unequivocally poses significant risk for limb loss. Its cessation is mandatory in patients with peripheral vascular occlusive disease.

PATHOPHYSIOLOGY

Whatever the pathogenesis of atherosclerosis, symptoms of vascular disease reflect interference in efficient blood transport to capillary beds due to arterial lumen obstruction. Symptoms occur with mild obstruction only when metabolic demands are increased as with exercise or infection. More severe disease compromises perfusion at rest. Consequently, peripheral vascular occlusive disease may be asymptomatic or symptomatic with exercise or at rest, depending on the reduction in capillary perfusion and the metabolic demands of compromised tissue.

In patients with large artery stenosis or occlusion, nutritive blood must travel via collateral networks of vessels to bypass obstruction. Collateral vessels are pre-existing arterial branches proximal to stenosis that enlarge under conditions of greater pressure in the arterial circulation proximal to obstruction. These vessels are smaller, longer, and more circuitous than vessels they replace. Despite such enlargement, resistance in collateral vessels is always greater than that of the primary nondiseased circulation. At rest, collateral circulation usually provides adequate blood flow to meet tissue demands. With exercise, distal capillary resistance falls. Because resistance in the diseased artery and collateral circulation is fixed, flow to capillaries may be less than tissue energy requirements. In this case, ischemia and, sometimes, pain develop. With superficial femoral artery occlusion, calf claudication results, whereas proximal iliac artery occlusion may provoke thigh, hip, or buttock pain.

In multisegmental arterial disease (aortoiliac and femoral popliteal disease), compensatory decreases in capillary resistances may be insufficient to match loss of pulse pressure in the diseased proximal system. In this case, ischemic pain may occur at rest.

Sudden occlusion of vessels, without pre-existing severe stenosis may not allow time for the development of collateral circulation development. Without revascularization, severe ischemic pain and tissue loss will result. If sudden thrombosis occurs in chronically diseased segments where collateralization has occurred, patients may notice no change in symptoms or acute symptomatic exacerbation followed by gradual relief as collaterals develop further.

Progressive atherosclerosis usually spares collateral vessels. However, progressive atherosclerosis in more proximal vessels may flow in collateral vessels downstream. This progression may result in sudden deterioration of a previously stable situation. In the absence of new mechanical obstruction, factors that cause decreased cardiac output or increased blood viscosity may also decrease collateral blood flow.

DIAGNOSIS

Few ailments so lend themselves to diagnosis by history and physical examination as do vascular diseases. Most patients present with pain, tissue loss, or significant change in appearance, sensation, or function. Through application of problem-oriented history and physical examinations, primary care physicians can often predict peripheral vascular pathology before confirmation with more quantitative and invasive technology.

HISTORY

Patients with peripheral vascular disease most often present with one complaint (pain when walking, tearing back pain, nonhealing ulcers) that leads directly to diagnosis after a few pointed questions. For example, the most common presenting symptom in lower extremity arterial disease is pain. Pain is usually of sudden onset and does not vary in frequency, quality, or character. Pain, if ischemic, often is associated with neuromotor dysfunction over a similar motor or sensory distribution.

Chronic arterial insufficiency presents with either of two specific pain patterns—intermittent claudication or pain at rest. Intermittent claudication is recognized by its occurrence only with an invariable amount of exercise—i.e., leg cramping at walking one block. Pain does not occur at less than one block walking. Pain in the same muscle groups always occurs if one block is traversed. Claudication is always relieved by rest. Characteristically, ischemic rest pain is felt in toes or metatarsal heads. Elevation aggravates pain while dependency provides relief. One common variant is numbness induced by recumbency and relieved by dependency. Symptomatic improvement occurs due to gravity-related increases in capillary perfusion pressure.

Other forms of lower extremity discomfort rarely have arterial dysfunction as their etiology. Nocturnal leg cramps are related to muscle stretch rather than ischemia. The complaint of "cold feet" is common and innocuous. Numbness and paresthesias commonly occur with neurologic and skeletal disorders. Pain is often a manifestation of peripheral venous disease but is usually associated with superficial venous varicosities, swelling, and, possibly, findings suggestive of thrombophlebitis including superficial erythema and exquisite localized tenderness. Deep venous thrombosis of the lower extremity usually causes little or no pain unless there is associated inflammation. Elevation of the limb usually affords relief.

PHYSICAL EXAMINATION

Physical findings in patients with peripheral vascular occlusive disease compliment the history. Each lower extremity should be inspected for trophic changes (thinning of the skin, hair loss, nail changes, changes in skin color). Palpation of aorta and other major vessels is important to evaluate arterial diameter (aneurysm), pressure and character of all pulses, and capillary filling time. Auscultation of the entire vasculature is necessary to determine presence and distribution of bruits.

Ulcer is a common physical manifestation of severe lower extremity vascular disease. Chronic ulceration usually falls into one of three categories—ischemic, neurotrophic, and stasis. Each type has distinguishing characteristics that allow clinical diagnosis with little need for other diagnostic aids. Ischemic ulcers are located in the distal circulation usually in toes or foot. These lesions are painful but relieved by dependency. They occur in areas of mottled ruborous skin. Little bleeding occurs with debridement. These ulcers show little granulation tissue and have rarely epithelialized margins.

Neurotrophic ulcers occur in areas of pressure, friction, or chronic trauma such as plantar surfaces of metatarsal heads. These ulcers are deep, punctate, and surrounded by callous formation. Patients with these lesions usually have suffered from diabetes mellitus complicated by hypesthesia or anesthesia in the area of the ulcer. When debrided, neurotrophic ulcers bleed profusely.

Venous stasis ulcers are large, shallow, moist lesions with a base of granulation tissue. They occur in the "gaiter" distribution about the malleoli in areas of "brawny" hemosiderin deposition. Stasis ulcers often are associated with dull aching pain in dependency that is relieved by elevation.

Arterial examination is important in the evaluation of all extremity ulcers as the condition of the circulation can have important effects on ulcer healing.

NONINVASIVE STUDIES

Patients in whom vascular disease is suspected should be referred to a vascular diagnostic laboratory. The noninvasive vascular laboratory provides physiologic information and objective confirmation of the clinician's diagnosis. Data from the vascular laboratory also provide objective noninvasive means for following the course of therapy. Disease progression may be detected before clinical deterioration. This is of particular importance to patients who have undergone vascular reconstruction as deteriorating grafts are significantly easier to salvage than those that have failed. Noninvasive tests may help guide angiographers, calling attention to where particular diagnostic effort may be needed. Failure to demonstrate hemodynamically significant lesions consistent with the patient's complaint may obviate the need for further vascular evaluation.

Most laboratories employ multiple tests in each evaluation to improve accuracy. In many cases, arterial occlusions are well compensated at rest. Thus, exercise testing may be required to confirm the presence and extent of arterial insufficiency. Exercise testing should be performed only in laboratories where cardiac monitoring is the rule and resuscitative equipment is available.

When vascular disease is suspected at initial evaluation, a quick, simple screening test can be performed using the Doppler stethoscope to obtain bilateral systolic brachial, dorsal pedal, and posterior tibial arterial pressures. Ankle/brachial indices are determined by dividing systolic pressures obtained in each foot by the brachial pressure. The resulting value reflects occlusive disease severity within the extremity. Ankle/brachial indices equal to or greater than 1.0 are normal. Values below 0.95 are abnormal and indicative of proximal arterial obstruction. Although correlation between ankle/brachial indices and symptoms is inexact, patients with intermittent claudication usually have indices ranging from 0.5–0.8. Patients with pain at rest or arterial ulceration have indices of 0.4 or less. Symptoms may overlap at borderline ranges due to variations of up to 0.15 in ankle/brachial indices at repeated measurement. Another important limitation of this technique occurs among patients whose arteries are so calcified that they are incompressible. In this situation, which occurs most commonly among diabetics, ankle/brachial indices are meaningless. Systolic pressures usually are recorded as greater than 250 mm Hg below the calf using the Doppler stethoscope since the pulses cannot be obliterated.

Further information may be obtained by measurement of systolic blood pressures at upper and lower thigh, calf, and ankle with proper pressure cuffs. Detection of pressure gradients across specific arterial segments localizes disease and quantitates severity (29).

Pulse volume recording and analogue waveform analysis of arterial pulse characteristics provide other means to confirm, localize, and quantitate lower extremity arterial disease. Qualitative measurement of arterial waveforms have the advantage of assessing occlusive disease in patients with non-compressible vessels. Waveforms are normal when systole causes a sharp rise to a peak followed by a less rapid descent that displays the dicrotic notch. Mild disease with loss of vessel elasticity is characterized by absence of the dicrotic notch and downslope prolongation. More advanced disease demonstrates replacement of the sharp peak with a lower, more rounded systolic wave. The waveform of severe disease is flattened with long, slow, low up and down strokes.

"Duplex" ultrasonography, so called because it combines B-mode ultrasound imaging with Fourier analysis of shifts in sound wave frequency eminating from a phase-gaited Doppler, is now frequently being used to analyze atherosclerotic lesions in iliofemoral-popliteal arterial segments. This technology provides useful information regarding flow patterns within arteries and replacement bypass grafts. Duplex examination of bypass grafts also allows more accurate prediction of graft deterioration before graft failure than heretofore possible (14).

Although upper extremity vascular insufficiency is uncommon, the Doppler and ultrasound techniques described above can be helpful in evaluating the presence and location of such disease. The Doppler stethoscope can also be used to determine accurately the patency of the palmar arch with Allen's test.

DIGITAL SUBTRACTION ANGIOGRAPHY

Digital radiography uses computers rather than conventional film to produce images. This technology combines digital video processing with intravenous or intra-arterial contrast injection. The most extensive clinical experience with digital subtraction angiography (DSA) has been in the extracranial cerebrovascular circulation (Fig. 11.1A and B). However, its exact role in diagnosis and follow-up remains unclear. At Georgetown University Medical Center, intra-arterial DSA has been most useful in peripheral arterial evaluations in three settings: (a) in patients with severe lower extremity occlusive disease, quality images with standard arteriography often are difficult to obtain due to little dye flow in the distal ischemic limb. Computer-assisted imaging permits visualization of this distal arterial circulation often invisible to standard techniques. (b) DSA also allows screening visualization of other circulations during standard arteriography with little increase in dye load. Selected patients then may undergo evaluation of troublesome areas such as mesenteric circulation before aortic surgery, a luxury previously obtainable only with a second formal arteriogram. (c) Finally, intra-arterial DSA allows reduction in dye load if visualization of limited arterial segments can be accepted. In patients with dye allergy or renal compromise who would otherwise be subjected to standard arteriography, this significantly reduces dye-related complications.

Figure 11.1 A This digital subtraction arteriogram of the aortic arch demonstrates normal anatomy except for the occluded left subclavian artery remnant. **B.** From the same patient, this DSA diagnoses "subclavian steal" syndrome with its retrograde flow down the vertebral artery into the subclavian artery.

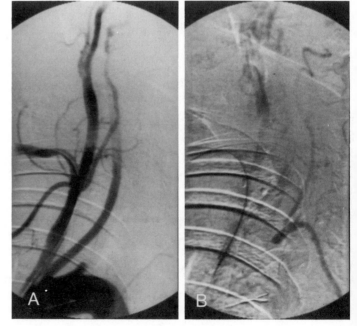

DSA can be performed with intravenous or intra-arterial injections. The particular advantage of the intravenous route is simplicity. No special training is required for intravenous cannulation. This method is less time-consuming than the intra-arterial method and avoids risk of arterial injury. No other angiographic technique provides the patient acceptance necessary to perform multiple or periodic studies. Data storage is greatly simplified with digital technology. Radiation exposure is similar to that of conventional angiography. However, allergic reactions to contrast agents are more frequent after intravenous injection (12).

DSA has other disadvantages. Any patient movement renders the study uninterpretable. Venous injection in the presence of diminished cardiac output is dispersed causing poor visualization. Vessels are opacified simultaneously, often making anatomy unclear when vessels overlap. Most machines have a small field of view necessitating multiple studies for an entire arterial tree. Unless performed using intra-arterial injection, much more dye is required than with standard angiography. Thus, the role of DSA in diagnosis of lower extremity vascular disease is, at least, restricted and remains to be clearly defined.

ARTERIOGRAPHY

Cost and accuracy of clinical and noninvasive examinations preclude the risk and expense of invasive radiologic studies until the anatomic specificity of such studies is required for therapeutic planning. Patients with peripheral vascular disease should be subjected to arteriography only after the decision for surgery or angioplasty has been made. The absolute indications for intervention are pain at rest or impending tissue loss due to ulceration or gangrene. Disabling claudication, a relative indication, will be discussed in more detail below.

Roentgenographic demonstration of vascular structures requires prodigious x-ray absorption. Iodine is a relatively nontoxic atom that possesses this property. Toxic responses to iodine administration are related to dose, duration of exposure, and specific tissue sensitivity. Untoward reaction to radiocontrast material occurs in 4-8% of patients. Fatalities occur in 0.002-0.009% of patients (43). There is no reliable "sensitivity" test.

Contrast media also are directly toxic to vascular endothelium. Patients with hemolysis or hypercoaguability suffer higher incidence of thromboembolic complications with angiography due to contrast-induced red blood cell damage.

Contrast-induced nephrotoxicity is a well known complication of arteriography. Precise mechanisms

causing this injury are unknown but damage is related to dose and previous agent exposure. Patients with compromised renal blood flow, diabetes mellitus, proteinuria, dehydration, or renal disease are at increased risk for renal failure after arteriography. Regardless of the situation, renal function should be evaluated in patients before arteriography. In addition, patients should be well hydrated before, during, and after study.

Cardiopulmonary complications can occur with arteriography, especially in patients with peripheral vascular disease due to the prevalence of heart disease within this group. Most cardiac complications are due to the volume load associated with high osmolarity of contrast media. Pulmonary edema, arrhythmias, and hypotension have been reported. Pheochromocytoma also may manifest itself through a hypertensive crisis provoked by arteriography.

Incidence of local catheter-induced complications is related to the artery used. Complications occur in 2-4% of patients when the axillary artery is used (17). Transfemoral catheterization causes significant morbidity in 0.5—1% of patients. Distal complications such as embolization, catheter breakage, and arterial disruption occur independent of approach.

Outpatient arteriography now has been shown generally safe and cost-effective (41). Smaller high flow catheters should be used, as diameter has been identified as a key in lowering complication rates. However, older patients with vascular disease, particularly those with hypertension or renal disease, require closely monitored hydration before, during, and after study to protect renal function. Pulmonary edema occurs more frequently in these patients due to their high incidence of significant cardiac disease. Any patient with even mild alterations in mental status or compromise may be less able to report or respond to wound complications. Thus, we remain reluctant to recommend these patients for outpatient arteriography.

PERIPHERAL VASCULAR DISEASE: THE REALITY

CHRONIC ARTERIAL INSUFFICIENCY

Functional limitation caused by lower extremity segmental atherosclerosis can be clearly defined and remains the determining factor in therapeutic planning. The hallmark of intermittent claudication is cramping pain in a muscle group, which occurs with constant repeatable amounts of exercise. Claudication pain subsides with rest. By definition, claudication does not occur at rest. Pain patterns can be changed by varying exercise intensity, but they remain exercise related.

In 1964, Widmer et al. (52) demonstrated that two-thirds of patients with proven arterial stensosis or occlusion reported no complaints. After detailed interviews, as many as one-third were symptom free. Prevalence of true symptomatic claudication among patients over 65 years old is approximately 6% (51). In this group, peripheral vascular disease is much more frequent among men. Pre-existing coronary artery disease, diabetes mellitus, and smoking increased significantly the incidence of claudication.

Among patients who present with claudication, one-half will worsen over 2 years (8). Approximately 10% of patients will require surgical intervention each year (23). If patients continue smoking, more than 11% will require amputation (42). If patients are diabetic, the risk of amputation increases fivefold (11). Seventy-five percent of claudicants will not require surgical intervention. However, life expectancy in these patients is very much decreased due to atherosclerosis. Annually, 5% die. Fifty percent of deaths in this group will be due to coronary artery disease, 15% to cerebrovascular disease, and 10% to abdominal atherosclerosis (21).

Accurate histories in these patients can exclude neurogenic or skeletal origins of complaints and define limitations imposed on patients by disease. Physical examination when confirmed by noninvasive vascular studies can determine accurately the anatomic extent and location of disease.

Indications for vascular reconstruction of ischemic lower extremities are pain at rest and impending tissue loss. The risk for amputation in such patients is three to five times higher than among claudicants without revascularization (30, 44). When disabling, claudication is also an indication for reconstructive surgery. At this point, the physician's judgment is crucial. An 80-year-old patient with claudication at two blocks who lives with his children and has no great need to shop will not require surgery in most instances. On the other hand, a 67-year-old retiree who can no longer enjoy travel or physical recreation may find surgical risks acceptable. Arterial reconstruction should not be performed unless patients are so handicapped that their life-style or occupation must be altered in an unacceptable way. Constant ischemic pain or ulceration demands operation because risk of arterial reconstruction is equal to or less than that of amputation.

Before surgical intervention, several less invasive treatment options are worth considering. Exercise to the onset of symptoms followed by rest with repetition has been demonstrated to improve collateral function, and, thus, exercise tolerance among claudicants (36). Recently, several drugs, pentoxifylline, ketanserine, naftidrofuryl, cinnarizine, flunarizine, buflomadol, and cyclandelate have been shown to increase pain-free walking distance in randomized, blinded trials (6, 10, 38, 45). In spite of these positive results it remains open to question whether statistical significance also means clinical relevance. Our experience with pentoxifylline typifies the guarded optimism with which these drugs should be treated. Nearly 20% of our patients were unable to tolerate the drug due to gastrointestinal upset and diarrhea. Among those without side effects, one-half noted sustained increase in exercise tolerance after 6 weeks of therapy. Approximately one-third of patients thought the amount of exercise increase did not justify the drug-related expense. However, for the first time, one-third of patients suffering claudication could be significantly helped by drug therapy.

Experience with percutaneous translumenal angioplasty (PTA) is now long enough to define its role in lower extremity revascularization. Significant incentives for use of PTA are its low risk and cost. Per patient, the cost of PTA is 20–30% that of surgical revascularization (13). Complications occur both at puncuture and dilatation sites. Although they have been reported to occur in as high as 50% of patients, most complications are minor. Surgical intervention is required in less than 5% of patients (28). The mechanism of PTA's action centers on fracturing weak points of atherosclerotic plaque causing subintimal dissection. Consequent vessel dilatation with plaque remodeling leads to an increase in flow (55) (Fig. 11.2).

PTA is most effective where surgery cannot be justified (in the claudicator with short, discrete stenosis) or cannot be tolerated (because of extreme operative risk). Long occlusive stenoses or multiple short stenoses in the same segment, single critical stenosis in a diffusely diseased artery, or those arteries with long complete occlusions do not lend themselves to successful long term-patency after PTA and are more effectively treated with surgical revascularization (40). Effective use of PTA can be achieved only with close cooperation among the primary care physician, angiographer, and vascular surgeon. Such cooperation ensures proper patient selection, appropriate combination or staging of procedures, and prompt treatment of complica-

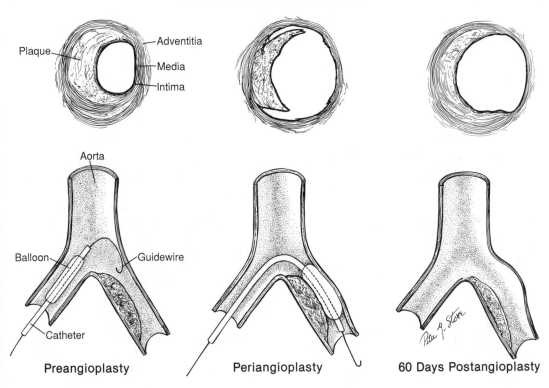

Preangioplasty   Periangioplasty   60 Days Postangioplasty

Figure 11.2. This figure depicts the plaque fracturing and remodelling that occurs with angioplasty in the iliac arteries.

tions. When PTA is performed by an experienced medicine-radiology-surgery team, it plays an important role in extremity revascularization.

The first principle of lower extremity surgical reconstruction is that satisfactory inflow must exist and be normal prior to the performance of any outflow procedure. In practical terms, this principle demands adequate aortoiliac blood flow into the femoral-popliteal and more distal arterial tree if femoral-popliteal reconstruction is considered. Inattention to aortoiliac segments will lead to prohibitive failure rates of distal reconstructions. In patients with both aortoiliac and femoral-popliteal occlusive disease, aortobifemoral reconstruction will improve lower extremity perfusion to such an extent that no additional procedure will be necessary in many patients (Fig. 11.3). With current techniques of anesthesia, cardiac monitoring, and fluid therapy, surgical mortality has been reduced to 1–2%. Five-year patency of aortobifemoral grafts exceeds 90% (4).

In elderly patients whose lower extremity ischemia is complicated by coronary or intra-abdominal disease, extra-anatomic arterial reconstructions can be performed. Axillobifemoral bypass grafts are the most frequently used alternative to intra-abdominal revascularization Patency rates for these grafts vary between 60% and 70% at 5 years (37). Therefore, extra-anatomic operations can bypass successfully aortoiliac occlusive disease in poor risk patients with minimal complications.

In patients with symptomatic peripheral vascular occlusive disease free of significant aortoiliac disease, reconstruction from femoral artery to popliteal or more distal arteries should be considered. Superficial femoral artery occlusions most commonly occur at the adductor hiatus above the knee and cause claudication. Although saphenous vein remains the conduit of choice for vascular reconstructions, results with prosthetic materials when employed in femoral-popliteal bypasses above the knee are nearly as good. Use of prosthetics speeds the operation, minimizes incisions, and preserves saphenous vein for use in coronary or more distal arterial bypasses. Aggressive reconstruction is justified in patients with severe ischemia of the lower extremity because the immediate limb salvage rate in this patient group is 86%.

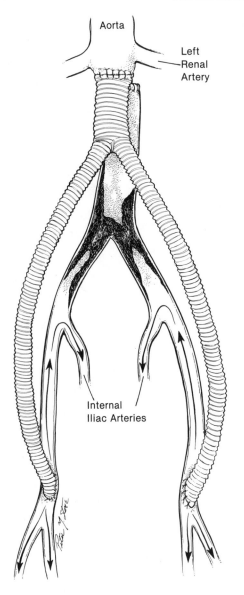

Aorta

Left
Renal
Artery

Internal
Iliac Arteries

Figure 11.3. This figure demonstrates an aortobifemoral bypass for bilateral iliac artery occlusive disease. Note the retrograde flow in the external iliac artery that supplies the pelvis.

In patients requiring arterial reconstruction with anastomosis below the knee, saphenous vein is required as the conduit if acceptable limb salvage and graft patency rates are to be achieved. In situ techniques of saphenous vein-femoral-distal artery bypass described by Hall and reintroduced by Leather appear most effective for long bypass grafts to distal lower extremity arteries. This operation consists of standard vascular anastomoses at femoral and dis-

tal arterial sites. The saphenous vein remains in its normal anatomic position. Venous valves are bisected using specifically designed instruments. All vein branches are ligated after minimal dissection (Fig. 11.4). At Georgetown University, graft patency of these long distal in situ bypasses has exceeded 85% (32). Success of this technique appears related to removal of the obstructive vein valves with consequent increases in flow and preservation of the vein's physiologic characteristics (5, 48, 49). The technique permits bypasses more distal than commonly performed in the past with improved success rates (Fig. 11.5).

The question then arises as to whether aggressive limb salvage surgery is warranted in patients whose 5-year mortality approaches 50%. Most patients who die within 5 years of lower extremity revascularization do so with intact limbs. Second, energy required to ambulate or transfer from bed to wheelchair for amputees is significantly higher than that for patients who have functional limbs. Clearly, in this patient group with its high incidence of coronary artery disease, any increase in cardiovascular work will tend to increase cardiac complications. Expenses for this aggressive approach to limb salvage are high. The mean cost for femoral-popliteal bypass is $19,000; for distal bypass, $29,000. These figures include physician, hospital, and rehabilitation costs, including those of reoperation. Mean total cost of below knee amputation, which results in failed rehabilitation and chronic institutional care or professional assistance at home in 26% of patients, is $27,000. Clearly, limb salvage surgery is expensive, but no more so than amputation. For many elderly patients, limb salvage is their only opportunity to maintain independence and avoid permanent admission to chronic care facilities (47).

ACUTE ARTERIAL INSUFFICIENCY

Acute arterial insufficiency may result from primary arterial thrombosis, trauma, or embolism. In most cases, thrombosis and embolism can be distinguished clinically. Both conditions present as emergencies requiring surgical intervention. Rapid and correct diagnosis is imperative as pathophysiology and natural history of ischemic episodes differ and indications for and magnitude of surgical intervention are dissimilar.

Following acute occlusion, soft coagulum forms proximal and distal to adjacent areas of stagnant blood flow. As a clot grows, ischemia progresses because collateral pathways are compromised. The extent of distal thrombus propagation greatly determines outcome. Failure to remove successfully a

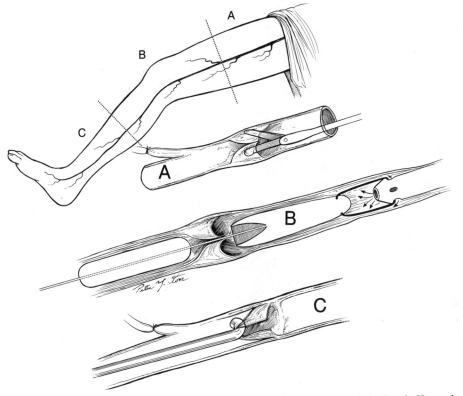

Figure 11.4. This figure demonstrates techniques for valve lysis while leaving the vein in situ. **A.** Karmody scissors are used to lyse proximal valves. **B.** The Leather valvulatome may be used for lysis of midleg valves. **C.** The Mills-Oschner valvulatome is used for most distal vein valves.

distally propragated clot will result in incomplete and, likely, inadequate restoration of distal perfusion.

Although most clinically significant emboli originate in the heart, about 90% of surgically treated emboli are carried to lower extremities. The most common sites of clot impaction are the aortic, femoral, and popliteal artery bifurcations. Upper extremity artery embolic occlusion occurs in only 3–11% of patients. Mesenteric and renal vascular beds are occasionally affected (18).

With embolic occlusion, distal tissues are deprived of oxygen. Since peripheral nerves are extremely sensitive to ischemia, pain and parethesias occur early in effected areas. Ischemia forces anaerobic metabolism, which results in a cold, swollen, pale, paretic, and anesthetic extremity. At this stage, tissue loss may be inevitable. Although many factors determine the rate at which ischemic damage occurs, the diagnosis must be made quickly and therapy instituted promptly in order to achieve salvage.

At first presentation, patients with complaints consistent with acute ischemia should be examined for presence and strength of arterial pulses in all extremities. Arterial pressures and flow should be evaluated by noninvasive techniques to confirm and quantitate ischemia and localize disease. Extremity color, temperature, sensation, and motor function should be evaluated. In addition, symptoms and signs indicating pre-existing vascular insufficiency should be noted. Virtually all elderly patients suffering arterial embolus have associated myocardial disease. Careful cardiac evaluation should proceed simultaneously with that of the lower extremity. Electrocardiography, chest roentgenography, echocardiography, serum myocardial enzyme determinations, and Holter monitoring are of value in the evaluation of the heart as the possible source of emboli. The abdomen should be palpated for the presence of aortic aneurysm.

Arterial thrombosis is usually distinguished by antecedent symptoms or signs of vascular insufficiency. The patient may present with excruciating chest or back pain of acute aortic dissection. In addition, the patient may have a history of intermittent claudication.

Once the diagnosis of acute arterial insufficiency

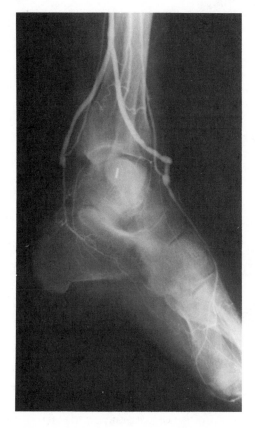

Figure 11.5. This is an arteriogram of a distal in situ saphenous vein bypass to the dorsal pedal and posterior tibial vessels. Luckily, the saphenous vein bifurcated allowing both anastomoses.

has been made, patients should be anticoagulated immediately with intravenous heparin. Anticoagulation prevents further clot propragation and embolization. Preoperative management should include improvement of the patient's overall condition with inotropes, diuretics, antiarrhythmic medication, and intensive care monitoring. If the condition of the limb permits, arteriography may be indicated to define anatomy of the distal lower extremity and discover emboli that are present but not, as yet, symptomatic. Embolectomy can be performed under local anesthesia with minimal patient discomfort. Postoperative anticoagulation reduces recurrence and mortality in this patient group.

Despite the technical ease of embolectomy, perioperative mortality among these patients remains substantial. Nearly 25% of patients die within the postoperative period, with more than 50% of fatalities directly attributable to cardiopulmonary complications (7).

After revascularization, swelling of the previously ischemic limb may cause a compartment syndrome and require surgical decompression. Fasciotomy is required in 10% of patients after embolectomy. Further management should focus on underlying pathology. Anticoagulation and control of atrial fibrillation are necessary to prevent recurrence.

Thrombolytic therapy for treatment of acute extremity ischemia remains controversial. Although thrombolytic therapy avoids surgery, drug cost, prolonged intensive care monitoring, and unpredictable but potentially disastrous complications, such as intracerebral hemorrhage, discourage its use in most cases. It remains the burden of those who urge against embolectomy to prove that other forms of therapy are as rapid, inexpensive, and safe as surgical intervention.

DIABETIC FOOT

The cornerstone of the management of diabetic foot problems is prevention. When problems do occur, all physicians must clearly understand that no infection in a diabetic's foot is trivial. All are potentially limb threatening. When diabetics present with pain at rest or foot ulceration, hospital treatment is mandatory. The foot should be washed, dried, and, after debridement, wounds are dressed. Special attention should be directed to interdigital spaces. Any evidence of cellulitis or lymphangitis mandates intravenous antibiotics. Smoking must cease. Bedrest is essential. X-rays should be obtained to demonstrate osteomyelitis. Noninvasive vascular examination will establish the condition of distal arterial circulation. If nonoperative therapy is unsuccessful, vascular reconstruction or amputation is necessary.

If pedal circulation is adequate, debridement, drainage of infection, and toe amputation should suffice to control disease. Care should be taken to protect the heel from pressure to avoid further injury during treatment.

Proximal vessel lower extremity arterial disease is more common among diabetics, occurs earlier in life, is more extensive, and differs in pattern of occurrence from that seen in nondiabetics. Moreover, the male predominance usually seen in peripheral vascular disease is lost. Prognosis for vascular disease is worse among diabetics than nondiabetics. Diabetics suffer perioperative myocardial infarction, gangrene, amputation, reamputation, and contralateral limb amputation more commonly than nondiabetic patients. Nevertheless, at least 50% of diabetics have vascular disease requiring operations. Indications for vascular reconstruction are not altered by diabetes mellitus. Among these patients, only diligent, compulsive, and frequent medical care will provide acceptable results in treatment of their peripheral vascular disease.

ANEURYSMS

Arterial aneurysms are local irreversible dilatations of arterial walls that result in abnormal vessel configuration, alterations in blood flow, and increased tendency toward thrombosis, distal embolization, and rupture. Any artery is susceptible to aneurysm formation. Aneurysms can be caused by trauma, infection, or congenital defects. Most commonly, aneurysms occur secondary to atherosclerosis. The incidence of aneurysm formation occurs in direct relation to age. Aneurysms occur most frequently in the aorta. Infrarenal abdominal aortic aneurysms are the most common aortic aneurysms.

Aneurysms result from vessel wall weakness secondary to loss of elastic fibers in arterial media. Decrease in tensile strength leads to stretching of remaining fibrous tissue. As aneurysms enlarge, turbulence occurs in blood flow causing clot formation in areas of low flow. This clot provides is a nidus for infection or distal embolization and does not in any way strengthen the arterial wall.

INFRARENAL ABDOMINAL AORTIC ANEURYSM

Greater disease awareness as well as an increasing number of elderly patients at risk are responsible for the increasing incidence of recognized arterial aneurysms, especially infrarenal aortic aneurysms. Most abdominal aortic aneurysms are discovered inadvertently by patient or physician. Aneurysms are also detected in increasing numbers during roentgenologic examination for other symptoms. These "incidental" aneurysms tend to be small and are often not apparent on physical examination. Many aneurysms can be detected by careful examination, but the method of palpation is important. In normally transmitted aortic pulsations, the aorta moves in an anterior-posterior direction. Typically, an aneurysm pulses with a lateral wall displacement. These are best felt using fingertips while palpating deep along the lateral margins of the mass. Most diagnostic errors made are in the estimation of size. Aneurysms usually are not as big as they feel. In many patients, especially those who are thin, lordosis or aortic ectasia can cause aortic pulsations to be disturbingly prominent.

Whether the clinical suspicion of abdominal aortic aneurysm has been based on physical findings or on incidental roentenographic observation, diagnostic confirmation should be obtained with ultrasonography or CT scanning (Fig. 11.6). Both

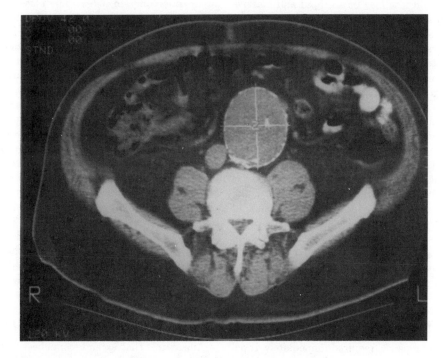

Figure 11.6.   This is an abnormal CT scan of a large infrarenal aortic aneurysm.

methods are accurate. Ultrasonography has the advantage of lower cost and wider availability. CT scanning provides more anatomic detail particularly with respect to renal artery origin.

Acute expansion of abdominal aortic aneurysms produces a characteristic set of symptoms. Almost without exception, pain draws the patient's attention. Pain is usually severe, constant, unrelated to posture, and boring in character. It is most commonly located in the lumbar region, midabdomen, or pelvis. From these primary sites, pain may be referred to thigh, testicle, or rarely, perineum. Since there is no extravasation of blood, the pain of aneurysm expansion is not accompanied by systemic signs, such as hypotension, fever, tachycardia, or leukocytosis. Errors in diagnosis in cases of aneurysmal expansion are related to failure to palpate the pulsatile mass. Soft tissue abdominal roentgenograms done in two planes will demonstrate calcium shadows typical of aneurysm in 70% of cases.

When aneurysms rupture, clinical presentations are remarkably consistent. The first phase may be expansion that precedes or accompanies at least 60% of cases. However, pain may be only momentary and rapidly overshadowed by manifestations of massive intra-abdominal or retroperitoneal hemorrhage. Typically, patients complain of severe, tearing back or midabdomen pain. Once rupture has occurred, blood loss may be so rapid and massive that patients lose consciousness. If bleeding continues, patients rapidly expire. Fortunately, most ruptures are contained. In these cases, patients will continue to complain of pain. Tachycardia, hypotension, and hemorrhagic shock present in varying degrees. Diagnosis should be made on clinical grounds and the patient rapidly transported to an operating room. Confirmation, if necessary, should be obtained with ultrasonography or CT scanning.

Errors in diagnosis can be traced to failure to palpate the pulsatile abdominal mass. The best means to avoid this is by cultivated awareness of such lesions, especially in men over the age of 50 years. In any patient, tachycardia, especially when associated with decreasing hematocrit, and especially in the absence of external signs of blood loss, demands that ruptured aneurysm be considered. Early vascular surgical consultation is essential for survival.

INDICATIONS FOR SURGERY OF ANEURYSMS

In cases of aneurysmal rupture or acute expansion, surgical repair is required immediately. If patients reach the hospital, surgical mortality remains approximately 30%. This large surgical mortality explains why any manipulation or diagnostic intervention that delays surgery threatens disaster.

Asymptomatic aneurysms (60% of abdominal aortic aneurysms) pose a different problem because patients are well but at great risk should aneurysms rupture. This is particularly true of the geriatric population. Risk of rupture is related to size. Large aneurysms rupture more frequently than small aneurysms, but small aneurysms may also rupture. Darling and his coworkers (9) have shown that 33% of aneurysms in patients dying of rupture were less than 5 cm in diameter. Thus, risk of rupture correlates with size but correlation is not sufficiently reliable to be used as an absolute criterion.

The issue then turns on the risk of elective aneurysm repair because the risk of emergency surgery after rupture of a previously asymptomatic aneurysm can be estimated. Risk factors of elective aneurysmectomy are those of any major abdominal operation. Pre-existing cerebrovascular, cardiovascular, pulmonary, or renal diseases increase risk of surgery significantly. Chronologic age is not a significant risk factor in aortic surgery. Previous intraabdominal procedures, abdominal radiation, or abdominal inflammatory disease greatly increase technical difficulty of aortic surgery. Even with these caveats, improvements in pre- and postoperative care have decreased mortality of elective aneurysmectomy to 3–5%. The classic study by Szilagyi et al. (46) on contribution of aneurysmectomy to the prolongation of life demonstrated considerable differences in survival between operated and nonoperated patients with aneurysms that were 6 cm or greater in size. With the current surgical mortality ratio, even patients with smaller aneurysms have significant survival advantage when compared to nonsurgical patients (46).

In general, *operation is advised if aneurysms are (a) 6 cm or greater in diameter, (b) associated with symptoms, (c) documented to be enlarging, (d) sources of distal emboli. Operation for aneurysms less than 6 cm in diameter is also recommended in any good risk patient regardless of age. The indication for aneurysmectomy is "presence."* It remains the physician's responsibility to find justifiable causes as to why aneurysms should not be repaired. Nonsurgical patients should be followed by ultrasonography or CT scanning and reviewed for surgery if enlargement is documented.

THORACOABDOMINAL AORTIC ANEURYSMS

Aneurysms that extend from chest to abdomen and are involved with the descending thoracic aorta and upper segments of abdominal aorta are known as thoracoabdominal aortic aneurysms. Arteriosclerosis and medical degenerative disease are main causes of these aneurysms. These aneurysms compress or erode into adjacent structures, such as nerves, lung, bowel, or chest wall. The most dreaded and ultimate complication is rupture.

Thoracoabdominal aneurysms produce a variety of symptoms before rupture. The most common complaint is pain in the chest, abdomen, flank, or back and is usually related to pressure on adjacent structures. Pulmonary complaints may be related to compression or erosion of the tracheobronchial tree with hemoptysis. Similar compression of esophagus may cause dysphagia or hematemesis. Recurrent la-

ryngeal nerve paralysis may produce hoarseness. Secondary infection of artheromatous debri and clot may occur, resulting in generalized sepsis. As with other anuerysms, distal embolization is common.

Thoracoabdominal aneurysms rarely are diagnosed by physical examination. Chest roentgenograms, the common means of diagnosis, usually demonstrate widening of the descending thoracic aortic shadow. They also demonstrate localized calcification and dilation. Diagnosis is confirmed by CT scanning or contrast aortography. Treatment consists of aortic and visceral arterial reconstruction. The procedure most commonly performed today is reconstruction by graft with visceral arterial reattachment (Fig. 11.7A and B). In experienced

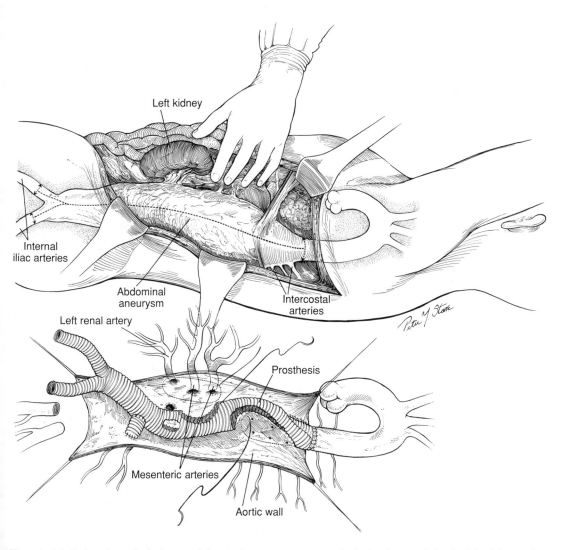

Figure 11.7 A. A typical thoracoabdominal aneurysm approached via thoracoabdominal incision and a retroperitoneal approach is depicted. **B.** The repair of the aneurysm is depicted.

hands, surgical survival rates range between 75% and 90%. Most common complications are related to ischemia of spinal cord (4%) or kidneys. There is also risk of stroke depending on distribution of the aneurysm (7).

DISSECTING ANEURYSMS OF THE AORTA

Acute aortic dissections are the most common catastrophic event involving the aorta. Acute aortic dissections occur two to three times more frequently than ruptured abdominal aortic aneurysms. Aortic dissections are three times more frequent in men than in women. Congenital heart disease and Marfan's syndromes are risk factors for aortic dissection. In patients with longstanding hypertension, aortic dissections are common.

The underlying cause of aortic dissections is destruction of the most medial layer. Commonly, tears originate either in ascending (62%) or descending aorta just distal to left subclavian artery (26%). Ascending aortic dissections usually proceed along the entire aorta whereas distal dissections proceed distally into distal thoracic and abdominal aorta. Either type may re-enter aortic lumen. Ascending dissections may proceed retrograde to involve coronary arteries or pericardium and may even rupture freely into mediastinum. This retrograde dissection may produce aortic insufficiency with acute pulmonary edema and cardiac failure. Only 10% of patients have involvement limited to ascending aorta or aortic arch. If coronary arteries are occluded by dissection, sudden death is likely from acute myocardial ischemia.

Acute aortic dissections most frequently present with catastrophic chest pain or sudden tearing pain in the chest or back. Pain may radiate into upper or lower extremities. At physical examination, patients are seriously ill and, often, in shock. Physical findings consistent with aortic insufficiency, acute pulmonary edema, or cardiac tamponade are common. Peripheral pulses may be absent, asymmetric, or normal. Neurologic findings are present in 30% of patients and are related to the extent of involvement. Murmurs or bruits may be heard, varying from aortic insufficiency to sounds over many aortic branches. Once aortic dissection is suspected, patients must be prepared immediately for arteriography or CT scanning to obtain objective data about origin, extent of dissection, and re-entry. Lethality of aortic dissection makes early diagnosis and treatment mandatory. The literature suggests a 15-min mortality of 20%; within 48 hours, 50% of patients are dead (2).

Intravenous nitroprusside should control blood pressure before, during, and after arteriography. An operating room should be ready. If ascending aortic dissection is diagnosed, patients should be brought to surgery immediately. In most cases, dissection involves the entire aorta. Graft replacement of ascending aorta is necessary, occasionally with coronary artery bypass. Operation on distal aorta and peripheral arteries for obstruction is rarely necessary acutely.

Descending aortic dissections are usually treated medically. Involvement of visceral vessels or rupture into pleural space are life-threatening complications and demand immediate surgical attention. During hypotensive therapy, continuing pain, development of neurologic deficit, pleural effusion, or ischemia of the lower extremities demands immediate surgery. Postoperatively, all patients require strict blood pressure control.

Chronic aortic dissections are those in which patients have survived two or more weeks after acute episodes. Some patients will develop complications such as enlarging aneurysm or back pain (33% within 5 years). Operative therapy in this group also is indicated.

Mortality in patients with aortic dissections who do not have surgery approaches 100%. Although 86% of patients survive early dissection with antihypertensive therapy, drug therapy alone is inadequate in treatment of acute ascending aortic dissections. Surgical mortality in the treatment of acute descending dissections should be about 20% with 5-year survival approaching 60%. With descending aortic dissections, mortality rates of medical and surgical treatment are similar.

Prognosis for these patients is related to the severity of aortic disease and visceral involvement at the time of dissection. With compulsive surgical care, antihypertensive therapy, and careful long-term follow-up, 50–65% of these patients will live 5 years (1).

AMPUTATION

Amputation is a formal means of providing wound care to the diseased limb when other less rigorous treatment regimens have failed to stimulate successful wound healing. Between 30,000 and 50,000 lower extremity amputations are performed in the United States annually. About 65% are performed on diabetic patients. Since 50% of amputees suffer symptomatic cardiorespiratory disease, the importance of careful preoperative physical examination cannot be overstressed (20). Systemic diseases should be noted because their presence may influence preoperative preparation and timing of operation. If limbs are grossly infected, patients considered for lower extremity amputation should be treated with broad-spectrum antibiotics for both aerobic and anaerobic organisms.

Ischemic rest pain is the most compelling indication for amputation. Characteristically, patients dangle their legs in dependent positions. Only if vascular reconstruction is deemed impossible by arteriogram or previous failure, should amputation be considered in patients without overwhelming lower extremity sepsis.

Dry gangrene is neither a surgical emergency nor the hallmark of an ominous clinical situation. Dry gangrene may be treated conservatively if circulation is adequate. However, infection complicating dry gangrene, especially in diabetic patients, is limb- and life-threatening. Antibiotic therapy alone is seldom adequate for wet or suppurative gangrene. Failure to institute prompt therapy results in rapid progression of infection, loss of salvageable tissue, and increases mortality.

The first step in management of gangrene is identification of the infecting organism. Specific organism identification by culture is usually impossible due to severity of illness. Gram stain is the only way to obtain accurate preliminary information regarding type of infecting organism. At that time, broad-spectrum antibiotic coverage should be initiated. If prompt response to antibiotic therapy is noted, it should be continued for maximum effect before definitive amputation. Absence of improvement with antibiotics or evidence of undrained pus demands immediate drainage and debridement of gangrenous tissue.

Appropriate amputation level selection is of critical importance. Too proximal an amputation deprives patients of significant opportunities for subsequent ambulation and rehabilitation. Too distal an amputation will heal inadequately and will require additional surgery. Unilateral below-knee amputation will require 25% more energy for ambulation than walking with an intact extremity. Unilateral above-knee amputation requires 50–70% more energy to walk (50). Patients with severe coronary artery disease and chronic obstructive pulmonary disease may be physically unable to provide additional energy for ambulation on above-knee compared to below-knee prostheses. The decision regarding adequacy of blood supply at the proposed amputation level is one of the most difficult problems facing surgeons.

Elective lower extremity amputation should be performed using objective testing to obtain the most distal amputation site where good healing can be expected. In most centers, experienced vascular surgeons use segmental systolic Doppler pressures. Xenon[133] skin clearance also has been useful. The techniques chosen depend on available equipment and the surgeon's experience. However, the importance of achieving the most distal healed amputation cannot be overemphasized.

Amputations should be considered as a form of reconstructive surgery. When carefully done among correctly chosen patients and when combined with aggressive rehabilitation, amputation should relieve pain and allow patients to continue satisfying and effective lives.

CONCLUSION

Atherosclerosis is endemic and epidemic in the United States. Atherosclerosis causes more than twice the morbidity and mortality of any other disease type. Prevention should be the hallmark of treatment through exercise, diet, blood pressure, weight and cholesterol control, along with mandatory cessation of smoking.

The geriatric population is at greatest risk for complications of atherosclerosis including occlusive disease and aneurysm as blood vessel walls progressively deteriorate with advancing age. Disease recognition is vital in this group since early diagnosis and treatment in all categories of disease using available modern technology can often prevent significant morbidity and mortality.

REFERENCES

1. Anagnostopoulos CE: *Acute Aortic Dissections.* Baltimore; University Park Press, 1975.
2. Anagnostopoulos CE, Prabhakar MJ, Kittle CF: Aortic dissections and dissecting aneurysms. *Am J Cardiol* 30:263, 1972.
3. Armstrong ML: Regression of atherosclerosis. In Paoletti R (ed): *Atherosclerosis Reviews,* Vol. I. New York, Raven Press, 1976.
4. Brewster DC, Darling RC: Optimal method of aortoiliac reconstruction. *Surgery* 84:739, 1978.
5. Bush HJ Jr, Graber JN, Jakubowski JA, et al: Favorable balance of prostacycline and the thromboxone A_2 improves early patency of human in situ vein grafts. *J Vasc Surg* 1:149, 1984.
6. Clyne CAC, Galland RB, Fox MJ, et al: A controlled trial of naftidrofuryl in the treatment of intermittent claudication. *Br J Surg* 67:347, 1980.
7. Crawford ES, Snyder DM, Cho GC, et al: Progress in treatment of thoracoabdominal aortic aneurysms involving celiac, superior mesenteric, and renal arteries. *Ann Surg* 108:404, 1978.
8. Croenwett JL, Warner KG, Zelenock GB, et al: Intermittent claudication: current results of nonoperative management. *Arch Surg* 119:430, 1984.
9. Darling RC, Messina CR, Brewster DC, et al: Autopsy study of unoperative abdominal aortic aneurysms. The case for early resection. *Circulation* 56:161, 1976.

10. De Cree J, Lempoels J, Genkens H, Verhaegen H: Placebo-controlled double-blind trial of ketanserine in treatment of intermittent claudication. *Lancet* 2:775, 1984.

11. Dormand JA, Mahir MS: The natural history of peripheral atheromatous disease of the legs. In Greenhalgh RM, Jamieson CW, Nicolaides AM (eds): *Vascular Surgery: Issues in Current Practice.* New York, Grune & Stratton, 1986.

12. Ereftmeyer L: Anaphylactoid reaction to radiocontrast materials. *J Allerg Clin Immune* March, 1985.

13. Freeman DB, Freeman MP, Spence RA, et al: Economic impact of translumenal angioplasty. *Angiology* 36:772, 1985.

14. Goldstone J: Use of digital subtraction angiographs in limb arterial evaluation. In Bergon JJ, Yao JS (eds): *Evaluation and Treatment of Upper and Lower Extremity Circulatory Disorders.* New York, Grune & Stratton, 1984.

15. Habushaw G, Donovan JC: Biomechanical considerations of the diabetic foot. In Kozak GP, Hoar CS, Rowbotham JL, et al: *Management of Diabetic Foot Problems.* Saunders, 1984.

16. Hertzer NR, Beven EG, Young JR, et al: Coronary artery disease in peripheral vascular patients. A classification of 1,000 coronary angiograms and results of surgical managements. *Ann Surg* 199:223, 1984.

17. Hessel SJ, Adams DF, Abrams HL, et al: Complications of angiography. *Radiology* 138:273, 1981.

18. Hight DW, Tilney N, Couch NP: Changing clinical trends in patients with peripheral arterial emboli. *Surgery* 79:122, 1976.

19. Hoeg JM, Gregg RE, Brewer HB: An approach to the management of hyperlipoproteinemia. *JAMA* 244:512, 1986.

20. Huston CC, Bivins BA, Ernst CB, et al: Morbid implications of above knee amputation. Report of a series and review of literature. *Arch Surg* 115:165, 1980.

21. Imparato AM, Kim G, Davidson T, Crowley SG: Intermittent claudication: Its natural course. *Surgery* 78:795, 1975.

22. Janett F: Lower extremity problems in diabetics. In Janett F (ed): *Vascular Surgery of the Lower Extremity.* St. Louis, CV Mosby, 1985.

23. Jeurgens JL, Barber NW, Hines EA: Atherosclerosis obliterans: Review of 250 cases with special reference to pathogenic and prognostic factors. *Circulation* 21:188, 1960.

24. Kannel WB: Update on the role of cigarette smoking in coronary heart disease. *Am Heart J* 101:319, 1981.

25. Kannel WB, Castelli WP, Gordon T: Cholesterol in the prediction of atherosclerotic disease. New perspectives based on the Framingham study. *Ann Intern Med* 90:85, 1979.

26. Kaplan NM: Hypertension: Prevalence, risks, and effective therapy. *Ann Intern Med* 98:705, 1983.

27. Knight RW, Kenney GJ, Lewis EE, Johnston GG: Percutaneous translumenal angioplasty: Results and surgical implications. *Am J Surg* 147:578, 1984.

28. Kozak GP, Rowbotham JL: Diabetic foot disease: A major problem. In Kozak GP, Hoar CS, Rowbotham JL, et al (eds): *Management of Diabetic Foot Problems.* Philadelphia, WB Saunders, 1984.

29. Mannick J: Current concepts in diagnostic methods. Evaluation of chronic lower extremity ischemia. *N Engl J Med* 309:841, 1983.

30. Martinez BD, Hertzer NR, Beven EG: Influence of distal arterial occlusive disease on prognosis following aortobifemoral bypass. *Surgery* 88:795, 1980.

31. National Center for Health Statistics: The Monthly Vital Statistics Report. Public Health Service, 32 (4) (Suppl.), 1983.

32. Neville RF, Gomes MN: Distal in situ saphenous vein bypass grafting for limb salvage. Presented at the Annual Meeting, Southern Medical Association, Atlanta, GA, Nov. 1977.

33. Optimal resources for the prevention of atherosclerotic disease by Atherosclerosis Study Group of the Intrasociety Commission for Heart Disease Resources. *Circulation* 157A, 1984.

34. Page LB: Epidemologic evidence in the etiology of human hypertension and its possible prevention. *Am Heart J* 91:527, 1976.

35. Peabody CN, Kannel WB, McNamara PM: Intermittent claudication. Surgical significance. *Arch Surg* 109:693, 1974.

36. Porter JM, Cutler BS, Lee BY, et al: Pentoxiphylline efficacy in the treatment of intermittent claudication: Multicenter controlled double-blind trial with objective assessment of chronic occlusive arterial disease patients. *Am Heart J* 104:66, 1982.

37. Ray LI, O'Connor JB, Davis CC, et al:Axillofemoral bypass: A critical reappraisal of its role in the management of aortoiliac occlusive disease. *Am J Surg* 138:117, 1979.

38. Rich T: Cyclandelate: Effect on circulatory measurements and exercise tolerance in chronic arterial insufficiency of the lower extremities. *J Am Geriatr Soc* 25:202, 1977.

39. Ross R: The pathogenesis of atherosclerosis—An update. *N Engl J Med* 314:488, 1986.

40. Rutherford RB, Pitt A, Kumpe DA: The current role of percutaneous translumenal Angioplasty. In Greenhalgh RM, Jamieson GW, Nicolaides AN (eds): *Vascular Surgery Issue in Current Practice.* Orlando, Grune & Stratton, 1986.

41. Saint-Georges G: Safety of outpatient angiography: A prospective study. *AJR* 144:235, 1985.

42. Schadt DC, Hines EA, Jeurgens JL, Barber NW: Chronic atherosclerotic occlusion of the femoral artery. *JAMA* 175:937, 1961.

43. Shehadi WH: Contrast media adverse reactions: Occurrence, recurrence, and distribution patterns. *Radiology* 143:11, 19, 1982.

44. Skinner JS, Strandness DE Jr: Exercise and intermittent claudication: Effect of physical training. *Circulation* 36:23, 1967.

45. Stassen AJ: Treatment of circulatory disturbances with flunarizine and cinnarizine: A multicenter, double blind and placebo-controlled evaluation. *VASA* 6:59, 1977.

46. Szilagyi DE, Smith RF, DeRusso FJ, et al: Contribu-

tion of abdominal aortic aneurysm in the prolongation of life. *Ann Surg* 164:678, 1966.

47. Veith FJ, Enrico A, Sushil KG, et al: Femoral-popliteal-tibial occlusive disease in Moore WS (ed): *Vascular Surgery: A Comprehensive Review.* New York, Grune & Stratton, 1983.

48. Walsh DB, Butterfield AB: Contractility: A technique for the study of vein grafts? In Hall WC (ed): *Surgical Research: Recent Developments.* New York, Pergamon Press, 1985.

49. Walsh BD, Downing S, Ahmed SW, et al: Venous valvular obstructions of blood flow through saphenous veins. *J Surg Res* 42(1):39, 1987.

50. Waters RL, Perry J, Antonelli D, et al: Energy cost of walking of amputees. The influence of level of amputation. *J Bone Joint Surg (Am)* 58:42, 1976.

51. Widmer LK, Boland L, DaSilva A: Risk profile and occlusive peripheral artery disease. Proceedings of the 13th International Congress of Angiology, Athens 9–14, June, 1985.

52. Widmer LK, Greensler A, Kannel WB: Occlusion of peripheral arteries—A study of 6400 working subjects. *Circulation* 30:836, 1964.

53. Wissler RW: Development of the atherosclerotic plaque. In Braunwald E (ed): *Myocardium. Failure and Infarction.* New York, HP Publishing, 1974.

54. Zarins CK: Hemodynamics in atherogenesis. In Moore W (ed): *Vascular Surgery: A Comprehensive Review,* 2nd ed. New York, Grune & Stratton, 1986.

55. Zarins CK, Lu CT, Gewertz BL, et al: Arterial disruption and remodeling following balloon dilatation. *Surgery* 92:1086, 1982.

CHAPTER 12

Clinical Geropsychiatry

NATHAN BILLIG

Most elderly people are mentally healthy. Of the population that is over the age of 65 years, 95% live in the community, not in institutions such as nursing homes or mental hospitals. And yet many people incorrectly continue to view older people as generally debilitated, frail, and demented. Only 10% of elderly people are severely affected in those ways. Older adults suffer with some of the same psychologic disorders that are common to younger people. They are subject to personality and adjustment disorders, schizophrenia, and substance abuse. The most common psychologic problems of the later years however are *affective disorders* and *organic mental disorders,* particularly dementia.

AFFECTIVE DISORDERS

Affective disorders are disturbances of mood. The more commonly occurring of these are major depression and bipolar disorder. Depression is not synonymous with old age. Depression in the later years, as at any age, is a pathologic condition that must be evaluated, diagnosed, and treated. It is the most common psychiatric problem at every age and one of the most treatable. Estimates of prevalence of depression in the elderly population range between 5% and 20%.

The elderly may have some special vulnerabilities that may make them more susceptible to depression and may make the consequences more serious. These vulnerabilities include losses, biologic changes, developmental issues, flexibility and coping, social issues, retirement, relocation, medical problems, medications, thoughts of death, and recurrent depression.

LOSSES

Inherent in the aging process is the concept and reality of multiple losses. Some bodily functions,

stamina, friends, loved ones, financial stability, and the acuity of the senses may be lost. Losses are inevitable; they are part of everyone's life experience. In an elderly person, the losses are cumulative and intense. The extent to which one deals with losses successfully may affect one's vulnerability to depression.

BIOLOGIC CHANGES

There are changes in the amounts of neurotransmitters as aging proceeds. The relative decreases in some and increases in others may have some role in predisposing the elderly to depression. Likewise, adrenal, pituitary, and thyroid hormones change in quality and quantity with age and may produce some further vulnerability.

DEVELOPMENTAL ISSUES

Erik Erikson, the noted psychoanalyst, views old age as a stage of life that involves the struggle between "ego integrity" and despair. By ego integrity, he means the acceptance of the fact that one's life is one's own responsibility. Successfully reaching old age means the mastering of earlier stages of development and coming to terms with the positive and negative experiences one has had, resigning oneself to the fact that they cannot be remade. If this level of integrity cannot be achieved, despair wins out.

FLEXIBILITY AND COPING

As one ages, he or she becomes less flexible in schedules, activities, diets, and general patterns of living. At the same time, some usually adaptive coping skills have been lost which had helped to deal better with stresses in the past. Hard work, athletics, and other physical sublimations may have to be adjusted to a level that is more suitable to an individual's physical status. Impairments in hearing, vision and taste, and decreases in stamina may add to a generalized feeling that coping ability is decreasing. These changes do not imply illness, but rather are challenges to coping skills and imply potential vulnerability.

SOCIAL ISSUES

The social system in which the older adult finds him- or herself is vital to the assessment of susceptibility to psychologic problems and to depression in particular. With the loss of loved ones and friends, the support system that had been available in earlier years may become considerably diminished. Widows and widowers may retreat into virtually solitary existence. Children and grandchildren develop their own lives, friends, and families, and the extended family no longer lives under one roof.

RETIREMENT

For many people, retirement offers an opportunity for "golden years" after many years of work. It allows for extended vacations that might not have been possible earlier, relative freedom from responsibilities for children, and an opportunity to spend time with one's spouse, friends, adult children, and grandchildren. Unfortunately for some people, retirement is not so golden. It may be another reminder of loss, may provoke marital tensions, and often necessitates relocation from a long-familiar environment. Retirement stresses can make one more vulnerable to depression.

RELOCATION

Many older adults have lived, for decades, in one environment or even in one apartment or house. The later years often require a move to a smaller house, a relative's home, a retirement community, or a nursing home. Whether the relocation is voluntary or required because of physical or emotional needs, the stresses and losses inherent in a move must be considered vulnerabilities to depression.

MEDICAL PROBLEMS

Illness is not pleasant to endure at any age, and, for the older adult, it is even more difficult. Although most older people are not sick, the prevalence of chronic illness is great. They cope less well than their children and grandchildren and they find it harder to recuperate. Hip fractures, cataracts, and the surgery required to treat them are stresses that may serve as focal points for the onset of depression. Similarly, there is evidence that more than 50% of

people who sustain strokes may become depressed in the 2 years after those insults.

MEDICATIONS

Medications play an important role in the lives of older adults. Medications are, in many cases, essential to survival and, at other times, are helpful in relieving symptoms. It now is understood that, at times, medications—alone or in combination—produce dangerous or at least unpleasant side effects including depression and cognitive impairment. The medications that are most commonly implicated include the antihypertensives, cardiac antiarrhythmics, anti-inflammatory agents, steroids, and β-blocking agents.

THOUGHTS OF DEATH

Although not necessarily consciously, many older people have some preoccupation with the knowledge that they are closer to death than they have ever been. Death is a probability in the not-too-distant future. These thoughts are rarely openly expressed, but many older adults welcome the opportunity to ventilate these concerns. Unexpressed thoughts of death can represent another cause of vulnerability to depression.

RECURRENT DEPRESSION

Many older people have been depressed for many years and are vulnerable to recurrences in late life. Some of these people have extensive family histories of depression with some indications of biologic predispositions to affective disorders. The stresses of old age may precipitate any given depressive episode, especially in those people who are sensitive to the extreme distress produced by loss.

A complex network of factors can conspire to produce or precipitate depression in the older adult. Fortunately they rarely all converge. In no other medical disorder is the interweaving of biologic (including genetic), sociocultural, medical, and psychologic issues so apparent.

DIAGNOSES OF DEPRESSION

"I'm not depressed. I just don't feel like living; I'm of no use to anyone."

"I don't know what you mean by "depressed." My problem is that my bowels aren't working right and my head aches all the time."

While the various affective disorders generally can be categorized in terms of signs and symptoms, as with other medical problems, the elderly often present in atypical ways. Older adults may not use the word "depressed"; they may even deny the feeling. They sometimes force us to see through a disguise of denial, physical symptoms, agitation, or subtle personality changes.

The affective disorders include major depression, bipolar disorder, dysthymic disorder, abnormal bereavement, and organic affective syndrome.

Major Depression

Major depression is the most common of the affective disorders in the elderly. The core symptoms of major depression are detailed in the *Diagnostic and Statistical Manual* of the American Psychiatric Association (DSM III). They include:

Dysphoric mood, including symptoms such as feeling depressed, sad, blue, hopeless, low, down in the dumps, and irritable. These feelings should be prominent and relatively persistent.

At least four of the following symptoms, present nearly every day for a period of at least 2 weeks:

1. Poor appetite or significant weight loss or gain
2. Insomnia or oversleeping
3. Psychomotor agitation or retardation
4. Loss of interest or pleasure in usual activities
5. Loss of energy, fatigue, or excessive tiredness
6. Feelings of worthlessness, self-reproach, or excessive or inappropriate guilt
7. Complaints or evidence of decreased ability to think or concentrate, such as slowed thinking or indecisiveness
8. Recurrent thoughts of death, suicide, wishes to be dead, or a suicide attempt

The DSM III criteria do not take into account the fact that many elderly patients do not complain of being depressed, sad, or blue. In addition, older people often demonstrate clinical depression through increased physical symptoms that do not result in the diagnosis of a physical disorder.

Bipolar Affective Disorders

Bipolar affective disorders, previously known as "manic-depressive illness," are less common than major depression, but they should not be overlooked in the older adult. Bipolar disorders commonly arise in early to middle adulthood and may persist into later life. They may also appear de novo in the elderly adult. "Bipolar" implies both manic and depressive episodes, occurring in alternating or periodic fashion, each episode lasting days, weeks, or months.

Manic symptoms include elation or euphoria, hyperactivity, decreased need for sleep, agitation, ir-ritability, grandiosity, pressured speech, or flight of ideas. Many of these manic symptoms appear to be the opposite of depression and, indeed, many of them are experienced as pleasurable by the affected patient. The symptom complex is disabling because it results in poor judgment, impulsiveness, highly erratic behavior, and distorted thought processes.

People with bipolar illness are more likely to have a family history of affective disorders, are more likely to have problems with alcohol abuse (sometimes in an effort to control manic symptoms or for sleep), and are at greater risk for suicide than are people with depressive symptoms alone.

Dysthymic Disorders

Dysthymic disorders, formerly referred to as depressive neuroses, are chronic disturbances of mood in which there is generalized loss of pleasure and interest in almost all usual life activities. The disturbance is not sufficiently severe nor does it have the necessary elements to qualify as a major depressive episode. People with dysthymic disorders do not have the vegetative symptoms of appetite and sleep disturbances, weight loss and somatic complaints, and do not have frankly psychotic symptoms, such as hallucinations or delusions. Dysthymic disorders have their origins early in adult life without a clear time of onset. Symptoms include insomnia, low energy or chronic tiredness, low self-esteem, decreased effectiveness, concentration and attention, pessimistic attitude about the future, and brooding about the past.

Abnormal Bereavement

What is normal grief after a long marriage? It may take up to several years to grieve the loss and regain full function after the death of a spouse of many years or a child. In the first 6 months to 1 year, there may be profound sadness, crying, insomnia, anorexia, anhedonia, and a taking on of attributes or habits of the mourned person.

Abnormal grief reactions may have many of the symptoms that are characteristic of a major depression with increased somatic symptoms, agitation, withdrawal from people and activities, thoughts of worthlessness, helplessness and hopelessness, suicidal thoughts, cognitive impairment, and almost constant ruminations about the loss. Some people are inconsolable and grieve for the rest of their lives. Others who are profoundly affected are literally unable to survive alone and die within the first year after a significant loss, such as a spouse.

It is difficult to determine exactly when normal

grief becomes abnormal. What is acceptable varies with different cultures and families and is tempered by the length and nature of the relationship with the deceased person. Many cultures accept 1 year of mourning, but after a long marriage, most people need a longer grief period before they can resume a normal life. We judge the mourning process as pathologic by the presence of symptoms of depression as well as the length of time. Symptoms of major depression that are present after the first 6 months or a suicidal preoccupation at any time require psychiatric consultation.

Organic Affective Syndromes

An organic affective syndrome is a mood disorder that results from a specific physiologic or structural, temporary or permanent brain dysfunction. It may be caused by disorders such as a stroke, Alzheimer's disease, toxic and medication reactions, metabolic and endocrine dysfunctions, system disorders, etc. They result in behavioral or psychologic abnormalities that resemble the diagnostic entities previously described in this chapter. The clinician must consider the organic etiologies that might be causing an affective disorder and thoroughly rule out those possibilities.

Suicide: A Special Problem

Suicide is more common in elderly white men than in any other age group. In women, the peak suicide risk is in the immediate postmenopausal period. The elderly population (12%) accounts for more than 25% of the suicides committed. When older adults attempt suicide, they more usually succeed than do people of other ages. Suicide attempts in the elderly should not be dismissed as gestures. They must be taken seriously; they always mean great distress. Most suicides are attempted by people who are depressed or who are just mobilizing from a serious depression. In view of these data, suicide must be reckoned with by the family and the clinician and seriously considered in any evaluation of a depressed older adult.

Suicidal feelings occur, at least fleetingly, in most depressed people and maybe in most people, but the idea of suicide as a solution to one's state of mind is a different matter. Even the actively suicidal state is usually temporary, lasting days or weeks, and it needs to be approached as a potentially treatable symptom that is part of a larger problem, usually depression.

Many of the vulnerabilities to suicide are the same as those discussed for depression, but there are also some special risk factors. Older adults who attempt suicide often do so impulsively and don't give a clear message of increased distress or of particular desperation. The loss of a spouse is a major risk factor for suicide and the risk may last for weeks or months, depending on the mourning process and the person's adaptation to widowhood. Older people may feel totally lost in the world without their spouse, unable to contemplate survival, or they may have some variant of the delusion of being called to the dead spouse's grave, "being called to join him (her)." These distinctions have to be made by clinicians because they give us some notion of how irrational and how extensive the feelings of loss may be.

The presence of dementia or other organic mental impairments increases the suicide risk, as does the abuse of alcohol and other drugs. Increased somatic complaints may herald potential suicide; it is well known that most patients who attempt suicide have seen their physicians in the prior month. Most have had physical complaints and have not mentioned suicide or even depression.

What is the role of the clinician in the face of some suicide risk or threat? Although the question is not always responded to honestly, it is worth asking a worrisome person whether he or she has thought about self-harm or suicide, and if so, how strong is that thought or feeling? Does he or she have a plan to do it? Can he or she talk about the distress? Most people in distress welcome and respond to care, concern, and support. Consultation with a psychiatrist and/or hospitalization is usually indicated.

What about the terminally ill patient who expresses the desire to die? It is perhaps surprising that most older people with terminal illnesses do not wish to die and certainly most do not wish to have their lives terminated prematurely by suicide or mercy-killing. Although this area has not been studied extensively, some research indicates that most of those people who wish for any early death are clinically depressed: they exhibit the signs and symptoms that are the criteria for the diagnosis of major depression. Suicidal thought is just one of those symptoms. When confronted by such a patient, clinicians treat the depression before considering issues related to rational suicide.

TREATMENT OF DEPRESSION

Once depression is diagnosed and found not to be secondary to a physical disorder, efforts should then be made to find the optimal treatment. Depression is one of the most treatable medical problems, but unfortunately, it often goes untreated because of a sense of therapeutic nihilism on the parts of physician, patient, and family. The understanding of the biology of depression and the available treatment options have advanced in the past decade to a point where over 75% of patients improve significantly as a result of a single or combined treatment approach.

What are the major treatment approaches for depression? Although there are dozens of treatment possibilities, the primary modalities include:

1. Psychotherapy ("talk therapy") of various kinds;
2. Psychopharmacologic therapies;
3. Electroconvulsive ("shock") therapy (ECT).

Psychotherapy

Psychotherapy is a generic term for the types of "talk therapy" approaches that have evolved over the past 50 years. Many elderly people feel that their troubles can be solved at the bridge table because their friends are "going through the same thing, and going to a psychiatrist is for crazy people." The psychiatrist or other mental health professional has the advantage of specific training that friends at the card table do not have.

Psychotherapy includes the dynamically or psychoanalytically oriented ("Freudian") approach, supportive, behavioral, and cognitive approaches. These therapies may be conducted in individual, group, or family settings. All are valid forms of treatment and any one is chosen in a given case because of the preference of the patient and therapist. Whatever type of psychotherapy is chosen, the relationship between the therapist and patient, the flexibility of the therapist and his or her knowledge of normal aging and the medical/psychiatric disorders that might possibly occur are vital to the success of the endeavor. In all situations, the therapy focuses on the strengths of the patient and efforts to help maximize his or her functional ability.

It is important for people with psychologic pain to talk. Although talking may not always be curative by itself, it is almost always relieving. The older adult has a wealth of experiences that demonstrate strengths and weakness, recurrent themes, and new concerns. The therapy can utilize reminiscence techniques, in which patients are encouraged to review their life experiences to draw on assets that may have been overlooked and to come to terms with difficult issues that may not have been worked through in the past. The therapy must focus on a range of considerations from early childhood worries to the real dilemmas, problems, and exaggera-

tions of old age. Depressed older adults can well use the support offered by an empathic therapist who attempts to build on the defenses that work well for the patient. The therapist can convey an optimistic view that the psychologic problem is treatable. He or she can help the patient understand the course of the disorder and recognize the changes that result from treatment.

Psychopharmacologic Therapies

The medications used in the treatment of depression in the older adult include:

1. Tricyclic antidepressants and related medications
2. Lithium
3. Major tranquilizers
4. Minor tranquilizers
5. Monoamine oxidase inhibitors
6. Stimulants

The *tricyclic antidepressants* are the most commonly used medications to treat depression. There are up to 20 different tricyclics or closely related medications. These include nortriptyline, desipramine, imipramine, amitriptyline, and doxepin. Trazodone is another commonly described antidepressant drug that is not a tricyclic. They all appear to work by affecting neurotransmitter activity in the brain. They are all effective in reducing depression and their adverse effects vary in intensity and number. Treating the elderly with medications requires a careful balance between maximizing effectiveness and minimizing side effects. Common side effects include drowsiness, tachycardia, blurred vision, dryness of the mouth, constipation, orthostatic hypotension, and urinary retention. Many of these decrease after a few days of medication use and others will necessitate reduction in dosage or substitution with another compound.

Although there is a great deal of individual variability, the secondary amines including nortriptyline and desipramine, have a lower side effect profile than the other tricyclics mentioned. In addition, trazadone has fewer anticholinergic effects, but may produce drowsiness in therapeutic dosages.

Older adults generally can benefit from dosages of tricyclics that are one-quarter to one-half of those used in younger patients. Most can be taken in single nighttime doses so that many of the unpleasant adverse effects occur during sleep. Treatment response can be judged clinically and tricyclic blood levels provide evidence of compliance and absorption.

Lithium is one of the miracle drugs of the 20th

century. Introduced in the late 1960s and popularized since the 1970s, lithium is vital to the treatment of both bipolar disorders and recurrent depression. In 70–80% of people suffering with bipolar disorders, lithium provides a permanent remission as long as the medication is continued. Others who are more resistant or who are "rapid cyclers" require regimens with multiple medications. Lithium is also effective in leveling the moods of cyclothymic patients who have cyclical mood swings that are not as extreme or intense as those of bipolar patients. Lithium is prescribed alone and as a potentiator with tricyclic antidepressants in people who are severely or chronically depressed.

Lithium treatment requires regular monitoring of blood levels with therapeutic levels between 0.5 and 1.5 ng/ml. In the elderly, maintenance blood levels between 0.5 and 1.0 ng/ml are the goals, in order to minimize adverse effects. Side effects include weight gain, muscle spasms, and a reversible hypothyroidism. High levels of lithium can result in confusion, slurred speech, ataxia, lethargy, and delirium. Patients who are also taking diuretics for hypertension or heart disease need careful electrolyte monitoring and all patients should maintain a normal diet (not low salt) with adequate fluid intake.

Lithium can be used with the tricyclics, major tranquilizers, and stimulants as the patient's symptomatology requires. Lithium is not prescribed frequently enough, particularly with elderly patients. When used and monitored with care, it is safe and highly effective as a treatment and prophylaxis for some of the most disabling and dangerous disorders that physicians treat.

Major tranquilizers such as thioridazine and haloperidol are used to treat severe agitation and/or psychotic symptoms—usually hallucinations or delusions—when they accompany depression. Although the combination produces increased anticholinergic side effects, the therapeutic benefits are significant, often making a remission of delusional depression possible.

Minor tranquilizers have little role in the therapy of depression, except for the treatment of insomnia and mild agitation. Alprazolam is a benzodiazepine that has both antianxiety and antidepressant effects and may be useful in the treatment of depression when tricyclics are contraindicated and where no psychotic symptoms are present. Some physicians are concerned about problems with withdrawal even after the slow tapering of the drug. More experience with alprazolam in the elderly is necessary.

Monoamine oxidase inhibitors are a class of antidepressants that increases the availability of neurotransmitters in the brain and are generally regarded as secondary choices for antidepressant treatment in the elderly. They have many of the same side effects as the tricyclics and require dietary and medication restrictions that sometimes prove to be prohibitive for the older adult.

Stimulants are not true antidepressants, but they have a valuable role in activating the lethargic, apathetic, depressed elderly patient. Stimulants, typified by methylphenidate, are useful in patients who are unresponsive to tricyclics or when these drugs are contraindicated. They are particularly useful in patients who have depression accompanying medical or postsurgical problems. There are some data showing that a positive response to stimulants may indicate an equally successful treatment with tricyclics. The stimulants are effective within 3–5 days and are sometimes utilized until the tricyclics begin to be effective. They are not recommended for long-term use and have drawbacks including a brief duration of action, side effects of insomnia, anorexia, hyperactivity, and tachycardia.

The skilled clinician who treats depression in the elderly may have the best success using a flexible approach that includes supportive psychotherapy and pharmacotherapy of various types. Several of the medications mentioned above can be used effectively in combination. In addition, thyroid hormone and some anticonvulsants have been tried in resistant cases. The treatment of the elderly with psychotropics requires a careful, cautious persistent approach with attention to polypharmacy, drug-drug interactions, adverse side effects, and clinical signs of improvement. Except after dramatic negative side effects, medications should not be switched rapidly, allowing for slow metabolic and symptomatic changes.

ECT is one of the most effective treatments for severe depression and may be life-saving in certain situations. It is almost always administered in a hospital setting, particularly in the older adult, and the technique used makes it safe, humane, and effective. Most patients have had previous trials on antidepressants before receiving ECT, but some research indicates that ECT is, in fact, the treatment of choice for delusional depression. It may be safer than tricyclic medications in patients with cardiac disorders and usually produces a response in a shorter time. Treatments are administered in a three per week series, using a muscle relaxant and short-acting anesthetic premedication. There is usually some short-term memory loss, but rarely longer range cognitive changes in people who were not previously demented.

DEMENTIA

The term dementia means a loss of brain function and refers to a set of symptoms and disorders produced by transient or permanent structural changes in the brain. Over time, these changes may result in a gradual but progressive deterioration of neurologic and psychologic functioning. Typical findings in a patient with dementia include memory impairment, loss of concentration, disorientation, loss of intellectual functioning, and later, the loss of the ability to perform activities of daily living such as toileting, feeding, and dressing oneself. In contrast to patients who are delirious, demented people are alert; they are not stuporous, semicomatose, or comatose.

The dementias are one group of disorders under the broader category of organic mental disorders. Other organic mental disorders include deliria, substance abuse and withdrawal states, and organic affective and amnestic syndromes. These will be dealt with in other sections of this text (see Chapters 13 and 14).

The behavioral symptoms of the dementias (Alzheimer's disease, multi-infarct dementia, or secondary dementias) include the gamut of psychopathology including depression, anxiety, agitation, paranoid ideation, hallucinations, delusions, somatization, insomnia as well as cognitive organic symptoms— amnesia, apraxia, agnosia, and agraphia—usually associated with these symptoms.

It is essential that every patient presenting with behavioral or cognitive signs or symptoms be evaluated fully to define an accurate diagnosis. The evaluation must include a history taken from both the patient and an interested family member or friend, a complete physical examination including neurologic and mental status components, and laboratory, x-ray, and special testing. This assessment should allow the clinician to define the presence of a treatable secondary dementia, or the existence of a primary dementia or functional psychiatric problem. Furthermore, it is crucial to identify the possibility of systemic illness that presents with neuro/psychiatric symptomatology, so that treatment of that specific disorder can be instituted.

OTHER PSYCHIATRIC SYNDROMES

SCHIZOPHRENIA

There is some debate about the incidence of schizophrenia in late life. Most people so diagnosed have been ill, either consistently or episodically, for many years and come to the attention of clinicians for continuing care, changes in psychotropic medications, and social interventions. The term "paraphrenia" has been used to describe paranoid illness of late life that may have some delusional, hallucinatory, and other thought disorder components, without the typical schizophrenic syndrome.

Regardless of their relationship, schizophrenia and other paranoid states of late life can be treated with a combination of pharmacotherapy, supportive psychotherapy, and attention to social and environmental needs. The phenothiazines and other major tranquilizers are usually the medications of choice to deal with the psychotic symptoms of these disorders. The judicious use of neuroleptics should include attention to the possibility of tardive dyskinesia, deliria, and drug-drug interactions.

Brief hospitalizations, day treatment, and other supportive efforts are usually necessary to help elderly people with severe chronic psychopathology function better in the community. Long-term continuity with mental health and/or social service personnel is essential.

HYPOCHONDRIASIS

Elderly people are often told by physicians that their physical symptoms are "all in their heads." Arthritis, indigestion, constipation, and fatigue are among the most common complaints that even "normal" older adults have and we accept the idea that with age some systems and functions will deteriorate and periodically or chronically result in some symptoms.

When elderly patients become preoccupied with physical symptoms for which no disease state can be found those people are often defined as hypochondriacal. In fact, there may be an exaggeration of chronic physical discomfort that represents a displacement of stress, anxiety, and/or depression onto the body. The clinician may be tempted to dismiss or write-off those patients as chronic complainers but, in fact, they may be presenting with a primary psychiatric problem with physical symptomatology. They need to be evaluated to make a diagnosis for a possibly treatable illness.

Patients with affective, anxiety, or personality disorders, psychotic phenomena, and organic syndromes may all present with vague physical symptoms. Suicidal patients frequently present to their physicians with physical complaints in the month before a suicide attempt. The physician cannot dissuade the patient from a psychiatric disorder by saying that he or she is physically fit or "it's all in your head." Rather, the physician must see the patient as in distress and attempt to establish a supportive relationship that has some therapeutic benefit. Consultation with or referral to a psychiatrist for diagnostic and therapeutic considerations may be indicated.

CONCLUSIONS

The elderly are subject to an array of psychologic disorders, although depression and dementia are the most common. The older adult deserves the benefit of the full range of therapeutic attempts because, indeed, experience teaches that when psychologic disturbances are properly diagnosed and treated, the responses are quite gratifying. The clinician who treats older patients has to consider the complex interweaving of physical, psychologic, and social issues that often conspire to produce pathologic states in the aged.

We must guard against the stereotyping of the old as impaired merely because of their age or ascribing pathologic states to "just being old." Being old has its difficulties and challenges, but it doesn't necessarily imply illness or psychologic impairment.

SUGGESTED READINGS

1. Billig N: *To Be Old and Sad: Understanding Depression in the Elderly.* Lexington, MA, Lexington Books, 1987.
2. Blazer D: *Depression in Late Life.* St. Louis, CV Mosby, 1982.
3. *Diagnostic and Statistical Manual of the American Psychiatric Association.* Washington, APA, 1980.
4. Jenike MA: Alzheimer's disease: Clinical care and management. *Psychosomatics* 27:407, 1986.
5. Mace N, Rabins PV: *The 36-Hour Day.* Baltimore, Johns Hopkins Press, 1981.
6. *Medical Letter on Drugs and Therapeutics:* Drugs that cause psychiatric symptoms. 28:721, 1986.
7. Robinson R, Price TR: Post-stroke depressive disorders: A follow-up of 103 patients. *Stroke* 13:635, 1982.
8. Salzman C: *Clinical Geriatric Psychopharmacology.* New York, McGraw Hill, 1984.
9. Schneck MK, Reisberg B, Ferris SH: An overview of current concepts of Alzheimer's disease. *Am J Psychiatry* 139:165, 1982.
10. Wells CE: Pseudodementia. *Am J Psychiatry* 136:895, 1979.
11. Winograd CH, Jarvik LF: Physician management of the demented patient. *J Am Geriatr Soc* 34:295, 1986.

CHAPTER 13

Alcoholism and Drug Abuse

WILLIAM E. FLYNN
GABRIELLE BEMIS BATZER

Alcoholism and drug abuse among the elderly have generally been ignored or minimized. In recent years, there has been greater awareness and understanding of these conditions in all segments of the population including the elderly. This has resulted in an increasing expectation that health care professionals be alert to the problems and knowledgeable in their care. This chapter will focus on the identification, medical complications, intervention, and treatment of these conditions.

The extent of the problem is estimated, roughly, at 2–10% of the elderly population. Studies of clinics and hospitalized patients give a much higher incidence of problems (20–40%) but other epidemiologic studies of broader groups of healthy elderly people suggest that the health problems of the elderly are generally overstated. However, the increasing size of our elderly population and their heavy use of medications of all kinds make these problems a significant concern for health care providers. (1).

Among the elderly, two different categories of substance abuse, which can be applied equally to problems with alcohol and drug abuse, are described. These subgroups include individuals with early onset and a lifelong pattern of abuse and those with late onset who had essentially no problem with these substances in their younger years (7, 11).

An example of the early onset, chronic abuser, is this case:

A 73-year-old woman was brought to the alcohol clinic by her husband and other members of her family with the report that she had been drinking excessively, had several falls, and appeared to be unable to control her drinking. Initial history revealed that the patient had several hospitalizations during her 40s and 50s for alcohol withdrawal and had been a chronic problem for her husband and her family. They had barely tolerated

her alcohol excesses but, in recent months, had become increasingly concerned because her 75-year-old spouse was less able to deal with her alcoholic outbursts. Their concern was more about the effect of her alcoholism on her husband and his declining health.

This woman can be described as a survivor in that her chronic alcoholism would have predicted a shorter life-span. Patients in this category tend to have the personality changes that are associated with lifelong abuse and also are more likely to have medical complications. They usually have worn down or so alienated the family support that they tend to be alone and relatively abandoned. Treatment approaches are not very different from the approaches for alcoholism in other age groups. Given the chronicity of the problem and the personality changes that have taken place, the chance of dramatic behavioral change is only fair (3).

About one-third of patients fit into the late onset group. Living alone, for whatever reason, appears to increase the chances of development of this condition. An example of the late onset, reactive abuser is this case:

A 69-year-old man came with his wife to the clinic because of increasing difficulties with alcohol. He was becoming drunk several days during the week, becoming more withdrawn and depressed, and beginning to have more difficulty sleeping. History from the patient and his wife indicated that he had been a moderate drinker all his life but upon retirement 2 years before, he had considerable difficulty adjusting to a different life-style. He spent a considerable amount of time sitting around the house doing nothing and gradually began to fill the time with increasing periods of drinking. His tolerance to alcohol had gradually increased and he was drinking increasing amounts every day.

The late onset alcoholics generally are seen as developing their problems in response to the changes associated with aging. These changes are identified as losses, such as the death of a spouse, family problems, loss of a child, medical illness, loneliness, and boredom. Also, retirement from work, as in the case illustration, and the resulting unstructured time has been identified as an important factor. These patients usually do not have the medical complications or personality changes associated with chronic alcoholism. Their support systems are generally intact and supportive and they see the alcoholism as a direct response to the difficulties of aging. They respond well to education and supportive intervention that helps them to establish more constructive patterns of adaptation. Specific attention must be paid to the structuring of their time and the necessity of changing patterns of behavior to avoid the use of alcohol or drugs. Increased information about the effects of alcohol and the manner in which dependency upon the use of alcohol develops are important aspects of the education of these patients. With all of these factors in mind, it follows that the prognosis for this group is much more favorable and the rationale for aggressive intervention is clearer.

ALCOHOL PROBLEMS

Alcohol is by far the most serious drug problem among the elderly. Unfortunately, many elderly individuals continue to view alcohol problems in a moral context; hence there are feelings of shame and weakness related to any problems with alcohol. Acceptance of alcoholism as a disease is minimal so there is a greater sense of guilt and less voluntary reaching out for help.

When the problem is relatively minor or in an early stage, the elderly patient may express some concern about what is happening and respond openly and frankly to questions about changes in their own response to alcohol. In the interest of improving health and functioning, they look for ways to control the developing dependence upon alcohol and respond favorably to education and support. As the problem intensifies and the complications begin to set in, there is an increased sense of frustration and guilt on the part of the patient and, frequently, increasing denial of the extent of the problem.

Such denial is both a refusal to see the extent of the problem and a failure to remember events that have taken place. A vicious cycle develops in which the alcohol causes confusion and memory impairment and the patient then takes more forgetting what has already been taken. This confusion and automatic repetitive consumption is present in all age groups, but is much more prevalent and destructive for the elderly.

A frequent alerting factor has been complaints by the family who may describe a problem that has not yet become clinically apparent. The elderly alcoholic has a markedly increased vulnerability to accidents of all kinds: falls, fires, auto accidents, misplaced money, etc. In addition, disruptive behavior, such as loud arguments, property destruction, and inappropriate sexual behavior can lead to intervention by police or other authorities with resultant eviction from homes, apartments, and nursing homes and sometimes can lead to embarrassing legal action. When the family's patience and tolerance have been pushed to the limit, they take action. Out of concern, frustration, and sometimes anger, they turn to the health professionals with a request for help. Without some form of help the social and physical deterioration continues until the individual is no longer able to function independently, at which point some form of custodial care may be arranged. This leads to a control of access to alcohol by the caring figures in the environment. These placements may be less than satisfactory and usually involve considerably less independence for the individual. In addition, constant vigilance is required so that there is not some accidental availability of alcohol that leads again to excesses and once more to the problems experienced previously.

An elderly person is at greater risk for difficulties with alcohol than a young person for several reasons. Both total body water and lean body mass are reduced as one ages. Even though it does not seem that ethanol metabolism per se is decreased in the elderly (unless there is some underlying condition), blood alcohol levels are proportionally higher in the older person than in the younger person when both are given equivalent amounts determined by body surface area. Thus, the same person as he or she ages can achieve higher blood alcohol levels with no increase in the amount ingested, all other factors remaining constant (8). These other factors, however, often do not remain constant. Illness, malnutrition, the administration of other hepatotoxic drugs or drugs that require hepatic breakdown may all further increase an elderly person's sensitivity to alcohol.

Important sequellae of alcohol abuse in any age group, of course, are the central nervous system (CNS) effects. The older person is even more vulnerable to the detrimental effects of alcohol on cognitive function than a younger person. This decrement in function occurs even with light "social" drinking. What confuses the picture is that qualitatively the cognitive defects caused by alcohol are similar to those associated with aging. Thus, alcohol can mimic or exacerbate those changes linked both with normal aging and Alzheimer's disease (1, 2, 4, 8).

Other CNS side effects of alcohol involve a wide spectrum of organic brain diseases. These include Wernicke-Korsakoff's syndrome (which is more prevalent in the elderly), depression, emotional lability, irritability, and during withdrawal, seizures and/or delirium (4). The risk of intracranial hemorrhage is also increased, independent of the rise in blood pressure.

Insomnia is perhaps the most insidious effect of alcohol use. Since sleep disorders are common among older persons, the elderly patient often becomes used to a chemical management of insomnia either in the form of alcohol or sedative/hypnotic drugs (see below). Alcohol does act to decrease sleep latency that increases with age. However, it tends to further reduce REM and stage 3 and 4 of NREM sleep, which is already decreased in the elderly. The net result is a virtual elimination of the restful and restorative portions of the sleep cycle. This can be further complicated by alcohol withdrawal occurring during sleep with concomitant sympathetic discharge and arousal (8).

Of course, the older patient is not immune from the more typical sequellae of alcohol that range from bone marrow suppression of all the cell lines, resulting in pancytopenia (although one may see a leukocytosis in acute withdrawal) to gastrointestinal disease including, but not limited to, gastritis, alcoholic hepatitis, cirrhosis, and resulting portal hypertension and pancreatitis. Cardiovascular effects involve various tachyarrhythmias, cardiomyopathy, worsening angina and hypertension. Myopathy and neuropathies may also be seen. Ethanol can decrease sexual drive in both sexes and can lead to testicular atrophy and organic impotence. Thus, combined with age-related changes, alcohol can sharply curtail or end an older person's sexual life (4, 8).

An important sign of alcohol problems in the elderly is an unexpected response to other medications. This can result from either decreased metabolism from acute alcohol ingestion or increased hepatic microsomal enzyme metabolism from chronic alcohol use. Thus, in the face of long-term use of alcohol, one may see decreased effectiveness of phenytoin, anticoagulants, and antidepressants.

Many liquid cold medications are actually tinctures with significant alcohol content. Most mouthwashes, cough syrups, and patent medicines also contain alcohol as do some geriatric tonics. There

will be patients who view the consumptions of these compounds as taking medicine rather than drinking. Thus, when a patient presents with all the signs and symptoms of alcohol abuse, but denies alcohol intake, the practitioner needs to question him or her vigorously and perhaps his or her family about these medications.

SEDATIVE-HYPNOTICS

Abuse of sedative-hypnotics, taken either for sleep or anxiety, is a prevalent form of drug abuse among the elderly (11). The fragile sleep patterns of older people and their attention to them lead to prescriptions for sleep medication. In recent years, primarily long-acting benzodiazepines have been prescribed. Initially there are good results, but a build-up of tolerance develops followed by a necessity to remain on the drug to prevent withdrawal. A frequent clinical pattern is that of the patient who attempts to stop the medication and experiences a sleepless night or a period of intense discomfort. This acts as a powerful reinforcer and the patient and, frequently, the family members strongly support maintenance of the medication. Prescriptions from several physicians or use of other people's medications allow for the development of a pattern of abuse.

Complications of these drugs may be related to the development of toxic levels, particularly of the long-acting benzodiazepines. Toxic levels result from the long half-lives of these compounds along with the slow metabolic breakdown in the elderly. Slowed response, hypersomnia, and increasing confusion are sometimes thought to relate to aging when actually they are symptoms of toxic drug levels. The short-acting benzodiazepines are less likely to cause a toxic buildup but have other limitations (11).

Another complication is withdrawal symptoms that occur when the medication is abruptly discontinued as the result of hospitalization or other change in life circumstances. Even in hospitalized patients, the misuse frequently is not diagnosed. These withdrawal symptoms can be severe and may include tachycardia, hyperthermia, hypertension, altered mental states, seizures, and opisthotonos (8, 10, 12). Constant vigilance is required to avoid the development of dependence on sedative-hypnotics.

NARCOTIC ANALGESICS

Abuse of analgesics is another serious problem in the elderly. According to Whittington (13), 10% of drug toxicity in the elderly is due to narcotic analgesics, particularly propoxyphene. There is a small group of elderly who use illegally obtained drugs and a much larger group of patients who become drug dependent while being treated for various medical illnesses, most commonly various forms of arthritis. When the medication is discontinued or unavailable for whatever reason, the patient feels very uncomfortable, has difficulty sleeping, some pain, and a sense of apprehension. Resumption of the medications leads to reduction of symptoms and reinforcement of the dependency. Consistent usage without problems may continue over a period of years and only be brought to light by a fall, hospitalization, or family concern. At that point, the patient's description of the amounts taken is often different from the family's accounts or the physician's own record of amounts prescribed.

A crisis sometimes develops when the family or the physician becomes alarmed about the extent of drug misuse and makes a demand for immediate termination of the drug. This can result in considerable withdrawal discomfort and, occasionally, seizures. A gradual tapering with supportive counseling about the difficulties in helping the body readjust to a drug-free status is the easier course for the patient. Over the time of drug use, the patient may have lost the ability to distinguish between physical pain and the normal discomforts of living, i.e., boredom, frustration, hunger, loneliness, etc. Re-establishing the ability to discriminate between these sensations and enhancing the ability to tolerate discomfort would be the goals of counseling.

As with the other CNS depressant drugs, opiates can produce signs of CNS toxicity such as mental confusion and physical clumsiness that may be dismissed as normal aging (1, 2, 13).

OVER-THE-COUNTER MEDICATIONS

Over-the-counter (OTC) medications are used more frequently by the elderly than younger patients and account for two of every five drugs taken by the elderly. Arthritis, insomnia, and constipation are the most frequently self-treated conditions in this age group. Furthermore, 80% of daily OTC users also use alcohol, prescription medications, or both.

It is ironic that this population, which is the largest consumer of these medications, is at greatest risk for developing toxicities from them. These difficulties take the form of increased sensitivity to side effects, such as sedation, anticholinergic effects, and metabolic derangements.

As with alcohol and the sedative-hypnotics, serious drug interactions with OTC and prescription drugs are possible. Furthermore, drug interactions

are more likely in this older population, being both the highest consumer of both classes of drugs and biologically more vulnerable to develop complications than younger people.

When taken in sufficient amounts, these drugs can present a variety of clinical problems, ranging from gastrointestinal disorders to CNS disorders (9). Most patients do not consider these drugs to be harmful and seldom make the connection between symptom and medication. Careful history regarding onset and other medications being taken is important and often information from collateral sources such as family and friends is essential.

INTERVENTION

The attitude of the clinician is the most important variable in the actions taken after diagnosis of alcoholism or drug abuse has been made. Optimism and expectation of success is essential to combat the natural pessimism of the elderly patient.

There needs to be an accurate assessment of the stage of the problem that would indicate the level of intensity of intervention required. Early stages are those that are relatively new, without major complications, and with no indications of previous assistance. These patients respond to education about medical effects along with information about the manner in which dependence upon alcohol and drugs can develop without the individual being aware of what is happening. In this manner, the patient is helped to recognize what has happened and then to take responsibility for the management of this condition.

Midstage problems are those in which there has been some attempt at help without success. The complications are more serious and the situation is not getting better. These patients may require referral for specific alcohol or drug abuse counseling or attendance at self-help groups such as Alcoholics Anonymous or Narcotics Anonymous. These groups can be a valuable source of information and aid in helping the patient both to confirm the presence of a problem and to strive for abstinence.

Later stages of these problems are identified when efforts at help have failed, the symptoms are becoming unmanageable or even dangerous, and the patient's denial may be complete. At this point, hospitalization for detoxification is necessary as well as more intensive education and restructuring of the patient's life-style.

Threats, exhortations, and dire predictions have not been found to be very effective. The use of the family with whatever leverage can be brought to bear is frequently the key factor in getting a patient reluctantly to accept necessary help. Contrary to popular myth, patients forced into treatment against their will frequently do very well, particularly when the noxious effects of the alcohol or the drug have been removed and the individual can get a clearer perception of his or her own situation. The clear message that the family has no intention of tolerating the gradual decline of their family member is also therapeutic.

TREATMENT

As in all other conditions, the elderly tend to get treatment for alcohol and drug problems from their primary care provider usually in the form of education and encouragement (6). The use of inpatient units specifically designated for alcohol or drug abuse is increasing, but slowly.

There is an underutilization of available treatment resources, which is particularly unfortunate since the elderly respond very well to these programs. The reasons for underutilization include resistance on the part of patients and their families and some perception that only younger people ought to make such an investment in their own health. Experience in the treatment field is contrary to this; indeed, there are increasing numbers of patients whose lives have greatly improved by appropriate treatment programs. This fact is coupled with the testimony of families who experience even a few months of their parent's sobriety before their death as compared to families who regretfully remember that the parent died without ever regaining sobriety. It appears that the length of recovery is less important than the fact of recovery.

Several major research projects are underway to document more clearly the role of structuring of time in retirement and the development of problems with alcohol and drug abuse (5). The treatment programs that emphasize this aspect report considerable success in helping elderly patients restructure their lives to exclude uses of alcohol or other drugs.

Alcoholics Anonymous groups with attention to needs of the aged are increasing with greater appreciation for their effectiveness. Health clinics, retirement communities, and senior citizen centers are encouraging the formation of these groups and there are increasing numbers of daytime meetings with smoking restrictions and good transportation access. Frequently it is not sufficient simply to refer a patient and family to Alcoholics Anonymous. It may be necessary that the referrer know the location of appropriate meetings and a contact person. It is then possible to encourage the patient to attend several different meetings and to return to discuss the meetings that were attended, often focusing upon indications of resistance. This extra bit of reinforcement frequently makes the difference in whether or not a patient follows up on the original referral.

Finally, it is important to help the patient to see alcoholism and drug abuse as chronic conditions with a propensity for relapse that necessitates constant vigilance. Relapse, when addressed quickly and appropriately, need not be seen as destroying the whole recovery process, but rather as a slight aberration that needs to be quickly corrected.

REFERENCES

1. Atkinson RM, Kofoed LL: Alcohol and drug abuse in old age. In Walsh CC (Ed): *Geriatric Medicine Vol. II: Fundamentals of Geriatric Care.* New York, Springer-Verlag, 1984.
2. Atkinson RM: Substance use and abuse in late life. In Atkinson RM (Ed): *Alcohol and Drug Abuse in Old Age.* Washington, D.C., American Psychiatric Association Press, 1984.
3. Blum L, Rosner F: Alcoholism in the elderly: An analysis of 50 patients. *J Nat Med Assoc* 75:489, 1983.
4. Cassem NH: Alcoholism. In Rubenstein E, Federman DD (Eds): *Scientific American Medicine.* New York, Scientific American, 1986.
5. Dupree LW, Broskowski H, Schanfeld L: The Gerontology Alcohol Project: A behavioral treatment program for elderly alcohol abusers. *Gerontologist* 10:510, 1984.
6. German PS, Shapiro S, Shinner EA: Mental health of the elderly: Use of health and mental services. *J Geriatr Soc* 33:246, 1985.
7. Gomberg ES: Alcohol use and alcohol problems among the elderly. In *Alcohol and Health Mongograph #4.* Special Population Issue. Rockville, MD, NIAAA, 1982.
8. Hartford JR, Damorajski T: Alcoholism in the geriatric population. *J Am Geriatr Soc* 30:18, 1982.
9. Kofoed LL: OTC drug overuse in the elderly: What to watch for. *Geriatrics* 40:55, 1985.
10. Miller F, Whitcup S, Sacks M, Lynch PE: Unrecognized drug dependence and withdrawal in the elderly. *Drug and Alcohol Dependence* 15:177, 1985.
11. Salzman, C. Treatment of insomnia in the elderly. *Clinical Geriatric Psychopharmacology.* New York, McGraw Hill, Inc., 1984, p. 149.
12. Speirs CJ, Navey FL, Broods DJ, Impallomeni MG: Opisthotonos and benzodiazepine withdrawal in the elderly. *Lancet* 2:1101, 1986.
13. Whittington FJ: Misuse of legal drugs and compliance with prescription directions. In Glantz MD, Peterson DM, Whittington FJ (Eds): *Drugs and the Elderly Adult.* Washington, D.C., National Institute on Drug Abuse, 1983.
14. Zimberg S. Alcoholism in the elderly: A serious but solvable problem. *Postgrad Med* 74:165, 171, 1983.

CHAPTER 14

Evaluation and Management of the Confused, Disoriented, or Demented Elderly Patient

WILLIAM REICHEL
PETER V. RABINS

One of the most common problems facing the physician today is evaluating and managing the elderly patient with cognitive and behavioral disturbances. This chapter focuses mainly on three neuropsychiatric disorders: the patient with acute confusion, disorientation or delirium; the patient with dementia or generalized cognitive loss; and the patient with an emotional or psychiatric disorder. Of course, there are often mixed forms or combinations of each of these clinical entities. Proper diagnosis of these specific neuropsychiatric disorders is essential to make specific treatment plans.

Additional recent information and perspectives on the epidemiology and etiology of the most common form of dementia—senile dementia of the Alzheimer type—are contained in an addendum at the end of this chapter.

The physician evaluating a person who complains of memory difficulty must identify correctly individuals with minor age-related memory impairments. These do not require an extensive evaluation but should be recognized as reflecting minor nondisease-related changes.

AGE-ASSOCIATED MEMORY IMPAIRMENT

What was previously called "benign senescent forgetfulness" has been called "age-associated memory impairment" (10). This condition is characterized by complaints of memory impairment in carrying out activities of daily life, supported by evidence of such impairment on psychologic performance tests. This term is applied to individuals over 50 years of age, although this does not mean that such problems are not possible in younger adults. It is characterized by difficulty in remembering names of individuals on meeting them; misplacing spectacles or keys; difficulty remembering tasks to be performed; and difficulty in remembering telephone numbers. The onset of memory loss is described as gradual, without worsening in recent months.

DELIRIUM OR ACUTE CONFUSIONAL STATE

The elderly patient often presents with acute confusion, delirium, disorientation, or other behavioral alterations (Table 14.1). When this is accompanied by an altered level of consciousness, that is, by

Table 14.1
Differential Diagnosis and Treatment of Delirium (or Acute Confusional State) and Dementia

Delirium or Acute Confusional State	Dementia
Differential diagnosis:	
May be secondary to:	Causes include:
Myocardial infarction	Senile dementia of he
Dehydration	Alzheimer type (pri-
Pneumonia	mary degenerative
Ischemia mainly in	dementia)
basilar-posterior	Multi-infarct dementia
cerebral artery	Normal pressure hy-
territory	drocephalus
Fecal impaction	Myxedema
Gastrointestinal	Hyper/hypopara-
hemorrhage	thyroidism
Electrolyte imbalance	Cushing's/Addison's
Urinary tract infection	disease
Pulmonary embolism	Pernicious anemia
Heart failure	Folic acid deficiency
Occult malignancy	Chronic hepatic en-
Drug intoxication	cephalopathy
Drug withdrawal	Chronic drug intoxi-
Alcohol intoxication	cation
Alcohol withdrawal or	Chronic subdural he-
abstinence states	matoma
Other hidden medical	Brain tumor
problems	General paresis
	Parkinson's disease
	Wilson's disease
	Pick's disease
	Huntington's chorea
	Creutzfeldt-Jakob
	disease
	Punchdrunk syndrome
	or dementia pugilis-
	tica
Treatment	Depression
Proper recognition and	Proper recognition and
management of the	management of the
underlying medical	underlying neuro-
disorder or drug	logic disorder
problem	
Reassurance, frequent	Recognition and treatment
reorientation, good	of associated medical
lighting, moderately	and behavioral
stimulating environment	disorders
	Family support

inattention, drowsiness, or hypervigilance, a diagnosis of delirium is made (2). Previously known as "acute brain syndrome," delirium is often accompanied by hallucinations, fluctuations in memory and behavior, and disordered sleep. Abrupt change in any patient from his or her customary state of sen-

sorium, intellectual function, or consciousness should be investigated thoroughly for a possible organic disorder.

The problem may result from almost any physical ailment or drug problem. For example, heart attack, dehydration, urinary tract infection, pneumonia, fecal impaction, pulmonary embolism, gastrointestinal hemorrhage, and many types of drug intoxication and drug withdrawal all cause delirium or acute confusional states. Such confusional states are often transient and reversible. The geriatric patient with relatively recent changes in mental status is not suffering from dementia or chronic brain syndrome (Table 14.1), which is characterized by the gradual deterioration of intellectual function, memory, or cognitive ability in a normally alert individual. In making the diagnosis of dementia, it is necessary to document intellectual decline and loss of memory over a period of months to years.

An illustration of an acute confusional state might be a 73-year-old woman who took care of her household, performing all her usual duties until 3 days prior to her presentation to a hospital emergency room. She appeared confused, agitated, and restless. There were no other medical complaints, but an electrocardiogram revealed an anteroseptal myocardial infarction. Following an initially difficult course in a coronary care unit, she eventually improved and at the time of discharge showed no signs of mental dysfunction.

DEMENTIA

In contrast, a case of dementia (2) is exemplified by an 80-year-old man who presents with a 1½-year history of significant memory loss and inability to care for himself. The family has been concerned about his recent failure to recognize his own relatives and an increased tendency to wander astray. Examination demonstrates that he is markedly forgetful, not remembering conversations from one minute to the next. He has no recall of recent events and recall of events in the remote past is blurred. Neurologic examination is normal. His affect is not blunted and he appears very pleasant. The patient is doing well in a nursing home setting.

In the symptom/sign complex of dementia (called chronic brain syndrome in DSM-I), the patient initially may experience diminishing ability to concentrate and recall recent events. As the illness progresses, judgment becomes impaired and conversation difficult. Family members may be the first to notice the disorder, but the gradual course of the disease often permits the patient some insight into his or her condition and may give rise to irritability, anxiety, or depression. He or she may become unable to perform usual occupational or household duties. Eventually, remote memory may be affected and the patient can no longer recognize family members or friends. In the final stages, the patient is rendered totally incapable of caring for himself.

TESTING COGNITIVE FUNCTION

It is imperative in testing for dementia that the physician or other health professional evaluate the intellectual functions of the patient. Remote memory is preserved to a greater degree than recent memory. Impairment of remote memory carries a more grave prognosis than the loss of recent memory alone. The mental acuity of the geriatric patient is also affected by socioeconomic factors and the accessibility of interpersonal communication and audiovisual stimuli, such as newspaper, radio, or television. In the absence of sufficient exposure to the external environment, it may be quite difficult for the elderly patient to answer common test questions, such as the identity of past or present American presidents.

The Mini-Mental State Exam, developed by Folstein et al. (18), is an easily administered screening exam that measures orientation, memory, concentration, and language (Table 14.2). Another instrument, the Short Portable Mental Status Questionnaire, developed by Pfeiffer (36), provides a screening examination that tests short- and long-term memory, capacity to perform serial mathematical tasks, and orientation. It is easy to perform and score, is portable, and requires little time to administer (Table 14.3).

In addition, it is imperative that the health professional be able to verify the answers provided by the patient to questions in the mental status examination. This goal is usually accomplished with the aid of the children, spouse, or other relatives or friends of the patient. If such substantiation is not possible, a different type of test becomes necessary. Asking the patient to repeat a short series of words or numbers in a limited time framework may be particularly efficacious, although this test evaluates a different form of memory. The health professional should also ask questions about home and work that can be verified by family. Questions about recent news or sporting events, or even the weather, can be very revealing.

DIFFERENTIATING EMOTIONAL DISORDER FROM DEMENTIA

In the interview, the health professional must differentiate from functional or emotional distur-

bances that resemble dementia. An individual experiencing depression after the loss of a spouse may present the appearance of dementia. On further examination, it becomes evident that the patient is extremely depressed. Hidden depression should be considered in the evaluation of all patients with apparent dementia.

It can be difficult to differentiate between dementia accompanied by some reactive depression and depression with some cognitive loss secondary to the depression. There are certain clinical situations in which it is simply too difficult to separate these two entities. When faced with this dilemma, a therapeutic trial with an antidepressant medication is useful in order to separate dementia and depression. However, in most cases, with skillful interviewing technique, the physician should be able to determine what diagnostic category or cluster is predominant. The cluster of symptoms and signs is usually clear. The physician's interviewing skills should, in most cases, determine whether he or she is dealing principally with a loss of intellectual capacity, with a functional disorder, or with some mixture of both.

A great deal of attention has been given to the condition called "pseudodementia" (48). Wells made the point that, in the past, the diagnosis of pseudodementia had been made largely after the unanticipated recovery of a patient who had previously been diagnosed as suffering from dementia. According to Wells, early recognition of pseudodementia allows the prediction of improvement or recovery in contrast to the negative prognosis of most patients with dementia. Wells (48) noted that in pseudodementia the history of previous psychiatric dysfunction is common. In pseudodementia, the onset of the illness can usually be dated with precision, and the symptoms are of short duration before medical help is sought. The patient usually complains to a greater degree of cognitive loss in pseudodementia than in dementia, and will communicate a strong sense of distress. Rabins et al. (39) also demonstrated that dementia due to depression can be recognized by its subacute onset, occurrence in persons with a past history of depression, coexistence with hypochondriacal depressive preoccupations, and weight loss.

Finlayson and Martin (16) suggested that the term pseudodementia has value in describing certain aspects of depression that deserve emphasis because of the common tendency to overlook a potentially treatable condition. Wells' 1979 paper (48) reported the occurrence of pseudodementia with a variety of psychiatric diagnoses. Other functional or emotional disturbances that may give the impression of organic dementia include paranoid states. On proper questioning, the patient with this prob-

CLINICAL ASPECTS OF AGING

Table 14.2
The Mini-Mental State Exam (MMS)

Maximum Score	Score	
		ORIENTATION
5	( )	1. What is the (year) (season) (date) (day) (month)?
5	( )	2. Where are we: (state) (county) (town) (hospital) (floor)?
		REGISTRATION
3	( )	3. Name 3 objects: 1 second to say each. Then ask the patient all 3 after you have said them.
		Give 1 point for each correct answer. Then repeat them until he learns all 3. Count trials and record.
		Trials
		ATTENTION AND CALCULATION
5	( )	4. Serial 7's. 1 point for each correct. Stop after 5 answers. Alternatively, spell "world" backwards, if cannot subtract.
		RECALL
3	( )	5. Ask for 3 objects repeated above. Give 1 point for each correct.
		LANGUAGE
9	( )	6. Name a pencil, and watch (2 points)
		7. Repeat the following "No ifs, ands or buts" (1 point)
		8. Follow a 3-stage command: "Take a paper in your right hand, fold it in half, and put it on the floor." (3 points)
		9. Read and obey the following: "Close your eyes" (1 point)
		10. Write a sentence. (1 point)
		11. Copy design. (1 point)

TOTAL SCORE

1. 1 point for each correct answer.

2. 1 point for each correct answer.

3. 1 point for each of the 3 object names that is correctly repeated the first time. Then repeat them until all 3 are repeated but give no further points.

4. 1 point for each correct subtraction. If the patient does not or cannot make any subtractions have him spell the word "world" backwards. If an attempted subtraction is made this is the preferred task.

5. 1 point for each object.

6. 1 point for each correctly named object. Give no points if an approximate but incorrect word is used.

7. 1 point if completely and correctly completed.

8. 1 point for each command followed.

9. 1 point only if the patient carries out the activity. No points if the sentence is read correctly but the act is not done.

10. Sentence should be grammatically correct and have subject, verb and predicate.

11. 1 point if each figure has 5 sides and the overlap is correct.

Table 14.3
The Short Portable Mental Status Questionnaire (SPMSQ)

SHORT PORTABLE MENTAL STATUS QUESTIONNAIRE (SPMSQ)
Eric Pfeiffer, M.D.

Instructions: Ask questions 1–10 in this list and record all answers. Ask question 4A only if patient does not have a telephone. Record total number of errors based on ten questions.

+	−	
		1. What is the date today?_____
		Month Day Year
		2. What day of the week is it?_____
		3. What is the name of this place?_____
		4. What is your telephone number?_____
		4A. What is your street address?_____
		(Ask only if patient does not have a telephone)
		5. How old are you?_____
		6. When were you born?_____
		7. Who is the President of the U.S. now?_____
		8. Who was President just before him?_____
		9. What was your mother's maiden name?_____
		10. Subtract 3 from 20 and keep subtracting 3 from each new number, all the way down.
		Total Number of Errors

To Be Completed by Interviewer

Patient's Name: _____ Date: _____

Sex: 1. Male   Race: 1. White
         2. Female   2. Black
                            3. Other

Years of Education: _____ 1. Grade School
                                    2. High School
                                    3. Beyond High School

Interviewer's Name: _____

INSTRUCTIONS FOR COMPLETION OF
THE SHORT PORTABLE MENTAL STATUS QUESTIONNAIRE (SPMSQ)

Ask the subject questions 1 through 10 in this list and record all answers. All responses to be scored correct must be given by subject without reference to calendar, newspaper, birth certificate, or other aid to memory.

Question 1 is to be scored correctly only when the exact month, exact date, and the exact year are given correctly. Question 2 is self-explanatory.

Table 14.3 *continued*

Question 3 should be scored correctly if any correct description of the location is given. "My home," correct name of the town or city of residence, or the name of hospital or institution if subject is institutionalized, are all acceptable.

Question 4 should be scored correctly when the correct telephone number can be verified, or when the subject can repeat the same number at another point in the questioning.

Question 5 is scored correct when stated age corresponds to date of birth.

Question 6 is to be scored correctly only when the month, exact date, and year are all given.

Question 7 requires only the last name of the President.

Question 8 requires only the last name of the previous President.

Question 9 does not need to be verified. It is scored correct if a female first name plus a last name other than subject's last name is given.

Question 10 requires that the entire series must be performed correctly in order to be scored as correct. Any error in the series or unwillingness to attempt the series is scored as incorrect.

SCORING OF THE SHORT PORTABLE MENTAL STATUS QUESTIONNAIRE (SPMSQ)

The data suggest that both education and race influence performance on the Mental Status Questionnaire and they must accordingly be taken into account in evaluating the score attained by an individual.

For purposes of scoring, three educational levels have been established: a) persons who have had only a grade school education; b) persons who have had any high school education or who have completed high school; c) persons who have had any education beyond the high school level, including college, graduate school or business school.

For white subjects with at least some high school education, but not more than high school education, the following criteria have been established:

0–2 ERRORS	INTACT INTELLECTUAL FUNCTIONING
3–4 ERRORS	MILD INTELLECTUAL IMPAIRMENT
5–7 ERRORS	MODERATE INTELLECTUAL IMPAIRMENT
8–10 ERRORS	SEVERE INTELLECTUAL IMPAIRMENT

Allow one more error if subject has had only a grade school education.
Allow one less error if subject has had education beyond high school.
Allow one more error for black subjects, using identical education criteria.

lem reveals his or her paranoid ideation. Similarly, the individual suffering from sensory deprivation may give the appearance of a demented state. Elderly patients living alone with no visitors, dim lighting, and no other means of communication may demonstrate abnormal behavior that improves with a resocialization program with increased psychologic stimuli.

IMPORTANCE OF DIFFERENTIATING VARIOUS NEUROPSYCHIATRIC DISORDERS

It is by means of a thorough history, interview, and physical examination that the various types of neuropsychiatric disorders may be differentiated. Is this syndrome representative of a delirious or acute confusional reaction with diminished alertness and recent onset caused by medical illness or drug toxicity? Does the history reveal a gradual and progressive decline in the intellectual function and memory? Is the presenting disorder chiefly functional or emotional, a disorder of affect, such as in the case of an elderly patient with recent onset of depression. It is essential for the physician to understand the underlying illness in order to be of benefit to the patient who presents with a neuropsychiatric disturbance. Treatment of the acute confusional state, dementia, or functional illness is based upon the proper recognition and management of the underlying problem. Of course, there are also mixed combinations of these three types of disorders. In mixed cases, the treatment is based upon the proper recognition and management of the several underlying problems.

COMMON DISEASE STATES WHICH CAUSE DEMENTIA

A careful consideration of the causes of dementia is appropriate (Table 14.1). In the past, many thought that most cases of dementia were arteriosclerotic in origin. In fact, it is now known that only one-fourth of all dementia is arteriosclerotic. The elderly demented individual merits complete evaluation to determine the cause of this problem. The most common form of dementia (approximately 60% of cases of organic dementia in the elderly) is senile dementia of the Alzheimer type, called primary degenerative dementia in DSM-III-R (2). The second most common cause is multi-infarct or arteriosclerotic dementia which comprises approximately 25% of the cases of dementia in the elderly. Some patients show clinical and pathologic features of both senile dementia of the Alzheimer type and multi-infarct dementia.

SENILE DEMENTIA OF THE ALZHEIMER TYPE

Senile dementia of the Alzheimer type is characterized by memory loss and a deficit of at least one other cognitive skill (33). At an ultrastructural level, the neuropathologist finds senile plaques and Alzheimer's neurofibrillary tangles.[1] The senile or neuritic plaque consists of a group of degenerating nerve processes including axons and dendrites surrounding an amyloid core, suggesting a role for immunologic processes in the pathogenesis of this lesion. The neurofibrillary tangle is an intracellular lesion consisting of a tangled mass of abnormal cytoplasmic fibrils. Both neurofibrillary tangles and neuritic (senile) plaques are found in small numbers in the hippocampus of most elderly individuals, but they are found with increased frequency in both the neocortex and hippocampus in patients suffering senile dementia of the Alzheimer type. Tomlinson and Henderson (47) demonstrated that the concentration of these lesions is strongly correlated with the degree of dementia.

In diagnosing different types of dementia, the computerized tomogram (CT) of the brain is extremely valuable. The CT scan is important in the diagnosis of multi-infarct dementia, normal pressure hydrocephalus, brain tumor, and subdural

hematoma. The CT scan provides information regarding the degree of atrophy of the brain, but this information is not diagnostic of Alzheimer's disease.

Although the CT scan was originally believed to provide an accurate assessment of the degree of atrophy of the brain, it is clear that dementia remains a clinical syndrome; the diagnosis must be based on history, evaluation of mental and behavioral status, and the evaluation of the total clinical picture. It has been recognized that there are patients with radiographic signs of atrophy and no dementia. In these individuals, the radiographic findings may represent gross pathologic alterations but are not accompanied by the ultrastructural changes of senile dementia of the Alzheimer type. Conversely, there are patients with dementia with absence of cerebral atrophy as noted by CT scan. Huckman et al. (26) pointed out that absence of brain atrophy in the demented patient should alert the physician to a potentially treatable cause of dementia. Ford and Winter (19) suggested that CT evidence of cortical atrophy in the elderly should not be accepted as evidence of senile dementia; specifically, the presence or absence of brain atrophy should not preclude a vigorous search for potentially reversible causes of dementia, nor should radiologic findings of atrophy or ventricular enlargement be considered pathognomonic of dementia. We do not yet have good longitudinal data on the CT scan of the brain in an aging population. More information will be required in the future to determine the usefulness of the CT scan in the diagnosis of clear-cut senile dementia of the Alzheimer type in the elderly population.

It is unclear whether onset of the Alzheimer type of dementia before age 60 years is different than the late onset form. While they are pathologically similar, the early onset cases may progress more rapidly and have a stronger family history (44).

MULTI-INFARCT DEMENTIA

Multi-infarct or arteriosclerotic dementia may occur after repeated cerebrovascular accidents. The symptoms of vascular disease are episodic, based on the history of recurrent stroke. The neurologic findings of vascular disease are focal, usually accompanied by signs of motor weakness, sensory loss, or reflex change. Hypertension and/or diabetes are often present and a CT scan may demonstrate multiple small subcortical infarcts. Repeated episodes of cerebral infarction are thought to be requisite for arteriosclerotic dementia. Gross examination of the brain shows evidence of cerebral softening secondary to the vascular insults.

---

[1]Alois Alzheimer first presented his clinical and neuropathologic findings regarding a 51-year-old woman at a meeting of the South West German Society of Alienists in Tübingen in November 1906. His report was noted by title only in the *Neurologische Zentralblatt* in 1906 and more fully in the *Allgemeine Zeitschrift für Psychiatrie* in 1907.

The woman's symptoms consisted of loss of memory and disorientation. Within 5 years, she suffered severe dementia and death. Her brain was found to be atrophied and, using a method of silver impregnation, a specific clumping and distortion of the cortical neurofibrils was noted which is now associated with Alzheimer's name.

PSEUDOBULBAR PALSY

The syndrome of pseudobulbar palsy may be found in the hypertensive patient who has suffered a series of small strokes. It is characterized by a labile facies with sporadic outbursts of laughter and weeping, and moderate dysarthria and dysphagia. Signs of a bilateral upper motor neuron paralysis can be found on neurologic examination.

OTHER CAUSES OF DEMENTIA

As mentioned previously, senile dementia of the Alzheimer type and multi-infarct or arteriosclerotic dementia are the two most common causes of intellectual loss. According to autopsy findings, approximately 60% of cases of organic dementia in the elderly are associated with the neuropathologic findings of senile dementia of the Alzheimer type. The second major cause of dementia among the aged is infarction of brain tissue due to cerebrovascular disease; this group comprises 25% of the cases of dementia in the elderly. Other causes of dementia include general paresis, Huntington's chorea, Pick's disease, Parkinson's disease, acquired immune deficiency syndrome, Wilson's disease, chronic drug intoxication, Creutzfeldt-Jakob disease, folic acid deficiency, myxedema, chronic drug intoxication, and pernicious anemia (Table 14.1). Obviously depression, folic acid deficiency, myxedema, chronic drug intoxication, and pernicious anemia are treatable causes of dementia.

NORMAL PRESSURE HYDROCEPHALUS

In 1965, Hakim, Adams, and associates at Harvard described a new form of dementia that is surgically correctable, at least in some cases. The classic triad of gait disturbance, progressive dementia, and urinary or fecal incontinence is found in normal pressure hydrocephalus. The diagnosis of normal pressure hydrocephalus should always be suspected if gait disturbance is a predominant feature in a demented patient. CT of the brain reveals significant ventricular enlargement, without cortical atrophy. Computerized axial tomography and the cisternal scan are useful diagnostically, but are not specific and diagnosis still can be difficult even when these two tests are performed. Severe apathy is common. The evaluation of the total clinical picture is the most important diagnostic measure. Striking improvement may follow a shunt operation, but response to shunt therapy is difficult to predict.

It should be noted that patients with normal pressure hydrocephalus secondary to head trauma, meningitis, or subarachnoid hemorrhage are more readily diagnosed and respond very well to shunt therapy, in comparison to patients with idiopathic normal pressure hydrocephalus, where the pathology is not known and response to therapy is often variable. Idiopathic normal pressure hydrocephalus is uncommon (27). It should also be noted that surgical outcome is better where the clinical picture is recognized early and conforms most closely to the classical triad of gait disturbance, dementia, and urinary incontinence.

Normal pressure hydrocephalus should be especially considered if there is a history of dementia following a head injury in an elderly individual. Trauma to the head can cause both chronic subdural hematoma and normal pressure hydrocephalus in the elderly.

SEARCHING FOR REVERSIBLE DISEASE

It is clear that there are certain correctable forms of dementia in the elderly. The physician must decide which cases of dementia are worth investigating for any of these possible causes, such as myxedema or normal pressure hydrocephalus. Failure to recognize a correctable cause may result in the establishment of an irreversible or end-state dementia. The physician may not wish to undertake a major evaluation if the situation offers little hope of correction. In an 85-year-old individual with a 4-year history of severe dementia and other serious illnesses and a history of absolutely poor general function preceding the onset of dementia, one may not feel compelled to aggressively pursue a major diagnostic workup. But certainly the physician should at all times be alerted to the possibility of a correctable disorder. Good judgment becomes the final arbiter in determining the appropriate extent of diagnostic evaluation. The tell-tale signs of myxedema, a history of recent head trauma, or the presence of low serum concentrations of vitamin B_{12} or folate would be signals for the practicing physician that the patient's dementia might be reversible (Tables 14.1 and 14.4).

It is difficult to prescribe a cookbook formula for the evaluation of reversible dementia. If the physician is alerted to the possibility of a correctable disorder, then good judgment and common sense will determine the extent of diagnostic assessment. It is most helpful if the physician has known the patient over a period of time.

A physician, integrating all available history, mental status examination, physical examination, laboratory and other clinical information, will rec-

Table 14.4
The Evaluation of Possible Reversible Dementia

Historical questions of diagnostic importance
  Duration and progression of illness
    Long-term
    Recent
    Recent on top of long-term
    Slow insidious progression versus step-wise
      progression
  Medication and alcohol use
  Gait disturbance and urinary incontinence
  Previous cerebrovascular accidents, head injury,
    subarachnoid hemorrhage, subdural hematoma
  Emotional or behavioral history
    Depression
    Paranoia
    Sensory deprivation
    Agitation
    Lethargy/listlessness
  Family history of dementia
  Other major associated illnesses
    Cardiovascular
    Pulmonary
    Hepatic
    Malignancy
    Neurologic
  Complete physical examination
  Basic diagnostic studies
    Psychologic or mental status evaluation
    Complete blood count
    Chemistry profile
    Chest x-ray
    Urinalysis
    Electrocardiogram
    CT brain scan
    Electroencephalogram
    Thyroid function studies
    Serologic test for syphilis
    Serum folate level
    Serum vitamin B_{12} level
  Special examinations in selected cases
  Magnetic resonance imaging
  Cisternal scan
  Lumbar puncture
  Heavy metals and or toxicology screening
  Blood ammonia level

ognize certain clusters suggesting reversible or irreversible dementia. Gait disturbance, dementia, and urinary incontinence suggest normal pressure hydrocephalus. Trauma and change in consciousness suggest subdural hematoma. A fluctuating state of consciousness, inconsistent neurologic findings, and a negative CT scan suggest a metabolic encephalopathy. Dementia and ataxia and peripheral neuropathy suggest the possibility of chronic alcoholism. Some very simple conditions in the elderly, such as hearing loss or sleep deprivation may mimic the presence of dementia.

Table 14.4 describes various tests that are helpful in assessing the patient for reversible dementia. The history is of major diagnostic importance. It is helpful if family members or other significant individuals can assist in providing a good history. Is the problem long-term or recent? Is it recent on top of a more long-term problem? How rapidly is the problem progressing? Is there history of head trauma? Gait disturbance? Urinary incontinence? Recent or past emotional disturbance, such as depression? Family history of dementia? Other major associated illness, such as cardiovascular or hepatic disease? Significant medications and/or alcohol use? Drug use remains one of the most common problems causing both acute confusional states and dementia.

In checking the psychologic or mental status evaluation, a screening test such a the Mini-Mental State Exam or the Short Portable Mental Status Questionnaire (as described previously) is useful. It can also be useful in following cognitive status over time.

Complete blood count with indices; chemistry profile, including serum calcium, electrolytes, liver function, glucose, blood urea nitrogen and creatinine; chest x-ray; urinalysis; and electrocardiogram are basic diagnostic studies in most new cases of dementia. At this time, CT brain scan, electroencephalogram (EEG), thyroid function test, serologic test for syphilis, serum folate and vitamin B_{12} levels are also indicated. (The EEG is most valuable in the diagnosis of a metabolic encephalopathy; if normal, the EEG certainly tends to exclude a metabolic encephalopathy and suggests the presence of another potentially treatable cause of dementia). In selected cases magnetic resonance imaging, heavy metal screens, toxicology screens, cisternal scan, lumbar puncture, and blood ammonia might be indicated. Again, it is very difficult to reduce this type of judgment to a fixed algorithm or protocol in a cookbook fashion.

A potentially important diagnostic tool in the future may be positron emission tomography (PET), a brain scan that allows the actual visualization of brain metabolic activity (40). PET imaging procedures have provided an accurate diagnosis of well-established Alzheimer's disease and multi-infarct dementia. However, PET facilities have principally been limited to research settings. Single photon emission CT, a CT nuclear medicine scan, may also provide an accurate test for the diagnosis of dementia and is more clinically available (4). SPECT may soon provide information similar to that provided by PET with increased use in many regional medical centers.

IRREVERSIBLE DEMENTIA: HELPING THE PATIENT AND FAMILY

What can be offered the patient with dementia in which reversible causes are not apparent? Here the physician and other health professionals face a complex and difficult situation. Although cure is not possible, the health professional can do much to improve the patient's and family's condition. Previously, many patients with dementia were committed to state mental institutions. At present, with prudent evaluation provided by both the physician or specialized geriatric evaluation services, one could hope to maintain the patient in his or her own home with certain supports or in the community at a nursing home or in a day care program.

A study carried out in Maryland (24, 41, 42) demonstrated the plight of the caregiver of patients with dementing illnesses and noted significant service gaps. Using survey instruments designed for 16 target populations in Maryland (caregivers; physicians; nursing homes; training institutions; public and private service agencies; law enforcement agencies; insurance companies; etc.), the study showed significant need in the areas of respite care out of the home and information and referral services. A highlight of the survey findings was the overwhelming judgment from all categories of respondents that in-home respite care was not adequately provided. Overall, those who reported inadequacy of the service outnumbered those who deemed it adequate by 10:1. Among caregivers, the ratio catapulted to over twice that magnitude. By more than a 3:1 ratio, respondents judged adult day care provisions to be inadequate. It was noted that at the time of the study, 11 of Maryland's 24 counties did have an adult day care program. In other words, 13 counties in Maryland did not have an adult day care center. It was also noted that the shortage of such a sought-after resource is, in part, a consequence of limited readiness of adult day care centers to admit victims with dementing illness. This is because they require closer supervision, entailing a higher staff ratio and greater staff stress. In addition, financial capability to purchase this service can be a barrier.

Throughout the United States, geriatric assessment programs are being developed in many cities, related to hospitals or long-term care facilities, county health departments, and even as independent organizations. In many hospitals, geriatric assessment programs are part of a full spectrum of geriatric services, including home care, day care, information and referral services, etc. There should be little difficulty in most metropolitan areas for a physician to find consultative support from a specialized geriatric evaluation service as a means of helping both the dementia victim and his or her family members or caregivers.

Important considerations in the evaluation include the presence of firearms and gas ovens in the home. Does the patient wander and get lost? Are there children in the family or in the neighborhood who might be harmed by the patient? How are medications handled in the home? Can they be locked up and dispensed under the control of another adult? The health of the relative or relatives of the elderly demented patient is an extremely important factor. Is the health of the spouse holding up under stress of caring for the patient? Is there a physician and/or nurse providing care to the patient? Finally, financial affairs must be considered and it may fall upon the family and personal physician to decide issues of guardianship and incompetency.

Should the patient with dementia be hospitalized, there are several practical aspects that should be noted. Restraining devices should be avoided if possible. At night, the bed rails should be left down, a light should be on, and the patient ideally should not be too far from the bathroom. Placing the patient where he or she can be observed by the nurse is helpful. Admission to the hospital is another opportunity to re-evaluate all previous medications. It is always helpful if one knows the basis for the patient's being started on such medications as digoxin, thyroid medication, or Dilantin. One is always reluctant to discontinue medication that has been in use for 15 or 20 years. In any case, the physician should attempt to reduce medications to those which seem necessary and logical at the time. Certain drugs, such as Dilantin, may have to be discontinued on a gradual or tapered basis.

One should be cautious in the use of psychotropic medications in dementia. Adverse effects may occur, including worsening of the patient's mental status, resulting in chronic oversedation with additional complications of dehydration, pneumonia, and bed sores. A vicious cycle of worsening of the patient's mental status, triggering further use of medications and restraining devices, should be avoided.

Social interaction should be made to help the patient maintain his orientation, utilizing newspaper, calendars, clocks, and radio and television wherever appropriate. The patient's name and the names of significant others should be used in conversation, in addition to reinforcing other aspects of time and location.

Understanding the impact of dementia on the family is of the greatest importance (38). The family faced with caring for a member with dementia will experience feelings of anger, depression, fatigue, guilt, and shame. The family may be struggling to cope with such problems as catastrophic reactions (uncontrolled agitation precipitated by task failure), communication disorders, waking at night, suspiciousness, significant memory failure, and wandering. Families may be troubled by a poor understanding of the disease; isolation and a trapped feeling; anger and fear about the patient's behavior; feelings of loss of self-identity; role reversal (where the adult child now is taking care of the parent in place of the parent looking after the child); fears about heredity; and simply handling a condition that has become unmanageable. Of course, the family having difficulty coping with such problems is similar to other families in crisis (29). There are similarities of families caring for the dementia patient with those families facing the care of a family member with chronic schizophrenia, substance addiction, cancer, and mental retardation. In all these situations, increasing the family's support system will be beneficial (8). Caplan (8) makes the point that families and individuals can be helped in mastering most types of stressful situations by receiving social support.

The physician and other health professionals are in a key position to help family members caring for patients with dementia. These families often turn to physicians for evaluation, advice, and emotional support. There are a number of appropriate interventions that can be readily provided to families experiencing the significant stress of becoming caregivers to a family member with dementia. All these interventions should maximize the patient's level of functioning and quality of life for both the patient and the family or caregiver.

A number of important functions in the physicians' management of dementia can be suggested (3, 14, 32, 43). Physicians should provide specific information to the family about the nature of dementing illness. Physicians can help the family understand that even the best efforts of health professionals may not lead to the patient's improvement. They can instruct the family to let the patient do all that he or she is able to do and encourage the family to increase the patient's activities. They can point out to the family ways to balance the patient's needs with the family's needs, e.g., encouraging the family to utilize community services, including adult day care centers, or home health aides or sitters in the home. They can teach the family more effective ways of communicating with the patient, e.g., not to overload the patient with instructions or complex series of tasks, but instead to offer the patient a simplified message; or to avoid logical arguments when these are no longer effective, but instead to respond to the emotional tone of the patient's message, rather than to the content (43).

Most of all, the patient with dementia needs a physician who will take charge of complicated medical, social, and emotional problems. Patients with senile dementia of the Alzheimer type may have other serious medical problems. Many of these can be handled by the personal physician; certain problems may require referral to other physicians or health professionals. The diagnosis of medical illness in persons who are already demented can be a major challenge.

Many patients can be evaluated for their dementia on an outpatient basis. Some will benefit from evaluation or assessment as an inpatient in the hospital. A great deal of help can be provided to the family by advising on the question of institutionalization in a long-term care facility. The physician can help assess the patient's various problems, including wandering, agitation, and incontinence, and the family's ability to cope with these problems. By addressing such specific problems as incontinence, depression, or sleeplessness, the physician may relieve some of the burden of the illness even though the degree of dementia is unchanged.

The physician may help provide counseling or referral of psychotherapy where family problems are evident. Referral of the family for often-needed legal and financial guidance may be necessary. It is very helpful if the physician can provide home visits in order to provide support for the family, in addition to arranging nursing visits or the services of homemakers or home health aides if needed. As part of the home visit, the physician will better understand the patient's actual environment and help advise on eliminating barriers and maximizing the patient's independence in his or her environment. The physician plays a key role in working with the family or caregiver, providing support, and helping the family cope effectively with the long-term stress in caring for the patient.

A national support group for patients with organic brain syndrome and their families is the Alzheimer's Disease and Related Disorders Association (A.D.R.D.A.), which has a network of over 55 chapters across the country. The national headquarters are located at 70 E. Lake St., Suite 600, Chicago, IL, 60601. Families may get information by calling 1-800-621-0379.

Barnes et al. (3) described a support group for caregivers consisting of 12 spouses and 3 adult children of Alzheimer's patients. This group met biweekly for 16 90-min sessions. Group participation was especially helpful for spouses who function as primary caregivers. Participation resulted in their feeling greater support and less isolation and helped members deal with many of the feelings brought about by the illness. The sessions also helped spouses to become more aware of their own needs and regain some feeling of self-identity. Barnes and associates offer much useful advice in developing a support group for families caring for Alzheimer patients.

A handbook that should be of great help to all families dealing with the problem of dementia is *The 36-Hour Day: A Family Guide for Persons With Alzheimer's Disease, Related Dementing Illness, and Memory Loss in Later Life,* by Nancy Mace and Peter Rabins (32). Not only families dealing with this problem but health professionals, too, will find an abundance of useful information in this book.

Many families are deeply concerned about avoiding the use of long-term care facilities. Physicians, of course, should use the prescription for a nursing home as cautiously as a prescription for cardiac medication or an antibiotic. However, many patients with Alzheimer's disease eventually reach a point in which they are simply not manageable in terms of their need for 24-hour/day, 7 day/week nursing care, medical interventions, and other safety considerations as far as their custodial care. When a family tells the physician early on that they never want their relative to be placed in a nursing home, it is important for the physician to tell the family that their loved one might conceivably some day require care in a nursing home facility.

A recent innovation in nursing home care has been the establishment of special units for the care of Alzheimer's patients (31). These units benefit persons with dementia by allowing appropriate resources to be concentrated in one area and by allowing an interested skilled staff to focus its efforts on a group of individuals most needy of their services. Drawbacks to such units include the high intensity of care needed; this is more costly and puts added emotional and physical strain on the staff who work on the unit. Such units also imply that Alzheimer's disease patients cannot be cared for in general nursing home units, an idea that is contradicted by the fact that between 70% and 90% of all nursing home residents suffer from some form of dementia.

Other innovative care approaches for those with dementia and their families include in-home visiting nurse or aide services. These allow the family to have some relief from care and provide for stimulation of the ill person. Day care centers are an important addition to the health delivery system. There are many that now serve both cognitively impaired and well elderly. These units provide stimulation and activity for the ill person and respite for the family.

In summary, in the case of irreversible dementia, the patient should be maintained, if at all possible, in his or her own home or in the community. Establishing a constant and familiar environment is most helpful, in addition to trying to maximize the patient's level of functioning. The impact of the patient's illness on the family or caregiver should be kept in mind. The family or caregiver could be helped through increased social support. Interventions should result in family members feeling less isolated and should improve the quality of life for both the patient and family or caregiver.

Additional Perspectives on the Etiology of Senile Dementia of the Alzheimer Type

EPIDEMIOLOGY

Any possible understanding of the etiology of senile dementia of the Alzheimer type must be based on solid epidemiologic information. Genetic theories, viral theories, an understanding of environmental risk factors, the role of trace elements, such as aluminum, and other causal hypotheses all benefit from a reliable epidemiologic data base.

A wide range of prevalence rates exists for senile dementia of the Alzheimer type. Dr. Jacob Brody (5,

6) of the National Institute on Aging reviewed the dementia syndromes in several major studies. He noted that, worldwide, approximately 4% of persons over 65 years of age have a malignant form of senile dementia and about 10–20% have mild forms. Prevalence rises sharply with age, approaching about 20% for severe forms at age 80 years. As life expectancy is increasing rapidly all the time (principally because of the decrease in the death rate from heart disease and stroke), a spiraling increase can be ex-

pected in the number of elderly in each decade past 60 years. One estimate, at the present, is that 1% of the population has senile dementia at age 65 years, 10% at age 75 years, and 25–30% at age 85 years.

Using data from hospitals and long-term care institutions, there appear to be predominance among women and among persons of low socioeconomic status. Others have shown an equal prevalence among men and women and have criticized the use of information largely gathered from institutional experience, noting the preponderance of female institutionalized patients. Very little is presently known about Alzheimer's according to race, rural versus urban, nationality in nations other than western Europe and the United States, and other cross-cultural comparisons. Hopefully, these questions will be answered within the next decade.

There is uncertainty that exists in the diagnosis of Alzheimer's disease and related disorders. Adolfsson and colleagues (personal communication, 1985) in Sweden studied 80 patients with progressive dementia. About one-third of the patients could not be classified as either dementia of the Alzheimer type or multi-infarct dementia, but showed signs and symptoms of both diseases. A clinical-pathologic correlation of 95 patients with progressive dementia demonstrated that pathologic studies confirmed the patients diagnosed as dementia of the Alzheimer type were correctly classified in 84% of cases, but patients with multi-infarct dementia were correctly classified in only 58% of cases. A 12-year clinical-pathologic study of "Alzheimer group diseases" by Daniel (11) in Australia concluded that it is virtually impossible to compartmentalize the disease into the various disease entities as described in medical and pathology textbooks. Finally, a Japanese report by Endo et al. (15) points out that there is a very large difference between Japan and other countries in that senile dementia represents only about 18% of the total number of demented patients while arteriosclerotic dementia represents about 70% of cases in Japan. All these varying reports point to the difficulties in clinical diagnosis and raise questions about diagnostic criteria, nomenclature, and, therefore, the existing demography and epidemiology of the dementias.

NEUROTRANSMITTER-RELATED STUDIES

In 1976, Davies and Maloney reported a significant reduction in the activity of choline acetyltransferase in the cerebral cortex of patients with senile dementia of the Alzheimer type in comparison to age-matched normal individuals. This finding has been confirmed by others. There is a clear correlation between this change in neurochemical activity and changes in cognitive loss and in brain pathology, particularly the number of neuritic plaques seen at autopsy. This reduction in the activity of choline acetyltransferase is not noted in multi-infarct dementia or depression (35).

Of course, this significant decrease in choline acetyltransferase raises several questions: Are there therapeutic measures that can be taken to restore the apparent deficiency of acetylcholine and will these measures benefit the patient with senile dementia of the Alzheimer type?

Whitehouse, Price, and colleagues (49, 50) found that the nucleus basalis of Meynert from patients with Alzheimer's disease demonstrated a substantial reduction of neurons when compared with age- and sex-matched controls. As the nucleus basalis provides diffuse cholinergic input to the neocortex, loss of this neuronal population may represent an important anatomic correlate of the markedly reduced activity of choline acetyltransferase in Alzheimer's disease. Demonstration of the selective degeneration of the nucleus basalis of Meynert neurons may provide the first documentation of a loss of a transmitter-specific neuronal population in a major disorder of higher cortical function, thus pointing to a critical subcortical lesion in Alzheimer's disease. Whether nucleus basalis cell death leads to neocortical abnormalities or is the result of these neocortical deficits is unanswered but the evidence now favors the cortex as the initial site of disease (34).

Since cholinergic activity in senile dementia of the Alzheimer type is diminished, it is logical to try to increase acetylcholine synthesis or to prevent its breakdown, or both. Senile dementia of the Alzheimer type might be compared to Parkinson's disease as far as the hope of chemical manipulation.

Many therapeutic possibilities have been considered. Since increased dietary choline results in increased synthesis of acetylcholine (requiring choline acetyltransferase), several clinical trials have utilized dietary choline supplements in the Alzheimer-type process. Another approach has been the use of lecithin, the dietary source of choline, which increases the level of choline in the blood more than through the administration of choline chloride. Early trials of choline, lecithin, and 2-dimethylaminoethanol (deanol) have not been successful. Another approach has been the attempt to increase cholinergic activity in the brain by slowing down the rapid breakdown of the neurotransmitter acetylcholine. Davis et al. (13) reported that physostigmine, which works by blocking the breakdown of acetylcholine, has a positive effect on memory, but the dosage required to accomplish this improvement varied a great deal from subject to subject and the improvement has been short lived.

More recently, Summers et al. (46) used an oral anticholinesterase drug, tetrahydroaminoacridine, in a trial of 17 persons with Alzheimer's disease. Using blood levels to assure that appropriate dosages were being administered and a double-blind, placebo-controlled, crossover methodology, they demonstrated significant improvement in both behavioral and cognitive measures. While the report is a preliminary one and has methodologic limitations, it offers the hope that pharmacotherapy might prevent, stabilize, or cure Alzheimer's disease.

If the "cholinergic" theory is correct, then it raises the question of possible harmful effects of anticholinergic drugs, including amitriptyline and thioridazine. A host of medications with anticholinergic properties are utilized in daily practice. Their use must be reconsidered.

Four other neurotransmitter deficits have been identified. Norepinephrine, serotonin, somatostatin, and corticotrophin releasing factor are all diminished in the brains of Alzheimer's disease victims (34). This suggests that replacement strategies might have to combine several drugs or that individual patients will require different treatment regimens based on their pattern of deficits.

A host of claims of efficacy for a wide variety of other drugs has failed to result in a specific treatment for dementia with major therapeutic benefit. Potential benefit might derive from the ergot derivative, Hydergine, as there is some evidence that patients on Hydergine therapy seem to improve more than those receiving a placebo (20). More recently, Yoshikawa and colleagues (52) have reported a collaborative study by 67 Japanese hospitals, investigating the optimal dose of Hydergine in 550 patients with cerebrovascular disorders. Comparing 3-mg and 6-mg doses of Hydergine, significant improvement was noted from the larger dose. It is not clear that Hydergine specifically improves cognitive loss, but it appears to enhance behavior, particularly affecting arousal and attention.

The practicing physician will be faced with many episodes in which family members and caregivers will make demands for the use of drugs that are receiving attention in the public press as possible cures for Alzheimer's disease. The physician will be obligated to urge a "wait and see attitude," as it will take drug trials on a much larger scale to determine the true efficacy and potential risks of these drugs.

GENETIC THEORIES

There is no question that there is a genetic component to Alzheimer's disease. The rate of occurrence of Alzheimer's disease in the presenium or senile dementia of the Alzheimer type appears to be increased in near relatives of patients (30). Numerous pedigrees suggest a dominant mode of transmission but this is found more commonly among presenile patients than in those with late-onset Alzheimer's disease. Folstein et al. (17) have suggested that the majority of Alzheimer cases are familial but this hypothesis is controversial. Of interest is that many Down's syndrome patients surviving into later age will eventually develop the typical Alzheimer lesions in the brain. Also of interest is an increased frequency of Down's syndrome and blood dyscrasias such as leukemia and Hodgkin's disease among the family members of Alzheimer patients (25).

This clue has led to recent work by St. George-Hyslop and coworkers (45) localizing the genetic defect in Alzheimer's disease on chromosome 21, the same chromosome that contains the gene for amyloid protein that accumulates abnormally in the brains of both Alzheimer's and Down's victims. If confirmed, this finding may provide a "genetic marker" for identifying those at risk for Alzheimer's disease, allow determination of how common the genetic form of Alzheimer's disease is, and lead to an understanding of the cause of Alzheimer's disease.

ALUMINUM STUDIES

Crapper and associates in 1973 (9) reported significantly elevated levels of aluminum in the brains of Alzheimer patients. Their findings have not been replicated elsewhere and it seemed likely that their results were due to high levels of aluminum in the environment where they did their studies. Recent work by Perry (34) in which aluminum silicates have been found in high concentrations in the core of neurofibrillary tangles, has revived interest in this theory.

VIRAL THEORIES

Several slow virus diseases—kuru and Creutzfeldt-Jakob disease in man and scrapie in sheep—are of tremendous interest as far as insights they may possibly offer into the dementing process.

The reader is referred to the fascinating report by Gajdusek et al. (21) that reviews Creutzfeldt-Jakob disease, kuru, scrapie, and transmissible mink encephalopathy. In this review, Gajdusek et al. (21) also discuss precautions that should be followed in the medical care of, and in the handling of materials from, patients with a possible transmissible virus dementia.

CREUTZFELDT-JAKOB DISEASE

Creutzfeldt-Jakob disease is a fatal disorder of the central nervous system that presents as a rapidly evolving dementia with myoclonic seizures, a characteristic EEG, and other neurologic signs including pyramidal, extrapyramidal, cerebellar, and lower motor neuron; the disease progresses swiftly to coma and death. More than 200 deaths each year probably occur in the United States and at least 10% of patients have a family history of presenile dementia. Corneal grafts and contaminated stereotactic EEG leads have been implicated in cases in which surgical transmission was certain. Three cases occurred within 2 years after operative procedures by a single neurosurgeon, suggesting surgical transmission. Thus, neurosurgery and ophthalmic surgery may iatrogenically cause infections, although the disease is clearly rare.

In the cases resulting from surgical transmission, 15–20 months elapsed between the surgical procedure and the onset in patients. The time elapsed between patients in affected families suggests incubation periods of several decades.

The viral agent has been found in brain, spinal fluids, cornea, cerebrospinal fluid, spleen and other organs. Several species of primates, including the chimpanzee and New and Old World monkeys, are susceptible by intracerebral, subcutaneous, and other routes of inoculation. Experimental incubation periods appear to range from 8 months to several years.

Gajdusek et al. (21) point out that caution must be taken to avoid accidental percutaneous exposure to a patient's blood, cerebrospinal fluid, or brain tissue. Blood and cerebrospinal fluid should be handled as potentially infectious. The same type of needle precautions utilized to prevent hepatitis B would serve to protect against the less likely chance of viral contamination from tissues of Creutzfeldt-Jakob disease.

KURU

Kuru, or "trembling with fear," is a progressive and fatal neurologic disorder that has occurred exclusively among natives of the Eastern Highlands of Papua, New Guinea. Difficulty in walking is usually the first sign to appear, with progression from a minor disturbance to marked, side-to-side lurching and staggering. As the disorder progresses, there is cerebellar involvement and, in later phases, dementia.

The disease has been reduced significantly, owing to the disappearance of cannibalism in New Guinea. The infectious origin of kuru was confirmed by the appearance of a kuru-like syndrome in chimpanzees. Inoculation by the intracerebral, intravenous, and other routes resulted in disease after periods of 11 months to 8.5 years. The slow virus of kuru has been found in high titers in the brains of patients and in other organs in lower titers.

SCRAPIE

Scrapie is a natural disease of sheep and goats. Both the clinical picture and pathologic findings show close resemblance to those of kuru. Scrapie may spread from infected sheep to uninfected sheep and goats. Experimental infection has been induced in sheep, goats, and mice by the oral route. Older sheep have been infected after prolonged contact with diseased sheep or after feeding in pastures that have been previously occupied by diseased sheep.

Scrapie has been transmitted to five species of monkeys, producing a syndrome clinically and pathologically indistinguishable from experimental Creutzfeldt-Jakob disease. However, intracerebral inoculation of infectious material has not succeeded in transmitting scrapie to chimpanzees.

ALZHEIMER'S DISEASE

All the above concerning transmissible virus dementia is of interest if it can be related to the etiology of the Alzheimer-type process. Gibbs and Gajdusek (22) reported the transmission to chimpanzees of a chronic, progressive, neurologic illness after the animals' brains were injected with tissue from the diseased brains of two patients with familial Alzheimer's disease. Attempts to reproduce and corroborate their initial findings have been unsuccessful, both in other laboratories and in their own laboratories (23). As of this time, one would have to conclude that no case of Alzheimer's disease has been shown to be transmissible. A variation on this hypothesis has been suggested by Prusiner (37). He suggests that a very small particle, the prion ("proteinaceous infectious particle") is the agent that causes Alzheimer's disease. Others have suggested this is a component of normal brain. Further work needs to be done before this hypothesis is accepted. Still, the resemblance in symptoms and the demonstration of familial occurrence of the Alzheimer-type disease and Creutzfeldt-Jakob disease is intriguing, as is the theory that a latent virus

may be responsible for the slowly progressive damage to the Alzheimer brain that produces the signs and symptoms of the disease only after a prolonged period of time.

Although currently in the infancy of understanding the causal factors in the Alzheimer-type process, various beachheads have been established. A strong likelihood exists that the Alzheimer-type process is the end-stage of more than one pathologic mechanism. Surely the next decade will see enormous progress in understanding this devastating disease. Hopefully, with an improved understanding of the etiologic factors in this disease, specific preventive or therapeutic measures will be possible.

The practicing physician will be obligated to sort out different physiologic hypotheses regarding Alzheimer's disease. In medical and scientific journals, and in the lay press, the practicing physician will read that Alzheimer's disease has its origin in an immunologic disorder, a toxic effect of aluminum, a slow virus disorder, genetics, a neurotransmitter disturbance, etc. Wurtman (51) has compared the different pathophysiologic hypotheses to the tale of six blind men and the elephant. The original story (7) of the six blind men reads:

Once upon a time a king gathered some blind men about an elephant and asked them to tell him what an elephant was like. The first man felt a tusk and said an elephant was like a giant carrot; another happened to touch an ear and said it was like a big fan; another touched its trunk and said it was like pistle; still another, who happened to feel its leg, said it was like a mortar; and another, who grasped its tail, said it was like a rope. Not one of them was able to tell the king the elephant's real form.

Hopefully, scientific investigations will someday converge and the true "elephantness" of Alzheimer's disease will be understood.

REFERENCES

1. Adams RD, Fisher CM, Hakim S: Symptomatic occult hydrocephalus with normal cerebrospinal fluid pressure. A treatable syndrome. N Engl J Med 273:117, 1965.
2. American Psychiatric Association: Organic mental disorders. In: Diagnosis and Statistical Manual of Mental Disorders, Ed. 3, Revised, American Psychiatric Association, Washington, D.C., 1987, pp. 101–128.
3. Barnes RF, Raskind MA, Scott M, Murphy C: Problems of families caring for Alzheimer patients: Use of a support group. J Am Geriatr Soc 29:80, 1981.
4. Bonte FJ, Ross ED, Chehabi HH, Devous MD: SPECT study of regional cerebral blood flow in Alzheimer disease. J Comput Assist Tomogr 10:579, 1986.
5. Brody JA: An epidemiologist views senile dementia—facts and fragments. Am J Epidemiol 115:155, 1982.
6. Brody JA: An epidemiologist's view of the senile dementias—pieces of the puzzle. In: Senile Dementia: Outlook for the Future. New York, Alan R. Liss, 1984, p. 383.
7. Bukkyo Dendo Kyokai: The Teaching of Buddha. 72nd, Rev. Ed., Kosaido Printing, 1984, p. 75.
8. Caplan G: Mastery of stress: Psychosocial aspects. Am J Psychiatry 138:413, 1981.
9. Crapper D, Krishnan SS, Dalton AJ: Brain aluminum distribution in Alzheimer's disease and experimental neurofibrillary degeneration. Science 180:511, 1973.
10. Crook R, Bartus RT, Ferris S, Whitehouse P, Cohen GD, Hershon S: Age-associated memory impairment: Proposed diagnostic criteria and measures of clinical change. Devel Neuropsychol 2:261, 1986.
11. Daniel R: Twelve year clinico-pathological study of Alzheimer group diseases. Book of Abstracts of the XIIIth International Congress of Gerontology, New York, July 12–17, 1985, p. 163.
12. Davies P, Maloney AJF: Selective loss of central cholinergic neurons in Alzheimer's disease. Lancet 2:1403, 1976.
13. Davis KL, Mohs RC, Tinklenberg JR: Enhancement of memory by physostigmine. N Engl J Med 301:946, 1979.
14. Eisdorfer C, Cohen D: Management of the patient and family coping with dementing illness. J Fam Pract 12:831, 1981.
15. Endo H, Yamamoto T, Kuzuya F: Predispositions to arteriosclerotic dementia and senile dementia in Japan. Book of Abstracts of the XIIIth International Congress of Gerontology, New York, July 12–17, 1985, p. 163.
16. Finlayson RE, Martin LM: Recognition and management of depression in the elderly. Mayo Clin Proc 57:115, 1982.
17. Folstein MF: Inheritability of Alzheimer's disease. Am Fam Phys 25:56, 1982.
18. Folstein MF, Folstein SE, McHugh PR: Mini-mental state: A practical method for grading the cognitive state of patients for the clinician. J Psychiatr Res 12:189, 1975.
19. Ford CV, Winter J: Computerized axial tomograms and dementia in elderly patients. J Gerontol 36:164, 1981.
20. Gaitz CM, Varner RV, Overall JE: Pharmacotherapy for organic brain syndromes in late life. Evaluation of an ergot derivative vs. placebo. Arch Gen Psychiatry 34:839, 1977.
21. Gajdusek DC, Gibbs CJ, Asher DM, Brown P, Diwan A, Hoffman P, Nemo G, Rohwer R, White L: Precautions in medical care of, and in handling materials from, patients with transmissible virus dementia (Creutzfeldt-Jakob disease). N Engl J Med 297:1253, 1977.
22. Gibbs CJ, Gajdusek DC: Subacute spongiform virus encephalopathy: The transmissible virus dementias. In Katzman R, Terry RD, Bick KL (Eds): Alzheimer's Disease: Senile Dementia and Related Disorders, Aging Vol. 7. New York, Raven Press, 1978, p. 559.
23. Goudsmit J, Morrow CH, Asher DM, Yanagihara RT, Masters CL, Gibbs CJ, Gajdusek DC: Evidence for and against the transmittability of Alzheimer's disease. Neurology 30:945, 1980.
24. Governor's Task Force on Alzheimer's Disease and Related Disorders: The Maryland Report on Alzheimer's

Disease and Related Disorders. State of Maryland, June 30, 1985.

25. Heston LL, Mastri AR: The genetics of Alzheimer's disease: Associations with hematologic malignancy and Down's syndrome. *Arch Gen Psychiatry* 34:976, 1977.

26. Huckman MS, Fox J, Topel J: The validity of criteria for the evaluation of cerebral atrophy by computed tomography. *Radiology* 116:85, 1975.

27. Katzman R: Normal pressure hydrocephalus. In Katzman R, Terry RD, Bick KL (Eds): *Alzheimer's Disease: Senile Dementia and Related Disorders, Aging Vol. 7,* New York, Raven Press, 1978, p. 115.

28. Katzman R: Alzheimer's disease. *N Engl J Med* 314:964, 1986.

29. Kushner HS: *When Bad Things Happen to Good People.* New York, Schocken Books, 1981.

30. Larson T, Sjogren T, Jacobson G: Senile dementia: A clinical, sociomedical and genetic study. *Acta Psychiatr Scand* 39(Suppl 167):1, 1963.

31. Mace N: Do we need special care units for dementia patients? *J Gerontol Nurs* 11:37, 1985.

32. Mace NL, Rabins PV: *The 36-Hour Day: A Family Guide to Caring for Persons with Alzheimer's Disease, Related Dementing Illnesses, and Memory Loss in Later Life.* Baltimore, Johns Hopkins University Press, 1981.

33. McKhann G, Drachman D, Folstein M, Katzman R, Price D, Stedlan EM: Clinical diagnosis of Alzheimer's disease: Report of the NINCDS-ADRDA Work Group under the auspices of Department of Health and Human Services Task Force on Alzheimer's disease. *Neurology* 34:939, 1984.

34. Perry RH: Recent advances in neuropathology. *Br Med Bull* 42:34, 1986.

35. Perry EK, Tomlinson BE, Blessed G, Bergmann K, Gibson PH, Perry RH: Correlation of cholinergic abnormalities with senile plaques and mental test scores in senile dementia. *Br Med J* 2:1457, 1978.

36. Pfeiffer E, A short portable mental status questionnaire for the assessment of organic brain deficit in elderly patients. *J Am Geriatr Soc* 23:433, 1975.

37. Prusiner SB: Some speculations about prions, amyloid, and Alzheimer's disease. *N Engl J Med* 310:661, 1984.

38. Rabins PV, Mace NL, Lucas MJ: The impact of dementia on the family. *JAMA* 248:333, 1982.

39. Rabins PV, Merchant A, Nestadt G: Criteria for diagnosing reversible dementia caused by depression. *Br J Psychiatry,* 144:488, 1984.

40. Rapaport SI: Positron emission tomography in normal aging and Alzheimer's disease. *Gerontology* 32(Suppl 1):6, 1986.

41. Reichel W, Franch MS, Solon J: Survey research guiding public policy in Maryland: A case of Alzheimer's disease and related disorders. *Exp Gerontol* 21:439, 1986a.

42. Reichel W, Franch MS, Beacham E: Alzheimer's disease and related disorders: A growing challenge in *MD. Med J* 35:927, 1986b.

43. Reifler BV, Wu S: Managing families of the demented elderly. *J Fam Pract* 14:1051, 1982.

44. Seltzer B, Sherwin I: A comparison of clinical features in early- and late-onset primary degenerative dementia. *Arch Neurol* 33:217, 1976.

45. St. George-Hyslop PH, Tanzi RE, Polinsky RJ, et al: The genetic defect causing familial Alzheimer's disease maps on chromosome 21. *Science* 235:885, 1987.

46. Summers WK, Magorski LV, Marsh GM, Tachiki K, Kling A: Oral tetrahydroaminoacridine in long-term treatment of senile dementia, Alzheimer type. *N Engl J Med* 315:1241, 1986.

47. Tomlinson BE, Henderson G: Some quantitative cerebral findings in normal and demented old people. In Terry RD, Gershon S (Eds): *Neurobiology of Aging, Aging, Vol. 3,* New York, Raven Press, 1976.

48. Wells CE: Pseudodementia. *Am J Psychiatry* 136:895, 1979.

49. Whitehouse PJ, Price DL, Clark AW, Coyle JT, DeLong MR: Alzheimer disease: Evidence for selective loss of cholinergic neurons in the nucleus basalis. *Ann Neurol* 10:122, 1981.

50. Whitehouse PJ, Price DL, Struble RG, Clark AW, Coyle JT, DeLong MR: Alzheimer's disease and senile dementia: Loss of neurons in the basal forebrain. *Science* 215:1237, 1982.

51. Wurtman RJ: Alzheimer's disease. *Sci Am* 252:62, 71, 1985.

52. Yoshikawa M, Hirai S, Aizawa T, et al: A dose-response study with dihydroergotoxine mesylate in cerebrovascular disturbances. *J Am Geriatr Soc* 31:1, 1983.

CHAPTER 15

The Therapeutic Milieu: Social-Psychological Aspects of Treatment

DOROTHY H. COONS

This chapter will examine the impact of the total environment of treatment settings on older persons and will discuss social-psychological issues that influence the quality of care.

More than 40% of the aged who live in long-term care institutions are comprised of those in their 80s and 90s. According to current population projections, the number of persons living beyond age 85 may triple within the next few decades. Thus, we can expect to find our nursing homes, mental hospitals, and other long-term care facilities swelling with this population of the "old old." With this increase in age, there are predictions that the number of persons with dementing illnesses will reach epidemic proportions. (7) This forecast has significant implications for the current and future planning of treatment settings for the elderly. The urgent need for new methods of dealing with unsolved problems related to care is evident.

The model for long-term care facilities currently predominant is that of custodial care, which is an outgrowth of the hierarchial medical style of operation practiced in acute care hospitals. Many health professionals now view this model of health care as inappropriate for elderly persons in need of residential treatment, since it fosters the role of sick patient. In recent years new techniques and perspectives have been investigated to enable those working with the elderly to develop a comprehensive and therapeutic approach to treatment. The goal is to ensure a quality of life that will enable the mentally and physically frail elderly to maintain dignity and a maximum of independence. The essential changes necessary in a treatment setting to accomplish this goal will not occur, however, without a concerted effort by policy makers who are shaping long-term care for older persons and a commitment to the belief that the elderly in need of care are deserving of, and can benefit from, a *therapeutic program* rather than *custodial care*, regardless of their degree of illness.

Custodial care focuses on meeting the physical needs of residents and providing for their physical health and safety. The therapeutic milieu, that has been tested in both research and practice, can be characterized as an environment in treatment settings that emphasizes the well aspects of the individual and creates a climate encouraging individuality and enabling the elderly resident to maintain and integrate, to the greatest extend possible, relationships with past life.

Over a number of years the Institute of Gerontology has undertaken a planned series of research and demonstration projects in a variety of settings to test the effectiveness of different modes of environmental intervention in enhancing the self-concept and well-being of institutionalized elderly people. The research design adopted a humanistic approach, incorporated a program of work therapy and social activity, and offered a variety of normal social roles to residents.

The positive results and the experience acquired in the course of these studies directed the interest of the Institute to the development of techniques for more effective application of the principles that were the basis of a therapeutic milieu. These new studies resulted in an integrated approach that is adaptable to the differing needs of older people in nursing homes, in residential care settings, and in mental hospitals and defines the essential environmental factors in a variety of protected settings.

This chapter, in examining the social-psychological aspects of treatment, will compare the design and impact of a therapeutic milieu with that of custodial treatment. In order to define and develop the implications of each mode clearly, the author presents the two systems as though they were discrete and opposing models although, in reality, treatment programs often incorporate elements of both custodial care and a therapeutic milieu in varying degrees, and many gray areas lie between the two. The comparison examines four major components of the milieu: the program, the staff, the residents, and the physical environment.

BASIC CONCEPTS IN DESIGNING THE THERAPEUTIC MILIEU

The therapeutic milieu encompasses the total environment, and therefore all parts need assessment and often alteration to ensure that all foster well-being. While each part has its own influence on the life of the individual, the milieu fulfills its greatest potential for therapeutic impact only when all of its components mirror the therapeutic mode. For example, a home-like physical setting alone cannot ensure a therapeutic milieu. In fact, it may be rendered impotent if staff assume a highly custodial stance or the program lacks challenge and stimulation.

The following hypotheses form the basic concepts in designing the therapeutic milieu (4). The hypotheses hold that:

The resident makes the greatest gains when the environment offers opportunities and experiences for the individual to maintain continuity with the past and assume, to the fullest extent possible, the social roles normally available in the outside community.

Roles prescribe the patterns of behavior that are socially acceptable for each position or function in a group or society. If, for example, the only available role is "frail sick patient," the individual will conform to the expectations embodied in that role. If, however, a number of normal social roles that had had meaning to him or her in earlier life, such as friend, citizen, consumer, worker, or volunteer, are available and the individual is encouraged to choose freely among them, his or her behavior will be varied and far more therapeutic in its effects than when it is prescribed by the sick patient role. These roles enable even the very frail to respond and to function in an environment that is nurturing and enabling.

The resident makes the greatest gains when the treatment program is designed to provide a structured series of meaningful expectations.

Because people respond to the expectations placed upon them, it is essential for institutions to have expectations that foster well-being and independence. One element of well-being is success at increasingly challenging levels of achievement, for such success is integral to self-esteem and maintenance of personality function. Relevance, too, is an essential element, for it is meaningful rather than trivial expectations that elicit a healthy response.

The Cummings' (6) theory of crisis resolution as a therapeutic tool offers a theoretical explanation for the above hypothesis. In the Cummings' formulation, reorientation of personality and ego growth occurs as the individual successfully copes with tasks of graduated difficulty. The practical application of a "structured series of graded tasks" provides staff at all levels with treatment techniques that can enable residents to experience ego growth.

The resident makes the greatest gains when there is a degree of homogeneity among individuals according to their needs and abilities.

An environment designed to meet the needs of the mentally and physically frail elderly often provides services, care, and protection that are excessive for the alert, active elderly person, even though the latter may have a number of chronic illnesses. No single environment can meet the needs of both the mentally frail and the alert, or relatively well, older person. It is the sickest person for whom the limits are established. Doors are locked; materials and equipment are unavailable for maximum independence; and activities are often degrading and inappropriate for the alert, able person.

The resident makes the greatest gains when the milieu offers maximal autonomy and freedom of choice to the individual and provides environmental flexibility to accommodate individual needs and wishes.

The assumption in the therapeutic milieu is that the elderly resident is capable of making choices and of determining what is appropriate and desirable for his or her well-being. It offers, to the greatest extent possible, individual choice in times to get up or go to bed or bathe, participation in activities, dress, and selection of food. Flexibility of daily routines allows for adjustment to the special needs of residents and their individual life styles.

In a therapeutic milieu the use of physical restraints, except in dire emergencies, and the overuse of drugs are rejected. Both forms of control are infantalizing and dehumanizing practices that strip the elderly person of all autonomy, personality, and dignity. Research has provided evidence that physical restraints are not only degrading but are ineffectual techniques in reducing falls and accidents (1, 8).

The resident makes the greatest gains in a complex and stimulating sensory and social environment.

The therapeutic milieu offers a rich and varied selection of opportunities and experiences for residents that encourages involvement and retards deterioration. A complex and stimulating environment will be nonstressful if the resident has the right to accept or reject the opportunities offered. It is the absence of opportunities, as characterized by a sterile environment, that creates stress.

The physical environment through the inclusion of personal possessions and artifacts provides stimulation and continuity for residents. The environment also uses color, lighting, and sound both to stimulate and to accommodate sensory deficits.

The resident makes the greatest gains when there is an individualization in staff approaches, in the opportunities for involvement, and in elements of the physical environment.

The individual-centered approach adjusts expectations and methods to individual abilities rather than assuming that one set of norms, one style of staff approaches, and unvaried activities will apply to everyone (11). Individualization enables the resident to use his or her existing capabilities and to continue interests and skills that were rewarding to him or her in earlier life. The physical environment also can be individualized to help each person maintain identity and a sense of ownership and individuality.

These six hypotheses have been tested and confirmed in several experimental settings and repeat-

edly applied to good effect in a variety of other treatment facilities. The concepts, because they are so logical, may seem simplistic, yet they form a solid basis on which to define and design the environment. Complexity enters with the *application* of the concepts. It is not the theory but the implementation of a therapeutic milieu that provides the challenge.

CUSTODIAL CARE IN CONTRAST TO THE THERAPEUTIC MILIEU

PROGRAM IN CUSTODIAL CARE

The program in custodial care actively fosters dependency.

The program in a care setting may be described as the pattern of daily life for the residents. Thus, in custodial care a typical day might follow the routine outlined below for Mrs. J., an elderly resident.

At 5:30 AM she is awakened by the midnight staff before they go off duty. Staff selects her clothing and helps her dress. She is given her medication and then sits on her bed or a bedside chair to wait for breakfast. At 6:30 AM Mrs. J. is told to go to the dining room (or moved there if she is in a wheelchair) for breakfast. She sits with others but there is almost no conversation. Breakfast trays are served by staff with a minimum of communication. After eating breakfast, Mrs. J. is told to go to the dayroom, where she spends the morning dozing and waiting for midday medication and lunch, with an occasional trip to the bathroom. Silence in the dayroom is broken only by the sound of the staff conducting daily routines and by the incessant buzz of an untuned television set. After lunch, Mrs. J. returns to the dayroom or lies down for an afternoon nap. If it is bath day, she and the other residents may be processed through the showers. In the late afternoon Mrs. J. is given her medication, followed by supper at 5:30 PM. At 7:00 PM she is told it is bedtime and helped into her nightclothes. She may receive medication to help her sleep. Since she dozed much of the day, she will not sleep at night if left unmedicated.

This monotony may be broken occasionally by a group birthday party or a bingo game, but nothing happens during a typical day that is physically or mentally stimulating or that gives the resident a sense of satisfaction, accomplishment, or anticipation.

PROGRAM IN THE THERAPEUTIC MILIEU

The program of the therapeutic milieu incorporates all of the activities that make up the fabric of each person's day, including self-care to the extent possible, choices in daily life that accommodate individual differences and contrasting life styles, and those activities that enable the elderly to continue to get pleasure from life and maintain contact with family and friends and the greater community.

The specifics of the program in a therapeutic milieu will vary to meet the needs of the elderly residents and, at the same time, take into account the potential of staff and the resources existing at the particular institution. One constant, however, is the climate produced by the implementation of a therapeutic program. It fosters, enables and supports individual worth, and is aimed toward helping each resident and staff member achieve a maximal degree of success.

The opportunity-filled therapeutic program fosters a sense of individual worth and of normalcy, affirmation, and achievement. It generates a spirit of community through mutually recognizing and accommodating needs; and it demands recognition of the residents' human rights to satisfaction and dignity in their lives.

Because the therapeutic milieu is a total, integrated view, this climate invades all aspects of the institution, not just some specially designated therapeutic segment. Clearly, it is a 24 hour need that is always with the resident and not something that happens only in craft classes or a weekly group meeting.

The therapeutic milieu defines the long-term care facility as fundamentally a "home" that accommodates the diversity of individual needs and desires. Good medical care and treatment are essential and should aid, not impede, a favorable life. In the hospital version of long-term care, medical treatment becomes an end in itself. In the therapeutic milieu, as in the outside community, medical treatment becomes the means by which the individual is able to maintain the energy and capacity for continued life satisfaction.

Within the context of the therapeutic milieu, the variety of programs that meet resident needs, fit within available resources, and utilize staff and resident abilities is unlimited. A program designed with sensitivity and in response to resident ideas and individual differences can build a life, even for the very frail, that has meaning and worth.

STAFF IN CUSTODIAL CARE

The demands placed on staff by their custodial responsibilities dictate a style that erodes the independence and self-concept of the residents and provides job situations that are unrewarding and stifling to staff.

Staff shortages, rigid job descriptions, and an inflexible hierarchy of authority, red tape, and paper work are common products of the custodial system. They provide the staff of many long-term care centers with high-pressure, low-reward jobs. The qualities for which the traditional system rewards staff, such as efficient performance of custodial responsibility or cleanliness and quietness, may actually contribute to the tedium characteristic of these jobs.

Staff receive contradictory messages regarding policies and priorities. For example, an aide may be told that the institution's primary concern is with the patients. Yet the stress may be on other matters: "Is your area clean? You're wasting your time talking with a resident—don't you have a job to do?" A staff member may be required to conform to policies, even to an institutional style, that do not permit individual creativity, the expression of positive personality traits, or the use of personal skills. The "professional stance" demanded by the system may be defined as an avoidance of involvement with the residents. Cheerfulness, humor, and a relaxed, lighthearted approach may be out of keeping with the tone maintained, and commiseration with an unhappy resident may be seen as lowering morale or becoming too intimate with residents.

In the face of these built-in obstacles, it is easier and more expedient in the short run for a staff person to do a task for a resident. With this system, staff members are better able to meet the standards of performance in terms of cleanliness and conformity that institutions establish. This practice of doing for, rather than assisting or teaching, can induce total dependency in a short time.

Decision making in the custodial system adheres rigidly to the hierarchial pattern. Decisions are handed down from above, and the sphere of influence lessens at each level. For example, aides are seldom involved in the development of treatment plans, and the insights they gain from their contact with residents are without effect. Staff at many levels are left with feelings of impotency and powerlessness.

STAFF IN THE THERAPEUTIC MILIEU

Staff responsibilities extend beyond mere custodial care and medical treatment to the establishment of an environment that enables the elderly to live with dignity and with a sense that others care about and value them. All staff members act as friends, therapists, and teachers rather than caretakers. All staff members share knowledge and participate in decision making as it relates to the treatment program.

The quality of human relationships in any milieu becomes the major factor in defining the character and climate of the setting. Staff, therefore, hold the key to determining whether the elderly will live in an enabling environment in which they have opportunities to assume responsibilities for decisions about their own lives or an environment in which the residents lose all power and gradually the capacity to take responsibility. In a therapeutic milieu, staff give clear messages of warmth and understanding in their communication with residents and a recognition of the value and the capacities of the individual.

Enhancing the independence and self-actualization of residents through environmental intervention becomes the primary responsibility of all staff members in a therapeutic milieu. All are actively involved in planning, providing treatment, and developing opportunities. These new responsibilities are less easy to describe than custodial ones (bathe patient, make bed, complete form 707-C). In general, an aide's job will shift from doing tasks for the residents to assisting residents or teaching them the essential skills they need to perform the tasks themselves. Through modeling and training, supervisors provide aides with the knowledge and communication skills they need to become teachers and enablers rather than caretakers.

RESIDENTS IN CUSTODIAL CARE

The only role available to residents is the patient role; in this role, residents eventually become agents in their own deterioration.

The behavioral expectations for residents in the role of patient are that they will respond in sick ways. When this role is emphasized, it is assumed that residents will be dependent, confused, withdrawn, sometimes incontinent, forgetful, or even bizarre, and they may respond to these expectations because this is one way to get attention. It is sometimes easier for staff to cope with ill and inappropriate behavior than with normal well behavior in a setting where people are expected to be sick. Only the exceptional person will resist the numbing influence of the total environment, and that exceptional person is likely to be treated very critically.

RESIDENTS IN A THERAPEUTIC MILIEU

The residents are provided with opportunities to be involved in a variety of social roles and through

their participation become effective agents in their own treatment and that of other residents.

In the therapeutic environment, the life space of each resident is extended beyond his bed, his room, or his dining area to include the whole facility and all of the residents and staff. No longer is the resident's concern limited to the routine of his own bodily functions, taking medicines, and reporting ailments. In the enlarged environment with its multiple nonsick role opportunities, residents have their own affairs and their own expectations of what satisfaction will be derived from the day's activities and social transactions. The resident is in contact with other residents and often shares interests and activities with them.

In the role of friend, leader, teacher, consumer, volunteer, worker, and so on, the resident links the current life patterns with those of the past. Value and reward systems, long established, can still be retained, and continuity of personality is uninterrupted.

In a therapeutic milieu, residents are encouraged to select their own programs according to their wishes, for self-determination is a precious privilege of all persons. As in any society, this free selection operates with a set of built-in expectations: being up and dressed, taking care of one's possessions and living space, and being on hand for meals. But beyond these normal everyday expectations, the individual residents spend their time as they choose.

The extent to which the elderly in treatment settings can continue in social roles varies, of course, with the functioning level and energy of individuals. The objectives are to provide the opportunities for persons to enable them to get pleasure from each day and continue relationships and involvement to the greatest extent possible.

PHYSICAL SETTING IN CUSTODIAL CARE

The physical setting for custodial treatment is designed for hygiene, for the efficient accomplishment of routine physical care, and for security and safety.

Consider the response that is triggered by long, dimly lighted halls, locked doors, bare linoleum floors, and naked, mirrorless walls. In the midst of such sterility and suspicion, a healthy person would have difficulty maintaining a sense of interest, individuality, and worth. The effect of such an environment on a confused or disturbed person is shattering.

Even affluent settings may have a deadening effect on the elderly residents. A luxurious room that lacks personal possessions can be as barren as a sterile hospital room. The elderly, like everyone else, need their personal possessions to sustain their sense of identity, their interest in the things around them, and their self-sufficiency; but institutions often limit or deny them these possessions for reasons of administrative convenience.

Overemphasis on safety and security will cause further institutionalization. No one can question the need to protect persons in treatment facilities and to install appropriate devices for that purpose. But when accreditation and regulations are based solely on safety, security, and cleanliness with total disregard for the quality of life, there needs to be a reconsideration of policies.

PHYSICAL SETTING IN THE THERAPEUTIC MILIEU

The therapeutic setting is attractive and home-like and is designed to accommodate sensory changes and physical and social needs. It provides the materials and equipment essential for self-sufficiency and for the enhancement of the life of the elderly residents.

A therapeutic physical environment, in its use of color and such "unhygienic" but warming elements as carpeting, curtains, pictures, and artifacts shifts the emphasis from a sterile sickroom to one focusing on wellness (5). It provides residents easy access to equipment and materials essential for self-care and for involvement in activities of personal interest. This leads to greater independence and a sense of self-reliance and communicates staff confidence in residents.

The therapeutic milieu must include opportunity for each individual to have privacy—both auditory and visual privacy—but not isolation. This includes territory over which the individual holds the rights and can carry out those activities that he does not wish to share with others.

As a normal part of the aging process, gradual changes may occur in the sensory systems of vision, hearing, touch, taste, and smell. These changes take place at different rates, both among individuals and for different senses in the same individual. The ultimate result of decreased sensory acuity can be diminished ability to function in the physical environment, since the cues that give us the information we need about our environment are perceived through our senses. If the cues are not clear enough or are not organized in an understandable way, the person adapting to sensory changes can be left without the information needed to function at maximal capac-

ity. A colorful, stimulating, well-lighted environment and landmarks or prominent features marking a particular locality can help a person remain oriented.

The behavior of all people is influenced by the physical environment in which they find themselves. Whenever people are able to exert some control over the way their environment is designed, they organize space and possessions in ways that best meet their own special needs.

RESPONSE OF RESIDENTS TO A THERAPEUTIC MILIEU

For residents who have experienced years of traditional institutional life, motivation can be a major hurdle in implementing programs. Yet research data from various projects of the Institute of Gerontology demonstrate that residents, even those who have been long deprived of activity, will become intensively and consistently involved. Several necessary conditions for this have been discussed. For example, activities need to have relevancy and value for the older person. The depressed or withdrawn person may need time to consider what is involved and may require help and encouragement from staff to return step-by-step to the life of an active participant. Many residents have lost confidence in their own abilities, but a well-trained and optimistic staff and a careful selection of activities to ensure success can help the older person begin to test his or her abilities to cope with new and different expectations and opportunities.

A number of convincing examples of resident responses to a therapeutic environment could be cited from the experiences of pioneers in the field. The example described here has been selected because the population of elderly persons involved was viewed as a special challenge by staff and yet their response as a group exceeded all expectations.

The project[1] was a 2-year demonstration during which a specially designed residential care unit, called Wesley Hall, was established for persons with Alzheimer's disease or related disorders. The project came into being because a number of the residents who were living in the retirement home where Wesley Hall was eventually located were suffering from such severe memory loss that they were unable to cope with the scattered areas of the large home

---

[1]This project was documented in the videotape/film, *Wesley Hall: A Special Life,* produced by Inner Image Productions, Inc., and distributed by The University of Michigan Media Resources Center, Ann Arbor, Michigan, 1986.

and with the anger and frustration of alert residents who were annoyed and uncomfortable with the behaviors of their impaired neighbors. Nursing home placement was not considered an appropriate solution because the impaired persons were relatively well physically and most were so active that they would have presented serious problems to nursing home staff.

The Institute of Gerontology at The University of Michigan, working closely with the administration of the Chelsea United Methodist Retirement Home in Chelsea, Michigan, designed a small, intimate, homelike area for 11 residents (nine women and two men). The unit gave them the separation and privacy they needed to enable them to live with a degree of serenity, and the opportunities available and staff support helped them become active participants in the world around them. The intimacy of the area and the smallness of the numbers of staff and residents were crucial factors in creating a milieu that was therapeutic for this group.

The physical environment of Wesley Hall was greatly changed. Renovations included carpeting, increased lighting, many visual cues, and noninstitutional furnishings. The unit consisted of single occupancy rooms containing the furniture and memorabilia of each resident, a den, a living room with a small dining area, and a kitchen. All doors in the unit were unlocked, and residents had access to all areas and equipment, such as the coffee urn and the refrigerator for snacks or juice.

Staff notes written when the residents were still living in the large retirement home described the behaviors of several persons as agitated, verbally abusive, and, at times, combative. Four were incontinent; most wandered a great deal; and some frequently became lost. One of the men was locked out of his room daily to prevent his spending the entire day in bed. One person had a diagnosis of dementia secondary to viral encephalitis; the other 10 residents had the physician's presumed diagnosis of either Alzheimer's disease or multi-infarct dementia. On the Kahn Mental Status Questionnaire, one of a number of tests administered before and throughout the 2-year period, persons selected for the project scored in the range of eight to 10 errors, placing them in, or bordering on, the category of the severely impaired (9).

In the special unit, a variety of opportunities were made available to residents in order to create a rich environment in which they could become involved in many of the activities that they had overlearned and enjoyed in their earlier lives, including a number of housekeeping tasks (2). With the official approval of the Department of Public Health and with the support and assistance of staff, most were able to wash and dry dishes, set the tables, fold towels, and help with dusting or bed making. Although meals were catered from the central kitchen of the home, the residents were frequently involved with staff in preparing snacks.

Many of the activities generated by both staff and residents were unscheduled and spontaneous. Staff soon learned that flexibility in such activities as dressing and bathing enabled them to respond to resident moods and needs and helped to reduce stress. Staff made every effort to create a relaxed and lighthearted milieu that became a major ingredient in effecting the changes in the behaviors that had placed the residents in such unfavorable positions when they lived in the large retirement home. Restraints were never used and sedatives or psychotropic drugs were rarely used and only for short periods of time with careful monitoring by the physician and the nursing staff. Many of the routines were modified to give residents the time they needed to respond and to accommodate individual life styles. Breakfast, for example, was served over a period of several hours with some eating as early as 6 AM and others as late as 9 AM. This relaxed style also helped to reduce staff burnout characteristic of many settings caring for persons with dementia.

Although no approaches were consistently successful, staff nevertheless were able to help residents reduce significantly such behaviors as night wandering, combativeness, and incontinence (3, 4). The period after the evening meal was the most difficult to resolve. Staff tried a number of interventions, but one of the most effective was the introduction of a variety of activities generally involving the majority of residents. Sing-a-longs were popular, and occasionally residents were involved in tasks, carefully selected and structured to ensure success, such as folding flyers or stuffing envelopes for the American Red Cross. Gradually evening programs became quite absorbing to the point that most residents did not go to bed until 10 or 11 PM, tired and diverted from the problems that seemed to cause them so much stress at night.

Anger and combativeness had been described by staff of the retirement home as some of the most difficult behaviors with which they had to cope. The unit staff, however, developed a number of strategies that gradually helped to reduce the frequency and intensity of such episodes. As they became sensitive to resident moods, they often were able to anticipate explosive reactions and help residents avoid them. For each of the four residents who had been incontinent before moving to the new residential unit, an individualized toileting schedule and intervention plan was implemented. That, along with a decided increase in liquid intake to strengthen the signals in the bladder of the need to urinate, helped to greatly reduce the incidence of incontinence.

There was also a gradual change in the appearance of residents who, before coming to the area, looked bewildered, confused, ill, out of touch, and sometimes angry or depressed. Special efforts were made to help residents be well groomed, but there were other changes, more psychological in nature; for example, they gradually looked more alert, involved, and aware of their surroundings. They smiled and laughed easily and often, to the extent that visitors at first found it difficult to believe they were severely impaired.

Most of the staff on Wesley Hall had worked in either the nursing home or the retirement home of the facility prior to the establishment of the new unit. The staffing pattern for the project was higher than that of the retirement home, but lower than the nursing home area, placing daily costs to residents on Wesley Hall approximately halfway between the retirement home costs and those in the nursing home.

There were a number of factors that contributed to the success of the special area. Two of the key components, however, were a strong *coordinator* who was effective in problem solving and in providing constant support to staff and *staff training* designed specifically to prepare them to work with persons with dementia.

The extent to which the elderly in treatment settings can continue in social roles varies, of course, with the functioning level and energy of individuals. However, in this project the enthusiasm with which residents responded to the environment, roles, and opportunities available to them took on dimensions that demonstrated, without question, the capacities and needs of the elderly to continue to live normal and fulfilling lives even though ill.

TRANSITION TO A THERAPEUTIC MILIEU: ORGANIZATIONAL CHANGE

With careful planning, the establishment of a therapeutic milieu can transform the lives of elderly residents in a long-term care facility and provide rewarding and stimulating jobs for staff. The systematic implementation of a therapeutic milieu can be viewed as a five-step process: administrative commitment, dealing with potential problem areas, training of staff, implementation, and evaluation.

ADMINISTRATIVE COMMITMENT

The support of the administration of an institution is fundamental to change. With such administrative support, new policies can be planned and clarified, existing practices can be reviewed and altered; as needed new programs and methods can be tested, and the total system can be modified to advance therapeutic objectives. Transformation to a new system is likely to appear risky to staff members who may not feel that it represents a change for the better or who see the change as a threat to their authority. It becomes the responsibility of the administration to assure staff and provide them with the essential supports to help them feel comfortable with the transition.

TRAINING OF STAFF

Staff training that deals with the principles of a therapeutic milieu has four purposes: (1) to ground staff in the concepts of a therapeutic milieu; (2) to provide them with the knowledge, tools, and techniques they need to design and conduct a program; (3) to teach them about the processes and effects of aging to help them better understand the residents with whom they work; and (4) to give them basic skills to begin the development of an effective staff team.

This training has been found to be most effective and conducive to change when the participants represent a broad cross section of institutional staff—physicians, administrators, nurses, social workers, physical and occupational therapists, activity directors, aides, and housekeeping personnel. This enables staff and employees at all levels to gain a better understanding and appreciation of others' responsibilities. It can create a climate in which staff learn to work as a team rather than at cross-purposes, and in which each person can have influence over the action taken.

Consideration of effective teaching methodology is especially important when the trainees represent a wide range of institutional personnel. The use of a variety of teaching methods—lectures, audiovisual materials, simulations, skill exercises, fantasies, and role playing—enables each person to gain from the methods which provide the best learning experiences for him or her.

IMPLEMENTATION OF THE PROGRAM

Well-established and tested principles of management apply to treatment settings as well as industry. For example, staff at all levels need to participate in the planning after they have grasped the fundamentals of the change to be instituted. This involvement increases the participants' understanding of the new program, and it ensures that maximal amounts of expertise, awareness, and insight have gone into the decisions. If staff are involved in finding solutions to the inevitable problems that arise in making changes, even some of the most resistant staff will become supportive of plans that they have helped to formulate.

The sequencing and pacing of program implementation are crucial. To introduce too many changes and too many programming activities simultaneously can bring chaos. Reasonable goals need to be set and sufficient time allowed to test out each phase of programming.

Even best laid plans will go awry, however, without strong leadership. The leader's role throughout is one of support, encouragement, clarification, and training. It is the leader who can model behavior, demonstrating that it is rewarding and exciting to work with the elderly; that follow-through is essential in effective programming; that staff at all levels are valued and essential members of the team. It is the leader, too, who can establish a climate in which it is safe to test out new techniques and programs *and fail* and in which the failure itself becomes a learning experience to insure the effectiveness of future efforts.

REGULAR EVALUATION AND REVISION

The continued effort of evaluation and revision accommodates the program to the changing institution. Because of staff turnover, the changing needs of residents, and the successes and failures of the program, alterations will be needed to keep the program directed toward its objectives.

CONCLUSION

Only by constant examination of practices in treatment settings will we be able to improve the quality of care of the sick elderly. The humanistic approach is elusive and one that we probably can identify only by fantasizing our own reactions if we were in situations similar to those that the elderly are forced to face at times when they are least able to cope. May Sarton (10) wrote her poignant book *As We Are Now* by imagining her own reactions to living in a nursing home she had visited. She captures the essence of the humanistic milieu in the statement made by the principal character, a nursing home resident, who, after a very stressful period with hostile staff, finds comfort in her relationship with a warm and sympathetic aide: ". . . it is being cared for as though I am worthy of care. It is being not humiliated but treasured."

REFERENCES

1. Cape RDT: Freedom from restraint (abstract). *Gerontologist* 23:217, 1983.
2. Coons DH: Memory loss and issues of reality. In Coons DH, Metzelaar L, Robinson A, et al (Eds): *A Better Life.* Columbus, OH., Source for Nursing Home Literature, 1986, pp. 149–158.
3. Coons DH, Weaverdyck SE: Wesley Hall: A residential unit for persons with Alzheimer's disease and related disorders. In Taira ED (Ed): *Therapeutic Interventions for the Person with Dementia.* New York, The Haworth Press, 1986, pp 29–53.
4. Coons DH: Designing a residential care unit for persons with dementia. Washington, DC, Congressional Office of Technology Assessment, Contract No. 633-19500, 1987.
5. Coons DH: Overcoming problems in modifying the environment. In Altman H (Ed): *Alzheimer's Disease: Problems, Prospects, and Perspectives.* New York, Plenum Corporation, 1987.
6. Cumming J, Cumming E: *Ego and Milieu.* New York, Atherton Press, 1963.
7. Cummings JL, Benson, DF: *Dementia: A Clinical Approach.* Boston, Butterworth Publishers, 1983.
8. Frengley JD, Mion LC: Incidence of physical restraints on acute general medical wards. *J Am Geriatr Soc* 34:8, 1986.
9. Kane RA, Kane RL: *Assessing the Elderly: A Practical Guide to Measurement.* Lexington, MA: Lexington Books, DC Heath and Company, 1981.
10. Sarton M: *As We Are Now.* New York, WW Norton and Co, 1973.
11. Woods RT, Britton PG: *Clinical Psychology with the Elderly.* Rockville, MD, Aspen Systems Corporation, 1985.

CHAPTER 16

Neurologic Diseases in the Elderly

STANLEY L. COHAN

Almost all the common neurologic diseases are primarily diseases of the elderly and include stroke, dementia, and parkinsonism, with a large number, if not the majority, of peripheral neuropathies also making their appearance in old age. Neurology has always been the practice of geriatric medicine and elderly patients are the group with which most neurologists have the greatest affinity; the elderly have been the wisest teachers.

Much of the progress made in diagnosis and treatment of neurologic diseases has benefited elderly patients. Development of less invasive diagnostic methodologies has permitted more thorough evaluation of disease that would have been prohibited by risks entailed in older diagnostic methods. In addition, improved surgical and pharmacologic managements have presented treatment opportunities heretofore not available to the elderly patient, but these expanded opportunities have magnified the necessity to individualize the needs assessment of each elderly patient carefully. Whereas age cannot be the sole determinant in medical management decisions, one should not lose sight of the objective, which is to preserve or improve the medical well-being of the patient. Thus, one may be compelled not to pursue diagnosis or treatment if risk is excessive or if successful outcome will not improve the patient's quality of life. In the following discussion of neurologic diseases, diagnosis and treatment must be considered within the context of these management principles.

Although one could provide a list of the major neurologic illnesses affecting older patients, it seems more instructive where possible to categorize neurologic disease of the elderly according to types of disability produced.

DEMENTIA

Dementia is the presence of significant cognitive and intellectual impairment, due to organic brain dysfunction, usually in the presence of normal sensorium or level of alertness. Dementia is primarily a disease of the elderly and is a problem of growing dimensions as the percentage of elderly individuals increases in modern societies (49, 67). In its mildest forms, memory deficits such as forgetting names, impaired recall of information recently acquired, and increased misplacing of familiar objects may all occur. More advanced dysfunction may include loss of ability to perform simple calculations, difficulty in managing simple financial affairs, inability to remember the date, and in more severe cases, the day, month, or year. Demented patients may be the first to recognize their symptoms, particularly if the primary manifestations are difficulty with memory. Seeking medical attention, writing lists of information so as not to depend on memory, and enlisting the assistance of family members may be employed to combat the difficulty. More severe cognitive impairment may not be apparent to the patient and the symptoms may initially be manifest by errors or deterioration in performance at work, serious financial or social problems created by inability to manage a bank account properly, pay bills, or file tax returns. Patients may become lost when walking or driving if spatial or geographic disorientation occurs. Severely demented individuals may require assistance with dressing, preparation of meals, and personal hygiene.

In moderate to severe forms of dementia, there is often a progressive withdrawal from social contacts and diversions; often such patients will no longer leave the house, read books or listen to music. Although many such individuals become apathetic with blunting of affect, others may demonstrate increased irritability, reduced tolerance of frustration or confusion, and become belligerent and uncooperative. Increased suspiciousness, paranoid delusions, and visual hallucinations may occur in some patients with severe dementia. The most severe cases of dementia may be characterized by marked paucity of language, or complete mutism, marked impairment or inability to understand others, and total dependence on others for personal care (21, 49, 67).

Dementia encompasses a spectrum of severity and patients may vary widely in their degree of impairment. Some demented patients may experience gradual progression from the mildest forms of memory impairment to the most severe stages of cognitive and intellectual impairment, while others develop impairment suddenly and either remain stable or experience further impairment in a step-wise or episodic fashion. The features of onset and the pattern of progression are frequently critical information in differential diagnosis (42, 43, 66, 67).

The neurologic exam in demented patients will reveal abnormalities in mental status, particularly in short-term memory and immediate recall, orientation to place and time, abstract thinking, simple calculation, knowledge of current events, and ability to draw geometric shapes or common objects. Tests of language function may reveal paucity of vocabulary, difficulty in word finding, impaired comprehension of spoken language, and impaired ability to read. Word substitutions or neologisms (paraphasia) and, in the most severe cases, complete loss of ability to comprehend or communicate may be elicited. Other objective neurologic features may include loss of fine motor coordination, unsteady wide-based gait (ataxia) or shuffling, or frozen gait (gait apraxia). Abnormal deep tendon reflexes, and motor tone, frontal release signs such as the snout reflex and Babinski reflexes may be present. Sensory loss, particularly in a distal distribution in the extremities (stocking-glove sensory loss) may also be seen, particularly in dementia associated with metabolic diseases and intoxication.

There are many known causes of dementia but the majority of cases are due to only several important disease entities. Alzheimer's disease and cerebrovascular disease are the most common, with chronic intoxication, brain tumor, trauma, and communicating hydrocephalus being less frequent but important causes of dementia (49). Hypovitaminosis-malnutrition, endocrinopathy, syphilis, and chronic fungal infections are infrequent but important because of the potential for treatment.

ALZHEIMER'S DISEASE

Although long recognized as a cause of dementia in middle-aged and elderly patients, it is only over the last 10–15 years that Alzheimer's disease (AD) has been identified as the most common cause of dementia in the elderly, comprising 50–60% of cases over the age of 65 years (49, 67, 75). There are examples of familial occurrence and, in some cases, there is the possibility of genetic transmission (49). Recent studies also point to potential importance of history of severe head trauma (57), however, no definite etiology for AD has been established. AD is a progressive neurologic disease, which usually begins with forgetfulness and short-term memory disturbance, and extends eventually to all areas of observable cognitive function (67). Generally over a period of 2–5 years patients become increasingly dependent upon others for their care as memory loss, frank confusion, and disorientation render them incapable of managing their personal affairs. Patients may become lost when outside their home and eventually cannot operate an automobile. Vivid visual hallucinations, delusions, sometimes insisting that their spouse is someone else, and occasional intemperate or violent outbursts may occur. The loss of previous occupational skills and recreational interests combined with confusion and intellectual decline have the effect of progressively contracting the person's social sphere. Paucity of interests and apathy lead to ever diminishing levels of activity until they are reduced to remaining in their room, sitting in a chair, or remaining in bed if left alone. Loss of concern for and eventually severe deterioration in dressing, eating, and personal hygiene increase the dependency of the patient on family members, friends, or social service support. Urinary and fecal incontinence, eventual inability to communicate verbally, loss of ability to ambulate, and difficulty in swallowing characterize the most advanced stages of this disease. Patients may die during this stage, if not sooner, from intercurrent pulmonary or urinary tract infection, sepsis, or severe malnutrition and dehydration.

In any patient with a progressive dementia, the diagnosis of AD must be considered, however, there are no pathognomonic signs or symptoms that allow definitive diagnosis. Neither computed axialtomography (CAT) which invariably demonstrates atrophy (26), nor the electroencephalogram (EEG), which will demonstrate abnormal diffuse slow wave activity (58), establish the diagnosis. Definitive diagnosis requires brain biopsy or autopsy examination. Pathologically distinctive abnormalities include the presence of neurofibrillary tangles of abnormal proteins within neurons, senile plaques which are degenerating synapses, granulovacular, and Hirano bodies (75, 77). These findings are most prominent in the temporal lobes and hippocampus. In addition, there is a loss of large neurons throughout the cerebral cortex, as well as a loss of cholinergic neurons arising in the forebrain (nucleus basalis) that project to the cortex (20, 25, 49, 84) and may be responsible for problems in memory and recall in patients with AD. Loss of other cell groups arising in the brainstem and projecting to the cerebral cortex include noradrenergic neurons of the locus coeruleus (77, 78) and serotonergic neurons of dorsal tegmentum (49) that may account, in part, for the mood and behavioral disturbances in AD. In addition, a marked decrease in the peptide neurotransmitter, somatostatin, has also been demonstrated (24).

The loss of cholinergic neurons that project to the cortex, the demonstrated loss of the acetylcholine synthesizing enzyme, choline acetyltransferase (14), and the ability to produce memory disturbances in normal controls similar to those observed in AD patients by use of anticholinergic drugs (27) has resulted in attempts to treat AD with compounds that might increase cholinergic activity in the central nervous system (CNS). The acetylcholine precursors, choline or phosphatidylcholine (lecithin), have not resulted in improved memory function (37), but the parenterally administered centrally acting acetylcholinesterase inhibitor, physostigmine, does transiently improve memory (6, 18). Recent studies of the centrally acting cholinergic agonist tetrahydroaminoacridine (74) has also demonstrated significant benefit in memory function in patients with AD.

Although there has been some promise shown for drugs with cholinergic activity, these drugs address only part of the symptom complex. Therapy for patients with AD is symptomatic and social, maintaining adequate nutrition and personal hygiene, preventing and treating infection, and providing a social context within which the patient may function consistent with the patient's abilities and disabilities. Use of medication to treat depression, agitation, hallucinations and other psychotic thought disorders, and sleeping medication to prevent patients from being awake all night may also be necessary. Parallel to the symptomatic and supportive care provided to the patient, a support system must be present to assist the family, which must provide most of the care for the patient throughout all but the terminal stages of his or her illness, when most patients require a chronic care facility. The physical and emotional stress attendant to caring for a patient with AD cannot be overemphasized nor can the need for psychologic and social service support and counseling for family members.

MULTI-INFARCT DEMENTIA

Although multi-infarct dementia (MID) may be discussed in a section on cerebrovascular disease, MID produces a syndrome that is part of the differential diagnosis of dementia (43) and is second only to AD as a cause of dementia in the elderly, causing up to 20% of the cases (49). MID is the result of repeated strokes. Although MID is progressive in nature, its onset is more likely to be sudden and its progression episodic rather than the gradual progression seen in AD (43). Frequent, multiple infarctions arising from emboli within the heart or carotid arteries, large bilateral hemisphere infarctions secondary to carotid or middle cerebral artery occlusion, and scattered, small deep infarctions (lacunes) in association with hypertension and/or diabetes mellitus are all mechanisms by which these may occur. Unlike AD, the CAT scan may be diagnostic, demonstrating multiple focal areas of brain loss in the cortex and/or deep in the cerebral hemispheres. In addition to dementia and an episodic course, focal neurologic deficits such as hemiparesis, cerebellar ataxia, and brainstem dysfunction may assist in making the diagnosis of MID (43). Although functional loss due to infarction is irretrievable, progression of disease may be halted or slowed by addressing the underlying etiology of the infarction with use of anticoagulants, antiplatelet drugs, antiarrhythmics, antihypertensives, or carotid artery surgery where appropriate (see Cerebrovascular Disease).

HEAD TRAUMA

Head trauma frequently occurs when the elderly person falls at home (tripping over furniture, falling in bath tubs, at the toilet, or down steps) or falls when outdoors in inclement weather, trips over the pavement, is struck by a vehicle or is a victim of assault. The most severe forms of head trauma including depressed skull fractures, cerebral laceration, and intracerebral hemorrhage, are associated with high mortality or severe morbidity. Lesser degrees of trauma that result in contusion or concussion may produce dementia, either resulting directly from blunt trauma to the frontal and temporal lobes or indirectly resulting from the development of a chronic subdural hematoma. In dementia secondary to contusion, varying degrees and patterns of cognitive impairment may be present depending upon the sites and degree of brain damage. Because of the particular vulnerability of the temporal and frontal lobes, impairment in memory and recall, mood disturbances and blunted affect often predominate and may be associated with gait apraxia. These features may be apparent immediately or become so during convalescence. A more insidious progressive pattern of dementia may also occur, at times manifest weeks to months after the trauma and resulting from the development of a chronic subdural hematoma. The hematoma may enlarge progressively and, as a space occupying lesion, lead to increased intracranial pressure as well as focal brain compression, although the focal features may not be apparent on examination because the hematoma lies outside the parenchyma of the brain. Frequently the history of trauma is not obtained and, thus, a hematoma is not suspected. Although progressive or intermittent lethargy frequently accompanies the enlargement of the hematoma due to increasing intracranial pressure, disturbances in level of consciousness may not be apparent. Thus, subdural hematoma must always be considered in patients with dementia, particularly when the dementia has progressed over weeks to several months. The diagnosis can be made reliably by CAT scan, with rewarding results after surgical evacuation of the hematoma, although spontaneous resorption of the hematoma may occur in some patients on bed rest (9).

COMMUNICATING HYDROCEPHALUS

Communicating hydrocephalus (CH) may be associated with the triad of dementia, which is slowly progressive, apractic shuffling gait, and urinary incontinence. The CH arises from impaired reabsorption of cerebrospinal fluid (CSF) in the subarachnoid space by the arachnoid villi. This results in reflux of CSF back into the ventricles where it was produced and leads to progressive ventricular distention. Although there is a history of meningitis, subarachnoid or cerebral hemorrhage, or trauma in some patients, the cause of CH is unknown in most patients (2). The diagnosis is supported by a CAT scan demonstrating distention of the lateral ventricles without appropriate atrophy of the overlying cerebral hemispheres. The diagnosis is verified by radionuclide cisternography, in which radioactive tracer is instilled into the lumbar subarachnoid space. In normal individuals, the tracer would pass over the cerebral hemisphere with normally circulating CSF, but in CH, the tracer will accompany the CSF reflux into the ventricles. Treatment of CH by ventricular shunting is successful in halting the progression of dementia, or even improving mentation and ambulation in some patients (2). The reasons for failure of shunting in the remaining patients is unknown. Concurrent disease such as AD or cere-

brovascular disease, poor shunt function, or permanent brain damage from the hydrocephalus are possible explanations. It is probable that the earlier the diagnosis, the greater the likelihood of a good clinical response to shunting.

DEMENTIA SECONDARY TO SYSTEMIC DISEASE

Infectious etiologies of dementia include neurosyphilis, which should always be considered in the differential diagnosis of dementia, even if serum serology is negative. Spinal fluid examination, which is essential in all demented patients, should include Venereal Disease Research Laboratory test for syphilis (VDRL), cell count, protein and sugar. A positive CSF VDRL is diagnostic for neurosyphilis. Neurosyphilis is treated with intravenous penicillin, erythromycin, or tetracycline (63).

Cryptococcal meningitis may produce dementia that is slowly progressive and may persist for many years although rapid onset and progression of dementia may also be seen. Examination of CSF usually will reveal an elevated white blood cell (WBC) count, elevated protein, and normal glucose. The organisms are frequently not seen but tests for cryptococcal antigen will be positive in virtually all cases of active disease. Cryptococcal meningitis is treated with intravenous amphotericin B and 5-flurocytosine (10).

Endocrinopathy can also produce dementia that is usually slowly progressive. Hypothyroidism, in particular, should be ruled out by measuring thyroid hormone and thyroid stimulating hormone (TSH) levels and is treated by thyroid hormone administration. Hyperparathyroidism, usually due to a parathyroid tumor, may also produce dementia and is suggested by an elevated serum calcium level and confirmed by measurement of serum parathormone levels. Removal of parathyroid tumors may result in dramatic improvement in dementia.

Hypovitaminosis and malnutrition are extremely important potential causes of dementia in the elderly, with deficiency in thiamine (Wernicke-Korsakoff psychosis), niacin (pellagra), and B_{12}-folate (subacute combined degeneration), occurring singly or as part of polyhypovitaminosis (64, 81). This may be compounded by inadequate oral intake of protein to produce amino acid deficiency in the CNS. The presence of peripheral neuropathy manifested by diminished or absent tendon reflexes and loss of sensation distally in the extremities, may suggest malnutrition as causes of dementia. Anemia, hypoalbuminemia, and, in the case of B_{12} and/or folate deficiency, macrocytosis may suggest malnutrition (56, 64). In addition, serum B_{12}, folate, and thiamine levels can be measured.

Drug intoxication is an extremely important, reversible cause of dementia that may result from improper use of a wide variety of drugs, including but not restricted to, sedatives, neuroleptics, sleeping medication, opiates and nonopiate analgesics including aspirin, diuretics, nondiuretic antihypertensives, cardiac glycosides, and antiarrhythmics. Confusion about dosage, purposeful abuse, use of medication prescribed by several different physicians or clinics unknown to each other, failure to cease old medication when new drugs are prescribed, improper prescribing, or poor tolerance of adverse side effects are all possible reasons for drug intoxication. Careful history-taking from the patient and relatives, with review of all drugs in the patient's home, and if necessary, drug screening of urine to determine all drugs being used may be necessary.

Lastly, chronic alcohol abuse may also be associated with dementia, probably due to the combination of malnutrition and direct toxic effect of ethanol. A characteristic dementia, Korsakoff's psychosis, may be seen in which striking loss of short-term memory and recall, disorientation to place and time, and confabulation are seen and is thought to result primarily from thiamine deficiency (81).

The diagnostic workup of the demented patient should include CAT scan and EEG, thyroid function tests, complete blood count (CBC), serum electrolytes, including calcium and magnesium, serum VDRL, B_{12}, folate levels, and serum albumin. Spinal tap with CSF examination for protein, sugar, VDRL, cell count, and cryptococcal antigen are also necessary. When indicated, a broad drug screen (not just drugs of abuse) should be performed on a urine sample.

PARKINSONISM

Parkinson's disease (PD) is a degenerative disease of the CNS of unknown cause. A small percentage of cases are attributed to encephalitis that occurred during the influenza pandemic of 1914–1919; in these cases, the onset of PD occurred approximately 10 years after recovery from the encephalitis. Toxic side effects of certain drugs, particularly neuroleptics such as chlorpromazine or haloperidol, may produce some of the features of PD. The characteristic features of the disease include stooped posture, blunted, expressionless face (masked facies), and slow, small-stepped or shuffling gait that, in its more advanced stages, may evolve into a frozen stance on attempted ambulation. Patients also have postural instability, with a tendency to fall backward and a failure to make adjustments necessary to maintain balance. They usually have difficulty arising from a chair or rolling over in bed and may develop dysarthria or hypophonia. Patients have a characteristic tremor, particularly of the hands (pill-rolling tremors) with rigidity, slowness of movements (bradykinesia) and impaired fine motor coordination, difficulty writing, and a characteristic small-lettered tremulous penmanship (micrographia). The rigidity, bradykinesia, tremor, and impairment of fine motor coordination in the extremities almost invariably begin on one side, but eventually become bilateral. Mood disorders, particularly depression, are common in patients with PD (54). Dementia is also seen in many patients (27, 44), with some pathologic biochemical features similar or identical to those found in AD (12, 70).

Pathologically, the major feature of PD is loss of pigmented neurons in the substantia nigra that project to the basal ganglia (nigrostriatal system). These neurons synthesize dopamine that is released at synapses in the striatum. Many of the clinical features of PD can be attributed to dopamine deficiency in the brain. Pathologic features of AD are also seen in many parkinsonian patients who have dementia, with neurofibrillary tangles and senile plaques in the cortex, as well as loss of cholinergic neurons from the nucleus basalis of Meynert (12). The treatment of PD aims at restoring dopaminergic function (19, 73). Dopamine cannot be administered because it will not cross the blood-brain barrier, but its precursor, L-dihydroxyphenylalanine (levodopa) is transported into the brain where the enzyme, dopa-decarboxylase, converts it to dopamine (19). Most levodopa ingested does not enter the brain, being metabolized peripherally in liver, adrenals, blood vessels, and peripheral nerve endings. Levodopa has significant side effects, among which nausea and abdominal discomfort are largely due to systemic effects (19). The addition of d-methyldopahydrazine (carbidopa), a peripheral dopa decarboxylase inhibitor that cannot cross the blood-brain barrier, results in reduced peripheral conversion of dopa to dopamine and in higher percentages of levodopa entering the brain. This permits use of a lower dosage of levodopa and fewer peripheral side effects (53). Other toxic side effects of levodopa, which are centrally mediated, include restlessness, confusion, agitation, frank psychosis with hallucinations, excessive motor activity (hyperkinesia) and orthostatic hypotension that may result in lightheadedness or faintness, and in the most severe cases, syncope upon standing (17). Treatment with levodopa or levodopa plus carbidopa results in significant improvement in most of the motor features of the disease (19, 73), hand tremor being the least responsive. Improved postural stance and stability, improved speed of ambulation, increased ability to rise from a chair, and reduced rigidity and bradykinesia may all be seen (19, 73). Unfortunately, PD is a progressive disease and patients usually require increasing medication doses; a point eventually is reached where increased dosage produces increased side effects with little improvement in symptoms (23, 73). At that point, the addition of a direct dopamine agonist is indicated, bromocriptine being the prototype for this group of drugs (48). Whereas levodopa, a precursor of dopamine, requires some functioning neurons for its enzymatic conversion, bromocriptine, requiring no conversion, can act directly on dopamine receptors in the brain. Bromocriptine can be used in combination with levodopa, and, in some cases, as the sole medication. Anticholinergic drugs, such as trihexiphenidyl and benztropine, may be of transient benefit in the treatment of PD and possibly reduce the dosage requirement of levodopa or bromocriptine but are to be considered secondary drugs. Amantadine, an antihistamine, may be of transient benefit and but no significant role in the long-term drug management of most patients with PD. The anticholinergics, sometimes with the addition of amantidine, are occasionally used in patients who cannot tolerate dopaminergic drugs, but the clinical response is largely unsatisfactory. Anticholinergics may also impair memory (21), and because many patients with PD have dementia, anticholinergic use may be contraindicated (70). Many patients with PD, particularly those treated for many years, may develop periods of marked overactivity alternating in often unpredictable patterns with marked bradykinesia (on-off phenomenon) (30, 61). Although related at least in part to impairment of gastrointestinal absorption and uptake by the brain of levodopa (61), other factors, at present not understood, are also probably responsible. Management of this situation requires gradual reduction in dosage, careful observation of the time of onset of bradykinesia or hypokinesia in relationship to time of medication and timing of meals, because amino acids in food may block uptake of levodopa from intestines and high plasma amino acid levels may block uptake of levodopa by the brain. Measurement of plasma levodopa and amino acid levels at various intervals may aid in the selection of proper drug dose and intervals of administration (61). In addition to motor impairment, PD is associated with serious psychosocial problems for both the patient and other family members. Loss of self-confidence, dependency upon others, and resentment of well-meaning family members are all problems that require the attention, advice, and reassurance of physicians, nurses, and social service personnel. Adequate transportation and proper placement of furniture, hand rails, and bathroom appliances to reduce possible injury from falls, may permit maximum self-care and freedom of activity, both of which are extremely important. Physical therapy may also make an important contribution to the rehabilitation of the patient with PD. Although levodopa and other dopaminergic agents may increase the patient's potential motor performance greatly, the physical therapist's assistance in postural stability and gait training, in relearning fine motor skills, and regaining self-confidence cannot be overemphasized. Depression is common and may require psychotherapy including the use of antidepressants (54). Depression may be manifest primarily by perception of increased motor impairment or reduced tolerance to anti-Parkinson drugs, confounding the clinical management of the patient's PD. Dementia is an extremely serious complication of PD, often associated with adverse behavioral responses to anti-Parkinson medication and frequently resulting in the need for chronic care facility placement.

NEUROMUSCULAR DISORDERS

Myopathy classically presents as proximal muscle weakness of the extremities with loss of deep tendon reflexes and preservation of sensation. Although most myopathies occur in children and younger adults, several myopathic disorders are found in older patients, the most important being the myopathy that can occur as a nonmetastatic effect of carcinoma (72). Progressive, insidious weakness of proximal extremities, sparing the muscles supplied by cranial nerves, in an elderly patient should always prompt a search for a neoplasm, particularly of the gastrointestinal tract, pancreas, and lung.

An inflammatory myopathy (polymyositis), which is frequently associated with muscle aching or pain, usually presents as proximal muscle weakness and is only rarely associated with neoplasia (69). High circulating levels of muscle enzymes (creatinine phosphokinase and aldolase) and elevated sedimentation rate are usually found. Muscle biopsy reveals inflammatory muscle fiber necrosis. Polymyositis is treated with steroids, usually prednisone 100 mg/day, with dosage being gradually diminished as clinical and laboratory evidence of muscle necrosis diminishes. Successful treatment results in partial or complete return of motor strength and resolution of the myalgia. Unfortunately re-exacerbation is common and some patients lose steroid responsiveness and require treatment with cytotoxic agents (11).

All patients presenting with a myopathic picture should have electromyography and nerve conduction studies, as well as muscle biopsy before any consideration of therapy.

Neuropathies may be manifest as loss of sensation, with diminished or absent tendon reflexes, particularly distally. In more pronounced cases, there is also distal weakness and atrophy of muscles. This pattern is referred to as polyneuropathy and is extremely common in the elderly and usually the result of metabolic disease and/or chronic intoxication. Among the most common causes of polyneuropathy in the elderly is diabetes mellitus (76). Nutritional deficiency and associated polyvitamin B deficiency are also important causes of neuropathy (56, 64). Collagen vascular disease (51), syphilis (56), uremia (28), and drug toxicity may also result in polyneuropathy (56). Guillain-Barré syndrome, a dysimmune radiculoneuropathy (5), may also present with distal sensorimotor symptoms, although proximal muscle weakness is a common presentation. Polyneuropathy may also occur as a remote effect of carcinoma, in many cases appearing months to years before the tumor is discovered (55).

The diagnostic workup in a patient with polyneuropathy usually includes electromyography and nerve conduction studies, as well as the appropriate laboratory studies to establish a toxic or metabolic etiology. If an etiology is not established, workup for neoplasm should be considered (55). Physical therapy to improve motor strength and ambulation, including use of appropriate orthotic devices and especial attention to care of joints and skin are essential.

Mononeuropathies and plexopathies are also peripheral nerve disorders that affect large nerve trunks or plexi in contrast to the small distal fibers affected in polyneuropathy. Acute or chronic compressive neuropathy (38) involving ulnar, radial, sciatic, and peroneal nerves is common as is entrapment of the median nerve at the wrist (carpal tunnel syndrome). Blunt trauma, entrapment by degenerative joint hypertrophy, compression by tumor, or body position are common causes of mononeuropathy. Diabetes (55), and collagen vascular disease (51) may also cause mononeuropathy and, in some cases, diabetes may be associated with plexopathy with proximal muscle weakness that can be mistaken for myopathy but is distinguished by presence of neuropathic rather than myopathic changes on muscle biopsy, electromyograph/nerve conduction velocity (EMG/NCV), and usually some associated sensory changes which would not be seen in myopathies. In many instances, performance of EMG/NCV is unnecessary. An elderly patient with obvious polyneuropathy manifested by distal sensory loss in the extremities and loss of distal tendon reflexes, is not well-served by performing EMG/NCV. The tests are very uncomfortable, expensive, and unless the results of EMG/NCV influence therapy or prognosis, they are unnecessary.

Myasthenia gravis is a disease of neuromuscular transmission in which impaired interaction between acetylcholine, released by the motor nerve, and its receptor on muscle is impaired due to the presence of antibodies to the receptor (the nicotinic acetylcholine receptor) (31, 50). Although myasthenia gravis can occur at any age, it is seen more commonly in younger females and older males. Extraocular muscle weakness producing diplopia and ptosis is a common presenting symptom but symptoms may begin with weakness of the proximal extremities. Facial weakness, nasal speech, and difficulty swallowing may also develop. The most serious complication of myasthenia gravis is respiratory failure. Therefore, respiratory status must be closely monitored. Patients with myasthenia have preserved tendon reflexes and no loss of sensation, distinguishing them from patients with myopathy or neuropathy (41). Patients should be studied by EMG/NCV with repetitive stimulation, which in myasthenia results in a decremental motor response that is reversed by anticholinesterase medication. Most myasthenic patients have elevated acetylcholine receptor antibodies in the blood. Myasthenia gravis must be distinguished from the Eaton-Lambert syndrome in which patients with neoplasia, usually oat cell carcinoma of the lung, develop proximal muscle weakness due to impaired release of acetylcholine (29). These patients have reduced tendon reflexes, and on EMG repetitive stimulation, have augmentation rather than decrement in the motor response.

Most patients with myasthenia gravis respond to treatment with oral anticholinesterases, pyridostigmine being most commonly used. However, progression of symptoms, despite increasing drug dose, frequently requires the addition of steroids (41). Some patients continue to deteriorate despite steroids and anticholinesterases and may be helped by plasmapheresis that removes acetylcholine receptor antibodies from blood (22, 23). Intermittent plasmapheresis combined with steroids and anticholinesterases should control even the most severely impaired patients.

Amyotrophic lateral sclerosis (ALS) is a progressive illness characterized by weakness due to degeneration of motor neurons in the spinal cord ("anterior horn cell disease"), brainstem ("bulbar palsy"), and cerebral hemipheres (59). The cause of the disease is unknown, but has been associated with chronic lead poisoning (13) or autoimmune disease in a small number of cases (65). There are also examples of hereditary ALS where the disease appears in consecutive generations, but the majority of cases do not follow any pattern of genetic inheritance. Atrophy, weakness, and a characteristics twitching of muscles (fasciculations) in the hands are the most common presenting features and are due to dysfunction of anterior horn cells (59). Anterior horn cell dysfunction invariably progresses and is eventually seen throughout the muscles of upper and lower extremities, the tongue, and facial muscles. These are the lower motor neuron features of the disease. In addition, degeneration of the corticospinal and corticobulbar tracts further contribute to weakness, hyper-reflexia, and Babinski reflexes (59). These are the upper motor neuron features of the disease. In most cases, upper and lower motor neuron features occur simultaneously. Eventually, impaired swallowing leads to malnutrition, enhancing the rate of deterioration in muscles. Weakness of respiratory effort leads to hypoxia, CO_2 retention, and increased respiratory drive by the brain to already weakened muscle. Respiratory status is placed at further risk by aspiration of food and saliva. ALS must be distinguished from other illnesses producing both upper and lower motor neuron impairment, especially degenerative spine disease in which spondylosis leading to nerve root compression in cervical and lumbar regions would produce weakness, atrophy, and fasciculations; cervical spinal cord compression would produce corticospinal tract impairment. Cervical and lumbosacral spondylosis and stenosis are common in the elderly and its differentiation from ALS is essential because spondylosis is not a life-threatening disease and can be treated. The presence of fasciculations in tongue or face and other signs of brainstem motor dysfunction will differentiate ALS from spinal cord dysfunction due to vertebral disease, but when clinical signs of bulbar dysfunction are not yet present in patients with ALS, the differentiation can be very difficult. In ALS, EMG recording demonstrates fibrillation. When fibrillation is present in the tongue and upper and lower extremities, this should establish the diagnosis. Unfortunately, ALS is a progressive disease, and although the rate of progression is variable,

most patients die within 2–5 years of onset of symptoms (59).

Significant resources must be expended to care for the patient with advanced ALS. Impairment of swallowing and poor nutrition accelerate the process of muscle degeneration and patients will eventually require a nasogastric tube, gastrostomy, or esophagostomy for feeding. Because of marked soft tissue loss and immobility, skin breakdown is also a serious concern. Most patients with ALS probably die from respiratory failure or inability to clear airway obstruction due to aspiration. Therefore, tracheostomy and mechanical ventilation are eventually necessary to keep the patient alive. Many patients, even in the terminal stages of their disease can be managed at home with portable miniventilators and visiting ventilator and respiratory care technicians. The physical and emotional toll on family are considerable and, if the patient is cared for by an elderly spouse, serious adverse effects of fatigue from the lack of sleep and physical exertion necessary to provide total care will cause the support system to break down. Professional nursing assistance is required for at least one 8-hour shift per day, preferably at night, so that family members can sleep. Alternatively, many patients do not want to live under the conditions of almost total paralysis and dependence imposed by ALS and will refuse permission for tracheostomy and feeding tubes.

NEOPLASIA

Tumors of the nervous system may be primary or metastatic. Meningiomas are common primary brain tumors in the elderly. The location and, thus, the neurologic findings vary, with progressive weakness, headache, and seizures being common presentations. Meningiomas may also arise in the spine, producing both spinal cord compression and focal lower motor neuron weakness due to nerve root involvement. Usually benign and slowly growing, meningiomas should be surgically removed when accessible, the exception being small asymptomatic tumors that are best followed conservatively by serial CAT scans.

Glioblastomas, malignant intracerebral tumors, usually occur before the seventh decade but are occasionally seen in older patients. The prognosis for these tumors is extremely poor even with radical surgery and follow-up radiation therapy, survival rarely exceeding 2 years from time of diagnosis (47), thus, the surgical management of these tumors is rarely justified in the elderly.

A wide variety of tumors metastasize to the brain (45), the numbers increasing as chemotherapy becomes more effective systemically, using drugs that do not effectively penetrate the CNS. Depending on location, metastases may present as progressive weakness, seizures, lethargy, headache, ataxia, or behavioral change. In most cases, metastases are in multiple locations, are readily detected by CAT scan, and are usually treated with whole-head radiation and steroids (16, 46). In cases where solitary metastases are seen on CAT scan, there is debate whether these should be removed surgically or treated solely by radiation. Metastatic cells may involve the meninges and produce a meningitis-like picture with headache, stiff neck, and lethargy, however multiple progressive cranial nerve abnormalities, or distal spinal root (cauda equina syndrome) dysfunction with weakness, sensory loss, and areflexia in the legs may also be present (62). The diagnosis is established by finding tumor cells in the CSF and patients are treated with intrathecal medication or by placing a cerebral shunt (Ommaya reservoir) through which medication, usually methotrexate, can be injected (39).

INFECTIONS

The most common CNS infection in the elderly is bacterial meningitis, which may be caused by *Pneumococcus, Staphylococcus, Streptococcus,* or *Haemophilus* (63). In immunocompromised, malnourished, and hospitalized patients, *Klebsiella, Pseudomonas,* tuberculosis, and fungal meningitis, particularly *Cryptococcus,* may also cause meningitis. Clinically, the patients are typically, but not invariably, febrile and have lethargy, confusion, or frank stupor, and a stiff neck. Spinal tap will establish the diagnosis with increased CSF WBC count, elevated CSF protein, and lowered sugar (36). Organisms may be seen on microscopic examination but more commonly are diagnosed on culture. Patients are treated with appropriate antibiotics. Occasionally, patients develop brain abscess, usually from a septic embolus to the brain arising from bacterial endocarditis. Brain abscess is readily seen on CAT scan. Patients with brain abscess should not have lumbar puncture to avoid brain herniation. In any patient with symptoms consistent with CNS infection, CAT scan should be done before lumbar puncture, particularly if focal findings or endocarditis are present. The treatment of brain abscess traditionally has been surgical removal and weeks of systemic antibiotics; increasingly, however, antibiotic therapy alone is being employed with monitoring the abscess by CAT scan (15).

Among viral infections of the nervous system, herpes zoster is the most important (7). This infection usually presents acutely as a painful cutaneous eruption (shingles) in the distribution of the nerve root they have invaded, most commonly unilaterally over the face, thorax, or abdomen. Herpes zoster has a chronic phase in which the crusted, erythematous eruptions are replaced by brown flat lesions and there is depigmentation of skin in the distribution of the affected nerve root. During the acute phase of illness, tenderness of skin is so pronounced that the patient cannot tolerate light touch. In spite of this hyperalgesia, the patient has decreased sensation to pin-prick. In the chronic phase of disease, patients retain decreased sensitivity to pin-prick, but hyperalgesia and hyperesthesia are no longer present. An exception to this is postherpetic neuralgia in which patients have chronic pain and hyperalgesia. The cause of this chronic syndrome is unknown, but persistence of viral infection is a possibility. Until recently, therapy was symptomatic and largely unsatisfactory with analgesics rarely providing adequate pain control. Acyclovir, an antiviral drug that is well-tolerated, is of significant benefit, usually resulting in reduction of pain and more rapid resolution of the infection (7).

TRIGEMINAL NEURALGIA

This is a syndrome of severe facial pain that may occur in frequent shock-like bursts for several days at a time. The patient's face is hypersensitive to touch and patients usually have a trigger point that may set off the attacks. Pain may be so severe that they are unable to wash their face, brush their teeth, or chew. Even a breeze touching their face may produce intolerable pain. The cause of trigeminal neuralgia is unknown although vascular compression of the trigeminal nerve as it leaves the brainstem is one possible cause (4). Treatment of this disease is unsatisfactory in many cases. Although most patients initially will respond to the anticonvulsant carbamazepine, with or without the addition of phenytoin (40), these drugs cease to be effective in many patients. Baclofen and tricyclic antidepressants are also of marginal value. Surgical interruption of the trigeminal nerve, its ganglia or its preganglionic roots may all produce relief of pain. Unfortunately, relief of symptoms is often temporary. In some cases, insulating the trigeminal nerve root from adjacent blood vessels has been reported to reduce symptoms (4, 89).

CEREBROVASCULAR DISEASE

Stroke-related death is a major cause of mortality in the United States, particularly among the elderly.

In addition, millions of elderly people live with severe disabilities as a result of stroke. Major risk factors for stroke include age, hypertension, diabetes, coexistent heart disease, cigarette smoking, and elevated plasma lipids (86, 87). There are many known mechanisms by which cerebral infarction may occur but the vast majority of strokes may be attributed to several causes.

Atheromatous degeneration with stenosis and/or ulceration of the common and internal carotid arteries in the region of the common carotid bifurcation probably accounts for more than half of cerebral hemisphere strokes (33). Degenerative stenosis or occlusion of the middle cerebral artery or intracranial portions of the internal carotid artery is responsible for less than 1% of strokes. Progressive narrowing of the carotids may eventually result in decreased blood flow to the ipsilateral hemisphere and in cerebral infarction, usually deep within the hemisphere, and result in contralateral weakness with maximum involvement of the face and upper extremity. Stroke in the left hemisphere may produce aphasia if the lesion extends to the overlying cortex. The precise location and size of an infarct, and thus the severity of neurologic impairment, is determined in part by the degree of stenosis and the degree of collateral flow available through the circle of Willis at the base of the brain, branches of the external carotid artery and meningeal and cortical anastamoses. Parenthetically, the internal carotid artery must be 75% or more stenotic for a reduction in blood flow to occur at normal cardiac output. The vascular bed of brain tissue receiving reduced blood flow will dilate, increasing local brain blood volume as well as oxygen and substrate extraction. In this way, brain tissue may remain viable despite significant reduction in blood blow (1). The combination of focal vasodilatation plus collateral flow may explain, in part, the frequent finding of complete carotid occlusion in patients without stroke.

In addition to stenosis or occlusion reducing blood flow, emboli may arise from degenerating the carotid and occluded cerebral vessels, usually in the cortex, producing small focal strokes (33, 83). Some emboli may temporarily occlude vessels, with vasodilatation or lysis of emboli restoring cerebral blood flow, producing only temporary neurologic impairment or transient ischemic attacks (TIA). TIAs resolve in less than 24 hours, most commonly within minutes to several hours. The neurologic deficit produced depends upon the location of the embolic infarction, but typically produces more limited degrees of impairment than the deeper lesions produced by high-grade stenosis or occlusion of the carotids. On occasion, large emboli, particularly those arising from the heart, lodge in the distal intracranial carotid rather than passing on to the smaller cortical arteries. This results in large deficits in which complete hemiplegia, visual field, and hemisensory loss combined with decreased level of consciousness occur.

Stroke also occurs in the distribution of the vertebrobasilar system. Atheromatous degeneration of the basilar artery may result in brainstem or cerebellar infarction. Accounting for less than 10% of strokes, brainstem infarction may be manifest as extraocular muscle weakness, pupillary dysfunction, facial weakness or sensory loss, dysarthria, unilateral hearing loss or tinnitus, and difficulty swallowing. Vertigo, nystagmus, gait ataxia, or limb ataxia may result from cerebellar lesions. If infarction extends to the long motor tracts of the brainstem, hemiparesis, hemiplegia, or quadriplegia may occur. If infarction extends deep into the central gray of the brainstem, impairment of consciousness, including coma, may occur. Since the visual cortex of the occipital lobes is supplied by the terminal branches of the basilar artery (the posterior cerebral arteries), basilar artery occlusion can result in visual field defects. Embolic infarction and TIAs in the distribution of the vertebrobasilar system also occur. These emboli probably arise in the vertebral arteries and produce various combinations of cranial nerve, sensory, and motor abnormalities, depending on which branches are occluded. On occasion, an occlusion of the basilar artery may be followed by progressive propagation of thrombus along the length of the basilar artery, with progressive occlusion of more branches of the basilar artery with a resultant stepwise increase in neurologic deficit. This may occur over hours to days and is referred to as a stroke-in-evolution.

Spontaneous nonembolic occlusion of smaller deep vessels of the cerebral hemispheres, brainstem, and cerebellum may result in multiple, disseminated small infarctions (lacunar infarction). Lacunar infarction is seen primarily in patients with diabetes and/or hypertension and is characterized by stepwise progression in neurologic impairment or insidious progressive neurologic impairment punctuated by acute episodes of new neurologic impairment (34).

Another important cause of stroke is cardiac disease. Cardiac arrhythmias (particularly atrial fibrillation with or without concurrent mitral stenosis), endocarditis, prosthetic valves, ventricular wall motion abnormalities due to infarction, and ventricular thrombi may all be associated with embolization to the brain (85), which receives 20% of the cardiac output, mostly through the carotid arteries. In addition, decreased cardiac output and hypotension due to heart failure, ventricular arrhythmias, or heart block may produce a global ischemic insult with resulting loss or diminished level of consciousness. However, if there is pre-existing carotid stenosis, and particularly if compensatory focal cerebral vasodilation and increased oxygen extraction are taking place (1), decreased cardiac output or, for that matter, hypoxia or hypoglycemia, can produce focal rather than global ischemia or infarction. Similarly, hypotension due to acute blood loss or excessive use of antihypertensive medication can produce a focal stroke.

Other, less common causes of stroke include hyperviscosity of blood due to polycythemia, pathologic elevation of platelets (thrombocytosis), syphilis, lupus, and vasculitis, diagnoses that should all be considered in patients with evidence of multifocal infarctions. Giant cell cranial arteritis, usually referred to as temporal arteritis, is of particular importance. Usually manifested by temporal headache, jaw claudication, and occasionally associated with muscle aches and fever (polymyalgia rheumatica), the patients almost always have an elevated erythrocyte sedimentation rate and tenderness of cranial arteries. The diagnosis can frequently be established by temporal artery biopsy. Although cerebral infarction is unusual, infarction of the eye is common. Giant cell cranial arteritis should be suspected in any elderly patient with headache. High dose steroid therapy should be started as soon as the diagnosis is established.

THERAPY

Most therapy currently in use for cerebrovascular disease is prophylactic, in an attempt to reduce the incidence of future stroke in patients at risk.

a) In patients with carotid stenosis, with or without ulceration, who have had TIAs, or who have had a stroke but with good recovery of function, surgical repair of the artery by endarterectomy should be considered (33, 83). Several criteria must be met. The artery should be ipsilateral to the ischemic episodes, not be completely occluded, and the area of stenosis not extend intracranially (33). Surgical treatment may not be possible. Medical treatment should then consist of daily aspirin administration (32). Daily dose requirements have not been established, but 1 adult aspirin tablet each day is recommended, and should be well-tolerated by all patients. Aspirin reduces platelet aggregability that is believed to be the basis of its therapeutic benefit (32, 82).

Addition of other antiplatelet drugs has not been shown to provide additional protection (33, 82).

The use of anticoagulants is not indicated in the treatment of a completed stroke but, on occasion, may be required in the treatment of patients with recurrent embolic ischemia arising from the carotid artery.

b) Patients with completed brainstem or cerebellar strokes should be treated with aspirin, with one exception: stroke in evolution of the brainstem should be treated by anticoagulation with intravenous heparin, switched to oral anticoagulants for approximately 4-6 weeks and then treated chronically with aspirin.

c) Patients with lacunar state should be treated with aspirin.

d) Patients with cardiogenic embolization should be treated initially with heparin and switched to oral anticoagulants (85). In cases of atrial thrombi, valvular disease, and intraventricular clots, which are not going to be corrected surgically, and in patients with atrial fibrillation, even in the absence of mitral stenosis, anticoagulant therapy should be permanent. Caution must be sounded on the use of anticoagulants in patients who have had an embolic infarction and are at risk for additional emboli. Anticoagulation may result in bleeding into the infarction (71). Although it cannot be predicted with absolute certainty, anticoagulation is more likely to result in hemorrhage in strokes associated with large areas of edema seen on CAT scan (71). Thus, a CAT scan done within the first 48 hours after a stroke that demonstrates a large amount of edema should contraindicate anticoagulation. Needless to say, the presence of hemorrhage seen on a CAT scan would also dictate against the use of anticoagulants.

Lastly, one must consider the likelihood of serious hemorrhagic complications due to improper dosing in the forgetful, confused, or demented patient whose medication use is not supervised, as well as the likelihood of the patient having hemorrhage from trauma, particularly from falls. If these pose significant risks to the patient anticoagulants should not be employed even if otherwise clinically indicated.

CEREBRAL HEMORRHAGE

Intracerebral hemorrhage occurs most commonly into the basal ganglia, but is also seen with less frequency in the thalamus, pons, and midline cerebellum (35, 60, 79). A history of hypertension is found in the majority of these patients and the incidence of cerebral hemorrhage relative to nonhemorrhagic stroke has diminished over the past 30 years with the advent of effective antihypertensive medication (8, 88).

Cerebral hemorrhage presents clinically with the sudden onset of neurologic impairment, usually with hemiparesis or hemiplegia, headache, progressive decrease in level of consciousness, and hypertension. Although the presentation may be similar to a nonhemorrhagic deep stroke, patients frequently appear "toxic," with progressive deterioration, which may be an early hint that the patient has had a hemorrhage. CAT scan of the brain will establish this diagnosis. Spinal tap should never be done in a patient suspected of intracerebral hemorrhage for fear of increasing the risk of brain herniation (46).

It is generally agreed that cerebellar hemorrhage should be treated surgically (35). The proper management of cerebral hemispheric hemorrhage is less certain. Older studies pointed to a poor outcome for most patients irrespective of management (60), although more recent studies have suggested improvement in morbidity and mortality after surgical evacuation of hematomas (46, 79). Overall mortality is 40-50% in patients with intracerebral hemorrhage and severe neurologic impairment is common in the majority of survivors (46).

Subarachnoid hemorrhage is usually the result of ruptured berry aneurysm although arteriovenous malformations may also cause bleeding into the subarachnoid space (3, 52, 68). The symptoms of subarachnoid hemorrhage initially may consist solely of severe headache, frequently associated with stiff neck secondary to meningeal irritation by blood. Lethargy, hemiparesis, or cranial nerve abnormalities may also be seen if there is accompanying bleeding into the brain parenchyma or subarachnoid blood-induced vasospasm producing brain infarction. In the majority of cases, a CAT scan will demonstrate blood in the subarachnoid space obviating the need for spinal tap to determine if there has been subarachnoid hemorrhage. All patients with subarachnoid hemorrhage should have a cerebral angiogram to identify the aneurysm and all aneurysms should be treated surgically, if not otherwise contraindicated, because of the high propensity of aneurysms to rebleed (3). Mortality from aneurysmal hemorrhage is approximately 40% with mortality increased by each recurrent hemorrhage (3, 68). Contraindications to surgery include comatose state or hemiplegia as well as systemic bleeding disorders. In some centers, antifibrinolytic drugs, such as amino-epsilon-caproic acid, are used to decrease the incidence of recurrent hemorrhage, providing more time to improve the patient's clinical status and improve the chances of successful surgical management (80).

Arteriovenous malformations (AVMs) should also be treated surgically if they have bled and are readily accessible. AVMs that are deep in location or have multiple feeding vessels, making surgical removal impossible, should be treated by embolization via selective catherization in order to occlude the lesion partly or completely (52), provided that there has been hemorrhage or progressive neurologic impairment from these deeply placed lesions. Although the majority of symptomatic AVMs are encountered in patients under the age of 50 years, they are, on occasion, found in elderly patients. If the patient's general medical status and degree of neurologic impairment are not contraindications, the patient's age should not dictate against surgical removal or embolic occlusion of the lesion.

REFERENCES

1. Ackerman RH, Alpert NM, Correia JA, et al: Positron Imaging in ischemic stroke disease. *Ann Neurol* 15 (Suppl):S126, 1984.
2. Adams RD, Fisher CM, Hakim S, et al: Symptomatic occult hydrocephalus with "normal" cerebrospinal fluid pressure. A treatable syndrome. *N Engl J Med* 273:117, 1965.
3. Aoyagi N, Hayakawa I: Analysis of 223 ruptured intracranial aneurysms with special references to rerupture. *Surg Neurol* 21:445, 1984.
4. Apfelbaum RI: A comparison of percutaneous radio frequency trigeminal neurolysis and microvascular decompression of the trigeminal nerve for the treatment of tic doloreaux. *Neurosurgery* 1:16, 1977.
5. Arnason BGW: Inflammatory polyradiculoneuropathies. In Dyck PJ, Thomas PK, Lambert EH (Eds): *Peripheral Neuropathy*. Philadelphia, WB Saunders, 1975.
6. Ashford JW, Soldinger S, Schaeffer J, et al: Physostigmine and its effects on six patients with dementia. *Am J Psychiatry* 138:829, 1981.
7. Barnes DW, Whitley RJ: CNS diseases associated with varicella zoster virus and herpes simplex virus infection. Pathogenesis and current therapy. In: Booss J, Thornton GF (Eds): *Neurologic Clinics: Infectious Diseases of the Central Nervous System*. Philadelphia, WB Saunders, 1986.
8. Baum HM, Goldstein M: Cerebrovascular disease type specific mortality: 1968-1977. *Stroke* 13:810, 1982.
9. Bender MB, Christoff N: Nonsurgical treatment of subdural hematomas. *Arch Neurol* 31:73, 1974.
10. Bennett JE, Dismukes WE, Duma RJ, et al: A comparison of amphotericin B alone and combined with flucytosine in the treatment of cryptococcal meningitis. *N Engl J Med* 301:126, 1979.
11. Benson MD, Aldo MA: Azothioprine therapy in polymyositis. *Arch Intern Med* 132:547, 1973.
12. Boller F, Mizutani T, Roessmann U, et al: Parkinson disease, dementia, and Alzheimer disease: Clinicopathological correlations. *Ann Neurol* 7:329, 1980.
13. Boothby J, DeJesus PV, Rowland LP: Reversible forms of motor neuron disease: Lead "neuritis." *Arch Neurol* 31:18, 1974.
14. Bowen DM, Benton JS, Spillane JA, et al: Choline acetyltransferase activity and histopathology of frontal neocortex from biopsies of demented patients. *J Neurol Sci* 57:191, 1982.
15. Britt RH, Enzmann DR: Clinical stages of human brain abscesses on serial CT scans after contrast infusion. Computerized tomographic, neuropathological,

and clinical correlation. *J Neurosurg* 59:972, 1983.

16. Cairncross JG, Chernik NL, Kim J-H, et al: Sterilization of cerebral metastases by radiation therapy. *Neurology* 29:1195, 1979.

17. Calne DB: Hypotension caused by L-Dopa. *Br Med J* 1:474, 1970.

18. Christie JE, Shering A, Ferguson J, et al: Physostigmine and arecoline: Effects of intravenous infusions in Alzheimer's presenile dementia. *Br J Psychiatry* 138:46, 1981.

19. Cotzias GC, Van Woert MH, Schiffer LM: Aromatic amino acids and modification of Parkinsonism. *N Engl J Med* 276:374, 1967.

20. Coyle JT, Price DT, DeLong MR: Alzheimer's disease: A disorder of cortical cholinergic innervation. *Science* 219:1184, 1983.

21. Cummings H, Benson DF: *Dementia: A Clinical Approach.* Boston, Butterworth, 1983.

22. Dau PC: Plasmapheresis therapy in myasthenia gravis. *Muscle Nerve* 3:468, 1980.

23. Dau PC, Lindstrom JM, Cassel CK, et al: Plasmapheresis and immunosuppressive drug therapy in myasthenia gravis. *N Engl J Med* 297:1134, 1977.

24. Davies P, Katzman R, Terry RD: Reduced somatostatin-like immunoreactivity in cerebral cortex from cases of Alzheimer disease and Alzheimer senile dementia. *Nature* 288:279, 1980.

25. Davies P, Maloney AJF: Selective loss of central cholinergic neurons in Alzheimer's disease. *Lancet* 2:1403, 1976.

26. de Leon MJ, Ferris SH, Blau I, et al: Correlations between CT changes and behavioral deficits in senile dementia. *Lancet* 2:859, 1979.

27. Drachman DA, Leavitt J: Human memory and the cholinergic system: A relationship to aging? *Arch Neurol* 30:113, 1974.

28. Dyck PJ, Johnson WJ, Lambert EH, et al: Segmental demyelination secondary to axonal degeneration in uremic neuropathy. *Mayo Clinic Proc* 46:400, 1971.

29. Eaton LM, Lambert EH: Electromyography and electric stimulation of nerves in diseases of motor unit: Observations on myasthenia syndrome associated with malignant tumors. *JAMA* 161:1117, 1957.

30. Fahn S: "On-off" phenomenon with levodopa therapy in parkinsonism: Clinical and pharmacological correlations and the effect of intramuscular pyridoxine. *Neurology* 24:431, 1974.

31. Fambrough DM, Drachman DB, Satyamurti S: Neuromuscular function in myasthenia gravis: Decreased acetylcholine receptors. *Science* 182:293, 1973.

32. Fields WS, Lemak NA, Frankowski RF, et al: Controlled trial of aspirin in cerebral ischemia. *Stroke* 8:301, 1977.

33. Fields WS, Maslenikov V, Meyer JS, et al: Joint study of extracranial arterial occlusion. V. Progress report of prognosis following surgery or non-surgical treatment for transient cerebral ischemic attacks and cervical carotid artery lesions. *JAMA* 211:1993, 1970.

34. Fisher CM: Lacunes: Small, deep cerebral infarcts. *Neurology* 15:774, 1965.

35. Fisher CM, Picard EH, Polak A, et al: Acute hypertensive cerebellar hemorrhage. Diagnosis and surgical treatment. *J Nerv Ment Dis* 140:38, 1965.

36. Fishman RA: *Cerebrospinal Fluid in Diseases of the Nervous System.* Philadelphia, WB Saunders, 1980.

37. Fisman M, Merskey H, Helmes E, et al: Double blind study of lecithin in patients with Alzheimer's disease. *Can J Psychiatry* 26:426, 1981.

38. Gilliat RW, Harrison MJG: Nerve compression and entrapment. In Ashbury AK, Giliat RW (Eds): *Peripheral Nerve Disorders.* London, Butterworths, 1984.

39. Glass JP, Shapiro WR, Posner JB: Treatment of leptomeningeal metastases. *Neurology* 28:350, 1978.

40. Graham JG, Silkha KJ: Treatment of trigeminal neuralgia with carbamazepine: A follow-up study. *Br Med J* 1:210, 1966.

41. Grob D, Brunner NG, Namba T: The natural course of myasthenia gravis and effect of therapeutic measures. *Ann NY Acad Sci* 377:652, 1981.

42. Hachinski VC: Differential diagnosis of Alzheimer's dementia: Multi-infarct dementia. In Reisberg B (Ed): *Alzheimer's Disease.* New York, Free Press, 1983.

43. Hachinski VC, Lasser NA, Marshall J: Multi-infarct dementia: A cause of mental deterioration in the elderly *Lancet* 2:207, 1974.

44. Hakim AM, Mathieson G: Dementia in Parkinson disease: A neuropathologic study. *Neurology* 29:1209, 1979.

45. Henson RA, Urich H: Metastases to the brain. In Henson RA, Urich H (Eds): *Cancer and the Nervous System.* London, Blackwell, 1982.

46. Janny P, Colnet G, Georget AM, et al: Intracranial pressure with intracerebral hemorrhages. *Surg Neurol* 10:371, 1978.

47. Jelsman R, Bucy PC: Glioblastoma multiforme. Its treatment and some factors affecting survival. *J Neurosurg* 27:388, 1967.

48. Kartzinel R, Shoulson I, Calne DB: Studies with bromocriptine. Part 2. Double-blind comparison with levodopa in idiopathic parkinsonism. *Neurology* 26:511, 1976.

49. Katzman R: Alzheimer's disease. *N Engl J Med* 314:964, 1986.

50. Lennon VA, Lambert EH: Myasthenia gravis induced by monoclonal antibodies to acetylcholine receptors. *Nature* 285:238, 1980.

51. Lisak RP, Levinson AI: Neuropathy in connective tissue disorders. In: Asbury AK, Gilliat RW (Eds): *Peripheral Nerve Disorders.* London, Butterworths, 1984.

52. Locksley HB: Report of the Cooperative Study of Intracranial Aneurysms and Subarachnoid Hemorrhage. Section V, Part I Natural history of subarachnoid hemorrhage, intracranial aneurysms and arteriovenous malformations. *J Neurosurg* 25:219, 1966.

53. Marsden CD, Parkes JD, Rees JE: A year's comparison of treatment of patients with levodopa combined with carbidopa versus treatment with levodopa alone. *Lancet* 2:1459, 1973.

54. Mayeux R, Stern Y, Rosen J, et al: Depression, intellectual impairment, and Parkinson disease. *Neurology* 31:645, 1981.

55. McLeod JG: Carcinomatous neuropathy. In Dyck PJ, Thomas PK, Lambert EH (Eds): *Peripheral Neuropathy.* Philadelphia, WB Saunders, 1975.

56. McLeod JG, Pollard JD: Neuropathies in systemic diseases: Hidden and overt. In Asbury AK, Gilliat RW (Eds): *Peripheral Nerve Disorders.* London, Butterworths, 1984.

57. Mortimer JA, French LR, Hutton JT, et al: Head in-

jury as a risk factor for Alzheimer's disease. *Neurology* 35:264, 1985.

58. Muller HF, Schwartz G: Electroencephalograms and autopsy findings in geropsychiatry. *J Gerontol* 33:504, 1978.

59. Muller R: Progressive motor neuron disease in adults: A clinical study with special reference to the course of the disease. *Acta Psychiatry* 27:137, 1950.

60. Mutlu N, Berry RG, Alpers BJ: Massive cerebral hemorrhage. *Arch Neurol* 8:644, 1963.

61. Nutt JG, Woodward WR, Hammerstad JP, et al: The "on-off" phenomenon in Parkinson's disease. Relation to levodopa absorption and transport. *N Engl J Med* 310:483, 1984.

62. Olsom ME, Chernik NL, Posner JB: Infiltration of the leptomeninges by systemic cancer. *Arch Neurol* 30:122, 1974.

63. Overturf G: Pyogenic bacterial infections of the CNS. In: Booss J, Thornton GF (Eds): *Neurologic Clinics: Infectious Diseases of the Central Nervous System.* Philadelphia, WB Saunders, 1986.

64. Pallis CA, Lewis PD: *The Neurology of Gastrointestinal Disease,* Vol 3. Major Problems in Neurology. Philadelphia, WB Saunders, 1974.

65. Patten BM: ALS of autoimmune origin. *Neurology* 35 (Suppl 1):251, 1985.

66. Reifler BV, Larson E, Hanley R: Coexistence of cognitive impairment and depression in geriatric outpatients. *Am J Psychiat* 139:623, 1982.

67. Reisberg B: Clinical presentation, diagnosis, and symptomatology of age-associated cognitive decline and Alzheimer's disease. In: Reisberg B (Ed): *Alzheimer's Disease.* New York, Free Press, 1983.

68. Reynolds AF, Shaw C-M. Bleeding patterns from ruptured intracranial aneurysms: An autopsy study of 205 patients. *Surg Neurol* 15:232, 1986.

69. Rowland LP, Sagman D, Schotland DL: Polymyositis: A conceptual problem. *Trans Am Neurol Assoc* 91:332, 1966.

70. Ruberg M, Ploska A, Javoy-Agid F, et al: Muscarinic binding and choline acetyltransferase activity in parkinsonian subjects with reference to dementia. *Br Res* 232:129, 1982.

71. Shields RW, Laureno R, Lachman T, et al: Anticoagulant-related hemorrhage in acute cerebral embolism. *Stroke* 15:426, 1984.

72. Smith B: Skeletal muscle necrosis associated with carcinoma. *J Pathol* 97:207, 1969.

73. Stern PH, McDowell F, Miller JM, et al: Levodopa therapy effects on natural history of parkinsonism. *Arch Neurol* 27:481, 1972.

74. Summers Wk, Majovski LV, Marsh GM, et al: Oral tetrahydroaminoacridine in long-term treatment of senile dementia, Alzheimer type. *N Engl J Med* 315:1241, 1986.

75. Terry RD. Morphological changes in Alzheimer's disease—senile dementia: Ultrastructural changes and quantitative studies. In Katzman R (Ed): *Congenital and Acquired Cognitive Disorders.* Association for Research in Nervous and Mental Disease. Vol. 57. New York, Raven Press, 1979.

76. Thomas PK, Eliasson SG: Diabetic neuropathy. In Dyck PJ, Thomas PK, Lambert EH (Eds): *Peripheral Neuropathy.* Philadelphia, WB Saunders, 1975.

77. Tomlinson BE, Blessed G, Roth M: Observations on the brains of demented old people. *J Neurol Sci* 11:205, 1970.

78. Tomlinson BE, Irving D, Blessed G: Cell loss in the locus coeruleus in senile dementia of Alzheimer type. *J Neurol Sci* 49:419, 1981.

79. Van Der Ark GD, Edgar A, Kahn EA: Spontaneous intracerebral hematoma. *J Neurosurg* 28:252, 1968.

80. Vermeulen M, Lindsay KU, Murray GD, et al: Antifibrolytic treatment in subarachnoid hemorrhage. *N Engl J Med* 311:432, 1984.

81. Victor M, Adams RD, Collins GH: *The Wernicke-Korsakoff's Syndrome.* Philadelphia, FA Davis, 1971.

82. Weksler BB: Antithrombotic therapies in the management of cerebral ischemia. In Plum F, Pulsinelli WA (Eds): *Cerebrovascular Diseases. Fourteenth Research Conference.* New York, Raven Press, 1985.

83. Whisnant JP, Sandok BA, Sundt Jr TM: Carotid endarterectomy for unilateral carotid system transient cerebral ischemia. *Mayo Clin Proc* 58:171, 1983.

84. Whitehouse PJ, Price DL, Struble RG, et al Alzheimer's disease and senile dementia: Loss of neurons in the basal forebrain. *Science* 215:1237, 1982.

85. Wolf PA, Dawber TR, Thomas HE, et al Epidemiological assessment of chronic atrial fibrillation and risk of stroke. *Neurology* 28:973, 1978.

86. Wolf PA, Kannel W: Controllable risk factors for stroke: Preventive implications of trends in stroke mortality. In Meyer JS and Shaw T (Eds): *Diagnosis and Management of Strokes and TIA's.* Menlo Park CA, Addison-Wesley, 1982.

87. Wolf PA, Kannel WB, Dawber TR: Prospective investigations; the Framingham Study and the epidemiology of stroke. In Schoenberg BS (Ed): *Advances in Neurology. Vol 19 Neurological Epidemiology: Principles and Clinical Applications.* New York, Raven Press, 1978.

88. Wylie CM: Recent trends in mortality from cerebrovascular accidents in the United States. *J Chron Dis* 14:213, 1961.

89. Zorman G, Wilson CB: Outcome following microsurgical vascular decompression or partial sensory rhizotomy in 125 cases of trigeminal neuralgia. *Neurology* 34:1362, 1984.

CHAPTER 17

Rehabilitation and the Aged

JOHN B. REDFORD

Medical rehabilitation has been defined most simply as the process of restoring persons to the highest possible level of physical, emotional, and social capability. It implies a creative procedure that includes a cooperative team approach to care: various medical specialists and their associates in allied health fields provide personal services with an emphasis on learning and behavioral change rather than the traditional medical model of care. The traditional medical model presumes that some adverse circumstances or special etiology produced the pathologic change of disease or disorder. The physician diagnoses the disease from symptoms and signs, then prescribes treatment to reverse the process and the patient obeys.

In the rehabilitation model of care, the patient must participate in relearning tasks and improving his or her own function and not be simply a passive recipient of medical or surgical care (9).

Traditional medical education has rarely included effective management of irreversible consequences of disease or functional limitations. Yet, teaching the patient to cope with functional disabilities is the essence of rehabilitation. Education is critical in today's care for elderly patients. The ravages of time and disease may be irreversible but ignoring the possibility of functional improvement through retraining the patient leads to despair and even early death.

In considering rehabilitation of the aged, the terms impairment, disability, and handicap are frequently confused and used interchangeably. The World Health Association (WHO) of the United Nations has attempted to clear up this confusion by publishing the first "International Classification of Impairment, Disability, Handicap." This was a much needed response to a lack of any classification of the effects of disease on human performance.

These terms have not just medical but also psychologic and social implications (15).

Impairment is "any loss or abnormality of psychologic, physiologic or anatomical structure or function." Impairment may be considered as a disturbance at the organic level, such as limitation of joint motion, muscle weakness, amputation, reduced cardiac reserve, or seizure. The AMA Guide to Impairment (1) is a good example of attempts to objectify impairment and is widely used for this first step in assessing disability.

Disability is a more functionally oriented concept: "Any restriction or lack of ability to perform an activity in the manner or within the range considered normal for every human being." Thus, disability represents a disturbance at the personal or individual level; the same impairment to two different persons may produce great differences in the degree of disability. In general, managing a person's disability requires much more time and rehabilitative effort than dealing only with the impairment. For example, manufacturing an artificial leg to replace a below-knee amputation is relatively easy compared with calming fears or helping with expectations of the amputee who has limited learning capability and suffers from unfavorable social and economic circumstances.

Handicap should not be equated with disability; it is preferably defined in a social context as "a disadvantage for a given individual resulting from an impairment or disability that limits or prevents fulfillment of a role that is normal (depending on age, sex, social, and cultural factors) for that individual." Handicap is determined by such factors as environmental barriers, legal constraints, and community acceptance.

These three concepts of impairment, disability, and handicap may form a sequence after the onset of a disease or disorder that cannot be reversed. The disease creates the impairment; this is largely the concern of conventional medical services. Impairment, then, can secondarily lead to a disability as the person reacts unfavorably to its consequences. Here, rehabilitation plays a role because it seeks to minimize disability through functional assessment and restoration. The next stage, handicap, often follows disability because after the shelter of a rehabilitative institution, a person may encounter social and economic policies or environmental barriers that restrict living. For example, an epileptic who is capable of driving may be prevented from doing so by restrictive driving laws. Many elderly persons have handicaps: inadequate housing, limited household services, poor transportation, and lack of personal protection are causing handicaps in spite of even minimal impairment or disability. Overcoming handicaps are often beyond the realm of medical intervention but can be addressed by social policy and welfare provisions.

GERIATRIC REHABILITATION

Rehabilitation is incomplete until all aspects of a patient's problems, namely, impairment, disability, and handicap, are tackled. This process of rehabilitation includes: (a) an inventory of the medical problems with particular attention to those producing chronic impairment; (b) a dynamic assessment of a patient's psychologic and social resources along with an assessment of preserved skills; or, in other words, a functional assessment of the disability taking into account both physical and psychologic factors; (c) an environmental survey including not only the physical environment but also the social and economic conditions to which the patient may return. Based on these assessments, goals are set and various therapies begun.

Rehabilitation, from the above standpoint, has been described as the third phase of medical care—the first two being prevention and definitive surgical sequence with rehabilitation beginning when definitive treatment ends. Rehabilitation should be a continuous process encompassing all the aspects of medical care (7). This is particularly true of elderly care where a long stay in the hospital without attention to preventing disability may result in marked decrease in muscle strength as well as adverse cardiovascular, pulmonary, and metabolic effects. In fact, much geriatric rehabilitation consists of attempts to undo the changes caused by prolonged rest and neglect.

Limitation of activity in the elderly can be summarized as fundamental deficiences in one or more body systems concerned with motion: the nervous, musculoskeletal, cardiovascular, and pulmonary systems. Since impairments may arise in multiple systems in aged patients and these interact with each other, even more disability may occur than from a single disorder, that might, for example, be treated surgically. In such circumstances, getting out of bed and moving about as soon as possible after surgery or even an acute illness is the best way to avoid disability. Furthermore, before a surgical procedure is performed, the debilitated older patient should be taught deep breathing exercises and how to preserve and increase mobility both in and out of bed. Therefore, although most rehabilitation occurs after specific medical or surgical treatment, it should begin in parallel and not in series with acute medical care.

Although preventive care is an important aspect of rehabilitation, maintenance of functional mobility after hospitalization on a rehabilitation unit is perhaps even more significant. Much of the past criticism of rehabilitation efforts has been the lack of follow-up—the paraplegic patient goes home and sits; the stroke patient reverts to total dependency on the family. Certainly, many old people need lifelong follow-up after a devastating illness and disability. If this cannot be done actively by the hospital rehabilitation team, communication with the family physician and community services should be such that continuity of success is ensured. Accrediting agencies for rehabilitation programs are now insisting that functional gains from rehabilitation must be reassessed for a specific time period following discharge from the rehabilitation center (6).

Although rehabilitative principles in prevention of illness and maintaining function are significant, the key to rehabilitation is setting goals and attaining them with a well-coordinated rehabilitation team. In a typical rehabilitation unit, the focus is primarily on disorders of locomotion caused by neuromuscular or musculoskeletal problems. Today's demand for economy in health care services requires that goals be specific and met within a certain time frame; otherwise, questions may be raised about unjustifiable expense.

Because vocational considerations are not as paramount in rehabilitating elderly persons as in the young, the main goal in geriatric rehabilitation is to return people home. To most elderly persons, confinement to a nursing home or other institution is a dreadful prospect. Often, in the elderly person, minor or temporary functional losses, such as a fracture of the patella or in an arthritic, hospitalization for pulmonary infections are enough to fragment a fragile family support system and prevent the patient from returning home.

Unlike rehabilitation efforts in the young, goal setting for older persons may have to be quite limited. Small gains derived from a rehabilitation program may make the difference between returning home and institutional placement. Although the limited and very specific goals may need frequent altering or even downgrading as restoration progresses, the improvements achieved usually justify the time and expense. Although multiple therapies, team meetings, and special consultations from different specialists are expensive, rehabilitation has proven the most effective method of cost reduction in chronic disability (10).

FORMAL REHABILITATION SETTING

The practical application of concepts of inpatient rehabilitation for the elderly involves a number of elements. Of prime importance is the skill of various members of a rehabilitation team that, in a medical setting, is generally directed by a physiatrist, a physician specializing in rehabilitation medicine. In other settings, the team can be directed by a geriatrician, particularly if all the patients are in the elderly age group. In addition to one or more medical specialists, the elderly patient may require help from rehabilitation nurses, nutritionists, physical therapists, occupational therapists, speech therapists, social workers, and psychologists; other services may also be needed such as prosthetics and orthotics, recreation programs, and vocational counselors. The advantages of treating a disabled patient in a structured rehabilitation setting are: (a) availability of expert medical care for dealing with certain specific mobility problems, such as amputations, strokes, or other neurologic disorders characterized by paralysis; (b) easy access to medical consultation and support services, e.g., orthopaedics, neurosurgery, rheumatology, etc., (c) use of special equipment for therapeutic purposes not usually available in the home or in skilled nursing facilities; (d) close cooperation and comprehensive evaluation and treatment by a multidisciplinary team of allied health personnel working together who create a special atmosphere; (e) a planned gradual withdrawal of assistance and support that occurs through team conferences and resetting goals as the patient becomes more independent; (f) an educational environment that is essential in teaching patients their personal care. Patient education is greatly stressed in all rehabilitation units because

many of them are a part of large educational institutions such as a teaching hospital (14).

There are certain disadvantages for the elderly person. In many instances, the patient's displacement from his usual home setting may be more critical than any gains that may occur through functional restoration. Because of this disadvantage, a careful analysis of the value of the home rehabilitation setting with home care or outpatient programs must be weighed against the advantage of a formal inpatient setting. The shelter and security offered by an inpatient rehabilitation program is often unrealistic. Patients may be faced with a rude awakening once they leave the comfortable atmosphere of a rehabilitation unit with all the available extra support and interaction, not only with team members but others with similar disabilities. This can be alleviated in some degree by home passes whenever possible. Weekend passes were a common practice until cost-cutting measures have eliminated them for almost all rehabilitation units. Use of homelike settings and special self-care apartments for selective patients before discharge from the rehabilitation unit also help. Another disadvantage is cost; although the long-term gains may be undoubtedly worthwhile, patients with limited economic means may have no way of financing their care in a rehabilitation setting.

BODY SYSTEMS IN AGING AND DISEASE

Before illustrating how a rehabilitation team treats a typical case, some consideration is needed of physiologic changes that affect performance of elderly patients, particularly changes in the nervous, musculoskeletal, and cardiovascular systems. Classifying disorders of elderly persons by the system at fault is somewhat simplistic because all systems interact: a disorder in one system affects all the others and the person's overall functional abilities. Therefore, although diagnostic categorization is important, functional classification is more significant in considering rehabilitation possibilities. In other words, the major question in rehabilitation is: "What can the patient do for himself or herself?" This is more significant than: "What chronic diseases does this patient have?"

NERVOUS SYSTEM

Although it has been said that man is as old as his arteries, the real key to aging perhaps lies in the nervous system, which is composed of nonmitotic irreplaceable cells. It is well known that during aging, the number of nerve cells decrease and the central nervous system actually shrinks in size. Associated with these changes are slower learning capability, easier fatigue, decreased motor skills, and altered sensory perception. Particularly significant are the losses in special senses of vision and hearing.

As restorative techniques involve primarily learning skills to replace lost ability, more detailed instruction and more time for repetition must be allowed in elderly persons. When cognitive or behavioral problems arise in rehabilitation treatments, psychologic testing with assessment of learning capabilities and emotional responses may be essential in planning treatment goals. In fact, treatment goals are often more limited by cognitive and emotional factors than by organic impairment such as paralysis.

Rehabilitation personnel need special attitudes and communication skills in working with older people, particularly those with deficient vision and hearing or other senses. Although tight schedules sometimes force rationing of time for special treatments and care in some rehabilitation settings, every effort should be made to give extra time for the elderly.

Major contraindications to application of rehabilitation techniques are irreversible brain changes such as memory loss and behavior disorders, but, unless the mental problems are very severe, all elderly disabled deserve a limited trial of rehabilitation.

Loss of balance control is probably the most significant change in the aging nervous system affecting mobility as this may lead to a fall that results in prolonged immobility or ultimately death. A host of causes may be at fault including neurologic or cardiovascular disease, drugs, or external environmental factors. Unless the cause can be found and corrected, the patient may be unable to resume independent ambulation or exercise programs. Rehabilitation techniques to improve righting reflexes as well as muscle strength and coordination play a vital role in preventing falls. In patients with falling tendencies, provision of special wheelchairs or walking aids form an essential part of any rehabilitation program.

MUSCULOSKELETAL SYSTEM

Musculoskeletal complaints are so prevalent in the elderly that they seem almost characteristic of aging. By age 70 years, 80% of persons have rheumatic complaints such as muscle pain or weakness. Most patients refer to their complaints as "just a little arthritis or rheumatism." Deciding how extensively to investigate such complaints often poses a dilemma; but usually a careful history and thorough physical examination will distinguish the few more serious causes of these complaints from the common ones. The usual causes associated with "wear and tear" changes will respond well to rest, heat, or other simple physical modalities along with exercise and mild analgesics.

Although muscle weakness without pain is not so common, weakness of neurologic origin should be distinguished from intrinsic muscle disease, which is less common. In this regard, physiatrists are skilled not only in recommending management of such disorders but can provide a differential diagnosis in such cases by electromyographic studies. These may be helpful not only in diagnosis but also for kinesiologic assessment and treatment, such as electromyographic biofeedback.

Persons who are robust physically and undertake regular exercise programs to keep fit, retain muscle bulk and strength well into the sixth and seventh decades. Studies have shown that muscles in healthy persons, even in the seventh and eighth decades, respond to graduated resistive programs just as in younger persons (8). The same principle may be said to apply to other aging tissues or, to quote an old adage "If you don't use it, you lose it." Appropriate and regular exercise can contribute to longevity of muscle cells that like nerve cells, are not replaceable during life. Inadequate exercise tends to decrease longevity. Changes in the connective tissues or in the cardiovascular system and not actually muscle deterioration probably determine the diminution of physical capacity associated with aging (13).

Because capacity to produce or conserve energy declines with age, onset of fatigue occurs much earlier than in the young. Endurance, the maximum duration of a sustained effort without fatigue, is intimately linked to energy consumption. Consequently, many older people, especially those deconditioned by sedentary living habits or cardiovascular disease slow down their actions and may not reach standards of physical activity within the time frame considered appropriate by treating personnel. Thus, for success in geriatric rehabilitation, particularly if there is a history of heart disease, one must establish realistic time schedules, limit duration of individual treatment, and frequently reset goals if progress is slow (13).

In considering strategies for treating musculoskeletal deficiencies in elderly patients, several points need emphasis. All patients, prior to rehabilitation, need assessment of range of motion and muscular strength as part of the functional assessment and certain areas need particular attention. Table 17.1 illustrates some of the key elements in assessment and treatment.

Table 17.1
Key Elements in Assessment and Treatment

Region/ Joint	Common Pathologic Problems	Functional Deficiency	Physical Treatment
Neck	Cervical spondylosis, chronic neck tension syndromes	Limits mobility to perform, particularly upper extremity tasks and may cause balance problems	Thermotherapy plus relaxing and mobilizing techniques for the neck including cervical traction
Shoulder	Age changes in the rotator cuff	Pain and reduced shoulder mobility causing loss of reaching, dressing, and lifting activities	Active assistive exercises with stretching and strengthening exercises after application of deep heat
Lumbar spine	Degenerative disc changes and osteoarthritis aggravated by prolonged immobility such as excessive sitting or bedrest	Inability to roll or sit up in bed Defective sitting and standing posture Inability to bend to dress lower extremities, use the toilet facilities, etc.	Trunk and hip mobilizing exercises on gym mats and often in group settings, usually preceded by various heating modalities
Hip	Hip flexion contracture from prolonged poor sitting or lying posture with hips flexed Degenerative joint disease	Poor upright posture with back pain and limitation of hip extension Decreased stride length causing reduced walking capacity	Deep heating modalities to hip joint followed by prolonged stretch hip flexors and strengthening of hip extensor and abductor muscles.
Knee	Flexion contractures (often accompanied by varus deformity) due to prolonged sitting, squatting, or degenerative joint disease	Reduced stride length and knee pain on prolonged standing or walking	Stretching and strengthening exercises, particularly directed at the hip and knee extensors Use of cane in opposite hand
Foot	Collapse of normal supporting structures often from poor footwear	Painful foot joints on weight bearing or abnormal callus formation Inability to tolerate walking any distance	Footwear that supports and reduces pressure in critical weight bearing areas Treatment of nail or skin problems Foot baths and simple mobilizing exercises Use of a cane

EXERCISE

Exercise programs are the mainstay of most rehabilitation programs. The emphasis in exercise should be task specific, that is, concentrating on functions that are expected to be achieved. All exercise programs must alter behavior. They have to become part of the regular routine of the patient or the family or they will not help. The teaching of exercise, by physicians or therapists, is undoubtedly the most significant aspect of physical rehabilitation.

Detailed discussion of exercises, especially for conditions such as a stroke, are beyond the scope of

this chapter. They can be reviewed in several texts (2, 3). Terms commonly used in prescribing exercises are given in Table 17.2

PHYSICAL MODALITIES AND THERAPEUTIC EQUIPMENT

Although exercise is the mainstay of most rehabilitation programs, there should be some use of physical modalities and equipment in geriatric rehabilitation. Most physical therapy departments have an impressive array of physical agents and gadgets and every year American ingenuity dreams up many

Table 17.2
Types of Exercise

Form	Application	Effects	Indications	Contraindications
Passive	Either by patient or therapist Continuous passive motion machines	Prevent contractures Maintain awareness of joint motion and position	Complete paralysis	Fractures or other severe injuries
Active	Patient performs activity alone	Maintain range of motion and improve training	Any situation where patient has normal range of motion and varying degrees of paralysis but sufficient to contract muscle	Fracture or other severe injuries
Active-assistive	Patient actively contracts muscle but therapist or apparatus assists	Assists muscles unable to complete range of motion	Conditions with combination of muscle weakness with and without joint problems May be accompanied by mild stretching of joints; for example, to prevent contractures of arthritis	As for active
Resistive	Manual or apparatus is used to apply resistance to muscle contraction	Increased muscle strength	Any condition where the aim is to increase strength, but not indicated if patient has undue fatigue or pain	Severe cardiac patients or others with very debilitated state Inability to comprehend instructions
Isometric	Form of active exercise where the parts do not move but muscle shortens	Maintain muscle bulk and awareness of muscle	Any situation where active joint movement is undesirable	Cardiac or other conditions with risk of arrhythmias
Isotonic	Active contraction through range of motion joints with or without resistance	Preserve range of motion and build up strength	Most commonly used exercise for muscle building, such as pulley and weight exercises for the shoulders	As for passive or other active exercise
Conditioning or aerobic exercise	Usually to all affected and unaffected segments by patient's own volition	Prevents debilitating effects of immobilization and disuse and prepares parts for added stress or coordination in restoring function.	All general medical conditions where deconditioning has been a problem such as cardiac disease, pulmonary disease, infection, etc.	Very acute medical conditions

more, often very expensive ones. Yet for most elderly patients, the simplest physical agents that can be used at home along with orthotic and self-help devices may be equally effective to many expensive treatments and gadgets.

In treating the elderly, particular care should be taken with the use of the deep heating modalities, such as shortwave and ultrasound. The possibility of impaired circulation or decreased sensation in the part being treated should not be overlooked. There is little way of measuring how much energy is delivered to the tissues by these deep heating modalities so the sensibility of the patient is critical. Furthermore, because extensive deep or even extensive superficial heating may considerably affect the autonomic nervous system in elderly patients, the excessive environmental stresses produced by these agents should be avoided. As a general rule, it is better to use cold or local superficial applications of heat for limited periods of time for relieving pain than relying on diathermy or ultrasound.

A new modality that has had widespread effectiveness for pain has been the introduction of equipment for transcutaneous electric nerve stimulation. These devices have made a significant difference in relieving both acute and chronic pain in older people, transcutaneous electric nerve stimulation can even be used to reduce joint pain during exercise routines. For example, electric currents can be passed across a painful shoulder joint during an active assistive exercise program and relieve some of the induced discomfort. Usually a trial lasting 3–4 days should always be made before considering these units for more prolonged use. The patient should always be carefully instructed in placement and maintenance of the electrodes of the electric stimulator. Contraindications are few; they should not be used on patients with cardiac pacemakers or other internally placed electric devices and avoided in patients with skin disorders or those sensitive to the electrode pastes. Of course, transcutaneous electric nerve stimulation units cannot be supplied to patients incapable of understanding their application and use.

Along with exercise treatment and modalities, often simple splints or orthoses of thermoplastic material put joints at rest or support various body parts, especially during exercise. These are particularly useful in arthritic joint protection. Occupational therapists are specifically trained in making and instructing patients in the principles of minimizing stress on painful joints or use of environmental adaptations to reduce energy consumption or stress.

For more complicated orthotic devices, an orthotist should be consulted rather than a therapist, especially for spinal or lower limb orthoses. All rehabilitation departments have on hand various pieces of adaptive equipment that can be tried on patients and then prescribed for home use, if necessary. Often, the patient must be instructed in special use of this equipment; much of it is only as good as the instruction and the capability of the patient to understand its purpose. For further information, the physician should consult the extensive literature available on orthotics and various types of self-help aids and devices (5, 11). In addition, local hospital equipment providers and many voluntary health agencies for various diseases (e.g., arthritis, Parkinson disease) give families and therapists free guides to equipment available (12).

GENERAL PRINCIPLES

In any treatment program for elderly patients with musculoskeletal problems, the emphasis must be placed on balancing rest against activity. A good general rule for prescribing exercise programs, for example, is to heed carefully the patient's complaints of pain and discomfort. Any functional activity or exercise program producing persistent pain for more than 2 or 3 hours is always a sign of overfatigue of muscles or overuse of damaged joints. Any patient complaining of increased pain 24 hours after physical modalities or exercise should be checked immediately by the attending physician.

Fatigue is often a prominent complaint of elderly patients in rehabilitation. Along with review of medical factors as to cause, this complaint may be managed by scheduled periods of rest during the day with special attention to adequacy of sleep at night. Elderly patients with "sundown syndrome" (awake and restless all night—with a tendency to nap or sleep during the day) present particular problems on rehabilitation units. Careful balance of activity and rest during daylight hours along with special visits from relatives to allay fear and anxiety at night may be necessary before such patients can be treated effectively.

In the use of physical modalities or exercises, safety is a prime consideration. All rehabilitation programs must have policies and procedures relating to the ordering and use of physical treatment. Equipment must be checked routinely for electrical safety, accuracy of recording, meters, or any other unusual hazards. Routine use of safety belts around the waists of patients being transferred or when walking is particularly helpful in avoiding accidents.

As wheelchairs usually are the means of transport, they should be kept in good repair with particular attention to brakes and moving parts. All baths, showers, and toilets should be equipped with safety rails and adapted for safe use by the disabled. This not only helps provide safety on the rehabilitation unit, but also serves as an example to patients in adapting their homes when they leave the institution.

PROCESS OF REHABILITATION

Rehabilitation in a hospital setting ideally begins when the patient is first admitted to the acute care ward. Any elderly person with an illness or injury, which might subsequently result in a functional impairment, should be referred for rehabilitation evaluation as soon as possible. In many hospitals, the current practice is for the physician who will subsequently be caring for the patient to evaluate potential and make recommendations for transfer to the Rehabilitation Unit while the patient is on an acute ward. Psychosocial resources are a particularly important part of this assessment; review of these resources is generally performed by a social worker.

In most hospitals, the criteria for admission are that the patient has a significant functional impairment and is considered medically stable, that is, without further need for intensive medical or surgical treatment.

Once the decision is made to accept the patient after discharge from the acute setting, an important step is to orient the patient and family to rehabilitation. This is often done by conducting a tour of the rehabilitation unit, describing the role of various persons on the rehabilitation team. Often, elderly patients become quite disoriented when they are first admitted to a rehabilitation setting. Providing a written description or even showing a representative television tape helps to improve adaptation to a new environment. Also appealing are having daily activities scheduled in writing and reality orientation, such as bringing familiar objects from home. Pictures of family and staff are often useful in this process. When possible, the same team (nurse, physical therapist, occupational therapist) should be assigned to work with the patient daily to overcome the feeling of strangeness. It is particularly critical for the patients to learn that they are on rehabilitation to assist themselves in their own care and not expect others to constantly wait upon them as in the acute care setting.

Conditions that might be referred for treatment in rehabilitation facilities are listed in Table 17.3

To illustrate this process of management by a rehabilitation team of an elderly patient, we will consider Mr.

Table 17.3
Condition for Treatment in a Rehabilitation Facility

1. Any medical condition that results in immobilization (e.g., extensive surgery for cancer, prolonged bed rest after severe infection) inactivity, deconditioning, malnutrition, etc. producing a secondary disability (e.g., extensive surgery, etc.)
2. All forms of disabilities caused by stroke
3. Parkinson's disease and other motor control disorders such as cerebellar ataxia
4. Arthritis, all forms, with pain and significant reduction of joint mobility
5. Back pain and impairment due to various causes such as trauma, disc disorders, inflammatory arthritis, spinal stenosis, and postural abnormalities
6. Neck pain with and without upper extremity nerve root involvement
7. Aftercare of all forms of fractures in the elderly, particularly hip fractures
8. Patients with prosthetic joint replacements
9. Peripheral vascular disease, particularly arterial but also conditions accompanied by venous insufficiency or lymphedema
10. All forms of upper and lower extremity amputation
11. Cardiovascular conditions accompanied by decreased mobility and deconditioning
12. Chronic pulmonary disorders associated with restrictive or obstructive lung disease

J.D., a 70-year-old man with hemiparesis who, when admitted to the hospital, had a nonhealing ulcer on his right foot. Six months before his admission, a stroke had caused right hemiplegia and mild aphasia. He had almost fully recovered his speech and, except for some clumsiness in his right hand, he had almost totally resumed use of right arm. He also had developed a very satisfactory gait pattern; he had walked with a plastic ankle-foot-orthosis to stabilize his ankle but he occasionally stumbled when his knee flexed unexpectedly because he had some persisting spasticity in the right hamstring muscles. The patient reported that every morning he had to stretch out these muscles on arising and also after prolonged sitting but, once the spasticity had been released by stretching, the knee problem bothered him very little. Unfortunately, the arterial circulation in his right foot had progressively deteriorated. Pressure from the hard plastic brace had led to a nonhealing ulcer on the lateral border. A molded plastic brace provides excellent ankle and foot control to improve gait in hemiplegia but, with lack of sensation and poor circulation in the limb, skin problems may arise as in this case.

After admission, an attempted bypass graft to the right femoral artery did not improve foot circulation. Subsequently, Mr. J.D. had a right below-knee amputation. Immediately postoperatively, a plaster cast was applied to the stump to control edema and prevent flexion deformity of the knee. Amputee fitting has proved very successful when postoperative fitting of plaster is performed and the patient is closely followed up. With immediate plaster dressing, the control of edema allows the stump to heal more quickly than with a standard dressing. This technique considerably shortens time from amputation to prosthetic walking as early fitting of temporary prostheses and subsequent successful prosthetic ambulation becomes much more likely (4).

Unfortunately for Mr. J.D., the cast had to be removed within the first 24 hours after amputation as the operation apparently had increased the latest spasticity and the spastic contraction of the hamstring muscles caused intolerable pressures inside the plaster cast. The increased spasticity was probably a direct result of the surgical wound because it is widely recognized that surgery or pressure sores usually increase spasticity.

Within a week after surgery, the Rehabilitation Team was consulted and agreed that in spite of the persistent neurologic findings with the accompanying knee contracture, the patient had potential for fitting with an artificial limb and he was admitted to the Rehabilitation Ward. A multidisciplinary assessment was carried out shortly after admission. Within a week of admission, a team conference was held directed by the physician. Each discipline outlined findings and suggested short-term goals. The following is a summary of the role of each team member and his/her report on this case.

The physician reviewed the clinical statue with special attention to undetected diseases and other problems. In addition to the right below-knee amputation and residual spasticity from hemiparesis, the patient had a history of hypothyroidism that was well-controlled on thyroid replacement. He also had some mild prostatic obstruction, requiring a catheter after surgery. He was taking a postoperative prophylactic antibiotic (a cephalosporin) and pentoxyfilline to prevent occlusion of other arteriosclerotic vessels. The long-term goals were set to increase fitness and muscle strength, to relieve spasticity, and to regain enough knee extension to return home walking independently with a prosthesis.

The nursing staff assessed motivation, self-help, skin care, continence, and ability to manage medications. They reported that the patient seemed well motivated to care for himself. The incision line was not quite healed but no growth was cultured from the drainage and skin pressure areas caused by the plaster cast had improved. The postoperative urinary retention that had required a catheter had cleared so he was voiding adequately and was having no difficulty with taking medications.

The dietitian or nutritionist assessed the adequacy of a patient's diet and ability to plan menus. She reported that this patient who had an adequate diet before surgery had lost weight immediately before and after surgery but was now eating well. No special diet had been ordered as nothing suggested that his widespread atherosclerosis might respond to any dietary manipulation.

The physical therapist assessed strength, range of motion, mobility, endurance, and gait. He reported that the patient's flexion contracture of the right knee had improved about 5° degrees with stretching exercises. These were done both passively by the therapist and actively by the patient contacting his quadriceps muscle. A splint of molded thermoplastic had been applied behind the right knee to keep it in extension and so reduce the flexion contracture of the knee by prolonged stretch. (This is much more effective than short passive stretches performed once or twice a day.) The patient transferred independently from wheelchair to bed and was able to manage his own wheelchair. On admission, a walker was used but now, although he was attempting crutch walking with standby assistance, he was still very unsteady. Strength in his arms seemed adequate although coordination in the right upper limb was decreased.

The occupational therapist assessed the activities of daily living regarding personal care, need for any adaptive equipment, or home adaptations. She reported that the patient was feeding himself independently, dressing the upper body alone, but needed minimal assistance in lower body dressing. He was independent in his personal hygiene but needed a little help with setup. Although the patient had some clumsiness with his right hand, this was not interfering significantly in self-care skills.

Social Service workers assess the person's need for family and social support and degree to which this is available. The social worker reported that the patient had lost his wife about 6 months before hospital admission. He owned his own home and would return there to live with his daughter upon discharge. Although he was still mourning his wife's death, his grief did not significantly interfere with his desire to help himself and live independently. There were no particular financial problems and the patient's hospitalization was covered by Medicare with a special tie-in plan for uncovered services.

Specialists in speech and audiology assess communication disorders and can report on disorders of memory and other cognitive factors functions. The speech pathologist reported that Mr. J.D. had no residuals from his original dysphasic disturbance other than some word finding difficulty. This did not significantly interfere with his rehabilitation. Although he was confused before amputation, he now exhibited no problems with cognition and no special treatment was recommended.

A further length of hospital stay was estimated at 4 weeks. The conclusions of the team conference were:

1. *Nursing:* Have patient continue use of the thermoplastic splint but also, for wound care, wear a removable plaster cast dressing to accelerate healing and, by continual changing of stump socks, prepare the stump for a prosthesis.

2. *Physical therapy:* Provide exercises in the gymnasium for two periods a day with push-ups and balancing exercises on the mats, strengthening of quadriceps and hip extensor muscles, and stretching of hamstring muscles of stump and practicing standing balance and endurance with crutch walking.

3. *Occupational therapy:* Teach functional activities of daily living combined with special tasks to increase right hand coordination.

4. *Prosthetist:* Fit patient with temporary prosthesis as soon as stump contracture has been minimized.

These plans for Mr. J.D.'s rehabilitation were set back by a small arterial embolus causing local skin necrosis on the sole of his right foot. He was placed on anticoagulants and ceased walking for over a week while this area healed.

The contracture in his left stump gradually improved and during the fourth week, he was fitted with a preparatory prosthesis made of Scotchcast (16). This preparatory prosthesis is achieved by direct formation of the socket on the residual limb using a special lightweight cast material which is wrapped around the stump and hardens shortly after application. The temporary limb was placed on an alignment unit consisting of a metal pylon with adjustable jig to line up the prosthetic foot under this cast. This limb was suspended by using a thigh cuff above the knee and a waist belt around the hip attached to this cuff.

After this prosthesis was fitted, the patient still had some difficulty with the knee buckling but learned to walk with a cane within 10 days of prosthetic application and was discharged home, still maintained on anticoagulants and pentoxyfilline. He was advised still to wear the plaster, removable dressing at night to keep the edema from recurring in the limb and to return in 6 weeks for consideration of a permanent type of prosthesis.

Before discharge, a family conference had been held with Mr. J.D., his daughter, and the rehabilitation team for a discussion of future plans and prognosis. In many cases, after the family conference, a plan for home care services are initiated but in this patient, home care was deemed unnecessary. As good social and economic support were available, no need for special follow-up existed except for further prosthetic care and continued medication for prevention of further ischemic episodes. The physiatrist sent a discharge summary outlining these conclusions to his referring family physician.

As well as illustrating the rehabilitation process in action, this case demonstrates several points about the amputee rehabilitation: (a) Prescribing orthotic devices for elderly patients with poor sensation and circulation may be harmful. These conditions may lead to skin breakdown and an ultimate amputation, as in this case. (b) Amputation on the hemiplegic side of a patient does not preclude the wearing of prosthetics. The chances of walking are distinctly better with a below-knee amputation and this should be attempted whenever possible. If the patient has enough cognitive ability to cooperate and exhibits good emotional stability and motivation, he or she will require only a moderate recovery of strength to walk with an artificial limb. A knee flexion contracture will complicate the problem and must be reduced before walking can be attempted, because with much flexion deformity, prosthetic alignment cannot be made adequate to permit weight bearing. (c) Reducing flexion contractures in any limb may be performed not only by exercise and intermittent stretching but also by plaster casting or use of plastic orthoses to stretch out a

contracture by continuous force. (d) Training and fitting with a prosthesis in a rehabilitation hospital setting is justified for complicated below-knee amputations. If it had not been for the intensive therapy and walking with a preparatory prosthesis, it is unlikely that Mr. J.D., would ever use a below-knee prosthesis and would have spent the rest of his life in a wheelchair or using crutches. With good rehabilitation follow-up, more than 80% of below-knee amputees—whether unilateral or bilateral, can learn to walk with prostheses. (e) Medical supervision, not just a physical therapist and prosthetist working together is essential to ensure good postoperative management in amputees. In this case, the problems of wound healing, treating the knee contracture, the complication of an embolus and the need for special medication, and the fitting of a temporary prosthesis all had to be coordinated and supervised by a physician interested in amputee care.

The home environment did not present a problem in this case. In other patients, especially those with bilateral amputations, a special wheelchair might have been prescribed. Then it would also have been necessary to adapt the home for a wheelchair access by using a ramp and probably modifying the bathroom because it is impossible to roll wheelchairs through bathroom doors in most housing. If a wheelchair is needed at home for an amputee, it should be used on a temporary basis unless cardiac or other complications make walking outside for any distance impossible. A wheelchair is not just "a chair with wheels." Matching the needs of the patient to the type of chair is an essential part of rehabilitation. Chapter 13 in Redford's *Orthotics Etcetera* (11) provides further information on prescribing wheelchairs.

SUMMARY

The process of rehabilitation consists of restoring patients to the optimal level of physical, emotional, and social ability. In the elderly, this usually means returning the individual to a suitable and safe environment that fosters independence. For patients with complex problems, such as neurologic disorders, this is often a slow process involving medical assessment, treatment, multiple therapies, and special attention to environmental and social factors. Rehabilitation is an educational process and is care-oriented rather than cure-oriented. It should be conducted in a rehabilitation unit if the patient's disability is at all complicated. Figure 17.1 illustrates the process of rehabilitation in a summary form.

Most rehabilitation treatment is empirically based but is founded on application of principles of neurophysiology, psychology (particularly learning theory), energy conservation, and kinetics of human motion. Along with physical treatment and exercises, many devices are now available to substitute for lost function. The environment can be changed

Initial diagnosis and definitive treatment
↓
Comprehensive assessment by the rehabilitation team to:
↓
—uncover problem
—identify assets
↓
Rehabilitation Team Meeting to:
—set goals (short and long term)
—develop solutions
↓
Tasks assigned and program executed
↓
One or more further team meetings conducted on a
bi-weekly basis to:
—plot progress
—re-evaluate goals
—reallot tasks
↓
Discharge summary to family physicians and home
care agency

Figure 17.1. The rehabilitation process.

to accommodate many patients with disability using skilled application of these principles. No longer should the elderly, impairing patient suffer severe disability and subsequently return to an environment where he or she is handicapped by environmental problems or short-sighted social policies. Rehabilitation therapy and rehabilitation technology today can "add life to years" and should be given careful consideration for all elderly persons suffering from permanent impairments.

REFERENCES

1. American Medical Association: *Guide to the Evaluation of Permanent Impairment, 2nd Edition,* Chicago, American Medical Association, 1984.
2. Bobath, B: *Adult Hemiplegia: Evaluation and Treatment.* London, Heinemann, 1978.
3. Brunnstrom S: *Movement Therapy in Hemiplegia.* New York, Harper & Row, 1970.
4. Burgees EM: Amputation surgery and post-operative care. In Banerjee SN (Ed): *Rehabilitation Management of Amputees.* Baltimore, Williams & Wilkins, 1982, p. 17.
5. Cestaro JM (Ed): *Pictorial Reference Manual of Orthotics and Prosthetics,* Alexandria, The American Orthotic and Prosthetic Association, 1986.
6. Commission on Accreditation of Rehabilitation Facilities: *Standards Manual for Facilities Serving People With Disabilities,* Tucson, Commission on Accreditation of Rehabilitation Facilities, 1985, p. 33.
7. Clark GS, Bray GP: Development of a rehabilitation plan. In Williams TF (Ed): *Rehabilitation in the Aging.* New York, Raven Press, 1984, p. 125.
8. DeVries H: Physiological effects of an exercise training regimen upon aged men. *J Gerontol* 25:325, 1970.
9. Fordyce WE: Psychological assessment and management. In Krusen FH, Kottke FJ, Ellwood PM (Eds): *Handbook of Physical Medicine and Rehabilitation.* Philadelphia, WB Saunders, 1971, p. 125.
10. Lehmann JF, DeLateur BJ, Fowler RS, Warren CG, Arnhold R, Schertzer G, Harka R, Whitmore JJ, Masock AJ, Chambers KH: Stroke: Does rehabilitation affect outcome? *Arch Phys Med Rehabil* 56:375, 1975.
11. Redford JB (Ed): *Orthotics Etcetera,* 3rd Edition. Baltimore, Williams & Wilkins, 1986.
12. Robinson MB: *Aids, Equipment and Suggestions to Help the Patient With Parkinson's Disease in Activities of Daily Living.* New York, The American Parkinson Disease Association (undated).
13. Wenger NK: Cardiovascular status: Changes With aging. In Williams TF (Ed): *Rehabilitation in the Aging.* New York, Raven Press, 1984, p. 1.
14. Wolcott LE: Rehabilitation and the aged. In Reichel, W(ed): *Clinical Aspects of Aging,* 2nd Edition. Baltimore, Williams & Wilkins, 1980, p. 184.
15. World Health Organization: *International Classification of Impairments, Disabilities, and Handicaps—A Manual of Classification Relating to the Consequences of Disease.* Geneva, WHO, 1980.
16. Wu Y, Krick H: Removable rigid dressing for below-knee amputees. *Clin Prosthet Orthot* 11:1, 33, 1987.

CHAPTER 18

Gastro-intestinal Diseases in the Aged

JUNETTE C. GIBBONS
SUSAN M. LEVY

Gastrointestinal disorders are common among the elderly. They may indicate a local gastrointestinal problem or be a manifestation of a more widespread systemic disease. Many medications prescribed for older patients have significant gastrointestinal side effects (29).

The approach to and management of gastrointestinal disorders is influenced by advancing age. Gastrointestinal disease may present atypically in older patients. The differential diagnosis of a given symptom is often different in younger versus older patients. The increased frequency of gastrointestinal malignancies with age raises this as a concern more readily when an older person presents with a new symptom. There are also many benign gastrointestinal conditions that increase with age and functional complaints continue to be a major problem.

Obtaining an adequate gastrointestinal history may be limited by older persons' tendency to underreport symptoms. Diagnostic evaluation of the gastrointestinal tract is generally considered to be more difficult in older persons. Complication rates from diagnostic studies are felt to be higher. The use of potent purgatives in preparation for studies may result in dehydration. The actual performance of basic barium studies may be limited by an older person's immobility.

The availability of several new drugs has influenced the management of gastrointestinal diseases. There have also been advances in the nonoperative management of some gastrointestinal problems. Although these medications and procedures have some adverse effects, they may offer a safer alternative to major surgery in a frail older person.

The purpose of this chapter is to review some of the "normal" changes that occur in the gastrointestinal tract with aging. Discussion of diseases will be limited to those disorders that are either prevalent or limited to the elderly. A few of the more common symptomatic problems will also be discussed.

ANATOMIC AND PHYSIOLOGIC CHANGES WITH AGING

Good studies determining normal aging changes in the gut are limited. Many are biased by the inclusion of subjects suffering from systemic diseases that affect gastrointestinal function. However, decreased rates of cell division along with years of recurrent surface damage results in the tendency toward an atrophic mucosa on many gut surfaces. Degeneration in the submucosal nerve plexus may occur and contribute to some of the changes in gastrointestinal motility that are seen. More specific changes have been reported in different regions of the gastrointestinal tract (12).

The term "presbyesophagus" was coined by Soergel and others to describe in a group of nonagenarians the abnormal esophageal motility that they attributed to aging (26). Unfortunately, many of the study group suffered from diseases known to affect the nervous system and these disorders impact on esophageal motility. Subsequent studies on "healthier" older subjects suggest that more subtle changes in motility do occur (11). The strength of peristaltic contraction seems to be weaker in older subjects and disordered contractions may be more likely to occur. Because some motility changes may be normal in older patients, the findings of manometric studies must be carefully interpreted in the older age group.

Both basal and stimulated levels of gastric acid secretion decline with age and are associated with an increase in basal gastrin blood levels. These changes in gastric acid secretion may reflect changes in the structure and/or function of the parietal cell. However, these findings are not universal. Clearly, hyperchlorhydric syndromes continue to occur in older patients. Gastric emptying also seems to be impaired in older patients.

Small intestinal biopsies demonstrate broadening and shortening of jejunal villi in a number of older persons. Subclinical changes in absorption of nutrients has also been reported. Lactase deficiency occurs commonly, but is by no means consistently present. Changes in fat absorption reflect both intestinal and pancreatic aging. Gastric hypochlorhydria may contribute to decreased iron absorption from the duodenum. However, the development of frank iron deficiency should not be attributed to aging and warrants a thorough evaluation of the gastrointestinal tract for a site of occult blood loss. Although the absorption of many vitamins may be slightly diminished with aging, the presence of a true deficiency indicates decreased intake or other intestinal pathology. One important exception is the decrease in vitamin D and calcium absorption with age. The combination of decreased sun exposure, decreased renal conversion of vitamin D, and decreased intestinal absorption of vitamin D results in diminished calcium absorption from the aging gut. As a result, daily requirements for calcium intake are increased and physiologic supplementation of vitamin D in the form of a multivitamin is often prudent. Changes in calcium and vitamin D absorption impact on the development of osteoporosis with aging.

Colonic transit time has been shown to be decreased in many older subjects. Using radiodense markers, Brocklehurst and Khan (7) demonstrated that this is related more to immobility than to aging.

Liver weight diminishes with age and appears to correlate with a decline in the number of hepatocytes. Some of the changes in drug pharmacokinetics that occur with age are attributable to aging changes in the liver. Decline in hepatic blood flow along with changes in hepatic enzymes responsible for drug metabolism are two of the major factors. In the face of these changes that occur in the liver with aging, commonly performed liver function tests change very little (5).

The concentrating ability of the gallbladder does not appear to be affected by age. There is an increase in lithogenicity of bile. Slight dilatation of the common bile duct occurs with aging and must be considered in the interpretation of biliary tract studies.

The pancreatic ducts become dilated with age but otherwise retain their normal appearance. Fibrosis and fatty infiltration are commonly found. Although repeated stimulation of pancreatic secretion may result in a more rapid decline in the rates of secretion in older individuals, these changes do not bear major clinical significance.

ESOPHAGEAL DISEASE

Complaints of difficulty or pain on swallowing along with classic heartburn suggest esophageal pathology in all ages. Dysphagia may be caused by either an anatomic or a motility problem. The traditional approach to dysphagia is to separate the causes into oropharyngeal or esophageal.

Oropharyngeal dysphagia implies problems in moving food from the mouth to the upper esophagus. Normal swallowing requires coordination between the sensory receptors in the mouth and pharynx, the corticobulbar tracts, the medullary swallowing center containing nuclei of the 5th, 7th, 9th, 10th and 12th cranial nerves, and the appropriate skeletal muscles. Many neuromuscular diseases can result in impaired swallowing. Damage to the corticobulbar tracts from frontal lobe or brainstem disease results in pseudobulbar palsy. Bulbar palsy refers to damage of the cranial nerves themselves including the nuclei in the brainstem or in their subsequent course to the periphery. In both cases, dysphagia results and is commonly associated with dysarthria. Both are commonly the result of cerebral vascular accidents. Demyelinating disease, Parkinson's disease, other degenerative neurologic conditions, as well as brain tumors can result in oropharyngeal dysphagia. Other neuromuscular diseases, such as myasthenia gravis, peripheral neuropathy, myopathy, oropharyngeal muscular dystrophy can all result in oropharyngeal dysphagia. Mechanical obstruction either from tumor, abscess, or previous surgery can also result in dysphagia.

Upper esophageal dysphagia is usually greater for liquids than solids in contrast to lower esophageal pathology. Pulmonary complications may be the initial manifestation including aspiration, pneumonia, and lung abscess. Diagnostic evaluation includes cineradiography, esophageal manometry, and laryngoscopy. Both diagnosis and treatment may require a team approach with involvement of a neurologist, gastroenterologist, and otolaryngologist. Dysphagia, secondary to stroke, may improve over time. Rehabilitative efforts by a speech therapist addressing both the speech and swallowing problems may be helpful. Initiating feeding with foods of soft consistency, such as applesauce, along with feeding only in the erect position with the head tilted forward helps to improve swallowing in the poststroke victim. Drug therapy for some conditions such as Parkinson's disease may result in improvement. If the primary problem results in incoordination of the cricopharyngeal muscle, cricopharyngeal myotomy may be indicated in severely symptomatic patients. Although the response to myotomy is variable, the majority demonstrate improvement regardless of specific etiology. The only absolute contraindication to cricopharyngeal myotomy is gastroesophageal reflux (6).

Esophageal dysphagia may result from intrinsic or extrinsic compression of the esophagus. An example of the former is carcinoma of the esophagus, a devastating disease with a dismal 5-year survival rate. Nonoperative management of squamous cell carcinoma of the esophagus now includes laser therapy and the insertion of an esophageal prosthesis for palliation. These modalities are usually combined with radiation therapy.

Benign stricture of the esophagus, which is usually a result of chronic gastroesophageal reflux, also produces progressive dysphagia. It usually can be treated with esophageal dilation that may require repeated procedures over time.

The evaluation of dysphagia with a barium swallow may show a typical "bird beak" esophagus suggestive of achalasia. The initial presentation of primary achalasia is uncommon in persons over the age of 50 years. Such findings in an older patient should prompt upper endoscopy to rule out "secondary" achalasia that results from a tumor in the cardia of the stomach with submucosal invasion of the esophageal nerve plexus. "Tertiary" achalasia may also be found relating to more distant neoplasms of the lung and pancreas (6).

The other major motility problem that is seen in the esophagus is diffuse esophageal spasm. This can occur with or without acid reflux. The typical presentation is that of chest pain, which is often very difficult to differentiate from angina. Like angina, the pain may be precipitated by eating or emotional factors. Gastroesophageal reflux may also precipitate the pain. Evaluation includes esophageal manometry, which may or may not demonstrate abnormalities, and provocative testing may be required.

The Bernstein acid perfusion test should be included to evaluate the role of reflux in initiating the problem. Treatment is aimed at smooth muscle relaxation, use of short- and long-acting nitrates, and more recently, additional success has been obtained with calcium channel blockers. If gastroesophageal reflux is a precipitating event, treatment aimed at this problem is also needed.

Hiatal hernias increase in frequency with age and, in one study, 70% of patients over the age of 70 years were found to have a hiatal hernia (19). Symptoms are actually related to associated reflux esophagitis from an incompetent lower esophageal sphincter and not the hiatal hernia. Symptoms of esophageal reflux include substernal burning and regurgitation. Dysphagia may be associated with reflux symptoms indicating the development of a stricture or the presence of a predisposing esophageal motility disorder. Treatment is aimed at relieving symptoms and preventing chronic reflux and esophagitis. Elevating the head of the bed, refraining from eating before lying down, avoiding large meals, and stopping smoking are all important measures. Weight reduction and avoidance of fats, chocolate, and alcohol, with their adverse effects on lower esophageal sphincter pressures, are also indicated. Medication in older patients should be reviewed because many drugs prescribed for other diseases affect lower esophageal sphincter pressure and lead to reflux. Addition of antacids may be helpful in controlling symptoms. Bethanecol increases lower esophageal sphincter pressure but may be associated with adverse cardiovascular effects as well as urinary retention. The H_2 blockers, are also useful, but may produce mental confusion. Metoclopramide may produce extrapyramidal reactions in older patients.

Medication-induced esophageal injury should not be overlooked as a cause of esophageal symptoms. Over 200 cases of pill-induced esophageal injury were reported by Kikendall and colleagues (15) implicating 26 different types of medication. Esophagitis and frank esophageal ulceration were found. Antibiotics were responsible for over half the cases, with doxycycline the most commonly implicated medication. In this country, potassium chloride tablets, iron tablets, quinidine, along with various steroidal and nonsteroidal anti-inflammatory preparations were implicated. It is important that medications be taken with adequate amounts of fluid and in the upright position. Bedridden older patients should be expected to be at higher risk for medication-induced esophageal disease.

Esophageal infections with *Candida* organisms or *Herpes* virus should not be forgotten as causes of esophageal symptoms. Esophageal candidiasis may occur in the absence of the typical predisposing problems, such as malignancy, diabetes, malnutrition, or recent treatment with antibiotics or immunosuppressants. Oral lesions may not be present. Definitive diagnosis can only be made by demonstrating the organism in tissue through biopsy. However, a double contrast barium swallow can be diagnostic in 88% of cases (17). Treatment can be initiated with nystatin troches or ketoconazole although invasive disease may require systemic therapy with amphotericin B or 5-fluorocytosine (6). *Herpes* virus infections are less common and usually restricted to the debilitated immunocompromised patient.

DISEASES OF THE STOMACH

Abdominal pain, bloating, dyspepsia, weight loss, and gastrointestinal blood loss may be the presenting symptoms of a gastric disorder in an older person. Although the incidence of peptic ulcer disease in the United States is declining, complication and mortality rates have remained stable. Duodenal ulcers are found more commonly in younger patients with gastric ulcers being more problematic in the older population. At necropsy, 35% of those under the age of 50 years and 80% of those over 80 years of age had gastric ulcers (2). Older patients may present with symptoms for the first time in late life or may have a long history of recurrent ulcer disease. Because of the tendency to present with the more severe symptoms of massive bleeding or perforation, hospitalization is more frequently required in older patients with peptic ulcer disease. Gastric outlet obstruction appears more often in those who have had a longstanding history of ulcer disease. Giant duodenal and gastric ulcers are generally restricted to older age groups. The former typically presents in males in their 70s with severe abdominal pain and weight loss raising concerns about gastrointestinal malignancy. Hemorrhage is a major complication of giant gastric ulcers although atypical pain is also usually present (27).

Improved understanding of the role of hydrogen ion production on mucosal defenses at a cellular level has led to the development of new classes of drugs to treat ulcer disease. Currently H_2 blockers, antacids, and sucralfate are all available for treatment. Anticholinergics may be used as adjunctive therapy. Undergoing investigation is omiprazole, a representative of the new class of hydrogen ion/potassium ion ATPase inhibitors being evaluated for the treatment of peptic ulcer disease.

Antacid regimens used in the treatment of ulcer disease are limited because of the need for frequent dosing, the risk of sodium overload, the effect on bowel habits, as well as their interaction with other medications locally that prevent their absorption. The use of cimetidine can result in mental confusion in older patients, arrhythmias, and multiple drug interactions. These problems may be averted with appropriate reductions in dosage. The newer H_2 blocker, ranitidine, seems to be associated with fewer adverse effects in the elderly. Sucralfate is well tolerated with few side effects except constipation and may have cytoprotective benefits. In addition to medications, abstinence from alcohol, smoking, aspirin, and other nonsteroidal anti-inflammatory agents should be encouraged. Diet appears to play little role in the management of peptic ulcer disease.

Long-term maintenance therapy for peptic ulcer disease remains controversial. Most, including the authors, treat for 12 months when the risk of recurrence and mortality is the highest. Others prefer intermittent courses of treatment. Long-term treatment with nocturnal low dose H_2 blockers or sucralfate is often indicated particularly in elderly patients with multiple system diseases.

Atrophic gastritis is a major concern because of its malignant potential. Type A gastritis is usually diffuse with some relative antral sparing. It is associated with the presence of parietal cell antibodies and other autoimmune diseases, with decreased absorption of vitamin B_{12}. Type B gastritis is more of a focal antral process, is usually related to environmental factors, and is not typically associated with B_{12} malabsorption. Development of pernicious anemia with its associated hematologic and neurologic symptoms may be the initial presentation of type A gastritis. Linkage with gastric carcinoma is highest with type A gastritis and these patients require periodic screening. Type B gastritis may just present with dyspeptic symptoms. Its linkage with cancer is less direct (30).

Frequent use of salicylates and other nonsteroidal anti-inflammatory agents in the management of common arthritic symptoms in older persons is often associated with the development of drug-induced gastritis. A degree of occult blood loss is the rule in patients who are ingesting aspirin because of its irritant effects. Mucosal injury is diminished by the use of enteric-coated preparations. Virtually all of the nonsteroidal anti-inflammatory agents have some intestinal side effects. The best approach to selecting an agent with the least effects often requires trial and error. The role of corticosteroids in the development of frank ulceration is commonly debated. However, it is clear that steroids do mask symptoms of ulcer disease resulting in more serious complications. When agents are prescribed that are known to result in the development of gastritis in the high risk patient, concomitant administration of H_2 blockers or sucralafate may be indicated.

Although gastric malignancy is on the decline, there is some controversy over the incidence of stump carcinoma developing in the stomach remnant after partial gastrectomy. Previously it was believed that patients 10 years after surgery were at increased risk. However, reports since 1982 show no increased risk in the development of gastric cancer over the general population. Prudent indications for surveillance include screening those patients who had surgery 15 or more years previously, symptomatic patients 5 or more years after surgery, patients who had surgery initially for benign gastric ulcer, and patients who had surgery prior to the age of 40 years.

DISEASES OF THE GALLBLADDER

The presentation of biliary tract disease in older persons may be variable. Chronic cholecystitis can be responsible for unexplained fevers and weight loss. Although acute cholecystitis typically presents with right upper quadrant pain, nausea, and vomiting, the initial presentation may be with unexplained sepsis associated with abnormal liver function tests, particularly an elevated alkaline phosphatase and bilirubin. Ultrasonography makes the diagnosis of gallstone disease in 90% of cases. Nuclear medicine scanning with biliary imaging agents (HIDA, PIPIDA, DECIDA) has generally replaced the need for intravenous cholangiogram in the diagnosis of acute cholecystitis.

The prevalence of gallbladder stones rises with age. In the majority of cases, older patients are asymptomatic and do not develop the complications of acute or chronic cholecystitis. Gallstone disease tends to remain stable and infrequent minor attacks of cholecystitis usually do not progress to more severe disease. Unfortunately, this must be tempered with knowledge that morbidity and mortality from severe gallbladder disease is much higher in older patients. In the symptomatic gallbladder, elective cholecystectomy should be done in the older person and can be performed with minimum mortality. Diabetics, regardless of age, generally are managed best with elective surgery (22).

Severe or frequent symptoms in a nonsurgical candidate is an indication for chenodiol (chenodeoxycholic acid) therapy. The National Cooperative Gallstone Study established the efficacy and safety of chenodiol in the dissolution of cholesterol gallstones (21). Chenodiol decreases hepatic synthesis of cholesterol by an unknown mechanism. It also desaturates bile, decreases its lithogenicity, and solubilizes cholesterol leading to gallstone dissolution. The initial study dosage of 750 ml/day showed a dissolution rate of 13.5% in 2 years and about 25% in 4 years of therapy. Increasing the dosage to 12–15 mg/kg/day improves response rates. However, the safety of this larger dose has not been established.

The prerequisites for administering chenodiol include a functional gallbladder with radiolucent stones on oral cholecystogram. The presence of small stones (less than 10 mm in diameter), multiple stones, and "floating stones" show improved response to chenodiol therapy. Response is also better in thin women with elevated serum cholesterols. Side effects of treatment include hepatic dysfunction with elevated serum transaminases in about 30% of cases. Clinically significant liver disease occurs in less than 3% of patients and resolves on withdrawal of therapy. Diarrhea is another bothersome side effect that is reported in 40% of patients and may require reduction in dosage. Theoretical side effects including an increased risk of colorectal cancer and atherosclerosis have not been proven (21, 22).

Other nonsurgical approaches to gallbladder disease continue to be investigated. These include endoscopic retrograde cholangiopancreotography (ERCP) with papillotomy and stone removal, percutaneous transhepatic stone removal, transhepatic dissolution of gallstones with either methyl tert butyl ether or monooctanoin, lithotripsy, laser, and percutaneous transhepatic papillotomy.

PANCREATIC DISEASES

The development of abdominal pain, weight loss, symptoms of diabetes, or chronic diarrhea may raise concerns about the development of pancreatic disease. Acute pancreatitis presents similarly in younger and older age groups except for more subtle abdominal findings in older patients. The etiology in the elderly is usually related to gallstones. Although alcoholic pancreatitis is seen, alcohol is the more typical etiologic factor in younger patients. Other types of pancreatitis seen in older patients include: pancreatitis secondary to hyperparathyroidism; postoperative pancreatitis usually related to abdominal surgery; pancreatitis related to duodenal disease, such as duodenal diverticula or obstruction; or pancreatitis as a complication of endoscopic evaluation. Drug-induced pancreatitis has certainly been reported with some drugs that are commonly prescribed in the elderly, such as thiazide diuretics and tetracycline. Although drugs are an uncommon cause of pancreatitis, it is generally advisable to withdraw any drugs that have been reported to cause pancreatitis when the disease develops. Acute pancreatitis may be the initial presentation of primary or metastatic carcinoma.

Biliary pancreatitis is thought to be related to ampullary obstruction by gallstones with subsequent reflux of bile into the pancreatic duct resulting in acute inflammation. Previously, urgent surgical treatment was necessary in the severely ill patient particularly with evidence of worsening pancreatitis. Mortality was frequently quoted as high and attempts to delay surgery several days were thought to result in improved survival. With the development and improvement in ERCP techniques, gallstones obstructing the ampulla can be removed and a transduodenal sphincterotomy performed to decompress the biliary tract and allow for resolution of the pancreatic inflammation.

Chronic pancreatitis is a less common problem in older patients, probably reflecting earlier mortality of those with chronic alcoholic pancreatitis. However, idiopathic chronic pancreatitis may present in the elderly as chronic abdominal pain with varying degrees of malabsorption. Treatment includes replacement of pancreatic enzymes which results in remarkable resolution of symptoms.

Pancreatic cancer is a devastating disease with 90% of cases diagnosed in patients over 50 years of age. Peak incidence is in the sixth decade and survival from the time of diagnosis is usually less than 1 year. Presentation is related to the location of the tumor in the gland. Tumors of the head of the pancreas typically present earlier with obstructive jaundice. The development of embolic disease, depression, diabetes, or symptoms of chronic pancreatitis are some of the syndromes associated with pancreatic cancer. Diagnosis may require a combination of tests including ultrasound, computed tomography, percutaneous biopsy with a skinny needle, ERCP with brush cytology, and pancreatic secretin testing. Palliation of biliary tract obstructive symptoms may be provided through transhepatic or endoscopic placement of a biliary stent (that is, a catheter used to assure patency). Treatment with surgery, radiation therapy, and/or chemotherapy have not affected the dismal survival rate (14).

LIVER DISEASES

The development of hepatic jaundice raises the differential diagnosis of obstructive versus intrinsic hepatobiliary disease in all age groups. The common causes of extrahepatic obstruction seen in older patients have already been discussed. Although obstructive causes of jaundice are more common than hepatocellular disease in older patients, the latter warrants discussion.

Acute viral hepatitis is thought to be less common in older patients. However, the possibility of outbreaks of hepatitis A virus, particularly in institutional settings, should not be overlooked. Also, improved surgical techniques have resulted in many older persons undergoing extensive surgical procedures requiring multiple transfusions with a subsequent risk of posttransfusion hepatitis. Viral hepatitis is generally a more serious disease in older patients with a higher mortality, and often is associated with a more protracted and morbid course.

Acute and chronic drug-induced liver disease should not be overlooked as a common cause for jaundice in older patients. Drugs may cause dose-related and predictable hepatic dysfunction or idiosyncratic reactions. The picture may be varied and include evidence of either cholestatic or hepatocellular injury. Granulomatous hepatitis may also be seen with a number of drugs. Extensive reviews of drug-induced liver disease are available (18).

Cirrhosis continues to present in older age groups. Similar etiologies should be sought as in younger patients including alcohol, drug or toxin-inducement, postinfectious, metabolic, and vascular disease including chronic heart failure. Biliary cirrhosis may initially present in elderly females in its primary form (16). Pruritus and jaundice are the typical symptoms with the former preceding the latter frequently by months to years. An elevation in the alkaline phosphatase in an otherwise asymptomatic patient may also be the initial presentation. Diagnosis is made by finding a positive antimitochondrial antibody and confirmed with liver biopsy. The disease is considered to be autoimmune and, logically, therapy should be aimed at immunosuppression. However, most studies have shown no proven benefit for treatment with steroids, which are contraindicated because of the adverse side effects. Treatment with penicillamine may be tried in symptomatic patients but, again, no definitive benefit has been demonstrated.

Cardiac failure is commonly associated with hepatic congestion. Variable patterns of abnormal liver function tests may be seen probably related to a combination of backward congestion of the liver as well as the decreased perfusion of the liver secondary to a decline in cardiac output. Hepatic encephalopathy may contribute to the altered mentation seen with severe congestive heart failure. However, decreased cerebral perfusion, hypoxemia, and electrolyte imbalance are usually the major contributors to the confused state that can be seen in patients with severe congestive heart failure (9).

DISEASES OF THE COLON

Abdominal pain, lower gastrointestinal bleeding, weight loss, and complaints of change in bowel movements are some of the manifestations of lower bowel disease. Diverticular disease affects one-third of all Americans over the age of 60 years and accounts for 200,000 hospitalizations a year. The typical low fiber American diet results in low fecal volumes in the left colon requiring increased intraluminal pressure for evacuation. Herniations of the mucosa through defects in the muscular wall result in the subsequent development of diverticula. Diverticuli may become symptomatic through lower gastrointestinal bleeding or the development of diverticulitis. The latter may present with evidence of gastrointestinal obstruction, perforation, the development of fistulae, and/or abscess formation. Treatment with a high fiber diet may result in improvement of symptoms in patients with established diverticular disease. Surgery is indicated in more severe cases to alleviate serious sequelae. A one-stage procedure with resection of the affected area is the preferable operative approach. Elective surgery in appropriately selected cases is associated with a lower mortality than emergent intervention for acute abdominal complications (13).

Inflammatory bowel disease including ulcerative colitis and Crohn's disease are reported to have a second peak in incidence after the age of 65 years. Brandt (3, 4) has recently questioned this finding, suggesting that many older patients diagnosed as having new onset of inflammatory bowel disease when carefully evaluated are frequently suffering from ischemic colitis. This incorrect diagnosis may explain some of the atypical features that are frequently reported to occur in older patients with inflammatory bowel disease. True cases of inflammatory bowel disease present similarly in younger and older patients. However, when ulcerative colitis does develop in an older patient, it seems to be a more serious disease. In evaluating studies of inflammatory bowel disease in older patients, it is important to differentiate between patients who have been symptomatic from their earlier years versus those who have true new onset disease. Treatment includes appropriate medical therapy along with surgery for certain complications.

Colonic ischemia may present with a wide spectrum of symptoms from mild pain and bleeding, to symptoms of frank gangrene and/or bowel perforation. The vascular disease is generally nonocclusive and usually reversible. The splenic flexure is involved in about 40% of the cases, descending colon 20%, rectosigmoid 25%, and rectum in 10% of cases (3). Diagnosis may be difficult in that nonspecific findings frequently will be seen on barium studies and endoscopy. In more severe disease, the mucosa wall edema will result in the findings of thumbprinting or nodularity on barium enema. Endoscopically, edema, friability, and submucosal hemorrhage may be seen. The clinical course is variable and the early lesions of hemorrhage and edema may resolve quickly or may develop into a frank colitis. Healing may subsequently occur with or without the development of a stricture.

When the diagnosis of colonic ischemia is suspected, it is important to exclude initially acute mesenteric ischemia, which is a more serious and life-threatening disease in the differential diagnosis. In the absence of frank colonic gangrene, treatment is expectant including careful observation, bowel rest, and intravenous hydration. Persistent or worsening symptoms are indications for surgical intervention with local colonic resection. It is always important to exclude obstructing lesions of the bowel as precipitants for the ischemia. Conservative management is supported by low recurrence rates (3).

Another important cause of lower gastrointestinal bleeding in older patients are angiodysplasias. These lesions are thought to represent a degenerative process and are usually localized in the cecum and the ascending colon. Frequently, there is associated cardiac disease and there appears to be an increased association with aortic stenosis. Bleeding from these lesions is typically slow and chronically recurrent. Massive lower gastrointestinal hemorrhage is not uncommon (4).

The initial management of gastrointestinal bleeding in all patients includes hemodynamic stabilization. Because an upper tract source may be present in 10% of patients presenting with massive rectal bleeding, a nasogastric tube should be inserted. If bile-stained gastric contents are returned without evidence of bleeding, an upper source is much less likely. Massive bleeding may require colonoscopy, upper endoscopy, as well as angiography to determine the source. Although colonoscopy is difficult in the setting of massive bleeding, it can be helpful in determining left- versus right-sided colonic bleeding. Angiography may be diagnostic as well as therapeutic with the infusion of vasopressin into the bleeding vessel or even thrombosing the vessel with Gelfoam. A technetium sulfur colloid scan or a technetium red blood cell-tagged scan is helpful before diagnostic angiography to determine the rate of bleeding as well as its localization. Therapeutic colonoscopy is limited to electrocautery or laser therapy of angiodysplasias. If bleeding polyps are identified, these may also be removed.

Although vascular angiodysplasias are important causes of lower gastrointestinal bleeding in the elderly, the most common cause of massive blood loss from the lower tract is bleeding diverticula. Although most diverticula are in the sigmoid region of the colon, bleeding is from right-sided diverticula in 70% of episodes. When lower gastrointestinal bleeding cannot be controlled and localization is not possible, a subtotal colectomy is recommended. Ideally, this should be performed when the patient has been hemodynamically stabilized and on an urgent rather than an emergent basis (13, 20).

Colonic neoplasms occur with increasing frequency in the elderly. Benign adenomas are recognized as precancerous lesions and usually are asymptomatic and are found during an evaluation of occult gastrointestinal blood loss. Polyps may be removed at the time of lower endoscopy and submitted for pathologic evaluation. For benign lesions, follow-up colonoscopy is indicated at 1 year with periodic surveillance thereafter.

Colonic malignancies are one of the major causes of cancer deaths. Right-sided lesions seem to increase in frequency with advancing age. In spite of the development of simple screening procedures, most patients with colon cancer continue to present later in the course of the disease when the chance for cure is diminished. Currently, annual screening of stool specimens for occult blood is considered prudent. Although the yield of routine sigmoidoscopy in finding malignant lesions may be small, the removal of the more commonly found benign polyp at the time of sigmoidoscopy may prevent the development of subsequent malignant lesions.

FUNCTIONAL BOWEL DISEASE

The previous sections have emphasized common gastrointestinal disorders that are found in older patients. Generally, the development of a new gastrointestinal symptom warrants careful evaluation for gastrointestinal or systemic pathology. However, in some cases, no organic disease can be identified through the usual diagnostic evaluation. The possibility of a functional bowel disorder may then be appropriately entertained. Although it is generally taught that functional bowel disease is less likely in those over the age of 50 years, in reality, this may not be the case. In a previous edition of this text, Sklar

(24) reviewed his experience with a group of 900 patients over the age of 65 years managed in different clinical settings who presented with gastrointestinal complaints. After the initial evaluation and follow-up of a minimum of 1 year, the most frequently established diagnosis was that of functional bowel disease. In fact, this was almost twice as common as any other gastrointestinal diagnosis (24).

The presenting symptoms of functional bowel disease are similar to many serious pathologic conditions. Although there are no diagnostic hallmarks, clues to the functional problem can be found in the history and presentation. Commonly, complaints are longstanding, symptoms are intermittent, weight is usually stable, and symptoms do not typically awaken the patient at night. Symptoms often may be precipitated by specific dietary indiscretions or various life stresses. The possibility of an underlying depression often should be sought. Some patients with senile dementia seem to focus on various somatic complaints.

Treatment is multifaceted. Frequently, extensive gastrointestinal evaluation is warranted in order to provide the patient with adequate reassurance that a serious disease is not present. Additional treatment modalities include dietary manipulation because symptoms sometimes improve on a high fiber diet. Antacids and antispasmodics may offer symptomatic relief. The latter includes such agents as Donnatal or tincture of Belladonna. If antispasmodics are instituted, they should be monitored for atropine-like side effects. Anxiolytics in small doses may be helpful, although long-term use of benzodiazepines should be avoided. Supportive psychotherapy is important in the overall treatment plan. The use of antidepressants may be indicated particularly in some difficult cases that do not respond to other treatment modalities. Unfortunately, the anticholinergic effects of antidepressants may result in additional gastrointestinal side effects, such as dry mouth and constipation.

CONSTIPATION

Preoccupation with regular bowel movements seems to be common in many older persons. Frequently these concerns stem from the patient's youth when the theory of autointoxication was used to explain ill health (25). The complaint of constipation may reflect a decrease in the size or frequency of bowel movements, discomfort associated with failure to have a regular bowel movement, or actual pain with the bowel movement.

Defining what represents constipation implies

the knowledge of "normal" bowel habits in the population. The survey by Connell et al. (8) of nearly 1500 adult patients indicated that 99% reported anywhere from three bowel movements per day to three bowel movements per week. No significant differences were demonstrated between older and younger patients. Fewer than 10% considered themselves constipated and this complaint often had no relationship to the bowel frequency or stool consistency of those individuals. Historic features that raise concern about serious underlying pathology include recent changes in bowel patterns, severe pain with defecation, and bleeding. Additional evaluation includes a digital examination, sigmoidoscopy, examination of stool specimen for occult blood, and in all but the most chronic of cases, a barium enema and/or colonoscopy.

Constipation has been divided into two types (24). Spastic constipation is associated with small hard stools and is believed to reflect an irritable colon. Atonic constipation seems to be more prevalent in older patients and is probably related to decreased colonic motility. Usually the rectal vault is empty until immediately before defecation. In older patients, digital examination may reveal feces in the rectal vault in the absence of the sensation to defecate. With failure to expel feces in the rectum, accumulation of fecal material continues filling the rectosigmoid and the more proximal parts of the colon. This had led to the use of the term "terminal reservoir syndrome." Immobility seems to be a major predisposing event for this form of constipation (7).

A number of additional factors contribute to constipation in older patients. Obviously pathology in the lower bowel or perineum must be considered. Normal defecation depends on intact nervous innervation of the internal and external anal sphincters and many neurologic diseases may interfere and result in increased constipation. Hypothyroidism should be considered. Depression is also commonly associated with constipation. Many medications predisposed to constipation include those with cholingeric activity, some antihypertensives, diuretics, analgesics, and aluminum-containing antacids. In addition to problems with mobility, many older persons do not take in adequate amounts of fluid, and their diets are deficient in fiber. Frequently, constipation is multifactorial.

Treatment of constipation in older patients is multifaceted. Perineal problems, such as hemorrhoids or fissures, should be adequately treated. Surgery is indicated in cases where bowel obstruction is the major etiologic factor. An adequate diet with fiber supplementation and an increase in fluid intake is required for successful treatment in many cases. Assistance with toileting and attention to proper posture at the time of defecation is important. The squatting position is more physiologic for normal defecation. Elevated toilet seats used by older patients with limited mobility frequently interfere with proper positioning. In these cases, a footstool should be provided to allow for a more physiologic position. Since immobility is associated with a decrease in bowel transit time, an exercise program may be initiated along with specific efforts to strengthen abdominal and pelvic muscles. Medication regimens should be reviewed and unnecessary medications that may interfere with bowel motility should be stopped or alternative medications selected. Increasing dietary fiber with bran supplementation may be effective in managing constipation.

Although chronic laxative use is commonly frowned upon, this may be needed to avoid symptoms of constipation. Bulk laxatives stimulate colonic motor activity and lubricate the stool. One example is psyllium (Metamucil, Konsyl). However, it is imperative when bulk laxatives are used that fluid intake is adequate. Some believe that stool softeners have little role in the treatment of chronic constipation. Potent stimulant cathartics should be avoided on a long-term basis and are associated with melanosis coli. Mineral oil is relatively contraindicated in older patients because of its effect on vitamin D absorption as well as the increased risk of aspiration pneumonia. Saline cathartics are among the most popular laxatives. Lactulose is effective, has relatively few side effects, and has been found to be particularly useful in older patients. In some cases, particularly in the institutionalized population, regular evacuation of the bowel with enemas may be the only successful program.

Fecal impaction is a serious complication of untreated constipation. This may result in fecal incontinence that may present with paradoxical diarrhea because of the seepage of fecal fluid around the bolus of unexpelled feces. Stercoral ulceration is another serious complication of impaction related to pressure necrosis of the fecal mass on the rectal bowel mucosa. Bleeding and perforation can result. Fecal impaction is particularly common in patients with neuropsychiatric disorders and is liable to recur if careful monitoring of bowel habits is not instituted. Treatment of fecal impaction requires rigorous cleansing of the colon with various combinations of cathartics, saline enemas, and in some cases, digital disimpaction. The latter must be done carefully as perforation can result. Once the impaction is resolved, a routine bowel program must be instituted to prevent recurrence.

FECAL INCONTINENCE

Fecal incontinence, as noted in the preceding section, is usually a complication of longstanding constipation and/or fecal impaction. Like its counterpart, urinary incontinence, it can result in social isolation and may be one of the factors that precipitates institutionalization. Adequate diagnosis is necessary in order to develop an appropriate treatment plan. Abnormal function of the anal sphincters and/or pelvic floor is usually implicated, which may be a result of direct trauma, rectal prolapse, medications, or various neurologic conditions. Diabetic neuropathy is not uncommonly implicated (10).

Although careful history and physical examination including digital examination and sigmoidoscopy along with a careful neurologic examination may result in the diagnosis, additional investigation may at times be indicated, which may include a combination of manometry, electromyography, and nerve stimulation techniques. Medical management includes treatment of constipation and impaction if these are implicated. In milder cases, treatment with constipating agents may restore continence. Biofeedback techniques have also proven useful. Surgery, including postanal repair and correction of previous anal sphincter damage, may be effective and successful in appropriate selected patients (10).

DIARRHEA

Diarrhea is defined by increased frequency and liquidity of stools. In one recent study of older patients hospitalized for evaluation of diarrhea, fecal impaction was the most common diagnosis via the mechanism described previously. However, certain diarrheal syndromes occur with increased frequency in the older population and warrant consideration.

Acute diarrhea generally raises the possibility of an infectious process and raises particular concern in the institutional setting where an infection may spread among the resident population. Infectious diarrhea tends to be more serious in older patients because of the more rapid development of dehydration with its sequelae.

Many medications can be associated with the development of diarrhea. The use of magnesium-containing antacids along with the overzealous use of laxatives is often implicated. Antibiotics may result in the development of mild diarrhea or frank pseudomembranous colitis. Virtually all antibiotics except the aminoglycosides have been implicated and the association with *Clostridium difficile* has become clear in recent years. Carriage rates of the organism and the presence of the cytopathic toxin are increased even in patients with no bowel symptoms who are institutionalized (1). Treatment with oral vancomycin or metronidazole is effective although relapse may occur.

Organic causes of chronic diarrhea are multiple. A not infrequent cause of diarrhea is that of lactose intolerance, which has been previously mentioned. This usually responds to an elimination of lactose from the diet. The differential diagnosis of various malabsorptive syndromes is extensive. These tend to be more prevalent in younger age groups. However, decreased gut motility and the increased development of small bowel diverticula in some older persons predisposes to the development of bacterial overgrowth syndromes. Treatment with a broad-spectrum antibiotic, such as tetracycline, is effective.

ANOREXIA

Anorexia is generally defined as the loss of appetite and is a common problem in older patients. It is one of the main factors that contributes to eating difficulties that are so common among frail dependent older persons. Eating disability is a common symptom of gastrointestinal disorders and systemic illnesses. Adequate nutritional intake is necessary for survival. Throughout life, eating is generally considered a pleasurable experience and is frequently the center of social gatherings. Intact taste and smell contribute to the pleasure and stimulate appetite. These senses diminish with age and influence appetite in older persons. Decreased salivation and dental disorders also influence an older person's eating behavior.

Hunger centers in the hypothalamus receive and respond to input from the environment and the gut. Damage to these areas of the brain can result in changes in appetite. Some medications may influence these centers directly and result in anorexia.

Recently, Siebens et al. (23) divided the act of eating into five components including: (a) behavioral/cognitive; (b) upper extremity function; (c) oral-motor; (d) pharyngeal; and (e) esophageal. A number of problems that are common in older persons can interfere in any of these areas and result in difficulties in eating. The study by Siebens et al. in a nursing home population confirmed the high incidence of eating dependency in institutionalized older persons and its association with early mortality (23).

Dementia and depression are commonly associated with eating problems. In the former, memory loss may result in patients simply forgetting to eat. With both these conditions, changes in central neurotransmitters may be responsible for a change in appetite. In stroke patients, eating problems may be related both to difficulties in using a weakened upper extremity as well as associated swallowing disorders. The latter has been discussed previously in this chapter.

After serious pathology has been excluded, including careful evaluation of the mouth and dentition as well as a high index of suspicion of swallowing disorders, often there remains a patient who is physically capable of eating but persists with a diminished appetite. In such cases, providing more varied selection of foods, a more socially acceptable milieu for meals, and/or withdrawal of medication that may diminish appetite can be helpful. In many cases, a trial of antidepressant treatment is indicated.

REFERENCES

1. Bender RS, Laughon BE, Gaydos C: Is *Clostridium difficile* endemic in chronic-care facilities? *Lancet* 2:11, 1986.
2. Boyd E, Wormsley K: Etiology and pathogenesis of peptic ulcer. In Berk JE (Ed): *Bockus Gastroenterology.* Philadelphia, WB Saunders, 1985.
3. Brandt LJ: Ischemic disorder of the intestine. In Brandt LJ (Ed): *Gastrointestinal Disorders in the Elderly.* New York, Raven Press, 1984, p. 368.
4. Brandt L.J: The colon. In Brandt LJ (Ed): *Gastrointestinal Disorders of the Elderly.* New York, Raven Press, 1984, p. 261.
5. Brandt LJ: The Liver. In Brandt LJ (Ed): *Gastrointestinal Disorders of the Elderly.* New York, Raven Press, 1984, p. 489.
6. Brandt LJ: The oropharynx and esophagus. In Brandt LJ (Ed): *Gastrointestinal Disorders of the Elderly.* New York, Raven Press, 1984, p. 29.
7. Brocklehurst JC, Khan Y: A study of fecal stasis in old age and the use of Dorbanex in its prevention. *Gerontol Clin* 2:293, 1969.
8. Connell AM, Hilton C, Irvine G, et al: Variation of bowel habits in two population samples. *Br Med J* 2:1095, 1965.
9. Dunn GD, Hayes P, Breen KJ: The liver in congestive heart failure: A review. *Am J Med Sci* 265:175, 1973.
10. Henry MM: Pathogenesis and management of fecal incontinence in the adult. *Gastroenterology Clin North Am* 16:35, 1987.
11. Hollis JB, Castell DO: Esophageal function in elderly men: A new look at presbyesophagus. *Ann Intern Med* 80:371, 1974.
12. Holt P: Aging and the gut. *Geriatr Med Today* 4:44, 1985.
13. Johnson H Jr, Block M: Diverticular disease, current trends in therapy. *Postgrad Med* 78:75, 1985.
14. Kaiser M, Smith F, Schein P, et al: Exocrine tumors of the pancreas. In Berk JE (Ed): *Bockus Gastroenterology.* Philadelphia, WB Saunders, 1985.
15. Kikendall JW, Friedman AC, Oyewole MA, et al: Pill-induced esophageal injury: Case reports and review of the medical literature. *Dig Dis Sci* 28:174, 1983.
16. Lehamnn A, Bassendine MF, James OFW: Primary biliary cirrhosis: A disease increasingly recognized in the elderly. *Geriatric Med Today* 3:64, 1984.
17. Levine MF, Macones AJ, Laufer I: *Candida* esophagitis: Accuracy of radiographic diagnosis. *Radiology* 154:581, 1985.
18. Ludwig J, Axelson R: Drug effects on the liver: An updated tabular compilation of drugs and drug-related hepatic diseases. *Dig Dis Sci* 28:651, 1983.
19. Pridie RB: Incidence and coincidence of hiatus hernia. *Gut* 7:188, 1966.
20. Rodkey GV, Welch C: Changing patterns in the surgical treatment of diverticular disease. *Ann Surg* 200:466, 1984.
21. Schoenfield LJ, Lachin JM, et al: Chenodiol for dissolution of gallstones: The NCGS. A controlled trial of efficacy and safety. *Ann Intern Med* 95:257, 1981.
22. Schoenfield LJ, Marks JW: Cholelithiasis: Nonsurgical management. In Berk JE (Ed): *Bockus Gastroenterology.* Philadelphia, WB Saunders, 1985.
23. Siebens H, Trupe E, Cook F, Anshen S: Correlates and consequences of eating dependency in institutionalized elderly. *J Am Geriatr Soc* 34:192, 1986.
24. Sklar M: Gastrointestinal diseases in the aged. In Reichel W (Ed): *Clinical Aspects of Aging.* 2nd ed. Baltimore, Williams & Wilkins, 1983, p. 205.
25. Smith JL: Sir Arbuthnot Lane, chronic intestinal stasis and autointoxication. *Ann Intern Med* 96:365, 1982.
26. Soergel KH, Zboralske FF, Amberg JR: Presbyesophagus: Esophageal motility in nonagenarians. *J Clin Invest* 43:1472, 1964.
27. Strange SL: Giant innocent gastric ulcer in the elderly. *Gerontol Clin* 5:171, 1963.
28. Strodel WE, Nostrant TT, Eckhauser F, et al: Therapeutic and diagnostic colonoscopy in non-obstructive colonic dilatation. *Ann Surg* 197:416, 1983.
29. Woodhouse KW: Drugs and the ageing gut, liver and pancreas. *Clin Gastroenterol* 14:863, 1985.
30. Villardel F: Gastritis. In Berk JE (Ed): *Bockus Gastroenterology.* Philadelphia, WB Saunders, 1985, p. 944.

CHAPTER 19

Infectious Disease Problems in the Elderly

VINCENT F. GARAGUSI

With the steady advances being made in medicine, patients are living longer. Infection is a frequent cause for hospital admission and remains an important cause of death in geriatric patients. Although most types of infections may be seen in the elderly, there are many infections that are more indigenous in this age group. These infections are discussed in this chapter.

PROBLEMS IN EVALUATING INFECTIONS

Geriatric patients may have serious infections with little or no fever due to an impaired thermoregulator system, the antipyretic effect of prescribed anti-inflammatory drugs or the uremic syndrome. A change in sensorium with confusion or lethargy may be the earliest signs of sepsis. Elderly patients may be unable to describe their present illness, past history, or list of medications. A complete physical examination may be impaired by the patient's uncooperativeness, neurologic deficits, or contracted limbs. Unfortunately, some physicians do not give the same care to geriatric patients as they do to their younger patients. Diagnostic studies and cultures are omitted, and shotgun antibiotic therapy is employed. If this type of treatment fails, the likelihood of finding the causative agent diminishes.

CELLULAR AND HUMORAL IMMUNOLOGY

Contrary to common belief, the geriatric patient's cellular and humoral immunity remains intact unless there is some debilitating or chronic disease, or if the patient is receiving immuno-

suppressive therapy. The incidence of viral upper respiratory infections and viral influenza decreases with age. However, when the geriatric patient develops these infections they tend to be of a more serious and debilitating nature, and associated with a higher mortality due to bacterial superinfections (3, 4, 7).

The aging process at the tissue-cellular level may lead to increased susceptibility to infection due to atrophic skin, achlorhydria, and a decreased cough-gag reflex as well as decreased bronchiolar elasticity and mucociliary activity (5). The most important determining factors of how well geriatric patients can handle infections are related to their underlying mental and physical disabilities, nutritional status, and the existence of chronic disease, i.e., renal and cardiac impairment and peripheral vascular insufficiency.

ENVIRONMENTAL INFECTIONS

In many elderly with evidence of impairment and decline or with evidence of dementing illness, personal hygiene suffers either through indifference or the loss of manual dexterity, body mobility, or vision. It is not uncommon to see the unmanicured, brown fingernail sign (feces under the nails) or vagabond dermatitis (uncleaned skin). Patients are no longer able to cut their nails and adequately clean certain parts of the body. Mosquito or flea bites on chronic atrophic dry skin lead to itching and scratching and subsequent cellulitis of the skin. Household trauma with breaks in the aging skin leads to an increased incidence of secondary infection. Elderly patients who have pet cats and dogs may sustain scratches or bites leading to primary infections with *Pasteurella multocida*. The latter infection has an abrupt onset, usually within 24 hours of the bite, and is characterized by localized pain and rapid-spreading cellulitis; it usually responds to penicillin or erythromycin. Gardening may result in an indolent skin-eschar as the first manifestation of sporotrichosis. A similar lesion may be seen with *Mycobacterium marinum* in patients who own and clean tropical fish tanks.

HEAD AND NECK INFECTIONS

Entropion, exotrophia, and Sicca syndrome are common phenomena of aging and are associated with *Staphylococcus aureus* and *Staphylococcus epidermiditis* conjunctivitis. Surgical correction, topical antibiotics, and artificial tears are indicated.

Extraction of cataracts may lead to postoperative endophthalmitis in 0.5% of cases. Contact lenses should not be prescribed for elderly patients unless they can demonstrate clearly the mental acuity and manual dexterity necessary for their care. Increasing incidence of infections with bacteria, fungi, and Acanthamoeba are being reported with their use.

The usual bacteria causing sinusitis continues throughout life, especially in the elderly when atrophic mucous membranes lose their mucociliary action. In poorly controlled diabetic patients, mucormycosis of the sinuses may be rapidly destructive to bony structures, with invasion into the carotid sheath, orbit, and brain. Mucormycosis is diagnosed rapidly by submitting biopsied tissue for histologic examination and for fungal cultures.

Oral hygiene may suffer in the geriatric patient. Recession of the gingiva, ill-fitting dental plates and bridges, and periodontal disease may lead to Ludwig's angina, actinomycosis of the soft tissue and osteomyelitis of facial bones, brain abscess, cavernous sinus thrombosis, or mediastinitis.

Hospitalized patients who require nasogastric suction or feeding tubes are more prone to develop acute *S. aureus* parotitis. This is characterized by acute erythematous painful swelling of the parotid. Pus may be seen exiting from Stenson's duct and may be associated with bacteremia. Occasionally, *Klebsiella pneumoniae* may be the etiologic agent. Nasogastric tubes may also lead to acute sinusitis by obstructing the nasal sinus ostia, and aspiration pneumonia.

Malignant otitis externa is a rapidly advancing infection of the auditory canal due to *Pseudomonas aeruginosa* and leading to osteomyelitis of the temporal bone with meningeal and brain invasion in poorly controlled diabetic patients. Blood cultures are usually negative. Poorly controlled diabetics should be cautioned against swimming in recreation pools or sitting in hot tubs or jacuzzis, and from removing cerumen from their ear. Cerumen acts as a natural barrier against this infection. Impacted cerumen should be removed preferentially with gentle lavages of hydrogen peroxide instead of using surgical instruments that could traumatize the auditory canal.

Nasal hairs should be clipped and not manually pulled out. Many patients are nasal carriers of *S. aureus* and may develop folliculitis from the pulled hair, resulting in bacteremia and metastatic osteomyelitis of the spine and other sites.

PULMONARY INFECTIONS

Pulmonary infections are one of the most common causes of death in the geriatric patient. The respiratory tree is said to be an extracorporeal organ where one breathes in and out a host of noxious agents from birth to death. With advancing age, the respiratory tract is compromised by previous lung damage that has led to fibrosis, emphysema, or bronchietasis. In the aging lung, mucociliary action and elasticity of the bronchiolar musculature decreases. Vertebral arthritis, kyphoscoliosis, neurologic disease with decreased gag and cough reflex, and large hiatal hernias all contribute to increased pulmonary ventilatory problems.

In the geriatric patient with bacterial pneumonia, no classic radiographic patterns of pulmonary infiltrates may occur. A roentgenogram density may be caused by any of the common bacteria associated with penumonia: i.e., *Streptococcus pneumoniae, Hemophilus influenza, S. aureus, Legionella pneumophilia, Klebsiella pneumoniae*, etc. In patients with emphysema, the classic lobar pneumonia of *Pneumococcus* may not be seen; instead, nodular infiltrates may be seen suggesting a staphylococcal infection.

In dehydrated patients, an infiltrate by roentgenogram may not become apparent until the patient is hydrated. Unfortunately, the etiologic agent causing the pneumonia is not identified unless there are concomitant positive blood cultures. Therefore, blood cultures should be obtained in every patient with pneumonia. It is extremely uncommon to obtain an adequate specimen of sputum of Gram stain and culture in the geriatric patient. These patients rarely can bring up sputum, especially if they are feeble, debilitated, or have neurologic deficits. Aggressive measures of obtaining sputum by transbronchial aspiration, bronchoscopy, or needle aspiration of a pulmonary infiltrate may or may not yield the causative agent. In many cases, these procedures cannot be done because of severe arthritis of the neck and the risk factors of pneumothorax or hemorrhage. In any case, all attempts should be made when possible to identify the causative organism in those patients who are not responding to the initially prescribed antimicrobial therapy.

Community-acquired pneumonia in a relatively healthy geriatric patient should be worked up diagnostically as in any other patient. The course of treatment will be the same, usually using a single antibiotic agent as dictated by the clinical history, roentgenogram, Gram stain, and culture of sputum. Debilitated patients or patients admitted to a hospital from a nursing home with pneumonia should not be classified as community-acquired pneumonia, but should be considered under the category of hospital-acquired pneumonia and treated with broad-spectrum antibiotics to cover for Gram-positive, Gram-negative (aerobic-anaerobic) and *Legionella* bacteria. This may require two to three antibiotics, i.e., cephalosporin, aminoglycoside, and erythromycin, until the etiologic agent has been identified.

Aspiration pneumonia is most commonly due to aspiration of saliva, food, or vomitus, and is due to polymicrobial organisms; i.e., aerobic and anaerobic Gram-positive and -negative bacteria. Aspiration pneumonia is frequently the last event leading to the demise of a patient. Aspiration pneumonia is common in patients who have had a brainstem stroke and are unable to swallow their saliva, in patients who regurgitate around their nasogastric feeding tubes, or when the nasogastric tube has been misplaced into the trachea. Every patient who has had a cerebral vascular accident should be supervised closely to make sure they can swallow their own saliva and handle clear liquid feedings. The most common cause of aspiration pneumonia in these patients is the initiation of early feedings without careful evaluation of their gag and swallowing reflexes. Patients who develop aspiration pneumonia should be treated with antimicrobial agents that cover Gram-positive, Gram-negative aerobic and anaerobic organisms; i.e., penicillin, clindamycin, cefoxitin or cefotetan, and an aminoglycoside.

Geriatric patients should be immunized prophylactically against viral influenza and the *Pneumococcus* organism (Pneumovax). In epidemics of Type A influenza, amantidine or rimantidine may be used as prophylaxis.

Pulmonary physical therapy such as chest clap-ping, postural drainage, breathing exercises, etc., may be an adjunct in caring for geriatric patients with pneumonia; it is less effective in the semicomatose patient. In patients with chronic lung disease with carbon dioxide retention, the administration of oxygen must be carefully performed with frequent monitoring of blood gases in order to prevent apnea.

In geriatric patients with fever of unknown origin, pulmonary or extrapulmonary tuberculosis must be considered. Reactivation of dormant tuberculosis may occur with late-onset diabetes or debilitation. Anergy to tuberculin protein skin testing may be present in those patients who have had two negative tuberculin skin tests a week apart. Some patients who were exposed to tuberculosis early in life may have cured their infection with a resulting loss of tuberculin protein skin sensitivity. These patients are susceptible to another primary infection with this disease if exposed to an infected person. Primary tuberculosis may occur in elderly patients who may never have had exposure to tuberculosis. Tuberculosis in the elderly may be manifested by very subtle signs and symptoms, and some patients may be totally asymptomatic. These patients are a risk to other people, especially if they have young grandchildren. Any geriatric patient entering a nursing home should have a chest x-ray and a tuberculin skin test. An epidemic of tuberculosis in a geriatric nursing home has been reported (8). The best treatment regimen is a combination of isoniazid and rifampin. Patients placed on this therapy must be closely monitored for liver toxicity. In patients over the age of 50 years, there is a 2% incidence of liver toxicity with isoniazid.

BACTERIAL ENDOCARDITIS

The presentation of bacterial endocarditis in the geriatric patient may be atypical, in that a fever or heart murmur may not be present. Malaise, myalgia, sensorial changes, or fatigue may be the only manifestations. Unexplained anemia, uremia, or embolic phenomena may be the first manifestations of this infection. Any patient with an organic heart murmur or a prosthetic heart valve and a fever for longer than 1 week should be considered to have endocarditis (2). The organism most commonly associated with endocarditis after the age of 40 years is *group D streptococcus*. *Streptococcus fecalis* endocarditis usually arises from bowel instrumentation, diverticulitis, or a urinary tract infection. Patients with *nonenterococcal group D streptococcus bovis* endocarditis are frequently found to have some primary bowel pathology; viz., colonic carcinoma, polyps, or inflammatory bowel disease (6). During treatment for this infection, the patient's bowel should be carefully evaluated. *Streptococcus viridans* endocarditis becomes a lesser problem in edentulous patients, unless they have poorly fitting dental plates that have caused gingival or mucosal erosions.

Every geriatric patient with unexplained fever should have blood cultures. Antibiotic treatment will be dictated according to the organism isolated and its sensitivity pattern. If the organism isolated requires a treatment combination of antibiotics for synergistic killing effect, i.e., *Streptococcus fecalis*, the addition of an aminoglycoside to either penicillin, ampicillin, or vancomycin should not be streptomycin but gentamicin. Streptomycin is not well-tolerated by the geriatric patient; otovestibular dysfunction occurs rapidly, usually within 2 weeks. Although gentamicin is better tolerated with fewer side effects, monitoring for renal and auditory toxicity is mandatory.

GASTROINTESTINAL INFECTIONS

With loss of gastric acidity and the medical need for antacids or histamine receptor antagonists, or previous gastrectomies, the geriatric patient is more prone to bacterial gastroenteritis. Nursing home epidemics of salmonellosis and shigellosis have occurred. Elderly patients should not be fed raw eggs or unpasteurized eggnogs. Bacterial gastroenteritis may be fatal to geriatric patients because of bacteremia, severe dehydration, and electrolyte loss.

Patients who have cholelithiasis or have had cholecystectomies in the past may present with a history of episodic fever and chills along with abnormal liver function tests. These episodes may last only for 1 or 2 days and be recurrent. One should think of ascending cholangitis due to a common duct stone.

Diverticulitis is the most common intestinal disorder in the geriatric patient and is characterized by episodic fever preceeded by constipation or diarrhea and lower left quadrant pain. The ingestion of nuts is a common predisposing factor in causing diverticulitis. Doxycycline has proven to be very effective in treating acute flares of diverticulitis. A patient with a history of diverticulitis who presents with chronic, low grade fever should be suspected of having a pelvic-colonic abscess. Tenderness on palpation may not be present. Barium enema, sonogram, gallium, or computerized axial tomography (CAT) scan will aid in the diagnosis. Fortunately, most perforations occur below the peritoneal reflection so that generalized peritonitis does not occur.

Chronic constipation may lead to impaction of stool with pressure necrosis of the bowel mucosa leading to perforation and generalized peritonitis. Prevention of constipation is most important especially if related to constipation-inducing medications.

Fever, nondeforming arthritis, marked diarrhea, weight loss, and generalized lymphadenopathy should suggest intestinal lipodystrophy (Whipple's disease). The disease is more common in males. The diagnosis is made by small bowel biopsy in which periodic acid-Schift-positive macrophages are seen in the lamina propria along with numerous small bacilli. These organisms have not yet been identified. Patients respond well to oral penicillin or tetracycline.

URINARY TRACT INFECTIONS

Urinary tract infections are common in the elderly. In females, urethral strictures from previous infections or surgery, neurogenic bladder and stress incontinence are all factors leading to a high degree of bacteriuria with or without infection. Many elderly females will have asymptomatic bacteriuria. In males, obstructive uropathy secondary to benign prostatic hypertrophy or urethral strictures are the most common causes of urinary tract infections.

Unfortunately, there are no adequate external catheters for females who are incontinent of urine. There should be clear-cut indications before an indwelling urinary catheter is placed in any patient's bladder. Urosepsis is most commonly associated with indwelling catheters and is the most common cause of hospital-acquired nosocomial infections. The care of the indwelling catheter is most important. It should be cleaned daily with soap and water where it enters the urethra. The indwelling catheter should be connected to a closed collection system. Indwelling catheters should be changed aseptically every month in those patients who require continuous catheterization. Fever, pyuria, and bateriuria, with or without dysuria, indicate a urinary tract infection. Parenteral or oral antibiotics are indicated after appropriate urine cultures have been obtained. Chronic suppressive antibiotic administration to patients who have chronic indwelling catheterization is not recommended since it will lead to the emergence of antibiotic-resistant organisms and superinfection.

Urosepsis may lead to Gram-negative lumbar osteomyelitis, either through bacteremia entering the central circulation or by the retrograde flow of bacteria through the veins of Batson. High fever, increasing back pain, and lumbar muscle spasm are the most common findings of this entity. The most serious manifestation of urinary tract infection is Gram-negative bacteremia and the shock syndrome. The mortality associated with this entity is high unless recognized and treated early with intravenous antibiotics.

Patients who require continuous indwelling urethral catheters and who have been treated with various antibiotics for urinary tract infections may develop *Candida albicans* or *Torulopsis glabrata* cystitis or pyelonephritis. If only yeast forms and pyuria are seen, it usually indicates a cystitis. If mycelia and yeast forms are seen with pyuria, pyelonephritis should be considered. If there is only cystitis, the patient's catheter should be changed. Amphotericin, 15 mg in 100 ml of saline (this will form a suspension) should be instilled into the bladder once per day through the catheter, retained 1 hour, and then released. This should be repeated daily for 7–14 days. If pyelonephritis is suspected, the patient should receive 75 mg/kg of 5-fluorocytosine by mouth in four divided doses per day for 14 days.

MENINGITIS

The clinical bedside evaluation of meningitis in the elderly patient is sometimes difficult. Geriatric patients frequently will develop stupor, lethargy, a change in sensorium and meningismus with any type of fever. Nuchal ridigity may be a false-diagnostic sign because of cervical osteoarthritis or rheumatoid disease. Whenever there is a clinical doubt as to whether meningitis is present and there is absence of papilledema, one should proceed with a diagnostic spinal tap. Especially in those patients who have papilledema or in patients with cataracts in whom the optic disc cannot be visualized, head (CAT) scan is an important procedure in ruling out brain tumor, hemorrhage, and abscess. In those patients with papilledema, if the head (CAT) scan is negative for the already mentioned conditions, a diagnostic cisternal tap for cerebral spinal fluid may be obtained by a neurosurgeon.

All of the common bacterial organisms responsible for meningitis may be seen in the geriatric patient, i.e., *S. pneumoniae, Neisseria meningitidis, Haemophilus influenzae,* etc. The portal of entry to the meninges is a primary infection of the nasopharynx, nasal sinuses, lung, genitourinary tract, or bowel. Aerobic Gram-negative meningitis carries a high mortality and frequently will require large doses of intravenous therapy with ampicillin, chloramphenicol, cefuroxime, cefotaxime, ceftriax-

one, or ceftazidime along with parenteral aminoglycosides and intrathecal or intraventricular aminoglycoside administration through an Ommaya shunt. Tuberculous meningitis usually is insidious in onset and the laboratory findings in cerebrospinal fluid will be that of aseptic meningitis, except for a low cerebrospinal fluid sugar. *Cryptococcus neoformans* and *Listeria monocytogenes* meningitis are usually seen in geriatric patients who are on steroids or who are undergoing chemotherapy. Cryptococcal meningitis is an aseptic type of meingitis with 50% of the cases showing a reduction of cerebrospinal fluid sugar. Although *L. monocytogenes* is a Gram-positive rod bacteria, it may present as an aseptic or atypical bacterial meningitis. The cerebrospinal fluid sugar may be normal or depressed, the protein mildly elevated, and the cellular response may be either polymorphonuclear cells, lymphocytes, or monocytes.

The increasing use of nonsteroidal anti-inflammatory therapeutic agents in the treatment of musculoskeletal pain may be associated with drug-induced hypersensitivity meningitis. The cerebrospinal fluid will reveal an increased polymorphonuclear response, a mild elevation of the protein, normal sugar, negative Gram stain and culture, and a rapid clinical response and improvement with steroid therapy.

INFECTIONS OF THE MUSCULOSKELETAL SYSTEM

Years of wear and tear take their toll on the musculoskeletal system. Arthritis, hip fractures, and aseptic necrosis are common. Septic arthritis may occur hematogenously from a distant primary focus of infection, or secondary to intra-articular injections of steroids for arthritis. Infections after intra-articular injections of steroids are usually due to *S. aureus* and *S. epidermidis*. These organisms may be resistant to the β-lactamase-resistant penicillins and cephalosporins, but are usually sensitive to vancomycin. Patients with orthopaedic prosthetic devices are at risk of these prostheses becoming infected years after insertion. Transient bacteremia from abscessed or extracted teeth, urinary tract infections, pyoderma, etc., may settle in the prosthesis and lead to septic arthritis. In some cases, debridement drainage and half-strength povidone iodine irrigations into the joint along with systemic antibiotics may cure a prosthetic infection. In most cases, the prosthesis has to be removed in order to cure the infection. A new prosthesis should not be considered until 6–12 months have passed and the physician is confident that no latent infection persists. All patients who have orthopaedic prostheses should receive the same prophylactic antibiotics as those patients with organic valvular heart disease or cardiac prostheses who are undergoing dental work, genitourinary manipulation, etc. All patients with orthopaedic prostheses who develop a bacterial infection should be treated promptly. Under no circumstances should an orthopaedic prosthesis be placed in a patient who has any evidence of infection or has significant bacteriuria. These infections should be treated and cured before surgery is contemplated.

Orthopaedic aids such as braces, crutches, casts, etc., must be carefully adjusted and frequently inspected for any pressure points and skin necrosis. This is most important in the diabetic or patient with sensory nerve deficits.

DERMAL TRAUMA AND INFECTION

The most common infection requiring hospitalization of the diabetic is an infection of the foot. Due to sensory neuropathy and peripheral arterial-vascular insufficiency, the diabetic patient is unable to sense pain. Minor injuries from trauma, tight shoes or socks, improper cutting of the nails or self-removal of corns or calluses may result in secondary infection. Once infection becomes established it progresses rapidly, leading to cellulitis or deep penetrating ulcers with osteomyelitis of the foot bones. The single most common organism isolated from the infected diabetic foot is *S. aureus*, although polymicrobial organisms, including anaerobes, may also be found. The very first infection of a diabetic's foot may lead to an amputation. All physicians caring for diabetics should routinely inspect the patient's feet and check to see if their toenails have been correctly cut and they are wearing properly fitting shoes and socks. The most neglected aspect of diabetic care is the diabetic foot.

A decubitus of the skin over bony prominences is a common dilemma of the elderly patient who is immobile or paralyzed. Decubiti ulcers may develop rapidly in the immobilized patient. They are most common over the bony prominences of the occiput, elbows, dorsal spine, sacrum, the greater trochanter, and the heels. Sacral and trochanter ducubiti are more prone to infection due to bacterial contamination from urinary and fecal incontinence. These infections are due to polymicrobial aerobic and anaerobic bacteria normally found in feces. Infected decubiti may lead to localized cellulitis, bacteremia and sepsis, osteomyelitis of the underlying bone and the dreaded, rapidly spreading Fornier's gangrene or *Clostridia* myonecrosis. Incontinence of urine and feces may result in urea-splitting organisms from the feces with ammonia formation leading to severe excoriation of the perineal area and secondary infection. Obviously the prevention of decubiti requires frequent movement of the patient with soft padding over bony pressure areas. Patients with incontinence of urine and feces must be promptly cleaned with a mild soap and water followed by an emollient.

The elderly patient who has had a radical or simple mastectomy may develop chronic lymphedema of the upper extremity. Patients with lymphedema are more prone to develop *Streptococcus* or *Staphylococcus* cellulitis after minor trauma to the arm, i.e., insect bites, nicks, cuts, etc. Penicillin, anti-β-lactamase penicillins or erythromycin are usually effective. Patients should be instructed that with any trauma to the arm, the site should be cleaned with soap and water followed by a topical antiseptic, preferably povidine iodine. If repeated episodes of cellulitis of the arm occur, the patients should be instructed to clean the arm once per day with hexachlorophene or chlorhexidine. These two agents have a lasting effect and markedly diminish the normal bacterial flora of the skin.

Herpes zoster (HZ) is a common infection in the elderly, either with or without malignancy. HZ may appear in any sensory dermatome of the skin and, in rare cases, may cause a disseminated varicella eruption or meningoencephalitis. In some cases, motor nerves may be involved, leading to paresis or paralysis. Ophthalmic (HZ) may involve the cornea when maculovesicular lesions follow the path of the nasociliary nerve. Complications of ophthalmic (HZ) include meningoencephalitis, cerebral vasculitis, and optic nerve blindness.

In mild cases of HZ, topical acyclovir may be used and applied to the lesions five times per day. HZ that involves the ophthalmic branch of the 5th nerve, or which is associated with cutaneous dissemination, pneumonia, or meningoencephalitis, should be treated with intravenous acyclovir.

In prospective studies, the routine use of steroids in the early treatment of HZ has been said to decrease the incidence of postherpetic neuralgia. However, the routine use of steroids in patients with HZ may result in disseminated disease and progression of the local dermatome lesion. Steroids may also lead to an increased susceptibility to secondary bacterial infection.

ACQUIRED IMMUNE DEFICIENCY SYNDROME

Older patients are now being seen with the acquired immune deficiency syndrome (AIDS) secondary to previous blood transfusions. Their presentation is similar to younger patients with AIDS, viz., opportunistic infections such as *Pneumocystis carinii* pneumonia, etc. It is important to inquire about previous blood transfusions when taking a medical history in geriatric patients who present with opportunistic infections.

With the improved screening of blood donors and the routine testing for hepatitis B antigen and the human immunodeficiency viral antibody, these infections from blood products should become extinct. There is, however, a slight risk that both of these viral infections can still be contracted through infected blood, since donors who have contracted these viral infections may not have developed detectable antigens or antibodies in their blood at the time of donation. Non-A non-B hepatitis and cytomegalic viral infections are still a risk with blood transfusions. At present, there are no blood donor screening tests for non-A non-B hepatitis antigen, and cytomegalic viral antigen and antibody testing are not done routinely in blood banks.

It is important that physicians not transfuse patients indiscriminately. Blood loss at surgery should be carefully monitored. If a patient is to have elective surgery and there is a possibility that blood transfusions will be required, the patient should have a unit or more of his blood removed and stored in a blood bank before surgery.

ANTIBIOTIC TREATMENT

There is little doubt that intelligent antibiotic treatment will prolong life in geriatric patients who develop acute infections. Appropriate cultures should be obtained before antibiotic therapy is instituted.

Many geriatric patients give a past history of penicillin allergy. Frequently, these allergic reactions occurred with the earlier penicillins. Some patients lost their allergenicity to penicillin when the initial reaction occurred many years before. In some cases, penicillin is the only effective treatment to cure the infection. If penicillin is required, an allergist should evaluate the patient with skin testing with penicilloyl (major determinant) and benzyl penicillin (minor determinant). If the skin tests are negative, penicillin may be administered under close supervision with aqueous adrenalin 1:1000, hydrocortisone, and an airway at the bedside. In some cases, if penicillin is the only antibiotic of choice and the patient reacts positively to the penicillin skin testing, desensitization may be accomplished with penicillin over a 3 hour period.

In patients who give a history of delayed hypersensitivity reaction to penicillin, a cephalosporin may be safely substituted. There is only a 10% crossover sensitivity between penicillin and cephalosporins. If there is a history of anaphylaxis to penicillin, cephalosporins should be avoided.

The use of long-acting sulfonamides should be monitored carefully in the elderly because there is a higher incidence of fatal Steven-Johnson syndrome.

Vancomycin, used in the treatment of infection or in dental prophylaxis in penicillin-allergic patients, should be given over a 1-hour period. Rapid infusion leads to a histamine-type reaction with rash, burning in the neck, and hypotension. The latter reaction is liable to be confused with an allergic reaction.

Erythromycin may cause upper gastrointestinal irritation due to stimulation of the smooth muscle of the gastrointestinal tract. After 3 days, this phenomenon lessens and the patient may be able to continue with its use. Rapid intravenous infusion of erythromycin lactobionate, e.g., in the treatment of *Legionella* pneumonia, may lead to acute but reversible hearing loss. Intravenous erythromycin should be given over a 1-hour period.

The use of tetracyclines in the geriatric patient is relatively safe. In patients with renal insufficiency, there may be a rapid rise in the blood urea nitrogen due to the antianabolic effect of tetracycline. This side effect is not seen with doxycycline. Patients should be instructed not to take outdated tetracyclines that may have been sitting in their medicine chest because it may lead to a temporary renal Fanconi syndrome. Minocycline should be avoided in the elderly patient because it may lead to tinnitus and vertigo. Minocycline-induced vertigo has been associated with traumatic falls that have resulted in fractures of the arm and hip.

Although demeclocycline is the most common tetracycline associated with solar photosensitivity, it may be seen with all the tetracyclines. Geriatric patients who have been given doxycycline in order to prevent traveler's diarrhea should be warned of this side effect.

Clindamycin may be associated with diarrhea in 20% of patients. In 1–10% of patients, pseudomembranous colitis may result due to the overgrowth of *Clostridia difficile* with toxin production. Antibiotic-associated pseudomembranous colitis may occur with many other antibiotics. The diagnosis should be suspected in patients with severe diarrhea, foul-smelling stools, abdominal cramps, chills, and high fever. The diagnosis is made by obtaining stool specimens for *Closteridium difficile* toxin assay. Fifty percent of these patients will demonstrate fecal leukocytes. The treatment of choice is oral vancomycin or metronidazole. Because the oral treatment with vancomycin is very expensive, the initial treatment should be started with the less costly metronidazole.

In patients requiring large doses of cefamandole, cefoperazone, moxalactam, or cefotetan, a bleeding diathesis may occur. These patients will be found to have abnormal prothrombin and partial thromboplastin times. It appears that the phenomenon is due to the tetrazole side chain and can be reversed with the administration of vitamin K. Patients on these antibiotics should receive prophylactic vitamin K, 10–15 mg intramuscularly, once per week. They should not be used in patients who are receiving anticoagulation therapy.

Nitrofurantoin therapy should be avoided in the geriatric patient because it may lead to degenerating sensorimotor peripheral neuropathy.

Patients who are receiving metronidazole or one of the cephalosporins containing the tetrazole radical should be instructed to abstain from alcohol in order to prevent a disulfiram (Antabuse)-like effect. Alcohol can usually be imbibed safely 3 days after cessation of these antibiotics.

Aminoglycosides are excellent antibiotics in treating Gram-negative infections, especially Gram-negative sepsis and bacteremia, but may be associated with otovestibular toxicity and nephrotoxicity. These toxic effects are the most common cause of medicolegal malpractice suits initiated by the patient against the prescribing physician. The patient should be monitored carefully for toxic side effects. When using aminoglycosides, the patient should be kept well hydrated, diuretics should be avoided, the creatinine should be checked every 2 or 3 days, peak and trough serum levels should be obtained once or twice per week and, if available, audiograms performed weekly. When needed, aminoglycosides are not contraindicated in patients with renal insufficiency, but their dose and interval of administration must be modified (1). The Physicians' Desk Reference (PDR) offers at least two types of dosage schedules and intervals of administrating aminoglycosides to patients with renal insufficiency.

Before prescribing any antibiotic, the physician should check the medications the patient is receiving in order to avoid drug interactions. Competitive metabolisms may result in toxic levels of one or more drugs, prolongation of half-life, or ineffectiveness of the antibiotic or other medications. Drug interaction information may be found in the PDR and hospital drug information services.

IMMUNIZATIONS

Geriatric patients should maintain an active immunization schedule against viral influenza, *Pneumococcus*, and tetanus. Tetanus antibodies may wane in later life, leading to the development of tetanus. Cases of tetanus have occurred in elderly patients who have undergone bowel surgery or amputation of a limb. Patients requiring bowel surgery or amputation because of arterial insufficiency and gangrene should receive a booster of tetanus toxoid, especially if their past tetanus immunization history is unknown.

DYING PATIENT

In patients who have a no-code status and who are at the end stage of life, one frequently observes the discontinuation of all medications except antibiotics. Frequently, antibiotics will be started when fever appears. As long as the patient is receiving the necessary supportive care for a comfortable demise, antibiotics should not be maintained or started. Death from infection is usually a painless cause of death. Once death is clearly inevitable, there are instances of prolongation of life with the use of costly antibiotic therapy that would only prolong the agony and the suffering of the patient and loved ones. These issues are discussed in greater detail in the chapter on Termination of Treatment (Chapter 53).

REFERENCES

1. Garagusi VF: Antimicrobial therapeutic drug monitoring. In Henry JB (Ed): *Symposium on Therapeutic Drug Monitoring. Clinics in Laboratory Medicine.* Philadelphia, WB Saunders, 1981, p. 585–597.
2. Garagusi VF: Management of complicated infective endocarditis. In Rackley CE, Brest AN (Eds): *Advances in Critical Care Cardiology.* Philadelphia, FA Davis, 1986, p. 153–162.
3. Gardner ID: The effect of aging on susceptibility to infection. *Rev Infect Dis* 2:801, 1980.
4. Garibaldi RA, Nurse BA: Infections in the elderly: Symposium on special problem cases in infection. *Am J Med* 81(1A):53, 1986.
5. Goodman R: Decline in organ function with aging. In Rossman R (Ed): *Clinical Geriatrics,* 2nd edition. Philadelphia, Lippincott, 1979, p. 23–59.
6. Klein RS, Reuco RA, Catalano MT, et al: Association of *Streptococcus bovis* with carcinoma of the colon. *N Engl J Med* 297:800, 1977.
7. Phair JP: Host defense in the aged In Gleekman RA, Ganty NM (Eds): *Infections in the Elderly.* Boston, Little, Brown, 1983, p. 1–12.
8. Stead WW: Tuberculosis among elderly persons: An outbreak in a nursing home. *Ann Intern Med* 94:606, 1981.

CHAPTER 20

Nutrition and Health in the Elderly

B. LYNN BEATTIE
V. Y. LOUIE

Mark Twain said, "The only way to keep your health is to eat what you don't want, drink what you don't like, and do what you'd druther not." Nutrition, health, and aging are a critical triad (133). Aging occurs throughout life, and so good nutrition and health practices must also. The objective of this chapter is to provide some understanding of the role of nutrition in aging, health, and disease, along with some practical guidelines for assessment and thoughtful intervention. These comments are hopefully more useful than Mark Twain indicated since "nutrition is the environmental factor most subject to human control in contributing to the health of the aging and aged" (64).

Fries (40) speculated that the goal of a long and vigorous life may be attainable as a result of the compression or telescoping of morbidity from chronic disease into the very latter part of human life. There is evidence in North America today that mortality from "lifestyle diseases," such as heart disease and stroke, is declining (41, 95, 101, 132). Is personal responsibility for health producing the impact? How much of this responsibility is related to nutrition?

Exton-Smith (34) observed that individual dietary patterns in the majority of old people remain similar to those that have been acquired by habit established at a younger age. Nutritional health education is, therefore, an early responsibility in life. Exton-Smith (35) also stated that there is a great need for longitudinal studies that measure dietary intake and incorporate clinical examination and laboratory investigation. These surveys must be standardized and repeated in order to develop meaningful descriptions of the specific needs of the elderly population. The American Dietetic Association (2) position statement emphasizes the relationship between nutrition, aging, and health and the need for nutritional well-being for quality of life of the elderly. Good health with increased physical activity stimulates appetite and thereby promotes better intake of nutrients.

Aging brings progressive loss of tissue function along with possible accumulation of diseases including osteoporosis, atherosclerosis, cancer, obesity, diabetes mellitus, and hypertension. Application of current knowledge of nutritional factors may influence the impact these diseases have on our society. Hazzard (53) commented in legal prose:

"Whereas all age-related diseases are (by definition) time-dependent; and
Whereas all such processes are multifactorial in origin; therefore:
Single modality intervention late in life is unlikely to yield appreciable benefit;
Intervention should be multifactorial and begin at an early age.

NUTRITION AND LONGEVITY

Knowledge of the relationships between nutrient intake and duration of life span is expanding. Dietary restriction in laboratory animals can be brought about by reducing daily intake of a nutritionally adequate diet (one that supports maximal growth), intermittently feeding a nutritionally adequate diet (e.g., feeding every second, third, or fourth day) and feeding ad libitum a diet containing insufficient amounts of protein to support maximal growth (16).

McCay et al. (88, 89) showed that although growth was retarded, the life span of rats was increased with dietary restriction. Barrows and Kokkonen (16) reviewed the current information and noted that dietary restriction imposed on young growing animals and also on adult animals is effective in prolonging life. Dietary restriction in animals also appears to delay the onset of a variety of diseases.

It is postulated (119) that food-restricted rats live longer because they retain an improved ability to utilize or metabolize fat. Masaro (87) showed that restricting food intake delays a decline in responsiveness of adipocytes to the hormones glucagon and epinephrine. Food restrictions also may tend to decrease the volume of substances passing through the mitochondrial enzyme system and to decrease free radical formation. It has been proposed (16) that reduction of protein synthesis as a result of dietary restriction delays the transfer of genetic information during early life and reduces the use of the genetic code minimizing imperfections of later life.

There is an urgent need for research into levels of specific nutrients required that will optimize physical and mental development in youth, physiological performance during adulthood, and retention of health and vigor in senescence (16). This research needs to be extended from laboratory animals to man.

NUTRITION AND AGING

With aging, physiological changes may affect ingestion and enjoyment of food. The sense of taste changes with aging. The number of taste buds on the lateral surfaces of the tongue that detect sweet and salty tastes decrease, leaving the central taste buds, which identify sour and bitter tastes, to predominate. The sense of smell tends to decline also, and the combined loss of gustatory and olfactory senses may lead to less interest in food. Decreased salivary flow, poor dentition, and decreased power of mastication that accompany the aging process may limit amount and variety of foods eaten. The superimposition of various pathological conditions may emphasize these physiological changes.

Ingestion may be hampered by gingival lesions, mucous membrane erosions, or difficulty swallowing. The most common age change in the digestive tract is achlorhydria (78), as it occurs in 25% of subjects over age 60. Lactase deficiency may be age related but to date no systematic study has been undertaken.

Digestion tends to be slower. With aging, there is a reduced capacity to regulate metabolism, hormonal induction of enzymes requires more time, and reduced numbers of hormone receptors are evident

on cell surfaces. These factors may be increasingly significant in the face of pathological changes such as hiatus hernia, reflux, and/or atrophic gastritis. Absorption appears to be little affected by aging, but many factors including quality of nutrients, the presence of medications, and the presence of various disease states may affect this function.

The cumulative effects of the changes of aging are more prominent as the years go on. Pathology may be superimposed. Awareness of both kinds of change is necessary when assessing nutritional vulnerability.

ASSESSMENT OF NUTRITIONAL STATUS

Nutrition assessment and intervention are essential components of nutrition services and integral to the continuum of health care for the elderly (2).

Nutritional status is the health condition of an individual as influenced by his or her intake and utilization of nutrients. Its assessment requires the corroboration of data from clinical, dietary, anthropometric, and biochemical evaluations. Simultaneous use of these techniques serves to substantiate and increase the sensitivity by which individuals at risk for protein-calorie malnutrition, nutrient deficiencies, or overnutrition may be identified. In the elderly, the assessment of nutritional status is complicated by age-related changes in routinely measured parameters and by lack of appropriate standards for interpretation of most measurements (93). The diagram (Fig. 20.1) from Blackburn et al. (21) illustrates the major parameters for assessment with corresponding components of body composition. The parameters must be judged against appropriate age and sex standards.

CLINICAL HISTORY

When addressing nutritional assessment, it is important to assess attitude and interest in life and the activities of daily living. The role physical disabilities may play in either procurement or preparation of foods is significant. Problems in ingestion and digestion must be addressed. Noteworthy are food avoidances and preferences. A history of bone fracture(s) or abdominal surgery may be relevant. A complete drug history including prescribed medications, over-the-counter medications, and laxatives is significant. Bowel and urinary habits may influence personal eating habits. The health of nails, hair, and skin and the predisposition to infection and ability to heal are important.

The physician may assess nutritional risk through review of clinical status by history, physical

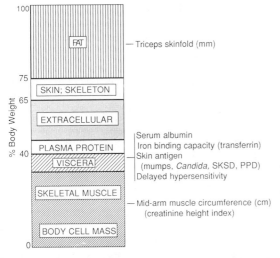

Figure 20.1 Parameters for the assessment of nutritional status with corresponding components of body composition. *SKSD.*, streptokinase-streptodornase; *PPD*, purified protein derivative. (Reproduced with permission from Blackburn GL, Bistrian BR, Maine BS, Schlamm HT, Smith MF: Nutritional and metabolic assessment of the hospitalized patient. *J Parenteral Enteral Nutr* 1:11, 1977.

examination and assessment of the general intake of the major food groups. Baker et al. (13) studied the effectiveness of clinical evaluation of nutritional status, and examiners agreed in 81% of cases. This clinical evaluation correlated well with objective measures, although the oldest patient was 76 years. Subsequent referral to a dietitian for a more extensive dietetic history is indicated when risk is evident and when intervention is recommended.

DIETARY ASSESSMENT

Dietary assessment is important as an indicator of nutritional status. It offers the most practical means of predicting an individual's nutritional risk. The estimated food and nutrient intake of an individual is evaluated against appropriate dietary standards.

There are a number of methods developed for the collection of data on food intake. The 24-hour recall provides a retrospective account of foods actually consumed in the previous 24 hours. It is a simple and rapid means of obtaining information at an interview. Because the accuracy of the information obtained is dependent on memory capabilities, the 24-hour recall may yield unreliable data from older individuals, particularly older men. Nevertheless, the method is a tool for securing the mean nutrient intakes of large groups of 50 or more individuals although it tends to underestimate caloric intake (83).

A more extensive diet history, which attempts to describe the general pattern of food usually consumed over a period of time, also can be recalled at an interview. The method incorporates the 24-hour recall, but it utilizes a checklist of predetermined foods to ensure the completeness of recalled information and subsequently verifies the data against a 3-day record of actual food intake.

Generally, more accurate data presume a well-defined dietary pattern and, while the extensive dietary history takes into account seasonal variation in food intake, it is time consuming, it requires skilled interviewers, and it is dependent on recall abilities of subjects.

The method that affords the greatest accuracy is the weighed food record, which records present intake of foods through accurate weighing and correction of plate wastes.

Direct observation of the elderly at mealtimes may be the method of choice for the collection of food consumption data (22). This method may be limited to institutions and nursing homes and to the study of individuals or small groups.

Following data collection, the interpretation of the actual nutrient intake is by means of comparison with the dietary standard. The standards of adequacy applied have varied from 100% of the Recommended Dietary Allowances (RDAs), to 67%, to as low as 40% (103). This makes comparison of survey data difficult and recommendations for individuals arbitrary.

Dietary assessment is often dependent on recall and good interview techniques. Presence of a relative or significant other and use of a checklist may be helpful. Data collected are compared against the RDAs as the nutritional standard.

CLINICAL ASSESSMENT

Clinical evaluation involves assessment of the mouth, skin, hair, eyes, nails, lower extremities, and various organs.

Angular stomatitis or cheilosis may be associated with niacin, riboflavin, or pyridoxine deficiency but also are seen with ill-fitting dentures. Poor oral hygiene and periodontal disease produce changes that are indistinguishable from deficiency glossitis and gingivitis. The raw appearance of the tongue with filiform papillary atrophy is associated with niacin deficiency and a magenta color reflects riboflavin deficiency although irritants, systemic antibiotics, and uremia also may be possible causes for the discoloration. Soft and spongy bleeding gums are indicative of ascorbic acid deficiency. The condition of the skin may be a reflection of an individual's nutritional status. Dry, inelastic skin may be associated with aging alone, dehydration or follicular hyperkeratosis of vitamin A deficiency, nasolabial seborrhea with lack of pyridoxine, and skin lesions of the exposed parts of the body with niacin deficiency. Dryness, thickening, and opaqueness of the conjunctivae are observed with progressively advanced vitamin A deficiency. Pale mucous membranes and the cupping of the nails are suggestive of inadequate iron. Lack of luster, depigmentation, and easy pluckability of the hair may accompany protein deficiency. Edema of the extremities may be associated with thiamine lack or protein deficiency from many causes. Enlargement of the liver or the thyroid, petechiae, ecchymoses, and other nonspecific findings should be considered in the overall assessment.

Clinical assessment is highly subjective and physical signs may indicate multiple nutrient deficiencies or may be due to nonnutritional influences.

ANTHROPOMETRY

Anthropometry is a useful, noninvasive means of evaluating nutritional status from measurements of body composition. It allows the assessment of an individual's muscle mass (protein) and energy reserve (fat). The most common measurements are height, weight, triceps skinfold thickness, and upper arm circumference.

Accurate estimates of height are important for use in computing several indices of nutritional status. Measurement of standing height may be obtained directly or by measurement from crown to heel in the supine position (45). The presence of kyphosis or flexion contractures of the legs may invalidate these estimates. Age-related bone loss also contributes to progressive loss in stature. Alternate means of predicting full adult height have been proposed, but these must be validated for all heights and races (72).

Body weight should be measured under standard conditions to minimize errors introduced by diurnal variation, clothing, different weighing scales, and other considerations such as dressings, casts, or artificial limbs. Appropriate standards of weight for height in the elderly are limited. The 1983 Metropolitan Height and Weight Tables show the average weights of young men and women associated with the lowest mortality. Average weights of the elderly up to age 74 years have been compiled by Frisancho (38) as percentile distributions based on data from the first and second National Health and Nutrition Examination Surveys. There are questions whether the standard applies to all races and if the criteria for assigning frame size are justified (72). Information on the rate and extent of weight loss/gain as well as the current weight relative to the usual body weight and the average weight for the population provide some estimate of the presence or risk of developing malnutrition. Weight also may be measured against the Age-Specific Gerontology Research Center Recommendations (96). Arbitrarily, weight 20% above the desirable weight is considered as evidence of overnutrition, while weight which is 20% or more below the desirable weight is considered presumptive of undernutrition (24). Roy et al. (120) emphasized the significance of weight loss of greater than 6% in preoperative assessment predicting postoperative complications.

Skinfold measures of subcutaneous fat at different body sites are useful for the estimation of total body fat. The reliability of these measures may be undermined by age-related changes in loss of lean body mass, increased fat deposits laid down truncally, and alterations in skin thickness, elasticity, and compressibility. Estimates of lean body mass are derived mathematically from triceps skinfold thickness and midupper arm circumference. Standards for these measures again are available up to age 74 based on data from the HANES I and II (38). However, the standards were based on cross-sectional rather than longitudinal studies. The mathematical formulae used to compute total body fat and protein were developed for younger populations. Although skinfold measures are insensitive to changes in body composition over the short-term period, they are useful in providing baseline information for subsequent comparisons.

Other indices of nutritional status based on height and weight for the estimation of body composition are the Quetelet or Body Mass Index (BMI) and the Creatinine Height Index (CHI). The BMI (wt/ht^2) is an index of obesity. Andres et al. (8) determined the range of values for BMI that is associated with lower mortality from a U-shaped curve relationship between BMI and mortality. The CHI provides an estimate of muscle protein from the total 24-hour creatinine excretion of an individual compared to the standard healthy individual of the same height. This tool is most practical in a research setting.

Recording of serial weight measurements is often the most practical means of assessing significant fluctuations in nutritional status or change in chronic disease states. Age- and sex-specific standards must be applied when estimating the upper arm parameters. Chronic functional disability may be associated with redistribution of body fat.

LABORATORY ANALYSIS

Laboratory evaluation provides the most objective means of assessing nutritional status. The selective use of biochemical analysis provides data to substantiate clinical judgment and dietary evaluation. The measurements may not accurately identify a subclinical deficiency state but they may have prognostic value.

The initial laboratory evaluation should include hemoglobin, hematocrit, red cell morphology, WBC with differential, total proteins, and albumin. Further evaluation, when indicated, should include serum iron, transferrin, red blood cell folate, serum B_{12}, calcium, phosphorus, alkaline phosphatase, BUN, creatinine, and serum lipids. Finally, specific tests may be indicated. These would include urinary vitamin levels, studies of absorptive capacity, measurement of trace elements, and assessment of the immune system. Michel et al. (92) recommend plasma thyroxine-binding prealbumin and retinol-binding protein as truer indicators of subclinical malnutrition and of response to enteral and parenteral nutrition. Practically, clinical status and weight changes are most useful.

Care must be taken in interpreting results of some of the vitamins and trace mineral assessments. Serum (plasma) ascorbate levels, for example, are likely to reflect recent dietary intakes of vitamin C and not the state of the body's reserve of the vitamin. With vitamin C deprivation, serum ascorbate levels fall rapidly to near zero while reserves are depleted only 50% (60). Because the white blood cell ascorbate levels relate to tissue stores of the vitamin, the levels fall more slowly, and only when the reserve is down to 20% of normal do symptoms of scurvy occur. Ascorbic acid saturation tests, which determine the extent of tissue saturation, may be used for further corroboration (122).

Zinc, on the other hand, is involved in enzymatic reactions that are predominantly intracellular. Plasma zinc is a poor measure of body zinc and a small shift from intracellular fluids may markedly increase the plasma concentration. Although low plasma zinc is found in zinc deficiency states, it may be associated with infection, trauma, myocardial infarction, neoplasm, or low dose estrogen treatment. Zinc levels can be measured in hair samples. A low concentration may indicate zinc deficiency. With prolonged zinc deficiency, there is decreased hair growth but a relative increase in hair zinc. A single observation may not be relevant to zinc status. Serial measurements, after zinc supplementation, may indicate a therapeutic response (122).

Radiological studies may reveal significant bone changes including osteoporosis and osteomalacia. Other studies, such as those of gastrointestinal tract, may point to specific problems.

Laboratory analysis may confirm suspicions based on clinical and dietary history and physical examination or may be used to monitor clinical management.

DIETARY STANDARDS

The RDAs (114) have been defined by the Food and Nutrition Board of the National Academy of Sciences of the United States as the levels of intake of essential nutrients considered, on the basis of available scientific knowledge, to be adequate to meet the known nutritional needs of practically all healthy persons.

The RDAs reflect the current knowledge derived from epidemiological findings, food consumption patterns, animal research, and metabolic studies on nutrient requirements, and they are subject to periodic revision. Set above the average physiological requirement, the levels cover variations in the needs of nearly all individuals in each category of the population (52). The probability is high that an individual's needs will be met and that the risk of deficiency is unlikely when nutrients are consumed at the recommended level (17). The RDAs are not guaranteed to represent complete nutrient needs for any one individual, particularly when additional demands are engendered by illness, injury, or surgery.

The standards in the United States and Canada differentiate energy requirements only for age groups after 50 years. Fewer calories are required to maintain the basal metabolic rate in the older individual, but there is little quantitative data, and age-associated adjustments in calorie intake are not absolute (16). Current assumption is that even though caloric requirements decrease after age 50, most nutrient levels should remain relatively constant, with the exception of a decrease in iron for postmenopausal women.

Leverton (79), in her commentary "The RDAs Are Not for Amateurs" pointed out that effective application of the RDAs requires understanding, skill, restraint, and even tolerance. She noted that their existence has been a potent factor in coordinating and directing dietary planning and nutritional teaching. She cautioned against the use of the RDAs as the basis for fabricated, contrived, or synthetic foods.

The RDAs are reviewed and updated at regular intervals. The anticipated release of RDAs in 1985 was delayed (111) and Guthrie (51) stated this was due to a healthy difference of opinion. Schneider et al. (123) contended that the delay in publication of age-related recommendations was unfortunate. Schorah and Hay (124) suggested that RDAs were less important than increased efforts to define elderly at risk for undernutrition and then assess whether dietary advice and treatment lead to any improvements in their health.

The RDAs are given in terms of nutrients, and these can be hard to interpret because we eat foodstuffs composed of various combinations. Thus, food groups that will supply the nutrients must be identified. These are described as Canada's Food Guide or the American Red Cross Food Wheel (51). The revised "Dietary Guidelines for Americans" outline the basic principles of a sound diet: Eat a variety of foods; maintain desirable weight; avoid too much fat, saturated fat, and cholesterol; eat foods with adequate starch and fiber; avoid too much sugar; avoid too much sodium; and if you drink alcoholic beverages, do so in moderation. The challenge for the aging population is to maintain nutrient content with a decrease in the amount of energy or calories.

PROTEIN

Young et al. (140) postulated that the decline of lean body mass with age should lead to a reduced need for dietary protein. They also suggested that with advancing years a fall in the rate of total body protein synthesis per unit of body weight occurs. Further, a redistribution in total protein synthesis occurs with the metabolically active visceral organs making a more important contribution to nitrogen metabolism. Other studies (97) showed that on adequate protein intake, the total rate of albumin synthesis in the elderly is less than in younger adults. The Boston collaborative study (46) has clearly indicated the decrement of serum albumin with increasing age. Gersovitz et al. (42) noted in a 30-day metabolic nitrogen balance study that where energy intake approximates requirement, the current RDA is inadequate for male and female subjects 70 years and above.

Young and Pellett (139) reviewed available information and concluded that for the elderly a somewhat higher recommendation for protein be made. The daily intake should be not less than 12–14% of caloric intake. At the same time speculation regarding the role of protein intake in kidney dysfunction has been raised. With current knowledge, however, restricting protein intake should probably be limited to patients with early and late chronic renal failure.

Recommended dietary allowances for protein are uncertain. The decrement in lean body mass and altered rate of protein synthesis with increasing age enhance the uncertainty for the elderly. Requiring further investigation are the data showing that older people, particularly those with chronic disease, may need more protein than do young adults to achieve nitrogen balance (97).

CARBOHYDRATES

There is evidence that glucose tolerance changes with increasing age. It is estimated that approximately 20% of the elderly over age 80 years have diabetes mellitus, predominantly type II, non-insulin dependent (19). However, advancing age alone may account for only 1–6% of the variances in insulin response among the elderly. Other age-related environmental factors such as obesity, physical inactivity, and use of potentially diabetogenic drugs may play significant roles (141).

Treatment of diabetes in the elderly is similar to that for younger diabetics (118). Diet remains the cornerstone of therapy to achieve euglycemia in both insulin- and non-insulin-dependent diabetes (IDDM and NIDDM, respectively) (1). The recommended diet provides as proportions of total calories 55–60% carbohydrate, <30% total fat, and 12–20% protein. The dietary prescription is consistent with the fundamentals of good nutrition as outlined in the Recommended Dietary Allowances, the Dietary Guidelines for Americans, and with the recommendations of the American Heart Association and the National Cancer Institute (1). Attempts should be made to alter life-style within an acceptable degree to encourage compliance with diet (137). Diet should be complemented by exercise within the limits of individual capacity.

With diet, weight control is the priority, despite the difficulties related to limited availability of standards for the elderly. It is not known whether elderly diabetics tend to be overweight compared to healthy nondiabetic elderly subjects (118). Rosenthal et al. (118) have emphasized that institutionalized elderly diabetics are more commonly underweight. Total calories may at first be aimed at weight reduction but must then be adjusted once this has been achieved. As with all prescriptions, adequate follow-up and education are important.

Classification of foods by their glycemic effects may be used but there are inconsistencies that suggest this is not the time for general application (1). Hollenbeck et al. (61) have taken issue with the clinical utility of glycemic index in the control of postprandial hyperglycemia. They maintain that studies have shown adverse metabolic effects of sucrose ingestion on carbohydrate and lipid metabolism. In particular, elevation of triglycerides and very low density lipoproteins are both risk factors for coronary artery disease. Although it is established that different carbohydrate-containing foods elicit variable glycemic responses in individuals with IDDM and NIDDM, studies have shown that the glycemic effect of a single food is mitigated when it is consumed as part of a complete meal. In some individuals, modest amounts of sucrose or other refined carbohydrates may be acceptable contingent on metabolic control and body weight (37). The revised Exchange Lists for Meal Planning (37) will facilitate menu planning for a high-carbohydrate, high-fiber, fat-modified diet.

Podolsky and El-Beheri (109) emphasized the potential of hyperglycemia in elderly patients on thiazides. Close observation of potassium is necessary and advice for foods such as bananas, orange juice, and apricots is given. They noted that hypokalemia can worsen hyperglycemia in non-insulin-dependent diabetics.

FATS

The accumulating evidence supports a causal role for cholesterol in the pathogenesis of coronary heart disease (CHD) and atherosclerotic vascular disease (130). Elevated plasma levels of total cholesterol (TC) and low density lipoprotein cholesterol (LDL) among middle-aged men are associated with increased risk. High density lipoprotein cholesterol (HDL) is inversely associated with CHD. Elevated triglyceride or triglyceride rich very low density lipoprotein (VLDL) may be an independent risk factor for CHD in the presence of a high TC/HDL ratio (26).

The Lipid Research Clinics Prevalence Study confirmed the relationship between elevated LDL, decreased HDL, and CHD in a freeliving asymptomatic population of older men up to age 69 years (121). Framingham data (65) suggest that TC levels in men tend not to rise beyond age 60 but in women they rise to age 70 and women tend to have higher values than men in advanced age. Mean levels of protective HDL do not appear to decline with advancing age in men although they may in women in advanced age (65). Grundy et al. (50) contend, however, that there is an increase in TC with increasing age and related CHD with increasing age. Grundy (48) stated that the linkage between TC and risk for CHD can be expressed according to the expected age of onset of CHD. A TC level of 200 mg/dl without other risk factors predicts critical atherosclerosis by age 70. If the TC level was 250 or 300 mg/dl, this degree of atherosclerosis would be achieved by ages 60

and 50, respectively. With the rise in TC with increasing age, probably secondary to increasing production of LDL and decreasing fractional clearance of LDL possibly due in part to age-dependent decline in activity of LDL receptors, the risk of CHD remains. Stamler et al. (127), based on data from the Multiple Risk Factor Intervention Trial, contend that TC levels and risk from CHD are continuous and graded and not threshold. Their data are on men who entered the study up to age 57. Again whether this is true for those over 65 years is speculative.

The risk of CHD increases as well with the addition of other factors including smoking, hypertension, and diabetes (48) as well as coffee consumption (73), inactivity, and obesity. Decreasing the risk of CHD must address all risk factors, not just TC alone.

CHD primary and secondary prevention treatment trials have been undertaken for adults. In primary prevention, dietary and/or drug regimes including combination drugs (138) have been shown to lower CHD development. As well, similar regimes have been demonstrated for secondary prevention (9) to decrease or modify consequences of established CHD. Trials have usually excluded individuals over the age of 65 years and whether specific regimes may be extrapolated to the elderly, particularly over age 70, is unknown. In addition, the cost of screening for primary prevention may be prohibitive for large populations. However, it is reasonable to recommend modification of lifestyle and treatment for known risk factors including obesity, hypertension, and diabetes. Again, there is no data on secondary prevention or treatment, particularly drug interventions in those over 70 years. Besides questionable efficacy in the elderly, there will likely be marked individual variability in response, altered drug tolerance, compliance considerations, toxicity, and cost factors. The availability of highly effective drugs such as reductase inhibitors which decrease cholesterol production, and the interest of the pharmaceutical companies in these products that may be presented to 15–20% of the population estimated to have hypercholesterolemia (48), provide a major challenge to the medical community. The availability of these drugs must not preclude appropriate dietary and life-style management.

For prevention of CHD in later life (after 65 years) maintaining TC as low as realistic is a goal. Dietary prudence in middle age may well reduce the burden of atherosclerosis in older age.

The ideal diet aims at reducing the intake of saturated fatty acids and cholesterol and maintaining desirable body weight. There is controversy about substituting carbohydrates, monounsaturated fatty acids, or polyunsaturated fatty acids for saturated fatty acids, but moderate introduction of all three may be viable.

The National Institutes of Health Consensus Development Panel (99) recommended a diet that provides 30% of energy as fat, divided equally between saturated (S), polyunsaturated (P), and monounsaturated fats and limits cholesterol intake to 250–300 mg/day. Further dietary restrictions may be necessary to achieve the desired blood cholesterol levels in individuals. The suggested guidelines are consistent with those of the American Heart Association (44). Modest restrictions of total fat intake at a P:S ratio of >1 appears most effective in lowering LDL without a concomitant rise in VLDL or a similar fall in HDL (100). The cholesterol-lowering effects of n-6 polyunsaturates (100) and monounsaturated fats (49) as substitutes for saturated fats are established. Recent research on n-3 polyunsaturates from marine fish show a potential for CHD prevention but specific clinical use is not yet established.

The evidence that elevated TC is related to CHD is established. The Lipid Research Clinics Coronary Prevention Trial revealed definite evidence for benefit from lowering cholesterol in individuals with elevated cholesterol. Nevertheless questions remain: when to treat; at what cholesterol level; at what age; men, women, or both; young or old; and diet or drug (80). It is well to consider that although the decline in CHD mortality in all age groups including the elderly is encouraging, there is deficient knowledge on how nutrition affects risk factors once old age is achieved (65).

Minor modifications in eating patterns probably provide the best chance of obtaining optimal mean concentrations of cholesterol and low density lipoproteins. This focus must be supported by other factors including restricted smoking and increased physical activity. Specific dietary restriction may be recommended for individuals with hyperlipidemic states. No studies to date demonstrate the effectiveness of attempting to lower serum lipids in the elderly. However, the potential benefit of this approach should not be precluded.

WATER

The aged, through custom or distaste, may consume less than optimal quantities of water (134). It is often more acceptable in soups, juices, tea, coffee, soft drinks, or milk products. The water content of diets has received increased attention with respect to its effect on utilization of other nutrients but such

effects have not been investigated in controlled studies in aged men (134).

Thirst responses tend to be impaired with increasing age (77, 107), and temperature regulation is less efficient in the elderly. These two homeostatic malfunctions, together with high ambient temperature, impaired mental function, or drugs such as chlorpromazine, may quickly lead to dehydration.

A daily intake of at least 1500 ml of fluid is recommended. Monitoring of diuretic therapy and prevention of unintentional diuresis from drugs, such as Dilantin, the tetracyclines, and some oral hypoglycemics, is necessary (63). In institutions, provision of fluid in bedside containers does not ensure adequate hydration. These liquids must be actively offered at frequent intervals by concerned staff. Consistent adequate fluid intake is a preventive measure for constipation, a very common problem in the elderly.

Water is an important nutrient for every age group including the elderly. Awareness of changes in homeostatic regulation for the elderly and monitoring and controlling factors, such as environment and drugs, can prevent significant morbidity.

CALCIUM AND PHOSPHORUS

The current RDA for calcium in adults is 800 mg/day. The level of dietary intake that meets the calcium requirement remains a controversial issue (102). Whether calcium deficiency results in osteoporosis is central to the controversy (43, 102). Previous estimates were erroneously based on metabolic studies performed in young adults at zero calcium balance. In elderly men and women, there is an age-related reduction in calcium absorption due to impaired production of 1,25-dihydroxyvitamin D or secondary to relative hyperparathyroidism (55, 115).

Recent studies estimated the daily calcium allowances to be 1000 mg for estrogen-replete women and 1500 mg for estrogen-deprived women as a result of hormonal changes across menopause (57). The National Institutes of Health (98) sponsored a Consensus Development Conference on Osteoporosis and recommended that calcium allowance for premenopausal and untreated postmenopausal women to be increased accordingly. Similarly, the 1985 RDA Committee proposed higher recommendations: 800 mg for men and 1000 mg for women of ages 55 and older (51). It is not known whether the calcium requirment of older elderly individuals exceeds 1000 mg per day.

Osteoporosis is a heterogeneous, multifactorial disorder (115). Calcium deficiency may contribute to the pathophysiology of bone loss by reducing the maximal adult bone mass accumulated at skeletal maturity. Lower initial bone mass coupled with age-related bone loss results in reduced bone mass and increased fracture risk (91). Risk factors for osteoporosis in descending order of importance are: female sex, white or Asian, positive family history, lifelong low calcium intake, early menopause, inactivity, nulliparity, alcohol abuse, high sodium intake, cigarette smoking, high caffeine intake, high protein intake, high phosphorus intake, steroid use, and hyperthyroidism (81). Among the experts on osteoporosis, there is consensus that older age, early menopause, corticosteroid use, extreme immobility, white race and petite female habitus are well-established risk factors, while low calcium intake, cigarette smoking, and moderate alcohol consumption are relatively implicated (28). Other confounding factors include gastric or small bowel resection, long-term use of anticonvulsants, and hyperparathyroidism (115). It has been demonstrated that estrogen stimulates bone formation and estrogen cessation in susceptible women is a major pathophysiological factor in osteoporosis (90).

Marcus (85), Parfitt (105), and Heaney (55, 56) reviewed the dietary risk factors for age-related bone loss. It is well established that protein increases urinary calcium because the acid load of protein decreases renal tubular resorption of calcium. The effect is not mitigated by higher phosphorus intake, which accompanies protein consumption. Some studies have estimated that urinary calcium is increased by 50% when protein intake is doubled. Other studies have shown no effect on calcium balance from variations in phosphorus intake or calcium to phosphorus ratio of diet.

Sodium induces hypercalciuria by competing with calcium for renal tubular resorption. Similarly, caffeine has been shown to increase urinary calcium and digestive juice calcium. Both sodium and caffeine may have important implications at higher levels of intake. In addition, alcohol alters calcium and bone metabolism and chronic alcohol abuse is associated with osteoporosis (126).

The effect of calcium supplementation on bone loss in clinical trials involving postmenopausal women with and without osteoporosis was critically reviewed by Martin and Houston (86). They concluded that the evidence is inconclusive to support calcium supplementation in these women.

The RDA for calcium is currently under review. There is evidence to support higher intakes to maintain calcium balance in the elderly. Inclusion of milk, dairy products, and calcium-rich foods is an important consideration throughout life (see Table 20.1). Recker and Heaney (113) concluded that milk and milk products recommended as sources of calcium may have an advantage as they do not suppress bone remodeling as severely as calcium carbonate. Recker (112) suggested that calcium absorption from carbonate is impaired in achlorhydria and may not be the ideal supplement.

Interest in the calcium deficiency hypothesis of hypertension has been raised. Kaplan and Meese (67) suggest that with information now available that calcium deficiency should not be accepted as a mechnism and calcium supplements should be used with caution for specific treatment of hypertension.

Preventive measures against osteoporosis must be begun early in life to ensure that the maximal bone mass is attained at skeletal maturity. Both weight-bearing physical activities and calcium nutrition play some role in the complex bone physiology. It is controversial whether calcium supplements or exercise can prevent age-related bone loss and osteoporosis, but it is reasonable to presume need

Table 20.1
Calcium Content of Some Foods

Food Sources	Quantity		Calcium
			mg
Dairy products			
Milk Low-fat (2%)	250	ml	314
Skim	250	ml	318
Buttermilk	250	ml	300
Cheese Cheddar	45	g	324
Swiss	45	g	432
Processed	45	g	277
Cottage cheese, low-fat	250	ml	142
Yogurts, plain low-fat	175	ml	348
Ice cream	125	ml	92
Nondairy products			
Beans Red kidney	250	ml	102
Soya	250	ml	115
Broccoli	1	stalk	158
Nuts Almond	125	ml	175
Brazil	125	ml	128
Salmon, canned with bones	100	g	258
Sardines, with bones	7	medium	393
Scallops	6		115
Sesame seeds	125	ml	76
Tofu (processed with calcium sulfate)	125	ml	145

Modified from Pennington JAT, Church HN: *Bowes and Church's Food Values of Portions Commonly Used,* ed 14. New York, Harper & Row, 1984.

for maintenance of calcium intake at least at current RDA recommendations throughout life.

VITAMINS

Vitamins are chemicals as well as nutrients. Vitamin D acts as a hormone, while B vitamins act as coenzymes, combining with protein apoenzymes, to form holoenzymes. The cellular capacity for vitamins is saturated at levels of the vitamin in the range of the RDAs. Undesirable effects of megadoses of vitamins have been recorded (33, 58). Vitamins A and D have been implicated and niacin and possibly ascorbic acid as well.

Baker et al. (11) examined vitamin profiles in elderly institutionalized individuals and in healthy volunteers, and detected subclinical vitamin deficits, particularly for B vitamins. They have recommended (12) parenteral multivitamin supplementation to bring levels to normal in some cases.

There are no data demonstrating that healthy people eating a well-balanced diet need vitamin supplements. Vitamin supplements are recommended for vulnerable individuals who have inadequate intake, disturbed absorption, or increased tissue requirements (47).

SALT

Burstyn et al. (23) stated that the small reductions in sodium intake and increase in potassium intake that might be achieved through public information and changes in food processing are unlikely to lower mean blood pressure in Western societies. Such maneuvers may be useful only to people who are genetically susceptible to salt-induced hypertension or whose salt intake is unusually high.

Carruthers (25) expressed concern that physicians and their patients have accepted too readily the option of long-term medication for hypertension rather than the review and revision of nutritional habits. He maintained that there is unequivocal evidence of a clear correlation between average daily sodium chloride intake of a population and the prevalence of hypertension in that population. He postulated that the correlation between obesity and hypertension may be the association between high sodium intake and excessive caloric intake.

The control of dietary salt intake may be offset by the presence of sodium in many foodstuffs and in medications. Fast foods and processed foods such as canned soups are notorious for salt content. Medications also may add substantial salt intake (Table 20.2).

Awareness of the potential preventive aspects of limiting salt in the diet should be maintained. Restaurants and fast food outlets should use less salt; customers should be allowed to determine their own salt preference. Not salting food discourages the expectation of saltiness and because the taste preference for sodium diminishes after a few months of restriction, good adherence is achievable (66). Hypertensive patients should use less salt. The effectiveness of thiazide therapy in hypertension will be enhanced by reduced salt intake.

FIBER

The human digestive tract does not contain enzymes necessary for the breakdown of dietary fiber. Hydrochloric acid in the stomach affects the cellular structure of plant material leaving the fiber constituents: cellulose, hemicellulose, pectin, gums, mucilages, and lignin. These constituents pass through the small intestine to the colon where they are acted on by intestinal bacteria. Digestion and metabolism of hemicellulose produces fatty acid, carbon dioxide, water, and methane. Kelsay (68), and Cummings and Stephen (29), have reviewed effects of fiber intake on man.

As little as 2–4 g of fiber can alter bowel behavior. Ten to 15 g of fiber affect stool volume possibly by increasing bulk from water absorption. This amount of fiber promotes peristalsis and decreases transit time. It produces fatty acid and sequesters bile salts in the small intestine with a subsequent additional cathartic effect. Dietary fiber supplementation, particularly for institutionalized individuals, is a popular mode for alleviating constipation (62).

The type and amount of fiber ingested may influence colonic bacterial flora and account for protection against colonic cancer (39). Lack of fiber has been implicated in diverticular disease and gallstones.

The potential of fiber for influencing carbohydrate absorption and insulin response curves in management of diabetes mellitus is being considered. Anderson and Sieling (4) reported favorable results of high carbohydrate, high fiber diets on glucose metabolism on older diabetic patients. They noted that patients who have well-controlled diabetes mellitus on oral agents or who are taking less than 40 units of insulin respond especially well.

Dietary fiber may have untoward effects by decreasing the apparent digestibility of other nutrients or by causing abdominal distress through increasing intestinal transit time. It may bind trace elements making them unavailable for absorption.

The role of dietary fiber is not yet defined clearly enough to transpose with assurance the clinical and

Table 20.2
Sodium Content of Selected Antacids and Drugs[a]

	Unit	mg	mEq
Antacids			
Aluminum hydroxide gel, Dried	15 ml	5.4	0.23
Amphojel			
Aluminum hydroxide with magnesium hydroxide	15 ml	24.0	1.04
and calcium carbonate			
Gelusil			
Magaldrate	15 ml	3.5	0.15
Riopan			
Rolaids	1 tablet	53.0	2.00
Drugs (injectable)			
Ampicillin sodium	1 g	71.8	3.12
Carbenicillin disodium	1 g	108.1	4.70
Cloxacillin sodium	1 g	52.0	2.26
Erythromycin Stearate	250 mg	70.0	3.04
Film-coated tablet			
Penicillin G potassium	1 million	7.6	0.33
Penicillin G sodium	1 million	46.0	2.00
Phenytoin sodium	1 g	88.0	3.83
Drugs (oral)			
Alka-Seltzer	1 tablet	521	22.65
Erythrocin Stearate Filmtab	1 tablet	250	10.89
Metamucil Instant Mix	6.5 g	300	13.04
Metamucil Powder	6.1 g		
Food supplements			
Carnation Slender	300 ml	440	19.13
Meritene Powder[b]	30 ml	113	4.91
Ensure[c]	1000 ml	845	36.8
Isocal[d]	1000 ml	532	23.1
Sustacal[d]	940 ml	1036	44.8
Other			
Fleet Enema	130 ml	5000[e]	217.39

[a]Modified from Knoben JE, Anderson PO, Watanabe AS: *Handbook of Clinical Drug Data*, ed 4. Hamilton IL, Drug Intelligence Publication, 1978; and Koda-Kimble MA, Katcher BS, Young LY: *Applied Therapeutics for Clinical Pharmacists*. San Francisco, Applied Therapeutics, 1978. Label information was provided by Ross Laboratories, Columbus, OH; Sandoz Canada; Dorval, Province of Quebec, and Mead Johnson, Evansville, IN.
[b]Sandoz Canada.
[c]Ross Laboratories.
[d]Mead Johnson Laboratories.
[e]275–400 mg (12–17 mEq) absorbed.

experimental studies to physiological needs (5). Fiber content of a variety of foods is included in Table 20.3. Laboratory measurements of crude fiber, dietary fiber, or total fiber are not precisely reproducible. The determinations of the fiber constituents of cellulose, hemicellulose, and lignins are available. However, few analyses of these constituents have been published (131). The equivalent of up to 10 g of bran per day to the diet has been recommended for maintenance of normal bowel function. This supplement must be accompanied by adequate fluid intake.

MALNUTRITION

Malnutrition is a sequitur of disease whether physical, metabolic, emotional, or attitudinal (133). Malnutrition in the broad sense may describe popu-

Table 20.3
Fiber Contents of Some Foods[a]

Food (dried)	Total Fiber
	g/100 g
Legumes	
Kidney beans	10.4
Canned white beans (drained)	8.8
Canned peas (drained)	7.9
Peanuts (roasted)	9.3
Cereal products	
Rolled oats	12.0
Polished rice	2.4
White bread	2.7
Whole wheat bread	5.1
Rye bread	3.0
Wheat bran	30.1
Vegetables	
Potatoes	2.8
Curled kale	3.7
White cabbage	3.4
Carrots	3.3
Onions	2.1
Fiber Enrich[b]	1.3

[a]Modified from Anderson JW, Chen W-JL, Sieling B: *Plant Fiber in Foods.* Lexington KY, HCF Diabetes Research Foundation Inc, 1980.
[b]Ross Laboratories, Columbus, OH.

lations either undernourished or overnourished. Acute illness and accidents require immediate attention to nutrition as well as other factors if needless morbidity and mortality are to be avoided.

O'Hanlon and Kohrs (103) reviewed 28 surveys assessing the intake of older Americans. They found that food energy and calcium were the nutrients most frequently below standards and protein and niacin were most frequently adequate. They noted difficulties in comparing results of studies because of differences in methodology and standards used.

OVERNUTRITION

Obesity is the common form of overnutrition. For most adults, a gain in weight is associated with a gain in excess fat. There is progressive loss of lean body mass and increase in fat with increased age. The rate of fat accumulation is slower in physically-active individuals. Moderating calorie intake and maintaining physical activity levels are the keys to successful weight control.

Andres (7) has concluded that the major population studies of obesity and mortality fail to show that overall obesity leads to greater risk of early mortality. He recommends, therefore, a need for reappraisal of advice on the subject of obesity and re-

search into the possible associated benefits of moderate obesity. On the other hand, the Framingham Study (31) related a clear-cut relationship between weight (obesity) and coronary artery and cerebrovascular disease. The relation of specific dietary components, resultant chemical structure of body fat, and metabolic consequences is not known.

Paganini-Hill et al.(104) concluded that individuals at least risk for significant osteoporosis and hip fracture are those who tend to be overweight. The role of adipocyte production of estrogen is entertained. De Waard (32) has suggested that perhaps calorie restriction and weight loss would be an adjunct to hormonal or chemotherapy for breast cancer in obese postmenopausal women. He based this on the assumption that diet and/or nutritional status contain promoting factors for breast cancer.

One should be cautious when advising healthy elderly people to lose weight and be conservative about weight goals. Individuals with high blood pressure or diabetes mellitus, however, will likely benefit by weight loss. Very restrictive diets of 600–1000 calories should seldom be considered for elderly people, particularly those who participate in physical activities. A 1200–1500 calorie diet may be preferable, allowing a flexible meal pattern that is adequate in the RDAs. Sedentary individuals who require more calorie restriction should have vitamin and mineral supplements considered.

UNDERNUTRITION

Many interrelated factors contribute to the nutritional vulnerability of the elderly, including physical, psychological, socioeconomic, and cultural considerations. For many, aging is coping with losses. Loved ones and contemporaries die or live significant distances away. Retirement may impose loss of social and economic status. Inflation may add to this burden. Decline in physical and mental health may restrict activity, particularly that associated with procurement and preparation of food. Any combination of isolation, relocation, loneliness, depression, economic constraint, and disability may lead to loss of appetite, impaired quality and variety of available foods, and subsequent marginal status. The advent of an acute episode such as bereavement or physical illness may tip the balance in favor of overt malnutrition.

Health care workers and other professionals as well as families should be aware of risk factors that may lead to malnutrition and should be alerted to the need for preventive intervention. Housebound individuals are often already known to health and social service agencies. Help with shopping, assistance in preparing meals, Meals on Wheels programs, luncheon clubs, and day centers are some measures that can be taken. "Health foods" and dietary supplements should be monitored because such products tend to needlessly erode purchasing power and do not guarantee a balanced diet.

PROTEIN CALORIE MALNUTRITION

The definition of protein energy undernutrition is the loss of lean body mass (protoplasm, extracellular fluid and bone) and adipose tissue because of inadequate intake of amino acids and calories. Existing amino acids are oxidized as fuel instead of being used for protein synthesis. With decreased intake, there is depletion of triglyceride in adipose tissue and decreased protoplasmic protein in muscle, liver, kidneys, gastrointestinal tract, pancreas, and skin. Weight loss occurs but may be masked by edema. For individuals in acute care situations, the problems may be immediate. It has been estimated that 25–50% (59, 135) of patients in hospital for 2 weeks or longer suffer protein calorie malnutrition. The elderly are particularly vulnerable, in hospital and at home (18a). Linn (82) observed that malnourished hospitalized patients are at high risk for long-term health problems, probably through continued or recurring episodes of malnutrition. Implied with malnutrition is a greater susceptibility to infection together with impaired mechanical, cellular, and humoral immunologic defenses. The natural history outlined in Figure 20.2 summarizes the potential downhill course, the finale of which may be witnessed in a long-term care facility.

A prominent nutrition problem in patients who are chronically or seriously ill is not that they cannot eat but that they do not willfully eat enough. Frequent encouragement with deference to personal preferences may not be adequate intervention. The physiologic advantage of enteral nutrition is maintenance of structural and functional integrity of the small intestine. The use of enteral feeding solutions that are more nearly nutritionally complete than intravenous solutions may be considered.

Bernard and Rombeau (20) reviewed aspects of nutritional support for elderly patients including oral liquid supplementation, enteral feeding by tube, and parenteral feeding. There are many commercially available enteral feeding solutions. Because of the vast array and expense of provision of these substances, it may be useful for institutions to have a formulary with one standard meal replacement formula, one high protein meal replacement formula, two hypercaloric formulas, and one elemental diet plus a protein, fat, and carbohydrate module (125).

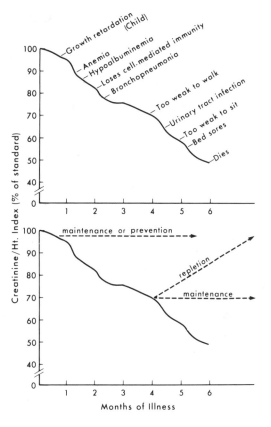

Figure 20.2 The natural history of protein-energy starvation (*top*) and prevention or correction by maintenance or repletion programs (*bottom*). Reproduced with permission from Heymsfield SB, Bethel RA, Ansley JD, Nixon DW, Rudman D: Enteral hyperalimentation: an alternative to central venous hyperalimentation. *Ann Intern Med* 90:63, 1979.

This approach will also allow for lessening of the potential confusion from the many choices. Potential complications of enteral feeding and their management should be understood. Reading mixing and diluting instructions for enteral feeding is mandatory (110). Total parenteral nutrition may be a consideration in specific patients but it is beyond the scope of this chapter.

Identification of individuals at risk for malnutrition is important whether they are at home or in acute or long-term institutions. The elderly are especially vulnerable. Prevention requires attention to nutritional status. Treatment of acute medical or surgical illness requires early intervention, possibly with enteral nutritional supplements, to modify or prevent the downhill course of nitrogen depletion (59, 129).

NUTRITION AND THE INSTITUTIONAL MILIEU

The need for institutionalization is often precipitated by a deterioration in the capacity for self-care or the loss of caretakers. Very few elderly view placement in an institution as an acceptable alternative living arrangement. The loss of independence and privacy and the inability to assume previous lifestyles make the adjustment more difficult. Adaptive capacities may be diminished by illness.

The food service in an institution has the monumental task of providing attractive and nutritious meals that are pleasing to the palate. The quality of food service in any institution is constrained by budgetary restrictions necessitated by spiraling food and labor costs. Nevertheless, a dietitian's skills can be utilized to translate the resident's nutritional needs into an individualized plan.

Retraining residents to feed themselves should be encouraged wherever possible. Follow-up is critical to any implemented plan. In this case, observation of meal service allows the dietitian, nurse, or other staff to evaluate actual intake and alter the diet if necessary. Table 20.4 identifies some nutrient intake problems and possible solutions to be considered.

Food acceptance itself is a complex reaction determined by the physiological, psychological, biochemical, social, educational, and sensory reactions of individuals moving in a framework of race, religion, tradition, economic status, and environmental conditions. Some degree of dissatisfaction is inevitable. Food preferences fall into distinct patterns and knowledge of these patterns for an institutionalized group may minimize dissatisfaction and increase consumption.

Table 20.4
Problems of Nutrient Intake and Potential Solutions[a]

Problems	Potential Solutions
Poor appetite and poor intake	Reassess eating capabilities and diet consistency
	Provide small portions, more frequent meals
	Tailor diet to personal preferences and food intolerances
	Offer selective menu
	Capitalize on breakfast, usually the best eaten meal
	Consider use of high-caloric density supplements or complete meal-replacement formulas
	Schedule aperitifs
	Allow sufficient time for meals
	Maintain oral hygiene and personal grooming
	Plan seating arrangements for compatibility
	Appeal to the senses by describing the aroma, taste, and visual appeal of a meal
	Remove from other residents with highly objectionable eating habits
	Establish patient rapport
	Maximize comfort and tolerance by proper positioning and management of pain and energy level
	Encourage use of dining room to increase socialization
	Encourage families to bring in favorite home-cooked or ethnic foods
	Use outings and catering activities to encourage participation
Low energy level	Keep food warm by using heat-retaining dishes
	Use high-caloric density supplements
	Offer smaller portion, more frequent feeding
	Place liquids and beverages in paper cups and styrofoam
	Set up tray by making foods easily accessible, e.g., removing lids and opening packaged items; spreading butter and jam
	Allow sufficient time for meals by providing early trays
	Assist with feeding as necessary
Impaired vision	Ensure lighting is adequate
	Orient to tray or table setting
	Help set up tray
	Place food in reach
	Place tray in field of vision

Barr et al. (15) studied nutrient intakes of the old old in a care facility. They found that only 75% of the food provided was consumed with mean intake of vitamin C, iron, niacin, and riboflavin adequate as, compared with RDAs, but average intakes of protein, calcium, vitamin A, thiamine, and zinc were lower than the standards. Advanced age was negatively correlated with overall dietary adequacy.

Mealtime tends to be a reference for the time of day for some individuals and may be the highlight activity of the day for others. Intake of food produces a psychologic need for social interchange. Many times the feeding situations in early life have a strong influence. The first sustained human contact and socially important transaction is feeding. It makes the world dependable, comforting, satisfying, and nonthreatening (18).

For the institutionalized aged, food may again become a symbol of security. The patient may reject food to manipulate the staff or concerned family. Staff attitudes may inadvertently promote dependency. Staff must be encouraged to patiently accommodate individual needs. If food on trays is attractively presented and judiciously chosen, monitoring of returns on trays may indicate a spectrum of problems from quality of food preparation to failure to address mental and physical handicaps of consumers. Table 20.5 describes considerations for planning institutional food services.

Asplund et al. (10) assessed psychogeriatric institutionalized patients. They found energy and/or protein undernutrition in 30% and obesity in 4% of the patients. Undernutrition did not correlate with duration of stay and was less frequent in subjects with their own teeth compared with edentulous individuals. Because food intake was similar in patients

Table 20.4 *continued*

Problems	Potential Solutions
Mastication	Assess need for dentures
	Ensure properly fitting dentures
	Modify food consistency, avoiding pureed whenever possible
	Offer pureed as a last resort
Hemiparesis	Offer bite-size portions, finger foods
Poor hand-to-mouth coordination	Help set up tray; place beverage to resident's functional side
	Use mechanical aides or adapted eating utensils
Dysphagia	Suction excess saliva before meals
	Allow sight and smell of food to stimulate salivation and prepare swallowing reflex
	Seat in an upright position with the head flexed slightly forward
	Encourage thorough chewing of food
	Offer solid foods—soft, moist, full-bodied, and held together well, e.g., fish, souffle, canned pears, ripe bananas
	Exclude pureed, sticky, stringy, grainy, acidic, or dry foods
	Provide thickened fluids, e.g., tomato juice, fruit nectar, eggnog
	Serve jello, sherbet, frozen juice, etc. if imbibing fluids is a problem
	Serve cold foods cold and hot foods hot to stimulate the senses
	Suggest exercise to improve swallowing, e.g., sucking on ice chips, frozen fruit juices
Objectionable behavior	Permit staff to role model desirable behaviors
	Seat according to compatibility and level of function
	Allow ample time to eat and provide flexible time of meal service
	Maintain calm, relaxed atmosphere; reduce background noise; minimize distraction by serving one food at a time
	Provide special plates and adapted utensils to maintain independence
	Encourage peer interaction and support
	Offer praise and encouragement for improvements

[a]The authors acknowledge the contribution of members of the Gerontological Practice Group of the British Columbia Dietitians' and Nutritionists' Association, British Columbia, Canada.

Table 20.5
Components of Institutional Food Service and Considerations for Planning[a]

Component	Consideration for Planning
Menu design	Provide attractive meals based on the four food groups to meet the nutritional needs of residents
	Consider day-to-day variations in color and visual appeal, texture, consistency, size, shape, and flavor combination in each meal
	Survey ethnic, religious, and regional preferences
	Note personal preferences on residents' menus when a selective daily menu is not available and update
	Plan for longer menu cycle; 4 or more weeks in length are more desirable
	Consider the type of meal pattern, the number of food items offered, and the times meals are served, e.g., a choice of three-meal-a-day, or four-meal plan consisting of a continental breakfast, late morning brunch, main meal in the late afternoon, and a substantial snack in the evening or five-meal plan
	Choose a meal pattern that will be compatible with the sleeping habits of residents (i.e., early risers, early retirers)
	Ensure that no more than 15 hours elapse between the last meal of one day and the first meal of the following day
	Adjust menu to reflect holiday items, special occasions, and social activities
	Offer alternates compatible with therapeutic dietary modifications
	Semiannually review menu based on quality review standards, production efficiency, and cost factor
	Revise menu to allow seasonal fruits and more economical food items to be incorporated
	Establish daily feedback for updating of preferences, assessing acceptability of menu selection, and monitoring of residents' nutritional intake
	Select china for stability and ease of eating; consider use of plate guards and rimmed plates
Type of meal service and staffing	Waitress service
	Family style dining, i.e., delivery of bulk food to be distributed
	Buffet—smorgasbord service, self-served selection
	Encourage socialization of dietary staff with residents during mealtimes to provide individual attention and maintain rapport
	Adopt a policy for dietary and nondietary staff to help with serving, tray returns, etc.

with and without undernutrition, possible interactions between malnutrition and chronic psychiatric disorders in the elderly were considered, such as "generalized dysmetabolism" in handling of substrates. Morgan et al. (94) observed that women in a psychiatric hospital suffering from severe dementia weighed 15 kg less as a group than a group of active elderly women living in the community consuming a similar calorie intake.

Anderson (3) compared a group of institutionalized veterans with a group of clinic patients. The greatest dietary difference between the clinic and domiciliary patients was not related to the use of dentures. Findings suggested that regardless of earlier diet, older persons in institutions will eat nutritionally important foods if given the opportunity.

Staff attitudes are important for institutional food services. If staff expect old people to be dependent and conforming (18), they may inadvertently extinguish independence. There is a nutritional bill of rights[1] in which the resident has a right to be as independent as possible in eating.

Institutional food is simply not everyone's home-cooked meal. The residents can be involved in menu revision. They may be solicited for menu suggestions and feedback once these are implemented. A representative of the dietary department should be identified to whom the resident may direct criticism and communicate changing food preferences. The dietitian or delegate must maintain a high profile in

[1]American Dietetic Association, 1976.

Table 20.5 *continued*

Component	Consideration for Planning
Atmosphere of dining room	Create a comfortable home-like environment with subdued painted walls and good lighting
	Partition room with mobile dividers for intimacy
	Provide soft, nonobtrusive background music
	Arrange for attractive table setting that highlights the season and special events or themes
	Group no more than six residents around small tables
	Make tables available for singles or couples
	Position tables for ease of movement
	Offer choice of seating companion to stimulate socialization
	Organize seating arrangements based on the need for supervision, assistance, and level of orientation
	Encourage use of dining room for group-related cooking activities
	Minimize background noise emanating from television, trolley, clatter of cutlery and plates, staff talk and consider use of thick wall hangings, baffles and padded placemats
	Separate noisy and difficult residents and those with objectionable table manners
Food-related activities	Meal preparation, baking session
	Men's Group; Ladies' Friendship Tea
	Reminiscence Group (to discuss favorite, traditional, "by-gone" foods)
	Pub Nites, Family Nites
	Outings to restaurants
	Outdoors picnics, barbecue
	Champagne breakfast
Cooking facility for residents' use	Small kitchenette with storage facilities
	Sink, stove, oven, refrigerator
	Electric kettle, toaster, pots and pans
	Plates, bowls, teacups and saucers
	Supply of tea, coffee, sugar, cream, bread, butter, cheese, cookies, milk, juice

[a]Modified from Beck C: Dining experiences of the institutionalized aged. *J Gerontol Nurs* 7:104, 1981; Davies L, Holdsworth MD: An at-risk concept used in homes for the elderly in the United Kingdom. *J Am Diet Assoc* 76:264, 1980; Mahaffey MJ, Mennes ME, Miller BB: *Food Service Manual for Health Care Institutions*. Chicago, American Hospital Association, 1981.

order to establish, observe, direct, encourage, and educate both residents and staff. Training dietetic staff to monitor and note tray returns as part of their cleanup procedure is an asset.

NUTRIENT DRUG INTERACTIONS

Lamy (76) suggested that food-drug interactions are probably more common than indicated in the literature.

Some associations between nutritional status and drugs include reduced albumin with consequences for highly protein-bound drugs (antimicrobials, cardiac drugs), changes in microsomal liver enzymes with alterations in effects of drugs metabolized in the liver (digitoxin, tricyclics), effects on urinary pH with change in the execretion patterns of drugs (urinary antimicrobials) and altered absorption (chelation of iron, calcium) (74, 75).

Many commonly used drugs affect vitamin and mineral status (116, 117). The elderly, particularly those with chronic illness, may be vulnerable to sublinical deficiencies. Drugs may stimulate (tricyclic antidepressants) or depress (digoxin) appetite and thereby induce over- or undernutrition.

Ethanol has many effects. It can stimulate appetite as an aperitif. Excessive ethanol ingestion may impair pyridoxine or folate metabolism or promote zinc and magnesium losses.

Pharmacotherapy in the elderly is a common situation. Awareness of potential drug-food interactions may allow interventions that will preclude undesirable side effects.

DIET AND CANCER

Farber (36) reviewed some aspects of nutrients and cancer. Diet may influence the incidence of cancer in some sites, such as the colon, breast, and endometrium. Carcinogens may occur in food as natural substances, as contaminants, or as products of food preparation methods. Balducci et al (14) suggested that dietary prevention of cancer may be effective in advanced age and that the dietary guidelines of the National Academy of Sciences should be implemented in this population.

Micronutrients have a role in the endogenous formation of carcinogens. Dietary amines or drugs such as oxytetracycline or chlorpromazine, for example, can react with nitrous acid generated in the stomach to form nitroso compounds. These compounds are carcinogenic to laboratory animals and may be effectively inhibited by dietary ascorbic acid and vitamin E. Fiber content plus vitamins C and E are being considered as modulators of carcinogens generated in the feces.

Plumlee et al (108) reviewed the harmful effects of cooking methods that produce carcinogens (e.g., benzo[a]pyrene). They described their process for setting priorities for food items to be tested for possible mutagen information when cooked.

Weisburger (136) addressed the role of the food type, quality, and mode of cooking in the etiology of carcinoma in the gastrointestinal tract and endocrine-sensitive organs. If current concepts are correct, risk for gastric cancer can be reduced by ensuring that appropriate amounts of food containing vitamin C are eaten with each meal and by reducing salt, which acts as an adjuvant. Reduced intake of fried foods and fat will lower risk for colon, breast, and prostrate cancer.

The promotion and prevention of carcinogenesis by micronutrients is an intriguing field ripe for study.

SUMMARY

Consumption of a nutritionally adequate diet is recommended for optimal health. This must be individualized to suit individual needs. Energy (calories) without nutrients is discouraged. Standards must be continuously monitored and the relation between nutrition, environment and life-style must be researched more thoroughly.

Education and personal responsibility for health are lifetime pursuits. Knowledge and application of the principles of good nutrition may go a long way toward successful aging. We should not be misled by extremists, professional or otherwise, who would consign us to a life of spartan diets and galley-slave exertion as a recipe for long life. Moderation has been touted for generations as a prescription for good health. There is no current evidence that this advice is out of date.

Acknowledgments—The authors gratefully acknowledge the cooperation of Lynn Trottier, Dr. Maria Chung, and Dr. Willliam McArthur.

REFERENCES

1. American Diabetes Association: Nutritional recommendations and principles for individuals with diabetes mellitus: 1986. *Diabetes Care* 10:126, 1987.
2. American Dietetic Association: Position of the American Dietetic Association: nutrition, aging and the continuum of health care. *J Am Diet Assoc* 87:344, 1987.
3. Anderson EL: Eating patterns before and after dentures. *J Am Diet Assoc* 58:421, 1971.
4. Anderson JW, Sieling B: High-fiber diets for diabetics: unconventional but effective. *Geriatrics,* 36:4, 1981.
5. Anderson JW: Health implications of wheat fiber. *Am J Clin Nutri* 41:1103, 1985.
6. Anderson W-JW, Chen JL, Sieling B: *Plant Fiber in Foods.* HCF Diabetes Research Foundation Inc., Lexington, KY, 1980.
7. Andres R: Effect of obesity on total mortality. *Int J Obes* 4, 381, 1980.
8. Andres R, Elahi D, Tobin J, Mueller DC, Brant L: Impact of age on weight goals. *Ann Intern Med* 103, 1030, 1985
9. Arntzenius AC, Kromhout D, Barth JD, Reiber JHC, Bruschke AVG, Buis B, van Gent CM, Kempen-Voogd N, Strikwerda S, van der Velde EA: Diet, lipoproteins, and the progression of coronary atherosclerosis: the Leiden intervention trial. *N Engl J Med* 312:805, 1985.
10. Asplund K, Normark M, Pettersson V: Nutritional assessment of psychogeriatric patients. *Age Ageing* 10:87, 1981.
11. Baker H, Frank O, Thind I, Jaslow SP, Louria DB: Vitamin profiles in elderly persons living at home or in nursing homes, *versus* profile in healthy young subjects. *J Am Geriatr Soc* 27:444, 1979
12. Baker H, Frank O, Jaslow SP: Oral *versus* intramuscular vitamin supplementation for hypovitaminosis in the elderly. *J Am Geriatr Soc* 28, 42, 1980.
13. Baker JP, Detsky AS, Wesson DE, Wolman SL, Stewart S, Whitewell J, Langer B, Jeejeebhoy KN: Nutritional assessment: a comparison of clinical judgment and objective measurements. *N Engl J Med* 306:969, 1982.
14. Balducci L, Wallace C, Khansur T, Vance RB, Thigpen JT, Hardy C: Nutrition, cancer, and aging: an annotated review I. Diet, carcinogenesis, and aging. *J Am Geriatr Soc* 34:127, 1986
15. Barr SI, Chrysomilides SA, Willis EJ, Beattie BL: Nutrient intakes of the old elderly: a study of female

residents of a long-term care facility. *Nutr Res* 3:417, 1983

16. Barrows CH, Kokkonen GC: Relationship between nutrition and aging. In Draper HH (ed): *Advances in Nutritional Research,* Vol. 1, Plenum, New York, p. 253, 1977.

17. Beaton GH: Uses and limits of the use of the Recommended Dietary Allowances for evaluating dietary intake data. *Am J Clin Nutr* 41:155, 1985.

18. Beck C: Dining experiences of the institutionalized aged. *J Gerontol Nursing* 7:104, 1971.

18a. Bender AE: Nutrition of the elderly. *R Soc Health J* 3:115, 1984.

19. Bennett, PH: Diabetes in the elderly: diagnosis and epidemiology. *Geriatrics* 39:37, 1984.

20. Bernard MA, Rombeau JL: Nutritional support for the elderly patient. In Young EA (ed): *Nutrition, Aging, and Health,* Alan R. Liss, Inc., New York, p. 229, 1986.

21. Blackburn GL, Bistrian BR, Maini BS, Schlamm HT, Smith MF: Nutritional and metabolic assessment of the hospitalized patient. *JPEN* 1:11, 1977.

22. Brogdon HG, Alford BB: Food preferences in relation to dietary intake and adequacy in a nursing home population. *Gerontologist,* Part 1, 355, Autumn, 1973.

23. Burstyn P, Hornall D, Watchorn C: Sodium and potassium intake and blood pressure. *Br Med J* 281:537, 1980.

24. Butterworth CE, Weinsier RL: Malnutrition in hospital patients: Assessment and treatment. In Goodhard RS, Shils ME (eds): *Modern Nutrition in Health and Disease,* Lea & Febiger, Philadelphia, p. 667, 1980.

25. Carruthers SG: Nutrition and hypertension. *J Can Diet Assoc* 41:274, 1980.

26. Castelli WP: The triglyceride issue: a view from Framingham. *Am Heart J* 112:432, 1986.

27. Committee for the Revision of the Dietary Standard for Canada: Recommended Nutrient Intakes for Canadians. Supply and Services Canada, Ottawa, 1983.

28. Culliton BJ: Osteoporosis reexamined: Complexity of bone biology is a challenge. *Science (Wash DC)* 235:833, 1987.

29. Cummings JH, Stephen AM: The role of dietary fiber in the human colon. *Can Med Assoc J* 123:1109, 1980.

30. Davies L, Holdsworth MD: An at-risk concept used in homes for the elderly in the United Kingdom. *J Am Diet Assoc* 76:264, 1980.

31. Dawber TR: *The Framingham Study: The Epidemiology of Atherosclerotic Disease.* Harvard University Press, Cambridge, MA, 1980.

32. De Waard F: Premenopausal and postmenopausal breast cancer: one disease or two? *JNCI* 63:549, 1979.

33. DiPalma JR, Ritchie DM: Vitamin toxicity. *Annu Rev Pharmacol Toxicol* 17:133, 1977.

34. Exton-Smith, AN: Malnutrition in the elderly. *Proc R Soc Med* 70:615, 1977.

35. Exton-Smith AN: Nutritional status: Diagnosis and prevention of malnutrition. In Exton-Smith AN, Caird FI, (ed): *Metabolic and Nutritional Disorders in the Elderly,* A. John Wright and Sons, Distributed by Year Book Medicine Publishing, Chicago, p 66, 1980.

36. Farber E: Chemical carcinogenesis. *N Engl J Med* 305:1379, 1981.

37. Franz MJ, Holler H, Powers MA, Wheeler ML, Wylie-Rosett J: Exchange lists: revised 1986. *J Am Diet Assoc* 87:28, 1987.

38. Frisancho AR: New standards of weight and body composition by frame size and height for assessment of nutritional status of adults and the elderly. *Am J Clin Nutr* 40:808, 1984.

39. Freeman HJ: Dietary fiber and colonic neoplasia. *Can Med Assoc J* 121:291, 1979.

40. Fries JF: Aging, natural death, and the compression of morbidity. *N Engl J Med* 303:130, 1980.

41. Garraway WM, Whisnant JP, Furlan AJ, Phillips LH, Kurland LT, O'Fallon WM: The declining incidence of stroke. *N Engl J Med* 300:449, 1979.

42. Gersovitz M, Motil K, Munro HN, Scrimshaw NS, Young VR: Human protain requirements: assessment of the adequacy of the current Recommended Dietary Allowance for the dietary protein in elderly men and women. *Am J Clin Nutr* 35:6, 1982.

43. Gordan GS, Vaughan C: Calcium and osteoporosis. *J Nutr* 116:319, 1986.

44. Gotto AM, Bierman EL, Connor WE, Ford CH, Frantz ID, Glueck CJ, Grundy SM, Little, JA: Recommendations for the treatment of hyperlipidemia in adults. *Circulation* 69:1067A, 1984.

45. Gray DS, Crider JB, Kelley C, Dickinson CC: Accuracy of recumbant height measurement. *JPEN* 9:712, 1985.

46. Greenblatt DJ: Reduced serum albumin concentration in the elderly: a report from the Boston collaborative drug surveillance program. *J Am Geriatr Soc* 27:20, 1979.

47. Greengard P: Introduction: the vitamins. In Goodman LS, Gilman A (eds): *The Pharmacologic Basis of Therapeutics:* Ed. 5. New York, Macmillan, p. 1544, 1975.

48. Grundy SM: Cholesterol and coronary heart disease: a new era. *J Am Med Assoc* 256:2849, 1986.

49. Grundy SM: Monounsaturated fatty acids, plasma cholesterol, and coronary heart disease. *Am J Clin Nutr* 45 (Suppl), 1068, 1987.

50. Grundy SM, Arky R, Bray GA, Brown WV, Ernst ND, Kwiterovich PO, Mattson F, Weidman WH, Schonfeld G, Strong JP, Weinberger M: Coronary risk factor statement for the American public: a statement of the Nutrition Committee of the American Heart Association. *Arteriosclerosis* 5:678A, 1985.

51. Guthrie, HA: Comment by Helen A. Guthrie. *J Nutr Educ* 17:194, 1985.

52. Harper AE: Recommended dietary allowances: are they what we think they are? *J Am Diet Assoc* 64:151, 1974.

53. Hazzard, WR: Aging and atherosclerosis: interactions with diet, heredity and associated risk factors. In Rockstein M, Sussman C (eds): *Nutrition, Longevity and Aging, Proceedings of Symposium on Nutrition, Longevity and Aging, Miami 1976,* New York, Academic Press, 1976, p. 143.

54. Health and Welfare Canada: Recommended Nutrient Intakes for Canadians. Bureau of Nutritional Sciences, Health Protection Branch, Department of Health and Welfare, Ottawa, Canada, 1983.

55. Heaney RP: Calcium intake, bone health, and aging. In Young EA (ed): *Nutrition, Aging, and Health.* Alan R. Liss, Inc., New York, Alan R. Liss, 1986, p 165.

56. Heaney RP, Gallagher JC, Johnston CC, Neer R,

Parfitt AM, Whedon GD: Calcium nutrition and bone health in the elderly. *Am J Clin Nutr* 36:986, 1982.

57. Heaney RP, Recker RR, Saville PD: Menopausal changes in calcium balance performance. *J Lab Clin Med* 92:953, 1978.

58. Herbert V: The vitamin craze. *Arch Intern Med* 140:173, 1980.

59. Heymsfield SB, Bethel RA, Ansley JD, Nixon DW, Rudman D: Enteral hyperalimentation: an alternative to central venous hyperalimentation. *Ann Intern Med* 90:63, 1979.

60. Hodges RE, Hood J, Canham JE, Sauberlich HE, Baker EM: Clinical manifestations of ascorbic acid deficiency in man. *Am J Clin Nutr* 24:432, 1971.

61. Hollenbeck CB, Coulston AM, Reaven GM: Glycemic effects of carbohydrates: a different perspective. *Diabet Care* 9:641, 1986.

62. Hull C, Greco RS, Brooks DL: Alleviation of constipation in the elderly by dietary fiber supplementation. *J Am Geriatr Soc* 28:410, 1980.

63. Hunt TE: Homeostatic malfunctions in the aged. *Br Columbia Med J* 22:379, 1980.

64. Justice CL, Howe JM, Clark HE: Dietary intakes and nutritional status of elderly patients. Study in a private nursing home. *J Am Diet Assoc* 65:639, 1974.

65. Kannel WB: Nutritional contributors to cardiovascular disease in the elderly. *J Am Geriatr Soc* 34:27, 1986.

66. Kaplan NM: Non-drug treatment of hypertension. *Ann Intern Med* 102:359, 1985.

67. Kaplan NM, Meese RB: The calcium deficiency hypothesis of hypertension: a critique. *Ann Inter Med* 105:947, 1986.

68. Kelsay JL: A review of research on effects of fiber intake on man. *Am J Clin Nutr* 31:142, 1978.

69. Keys A, Fidanza F, Kavonen MJ, Kimura N, Taylor HL: Indices of relative weight and obesity. *J Chronic Dis* 25:329, 1972.

70. Knoben JE, Anderson PO, Watanabe AS: *Handbook of Clinical Drug Data,* ed. 4. Hamilton, IL Drug Intelligence Publication, 1978.

71. Koda-Kimble MA, Katcher BS, Young LY: *Applied Therapeutics for Clinical Pharmacists.* San Francisco, Applied Therapeutics, 1978.

72. Kohrs MD, Czajka-Narins DM: Assessing the nutritional status of the elderly. In: *Nutrition, Aging, and Health,* Young EA, editor. New York, Alan R. Liss, Inc., 1986, p 25.

73. LaCroix AZ, Mead LA, Liang K-Y, Thomas CB, Pearson TA: Coffee consumption and the incidence of coronary heart disease. *N Engl J Med* 315:977, 1986.

74. Lamy PP: Drug interactions and the elderly—a new perspective. *Drug Intell Clin Pharmacy* 14:513, 1980.

75. Lamy PP: Nutrition and the elderly. *Drug Intell Clin Pharmacy* 15:887, 1981.

76. Lamy PP: The elderly and drug interactions. *J Am Geriatr Soc* 34:586, 1986.

77. Leaf A: Dehydration in the elderly. *N Engl J Med* 311:791, 1984.

78. Lemming, JT, Webster SPG, Dymock IW; Gastrointestinal system. In Brocklehurst JC (ed): *Textbook of Geriatric Medicine and Gerontology,* Edinburgh, Churchill Livingstone, 1973, p 321.

79. Leverton RM: The RDAs are not for amateurs. *J Am Diet Assoc* 66:9, 1975.

80. Levy RI: Primary prevention of coronary heart disease by lowering lipids: results and implications. *Am Heart J* 110:1116, 1985.

81. Lindsay R: Managing osteoporosis: current trends, future possibilities. *Geriatrics* 42:35, 1987.

82. Linn BS: Outcomes of older and younger malnourished and well-nourished patients one year after hospitalization. *Am J Clin Nutr* 39:66, 1984.

83. Madden JP, Goodman SJ, Guthrie HA: Validity of the 24-hour recall. *J Am Diet Assoc* 68:943, 1976.

84. Mahaffey MJ, Mennes ME, Miller BB, *Food Service Manual for Health Care Institutions.* American Hospital Association, Chicago, 1981.

85. Marcus R: The relationship of dietary calcium to the maintenance of skeletal integrity in man–an interface of endocrinology and nutrition. *Metabolism,* 31:93, 1982.

86. Martin AD, Houston CS: Osteoporosis, calcium and physical activity. *Can Med Assoc J* 136:587, 1987.

87. Masaro EJ: Aging and fat metabolism (Abstr.) Presented at the 145th Annual Meeting of the American Association for the Advancement of Science, Houston, Tex, January 3–8, 1979.

88. McCay CM, Crowell MF, Maynard LA, The effect of retarded growth upon the length of life span and upon the ultimate body size. *J Nutr* 10:63, 1985.

89. McCay CM, Sperling G, Barnes LL: Growth, ageing, chronic diseases and life span in rats. *Arch Biochem* 2:469, 1943.

90. McKenna MJ, Frame B: Hormonal influences on osteoporosis. *Am J Med* 82 (Suppl IB):61, 1987.

91. Melton III JL, Wahner HW, Richelson LS, O'Fallon WM, Riggs BL: Osteoporosis and the risk of hip fracture. *Am J Epidemiol* 124:254, 1986.

92. Michel L, Serrano A, Mait RA: Nutritional support of hospitalized patients, *N Engl J Med* 304:1147, 1981.

93. Mitchell CO, Lipschitz DA: Detection of protein-calorie malnutrition in the elderly. *Am J Clin Nutr* 35:398, 1982.

94. Morgan DB, Newton HMV, Schorah CJ, Jewitt MA, Hancock MR, Hullin RP: Abnormal indices of nutrition in the elderly: a study of different clinical groups. *Age Ageing* 15:65, 1986.

95. Morgan PO, Wigle DT: Medical care and the declining rates of death due to heart disease and stroke. *Can Med Assoc J* 125:953, 1985.

96. Morley JE, Silver AJ, Fiatarone M, Mooradian AD: Geriatric grand rounds: nutrition and the elderly. *J Am Geriatr Soc* 34:823, 1986.

97. Munro HN, Young VR Protein metabolism and requirements. In Exton-Smith AN, Caird FI (eds): *Metabolic and Nutritional Disorders in the Elderly.* A. John Wright and Sons Ltd., Distributed by Year Book Medical Publications, Chicago 1980, p 13.

98. National Institutes of Health Consensus Conference: Osteoporosis. *JAMA* 252:799, 1984.

99. National Institutes of Health Consensus Development Conference: Lowering blood cholesterol to prevent heart disease. *Arteriosclerosis* 5:404, 1985.

100. Nestel PJ: Polyunsaturated fatty acids (n-3, n-6). *Am J Clin Nutr* 45 (Suppl):1161, 1987.

101. Nicholls ES, Jung J, Davies JW: Cardiovascular disease mortality in Canada. *Can Med Assoc J* 125:981, 1981.

102. Nordin BEC, Polley KJ, Need AG, Morris HA, Marshall D: The problem of calcium requirement. *Am J Clin Nutr* 45:1295, 1987.

103. O'Hanlon P, Kohrs MB: Dietary studies of older Americans. *Am J Clin Nutr* 31:1257, 1978.

104. Paganini-Hill A, Ross RK, Gerkins VR, Henderson BE, Arthur M, Mack TM: Menopausal estrogen therapy and hip fractures. *Ann Intern Med* 95:28, 1981.

105. Parfitt AM: Dietary risk factors for age-related bone loss and fractures. *Lancet* 1:1181, 1983.

106. Pennington JAT, Church HN, Bowes and Church's Food Values of Portions Commonly Used. 14th Ed. New York, Harper and Row, 1984.

107. Phillips PA, Rolls BJ, Ledingham JGG, Forsling ML, Morton JJ, Crowe MJ, Wollner L: Reduced thirst after water deprivation in healthy elderly men. *N Engl J Med* 311:753, 1984.

108. Plumlee C, Bjeldanes LF, Hatch FT: Priorities assessment for studies of mutagen production in cooked foods. *J Am Diet Assoc* 79:446, 1981.

109. Podolsky S, El-Beheri B: The principles of a diabetic diet. *Geriatrics* 35:73, December, 1980.

110. Posner GF, Hickisch SM: Dilution factors for commercial enteral formulas. *J Am Diet Assoc* 84:1219, 1984.

111. Press F: Letter from Frank Press, NAS. *J Nutr Ed* 17:191, 1985.

112. Recker RR: Calcium absorption and achlorhydria. *N Engl J Med* 313:70, 1985.

113. Recker RR, Heaney RP: The effect of milk supplements on calcium metabolism, bone metabolism and calcium balance. *Am J Clin Nutr* 41:254, 1985.

114. Recommended Dietary Allowances, Ed 9: Food and Nutrition Board, National Research Council, National Academy of Sciences, Washington, D.C., 1980.

115. Riggs BL, Melton III LJ: Involutional osteoporosis. *N Engl J Med* 314:1676, 1986.

116. Roe D: Therapeutic significance of drug-nutrient interactions in the elderly. *Pharmacol Rev* 36:109S, 1984.

117. Roe D: Therapeutic effects of drug-nutrient interactions in the elderly. *J Am Diet Assoc* 85:174, 1985.

118. Rosenthal MJ, Hartnell JM, Morley JE, Mooradian AD, Fiatarone M, Kaiser FE, Osterweil D: UCLA geriatric grand rounds: diabetes in the elderly. *J Am Geriatr Soc* 35:435, 1987.

119. Ross MH: Nutrition and longevity in experimental animals. In Winick M (ed): *Nutrition and Aging.* John Wiley & Sons, New York 1976, p 3.

120. Roy LB, Edwards PA, Barr LH: The value of nutritional assessment in the surgical patient. *JPEN* 9:170, 1985.

121. Rubenstein C, Romhilt D, Segal P, Heiss G, Chambless LE, Boyle KE, Ekelund L-G, Adolph R Sheffield LT: Dyslipoproteinemias and manifestations of coronary heart disease: the lipid research clinics program prevalence study. *Circulation* 73 (Suppl I): I-91, 1986.

122. Sauberlich HE, Dowdy RP, Shala JH: *Laboratory tests for the assessment of nutritional status.* Cleveland, Ohio, CRC Press, 1974.

123. Schneider EL, Vining EM, Hadley EC, Farnham SA: Recommended dietary allowances and the health of the elderly. *N Engl J Med* 314:157, 1986.

124. Schorah CJ, Hay AWM: Recommended dietary allowances for the elderly. *N Engl J Med* 314:1708, 1986.

125. Slattery PJ, Swalling MJ: Share the wealth: selection of an enteral feeding formulary. *British Columbia Dietary and Nutritional Association Newsletter,* October, 1986, p 1.

126. Spencer H, Rubio N, Rubio E, Indreika M, Seitam A: Chronic alcoholism. *Am J Med* 80:393, 1986.

127. Stamler J, Wentworth D, Neaton JD: Is relationship between serum cholesterol and risk of premature death from coronary heart disease continuous and graded? *J Am Med Assoc* 256:2823, 1986.

128. Stare FJ: Three score and ten plus more. *J Am Geriatr Soc* 25:529, 1977.

129. Steffee WP: Malnutrition in hospitalized patients. *JAMA* 244:2630, 1980.

130. Steinberg D: Lipoproteins and atherosclerosis: some unanswered questions. *Am Heart J* 113:626, 1987.

131. Vahouny GV: Conclusions and recommendations of the symposium on dietary fibers in health and disease, Washington, D.C., 1981. *Am J Clin Nutr* 35:152, 1982.

132. Walker WJ: Changing United States life-style and declining vascular mortality: cause or coincidence? *N Engl J Med* 297:163, 1980.

133. Watkin DM: Logical bases for action in nutrition and aging. *J Am Geriatr Soc* 26:193, 1978.

134. Watkin DM: Nutrition for the aging and the aged. In Goodhart RS, Shils ME (eds): *Modern Nutrition in Health and Disease,* Philadelphia, Lea & Febiger, 1980, p 781.

135. Weinser RL, Hunker EM, Krumdieck CL, Butterworth CE Jr: Hospital malnutrition—prospective evaluation of general medical patients during the course of hospitalization. *Am J Clin Nutr* 32:418, 1979.

136. Weisburger JH: Mechanism of action of diet as a carcinogen. *Cancer (Phila)* 43:1987, 1979.

137. Wheeler ML, Delahanty L, Wylei-Rosett J: Diet and exercise in noninsulin dependent diabetes mellitus: implications for dieticians from the NIH Consensus Development Conference. *J Am Diet Assoc* 87:480, 1987.

138. Witztum J: Intensive drug therapy of hypercholesterolemia. *Am Heart J* 113:603, 1987.

139. Young VR, Pellett PL: Protein intake and requirements with reference to diet and health. *Am J Clin Nutr* 45 (5 Suppl), 1323, 1987.

140. Young VR, Perera, WD, Winterer JC, Scrimshaw NS: Protein and amino acid requirements of the elderly. In Winick M (ed): *Nutrition and Aging,* New York, John Wiley & Sons, 1976, p 77.

141. Zavaroni I, Dall'Aglio E, Bruschi F, Bonora E, Alpi O, Pezzarossa A, Butturini U: Effect of age and environmental factors on glucose tolerance and insulin secretion in a worker population. *J Am Geriatr Soc* 34:271, 1986.

CHAPTER 21

Medical Renal Disease in the Aged

PIERRE F. FAUBERT
WARREN B. SHAPIRO
JEROME G. PORUSH
ALVIN I. KAHN

The kidney in the elderly is affected by involutional processes, probably secondary to time-related phenomena that are independent of specific diseases such as atheroscelerosis. The degenerative component is reflected in many ways. The blood urea nitrogen at ages 30–40 averages 13 mg/dl, and at age 70, 21 mg/dl. Glomerular filtration rate and renal plasma flow at age 90 are approximately 50% below the value found at age 20, with major changes beginning at about age 40. Tubular function is also compromised, characteristically demonstrated by a reduced ability to concentrate the urine. Also, the renal compensation for ammonium chloride-induced acidosis is much slower in the aged than in younger individuals. Another involutional abnormality is a change in diurnal excretory pattern with the development of nocturia. These involutional changes are usually not in themselves significant enough to lead to symptoms or require any therapeutic manipulation. However, they may add diagnostic and therapeutic problems when other illnesses ensue in the elderly and they may worsen the prognosis for renal and other diseases. Although the average glomerular filtration rate declines significantly with age, renal function remains unchanged in over a third of the elderly.

In addition to the progressive diminution in renal function and renal blood flow that may take place as part of the aging process, the elderly male has an increased likelihood of developing bladder neck obstruction. Moreover, there is a generally increased susceptibility of the urogenital system to infection in older individuals. Further acute impairment of renal function also may result from the following problems, which are more common in the elderly: inadequate fluid intake; fluid loss due to vomiting diarrhea or injudicious use of diuretics; hemorrhagic shock; acute or chronic cardiac failure; septicemia due to Gram-negative and Gram-positive bacteria.

CLINICAL EVALUATION OF RENAL FUNCTION

In order to produce urine, the kidneys are supplied with approximately 1 liter of blood/min, representing about one-fifth of the total cardiac output. Each kidney contains approximately 1 million nephrons that produce 180 liters (125 ml/min) of filtrate per day from the plasma passing through the glomerular tufts. This glomerular filtrate is concentrated by the tubules between 5 and 100 times, depending upon fluid intake and urine concentrating ability. By modifying the composition of the urine during its passage through the tubules, the kidney is able to control body water, electrolyte, and acid-base equilibrium.

URINALYSIS

There are many tests of renal function, but a simple urinalysis, preferably done by the physician, will always give valuable information. In some instances a well-performed urinalysis may prove to be more useful than complicated clearance and other studies. Proteinuria and an abnormal sediment are among the earliest signs of renal disease, and these findings are often evident long before azotemia or impaired concentrating ability can be detected.

Examination of the urine should be done on a fresh morning specimen preferably after a 10-hour fast. The specific gravity of a solution is a function of the number and size of the particles, although the osmolality is related only to the number of particles in solution. In urine, which is composed of organic and inorganic substances, the specific gravity correlates with the osmolality:

Specific Gravity	Osmolality
1.000	50
1.010	300
1.020	800
1.022	900

A urine osmolality of 900 is considered normal after 10 hours of fluid deprivation.

The tests for glucose and protein are well known and have been greatly simplified by the "dip stick" methods. Most of the dip stick tests are specific for glucose and will not react with fructose, galactose, or pentose. On occasion, urines contain peroxidases that give the same dip stick reactions as glucose. The dip stick test for protein uses a paper strip impregnated with the pH -indicator dye, tetrabromphenol, and a buffer to maintain the pH in the paper at 3.0. The test is based on the capacity of proteins to change the color of tetrabromphenol when the pH is maintained at a constant level, with the degree of color change roughly proportional to the amount of protein present. The dip stick is designed to detect anionic proteins such as albumin and may, therefore, fail to detect the presence of cationic light chains even when the excretion is high. Precipitation tests using 5% sulfosalicylic acid added to an aliquot of urine will precipitate albumin, globulin, and light chains. Thus a negative dip stick test and a positive sulfosalicylic acid test should alert the physician to the possibility that light chains are being excreted in excess, pointing to a diagnosis of multiple myeloma.

In elderly individuals, 1+ proteinuria in the presence of a negative sediment may be accepted as being of no diagnostic significance most of the time. However, the only foolproof method is to collect a 24-hour urine for total protein. Amounts over 200 mg/24 hours are abnormal.

As described above, a concentrated urine is preferable for examination of the sediment. If the urine is not examined at once, it should be acidified with a drop or two of salicylic acid or refrigerated since some casts tend to degenerate as the urine pH moves toward the neutral or alkaline range due to bacterial contamination.

Hematuria constitutes one of the cardinal signs of glomerular disease but it may also result from disease of the urinary tract. When present, red blood cell casts represent a sure sign of the glomerular source of hematuria. It has been recently suggested that glomerular hematuria can be distinguished from urinary tract bleeding by examination of the red cells either by phase contrast microscopy or simple staining of the urinary sediment. Eythrocytes entering the urine from the urinary tract have uniform normal morphology, whereas those entering the urine from a source within the kidney are dysmorphic with variations in size and shape. By studying the red cell morphology it is possible to correctly diagnose a patient as having either glomerular or urinary tract bleeding in 85% of the cases. An incorrect diagnosis was made in only 4% of the patients. In the remaining 11% no definite diagnosis could be made. The presence of more than 3–5 white cells in the urine is usually associated with infection somewhere in the urinary tract. Although increased numbers of leukocytes are found in the urine in association with fever, exercise, or congestive heart failure, urine cultures should be obtained in all patients with pyuria. Pyuria with negative routine cultures should signal the possibility of tuberculosis. In acute interstitial nephritis the white cells in the sediment may be eosinophiles. The urine sediment should be stained with Wright's or Hansel's stain when interstitial nephritis is suspected.

Casts, because of their mass, will concentrate at the edge of the coverslip. Casts originate within the renal tubules and are washed down into the bladder. Their presence excludes uncomplicated cystitis or urethritis in which no casts should be noted. Red blood cell casts suggest the presence of a glomerulitis and white blood cell casts most often indicate purulent disease within the kidney. Casts containing tubular epithelium suggest a destructive process, e.g., acute tubular necrosis. Waxy casts (homogenous with high refractive index and wavy outline) are generally seen only in chronic renal disease. Red-colored casts in urine with a positive test for blood but no red blood cells may indicate the presence of myoglobin seen after muscle breakdown, or free hemoglobin seen after hemolysis from any cause. The presence of fat droplets in tubular cells (oval fat bodies) or in cellular casts suggests fatty tubular degeneration. These, as well as free fatty droplets, which are birefringent under polarized light, strongly point to the diagnosis of nephrotic syndrome. Uric acid and calcium oxalate crystals are frequently seen and do not indicate the presence of disease. Cystine crystals are seen in patients with cystinuria. Phosphates may be seen as amorphous material when the urine pH is alkaline. If they obscure other formed elements on the microscope slide, they can be dissolved with a drop of acetic acid. Sulfa crystals may be seen in patients on a sulfonamide and suggest that the dose should be decreased or the drug discontinued.

BLOOD CHEMISTRY

Actually every test, even endocrine and liver function tests, may contribute to the understanding of a renal problem, but some of the analyses are of special importance and merit separate emphasis.

The most important blood tests for evaluating renal function are the blood urea nitrogen (BUN) and serum creatinine. The BUN reflects the interaction between the patient's diet and his renal function. By limiting protein in the diet, an elevated BUN may be appreciably reduced. With a normal protein intake, a statistically significant rise in the BUN does not occur until 65% of renal function has been lost. Serum creatinine correlates better with renal function than the BUN, (see "Tests of Glomerular Function"). A disproportionate rise in the BUN compared to serum creatinine is suggestive of prerenal azotemia, usually the result of dehydration, rapid blood loss (especially in the gastrointestinal tract), hypotension, or hypercatabolism. Early in postrenal obstruction, because of renal ischemia, the elevation of BUN may be disproportionately greater than that of serum creatinine. Uric acid rises along with the BUN in most azotemic states. In intrinsic renal disease with acute or chronic renal failure without a hypercatabolic state, creatinine rises in proportion to BUN. In chronic renal failure, phosphorus tends to be elevated and calcium depressed. If the serum calcium is high or even normal in a patient with chronic renal failure with a serum creatinine of 3.5 mg/dl or greater, one must think of primary hyperparathyroidism with nephrocalcinosis as the cause of the uremia.

In a study of renal disease of the aged, it was noted that 60% of the subjects had a serum creatinine of less than 1.0 mg/dl even though the glomerular filtration rate (GFR), as measured by creatinine clearance, was decreased in all of the subjects, often as low as 35% of normal. This suggests that there is a decreased production of creatinine in the aged probably due to muscle atrophy and disuse. Therefore, one should be cautious in evaluating renal function based on serum creatinine alone in aged people, and should always obtain both the BUN and creatinine. Ideally, a creatinine clearance should be done, particularly if the exact level of renal function is necessary, as when using potentially nephrotoxic drugs or drugs requiring the kidney for excretion.

TESTS OF GLOMERULAR FUNCTION (CLEARANCE)

Because approximately 60% of glomerular filtration may be lost without an increase in BUN or creatinine, it is extremely important to perform other tests when renal disease is suspected or reduced filtration may be present, as in the elderly.

There is no technique for the direct measurement of GFR. All tests of GFR depend on the estimation of the clearance rate of substances excreted by glomerular filtration and neither reabsorbed nor secreted by the tubules. Inulin, a fructose polymer, fulfills these criteria best, but an inulin clearance is too difficult to perform routinely. Creatinine clearance, using endogenously produced creatinine, is a simpler clinical method of determining GFR. Creatinine clearance fairly accurately approximates inulin clearance until an inulin clearance of 30 ml/min is reached. Below that creatinine secretion becomes such a large part of total creatinine excretion that the creatinine clearance is falsely elevated above the inulin clearance. At this point, the average of the creatinine and urea clearance correlates best with the GFR, as measured by inulin clearance. This is important in clinical research but the creatinine clearance is adequate for most clinical purposes, even with advanced renal failure.

Urea clearance utilizes endogenously produced urea as the test substance. Urea is filtered at the glomerulus but large amounts may be reabsorbed in the tubule. Urea clearance is not as accurate or reproducible as creatinine clearance, and the need to perform the test after fairly vigorous hydration may be dangerous in older people or those with advanced renal disease.

All clearance tests require the collection of a timed urine specimen and, preferably, a midpoint blood sample. In clinical practice, 24-hour urine collections are advisable because this will minimize the problems due to incomplete bladder emptying. This should be done by starting the collection after the first morning voiding the following day. Blood may be obtained at any time in this 24-hour period. If a patient has an indwelling catheter, shorter timed periods may be used.

A formula derived by Cockcraft and Gault predicts creatinine clearance (C_{cr}) from serum creatinine (S_{cr}) utilizing age and weight. It takes into account the above discussed difficulties of using creatinine in the aged:

$$C_{cr} = \frac{(140\text{-}age) \times (wt\ in\ kg)}{72 \times S_{cr}(mg/100\ ml)}$$

This formula is for men. For females, multiply by 0.85.

TESTS OF TUBULAR FUNCTION

Urine concentration varies as a function of water intake. A random urine osmolality or specific gravity yields little information about urinary concentrating ability and, therefore, in order to assess the concentrating ability the patient should be deprived of fluids for at least 12 hours. The specific gravity will increase to 1.020–1.022 in 90% of normal individuals (800–900 m Osm/kg/H_2O osmolality). As already noted, in older individuals concentrating ability may be lost to some extent solely due to the involutional process. The patient should not be on diuretics and should have received adequate protein in his or her diet when tested. Results must be corrected for the presence of sugar and albumin. If the specific gravity of the urine does not rise above that of the plasma (1.010–1.012) or osmolality (280–300 m Osm/kg/H_2O), this is referred to as isosthenuria, and is characteristic of tubular disease, diabetes insipidus, obstructive uropathy, or advanced renal failure of any etiology.

IMAGING TECHNIQUES

Plain radiography (flat plate) and tomography of the kidneys can give a good estimate of renal size. Intravenous pyelography (IVP) can be utilized to visualize the kidney and excretory system. The numerous reports of acute renal failure following infusion (high dose) IVP in patients with reduced renal function (particularly diabetics) have resulted in a decrease in the use of the infusion IVP. However, routine IVP in patients with normal renal function appears to be quite safe.

Radionuclide tracers for renal imaging, such as technetium-99m, bind to a variety of ligands and injected intravenously, can be used to estimate renal blood flow, size, shape, position, and function of each kidney, as well as the presence of lesions in the kidney and/or lower urinary tract. These radionuclides are safe, emitting only γ-radiation with a 6-hour half-life and do not interfere with normal renal function.

Ultrasonography utilizes ultrahigh frequency sound waves generated at the skin surface to produce an image of the kidneys. Echoes returning from the kidneys (and other structures such as the liver, gallbladder, aorta, vena cava) are displayed on an os-

cilloscope. Cross-sectional views of the kidneys can be obtained and are particularly valuable in diagnosing urinary tract obstruction, renal masses, aortic aneurysms, and vena caval obstruction and for delineating renal size. The procedure is noninvasive and safe.

Computerized tomography (CT) utilizes the computer to enhance differences in tissue radiodensity allowing for accurate delineation of renal parenchymal, pararenal, retroperitoneal, and pelvic structures. Radiodensity differences in tissue can be further enhanced by the infusion of iodine containing radiocontrast materials. CT is a useful tool for investigating renal masses and the extent of injury after trauma. CT is probably more accurate than sonography for detecting calculi, infected cysts, tumors, and urinary tract obstruction in patients with coexisting polycystic kidney disease. The procedure may also be helpful in distinguishing clots and diagnosing urothelial carcinomas, fungus balls, vena caval or renal venous disorders including anomalies, clots, and tumor thrombi.

Digital subtraction angiography demonstrates the arterial system by using a venous injection of iodinated radiocontrast material. X-ray images prior to and after the radiocontrast injection are converted to digital impulses and subtracted from one another leaving the arterial supply outlined. Overall accuracy compared to standard arteriography is about 70%, while specificity and sensitivity exceed 90%. Accuracy decreases in the presence of obesity, severe proximal atherosclerotic disease, or anatomic tissue juxtaposition.

Magnetic resonance imaging (MRI) utilizes magnetic fields and pulsed radio frequencies to transiently alter the spin and magnetic dipole behavior of nuclear elements, bearing odd numbers of protons or neutrons, within tissue molecules (i.e., the hydrogen atom). As the nuclear elements resume their prior alignments between pulses, they release energy that is detected and recorded. This technique is relatively new and its potential as a diagnostic tool has yet to be determined. However, MRI offers several advantages over conventional imaging methods: absence of ionizing radiation; ability to visualize the vasculature without use of contrast agents; ability to distinguish renal cortex from medulla; elimination of bone artifacts, and very high contrast resolution.

TUBULOINTERSTITIAL DISEASE

PYELONEPHRITIS

The incidence of urinary tract infection increases with age in both sexes, with women outnumbering men. Sexual activity, previous childbearing, and relaxation of the pelvic floor may be responsible for the increasing rate of infection with age in women. In the elderly man, urinary infection is common due to bladder outlet obstruction secondary to prostatic enlargement. Obstruction to the flow of urine is an important predisposing factor in pyelonephritis. Experiments have shown that the normal kidney is resistant to bacterial infection when compared to the experimentally obstructed kidney. Other predisposing factors in the elderly are the increased use of bladder catherterization and colonization of the skin by Gram-negative bacilli.

Acute pyelonephritis may be responsible for a decrease in renal function in patients with underlying renal disease and if treated effectively, renal function will improve. The pathogenesis of chronic pyelonephritis is not clear. It is not certain whether active bacterial infection must be continually present for the disease to be progressive or if autoimmune mechanisms come into play.

Bacterial colony counts have been helpful in demonstrating that serious infection may be present in the absence of fever, dysuria, frequency, or pyuria. Counts up to 10,000 colonies/ml may reflect the presence of microorganisms that live as saprophytes in the terminal part of the urethra or may represent accidental contamination of the specimen. Counts of 100,000 colonies/ml or more are believed to be indicative of active infection involving the kidneys, bladder, or urethra. The technique of colony counting makes a midstream urine acceptable for bacteriologic examination, provided that cultures are made within an hour after voiding and no obstruction is present. If meticulous technique is observed, catheterization can be avoided. In the catheterized patient a urine culture showing growth of 10^4 organism/ml may be significant. In the clinical setting of infection, one can use the culture and sensitivity testing results as the basis for antimicrobial therapy.

The most common bacterial pathogens are *Escherichia coli, Proteus, Klebsiella,* and *Enterobacter* genera, although Gram-positive organisms, particularly staphylococcus, are found with increasing frequency. The bacterial flora and antibiotic sensitivities will vary depending upon geography and from institution to institution and may change depending upon previous antibiotic use.

Tuberculosis of the kidney, although rare, must still be considered in all cases of chronic pyelonephritis, particularly if routine urine cultures remain sterile in the presence of persistent pyuria. Three morning urine specimens should be sent for inoculation on special media.

Adequate therapy requires, first and foremost, correction of the causative factors that have led to the bacterial infection. This calls for the relief of obstruction, the control of diabetes when present, and the improvement of general health. Indiscriminate use of antibiotics in a patient with urinary tract obstruction will produce only resistant organisms. The possible causes of obstruction are many and include phimosis, urethral stricture, bladder neck fibrosis, prostatic hypertrophy, prostatic carcinoma, interstitial cystitis with contraction of the bladder, bladder tumor, ureteral stricture, ureteral calculi, pelvic tumor, ureteropelvic obstruction, and tumor of the renal pelvis. A urologic examination is mandatory in every male patient with infection and in female patients with recurrent infection, particularly if kidney function is depressed.

Following sensitivity studies, the patient should be placed on specific antibiotic therapy. The presence of tuberculosis calls for 1 year of therapy with isoniazid, combined with either rifampin or ethambutol. Most antibiotics and chemotherapeutic agents are not excreted in high concentration in the urine once azotemia develops, so care must be taken to use agents that can reach therapeutic levels in the urine in patients with renal insufficiency. Such antibiotics as tetracycline and the aminoglycosides (gentamicin, tobramycin, and amikacin) are nephrotoxic, but when used in appropriately reduced doses depending on the GFR (frequently reduced in the aged), they usually will not worsen renal function. When used in patients with decreased renal function, peak and trough antibiotic blood levels should be monitored as well as renal function. If levels of these antibiotics are not reduced, then vestibular damage and deafness (with aminoglycosides) or acute renal failure may occur. The dosage of penicillin also should be reduced in patients with renal insufficiency in order to avoid central nervous system complications such as seizures.

In order to determine the dosage for tobramycin or gentamicin in patients with a creatinine clearance of 70 ml/min or less, the following approach is used. After an initial loading dose of 1–2 mg/kg, the patient is given a maintenance dose every 8 hours, calculated by multiplying the usual maintenance dose of 1 mg/kg by the creatinine clearance divided by 100. A 70-kg man with a creatinine clearance of 10 would receive a 70- to 140-mg loading dose followed by 7 mg every 8 hours.

The above regimen is most accurate when renal function is stable and the creatinine clearance is calculated either by a timed urine collection or the formula of Cockcroft and Gault described earlier. Another approach is to use the same 1- to 2-mg/kg loading dose and give maintenance doses of 1 mg/kg at intervals determined by multiplying the serum creatinine by 8. It must be remembered that these are only rough estimates of dosage and do not take into account the pharmacodynamics of the amino-glycosides, i.e., the volume of distribution and elimination rates. The most accurate method of determining the correct dosage would be to measure the peak and trough levels and adjust the dosage accordingly.

The antibiotics of choice for urinary tract infections include ampicillin, cephalosporins, aminoglycosides, and sulfa-methoxazole-trimethoprim combinations. Furadantin and nalidixic acid should not be used in the treatment of acute disease but may be used as suppressive agents in chronic infections. One should appreciate that in the presence of diminished renal function they may not be excreted in sufficiently high concentration and, in the case of sulfonamides, may be toxic due to intrarenal crystal deposition. Methenamine salts also are effective in this respect with acidification being required only in infections with urea-splitting organisms. Once the urine is sterile, therapy should be continued for about 2 weeks in acute cases. In recurrent disease, either longer periods of therapy (for example a 6-week course) or long-term prophylactic therapy should be considered. Frequent urine cultures should be obtained thereafter because relapses are common once antibiotics are discontinued.

In general, infectious renal disease in the aged should be treated with the same vigor as in younger patients. However, the physician should be alert to the occurrence of strains of organisms resistant to particular antibiotics.

Failure of the fever to defervesce or the persistence of leukocytosis after what would otherwise be adequate treatment for pyelonephritis should alert the physician to the presence of complications such as: (a) Perinephric abscess, which most commonly arises from rupture of an intrarenal collection into the perinephric space. On a plain film of the abdomen the kidney is often enlarged and displaced. Gas may be seen in the abscess (small bubbles). Calcification may occur in an old abscess. Renal ultrasound and CT are the most accurate diagnostic procedures for making the diagnosis and localizing the collection. (b) Obstruction of an infected kidney. (c) Papillary necrosis (more prevalent in the diabetic).

ACUTE INTERSTITIAL NEPHRITIS

Acute interstitial nephritis (AIN) is usually secondary to drugs or infection. The most common drugs are antibiotics, anti-inflammatory agents, and anticonvulsants. The patient usually presents with a hypersensitivity response consisting of rash and fever. The patient may be oliguric. Leukocytosis with eosinophilia is frequently observed and eosinophiluria (diagnosed using Wright's or Hansel's stain) is common.

The above manifestations occur in only 20% of the patients who develop AIN secondary to nonsteroidal anti-inflammatory agents. In these patients signs related to nephrotic syndrome (edema) and renal failure are more prominent. Microscopic hematuria can be present as well making the differential diagnosis from acute glomerulonephritis difficult if a history of drug ingestion is not obtained. The renal failure can be severe and prolonged with up to one-third of the reported patients requiring dialytic therapy. Kidney biopsy reveals interstitial infiltration with lymphocytes, histiocytes, and eosinophiles. Fusion of the foot processes is seen in the patients with proteinuria. Withdrawal of the offending agent usually results in reversal of the nephritis; however, corticosteroids may both hasten the recovery and diminish renal damage. Table 21.1 provides a list of drugs that may cause AIN.

CHRONIC TUBULOINTERSTITIAL NEPHRITIS

Cast Nephropathy (Myeloma Kidney)

Multiple myeloma should be ruled out in any elderly patient with unexplained acute or chronic renal insufficiency. A low anion gap and proteinuria in the presence of anemia and/or renal failure should also

Table 21.1
Drugs Suspected of Causing AIN

Nonsteroidal anti-inflammatory drugs
    Fenoprofen (Nalfon)
    Ibuprofen (Motrin, Advil)
    Naproxen (Naprosyn)[a]
    Sulindac (Clinoril)

Antibiotics
    Penicillins (Methicillin, Ampicillin)
    Rifampin
    Sulfonamides

Diuretics
    Furosemide
    Thiazides

Others
    Allopurinol (Zyloprim)
    Cimetidine (Tagamet)
    Phenytoin
    Azathiaprin

[a]Most commonly involved.

alert one to the possibility of myeloma. There is usually a strong relationship between the occurrence of renal insufficiency and the presence of Bence Jones proteinuria. The latter may be identified by electrophoresis of concentrated urine. Bence Jones protein is a low molecular weight monomer or dimer of immunoglobulin light chains that is easily filtered by the glomerulus. Renal damage from Bence Jones protein may be secondary to either direct toxicity to the tubule (light chains of high isoelectric point may be more nephrotoxic) or tubular obstruction. Precipitation is more likely to take place in the patient with volume contraction, hypercalcemia, or after exposure to radiologic contrast material. Tubular dysfunction, manifested by proximal tubular acidosis, impaired proximal tubule calcium, uric acid, and phosphorus reabsorption (Fanconi syndrome), amino aciduria, and renal glycosuria have been described. The development of nephrotic syndrome in a patient with multiple myeloma is usually the consequence of either light chain nephropathy or amyloidosis. The histopathology of the myeloma kidney consists of atrophy of the renal tubules with precipitation of protein within the tubules. The tubular casts are dense and eosinophilic and are frequently associated with a giant cell reaction. The casts contain κ- and/or λ-light chains on immunoflourescence.

Cast nephropathy is usually treated with prednisone and cyclophosphamide. Improvement in kidney function, even in patients with advanced renal failure, has been reported. Thus, in our opinion all patients should have a trial of chemotherapy. In addition all patients should be kept well hydrated and aggressively treated for hypercalcemia and infection when present.

Drug-Induced Chronic Interstitial Nephropathy

Analgesic abuse is probably the most common cause of chronic interstitial nephropathy worldwide. Phenacetin usually combined with acetyl salicylic acid has been implicated as the causative agent in the majority of cases. Epidemiologic studies have shown that the patient is usually female with a chronic history of headache and daily ingestion of analgesics over a period of 2–3 years, resulting in a total dose of over 1 kg. A careful history of analgesic abuse should be sought in any elderly patient presenting with renal insufficiency and moderate proteinuria (500–1500 mg/24 hours). Besides proteinuria, pyuria is commonly found and hypertension is present in 50% of the cases. There is an increased risk of urinary tract carcinoma and papillary necrosis in these patients.

Because the disease affects the interstitium, especially the renal papilla, patients lose the ability to concentrate the urine. Thus, if salt intake is curtailed, acute volume depletion and worsening of renal function may occur. Renal function may be dramatically improved by volume expansion. In addition to analgesics, antineoplastic agents such as cis-platin and lomustine have been associated with chronic tubulointerstitial nephropathy. Renal failure associated with these drugs is more likely to progress if the agents are continued, although many patients who apparently discontinue analgesics still experience a progressive decline in renal function.

Uric Acid Nephropathy

Acute uric acid nephropathy is a potential complication in patients with myeloproliferative disease. It is more common when these diseases are treated with chemotherapeutic agents that cause an acute increase in both serum uric acid and uric acid excretion resulting in precipitation of uric acid crystals in the collecting ducts. This problem can be prevented by treating the patient with allopurinol, increasing urine flow and alkalinizing the urine prior to and during chemotherapy.

Chronic tubulointerstitial nephropathy can develop in a small proportion of patients with chronic gouty arthropathy. In practically all cases renal insufficiency results from hypertension, vascular disease, or other renal diseases. In some patients lead may play a role by causing gout, hypertension, and interstitial nephritis. This can be demonstrated by measuring the 24-hour lead excretion following a 3-day diagnostic lead chelation study with EDTA. Treatment of hyperuricemia with allopurinol, although appropriate for the resolution of tophi and improvement of arthropathy, cannot be expected to reverse the renal insufficiency once present.

POLYCYSTIC RENAL DISEASE

Although the diagnosis of autosomal dominant polycystic renal disease (PKD) is usually made prior to the 6th decade of life, a small percentage of patients are not discovered until after the age of 60. A family history may or may not be present. The presenting symptoms and signs are those of renal insufficiency and/or hypertension with or without a history of gross hematuria. On physical examination the enlarged kidneys may be palpable. Microscopic hematuria is frequently present along with proteinuria, which is usually less than 1g/24 hours. Renal sonography confirms the diagnosis. The renal failure tends to be progressive but careful attention to control of hypertension, fluid and electrolyte balance, bleeding, and infection may prolong the course.

PRIMARY GLOMERULAR DISEASES

ACUTE GLOMERULONEPHRITIS

Glomerulonephritis in the aged will usually be seen only as a chronic disease, but acute glomerulonephritis can occur even in the 8th decade of life. Infections with nephritogenic streptococci cause acute glomerulonephritis. Acute glomerulonephritis may begin with nonspecific symptoms such as headache, fever, nausea, vomiting, and abdominal pain. The latter two may be so severe than an acute surgical abdomen is simulated. The more specific signs include an acute "nephritic syndrome" manifested by oliguria, edema (usually periorbital), smoky or grossly bloody urine (the latter is rare), hypertension, and proteinuria. The sedimentation rate in glomerulonephritis is always elevated. Within 2 weeks following an acute streptococcal infection there is a rise in antistreptolysin O titer in 56% of the patients, although occasionally no rise will occur for 4 or 5 weeks. When the streptococcal infection is of dermal origin, the antibody response may be blunted and the antistreptolysin O titer may not rise. Studies of various streptococcal infections indicate that this immunologic response is not impaired in the aged. The blood urea nitrogen may rise rapidly and serum complement levels are depressed (C_3, C_4, CH_{50}). Cerebral edema may cause headache, convulsions, paralysis, aphasia, and coma. Water and salt retention may cause congestive heart failure, particularly because the heart may already be damaged by accompanying arteriosclerotic heart disease and involutional changes due to age.

The differential diagnosis of acute glomerulonephritis includes the following: (a) nonglomerular diseases such as acute interstitial nephritis, acute tubular necrosis, thrombotic thrombocytopenic purpura, hemolytic uremic syndrome, atheroembolic disease, and malignant hypertension; (b) multisystem and hereditary diseases such as systemic lupus erythematosus, Henoch-Schönlein-purpura, vasculitis, Goodpasture's syndrome; (c) idiopathic diseases with primary glomerular involvement such as Berger's disease (IgA nephropathy), focal glomerulonephritis, mesangiocapillary glomerulonephritis, and mesangioproliferative glomerulonephritis.

Nonstreptococcal infections may be associated with some features of acute glomerulonephritis. Staphylococcus, pneumococcus, *Klebsiella,* meningococcus, *Salmonella*, toxoplasma, and *Plasmodium falciparum* have been implicated. This nephritis is usually mild (hematuria, proteinuria) and not associated with edema, hypertension, or vascular congestion. In most cases the nephritis is not progressive and recovery is the usual outcome. On occasion a rapidly progressive glomerulonephritis can develop especially with chronic infections such as bacterial endocarditis, abdominal abscess, and osteomyelitis.

Treatment of acute glomerulonephritis in the aged does not differ significantly from that in younger persons. Prolonged bed rest in the elderly should be avoided because older patients are more prone to develop osteoporosis, phlebothrombosis, and pulmonary embolism when immobilized. During active disease, salt should be restricted as well as fluids for control of edema and hypertension. Dietary protein supplementation and a liberal carbohydrate intake may have additional value when the patient is acutely ill and catabolic. Digitalis, antihypertensive agents, and diuretics should be used only with clear indications and considerable caution in the older patient. Recovery of renal function is generally the rule except for the patient presenting with severe impairment of renal function, persistent proteinuria, or the nephrotic syndrome in cases in which impairments of kidney function can persist.

Rapidly progressive glomerulonephritis (crescentic or extracapillary glomerulonephritis) is another form of acute glomerular disease also found in the elderly. The patient usually presents with acute renal failure associated with hematuria and red cell casts in the urinary sediment. This form of acute glomerulonephritis may be idiopathic, secondary to streptococcal infection or seen in association with other diseases such as membranous nephropathy, infectious endocarditis, lupus erythematosus, mixed cryoglobulinemia, Wegener's granulomatosis, vasculitis, Henoch-Schönlein purpura, Berger's disease, and mesangiocapillary glomerulonephritis. Kidney biopsy reveals compression of the glomerular tuft by epithelial cell proliferation (crescents). The glomeruli are usually negative on immunofluorescent microscopy, but linear deposits of IgG in the glomerular capillary may be seen, particularly when this form of glomerulonephritis is seen with pulmonary hemorrhage in Goodpasture's syndrome. At present there is no definitive therapy for the disease even though successes are now being reported with the use of steroids, cyclophosphamide (Cytoxan), and plasmapheresis. Beneficial results also have been reported with the use of intravenous steroids in very large doses (equivalent to 1000 mg of prednisone) for 3–5 days (pulse therapy) followed by steroids at more usual doses with or without cyclophosphamide.

CHRONIC GLOMERULONEPHRITIS

This is an all-encompassing term lumping together a variety of primary glomerular diseases that are persistent. Patients often present with nephrotic syndrome, which may be associated with hypertension, an abnormal urinary sediment, and various degrees of renal insufficiency. The progression of acute glomerulonephritis to chronic nephritis has not been convincingly proven, although there have been reports professing this to occur. Certainly there is much more chronic glomerulonephritis than can be accounted for by progression of classical acute glomerulonephritis.

Two diseases that are immune mediated and often associated with a long course, abnormal urine, nephrotic syndrome, and azotemia are membranous nephropathy and mesangiocapillary glomerulonephritis.

Membranous nephropathy (membranous glomerulonephritis) usually presents as nephrotic syndrome. It is the most common cause of nephrotic syndrome in the elderly and may be associated with a long chronic course and slowly progressive azotemia. In approximately 25% of patients a spontaneous remission may occur. This entity has many causes including an association with hepatitis (hepatitis-antigen positive), syphilis, malaria, and carcinoma, especially that of the colon (with circulating carcinoembryonic antigen). On immunoflourescence microscopy, the antigen of the causative disease may be shown to be deposited on the glomerular basement membrane in some cases. In most patients, deposits of IgG and the third component of complement are seen on the glomerular basement membrane. Light and electron microscopy both show deposits on the epithelial side of the basement membrane that, in the latter stages, is markedly thickened and irregular in appearance. Any elderly patient with membranous nephropathy should have a chest x-ray and stool guaiac screen for possible malignancy. If clinically indicated (i.e., acute decrease in GFR or signs and symptoms of pulmonary embolization), renal vein thrombosis should be ruled out by sonography and/or renal vein angiography. A course of steroids consisting of 120 mg of prednisone every other day for 2 months with gradual tapering over an additional 1–2 months is used by the authors to treat early membranous nephropathy. This regimen is generally well tolerated by the elderly. Depending upon the response, particularly with regard to the degree of proteinuria, a longer course of therapy may be indicated.

Mesangiocapillary (membranoproliferative, lobular) glomerulonephritis often presents as acute glomerulonephritis with hypocomplementemia and nephrotic syndrome. It is not very common in the elderly and may resolve in 10% of patients but more often remains as a chronic disease with progressive renal failure and hypertension. It also may present as renal failure and hypertension or as a chronic disease first picked up on a routine urinalysis as proteinuria and/or hematuria. Mesangiocapillary glomerulonephritis is often associated with chronic depression of serum complement levels, particularly those associated with the alternate pathway of complement activation. On light microscopy the mesangial cells and matrix are markedly increased and the basement membrane appears to be split, although under electron microscopy these so-called splits, or tram tracks, are actually invasions of the mesangium under the basement membrane. Subendothelial deposits are seen on electron microscopy (type I). The type II form, in which dense intramembranous deposits are seen on electron microscopy, has not been reported in the elderly. Immunoflourescence microscopy shows complement components either alone or with immunoglobulins. Dipyridamole and aspirin have been shown to be of some benefit, however, long-term follow-up as well as studies in large groups of patients are needed before this form of therapy is routinely accepted.

GLOMERULAR DISEASES ASSOCIATED WITH SYSTEMIC DISEASES

DIABETIC NEPHROPATHY

Diabetic nephropathy (DN) is the most frequent cause of glomerular disease associated with systemic illness in the elderly. Although the incidence of isolated DN is not known, together with hypertension it is the major cause of end-stage renal disease in patients over 45 years of age, representing almost 50% of those patients in the United States. The diagnosis of DN can be made clinically in the presence of a long-standing history of diabetes mellitus (usually over 10 years), proteinuria (usually in the nephrotic range with or without renal insufficiency), diabetic retinopathy (over 90% of the patients), and hypertension.

When nephrotic proteinuria appears, the disease usually follows an inexorable downhill course, eventuating in end-stage renal disease and the need for dialysis or transplantation. Great effort should be made to control the blood pressure because that intervention appears to slow the rate of deterioration in renal function. Tight control of the blood glucose does not appear to alter the course of DN once clinically detectable renal insufficiency has occurred. Recent studies have indicated that treatment with angiotensin enzyme inhibitors (captopril or enalopril maleate) may be more beneficial than control of hypertension with other agents, as they may have specific effects on intraglomerular hemodynamics. Long-term studies are needed before treatment with these drugs can be universally recommended, however. If converting enzyme inhibitors are utilized, the serum potassium must be carefully monitored as treatment with these drugs may result in significant hyperkalemia.

Bladder dysfunction secondary to neuropathy should always be looked for in the diabetic patient presenting with urinary tract infection or acute worsening of kidney function.

Papillary necrosis, another complication found in diabetic patients, is characterized by infarction and necrosis of one or more renal papillae with sloughing of medullary tissue in association with pyelonephritis. The medullary tissue sometimes may be found in strained urine specimens and may cause ureteral obstruction. Papillary necrosis appears to be the result of many factors, foremost of which are infection, vascular disease, and urinary tract obstruction. Poor control of diabetes also may play a role. Although this complication is commonly associated with diabetes, necrotizing papillitis also has been seen with chronic alcoholism, sickle cell disease, ureteral obstruction, and analgesic abuse. Papillary necrosis in the diabetic is a serious disease that runs a fulminating course with high fever and severe renal insufficiency and frequently terminates in death. It is best prevented by controlling the blood sugar, avoiding analgesic abuse, relieving urinary tract obstruction, and vigorously treating urinary tract infection.

AMYLOIDOSIS

Amyloidosis is characterized by the deposition of extracellular proteinaceous material in various organs. These deposits have a fibrillar structure on electron microscopy and green birefringence with congo red stain under the polarizing microscope. The two most common forms of amyloidosis are

1. AL amyloidosis, also called primary amyloidosis or light chain amyloid (κ or λ), is related to plasma cell dyscrasias such as monoclonal gammopathy, macroglobulinemia, and multiple myeloma.
2. AA amyloidosis (amyloid A), also called secondary amyloidosis, is found in patients with chronic infections, inflammatory conditions, and malignancies. The renal manifestations of both forms of amyloidosis are identical. Proteinuria is the most common finding with

nephrotic syndrome present in 35% of cases. Renal insufficiency is present in 25–43% of patients at the time of diagnosis. Renal disease due to amyloidosis is usually progressive with practically all patients reaching end stage or dying from complications within 1–3 years after diagnosis.

The development of flank pain, hematuria, pulmonary embolism, or rapidly decreasing renal function should alert the physician to the possibility of renal vein thrombosis. Treatment of amyloidosis is still in the experimental stage. There are a few case reports of the disappearance of amyloid A deposits after treatment of chronic infection or removal of a renal cell carcinoma. D-penicillamine alone or combined with chlorambucil has been used in patients with rheumatoid arthritis-related amyloid A. Colchicine has been useful in reducing the frequency of attacks in patients with familial Mediterranean fever and may delay the development of amyloidosis. Dimethyl sulfoxide has not been successful as a treatment for AL amyloidosis. At present, melphalan and prednisone are the drugs of choice for this form of the disease.

VASCULITIS

This term refers to a heterogenous group of primary disorders having inflammation and necrotizing lesions of blood vessel walls in common and not associated with other systemic diseases such as lupus erythematosus, essential cryoglobulinemia, etc. Systemic manifestations include fever, weight loss, arthritis, abdominal pain, polyneuritis, myopathy, and cardiac and central nervous system dysfunction. In some of these diseases sufficient clinical associations are present to classify them into specific disorders, i.e., periarteritis nodosa or Wegener's granulomatosis. In other cases the presenting signs and symptoms are not specific for any one disease and so the term "overlap syndrome" is utilized. The renal manifestations of vasculitis are more or less the same for all types with hematuria, with or without red cell casts, an almost universal finding. Kidney function is normal in almost 50% of the patients. If renal insufficiency is present, patients may evolve to end stage requiring dialysis in a relatively short period of time.

Histologically, both vascular and glomerular structures may be involved singly or in combination. The vascular lesion is characterized by fibrinoid necrosis of the vessel wall and infiltration with polymorphonuclear, eosinophilic, and mononuclear cells. The glomerular lesion may include necrotizing glomerulitis with crescent formation involving a variable number of glomeruli.

The treatment of choice for the various vasculitides is prednisone and cyclophosphamide (with the exception of Henoch-Schönlein purpura, which usually does not require treatment). In the presence of rapidly progressive renal failure and/or pulmonary hemorrhage, pulse methyl-prednisolone therapy should be attempted (as described above) in conjunction with cytotoxic therapy.

LUPUS NEPHRITIS

Systemic lupus erythematosus can occur in the elderly. The clinical manifestations in that age group do not differ much from those in the younger patient except perhaps for a higher incidence of polyserositis. Most authors agree that in the elderly the disease seems to follow a more benign course; however, there is some controversy as to how commonly the kidneys are involved. In our experience, the incidence of clinically evident renal disease is identical in both age groups.

GLOMERULAR DISEASE ASSOCIATED WITH CANCER

As noted earlier, membranous nephropathy has been reported in association with some solid tumors involving the lungs and the gastrointestinal tract. Patients with lymphomas can also develop minimal change disease (lipoid nephrosis), which may remit after successful treatment of the lymphoma. More and more cases of glomerular diseases are being reported in association with chronic lymphocytic leukemia. Various forms of glomerulopathy have been found in leukemic patients and include in order of frequency mesangiocapillary glomerulonephritis, membranous nephropathy, focal glomerulosclerosis, and minimal change disease. It is not clear from the reported cases whether treatment of the leukemia will alter the natural history of the glomerular disease.

GLOMERULAR DISEASE ASSOCIATED WITH DRUGS

In our discussion of interstitial nephritis, we noted that proteinuria in the nephrotic range may be seen as a complication of nonsteroidal anti-inflammatory drugs. The only glomerular abnormality found on electron microscopy was fusion of the foot processes. Drugs such as gold, penicillamine, and captopril can also induce glomerular injury, however, subepithelial electron dense deposits (similar to those seen with membranous glomerulopathy) are detected on examination of kidney tissue in such patients. Clinical manifestations include proteinuria with minimal to moderate impairment of kidney function. Such complications tend to be dose related for both penicillamine and captopril (requiring a dose of 300–400 mg for the latter). Gold-induced proteinuria is not dose related. Instead, a genetic predisposition and the method of administration, oral versus parenteral, seem to play a role. With discontinuation of the drugs, the proteinuria usually disappears after a variable period of time.

VASCULAR DISEASE

ATHEROSCLEROSIS

Atherosclerosis in the kidney is pathologically no different from that seen elsewhere in the body. The lesion of atherosclerosis is the fibrous plaque, which is a raised, gray lesion in the intima consisting of a core of proliferating and degenerating smooth muscle cells and lipid-laden foam cells covered by fibrous tissue and collagen from endothelial cells. The plaques tend to develop at sites of mechanical stress or altered flow such as occur at vessel bifurcations. It is estimated that 50% of the population over age 60 will have renal vascular disease, yet only a minority will develop clinical manifestations. One or both renal arteries may be involved. The occlusion is most frequently located in the proximal portion of the renal artery and is frequently manifested by the development of accelerated hypertension or hypertension resistant to the usual medications. The diagnosis should be suspected in any patient in whom hypertension begins after the age of 50. The patient may also present with a history of long-standing hypertension and sudden worsening of renal function, particularly in the presence of bilateral disease. On physical examination the auscultation of an abdominal bruit (particularly if both systolic and diastolic), high pitched and radiating laterally, is strongly suggestive of the diagnosis of renovascular disease. The workup of the patient suspected of having renovascular disease should include electrolytes (hypokalemia and/or metabolic alkalosis secondary to elevated renin and aldosterone are frequently seen), creatinine clearance, and timed IVP or renal scan. If either the IVP or renal scan demonstrates a discrepancy between kidneys in function or size, an angiogram is warranted. These tests are of limited value in the patient with advanced renal disease or bilateral renovascular disease of equal severity. The definitive diagnosis is made by renal angiography and when the index of suspicion is high, one should go directly to this test. Digital subtraction angiography eliminates the need for arterial injection (see "Clinical Evaluation of Renal Function"). A critical evaluation of this procedure in terms of both false-positives and -negatives is not as yet available.

The renal vein renin assay has been proposed as a method for predicting the outcome of transluminal angioplasty or surgical intervention for the treatment of renovascular hypertension. Several modifications, such as the administration of furosemide and/or a converting enzyme inhibitor prior to the cannulation of the renal veins, have been proposed in order to enhance the reliability of the test. It should be noted, however, that angioplasty or surgery may be useful in some patients despite the absence of lateralization of renin production, particularly if renal insufficiency is present due to bilateral disease.

Once the diagnosis of renovascular hypertension secondary to atherosclerosis is made, the question then becomes which therapeutic modality to offer to the patient. The use of medical therapy may be successful in decreasing the blood pressure, but drugs do not alter the underlying renovascular pathology, so that the patient remains at risk of developing progressive renal failure particularly if bilateral disease or a solitary kidney is present. Indeed, there is evidence to suggest that in this group of patients deterioration of renal function can occur despite acceptable medical control of blood pressure. Therefore, our personal bias is toward interventional therapy with either surgery or transluminal angioplasty. The latter modality is preferred in patients who have significant cardiac or pulmonary disease, although the results are not as good as with surgery.

Patients with renovascular disease (especially bilateral disease) frequently have additional atherosclerosis at other sites such as the cerebral and/or coronary arteries. Surgery in such patients is associated with a high mortality and failure rate and probably should not be offered. The duration of hypertension is an important predictor of the outcome of renovascular surgery. In one study of patients treated with surgery, those with less than a 5-year history of hypertension had an improvement rate of 67% compared to 13% in those patients with hypertension for longer periods of time.

As noted, when surgical treatment of renovascular disease is not possible or advisable, percutaneous transluminal angioplasty (PTA) may be useful. This technique utilizes a catheter with a balloon at the end, which is passed into the vessel and inflated, displacing the atheromatous plaque into the intima and thereby enlarging the lumen. A long-term study of PTA in a large number of patients with atheromatous renovascular hypertension has recently been reported. Following successful angioplasty, hypertension improved or was cured in 84% of patients. The procedure was successful in 57% of patients with unilateral disease and only 10% of those with bilateral disease. In those patients with 50–80% occlusion undergoing successful PTA, the recurrence rate was 35% within the first year. A second dilatation is often effective and should be attempted. At present there is no clear strategy for treating those patients who are either poor surgical risks or PTA failures.

ARTERIOLAR NEPHROSCLEROSIS—BENIGN AND MALIGNANT

The small arteries and arterioles of the kidney are frequently affected by elevations in the systemic blood pressure. Renal arteriolar involvement in hypertension has been divided into two types: benign and malignant arteriolar nephrosclerosis with the major determinant of the type of involvement being the severity of the hypertension itself.

Benign Arteriolar Nephrosclerosis

Patients with mild to moderate blood pressure elevation have few symptoms attributable to the rise in pressure itself. Morning headaches may be present and are typically located occipitally. The major physical findings (aside from elevated blood pressure) are hypertensive changes in the retinal vessels consisting most commonly of arteriolar narrowing. Less frequently one sees hemorrhages (flame-shaped) and hard exudates. On cardiac examination, a fourth sound may be present that represents early evidence of cardiac enlargement and decreased left ventricular compliance.

The most characteristic histological change associated with benign nephrosclerosis is an arteriosclerotic process that, in the larger arteries, is characterized by fibrosis and thickening of the intima resulting in decreased luminal size. In the afferent arteriole, patchy hyaline thickening of the entire wall of the arteriolae is frequently seen, which is more severe proximally.

There have been many studies showing that patients with untreated hypertension have a higher incidence of proteinuria, impairment of renal function, uremia (usually associated with an accelerated or malignant phase), cardiac hypertrophy, congestive heart failure, and coronary artery disease. The mortality in untreated hypertension has been found to be directly related to the extent of vascular disease present on the initial examination.

Treatment of the hypertension can decrease the risk of death and vascular complications such as stroke, congestive heart failure, renal failure, and accelerated hypertension. Recent studies, Multiple Risk Factor Intervention Trial (MRFIT) and Hypertension Detection and Follow-Up Program (HDFP), have shown that drug therapy for mild hypertension results in protection from stroke, but protection from heart attacks has not been clearly demonstrated. On the other hand, the same studies indicate that further lowering of the blood pressure was associated with an increased death rate from coronary disease (sudden death) in patients entering the study with abnormalities in the resting electrocardiogram (ECG) (high T waves and ST-T wave changes). The reason for this increased death rate from coronary events in unknown, but it is possible that this excess coronary disease mortality among men with ECG abnormalities may have been caused by a combination of increased left ventricular mass in the presence of coronary atherosclerosis and hypokalemia caused by compliance with diuretic therapy. Thus, there is still uncertainty about the value of antihypertensive therapy in reducing the risks of premature coronary artery disease although the risks of stroke seem clearly to be reduced.

Malignant Arteriolar Nephrosclerosis

In 1–8% of patients (male > female and most in their 4th decade) with essential hypertension, an accelerated or malignant phase will occur with diastolic blood pressure in excess of 130 mm Hg and histological changes including (a) proliferative endarteritis (onion skin) of the afferent arterioles and interlobular arteries, (b) necrotizing arteriolitis of the afferent arteriole with fibrinoid necrosis in the wall, and (c) glomerulitis with necrosis similar to that seen in the afferent arteriole. Other diseases associated with hypertension such as primary renal disease, pheochromocytoma, and renovascular disease may lead to malignant nephrosclerosis. Plasma renin and aldosterone levels are elevated and hypokalemic alkalosis may be present (secondary hyperaldosteronism). Microangiopathic hemolytic anemia characterized by fragmented red blood cells has been described. Albuminuria (0.4–12 g/24 hour) is frequently present although creatinine clearance may be normal at the onset of the malignant hypertensive state. Hematuria, both gross and microscopic, as well as red blood cell casts have been described. Mortality is very high (80% of untreated patients die within 1 year) with the majority dying of cardiac or renal failure (prior to dialysis). There is no doubt that lowering the blood pressure is lifesaving with as high as 85% survival at 1 year in treated patients. Renal function may improve sig-

nificantly, but rarely will function return to normal once it is diminished. Progressive deterioration is prevented by prompt and adequate control of the blood pressure. In some patients with malignant hypertension and renal failure severe enough to require dialysis, control of blood pressure has resulted in sufficient improvement in renal function so that dialysis is no longer necessary.

SCLERODERMA

The elderly patient with the diagnosis of scleroderma may present with a picture characterized by a sudden rise in blood pressure, hypertensive retinopathy, and rapid deterioration of renal function. In this disease, as in malignant hypertension, blood pressure must be controlled. There are reports suggesting that renal function may improve when a converting enzyme inhibitor is included in the drug regimen.

RENAL ARTERIAL EMBOLI

Renal arterial occlusion from emboli is not uncommon, with the source usually being the heart. The patient may present with a clinical picture mimicking that of acute pyelonephritis. Fever, flank pain, leukocytosis, hematuria, and renal functional impairment are common. Urine culture, however, is negative. Serum lactic dehydrogenase and serum glutamic oxaloacetic transaminase are elevated in most of these patients and the ECG may show atrial fibrillation. The diagnosis is confirmed by renal scan and angiography. Prognosis is good with long-term anticoagulation. Renal embolization can also occur secondary to intraarterial accumulation of cholesterol containing fragments that break off from aortic atheromatous plaques. These emboli frequently occur after aortic surgery or major vessel angiography in patients with diffuse atherosclerosis. They may also occur spontaneously or be induced by renal transluminal angioplasty. The patient may present with purpura, livido reticularis, gastrointestinal bleeding, and/or renal failure, making it difficult to distinguish from systemic vasculitis; however, fever, joint pain, red cells, and/or red cell casts and proteinuria, which are common features of the vasculitides, are rare with cholesterol embolization.

In elderly patients with obscure or even chronically progressive renal failure, spontaneous cholesterol embolization should be considered, particularly if there is evidence of aortic atherosclerosis (such as an aneurysm).

The definitive diagnosis is made through the

demonstration of cholesterol crystals (actually clefts left after the crystals have been dissolved by the solvents used in preparing the tissue for microscopy) in the small vessels of the kidneys or other clinically involved organs on biopsy. Occasionally, the diagnosis may be confirmed by finding the cholesterol emboli on retinal examination. Renal failure is not always severe or irreversible and some patients develop mild renal insufficiency with subsequent improvement. In others, recovery can occur even after dialysis has been instituted. There is no known treatment for cholesterol embolization.

RENAL CALCULI

The consideration of renal stones is particularly important in the aged because these calculi may be responsible for either acute or chronic renal syndromes, and, if unrecognized, may lead to the loss of one or both kidneys. Many of the constituents of calculi, particularly calcium, are present normally in the urine as supersaturated solutions and are maintained as such by protective colloids. The mechanism by which precipitation in supersaturated solutions is prevented is very delicate. If either the concentration or the pH changes, precipitation may result. At an alkaline pH, phosphates and carbonates are insoluble; acid pH will favor precipitation of uric acid and cystine. Oxalates precipitate easily even in neutral solutions. Uric acid and calcium oxalate stones grow slowly. Cystine and calcium phosphate stones tend to grow rapidly, filling the cavity in which they formed, thereby producing the typical staghorn or dendritic calculi of the renal pelvis. Stasis produced by a stone favors its continued growth because of (a) changes in concentration, (b) deterioration of protective colloids, and (c) infection.

Obstruction of the urinary tract must be corrected or proper drainage established as the risk of infection and sepsis is great. Infection with a urea-splitting organism will increase alkalinity and cause precipitation of phosphates, adding these substances to whatever salts the stone may have originally contained. Urinary tract infection may be the presenting symptom and, on occasion, the only sign of a renal calculus. Triple phosphates practically always mean infection with a urea-splitting organism.

CALCIUM

An individual on a normal American diet will excrete approximately 150 mg of calcium/day. If excretion is between 150 and 250 mg/day, a person is considered to have borderline hypercalcuria; if over 250 mg/day, definite hypercalcuria. The identifica-

tion of calcium as a component of a calculus should give rise to a search for diseases associated with hypercalciuria. Most urologists routinely order at least one determination of the serum calcium, phosphorus, and alkaline phosphatase in patients with calcium renal stones. Although a high serum calcium is the most consistent finding in hyperparathyroidism, this may not always be evident. In addition, each physician must be aware of what constitutes normal and high values for his particular laboratory. The search should not end with the exclusion of hyperparathyroidism. Other hypercalciuric syndromes include thyrotoxicosis, Paget's disease, sarcoidosis, malignancies, hypervitaminosis D, milk-alkali syndrome (Burnett), renal tubular acidosis, berylliosis, and idiopathic hypercalciuria.

Two weeks of immobilization, particularly when due to paralysis or a fracture requiring a large body cast, may produce a urinary calcium excretion in excess of 500 mg/day and thereby lead to calcium stone formation. In the aged, this reaction to immobilization is even further exaggerated. Chronic diarrhea favors the formation of calcium stones without either hypercalcemia or hypercalciuria. In these instances, increased urine concentration of calcium with increase in oxalate excretion (due to increased gastrointestinal absorption) as the result of dehydration is probably the decisive factor.

Idiopathic hypercalciuria with stone formation can be treated with a number of regimens. The most important treatment is a high fluid intake during the waking hours (2–3 liters/day). Thiazides (with modest salt restriction) have proven to be an effective treatment. Potential side effects include hypercalcemia, hyperglycemia, hyperuricemia, and hypokalemia. If, in spite of this regimen, hypercalciuria persists, the combined use of thiazide and amiloride may be therapeutically advantageous because their hypocalciuric effects are additive. In addition, the possibility of hypokalemia due to the thiazide is prevented by amiloride.

Chronic bowel disease such as ulcerative colitis or regional ileitis, especially with ileostomy, colostomy, or intestinal bypass surgery, is associated with increased incidence of calcium oxalate and uric acid stones. The hyperoxaluria present in the former can be treated with cholestyramine.

URIC ACID

Uric acid stones form when the urinary concentration of undissociated uric acid exceeds its solubility limit. This limit is pH dependent, i.e., the lower the pH, the lower the solubility of uric acid. Thus, low urine pH (<5.5) is characteristically found in uric acid stone formers. Among the causes of low urinary pH are malabsorptive states (as described above) and excessive purine intake (meat products). Therapy in such patients should be directed at increasing the urinary pH by providing alkali, preferably in the form of potassium citrate, at a dosage of 30 to 80 mEq per day in three to four divided doses. Overly aggressive urinary alkalinization should be avoided in order to prevent the formation of calcium stones. Hyperuricosuria (uric acid excretion > 1000 mg per day) may, in itself, constitute a risk for the development of calcium oxalate stones. The treatment of hyperuricosuric calcium oxalate stones is allopurinol in addition to a thiazide, as noted above.

ACUTE RENAL FAILURE

The inability of the kidney to excrete the normal load of metabolites produced within the body is designated as renal failure, which may be acute or chronic. The acute forms usually present as oliguria, i.e., a daily output less than 400 ml. Thus, to diagnose acute renal failure as rapidly as possible, any output of less than 20 ml/hour must be immediately investigated.

Acute renal failure may be classified into three broad categories: prerenal, renal, and postrenal. Clinically, the presentation may be identical, but the outcome quite different. The renal failure in the prerenal and postrenal varieties improves rapidly after the correction of the underlying problem (ischemia and obstruction of the urinary tract, respectively), whereas in intrinsic renal failure, improvement does not necessarily take place when the precipitating event is removed. The response will depend upon the nature of the renal lesion, its severity, the age of the patient, and other well- and not well-defined parameters.

OBSTRUCTIVE UROPATHY OR POSTRENAL FAILURE

Postrenal failure may present with oliguria or anuria. Early in the course of postrenal failure, renal ischemia may occur leading to a blood picture indistinguishable from prerenal azotemia (see below). The location of the obstruction can be at the urethral terminous (male or female) or at any point proximal.

Bladder neck obstruction due to prostatic disease, benign or malignant, is the most common cause of obstructive uropathy in the male. Renal failure may be the presenting manifestation; however, upon questioning, there is usually a history of frequency, nocturia, urgency, and/or dysuria. The bladder may not necessarily be enlarged, and in the case of prostatic carcinoma the obstruction may actually be at the ureteral orifices secondary to tumor infiltration. In the female patient, pelvic malignancies are the most common cause of postrenal failure (usually a late occurrence). Other causes of ureteral obstruction include carcinoma of the bladder, bilateral renal calculi, retroperitoneal fibrosis, and metastatic carcinoma. Catheterization of the bladder should be the first step in the workup of oliguria. This should be followed by an x-ray of the abdomen, which may show calcifications, discrepancy in kidney size (particularly enlargement of one kidney although enlargement of both kidneys favors the diagnosis of obstruction at the level of the bladder or distal), or even a distended bladder. This should be followed by an ultrasound study, which has become the definitive noninvasive test for obstructive uropathy. False-negative and false-positive ultrasonography are rare, so that if obstruction is seen, cystoscopy with retrograde pyelography should be undertaken.

In bilateral obstructive disease or when there is one kidney obstructed and one nonfunctioning, rapid decompression is potentially dangerous, particularly in the aged. There is usually a substantial diuresis accompanied by massive electrolyte losses that may result in sudden deterioration of renal function. This often occurs after an initial improvement in renal function. Accurate replacement of fluid and electrolyte losses is mandatory.

PRERENAL AZOTEMIA

Prerenal azotemia is the most common form of acute renal failure in the elderly. It usually results from a decreased circulating blood volume, e.g., dehydration associated with vomiting or diarrhea, hemorrhage, burns, or a decrease in blood pressure or cardiac output. In patients with congestive heart failure, overzealous use of diuretics not infrequently leads to dehydration and prerenal azotemia.

In order to maintain the circulation and tissue perfusion, a variety of events takes place including an increase in vasoactive hormones, antidiuretic hormone, and aldosterone leading to vasoconstriction and salt and water retention. At the glomerular level, the vasoconstrictive effects of angiotensin II and the autonomic nervous system are opposed by increased renal production of vasodilator prostaglandins so that a balance between these two vasoactive forces serves to maintain renal blood flow and glomerular filtration rate at their new steady state. The diagnosis of prerenal azotemia is usually established in the presence of

1. A history or presence of fluid and electrolyte losses and/or signs of volume contraction, hypotension, or congestive heart failure;
2. Oliguria, i.e., urinary output less than 20 ml/hour;
3. Markedly diminished urinary sodium concentration— less than 10 mEq/liter. Aged individuals, despite the tendency to urinary sodium losses may still respond to renal ischemia by making urine with a low sodium concentration. The fractional excretion of sodium (the relationship of sodium excretion to GFR) will be less than 1%.
4. Increased concentration of urine-specific gravity above 1.020 as the result of antidiuretic hormone effect. As in the case of urinary sodium, there is a limited capacity to concentrate the urine in the elderly. Nevertheless, under the stress of ischemia, a concentrated urine may be formed.
5. BUN elevation with normal or relatively smaller increase in serum creatinine level.

In general, the diagnosis of prerenal azotemia is more difficult in the elderly, since the diagnosis is somewhat dependent upon the urinary findings, which may be modified by the underlying renal functional defects of the elderly as described above. Furthermore, if the GFR is already substantially reduced and/or protein intake limited the BUN, creatinine ratio may remain close to normal (10–15:1) mimicking intrinsic renal disease (or obstructive uropathy).

Prerenal failure, if not rapidly treated, may develop imperceptibly into acute tubular necrosis. This is more frequent in the elderly, in whose case the incidence is twice as high as in younger patients. In most cases, however, restoration of blood pressure, blood volume, or cardiac output will quickly establish urine flow again. Careful monitoring of fluid volume status either clinically or by the central venous pressure or pulmonary artery and wedge pressures are mandatory to avoid excessive fluid replacement and pulmonary edema.

ACUTE TUBULAR NECROSIS

This form of acute renal failure differs from the first two discussed in that there is no way that the physician can reverse the lesion once it occurs. The damage to the kidney, no matter what the cause, must heal itself if possible. The hallmark of this syndrome is a marked decrease in GFR with a proportionately smaller decrease in renal blood flow.

In contrast to prerenal azotemia in which tubular functions are operating normally, i.e., increased urinary concentration and decreased fractional excretion of sodium, acute tubular necrosis (ATN) by definition indicates the presence of tubular damage. This damage may be manifested by the presence of dirty brown casts, a fractional excretion of sodium greater than 1% (and frequently greater than 3%), and loss of urinary concentration (specific gravity of 1.010). However, in some patients with established ATN (perhaps as high as 20%), the above parameters may incorrectly indicate prerenal failure.

The exact pathogenesis of ATN is not clear. Some of the theories are:

1. Renal blood flow and glomerular filtration rate are decreased because of an increase in renal vascular resistance (vasoconstriction);
2. An alteration in glomerular capillary permeability may be the cause of the decrease in filtration rate;
3. Renal tubules may be obstructed by debris or cell swelling leading to a decrease in filtration rate and renal blood flow;
4. Back diffusion of filtrate through damaged tubules may be responsible for the renal failure.

ETIOLOGY OF ATN

The major causes of ATN are shown below. Renal ischemia is the most common cause of ATN, usually in a surgical and/or trauma setting. Nephrotoxins are another major cause of ATN, especially industrial poisons such as mercury, arsenic, and other metals. Recently medicinal products such as drugs (especially antibiotics) and radiocontrast agents are more frequently responsible.

1. Ischemic
   a. Skin, gastrointestinal, renal volume loss
   b. Hemorrhage (surgery, trauma)
   c. Sepsis
2. Nephrotoxic
   a. Antibiotics—such as aminoglycosides, cephalosporins, tetracyclines, amphotericin B
   b. Metals—including mercury, arsenic, platinum, bismuth
   c. Organic solvents such as carbon tetrachloride
   d. Radiocontrast agents (iodine containing)
   e. Other agents such as acetaminophen
3. Multiple contributory events—In up to 10% of patients with ATN more than one precipitating factor will be identified at the time of diagnosis, i.e., sepsis, nephrotoxins, and stones.

The course of ATN generally may be divided into three phases, which are detailed below.

Oliguric or Anuric Phase

This may last anywhere from 1 day to several weeks. During this phase, the BUN will rise 10–40 mg/dl and the creatinine 1–3 mg/dl/day, depending upon the degree of catabolism and protein intake. Other findings include elevated serum potassium (especially in oliguric and acidotic patients), elevated phosphorus and magnesium, depressed total CO_2, low pH and calcium. It should be noted that a nonoliguric form of renal failure occurs in 19–30% of elderly patients with ATN, particularly when related to aminoglycoside nephrotoxicity and following trauma and surgery.

Potassium Control. Potassium control is important to patient survival. The elevated serum potassium is the result of catabolism (release of potassium from cell breakdown), acidosis (with shift of hydrogen into and potassium out of the cell), and lack of excretion (in oliguria or anuria). If there is significant urine output, potassium control becomes simpler. The serum potassium should be monitored daily and when an elevation is found, an ECG should be performed to evaluate cardiotoxicity. Calcium infusions will reverse the cardiac manifestations of hyperkalemia immediately but only transiently. Infusions of sodium bicarbonate (44–88 mEq) when feasible (in the absence of congestive heart failure) with careful attention to serum calcium and the possibility of tetany are the best means of combating hyperkalemia. Ten percent glucose solution, with 10 units of regular insulin per 250 ml of solution is also a useful but transient adjunct. Sodium-potassium exchange resins (Kayexalate) should be given by mouth and/or by rectal enema with the understanding that significant amounts of sodium (two molecules of sodium enter the body for every molecule of potassium removed) may be absorbed and that exchange occurs slowly. If a patient with hyperkalemia is in congestive heart failure (or fluid overload) and has a significant acidosis, dialysis (either hemo or peritoneal) should be instituted and all three complications corrected.

Water Replacement. Water replacement should be extremely conservative. Overhydration, especially in the aged, has been a frequent cause of rapid deterioration, adding the problems of congestive heart failure and cerebral edema to those of uremia. The catabolism of fat, carbohydrate, and protein so frequently seen in ATN produce increased amounts of endogenous water of metabolism so that net insensible loss of water is lower in these patients.

The weight of the patient is most helpful in judging fluid replacement. While anuric, the patient should lose 0.3–0.4 kg/day. This generally will allow for the administration of 400 ml fluid/day in addition to what is required to cover urine loss, diarrhea, vomitus, or nasogastric drainage. The fluid whenever possible should be given by mouth and made of any one of the widely available calorie-containing feeding preparations. Intravenous solutions should supply at least 800 calories/day, which minimize protein catabolism. More complete nutrition, including the use of essential amino acids, has been recommended in an attempt to prevent catabolism of protein and to bring about positive nitrogen balance. These substances can be administered orally, through a nasogastric tube, or intravenously, through a central venous line. Volume, as discussed above, is the limiting factor in nutritional maintenance whether oral, enteral, or parenteral. Dialysis with fluid removal will allow for more complete nutritional care. All necessary medications, particularly digitalis and antibiotics, should be given at appropriately reduced dosages. Sedation should be used with great caution. Anemia, when present, is refractory to all hematinics. Nevertheless, transfusions should be given only to correct depressed blood volume or in the face of coronary insufficiency. Administered blood should be fresh to avoid potassium intoxication.

Early Diuretic Phase

As kidney function improves, urine output increases, sometimes enormously, with the urine concentration fixed at isotonicity. Salt and potassium loss may be excessive in this stage (glomerular function often returns before tubular function) and careful measurement of urine sodium and potassium is necessary in order to calculate replacement. After a period varying from days to weeks, urine output decreases but normal urine concentration may not return for many months or even years.

Convalescent Phase

The patient gradually returns to a normal state during which a chronic low grade azotemia may persist. High risk patients (postoperative or post-trauma) have a mortality rate of 60–65% or more, which has not been changed appreciably by dialysis.

The exact role of dialysis in altering the course of acute renal failure is not known. Dialysis is important in controlling fluid, potassium, and acid-base balance and should certainly be used in those patients who are oliguric and hypercatabolic. However, the use of dialysis therapy is not without danger. Hemodialysis requires access to the vascular system (via peripheral and/or central veins and/or an artery) and either systemic or regional heparinization while peritoneal dialysis involves entering the peritoneal cavity, which may result in trauma to the abdominal organs, bleeding, and/or infection. In addition, hemodialysis is frequently associated with hypotension (in as many as 25% of treatments), which may decrease renal perfusion, theoretically resulting in additional renal damage and prolongation of the course of ATN.

There is no formula for predicting when dialytic therapy should be instituted (with the exception of intractable hyperkalemia, acidosis, and volume overload). Those patients with oliguria and a hypercatabolic state should be treated with early and aggressive dialytic therapy (daily, if needed) while those who are less catabolic may (with close observation) be treated more conservatively.

Occasionally, the cause of declining renal function cannot be readily ascertained, or the course of acute renal failure is atypical. Under these circumstances, additional information is necessary. For example, in the patient with severe atherosclerosis disease and acute renal failure, in which case renovascular occlusion is a strong possibility, renal angiography should be undertaken. In patients with atypical clinical features such as gradual onset of acute renal failure, significant hypertension, marked proteinuria, hematuria, or underlying systemic disease, a renal biopsy may be necessary to make a definitive diagnosis of glomerulonephritis. In an analysis of 22 such elderly patients reported recently, ATN or interstitial nephritis was diagnosed in 41% (9 patients). The remaining 59% (13 patients) had a glomerular disease with acute crescentic glomerulonephritis accounting for 9 cases and various other glomerulonephritides for the other 4.

CHRONIC RENAL FAILURE

Chronic renal failure results from damage to both kidneys from a wide variety of causes. It usually occurs gradually with or without persistence of the inciting disease. Elderly patients, however, are particularly prone to developing irreversible (chronic) renal failure, such as occurs in multiple myeloma or irreversible ATN or rapidly progressive (extracapillary or crescentic) glomerulonephritis. Up to 90% or more of kidney function may be lost without any significant morbidity. In fact, the disease is usually silent for many years. When present, no matter the cause, the physician's primary role is to prevent worsening of the condition secondary to hypertension, infection, obstructive uropathy, congestive heart failure, or dehydration. The patient must be seen frequently and made aware of his condition. Occasionally, the patients are profound salt-losers and must be prevented from becoming dehydrated by administering sodium, particularly in the form of bicarbonate, if there is accompanying acidosis. Phosphorus retention can be combated with proper diet and phosphate binders (aluminum-containing antacids).

Calcium carbonate may also be used to lower the serum phosphorous (in addition to treating hypocalcemia), but care must be taken not to raise the serum calcium at a time when the phosphorus is still high. Therefore, it may be prudent to use aluminum hydroxide at first and once the serum phosphorus decreases or normalizes, calcium carbonate may be substituted for the aluminum hydroxide. Use of the latter should be minimized because it has been shown that aluminum can be absorbed from the gastrointestinal tract and cause toxicity (aluminum-induced osteomalacia and brain disease).

Acidosis is best controlled with sodium bicarbonate tablets that contain 7 mEq sodium and bicarbonate/10 grains sodium bicarbonate. The goal is to keep the plasma bicarbonate above 18–20 mEq/liter. When the GFR falls below a critical level, the rate of loss of renal function becomes constant even when hypertension, infection, calcium metabolism, and fluid and electrolyte balance are carefully controlled. Recently, a hypothesis has been proposed to explain this inexorable deterioration in function. The theory (based in part on animal experiments) proposes that as nephrons are lost, those remaining are subjected to excessive intraglomerular pressure and flows, i.e., glomerular hypertension, which results in their destruction leading to deterioration in renal function. The degree of glomerular hypertension appears for a large part to be directly mediated by protein intake. Based upon these theories clinical trials have been instituted utilizing a low protein diet, sometimes supplemented with essential amino acids or their keto analogues. In addition to its effect on glomerular hemodynamics, this diet, which is also low in phosphorus, may provide additional benefits by preventing the deposition of calcium, phosphate, and oxalate crystals in the kidney tissue. Some of the early results are promising. In patients with nephrosclerosis, for example, the rate of decline in renal function has been decreased, thus postponing the need for dialysis, albeit for a limited time. The diet most often utilized consists of: protein, 0.6 g/kg/day; phosphorus, 700 mg/day; calories, 40/kg/day; and a calcium supplement, 1000–1500 mg/day. The ideal time to institute this rather restrictive diet is not known, but it should probably be relatively early in the course of chronic renal failure, when the serum creatinine is approximately 2 mg/dl.

The use of diet therapy in chronic renal failure is still very new and important questions remain unanswered: (a) What is the long-term effect of this diet on the patient's nutritional state? (b) How acceptable will it be to the population of patients with chronic renal failure? (c) How does one handle a patient with renal failure and nephrotic syndrome, particularly with very large amounts of urinary protein loss? Thus, until the results of ongoing studies in the United States and elsewhere are made available, the dietary treatment of chronic renal failure should be approached with some caution.

Once the patient requires chronic dialysis therapy, the recommended diet should include more liberal protein intake, but strict sodium, potassium, and phosphorus restriction, as outlined below.

Hypertension, which is a common finding in patients with chronic renal failure (70% or more in the elderly), should be treated aggressively. In theory the converting enzyme inhibitors (and possibly the calcium channel blockers) may have an additional, as yet unproven, beneficial effect on renal function by decreasing intraglomerular pressure. Trials utilizing these agents in chronic renal failure patients both with and without hypertension are now in progress. The point at which chronic renal failure can no longer be treated by conservative means is not clear. Some physicians believe that when creatinine clearance drops below 8–10 ml/min, dialysis must be instituted. However, most patients are not dialyzed until the creatinine clearance is less than 5 ml/min. If uremic complications such as neuropathy, gastrointestinal bleeding, bone disease, pericarditis, or seizures intervene, then dialysis has been postponed too long. These complications are reversible, however, once adequate dialysis is instituted.

In the elderly, uremic symptoms may being at a higher creatinine clearance than in younger patients so that dialysis is often instituted with a creatinine clearance of 10 ml/min, or even slightly greater. If heart failure is present in addition to severe renal insufficiency, it may be useful to start dialysis before uremic symptoms occur. Once the patient requires chronic hemodialysis therapy, the recommended diet should include: protein, 1–1.5 g/kg/day; calories, 30–40 kg/day; sodium, 2 g; potassium, 2 g; and phosphorus, 1500 mg/day.

Elderly patients constitute the largest group of new patients entering the end-stage renal disease program. Presently, all three major treatment options, transplantation, hemodialysis, and continuous ambulatory peritoneal dialysis (CAPD), are available to the elderly. The choice of treatment modality should be made on an individual basis. The 1-year survival of elderly patients receiving a cadaver allograft is not much different from those on dialysis; however, the 3-year survival for the elderly transplant recipient receiving a cadaver graft is higher than dialysis. Live related donor recipients fare better at both 1 and 3 years. In general, more stringent selection criteria are used for the elderly undergoing renal transplantation so that survival rates in this select subpopulation are difficult to compare to overall survival rates in transplantation. In Table 21.2, the percentage survival of the elderly patient on dialysis at 1, 3, and 5 years is compared to the survival rate for all ages on hemodialysis.

CAPD is a relatively new treatment modality. So far, the statistics indicate that patients over 65 years of age appear to have a survival rate similar to that of younger adults.

The most common cause of death in elderly patients on dialysis is the same as for younger adults, namely, cardiovascular disease. Access problems, infections, and bleeding are the most common cause of hospitalization, similar to that of younger patients.

SUGGESTED READINGS

1. Bennett WM, Aronoff GR, Morrison G, et al: Drug prescribing in renal failure: Dosing guidelines for adults. *Am J Kid Dis* 3:155–193, 1983.
2. Brenner BM, Lazarus JM: *Acute Renal Failure*, ed 1. Philadelphia, WB Saunders, 1983.

Table 21.2
Survival of Patients Treated with Hemodialysis

Age in Years	No. of Patients	1 Year	3 Years	5 Years
All ages (overall)	74,547	81	57	44
65–74	14,273	74	45	30
75+	4,491	64	33	22

3. Brenner BM, Rector FC Jr: *The Kidney,* ed 4. Philadelphia, WB Saunders, 1986.
4. Brown WW, Davis BB, Spry LA, et al: Aging and the kidney. *Arch Intern Med* 146:1790–1796, 1986.
5. Churg J, Sobin LH: *Renal Disease. Classification and Atlas of Glomerular Diseases.* Tokyo, Igaku-Shoin, ed 1. 1982.
6. Drucker W, Parsons FM, Maher J: *Replacement of Renal Function by Dialysis,* ed 2. The Hague, Martinus Nijhof, 1983.
7. Frochet A, Fillet H: Renal disease in the geriatric patient. *J Am Geriatr Soc* 33:28, 1985.
8. Kokko JP, Tannen RL: *Fluids and Electrolytes,* ed 1. Philadelphia, WB Saunders, 1986.
9. Moorthy AV, Zimmerman SW: Renal disease in the elderly: Clinicopathologic analysis of renal disease in 15 elderly patients. *Clin Nephrol* 14:223–229, 1980.

CHAPTER 22

Application of Fluid and Electrolyte Balance Principles to the Older Patient

ROBERT D. LINDEMAN

The ability to maintain, within narrow limits, fluid volumes and electrolyte concentrations in the various body compartments is necessary for survival. Older persons retain a remarkable capacity to maintain the chemical and physical composition of the body fluids within a narrow normal range under basal conditions. However, they do require a longer period of time to return abnormal blood levels to the normal range when deficits or excesses are imposed by disease or environmental stresses.

The capacity of any individual to return fluid and electrolyte composition to the normal range diminishes proportionately with a decrease in renal function. Since the average 80-year-old person has approximately one-half the renal function (glomerular filtration rate) of that of the normal 30-year-old person, it takes him considerably longer to correct any induced fluid or electrolyte abnormality.

EFFECTS OF AGE ON BODY FLUIDS AND SERUM ELECTROLYTES

TOTAL BODY WATER, EXTRACELLULAR FLUID AND INTRACELLULAR FLUID

The total body water content diminishes significantly with age (25). Extracellular fluid volume, however, tends to remain remarkably constant with age and, therefore, constitutes a larger percentage of total body water in the older person. The reduction in total body water then is a reflection of decreased intracellular water presumably due to tissue loss with age. Further confirmation of an age-related decrease in lean protoplasmic mass is obtained if one studies total body potassium or exchangeable potassium in young versus old subjects.

BLOOD, PLASMA, AND RED CELL VOLUMES; PLASMA PROTEINS

Although the range of individual variation in plasma, blood, and red-cell volume is large, it appears that these values remain essentially unchanged with age (25). The total plasma proteins, which play an important role in regulating the osmotic pressure of the blood and in maintaining blood volume, also remain unaltered with age (25, 5). Serum albumin levels, however, do appear to decrease slightly with age while serum globulin levels tend to increase.

SERUM ELECTROLYTE CONCENTRATIONS

Sodium, potassium, chloride, and bicarbonate levels are not significantly altered with age under basal conditions (5, 25). Blood pH, bicarbonate, and PCO_2 values also fail to show significant changes with age (26). When challenged with an acid load, however, older persons do take longer to return serum bicarbonate levels to basal levels. The interval necessary to correct an imposed acidosis is inversely proportionate to the level of residual renal function (1).

DISTURBANCES IN SODIUM AND WATER BALANCE

The serum sodium concentration alone fails to reflect total body sodium; the clinical assessment of extracellular fluid volume (ECFV) is equally important and generally much more difficult. Total body sodium then is approximately the product of the serum sodium concentration and ECFV. The various disturbances in salt and water balance can be visualized in Figure 22.1.

DEHYDRATION

Dehydration by definition is a decrease in body water. ECFV depletion can result from excessive water loss (without salt) with inadequate replacement (water depletion or simple dehydration); more commonly it results from a loss of sodium with osmotically obligated water (primary salt depletion). Serum sodium concentration and osmolality are increased in water depletion and tend to be decreased in sodium depletion (Table 22.1).

Simple Dehydration

The minimum intake of water necessary to prevent dehydration is that amount necessary to replace losses through the lung, skin, gastrointestinal tract, and kidneys, minus water generated by metabolism. Older persons lose some of their ability to concentrate their urine (18) so they may become dehydrated more easily when faced with inadequate water intake.

In normal persons with free access to water, the thirst mechanism ensures that the individual maintains an adequate intake of fluids. Simple dehydration may result from inadequate intake of fluids in unconscious or neglected persons with nervous system or mental diseases when they become unable to ingest fluids or refuse them, or in persons with obstructive lesions of the upper gastrointestinal tract.

Table 22.1
Dehydration Due to Primary Loss of Sodium versus Water[a]

	Salt Depletion	Water Depletion
Clinical Features		
Thirst	Not remarkable	Marked
Skin turgor	Decreased	Normal
Pulse	Rapid	Normal
Blood pressure	Low	Normal
Laboratory Findings		
Urine volume	Not remarkable	300–500 ml/day
Urine concentration	Not remarkable	Maximal
Serum proteins	Increased	Normal
Hematocrit	Increased	Normal
BUN	Increased	Normal
Serum sodium	Reduced	Elevated
Treatment	Salt	Water

[a]With weight loss of 3–5% of body weight in both conditions assumed.

SALT and WATER DISTURBANCES

SERUM SODIUM CONCENTRATION			
LOW	DEHYDRATION (Primary Salt Loss) Na⁺ Loss > H₂O Loss	PSEUDOHYPONATREMIA Hyperglycemia Hyperlipemia Hyperproteinemia	DILUTIONAL HYPONATREMIA Congestive Heart Failure Cirrhosis Nephrotic Syndrome INAPPROPRIATE A D H WATER INTOXICATION H₂O Retention > Na⁺ Retention
NORMAL	DEHYDRATION Na⁺ Loss = H₂O Loss	NORMAL	UNCOMPLICATED EDEMA H₂O Retention = Na⁺ Retention
HIGH	DEHYDRATION (Primary Water Loss) H₂O Loss > Na⁺ Loss	HYPERALDOSTERONISM HYPERCORTISONISM	STEROID EXCESS SALT INTOXICATION Na⁺ Retention > H₂O Retention
	LOW	NORMAL	HIGH
	EXTRACELLULAR FLUID VOLUME		

Figure 22.1. Abnormalities in salt and water balance. Total body sodium is the product of serum sodium concentration times extracellular fluid volume.

An occasional patient with neurologic disease may have an impaired thirst mechanism that makes him susceptible to dehydration, e.g., surgical intervention in patients with aneurysms of the circle of Willis may result in damage to the thirst center. Such individuals, unless required to ingest a measured quantity of fluids daily, are prone to develop progressive dehydration and hypernatremia. Stroke patients fed high protein formula diets by nasogastric feeding tubes without adequate water also may develop simple dehydration. The increased solute load increases losses of fluid in the feces and urine.

Simple dehydration also may result from excessive loss of water from the kidneys. Renal losses are most marked in patients with diabetes insipidus, but simple loss of concentrating ability due to such entities as hypercalcemia, hypokalemia, or advanced renal disease also may contribute to the development of dehydration. Patients with increased urinary solute, most notably individuals with uncontrolled diabetes melitus, lose water in excess of sodium (nonketotic hyperosmolar coma). Pituitary diabetes insipidus in the older age groups is most often due to an intracranial neoplasm, either primary or metastatic; but traumatic, postoperative, infectious, granulomatous, and vascular origins must be considered. Idiopathic diabetes insipidus would have become manifest at an earlier age. Nephrogenic diabetes insipidus is an uncommon disease in the older age groups, but may occur as an acquired lesion due to amyloidosis, potassium deficiency, or interstitial disease.

Thirst is the earliest symptom of water loss. In patients with impaired thirst, dessication may be manifested as fever, flushing, loss of sweating, and dryness of the tongue and mucous membranes. A tachycardia develops and personality changes occur. With severe dehydration, hallucinations, delirium, manic behavior, convulsions, and coma may develop. It should be noted that older patients often are less perceptive of mild states of dehydration and fail to appreciate thirst for a variety of reasons, one of which may be vascular disease in the area of the thirst center.

Treatment is aimed at replacing water orally or parenterally with 5% dextrose and water. Preventive precautions need to be considered in susceptible persons.

Primary Salt Depletion

Patients with primary salt depletion, in contrast, maintain normal serum sodium concentrations and osmolalities until volume depletion becomes sufficient to stimulate antidiuretic hormone (ADH) release. At this time, water is retained and hyponatremia begins to occur. Hyponatremia with decreased ECFV will be discussed in more detail in a subsequent section.

OVERHYDRATION

The excessive retention of body fluids may result from primary salt retention with its osmotically obligated water (simple edema), or from retention of water in excess of salt (water intoxication, dilutional hyponatremia, or syndrome of inappropriate ADH [SIADH]). Dilutional hyponatremia, water intoxication, and the SIADH are discussed under the section of hyponatremia with expanded ECFV. Salt retained with osmotically obligated water leads to the formation of edema with maintenance of normal serum sodium concentrations and osmolalities. This occurs with increasing frequency with age primarily as a result of congestive heart failure but, in some instances, due to cirrhosis, nephrotic syndrome, or renal insufficiency. Treatment is aimed at the underlying disease, at reducing salt intake, and increasing urinary salt excretion with diuretic therapy.

The thiazide diuretics working in the distal diluting site of the nephron are most frequently used to initiate therapy for simple edema. Although numerous thiazide diuretics are available, the only advantage of one over the others appears to be the duration of effect. Since the potassium-losing effects of the various thiazide (and loop) diuretics are dependent on the increase in sodium load delivered to the distal sodium-potassium exchange site, there appears to be no advantage of one over the other in preventing potassium loss while accomplishing a desired natriuresis. Hydrochlorothiazide is probably the most frequently used thiazide and the 50-mg tablets can be given once or twice daily. Additional doses only have minimal efficacy in enhancing the diuresis.

If a stronger diuretic is needed, one should then utilize a loop diuretic, such as furosemide. One can start with 40 mg, orally or intravenously, and progressively increase the dose up to as much as 2 g daily to achieve a desired diuresis.

The potassium-sparing diuretics, spironolactone and triamterene (working in the distal sodium-potassium exchange site), are used primarily in combination with the above diuretics to decrease potassium loss in the urine.

HYPONATREMIA

A low serum sodium may result from: (a) a loss of sodium in excess of osmotically obligated water (primary salt depletion); (b) a retention of water in excess of sodium (water intoxication, dilutional hyponatremia, SIADH); or (c) a combination of both. It also may result from displacement of plasma water with large molecular weight solute (lipids, proteins) or addition to the ECFV of an uncharged solute (glucose) that draws water from the intracellular spaces into the extracellular spaces thereby diluting the sodium present.

In considering the circumstances in which hyponatremia may be encountered in elderly persons, one can divide them for purposes of this discussion into three general categories, specifically (a) with extracellular volume depletion, (b) with normal extracellular volume, and (c) with ECFV expansion, as shown in Table 22.2. Such a division may be difficult to make clinically.

HYPONATREMIA WITH CONTRACTED ECFV (PRIMARY SALT DEPLETION)

A decrease in intravascular volume is a more potent stimulus to ADH release than an increase in plasma tonicity. Thus, in the presence of hypovolemia, ADH release may persist or increase as hypoosmolality and hyponatremia develop. In patients with evidence of volume depletion clinically (weight loss, thirst, orthostatic hypotension, decreased skin turgor and sweating), the retention of water due to persistent secretion of ADH leads to hyponatremia. If the urinary sodium concentration is less than 10 mEq/liter, one can suspect decreased salt intake, excessive sweating, and/or gastrointestinal salt losses. If the urinary sodium excretion is greater than 10 mEq/liter, inappropriate renal losses of sodium and water should be suspect as the cause of the hypovolemia. The excessive use of diuretics, adrenal or pituitary insufficiency, or intrinsic renal disease (salt-losing nephritis, advanced renal failure, or renal tubular acidosis) need to be considered as possible etiologies. In severe vomiting with metabolic alkalosis and bicarbonate wasting, urinary sodium concentrations may be elevated despite hypovolemia and hyponatremia. Treatment would be with isotonic or hypertonic saline. If it is unclear whether one is dealing with primary salt depletion (contracted ECFV), a dilutional hyponatremia, or a SIADH (expanded ECFV), and this differential can be difficult as shown in Table 22.3, it is wise to place a central venous pressure (CVP) catheter to monitor right heart pressures. One can then give hypertonic or normal saline until the CVP climbs above 8 cm H_2O. If the patient has left heart failure, as many older patients do, a Swan-Ganz catheter would provide added safety. If one calculates the replacement needs on the basis of replacing only extracellular vol-

Table 22.2
Hyponatremic Syndromes

I. Hyponatremia with contracted ECFV[a]
  A. Urinary sodium <10 mEq/liter
    1. Inadequate intake
    2. Excessive sweating
    3. Excess gastrointestinal loss
      a. Diarrhea
      b. Fistulous tracts (bowel, biliary)
  B. Urinary sodium >10 mEq/liter
    1. Severe metabolic alkalosis due to vomiting (bicarbonaturia)
    2. Excessive urinary losses
      a. Adrenal insufficiency (Addison's hypoaldosteronism)
      b. Renal salt wasting (RTA, interstitial nephritis, end stage renal disease)
      c. Diuretic-induced
II. Hyponatremia with normal ECFV
  A. Displacement syndromes
    1. Hyperglycemia
    2. Hyperlipemia
    3. Hyperglobulinemia
III. Hyponatremia with expanded ECFV
  A. Dilutional hyponatremia (low solute excretion)
    1. Congestive heart failure
    2. Cirrhosis
    3. Nephrotic syndrome
    4. Renal insufficiency
  B. SIADH
    1. Malignancies (lung, pancreas)
    2. Pulmonary diseases, including positive pressure breathing
    3. Cerebral conditions (trauma, infection, tumor, CVA)
    4. Drugs (sulfonylureas, thiazides, antitumor agents)
    5. Myxedema
    6. Porphyria
    7. Idiopathic
  C. Water intoxication

[a]The abbreviation used is ECFV, extracellular fluid volume.

ume depletion, i.e., 140 mEq/liter, minus the observed serum sodium concentration times 20% of body weight (ECFV), this will be inadequate for two reasons. First, there will be some increase in ECFV, i.e., volume repletion with a volume of fluid having a sodium concentration of 140 mEq/liter; second, as extracellular osmolality increases, water will move from inside the cell into the ECFV rediluting the sodium. It is therefore best to give sodium and water and monitor serum sodium concentrations and CVP at frequent intervals until correction is achieved. If overhydration should occur with pulmonary edema, furosemide can be given as described later.

Table 22.3
Differential Diagnosis Between Salt Depletion and Inappropriate ADH Syndrome

	Salt Depletion	Inappropriate ADH Syndrome
Laboratory finding		
Serum sodium	Low	Low
Serum osmolality	Low	Low
Urine sodium	Variable	High
Urine osmolality	High	High
Skin turgor	Decreased	Normal
Pulse	Rapid	Normal
Blood pressure	Low	Normal
Serum proteins	Increased	Normal
Hematocrit	Increased	Normal
BUN	Increased	Decreased
Treatment	Salt	Water restriction

HYPONATREMIA WITH NORMAL EXTRACELLULAR FLUID VOLUME (PSEUDOHYPONATREMIA)

A decrease in serum sodium concentration does not always indicate a decrease in osmolality of body fluids. In cases of hyperglycemia, the main cause of the hyponatremia is the glucose-related increase in osmolality in the extracellular fluid followed by a movement of water from the intracellular to extracellular fluid compartments and a subsequent loss of excessive extracellular fluid and electrolytes. The serum sodium concentration in hyperlipemia and hyperproteinemia is diminished because of the volume occupied by the lipids or proteins. If the lipids or proteins are removed from the plasma, the sodium concentration in the remaining plasma water is found to be normal. No treatment is needed for these entities.

HYPONATREMIA WITH EXPANDED EXTRACELLULAR FLUID VOLUME

The three entities responsible for hyponatremia with expanded ECFV are: (a) dilutional hyponatremia, (b) SIADH, and (c) water intoxication, as shown in Table 22.2.

Dilutional Hyponatremia

Impairment in water excretion occurs commonly in situations where urinary salt excretion also is severely impaired. Patients with advanced cardiac, hepatic, and renal disease with gross edema are severely limited in their ability to eliminate both salt and water in the urine. The universal practice of sharply restricting salt intake but placing no limitations on fluid intake in edematous patients is probably appropriate in most patients. However, once hyponatremia begins to develop, it also may be necessary to restrict water intake.

Although the total blood volume is increased in most patients with cardiac, hepatic, and renal failure, the blood volume in the arterial vascular system tends to be decreased. In patients with congestive heart failure, the decrease in cardiac output is interpreted by baroreceptors in the arterial system as a decreased effective blood volume stimulating salt and water retention. With hepatic cirrhosis, the decrease in total peripheral resistance, the portal obstruction and hypertension leading to ascites with impingement of blood return through the inferior vena cava, and hypoalbuminemia contribute to a decreased effective blood volume in the arterial system. In the nephrotic syndrome, hypoalbuminemia is the major cause of the hypovolemia these patients develop. In all these entities, concurrent decreases in glomerular filtration rate and increased tubular reabsorption in the proximal tubule limit water excretion by decreasing delivery of tubular fluid and salt to the distal diluting segment of the nephron. If essentially no salt and water reaches the distal nephron, the patient is unable to dilute his urine below isotonic levels. Since the intake of total salt and water is usually very hypotonic, this has to result in the development of hyponatremia. Since a decrease in intravascular volume is a potent stimulus to ADH release, secretion of ADH also plays a role in the pathogenesis of the hyponatremia in these patients. ADH is released in response to a decrease in left atrial volume and pressures in the carotid and aortic arch baroreceptors.

Patients with cardiac and hepatic failure, unless receiving diuretics, exhibit marked sodium retention (urine sodium concentrations <10 mEq/liter). If urinary sodium excretions are not low in such patients (unless they are receiving diuretics), then their cardiac and liver disease cannot be incriminated as the cause of the hyponatremia. Treatment is with diuretics and fluid restriction in addition to treatment of the underlying disease. Furosemide is the preferred diuretic as it promotes loss of a dilute urine (more water relative to salt) in contrast to the thiazides that do not have this effect.

Syndrome of Inappropriate Antidiuretic Hormone

A diagnosis of SIADH can be made only when other causes of hyponatremia have been eliminated.

The following criteria must be met: (a) the extracellular fluid osmolality and sodium concentration must be decreased; (b) the urine must be hypertonic to serum; (c) sodium excretion in the urine continues to exceed 10 mEq/liter, despite hyponatremia; (d) adrenal, renal, cardiac and hepatic function must be normal; and (e) the hyponatremia must be corrected by water restriction.

A persistent high level of circulating ADH is considered inappropriate when neither hyperosmolality of the serum nor volume depletion, the usual stimuli to ADH release, is present. Inability to excrete water leads to volume expansion which, by multiple renal mechanisms, leads to increased urinary salt loss. The SIADH secretion is seen most frequently in patients with pulmonary neoplasms, most notably oat cell carcinomas, but it may be seen associated with a number of other entities as seen in Table 22.2.

Surveys of older patients in acute and chronic care facilities show a high prevalence of hyponatremia. For example, Kleinfeld et al. (11) showed that 36 of 160 chronically ill patients (23%) had a serum sodium concentration below 132 mEq/liter (mean 120 mEq/liter). In most, the low serum sodium concentration was not readily explained except by the presence of debilitating disease and old age.

Elderly patients appear prone to develop the SIADH. Antidiuresis and hyponatremia in the postoperative period have been observed primarily in elderly patients (4). SIADH in patients receiving sulfonylureas is seen almost exclusively in older persons (28). Diuretic-induced hyponatremia also was observed mostly in elderly patients (6).

Other observations (9) may bear on the increased susceptibility of older patients to develop hyponatremia. Older subjects increased serum vasopressin concentrations more after a standardized hypertonic saline infusion designed to increase serum osmolality from 290 to 306 mOsm/liter, than did younger subjects. Despite comparable baseline arginine vasopressin concentrations, older subjects increased vasopressin concentrations more than twice those observed in young subjects. In contrast, ethanol infusion, known to inhibit ADH secretion produced a more prolonged decrease in serum vasopressin concentrations in young than in old subjects. Thus, these two observations suggest an increasing osmoreceptor sensitivity with age associated with a greater production of vasopressin and water retention. Rowe et al. (20) reported studies designed to determine if this hyper-responsiveness in elderly subjects was a generalized age-related increase in vasopressin responsiveness or was specific only for osmotic stimulation. They found that older subjects, following quiet standing, failed to increase their serum vasopressin concentrations as much as younger subjects, suggesting that volume-baroceptor responsiveness is decreased in old compared with young subjects. One might speculate that continuing stimuli to baroreceptors in older persons (? related to systolic hypertension or decreased arterial distensibility) might result in a resetting of the threshold necessary to stimulate release of arginine vasopressin. The osmoreceptors, in turn, might compensate by becoming more responsive in older persons.

The problem frequently arises in the nonedematous patient of differentiating salt depletion hyponatremia from SIADH. As seen in Table 22.3, serum osmolality and sodium concentrations are low, urine osmolalities are hypertonic, and sodium excretions are variable but often fairly significant. In salt depletion states, volume depletion appropriately stimulates ADH; in SIADH, the increased ADH levels are often unexplained. Generally, blood urea nitrogen (BUN) concentrations tend to be elevated in salt depletion; they are often subnormal in SIADH. Monitoring the CVP may be necessary if one remains unsure clinically which entity he is dealing with. If the CVP is less than 4 cm H_2O, isotonic or hypertonic saline can be infused until the CVP increases above 8 cm H_2O. If the CVP is high initially, then water restriction is the appropriate treatment. The hyponatremia can be corrected most safely by water restriction alone. If there is thought to be some urgency in correction of the hyponatremia or if water restriction alone proves ineffective, one can administer a loop diuretic, such as furosemide (1 mg/kg/body weight intravenously or intramuscularly followed by additional doses as necessary), which will promote excretion of a dilute urine along with a natriuresis and follow with a replacement infusion of hypertonic saline (3%). One must be aware that as the serum sodium concentration is increased, water moves from the intracellular to extracellular compartments expanding the latter. If urine volume does not substantially exceed fluid intake, an individual can become overhydrated easily and develop congestive failure. Older subjects are especially susceptible.

Water Intoxication

It is difficult, if not impossible, for the normal person to drink sufficient water to become symptomatically hyponatremic. Vomiting prevents this from developing. Patients with schizophrenia, on the other hand, do appear to be capable of drinking sufficient water to become symptomatic. Treatment is merely restriction of water.

HYPERNATREMIA

Hypernatremia most frequently occurs in persons who, because of inability to communicate, are unable to obtain sufficient water to replace losses. Patients with a large urinary solute load (glucose) also may develop the simple dehydration previously described. Hypernatremia with normal or expanded ECFV may be seen in persons with excessive circulating corticosteroids (Cushings' syndrome) or aldosterone. Hypernatremia (salt intoxication) resulting from ingestion of large, hypertonic quantities of sodium chloride or bicarbonate produces psychiatric aberrations with cerebral hemorrhages. Treatment is rehydration with oral water or 5% glucose and water, regardless of cause. Providing the individual does not have renal failure, this replacement can be accomplished rapidly.

DISTURBANCES IN POTASSIUM BALANCE

Potassium is the primary intracellular cation; only about 2% of total body potassium is contained in the extracellular fluid compartment. Therefore, the serum concentration of potassium may fail to reflect accurately total body potassium stores. A potassium flux into cells occurs with cell growth, with intracellular nitrogen and glycogen deposition, and with increases in extracellular pH; potassium leaves the cell with cell destruction, glucose utilization, and decreases in extracellular pH. In interpreting any given serum potassium concentration, consideration must be given to these factors affecting the ratio of intracellular to extracellular concentration, as a steep concentration gradient must be maintained. A dramatic example is provided by the patient with diabetic ketoacidosis who, prior to treatment, has high serum potassium levels, but with rehydration, correction of the acidosis and treatment of the hyperglycemia with insulin shows a dramatic decrease in plasma potassium concentrations as the cation moves intracellularly.

HYPOKALEMIA

Isotopic dilution studies and muscle biopsies have been utilized to demonstrate that intracellular stores of potassium can be decreased in a variety of clinical conditions (diabetic ketoacidosis, chronic respiratory acidosis, chronic congestive heart failure, cirrhosis, and uremia) while serum potassium concentrations remain within normal limits. It appears appropriate to identify two types of intracellular potassium deficit. The first would be that restorable by administration of supplemental potassium (potassium deficiency); the second would be that portion not restorable, but decreased, due to cellular metabolic disturbances that impair the ability of the cell to maintain a high intracellular to extracellular concentration gradient (potassium depletion). The serum potassium concentration tends to be low in the first condition and normal in the second.

The serum potassium concentration is the only clinically practical measure of potassium stores in the body. Along with a skillful evaluation of the clinical status of the patient, it can be used to estimate satisfactorily total body potassium. A serum potassium concentration of 3 mEq/liter implies a deficit in the range of 100–200 mEq; below 3 mEq/liter each mEq/liter decrease in serum potassium concentration indicates an additional deficit of 200–400 mEq. One can correct for any deviation in acid-base balance by recognizing that for every 0.1 unit change in pH, there is an inverse change in the plasma potassium concentration of 0.6 mEq/liter.

The functional and structural defects associated with hypokalemia can be divided into involvement of four organ systems, specifically: (a) the kidney, (b) the myocardium and cardiovascular system, (c) the neuromuscular and central nervous system, and (d) the gastrointestinal tract (Table 22.4). There also is impairment in carbohydrate metabolism and protein synthesis.

The potential causes of hypokalemia are outlined in Table 22.5. Although the normal kidney is not as effective in conserving potassium as it is sodium, it can reduce excretion to between 3 and 15 mEq/day when potassium deficiency is induced even in the presence of an alkalosis or acidosis. Normally, little potassium is lost from the gastrointestinal tract. This means it would take 2–3 weeks on virtually a potassium-free intake for a person to lower his serum potassium to 3 mEq/liter, if all organ systems were functioning normally. An example where this might occur would be the patient with anorexia nervosa.

The serum potassium concentration may decrease with dilution of the extracellular space, movement of the cation into cells (glucose, insulin or sodium bicarbonate administration, familial periodic paralysis), or from loss from the body via sweat glands, the gastrointestinal tract, or the kidney in quantities greater than that replaced. Patients with persistent vomiting develop hypokalemia for five reasons: (a) the ingestion and retention of potas-

Table 22.4
Functional Consequences of Potassium Depletion

I. Myocardium and cardiovascular system
  A. Electrocardiographic changes 2° to myocardial necrosis
    1. Depressed S-T segment, inversion of T waves
    2. Accentuated U waves
  B. Arrhythmias
  C. Potentiation of digitalis toxicity
  D. Salt retention
  E. Hypotension
II. Neuromuscular and psychiatric
  A. Muscle weakness to flaccid paralysis
  B. Muscle pain and tenderness 2° to muscle necrosis
  C. Depressive reaction (anorexia, constipation, weakness, lethargy, apathy, fatigue, and depressed mood)
  D. Acute brain syndrome (memory impairment, disorientation, confusion)
III. Kidney
  A. Defect in urine-concentrating ability with polyuria
  B. Paradoxical aciduria
  C. Sodium retention
IV. Gastrointestinal
  A. Decreased motility and propulsive activity of intestine
  B. Paralytic ileus
V. Metabolic
  A. Carbohydrate intolerance (delayed release of insulin)
  B. Growth failure due to impaired protein synthesis

Table 22.5
Potential Causes of Hypokalemia

I. Inadequate intake
II. Dilution of ECFV
III. Excessive sweating
IV. Intracellular shift of potassium
  A. Alkalosis (increase in blood pH)
  B. Glucose and insulin
  C. Rapid cellular regeneration and growth
  D. Familial hypokalemic periodic paralysis
V. Excessive gastrointestinal loss
  A. Vomiting
  B. Biliary, pancreatic and intestinal drainage, fistulas and ostomies
  C. Diarrhea
    1. Chronic infectious and inflammatory lesions
    2. Malabsorption
    3. Villous adenomas of colon and rectum
    4. Catechol-secreting neural tumors
    5. Abdominal lymphomas
    6. Non-α, non-β islet cell tumors of the pancreas
    7. Excessive use of enemas and purgatives
  D. Ureterosigmoidostomy
VI. Increased urinary loss
  A. Pituitary-adrenal disturbances
    1. Primary aldosteronism (adenoma, carcinoma)
    2. Secondary aldosteronism
      1. Accelerated hypertension, renal artery stenosis and interstitial nephritis
      b. Volume depletion (heart failure, cirrhosis, nephrotic syndrome)
    3. Cushing's syndrome
      a. Adrenocortical tumors
      b. Pituitary ACTH hypersecretion
      c. Pituitary ACTH secretion 2° to tumor
    4. Congenital adrenal hyperplasis (11, 17, and 21-hydroxylase deficiency)
  B. Renal disorders
    1. Renal tubular acidosis, proximal or distal
    2. Renin-secreting renal tumor (hemaniopericytoma)
    3. Salt-losing nephritis
    4. Diuretic phase of acute tubular necrosis, postobstruction diuresis
    5. Chronic lysosomuria (myelogenous leukemia)
  C. Drug-induced disorders
    1. Diuretic (thiazide and loop diuretics)
    2. Licorice extracts (glycorrhizic acid)
    3. Nonreabsorbable anions (penicillin, carbenicillin)
    4. Acetylsalicylic acid (respiratory alkalosis)
  D. Idiopathic and other pathology
    1. Bartter's syndrome
    2. Liddle's syndrome
    3. Idiopathic or familial
    4. Hypomagnesemia or hypercalcemia
    5. Thyrotoxicosis

sium is impaired, (b) gastric and small bowel fluids containing low concentrations of potassium are lost, (c) the acid secretion into the stomach produces a metabolic alkalosis which augments renal potassium excretion and shifts potassium intracellularly, (d) volume contraction enhances tubular bicarbonate reabsorption also producing a metabolic alkalosis, and (e) volume contraction produces a secondary hyperaldosteronism which increases urinary potassium losses. A number of other gastrointestinal disturbances increasing potassium loss are listed in Table 22.5.

A reasonable criterion for establishing a diagnosis of renal potassium wasting when the plasma potassium concentration falls below 3.5 mEq/liter would be the daily excretion of more than 20 mEq/day. The causes of excessive urinary potassium loss have been separated into four categories: (a) pituitary-adrenal disturbances, (b) renal disturbances, (c) drug-induced losses, and (d) idiopathic and other causes.

An aldosterone-secreting tumor (adenoma or carcinoma), in addition to renal potassium wasting, causes salt and water retention and hypertension. Serum sodium concentrations are normal or increased, urinary aldosterone excretions are increased, and plasma renin levels are decreased. Secondary aldosteronism results from the stimulation of the juxtaglomerular apparatus and/or macula densa with an increase in circulating plasma renin concentrations. Patients with malignant hypertension, renal artery stenosis, and some cases of interstitial nephritis (pyelonephritis) develop secondary aldosteronism presumably because blood flow to the juxtaglomerular apparatus is reduced. Hypertension is usually present in such patients. Patients with volume depletion and decreased perfusion of the kidney due to congestive heart failure, cirrhosis, and nephrotic syndrome often have low blood pressures and the renin-angiotensin-aldosterone system is stimulated in an attempt to expand intravascular volume and improve renal perfusion.

Hypokalemia also may result from Cushing's syndrome due to adrenal tumors (adenomas, carcinomas), from bilateral adrenal hyperplasia, or from iatrogenic administration of adrenocorticotropic hormone (ACTH) or corticosteroids. The increased ACTH levels producing bilateral adrenal hyperplasia may result from idiopathic pituitary stimulation of ACTH release or from ectopic production of ACTH-like material from "nonendocrine" tumors (oat cell tumor of lung, pancreas, thymus, colon, ovary, esophagus, and gall bladder). In one series (3), only 12 of 42 patients with Cushing's syndrome developed hypokalemia; aldosterone secretions were normal or low. Later studies (21) showed that only those subjects with increased levels of the nonaldostrone mineralocorticoids desoxycorticosterone and corticosterone (compound B) developed hypokalemia.

In certain types of renal disease, there is an inability to conserve potassium. Distal renal tubular acidosis may be due to a hereditary defect but more commonly it is acquired from a variety of drugs (amphotericin B, toluene, vitamin D) or disease states (hyperglobulinemia, cirrhosis, pyelonephritis, amyloidosis). Proximal renal tubular acidosis also can be hereditary or acquired (outdated tetracycline). Potassium-losing nephritis and renin-secreting hemangiopericytomas are rare causes of hypokalemia. Potassium loss can be substantial during the diuretic phase of acute tubular necrosis or the diuresis observed following relief of urinary tract obstruction.

Diuretic therapy undoubtedly remains the most frequent cause of hypokalemia. Licorice extract used in the management of ulcer disease (carbenoxolone sodium), as an additive to alcoholic drugs and as a flavoring for drugs (PAS) contains glycyrrhizic acid, a substance with a structure and action similar to aldosterone. Medications containing large amounts of anion (penicillin, cabenicillin) that is poorly reabsorbed in the renal tubules can precipitate hypokalemia.

Since the last group of entities is uncommon in older patients, they are not discussed in detail except to mention that unrecognized hypomagnesemia or hypercalcemia can cause hypokalemia. It should be emphasized that, in many patients, multiple factors contribute to the development of hypokalemia. For example, in Figure 22.2, an elderly, psychoneurotic patient with anorexia, vomiting, and abuse of diuretics and purgatives developed hypokalemia through the mechanisms shown.

THERAPY

Since an alkalosis (chloride depletion) usually accompanies hypokalemia, replacement therapy should be with potassium chloride rather than with other potassium salts. Intravenous repletion may be necessary but can be hazardous; rates over 20 mEq/hour and concentrations in excess of 40 mEq/liter should be utilized only when a good urine output is established and with electrocardiographic monitoring. Care must be exercised in administering glucose, insulin, and bicarbonate parenterally to hypokalemic patients as these agents will potentiate the deficiency even when supplemental potassium is included in the infusion solution. This is particularly

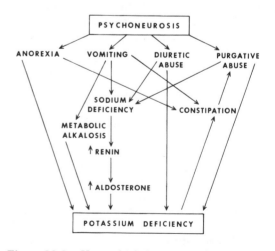

Figure 22.2. How multiple factors contribute to the development of potassium deficiency in an elderly psychoneurotic patient.

true in patients receiving digitalis glycosides as toxicity can be easily precipitated.

The use of foods rich in potassium (citrus and tomato juices, bananas, meats, vegetables) is the best way to administer potassium, but when additional replacement is needed, the potassium should be dispensed separately from thiazide diuretics as the chloride salt in liquid form. Most commercial preparations, e.g., Kaochlor, 10%; Kay Ciel Elixir; Klorvess, 10%, contain 20 mEq/15 ml, which should be given two to four times daily. Enteric coated tablets, especially with the diuretics, may cause small bowel perforation, stenosis, obstruction, or hemorrhage. Most of these have been removed from the market for this reason. Another preparation with potassium imbedded in wax (Slow-K) may produce the same complications. Each tablet contains 8 mEq of potassium. Even uncoated tablets may pass through the gastrointestinal tract without being absorbed. Spironolactone or triamterene also may be used to minimize potassium loss.

One can question the need for routine replacement therapy in hypertensive and edematous patients receiving diuretic therapy. Only when the serum potassium falls below 3.5 mEq/liter, and symptomatology suggesting potassium deficiency (weakness) develops, is therapy clearly indicated. There also is controversy over whether or not failure to replete potassium adequately leads to an increased incidence of ventricular arrythmias, some potentially lethal. The Boston Collaborative Drug Surveillance Program (13) reported on adverse reactions to potassium replacement therapy. Of 16,000 patients monitored, 5000 received potassium; adverse reactions were seen in 283 (5.8%) with seven deaths directly attributable to this therapy. The incidence of life-threatening hyperkalemia was greatly increased in the elderly patient, especially if renal function was decreased. Elderly individuals on both restricted and unrestricted sodium intakes have lower plasma renin activities and urinary aldosterone excretions than do comparable young subjects providing a plausible explanation for this observation.

HYPERKALEMIA

The clinical manifestations of hyperkalemia are subtle and appear late, often only shortly before death from cardiac arrhythmias. Anxiety, restlessness, apprehension, weakness, stupor, and hyporeflexia should alert one to the possible existence of this imbalance. Characteristic electrocardiographic changes (peaking of the T waves followed by loss of P waves and widening of the QRS complex) also may be present. Because the distal nephron has such a large capacity for secreting potassium even in advanced renal failure, hyperkalemia develops only when there is some associated factor such as: (a) oliguria, e.g., acute renal failure, (b) excessive potassium load (tissue catabolism, potassium supplementation, administration of excess potassium in some other form, e.g., as potassium penicillin G), (c) severe acidosis, (d) spironolactone or triamterene diuretic therapy, or (e) a deficiency of endogenous steroid (aldosterone, cortisol). As mentioned earlier, poorly monitored potassium supplementation to patients receiving thiazide diuretic therapy leads to lethal hyperkalemia with frightening frequency especially in older patients and patients with renal impairment that is not yet severe enough to produce significant azotemia (13).

Therapy should be started once the serum potassium concentration exceeds 5.5 mEq/liter; a true medical emergency exists when the serum potassium concentration exceeds 7.0 mEq/liter. Acute treatment is with glucose, insulin, and sodium bicarbonate (to shift potassium intracellularly) and with calcium and sodium salts (physiologic antagonists). For each 500 mg of 10% glucose infused, 15 units of regular insulin (1 unit/3–4 g glucose) and one to two ampoules of sodium bicarbonate (44–88 mEq) may be added. If serum sodium or calcium concentrations are depressed, more normal or even hypertonic saline and calcium salts (10 ml of 10% calcium gluconate) can be added. This infusion must be continued until other means are used to permanently remove potassium from the body.

Sodium polystyrene sulfonate (Kayexalate) resins are used to remove excess potassium from the body permanently. Although three forms of the resins are made, the most readily available commercial resin is the sodium-containing resin. Twenty-gram doses of Kayexalate may be given orally two to four times daily. If complete exchange is accomplished, each gram of resin exchanges more than 2 mEq of sodium for each 1 mEq of potassium (other cations exchanged onto the resin account for the other 1 mEq). Salt and water retention may limit the amount of the resin which can be given in patients under treatment. To avoid constipation and fecal impaction, 30 ml of 50–70% sorbital can be given with each dose of Kayexalate and the amount varied thereafter to assure passage of several semiformed stools daily. If oral intake cannot be tolerated, 60 g of resin in 200 ml of tap water or diluted sorbital solution (50 ml 70% sorbital plus 150 ml tap water) should be given as an enema to be retained at least one-half hour as often as necessary (up to every 2 hours if necessary). When hyperkalemia can be attributed to mineralocorticoid deficiency, correction can be achieved with 0.1 mg daily of 9 α-fluoro-hydrocortisone (Florinef). If all else fails, peritoneal dialysis or hemodialysis can be used to remove excessive potassium but rarely is this necessary.

DISTURBANCES IN CALCIUM AND PHOSPHATE BALANCE

The routine screening of blood samples for calcium and phosphate concentrations with automated multichannel autoanalyzers (Technicon Instruments Corporation) has identified many patients with unsuspected abnormalities. A finely tuned endocrine system exists to maintain calcium balance and acts in concert to control intestinal absorption, bone exchange, and renal excretion. Whenever serum calcium concentrations decrease, parathyroid hormone secretion increases resulting in mobilization of calcium from bone, increased urinary phosphate excretion (serum phosphate concentrations decrease), and increased tubular calcium reabsorption. Whenever serum calcium concentrations increase, serum thyrocalcitonin concentrations increase and produce effects counter to those of parathormone. Vitamin D is converted by the liver to the carrier metabolite, 25-OH-cholecalciferol, and by the kidney to the active metabolite, $1,25-OH_2$-cholecalciferol. The latter acts primarily to increase calcium absorption in the intestine but, secondarily, it also increases bone resorption of calcium and decreases urinary calcium and phosphate excretion.

Serum calcium exists in two states—ionized and unionized. Only the ionized portion is physiologically active. The unionized portion is either bound to serum proteins, primarily albumin, or complexed with various anions, e.g., citrate. The degree of protein binding is dependent upon the concentration of serum protein (albumin) and the blood pH, the calcium binding increasing as the pH increases. Since one usually measures only total serum calcium concentrations in the clinical laboratory, these factors must be kept in mind when one evaluates a specific serum calcium concentration.

HYPOCALCEMIA

Hypocalcemia is not a problem seen more commonly in elderly than in young persons. It is seen primarily in patients with hypoparathyroidism (or pseudohypoparathyroidism), renal insufficiency, gastrointestinal disorders (malabsorption or small bowel bypass), osteomalacia due to vitamin D defi-ciency or resistance, acute pancreatitis, and calcitonin-producing tumors (medullary carcinoma of the thyroid). Patients with the first two entities have high serum phosphate concentrations; the others tend to have normal or low values. Patients with hypomagnesemia often develop hypocalcemia due to a peripheral resistance to parathormone and decreased release of parathormone in response to the hypocalcemic stimulus.

The prominent acute symptom of hypocalcemia is increased neuromuscular excitability that may proceed to tetany. Long-term manifestations include lenticular opacities, abnormalities of the nails, skin, and teeth, and mental and growth retardation.

Acute correction of symptomatic hypocalcemia can be accomplished with calcium gluconate administered parenterally (10 ml of a 10% solution contains 50 mEq of calcium). Intravaneous calcium should not be administered at a rate exceeding 50 mg (2.5 mEq)/min for a total of 2 g (100 mEq) without a repeat determination of serum calcium concentration, unless evidence of tetany persists, especially when given to a patient receiving digitalis glycosides. Oral calcium carbonate (650 mg), calcium gluconate (500 mg or 1-g tablets) or lactate (300- or 600-mg tablets) may be used to treat mild or latent hypocalcemic tetany. Up to 8 g of oral calcium gluconate (1 g or 50 mEq of calcium) daily is well tolerated.

Vitamin D and its metabolites increase serum calcium concentrations by increasing intestinal absorption and bone resorption of calcium, and increasing urinary phosphate excretion. Vitamin D can be given orally as ergocalciferol (vitamin D_2) in 25,000 or 50,000 IU capsules or tablets with maintenance therapy being 25,000–100,000 IU daily; as dihydrotachysterol (Hytakeral, Winthrop, 0.125-mg capsules) with maintenance therapy being 0.25–1.75 mg weekly; or, in patients with renal failure, as calcitriol (Rocaltrol, 0.25 and 0.5 μg, Roche) with maintenance therapy starting at 0.25 μg daily and increasing in increments of 0.25 μg at 2- to 4-week intervals. Serum calcium concentrations must be monitored frequently to insure that hypercalcemia does not develop.

HYPERCALCEMIA

The most frequent cause of hypercalcemia in elderly patients is malignant disease. A number of mechanisms are involved both with and without bony metastases (24). Other causes of hypercalcemia include hyperparathyroidism, sarcoidosis, tuberculosis, vitamin D intoxication, milk-alkali syndrome, and thiazide administration. Symptoms often are vague and nonspecific but include anorexia, nausea, vomiting, constipation, fatigue, somnolence, muscle weakness, pruritis, and psychiatric disturbances. Nephrolithiasis and nephrocalcinosis are manifestations of chronic hypercalcemia. Polyuria with dehydration and azotemia is common. A serum calcium concentration above 15 mg/dl can produce cardiac arrhythmias and should be considered a medical emergency, especially when a patient is receiving digitalis.

The initial therapy for patients with hypercalcemia should be rehydration with normal saline. This generally produces an increase in urinary calcium excretion and decreases serum calcium concentration by hemodilution. Loop diuretics (furosemide, ethacrynic acid) can further increase urinary calcium excretion; thiazide diuretics, in contrast, decrease calcium excretion and may potentiate hypercalcemia. Up to 80 mg of furosemide intravenously every 2 hours, as necessary, to sustain a diuresis for 6–48 hours is effective therapy provided that noncalcium (sodium and potassium) ionic losses and fluid volume are adequately replaced.

Although intravenous phosphate therapy may be employed to lower serum calcium concentrations acutely, it is safer but slower to use oral phosphates (a therapeutic effect may not be appreciated for 24 hours or longer). A stable mixture of the sodium and potassium salts, e.g., 2–4 capsules of Neutra-Phos provides 0.5–1.0 g phosphorus every 8 hours and is usually well tolerated orally, although it may cause some gastrointestinal disturbances and diarrhea. Other preparations providing an initial therapy of 2 g of phosphorus are available in liquid (Phospho-Soda, 3 teaspoons daily), and powder (Neutra-Phos, 2 teaspoons daily).

Forty milligrams of prednisone daily for 7–10 days will correct the hypercalcemia (by decreasing vitamin D-mediated calcium absorption from the intestine) in most cases of sarcoidosis, multiple myeloma, and vitamin D intoxication, and in about one-half the cases of nonosseous malignancy. It is less effective when there is extensive bone invasion by malignancy and only rarely is it effective in hyperparathyroidism.

Mithramycin appears to be the drug of choice in the treatment of the hypercalcemia associated with malignancy that is unresponsive to other therapies. This antitumor agent acts by inhibiting bone resorption and blocking vitamin D action. Most cases can be maintained normocalcemic on one or two doses weekly of 25 μg/kg body weight. Transient nausea and vomiting and bone marrow suppression are the major adverse effects. Frequent monitoring of serum calcium concentrations is necessary to determine the frequency of administration needed.

Other agents that can prove to be useful in selected situations include the phosphonates, calcitonin, indomethacin and the chelating agent EDTA. Finally, if all else fails or if renal failure is present, dialysis is effective in acutely lowering serum calcium concentrations.

PHOSPHATE DEPLETION

Selective phosphorus deficiency induced in normal subjects by a deficient diet and/or ingestion of large quantities of phosphate-binding antacids leads to a distinct clinical syndrome characterized by anorexia, weakness, and bone pain. Symptoms appear primarily when the serum phosphorus concentration falls below 1 mg/dl and clinical improvement occurs rapidly when phosphorus is restored to the diet. Severe hypophosphatemia has been documented in association with alcohol withdrawal, diabetes mellitus, excessive antacid ingestion, recovery from severe burns, hyperalimentation, nutritional recovery syndrome, and severe respiratory alkalosis (12). Patients with severe hypophosphatemia may develop a metabolic encephalopathy (irritability, muscular weakness, hypesthesias and parasthesias, dysarthria, confusion, seizures, and coma), rhabdomyolysis, hemolysis, leukocyte dysfunction (abnormal phagocytic, chemotactic, and bacteriocidal activities of granulocytes), and platelet dysfunction.

Milk contains approximately 1 g of phosphorus per quart and is the best dietary source of phosphorus. Two capsules of Neutra-Phos four times daily provides 2 g of phosphorus. Other forms of phosphorus replenishers are available for oral administration or, in patients unable to take phosphorus orally, for intravenous infusion.

DISTURBANCES IN ACID-BASE BALANCE

Alterations in acid-base balance are generally described in terms of changes in the CO_2-bicarbonate system, as these changes mirror shifts in all other buffer systems in the blood and tissues and can be easily quantified. Measurement of two of the three parameters (pH, PCO_2, and HCO_3^-) will allow one to calculate the third using the Henderson-Hasselbalch equation.

Since most clinical laboratories measure pH and PCO_2 with highly accurate and reproducible electrodes and then read HCO_3^--concentration from a nomogram, it makes sense to plot these two measurements on the ordinate and abscissa (Fig. 22.3). Use of the hydrogen ion concentration (H^+) rather than pH makes it possible to rearrange the Henderson-Hasselbalch equation so that a logarithmic calculation is no longer necessary. When the pH is 7.4 or normal, the H^+ is 40 nEq/liter. There is a sufficiently linear relationship between H^+ and pH between pH values of 7.1 and 7.5 that for each 0.01-unit change in pH, there is an inverse change in H^+ of 1 nEq/liter, e.g., when the pH falls from 7.40 to 7.30, the H^+ increases from 40 to 50 nEq/liter. A normal subject would balance the following equation with an H^+ of 40 nEq/liter, a PCO_2 of 40 mm Hg and a serum bicarbonate (HCO_3^-) of 24 mEq/liter.

$$H^+ = 24 \times \frac{PCO_2}{HCO_3}$$

This equation clearly illustrate the interdependence of these three parameters. The purpose of the bicarbonate buffers is to protect pH or H^+ in the body so that for every primary disturbance, there are compensatory changes to minimize the change in H^+. When the PCO_2 increases with a respiratory acidosis or decreases with a respiratory alkalosis, the HCO_3^- also respectively increases or decreases to minimize the change in the H^+. Generally, the change in the latter is less than that of the former, so that compensation is not complete. Similarly HCO_3^- increases with a metabolic alkalosis and decreases with a metabolic acidosis so that PCO_2 changes parallel directly the changes in HCO_3^-. The normal compensatory changes in acid-base disturbances are shown in Table 22.6. If these relationships fail to hold true, one should suspect a combined metabolic and respiratory disturbance. The ranges of normal variation for single primary acid-base disturbances are illustrated in Figure 22.3. Points that fall outside these ranges represent mixed acid-base disturbances.

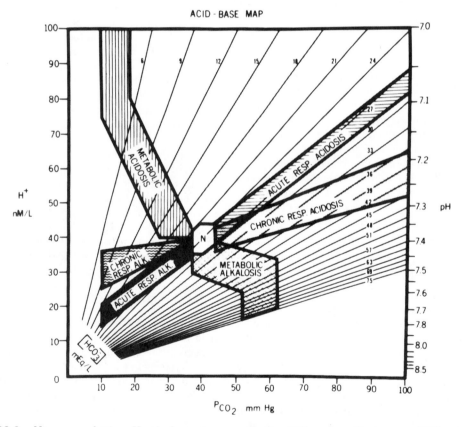

Figure 22.3. Nomogram plotting pH or hydrogen ion concentration (H^+) on the ordinate versus PCO_2 on the abscissa. The ranges of normal values for primary or single acid-base disturbances with their normal compensatory changes are shown based on actual values from an accumulated experience. (Reproduced by permission from Goldberg M, et al: 223:262, 1973. *JAMA* copyright 1973, American Medical Association.)

Table 22.6
Normal Compensatory Adjustments in Acid-Base Disturbances[a]

1. Metabolic acidosis
    Expected $pCO_2 = 1.5 \times HCO_3^- + 8$
2. Metabolic alkalosis
    Expected $pCO_2 = 0.9 \times HCO_3^- + 15.6$
3. Acute respiratory acidosis and alkalosis
    ΔH^+ (nEq/liter) $= 0.8\ (\Delta PCO_2)$
4. Chronic respiratory acidosis
    $\Delta H^+ = 0.3\ (\Delta PCO_2)$
5. Chronic respiratory alkalosis
    $\Delta H^+ = 0.17\ (\Delta PCO_2)$

[a]Modified from R. G. Narins and M. Emmett, 1980.

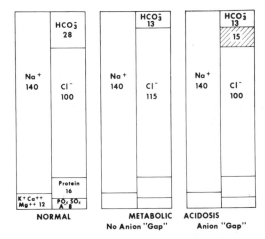

Figure 22.4. The serum sodium, chloride, and bicarbonate concentrations in a normal subject and two patients with a metabolic acidosis are shown. The second graph shows a patient with a hyperchloremic acidosis and a normal anion gap; the third graph shows a normochloremic acidosis with an abnormal anion gap.

ACIDOSIS AND ALKALOSIS

The body jealously guards pH and maintains it within a narrow normal range. Only small changes in pH (6.9–7.7) remain compatible with life. Generally, an acidosis is better tolerated than an alkalosis. Fundamentally, an acidosis results from introduction of an excess of acid into the body fluids whereas an alkalosis develops from excessive loss of acid. The body must cope with two types of acids:

1. Carbonic acid derived from hydration of CO_2. The lungs remove the volatile CO_2 generated during metabolism. Retention of CO_2 results in an acidosis; excessive loss of CO_2 results in an alkalosis.

2. Fixed hydrogen ion. The hydrogen ion and its associated organic (lactate, pyruvate, acetoacetate, β-hydroxybutyrate) and inorganic (phosphate, sulfate, chloride) anions are buffered in body fluids and can be excreted only by the kidney or in other fluids such as those lost via the gastrointestinal tract.

METABOLIC ACIDOSIS

A metabolic acidosis can arise from: (a) addition of acid to or loss of alkali from the body fluids more rapidly than the kidney can excrete the acid load; (b) impairment in the capacity of the kidney to excrete acid; or (c) very commonly, a combination of both.

Causes of Metabolic Acidosis

It is useful in any given patient with a metabolic acidosis to determine if an "anion gap" exists. In the normal person, the differences between sodium concentration and the sum of the chloride and bicarbonate concentrations is less than 12 mEq/liter. This difference represents anions in the plasma not commonly measured (Fig. 22.4). When the difference is larger, an anion gap exists indicating exces-

sive accumulation of organic (lactate, acetoacetate, salicylate, formate) or inorganic (phosphate, sulfate) anions. If no anion gap exists, the serum chloride concentration increases as the serum bicarbonate decreases (hyperchloremic acidosis). The classification of a metabolic acidosis can be divided into two groups, one with an anion gap and one without a gap, as follows:

I. With anion gap
   A. Azotemic renal failure
   B. Diabetic and starvation ketoacidosis
   C. Methyl alcohol intoxication
   D. Paraldehyde intoxication
   E. Ethylene glycol intoxication
   F. Salicylate intoxication
   G. Lactic acidosis
       1. Phenformin administration
       2. Circulatory insufficiency and shock
       3. Primary
II. Without anion gap
   A. Diarrhea and fistula drainage (loss of bicarbonate)
   B. NH_4Cl ingestion or infusion
   C. Renal tubular acidosis, congenital and acquired
   D. Ureterosigmoidostomy

If an anion gap exists, a careful history, a BUN concentration, a urinary ketone excretion, and toxicology screen will eliminate all but the lactic acidosis. If no anion gap exists, one can generally exclude all but renal tubular acidosis with the history and that can be confirmed by finding a urine pH greater than 6 in the face of an acidosis.

A metabolic acidosis is generally asymptomatic until the CO_2 content falls below 15 mEq/liter. The patient may then complain of weakness, malaise, dull headache, nausea, vomiting, and abdominal pain. Characteristic deep respirations (Kussmaul breathing) are usually present. The rest of the clinical picture usually depends on the cause of the acidosis.

Treatment varies with the cause of the acidosis. In renal failure, an attempt is made to limit exogenous protein intake by dietary limitations, and endogenous protein catabolism by high carbohydrate and fat intake. Since most of the 60–80 mEq of hydrogen ion accumulated by the body daily comes from protein catabolism, i.e., oxidation of sulfur and phosphorus, these dietary maneuvers are useful in decreasing the acid load presented to the kidneys. Sodium bicarbonate can be administrated orally or parenterally to correct the acidosis, but often one is limited in its use by the overhydration from salt and water retention that may develop. Peritoneal or hemodialysis may be required if this occurs. The treatment of diabetic acidosis is discussed elsewhere.

METABOLIC ALKALOSIS

A metabolic alkalosis results from excessive intake of alkali or abnormal losses of acid, e.g., pernicious vomiting. The kidney has the capacity to excrete large amounts of bicarbonate with associated cation so that significant alkalosis usually occurs only after sufficient dehydration to impair renal function. Volume contraction produces a metabolic alkalosis by increasing bicarbonate reabsorption in the proximal tubules. Alkalosis also occurs with potassium depletion due to: (a) a shift of acid from the extracellular to intracellular compartments in exchange for potassium, and (b) an increase in the exchange of hydrogen ion for sodium ion in the distal nephron. Since a competition exists between potassium and hydrogen ion for secretion in the distal nephron in exchange for the sodium reabsorbed, the decrease in available potassium seen in hypokalemia results in an increase in hydrogen ion secretion.

For diagnostic and therapeutic purposes, the state of metabolic alkalosis should be subdivided on the basis of the amount of chloride in the urine and whether or not the alkalosis can be corrected with chloride administration. Chloride responsive alkalosis (urine chloride concentration <20 mEq/liter) is generally due to excessive vomiting or diuretic administration; chloride unresponsive alkalosis (urine chloride concentration >20 mEq/liter) is generally due to hypokalemia induced by mineralocorticoid excess.

Correction of the metabolic alkalosis due to the former can be accomplished by expansion of the depleted extracellular fluid volume with normal saline. Chloride is retained and the excess sodium is excreted in the urine as sodium bicarbonate. Ammonium chloride can be given orally or parenterally but is usually unnecessary. The correction of the alkalosis may be difficult to accomplish if hypokalemia is present until potassium is simultaneously repleted. Potassium should be give as the chloride salt in order to more quickly correct the alkalosis.

RESPIRATORY ACIDOSIS

Respiratory acidosis results from CO_2 retention. Pulmonary disease with impaired ventilation-perfusion dynamics and hypoventilation due to respiratory center pathology or use of respiratory center depressants, e.g., morphine, may produce CO_2 retention. Inhalation of high concentrations of oxygen by patients with chronic pulmonary insufficiency may accentuate the respiratory acidosis. The fall in pH is partially compensated by increasing urinary loss of ammonium chloride.

Treatment consists of aiding the ventilation with any of a variety of mechanical devices. Caution must be exercised to ensure that acute hyperventilation without replacement of lost chloride does not result in a lethal alkalosis. Potassium replacement may also be necessary.

RESPIRATORY ALKALOSIS

Respiratory alkalosis is produced by hyperventilation and is seen primarily in patients with emotional disturbances, central nervous system lesions, and cirrhosis. Anxiety with hyperventilation is common at all ages, and patients may complain of dyspnea or "smothering," lightheadedness (or even syncope), numbness and tingling in the extremities, and chest pain or discomfort. Severe hyperventilation and alkalosis may result in tetany. Difficulty may be encountered in differentiating this "hyperventilation syndrome" from organic pathology such as congestive heart failure or pulmonary insufficiency. Treatment is aimed at relieving the anxiety in the patient by assuring him that, while his symptoms may be real, they are not life-threatening.

REFERENCES

1. Adler S, Lindeman RD, Yiengst MJ, Beard ES: The effect of acute acid loading on the urinary excretion of

acid by the aging human kidney. *J Lab Clin Med* 72:278, 1968.

2. Bartter FC, Schwartz WB: The syndrome of inappropriate secretion of antidiuretic hormone. *Am J Med* 42:790, 1967.

3. Christy NP, Laragh JH: Pathogenesis of hypokalemic aldalosis in Cushing's syndrome. *N Engl J Med* 265:1083, 1961.

4. Deutch S, Goldberg M, Dripps RD: Postoperative hyponatremia with the inappropriate release of antidiuretic hormone. *Anaesthesia* 27:250, 1966.

5. Elkinton JR, Danowski TS: *The Body Fluids, Basic Physiology and Practical Therapeutics.* Baltimore, Williams & Wilkins Co., 1955.

6. Fichman MP, Vorherr H, Kleeman CR, Telfer N: Diuretic-induced hyponatremia. *Ann Intern Med* 75:853, 1971.

7. Fuisz RE: Hyponatremia. *Medicine* 42:149, 1963.

8. Goldberg M, Green SB, Moss ML, Marbach CB, Garfinkel D: Computer-based instruction and diagnosis of acid-based disorders. *JAMA* 223:269, 1973.

9. Helderman JH, Vestal RE, Rowe JW, et al: The response of arginine vasopressin to intravenous ethanol in man: The impact of aging. *J Gerontol* 33:39, 1978.

10. Kassier JP: Serious acid-base disorders. *N Engl J Med* 291:773, 1974.

11. Kleinfeld M, Casimir M, Borra S: Hyponatremia as observed in a chronic disease facility. *J Am Geriatr Soc* 27:156, 1979.

12. Knochel JP: The pathophysiology and clinical characteristics of severe hypophosphatemia. *Arch Intern Med* 137:203, 1977.

13. Lawson DH: Adverse reactions to potassium chloride. *Quart J Med* 43:433, 1974.

14. Leaf A: The clinical and physiologic significance of the serum sodium concentration. *N Engl J Med* 267:24, 1962.

15. Levinsky NG: Management of emergencies. VI. Hyperkalemia. *N Engl J Med* 274:1076, 1966.

16. Lindeman RD: Hypokalemia: Causes, consequences and correction. *Am J Med Sci* 272:5, July/Aug 1976.

17. Lindeman RD, Papper S: Therapy of fluid electrolyte disorders. *Ann Intern Med* 82:64, 1975.

18. Lindeman RD, Van Buren HC, Raisz LG: Osmolar renal concentrating ability in healthy young men and hospitalized patients without renal disease. *N Engl J Med* 262:1306, 1960.

19. Narins RG, Emmett M: Simple and mixed acid-based disorders: A practical approach. *Medicine* 59:161, 1980.

20. Rowe JW, Minaher KL, Sparrow D, Robertson GL: Age related failure of volume-pressure mediated vasopressin release. *J Clin Endocrinol* 54:661, 1982.

21. Schambelan M, Slaton PE Jr, Biglieri EG: Mineralocorticoid production in hyperadrenocorticism. Role in pathogenesis of hypokalemic alkalosis. *Am J Med* 51:300, 1971.

22. Schrier RW, Berl T: Hyponatremia and related disorder. *Kidney* 7:1, 1974.

23. Schwartz WB, Relman AS: A critique of the parameters used in the evaluation of acid-base disorders. *N Engl J Med* 268:1382, 1963.

24. Sherwood LM: The multiple causes of hypercalcemia in malignant disease. *N Engl J Med* 303:1412, 1980.

25. Shock NW: Physiological aspects of aging in man. *Annu Rev Physiol* 23:97, 1961.

26. Shock NW, Yiengst MJ: Age changes in acid-base equilibrium of the blood of males. *J Gerontol* 5:1, 1950.

27. Slayton RE, Shnider BI, Elias E, Horton J, Perlia CP: New approach to the treatment of hypercalcemia. The effect of short term treatment with mithramycin. *Clin Pharmacol Ther* 12:833, 1971.

28. Weissman PN, Shenkman L, Gregerman R: Chlorpropamide hyponatremia: Drug-induced inappropriate antidiuretic hormone activity. *N Engl J Med* 284:65, 1971.

29. Welt LG, Hollander W Jr, Blythe WB: The consequences of potassium depletion. *J Chron Dis* 11:213, 1960.

CHAPTER 23

Common Lower Urinary Tract Problems in the Elderly

LOUIS BRESCHI

In order to discuss the topic of common lower urinary tract problems in the elderly, it is necessary to clarify the population one is discussing. The common problems of the lower urinary tract in the elderly hospitalized patients generally will be of a more acute and surgically oriented type than the common primary problems in patients in nursing homes. Both these populations will differ somewhat with those common problems encountered in the outpatient, office, or clinic setting. The following discussion will try to emphasize the problems in the outpatient, office, or clinic setting.

It is unfortunate that not enough studies are available focusing on this group of elderly patients. However, based on the author's experience together with those articles that are available, sufficient information can be produced that can provide a good overview of common lower urinary tract problems in the elderly. Urinary infections, prostatic disorders, urinary retention, hematuria, and disorders of the external urogenitalia comprise the common reasons for complaints and consultation for urologic problems. Included in the last category would be the increasingly overt concern of elderly males about impotency. But probably the most frequent complaint in the elderly age group is that of urinary incontinence.

LOWER URINARY TRACT INFECTIONS

Comprehensive studies of urinary tract infections in the elderly have shown a marked increase of infection with advancing age (3, 16). These studies have shown also nearly 5:1 ratio of frequency of lower urinary tract infection in women over men. The increase in prevalence of infections correspond with the onset of menopause and prostatism. More specific factors that may explain these developments may be: poor emptying of the bladder in old age that may predispose to infection; perineal soiling by elderly women with fecal incontinence; obstructive uropathy in men caused by prostatic disease; instrumentation of lower urinary tract of both men and women; ischemia of the bladder wall secondary to overdistention; impaired mental status in the bedridden elderly patient causing incomplete emptying of the bladder with loss of sensation (1, 7).

Symptomatic urinary tract infections should be treated in patients of any age. But the necessity of treating asymptomatic bacteriuria in the elderly patient remains controversial.

Symptomatic urinary tract infections are documented by midstream urine culture in both men and women. While awaiting the results of the urine cultures, empiric treatment to alleviate the patients' symptoms is appropriate. Using some urinary analgesic (Pyridium, Urised) usually will reduce the painful symptoms of dysuria and burning when present. At the same time, initiating oral antibiotics usually will improve the patients' condition. The choice of oral antibiotic will be each physician's preference based on experience. For women, the use of one of the synthetic penicillins (ampicillin or amoxicillin), sulfamethoxazole/trimethoprim, nitrofurantoin, or carbenicillin would be good empiric choices. If the cultures and sensitivity of urine support the initially chosen drug, the treatment is continued for the usual 7- to 10-day course. The place for single "megadose" therapy needs to be mentioned here. Single dose treatment using 3 g amoxicillin orally, or 2 g sulfamethoxazole have been advocated in treating acute uncomplicated bladder infections especially in women (4, 13). However, later studies of single dose therapy has proved relatively ineffective in "geriatric women as opposed to younger population" (15).

It is, therefore, safe to conclude that in an elderly patient population, if acute lower urinary tract infection appears for the first time in a patient, a trial with single dose therapy may be undertaken. However, in the geriatric age group, a treatment success rate may be as low as one-third of that seen in younger patient populations. Further therapy would then be needed. Persistent or rapid recurrence of symptoms along with the infection, would require a . urologic workup.

The management of asymptomatic bacteriuria is more controversial. There are studies and proponents (6) of the importance of bacteriuria and reduced survival. At this time, there may be more sentiment toward the concept of asymptomatic bacteriuria being a benign condition rather than a cause of increased mortality in the aged (3, 16). The author agrees with the latter sentiment. Management of patients with asymptomatic bacteriuria should include: regular follow-up visits; encouragement of good fluid intake, which is conducive to higher fluid output; and acidification of urine with either noncitrus juices and/or vitamin C therapy in appropriate amounts to cause urine pH to be under 7.0.

The common experience of clinicians who treat and manage urinary tract infections in all age groups is the inevitability of frequent recurrences. There are essentially two schools of thought in the management of recurrent infections.

The one group holds that symptomatic infections should be treated as they occur. Furthermore, this school of thought downgrades the effect of long-term suppressive therapy. Of greater concern to this group is the overgrowth of resistant bacteria and the possibility of ultimately developing side effects, not to mention the attendant expense.

The opposite opinion that many authors hold is that continued suppressive therapy in sufficient minimum doses for up to 4-6 months (5) or longer is effective. Furthermore, the decreases in patient morbidity, lost employment, and general well-being, offset by far the concerns of those who oppose long-term therapy. The author strongly favors the approach of long-term therapy. The author has used several modes of therapy tailored to each individual patient. These include: once daily dose; every other day; three times weekly; 1 week each month; two doses after intercourse; or any combination of above. All have proven extremely successful.

The patient with an indwelling Foley catheter is a subset of the bacteriuric patient. Here too, so long as the patient is asymptomatic, bacteriuria should be managed by the same principles of hydration causing high urinary output and acidification with juices or vitamin C. In addition, cleanliness around the catheter with a weakly acidic solution would be satisfactory management.

DISEASES OF THE FEMALE URETHRA

The female urethra is normally approximately 3-5 cm in length. As in women of younger ages, the urethra in the elderly female also is subject to various inflammatory and anatomic changes. There are, in addition, several disease entities that are peculiar to the elderly female urethra. An entity that is not often mentioned, but is believed by the authors to be an important factor in urethritis and recurrent urinary tract infections in females, is the hypospadiac female urethra. In this condition, the urethral meatus is recessed inside the vaginal vault rather than being more exterior and parallel to the vagina (Figs. 23.1 and 23.2). This anatomic situation could then predispose to recurrent trauma to the meatus and irritation resulting in ascending urethritis and/or cystitis. The recessed urethra also can cause some degree of local vaginal irritation by means of some of the urinary stream entering the lower portion of the vagina, resulting in irritating effects.

Urethral prolapse is a common finding in the postmenopausal female. The presenting appearance

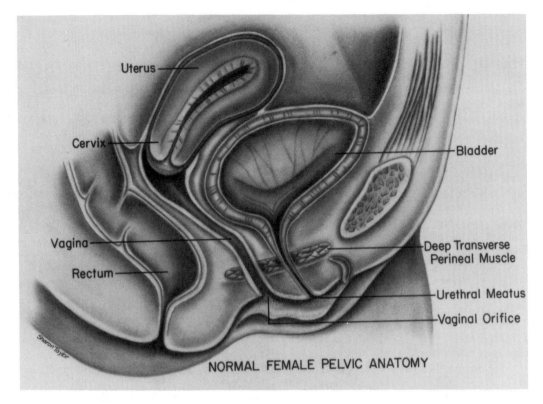

Figure 23.1 The normal anatomic relation of the urethra and vagina.

on examination may range from a slight out-pouching of the urethral meatus to obvious urethral prolapse of the mucosa, which is a deep red color. The presence of the prolapse to an extreme degree at the 6 o'clock position of the urethra, is often nodular in appearance (Fig. 23.3). This localized area is referred to as a urethral caruncle. Other complaints in the presence of a urethral caruncle are burning on urination, occasional dysuria, and even hematuria. Although almost always benign, occasional associated urethral carcinoma at this site has been encountered. The treatment of urethral caruncle may entail periodic urethral dilatation for the very mild cases of urethral prolapse to excision of the urethral caruncle in those cases that are of a suspicious nature or causing recurrent symptoms.

Another anatomic change of the elderly female urethra is the formation of a urethrocele. A urethrocele may simply be secondary to contiguous prolapse of the supporting structures of the urethra causing a bulging anywhere from the meatus up to the bladder neck. It also may be in conjunction with a cystocele and, therefore, referred to as a urethrocystocele. The very presence of a urethrocele does not necessarily demand therapy unless it results in a func-

tional stenosis of the urethra. A urethrocele, if severe, potentially could cause chronic urinary retention, although this is a rare occurrence.

A urethral diverticulum is also a finding noted in the female urethra. Most often, this is secondary to an infection involving a periurethral gland that results in that particular gland enlarging in size and forming a cavity. Suspicion for existence of a urethral diverticulum may come in any one of several forms. A patient may describe a history of recurrent urinary tract infections as her only obvious symptom. But more often the patient will describe occurrences of urethral discharge between urinations. She will often describe associated urethral discomfort, either burning, dysuria, or both. Another common complaint in women with urethral diverticula is that of spontaneous passage of urine once the woman has apparently finished urinating and has stood up. Upon taking the erect position and perhaps taking a step or two, she has noted the passage of additional amounts of urine uncontrollably. If this occurs repeatedly, suspicion of a urethral diverticulum is strong. A symptomatic urethral diverticulum requires excision. Although most often easily performed, there is concern when the diverticulum may

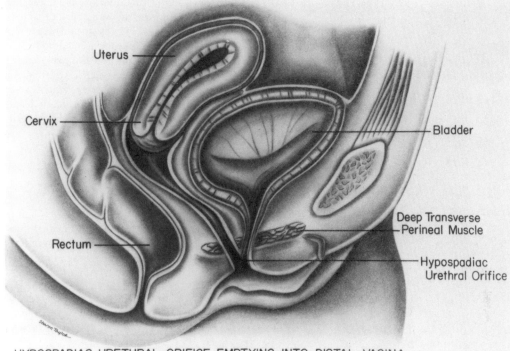

HYPOSPADIAC URETHRAL ORIFICE EMPTYING INTO DISTAL VAGINA

Figure 23.2 The location of the urethra frequently found in elderly women. Note that the urethral meatus is recessed into the anterior vaginal wall.

exist in proximity to the bladder neck and the sphincter mechanism of the bladder.

Senile urethritis is also an entity that in some women causes considerable distress. As the name implies, this is a condition seen in postmenopausal females in which there is a combination of very low estrogen level together with irritative symptoms. The findings on urethroscopy are those of a reddened "cobblestoning" appearance of the urethra with perhaps some tiny varices of the urethra. This differs from a standard inflammatory urethritis that is more of an edematous reddened surface. Most often, cultures of the urine fail to reveal bacteria. At times, symptoms are sufficiently controlled by the use of a mild urinary acidifier (Uro-Phosphate, mandelamine) or at other times by the administration of a urinary analgesic either alone or in combination with a mild antispasmodics (methylene blue, Pyridium, or Urised).

Urethral stenosis, a common finding in any age group, is likewise not a rarity in the elderly female. Etiologic causes may range from a life-long asymptomatic condition, postmenopausal estrogen deprivation with secondary tightening of the periurethral

tissue, recurring infections, the previous use of indwelling Foley catheter, iatrogenic causes such as urethral plication, or other types of vaginal trauma. The dilatation of the urethra in patients who are symptomatic with urethral stenosis will often relieve their symptoms, but this problem in the elderly may require periodic dilatation because of the tendency to recurrent constriction of the stenotic area. Symptoms of urethral stenosis are most often hesitancy, slowness of urinary stream, and a feeling of incomplete emptying. It is important to note, however, that not all patients with urethral stenosis are symptomatic.

DISEASES OF THE FEMALE BLADDER

By far, the most common urologic complaints of the elderly female patient will be the symptoms of a bladder infection. The treatment of lower urinary tract infections has been addressed elsewhere in this chapter. But what is also important in evaluating the elderly female patient beyond the treatment of the acute infection is the uncovering of any causes of persistent or recurring symptoms of infection in this

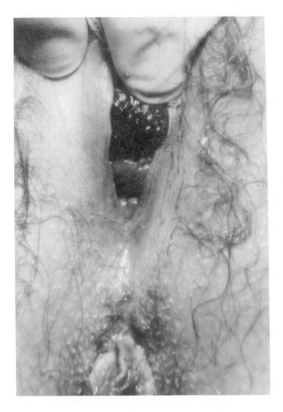

Figure 23.3. The nodular deep-colored tissue immediately below the gloved finger is the prolapsed urethral mucosa.

group of patients. Also, elderly women will complain of other problems not necessarily associated with infection that deserve discussion.

CYSTOCELE

The prolapse of the anterior vaginal wall is a common finding in the elderly female patient. Frequently, mild degrees of cystocele are not symptomatic. The symptomatic woman with a cystocele may complain of palpation of a protruding mass from the vagina, the feeling of heaviness or sensation of pelvic organs pulling down through the vagina, or difficulty in emptying the bladder. This latter complaint may require the woman to elevate her vagina manually or to lean forward in order to void.

A cystocele may be associated with stress urinary incontinence. The awareness of stress incontinence along with the cystocele, is most important in planning the nature of management. A cystocele without stress incontinence may be managed possibly by a pessary. If the patient is an appropriate surgical candidate, plication of the anterior vaginal wall could also be done. However, this surgical approach would not be satisfactory when stress incontinence is present. Anterior urethral plication, in addition to vaginal plication, would be the necessary surgical procedure if correction of both problems is desired. Again, the recommended course of management would be dictated by the same factors in the elderly female as in other areas of surgery.

URINARY RETENTION

The female of any age group must be evaluated to rule out chronic urinary retention as part of any evaluation of the lower urinary tract for recurrent or continued symptoms. Whether the problem is recurrent cystitis, urinary frequency, urinary incontinence, dyspareunia, or abdominal distention, the postvoid catheterization can be very revealing and possibly suggest the primary underlying cause for the patient's complaints. A residual urine of up to 30 ml is considered normal. Some authorities would accept a high level of residual, up to 90–120 ml for some conditions, especially in a neurogenic bladder. But,in dealing with patients with recurrent urinary infections, frequency, and even incontinence, a residual urine more than 30–60 ml is not acceptable and usually is a significant factor in the patient's urologic problem.

The management of chronic retention may require catheterization if large in quantities or respond to use of Bethanechol, or a combination of both modalities. A cystometrogram normally would contribute to the appropriate planning of the management course for such a patient.

DISEASES OF THE PROSTATE

PROSTATITIS

Infection of the prostate is not peculiar to the elderly male prostate gland. In fact, infection can be seen in the teenage years when the prostate gland is barely the size of a quarter. But there is no question that, as the male becomes older, and with enlargement of the gland, there is an increased incidence and likelihood of infection of that same gland.

Many factors are involved in the development of prostatitis. The most common site of bacteria entering the prostate gland is from the distal urethra. An ascending urethral infection is then most often associated with sexual contact from an infected source. Urethral cultures taken from male sexual partners of women whose vaginal secretions contained pathogenic bacteria showed at least a transient coloniza tion with these bacteria (18). The likelihood of a gonococcal infection as an initiating cause for an infection of the prostatic urethra also is well known. Other factors that may predispose to, or be the source of, infections include: instrumentation of the urethra; the use of, or presence of an indwelling Foley catheter; significant phimosis; poor genital hygiene especially in the uncircumcised male; and, on occasion, hematogenous spread from distant sources of infection in the body.

The pathologic organisms normally responsible for prostatitis are generally similar to the bacteria responsible for infection elsewhere in the urinary tract. Again, approximately 80% of infections are due to the various Gram-negative organisms such as *Escherichia coli*, *Klebsiella* species, *Enterobacter*, *Proteus*, and *Pseudomonas* species. *Chlamydia trachomatis* has recently been identified as an important contributing factor in the development of prostatitis. This is certainly true in the sexually active male, but sources other than sexual contact become increasingly more important as the etiology of prostatitis in the elderly male.

Acute prostatitis is generally bacterial and characterized by sudden onset of a moderate-to-high fever, chills, perineal pain, urinary frequency, malaise, possibly myalgia, and varying degrees of bladder outlet obstruction. Rectal examination reveals an exquisitely tender swollen prostate gland, either partially or totally involving the gland. The patients with this suspected diagnosis should not have their prostate gland massaged. In patients with acute prostatitis, bacteremia is very likely to result from vigorous rectal examination.

Patients with acute bacterial prostatitis and who are in an elderly age group should be considered for hospitalization. This is especially true if the degree of outlet obstruction caused by the swelling of the prostate gland requires catheterization. Various regimens of antibiotic therapy can be instituted depending on the severity of the illness and the overall health of the patient. Successful treatment of acute bacterial prostatitis by the use of oral doxycycline and trimethoprim-sulfamethoxazole has been reported. However, these reports deal primarily with young and middle-aged men who are probably in otherwise good general health. The elderly male may not tolerate the slowness of absorption of oral antibiotic and may deteriorate more rapidly. Therefore, the consideration for hospitalization and intravenous antibiotic therapy empirically treating for a Gram-negative organism with the use of intravenous ampicillin, cephalosporins, and aminoglycosides, is appropriate.

Chronic prostatitis is by far the most commonly encountered inflammatory condition in the elderly male. Symptoms may include any or all of the following: burning on urination; frequency of urination; suprapubic discomfort; inguinal discomfort; testicular discomfort; distal penile discomfort; low back pain; nocturia; increased daytime frequency; urgency; feeling of incomplete emptying; and also, occasionally, arthralgias. Rectal examination of these patients may or may not reveal any degree of tenderness of the prostate. The gland may show varying degrees of swelling. Urinalysis may reflect associated bladder involvement in this condition, but cannot be relied upon to exclude cystitis from prostatitis. Massaged prostatic secretions are also a helpful guide in determining the presence of prostatitis. It does not, however, distinguish bacterial from abacterial prostatitis.

The treatment of chronic prostatitis is associated with varying degrees of success with various types of medications. A urologist is always careful to warn a patient with prostatitis that the chances of cure are minimal. Basically, the reason for this is the well known fact that few antibiotics diffuse in sufficient concentration into the prostatic fluid and prostatic tissue to completely eradicate the bacteria that may be present therein. Drugs that have had varying degrees of success in treatment of prostatitis included sulfisoxazole (Gantrisin), sulfamethizole (Thiosulfil), and sulfamethoxazole (Gantanol), nitrofurantoin, nalidixic acid, trimethoprim-sulfamethoxazole (Bactrim or Septra), and carbenicillin. The length of therapy has varied. For the first episode, treatment for a period of 10–14 days is common. Continuation of the therapy beyond 2 weeks may be appropriate, especially in frequently recurring episodes.

The lack of response of the patient to any form of therapy mentioned above raises the possibility that one is dealing with other forms of prostatitis. The most common of these is nonbacterial prostatitis or prostatosis. The symptoms may be precisely the same, but the response to therapy is not nearly as good. Some of these patients may improve with anti-inflammatory agents such as phenylbutazone (Butazolidin) or indomethacin (Indocin). Periodic prostatic massage, sitz baths, and avoidance of dietary products such as coffee, colas, and alcoholic beverages are more often effective. It has been the authors' opinion, in fact, that in many cases the chemical irritants contained in coffee and colas are a frequent cause of persistent or recurring symptoms, when taken in daily, large amounts. Viral prostatitis has been reported. The exact frequency of viral prostatitis is difficult to determine but may be present if the patient describes the onset of the symptoms immediately with or after a flu or flu-like syndrome. Parasitic prostatitis may be attributed to those men in whom *Trichomonas vaginalis* is a common finding in the prostatic secretions. Although *Trichomonas* urethritis is more common than *Trichomonas* prostatitis, it is likely that this plays a part in a small group of men. The appropriate therapy using metronidazole (Flagyl) has been successful.

PROSTATIC OBSTRUCTION

Perhaps no other organ in the body increases in size and bulk, with the possible exception of body fat, as does the prostate gland. It is thought to begin its increase in size in the third decade of life. Many factors contribute to the growth of the prostate including testicular androgens, the adrenal glands, and the pituitary gland.

Symptoms of prostatic obstruction that are first noted by patients most often include hesitancy on urination, decreasing force and size of the urinary stream, and nocturia. These symptoms may be only mildly annoying at first but as the obstructive uropathy increases, the symptoms likewise worsen. As the obstructive uropathy becomes more pronounced, the patient relates that the hesitancy is increasing and that the stream is intermittent. At that point, abdominal pain from bladder distention may be apparent. If assistance is not sought by the patient, total retention of urine with possibly some involuntary overflow in voiding is the ultimate result.

Examination of the patient may disclose suprapubic tenderness or even a palpable bladder. The examination of the prostate gland rectally may show any variation in size from a relatively small gland to the size of a tennis ball or larger. Most often the gland, unless infected, is not tender. The absence of significant prostatic enlargement does not rule out an obstructing prostate. As an example, enlargement of the median bar or median lobe of the gland may not be palpable and would not be of significant size on rectal examination. This determination can only be made on cystoscopic evaluation.

Further diagnostic tests should include determination of renal function such as a creatinine and/or blood urea nitrogen. X-ray studies, including an intravenous pyelogram, are appropriate, although not mandatory in all cases. Cystoscopic examination is the next step in the evaluation of a possible outlet obstruction. Although the patient with urinary retention would require immediate catheterization, the routine catheterization of a patient that may be mildly symptomatic for determination of residual

urine is questionable. The possibility of introducing bladder infection by this maneuver is always of concern. The authors believe that this determination should be reserved more properly for the time of cystoscopic examination when further definitive procedures would probably follow.

A patient with a longstanding history of outlet obstruction and with a palpable bladder must be observed for possible electrolyte imbalance. This occurs when an indwelling catheter is inserted and a longstanding obstruction is relieved. Postobstructive diuresis can result in electrolyte imbalance and require hospitalization for intravenous replacement and electrolyte corrections. In an elderly male, this could be catastrophic if not carefully monitored.

Upon determination of the need for surgical correction of prostatic obstruction, one of two general approaches is indicated. Currently, about three of four patients can be properly managed by transurethral resection. The other 20–25%, in the hands of most urologists, are better managed by open prostatectomy. The two most common forms of open prostatectomy currently performed are suprapubic prostatectomy and retropubic prostatectomy.

An additional indication for open prostatectomy may occur in those men in whom large bladder calculi are associated with large prostate glands. The introduction of the ultrasonic and electrohydrolic lithotripsy units has increased the successful management of bladder calculi by the transurethral approach. This can then be followed by a transurethral prostatectomy.

The potential complications of any form of prostatectomy need to be outlined clearly to the patient before undertaking surgical correction. The most frequent problems encountered with prostatectomy of any type are: hematuria in the immediate postoperative period; urinary incontinence once the Foley catheter is removed; and urinary infection. If injury occurs to the urethral sphincter, the incontinence may be an ongoing and long-lasting problem requiring some secondary surgical correction. The incidence, however, of true urinary incontinence after surgery for benign prostatic hypertrophy is in the order of 0.5–1%. Urinary infections are mostly a problem in patients with longstanding urinary tract infections before the surgery or in those individuals in whom an indwelling Foley catheter was required for a long period of time before submitting to corrective surgery. In these cases, the probability of sterilization of the urinary tract are very low. In most other instances of prostatic surgery in which infection was not a preceding associated problem, chances of sterilization of the urinary tract following removal of the catheter and a period of immediate postoperative therapy are excellent.

Another problem that is necessarily addressed before the undertaking of prostatic surgery is the question of impotence associated with prostatectomy. What can be stated with relative certainty is that alteration in the ejaculatory ability at the time of intercourse will certainly result after prostatic surgery. Obviously, this is the result of removal of the glandular tissue that is responsible for a large portion of the seminal fluid. In addition, it also is known that in a normal situation, at the time of ejaculation, the bladder neck closes causing the ejaculate to pass from the proximal urethra into the distal urethra and meatus. After prostatectomy, the bladder neck very often is wide open. Therefore, any ejaculation that occurs postprostatectomy will result in the seminal fluid passing into the bladder. Impotence is not a postoperative complication as many series have shown. Just as many patients will claim an improved sexual capability as will those who claim decreased sexual ability. The majority are unaffected one way or the other postprostatectomy. One operative procedure that is associated with a slightly higher incidence of impotence postoperatively is the perineal prostatectomy. This is an open-type prostatectomy that is still used occasionally for benign disease.

CARCINOMA OF THE PROSTATE

Carcinoma of the prostate is the second most common malignancy of adult males. Therefore, proper and important attention must be directed to a discussion of this problem. The etiology of carcinoma of the prostate, like so many other malignancies, is still obscure. Some facts that are known are the relative infrequency of this malignancy before the fourth decade of life and rapid increase of frequency beginning with the sixth decade. The importance of prostatitis as a preceding cause for carcinoma of the prostate remains unproven. Some authors recently have alluded to the fact that irregular ejaculation and chronic congestion of the prostate gland may contribute in some way to an increased incidence of carcinoma of the prostate. All these conjectures remain to be proven and supported by significant studies.

The symptoms of prostatic carcinoma may vary from an asymptomatic nodule noted on rectal examination to urinary retention of a rather sudden onset. Symptoms may present in other parts of the body as evidence of metastasis rather than causing difficulty in the prostate gland itself.

Urologists have often received requests for consultation on a patient who first presented with metastatic signs and symptoms and in which the prostate was the site of origin. Among the more frequent occurrences has been in those patients in whom x-rays have shown osteoblastic disease, but in whom there are no obvious symptoms of prostatic obstruction uropathy (Fig. 23.4). In others, the patient may present on a neurology or neurosurgical service with a rapid onset of paraplegia. The findings on x-ray suggest osteoblastic disease and a decompression laminectomy produces material consistent with adenocarcinoma. Still other patients presenting on the medical or surgical services with abdominal masses in the lower abdomen have been found to have metastatic carcinoma to inguinal, or even iliac, nodes. In many instances, in which the first findings are those of distant metastases, the prostate itself may not have the classic finding of hardness that is attributable to carcinoma of the prostate. The fact that the gland is not strongly suspicious should not exclude the need for biopsies of the prostate for diagnostic purposes.

The routine rectal examination of all males over the age of 50 years, on an annual basis, is a simple but rewarding examination in early detection of this particular tumor. A prostate gland that presents with a hard, occasionally irregular nodule, or that is uniformly hard with ill-defined margins, is carcinoma of the prostate until proven otherwise. However, an area of inflammation or questionable nodularity should raise suspicion of early carcinoma. It is with this group of patients that adjunctive, if possible, noninvasive techniques, would be helpful, before subjecting the patient to the risks of prostatic biopsy. It appears that several new modalities are now appearing to help physicians in their attempt at earlier detection of this common malignancy.

Prostatic acid phosphatase (PAP) has been available as an adjunctive test for several years. When elevated, this usually indicates metastatic disease of the prostate. Occasionally, elevated serum levels may represent an extensive local lesion. Occasionally, false-positive elevations may occur transiently after manipulation of the prostate gland. Other occasional causes of false elevation of PAP may be: hemolyzed blood samples; Paget's disease of bones; hyperparathyroidism; other primary hematologic disorders.

One of the earliest descriptions of the use of rectal ultrasonography in the diagnosis of cancer of the prostate appeared in 1976 in a paper by Boyce et al. (2). The technique continues to be perfected to the point where some authors tout this modality as a

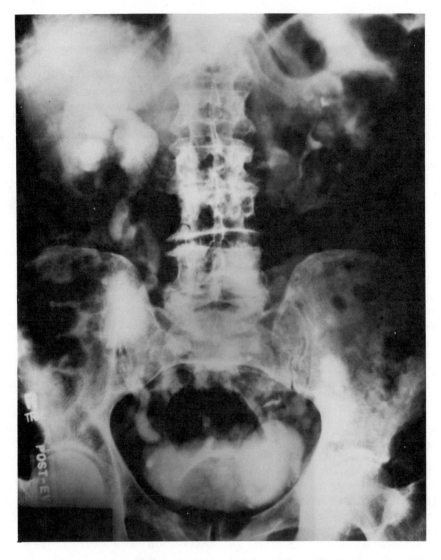

Figure 23.4. This x-ray demonstrates diffuse osteoblastic metastases. The stark white areas on the various bones are the metastatic sites.

screening mechanism for cancer of the prostate. But the results thus far are not reproducible as to accuracy, in multiple centers. However, it is highly probable that rectal ultrasonography has reached the stage of being an adjunct in the workup of a susceptible prostatic lesion.

Histopathologic diagnosis remains the only certain confirmation of cancer of the prostate. Standard core biopsies of the prostate, either by the transperineal approach or transrectal approach, are certain confirmation of 90% of carcinomas of the prostate. However, the need for anesthesia for good biopsy results, the not insignificant risk of sepsis,

and the potential for bleeding from this biopsy technique cause many urologists to hesitate in performing this procedure, especially in an elderly male who is an anesthesia risk, or in whom overall medical conditions may not change the course of management if a diagnosis is confirmed.

On the other hand, recent advances in transrectal fine needle aspiration biopsy may make the risky process of standard needle biopsy frequently unnecessary. This modality requires no anesthesia, entails very low risk of infection or bleeding, and according to its proponents is little more than an office procedure. If more generalized use of this diagnostic modality proves satisfactory, the diagnosis of carcinoma of the prostate will be made more effective especially in the early or suspicious prostate gland.

The treatment of carcinoma of the prostate will depend on many factors: the age of the patient; overall general medical condition; and the presence or absence of metastasis. There are very few unequivocal statements that may be made concerning this malignancy. Carcinoma of the prostate in a younger man has, unquestionably, a uniformly poor prognosis as compared to the onset of this same malignancy in a man in his eighth decade of life. All other factors concerning this malignancy, its treatment and prognosis, remain in a state of flux and require frequent re-evaluation. The reader is referred to the many current articles on prostatic carcinoma in the literature for in-depth reviews and opinions.

ANTERIOR AND POSTERIOR URETHRA

The prostatic urethra and prostate comprise, by far, the major cause of urinary difficulty in the male of any age and especially in the elderly male. However, the urethra is a conduit that has other sites for possible difficulty and these sites and their potential

difficulties must be considered. Figure 23.5 shows the urethra divided into an anterior and posterior part. The posterior urethra comprises the prostatic and the membranous urethra. The membranous urethra is contained in the urogenital diaphragm and is the least distensible. Its length is approximately 1 cm. An injury to this area, whether by trauma or by iatrogenic means, is the main source of urinary incontinence. Unfortunately, this is also a common area of inflammatory stricture both from Foley catheters and instrumentation of any type.

The anterior urethra is the longer of the two segments. It begins distal to the membranous urethra and includes the bulbous urethra and pendulous urethra. The distal portions of the pendulous urethra include the fossa navicularis and the urethral meatus. Along any portion of this urethra, strictures may be encountered and may be a cause of difficulty in urination or a cause of difficulty in insertion of a Foley catheter. Previously, the most frequent cause for strictures of the urethra was gonococcal urethritis. This has diminished in recent years due to the more adequate means of therapy for this inflammatory process. At the present

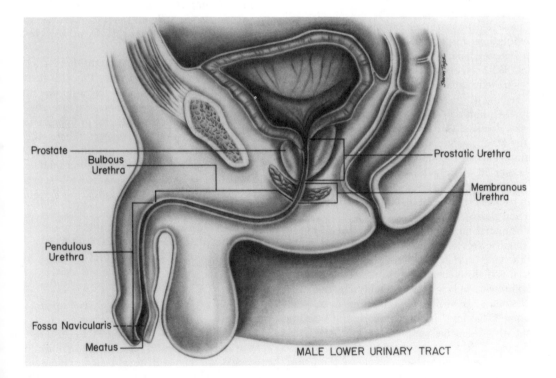

MALE LOWER URINARY TRACT

Figure 23.5. The various portions of the male lower urinary tract are identified. The prostatic and membranous urethras comprise the posterior urethra. The bulbous and pendulous urethra are referred to as the anterior urethra.

time, strictures are more often caused by trauma or iatrogenic means.

Carcinoma of the urethra in the male is uncommon. It is most often found in areas of stricture. Any mass associated with a stricture should be suspected of containing a possible malignancy and a biopsy should be performed.

Urethritis in the elderly is certainly seen, but with far less frequency than in the more sexually active younger male.

DISEASES OF THE PENIS

The commonly encountered problems of the penis and external genitalia in the elderly include such problems as phimosis, paraphimosis, balanitis, and balanoposthitis. Phimosis is the tightness of the foreskin around the glans causing varying degrees of difficulty in retracting the foreskin, or not being able to retract the foreskin at all. Paraphimosis is used to describe the foreskin that is trapped proximal to the corona (Fig. 23.6). This causes considerable swelling and pain and edema of the foreskin in this position and if left untreated would result in necrosis of the foreskin and infection.

Balanitis and balanoposthitis refer to the inflammation of the foreskin (balanitis) and the foreskin and glans (balanoposthitis). It is most often noted in two situations in particular: (a) in male patients with diabetes, balanitis and balanoposthitis are frequent. With recurring flareups, the foreskin becomes more inflamed and contracts and then tears. The healing of the torn foreskin causes increasing tightness (phimosis) and the process continues until either a dorsal slit or a circumcision is performed; (b) the other major cause of balanitis and balanoposthitis encountered in the elderly male occurs in those men in whom external urinary drainage devices (condoms, catheters) are used. These devices often result in significant inflammation of the foreskin and glans.

The management of balanoposthitis depends on the condition of the patient, the goals to be obtained and the long-term expected results. The treatment of balanoposthitis consists of cleaning the penis and foreskin twice daily with mild bland soap, then, the application of an antibiotic-steroid-ointment combination (Mycolog). If the balanoposthitis recurs frequently, definitive surgical therapy is usually necessary.

Another common problem involving the penis, usually encountered in men in their 50s, but not infrequently seen in later years, is Peyronie's disease. Peyronie's disease, or fibrous cavernositis, is the formation of single or multiple fibrous plaques that envelop the cavernous sheaths of the penis. The condition is well established, but its etiology remains a mystery. The only fact that stands out in multiple studies concerning this illness is its frequent association with Dupuytren's contracture. No other etiologic or associated illness has been found to explain this condition. The most common fear of the patient is that of malignancy. This can be rapidly dispelled by reassurance. The condition causes curvature on erection, pain on erection, and flacidity of the erection beyond the point of this plaque. The onset may be rapid but the resolution of this condition is even slower.

Therapy is difficult because of the uncertainty of its etiology. At times, surgical removal of the fibrous plaques with utilization of skin graft has been done, but this is not advocated in general for the smaller or nonprogressive condition. The use of p-aminobenzoate (Potaba) is probably the most widely used medication for this purpose. Some benefit may also be gained by use of vitamin E.

Premalignant lesions of the penis include leukoplakia, erythroplasia of Queyrat, and Bowen's disease. The last two, erythroplasia and Bowen's disease, are probably the most likely premalignant lesions encountered. These lesions are often present on the glans especially on the uncircumcised male and appear velvety or actually have red plaques. They may be tender.

Carcinoma of the penis is a condition that occurs in the age group from 31–85 years, but with an average age of 63 years (11). The diagnosis was made upon examination of the glans or the foreskin and finding a lesion that was enlarging or appeared elevated, or in some way was suspect. There still remains a significant instance of carcinoma of the penis in uncircumcised males. A large number of these malignancies may be managed by local or partial excision but once metastasized are extremely difficult to manage and cure.

DISEASES OF THE SCROTUM AND SCROTAL CONTENTS

EPIDIDYMITIS

The most frequently encountered acute problem of the scrotum in the elderly male is epididymitis. Usually, epididymitis is secondary to an intercurrent urinary tract infection with the organism proceeding down the vas deferens causing epididymitis and/or epididymo-orchitis. Another cause of epididymitis follows instrumentation and/or surgery of the lower urinary tract. Patients normally present with a tender, enlarging hemiscrotum, although bi-

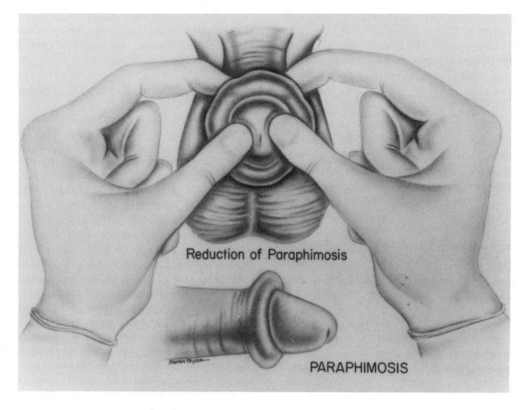

Reduction of Paraphimosis

PARAPHIMOSIS

Figure 23.6. Paraphimosis is often misdiagnosed as penile edema. If necrosis of skin is not too severe, the condition is quickly improved by reduction of foreskin in the manner shown.

lateral involvement can occur. Patients are usually febrile and in considerable pain and frequently are unable to walk. A history of either symptoms of urinary tract infection or instrumentation are frequently obtained.

Treatment involves bed rest, scrotal elevation, ice packs to progression to heat as pain subsides, and appropriate antibiotic therapy. Although normally a controllable condition, if attention is not properly paid to this condition, septicemia and death have been reported on occasion.

HYDROCELE

A frequent finding on physical examination of the elderly male is cystic enlargement, usually unilateral, of the scrotum. If there is a minimal amount of fluid present, the testicle is readily palpable. However, if enough fluid is contained within the tunica vaginalis, the testis may not be palpated with certainty. The diagnosis of hydrocele is further supported by transillumination of the scrotal wall. Surgery is indicated only if the patient is clinically symptomatic or possibly having local hygiene prob-

lems. In the differential diagnosis of hydrocele is a large, direct inguinal hernia and a spermatocele.

SCROTAL HERNIA

Another frequently encountered cause of scrotal swelling in the elderly male is a large direct inguinal hernia. Differentiating features from that of a hydrocele are that a hernia usually does not transilluminate, the testis is palpable at the very base of scrotum, and fullness of external ring where the abdominal content has tranversed into the scrotum. Not all large hernias of this magnitude need to be surgically repaired. A general surgical opinion is advised.

SPERMATOCELE

A spermatocele is an intrascrotal cyst resulting from a partial obstruction of the tubular system that transports sperm. It differs from a hydrocele in that it usually lies at the upper pole of the testis. Like the hydrocele, it transilluminates. Occasionally, spermatoceles reach such size as to appear like hydroceles. Spermatoceles may also occur concurrently with a hydrocele.

Small spermatoceles seldom need surgical removal. However, larger size spermatoceles and those that cause increasing discomfort may be removed surgically.

CANCER OF TESTIS

Malignancy of the testis is normally a disease of the young adult. In the elderly male, testicular tumors are seen, but are generally secondary to metastatic disease including lymphoma and, not infrequently, metastatic carcinoma from the prostate.

HEMATURIA

One of the most frequent causes for referral to a urologist is hematuria. This is true of all age groups. Whereas there is increasing conservatism in the workup of the child and young adult for microscopic hematuria especially (10), the same is not forcefully supported in the elderly. Nevertheless, it remains difficult to have a logical and uniform approach to the evaluation of the elderly with hematuria. An effort to do this for the reader will be made, being fully aware that no system will be totally infallible.

Three scenarios are most common with hematuria: gross painless hematuria; microscopic painless hematuria; hematuria either gross or microscopic, but associated with symptoms. Gross painless hematuria reliably documented should have a primary urologic evaluation in every case. This evaluation should consist of an intravenous urogram and, most likely, a cystoscopy. In cases of allergy to the dye, a KUB x-ray and renal sonogram together with a cystoscopy, would be a secondary method of evaluation.

Symptomatic hematuria, whether gross or microscopic, can be very appropriately treated first. Such causes as cystitis or urethritis in the female, or prostatitis in the male, may be treated until symptomatically clear. If hematuria persists after all other symptoms have disappeared, then urologic evaluation is indicated.

The final category of patients is most likely to cause a dilemma. Asymptomatic microscopic hematuria (defined as more than 2-3 red blood cells per high powered field), does not need full urologic workup in all age groups. Several studies (10, 18) have shown that the child, adolescent, and young adult, have a very poor yield from a urologic workup. However, these studies do show an especially significant finding or urologic pathology over age 69 years. Therefore, it is reasonable, at least, to perform an in-

perform an intravenous urogram and urine cytology as a primary workup. In most cases, a cystoscopy should be also considered if the information is not obtained by the initial tests.

IMPOTENCE AND SEXUALITY OF AGING

Sexual problems are of increasing importance in any practice treating the elderly male. There are two principal reasons for this development. More people are reaching middle and later years in a state of greater physical health than in the past. With the age of sexual enlightenment that has occurred in the last decade, these men are also questioning changes in their own body functions and looking for corrective answers if at all possible. Indeed, some specialists in the field of sex counseling have remarked that the family practitioner will see this to be second only to alcoholism as a major health problem in the very near future in the elderly patients coming to the office. It is certainly not within the purview of this treatise to explore exhaustively all the psychologic as well as organic causes for impotence and sexual dysfunctions in the elderly male. Rather, it is important to look at the principal causes and do a good initial evaluation of the patient's health and background, and also to obtain some ideas of the patient's impressions of this malady.

It has by now become a cliché in medicine, but it is most important that the treating physician be comfortable in discussing the problems of sex and marital relations with the patient. Also, the physician must now accept the idea that the old concept of "well it's because you are getting old and those things happen" is no longer acceptable in this area of sexuality and sexual dysfunction. It is necessary to treat this complaint as one would any other illness. Indeed, sexual dysfunction may be the underlying reason for a patient's minor psychosomatic complaints.

The physician should obtain a full and complete history. There are specific questions that need to be asked of the patient concerning the problem of impotence. The physician should ask whether the problem is that of inability to obtain an erection or an inability to maintain an erection during intercourse, or a combination of both. It is important to determine whether it is a matter of partial erection versus full erection or is there only partial turgidity versus full turgidity of the penis. The physician should inquire whether the impotence pattern changes with the circumstances. By this it is meant does the impotence occur with one partner, but not with others; or is there an ability to obtain erection with masturbation; or are there erections in the morning on arising, but not at other times. It is also very important to inquire about the recollection of the circumstances at the time of the erectile loss. And finally, it is most important to ask the patient the question of whether it is a matter of loss of ability or is it a loss of desire or libido. If the patient answers in the affirmative concerning the loss of libido, then one is probably faced with more of a psychologic impotence, which is probably more difficult to treat and may rest in the area of sexual counseling by a specialist in this area.

However, the patient in many instances does not indicate a loss of libido, but indicates a loss of ability to perform sexually. In these cases, it is necessary to inquire into the history of diabetes, alcoholism, or drug abuse. It is important to know the presence of other medical problems such as hypertension or vascular disease. It is important to inquire about a possible history of thyroid or neurologic diseases. Urologic problems that may be important are the presence of Peyronie's disease.

Medications are a common cause of impotence in the elderly. As the pharmacologic armamentorium has grown for all illnesses, so has the likelihood of these medications interfering with sexual potency in the male. Major drug categories with some common examples will be listed. For a complete list of all drugs, the reader is referred to the article by Van Arsdolen and Wein (19).

Antihypertensive drugs are the most common medications seen in this age group. They would include the diuretics such as the thiazides and spironolactones; reserpine-containing compounds; guanethidine; the α-adrenergic blockers, such as phentolamine and phenoxybenzamine; and even the β-blockers, such as propranolol and metoprolol.

Many psychotropic drugs can be agents that affect sexual function. The tricylic antidepressants, such as amitriptyline, imipramine and doxepin, the phenothiazines, and the benzodiazopines are major drug categories in this group.

Another large category of drugs often seen in use in the elderly are anticholinergics. These include the bella donna drugs, anti-parkinson agents, antihistamines, and muscle relaxants.

Other individual drugs that are known to cause effect on libido and impotence include cimetidine, estrogens (as when used in treatment of carcinoma of prostate), lithium, and indomethacin. This listing is only an overview and is by no means exclusive.

Patients with a past history of vascular disease are very likely to have progressive loss of potency.

Patients with aneurysms of the abdominal or iliac vessels and those patients who have previously undergone vascular bypass for these disorders are very likely to be impotent.

Physical examination of the impotent patient should include the examination of the abdomen and blood pressure. The abdomen should be examined specifically for abdominal bruits and also for evidence of previous surgery including aortic or femoral surgery. Other types of operative procedures that may induce impotence include surgery for carcinoma of the colon, in which dissection in the pelvic area might have the potential for disrupting the nervi erigentes and the pudendal nerve. Examination of the inguinal areas should include the femoral pulsations to determine circulatory potential to the lower extremities as well as the genitalia. The determination of penile circulation can be specifically measured by the use of the Doppler flowmeter. This assessment significantly improves this part of the evaluation of the penis. Examination of the genitalia should reveal any evidence of phimosis that may be restrictive of the ability for erection. The penis should also be examined for the presence of plaques of Peyronie's disease. An examination of the testes should be done to determine if they are reasonable in size taking into account that the testes may be somewhat smaller with age. If the testes are atrophic, hypogonadism as a contributing factor to the impotence is then likely.

Examination of the rectum and prostate is important. If, for instance, the examination of the rectal sphincter reveals poor rectal tone, there would be concern about the innervation of the pudendal nerve. The prostate gland may be congested or be otherwise inflamed and that may be a contributing factor to the problem of impotence.

Once the history and physical examination has been completed, the next step includes the appropriate diagnostic tests. A basic test that should be obtained would be a fasting blood sugar and if necessary, a glucose tolerance test. Also, a serum prolactin and serum testosterone should be measured. If there has been a history of alcoholism, liver function tests would be appropriate. More recently, the development of the penile tumescence testing devices have been developed and are available to aid in determining those men in whom the likelihood that the impotence problem is circulatory in nature.

TREATMENT

Because of the multiplicity of causes for impotence, there are available an increasingly wide array of treatments for impotence. Only an overview of approaches can be addressed here. In those patients in whom the history suggests a causal relationship with illness or medications, there is the potential for correction. As an example, in the case of the patient on antihypertensive drugs, changing the patient to another form of antihypertensive management, if possible, may result in improvement of potency. With the alcoholic, one is faced with accelerated destruction of male hormone by the liver along with other altered functions caused by the alcoholism. Therefore, the treatment of the alcoholism is paramount.

Penile Revascularization

The findings of iliac and/or aortic disease causing ischemia of the lower extremities and ischemia of the genitalia are of some concern. Until recently, there was no hope for reversal of this problem. Some authors have indicated that revascularization of the internal iliacs could improve these patients. The evolution of microvascular surgery has enhanced this possibility.

When the patient's impotence is due to previous surgery, whether it be from vascular surgery, or when the neurologic axis has been interrupted in such operations as an abdominoperineal resection, or when radical prostatectomy or cystoprostatectomy has been performed for malignancies and in the longstanding diabetic, one is left with no possibility for return of erectile function. The physician and the patient then need to discuss the various forms of artificially induced methods of creating erections.

Penile Prosthesis

Prosthetic placements or penile implants, have become frequently used modalities of creating artificial erections. This surgery began first with the use of the solid and, more recently, a hinged prosthesis has been developed that makes the erection more comfortable and easier to conceal.

Further refinement in the area of implanted penile prosthesis has led to the use of either a hydraulic prosthesis or an inflatable prosthesis. The inflatable prosthesis uses a reservoir away from the penis to store the fluid for inflation. The hydraulic prosthesis, a more recent development, stores the fluid in the base of the penile prosthesis itself. Both forms of inflatable prosthesis make it easier to conceal the penis in the noninflatable state.

Pharmacologic Injection

The injection of vasodilators, Papavarine and Phentolamine, into the corpora cavernosa has been developed and used successfully to induce temporary erections (20). As this method has spread in usage, its limitations and side effects have become more evident. At this point, the proper parameters for the use of Papauarine-Phentolamine injections remain to be defined.

Other Pharmacologic Treatment

The oral or intramuscular injection of testosterone has been in use for some time. Currently, it is believed that the appropriate use of these agents is only when serum levels demonstrate a low testosterone level. In those cases, either methyl testosterone buccal tablets, fluoxymesterone oral tablets, or testosterone cypionate intramuscular injections are helpful.

An intriguing old drug has been in use for approximately 5 years and is a nonhormonal compound. The drug, yohimbine, an α-adrenergic blocking agent, has had some degree of success in various types of organic impotence. This drug, in doses of 6 mg, three to four times daily, is worth a trial because of low incidence of side effects.

Psychotherapy

Not too many years ago, this form of treatment was recommended in some form of offhand remark by many physicians. Today evidence is strongly in favor of organic causes as being the major cause for impotence. Furthermore, the use of various penile tumescence and sleep laboratory testings have helped to point out those patients that would benefit most from counseling and behavior modification.

In summary, it becomes apparent that impotence is not a simple problem of aging. It is a much more complex problem with some answers, partially correctable, and other questions yet to be answered. It is, therefore, incumbent upon the physician not to indicate to the patient that the problem is one of becoming old.

REFERENCES

1. Boscca J: Impaired elderly more prone to bacteriuria. *Med World News*, November 28, 1985.
2. Boyce H, et al: Ultrasonography as an aid in the diagnosis and management of surgical diseases of the pelvis: Special emphasis on the genitourinary system. *Ann Surg* 184:477, 1976.

3. Brocklehurst JC, Dillane JB, Griffiths L, Fry J: The prevelance and symptomatology of urinary infections in an aged population. *Gerontol Clin* 10:242, 1968.
4. Buckwold J, et al: Therapy for acute cystitis in adult women: Randomized comparison of single dose sulfasoxazole vs. trimethoprim-sulfamethoxazole. *JAMA* 247:1839, 1982.
5. Corson C: How to treat urinary tract infections. *Drug Ther* Nov:32, 1982.
6. Dontas S: The effect of bacteriuria on survival in old age. *Geriatr Urol* 2:74, 1983.
7. Kaye D: Problems concerning bacteriuria in the elderly. *Infect Dis* 12:4, 1982.
8. Kurtz B: UTI in the elderly: Seeking solutions for special problems. *Geriatrics* 35:97, 1980.
9. Mayer R: UTI in the elderly: How to select treatment. *Geriatrics* 35:67, 1980.
10. Mohn DN, et al: Asymptomatic micro-hematuria and urologic disease. *JAMA* 256:224, 1986.
11. Persky L, Dekernion J: Carcinoma of the penis. *CA* 26:130, 1976.
12. Romano J, Kaye D: UTI in the elderly: Common yet atypical. *Geriatrics* 36:113, 1981.
13. Rubin RH, et al: Single-dose amoxicillin therapy for urinary tract infection. *JAMA* 244:561, 1980.
14. Schaeffer AJ, Childs SS: Bladder defense: Current concepts of UTI management. *Infect Surg* 4:271, 1985.
15. Single Drug Dose Fails to Halt Cystitis: Medical World News for Obstetricians, Gynecologist and Urologists: p. 7, March 13, 1986.
16. Smith IM: Infections in the elderly. *Hosp Pract.* July, 1982, p. 69–85.
17. Sourander LB: Urinary tract infection in the aged—an epidemiological study. *Drs Intern Med* (Suppl 45) 55:7, 1966.
18. Stamey JA: *Urinary Infections.* Baltimore, Williams & Wilkins, 1972.
19. Van Arsdalen KM, Wein AJ: Drug induced sexual dysfunction in older men. *Geriatrics* 39:63, 1984.
20. Zorgniotti AW, Lefleur RS: Auto-injection of the corporo cavernosum with a vasoactive drug combination for vasculogenic impotence. *J Urol* 133:39, 1985.

Urinary Incontinence

M. JANETTE BUSBY

One of the most common and difficult problems involving the urinary tract in elderly patients is urinary incontinence or involuntary loss of urine. In this section, the epidemiology, pathophysiology, classification, diagnosis, and treatment of this important geriatric problem will be examined.

EPIDEMIOLOGY

Recent prevalence studies have shown that urinary incontinence affects approximately 50% of all elderly patients in long-term care facilities, 35–40% of all geriatric patients in acute care hospitals, and approximately 15–20% of community dwelling elderly in the United States. Over one-half of all cases of urinary incontinence are undiagnosed. Patients who are female, immobile, who have neurologic disease or who have a history of gynecologic or urologic surgery, are more at risk for developing incontinence.

PATHOPHYSIOLOGY

Urinary incontinence is not an inevitable consequence of the aging process. Rather, its presence reflects an underlying disorder that is structural, functional, or iatrogenic in origin.

The basic structure of the lower urinary tract consists of the bladder (detrusor muscle), and the urethra with its internal and external sphincters. The bladder maintains a variable volume, yet remains a constant low pressure storage system. The internal sphincter is formed by the smooth muscle layers of the urethra and is important in preserving continence. The external sphincter is composed of urethral striated muscle that may be voluntarily contracted to interrupt voiding.

Neurologic innervation of the lower urinary tract system is cholinergic, adrenergic, and somatic. Coordination of bladder and sphincter function occurs via the cholinergic inhibitory centers of the central nervous system that are located in the frontal lobes and basal ganglia. The basic reflex controlling micturition occurs through the parasympathetic (cholinergic) S2-4 sacral nerve roots. During bladder filling, urine storage is enhanced by (a) stimulation of β-adrenergic receptors, inhibiting cholinergic effects on the bladder and causing relaxation and (b) stimulation of α-adrenergic receptors, thus constricting the internal sphincter. Somatic innervation through the pudendal nerve allows voluntary contraction of the external sphincter, which protects against urine loss with sudden increases in abdominal pressure.

For normal voiding to occur, intravesical pressure must overcome bladder outlet and urethral sphincter resistance. Continued bladder filling increases cholinergic tone, stimulating involuntary contraction of the bladder. Simultaneously adrenergic blockade occurs, acting on β-adrenergic receptors in the bladder and α-adrenergic receptors in the internal sphincter. Detrusor constriction is enhanced while the internal sphincter relaxes. Unless central inhibition occurs, the consequence of this sequence of events is normal micturition.

Normal micturition is thus a complicated process requiring the integration of musculoskeletal and neurologic responses to stimuli from the lower urinary tract. If any component of this intricately balanced physiologic mechanism is disrupted, urinary incontinence may occur.

CLASSIFICATION

The initial distinction to be made by the clinician is whether the patient has temporary or established incontinence. Temporary incontinence generally occurs suddenly, is associated with an acute medical or surgical illness (myocardial infarction, pneumonia, hip fracture) or drug therapy (diuretics, sedatives, hypnotics, anticholinergics) and is reversible. Extensive, inconvenient, uncomfortable, and costly evaluation and treatment can be avoided with proper identification of temporary incontinence. Established incontinence is usually chronic, not related to acute illness, requires investigation, and may be reversible with proper diagnosis and treatment.

Classification of the types of established incontinence can be useful for directing proper workup and treatment of this problem. The categories described by Williams and Pannill, based on underlying pathophysiology, seem to be the most useful: detrusor instability; overflow incontinence; sphincter insufficiency; functional; and iatrogenic causes.

DETRUSOR INSTABILITY

Detrusor instability (unstable bladder, spastic bladder, uninhibited bladder) results from unsuppressed cholinergic bladder contractions that are strong enough to overcome outlet resistance. Therefore, any insult to the structural integrity of the cholinergic inhibitory centers of the CNS can cause detrusor instability. Alzheimer's disease, cerebrovascular atherosclerosis, multiple sclerosis, Parkinson's disease, spinal cord tumors, or cervical spondylosis among others may result in incontinence by this mechanism. Alternatively, increased sensory stimulation that overrides central inhibition may occur in the presence of local, irritating processes such as fecal impaction, enlarged prostate, or inflammation from radiation or chemotherapy. Increased detrusor tone that is unsuppressed may also result from frequent, low volume voiding that may be begun by a patient in an effort to avoid an accident.

OVERFLOW INCONTINENCE

Overflow incontinence may result primarily from two causes: outlet obstruction or insufficient detrusor tone due to neurologic disease (atonic or neurogenic bladder). Outlet obstruction is more common in men than in women and is usually due to prostatic hypertrophy. Urinary incontinence of this type may be precipitated by drugs that block the cholinergically induced contraction of the detrusor muscle. Insufficient detrusor tone may result from low spinal cord lesions, diabetic or alcoholic neuropathy, or the chronic use of muscle relaxants. Diabetes mellitus or tabes dorsalis may cause a decrease in sensory input from the bladder; however, central inhibition remains intact so patients may be able to maintain volitional bladder control by voiding at scheduled times. A functional obstruction may occur with uncoordinated contractions of the bladder and external sphincter. This bladder-sphincter dyssynergia is uncommon in the elderly and primarily occurs with spinal cord injury.

SPHINCTER INSUFFICIENCY

Almost one-third of all incontinent women have internal sphincter insufficiency (stress incontinence). Sphincter weakness may result from local urethral inflammation, multiparity, neurologic disease, radiation therapy, or sympatholytic drugs. In men, this condition occurs much less frequently, usually in those who have had a prostatectomy.

FUNCTIONAL

Functional incontinence primarily results either from the inability of otherwise continent persons to reach the toilet in time or from psychologic factors. Joint pain, muscle weakness, inconveniently located toilets or physical restraints can lead to functional incontinence. Depression or hostility, especially occurring after institutionalization, are two psychologic factors that may result in incontinence.

IATROGENIC

Iatrogenic incontinence may be the most important type of incontinence because it occurs frequently and is usually completely reversible. Orders for physical restraints and drugs are the two primary ways in which physicians may help precipitate urinary incontinence in their patients. Table 23.1 lists some common drugs implicated in this problem.

CLINICAL PRESENTATIONS

The patient with detrusor instability usually presents with symptoms of frequency and nocturia with a loss of large urine volumes (>100 ml). Many pa-

Table 23.1
Common Drugs That May Be Implicated in Urinary Incontinence

Detrusor instability	
Sedatives/hypnotics	Flurazepam
	Diazepam
	Ethanol
Overflow	
α-Adrenergic agonist	Pseudoephedrine
Antiarrhythmics	Disopyroamide
Antispasmotics	Belladonna/Phenobarbitol
	(Donnatal)
	Dicyclomine
Antiparkinsonian agents	Benztropine mesylate
	Trihexyphenydyl
Opiates	Diphenoxylate
	Meperidine
	Morphine
Psychotropics	Amitryptyline
	Chlorpromazine
	Imipramine
Sphincter insufficiency	
α-Adrenergic antagonist	α Methyldopa
	Prazosin

tients also complain of urgency, which has led some authors to label this condition "urge incontinence." People with overflow incontinence usually strain to void and have very small urine volumes. With sphincter insufficiency (stress incontinence), small amounts of urine are lost with laughing, coughing, straining, or a change in position. Nocturia is uncommon. Complaints of intermittent daytime incontinence usually when the patient is attempting to reach the toilet are common for functional incontinence. Depressed or hostile patients may have no complaints.

EVALUATION

An incontinence record can be a valuable adjunct to a good history for documenting onset and duration, frequency, amount of urine lost per episode, and associated factors (cough, laugh, urge, after receiving medication). Symptoms of dysuria and hematuria may suggest infection. A decrease in force of the urine stream and strain with urination suggests obstruction; inability to stop urine flow voluntarily suggests pelvic muscle weakness.

Abdominal, rectal, genital, and neurologic examinations are the focus of physical diagnosis for urinary incontinence. With a full bladder, the patient should cough, laugh, or strain in order to induce urine leakage. The patient then voids and the urine volume is measured. A palpable bladder strongly suggests overflow incontinence. The rectal exam may reveal fecal impaction, pelvic mass, or enlarged prostate gland. The size of the prostate, however, does not correlate well with obstruction. Assessing perianal sensation, constriction and relaxation of the sphincter will test innervation.

During pelvic examination, prolapse of urethra, bladder, or uterus or pelvic mass should be sought. Atrophic vaginitis reflects lack of estrogen, which is important for maintaining the thickness of the urethral mucosa. Sphincter insufficiency should be checked by placing a finger just inside the vagina on either side of the urethra while the patient coughs. Pressure against the fingers may be felt and urine loss may occur with stress incontinence. If upward pressure of the fingers stops urine leakage (positive Bonney test), this is also strongly suggestive of stress incontinence.

LABORATORY EVALUATION

Initial diagnostic testing should include urinalysis and urine culture (infection, neoplasm) as well as serum electrolytes, urea nitrogen, calcium, and glucose (renal insufficiency, polyuric syndromes). The urine studies may be obtained in conjunction with measurement of postvoid residual volume 10 to 15 minutes after the patient has emptied the bladder. A residual volume of 100 ml or greater indicates either obstruction or atonic bladder and is an indication for further urologic evaluation.

Sphincter insufficiency is the only type of urinary incontinence that can be reliably diagnosed by medical history and physical examination given clear-cut symptoms. Once simple sphincter insufficiency and acute medical (temporary), metabolic, functional, and iatrogenic causes of urinary incontinence have been eliminated, most patients will need cystometry with full-bladder provocative testing for accurate diagnosis.

TREATMENT

The most important aspect of treating urinary incontinence is accurate diagnosis. Then with appropriate therapy, most patients will improve in terms of reduced incontinence or increased comfort.

Treatment of detrusor instability is directed toward decreasing or blocking uninhibited contraction. Anticholinergic drugs, such as oxybutynin (Ditropan) and imipramine (Tofranil) have been found to be effective in controlled studies in at least 50% of patients tested. Oxybutynin may be given in an initial dose of 5 mg bid, which may be increased to tid. Improvement is generally seen within 1 week. Starting dose for imipramine is 25 mg at night, which may be increased every third night by 25 mg to a total of 150 mg. Both drugs may cause classic anticholinergic side effects including dry mouth, drowsiness, constipation, or urinary retention (especially with partial obstruction or benign prostatic hypertrophy). Confusion is more commonly seen with oxybutynin, while postural hypotension occurs primarily with imipramine. As with most drugs prescribed for the elderly patient, the lowest dose possible with the fewest side effects should be used.

Bladder-sphincter biofeedback in association with bladder retraining has been successfully used in selected patients to teach voluntary inhibition of detrusor contractions. This approach is most successful with patients who are mobile and who have minimal cognitive impairment.

Therapy of overflow incontinence is aimed at achieving a completely drained bladder. Overflow incontinence caused by obstruction should be treated by surgery. If the underlying cause is hyporefexia of the bladder, bethanechol chloride (10–30 mg tid-qid) may improve bladder contraction. This drug is a cholinergic agonist that may cause hypotension, bradycardia, bronchoconstriction, and increased gastric acid secretion. Functional outlet obstruction caused by bladder-(external) sphincter dyssynergia may be improved with an antispasmodic drug such as Baclofen (5 mg bid-tid), whose side effects are drowsiness and weakness. Intermittent catheterization using clean (sterile) technique may be used to keep the bladder drained if other treatment fails and is preferable to an indwelling catheter.

Sphincter insufficiency (stress incontinence) may respond to several treatment approaches. For mobile, alert patients, Kegel's exercises to strengthen pelvic floor muscles may be very beneficial. The patient is instructed to contract the vaginal muscles to interrupt urination, then to repeat the exercise throughout the day. Bladder-sphincter biofeedback, in conjunction with Kegel exercises and bladder retraining has been successful in treatment of this condition. If atrophic vaginitis is present, treatment with estrogen as a topical cream or oral Premarin may be beneficial through its effects on urethral mucosa integrity. If long-term therapy is planned, cyclic low-dose estrogen plus progesterone should be given. Complications of estrogen therapy include gallbladder disease and endometrial carcinoma (low risk).

Surgical bladder neck suspension, which may now be done under local anesthesia, has been highly successful in both younger and older women for treatment of sphincter insufficiency. Urinary retention, usually temporary, may occur after surgery. Implantation of artificial urinary sphincters has also been tried with some success in elderly patients. Complications of this approach include infection, erosion of the inflatable cuff, and loss of cuff compression, all of which require prosthesis revision.

Successful treatment of functional incontinence relies on the re-establishment of the normal pattern of voiding. This goal is accomplished by improving access to toilets (bedside commode if patient has restricted mobility), treatment of psychologic disorder if possible, and bladder retraining program.

Iatrogenic incontinence may be reversed by careful attention to the patient's drug regimen and possible side effects and interactions.

SUMMARY

Urinary incontinence is a frustrating, embarrassing, common, and costly problem in elderly patients. However, new therapeutic approaches are now available that can lead to more satisfactory management of this important clinical problem.

SUGGESTED READINGS

1. Benson JT: Gynecologic and urodynamic evaluation of women with urinary incontinence. *Obstet Gynecol* 66:691, 1985.
2. Burgio KL, Whitehead WE, Engel BT: Urinary incontinence in the elderly. *Ann Intern Med* 103:507, 1985.
3. Diokno AC, Wells TJ, Bunk CA: Urinary incontinence in elderly women: Urodynamic evaluation. *J Am Geriatr Soc* 35:940, 1987.
4. Goldwasser G, Furlow WL, Barrett DM: The model AS 800 artificial urinary sphincter: The Mayo Clinic experience. *J Urol* 137:668, 1987.
5. Hadley EC: Bladder training and related therapies for urinary incontinence in older people. *JAMA* 256:372, 1986.
6. Harris T: Aging in the Eighties, Prevalence and Impact of Urinary Problems in Individuals Age 65 Years and Over. Advance Data from Vital and Health Statistics No. 121: DHHS Pub No (PHS) 86-1250. Public Health Service. Hyattsville, Md, 1986.
7. Kane RL, Ouslander JG, Abrass IB: Incontinence. In: *Essentials of Clinical Geriatrics.* New York, McGraw-Hill Book Co., 1984, pp. 107–135.
8. Resnick NM: Urinary incontinence in the elderly. *Med Grand Rounds* 3:281, 1984.
9. Starer P, Libow L: Obscuring urinary incontinence: Diapering of the elderly. *J Am Geriatr Soc* 33:842, 1985.
10. Williams ME, Pannill FC: Urinary incontinence in the elderly. *Ann Intern Med* 97:895, 1982.

CHAPTER 24

Geriatric Gynecology

GERALD A. GLOWACKI

The gynecologic problems of the geriatric female have a broadbased derivation from a multiplicity of etiologic factors.

Heredity, the parental genetic inheritance, bears an important relationship to tissue integrity and hormonal constitutionality. Racial and ethnic background seem to have a definite correlation with the incidence of pelvic and vaginal relaxation and ultimate genital prolapse. For example, in the black African race, genital prolapse is an uncommon occurrence. Similarly, birth trauma plays a major role in various degrees of pelvic relaxation. In this era of smaller family size, the degree of relaxation in younger women is beginning to show signs of being reduced. Improved obstetrical care and controlled deliveries, as well as the repair of obstetrical lacerations, have made the most significant contribution to this reduction.

Hormonal influence is another factor crucial to the promotion and maintenance of pelvic tissue integrity. From puberty to the onset of menopause, the pelvic structures are continuously sustained and regulated by means of a cyclic abundance of estrogenic products. The reduction of estrogens to subsupportive levels during the climacteric gradually imparts to the postmenopausal female a number of pelvic deformities leading to symptomatic alterations of pelvic physiology.

GERIATRIC EVALUATION

In taking a history from the geriatric gynecologic patient, the physician must adopt an approach that will encompass the problems peculiar to this phase of social and physiologic alteration. As the pubertal female requires questioning pertinent to her particular social and physiologic state, the geriatric patient deserves similar consideration. Conducted in this fashion, the history-taking process provides an accurate historical documentation of the patient's reproductive career, beginning with developmental maturation and proceeding through the menstrual experience, reproductive period, climacteric alterations, menopausal alterations, and current state of gynecologic health.

A detailed reproductive history can be of significant value in evaluation of the etiology of pelvic abnormalities. Many patients suffering from these disorders will be of high parity, consistent with either unattended and/or midwife-attended childbirth. The degree of difficulty encountered in childbirth can usually be vividly recalled and reiterated. Should infertility and/or sterility have arisen subsequently, it may prove useful to correlate the history of present pelvic abnormalities with previous reproductive events or episodes of illness.

An individual's age at menarche is unrelated to the age of onset of menopause except in cases of true precocious puberty associated with hypothalamic or pituitary abnormalities and/or other atrophic influences on the ovary. It has been shown conclusively that early menarche does not herald an early menopause.

It is well documented that regular menstrual periods are indicative of regular ovulation and, thereby, a normal physiologic balance of hormonal relationships. Conversely, markedly irregular menstrual periods may, and probably do, portend irregular ovulation and a concomitant imbalance in the secretion of estrogen and progesterone. A significant increase in endometrial and breast cancer has been reported among the latter group of patients. Whether or not these patients continue at high risk past the reproductive period has not been conclusively established. Current speculative evidence suggests that they are at increased risk due to basic alterations in their estrogen metabolism.

The age of onset of the climacteric, with its attendant somatic complaints of hot flushes, insomnia, irritability, and menstrual irregularity, is highly variable. Onset of menopause past 50 years of age has been shown to be associated with a higher incidence of endometrial carcinoma. The prolonged unopposed influence of estrogen on the uterus is indeed an etiologic factor in the susceptible patient. Therefore, it is important to determine if any hormonal therapy has been used in the treatment of the climacteric period.

A certain percentage of these individuals require endometrial sampling for irregular and prolonged peri-menopausal bleeding abnormalities. A common practice during the early part of the century was the insertion of radium sources into the uterine cavity for the amelioration of these disorders. These radium sources were placed so that they could be left in situ for a therapeutic tissue effect in the event of the subsequent discovery of an endometrial neoplasm. If the tissue was benign, the sclerosing effect averted further bleeding. However, a high incidence of a relatively rare mixed mesodermal tumor of the uterus has been seen in these patients 15 or more years after their treatment with the radium devices. An enlarged uterus in this group should be investigated.

A significant impediment to thorough history-taking is the failure of many of our contemporaries, as well as predecessors, to document adequately the course of a patient's medical and/or surgical therapy and the potential subsequent side effects of this treatment. It is not uncommon in history-taking to find that the patient has only a partial awareness of previous gynecologic procedures. In fact, the patient may not even be certain as to which organs were altered or removed. A record of valid informed consent, as well as a complete operative review of surgical procedures and findings, will help to alleviate this problem in the future. If medical records are no longer available due to the passage of time, one must speculate upon the actual course of events by reconstructing the signs and symptoms that led to surgical intervention.

An ideal review of gynecologic symptomatology for the geriatric patient can be obtained by pursuing a line of questioning that simulates a normal pelvic examination. That is, beginning with complaints of vulvar symptomatology, the interviewer proceeds to inquire about maladies associated with vaginal, cervical, uterine, tubal, ovarian, and general pelvic problems. An extensive evaluation of the urinary system also must be included in any investigation of vulvar or vaginal problems.

No gynecologic history is complete, especially in the geriatric population, without a detailed sexual history. It is too often presumed that his age group is either sexually inactive or will be too embarrassed by such questioning. Many somatic complaints in the form of vulvar or vaginal irritation and even postmenopausal spotting may be directly related to sexual activity, discussed below.

To facilitate examination of the geriatric patient, many of whom have a great deal of difficulty in assuming the lithotomy position, an automated examination table can be utilized. Such an automated table, produced by Midmark, assumes the initial position of a chair and subsequently can be positioned into a total lithotomy position with the head elevated to any level to accommodate the patient. Similarly, a wide variety of vaginal specula need to be available to visualize the vagina and cervix properly. A Pederson narrow bivalve speculum is useful for the patient with vaginal stenosis. Small, medium, and large Graves specula are used for patients with varying degrees of vaginal caliber and/or degrees of vaginal relaxation.

VULVA

In the postmenopausal female, atrophy of the external genitalia is demonstrated by the paucity of pubic hair distribution over the mons pubis and labia majora. There also is a decrease in subcutaneous fatty tissue that in some individuals, causes this area to become pendulous. With the decrease in endogenous hormonal support, a host of dystrophic maladies occurs in the vulvar area. Coincidentally, the individuals with urinary incontinence expose the vulvar zone to a constantly moist atmosphere, with subsequent skin maceration and infection.

Probably the most common inflammatory processes noted in the vulva are those associated with candidiasis. This finding is both logical and consistent with the available evidence, since diabetes mellitus has a peak incidence among the older age groups and is highly correlated with monilial infections. Conversely, the patient also may present with a chief complaint of vulvar irritation and a subsequent diagnosis of monilial vulvar vaginitis, which, in turn, provides a basis for the diagnosis of diabetes. The diagnosis of monilial vaginitis can generally be confirmed by means of a 10% KOH smear of the vaginal discharge or vulvar encrustations. Therapeutic success can usually be achieved with any of the following: nystatin vaginal tablets twice daily for 2 weeks, miconazole nitrate 2% cream at bedtime for 1 week, or clotrimazole 1% cream or tablets at bedtime for 7 days.

Newer regimens include butoconazole nitrate 2%

vaginal cream (Femstat) and micanozole nitrate 2% cream (Monistat Dual-Pak) reduce the therapeutic treatment to 3 days of therapy. Additionally, clotrimazole 500 mg vaginal tablets (Mycelex-G) is a 1-day treatment regimen. For the recurrent vulvar vaginal candidiasis, ketoconazole (Nizeral) can be used in a therapeutic oral regimen of 200 mg twice daily for 5-7 days. Chronic suppression with 200 mg daily has been effective when used for prolonged periods of up to 1 year with a recurrence rate of less than 5%. Because of the risk of hepatotoxicity, caution is essential when selecting patients for long-term ketoconazole therapy and in following patients undergoing such treatment (Table 24.1). Immediate vulvar relief can often be accomplished by the topical application of a 0.1% fluorinated lydiocortisone cream to the affected area.

In those cases in which diabetes can be identified as an underlying etiologic factor, proper diabetic management can often reduce the recurrence rate of monilial infections. Application of the miconazole vaginal cream or nystatin tablets two times per week serves to lower the incidence of acute exacerbation. An economical alternative for prophylaxis is the use of boric acid douches (2 tablespoons of boric acid crystals in 1 pint of warm water) used on an as needed basis.

Trichomonal vaginitis may trigger the onset of acute vulvar inflammation. Metronidazole therapy (2 g as a single dose) is the most effective form of treatment for this disease process. Chronic vulvar dermatitis with associated pruritis can sometimes cause secondary infections in this area as a consequence of excessive scratching. It may be necessary occasionally to use systemic antibiotics to reduce the inflammation. The basic etiologic factors for the dermatitis must always be delineated at the outset. The majority of these acute dermatidities are effectively treated initially with 0.1% fluorinated hydrocortisone cream. The only exceptions are those lesions of viral etiology, such as herpes. Vulvar pruritis of unknown etiology has been one of the most enigmatic therapeutic problems. In cases when local steroid therapy has been unsuccessful, local application of either estrogens and/or androgens have, at times, proved effective. A preparation that can be made up by most pharmacies, 5% concentration in petrolatum, can be applied on a twice daily (every morning and bedtime) basis. Should these conservative forms of therapy fail, local alcohol injection or denervative surgery may be the only means of resolving the problem.

Lesions of the vulva in elderly patients should be highly suspect for vulvar carcinoma, as the peak incidence of that neoplasm occurs in this age group. Lesions that appear to be ulcerative and that do not respond to therapy and those that simply look suspicious should be promptly biopsied. Whitish lesions of the vulva are not necessarily precancerous lesions simply on the basis of their white appearance. To determine the exact nature of the underlying process, a tissue diagnosis is generally advisable.

Lichen sclerosis, a very common vulvar dystrophy, is characterized by a thin parchment-type appearance of the vulvar area. It is highly pruritic and excoriation, secondary to itching, is common. About 5% of these lesions show various degrees of atypia. Suspicious areas, such as whitish, reddish, bluish, or ulcerated areas, should be biopsied. Most lesions can be biopsied in the office with the use of local anesthesia and the use of vulvar biopsy instruments, such as the Keyes instrument. These lesions are best treated with local applications of testosterone cream. Corticosteroids can be used adjunctively to reduce inflammation and swelling.

Reddish lesions, indicative of Paget's disease, should arouse similar suspicion and prompt biopsy. Ulcerative and/or bluish lesions of the vulva may herald basal cell carcinoma and similarly require prompt biopsy.

Table 24.1
Monilial Vaginitis Treatment Regimens

Drug	Dosage	Treatment Cycle
Femstat	2% Creme	3 days (at bedtime)
Monistat	3 DS-Suppositories	3 days (at bedtime)
Monistat	Dual-Pak	3 days suppositories
	3 suppository	at bedtime
	Creme	External creme, twice daily (7–10 days)
Myeclex G	500 mg	1 day at bedtime
Nizeral	200 mg	Twice daily (orally) 5–7 days
		Chronic administration
		one tablet daily (oral)

Venereal diseases are seldom seen in this age group. Herpes, chancroid granuloma inguinal, lymphogranuloma inguinale, and syphilitic lesions are uncommon but must certainly be included in any thoughtful differential diagnosis. The elderly rape victim, who has not revealed an episode of sexual assault because of embarrassment, is a very likely candidate for venereal disease exposure.

VAGINA

Most of the previously discussed vulvar inflammatory processes are related to precursory conditions in the vagina. Monilial and trichomonal infections are the most common vaginal inflammatory processes with such a correlation.

Postmenopausal senile vaginitis, with its accompanying increased vascular fragility, is the leading cause of postmenopausal bleeding. On physical examination, this entity is readily recognized by the absence of the normal rugal folds of the vaginal epithelium. With or without intercurrent infections, this area bleeds easily from spontaneous vessel rupture or, more commonly, after douching and/or coitus. Dyspareunia, in the form of vaginal burning, is often secondary to senile vaginitis. Without adequate estrogen support, the epithelium becomes highly susceptible to trauma and infection. There is a reduction in the size of the vaginal outlet and a decrease in the elasticity and concomitantly, to the compliance of the vaginal vault. Local estrogen therapy can be provided in the form of creams or suppositories on a once nightly basis for a 1- to 2-week period. It must be kept in mind that this form of estrogen is readily absorbed into the general circulation and can cause such effects as proliferation of endometrial tissue and subsequent bleeding. The vagina will generally demonstrate a remarkable response to this therapy by re-establishing its rugal folds. Should intercurrent infection be present in conjunction with or secondary to epithelial atrophy, concurrent treatment will hasten estrogenization and recovery. It should be mentioned that lubricants, cortisone creams, and local anesthetic creams offer only temporary relief, but do not resolve the underlying problem of atrophy. Furthermore, the vagina will become less susceptible to minor irritation after a regimen of estrogen cream used prophylactically on a once weekly basis.

Vaginal relaxation, in the form of cystocele, cystourethrocele, urethrocele, enterocele, and rectocele plays an important role in the evaluation of symptoms of stress incontinence. As the competency of the urethra diminishes, varying degrees of stress incontinence develop. Many of these patients must wear perineal pads because of the constant involuntary loss of urine. When stress incontinence begins to interfere with the patient's ability to function socially, surgical intervention and repair should be seriously considered. Of course, the patient's overall medical status and possible associated pelvic abnormalities must be carefully evaluated. A significant percentage of patients with stress urinary incontinence will have a component of urgency and urge incontinence. All such patients should be thoroughly investigated by urodynamic studies before surgery is seriously contemplated to determine the exact etiology of the problem. In this group of patients, a variety of conditions can and do exist. When severe stress incontinence is present, the patient learns to empty her bladder frequently so that large volumes are not lost with activities. Over a period of time, this causes a reduced bladder capacity and symptoms of urgency.

Urge incontinence is generally a symptom of a neurologically unstable bladder. The patient states, "when I have to go, I must go immediately or I lose urine." It is not uncommon for this to occur during sleep with the symptoms waking up the patient. On urodynamic study, the findings are those of involuntary bladder contractions. These give the patient the symptoms of urgency. When intravesicle pressure exceeds the intraurethral pressure, urine is lost. A variety of causes of urge incontinence may be present singularly or additively. Diabetes, atherosclerosis, or spinal osteoarthritis or osteoporosis can cause damage to the delicate spinal neural components of micturition. As these reflex arcs become hyperreflexic, urgency and urge incontinence result. These can masquerade as stress incontinence when coughing, sneezing, or even walking cause the unstable bladder musculature to contract. Parkinson's disease causes similar symptoms. Therapeutic benefit is obtained when levodopa therapy replaces the needed neurotransmitter.

Since bladder instability is triggered through cholinergic nerve pathways, a variety of anticholinergic drugs can be used to reduce or alleviate these symptoms. In many of the patients with urge incontinence, surgery may exaggerate rather than alleviate the condition. Table 24.2 lists the appropriate drugs and their dose ranges. They should not be used in patients with glaucoma.

If the patient is not a surgical candidate because of intercurrent medical problems, vaginal pessaries (either pneumatic or stable) can be used to relieve stress urinary incontinence. A patient with total urinary incontinence secondary to a neurologic deficit

Table 24.2
Drugs Used for Urge Incontinence

Generic Name	Trade Name	Dose Range
Oxyphencyclimine hydrochloride	Daricon	10–30 mg daily
Dicyclomine hydrochloride	Bentyl	10–80 mg daily
Propantheline bromide	Pro-Banthine	15–75 mg daily
1-Hyoscyamine	Cystospaz	1–2 tablets four times daily
Oxybutynin chloride	Ditropan	5–30 mg daily
Imipramine hydrochloride	Tofranil	75–150 mg daily

should be considered as a candidate for microvoltage vaginal pessaries for constant bladder neck stimulation. Although their efficacy has been demonstrated in only a small percentage of the incontinent population, when successful, these devices generally enable the patient to resume a full and active schedule.

Urethroceles, either in conjunction with cystoceles or as isolated entities, are generally productive of symptoms associated with postmicturition dribbling. Exaggeration of urinary stress incontinence can be seen with this abnormality. Chronic urethritis, with attendant bladder and urethral functional disorders, are associated entities.

Vaginal pessaries, at best, should be considered a temporary mechanism for reduction of vaginal or uterine prolapse. Good peritoneal support must be present at the forchette so that the pessary is retained in the vaginal vault. The highest degree of success can be obtained with a cube-type vaginal pessary produced by the Milex Corporation. These come in four sizes. They create a suction-type effect against the vaginal tissues and are thereby well retained. These should be left in the vaginal vault for no more than 7 days without removal and cleansing. They are used most satisfactorily when inserted during the daytime and removed at bedtime. Although several other varieties of pessaries are available, they are generally less effective when used for vaginal or uterine prolapse.

Before contemplating corrective surgery and/or employment of a vaginal pessary, the physician must provide for adequate estrogenization of the vaginal mucosa and its underlying tissues. This approach has been shown to be extremely effective. In several series, as high as 70% of postmenopausal populations with urinary stress incontinence have shown remarkable improvement with simple estrogenization of these tissues. Although total urinary continence is seldom achieved, it is usually possible to accomplish an acceptable functional compromise. In the event that subsequent pessary placement proves necessary, the increased tissue resistance secondary to estrogen therapy often prevents irritation and ulceration. The choice of an appropriate operative procedure, e.g., vaginal anterior repair, suprapubic urethropexy, or a combined approach, should be determined on the basis of the anatomical deformity as well as the degree of incontinence. Many of these patients will have experienced previous attempts at surgical repair. Scarring or other associated pathologic conditions might alter the approach necessary to correct the recurrent problem.

In general, enteroceles and rectoceles are associated with varying degrees of tenesmus. This symptom complex develops so gradually and is associated with such a high incidence of constipation in this population that its presence is usually elicited only on direct questioning. Surgery should only be considered when these symptoms become a major hindrance to normal bowel physiology. In view of the fact that some 50% of the female population has undergone a hysterectomy by the onset of menopause, it has been documented that approximately 10% of these individuals undergoing either abdominal or vaginal hysterectomy will subsequently develop vault prolapse. Prolapse of the vaginal vault with associated ulceration should be managed according to the previously described protocol concerning anterior vault relaxation. Once again, the patient's general condition must be fully evaluated before surgical assessment. In those individuals who are still sexually active, the procedure of choice is resuspension of the vault with a combined abdominal and vaginal approach. For those individuals not desirous of further vaginal sexual competency, obliteration of the vaginal vault through colpocleisis offers a high degree of success. Either of these surgical approaches will serve to relieve related symptoms of pelvic pressure, that is, a bulging from the vagina, referable to vaginal vault relaxation. When total uterine and vaginal prolapse are accompanying maladies, vaginal hysterectomy combined with vaginal supportive measures (as indicated above) can accomplish total correction of the abnormality.

Although primary vaginal carcinoma makes up less than 1% of all female cancers, adequate visualization of the vaginal epithelium at the time of pelvic examination is mandatory. This inspection is particularly crucial to the evaluation of cases of postmenopausal bleeding. Cytologic sampling of the vaginal epithelium will facilitate the visualization of these lesions which are not identifiable by the naked eye. Ulcerated and/or exfoliated vaginal lesions require biopsy. There is an increased incidence of vaginal dysplasias among those patients who have demonstrated cervical and/or vulvar dysplasias. Adequate cytologic evaluation of these patients on a yearly basis is advisable. If cytologic studies are suspicious in the absence of gross vaginal lesions, colposcopy is the best method to delineate the source of the abnormal cells.

CERVIX

Proper evaluation of the cervix classically has meant not only the visual inspection, but the performance of a Pap smear. There is no doubt that cervical cytology is the most valuable means of determining occult dysplasia or carcinoma. Squamous cell carcinoma of the cervix, the most common form of cervical cancer, has been shown to be predominantly a venereally transmitted disease process. Therefore, in the geriatric patient who is no longer sexually active, the yield of abnormal smears will be significantly less. There is, however, the consideration that adenocarcinoma of the endocervix or endometrium can be picked up in a significant number of these patients. Occasionally, an exfoliative ovarian or fallopian tube carcinoma will be manifested in this fashion. The decision to perform the Pap smear then becomes simply one of economics. The cost-benefit ratio must be determined on an individual case by case basis.

Postmenopausally, the cervix usually regresses in size and volume, and becomes flush with the vaginal vault. After postmenopausal loss of estrogenic support, the cervical canal becomes quite atrophic and may conceal significant endocervical lesions. As stated in the preceding section on the vagina, with the presence of cytology indicative of a squamous lesion of cervix and/or vagina without a gross lesion, colposcopic investigation of both cervix and vagina is recommended. Should the suspicious cytology not be fully explained by colposcopy, endocervical curettage and/or cone biopsy of the cervix may be necessary.

Cervical polyps protruding from the endocervical canal are a common cause of postmenopausal bleeding. Office excision is generally sufficient therapy. However, they must always be submitted for pathologic sectioning and evaluation. In the case of an undetermined source of postmenopausal bleeding with a demonstrated patent cervical canal, sampling of the uterine cavity is mandatory to rule out an endometrial lesion.

UTERUS

By convention, the menopause is defined as the period commencing 1 year after cessation of menstrual function unassociated with pregnancy. Physiologically, this state is evoked by the failure of endometrial proliferation in response to decreased circulating estrogenic substances. Objectively, an elevated follicle stimulating hormone (FSH) and luteinizing hormone (LH) level in excess of 75 IU/ml are confirmatory of the menopause.

Postmenopausal bleeding has as its etiology a myriad of pathologic entities. As previously stated, the vagina and cervix are potential problem sources. When these structures have been thoroughly evaluated and eliminated as lesion sites, the endometrium and fallopian tubes are next in line for investigation. Cytology, routinely obtained by a combined cervical and vaginal pool smear, is only accurate in detecting approximately 60% of endometrial and a lesser percentage of fallopian tube abnormalities. Consequently, several methods of endometrial sampling have been developed. The endometrial brush and endometrial biopsy (with or without aspiration) are among the office procedures designed for such sampling. In combined studies with dilatation and curettage (D & C) on confirmed cases of endometrial cancer, these screening procedures have proved to be approximately 90% accurate. Their facility for delineating early lesions of the endometrium in the form of hyperplasia has been adequately studied and proven to be highly reliable. Needless to say, when outpatient diagnostic studies have not satisfactorily explained the etiology of a case of postmenopausal bleeding, fractional D & C (fundus and endocervical canal) is mandatory. Statistically, 10% of patients with postmenopausal bleeding subsequently will demonstrate endometrial carcinoma. The remainder will have bled as a function of the atrophic nature of the endometrium, estrogen-related therapy, or benign endometrial factors, including endometrial polyps of hyperplasia.

Endometrial cancer occurs spontaneously in 1 woman/1000/year postmenopausally. The women at highest risk for endometrial cancer are classically described with the triad: obese, hypertensive, and diabetic. Obesity is the culprit in the triad; the other two are there by association rather than as contributors to endometrial cancer. To understand where obesity contributes etiologically to endometrial cancer, we must investigate the sources of estrogen in the postmenopausal female. In the postmenopausal female, the mean circulating levels of estrogen are similar to levels seen in ovariectomized premenopausal women. The ovaries in the postmenopausal woman are not the main source of estrogen production (30%). The primary source is the adrenal gland (70%) by production of estrone and precursor steroids (androstenedione and dehydroepiandrosterone sulfate), which undergo extraglandular conversion by aromatization to estrone. This conversion occurs in fat, muscle, liver, kidney, and adrenal glands. Because the conversion is proportional to body size, the heavier woman would have higher circulating levels of estrogen. When this constant estrogen production stimulates endometrial growth and is unopposed by progesterone, it is believed to lead initially to endometrial hyperplasia. If still unopposed at this level, a certain percentage, not fully defined, will develop further atypicalities of this lesion and ultimately endometrial carcinoma. The obese female patient is, therefore, a high risk individual in the postmenopausal age group to develop endometrial cancer.

Gusberg published data in 1975 that showed that women 25–50 lb above their ideal body weight had a threefold increase risk of developing adenocarcinoma of the endometrium, whereas those who were greater than 50 lb over their ideal body weight had a ninefold risk.

Based on the above concept of unopposed estrogen stimulation to the postmenopausal endometrium, it is not difficult to envision why postmenopausally exogenous estrogen therapy could cause endometrial cancer. Several retrospective studies have shown that the relative risk ratio of postmenopausal females developing endometrial carcinoma while taking estrogen is between 4.5 and 6.5 times higher than a control population of similar females not on estrogen therapy. Translated in the previous statistic for the spontaneous occurrence of endometrial cancer, 1 case/1000 postmenopausal women/year would mean 4–8 women/1000/year on estrogen would develop endometrial cancer. Because this is a gradual process, several epidemiological studies show that it generally takes a minimum of 2–3 years to develop endometrial cancer on constant estrogen therapy. Dosage of estrogen, type of estrogen and compound, and dosage regimens (cyclic versus constant) have not been shown to alter the incident of postmenopausal women on estrogen replacement therapy in developing endometrial cancer.

Progestin administration, when added to the estrogen regimen for from 10–14 days in the cycle pattern, has been shown conclusively to reduce the incidence of endometrial carcinoma to or below the rate for the control population not receiving estrogen-progestin replacement therapy.

The majority of estrogen-induced endometrial cancers are histologically low grade with minimal myometrial invasion. Careful surveillance of patients on estrogen therapy by endometrial sampling can limit the risk of developing adenocarcinoma or can detect it at an early, highly curable stage. It is generally held that sampling should be done before initiating estrogen therapy to assure that there is no pre-existing lesion, and thereafter only if patients bleed during the estrogen or early progestational portion of the replacement cycle.

FALLOPIAN TUBES

Although the fallopian tubes are of major importance during the female reproductive span, it is seldom an organ of major consequence in the geriatric population. Carcinoma of the fallopian tube as a primary lesion is an extremely rare tumor. As a causative factor among those individuals with postmenopausal bleeding, it represents an extremely small percentage. Nevertheless, it must be considered in evaluating those individuals who demonstrate positive vaginal cytology with a negative investigation of vagina, cervix, and uterus since passage of malignant tubal epithelium can and does appear in the Pap smear obtained from the vaginal pool. As a source of an adnexal mass, it is extremely rare.

OVARY

Steroidogenesis is known to occur in the ovary for a significant period of time beyond the menopause. The exact length of this process is variable. By the sixth decade, the ovary is not the major source of estrogen production. Possibly because of the increased influence of FSH at that time, the ovary becomes a prime site of neoplastic development. It has been variously quoted that at 5 years postmenopause, the ovary should no longer be palpable. In one small study, 60% of a postmenopausal population with palpable ovaries had ovarian cancer on exploration. It is obvious, then, that all ovarian enlargement in the postmenopausal patient deserves prompt investigation to determine the etiology. Among these investigatory procedures are sonography, magnetic resonance imaging, CT scanning, and laparoscopy.

Currently, only one in four patients who undergoes laparotomy for ovarian enlargement in which ovarian carcinoma is found survives for longer than 5 years. Three of four are surgically incurable at initial laparotomy. Before achieving significant enough size to produce subjective symptoms, these lesions have metastasized beyond the scope of surgical, radiotherapeutic, and chemotherapeutic cure.

Since many of the causative factors for benign enlargement of the ovary have either been previously investigated or are no longer functionally operative in the geriatric age group, a higher proportion of cases of ovarian enlargement (40%) represent ovarian cancer. In the postmenopausal patient being treated for benign and/or malignant abnormalities of the uterus or cervix, there is no place for ovarian conservation. At present, diagnostic studies to elicit early lesions of the ovary still rely on a meticulous bimanual pelvic examination.

ESTROGEN THERAPY

The consideration of estrogen replacement therapy must begin with the conceptualization of the term and meaning of menopause. Menopause is the cessation of menstrual function, but it is technically much more. It is the cessation of reproductive capability as a consequence of ovarian aging and failure to produce both ova for reproduction and estrogen and progesterone for hormonal support. This is a phenomenon virtually unique to the human. From an evolutionary basis, this biologic and physiologic event of the menopause now requires that women live virtually one-third of their life after reproductive senescence and in hormonal deficiency. Is this hormonally deficient state to be envisioned as a selected or unselected event associated with reproductive senescence? It would seem to be an unselected event due to the fact that 2–3 decades of presumably desirable longevity is spent beyond the reproductive years. Reproductive senescence has biologic validity. It is well documented that with increasing age, chromosomal aberration occurs as a function of the aging process within the ovary. Reproductive errors in the ova in the third and fourth decades of life of the female make the event of the menopause, from the standpoint of reproductive failure, evolutionarily plausible and acceptable. Should it be assumed then that the associated consequences of ovarian hormonal deficiency is a natural event and should not be treated or is it more prudent to treat this failure with physiologically effective substitution?

The era in which ovarian hormonal replacement was used has concluded, at least conceptually, as a mechanism of stopping or at least slowing the aging process. Hopefully, this has been laid to rest. At present, study should be attempted to determine if and how substitutional therapy can be made safe and effective. As Romero (29) has aptly stated:

"It is paradoxical that, although we witness the manifestations of biologic aging daily in our lives and our surroundings, we still have such limited understanding of the basic mechanisms and causes of this universal process. Perhaps one of the greatest difficulties that face the science of gerontology is arriving at a concrete definition of aging that would then be the basis of and departure point for the investigation of the physiologic basis and etiology of this process."

The term "ovarian hormone replacement" has been used continually for good reason. In the physiologic reproductive state, both estrogen and progesterone are produced sequentially and simultaneously. As pointed out in the section on the uterus, endometrial carcinoma is a concern with prolonged unopposed estrogen replacement. This concern only exists if the uterus remains in situ since similar concerns about the effects of estrogen on other organ systems have not been established. Why consider estrogen replacement? It has been well established that estrogen is the most effective agent for the relief of hot flushes at menopause. These symptoms are significantly distressing to a high percentage of women. Several double-blind crossover studies have conclusively demonstrated this effective versus placebo. It is therefore a truly physiologic and not solely a psychologic phenomenon. Judd et al. (17) associated with the hot flush with spikes in the serum levels of LH. Estrogen effectively dampens these surge releases of LH by the pituitary through the biologic feedback mechanism.

Estrogens also support the vaginal tissues which, postmenopausally, undergo atrophic change and can lead to sexual and anatomic disorders. As the vaginal epithelium has inadequate estrogen stimulation, the mitotic activity and maturation of this epithelium changes as demonstrated by the maturation index. This index shows, based on vaginal epithelial sampling, that basal and parabasal cells are being produced with a deficiency of the more mature superficial keratinized squamous variety of cells. These superficial cells are more resistant to trauma and infection. Based on these atrophic changes, the common vaginal pathogens are more likely to produce vaginal irritation and be more difficult to eradicate. Dyspareunia is a common symptom of the postmenopausal female who has atrophic changes in the vagina.

Possibly most importantly is the concern over the process of osteoporosis. This represents the great health hazard to the postmenopausal female of all the consequences of ovarian failure. Hot flushes dissipate in time; genital atrophy is disabling; but osteoporosis can lead to ensuing complications such as hip fractures, vertebral compression fractures, and associated complications including death.

It has been well established that after the fifth

decade, demineralization of bone occurs at a more rapid rate in women than men. Women over age 50 years and still menstruating lose bone mass at a rate comparable to men. Is estrogen the reason for this decrease in bone loss, and will replacement prevent this phenomenon in postmenopausal women? Between 1957 and 1968, Aitken et al. (1) conducted a double-blind study to investigate this hypothesis. Using 23 µg of mestranol (3-methyl ester of ethinyl estradiol) daily, they studied the metacarpal density by photon absorptiometric measurement in 114 women annually who underwent premenopausal oophorectomy. Because it has been previously established that the postmenopausal female and the castrate are virtually identical hormonally, this comparison should be valid. The authors found the bone density was either maintained or increased in women who began the replacement regimen after 3 years of castration. The placebo group had statistically significant lower bone density. The next subgroup studies were in women who did not enter the study until 6 years after castration. In this estrogen-replaced group, a substantial increase in bone mass was noted over the next 5 years at which time it plateaued but at a lower level than the group who were begun on estrogen at 3 years. The placebo group continued to lose bone mass. This lends credence to the indication of estrogen replacement therapy within a 3- to 4-year period postmenopausal. A third group was studied that discontinued estrogen therapy after 4 years of use. The women immediately began bone demineralization at a rate identical to the castrated women. At 4 years after cessation of estrogen therapy, they were virtually identical in bone loss to the group not on replacement estrogen therapy for 8 or more years after castration. In contrast, a group maintained on estrogen over this 8-year period maintained bone density at the pre-castration level. These studies have led most investigators and the Food and Drug Administration (FDA) to accept the concept that estrogen effectively prevents osteoporosis.

The most significant consequence of osteoporosis, therefore, is increased rate of fracture. In the series by Aitken et al. (2), 2 of 66 controls sustained fractures, but none of the 68 estrogen-treated women suffered a fracture. Several other studies on either postmenopausal or estrogen-deficient groups report reduced rates of fractures far below expected numbers when estrogen replacement therapy was used. By statistical technique, Hutchinson et al. (16) computed from a retrospective case control method, the relative risk ratios for women who began estrogen therapy within 5 years of the menopause. These

women were 3.8 times more likely to remain free from fracture than their counterparts not on estrogen therapy.

The specific mechanism by which estrogen promotes bone formation or reduces its absorption is not known. Parathormone, calcitonin, and vitamin D are the main regulators of bone formation and resorption. It is believed that estrogens stimulate osteoblastic proliferation and inhibit the action of parathormone on osteoclasts. This evidence is indirect and speculative. It is well established that estrogens are much more effective in promoting positive calcium balance than androgen in postmenopausal women.

The economic impact of osteoporosis, as well as the health risks, are well known in our geriatric society. Wylie in a 1977 article on "Hospitalization for Fracture and Bone Loss in Adults" stated that 10% of Medicare enrollees sustain hip fractures per year (35a). This is a 10-fold higher rate than cancer of the endometrium and is associated with higher costs, morbidity, and mortality. Approximately one-sixth of all patients sustaining hip fractures die within 3 months of their injury. The estimated health care cost in caring for fractures secondary to osteoporosis is $9 billion annually.

A number of studies have been done on calcium supplementation, fluoride therapy, 1α, 25-dihydroxyvitamin D_3 therapy, and thiazide therapy with and without estrogen replacement.

No study that did not include estrogen replacement therapy as the principal mechanism of prevention of osteoporosis has been effective. Studies of estrogen and calcium replacement at a level of 1000–1500 mg of calcium carbonate per day have shown a 50% reduction in fracture rate. Studies including estrogen, calcium, and sodium fluoride (20–40 mg/day), have shown an additional 75% reduction in fracture rates. The vast majority of patients do not tolerate sodium fluoride therapy over extended periods of time due to gastrointestinal distress. Its use in the severely osteoporotic patient, over a 3- to 6-month period, has shown to be of some benefit. 1α, 25-dihydroxyvitamin D, a synthetic metabolite of vitamin D, has been used in experimental protocols to enhance calcium absorption from the gastrointestinal tract. To date, these studies are encouraging, but not definitive. Recently, studies on the chronic use of thiazide diuretics in relationship to postmenopausal bone mineral content in both estrogen-treated and untreated groups have been reviewed. Administration of thiazide over a period of years was associated with a significantly higher bone mineral content. Long bone fracture prevalence was decreased by one-half compared to a control group with no thiazide therapy. Thiazide apparently caused greater bone mineral content at both trabecular and cortical sites, while estrogen was associated with greater bone mineral content in sites containing trabecular bone only. This is of significant interest because the head of the femur, where hip fractures occur, is cortical bone and, therefore, is relatively unaffected by estrogen therapy. Thiazide apparently exerts its influence by causing decreased urinary calcium excretion and, therefore, maintains a lower rate of calcium resorption. Because hip fractures are the major factor contributing to the morbidity and mortality related to osteoporosis in the aging population, thiazide therapy may be an additional tool in the armamentarium in the prevention of nontraumatic hip fractures.

For a significant period of time, there has been speculation concerning the beneficial effects of estrogen in prevention of coronary artery disease. As early as 1968, Furman published in the Annals of the New York Academy of Science a graphic representation of the discrepancies in death rate from coronary artery disease between white males and females through age 85 years (10a). That graphic representation lent credence to the protective mechanisms of estrogen in the premenopausal age group of women. In the postmenopausal white female, the increased death rate in postmenopausal white females gradually approached that of their male counterpart by age 75 years. With the correlation of cholesterol, high and low density lipoproteins (HDL, LDL) and triglycerides as either increasing or decreasing the incidence of coronary artery disease, several studies on estrogen replacement therapy and lipid values have been conducted. These studies clearly elucidate that estrogen replacement therapy in the postmenopausal female decrease cholesterol, LDL, and triglycerides. Estrogen enhances the HDL fraction.

Recent work from Henderson (15a) from the Leisure World Community in California has shown a reduction in the overall death rate in postmenopausal women who were ever users of estrogen replacement therapy to have a 0.78 risk ratio as opposed to the never user of estrogen replacement therapy. The acute myocardial infarct death rate in the ever user of estrogen replacement therapy was 0.55 as opposed to the never user. These statistics were based solely on the use of Premarin as the estrogen replacement drug.

Levels of LDL of less than 150 mg/dl and levels of greater than 40 mg/dl of HDL have been shown to decrease the risk of cardiovascular disease. An LDL:HDL ratio of less than 4:1 has been shown to be exceedingly beneficial in prevention of coronary artery disease. With each percent decrease in LDL levels, there is a 2% decrease in coronary heart disease risk.

The addition of the commercially available oral progestins to the estrogen replacement regimen for patients with a uterus in situ remains controversial in relationship to their ameliorating effects on the induction of increases in high density liproproteins. As previously stated, there is no question that they are beneficial in reducing the incidences of endometrial hyperplasia and carcinoma. Medroxyprogesterone acetate does not decrease LDL levels significantly. The 19 nor progestins have more of an effect in lowering these levels. Several new products including micronized progesterone are now being investigated to determine their effects on lipoproteins. There is no conclusive evidence that oral progestins, when added to the estrogen regimen, afford a protective factor against breast cancer.

Based on the aforementioned evidence, it could be concluded that estrogen supplementation of the postmenopausal women within 3 years of the occurrence has defined merits, both to the individual as well as to the national economic health care cost. There are definite contraindications to estrogen therapy: estrogen-dependent neoplasms of breast or endometrium, history of thrombophlebitis or thromboembolism, and active or severe liver disease. Before the initiation of therapy, it is mandatory to review with the patient the benefits and risks of estrogen therapy as previously outlined in this section.

The threshold dose of estrogen replacement at which osteoporosis, genital atrophy, and uterine bleeding can be prevented has not been fully defined at this time. Although the oral route of administration has been the most common and most studied, the impact of the enterohepatic conversion of estrogen has not been fully elucidated. It may be preferable at some time in the future to look to the vaginal route for replacement since this route bypasses the enterohepatic system before having its end organ effect. The injectable and pellet forms of estrogen therapy have disadvantages—variability of absorption and length of action, and the fact that therapy cannot be terminated because the medication is not easily retrievable.

Before initiating therapy in the patient with a uterus in situ, a progesterone challenge test or endometrial sampling should be considered. A progesterone challenge can be done by using 100 mg of progesterone in oil intramuscularly, or medroxyprogesterone acetate (Provera) 10 mg daily for 10 days, or similar progestines to test for uterine bleeding. If bleeding occurs, endometrial sampling is advised. Endometrial sampling thereafter should be reserved for those individuals with irregular bleeding on estrogen-progestin replacement.

There does appear to be a significant advantage of oral estrogen replacement therapy over transdermal as well as transvaginal vehicles of administration. The oral products, because of their gastrohepatic absorption and transport, reduce hepatolipase lactate activity. In so doing, it is believed to be one of the mechanisms for the increase in HDL levels. Conjugated estrogen, with its equilin component, appears to induce the most cardioprotective lipoprotein configuration.

As little as 0.3 mg of conjugated estrogen or 0.01 mg of ethinyl estradiol are effective for postmenopausal osteoporosis prophylaxis. However, most beneficial lipoprotein profiles have been obtained with dosages of 1.25 mg of conjugated estrogen and 0.02 mg of ethinyl estradiol. In none of these dosage regimens are coagulation profiles adversely affected.

In the following table are listed the various estrogen and progestin regimens. In those regimens utilizing continuous progestin therapy, the aim is to ameliorate, if not obliterate, withdraw bleeding.

This, however, may have adverse effects on lipoprotein profiles.

A variety of noninvasive techniques have been utilized for the measurement of bone mass. Plain radiographs are a very insensitive method of determining osteoporosis. As much as 65% of bone mass must be lost before this modality is sensitive as a diagnostic tool. Quantitative radiographic methods utilizing a step wedge aluminum equivalent measuring the third metacarpal bone were among the original methods to quantify bone density. Newer methodologies to include single and dual photon/absorptiometry have been utilized. Both single and dual photon absorptiometers measure both trabecular and cortical bone, but are unable to differentiate mineral loss between these two entities. Single photon absorptiometry utilizes either radius-ulna or os calcis to measure bone density. Good quantified relations between bone density and fracture risk rates in these structures have not shown good quantified relationships. On the other hand, dual photon absorptiometry, measuring lumbar spine, femoral neck, and trochanter have demonstrated excellent quantitative relationships between bone mineral content and fracture rates in the structures measured. Both single and dual photon densiometry deliver less than 10 mrem levels of radiation. The average cost of a single photon absorptiometry study is about $125.00. A dual photon absorptiometry study including spine and femoral head range

ALTERNATE HORMONE THERAPY REGIMENS

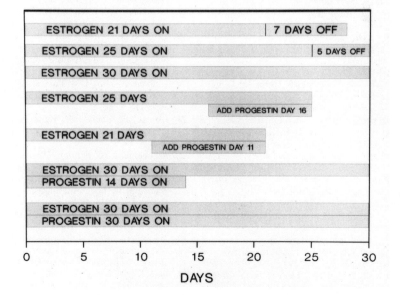

from $125.00–250.00. CT, of the single or dual energy sources, afford excellent evaluation of bone mineral density in both cortical and trabecular bone. Quantified risks ratio for fractures and bone mineral density are excellent. They do require higher levels of irradiation (between 250–500 mrem). Cost is generally in the range of $250.00. Neutron activation analysis affords excellent analysis of bone mineral density in both cortical and trabecular bone in all skeletal sites. It does require high levels of irradiation between 150–2000 mrem. Neutron activation is basically a research technique.

The benefits and risks of estrogen therapy have been reviewed. Postmenopausal women should have the benefit of this information to make an informed judgement on the subject. The exaggerated risks of endometrial cancer have overshadowed the potential beneficial effects in ameliorating the consequences of osteoporosis. Although not previously mentioned, there is no established evidence that estrogen therapy is causally associated with the development of breast cancer. Estrogen, when used, should be used in the lowest effective dose. Vaginal bleeding must be reported and investigated promptly. Due to the low incidence of endometrial cancer developing, especially when progestins are added to the regimen, endometrial sampling at 1- or 2-year intervals must be evaluated and discussed with the patient from the risk, inconvenience, and cost perspective.

SUGGESTED READINGS

1. Aitken JM, Hart DM, Lindsay R: Oestrogen replacement therapy for prevention of osteoporosis after oophorectomy. *Br Med J* 3:515, 1973.
2. Aitken JM, Hart DM, Anderson JB, Lindsay R, Smith DA, Speirs CF: Osteoporosis after oophorectomy for nonmalignant disease in premenopausal women. *Br Med J* 2:325, 1973.
3. Aloia JF, Zanzi I, Vaswani A, Ellis K, Cohn SH: Combination therapy for osteoporosis with estrogen, fluoride and calcium. *J Am Geriat Soc* 30:13, 1982.
4. Antunes CMF, Stolley PD, Rosenshein NB, Davies JL, Tonascia JA, Brown C, Burnett L, Rutledge A, Pokempner M, Garcia R: Endometrial cancer and estrogen use: Report of a large case-control study. *N Engl J Med* 300:9, 1979.
5. Arthes FG, Sartwell PE, Lewison EF: The pill, estrogens and the breast. *Cancer* 28:1391, 1971.
6. Avioli LV, Baran DT, Whyte MP, Teitelbaum SL: The biochemical and skeletal heterogeneity of "postmenopausal osteoporosis." In: Barzel US (Ed): *Osteoporosis II.* New York, Grune & Stratton, 1979.
7. Boston Collaborative Drug Surveillance Program: Surgically confirmed gallbladder disease, venous thromboembolism, and breast tumors in relation to postmenopausal estrogen therapy. *N Engl J Med* 290:15, 1974.
8. Bullock JL, Massey FM, Gambrell RD: Use of medroxyprogesterone acetate to prevent menopausal symptoms. *Obstet Gynecol* 46:165, 1975.
9. Chetkowski RJ, Meltrum DA, et al: Biological effects of transdermal estradiol. *N Engl J Med* 314:1615, 1986.
10. Friedrich E: *Vulvar Disease.* Philadelphia, WB Saunders, 1976.
10a. Furman RH: Are gonadal hormones (estrogens and androgens) of significance in the development of ischemic heart disease? *Ann NY Acad Sci* 149:822–833, 1968.
11. Gambrill RD: The roles of hormones in the etiology of breast and endometrial cancer. *Acta Obstet Gynecol Scand* [Suppl] 88:73, 1979.
12. Gambrill RD: The menopause: Benefits and risks of estrogen-progestogen replacement therapy. *Fertil Steril* 37:457, 1982.
13. Gordon J, Kannel WB, Hjortland MC, McNamayer PM: Menopause and coronary heart disease: The Framingham study. *Ann Intern Med* 89:157, 1978.
14. Hammond CB, Jelovsek FE, Lee KL, Creasman WT, Parker RT: Effects of long term estrogen replacement therapy: 1. Metabolic effects. *Am J Obstet Gynecol* 133:525, 1979.
15. Hemsell DL, Grodin JM, Brenner DF, Siitevi PK, MacDonald PC: Plasma precursors of estrogens: II. Correlations of the extent of conversion of plasma androstenedione to estrone with age. *J Clin Endocrinol Metab* 38:476, 1974.
15a. Henderson BE, Ross RK, Paganini A, et al: Estrogen use and cardiovascular disease. *Am J Obstet Gynecol* 154:1181, 1986.
16. Hutchinson TA, Dolansky SM, Feinstein AR. Postmenopausal oestrogens protect against fractures of hip and distal radius: A case control study. *Lancet* 2:705, 1979.
17. Judd HL, Lucas WE, Yen SSC: Effect of oophorectomy on circulating testosterone and androstenedione levels in patients with endometrial cancer. *Am J Obstet Gynecol* 118:793, 1974.
18. Leis HP, Black MM, Sall S: The pill and the breast. *J Reprod Med* 16:5, 1976.
19. Lindsay R, Aitken JM, Anderson JB, Hart DM, MacDonald EB, Clark AC: Long-term prevention of postmenopausal osteoporosis by oestrogen. *Lancet* 1:1038, 1976.
20. Lindsay R, Hart DM, Forrest C, et al: Prevention of spinal osteoporosis in oophorectomized women. *Lancet* 2:115, 1980.
21. Lindsay R, MacLean A, Kraszewski A, et al: Bone responses to termination of oestrogen treatment. *Lancet* 2:1325, 1978.
22. MacDonald PC, Edman CD, Hunsell DL, Porter JC, Siiteri PK: Effect of obesity on conversion of plasma androstenedione to estrone in postmenopausal women with and without endometrial cancer. *Am J Obstet Gynecol* 130:448, 1978.
23. Meckeinburg RL: Mechamism and detection of osteoporosis. *Del Med J* 57:355, 1985.
24. Nachtigall LE, et al: Estrogen replacement therapy I: A 10 year prospective study in the relationship to osteoporosis. *Obstet Gynecol* 53:277, 1979.
25. Novak E, Woodruff D: *Novak's Gynecologic and Obstetric Pathology.* Philadelphia, WB Saunders, 1979.
26. Padwick ML, Prepe-Davies J, Whitehead MJ: A single

method for determining the optimal dosage of progestin in postmenopausal women receiving estrogen.
315:930, 1986.
27. Richelson LS, Wahner HW, Melton LJ, Riggs BL: Relative contributions of aging and estrogen deficiency to
postmenopausal bone loss. 311:1273, 1984.
28. Riggs BL, Hodgson SF, Hoffman DL, Kelly PJ,
Johnson KA, Taves D: Treatment of primary osteoporosis with fluoride and calcium. Clinical tolerance and
fracture occurrence. *JAMA* 243:446, 1980.
29. Romero JA: Biologic rhythms and sympathetic neural
control of pineal metabolism. *Adv Exp Med Biol* 108:
235, 1978.
30. Ross RK, Mack TM, Paganini-Hill A, et al: Menopausal estrogen therapy and protection from death from
ischaemic heart disease. *Lancet* 1:858, 1981.
31. Ryan KJ, Gibson DC: Menopause and Aging, Department of Health, Education and Welfare, Publications
No. (NIH) 73–319, United States Government Printing Office, Washington, D.C., 1971.

32. Utian WH: *Menopause in Modern Perspective, A
Guide to Clinical Practice.* New York, Appleton-
Century-Crofts, 1980.
33. Wasnick RD, Ross PD, Heilburn LK, et al: Differential
effects of thiazide and estrogen upon bone mineral
content and fracture prevalence. *Obstet Gynecol*
67:457, 1986.
34. Wasnick RD, Ross PD, Heilburn LK, et al: Predictions
of postmenopausal fracture risk with use of bone mineral measurements. *Am J Obstet Gynecol* 153:745,
1985.
35. Worley R (guest ed): Menopause. *Clin Obstet Gynecol.*
24: 1981.
35a. Wylie CM: Hospitalization for fractures and bone
loss in adults. *Public Health Rep* 91:33, 1977.
36. Ziel HK, Finkle WD: Increased risk of endometrial
carcinoma among users of conjugated estrogens. *N
Engl J Med* 23:1187, 1975.

CHAPTER 25

Common Disorders of Muscles in the Aged

DAVID GROB

Disorders of the muscles that occur in the aged may be divided into those that are the natural result of aging (13, 14) and those that result from disease (10).

MUSCLE DYSFUNCTION IN "NORMAL" AGED PERSONS

SENILE MUSCULAR WASTING

Wasting of skeletal muscles and general decrease in muscular strength, endurance and agility are common in the aged. There is a decrease in the number of muscle fibers and in their individual bulk, which is merely part of a general atrophy of organs and tissues and includes a 30% reduction in the number of anterior horn cells and nerve fibers (14). The process of regeneration is not active. Fibrous tissue replacement occurs secondarily. The age at which these changes in the muscles begin is highly variable. The changes are particularly conspicuous in the small muscles of the hands, which become thin and bony with deep interosseous spaces. The arm and leg muscles become thin and flabby. The atrophy may be so prominent as to suggest progressive muscular atrophy. However, this disease can be excluded by the absence of severe weakness, muscular fasciculations at rest, or progression of signs and symptoms. While some degree of weakness may occur in patients with senile muscular wasting, it is usually surprisingly little and not in proportion to the degree of wasting.

CHANGES IN POSTURE

In old age, the posture tends to become one of general flexion. The head and neck are held forward, the dorsal spine becomes gently kyphotic, the upper limbs are bent at the elbows and wrists, and the hips and knees are also slightly flexed. This flexed attitude of old age is due to changes in the vertebral column and in the intervertebral discs, to ankylosis of ligaments and joints, to shrinkage and sclerosis of tendons and muscles, and to degenerative changes in the extrapyramidal central nervous system.

These factors also contribute to an increase in muscular rigidity, sometimes referred to as senile or arteriosclerotic rigidity. This is demonstrable clinically by resistance to passive movement, especially in the limbs and neck. The legs tend to be more affected than the arms and proximal segments of the extremity more than the distal. In its more severe form, this increased rigidity may result in the aged individual assuming catatonic postures and allowing his limb to be retained in whatever position it is placed. Impairment of memory, especially for recent events, difficulty in concentrating, mental inattention, depression, apathy, perseveration, and dementia also may contribute to this phenomenon.

DISORDERS OF MOVEMENT

The aged person usually shows a decrease in movement, attributable mainly to impairment of the extrapyramidal system. He or she will have an impassive facial expression, infrequent blinking of the eyes, and a decrease in spontaneous and associated movements. When they occur, movements are characteristically slow. At times, a resting tremor may be present. The flexion attitude, rigidity, infrequency and slowness of movement, and tremor, when intense, constitute the parkinsonian state, attributable to degeneration of the extrapyramidal system. However, these signs are commonly seen in minor degree in normal old people, suggesting that this system is more vulnerable to the aging process than are other parts of the motor system.

DISORDERS OF REFLEXES

The tendon jerks tend to become decreased, particularly the ankle jerks, which are often unobtainable, due mainly to inelasticity of the Achilles tendon. Less marked decrease in other tendon jerks is probably due more to shrinkage and sclerosis of tendons and muscles than to changes in the spinal reflex arc. Loss of the abdominal reflexes is common, especially if there has been stretching of the abdominal musculature by adiposity or childbearing.

The plantar responses are often difficult to elicit, due mainly to deformities of the feet with valgus or equinovalgus deformities of the great toe, stiffness or ankylosis of the first metatarsophalangeal joint, and hardening of the sole. This results in a clear-cut flexor response being seen much less frequently than in younger individuals. However, a frank extensor response must be regarded as an abnormal finding, usually indicating a lesion of the upper motor neuron (pyramidal tract or motor cortex).

DISORDERS OF EYE MOVEMENTS

Defective upward movement and convergence of the eyes are common "normal" findings in the aged. It is not clear to what extent this is due to alterations in the central nervous system or in the muscles. The pupils tend to become miotic and sluggish in their reflex response to light and to accommodation. The pupils may even become unresponsive to light while still contracting on accommodation (Argyll Robertson pupils). These changes are believed to be the result of fibrosis, hyalinization, and lipoid infiltration of the smooth muscle of the pupillary sphincter. Lipoid infiltration of the cornea results in the presence of an arcus senilis, a familiar ocular evidence of aging.

MUSCULAR FASCICULATIONS

Spontaneous fasciculations, which are visible as flickering movements of muscles, usually occur in the presence of muscular weakness and wasting and are then a manifestation of slowly progressive destruction of anterior horn cells, cranial motor nerve nuclei, or less often, nerve roots or motor nerves. However, spontaneous fasciculations occasionally occur in normal individuals, including the aged. When marked, they are termed myokymia. They occur particularly in the calves, eyelids, hands and feet, and especially after fatigue or excessive loss of sodium chloride. The movements may resemble fasciculations due to anterior horn cell disease, but if the latter can be excluded by the absence of significant weakness and wasting, the movements are of no significance. Fasciculations occurring in normal individuals are usually more irregular in rate and size and shorter in duration than those in anterior horn cell disease.

Spontaneous fasciculations must be distinguished from contraction fasciculations, which may occur during voluntary contraction of muscle that has atrophied due to any cause, including senile atrophy. These probably represent the contraction of isolated groups of motor units, which stand out because adjacent units are not responsive.

MUSCLE CRAMPS

This disorder is characterized by sustained involuntary and painful contractions of muscle. Cramps usually occur in one muscle group of the calf, foot, thigh, hand, or hip, especially following unusual muscular effort and usually at night. They may occur at any age, but often become more troublesome with advancing age. They may occur as a result of peripheral vascular insufficiency, sodium deprivation or loss, decrease in the plasma concentration of calcium, hypoglycemia, certain toxins such as that of the tetanus bacillus and "black widow" spider, and rarely, anterior horn cell or peripheral nerve disease. In uremia, cramps and twitching may occur even in the absence of marked change in plasma calcium or sodium. Muscle cramps also occur in association with certain diseases of muscle, including the stiff-man syndrome, McArdle's syndrome (phosphorylase deficiency), congenital myotonia and, to a lesser degree, myotonic dystrophy, hypothyroid myopathy, and paroxysmal myoglobinuria. However, in the great majority of instances, cramps occur in apparently normal individuals and their mechanism is unknown.

Cramps may frequently be terminated by passive stretch. Their incidence may be diminished by a hot bath at bedtime, by orally administered quinine sulfate, which lengthens the refractory period of muscle, presumably by slowing repolarization, or by methocarbamol (Robaxin), cyclobenzaprine (Flexeril), or diphenhydramine (Benadryl), which may diminish spinal cord reflex activity.

RESTLESS LEGS

In this condition, the patient complains of paresthesias in the legs. Since the paresthesias are usually relieved by motion of the legs and reappear only when the legs have been quiet for a while, the patient tends to keep the legs in motion. The disorder may occur at any age, but tends to become more troublesome with advancing age. It may occur without evident cause or it may result from neuropathy due to diabetes, lumbar osteoarthritis (spondylosis) or other cause, or from hypoglycemia, hypocalcemia, or alkalosis due to hyperventilation or other cause.

MUSCLE DYSFUNCTION DUE TO DISEASE

Skeletal muscle dysfunction may result from impairment of any part of the path taken by the stimulus for voluntary movement (the motor unit), from the highest cerebral centers to the motor cortex, pyramidal (corticospinal) tract, motor nuclei of the brainstem and anterior horn cells of the spinal cord, peripheral motor nerves, neuromuscular junction, and muscle fibers. The manifestations of muscle dysfunction are limited.

Weakness occurs in almost all disorders of the neuromuscular system and is usually the presenting complaint (10). Weakness is accompanied by muscular wasting in diseases of the lower motor neuron (anterior horn cells and peripheral motor nerves) and in primary diseases of muscle. It is accompanied by stiffness or spasm in diseases of the upper motor neuron (motor cortex and pyramidal tract) or extrapyramidal system, and in tetany, tetanus, myalgias, scleroderma, and occasionally, myositis. Weakness is accompanied by muscle pain or tenderness in spinal cord tumor, intervertebral disc, trichinosis, myalgia, and, in some instances, of peripheral neuritis and myositis. Weakness is associated with abnormal movements such as fasciculations in progressive muscular atrophy, and occasionally in syringomyelia or hyperthyroidism, and with grosser abnor-

mal movements in some diseases of the extrapyramidal system.

The many causes of muscle dysfunction may be considered in the order in which they affect the passage of the motor stimulus, beginning in the frontal cortex and terminating in the muscle fibers (10).

DISORDERS ARISING PRIMARILY FROM THE NERVOUS SYSTEM

Emotional Disorders

The impulse for voluntary motor activity arises in the frontal cortex and any impairment in volition may result in symptoms of weakness or fatigue. This may take the form of local weakness or paralysis as in hysteria, generalized weakness and fatigue as in neurasthenia, weakness with catatonia as in schizophrenia, or weakness with wasting as in anorexia nervosa. Weakness or fatigue of emotional origin is frequently accompanied by a general increase in muscle tension associated with anxiety and by incomplete muscle relaxation during rest or sleep. The increased muscle tension may result in pain in the back of the neck or head, temporal or frontal headache or tightness, postural deformity, backache, pain in and around joints simulating rheumatism, and even generalized muscle soreness.

The diagnosis of weakness or fatigue of emotional origin can be made only after careful exclusion of the many other causes of weakness, but is often suggested by a history of anxiety and increased muscle tension, fatigue on awakening, early evening drowsiness, and improvement in symptoms following suggestion or placebo administration. However, it must be kept in mind that weakness of emotional origin may be superimposed on weakness due to other causes. In such instances, the major part of the disability may be relieved following hypnosis, placebo or other forms of suggestion, but evidence of the underlying disease process remains.

Upper Motor Neuron Disorders

Injury to the motor cortex or the pyramidal tracts results most commonly from vascular disease (thrombosis, hemorrhage, or embolism of cerebral or, rarely, spinal vessels), or, less commonly, from infection (encephalitis, meningitis, abscess, syphilis), disseminated sclerosis, pernicious anemia, amyotrophic lateral sclerosis, trauma, or brain or spinal cord tumor (1, 16). An upper motor neuron lesion can usually be identified by its characteristic manifestations: weakness on the side of the affected pyramidal tract, with spasticity that is greater in the flexors of the upper extremities and in the extensors of the lower extremities, exaggerated tendon reflexes, diminished abdominal and cremasteric reflexes, clonus and extensor plantar reflex.

Cerebral vascular disease is the most common cause of paralysis of one or more extremities. It usually results in hemiplegia, less often monoplegia, and least often quadriplegia as a result of bilateral damage. Weakness due to cerebral vascular disease almost always results from a lesion of the corticospinal tract or motor cortex, and hence is accompanied by upper motor neuron signs. On occasion, it may be due to a lesion of the extrapyramidal motor system, or there may be loss of purposive movement without paralysis (apraxia).

Sixty percent of cerebral vascular accidents are due to *arterial thrombosis*, 16% to *embolus*, 12% to *intracerebral hemorrhage*, 10% to *subarachnoid hemorrhage*, and 2% to other causes (1, 16). The onset of a cerebral vascular accident is usually fairly rapid, with maximum intensity of weakness attained within minutes to hours after onset. However, at least 15% of patients have premonitory manifestations for hours or days; these consist of headache, dizziness, drowsiness, mental disturbances, and focal neurologic signs, especially transient hemiparesis, aphasia, or paresthesia over half the body. Aspirin and dipyridamole (Persantine) may have some prophylactic value.

Headache is prominent at the onset of weakness in all patients with subarachnoid hemorrhage, 60% of those with intracerebral hemorrhage, 25% of those with cerebral embolus, and 6% of those with thrombosis. Vomiting at onset occurs in half of patients with hemorrhage and in 10% of those with embolus or thrombosis. Coma at onset occurs in half of those with hemorrhage and one-fourth of those with embolus or thrombosis, and convulsions (usually generalized, occasionally jacksonian) at onset occur in 15, 9, and 7%, respectively. Hence, the occurrence of headache, vomiting, coma, or convulsions at the onset of a cerebral vascular accident suggests that this is due to hemorrhage, but does not exclude embolus or thrombosis. Stiffness of the neck is usually, though not always, present after hemorrhage and is only occasionally present after embolus or thrombosis, but cervical osteoarthritis, which is common in the elderly, may simulate this sign. Cheyne-Stokes or labored respiration, pupillary changes, conjugate deviation of the eyes, quadriplegia, and bilateral extensor plantar reflexes are also more common after hemorrhage.

The spinal fluid is grossly bloody in all patients with subarachnoid hemorrhage, in 85% of those with intracranial hemorrhage (the remainder having encapsulated bleeding that can be seen by computerized tomography (CT) or magnetic resonance imaging (MRI)), and 15% of those with cerebral embolus (17). It is grossly clear in those with cerebral thrombosis, although there may be slight xanthochromia and red blood cells may be seen on microscopic examination. In patients with cerebral thrombosis the spinal fluid protein level is normal (below 45 mg/dl) in 69%, slightly elevated (46–99 mg/dl) in 29%, and more markedly elevated in only 2%.

Approximately one-fourth of patients with cerebral vascular accidents have extracranial thrombosis of the carotid, vertebral, or subclavian artery, which can be revealed by arteriographic studies. These must be undertaken before the hemiplegia is complete if arterial reconstruction is to have any value. The finding of a systolic bruit in the neck may provide supportive evidence of arterial stenosis.

It is frequently difficult to distinguish between cerebral thrombosis and embolus. Cerebral embolus should be considered whenever there is sudden onset of paralysis in a patient with bacterial endocarditis, fever of undetermined origin with a cardiac murmur, or auricular fibrillation, mitral valve disease, or recent myocardial infarction. Cerebral embolus may also arise from an arteriosclerotic plaque in the ascending aorta or carotid artery.

Approximately 60% of patients with subarachnoid hemorrhage (usually those below the age of 40 years) bleed from a ruptured berry aneurysm, 30% (usually those above the age of 50 years) from a ruptured arteriosclerotic vessel, and 10% from an arteriovenous aneurysm (before the age of 40 years), tumor, or following trauma.

The mortality of patients with cerebrovascular accident varies with the cause: about 20% after cerebral thrombosis, 30% after cerebral embolus or subarachnoid hemorrhage, and over 80% after cerebral hemorrhage. In about one-third, the cause of death appears to be cerebral, about one-third cardiac, and one-third respiratory infection, or, occasionally, pulmonary embolus (3). Aspiration of saliva and food results in pneumonia more commonly than is appreciated.

The development of slowly progressive hemiplegia or monoplegia, spreading from one part of the limb to another, is particularly suggestive of **brain tumor** or **subdural hematoma**, though in some patients the paralysis may set in rapidly. If increased intracranial pressure occurs, there may be headache, vomiting, papilledema, visual impairment, and diplopia due to sixth nerve palsy. Focal or generalized convulsions, ataxia, incoordination, pupillary inequality, sensory changes, personality change, or impairment of consciousness also may occur. The examinations of the greatest helpfulness and accuracy are CT and MRI, although at times carotid and vertebral angiography and other diagnostic procedures are necessary.

Lower Motor Neuron Disorders

Injury to the motor nuclei of the brainstem, to the anterior horn cells of the spinal cord, or to the anterior roots or motor nerves, results in the characteristic manifestations of a lower motor neuron lesion: weakness or paralysis of the muscles innervated by the affected neurons, accompanied by diminished tone, softness and wasting, and diminution or loss of tendon reflexes (2, 10). The distal parts of the extremities are more affected than the proximal. Slow degeneration of the anterior horn cells, as occurs in progressive muscular atrophy and occasionally in syringomyelia, herniated intervertebral disc or spinal cord tumor, results in fascicular twitching of muscle. Disease of the peripheral nerves may also result in sensory loss and, occasionally, in autonomic dysfunction.

Peripheral neuropathy of infectious or toxic origin is more common in younger individuals, while that due to deficiency of diet or absorption or to metabolic, vascular or neoplastic disease is more common in older individuals (5, 6). The most common form of polyneuropathy in elderly patients is that associated with diabetes mellitus of at least 10 years' duration. Occasionally, the neuropathy may take the form of a mononeuritis (affecting most commonly the third nerve), or a neuritis involving only the upper or lower extremities. Older individuals, particularly those who are thin or diabetic, are more prone to develop compression neuropathy of the peroneal nerve due to crossing the legs; to have late ulnar palsy several years after injury to the elbow; or to have compression of the median nerve in the carpal tunnel, due to osteoarthritis or local tenosynovitis at the wrist. Carcinoma may result in neuropathy due to local invasion or, more frequently, by an unknown mechanism.

Lesions of the sensory nerve fibers (most commonly due to diabetes mellitus or alcoholism) result in paresthesias, sensations of pain, burning, and numbness, tenderness, hypo- or hyper-esthesia, and loss of sensation for touch, pain, temperature, vibration, and position. The manifestations are predominantly distal, and are often of stocking or glove distribution. Vibratory sensation is usually impaired to a greater degree than position sense, in contrast to the effect of lesions of the spinal cord or brain, which tend to affect proprioception more than vibratory sensation.

Lesions of autonomic nerve fibers result in vasomotor changes (warmth or coolness, pallor or cyanosis) and trophic change, such as sweating and increased hair growth with incomplete lesions, or anhydrosis and decreased hair growth with complete lesions, pigmentation or depigmentation, irregular growth of nails, and skin ulcers. Lesions of splanchnic nerves, which occur especially in diabetic neuropathy, may result in postural hypotension, anhidrosis, impotence, and nocturnal diarrhea.

In diffuse neuropathy, weakness and wasting are predominantly distal in distribution, spinal fluid protein is usually increased, and sensory impairment is often present. These findings point to disease of the peripheral nerves or spinal cord rather than of muscle. However, if sensory impairment or elevated spinal fluid protein is not present, it may not be possible to distinguish by clinical examination between weakness, atrophy, flaccidity, and diminished tendon reflexes due to disease of the lower motor neuron and the effects of primary muscle disease. The differentiation may be made by demonstrating in the patient with neuropathy delayed motor or sensory nerve conduction, spontaneous fibrillations, fasciculations, or giant potentials, normal serum levels of some of the enzymes present in muscle, and "neurogenic" (grouped) distribution of muscle atrophy in the muscle biopsy.

The most common cause of generalized motor and sensory neuropathy of acute onset is the *Guillain-Barré syndrome*, which has an incidence of 1–2/100,000 population, higher in older persons. It may have an autoimmune basis. In two-thirds of the patients there is a flulike illness 1–3 weeks before onset. In one-half of the patients, the initial symptom is symmetrical weakness, most commonly in the lower extremities and less commonly in the upper extremities or face, whereas in one-half of the patients the initial symptom is numbness and paresthesias of similar distribution. Most patients develop both weakness and paresthesias. The weakness progresses in most patients to the other extremities and the face, and in half to the muscles of swallowing, speech, cough, and respiration, and increases in severity over a period of 1–3 weeks, during which the patient must be carefully observed. Tendon reflexes become diminished, and all sensory modalities usually decrease in glove-stocking distribution. Occasionally, there is evidence of autonomic dysfunction (e.g., orthostatic hypotension, transient hypertension, arrhythmias). Occasionally, ocular and pupillary muscles are affected, with or without limb weakness (Miller-Fisher syndrome). The protein content of the spinal fluid is elevated, usually between 50 and 100 mg/dl, while the cellular content is only occasionally and slightly increased. Nerve conduction is slowed. When the maximal degree and distribution of weakness is reached 2–3 weeks after onset, about 20% of patients require endotracheal intubation and assisted ventilation. While the mortality has been decreased by these measures and by frequent suctioning and other intensive care, mortality remains appreciable (5–15%) and results from aspiration or pneumonia, or less often, obstruction of or bleeding around the endotracheal tube, hypotension, arrhythmia, or pulmonary embolism secondary to venous stasis in the paralyzed extremities. Management relies on endotracheal intubation and assisted ventilation when needed, and measures to prevent or treat pneumonia and pulmonary embolism. Plasmapheresis appears to be of some value, but corticosteroids have been disappointing. Recovery occurs gradually over 2–12 months and is complete in 70%, while the remainder have varying degrees of permanent residual weakness, wasting, and hyporeflexia. About 10% of patients have one or more relapses during or after the period of recovery. A few patients have a chronic course with several recurrences in which the onset is less acute, but the weakness and sensory impairment last for months or years. In this chronic demyelinating polyneuritis, corticosteroids may help speed recovery and prevent relapse.

A number of chronic diseases affecting **anterior horn cells and cranial motor nerve nuclei** produce progressive weakness and atrophy of the extremities and of muscles innervated by cranial nerves (lower motor neuron signs), sometimes associated with upper motor neuron signs. In adults, the most common form is *amyotrophic lateral sclerosis*, which is a combination in varying proportions of three diseases: *progressive spinal muscular atrophy*, affecting mainly muscles of the trunk and limbs; *progressive bulbar palsy*, affecting mainly muscles innervated by cranial nerves, especially the tongue and pharynx; and *primary lateral sclerosis*, affecting mainly the pyramidal tracts. These diseases are only occasionally familial. The lower motor neuron lesion results in progressive weakness, decreased reflexes, atrophy and fasciculation of the muscles of the extremities, especially distally, and of the trunk and tongue, and impairment of swallowing and speech. The upper motor neuron lesion results in spasticity, mainly in the lower extremities, and extensor plantar reflexes. The mean duration of the disease to death is 3 years from the onset of peripheral muscle weakness, and 1½ years from the onset of bulbar weakness. Five-year survival is only 10%. The presence of fasciculations accompanying weakness and atrophy, and spontaneous electromyographic activity, aid in localizing the lesion to the lower motor neuron and to the anterior horn cells. Absence of sensory changes, of delayed nerve conduction, and of elevation of spinal fluid protein, and the progressive course of the disease help to distinguish the disease from polyneuropathy. The normal or only slightly elevated levels of serum enzymes derived from muscle, and evidence of neurogenic (grouped) muscle atrophy on biopsy help to distinguish the disease from myopathy.

A less common lower motor neuron disease, *chronic proximal spinal muscular atrophy*, differs from amyotrophic lateral sclerosis and progressive spinal muscular atrophy in the following ways: familial incidence is much higher (60%); juvenile onset is more common; proximal muscles are affected more than distal; fasciculations are less common (50%) and less pronounced; dysphagia and dysarthria are much less common (15%) and life-threatening dysphagia is rare; extensor plantar reflex is much less common (6%); and the course is much more prolonged (mean duration, 30 years). Since the main manifestations of the disease, slowly progressive proximal muscle weakness and atrophy with diminished tendon reflexes, resemble those of myopathy, diagnosis may be difficult when fasciculations are undetected. The electromyogram is helpful, revealing evidence of a lower motor neuron lesion in 97%, with spontaneous discharges in 50%, and giant potentials in 90%. Nerve conduction is normal. Spinal fluid is normal. The serum levels of enzymes derived from muscle are normal in 90% and slightly elevated in the remainder. Muscle biopsy shows neurogenic (grouped) atrophy in 68% and both neurogenic atrophy and myopathic changes (probably secondary to atrophy) in 19%. There is no treatment for any of the spinal muscular atrophies.

DISORDERS OF MOVEMENT

Bradykinesias

When movement is slow and reduced, and this is not attributable to musculoskeletal pain or weakness, the most common cause is **Parkinson disease**. This disease is recognized in 1/700 population and 1/200 over the age of 50 years. Subclinical manifestations are much more common in the elderly and contribute to changes in gait and posture with age. The disease is caused by degeneration of the substantia nigra, resulting in decreased concentration of dopamine, a neurotransmitter that normally inhibits and modulates the excitatory action of acetylcholine on the striatum. This change in the extrapyramidal motor system results in the classic triad of symptoms of Parkinson disease: muscle rigidity, decreased movement (bradykinesia), and tremor (hyperkinesia). While the earliest symptom noticed by the patient is usually tremor, others will have previously noticed slowing and decrease in movement, particularly of facial expression and blinking of the eyelids, slowness in getting up from a chair or sitting down, a tendency to sit or stand motionless for a long time, and loss of arm swing when walking. The posture becomes one of forward tilting and fixed flexion of the trunk, with slight extension of the neck, and flexion of the extremities. Gait becomes hesitant, with difficulty starting, short shuffling steps that gradually accelerate (festinate), and difficulty stopping. Speech and writing become hesitant and even frozen. Autonomic dysfunction also usually occurs, with excessive sweating, salivation and drooling, and decreased smooth muscle activity that may result in constipation, urinary retention, and postural hypotension.

Management of Parkinson disease is aimed at increasing the concentration and action of dopamine in the striatum, and decreasing the action of acetylcholine. Anticholinergic drugs such as Artane, Cogentin, or Pagitane may suffice when symptoms are mild, but when they are more marked dopaminergic drugs are needed. Dopamine does not cross the blood-brain barrier, but its precursor l-dopa does, and is converted by decarboxylase to dopamine in the brain. l-Dopa is also rapidly converted to dopamine by decarboxylase in extracerebral tissues, especially the liver, so that therapeutic levels require large doses of l-dopa, which may cause anorexia, nausea, vomiting and cardiac arrhythmias. Carbidopa inhibits decarboxylase in the extracerebral tissues, but not in the brain, since it does not cross the blood-brain barrier. Therefore, carbidopa is administered with l-dopa (as Sinemet), in a ratio of 1:4 (25 mg/100 mg) or 1:10 (10/100 or 25/250). The initial dose is usually 1 tablet of Sinemet 10/100 three times a day orally. This dose is increased by 1 tablet every 2 or 3 days until a therapeutic effect is achieved and then more slowly until maximal improvement occurs. This usually requires a daily dose of about 100 mg carbidopa and 1000 mg l-dopa. Adverse effects that require reduction in dose include involuntary choreiform or dystonic movements, such as blepharospasm or orofacial or generalized dyskinesia, confusion, depression, vomiting, postural hypotension, or cardiac arrhythmias.

Normal pressure hydrocephalus is a much less common cause of gait disorder. There is progressive dilatation of the ventricles (observable on CT or MRI) with no (or, at most, transient) increase in intracranial pressure. It is usually of unknown cause, but may follow head trauma or subarachnoid hemorrhage, which may interfere with resorption of ventricular fluid by the arachnoid villi. Symptoms consist of unsteady, broadbased "magnetic" gait, urinary urgency and incontinence, and dementia. Symptoms, especially the gait disorder, improve temporarily in about one-half of the patients after removal by lumbar puncture of 30 ml of cerebrospinal fluid, and in these patients for a longer period after shunting the ventricular fluid to the cisternal space, jugular vein, or pleural or peritoneal cavity.

About one-half of the patients in most geriatric facilities have some instability of posture or gait, and in about one-half of these it is incapacitating. These patients have the slow, unsteady, fearful, short-stepped, shuffling gait of the elderly. In about one-half of such patients, the gait disorder can be attributed mainly to Parkinson disease, normal pressure hydrocephalus, or stroke, but in the other half, a diagnosis cannot be made. Because antiparkinson drugs or ventricular shunting may be of help to some of these patients, they should be evaluated more carefully than is usually the case.

Hypothyroidism results in slowing of movement, speech, mentation, and contraction and relaxation response to percussion of the muscle or its tendon. Because these signs are reversible by hormone replacement, a high index of suspicion is warranted.

Depression and **dementias** are frequently overlooked causes of mental and physical slowing. Because depression is potentially reversible, it is particularly unfortunate that it is often overlooked and untreated.

Hyperkinesias and dyskinesias may result from disease or drugs or may be of unknown cause.

Tremors, the most common hyperkinesia, are involuntary, rhythmic, oscillatory movements of a limb, or part of a limb, or of the head, due to either alternating contractions of opposing muscle groups (agonists and antagonists) as in Parkinson disease (at 4–7/sec) or simultaneous contractions of opposing muscle groups as in essential tremor (at 8/sec). The tremor of anxiety or hyperthyroidism is finer, having a higher frequency and lesser amplitude, whereas that of intoxication by alcohol, barbituates, lithium, other drugs, or carbon dioxide retention tends to be coarser; i.e., of lower frequency and wider amplitude.

Essential tremor of the hands, and often of the head and voice, occurs in 1/500 population as an isolated phenomenon of unknown etiology. It is familial (autosomal dominant) in about half. Onset is usually during midlife, when it is called benign essential tremor, but less often begins in old age, when the term senile tremor is sometimes applied. The tremor is most pronounced when the arms are held outstretched (postural tremor) and diminishes at rest and during movement, in contrast to the tremor of Parkinson disease, which is present at rest and sometimes also during movement, or the (intention) tremor of cerebellar disease, which is absent at rest and appears during movement. Essential tremor often becomes worse when the patient is under stress, and may be misinterpreted as "nervousness." Essential tremor slowly gets more frequent and of greater amplitude with age and often then involves the head, with vertical or horizontal tremor that may become less on tilted the head to the side, and the thorax and diaphragm, with vocal tremor. Essential tremor usually diminishes after an alcoholic drink, which has led some patients to become alcoholics. A safer treatment is a β-blocker like propranolol, a sedative, a tranquilizer, Amantadine, or Primidone, each of which diminishes, but does not abolish the tremor.

Chorea consists of involuntary, repetitive rapid contractions of different groups of muscles. It is of central origin and occurs in adults in *Huntington's chorea*, a progressive hereditary (autosomal dominant) disease characterized by rapid, irregular, aimless involuntary movements of the muscles of the limbs, face and trunk, personality change, and dementia. Symptoms usually begin in the late 30s and increase with age. Similar movements may start late in life in the absence of a family history, in which case the term *senile chorea* may be applied.

Athetosis consists of slower and more sinuous, writhing, involuntary repetitive movements, and **dystonia** consists of even slower, more sustained, and more contortional involuntary repetitive movements. In the elderly, these dyskinesias are most

commonly seen after the use of antipsychotic (neuroleptic) drugs, such as phenothiazines, e.g., chlorpromazine (Thorazine); prochlorperazine (Compazine); butyrophenones such as haloperidol (Haldol); Mellaril, Navane, or Stelazine. Because dyskinesia due to antipsychotic drugs is more likely to occur after prolonged administration (especially at high doses), the term tardive (late) has been applied. The movements of *tardive dyskinesia* produced by antipsychotic drugs are involuntary, rapid, and repetitive, but, whereas choreiform movements move from one part of the body to another, those of tardive dyskinesia are repetitive and stereotyped; i.e., the same movements keep repeating themselves. The most common sites are the mouth, tongue (fly catcher darting out of mouth or moving around mouth), and jaws (chewing) and, less often, the fingers (piano playing), toes, back, or trunk (head or body rocking). If the patient is asked to keep the tongue protruded, he or she usually can do so, in contrast to patients with Huntington's chorea. On standing, the patient may march in place or, on walking, may lengthen the stride and swinging of the arms. The increased movements are opposite to the bradykinesia and akinesia of Parkinsonism, and may be due to supersensitivity of dopamine receptors in the brain.

The prevalence of tardive dyskinesia increases with age and is most common in elderly women. Unlike dyskinesia produced by l-dopa, which disappears when l-dopa is decreased in dose or discontinued, tardive dyskinesia produced by antipsychotic drugs may persist after the drug is stopped, may first appear within 3 months after the drug is discontinued, and may be permanent. Antipsychotic drugs may also produce tardive akathisia (waves of inner restlessness and a feeling of "jumping out of the skin"), Parkinsonism which is unresponsive to l-dopa, or dystonia with severe twisting movements of the limbs, trunk (opisthotonus), neck, tongue, face, or eyes (oculogyric crises).

Dyskinesias resembling those produced by antipsychotic drugs may appear spontaneously during mid or late life. The most common are *oromandibular dystonia* (sustained involuntary contraction of facial and jaw muscles) and *blepharospasm* (sustained contraction of orbiculares oculi). When they occur together, the name Meige syndrome is applied. *Hemifacial spasm* consists of sustained involuntary contraction of facial muscles, usually starting around the eye and then spreading to the other facial muscles of one side. Unilateral repetitive sustained (dystonic) movements of facial, neck, or shoulder muscles (*torticollis*) may be a tic and may be psychogenic. Bilateral movements may also be psychogenic (tic), but are more often of unknown etiology. Except when dystonic movements are psychogenic or related to drugs or local irritation (e.g., poorly fitting dentures provoking jaw, tongue, or buccal tics), there is no good treatment.

DISORDERS OF THE NEUROMUSCULAR JUNCTION

Myasthenia Gravis

Myasthenia gravis is a chronic disorder of neuromuscular transmission, characterized by weakness and abnormal fatigability (12). The muscles innervated by the cranial nerves are particularly affected, and usually those of the neck, trunk, and extremities. In severe disease, weakness of the muscles of respiration occurs. Smooth and cardiac muscle are not involved. The disease usually becomes generalized, but in 16% of the patients it remains localized to the extraocular muscles. While generalized myasthenia gravis is more common in females, ocular myasthenia gravis occurs more frequently in males.

Onset of the disease may occur at any age, but the peak is in the third decade in women and in the third through the seventh decade in men. The disease is more common in women, the ratio of females to males being 61:39, but after the age of 50 years, onset of the disease is more common in men.

The initial manifestations are most commonly referable to the extraocular muscles: ptosis in one-fourth of the patients, diplopia in one-fourth, and weakness of legs, difficulty in swallowing, or generalized weakness in the remainder. Older patients, particularly older men, tend to have a more severe and progressive form of the disease and fewer spontaneous remissions than young patients. Male patients are less likely to have spontaneous remissions than females. Mortality was reduced from 31% to 15% after the introduction of positive pressure, volume controlled respiration in the 1950s, and to 7% following the introduction of corticosteroids in the 1960s. Mortality remains highest in older patients. Death is usually due to pneumonia in patients with weakness of the muscles of respiration or cough, or less often to pharyngeal obstruction or aspiration in patients with impairment of swallowing.

Anticholinesterase compounds are administered for the amelioration of weakness in day-to-day management. The most useful of these are pyridostigmine (Mestinon, 60–180 mg orally every 4 hours) and neostigmine (Prostigmin, 15–30 mg orally every 33 hours or 0.5–1 mg intramuscularly every 2–3 hours). Another and shorter acting anticholinesterase compound, edrophonium (Tensilon) is useful in diagnosis (10 mg intravenously) and in evaluation of adequacy of dose of the longer acting compounds (2 mg intravenously). Atropine (0.4 mg intramuscularly) should be administered before edrophonium in older individuals to prevent bradycardia or heart block, and may be administered by any route every 6 to 8 hours if needed to treat or prevent diarrhea, abdominal cramps or excessive salivation that may be produced by any of the anticholinesterase compounds. The maximum strength obtained after optimal doses of any of these compounds is approximately the same. The compounds differ mainly in their duration of action (pyridostigmine > neostigmine > edrophonium), and in the severity of their parasympathomimetic side effects (neostigmine > pyridostigmine > edrophonium). The administration of graded doses of any of these compounds results in an increase in strength in muscles affected by the disease, but the maximal strength obtained is usually below normal, and may be far below normal.

Corticosteroids are administered to patients who are responding poorly to anticholinesterase medication. If the patient is severely ill, treatment should be initiated in an intensive care unit with prednisone (100 mg) or dexamethasone (15 mg) orally, daily for 10 days. Exacerbation of weakness occurs in about one-half of the patients during the first week, and may require intubation or assisted respiration. Improvement occurs in most patients, to a marked degree in about one-half, usually beginning during the second week. If improvement does not occur, repeated courses of corticosteroid should be reinstituted within 1 or 2 weeks until improvement begins, after which smaller doses of oral prednisone (35mg) or dexamethasone (4 mg) should be administered every other day. On this regimen, improvement persists for 3–6 months in about one-half of the patients, and over a year in one-fourth of the patients. If exacerbation of the disease recurs, higher doses of steroid should be reinstituted. In patients who are less severely ill, prednisone can be administered orally in smaller doses (50 mg on alternate days or 25 mg daily and gradually increased). This results in slower improvement, but a lower incidence of initial exacerbation, which, nevertheless, may be severe.

The complications of prolonged steroid treatment have included, in addition to initial exacerbation of the disease, a 10% incidence of upper gastrointestinal hemorrhage, osteoporosis with vertebral compression or aseptic necrosis of bone, glaucoma, or posterior subcapsular cataracts. Because of these complications, steroid should be reduced in dose as improvement occurs, and discontinued whenever possible. Most physicians have limited the prolonged use of steroid to patients with severe generalized myasthenia gravis, but administration of prednisone may also be helpful in refractory ocular myasthenia gravis.

In patients with severe myasthenia gravis who do not improve on steroid, addition of **plasmapheresis** or intravenous **immunoglobulin** may provide improvement of several weeks duration, while addition of daily **azathioprine (Imuran)** or **cyclophosphamide (Cytoxan)** may provide slower, but longer lasting improvement.

Thymectomy is followed by improvement in most myasthenic patients below the age of 60 years, sometimes over a period of months, but more often over many years. Its efficacy in older patients is uncertain. While the natural history of the disease is that of gradual improvement after the first 1–3 years, patients who have had thymectomy early in the disease do appear to have a somewhat more benign course. Therefore, thymectomy is recommended in most patients with generalized myasthenia gravis below the age of 60 years who are not able to carry out normal activity on anticholinesterase medication and well-tolerated doses of corticosteroid when needed.

Thymoma occurs in 10% of patients with myasthenia gravis, and is seldom seen before the age of 40. The tumor is usually asymptomatic. It is detected by x-ray or CT scan as a density in the anterior mediastinum and should be removed trans-sternally. Three-fourths of thymomas are fully encapsulated and can be totally removed, while one-fourth will be found to have invaded adjacent structures. Only 1% metastasize distantly. Thirty percent of patients with thymoma have or develop myasthenia gravis, 20% develop nonthymic cancer, and 3% develop red cell aplasia, leukopenia, or thrombocytopenia.

CARCINOMATOUS AND OTHER MYASTHENIC SYNDROMES

Muscular weakness and fatigue, with distribution and temporal characteristics similar to myasthenia gravis but with little or no response to anticholinesterase compounds, occasionally occurs without any detectable associated disease or in association with neoplastic disease, polymyositis, disseminated lupus erythematosus, peripheral neuropathy, or amyotrophic lateral sclerosis (12). The best studied of these myasthenic syndromes, the Eaton-Lambert syndrome, is usually associated with neoplasm, particularly small cell bronchogenic carcinoma. The syndrome resembles myasthenia gravis in symptomatology and usually in increased reactivity to *d*-tubocurarine and abnormal reactivity to decamethonium and succinylcholine. It differs from myasthenia gravis in that only a minority of patients respond to neostigmine and most respond to 3,4-diaminopyridine (40–200 mg orally a day).

DISORDERS OF MUSCLE DUE TO ELECTROLYTE DISTURBANCE

Hypokalemia

Hypokalemia may develop when there is deficient intake or absorption of potassium, substantial loss in vomitus, stool (as a result of steatorrhea, malabsorption, or cathartics) or urine, or marked intracellular movement of the ion (8, 15). Excessive potassium loss in the urine occurs as a result of renal tubular injury or disease, diuretic or corticosteroid administration, or protein catabolism, and is particularly important in the elderly person. Approximately one-half of patients who receive 50 mg hydrochlorothiazide twice daily for more than 2 months, as in the control of hypertension, develop a decrease in serum potassium concentration of at least 0.5 mEq/liter. There is sufficient reduction in whole-body potassium in most diabetic patients, particularly those who are poorly controlled, to require daily replacement even in the presence of normal serum potassium. Hypokalemia also may occur as a result of excessive movement of potassium into cells of the liver after the administration of large amounts of glucose and insulin in the treatment of diabetic acidosis, into cells throughout the body in alkalosis, or into muscle in hypokalemic periodic paralysis.

Hypokalemia due to any cause, if severe, may impair the function of skeletal, cardiac, and smooth muscle. This is more likely to occur after rapid reduction in plasma potassium concentration than after gradual reduction. Weakness may involve the muscles of one or all extremities, and the neck, trunk, and respiration, but seldom the muscles innervated by the cranial nerves. The tendon reflexes and muscular contraction in response to direct percussion are diminished. Severe loss of potassium may result in profound weakness, elevation of serum enzymes derived from muscle, and muscle degeneration, necrosis, and infiltration by macrophages (hypokalemic myopathy). Hypokalemia also may produce broadening and lowering of the T wave of the electrocardiogram, depression of the ST segment, extrasystoles, and other arrhythmias, and increased sensitivity to the arrhythmic effects of digitalis.

Treatment of potassium deficiency is accomplished by supplying potassium-containing medication, either orally or parenterally if necessary. For mild deficiency, at least 60 mEq of potassium chloride is required daily. Potassium-containing foods, such as orange juice (5 mEq/dl) or bananas (10 mEq/100 g), are seldom ingested in sufficient amounts to provide adequate replacement. For severe deficiency, several times this amount may be required. In the presence of normal renal function, the only practical limit to the amount of potassium given orally is the development of abdominal cramps or diarrhea, which occur at doses greater than 150 mEq of potassium per day. Potassium salts in tablet form, even when enteric coated, may cause local vasoconstriction, mucosal ulceration and, later, stenosis of the esophagus and small bowel, and should never be used. A wax-coated, slow-release tablet (Slow-K) has been introduced, but has been reported to produce esophageal ulceration and stricture. The organic anion compounds of potassium are more palatable than the chloride, but are somewhat less suitable, since most of the organic anions, such as gluconate or citrate, are converted to bicarbonate, and may aggravate the metabolic alkalosis accompanying hypokalemia. For intravenous treatment, potassium chloride (40 mEq/liter) is administered at a rate of 20 mEq/hour. There are occasional instances of severe hypokalemia, as in diabetic ketoacidosis after treatment with insulin, where potassium chloride needs to be administered more rapidly than 20 mEq/hour, with electrocardiographic monitoring.

Hyperkalemia

Hyperkalemia results mainly from deficient renal excretion of the ion due to anuria or oliguria, from excessively rapid potassium administration, from intravascular hemolysis, from acute acidosis, and from crush injuries (8). Hyperkalemia, if sufficiently severe, results in impairment of function of skeletal, cardiac, and smooth muscle. Weakness due to hyperkalemia clinically resembles that due to hypokalemia, but the electrocardiographic alterations are different, with peaked T waves, widening of the QRS interval, and atrioventricular dissociation. Patients with atrioventricular block appear to be particularly susceptible to the cardiac effects of hyperkalemia, which may increase the block, retard impulse propagation and depress the ventricular pacemaker with resultant asystole.

Emergency treatment of hyperkalemia consists of infusion of glucose (100 g), insulin (25 units) and sodium bicarbonate (50 mEq every 20 min), to produce an intracellular shift of potassium, and of calcium gluconate (1 g) to antagonize the cardiac toxicity of hyperkalemia. If the patient was previously digitalized, calcium should be omitted, since it increases digitalis toxicity. For longer lasting treatment the patient can be given peritoneal or hemodialysis, and sodium polystyrene sulfonate (Kayexalate) cation exchange resin (20–40 g, four times a day) orally or by enema.

Hypocalcemia

This may occur in osteomalacia, hypoparathyroidism, steatorrhea, and uremic phosphorus retention. Hypocalcemia, or reduced ionization of calcium without change in concentration, which occurs in alkalosis due to hyperventilation or sodium bicarbonate ingestion, results in increased irritability and spontaneous discharge of sensory and motor nerves and muscle, producing paresthesias, twitching, and muscular spasms (tetany). Most patients are not weak, but some with osteomalacia or hypoparathyroidism develop proximal muscle weakness, histologic changes compatible with myopathy, and increased serum enzymes derived from muscle. Improvement occurs after treatment with calcium and vitamin D.

Hypercalcemia

This may occur in primary or secondary hyperparathyroidism, sarcoidosis, administration of calcium and alkali or of vitamin D, and in malignant disease with or without bony metastasis. Hypercalcemia results in a moderate decrease in muscle strength and tone, decreased intestinal motility, drowsiness, and nephrocalcinosis. Some patients with primary or secondary hyperparathyroidism have more pronounced proximal weakness and wasting, myopathic potentials, and muscle fiber atrophy. Improvement occurs after removal of a parathyroid adenoma or alleviation of the cause of parathormone stimulation.

Sodium

Hyponatremia results from loss of sodium in the urine, as a result of renal disease, diuretic administration, or hypoadrenocorticism, or loss of sodium in the gastrointestinal tract or sweat, or from inappropriate secretion of antidiuretic hormone. Hyponatremia due to sodium loss by any route results in decreased plasma volume and hypotension (initially postural), especially in the elderly. Diuretics are the most common cause of postural hypotension, which should be suspected when the patient complains of syncope, light headedness, or even weakness, on standing. Hypernatremia may result from restriction of water intake, dehydration, hyperaldosteronism or certain lesions of the brain. Either hyponatremia or hypernatremia may result in lassitude or weakness, which, in severe hypernatremia, may progress to paralysis.

DISORDERS OF MUSCLE DUE TO ENDOCRINE DISTURBANCE

Weakness may occur when there is either deficient or excessive function of the thyroid, adrenal cortex, or anterior pituitary glands. It may also occur when there is hypocalcemia (with tetany), hypercalcemia, or hypoglycemia arising from any cause (8).

Hyperthyroidism

Approximately 70% of patients with hyperthyroidism have mild-to-moderate muscular weakness, with easy fatigability and a varying degree of muscle wasting and weight loss (9). This tends to be more severe in older patients. Weakness is usually most prominent in the muscles of the pelvic girdle and upper legs, with difficulty in climbing stairs. Muscle wasting tends to be more generalized, but the quadriceps and temporal muscles are often involved to a greater degree.

A smaller proportion of patients have more pronounced evidence of disturbance in muscle function. In *chronic thyrotoxic myopathy*, there is more marked weakness and symmetrical muscle wasting than occurs in the great majority of patients with uncomplicated hyperthyroidism. Most patients with chronic myopathy differ in other ways from those with uncomplicated hyperthyroidism. In patients with thyrotoxic myopathy, exophthalmos is usually not prominent, the thyroid gland may or may not be grossly enlarged, and the usual manifestations of hyperthyroidism, such as tachycardia, sweating, heat intolerance, tremor, and hyperkinesia, may or may not be noted or may be overshadowed by the marked weakness, muscle wasting, and weight loss that are usually the principal symptoms (9).

Some patients may be depressed and anorectic and may be said to have "masked" or "apathetic" hyperthyroidism. In these patients, who are usually in the older age group, the only clue to the diagnosis may be weakness or wasting, auricular fibrillation, or heart failure. Such patients may be thought to have the cachexia of malignant disease, but treatment will result in dramatic benefits once normal thyroid function is restored.

Rarely, patients with severe hyperthyroidism may develop *acute myopathy* or *encephalomyopathy*, characterized by the acute development of severe weakness, marked tremor, delirium, and sometimes dysphagia, dysarthria, and coma. Concomitant myasthenia gravis should be excluded by the edrophonium test. Management of thyroid "storm," with or without encephalomyopathy, relies on rapid institution of antithyroid treatment with potassium iodide and propylthiouracil, supplemented by propranolol, reserpine, and corticosteroid.

Ophthalmomyopathy

This is the most common myopathy associated with thyroid disease. The relationship to thyroid function is probably indirect, since the muscular symptoms may develop with or without thyrotoxicosis and have been ascribed to increased serum level of the thyroid-stimulating hormone (TSH) or, more likely, of long-acting thyroid stimulating globulin (LATS). Eye signs may develop before there is evidence of hyperthyroidism, may be severe when there is minimal thyrotoxicosis, or may progress after amelioration of thyrotoxicosis. The most severe instances of exophthalmic ophthalmoplegia develop in older patients after the relief of hyperthyroidism by thyroidectomy.

Hypothyroidism

The slowing of physical activity that characterizes hypothyroidism is due not only to the lethargy and mental sluggishness that occur in this disease, but also to alterations in skeletal muscle. Almost all hypothyroid patients complain of subjective weakness, usually of mild degree, and nearly one-third have objective weakness, primarily of the proximal muscles of the shoulder girdle and hips. The weakness is usually not marked. There also commonly occurs slowness of movement, which is due in part to retarded mental activity and also to an actual slowness of muscular contraction and relaxation. Hypothyroid patients often complain of muscular stiffness and, occasionally, have aching muscles, spasms, and even painful cramps, especially in calves and low back. The slowness of muscle movement that occurs in most hypothyroid patients is well seen in the characteristic retardation of the response to percussion of the muscle or its tendon, particularly in the relaxation phase.

In contrast to the muscular wasting that occurs in hyperthyroidism, hypothyroid patients have either normal or increased muscle bulk. The hypertrophied muscles are firmer than normal and may become even harder and more swollen after exercise, with aching and local tightening. The hypertrophied muscles are either of normal strength or are slightly to moderately weak. They are never of increased strength. The serum enzymes derived from muscle, including creatine phosphokinase, may be elevated.

In patients with severe and protracted hypothyroidism, coma may occur, accompanied by hypothermia and marked slowing of respiration and, in one-fourth, by convulsions. Mechanical ventilation may be required to prevent carbon dioxide narcosis. The mortality rate of patients with myxedema coma is high.

The term "masked hypothyroidism," like "masked hyperthyroidism," has been introduced in an attempt to draw attention to the atypical picture of the disease. There is an increasing belief that many older people may have unsuspected "subclinical" or mild hypothyroidism, with nonspecific complaints, such as weakness, muscle cramps, apathy (and occasional irritability), weight gain, constipation and menorrhagia.

Hypo- and Hyperadrenocorticism and Hypo- and Hyperpituitarism

Weakness is a prominent manifestation of hypoadrenalism (Addison's disease) and hypopituitarism (Simmonds' disease, Frohlich's syndrome) and also may occur in hyperfunction of the adrenal glands or pituitary gland (Cushing's syndrome, acromegaly). Muscle weakness occurs in 80% of patients with Cushing's syndrome and sometimes is accompanied by wasting of limb muscles, despite truncal obesity. Similar symptoms may be seen with prolonged corticosteroid therapy, and there may be increased creatinuria and, rarely, muscle necrosis.

DISORDERS OF MUSCLE DUE TO INFLAMMATORY DISEASE

Varying degrees of muscle weakness and wasting, associated with round cell infiltration, perivascular collections of lymphocytes, and degeneration, necrosis, and atrophy of muscle fibers, may occur in association with any of the inflammatory connective tissue or collagen diseases that have been attributed to hypersensitivity (7, 18). These changes are most severe in polymyositis, but also may occur in some patients with disseminated lupus erythematosus, periarteritis nodosa, scleroderma, or rheumatoid arthritis.

Polymyositis

This is the most common primary muscle disease of adults. It may begin at any age, with roughly equal distribution of onset from the first to sixth decades. In approximately one-third of patients, polymyositis occurs alone; in 40%, it is accompanied by dermatitis (dermatomyositis); in 20% by clinical and laboratory evidence of disseminated lupus erythematosus, polyarteritis, scleroderma or, less often, rheumatoid arthritis; and in 15%, by a malignancy, usually of lung, gastrointestinal tract, breast, ovary, or uterus (18).

The disease may begin insidiously or acutely. The initial symptom is weakness, usually of the legs, in half the patients, dermatitis in one-fourth, and muscle or joint pain or Raynaud's phenomenon in one-fourth. The main manifestation of the disease is muscular weakness, which occurs in all patients. Proximal muscles are affected more than distal. The proximal muscles of the legs become weak in almost all patients, and those of the arms in 80%, while only 35% develop weakness of distal muscles. The neck flexors are weak in 65%, and dysphagia occurs in 30%. Facial and extraocular muscles are seldom affected. Pain or tenderness of muscles occurs in one-half of the patients, but many with severe weakness have no other complaint. Severe atrophy and weight loss develop in one-half of the patients, and contractures in one-third. Tendon reflexes and the contractile response of affected muscle to direct percussion are usually diminished.

Approximately 40% of patients have an erythematous eruption that usually begins on the face or upper trunk, with edema, erythema, and a pink "heliotrope" hue. The periorbital areas are particularly involved, and malar erythema may occur, as in lupus erythematosus. The hands are frequently involved, especially the extensor surfaces and nail beds, and sometimes the feet. Pigmentation, hardness, and even calcinosis of the skin and subcutaneous tissues may occur as a late development.

Approximately one-third of patients have Raynaud's phenomenon, one-third have joint pains, and a few have arthritis that may be indistinguishable from rheumatoid arthritis. About 8% have significant intestinal hypomotility, and 2% have recurring pneumonitis. The heart is rarely affected. Fever is variable. Many patients have no fever, despite severe illness, while some, especially younger patients and those with an acute course, have either low-grade or high fever. The course of the disease is also variable, and may be progressive or characterized by spontaneous exacerbations and remissions.

During acute stages of the disease, the erythrocyte sedimentation rate is elevated, and there may be a neutrophilic leukocytosis, but anemia is uncommon. The α_2 and γ-globulins are elevated in the serum of about one-half of the patients, and the tests for circulating rheumatoid factor and antinuclear globulin are occasionally positive. There is usually increased creatinuria. The electromyogram is usually compatible with myopathy.

The serum enzymes derived from muscle, including creatine phosphokinase (CPK), are almost always elevated, sometimes markedly, during active stages of the disease, and usually decline toward normal levels with spontaneous improvement or after treatment with corticosteroids. Muscle biopsy, if it includes an involved area, is almost always helpful in diagnosis.

Treatment relies on *corticosteroids*, which are beneficial in most patients, particularly during the acute stage and during exacerbations (11, 18). Prolonged administration of relatively high doses of corticosteroid is usually required before muscle strength improves. The initial dose should be 60–120 mg of prednisone, or its equivalent, daily, by mouth, although occasionally higher doses may be necessary. After 1–4 weeks of corticosteroid administration, the level of serum enzymes derived from muscle, particularly CPK, will begin to fall and will gradually decline over a period of months. The enzymes usually begin to decrease 3–4 weeks before improvement in muscle strength begins, and the improvement may not be manifest until high doses of corticosteroid have been administered for 1–2 months. The dose of steroid should not be reduced until there is good evidence of improvement, as indicated by increased muscle strength, decreased muscle tenderness, decreased serum enzymes derived from muscle, and decreased creatinuria. When improvement is manifest, the dose of steroid should be reduced by about 10% every 1–2 weeks. Too rapid reduction in steroid dose may result in clinical relapse, which usually necessitates an increase in dose. A rise in the level of serum enzymes derived from muscle,

or in creatinuria, usually precedes clinical relapse by 3–6 weeks and may be a helpful sign. Unfortunately, there is not always a good correlation between these laboratory tests and the clinical condition of the patient, which is a more important guide to management. Occasionally, the serum enzymes are within normal range despite active myositis, particularly when muscle atrophy is extensive in longstanding disease. If the disease goes into remission, it may be possible to discontinue steroid, but if not, steroid administration is continued at the lowest dose that suppresses active manifestations. Since most patients require long-term administration of steroid, it is necessary that precautions be taken to observe for an attempt to prevent complications of steroid therapy, including steroid myopathy. Decrease in strength accompanied by a rise in serum enzymes derived from muscle is usually due to exacerbation of the disease, and warrants an increase in steroid dose. In patients who are receiving high doses of steroid for prolonged periods, decrease in strength without a rise in serum enzymes may be due to steroid myopathy. Unfortunately, there is no laboratory test for steroid myopathy, which can be diagnosed only if reduction in dose of steroid, or gradual discontinuation, is followed by improvement in strength.

The complications of corticosteroid therapy vary with the dose and duration of administration. The more serious effects include peptic ulceration (often gastric), osteoporosis with vertebral compression fractures or aseptic necrosis of bone, glaucoma and posterior subcapsular cataracts, cerebral edema, and superimposition of bacterial, fungus, and viral infections. Less serious effects include myopathy, psychiatric disorders, edema, elevation of blood pressure, hypokalemic alkalosis, hyperlipidemia, centripetal obesity, impaired wound healing, acne, and suppression of the hypothalamic-pituitary-adrenal system. Acute adrenocortical insufficiency may occur during or after withdrawal from corticosteroid treatment in the event of physiologic stress and requires immediate parenteral administration of hydrocortisone and saline.

Immunosuppressant therapy is employed in patients whose strength does not improve following the administration of at least 60 mg prednisone daily for at least 2–4 months, and in patients who are unable to tolerate the large doses of steroid that may be required to suppress the disease (11, 18). In the latter, it is usually possible to reduce the dose of steroid if supplemented by immunosuppressive medication. Methotrexate, a folic acid antagonist, has been used most. The initial dose is 10–15 mg, intravenously, intramuscularly, or orally, once a week, increased at weekly intervals if well tolerated to 0.5–0.8 mg/kg (30–50 mg). After several weeks, methotrexate administration is decreased to biweekly, triweekly or monthly intervals. Methotrexate may also be administered in smaller doses, e.g., 2.5 mg orally, daily for 5 days each week. It is necessary to perform preinjection blood counts and serum alkaline phosphatase activity, and to check for the occurrence of stomatitis, sore throat, skin rash, purpura, fever, gastrointestinal complaints, and hepatic dysfunction.

Other immunosuppressive drugs that have been employed with variable success include azathioprine and cyclophosphamide. Azathioprine (Imuran) is administered orally in doses of 2–3 mg/kg daily. Toxic effects requiring decrease in dose or discontinuation include leukopenia, granulocytopenia, pancytopenia, gastrointestinal distress, and superimposed infection. Patients should have weekly blood counts for the first 4 weeks and at least every 2 or 3 weeks thereafter. Cyclophosphamide (Cytoxan) is administered orally in an initial dose of 50 mg daily. If after 4 weeks there have been no therapeutic or toxic effects, the dose is increased to 100 mg daily, and if no effects after another 4 weeks, to 150 mg daily. Complete blood counts are obtained weekly, and the drug is withheld when the white blood count falls below 2500/mm^3. Other toxic effects include nausea, vomiting, diarrhea, reversible hair loss, thrombocytopenia, hemorrhagic cystitis, and amenorrhea or azoospermia.

Disseminated Lupus Erythematosus

Three-fourths of patients with lupus, polyarteritis, scleroderma, or rheumatoid arthritis develop histologic evidence of nodular myositis, but these lesions are usually without any clinical counterpart. However, about 20% of those with lupus erythematosus develop weakness and atrophy due to polymyositis. Usually clinical and laboratory evidence of lupus is already present (Chapter 26).

Since the patient may be receiving corticosteroids when weakness is noted, it is necessary to differentiate between steroid myopathy and other causes of weakness.

Scleroderma (Progressive Systemic Sclerosis)

Weakness and atrophy due to polymyositis occasionally accompany scleroderma, but in most patients, the limitation of motion and weakness that occur are due mainly to induration and thickening of skin (95% of patients), particularly of the hands and face, and to arthritis (61%). Other manifestations include Raynaud's phenomenon (83%), symptomatic disease of the esophagus (50%), lungs (30%), heart (20%), kidneys (20%), and intestine (10%), and gangrene of terminal digits due to arteritis (5%). Treatment relies on corticosteroids, but the results are poorer than in other collagen vascular diseases.

Polyarteritis Nodosa

Weakness and atrophy occur in over one-half of the patients with this disease: in 10% of patients it is due to polymyositis, and in 50% to polyneuritis, which is usually localized, but occasionally involves all extremities. Clinical and laboratory evidence of polyarteritis is usually already present: fever (85%), weight loss (50%), hypertension (60%), albuminuria (60%), hematuria (40%), abdominal pain (50%), asthma (20%), leukocytosis (80%), and eosinophilia (20%). Muscle biopsy usually reveals polyarteritic lesions, but this may require study of numerous serial sections and several biopsies. Treatment relies on corticosteroids.

Temporal Arteritis

This is a disease of older people, with onset after the age of 50 years, and usually after 65 years. Onset is characterized by headaches (80%), fever (80%), pain and tenderness, and sometimes swelling over the temporal arteries (50%), muscle aching and stiffness (60%), anorexia, weight loss (50%), ophthalmoplegia and ptosis (each in 30%) and occasionally, arthralgia, pain in the jaws on chewing, and visual disturbances (each in 50%) (4, 7). The temporal arteries are usually tender but as the disease progresses the pulsations may disappear. The sedimentation rate is almost always elevated to over 50 mm/hour Westergren or 25 Wintrobe and is usually much higher. The diagnosis is established by biopsy of the temporal artery, in several areas if necessary, which discloses giant cell arteritis. Treatment with corticosteroid is effective, and improvement is usually seen within 24 hours. Steroids should be promptly instituted, not only for symptomatic relief, but also to prevent occlusion of the ophthalmic or other essential artery. The initial dose of prednisone is 60 mg, and this is gradually reduced as improvement occurs. Treatment is continued at a low dose for a year, and may have to be resumed if active disease recurs.

Polymyalgia Rheumatica

This poorly understood syndrome, which is much more common in the elderly and in women, is characterized by aching and stiffness in the muscles of the shoulder and pelvic girdles, arthralgia, and usually low-grade fever and increased erythrocyte sedimentation rate. There is often subjective weakness, but little or no objective weakness and no wasting. There is no elevation of serum enzymes derived from muscle, nor is there electromyographic abnormality or histologic change in muscle. The syndrome has a very protracted course and is accompanied by much emotional stress, but is not disabling. Since some patients eventually develop manifestations of temporal arteritis (30%), rheumatoid arthritis, disseminated lupus erythematosus, polymyositis or polyarteritis nodosa, the syndrome is thought by some to be related to autoimmunity. Specific diagnostic criteria are lacking, however, and it is often difficult to distinguish polymyalgia rheumatica from systemic infections and emotional disorders. Small doses of steroid provide symptomatic relief so rapidly and effectively as to be of diagnostic help.

DISORDERS OF MUSCLE DUE TO OTHER CAUSES

Muscular Dystrophy

This is the most common primary muscle disease of children, and in adults ranks second to polymyositis. The cause is unknown. There are several types, which are usually familial, although sporadic cases are not uncommon. All are degenerative diseases of muscle manifested by weakness (7, 18). The tendon jerks of affected muscles are diminished or lost. Muscle atrophy, which may or may not be preceded by pseudohypertrophy, occurs, and later there may be contractures. The serum level of enzymes derived from muscle, including creatine phosphokinase, is usually elevated in children and normal or slightly elevated in adults. Diagnosis is made by muscle biopsy. Management is limited to physical therapy, avoidance of obesity, and careful attention to respiratory complications.

The severe, generalized, rapidly progressive (Duchenne) type, which is the most common, begins in early childhood and most patients become bedridden and die from respiratory infection or heart failure before they are adults. The mild, restricted, slowly progressive (facioscapular) type usually begins between the ages of 6 and 20 years, although occasionally as late as middle age. There is almost always weakness and atrophy of the muscles of the face, and usually of the shoulder girdle, with winging of the scapulae, and of the upper arms, pelvic girdle, legs and trunk. These changes may be asymmetrical. Pseudohypertrophy is rare. The course of the disease is slowly progressive, so that patients usually live to old age. The limb-girdle (Erb) type has similar age of onset and course, but involves symmetrically the muscles of the pelvic and shoulder girdles and the proximal muscles of the limbs, and spares the face. The ocular type of muscular dystrophy may begin at any age, and results in slowly progressive ptosis and ophthalmoplegia, weakness of facial muscles in 25% and of jaws, neck, and limb muscles in 10%. The myotonic type of muscular dystrophy is characterized not only by weakness and wasting, but also by myotonia, and frequently frontal baldness, cataracts, evidence of testicular or ovarian atrophy, and hyperostosis frontalis. There is no treatment for the weakness, but the myotonia can be improved by quinine (0.6 g) or procainamide (250 mg) orally, four times a day.

Diabetic Amyotrophy

Weakness and wasting of the muscles of one or several extremities, usually involving the distal musculature first, is common in patients with diabetes mellitus. Peripheral neuritis is the most common cause. Accompanying sensory changes may facilitate diagnosis. In some patients, however, the proximal muscles of the lower extremities are affected first, and histologic studies have provided evidence that muscle as well as nerve may be affected. These patients, who have been mainly elderly male diabetics, also have had myalgia with anterior thigh pain and marked muscle wasting and weight loss. The disease is self-limited and improvement or recovery usually occurs within a few months to several years.

Atherosclerosis

Atherosclerosis of the large arteries to the lower extremities may result in fatigue, weakness and intermittent claudication on effort, and cramps. The decrease in muscular power and endurance that occurs with advancing age is commonplace. The legs are traditionally the first of an athlete's assets to fail. Subjective or objective weakness of the legs that recurs on walking, with or without pain, and is relieved by bedrest, is usually due to atherosclerotic peripheral arterial insufficiency. Symptoms may be precipitated or aggravated by anemia, hypoxia, right heart failure, or reduced cardiac output after blood loss or myocardial infarction.

Recurring Subjective Weakness

Subjective weakness (usually without objective evidence at the time of examination after subsidence of the episode) may occur acutely or recurrently when there is a decrease in the blood supply to the brain or skeletal muscles from any cause (12). Such changes in blood supply may result from decreased venous return (postural hypotension), decreased blood volume, tachyarrhythmia, myocardial ischemia or infarction, and/or cerebral vascular disease. Sufficient decrease in blood supply to the brain results in giddiness and syncope, varying degrees of loss of consciousness and, finally, convulsions. Observation or history of these complaints facilitates identification of cerebral ischemia as the cause, but when the ischemia is mild or transient, the patient may complain only of weakness. The cerebral origin of the symptoms may not be readily recognized.

Acute, recurrent subjective weakness also can result from hyperventilation or hypoglycemia. Blowing off carbon dioxide and resulting alkalosis also causes giddiness, paresthesias, and sometimes tetany. Hypoglycemia may result in other central nervous symptoms: headache, giddiness, confusion, visual disturbances, including diplopia and, if severe and prolonged, coma, convulsions and paralysis. Both hyperventilation resulting from anxiety and hypoglycemia cause epinephrine release, which produces tachycardia, palpitations, sweating, and dilated pupils.

Subjective weakness and fatigue may also result from hypoxia or hypocarbia of any origin, including chronic obstructive or other pulmonary disease, or hypoventilation. The latter may result from upper airway obstruction, marked obesity, or reduced ventilatory drive due to muscle or cerebral disease. Nocturnal sleep apnea may occur, especially in older persons, and the resulting hypercarbia and nocturnal restlessness may result in daytime somnolence.

Emaciation and Cachexia

Generalized muscular wasting and weakness may result from chronic malnutrition, whether due to starvation or intestinal malabsorption, and is also seen in such "wasting" diseases as cancer, tuberculosis and thyrotoxicosis. Along with the loss of subcutaneous fat, the muscles become wasted and weakened, although usually not as weak as may be expected from the degree of atrophy. In addition, the muscles may show an unusual excitability to mechanical stimulus. A sharp blow to the belly of the muscle with a percussion hammer causes an imme-diate local contraction in the form of a visible ridge, which persists for several seconds and may give rise to a small wave which slowly moves along the muscle. This reaction is known as myedema or "idiomuscular contraction." The propagated contraction wave is electrically silent.

Senile Myosclerosis

Some aged persons who have been immobilized for a prolonged period develop progressive disuse atrophy and weakness of muscles, retraction of the wasted muscles and their tendons, and contractures of the limbs. The legs may be held in extreme flexion, and standing and walking may become impossible. The resulting picture, which has been termed senile myosclerosis, superficially resembles that produced by dermatomyositis. However, the disorder is not the result of a specific myopathy, but rather of immobility, disuse atrophy and secondary contractures.

REFERENCES

1. Barnett HJM, Mohr JP, Stein BM, Yatsu FM: *Stroke: Pathophysiology, Diagnosis and Management.* New York, Churchill Livingstone, Vol. 1, pp 1–641, Vol. 2, pp 643–1274, 1986.
2. DeMyer, W: Anatomy and clinical neurology of the spinal cord. In Baker AB, Joynt RJ, (eds): *Clinical Neurology.* Hagerstown, MD, Harper and Row, Vol. 3, No. 43, pp. 1-32, 1985.
3. Dimant J, Grob D: Electrocardiographic changes and myocardial damage in patients with acute cerebrovascular accidents. *Stroke,* 8:448, 1977.
4. Dimant J, Grob D, Brunner NG: Ophthalmoplegia, ptosis and miosis in temporal arteritis. *Neurology* 30:1054, 1980.
5. Dyck PJ, Thomas PK, Lambert EH, Bunge E: *Peripheral Neuropathies.* Philadelphia, WB Saunders, Vol. 1, pp 1-1166 and Vol. 2, pp 1167-2323, 1984.
6. Dyck, PJ, Law PA: Diseases of peripheral nerves. In Baker AB, Joynt RJ (eds): *Clinical Neurology,* Hagerstown, MD, Harper & Row, Vol. 4, No. 51, pp 1-126, 1985.
7. Engel AG, Banker BQ: *Myology.* New York: McGraw-Hill, Vol. 1, The Anatomy, Physiology and Biochemistry of Muscle, pp 1-1184, and Vol. 2. Diseases of Muscle, pp 1185-2159, 1986.
8. Grob D: Metabolic diseases of muscle. *Ann Rev Med* 14:151, 1963.
9. Grob D: Myopathies and their relation to thyroid disease. *NY State J Med* 63:218, 1963.
10. Grob D: Weakness. In Barondess J (ed): *Diagnostic Approaches to Presenting Syndromes.* Baltimore, Williams & Wilkins, pp 197-300, 1971.
11. Grob D: Uses of drugs in myopathies. *Ann Rev Pharmacol Toxicol* 16:215, 1976.
12. Grob D: Acute neuromuscular disorders. *Med Clin North Am* 65:189, 1981.

13. Gutmann E: Age changes in the neuromuscular system and aspects of rehabilitation medicine. In Buerger AA, Tobis JS (eds): *Neurophysiologic Aspects of Rehabilitation Medicine*, Springfield, Ill., Charles C. Thomas, pp. 42-61, 1976.

14. Kaldor G, DiBattista WJ (eds): Aging in muscle. *Aging*, Vol. 6, New York, Raven Press, 1978.

15. Nardone DA, McDonald WJ, Gerard DE: Mechanisms in hypokalemia. Clinical correlation. *Medicine* 57:435, 1978.

16. Toole JF, Cole M: Ischemic cerebrovascular disease. In Baker AB, Joynt RJ (Eds): *Clinical Neurology.* Hagerstown, MD, Harper and Row, 1985, Vol. 2, No. 15, 1-51.

17. Utterback RA: Hemorrhagic cerebrovascular disease. In Baker AB, Joynt RJ (Eds): *Clinical Neurology.* Hagerstown, MD, Harper & Row, 1985. Vol. 2, No. 16, 1-31.

18. Walton J: *Disorders of Voluntary Muscle.* Edinburgh, Churchill Livingstone, 1981, pp. 1-1069.

CHAPTER 26

Prevalent Joint Diseases in Older Persons

DAVID GROB

OSTEOARTHRITIS

Osteoarthritis (also called hypertrophic arthritis, senescent arthritis, and degenerative joint disease) is a noninflammatory disorder of movable joints, characterized by deterioration and abrasion of articular cartilage and by formation of new bone at the joint surfaces (13).

INCIDENCE

Histologic changes of osteoarthritis are present universally after the second decade of life and the degree increases with age. Radiologic changes are usually present after the age of 50, though only 5% of individuals over age 50 have clinical symptoms. After the age of 60, 15% of men and 25% of women have symptoms.

PATHOLOGY

The initial change appears to be injury to cartilage, which is followed by proliferation of adjacent bone (17). The cartilage first loses its elasticity, becoming dull and opaque, and later softened and frayed, denuding the underlying bone. Where the joint cartilage is thinned, the subchondral bone develops proliferation of fibroblasts and new bone formation takes place. At the joint margins, the periosteal bone proliferation forms bony spurs termed osteophytes. Subchondral cysts may develop. Small pieces of cartilage and bone may break off to form loose bodies in the joint. The joint capsule and synovium become thickened. Although the joint disease is not due to inflammation, trauma of the synovial membrane by bony spurs may give rise to transient inflammatory changes.

PREDISPOSING FACTORS

The main predisposing factor in osteoarthritis is advancing age. However, it is not clear to what extent this is the result of cumulative insults to the articular tissue or of senescent change in cartilage, with diminution in chondroitin sulfate content and "unmasking" of collagen. There is some evidence for diminished polymerization and hyaluronic acid content of synovial mucin. Injury to joints, whether major or minor, may predispose to osteoarthritis, perhaps as a result of irregular pressure. Abnormalities of joints associated with laxness of the ligamentous structures, such as congenital dysplasia of the hip, recurrent luxation of the patella or shoulder, genu recurvatum, and knock knees, predispose to local changes. Excessive use of a joint, for occupational or other reasons, accelerates local changes. Obesity may predispose to osteoarthritis. This is presumed to be due to the mechanical burden on joints undergoing abrasion, but the joints affected may include some that are not weight-bearing. A role for genetic factors is indicated by familial incidence of the disease, particularly with regard to involvement of terminal interphalangeal joints. The role of metabolic factors is poorly understood, but is suggested by the increased incidence and severity of osteoarthritis in patients with acromegaly or with ochronosis associated with alcaptonuria.

JOINTS INVOLVED

Osteoarthritis affects mainly the weight-bearing joints (knees, hips, lumbar spine), cervical spine, and terminal interphalangeal joints of the fingers (9). Less often there is involvement of the first metatarsophalangeal, temporomandibular, and proximal interphalangeal joints of the fingers. Except where one joint is subjected to chronic trauma, the disease seldom remains monarticular for a long time. On the other hand, generalized involvement with simultaneous symptoms in all of these joints is very rare. Involvement of the wrists, shoulders, elbows or feet (other than "bunion joint") is rare except after trauma.

CLINICAL MANIFESTATIONS

These are local, but are not well correlated with the degree of joint changes found either pathologically or radiologically. Only a small proportion of patients with joint changes have local symptoms. Systemic signs or symptoms do not occur, except for weakness and muscle wasting, which may result from immobilization.

The main symptom is joint pain that occurs on motion and weightbearing ("friction effect") and is relieved by rest. The pain is usually aching and is rarely intense. Stiffness after sitting ("articular gelling") or on arising may occur, but persists for only minutes, in contrast to the stiffness of patients with rheumatoid arthritis, which may persist for hours. Physical examination usually reveals crepitation on joint motion. There may be hard enlargement of the joint, due mainly to bony and cartilaginous overgrowth, particularly of the terminal interphalangeal joints (Heberden's nodes) and the knees. Although there may be some local tenderness and slight increase in synovial fluid, especially in the knees, effusion and signs of inflammation are usually mild except following trauma. Limitation of joint motion may occur as a result of pain, muscle spasm, contracture of capsule, fascia, or muscle, incongruity of joint surfaces, or osteophyte formation, but flexion deformities are much less severe than in rheumatoid arthritis. Abnormalities of posture and gait may occur and may cause muscle pain and soreness. The course of osteoarthritis is usually slowly progressive, without characteristic exacerbations or remissions. The clinical manifestations vary with the predominant site of involvement. In most instances, only one set of joints, or sometimes two, produce symptoms.

Interphalangeal Joints

Heberden's nodes may appear after trauma or may occur without preceding trauma, particularly in women. They may be asymptomatic or may cause local aching (especially on exercise), tenderness, redness, overlying cysts, clumsiness, and numbness

and tingling. The joint may become flexed or displaced laterally. Many patients do not develop symptoms elsewhere. Similar swellings occur less often at the proximal interphalangeal joints (Bouchard's nodes).

A small subset of patients, particularly middle-aged or older women, have a more acute, inflammatory joint disease involving particularly the joints of the hands, called *erosive osteoarthritis*. The interphalangeal joints, proximal and distal, become more red, tender, and enlarged than is usually the case in osteoarthritis, and the x-ray shows erosions of joint surfaces, in addition to osteophytes and subchondral sclerosis. This form of osteoarthritis may be progressive or may have remissions and exacerbations, resembling rheumatoid arthritis, but differing in distribution and in absence of rheumatoid deformities, prolonged morning stiffness, synovial hypertrophy and an elevated titer of rheumatoid factor above that seen in normal elderly persons.

Knees

The knee joints are frequently affected by osteoarthritis. The site of cartilage breakdown is usually the weight-bearing surfaces of the femoral and tibial condyles and the posterior surface of the patella. Focal involvement of these areas may produce symptoms despite negligible x-ray changes. Atrophy of the quadriceps may develop as a result of disuse secondary to pain.

Hips

Osteoarthritis of the hips, which has been termed malum or morbus coxae senilis, is the most disabling site of the disease. It is more common in men and is unilateral in approximately half of the patients. The pain, which occurs on motion, may be referred to the groin, buttock, sciatic region, or inner aspect of the thigh or knee. Limitation of motion of the hip, especially abduction, extension, and internal rotation, results from exostoses. The leg is often held in eversion, with the hip flexed and adducted. The gait is often awkward and shuffling, and even sitting, or arising from this position, may be difficult.

Spine (Spondylosis)

The spine is the most common site of radiologic change due to osteoarthritis in men, and second only to Heberden's nodes in women. However, symptoms are usually absent or mild (backache, stiffness, limitation of motion), except in the minority of patients who develop compression of nerve roots (radiculopathy) or of the spinal cord (myelopathy).

The primary pathologic process is degeneration of the intervertebral discs, which results in increased stress at the lips of the vertebral bodies and zygapophyseal joints, leading to osteophyte formation and narrowing of the intervertebral foramina. Osteophyte formation or protrusion of intervertebral discs may cause compression of nerve roots or spinal cord in the cervical spine, especially at C4–C7, and of nerve roots in the lumbar spine, especially at L4–L5 (the most common site of disc protrusion), L5–S1, and L3–L4. Narrowing of the spinal canal (spinal stenosis, usually congenital) can contribute to the compression syndrome of the cord and cauda equina.

Symptoms may occur acutely, particularly after trauma such as "whiplash" injury, or chronically. Compression of nerve roots results in pain, the distribution of which depends on the roots affected and may include the head, neck, shoulders, arms, digits, chest, back, or posterior aspect of the legs. The pain may be aggravated by active or passive movement of the spine and may be accompanied by muscle spasm. There also may be sensory changes (paresthesias, dysesthesias, and hypesthesia) and signs of lower motor neuron lesion (muscle wasting and weakness, diminished tendon reflexes, and occasionally fasciculations) in the dermatome innervated by the affected root.

Cervical disc protrusion is the most common cause of root pain extending from the neck down an upper extremity. It is accompanied by spasm of the neck muscles, loss of normal curvature of the cervical spine, and pain on motion of the neck. The tendon reflexes, particularly of the biceps or triceps, may be diminished, and paresthesias or dermatome hypalgesia may be present.

When the sixth cervical root is involved, the sensory symptoms are felt in the thumb and index finger, and when the seventh cervical root is affected, the middle finger. The spinalis, deltoid, biceps, brachioradialis, and supinator muscles are those most affected when there is compression of the fifth cervical root. In the case of the sixth cervical root, the muscles involved are the triceps, extensors of the wrists and digits, pectoralis major, and latissimus dorsi.

Compression of lumbar roots by osteoarthritis or disc protrusion results in recurring attacks of low backache, with or without pain in sciatic distribution, usually unilateral. The patient usually walks with a limp. Motion of the spine is limited by pain and spasm, and raising the extended leg may reproduce the pain. Advanced compression may result in diminished Achilles tendon reflex, hypalgesia and weakness in the distribution of the affected root, and mild atrophy of muscles of the lower leg.

Compression of the spinal cord may result in sensory symptoms and lower motor neuron signs at the level of compression, and upper motor neuron signs (weakness, spasticity, increased tendon reflexes, diminished abdominal reflexes, and extensor plantar reflexes) below the compression, mainly in the lower limbs. Occasionally, tactile or postural sensibility may be diminished below the level of compression. Sphincter control is usually unaffected unless there is severe paraplegia or quadriplegia. The cerebrospinal fluid is usually normal, but occasionally the protein content is slightly elevated and there may be delayed rise and fall of pressure in the Queckenstedt test when the neck is passively extended.

The vertebral arteries enter the cervical spine at the level of the sixth cervical vertebra and pass upward through a canal in the transverse processes. Cervical osteoarthritis may result in symptoms of cerebral ischemia, particularly if collateral circulation through the circle of Willis is impaired by atheromata in the vertebral or carotid arteries. Transient episodes of giddiness or syncope may occur at rest, on standing, or particularly after rotation or extension of the neck, or, less frequently, after flexion. A drop attack may occur, in which the patient suddenly falls, without impairment of consciousness. A persistent cerebral ischemic lesion (stroke) may occur after marked movement or manipulation of the neck.

Ribs

At the level of each costovertebral joint, the intercostal nerve leaves the spine and passes along the rib. Osteoarthritis of these joints, especially at T8, may occasionally produce pressure on the intercostal nerves and pain referred to the chest wall or upper abdomen (intercostal neuralgia).

ROENTGENOGRAPHIC MANIFESTATIONS

The principal changes are joint narrowing (due to degeneration and disappearance of articular cartilage), sharpening of articular margins and intra-articular structures (e.g., tibial tubercles), bony sclerosis (eburnation), osteophytes and marginal lipping, and bone cysts (9). However, there is frequently no relation between the clinical and radiologic picture, and the diagnosis should seldom be made on the roentgenographic findings alone. In a few patients, focal changes may produce symptoms despite a normal roentgenographic appearance.

More frequently, there are radiologic changes of osteoarthritis without symptoms. It is not infrequent for rheumatoid arthritis, gout, and other diseases to occur in persons with asymptomatic osteoarthritic changes. In evaluating a roentgenogram, the "normal" for the patient's age should be kept in mind.

In diagnosing neurologic effects of osteoarthritis of the spine, one utilizes radiologic studies to demonstrate sufficient narrowing of the spinal foramina by posterior osteophytosis (which produces pressure on the nerve roots), or of the spinal canal (which produces pressure on the cord).

LABORATORY FINDINGS

There are no specific laboratory abnormalities. The sedimentation rate, white blood count, hematocrit, and serum proteins are usually normal unless some other disease process coexists. When effusions are present, the synovial fluid shows normal cytologic and chemical values except for inconstant elevation of the mucin content. The presence of cartilage fragments and fibrils in the synovial fluid is characteristic of osteoarthritis. Occasionally, local inflammation may be sufficient to cause increased levels of leukocytes, mainly mononuclear, proteins (including immunoglobulin), and pyrophosphates in the synovial fluid (3).

Electromyography is helpful in documenting and localizing root or nerve injury.

TREATMENT

Rest

Since intraarticular physical stress plays an important role in pathogenesis, involved joints should be rested periodically and should not be subjected to excessive exercise. When weight-bearing joints are affected, local supports including the use of canes, crutches, or other mechanical devices, and intermittent rest in bed or on a couch are helpful. Patients with spinal disease should use a bed board for adequate support during recumbency. Unnecessary painful exercise and stair climbing should be avoided. Obesity should be treated by weight reduction. Poor body mechanics causing chronic irritation to joints should be corrected if possible. Faulty position should be corrected and proper support prescribed for pronated feet, genu valgum and varum, and curvatures of the spine. Faulty work habits should be corrected. However, excessive rest should be avoided, as this may cause articular gelling and stiffness and atrophy of cartilage and muscle.

Physical Therapy

Heat, massage, and mild exercise produce some symptomatic relief in most patients. Heat may be dry (electric pad, infrared, diathermy, or ultrasound) or moist. Massage should be gentle over joints, but may be more vigorous over muscles to help prevent atrophy. Isometric exercises are helpful in improving muscle strength and preventing atrophy.

Drugs

Except for the use of analgesics, most of which also have anti-inflammatory activity, drugs play a relatively minor role in management. Acetylsalicylic acid (aspirin, 0.6 g, enteric coated and after food) orally every 4 hours is useful in conjunction with rest and physical measures for relief of pain. When inflammation due to traumatic synovitis produces intractable pain, indomethacin (Indocin, 25 mg), phenylbutazone (Butazolidin, 100 mg), or ibuprofen (Motrin, 400 mg) may be administered three times a day, or sulindac (Clinoril), 100 mg twice a day after meals, provided the patient is followed closely for observation of toxic effects (nausea, vomiting, epigastric distress, upper gastrointestinal bleeding, rash, edema, anemia, leukopenia, thrombocytopenia) (2,11). Intraarticular injection of corticosteroid may provide temporary benefit, but repeated injection or systemic administration of corticosteroids or corticotropin may be harmful and should not be employed.

Traction

This may be helpful in patients with spondylosis and symptoms of nerve root or cord compression not relieved by bed rest. For cervical spondylosis, a simple rolled towel splint or a Thomas collar may be worn for several weeks. If this does not relieve symptoms, or if the disease is in the lumbar spine, the patient may be hospitalized for a few days of intermittent or constant head-halter traction or intermittent motorized traction.

Surgery

Few patients require surgical procedures, but these are occasionally performed when symptoms of hip, knee, or spine disease are severe and are not relieved by other measures. Since aged individuals are more likely to develop postoperative complications, they should be operated on only when this is deemed essential. In patients with severe restriction of hip motion, mobility may be improved by incision of the hip capsule or of the surrounding muscles (hanging-hip operation), and debridement. Severe hip pain can be relieved by arthrodesis (joint fusion), but this is practical only for unilateral disease. When there is extensive destruction of the femoral head and severe pain or limitation of motion, prosthetic arthroplasty and total hip replacement have given highly encouraging results, with pain relief in 96% of cases, improved range of motion in 90%, increased walking distance in 80%, and good stability and mobility.

Surgery for knee disease is less well defined, but some patients benefit from tibial osteotomy (section of bone to alter weight-bearing surfaces), patellectomy and debridement, arthrodesis, or prosthetic arthroplasty. Knee replacement has been mechanically less satisfactory than hip replacement, but pain relief and improvement in motion and walking distance occur in 80%. Complications of hip or knee replacement include adjacent osteomyelitis in 5%, usually requiring removal of the prosthesis, loosening of the prosthesis in 5% (hip) to 10% (knee), thromboembolism in 3%, and fat embolism in 2%.

Surgery on the cervical spine has major risks. It should be employed rarely and only in patients who are disabled by intractable symptoms of root or cord compression due to spondylosis or herniated intervertebral disc, and only after a thorough trial of conservative measures. In such patients, the nerve root can be decompressed by removal of foraminal osteophytes or of the posterior wall of the intervertebral canal. The cord or cauda equina can be decompressed by removal of degenerated disc material and spurs. Removal of a cervical disc or lumbar disc is by the anterior route, usually followed by fusion of the vertebrae. Surgery on the cervical spine risks damage to the vascular supply of the cord and should not be performed for relief of pain alone. It should be considered only if there are signs of lower motor neuron injury (weakness, wasting, fasciculation, or decreased tendon reflex) or cord compression.

SEROLOGIC AND HEMATOLOGIC ALTERATIONS IN NORMAL OLDER PERSONS

The serum level of a number of globulins thought to be autoantibodies is elevated in some normal older persons. This is perhaps due to alteration of some immune surveillance with age. The level of rheumatoid factor and of antinuclear antibody is elevated in 10–15% of normal people over the age of 60. Titers tend to be low, and the nuclear staining by antinuclear antibody tends to be of a diffuse or homogeneous pattern. The erythrocyte sedimentation rate may increase by up to 50% in normal people over the age of 60, and the hematocrit may fall slightly, though not below the lower limits of normal.

RHEUMATOID ARTHRITIS

Rheumatoid arthritis is a systemic disease of connective tissue in which joint inflammation is the predominant manifestation. The cause is unknown, but is probably related to hypersensitivity. In most patients the course of the disease is chronic and progressive, leading to characteristic deformities and disability (14).

INCIDENCE

The disease may begin at any age from the first year of life to the ninth decade, but usually begins between the ages of 20 and 60, with peaks at 35 and 45. In 2% of patients, onset is after the age of 65. Population studies suggest an incidence of approximately 0.5% in the general population, 1.5% in the population over the age of 30, and 2–3% in the population over the age of 55. The disease is two to three times as common in women as in men and there is a familial aggregation of the disease and of serologic abnormalities.

PATHOLOGY

The main lesion is inflammation of the synovial membrane, or synovitis, with exudation (effusion), cellular infiltration (mainly lymphocytes and later plasma cells), and proliferation of granulation tissue (6). The thickened synovium (pannus) spreads over the cartilage and erodes it and the subchondral bone, which becomes osteoporotic. Adhesions between opposing layers of pannus may lead to fibrous ankylosis of the joint. There is also edema and cellular infiltration of periarticular tissues, especially tendons and tendon sheaths, and foci of mononuclear cell infiltration in muscles. The most characteristic lesion is the rheumatoid nodule, consisting of a central zone of fibrinoid material surrounded by zones of large, palisaded mononuclear cells and smaller mononuclear cells. The nodules may be found in the connective tissue of almost any organ, but especially in synovia and in periarticular tissue, subcutaneously.

JOINTS INVOLVED

In most patients, the arthritis is polyarticular and involves the small joints of the hands and feet, whether or not major joints are also involved. The joints involved, in order of frequency, are the proximal interphalangeal; metacarpophalangeal; joints of the toes, wrists, knees, elbows, ankles, shoulders, and hips; temporomandibular; and cervical spine. The terminal interphalangeal joints are rarely involved except in the presence of psoriasis of the nails. The joints are usually involved symmetrically, but atypical cases occur with complete asymmetry.

LOCAL SIGNS AND SYMPTOMS

Onset of the disease is usually insidious, with joint aching and stiffness, followed by gradual swelling, warmth, redness, and tenderness. However, in about 20% of patients there is sudden onset of severe, multiple joint inflammation.

The patient complains of joint pain, especially on motion but also at rest, swelling, stiffness after inactivity (gelling), especially on awakening (morning stiffness), and limitation of motion due to pain and stiffness.

The typical joint presents a spindle-shaped appearance with thickening of the periarticular structures (soft tissue swelling) and atrophy of the contiguous muscle. This is best seen in the proximal interphalangeal joints. Involved joints may also be hot, red, and tender. Over a period of time flexion contractures may occur, because the flexor groups of most muscles are stronger. Progressive disease of the metacarpophalangeal joints leads to characteristic volar subluxation and ulnar deviation of the phalanges. Volar subluxation of the wrist seriously impairs hand function. Flexion contractures of hips and knees are also major causes of disability. The muscles of affected extremities may become severely weak and atrophied, to a greater degree than would be expected from disuse alone.

SYSTEMIC SIGNS AND SYMPTOMS

Fatigue, malaise, fever (usually low grade), tachycardia, weakness, wasting and weight loss, and mild or moderate anemia may occur. An acute, fulminating course with high fever is seldom seen in adults except as a "rebound phenomenon" following steroid withdrawal.

EXTRAARTICULAR MANIFESTATIONS

The commonest of these are subcutaneous nodules, which appear over pressure joints, especially the elbow, at some time in 25% of patients. Lymphadenopathy is common. Splenomegaly occurs in 10% of patients and may be associated with leukopenia (Felty's syndrome). Vasomotor instability may occur with cold, clammy hands and feet that sweat excessively. Erythema of the thenar and hypothenar eminences, resembling "liver palms," may occur. Less common manifestations, which occur in 10% of patients, include pericarditis, pericardial effusion, myocarditis, pleurisy, pleural effusion, and nodular pulmonary infiltrates resembling those seen in Caplan's disease of miners. Uveitis and aortic insufficiency may occur, but less commonly than in patients with ankylosing spondylitis. Other rare complications include necrotizing arteritis (resulting in skin ulcers, digital gangrene, or peripheral neuritis), softening and perforation of the sclera, and systemic lupus erythematosus (13).

Albuminuria occurs in 10% of patients with rheumatoid arthritis. In half of these, it is due to amyloidosis, glomerulitis, arteritis, or rheumatoid nodules, and in half to unrelated pyelonephritis or nephrosclerosis. Renal insufficiency may occur, but is rare. Secondary amyloidosis has been found in 20% of patients with rheumatoid arthritis at postmortem examination, but clinical effects occur in only a few of these patients.

Patients with rheumatoid arthritis appear to be more susceptible to peptic ulcer than other patients. This tendency is increased when the patient takes drugs that are ulcerogenic, such as aspirin and other nonsteroidal anti-inflammatory agents, and probably corticosteroids.

COURSE

The course may be episodic or sustained. Frequently the disease begins in episodes and ultimately becomes sustained. Remissions are more common early in the disease. One-fifth of patients achieve full remission, though many later relapse. After 3 years of sustained disease, complete remission is rare. Patients with sustained disease develop more incapacitation and a small proportion becomes completely incapacitated in 10–15 years. After 10 years of disease, 50% of patients are improved, including 15% in complete remission, 15% are stationary, and 35% are worse. The manifestations and course of the disease in the aged are not significantly different than in younger patients.

ROENTGENOGRAPHIC MANIFESTATIONS

Early in the disease there is fusiform periarticular soft-tissue swelling, rarefaction of underlying bone, and sometimes systemic decalcification. Later there is decrease of joint space, lipping and osteophytes, and punched-out areas of bone at the articular margins. Finally, subluxation, flexion deformity, or ankylosis may occur.

LABORATORY FINDINGS

The most important finding is elevation of the serum level of anti-γ-globulin, termed rheumatoid factor, in 76% of patients (3). It is indicated by agglutination by the serum of latex particles coated with human γ-globulin. The serum level of rheumatoid factor is also elevated in 20% of patients with systemic lupus erythematosus. However, this elevation is seen in only a few patients with psoriatic or ankylosing spondylitis, osteoarthritis, or gout. In the first few months of rheumatoid arthritis, the level of rheumatoid factor is usually not increased in the serum, but tends to rise during the first year of the disease. It may appear in the synovial fluid of affected joints before the serum (4).

During active phases of the disease, there also is elevation of the erythrocyte sedimentation rate and serum C-reactive protein and slight leukocytosis. A mild or moderate normocytic, hypochromic anemia is common, with low serum iron but no response to iron administration. Serum albumin is usually decreased and globulins increased, especially α- and γ-globulins. Synovial fluid of affected joints contains a high total count and proportion of polymorphonuclear leukocytes, which may contain inclusions of rheumatoid factor (4).

Elevated serum levels of antinuclear antibody are found in 25% and of anti–double-stranded DNA antibody in 5% of patients with rheumatoid arthritis, compared with 98% and 50%, respectively, of patients with systemic lupus erythematosus.

TREATMENT

The primary objectives are to reduce inflammation and the symptoms of inflammation such as pain, to preserve function, to prevent deformity, and to repair previous damage when necessary to restore function. The basic treatment consists of rest, physical therapy, and salicylates. This suffices during most of the course of the disease in most patients. When it does not suffice, additional measures are added to the basic regimen.

Rest

Rest, both systemic and local, is helpful to most patients. During acute flare-ups, complete bed rest may be warranted, while at other times 2–4 hours of rest each day may suffice. Local articular rest may be provided by well-fitted, lightweight splints or shells, which should be removable to permit daily motion and exercise of the affected extremities.

Physical Therapy

Exercise is necessary to preserve and restore joint motion and muscular strength and to retard muscular atrophy. Exercises of the active-assistive type should be performed, within the limits of pain, from

the onset of management. If pain lasts more than an hour after exercise, the exercise should be decreased but not discontinued. A proper balance of exercise and rest should be part of the patient's daily program until joint and muscle function have recovered. Then, a regular program of exercise to maintain general muscular fitness and reduce atrophy should be carried out.

The pain and swelling of acutely inflamed joints may be ameliorated by ice packs. Later, spasm can be reduced and mobility increased by local application of moist heat in the form of packs, bath, or paraffin. Therapeutic exercise is best done after the application of heat, when the patient is more comfortable and muscle spasm is reduced.

Drugs

Acetylsalicylic acid (aspirin) is the most useful drug in the management of rheumatoid arthritis and in a considerable proportion of patients is the only drug needed (10). It is analgesic and anti-inflammatory. In active disease, the dose is rapidly increased until pain is relieved or toxic symptoms develop (upper gastrointestinal distress, tinnitus, or deafness), and a maintenance dose, at a slightly lower level, is continued more or less indefinitely. The average maintenance dose of aspirin in adults is 0.6–0.9 g every 3–4 hours when awake, preferably after meals or milk to reduce gastric intolerance. Aspirin causes occult gastric bleeding in many patients and, occasionally, hemorrhagic gastritis, peptic ulceration, or temporary hearing loss. Elderly patients are usually less tolerant of the side effects of aspirin and other anti-inflammatory drugs than are the young. Gastric distress may be reduced by the use of antacids or enteric-coated tablets of aspirin. If this results in delayed or reduced absorption of salicylate, the dosage schedule may have to be altered. Long-acting preparations of aspirin may be taken at bedtime if needed to reduce early morning pain and stiffness.

Approximately half of patients will respond with improvement to a conservative program of rest, physical therapy, and aspirin carried out for at least 2 months. The remaining patients who have persistent symptoms may be treated with additional drugs, but since these are more likely to have toxic effects when administered for a prolonged period, they should be used only when necessary, and for as short a period as feasible.

Indomethacin (Indocin, 25 mg), phenylbutazone (Butazolidin, 100 mg), oxyphenbutazone (Tandearil, 100 mg), ibuprofen (Motrin, 400 mg) orally three or four times a day after meals, sulindac (Clinoril, 100 mg) twice a day. Nalfon, Naprosyn, and other **nonsteroidal anti-inflammatory drugs (NSAIDs)** may have a somewhat more anti-inflammatory effect than aspirin, but are less suitable for long-term use because of side effects. All NSAIDs cause gastrointestinal irritation, platelet dysfunction, and prolonged bleeding time, the combination of which can cause gastrointestinal hemorrhage, especially in elderly patients. All NSAIDs can also cause dizziness, anxiety, tinnitus, drowsiness, confusion, mild hepatic dysfunction, and, rarely, severe hepatitis. If any one of these drugs does not produce improvement within a week, it should be discontinued.

Corticosteroids have an impressive anti-inflammatory effect and often dramatically relieve pain and stiffness. However, since they promote demineralization and do not halt progression of the disease, they should be used only when other measures have failed or when there is evidence of vasculitis (5). The dosage should be as small as possible and administered for as short a time as possible. When needed, they may be given in addition to, but not as a substitute for, aspirin. The initial dose (usually 10-20 mg prednisone orally, daily, or the equivalent of related steroids), and the maintenance dose (usually 5-10 mg prednisone daily, or twice this amount every other day) should be the lowest dose needed for moderate symptomatic relief, and should not be increased to the dose necessary to completely relieve pain.

Clinical improvement occurs in three-fourths of patients, usually beginning within hours and reaching a maximum response in 3-4 weeks. In nearly half the patients, the clinical improvement may then diminish despite continuation of steroid administration. Although the steroids suppress inflammation and acute manifestations of the disease, they do not prevent joint destruction and deformities. Furthermore, unless the disease has entered into natural remission, discontinuation of steroid is followed by return of signs and symptoms that were present before steroid was initiated. If the drug is withdrawn rapidly, there is often a rebound, with more severe signs and symptoms than prior to treatment. Therefore, a gradual and prolonged tapering of dose is necessary when the drug is discontinued, usually at the rate of 1-2.5 mg monthly (16).

The side effects of corticosteroids are similar to the effects of spontaneous Cushing's disease, except that hypertension is much more common and more severe in the latter (1). The milder side effects include truncal obesity, moon facies, acne, ecchymo-sis, hirsutism, mild insulin-resistant diabetes, and euphoria. More serious side effects, which usually require discontinuation of steroid, include refractory or bleeding peptic ulcer, osteoporosis, aseptic necrosis of bone, psychosis, myopathy, cataracts, and increased susceptibility to infection. Since prolonged administration of corticosteroid suppresses adrenal function, patients undergoing surgery or comparable stress are usually given additional corticosteroid to avoid adrenal insufficiency in stress situations.

It has been suggested, though not proved, that patients with rheumatoid arthritis may be more prone to the development of peptic ulcer, particularly gastric, than other patients receiving corticosteroids. Therefore, antacids should be administered prophylactically after meals and ranitidine (Zantac, 150 mg) at bedtime. Patients with rheumatoid arthritis also may be more prone to develop osteoporosis, perhaps owing to their inactivity, and the less common complication of aseptic necrosis of the femoral or humeral head.

Once the arthritis has come under control, repeated efforts should be made to reduce the maintenance dose of steroid and to discontinue the drug. After several months of steroid administration, the harmful side effects of the drug are usually more significant than the benefit provided. Therefore, the long-term management of the disease relies on other measures, particularly rest, physical therapy, and aspirin, with steroids being reserved for use during as brief a period as possible in patients who have not responded to other measures.

Corticosteroids also may be administered intra-articularly when one or a few joints fail to respond to other therapeutic measures. Care must be used to maintain aseptic technique, and fluid should be removed from the joint prior to injection for examination and relief of pain. Repeated injections increase the risk of introducing infection and of causing changes resembling the Charcot joint.

In the minority of patients with persistent, active, severe inflammatory disease whose symptoms are not ameliorated by aspirin, other NSAIDs, and corticosteroid, a therapeutic trial may be carried out with gold salts, d-penicillamine, or antimalarial or immunosuppressant drugs. This is the usual order of trial, although there is not yet agreement on the role of each drug or the optimal sequence.

Gold salts (usually 50% aqueous solutions of gold sodium thiomalate or thioglucoside, 25-50 mg intramuscularly weekly for 4-6 months, after an initial test dose of 10 mg) may be useful in a small percentage of patients with persistent, active, inflammatory disease, producing improvement in over half beginning after 3–4 months of administration (10). Some physicians then give monthly injections, but the value of this in maintaining improvement is not clear. Unfortunately, approximately one-third of patients develop toxic effects due to gold, which are severe in 5%. Most common are dermatitis and stomatitis in 20%. Less common are colitis and renal injury with proteinuria or microscopic hematuria. Least common (less than 2%) are hepatitis and bone marrow depression (anemia, leukopenia, thrombocytopenia). An oral gold preparation auranofin (Ridaura), 3 mg twice daily) is less toxic than intramuscular gold, except for diarrhea in 25%, but it also appears to be less effective. The toxic effects of gold respond to the prompt withdrawal of the drug and to administration of corticosteroid and dimercaprol (BAL), except that severe bone marrow depression may be irreversible and fatal.

d-Penicillamine (Cuprimine) may be tried if necessary, before or after gold salts, in doses of 250 mg orally, daily, for 1 month, twice a day for 1 month, and then three times a day if tolerated (12). Toxic effects include fever, rash, aphthous ulcers, loss of taste, nausea, vomiting, neutropenia, thrombocytopenia, proteinuria, hematuria, and, rarely, renal insufficiency.

The antimalarial drugs, **chloroquine** (Aralen, 250 mg) or **hydroxychloroquine** (Plaquenil, 200–400 mg) orally, daily, may be useful in a small percentage of patients with persistent, active, inflammatory disease. Benefit is not observed for at least 4–8 weeks, but after that time over half the patients will show improvement. Larger doses should not be used. Toxic effects include skin lesions, loss or blanching of hair, anorexia, nausea, vomiting, peripheral neuropathy or neuromyopathy, headache, and, rarely, bone marrow depression. Corneal changes may occur, which may be asymptomatic or manifested by halos around lights, fuzziness of vision, and loss of corneal sensitivity. These changes are reversible with cessation of the drug. However, retinopathy occurs in 1/1000–2000 patients and is irreversible. Patients taking these drugs must be examined by an ophthalmologist every 3 months. Some physicians consider the risks of the drugs too great to warrant their use.

Immunosuppressant drugs, such as azathioprine (Imuran), cyclophosphamide (Cytoxan), or methotrexate may be beneficial in the few patients who do not respond to more conventional therapy, resulting in amelioration of symptoms and permitting reduction in steroid dose. The doses of these drugs, and their toxic effects, which may be fatal, are discussed in the section on polymyositis in Chapter 25.

Surgery

Surgery is needed in a very small number of patients. Chronically hypertrophied synovia may be removed from knees, wrists, and metacarpophalangeal joints, but the value of synovectomy is still under study, as the synovia may regenerate over a period of years. Painful, plantar subluxed metatarsal heads may be resected. Occasionally, fusion of wrist or elbow in a useful position may be necessary to stabilize a useless joint. Total hip or knee replacement is occasionally performed for intractable pain or severe limitation of motion. Prosthetic joint replacements also are being developed with metallic hinges for metacarpophalangeal and interphalangeal joints.

Rehabilitation

The patient's functional capacities may be considerably improved by a program of physical and occupational therapy carried out over a long-term period. The patient must be encouraged and motivated to make the most of his or her limited capabilities.

PSORIATIC ARTHRITIS

Seven percent of patients with psoriasis have arthritis at some time in the course of the disease, or less often, prior to onset of the skin disease. In half of these, the arthritis is a distinct type termed psoriatic arthritis. In the remainder the arthritis is classical rheumatoid arthritis, osteoarthritis, or gout. Psoriatic arthritis differs from rheumatoid arthritis in several respects:

1. The distal interphalangeal joints of the fingers and toes are most commonly involved, but some of the proximal interphalangeal and metacarpo- and metatarsophalangeal joints may also be involved. The cervical spine, hips, and sacroiliac joints also may be affected, but asymmetric involvement is more common than in rheumatoid arthritis, and pain and disability tend to be less severe.

2. Exacerbations and remissions of the joint manifestations may occur synchronously with those of the skin. Remissions tend to be more frequent, rapid, and complete than in rheumatoid arthritis.

3. The nails are involved in 80% of patients, compared with 30% in psoriatic individuals without arthritis.

4. Subcutaneous rheumatoid nodules are absent. Rheumatoid factor is present in the serum no more frequently than in the general population.

5. Radiologic examination often shows resorption ("whittling") of terminal phalanges, and de-

struction and ankylosis of the distal interphalangeal and other small joints. The severe osteolysis may progress to arthritis mutilans.

Treatment is similar to that for rheumatoid arthritis with the addition of measures for psoriasis. Local applications include crude coal tar (3–5%), salicylic acid (3–5%), anthralin (Anthra-Derm, 0.1–1%), and corticosteroid. Systemic medication for psoriasis and arthritis includes corticosteroid and immunosuppressive drugs, such as methotrexate, for severe disease. Antimalarial drugs and gold salts are not helpful, and may aggravate the skin disease.

ANKYLOSING SPONDYLITIS

Ankylosing (rheumatoid) spondylitis is a chronic and usually progressive disease of the sacroiliac joints, the synovial joints of the spine, and the adjacent soft tissues (15). The disease differs from rheumatoid arthritis in several respects:

1. Eighty to 90% of patients are male, and a similar proportion have HLA-B27 histocompatibility cellular antigens. The age of onset is usually between 16 and 40 years and especially between 17 and 25 years. Activity of the disease usually decreases after the age of 50, but limitation of movement of the spine persists.

2. Ligamentous calcification and ossification occur in later stages.

3. Subcutaneous rheumatoid nodules are absent. Rheumatoid factor is present in the serum no more frequently than in the general population.

4. Gold therapy, which produces improvement in half of the patients with rheumatoid arthritis, has no effect on ankylosing spondylitis.

CLINICAL MANIFESTATIONS

The onset is usually insidious, with episodes of low backache, stiffness, and sciatic pain, which last a few days at a time and subside. Later, local symptoms become more persistent and systemic symptoms such as fatigue, anorexia, weight loss, and low-grade fever may occur. Occasionally, thoracic girdle pains or radicular pains in the costovertebral angle, abdomen, or inguinal region may occur. Tenderness over the spine and sacroiliac region is frequently present. Evidence of spinal root or cord compression is rare, being much less common than in hypertrophic osteoarthritis of the spine (spondylosis). Involvement of the lumbar spine produces straightening of the lumbar spine, pain on motion, limitation of motion ("poker back"), paravertebral muscle spasm, and anterior stoop. Involvement of the thoracic spine produces thoracic girdle pains, chest pain on deep inspiration, diminished chest ex-

pansion, and thoracolumbar kyphosis. Involvement of the cervical spine causes limitation of motion in all directions and forward protrusion of the head. The postural deformity usually develops gradually over a period of 10–20 years, and disability is usually less severe than in rheumatoid arthritis.

Almost one-fourth of patients develop involvement of peripheral joints, especially shoulders and hips, indistinguishable from rheumatoid arthritis. The extraarticular manifestations of ankylosing spondylitis are similar to those of rheumatoid arthritis; in fact, iritis, posterior uveitis, aortic insufficiency, and pulmonary fibrosis are even more frequent. Iritis occurs in one-fourth of the patients, and may precede the arthritis.

Roentgenographic manifestations are characteristic. Changes in the sacroiliac joints are the earliest and most diagnostic, and are almost invariably present. They consist of bilateral blurring of the bony margins, then sclerosis and later ankylosis. Similar changes occur in the spinal apophyseal joints, but are less constant early in the disease. Later, calcification and ossification of the anulus fibrosus and paravertebral ligaments may occur, with bridging of adjacent vertebrae ("bamboo spine").

TREATMENT

Treatment is similar to that in rheumatoid arthritis, except that gold is ineffective and corticosteroids are less effective than in rheumatoid arthritis. Most patients can be managed with aspirin, other NSAIDs, and physical therapy. Only occasionally is corticosteroid needed. Although local roentgen therapy (600–800 roentgen units in divided doses) reduces pain, stiffness, and tenderness, especially in recently involved areas, this therapy is inadvisable or, at best, reserved for patients with severe symptoms who do not obtain relief from other measures, because of the possible increased incidence of leukemia and aplastic anemia in patients so treated.

Proper positioning of the body during rest and sleep is important in order to avoid positions that encourage flexion deformity. The mattress should be firm, supported by a bed board, and the patient should sleep on his or her back, without a pillow. Postural, abdominal, and breathing exercises should be regularly performed, preferably after the application of heat, but not to the point of producing persistent pain. The object is to maintain the best possible position of the vertebral column, strengthen the paraspinal and abdominal muscles, and increase breathing capacity. A back brace is occasionally helpful in patients with advanced disease. In a few patients with advanced and disabling deformity, spinal osteotomy can improve fixed flexion deformities, but the operation carries significant risk of neurologic complications.

The occurrence of iritis requires prompt treatment with topical corticosteroid and cycloplegic drugs, and severe iritis or posterior uveitis (choroiditis or chorioretinitis) also requires systemic corticosteroid.

DISSEMINATED LUPUS ERYTHEMATOSUS

The most common manifestations of this disease are arthralgia and fever, each occurring in 90% of patients. In one-third, the arthralgia progresses to arthritis, usually symmetric and of distribution similar to rheumatoid arthritis, but with little or no joint deformity or erosion. Erythematous eruption occurs in 85%; malar distribution (butterfly rash) in 50%; renal disease, pleurisy, and pericarditis, each in 50%; and pneumonitis, polymyositis, encephalopathy, and psychosis, each in 20%. Serologic findings include antinuclear antibodies (98%), anti-double-stranded DNA antibodies (50%), rheumatoid factor (25%), and false-positive VDRL (15%), as well as lowered complement activity during active phases of the disease. Hematologic findings include anemia (75%), hemolytic Coombs positive in 5%, leukopenia (50%), and thrombocytopenia (10%).

Disseminated lupus erythematosus is four times as common in females as in males and is most common in black females. In females the disease begins much more frequently during adolescence and early adult life than after the age of 50, but in males the disease is more common after this age. While patients with diffuse renal disease usually die within 5 years without treatment and within 10 years with corticosteroid or immunosuppressive treatment, the majority of patients live for decades, although their life expectancy is shortened by their increased susceptibility to infection, particularly during treatment. Lupus is, therefore, not uncommon among the elderly. However, it is often not diagnosed, as the disease tends to be milder, affecting mainly the joints and pleuropericardium, with a low incidence of renal disease and less marked serologic changes. These characteristics make lupus in the elderly resemble drug-induced lupus, which may occur at any age after the prolonged administration of procainamide, hydralazine, d-penicillamine, isoniazid, or diphenylhydantoin (13).

GOUT

Gout is a systemic disease characterized by recurrent episodes of acute, severe arthritis associated with urate crystals in the synovial fluid, and, in many patients, by the eventual appearance of urate deposits (tophi) in and about the joints, in the kidneys, and under the skin. Gout results from overproduction or retention (or both) of uric acid with resultant hyperuricemia. The great majority of patients have primary gout, which appears to be due to an inherited error of metabolism, whereas a minority have secondary gout due to increased turnover of nucleic acid, with overproduction of uric acid, as in myeloproliferative disorders (primary or secondary polycythemia, myeloid metaplasia, chronic granulocytic leukemia), lymphoma, multiple myeloma, sickle cell anemia and other hemoglobinopathies, or retention of uric acid in chronic renal disease.

INCIDENCE

The incidence in the general population is about 0.3%, in adults about 0.5%, and in patients at arthritic clinics about 5%. In primary gout, 90% of patients are male, and female patients are usually postmenopausal. The familial incidence is about 18%, and about 25% of relatives of gouty patients have hyperuricemia. The mode of inheritance, which was originally thought to be autosomal dominant with incomplete penetrance, is now known to be more complex. The incidence of gout increases with age. The first attack of gout may occur at any age, but onset before puberty is rare, and usually signifies another inborn error or metabolism such as Lesch-Nyhan syndrome or glycogen storage disease. The peak period of onset of primary gout in men is during the fifth decade, and in women after menopause.

Essential hyperuricemia has a much higher incidence than gout, occurring in 5% of the adult population and, like gout, increasing with age. The duration and degree of hyperuricemia appear to be important factors influencing the appearance of gout. In a study of hyperuricemic individuals, about 2% developed gout by the age of 34, but by the age of 58, 23% had developed gout. The prevalence of gout was 7% in those with serum urate levels of 8–9 mg/100 ml (upper limit of normal by the automated colorimetric method: 8 mg/100 ml in men and 7 mg/100 ml in women), 18% in those with levels of 9–10 mg/100 ml, and 83% in those with levels above 10 mg/100 ml.

PATHOGENESIS

Uric acid is derived mainly from the catabolism of purines formed in the de novo biosynthesis of nucleic acids, and to a lesser extent, from the breakdown of purines in the diet (18). At the pH of body fluids, uric acid is present in the ionized form as sodium urate. About two-thirds of the uric acid formed each day is excreted by the kidneys, almost entirely by tubular secretion. On a purine-restricted diet, this amounts to 420 ± 80 mg/24 hours. About half of patients with primary gout produce excessive amounts of uric acid, and most, but not all of these patients excrete more than the normal amount of uric acid in the urine. The other half produce normal amounts of uric acid, but have diminished renal tubular excretion of uric acid, especially at elevated plasma concentrations, and these patients may excrete less than the normal amount of uric acid in the urine.

The manifestations of gout are due to the deposition of sodium urate crystals in and around the joints and in the kidneys and subcutaneous tissues as a result of hyperuricemia, and of uric acid in the urinary collecting system as a result of hyperuricuria. The crystals of sodium urate in the synovia and synovial fluid are phagocytosed by neutrophilic leukocytes, which then release lysosomal enzymes that produce an inflammatory reaction and erosion of cartilage. At the customary urinary pH, uric acid is largely nonionized. Uric acid is less soluble than sodium urate and is markedly less soluble the more acid the pH and the more concentrated the urine. Uric acid stones occur in 15% of patients with gout and represent about 10% of all urinary calculi.

PRECIPITATING FACTORS

Acute gouty arthritis may occur without any apparent precipitating factor, or it may occur after trauma to a joint, a surgical procedure, or any event that elevates the serum urate level. The latter occurs whenever there is inhibition of tubular secretion of urate, which may result from prolonged fasting and accumulation of acetoacetic acid and β-hydroxybutyric acid, alcohol ingestion and accumulation of lactic acid, or administration of certain diuretics such as thiazides, furosemide, and ethacrynic acid. High dietary intake of purine, alone, has relatively little effect on serum urate levels, although it does increase uricosuria. Hyperuricosuria, diminished urine volume, and increased acidity of urine predispose to uric acid stone formation.

JOINTS INVOLVED

The disease is usually initially monarticular or limited to two or three joints and tends to involve the joints of the lower extremities, particularly the first metatarsophalangeal and tarsal joints, the ankles, and the knees. The big toe is the commonest site of initial involvement, and inflammation of the first metatarsophalangeal joint (podagra) occurs initially in 50% and at some time in the course of the disease in 90% of all patients. Later, other parts frequently affected include the finger joints, wrists, and elbows. Involvement of the shoulder and hip is uncommon, and of the sacroiliac and vertebral joints rare (7).

CLINICAL MANIFESTATIONS

Acute Gouty Arthritis

The onset of acute gout is very rapid, with maximal pain and swelling usually reached in several hours. The affected joint, usually the big toe or ankle, is exquisitely painful and tender, and the periarticular swelling and violaceous erythema are usually so severe as to resemble cellulitis or thrombophlebitis, particularly since low-grade fever, chilly sensations, and leukocytosis also may occur. Adjacent tissues, such as tendon (especially the Achilles tendon) and bursa, also may become painful, tender, and swollen. In the absence of treatment, the acute attack will last from several days to several weeks. As the inflammation subsides, the overlying skin may become desquamated and wrinkled, and may itch. After recovery from the initial attack, the patient usually remains free of symptoms for months or years but, in the natural course of the disease, attacks tend to recur with greater severity and at more frequent intervals.

Chronic Tophaceous Gout

Prior to the introduction of effective drugs for the control of hyperuricemia, about half of gouty patients developed clinically or radiographically detectable deposits of sodium urate (tophi) in and around their joints, usually beginning about 10 years after onset. These occur most commonly in the synovium and subchondral bone, in the olecranon bursa, in the infrapatellar and Achilles tendons, and in the subcutaneous tissue on the extensor surface of the forearm and over the joints. Occasionally, tophi occur in the ear cartilage, and rarely in the nasal cartilage, tongue, or vocal cords. Tophaceous deposits in the joints result in more frequent episodes of acute gouty arthritis, and may lead to persistent pain and tenderness, deformity, and disability.

EXTRAARTICULAR MANIFESTATIONS

The most important extraarticular manifestations are renal. Almost all patients with gout have histologic changes in the kidneys, consisting of urate deposits, infiltrative and tophaceous; acute and chronic pyelonephritis; fibrosis; giant cell formation; and nephrosclerosis. These abnormalities tend to be more severe as the disease progresses. Renal function is, in general, somewhat lower in gouty patients than would be expected for their age. Proteinuria occurs in 20% and hypertension in 40%. About 18% of patients develop renal insufficiency, and progressive renal failure contributes to death in 25% of these. Uric acid stones occur in about 15% of patients with gout and represent about 10% of all urinary calculi. They are characteristically radiolucent, though some stones may contain calcium salts and hence be radiopaque.

While tophi occur most commonly in and around the joints and in the kidneys, they occasionally also occur in tendons and bursae, subcutaneously on the extensor surface of the forearm, and in the cartilage, tongue, vocal cords, aorta, and myocardium. Patients with gout not only have an increased incidence of hypertension and renal insufficiency than nongouty individuals, but also have an increased incidence of cardiac and cerebral atherosclerosis, diabetes mellitus, and hypertriglyceridemia. Some of these associations may be related to the occurrence of obesity in half the patients.

ROENTGENOGRAPHIC MANIFESTATIONS

Roentgenograms usually show no changes early in the disease. After several attacks of acute gouty arthritis, usually over a period of several years, the first change appears, consisting of a localized area of osteoporosis adjacent to the affected joints, most often in the first metatarsal head. The subchondral bony cortex becomes eroded, and punched out areas (representing tophi) of 1- to 5-mm diameter, appear often with a shell-like margin of bone, most often at the base or head of the phalanges in the hands or feet. Although characteristic, these lesions are not diagnostic of gout, as similar lesions may occasionally be seen in rheumatoid arthritis, sarcoidosis, and even hypertrophic osteoarthritis. Marginal bone hypertrophy or spurring is also common in affected joints. Localized tissue swellings, with or without calcification, also may be seen, and calcification of cartilage (chondrocalcinosis) occurs in about 5% of patients. Later in the disease, ankylosis, deformity, and osteoporosis may occur.

LABORATORY FINDINGS

In patients with gout, the serum urate concentration is almost invariably at or above the upper limit of normal of 8 mg/100 ml by the automated colorimeter method for males and postmenopausal females, and 7 mg/100 ml for other females. An exception to this may occur in patients who are taking drugs that reduce the serum urate concentration, such as aspirin in large doses (4–6 g daily), phenylbutazone, corticosteroids, probenecid, sulfinpyrazone, and allopurinol, or who are under unusual stress. Some drugs can elevate the serum urate level; these include aspirin in low doses (less than 4 g daily), pyrizinamide, and some diuretics including thiazides and ethacrynic acid. To obtain a valid serum urate level, patients should abstain from any of these drugs and avoid unusual stress for at least 3 days. The serum urate level does not show any characteristic change during acute episodes of gouty arthritis, or following colchicine administration.

Most patients with gout have serum urate levels between 8 and 10 mg/100 ml, but higher levels are not infrequent, particularly with the development of renal insufficiency. It must be kept in mind that gout is one of the less common causes of hyperuricemia. Other causes, in addition to the drugs mentioned above, include azotemia, acidosis, hematologic disorders, lead poisoning, psoriasis, obesity, myocardial infarction, and essential hyperuricemia. Regardless of cause, the presence of hyperuricemia leads to increased risk of gouty arthritis, tophi, and uric acid stones, and the magnitude of the risk rises with the degree and duration of hyperuricemia.

The diagnosis of gout can be aided by the finding of crystals of sodium urate in synovial fluid or tophaceous material. These can be identified by their strongly negative birefringence in polarized light, and by chemical test. Other laboratory findings are less specific. During acute attacks, there is usually mild or moderate leukocytosis, elevation of the sedimentation rate, and sodium urate crystals in synovial fluid leukocytes. Anemia occurs only if there is renal insufficiency.

DIAGNOSIS

The diagnosis of gout should be suspected in any individual who develops acute arthritis, particularly if this involves the great toe or other joints of the feet, with a serum urate level at or above the upper limit of normal, and a dramatic response to colchicine. Family history of gout, or a history of uric acid stones, makes the diagnosis more likely. However, none of these features is pathognomonic of gout, and a similar acute inflammation can be seen in pseudogout and calcific tendinitis. The finding of crystals of sodium urate in synovial fluid or tophaceous material establishes the diagnosis most firmly.

TREATMENT

The two chief objectives of treatment are the control and prevention of acute attacks of gouty arthritis, and life-long reduction in hyperuricemia to prevent urate deposition and promote resolution of those tophi already present.

Acute Gouty Arthritis

There are several drugs that are effective in the management of acute gout.

Colchicine has the disadvantage of producing more side effects, particularly following oral administration, but has the advantage of aiding in diagnosis, and is usually employed at least until the diagnosis has been established. One 0.6-mg tablet is administered orally every 1 or 2 hours until pain is relieved, or diarrhea, abdominal cramps, nausea, or vomiting occurs, or a total dose of 6 mg is reached. Colchicine also can be administered intravenously, if necessary, in a dose of 2 mg, diluted with 20 ml of saline solution, injected slowly, and repeated after 12 hours if needed, to a total dose of not more than 4 mg in 24 hours. Extravasation causes tissue necrosis and severe local pain. If treatment is begun within 12 hours of onset of acute gouty arthritis, about 90% of patients have dramatic relief of pain and tenderness within 24-48 hours after oral administration, or 4-12 hours after intravenous injection. Swelling and erythema diminish more slowly over several days. Colchicine probably acts by inhibiting chemotaxis of leukocytes and ingestion of urate crystals. Dramatic response to colchicine supports the diagnosis of gout, as consistent and dramatic response rarely occurs in other kinds of arthritis, although some response may occur, especially in pseudogout. Failure to respond to adequate doses of colchicine should lead the physician to question the diagnosis of gout. Most patients find the gastrointestinal symptoms produced by therapeutic doses of colchicine sufficiently troublesome to prefer other drugs during recurrences of acute attacks of gout.

Colchicine also is helpful in preventing recurrences, and, in patients who have had two attacks within a year, should be continued for a year in a daily oral dose of 0.6 mg. This prophylactic dose may be resumed if attacks recur. Colchicine also should be administered in maximally tolerated doses for 1-2 days during initiation of therapy with uricosuric agents or allopurinol, which may induce an acute exacerbation. However, prolonged administration of therapeutic doses of colchicine should be avoided, as this may produce bone marrow depression and peripheral neuritis. The patient should be carefully instructed in the use of colchicine, since overdose can cause hemorrhagic gastroenteritis, vascular damage, shock, kidney damage, and paralysis. Since colchicine is excreted by the kidneys and liver, the oral or intravenous dose should be reduced in patients with renal or hepatic disease.

Indomethacin (Indocin, 50 mg), **phenylbutazone** (Butazolidin, 200 mg), or **oxyphenbutazone** (Tandearil, 100 mg) are as effective as colchicine in the relief of acute gout, and are preferred by most patients and physicians. Any of these drugs is administered orally three or four times a day for 1 or 2 days, and the dose then tapered over 3-5 more days. These drugs should not be used in patients with a history of peptic ulcer, hypertension, congestive heart failure, or blood dyscrasias, and the dose should be reduced in patients receiving probenecid.

Corticosteroids or corticotropin are occasionally necessary in those episodes of acute gout that fail to respond to other drugs. Some patients have a recrudescence of gout after discontinuation of corticosteroid or corticotropin, unless colchicine is administered prophylactically. When there is tense joint effusion, aspiration of fluid may relieve pain, and intraarticular injection of hydrocortisone or prednisolone will provide further relief if needed.

Hyperuricemia with Gout

Patients who have serum urate levels of more than 9 mg/100 ml, and frequent acute attacks of gout uncontrolled by colchicine prophylaxis, tophaceous deposits, chronic joint changes, or evidence of renal damage, should be treated with drugs that reduce the serum urate level (19). These drugs can precipitate acute attacks of gout during initiation of therapy, so that colchicine should be administered prophylactically at that time. None of them is effective in the treatment of acute gouty arthritis, though they help to prevent recurrences. Since hyperuricosuria increases the risk of nephrolithiasis, patients whose baseline excretion of uric acid exceeds 800 mg/day should maintain a high fluid intake of over 3 liters a day. Additionally, their urine should be alkalinized by the administration of potassium citrate, 2 g orally, four times a day.

Probenecid (Benemid, 500 mg orally, two to four times a day) is an effective uricosuric agent that blocks the renal tubular reabsorption of urate, thereby decreasing serum urate levels. To reduce the risk of nephrolithiasis, a high fluid intake should be maintained, and the urine alkalinized. Uricosuric agents should not be administered to patients with preexisting nephrolithiasis or impairment of renal function. Probenecid occasionally causes a rash. Its uricosuric effect is reduced by aspirin.

Allopurinol (Zyloprim, 300–400 mg orally, per day) reduces both serum urate and urinary uric acid levels by blocking the conversion of hypoxanthine and xanthine derived from purines to uric acid, and also by decreasing purine synthesis. It is preferred for patients with impaired renal function, who respond poorly to uricosuric agents, and for patients with a history of nephrolithiasis. The dose should be reduced in patients with renal insufficiency. Allopurinol may cause a rash, which requires prompt cessation of drug, as this may be followed by more severe hypersensitivity reactions such as vasculitis and toxic epidermal necrolysis. Gastrointestinal symptoms, elevated transaminase levels, or jaundice may also occur and, rarely, bone marrow depression, alopecia, or cataracts. The simultaneous use of uricosuric agents and allopurinol is seldom warranted.

Asymptomatic Hyperuricemia

The cause of hyperuricemia should be investigated, and removed, if possible. If hyperuricemia is due to use of thiazide diuretics, these may be administered every other day, if possible, or spironolactone substituted. If due to acidosis, hypertriglyceridemia, obesity, polycythemia, psoriasis, or renal insufficiency, treatment of the cause should be instituted. If hyperuricemia is not corrected, or if no cause is found, a urinary output greater than 2 liters/day should be maintained, the urine alkalinized, and hyperuricemic drugs and alcohol avoided. While foods high in purines, such as sweetbreads, anchovies, sardines, liver, kidney, and meat extractives have little effect on serum urate levels, they do increase uricosuria, and should be avoided. If there is mild or moderate hyperuricemia, with serum urate levels between 8 and 10 mg/100 ml, drug treatment is usually not necessary, although renal function should be evaluated annually. If there is persistent elevation of serum urate above 13 mg/100 ml, the risk of development of gout, uric acid stones, and renal insufficiency is great enough to warrant long-term administration of uricosuric agents, or allopurinol if nephrolithiasis or renal insufficiency have already occurred.

CHONDROCALCINOSIS AND PSEUDOGOUT

Calcification of joint cartilage is common in the elderly, especially in those with osteoarthritis. It is usually asymptomatic and requires no treatment. In a small number of patients, usually elderly, male or female, crystals of calcium pyrophosphate in the joint fluid may cause acute attacks of intense inflammation (pseudogout), usually of one joint but occasionally of two or more joints, lasting about 2 weeks and sometimes followed by low-grade chronic inflammation. The knee is by far the most frequently involved joint, but any large peripheral joint or the symphysis pubis may be affected. Joints of the hands and feet are less commonly involved. Roentgenographic examination of affected joints shows calcification of cartilage and often hypertrophic osteoarthritis, but the diagnosis of pseudogout requires identification in synovial fluid of calcium pyrophosphate crystals, which are weakly positively birefringent in polarized light. Symptoms can usually be relieved by aspiration of fluid from the inflamed joint. If this does not suffice, indomethacin or phenylbutazone can be administered orally, or corticosteroid instilled into the joint. Occasionally, there is a response to colchicine.

SUGGESTED READINGS

1. Axelrod L: Glucocorticoid therapy. *Medicine (Baltimore) 55:*39, 1976.
2. Bollet A: Analgesic and anti-inflammatory drugs in the therapy of osteoarthritis. *Semin Arthritis Rheum 11:*130, 1981.
3. Cohen AS: *Laboratory Diagnostic Procedures in the Rheumatic Diseases.* Boston, Little, Brown, 1985.
4. Cohen AS: *Rheumatology and Immunology.* The Science and Practice of Clinical Medicine, vol 4. New York, Grune & Stratton, 1986.
5. Garber EK, Fan PT, Bluestone R: Realistic guidelines of corticosteroid therapy in rheumatic disease. *Semin Arthritis Rheum 11:*231, 1981.
6. Glynn LE: Pathology, pathogenesis, and aetiology of rheumatoid arthritis. *Ann Rheum Dis 31:*412, 1972.
7. Grahame R, Scott JT: Clinical survey of 354 patients with gout. *Ann Rheum Dis 29:*461, 1970.
8. Gutman AB, Yu TF: Uric acid nephrolithiasis. *Am J Med 45:*756, 1968.
9. Hammerman D, Rosenberg LC, Schubert M: Diarthrodial joints revisited. *J. Bone Joint Surg 52A:*725, 1970.
10. Hollingsworth JW: *Management of Rheumatoid Arthritis and Its Complications.* Chicago, Year Book Medical Publishers, 1978.
11. Huskisson EC: Anti-inflammatory drugs. *Semin Arthritis Rheum 7:*1, 1977.
12. Jaffe IA: d-Penicillamine. *Bull Rheum Dis 28:*948–953, 1978.
13. Kelley WN, Harris ED Jr, Ruddy S, Sledge CB: *Textbook of Rheumatology.* Philadelphia, WB Saunders, 1985.
14. McCarty DJ: *Arthritis and Allied Conditions.* Philadelphia, Lea & Febiger, 1985.
15. McEwen C, DiTata D, Lingg C, Porini A, Good A, Rankin T: Ankylosing spondylitis and spondylitis ac-

companying ulcerative colitis, regional enteritis, psoriasis and Reiter's disease: a comparative study. *Arthritis Rheum 14:*291, 1971.

16. Nelson AM, Conn DL: Glucocorticoids in rheumatic disease. *Mayo Clin Proc 55:*758, 1980.

17. Peyron JG: Epidemiologic and etiologic approach to osteoarthritis. *Semin Arthritis Rheum 8:*288, 1979.

18. Wyngaarden JB, Kelley WN: Gout. In Stanbury JB, Wyngaarden JB, Frederickson DS, Goldstein JL, Brown MS: *The Metabolic Basis of Inherited Disease.* New York, McGraw-Hill, 1982, pp 1043-1114.

19. Wyngaarden JB, Kelley WN: *Gout and Hyperuricemia.* New York, Grune & Stratton, 1976.

CHAPTER 27

Common Metabolic Disorders of the Skeleton in Aging

URIEL S. BARZEL

OSTEOPOROSIS

The most prevalent metabolic disease of bone is osteoporosis (2–4). Osteoporosis is a condition that predisposes bone to fracture with little or no trauma, the result of absolute deficiency of bone tissue, and consequently diminished bone density. The bones involved, in decreasing order of frequency, are the spine, the femur, and the wrist. The ribs and other bones are less commonly involved.

Spinal osteoporosis has a protracted natural history and an unpredictable course. There are recurrent and unexpected fractures that cause severe pain, frequently require complete bed rest, and impose long periods of morbidity. The rate of fractures is markedly accelerated at the time of menopause. There may be intervals of freedom from fractures, but the progressive collapse of vertebrae leads to shortening of stature and the development of kyphosis, which is responsible for the all too frequent picture of the stooped old lady. Although spinal osteoporosis is not responsible for any significant mortality, the recurring and unpredictable attacks of pain and fracture and the progressive physical deformity severely affect the self-image and the quality of life of a large number of aging people. In the course of the disease, osteoporosis turns erect and independent citizens into bent, vulnerable, and dependent wards of society.

Hip fractures, on the other hand, begin at an earlier age than spinal fractures, double in rate every 5 years without any apparent effect of the menopause, may be associated with a fatal outcome in some 20% of cases, and doom nearly half of the survivors to long-term institutionalization.

Osteoporosis is encountered with increasing frequency in women over 45 years of age and in men over 55 years of age, and is estimated to affect 11 million aged in the United States. It is four times more prevalent in women, and is very common among Caucasians and especially women of northern European origin.

There are numerous cross-sectional studies that compare people of different ages and show that women have less bone, and less dense bones, than men throughout adult life. They show further that older age groups tend to have lesser amounts of bone and less dense bone. Prospective studies support the idea that there is an age-related bone loss, that the loss begins earlier for women, and that their rate of loss is faster than that of men. There is considerable uncertainty, however, as to whether osteoporosis is just the extreme manifestation of a normal process of senescence or whether it is a distinct pathologic process. Recently, it has been proposed that osteoporosis comprises at least two different syndromes, one due to aging, and the other the result of gonadal deficiency.

PHYSIOLOGIC CONSIDERATIONS

The skeleton is made up of two types of bone. One, cortical bone, is found in the shafts of long bones. The other, trabecular bone, is found at the end of the long bones, in the body of the vertebrae, in the pelvis, and in other flat bones. Bone is a dynamic, metabolically active organ. The outer surfaces of bones continue to grow slowly throughout life. Change and turnover are achieved in the adult by resorption on the inner surfaces of cortical bone and on surfaces of the trabecular bone, followed by formation at the same sites.

Bone turnover serves two major functions. One function is mechanical, the other metabolic. The mechanical function subjects the skeleton to constantly changing and varying stresses. It stimulates and controls bone remodeling, which continues throughout life. The metabolic function is subservient to the organism's need to maintain calcium homeostasis and, probably, acid-base balance. The maintenance of calcium homeostasis is a complex system of feedback controls and checks and balances involving vitamin D and parathyroid hormone.

Vitamin D is essential for absorption of calcium from the gut, for normal mineralization of bone, and also as a "cofactor" for the effect of parathyroid hormone on bone resorption. The vitamin may be synthesized from cholesterol in the skin upon exposure to ultraviolet light, or may be obtained from some food items. Whether synthesized in the skin or ingested, vitamin D is metabolized in the liver to 25-hydroxyvitamin D, which partly circulates in the blood and is partly stored in fat. 1-Hydroxylation in the kidney is responsible for the formation of 1,25-hydroxyvitamin D, which is the metabolite active in calcium absorption.

Age per se has a deleterious effect on the gastrointestinal absorption of calcium. The fractional absorption of calcium falls with age at all intake levels. As a result, the same dietary intake of calcium is likely to provide less calcium to an older person than to a young one.

The primary function of parathyroid hormone is the maintenance of serum calcium at a constant normal level. When serum calcium falls, parathyroid hormone is released in larger amounts. It stimulates bone cells to resorb bone and release calcium into the circulation, and, at the same time, it stimulates renal reabsorption of calcium. It also increases calcium absorption from the gut by stimulating renal production of 1,25 dihydroxyvitamin D. Thus, the original stimulus of low blood calcium may result in a more efficient absorption of calcium from food in addition to increased renal reabsorption of calcium and resorption of bone. These functions contribute to the return of serum calcium to normal. High levels of serum calcium will diminish or stop parathyroid hormone secretion. Calcium resorption from bone will cease, renal calcium reabsorption and phosphaturia will not be promoted, and if serum phosphorus is high enough, elaboration of 1,25-dihydroxycholecalciferol may stop. These changes may allow serum calcium to return to normal. Calcitonin, a hormone produced by the medullary cell of the thyroid, is actively excreted in response to high serum calcium and negates the effect of parathyroid hormone on bone resorption.

PATHOGENESIS OF OSTEOPOROSIS

Clinical and pathologic observations clearly demonstrate that bone in osteoporosis is qualitatively normal, but there is a marked reduction in the amount of bone as an organ. This quantitative reduction is due to an imbalance between bone formation and bone resorption. Radioisotope studies of calcium metabolism, studies utilizing special histologic techniques, and microradiographic studies all suggest that there is, in fact, excessive resorption of bone. Excessive resorption affects primarily trabecular bone, but it also affects the cortices of long bones. The end result is a long bone with slightly larger external diameter but thinner walls, and with markedly diminished trabecular bone in its ends. Vertebral bodies, which have a larger percentage of trabecular bone, are more severely affected by this process.

Histologic and histochemical analyses fail to provide any clues to the cause of this imbalance. The bone is histologically unremarkable, and the number and nature of osteoclastic cells does not appear abnormal. The ratio of calcified to uncalcified matrix is normal, and the ratio of mineral to organic matrix is also normal.

The mechanism responsible for the development of osteoporosis is unknown. A number of factors are implicated in its pathogenesis.

Gonadal Deficiency

Albright and his colleagues, who first described osteoporosis, noted its high frequency among postmenopausal women, and postulated a cause-and-effect relationship between the gonadal deficiency of menopausal women and osteoporosis. Women subjected to oophorectomy have a rapid loss of bone in the first few postoperative years, and this loss can be prevented by the use of replacement estrogen therapy. In a recent study, bone density at various sites was examined in a group of 54-year-old women, 22 years after bilateral oophorectomy, and was found comparable with that of 73-year-old women, 22 years after the onset of menopause, and well below that of perimenopausal women 52 years of age. This study demonstrates that gonadal deficiency has a much more significant impact on bone density than does age per se.

There is no evidence that estrogens have any direct effect on bone cells. The mechanism by which gonadal deficiency causes osteoporosis may be indirect. There is evidence that calcium absorption from the gut is markedly diminished in the postmenopausal woman. The average requirement of elemental calcium in menstruating women is estimated to be 850 mg/day. Postmenopausal women require approximately 1500 mg/day to maintain metabolic calcium balance. The administration of estrogen to the postmenopausal woman decreases the calcium requirement to the premenopausal level.

There is also a theory that in gonadal deficiency, a heightened end organ sensitivity to parathyroid hormone exists, which leads to excessive bone resorption. Measurements of blood levels of parathyroid hormone show no increase in osteoporosis.

Calcium Deficiency

It has been observed that in osteoporosis, calcium balance is often negative if calcium intake is less than 1.5 g/day. This may be a manifestation of the decreased fractional absorption of calcium seen with aging, or it may be due to a specific defect in osteoporotic patients. In any case, insufficient absorption of calcium through the gut will activate the homeostatic mechanism and lead to resorption of bone, which in chronic cases will lead to osteoporosis. This has indeed been demonstrated experimentally in rats, cats, and dogs, all of whom develop osteoporotic changes when given a diet adequate in vitamin D but low in calcium. Prior parathyroidectomy prevents the osteoporosis from developing. In some women, there is a deficiency in the 1-hydroxylation of 25-hydroxyvitamin D, resulting in deficiency of 1,25-dihydroxyvitamin D and thus in calcium malabsorption. The effect of estrogen in reducing calcium requirement may be due to the stimulation of production of this vitamin metabolite.

In a few cases, a renal calcium leak may be responsible for chronic calcium loss and the development of osteoporosis.

High Protein Intake

Human studies show a correlation between the level of animal protein intake and the development of osteoporosis. Animal proteins (and some cereals as well) contain large residues of phosphates and sulfates, and are known as acid-ash foods. Their ingestion increases urinary calcium loss, which may contribute to a negative calcium balance and the development of osteoporosis. This finding has been supported by animal studies. It has been shown experimentally that the chronic intake of acid (such as ammonium chloride) causes excess calciuria and leads to the development of osteoporosis. This experimental osteoporosis is identical histologically, biochemically, and physicochemically to human osteoporosis.

Immobilization

Another factor that may contribute to osteoporosis is immobilization. Classic studies in subjects with paralytic polio, and more recent observations on immobilization in conjunction with space flight, show immobilization to be an important mechanism for bone loss. This is reinforced by experimental observations using plaster casts and denervation, which cause local or segmental osteoporosis. Of theoretical and practical importance is the observation in long-term space flight personnel and in human immobilization models that bone is redeposited with remobilization.

The application of these observations to the relative immobilization of the retired elderly is still speculative, but severe disease with total and prolonged immobilization may well be responsible for some cases of osteoporosis.

SECONDARY DEVELOPMENT OF OSTEOPOROSIS

Osteoporosis or osteoporosis-like states can develop secondarily in a number of conditions.

Hyperadrenocorticism

Adrenal cortical steroids interfere with calcium absorption and bone matrix formation, and thus lead to the development of less bone, osteoporosis, and some degree of osteomalacia. This is seen in patients treated with large doses of corticosteroids and in patients with Cushing's disease. There are case reports of patients with Cushing's disease, all young people, in whom severe osteoporosis was the one and only clinical manifestation of their disease. Twenty-four hour urinary free-cortisol excretion appears to be the most sensitive test for the diagnosis of this condition.

Hyperthyroidism

Increased bone turnover with excessive bone loss may be observed in this disorder. Elevation of blood thyroxine level, blood alkaline phosphatase level, and at times blood calcium level, and increased urinary calcium excretion clearly separate this group from osteoporosis as defined.

Hyperparathyroidism

In rare cases, diffuse decrease in bone density may be the manifestation of excessive parathyroid hormone secretion. Blood calcium is likely to be elevated, and the blood level of parathyroid hormone inappropriate for the ambient calcium level.

Miscellaneous

Smoking, lean body weight, alcoholism, and diabetes are thought to be risk factors for the development of osteoporosis. Excessive exercise by young female athletes may cause amenorrhea and the development of skeletal osteopenia. Osteoporotic changes may be seen in anorexia nervosa, acromegaly, prolonged heparin therapy, and lipid storage disease.

Regional osteoporosis is seen around areas of malignant disease and osteomyelitis, around rheumatoid joints, and in sickle cell disease.

DIAGNOSIS

The diagnosis of osteoporosis is basically one of exclusion in which the finding of diminished bone density is not accompanied by any other demonstrable metabolic abnormality.

The single most important condition to be differentiated from osteoporosis is osteomalacia. In this disease, bone formation is defective because of vitamin D deficiency or resistance. The patient may have continuous and generalized bone pain and tenderness, rather than episodic attacks. There is elevation of serum alkaline phosphatase and urinary calcium excretion is low, and in more severe cases blood phosphorus and even blood calcium may fall.

In establishing the diagnosis of osteoporosis the physician should demonstrate adequate intake of vitamin D or sun exposure, absence of immobilization, no steatorrhea, and no corticosteroid ingestion. The finding of the following abnormal values— high alkaline phosphatase, elevated or lowered blood calcium, low blood phosphorus, low blood car-

bon dioxide, elevated blood thyroxine, abnormal blood protein electrophoresis, high urinary calcium excretion, high urinary hydroxyproline, high urinary 17-hydroxysteroid, or high urinary free-cortisol levels—*rules out* the diagnosis of osteoporosis, in which all of these parameters are normal. It must be noted, however, that serum alkaline phosphatase level rises shortly after a bone is fractured and remains elevated for many months, even in osteoporotic individuals.

The practitioner of geriatric medicine should be aware that there is generally nothing specific and pathognomonic in radiographs in early osteoporosis. The relative decrease in bone or the lesser density of bone should be best described as "osteopenia." The loose manner in which the term "osteoporosis" is used by some radiologists should not mislead the physician to accept it as an accurate diagnosis until the differential diagnosis is fully satisfied.

The radiologic picture is one of uniform loss of bone density with cortical thinning and endosteal resorption (Fig. 27.1). Because trabecular bone is more severely affected than cortical bone by increased resorption, an apparent relative increase in cortex of long bones and vertebrae is seen. In the vertebrae, transverse trabeculae are preferentially resorbed and the remaining vertical trabeculae appear accentuated.

With increasing severity, progressive changes may be seen. In the vertebrae one sees increasing biconcavity of the end plates due to pressure of the nucleus pulposus, and the so-called "fish mouth deformity" emerges (Fig. 27.1). The anterior aspects of vertebrae collapse, leading to wedging of the vertebrae. The ultimate lesion is complete vertebral collapse, which may be seen earlier in thoracic vertebrae and later in lumbar vertebrae. The intervertebral spaces are preserved, there is little osteophyte formation, and the aorta often appears heavily calcified. In the head of the femur, progressive loss of stress lines occurs (Fig. 27.2). Pseudofractures (Looser's lines, Milkman's fractures) and subperiosteal resorption are characteristically absent.

DENSITOMETRY

Early studies of bone morphometry relied on radiographs. Estimates of inner and outer edges of metacarpal bones served as the first approximations of bone density. Special radiographic techniques allowed some investigators to determine the degree of porosity of cortical bones. The absence of stress lines in the femoral neck (Singh index) was used as predictor of tendency to hip fracture.

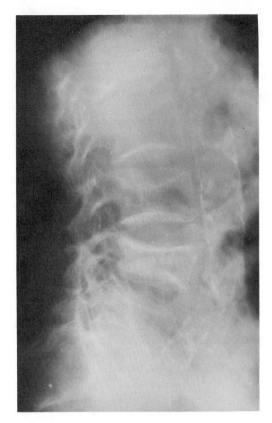

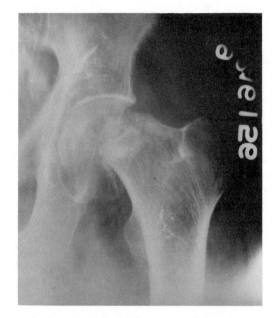

Figure 27.2. Head of the femur, osteoporosis. There is a marked decrease in the trabeculae that form the pressure lines in the normal hip. The head has been broken and the neck has slipped superiorly. The progressive decrease in stress lines of the neck of the femur can be correlated with the progression of the osteoporotic process.

Figure 27.1. Spinal osteoporosis. There is a loss of bone density, which makes the end plates relatively prominent. In reality, the end plates also are thinned and are deformed under pressure of the nucleus pulposus to give the typical "fish mouth" appearance. Various degrees of collapse of vertebrae are seen, most prominently in L4 and L1. Note the absence of osteophytes, and the prominence of the calcified aorta.

More accurate methods of determining bone density have been developed in the last two decades. The first to be developed utilizes monoenergetic radiation and depends on the differential absorption of the radiation by bone and soft tissue. Such monoenergetic absorptiometry continues to be useful for the measurement of bone density at the wrist, which is mostly trabecular bone, and at the cortical part of the radius. For the determination of density of the spine and of the proximal femur, dual photon absorptiometry has been developed. This technique allows the measurement of bone density independently of soft tissue thickness and composition. Quantitative computed tomography (CT) scanning has been developed more recently, and allows measurement of the trabecular portion of the vertebrae.

All of these methods have acceptable levels of re-

producibility and accuracy in dedicated research laboratories. However, since the determination of the bone edge is an arbitrary decision in all three methods, there is an inherent uncertainty as to the true bone density. In addition, dual photon absorptiometry measures all calcium in its path. The final report in this method includes the contribution of aortic calcification, osteophytes, and even calcium tablets in the gastrointestinal tract if they happen to be in the path of the radiation. CT scanning delivers a much higher radiation dose, and until recently had a built-in error related to the contribution of marrow fat to the final measurement. All three methods may be of value in population studies and, clinically, in the follow-up of individual patients. Claims that these analytic methods permit prediction of an individual's fracture risk are yet to be substantiated. There is definitely a very poor correlation between appendicular densitometry and vertebral osteoporosis.

Biopsy of the iliac crest correlates to some extent with densitometry of the spine. When prelabeled with tetracycline and processed without decalcification, such biopsy can not only give some insight into the quantitative aspects of the trabecular bone, but also some information on the dynamics of bone metabolism. (It is of interest that hip fracture patients do not have diminished trabecular bone volume on iliac crest biopsy.)

MANAGEMENT

Wrist fracture is treated with a cast, allowing callus formation and bone healing until union is complete. Hip fracture is treated with nailing or replacement of the head of the femur, early mobilization, and aggressive physiotherapy.

Collapse fracture of vertebrae requires complete bed rest and the use of analgesia. Stool softeners and high fluid intake should be encouraged to counteract the tendency to obstipation associated with bed rest. Codeine analgesia should be avoided since it causes constipation and increases the need to strain at stool, which in turn will increase the pain. The patients should be encouraged to get out of bed in the third week, and be fitted at that time with a light weight corset with steel ribs. The corset will serve the patient for approximately 8 weeks, during which time increased activity should be encouraged. With the return to normal daily activity, the corset can be discarded, but a maintenance program of back and anterior abdominal exercise should be maintained. Of available modes of activity, swimming (in heated pools) is probably the best year-round activity, and this, as well as other modes of activity, should be encouraged as part of a prophylactic program against future fractures.

It is generally believed that the maintenance of calcium balance is valuable for osteoporosis prophylaxis as well as for the prevention of further deterioration in the patient with established osteoporosis. Such balance can be achieved by means of an adequate calcium intake, approximately 1500 mg of *elemental calcium* per day in the postmenopausal patient. The efficacy of calcium supplementation in the prevention of osteoporotic fractures is yet to be demonstrated. Milk is the best source of calcium, providing approximately 1 g of calcium per quart of whole or skim milk. Milk also contains 400 units of vitamin D per quart, which is double the recommended daily dose for adults. Patients with lactase deficiency may find complete relief from milk intolerance by the use of lactase tablets, which are widely available over the counter in health food stores and pharmacies. Lactose-reduced milk is also available in some stores. Supplemental calcium can be ingested in tablet form. Calcium gluconate and lactate tablets are poorly soluble and often found (in metabolic studies) whole in the stool; 10–12 tablets are required to provide approximately the same amount of calcium as 1 quart of milk. Calcium carbonate is more efficiently absorbed; a 650-mg tablet provides 250 mg of calcium, and six tablets daily will therefore provide the entire daily requirement for a postmenopausal woman. Calcium carbonate depends on stomach acid for its solubility and absorption. In patients with achlorhydria, calcium carbonate may be absorbable if taken with food, but calcium citrate may be found to be a suitable alternative. It is wise to examine urinary and blood calcium from time to time during therapy to assure that the patient does not develop hypercalciuria or hypercalcemia.

Estrogen administration has been shown to lessen the amount of calcium intake required for the maintenance of a positive balance in the woman entering menopause. Estrogen was also shown to prevent the rapid fall in bone density that is observed in menstruating women who undergo oophorectomy. One epidemiologic study demonstrated a reduced rate of osteoporotic fractures in women who have "ever taken" estrogen. In most cases these women took estrogen in the early postmenopausal period. Cyclic therapy with estrogen and progesterone is now thought to confer an overall benefit that far outweighs the theoretical danger of uterine and breast cancer. However, there is no evidence that a woman with established osteoporosis, 15 or 20 years after the menopause, will benefit in any way from the administration of estrogen.

Pharmacologic amounts of vitamin D have been used experimentally and found to be detrimental, and are not recommended for the osteoporotic patient. *1,25-Dihydroxyvitamin D* supplementation may be appropriate in patients shown to be deficient in the production of this vitamin metabolite. *Hydrochlorothiazide* is indicated as primary therapy in patients whose osteoporosis is the result of hypercalciuria. *Fluoride* has been shown to stimulate bone formation, and therefore may find an important place in the treatment of osteoporosis. The dose and mode of its use are yet to be determined, and it must still be considered experimental. Preliminary data suggest that *anabolic steroids* may be of value in osteoporosis. Adequate studies of these drugs are not yet available. *Calcitonin* has been approved for use in osteoporosis. This salmon-derived analogue of the human hormone is a polypeptide that can be administered by injection only.

After complete healing of fracture or collapse, patients are often able to assume normal function, but recurrent episodes of fractures are the rule. These are unpredictable, and up to 7 and 10 years may pass between episodes. Eventually, recurrent collapse of vertebrae may lead to anterior kyphosis and forward bending of such a degree that the rib cage may come to rest on the iliac crests. The change in weight distribution in this situation may lead to cessation of fracture activity of the vertebrae (Fig. 27.3).

Active research may provide information both on the etiology and the treatment of osteoporosis in the next few years. Densitometry and computerized scanning will prove useful in the assessment of experimental therapeutic regimens in the treatment of this disease. We must remember, however, that no derivative measurement of bone metabolism or bone density can take the place of the final proof of therapeutic efficacy—the prevention of fracture activity.

OSTEOMALACIA

Osteomalacia is much less common than osteoporosis, but may superficially mimic it early in the course of illness. Since it is a disease of known etiology and is amenable to treatment and complete recovery, it is important to establish its presence in any patient with metabolic bone disease.

PATHOPHYSIOLOGY

The reader is referred to the previous section for a brief discussion of calcium metabolism. In osteomalacia, vitamin D deficiency or resistance is present, and in rare cases is due to phosphate diabetes. As can be readily appreciated, in the absence of or resistance to vitamin D, calcium absorption is defective and parathyroid hormone excretion may be stimulated with resultant increased bone resorption. At the same time, new bone formation is affected, as the newly deposited protein matrix fails to calcify. This is manifested by the finding on bone biopsy of increased width of the osteoid seam as well as increased bone resorption.

Clinically, the most important fact is the presence of generalized and unrelenting bone pain, which at times is accompanied by proximal muscle weakness. History must include careful questioning of the patient regarding eating habits, exposure to sun, and bowel function. In the United States it is difficult to develop vitamin D deficiency since vitamin D is present in milk and deep-sea fish, and is easily synthesized by the skin from solar ultraviolet radiation.

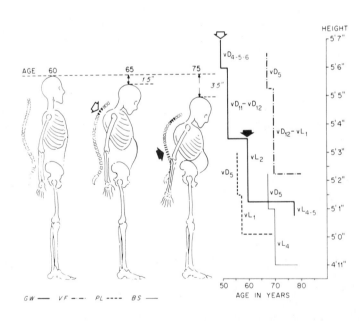

Figure 27.3. The natural history of spinal osteoporosis is illustrated diagrammatically in four patients observed for 10–20 years. In the early stages of the disease, there is asymptomatic loss of height due to changes in the upper thoracic vertebrae (*open arrow*), which account for the loss of 1–1½ inches. Later stages of the disease are characterized by painful collapse of lower thoracic and lumbar vertebrae (*black arrow*), which may account for the loss of 2–2½ inches/episode. Body weight remains stable between collapse-fractures. Significant loss of height ceases when the costal margins come to rest on the iliac crests. (From Urist MR, Gurvey MS and Fareed DO: Long-term observations on aged women with pathologic osteoporosis. In Barzel US (Ed): *Osteoporosis*, New York, Grune & Stratton, 1970, pp 3–37.)

However, among the geriatric population it is not unheard of that a patient's diet is poor and deficient in multiple factors, including vitamin D. In addition, some geriatric patients lead a very withdrawn life and rarely go out, thus depriving themselves of the benefit of exposure to sunlight. Some institutionalized elderly may also receive little or no sun exposure. In cases of marginal vitamin D intake, phenobarbital intake may cause increased degradation of cholecalciferol and thus may contribute to the development of osteomalacia. Vitamin D resistance may develop in adult age, as can phosphate diabetes and steatorrhea.

DIAGNOSIS

In the early stages, a high alkaline phosphatase and low urinary calcium may be the only findings. As the disease progresses, serum phosphorus falls, and eventually the patient develops not only hypophosphatemia but also hypocalcemia. This constellation of chemical findings is pathognomonic. Hormonal measurements can confirm the diagnosis: the blood level of 25-hydroxyvitamin D, which represents the state of repletion of the vitamin, can be measured; this test is available from commercial laboratories. A level below the normal range is strong evidence for vitamin D deficiency. The blood level of C-terminal parathyroid hormone will be elevated as a result of the physiologic response of the parathyroid gland to the deficiency. Absolute confirmation can be obtained by tetracycline prelabeled bone biopsy, which demonstrates in undecalcified sections the widened osteoid seams and the decreased rate of mineralization—the pathologic hallmark of this disease. If the intake of vitamin D is adequate, a search for occult steatorrhea should be instituted. This includes 72-hour stool fat on a 100-g fat diet, serum carotene level, and prothrombin time. Twenty-four-hour urinary phosphorus excretion also should be determined.

At the early stages of the disease, radiology is not helpful. Some decrease of bone density, with loss of trabecular bone and nonspecific thinning of cortices may be seen. In more advanced cases, pseudofractures (Looser's lines, or Milkman's fractures) may present as bilateral symmetric linear bands of radiolucency that can occur in the scapula, femur, pubis, ulna, radius, ribs, clavicles, and bones of the feet and hands.

CLINICAL COURSE AND MANAGEMENT

In simple vitamin D deficiency, repletion and maintenance of adequate intake lead to most gratifying results within a few weeks. Serum calcium and phosphorus return to normal within 2 weeks, and a number of weeks later the alkaline phosphatase returns to normal. The pseudofractures heal; the bone pain and the muscle weakness disappear. In cases of simple deprivation, 3000 units of vitamin D are given daily for the first month, followed by the daily administration of 200 units for life. In patients receiving barbiturate therapy, 5000 units/day may be required. Patients with vitamin D resistance require 50,000 and 100,000 units/day. Patients with steatorrhea may require 500,000 units/day. In all cases, therapy is given orally, medication is started at a low dosage, and 2–3 weeks are allowed to pass before a 10-fold increase in dosage is ordered. In patients with phosphate diabetes, large amounts of phosphate may be required either as sole therapy or in conjunction with vitamin D. In all cases, the aim is complete control of the process, and it is achievable in a large majority of patients.

Uremia is a special case in the spectrum of metabolic bone disease, and a detailed discussion of this is beyond the scope of this chapter. In uremia there is a combination of acidosis, hyperparathyroidism, and vitamin D resistance (although sensitivity to 1,25-dihydroxyvitamin D is normal). The treatment of this disorder depends on proper control of dietary calcium, phosphorus, and vitamin D and on proper dialysis, and is reversible by renal transplantation.

PAGET'S DISEASE

This disorder is characterized by an excessive and abnormal remodeling of bone. It is first seen in middle age in about 1% of the population, but may involve one out of nine persons at age 80. Paget's disease is more common in men than in women. The geographic distribution of the disease is spotty. It may appear in clusters, and occasionally in a number of family members. This distribution is similar to that seen in infectious diseases, and indeed there is electron microscope evidence that Paget's disease may be a slow virus disease.

PATHOPHYSIOLOGY

The disease may involve one or more bones, and generally is localized to part of the bone. The histologic picture is one of extreme osteoclastic activity with many large multinucleated osteoclasts in every section of bone that is involved with active disease. Virus-like clusters have been found in the nuclei of these osteoclasts. Osteoblastic activity is equally intense, and bone formation and resorption may be up to 20 or 40 times normal rates. However, the metabolic balance of calcium is generally normal.

The new bone is disorganized in its histologic appearance and is structurally deficient. Its growth is poorly controlled and does not conform to normal remodeling factors. Thus, it is prone to develop deformities and fractures easily. Furthermore, uncontrolled growth may cause the pagetic bone to invade neural foramina and to compress neural tissue in the spinal canal, with severe neurologic consequences. Hearing loss is a common complication due either to involvement of the ossicles in the middle ear or to compression of the eighth nerve.

The high turnover of bone is responsible for an elevation of alkaline phosphatase in the blood and for increased hydroxyproline excretion in the urine. The metabolic activity in this disease is so intense that in some cases increased cardiac output can be demonstrated and in a few cases a high-output heart failure develops.

DIFFERENTIAL DIAGNOSIS

The diagnosis is generally not difficult to make since the radiologic features are quite characteristic (Table 27.1). In the pelvis, cortical thickening and coarse trabecular patterns may be mimicked by metastatic osteoblastic disease. Similar changes can be seen in the long bones and in the vertebrae. The radiologic appearance of the skull as "cotton wool" is quite unique to this disease (Figs. 27.4–27.7).

The finding of elevated alkaline phosphatase with normal serum calcium and phosphorus, without evidence of liver disease, and the presence of typical radiologic changes, generally suffices for the diagnosis of Paget's disease. Determination of acid phosphatase levels may help in ruling out metastatic prostatic carcinoma.

CLINICAL COURSE

Paget's disease is frequently asymptomatic and need not be a cause for concern. It may involve a single bone (monostotic) or many bones (polyostotic). Bone pain, local heat, and deformity are frequently seen. Fracture, deafness, and neurologic deficits due to nerve compression, including paraplegia, may develop in the more severe cases. In all these cases treatment is indicated, as it is in patients with congestive heart failure due to high output.

In 1% of the cases, sarcomatous degeneration of pagetoid bone is seen. This is heralded by continuous pain and a marked rise in alkaline phosphatase.

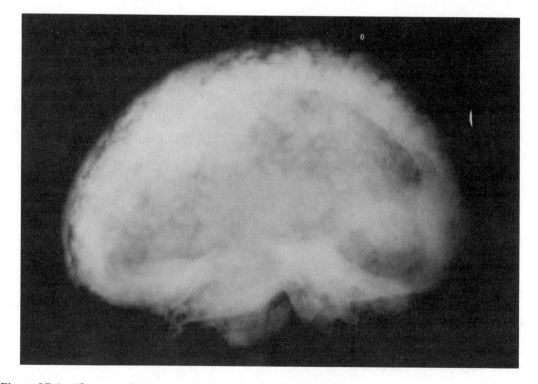

Figure 27.4. "Cotton wool" appearance of skull affected by Paget's disease.

Table 27.1
Some Typical Differential Features of Metabolic Bone Disease[a]

Condition	Symptoms	Serum			Urine			X-ray findings
		Calcium	Phosphate	Alkaline phosphatase	Calcium	Phosphate	Hydroxyproline	
Osteoporosis	Vertebral compression fracture	N	N	N	N	N	N	Generalized osteopenia
	Hip fracture							Cortical thinning and endosteal resorption
	Wrist fracture (*All with little or no trauma*)							Accentuated vertical trabeculae in vertebrae, and wedging
Osteomalacia	Generalized bone pain Proximal muscle weakness	N/L	N/L	H	L	H	VH	Generalized osteopenia Pseudofractures
Paget's disease	Localized areas of bone pain Deformity of bone Deafness	N	N	VH	N	N	VH	Adjacent areas of sclerosis and demineralization
Hyperparathyroidism	Bone pain, generalized or local Kidney stones	H	L	N/H	N/H	H	H	Subperiosteal resorption Absent lamina dura Bone cysts

[a]N, Normal; L, low; N/L, normal or low; H, high; VH, very high; N/H, normal or high.

Figure 27.5. Cortical thickening and coarse trabecular pattern of Paget's disease in the pelvis and the left femur.

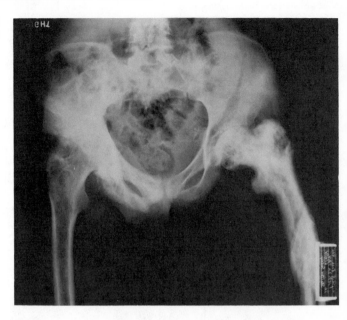

Figure 27.6. Bowing of the lower end of the involved femur.

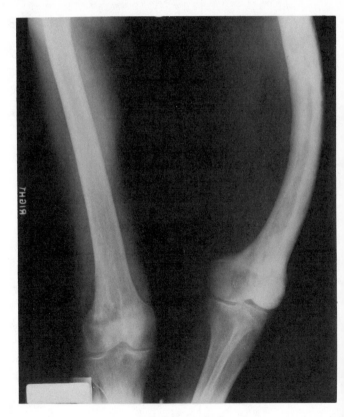

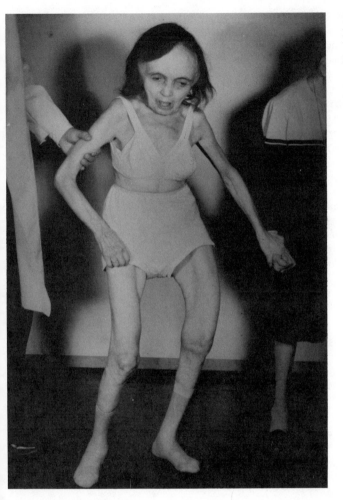

Figure 27.7. The marked deformity of the patient whose radiograms are shown in Figures 27.4–27.6. In addition to her obvious physical infirmity, the patient also suffered from total deafness. For 15 years she lived alone in an apartment, opening the door only to her sister, who shopped for her and who either came or called on the phone at a prescribed time daily to ascertain that the patient was not in need of help.

TREATMENT

In most patients with Paget's disease, the disease is asymptomatic and no treatment is indicated. Two products are available for treatment of the symptomatic patient: calcitonin and etidronate disodium.

Calcitonin, a hormone elaborated by the medullary cells of the thyroid, has been found empirically to be useful in the treatment of Paget's disease. Salmon calcitonin, an analogue of the human hormone, is a polypeptide and can be administered by injection only. It is used preferentially in cases with acute onset of neurologic complications and in cases with high-output congestive heart failure. Treatment is initiated by the daily injection of 100 MRC (Medical Research Council) units subcutaneously. In less severe cases, a dose of 100 or 50 units thrice weekly may suffice.

Complete relief of pain is reported by patients 2–6 weeks after initiation of treatment. Neurologic symptoms improve in some patients, although deafness is unaffected. Cardiac output may return to normal. These changes are associated with a fall in the alkaline phosphatase to 50% of the initial value, and a similar fall of urinary hydroxyproline. Side effects include transient nausea and vomiting. Flushing of the hands and face has been observed. The manufacturer recommends skin testing before use.

Etidronate disodium, disodium ethane-1-hydroxy-1,1-diphosphonate (EHDP), is available for the oral treatment of Paget's disease. Diphosphonate interferes with osteoclast function, and slows down bone turnover in Paget's disease. As with calcitonin treatment, serum alkaline phosphatase and urinary hydroxyproline return toward normal. The medication is taken 2 hours after a meal as a single daily dose of 5 mg/kg, for a period of 6 months. There are very few side effects to this treatment. Calcitonin and etidronate disodium can be used together in severe cases, especially those associated with neural complications.

After the initial remission, it is sometimes necessary to re-treat patients in whom the disease has become active again, and the results of re-treatment with either drug are generally good.

Mithramycin, an inhibitor of DNA-directed RNA synthesis, is an osteoclast poison. At a dose of 10–15 µg/kg once or twice weekly, mithramycin can bring about a clinical remission of the pagetic process. Because of its potential toxicity, however, this drug should be reserved for severe cases and for those in which other therapies have failed.

It is important for the treating physician to recognize that some pain in cases of Paget's disease is due to osteoarthritis of a joint of an involved extremity. Although the pagetoid lesions may respond to treatment, the osteoarthritic joint will continue to be symptomatic, and the patient should be so advised.

REFERENCES

1. Audran M, Kumar R: The physiology and pathophysiology of vitamin D. *Mayo Clin Proc* 60:851–866, 1985.
2. Barzel US (ed): *Osteoporosis.* New York, Grune & Stratton, 1970.
3. Barzel US (ed): *Osteoporosis II.* New York, Grune & Stratton, 1979.
4. Riggs BL, Melton LJ (eds): *Osteoporosis: Etiology, Diagnosis, and Management.* New York, Raven Press, 1988.
5. Singer FR: *Paget's Disease of Bone.* New York, Plenum Medical Books, 1977.
6. Smith P, Barzel US: Vitamin D deficiency osteomalacia in elderly persons. *Compr Ther* 10:24–32, 1984.
7. Zajac J, Phillips PE: Paget's disease of bone: clinical features and treatment. *Clin Exp Rheumatol* 3:75–88, 1985.

CHAPTER 28

Musculoskeletal Injuries in the Elderly

JOHN C. GORDON

Discussion of musculoskeletal injuries in elderly persons is not an isolated listing of cause, effect, and treatment. Such injuries evoke different responses in different age groups. The location and severity of injury, the quality of bone and soft tissues, and the healing process combine to dictate the recovery rate of an individual patient. Conditions such as deafness, blindness, impaired mental status, cardiovascular abnormalities, use of multiple medications, etc. may significantly affect treatment and rehabilitation. Progress and prognosis of orthopaedic injury in the older patient may be very different from those in the younger individual.

Aging itself makes the elderly patient different. As adults grow older, there are physical and psychologic alterations that affect function. Muscle fibers decrease in number and become atrophic. Slight flexion contractures of joints occur. Density of bone is decreased by demineralization, resulting in osteoporosis. Collagen, which comprises 40% of the body's protein, thickens and becomes less elastic and mobile that, in turn, affects the mobility and recovery capability of the skin, bone, cartilage, muscle, and joint surfaces. Changes in bone density and blood supply also affect healing response in an elderly patient.

Effects of injury on attitude and independence of the elderly patient must be assessed and treated, when possible, as must any disability from other medical and physical causes. Skeletal injury complicates and upsets an elderly person's already delicate balance of living and may worsen medical problems already present (4, 8). Injury may force the patient into health care systems he or she has avoided. Patients may equate hospitalization with dying and injury with loss of independence. They may try to recover that independence by minimizing problems and trying to avoid or shorten hospitalization. A practitioner must provide straightforward explanation, a positive yet realistic attitude, and much reassurance.

Ideal goals of orthopaedic treatment are restoration of preinjury function and prevention of further injury. Even these modest goals may be elusive in the elderly and extensive counseling for the patient and the family is necessary. One should not promise a restoration of normal function after injury if it was initially compromised by arthritis or other disease. Bones are thin, tissues are stiff, and recovery is slow in the elderly. Early rehabilitation is extremely important, both for restoring and maintaining the patient's physical independence. Prevention of further injury involves more than just "fixing" a fracture. Hospital discharge and postinjury planning is crucial. Home health aids, Meals on Wheels, visiting nurses, home therapists, and others are utilized to ease the transition and to speed acclimation at home. Home evaluation surveys to prevent recurrent or aggravating injuries are helpful, noting the need for wheelchairs, canes, bedside commodes, bathroom and stairway railings, and removal of scatter rugs.

INTERVIEW

When an elderly patient is seen in the office setting, the chief complaint is often pain, but may also include deformity, spasm, or joint stiffness. Reduction of function may cause frustration and resentment of a process over which the individual has little or no control. Resentment and/or the fear of lost independence may make an older person nervous and difficult to treat.

Extra gentleness and reassurance must be a part of every interview. The physician must not rush in or out, or leave the patient alone in the exam room for a long time. A hurried interview will make any patient more agitated and apprehensive. During history-taking, gently turning, touching, or massaging the injured area will often put the patient at ease and facilitate physical examination. It is necessary to explain the problems and proposed treatment in layman's terms. Patients do not remember all that the physician says and will remember even less if explanations are in complicated medical terms. Written instructions coupled with practical demonstrations are necessary to enable the older patient to carry out the recommended exercises. Reviewing the exercise in the office, before the patient leaves, may also reveal patient problems that preclude certain exercises. Instructions from a staff member or practical teaching by a physical therapist are helpful. In prescribing exercises, therapy, or medication for a certain injury, the physician must remain aware of the person as a whole, including previous injuries, past and present medical history, present medication, economic issues, psychosocial factors, and nutritional status.

The emergency room setting only exacerbates the anxiety and agitation the patient may feel. Often, he or she has been waiting for hours before the x-rays are taken, the diagnosis is made, and the specialist has arrived. A few extra minutes to reassure the patient and allay his or her anxieties is well-spent time and may facilitate the examination.

REHABILITATION

Rehabilitation attempts to return the patient to a preinjury level of functioning. Careful assessment must be made of the nature of injury or surgery and potential of each patient. Rehabilitation programs must begin immediately and be directed toward the whole patient. A hip fracture may necessitate non-weightbearing for 1–3 months, during which time independent mobility may be lost because of lack of upper body strength, instability of Parkinsonism, fear of falling, etc. Special problems affecting rehabilitation potential must be addressed preoperatively, if possible. Exercise programs and walker instructions are very beneficial before elective lower extremity surgery. Rehabilitation goals must be reassessed periodically while the patient is healing. It is important when treating the elderly to tailor a rehabilitation program to the individual patient and not order cookbook programs applicable to a younger patient. Reassurance, periodic evaluations,

home visits by physical therapists and social service workers and assessment of family or friend support systems are necessary. Fear, uncertainty, and even hostility may prevent a patient from following any rehabilitation program. Impaired mental status, deafness, and blindness may hamper a patient's progress, as may pulmonary or cardiovascular diseases.

HEALING FACTORS

Bone density and strength decrease with age. Osteoporosis and osteomalacia are common in the elderly and seem to be a function of increased bone resorption rather than of decreased bone formation (1). Calcium and protein intake and absorption are being studied as potential causes of loss of bone density, as well as effects of estrogens, exercise, and dieting in weight control. It is certain that the loss of mineral bone density in the elderly has multiple causes. With decreased density and strength, bones are more easily fractured as a result of falls and minor trauma. This fact, combined with the decreased mobility and stability of the elderly partially explains the high incidence of fractures and deformities in this age group. However, the elderly are quite capable of healing their fractures and do so with rapidity and voluminous callus. Unfortunately, the elderly are often osteoporotic before fracture and have bones already at risk. Immobilization and reduced activity secondary to fracture cause more osteoporosis and increase subsequent risk. Pain in the fracture area may increase both elements. Therefore, while the elderly may heal the fracture well, the underlying weak bone may require longer protection and more graduated rehabilitation than in a younger person.

TOTAL JOINT REPLACEMENT

As the older population increases, the effects of trauma, medical conditions, and normal wear and tear on joints are more pronounced. Many older persons are candidates for the pain relief and functional improvement afforded by total joint replacement (Fig. 28.1A and B).

Total joint replacements may loosen or wear out and need to be replaced in 2–10 years, depending on the joint replaced, the activity and weight of the patient, and the type of bone-cement-metal fixation. The patient is cautioned against having unrealistic expectations, such as complete restoration of former activity levels and life-style. Pain is the major reason for replacement, not the restoration of nor-

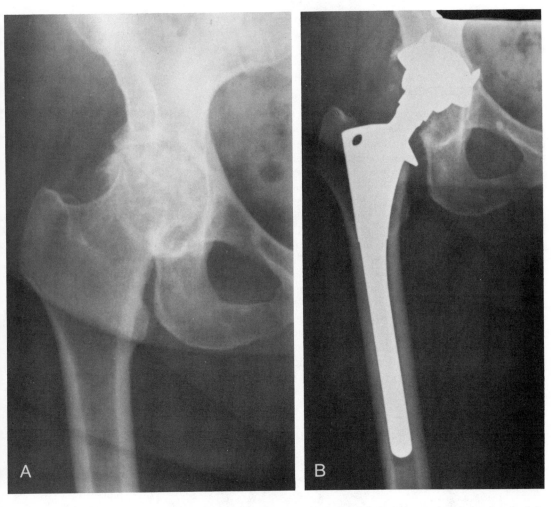

Figure 28.1A. Severe degenerative joint disease of hip; cartilage has been eroded, joint is nearly ankylosed, and pain is severe. **B.** Postoperative total hip replacement; function and length have been restored and patient now walks without pain.

mal movements nor the ability to play a certain sport or, for example, to jog. A middle-aged to elderly patient with restricted motion but no pain is better advised to wait until pain is a significant factor and interferes with his or her life-style and well-being before considering total joint replacement, other medical factors being equal.

While total hip replacement is an appropriate treatment for some acute femoral neck fractures, a cemented endoprosthesis is preferable in most cases. It provides good stability, less postoperative pain, and easy conversion to a total hip replacement if necessary. Endoprosthetic replacement entails considerably less surgery and reduces the incidence of the complications of embolism, infection, and

heterotopic bone formation. The morbidity and mortality rates of total hip replacements were twice as great as in endoprosthetic replacements in the acute fracture. With better techniques, anesthesia, and equipment, this ratio has been reduced, but a statistical difference still exists.

Today's state-of-the-art in joint replacement is quite good in total hips and good in total knees. Total shoulder replacement will relieve pain but all types compromise motion and strength to some degree. Total elbows, ankles, and wrists are salvage procedures at present and have been disappointing in long-term follow-ups. Finger joint replacement for rheumatoid arthritis and other medical and traumatic joint diseases has been quite good. The strength is less, the range of motion is moderate, but pain is relieved. Technical advancements continue to improve motion, pain relief, and compatibility of joint replacements.

UPPER EXTREMITY INJURIES

A principal purpose of the upper extremity is functional placement of the hand. Impaired mobility of the shoulder, elbow, or wrist can be compensated by the remaining two joints. Proper positioning and/or maintenance of a functional range of motion of the wrist, elbow, or shoulder after injury will prevent disability of the hand. Sufficient strength and range of motion are usually regained, allowing satisfactory function, but special attention to the adjacent uninjured joints is important in preventing stiffness, such as a frozen shoulder. Reflex sympathetic dystrophy (persistent vascular spasm) can occur and require aggressive physical therapy, nonsteroidal anti-inflammatory drugs (NSAIDs) and sometimes sympathetic nerve blocks. Constant motion of the extremity, elevation and compression to reduce edema, and the use of appropriate analgesics and NSAIDs can generally relieve these conditions. The physical function of the elderly may be restricted before the injury. Previous injury, ar-

thritic deformity of the fingers, flexion contractures of the elbow and decreased strength of the arm and hand, etc. must all be assessed by history and compared to the present evaluation. This will give a general direction to the goals of rehabilitation.

SHOULDER PAIN

Shoulder pain (Fig. 28.2) can be confusing to the examiner. Potential causes in the elderly include minor or major trauma, strains or overuse syndromes, arthritic changes, and degenerative changes secondary to medical disease. Soft tissue pain must be differentiated from degenerative joint pain and those from metastatic disease by the history and physical, x-rays and bone scan, etc. Subacromial bursitis, biceps tendinitis, adhesive capsulitis, and rotator cuff tears can mimic one another, cause significant pain and disability, and may be refractory to treatment.

Subacromial bursitis is caused by pinching and recurrent compression of the bursa between the edge of the acromion on one side and the rotator cuff and humeral head on the other. The patient has pain on attempted abduction of the arm against resistance and on direct palpation of the bursa.

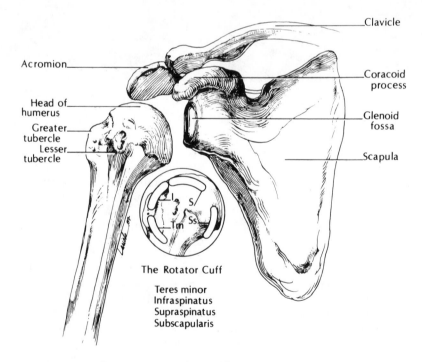

Figure 28.2.   Bony anatomy of the shoulder joint—anterior view.

Biceps tendinitis results from an irritation of the long head of the biceps tendon in the bicipital groove from trauma or degenerative disease. It causes significant pain in the region of the insertion of the pectoralis major, especially when the patient is trying to do overhead work. The patient avoids lifting heavy objects and tries to keep his or her arm by the side with the elbow flexed. Abduction is painful and other movements of the shoulder are limited. To test for biceps tendinitis, have the patient pronate the forearm and flex the elbow to 90°. Grasp the patient's wrist and ask him or her to supinate against resistance. When pain is localized to the anteromedial aspect of the shoulder, Yergason's sign for biceps tendinitis is positive.

Selective injection of Xylocaine into the bursa or along the tendon with resultant relief of pain will often distinguish one from the other. Ice, rest, NSAIDs, physical therapy and a sling for support while the irritation subsides are helpful. Physical therapy usually includes heat and phonophoresis (ultrasound with steroid cream). Recurrences are not uncommon, but may respond well to steroid injection and/or the above therapies.

Adhesive capsulitis is a progressive and painful tightening of the shoulder joint that restricts motion in all directions. Fifty percent of cases have a traumatic history, whereas the rest have no specific inciting incident. As motion becomes more painful, the patient self-limits his or her movement, setting up a vicious circle of pain and decreased motion. Eventually, the process will completely reverse, but this takes 2–3 years. The diagnosis is made by history and restricted movement in all directions. Treatment is aggressive physical therapy, NSAIDs, and reassurance for 1–6 months. Shoulders that are not responding to treatment within 4–10 weeks and are constantly painful may require closed manipulation under general anesthesia to break up the adhesions. This will usually start the patient on the road to recovery over 1–3 months.

Rotator cuff tears in the older population are usually extensive, happen with minimal trauma, and result from chronic irritation and thinning of the avascular area of the supraspinatus tendon under the acromion. The size of the tear and the activities of the patient will dictate how much instability ensues. Common problems are inability to work overhead and to abduct the arm with any strength. Pain is variable and located just below the acromion process. In a complete rupture, active abduction above 40° is impossible, passive abduction is full and usually painless, and once positioned, the arm can be held in a vertical position by deltoid contraction (abduction paradox). In partial ruptures of the supraspinatus, active and passive abduction are usually abandoned because of pain located at the insertion of the deltoid muscle that often radiates down the lateral aspect of the arm. It occasionally travels down the dorsal forearm as far as the wrist. Many older patients are able to adapt their life-styles and activities to limited motion and strength below shoulder level. Those with chronic pain and significant loss of motion may require decompressive acromioplasty and/or a rotator cuff repair. The results vary with the size of the tear and the quality of the tissues used in the repair. Full function is usually not regained in the older patient, but a painless and moderately functioning shoulder is possible.

Occurring primarily in middle-aged and older men, "Popeye" muscle deformities are caused by rupture of the long head of the biceps tendon just below the humeral head or at the radial attachment (Fig. 28.3). They are accompanied by a sharp pain in

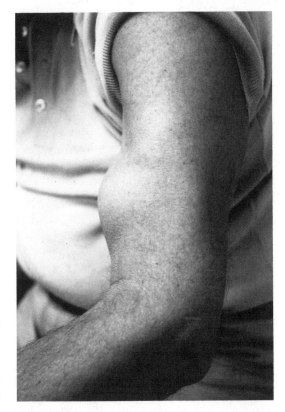

Figure 28.3. "Popeye" muscle—the tendon of the long head of the biceps is ruptured at the shoulder. Attempts at flexing the biceps caused the muscle to contract into a ball.

the upper arm and result in mild to moderate edema and ecchymosis. It is common for the elderly patient to appear at the doctor's office weeks or months after injury, wondering about the "bump" in the arm, but without complaining of any functional loss. Operative repair is rarely warranted and is only indicated in the first 2–3 weeks, after which scarring precludes an acceptable result. Even without surgical repair, the patient usually regains 90% of strength and a full functional range of motion with only a minor cosmetic deformity.

Thoracic outlet syndromes must be considered in the differential diagnosis of shoulder pain. Subclavian vessel and brachial plexus compression with certain positions of the upper extremity may cause weakness and aching. It is more common in middle-aged patients. Frequent causes of compression are scalene muscles, cervical ribs, and direct trauma to the base of the neck. Various degrees of sensory and/or motor and/or vascular abnormalities can occur in the affected extremity. Treatment is directed at relieving the offending pressure.

Differential diagnosis of shoulder pain must rule out neoplastic disease such as an apical lung neoplasm with either pain from the tumor itself extending to the arm, or metastatic lesions from breast or prostate. Pain and/or swelling and the absence of trauma must raise the suspicion of neoplasm. X-rays revealing pathologic fracture or bone destroying lesions confirm this suspicion. Definitive diagnosis is established on biopsy. Internal fixation to prevent pathologic fractures or to stabilize an existing fracture provides good palliation and comfort.

HUMERAL HEAD AND NECK FRACTURES

Humeral head and neck fractures are common in the elderly (Fig. 28.4). Bone in these areas lacks strength and is unable to withstand a fall on the outstretched arm. Impacted fractures are usually stable, minimally displaced, and may or may not be comminuted. Pain is not prolonged. Exercises are begun early and the overall result is good. Nonimpacted fractures are less stable, moderately displaced, and can be comminuted or noncomminuted. Pain is prolonged, exercises are delayed, and the fracture may require closed or open reduction. The end result is less satisfactory.

Some deformity and less operative treatment are acceptable in older persons and disimpaction of the fracture to achieve exact anatomic realignment rarely improves the functional result. Even malaligned but impacted fractures will be stable enough to begin careful range of motion exercises within

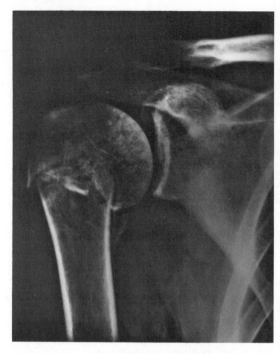

Figure 28.4. Comminuted, impacted, slightly angulated fracture of the humeral head. The articular surface is intact and the overall functional result should be good.

7–10 days. Careful instruction and counseling regarding the injury, the method of treatment, and the expected results are important. Generally, treatment is nonoperative, emphasizing protection and support in a Velpeau sling with early guarded mobilization. Pendulum (Codman) exercises, described in the next paragraph, should begin at 1–5 days depending upon the degree of pain and the status of the fracture. Overhead strength and mobility will be partially lost varying with the patient's age, type of fracture, and response to rehabilitation. However, ordinary activities of daily living, such as eating, dressing, hair combing, and others below 90° or shoulder level are almost always recovered.

Home exercises must be carefully taught and demonstrated to the patient and family or friends who will be with the patient. Long-term physical therapy is seldom necessary, but repeated instruction and encouragement by physical therapists early in the course of treatment are beneficial. The physician should inform the patient that edema and ecchymosis of the upper arm and even of the forearm and hand often occur with this injury. Range of motion exercises of the elbow and wrist are as necessary as those for the shoulder to prevent stiffness. The usual progression of home shoulder exercises begins with pendulum (Codman) exercises, advancing to pulley exercises, walking up walls with the fingers to improve abduction, and combing of the hair and scratching the small of the back repeatedly to improve rotation. Pendulum (Codman) exercises are designed to negate gravity and are done by bending over 90° at the hip, putting the good arm on a table for support and swinging the affected arm in gentle and increasingly larger circles for 1–5 minutes, 5–10 times per day. These exercises should start with the arm in a sling and then progress out of the sling as the range of motion increases and the arm feels better. Rope or pulley exercises are designed to allow the good arm to help elevate the injured one, thereby facilitating gradual protected range of motion exercises for the injured arm, joint, muscles, and bone. A rope or towel is placed over a hook or a door, both sides of the towel are grasped as high as possible, and each arm is alternately raised and lowered. As with many postfracture courses, improvement begins slowly, then progresses rapidly, and the last 15% of improvement can take up to a year. It is important for the practitioner to maintain an optimistic but realistic attitude during this time and to encourage the patient to do the same.

FRACTURE/DISLOCATION OF THE HUMERAL HEAD

Fracture/dislocation of the humeral head poses special problems in the elderly. Pre-existing arthritic changes and comminution of the humeral head may compromise any treatment that is carried out. Open reduction of the dislocation is often necessary because no leverage can be applied directly when the humeral head is comminuted and the shaft is broken at the surgical neck. Severe edema of the shoulder and comminution of the humeral head also frustrate reduction and alignment. Open reduction and internal fixation with wires, screws, or plates is difficult unless the fragments are of respectable size and the bone quality is sufficient. The underlying osteoporosis may thwart even this effort. Placing the fragments in good position with the articular surface turned toward the glenoid and treating the injury as an unimpacted, comminuted humeral head fracture may be all that is possible. Long-term prognosis remains guarded. When the comminution and displacement preclude a satisfactory result, early prosthetic replacement is worthy of consideration.

Dislocated shoulders with avulsion of the greater tuberosity occur equally in the elderly and young, but again, special difficulties occur in the elderly when the joint is arthritic and the head or the greater tuberosity is also fragmented because of the underlying osteoporosis. Treatment falls into two categories; those needing closed reduction and those needing open reduction and internal fixation. Fragments not displaced into the joint space usually will go back into close proximity to the original fracture site when the shoulder joint is reduced. This shoulder will function well when healed, although abduction may be limited by the position of the fragments under the acromion. If the avulsed greater tuberosity remains displaced inside the joint after closed reduction, open reduction and internal fixation is required.

Both of these injuries are then treated with a Velpeau sling followed by careful pendulum exercises in 7–10 days. Attention is again paid to elbow and wrist motion while the shoulder is healing. The prognosis depends upon the preinjury status of the glenohumeral joint, the degree of injury, and the response to rehabilitation. Partial loss of motion, especially above shoulder level, is not unusual.

DISLOCATIONS OF THE SHOULDER

More than 95% of all shoulder dislocations are anterior (Fig. 28.5) and occur when the person falls on the outstretched arm, forcing the shoulder into abduction and external rotation, and levering the

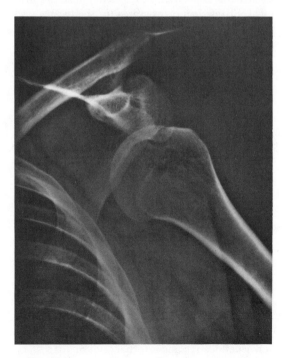

Figure 28.5. Anterior and inferior dislocation of the shoulder.

humeral head anteriorly out of the joint. The patient with an anterior dislocation typically presents after a fall with loss of the normal rounded contour, a prominent acromion, the arm held in internal rotation and pressed to the side, and all attempts at movement painful. Neurovascular integrity must be determined by checking pulses and testing sensory and motor distributions of the median, ulnar, and radial nerves. The most common complication is axillary nerve injury with loss of sensation near the insertion of the deltoid muscle and absence of deltoid and teres minor muscle contraction. An anteroposterior (A/P) and lateral or transthoracic x-ray should be obtained. An axillary view will also help identify the position of the dislocated humeral head.

Closed reduction uses three methods, all preceded by steady traction on the arm in abduction to reduce muscle spasm before any reduction is attempted. The method favored by the author is that described by Stimson. The Stimson, Kocher, and Hippocratic methods are well described in standard orthopaedic texts.

In the postreduction period, the shoulder is immobilized in a Velpeau sling for 3 weeks, then taken out of the sling and used actively for all motions below shoulder level or 90° of abduction for the next 3 weeks. For the entire 6 weeks, the patient should sleep in the Velpeau sling to prevent redislocation at night. Strengthening exercises for the biceps, pectoralis major, and anterior deltoid muscles are instituted early. Pendulum exercises are begun within 1 week to prevent stiffness, but range of motion exercises for the wrist and elbow are started immediately. The patient should refrain from abduction and external rotation movements as much as possible for 3–4 months to maximize the chances of preventing redislocation.

The frequency of recurrent dislocation in the elderly is dependent upon the severity of the dislocation and associated injuries around the shoulder, but is much less common than in the young. Ninety percent of those 20 years of age may experience recurrent dislocation, but less than 20% of those 50 years of age will redislocate. Recurrence in those older than 50 years is even less common. Complicating factors, such as a tearing of the anterior glenoid labrum (Bankhart lesion) or a compression fracture of the posteromedial portion of the humeral head (Hill-Sachs lesion) may lead to chronic instability requiring operative repair. Short- and long-term care, including operative treatment, is designed to restrict abduction and external rotation for a specified period of time. Operations include combinations of muscle/tendon shortening, bone blocks, and tendon transfers. Surgery is successful in preventing redislocations in over 93% of the patients, but range of motion and endurance of the shoulder is often decreased for over-the-head work.

Posterior dislocations of the shoulder in the elderly do occur, but are uncommon. The major problem of a posteriorly dislocated shoulder is that of misdiagnosis, because the A/P x-ray of a posterior dislocation can appear normal. Axillary or tangential views are used to verify the dislocation. Reduction of a posterior dislocation can be difficult and should be referred to the orthopaedic surgeon. After reduction, the shoulder must be immobilized in a sling and swathe. Chronic instability may necessitate operative repair.

An occurrence unique in the elderly is the long-term, dislocated shoulder, which may be unnoticed by nursing home personnel or family at home. It may not be reported by the patient, who is either unable to communicate the problem or considers it a minor disability or a sprain that eventually will get better. The humeral head is lodged beneath the coracoid and the patient has relatively little pain. The range of motion is surprisingly good, lacking primarily abduction beyond 60° and external rotation beyond 50°. There is an obvious defect in the shoulder where the humeral head should be. Edema may be present, but it is usually minimal in the chronic dislocations. Closed reduction without general anesthesia is difficult and sometimes impossible. Reduction often accomplishes very little. The range of motion may improve slightly, but the joint may become painful or begin to dislocate repeatedly. If the range of motion is moderate and painless, the dislocation has been present for more than 2 weeks and the patient can do most activities below shoulder level without difficulty, then aggressive efforts to reduce the dislocation by closed or open means are seldom warranted. If the patient has continuous pain and restricted motion to the point of disability, closed or open reduction under general anesthesia may be considered.

ACROMIOCLAVICULAR SEPARATIONS AND FRACTURED CLAVICLES

"Separated shoulders" are uncommon in the elderly and are often confused historically with shoulder dislocations. Questioning the patient regarding the method of injury usually will differentiate the two conditions. A separated shoulder refers to disruption of the acromioclavicular (AC) joint, involves the AC ligament and the coracoclavicular (CC) ligament, and occurs by falling directly on the acromion or point of the shoulder and forcing it downward. Three grades of injury thus occur:

Grade I   — Only the AC ligament is stretched;
Grade II — The AC ligament is torn, the CC ligament is stretched, and the tip of the clavicle may be slightly elevated;
Grade III— The AC ligament and CC ligament are ruptured and the tip of the clavicle is elevated giving a prominent bump to the shoulder.

Treatment is almost always nonoperative. Strength recovery is good and pain is usually minimal. If the AC joint becomes chronically painful and measures such as NSAIDs or local steroid injections give no relief, distal resection (Mumford procedure) of the clavicle can be effective.

A fracture through an osteoporotic clavicle is a common occurrence in the elderly from a fall striking the posterolateral surface of the shoulder, pushing the shoulder forward and snapping the clavicle that acts as a strut for the shoulder. Treatment with a figure-of-eight clavicle brace results in good healing in 3–8 weeks. Several simple tactics will make the patient more comfortable. A clavicle brace should be tightened periodically by the family over the first 4–5 days. It does not have to be tightened immediately and is much more comfortable if tightened gradually as the swelling and spasm decrease. Mark the clavicle straps to gauge the advancement of about 1 inch on each side per day until the brace is moderately tight or "comfortably uncomfortable." Have the patient sleep in a semi-sitting (semi-Fowler's) position either in a recliner chair or on a reading pillow for the first week for comfort. Place a folded sheet or narrow pillow between the shoulder blades to support the center of the back up to the occiput and prevent the bed from pushing the shoulders forward against the brace. Encourage the patient to put his thumbs under the brace, like thumbs under suspenders, to (a) push the shoulders back for comfort and healing; (b) relieve pressure on the neurovascular structures in the axilla; and (c) air out the axilla to prevent chafing from the brace. For the first 5–7 days, no motion will be comfortable; for the next 5–7 days, pain will occur with sudden and major movements; after that, the patient will be relatively comfortable. The clavicle brace should be worn full-time for 3 weeks and then may be removed for bathing and replaced. Clavicle fractures routinely heal in all age groups, but may take slightly longer in older patients than in younger patients and should be braced until healing is complete.

HUMERAL SHAFT FRACTURES

Fractures of the humeral shaft occur in the elderly with direct trauma or a fall, with or without twisting, resulting in various combinations and degrees of comminution and angulation. Splintering of osteoporotic bone is common. Appropriate immobilization allows union to occur rapidly within 3–6 weeks. A hanging cast is the traditional treatment for humeral shaft fractures and, while cumbersome for some, is an effective and proven modality. Hanging casts are only applicable in patients who can adjust to sitting up much of the time, allowing the cast to hang, thus pulling the fracture fragments into longitudinal alignment. Lying down causes loss of traction and the usefulness of the cast is negated. Repeated angulation of the fracture leads to a fibrous nonunion. A Velpeau cast or dressing is a useful alternative. A Velpeau cast is utilized to splint and secure the arm to the side of the body with pads and rolls of gauze around the arm and the torso. While effective and comfortable, it does require once-a-week changing to prevent skin breakdown under the arm and in the axilla. It is a less effective treatment for overriding and shortening fractures that lengthen with hanging cast treatment.

Intramedullary pin fixation is an effective method in a few displaced and noncomminuted mid and lower shaft fractures. This is most appropriately used in relatively nonosteoporotic bone when there is unstable displacement of horizontally fractured ends. Therefore, its use in the elderly patient is limited. This can achieve early alignment, early motion, good healing, and increased comfort. The pin is electively removed under local or general anesthesia after several weeks or months.

Another very effective treatment modality is the fracture brace, a form-fitted, heat-molded plastic brace that conforms to and supports the humerus. This can be used as a primary treatment, or after any of the above operative treatments in the mid and lower shaft fractures, allowing early protected motion and healing.

Complications of humeral shaft fractures are radial nerve injury, malunions, and delayed or fibrous nonunions. The radial nerve, which wraps around the humeral shaft, must be evaluated for injury, especially in displaced proximal one-third fractures of the humerus. Injury to this nerve is the most common nerve complication of humeral shaft fractures causing wrist drop and the inability to extend thumb and finger metacarpophalangeal joints fully. Spontaneous recovery of the radial nerve is the rule and the wrist, thumb, and fingers may be splinted until that recovery occurs. The humerus can tolerate malunions with shortening and angulation very well. Rotational deformities may cause problems and require derotational osteotomies because of the inability to get the hand toward the mouth or in certain directions. Delayed or fibrous nonunions are the most common complication of humeral fractures and may require operative fixation with bone grafting to heal the fracture. Fracture braces may be especially valuable in long-term nonoperative care.

SUPRACONDYLAR FRACTURES

Treatment methods for supracondylar fractures of the humerus depend upon the integrity of the elbow joint, i.e., the humeral/ulnar joint. If the distal humerus is split in a "T" fashion, open reduction and internal fixation are indicated. Evaluation of neurovascular status is critical before and repeatedly during treatment. Manipulation, reduction, and posterior splinting or casting will suffice for most pure supracondylar fractures. Use of olecranon pin traction for difficult fractures or those with moderately severe perielbow edema is an effective alternative. In the elderly, however, this type of treatment should not be used routinely. It requires a patient to be in bed too long and osteoporosis, stiffening of joints, and exacerbation of medical problems may result.

ELBOW DISLOCATIONS

Elbow dislocations are not uncommon in the older patient. They occur as the patient falls backward on the outstretched hand, hyperextending and dislocating the elbow posterolaterally. The olecranon is prominent posteriorly and the arm is held in semiflexion. The elbow should be packed in ice in a comfortable position until reduction is attempted. In uncertain cases, feel the points of the olecranon and the medial and lateral condyles. If the elbow is extended, these three points will be in a straight line. If the elbow is flexed to 90°, they should form an equilateral triangle. If not, then the elbow is dislocated. The dislocation and the reduction are confirmed with A/P, lateral, and oblique radiographs. Draw a straight line on the x-ray through the radial shaft and head and extend it through the center of the capitulum. If this line does not go through the center of the capitulum on *all views and at any angle*, then the elbow remains dislocated.

The complications of elbow injury in the elderly depend upon the status of the underlying tissues. Fragments of osteoporotic bone in the joint may require removal. Already delicate skin may tear or slough after elbow injury. Pre-existing arthritic changes and muscle stiffness may compromise the result. Although permanent neurovascular impairment is rare, the status of the arm should be assessed before treatment is instituted, after reduction, and during the first several days. The five "P's" of neurovascular compression (pain, pallor, pulselessness, paralysis, and paresthesia) should be recognized. However, the best indicator of an impending compartment syndrome, secondary to a fracture, is the sixth "P", painful passive extension of the fingers. If this occurs, compartment syndrome must be suspected until disproven. Immediately remove all splints and compressive dressings and extend the elbow to 10° or 15° of flexion. Elevate the arm. If there is no improvement, fasciotomy is necessary before irreversible muscle and nerve damage occurs. Volkmann's ischemic contracture is a disastrous and preventable sequel of unrecognized neurovascular compromise.

Early motion is essential in the treatment of dislocated elbows. Without it, the elbow will be stable but restricted. Within 7–10 days, the patient is taught active range of motion exercises in the sling in order to better extend and flex the elbow and rotate the forearm. Avoid passive stretching as it irritates elbow structures and actually decreases the range of motion regained. Loss of full extension is common, but this is rarely a functional disability.

OLECRANON INJURIES

Olecranon fractures occur from a direct fall or blow to the flexed elbow. Undisplaced olecranon fractures are treated with casting and early motion in 1–3 weeks, avoiding a long immobilization. A palpable "gap" in the bone indicates the more common displaced fracture which requires open reduction and internal fixation. Internal fixation allows early active range of motion within 3–7 days and nets excellent results. Minimal loss of full extension is a frequent but minor complication. Other complications, such as stiffness and pain, often depend upon the amount of comminution and the status of the reduction.

Traumatic olecranon bursitis is rare in the elderly. It is a contusion of the point of the elbow causing enlargement and fluid formation in the bursa. It may appear dramatically edematous and infected looking with induration and redness, but a culture of the aspirate is negative. The problem will resolve in several days to weeks when treated with ice, NSAIDs, time, and avoidance of further contusion. Rheumatoid arthritis and other medical diseases may inflame bursas. Treatment is directed to the underlying disease process. Chronically inflamed and enlarged bursas may be excised.

RADIAL HEAD AND NECK FRACTURES

Radial head and neck fractures occur when the patient falls directly on the hand and force is transmitted through the forearm to the radial head. Pain and edema occur over the radial head, accompanied by decreased flexion and extension and decreased pronation and supination because of pain or displaced fragments. Impacted radial head and neck fractures are treated with a short immobilization period and early active range of motion exercises. Displaced fractures require open reduction, excision, or prosthetic replacement if they physically restrict rotation of the forearm. A loss of some pronation is easily compensated, but loss of supination poses a larger problem and requires more aggressive treatment. Some mild loss of extension and full rotation is to be expected. If arthritic changes develop, later excision of the radial head will be helpful with relief of pain, although recovery of full motion is rare.

When the patient falls directly on the flexed forearm, the ulna may fracture and displace the radial head anteriorly. The treatment of this "Monteggia" fracture is by open reduction and internal fixation of the ulna and reduction of the radial head. Radial head reduction is again confirmed on x-ray by drawing a line through the radial shaft and the head that must pass through the capitulum.

FOREARM FRACTURES

Forearm fractures result from falls on the hand or direct trauma to the forearm. Edema and deformity may be clinically present at the fracture site, or the deformity may be much more subtle. In the elderly, nondisplaced distal and midshaft forearm fractures are treated with a long-arm cast, giving careful attention to the neurovascular status. Repeat the x-rays each week to detect any collapsing of the radius and ulna toward one another because this causes significant loss of forearm rotation. Displaced fractures require open reduction and internal fixation. Even then, some pronation-supination ability may be lost. Exact fracture management is described in several authoritative texts, for example, Rockwood and Green (12).

Rehabilitation for forearm and elbow fractures requires active and passive exercises, such as holding the wrist in a pronated position for 10 seconds with slight tension, then in supination, and repeat-

ing. This will gain rotation if it is carried out on a routine basis. Range of motion exercises for the wrist and shoulder should also be carried out.

WRIST

Wrist fractures from falls onto the outstretched hand are extremely common in the elderly. The distal radius and ulna are the weakest points of the upper extremity and have thin cortices with mostly cancellous bone. Colles' or posteriorly displaced fractures of the distal radius are the dinner-fork deformity fractures, so-called because the side view contour of the broken wrist resembles a dinner fork. Anteriorly displaced (Smith's) fractures and intra-articular (Barton's) fractures of the distal radius are less common, but not rare. Often associated with a fracture of the ulnar styloid, Colles' fractures are noted for a moderate degree of postreduction loss of position because the posterior cortex is often comminuted and provides little postreduction support. Fortunately, the wrist tolerates mild to moderate angulation while retaining a good functional result. In the majority of cases, closed manipulation and reduction under local or general anesthesia will restore alignment. A short- or long-arm cast is applied with the wrist in flexion and ulnar deviation and then trimmed to allow metacarpophalangeal joint motion. The fracture is immobilized 5–6 weeks, after which intensive range of motion exercises are started. In the more comminuted, unstable fractures, internal fixation or an external fixator is used. Physical therapy is helpful. Finger exercises, which were started immediately and continued during and after the immobilization period, are important for strengthening. Squeezing a rubber ball will increase gross hand strength and rough motion, but the patient must also squeeze a cloth or something very small while making a fist and get the fingers into the palm for closer grip strength and fine motion. "Silly Putty" works very well for this. The immediate and major postreduction problem is edema distal to the fracture site. Gordon's sling, a stockinette taped to the cast, will keep the hand elevated above the elbow at night, the time when postreduction edema most often develops. The stockinette is attached to a hook on the wall with the elbow resting on the bed and the hand elevated at right angles to the bed. Other techniques for preventing edema and postimmobilization stiffness include placing the hand on top of the head, reaching for the sky several times a day, and actively moving the fingers as if waving. Passive finger exercises are also important. Range of motion exercises for the elbow and the shoulder are included in the patient's instructions.

Besides stiffness of wrist and fingers and angular deformity of the wrist, a major complication is median nerve compression causing a carpal tunnel syndrome. If the patient has unremitting pain and numbness into the median nerve distribution of the hand, edema or a fracture fragment may be compressing the nerve in the carpal tunnel canal. Cast change, positional change, or a formal carpal tunnel release may be required early in the course of treatment. Late releases may also be required.

HAND INJURIES

Fractures of the metacarpals and phalanges are not common in the elderly and are usually minimally displaced when they do occur. Stiffness and functional loss often arise because the injury is superimposed upon a pre-existing deformity or arthritic change. Protected motion as early as possible reduces these problems. Treatment for extra-articular fractures of the metacarpals is short-term, handcast immobilization with active exercises in a buddy splint for the fingers (one finger taped to the other in two areas) for 2–3 weeks followed by a circumferential strapping for the metacarpals. Phalangeal fractures are treated with a finger traction hand cast for 2–3 weeks followed by active motion in a buddy splint. Buddy splinting for both injuries should be done in as much flexion as possible, for it is the grip that needs to be restored. Extension of the fingers will return and slight loss does not cause a functional disability. Loss of finger flexion, and therefore, grip strength, does cause functional loss. Intra-articular fractures require reduction with nearly anatomic alignment and/or open reduction with fixation. The postoperative course is the same as for a closed injury.

Fractures of the thumb are divided into impacted nondisplaced fractures and displaced fractures. Impacted, nondisplaced, or relatively nondisplaced fractures of the thumb can be treated with thumb spica immobilization for 2–3 weeks. The thumb has good mobility and compensates well for minor angulation and/or stiffness. Displaced thumb fractures require pin fixation by closed or open means especially for the displaced intra-articular fracture of the first metacarpal base (Bennett's fracture). This fracture is inherently unstable and will migrate proximally without fixation.

Proximal interphalangeal (PIP) joint dislocations are almost always posterior and should be reduced and held in a flexion splint for 5–10 days and then begun on flexion exercises with a buddy splint. Again, extension will be regained over time, but flex-

ion needs to be actively pursued. Permanent residual swelling around the PIP and the distal interphalangeal (DIP) joints is a rule, but usually does not interfere with function, only with the wearing of rings on that finger.

Mallet fingers, or baseball fingers, are avulsion fractures or ruptures of the extensor tendon at the base of dorsum of the distal phalanx, allowing unopposed flexion of the DIP joint. The DIP joint is splinted in extension for 3–6 weeks. The principal complications of treatment are stiffness and pain, especially in the already arthritic finger. Functional loss, with or without treatment, is minimal.

TRUNK INJURIES

Rib fractures are common in the older population, partly because of osteoporosis and partly because of increased frequency of falls in the older age group. Direct palpation over the fracture site will cause pain but remote palpation on the fractured rib will move the fracture and also cause pain at the fracture site. This will help distinguish a fractured rib from a contusion of the chest wall. Strapping may be used to support the rib cage, but should not mechanically impair respiratory excursion. When two or more ribs are fractured, admission to the hospital is advised for observation and stabilization. Treatment is usually symptomatic. Intercostal nerve blocks may be needed for severe pain. The physician must be aware of the adjacent internal structures. For example, an injury to the lungs or liver or spleen may lead to pneumonia and/or pneumothorax or internal bleeding. If there is any suspicion of internal injury, chest x-rays or serial hematocrits are obtained, as well as liver and spleen scans. Splinting of the rib cage from a fracture not uncommonly causes pneumonia. Incentive spirometry, deep breathing exercises, and mild analgesics may be required.

Falls and automobile accidents cause most of the pelvic fractures in this age group. Evaluation of the supporting columns, i.e., a weight-bearing line drawn through the hip joint, the ilium, the sacroiliac joint and up through the spine, dictates weight-bearing stability and mobilization factors. Most pelvic fractures are only mildly displaced. Bedrest from several days to 2 or 3 weeks and then gradual mobilization is usual. Major traumatic injuries to the pelvis are life-threatening with a 10–50% mortality rate from blood loss, cardiovascular failure, and local complications such as infection. Immediate care in a major trauma center is mandatory.

Complications of pelvic fracture include prolonged pain from ligament disruption and fragmentation of bone—especially around the symphysis pubis and sacroiliac joints. A walker or a cane, medication, and reassurance over time is tried at first. Treatment of these complications after prolonged local care may be operative, but is beyond the scope of this chapter.

SPINE FRACTURES

Acute onset of back pain in the elderly is vertebral compression fracture until proven otherwise. Osteoporotic bone in the vertebral column is particularly susceptible to this injury. A sudden blow or fall on the buttock may cause a compression fracture, but the cause may be far more subtle, such as a sudden twist of the body or a missed step. Typically, the pain of a vertebral compression fracture is acute, but gradually improves over 5–20 days. Often patients may not even seek medical help and old compression fractures are picked up on an x-ray done for some other reason. An appropriate period of bedrest, followed by stabilization with a brace or body cast, mild analgesics, and protected mobilization with a walker or cane is the usual sequence in treatment. If appropriate, early resumption of activities will lessen the increase of osteoporosis. Treatment of compression fractures necessitates the awareness of complications. Paralytic ileus, secondary to spine injury, occurs frequently, and is manifested by loss of bowel sounds, bloating, nausea and vomiting. A nasogastric tube or rectal tube for decompression and keeping the patient without food until the bowel sounds recur, are usually all that are necessary to treat this complication. Neurologic deficits must be detected and treated. X-ray evaluation of the neural canal must be correlated with clinical evaluation of the patient to assess neurologic compromise. Any questionable compromise of the spinal canal may require tomograms, CAT scans, or magnetic resonance imaging (MRI) for definitive diagnosis before treatment.

A new and accurate method of gauging a patient's vertebral bone density is the dual photon absorptiometry (DPA). DPA compares patients against an age-matched population and computes the relative risk of fracture. DPA provides a reliable and reproducible serial comparison and is the test of choice in evaluating the progress of any planned or ongoing treatment for osteoporosis.

COCCYDYNIA

Coccydynia represents pain from a fracture or contusion resulting from a fall directly on the coc-

cyx. With either diagnosis, treatment is nonoperative and often prolonged. The patient should sit on a pillow or a rubber ring at all times, use a high soft chair, do stretching exercises, take NSAIDs, and have patience. Because several months to a year or more may be necessary for the discomfort to resolve, these patients need constant reassurance of eventual relief. Coccygectomy is a salvage procedure and its results are equivocal.

FRACTURES OF THE ACETABULUM

Fractures of the acetabulum involve the posterior, medial, and superior surfaces and must be suspected after hip trauma without a fracture of the proximal femur. When there is direct horizontal trauma to the flexed knee while sitting or falling, the femoral head is driven posteriorly and punches out the posterior wall of the acetabulum. This is a common, so-called "dashboard" injury. The femoral head is typically displaced posteriorly to the acetabulum, so the patient presents with a thigh that is flexed, shortened, internally rotated, and virtually "locked" in that position. All attempts at movement are painful and meet with resistance. The pre- and postreduction X-ray evaluation of this injury is very crucial and sometimes difficult to achieve. The patient must lie on the affected side on the x-ray table. He or she is then turned approximately 45° anteriorly so that a tangential view of the posterolateral surface of the affected acetabulum can be taken. Reduction may require general anesthesia. Nondisplaced fractures can be treated closed and immobilized for several weeks with a Bermuda shorts walking cast that keeps the leg and hip straight and stable. If the posterior fragment is unstable, the femur will be unstable and dislocate posteriorly while sitting or bending over. This injury will require open reduction and internal fixation of the posterior fragment.

Medial wall fractures are the result of direct trauma to the greater trochanter or the lateral side of the femur, driving the femoral head medially into the acetabulum. Pain and restricted motion are present in all attempts at movement. Distal skeletal traction is the treatment of choice. If the nondisplaced fracture is not recognized and treated, the femoral head will migrate medially and protrude into the pelvis. Operative reduction may be necessary in these fractures or when the femoral head is locked inside the pelvis or the medial wall remains displaced after reduction of the femoral head.

Forces transmitted directly upward through the femur to the acetabulum, such as from jumping from a height, result in superior dome fractures that compromise the weightbearing capability of the hip joint. Full motion may be present, although painful. The treatment is nonweightbearing for 8–12 weeks and may include open reduction and internal fixation to restore the integrity of the dome. Inability of many elderly patients to comply with the nonweightbearing regimen compromises many long-term results because of displacement of the fracture fragments. Stiffness may ensue and some will develop arthritic changes within a short time. Periodic x-rays are necessary to identify any collapse or displacement because displacement of medial and superior surface fractures can necessitate difficult reconstructive total hip replacements.

LOWER EXTREMITY INJURIES

Lower extremity injuries involve more than just treatment of the affected area. In the elderly, a fracture or serious injury to the hip or leg may mark the end of independence or significantly decrease a patient's mobility. Upper body strength may not be sufficient for the use of crutches or a walker. The ability to drive, go up and down stairs, go to the toilet, or make one's dinner, and even the ability to answer the phone, may be compromised. Evaluation of the home and family support situations, use of Visiting Nurses Association or nurses aides, physical therapy, strengthening exercises for the upper extremities, Meals on Wheels, or temporary placement in a nursing home are among the many supports to consider when treating lower extremity injuries in this age group. In a significant number, acute disability will last 6–20 weeks. This must be foreseen and appropriate home and social services planning and referrals provided.

All of the problems and complications that occur in lower extremity injuries can be found in the treatment of hip fractures. Among these are shortening, rotation, infection, fibrous nonunion and non-weightbearing for several weeks or months. The strength of the arms and of the good leg is tested as well as balance, motor coordination and sensation, stamina, and judgment. Rehabilitation potential is also tested. Many studies have been done to try to develop preoperative rehabilitation predictors. Several preoperative factors have been shown to be of significance and were rated on a scale of 1–100 (3). Some of these are:

1. Mental awareness (status);
2. Independent ambulation;
3. Social interaction inside the home;
4. Social interaction outside the home; and,
5. Age.

In general, those who were mentally alert preoperatively were alert postoperatively. These patients better understood the nature of the injury and the demands for rehabilitation. Those who were independent ambulators before surgery most often achieved a comparable level of ambulation postoperatively. Those who had participated in outside activities and were active at home preoperatively, most often returned to preoperative activity levels after the surgery. Evaluation by age discerned a natural division between "young old" and "old old." Old old begins at 80–85 years and is characterized as less healthy, less productive, and less independent than the young old. They have greater needs in all areas and require more time to improve their level of functioning. The old old tend to have lower preoperative assessment and lower postoperative recovery scores. By evaluating these and other parameters, an estimate of the level of functional return can be given to the family and social worker to facilitate posthospital planning.

Immediate postoperative mortality is a concern in elderly patients with hip fractures. Six-month mortality estimates of 15–50% have been reported. In a 10-year Minnesota study of 456 persons over age 60 years (5), 32% of the women and 17% of the men sustained a hip fracture before age 90 years. The 4-month postoperative fracture mortality rate was 12% higher than an age-matched population without hip fractures. After 4 months, the mortality rate of both groups was the same. Other studies have verified that age is directly related to mortality rate (8). These mortality rates after hip surgery persist even though aggressive operative treatment has definitely decreased the mortality rate over nonoperative treatment. Historically, many patients with hip fractures and treated nonoperatively, would succumb to complications of pneumonia, emboli, pressure sores, and infections. Among those treated operatively, the mortality rate was less but still substantial, especially in the first 6 months after surgery. Advances in anesthesia, fixation devices and joint replacement metallurgy have helped reverse this statistic, giving the patient a 60–90% chance of a long-term, postoperative survival. The importance of preoperative and postoperative medical stability in keeping the mortality rate and morbidity rate down cannot be overemphasized. A significant number of the elderly admitted for hip fractures have medical problems that are untreated or require updated evaluation before they can tolerate the trauma of surgery (4). A recent study has even correlated lower serum albumin with fixation failures in hip fractures. While the stability of the fracture and the position of the hip screw were the direct causes of fixation failure, the high correlation of low serum albumin with those that did fail, suggests that nutritional supplementation may reduce the failure rate. Surgical fixation or hip replacement in the first 24–48 hours, followed by early mobilization, lessens the complications and allows for easier nursing care, faster recovery, and rehabilitation. The present attitude is more surgically aggressive toward these fractures, thus decreasing the mortality and morbidity inherent in long-term, nonoperative treatment.

HIP FRACTURES (PROXIMAL FEMUR FRACTURES)

Hip fracture is the "fracture of the elderly." It is the most common injury and reason for hospitalization in the elderly and causes more long-term disability than any other injury. Definitive treatment of hip fracture within the first 24–72 hours, early ambulation, and physical therapy have combined to reduce the morbidity, hospitalization time, and recovery time, but the problem is still significant.

Hip fractures usually result from falls. The patient has pain and inability to bear weight on the affected limb and all attempts at movement are painful. The leg is characteristically shortened, slightly flexed, and externally rotated.

Hip fractures are divided into three categories: subcapital, intertrochanteric, and subtrochanteric fractures (Fig. 28.6). Subcapital fractures involve the area of the femoral neck and are stable or unstable. Stable fractures are impacted in slight valgus, heal well, and internal fixation with threaded pins gives an excellent result. Unstable fractures are displaced in a varus position, roll posteriorly and shorten, and do not heal well. Unstable subcapital fractures are best treated by replacement with endoprostheses, that is, prosthetic hip joints without an acetabular replacement. Endoprostheses last for 2–10 years without the need for conversion to total hips to alleviate pain, depending upon the bone stock and the activity of the patient. Theoretically, ambulation can begin immediately. In practice, partial weightbearing for 4–6 weeks is advised. Painless, but somewhat decreased motion is usual in these patients. Femoral neck fracture in the elderly has its own special complication—aseptic necrosis of the femoral head. The blood supply to the femoral head is already reduced and is then further compromised by the fracture. Reasonable efforts should be made in the younger (55–70 years old) patient toward retaining his or her own hip, even with slight displacement and the increased chance of aseptic necrosis and further surgery. In a patient over 70 years of age with a displaced fracture, an endoprosthesis is the

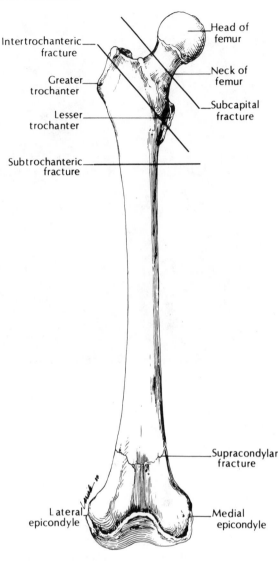

Figure 28.6. Anterior view of right femur showing anatomic designation and levels of hip fractures.

treatment of choice. Any patient who, for mental or physical reasons, would be unable to tolerate a nonweightbearing status and/or later surgery is also an excellent candidate for an endoprosthesis.

Intertrochanteric fractures involve the area along a general line between the greater and lesser trochanters of the femur (Fig. 28.7A). They are usually displaced and require open reduction and internal fixation, most often by a sliding hip compression screw and plate, which allows mechanical and functional impaction and fixation (Fig. 28.7B). Healing is prompt over 2½–3 months and fixation devices are of such quality as to protect most fractures from

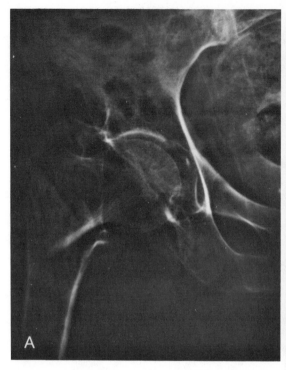

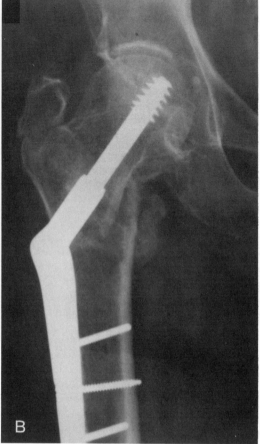

Figure 28.7A and B. Comminuted and displaced intertrochanteric fracture of the femur. Fracture fixed with sliding hip compression screw. Alignment has been restored.

displacement. The patient remains nonweightbearing for 8-10 weeks, during which time range of motion exercises of the hip are encouraged. Partial weightbearing with a walker and/or crutches then commences and should progress to full weightbearing by 12-16 weeks. Complications are uncommon, but would include delayed union, malrotation, and stiffness.

Subtrochanteric fractures, those below the lesser trochanter, are mechanically unstable and require either intermedullary fixation or a long side-plate fixation. These fractures need a longer healing time, closer follow-up, extended weightbearing protection and have a risk of refracture in the early stages. Delayed union is not uncommon in these fractures and may require later bone grafting.

FEMORAL SHAFT FRACTURES

Femoral shaft fractures usually result from significant direct trauma, for example, an automobile accident or a fall from a height, etc. The leg is edematous, shortened, and lies in external rotation. Femoral shaft fractures respond well to skeletal traction, followed by hip spica cast or a cast brace to give a solid and satisfactory union. This enforced immobilization, however, increases morbidity in the elderly. Internal fixation with intermedullary rods or compression plates, though preferable, has to be weighed against the condition of the patient and quality of the bone. Osteoporotic femurs may splinter from attempts at internal fixation, complicating an already difficult situation. The application of a cast brace, with or without surgical fixation, will allow earlier mobilization and reduced morbidity. Nonweightbearing and partial weightbearing continue for 4-9 months, depending upon the fracture, the fixation, and the quality of the bone. Delayed union occurs occasionally, but loss of hip and knee motion is more frequent. The most acute concern is blood loss. A femoral fracture allows the escape of 2 units of blood into the thigh at once. Vital signs must be monitored, fluid replaced, and blood pressure stabilized as needed.

SUPRACONDYLAR FRACTURES OF THE FEMUR

Supracondylar fractures of the femur (Fig. 28.6) occur as a result of direct trauma or by a fall with a twisting motion. Deformity and malalignment just above the knee are usually evident. Minimally displaced fractures can be treated with traction and cast bracing. Surgical treatment is preferred if alignment and displacement are a problem and after the usual factors of age, medical and physical condition, and bone stock are considered. Cast bracing after closed or open reduction enables earlier ambulation. Complications include malalignment and entrapment of the quadriceps in the healed fracture site. A displaced, intra-articular fracture must be internally fixed for the knee to be functional. Malalignment of a supracondylar fracture changes the normal tracking of the extensor mechanism and alters the weightbearing forces through the knee. The possible results are painful catching of the patella against the femoral condyle, early patellofemoral and/or knee compartment arthrosis and decreased extensor strength. When the muscle is caught in the fracture site, there is inability to flex the knee fully actively or passively, or to extend the knee fully actively (extensor lag). Extensor lag causes instability with walking on levels or declines, difficulty in ascending or descending stairs, and problems rising from a sitting position. Inability to flex the knee at least 90° impairs the ability to walk up the stairs or to sit easily. The patient has to step over the stair when climbing or kick the leg out in front of him to sit down, literally dropping into the chair.

These impairments can be devastating to the individual who was functioning independently before the injury. Early protected mobilization is helpful to reduce this complication, but closed manipulation may have to be considered when a significant loss of the range of motion is present at the 4- to 8-week level.

PATELLAR INJURIES

Patellar injuries in the elderly are usually the result of direct trauma from a fall or automobile accident. The knee area becomes very edematous and the patient is unable to extend the knee against gravity or any weight. There is often a palpable transverse defect in the middle of the patella. X-rays confirm a patellar fracture, ranging from nondisplaced to wide open and shattered.

Nondisplaced patellar fractures with good quadriceps function can be treated with a long-leg cast and knee immobilizer for 3 weeks, followed by grad-

ual knee flexion exercises for 4 weeks. The knee immobilizer is used for comfort during that time. Walking is encouraged during the first week after the fracture.

Displaced fractures require open reduction and internal fixation to restore strength and stability. Loose, comminuted fragments should be excised. If large fragments are present and provide a stable articular surface, they should be preserved and the extensor mechanism repaired. The inferior pole can be discarded, but if more than two-thirds of the patella is severely fragmented, a patellectomy may be necessary.

In an older person, forceful contraction of the quadriceps mechanism to prevent a fall may rupture the quadriceps just proximal to the patella. Inability to extend the knee and a palpable defect in the muscle just above the patella confirm the diagnosis and indicate a need for operative repair. Postoperatively, a knee immobilizer is used for 4–6 weeks. Graduated knee flexion exercises and quadriceps-setting exercises are begun at 2–3 weeks. Rehabilitation often takes 6 months or more but the results are usually quite good.

TIBIAL PLATEAU FRACTURES

Tibial plateau fractures are compression injuries that depress the central portion of the medial or lateral tibial plateau. These fractures occur when a sudden force is directed upward through the foot and the leg, compressing the knee joint at an angle, as with a fall from a height and landing directly on the foot. The lateral tibial plateau is more often affected than the medial plateau. X-rays may show an obvious fracture but, in some cases, the findings may be much more subtle. A lateral x-ray of the knee may show a double density where the plateau on the affected side is below the plateau on the noninvolved side instead of overlapping and is indicative of a tibial plateau fracture. Open reduction and internal fixation is considered if the depression is more than 8 mm, the resulting angulation is greater than 5° of valgus and 10° of varus or widening of the fracture line and displacement of the tibial plateau indicates fragment instability. The entire corticocancellous bone complex of the tibial plateau is elevated and fixed with a plate, or a long-leg screw and washer. After a closed or open reduction, the extremity is kept in a long-leg, bent knee cast for 3 weeks, followed by 3–5 weeks of range of motion exercises, before any partial weightbearing is allowed. Graduated weightbearing then progresses over the next 4–8 weeks. Exercises for the muscles of the upper arms and both legs are instituted immediately to prevent stiffening and loss of strength due to disuse atrophy. Valgus and varus deformities may result, compromising ambulation in the older person. Bracing, canes, proximal tibial osteotomies, or partial or total knee replacement may then be required to restore satisfactory ambulation.

TIBIAL SHAFT FRACTURES

Direct trauma to the tibia from falls or accidents cause most tibial shaft fractures in the elderly. X-rays will reveal nondisplaced fractures or confirm obvious deformities. Treatment of tibial shaft fractures depends upon the degree of displacement and whether they are compound or simple. Casting, especially with the newer synthetic or fiberglass casting materials, can provide excellent and lightweight stabilization during the healing process. Open reduction and internal fixation can be used in difficult, unstable or displaced fractures. Off-center or bayonet alignment and some shortening can be tolerated, but proper rotational or angular alignment is critical to allow the elderly patient continued ambulatory independence. In the elderly, careful assessment of the neurovascular status, the condition of the skin, and the quality of the bone is necessary. Delayed or fibrous nonunions of the tibia are present at any age, but the added complications of pressure ulcers, diabetic or vascular skin breakdown, and osteoporotic bone are far greater in the elderly.

ANKLE AND FOOT FRACTURES

Ankle and foot fractures are very common in the elderly. A stone, a slippery walk, or a rug may cause a mis-step and a broken ankle or foot. Deformity and edema are usually present. X-ray will confirm the clinical opinion and note the extent of the fracture. If the ankle joint or mortise is disrupted (the talus is displaced from under the tibia), then the bony integrity and the ligamentous attachments of the medial malleolus, the lateral malleolus, and the posterior malleolus must be evaluated. If both bone and ligament are intact with the mortise disrupted, then a fracture more proximal in the leg must be suspected, almost always of the proximal fibula. Good alignment is mandatory, especially of the fibular malleolus that supports the ankle mortise. Closed manipulation is usually very successful in the older patient, but marginal reduction or displaced articular fragments require internal fixation. Delayed union can occur and ankle stiffness is frequent. Early protected weightbearing can help reduce these problems.

Os calcis fractures occur from a direct blow to the calcaneus, usually from a fall, or as in jumping from a height. Os calcis fractures are usually impacted, comminuted, and often disrupt the subtalar joint. X-rays will outline the extent of the fracture and the displacement. Closed or open reductions are infrequent and have inconsistent results. Postfracture edema may be striking and long-term disability from pain may result. If long-term disabling pain is present, a subtalar fusion or triple arthrodesis may be required to restore ambulation and independence.

Fifth metatarsal base fractures are one of the most common fractures in the foot and also are one of the more common of all fractures in the elderly. This is an avulsion fracture, resulting from a sudden contraction of the peroneus brevis tendon attachment to the base of the fifth metatarsal when trying to straighten the foot, when the foot is suddenly inverted. Displacement is usually minimal and this fracture responds well to a short-leg walking cast for 3–4 weeks. Delayed or painful nonunion is a complication that may require surgical correction.

Fractures at the metetarsal shafts usually occur from direct trauma or twisting. Good alignment must be maintained and the tendency of the metatarsal shaft to collapse realized. Special attention to supporting the arch in the cast will prevent this complication. It may also be necessary to delay weightbearing in the more unstable metatarsal shaft fractures. Painful and persistent soft tissue edema on the dorsum of the foot after a fracture, dislocation, or serious soft tissue injury may lead to the devastating complication of reflex sympathetic dystrophy. In the author's experience, more than one-half of patients with reflex sympathetic dystrophy of the foot had no fracture present.

Toe phalangeal fractures and dislocations result from direct trauma or "catching" the toe on a furniture corner or a rug. Both injuries should be reduced into good alignment and treated with buddy-splint taping and with attention to circulation. When the taping becomes more of a nuisance than the toe injury, it is discontinued. Edema usually persists for a lengthy period and may never fully resolve. Rarely, the fracture or dislocation is nonreducible and requires operative treatment.

SUMMARY

Treatment of musculoskeletal system injuries in the elderly differs from that of the young in that the practitioner must be acutely aware of the effect of pre-existing medical problems, psychosocial impact of injury, and potential complications on the morbidity and mortality of this patient population. He or she must consider physiologic aspects of aging, drug metabolism in the elderly, and problems of healing with age, and realize that the precarious homeostatic balance of elderly patients is easily upset. He or she must draw on both medical and ancillary hospital and community-based support systems to care for the total person as he concentrates on specific treatment and rehabilitation.

Acknowledgments. I wish to acknowledge the contributions of James Hitzrot, M.D., whose tireless editing and encouragement made this chapter possible. I am also indebted to Ms. Hunt Gressitt-Young, for her technical and editorial assistance.

REFERENCES

1. Adams, P, Davies T, Sweetnam P: Osteoporosis and the effects of aging on bone mass in men and women. *Quart J Med* 601:39, 1970.
2. Boyd HB, Salvatore JE: Acute fracture of the femoral neck: Internal fixation or prosthesis? *J Bone Joint Surg* 1066:46A, 1964.
3. Carey RG, Posabac EJ: Manual for the level of rehabilitation scale (LORS). Park Ridge, IL, Office of Evaluation and Research, Lutheran General Hospital, 1977.
4. Furey, JG: Complications following hip fractures. *J Chron Dis* 103:20, 1967.
5. Gallagher TC, et al: Epidemiology of fractures of the proximal head. Rock, Minn. *Clin Orthop* 150:163, 1980.
6. Katz S, Heiple KG, Downs D, Ford AB, Scott CP: Long-term course of 147 patients with fractures of the hip. *Surg Gynecol Obstet* 1:124, 1967.
7. Katz S, Jackson BA, Jaffee MW, Littell AS, Turk CE: Multidisciplinary studies of illness in aged persons. VI. Comparison study of rehabilitated and nonrehabilitated patients with fractures of the hip. *J Chron Dis* 979:15, 1962.
8. Kenzora JE, McCarthy RE, Lowell JD, Sledge CB: Hip fracture mortality. *Clin Orthop Relat Res* 186:45, 1984.
9. Kohn RR: Human aging and disease. *J Chron Dis* 5:16, 1963.
10. Lukins L: Six months after hip fracture. *Geriatric Nursing* 7:202, 1986.
11. Miller CW: Survival and ambulation following hip fracture. *J Bone Joint Surg* 930:60-A, 1978.
12. Rockwood CA, Green DP: *Fractures.* Philadelphia, JB Lippincott, 1975.
13. Rowe CR: The management of fracture in elderly patients is different. *J Bone Joint Surg* 1043:47-A, 1965.
14. Sartoris DJ, Resnick D: Age-related skeletal changes; What to look for on radiologic studies. *J Musculoskel Med* 4:12, 1987.
15. Sherk HH, et al: The Rx of hip fractures in institutionalized patients: A comparison of operative and nonoperative methods. *Orthop Clin North Am* 5:543, 1974.
16. Villar RN, Allen SM, Barnes SJ: Hip fractures in healthy patients. Operative delay vs. prognosis. *Br Med J* 293:1203-04, 1986.

CHAPTER 29

Foot Health for the Elderly Patient

ARTHUR E. HELFAND

GENERAL CONSIDERATIONS

The ability to remain ambulatory and provide a significant level of self-care may well be the single dividing line between institutionalization and/or remaining an active and productive member of society, thus maintaining the dignity of age.

Most foot conditions present in the elderly are the result of long-standing problems and/or residuals of chronic disease. The utilization of podiatric services should be based upon the condition present and the necessity for care.

Foot health is needed by the individual geriatric patient to:

Increase personal comfort
Lessen the possibility of medical and/or surgical complications
Reduce institutional care
Reduce the likelihood of hospitalization as a result of foot infection
Remove some of the stress and strain associated with foot discomfort

There are also many factors that contribute to the development of foot problems in the elderly, including but not limited to the following:

The degree of walking
The duration of hospitalization or institutionalization
Previous types of foot care and management
The environment
Emotional adjustments
Current medications and therapeutic programs
Associated systemic and localized disease processes
Past foot conditions and/or manifestations of systemic disease

The aging patient is usually more susceptible to local infection because of the anatomic location of the foot itself and the decreased vascular supply that is a part of the normal aging process, again magnified by the presence of disease. The atrophy associated with degenerative neuromuscular and musculoskeletal disease and the avascular status and neuropathic changes associated with diabetes mellitus and arteriosclerosis further complicate patient management.

The elderly patient's ambulatory status is often limited and/or compromised by his or her physical deterioration and environment, and by the social poverty that most elderly are faced with. The elderly patient usually has one or more chronic systemic diseases and tends to be more prone to injure his or her lower extremities. Thus, a minor problem in the young is a major problem in the old, a problem that requires early diagnosis, appropriate treatment and care, continuing management, and proper health education to prevent exacerbations of pre-existing conditions. One might even conclude that functional disability and ambulatory dysfunction are eventual problems in most elderly, which are magnified when foot problems coexist.

In addition to all of this, there are known risk factors in the elderly that relate to foot problems, which include but are not limited to the diseases or conditions listed in Table 29.1.

In conducting a podiatric examination, a prior occupational history should be developed to include excessive exposure, geographic activity, the percentage of weight bearing and walking, and those environmental concerns, such as the type of flooring and surfaces, for which exposure can be documented.

Table 29.1
Known Risk Factors Relating to Foot Problems

Diabetes mellitus	Cardiac disease and congestive heart failure
Arteriosclerosis obliterans	Hypertension
Ischemia	Edema
Chronic indurated cellulitis	Posttrauma
Lymphedema—secondary to disease (e.g., Milroy's disease, malignancy, etc.)	Leprosy
	Neurosyphilis
Bürger's disease	Hereditary disorders
Chronic superficial thrombophlebitis	Mental illness
Venous stasis	Mental retardation
Peripheral neuropathies	Thyroid disease
Malnutrition	Hemophilia
Alcohol, chemical, and substance abuse	Patients on anticoagulant therapy
Malabsorption	Poststroke patients
Pernicious anemia	Degenerative joint disease
Carcinoma	Gout
Toxic states	Rheumatoid arthritis
Multiple sclerosis	Arteritis
Uremia	Scleroderma
Chronic renal disease	Intractable edema
Chronic obstructive pulmonary disease	

The skin of the foot should be evaluated for xerotic changes, hyperkeratotic lesions, and any dermatologic abnormality. The toenails should be inspected for dystrophies, diseases, and, in particular, vascular changes, such as periungual infarcts and subungual hemorrhages. Infections of the skin and toenails should be reviewed and special notation should be made when atrophy creates pressure areas and ulcerations.

The vascular status of the foot should be noted, including, but not limited to, pedal pulses, color changes, temperature, trophic changes, edema, varicosities, night cramps, claudication, fatigue, and burning. Appropriate function tests should be completed when indicated, such as Doppler ultrasound studies, skin temperature, venous filling time, plantar ischemia, and oscillometric readings, which must be related to the total vascular system. The relationship of hypertension, cardiac disease, and diabetes mellitus is of particular importance in relation to care and prognosis.

The foot orthopedic and orthodigital evaluation should include a review of the foot type, gait, postural changes and deformities, contractures, ranges of motion, angulation, atrophy, and symptoms and findings in relation to palpation and function. This segment of the podiatric examination should include, as indicated, appropriate radiographic examination, including weight-bearing and nonweight-bearing studies and comparisons to permit reviews for pathology, pathomechanics, and biomechanics as well as function.

The review of the neurologic status should focus on gait abnormalities, balance, reflexes (patellar, Achilles, and superficial plantar), ankle clonus, vibratory sense, position sense, and reactions to light and deep touch, pain, heat, and cold, as well as other related impressions.

A primary consideration in the treatment plan is to provide some immediate relief for the patient's pain or primary complaint and an assurance of comfort as a long-range goal for management.

It should also be assumed that the podiatric examination of the patient, particularly when institutional, should form a part of the total patient evaluation, treatment record, and plan and that free communication and referral exist between all practitioners and elements of patient care to enhance total patient service.

COMMON FOOT PROBLEMS

ONCHYIAL DISORDERS

Hypertrophy, thickness, and hardening, resulting in discomfort and an inability to provide self-care, are usually the initial chief complaint of the elderly patient. This singular condition becomes magnified by impaired vision, an inability to bend, obesity, and an unsteady hand. Debridement needs to be completed, usually every 60 days, and special concerns need to be focused on the "at risk" patient.

Sudden **trauma** to the toenail can result in a subungual hematoma. In the immediate posttrauma period, pain is a significant factor. The excessive bleeding can be easily identified through the translucent nail plate. If the trauma is recent and hemorrhage appears red, a small hole can be drilled through the nail plate to permit evacuation of the fluid. In any case, radiographic examination should be considered to rule out any possibility of fracture. The nail may auto-avulse or the color change may persist until the entire nail is replaced, which may take between 6 and 10 months. Should the nail become onycholysed (free at the distal end) or onychomadesed (free at the proximal end), the loosened nail should be debrided. The presence of a circular dark area subungually, particularly in the absence of any reported direct trauma, needs to be differentiated from a subungual heloma (corn), subungual ulceration, or the possibility of a melanotic lesion.

It should also be noted that following any trauma to the nail matrix (root), there will be a subsequent thickening of the nail plate in the future. A severe injury to the nail matrix area may also cause a loss of the nail, starting at the proximal end (onychomadesis).

Toenails may also exhibit **Beau's lines**, particularly in the elderly patient. These transverse striations occur when there has been a temporary interruption in nail growth, usually following some strong physical or emotional change. Postmyocardial infarction and poststroke patients are more prone to this condition. In addition, subungual hemorrhage without the presence of trauma is another dystrophic nail change, common in the diabetic patient, the patient taking anticoagulants, and those patients with chronic renal failure or on dialysis.

Onychauxis is a hypertrophic thickening of the nail and is associated with aging, nutritional disturbances, repeated trauma, inflammation, local infection, and various degenerative diseases where there is a decreased vascular supply to the nail matrix and bed. The nail thickening is accompanied by discoloration as the translucency of the nail is lost. Onychophosis (callus in the nail groove), subungual hyperkeratosis, and subungual debris are common. The nail becomes free at the distal portion (onycholysis), which further adds to the collection of debris. Onychomycosis (fungal infection of the nail) is more common and is associated with a loss of nail integrity.

Treatment consists of periodic debridement of the nail plate and measures to address the cause. Topical antifungal solutions are appropriate with mycotic involvement. Partial avulsion is appropriate when ulceration is noted. The use of emollients containing 10–20% urea can be of value as a keratolytic agent. Once thickening has taken place, a return to the normal nail structure should not be expected.

Onychogryphosis (ram's horn nail) is a large, deformed, and hypertrophic nail that has been permitted to grow. Without treatment, changes follow the curvature of the nail as a result of shoe pressure. The toenails may become so long that they penetrate the plantar surface of the foot. The management is similar to that of onychauxis. When the nail deformity is extensive, the total and permanent removal of the nail and matrix may be advised.

Onychophosis (callused nail groove) is usually the result of repeated microtrauma on the nail plate from some external pressure and some related nail or soft tissue deformity.

Onychocryptosis (ingrown toenail) occurs when a fragment of nail pierces the skin of the unguilabia (nail lip). It can occur as a result of improper self-treatment or from an external trauma. As the toenail grows forward, the spicule penetrates the skin, resulting in inflammation (onychia), swelling, and infection, and, if protracted, periungual ulcerative granulation tissue develops. The use of antibiotics to control the infection without removing the nail from the soft tissue does not resolve the condition. Initial management consists of drainage of the superficial abscess and partial avulsion or excision of the penetrating nail segment. Saline or povidone-iodine compresses can be utilized by the patient. In addition, culture and sensitivity tests should be completed as indicated, antibiotics utilized as indicated, and x-rays completed where there is significant infection. Topical antibiotics can also be used as part of the patient's self-care dressings.

Subungual heloma (hyperkeratosis) may result from pinpoint pressure on the nail bed. A subungual exostosis, spur or chondroma should also be ruled out by x-ray examination. The lesion usually appears as a dark spot beneath the nail plate and is painful on palpation. Management consists of debridement of the lesion and the removal of pressure, both external (from shoes) or internal. Subungual melanoma is the prime diagnosis to be differentiated.

Allergic manifestations in the ungual area may be due to repeated irritation, such as nail polish or shoe dyes. Inflammation (onychia) is usually present, followed by onycholysis (anterior separation of the nail from the nail bed). Treatment is directed toward eliminating the etiologic agent followed by anti-inflammatory agents and antibiotics, as indicated. Topical steroids are usually indicated along with mild astringent compresses. Subungual keratosis, when present, requires debridement and control with products such as Lac-Hydrin, Carmol 20, or Keralyt Gel.

In **poor nutritional states**, the nails usually become thin and brittle and lose their luster. Onychorrhexis (an exaggeration of the longitudinal line of nail attachment) is pronounced. Onychomadesis (separation of the nail from the bed proximally), and Beau's lines may also be present. Management should be directed toward better patient nutrition and the use of gelatin to help restore nail integrity.

Onychomycosis is a fungal infection of the nail that usually causes a severe disturbance of nail growth as the matrix and nail bed become involved. There is usually a significant amount of nail destruction with onycholysis. This condition is most common in the elderly patient and its etiology is related to not only the presence of the fungus, but to environmental factors, such as repeated microtrauma, darkness, and hyperhidrosis. The primary organisms are *Trichophyton mentagrophytes* and *T. rubrum*, and *Candida* to a lesser degree. Debridement and antifungals represent appropriate management.

In the superficial form, the dorsal surface of the nail plate serves as the invasive site. Small superficial white patches are generally well defined. These tend to coalesce and involve the entire nail plate. The dorsal surface of the nail plate then demonstrates trophic changes and a yellowish-brown color is noted.

Pyogenic nail infections can be caused by a wide variety of bacterial organisms. Inflammation, when present, demonstrates as onychia or paronychia. Management consists of compresses with povidone-iodine and appropriate antibiotics. The presence of chronic paronychia is also more common in the diabetic patient.

Neoplasms can also be domonstrated in the elderly patient in the onychial area. The differentials must also include verruca, subungual heloma, subungual exostosis, subungual chondroma, osseous spur, glomus tumor, fibroma, senile keratosis, and melanoma.

DERMATOLOGIC DISORDERS

The most common clinical signs associated with the geriatric skin of the foot include dryness, scaling, and atrophy. The etiologic factors are varied and multiple. They can be related to the normal aging process, systemic disease, and/or environmental factors. There is diminished sebaceous activity, diminished hydration and lubrication, metabolic and nutritional alterations, and dysfunction in keratin formation. There is an associated loss of hair and loss of skin elasticity, and the toenails become striated and brittle. There are multiple degenerative changes and pigmentary changes are common. The presence of any form of vascular occlusive disease, ranging from ischemia to cyanosis, may cause color changes. Increased deposition of hemosiderin is also frequently demonstrated. Adding to this is the stress of ambulation; keratin dysfunction becomes magnified as a reaction to pressure and as space replacement.

Pruritis is common in the elderly foot. It may be related to disturbed keratin formation, dryness, scaliness, decreased sebaceous activity, environmental changes, and defatting of the skin as a result of hot baths. It must be differentiated from chronic tinea and various forms of neurogenic and/or emotional dermatoses. Treatment should be directed toward moderation in bathing procedures and the use of emollients that lubricate and hydrate the skin. If tinea related, topical antifungals should be employed. Antihistamines in adjusted doses can also be employed to break the scratch reflex. Appropriate consideration should be given to male patients with prostate disease and those elderly patients taking multiple drugs in order to avoid drug interaction. Topical steroids are also of value in selected patients.

The complaint of **"dry skin"** is usually more often identified in the winter and colder climates. The use of emollients for hydration and lubrication provide relief. Oil and water baths are also of value. However, the patient should be cautioned that these products in bath water may make for a slippery tub, and caution must be taken to avoid falls.

Fissured heels can create a serious problem, particularly when there is an associated degree of vascular insufficiency and atrophy of soft tissue. Devitalized skin presents an excellent avenue for bacterial invasion and subsequent infection. Superficial tinea should be considered when there is diffuse keratosis in the marginal area of the calcaneal area. Atrophy of the skin and repeated microtrauma will also precipitate stress marks in the heel area, which provide the early signs of calcaneal fissuring. Management should be directed toward closing the fissures and preventing their recurrence. Emollients and the use of heel cups to reduce pressure should be employed, based upon the degree of soft tissue present and patient tolerance. Topical antifungals are indicated with mycotic infection. Antibiotics and reduced weightbearing should be considered with infection. With a diminished vascular supply, physical modalities can be employed to help local debridement and improve the local vascular status. Topical enzymes assist in the chemical debridement of the fissured areas. Local tissue stimulants may improve epithelization. Protection including the use of heel protectors and Plastizote sandals or shoes to reduce pressure and stress to the calcaneal areas during weightbearing and ambulation is also a consideration.

Hyperhidrosis is not as common in the elderly as in younger patients. When present, it may be associated with tinea, footwear, the use of stockings that do not absorb perspiration, shoe fabrics, and emotional factors. Local management involves daily foot hygiene and the use of an absorbent foot powder. Peroxide and alcohol swabbing and the use of 10% formalin solutions are also of value in resistant cases. Drysol (20% aluminum chloride) is another product that can be used topically with excessive perspiration.

Bromidrosis is a form of excessive sweating characterized by a fetid odor due to bacterial decomposition. The therapeutic approach is similar to hyperhidrosis. Deodorants and topical neomycin may be needed during the initial period of management. Shoes should also be changed daily and permitted to air dry in sunlight, when possible.

Superficial infections, or **pyodermas**, can be serious in the elderly and should be treated early in their development. Because of the various degenerative changes associated with aging, any break in the skin can result in infection. Treatment consists of tepid saline compresses, Betadine compresses, and appropriate antibiotics, topically and systemically.

Tinea pedis may present in any one of the clinical varieties: acute vesicular, subacute vesicular, chronic hyperkeratotic, and interdigital. Smears and cultures may be employed for identification but the clinical presentation should receive treatment. In the acute stages, astringent compresses and topical antifungals should be employed. Systemic antifungals tend to be more effective in the younger patient and in lesions other than the lower extremity. Castellani's paint or gentian violet are effective in interdigital areas but their color tends to mask the clinical signs. Clotrimazole, tolnaftate, undecylenic acid, iodochlorhydroxyquin, and haloprogin are examples of topical antifungals.

The vast majority of **ulcerative lesions** present in the feet of elderly patients are usually the result of pressure or biomechanical or pathomechanical dysfunction and are usually associated with a concomitant systemic disease, such as diabetes mellitus or peripheral arterial insufficiency. Associated angiopathy, dermopathy, and/or neuropathy are major contributing factors, as is atrophy of the plantar structures. Deformities related to joint change and degenerative joint disease are precipitating factors. Judicious debridement may be surgical or chemical, as indicated. Drainage should be established as indicated. The use of topical enzymes is of value when properly controlled. Antibiotics should be prescribed when infection is present and may be suggested as a prophylactic measure. Physical measures may be employed to assist in the healing phase. All attempts to remove weightbearing from the ulcerative site should be instituted. This may consist of the use of an orthosis, Plastizote sandals or shoes, surgical shoes, the Darby shoe, Thermold shoes, Extra Depth Inlay shoes, or molded shoes.

The ulcer in the diabetic patient is usually painless and accompanied by diffuse hyperkeratotic formation. The arteriosclerotic ulcer is generally very painful and will usually exhibit early and local necrosis and gangrene. The ultimate success of treatment depends on a proper diagnosis and management together with the full cooperation of all related health providers, the patient, and his or her family.

Localized pressure ulcerations may also be present and related to keratotic formation. There is usually a pressure area, subcallosal hemorrhage, and pain prior to the development of the ulceration. Local debridement and drainage, the removal of pressure, and the use of topical compresses such as tepid saline or Betadine promotes rapid healing. The key element is to employ methods to prevent such lesions from developing in the future.

BIOMECHANICAL AND PATHOMECHANICAL CONSIDERATIONS

Hyperkeratotic Lesions

Many of the most common foot complaints of the elderly patient are focused on the presence of hyperkeratotic lesions (corns and calluses). The types generally present include the heloma durum (hard corn), heloma molle (soft corn), heloma miliare (seed corn), heloma neurofibrosum (neurofibrous corns), heloma vasculare (vascular corns), and tyloma (callus). In the absence of overlying cutaneous disease, the lesions are usually symptomatic and secondary to some existing deformity or biomechanical or pathomechanical abnormality along with excessive pressure to a circumscribed and localized area. Lesions often develop as a result of incompatibility between the shape of the foot and direction of the foot, or flare, and the design of the last, or shaping mold, of the shoe. For example, most older people tend to walk with their feet in an outward-pointed position, which adds to stability and presents a wider base of support, similar to the young child.

Tyloma (callus) is a broad-based hyperkeratotic lesion that surfaces as a hyperplasia of the keratin layer and generally is associated with diffuse pressure. In any case, the formation of hyperkeratotic lesions represents the normal body reaction to external or internal forces that place stress on the skin of the foot as well as stress on the patient.

The degenerative loss of the plantar fat pad, digital contractures, spur and hyperostotic formation, arthritic changes, and functional adaptations are significant in the development of hyperkeratotic lesions. Usually, the initial skin lesion is tyloma (callus). Where the etiologic factor is permitted to continue and intervention and modification are not instituted to prevent, modify, or manage the problem, pressure becomes greater, a central nucleus develops, and a heloma (corn) is generated.

The heloma molle (soft corn) is an excellent example of such a progression. The usual etiologic factor is some change in the normal toe alignment that permits the head of one of the phalanges to be compressed on the base of an adjacent phalangeal or metatarsophalangeal articulation.

The approach to the management of hyperkeratotic lesions involves identifying the type of lesion, establishing the etiologic factors, and developing a proper long-range plan of therapy. As a result of degenerative changes that are part of the normal aging process, the residuals of chronic disease, and repeated microtrauma, management many times will include periodic debridement of the keratotic lesions. Weight-bearing radiographs are of value, when compared to non-weight-bearing positions. Initial management usually consists of debridement; the suggestion of an emollient to both hydrate and lubricate the skin and provide a mild keratolytic effect, such as Carmol 20 or Lac-Hydrin; and the use of protective padding to initially remove pressure. The involvement of the patient in a home care program is essential. The same is true for institutionalized patients.

Patients should be warned not to utilize any commercial "corn cure" products, which contain strong concentrations of acid for their keratolytic effect.

Various materials may be employed to help reduce pressure. These include the use of materials such as felt, foam rubber, sponge rubber, plastics, leather, and newer materials such as Plastizote, Spenco, Sorbathane, and other similar products that provide both weight diffusion and weight dispersion. Padding techniques of different types are employed for plantar orthotics, to help restore a neutral function of the foot. Crest padding and silicone molds may be utilized in the presence of digital deformities and contractures. Latex shields can also be employed for these deformities. If the patient is physically able, surgical revision should also be considered when the deformity is marked, when pain is persistent, and when such consideration can prevent future extension of the impairment and complications.

Footwear is also a consideration in the initial management of keratotic lesions, regardless of the etiology. When there is a clear shoe-related incompatibility, changes should be recommended.

Deformities

Digiti flexus, or hammer toe, may be present on any one or all of the lesser toes. The deformity results from a variety of factors that may include atrophy and/or contracture of the interossei, rotational deformities, enlarged interphalangeal joints, hyperostosis, and condylar prominence as a result of arthritic change. Pain is usually the result of inflammatory changes and may be associated with bursitis, capsulitis, and tendonitis. Heloma formation is common dorsally and distally and related to foot-to-shoe last incompatibility. Ulceration and possible sinus formation can be anticipated with continuous pressure to localized areas.

Management should be directed toward care of the keratotic and ulcerative lesions, changes in footwear, the use of protective orthotics, crest molds, silicone molds, and consideration of surgical procedures that revise and modify the deformity.

Hallux valgus is a complex of changes, symptoms, and deformities that are generally referred to as a *bunion deformity*. The condition usually involves some inward deviation of the first metatarsal (varus), outward deviation of the great toe (valgus), lateral displacement of the plantar sesamoids under the first metatarsal head, tendon contractures, adventitious bursa formation, rotation of the great toe, and some bony enlargement. In many cases, the rotational deformity coupled with the residuals of degenerative joint disease changes the stress of weightbearing and propulsion from the plantar surface to the medial aspect of the hallux, which increase the forces of deformity.

Management in the elderly patient should be directed toward the relief of pain and the restoration of maximum function rather than the cosmetic concern of the patient. Given the fact that the elderly female usually maintains a sense of style, patient concerns still need to be discussed so that an understanding can be reached that is best for the patient's total well-being. Because of the long-standing character of this condition in the elderly and its possible hereditary and degenerative etiology, conservative therapy should be considered initially. A bunion last shoe can be prescribed to help compensate and accommodate for the deformity. Orthotics and shields can be constructed to modify pressure to the joint. Local steroids and physical measures can be employed to manage the acute and subacute inflammatory process. Proper concern should also be directed to compensating, biomechanically, the associated rearfoot changes to help provide a more normal gait pattern. It should be noted that the longer the patient has the problem, the better chances are that the patient has made some adjustment in ambulation to compensate for the deformity. The various surgical procedures that have been identified to revise and modify the "bunion joint" comprise a text in themselves. Justification for surgical consideration should be based upon the symptoms present and the functional needs and general medical condition of the patient.

Hallux limitus appears clinically and radiographically as a monoarticular degenerative arthritis of the first metatarsophalangeal joint. When no motion is demonstrable in the hallux joint, the condition is termed *hallux rigidus*. It is many times associated with hallux valgus. Clinically there is a marked limitation of extension of the great toe due to dorsal and/or lateral lipping and spur formation at the periarticular segments of the joint. Movement creates a chronically inflamed joint, resulting in pain on movement, especially during the propulsive phase of gait.

Treatment, after appropriate radiographic examination, includes the use of analgesics, nonsteroidal anti-inflammatory drugs, physical modalities for pain, local steroid injections, and orthotics and shoe modifications to limit dorsiflexion or extension and trauma to the first metatarsophalangeal joint. A steel plate can also be prescribed for placement in the shoe, between the outsole and the insole, from the sulcus posterior to the head of the proximal phalanx to the sulcus posterior to the head of the first metatarsal head, which will limit motion in that area. An orthotic with the same configuration can also be utilized in place of the shoe modification. Surgical revision should be considered when conservative measures fail, in keeping with the functional needs of the patient.

Sesamoiditis can generally be managed with local steroid injections and physical modalities during the acute phase, together with the use of analgesics, mild heat, padding, and/or orthotics to suspend pressure and weightbearing from the area of involvement. The "dancer's pad," a $\frac{1}{4}$-$\frac{3}{16}$-inch felt pad applied to the foot, usually provides immediate relief. Thermold and Extra Depth Inlay shoes are excellent choices for footwear modification to provide for weight diffusion and weight dispersion.

Digiti quinti varus or tailor's bunion involves an inward deviation (varus) of the small or fifth toe and an outward deviation (valgus) of the fifth metatarsal, along with an enlargement of the fifth metatarsophalangeal joint. It is similar to the pathology involved in hallux valgus except for its anatomic location. The principles of management are similar to that of hallux valgus.

Foot Pain

Many patients will complain of diffuse pain in the ball of the foot. The term **metatarsalgia** has been utilized to describe the problem of pain in the metatarsal head area. An attempt should be made to identify the etiologic aspects of the symptoms. Some of the causes include a short first metatarsal segment or ray, hypermobility of the first segment, the loss of the anterior metatarsal fat pad, traumatic anterior metatarsal bursitis, tendonitis, tenosynovitis, capsulitis, and fasciitis, as well as the residuals of rheumatoid and degenerative arthritis. Gout, with which pain is severe enough to keep the patient awake at night, may also be a factor. Forefoot and rearfoot compensatory factors are also part of the etiologic considerations.

Management should be directed toward the cause, and in this case comparative weight-bearing and non-weight-bearing radiographs are of marked value. Physical modalities are indicated during the acute phase. Analgesics, nonsteroidal anti-inflammatory drugs, local steroid injections, and orthotic compensation for the biomechanical or pathomechanical changes will help reduce trauma and prevent future exacerbations of pain.

Where there are changes in the metatarsal length configuration, which produce a maldistribution of weight transmission during function, orthoses or molds that are functional in nature and either diffuse or redistribute weight may be utilized as the ultimate vehicle of choice.

Interdigital neuritis and neuroma (Morton's neuroma) may produce a burning pain that is exaggerated by compression, usually related to specific footwear. The patient generally complains of pain, radiating from the metatarsal head area to the distal portion of the toe, that is like an electric shock. Neuritis generally responds to conservative management. The neuroma will usually not respond to conservative management and requires surgical excision.

Heel pain in the elderly may be the result of multiple factors, one of which is an exaggeration and hyperostosis of the posterosuperior surface of the calcaneous, known as Haglund's disease. Pressure from the counter of a shoe tends to produce a bursitis (pump bump) between the tendoachillis and the posterior surface of the calcaneous. Plantarly, calcaneal spurs can be demonstrated on x-ray, and usually involve the medial plantar tuberosity, with an associated plantar myofasciitis.

The management of heel pain in the elderly patient includes the use of physical modalities, local steroid injections, analgesics, nonsteroidal anti-inflammatory drugs, and muscle relaxants when indicated, to control pain and spasm. Heel pads, heel cups (plastic or polyfoam), heel lifts, shoe modifications, and orthotics to reduce the percentage of weightbearing on the medial tuberosity of the calcaneous are also indicated. The primary aim of the biomechanical considerations is to provide some elevation in a superior, lateral and posterior direction, and the method and materials choices are secondary to the principle.

Traumatic Fractures

Trauma may produce fractures of the foot. Management consists of appropriate radiographic review followed by immobilization. Postfracture care is most important in the elderly because any degree of immobilization and prolonged disuse usually produces some degree of patient decompensation, functional disability, and ambulatory dysfunction. In many cases, fractures involving the foot that are not compound or significantly displaced can be immobilized by material other than plaster casts. Included in such considerations are surgical shoes, the Darby shoe, padding with shoe modification, splinting, and silicone molds, as well as the use of rigid protective materials. The use of isometric exercises in the cast, as indicated, will help reduce disuse atrophy and maximize the patient's recovery period. Key elements in the management of fractures involving the foot in elderly patients are future functional needs and their ability to adapt to treatment while maintaining their dignity and ability to function for themselves.

Miscellaneous Conditions

There are a variety of conditions present in the elderly that are residuals of earlier time periods and occupational activities. Some of these conditions have been classed under various clinical entities such as pes planus, pes valgo planus, imbalance, subtalar or calcaneal varus, forefoot varus, equinus, and plantar flexed first ray. When not of a congenital or inherited etiology, these acquired biomechanical and pathomechanical changes cause pain and discomfort that are modified by the functional needs of the patient. In most cases, physical modalities and exercises are of marked value.

Shoes and Orthotics

Shoe selection should meet the functional needs of the elderly patient and change to meet their desired use. Orthotics should be functional in character and provide accommodation and compensation for the existing conditions noted. Care must be taken to also provide for the loss of soft tissue, common in the elderly patient. When recommending a shoe for the elderly patient, one of two types of patients must usually be considered: the person who lives at home and goes about some form of normal life-style and community activity, and the patient who is confined to either his/her home or an institution and whose activity is significantly limited to residential necessities.

It should be noted that the "orthopedic shoe" is not corrective but rather compensatory in a limited manner, particularly for the elderly patient. Care must be exercised in the use of these shoes so that they do not become the "catchall" for other forms of appropriate therapy. Where deformity is extensive, as with the residual of advanced arthritic changes, and surgical revision is not possible to maintain the patient in some functional form, the Thermold shoe, the Ambulator, the Extra Depth Inlay shoe, or other similar shoes may be of marked value and provide a viable alternative.

When deformities such as hallux valgus or bunion exist, special shoes or modifications should be suggested to compensate for the deformed and altered foot contours. The "bunion last" is the best example of such a shoe. It provides a modified shape and additional soft leather, over the hallux joint, to permit the deformity to be housed without excessive pressure. The most important factor in shoe fit is a foot-to-shoe last (shape) compatibility.

Additional mention should be also made of the "molded shoe," which is a made-to-order shoe useful when special sizing and modifications are needed.

Its basic advantages are to reduce shock, provide a shape to fit the deformed foot, and provide a greater distribution of stress to help compensate for painful conditions. The Thermold shoe has similar qualities.

PEDAL COMPLICATIONS OF SELECTED SYSTEMIC DISEASES

It should be recognized that, although many diseases present foot symptoms as initial complaints, the usual response in the elderly is toward the overt abnormalities and a varied and sometimes confusing set of complaints and symptoms. The patient is often faced with complications arising from various and multiple sources all at the same time, which makes primary podiatric care for the elderly anything but "routine," no matter how common the condition. Foot problems, especially those related to systemic manifestations and complications, should not be taken lightly and should be managed to maintain the functional activity and total health of the patient.

Foot infection, with and without necrosis or gangrene, is by far the major complication in the elderly patient. In general, most of the etiologic aspects of foot infection can be classed in a reasonable number of categories:

Trauma, such as a cut, abrasion, or the result of crushing, blistering, or pinching that causes a break in the skin.
Neglectful acts, such as poor hygiene, poor-fitting footwear, foot-to-shoe last incompatibilities, and a lack of self-care due to functional disability and/or poor vision.
Changes due to the aging process of the skin, such as fissuring, dryness, hyperkeratosis, and atrophy.
Metabolic changes associated with systemic diseases, such as those seen in diabetes mellitus, peripheral vascular insufficiency, advanced arteriosclerosis, chronic renal failure, and decompensation.
Primary and secondary skin diseases.
The end result of *surgical procedures*, particularly when vascular impairment develops as a complicating factor.

Osteoarthritis or degenerative joint disease can usually be identified in the elderly patient in its primary form or secondary to trauma, inflammation, or metabolic changes. The primary findings in the foot include pain, stiffness, swelling, limitation of movement, and deformity. This usually provides some degree of functional disability and ambulatory dysfunction. Clinically, diagnostic associations may include plantar fasciitis, calcaneal erosions and/or spur formation, periostitis, osteoporosis, stress fractures, tendonitis, and tenosynovitis. When osteochondritis and avascular necrosis were present in youth, the end result is an arthritic joint in old age.

Existing deformities such as pes planus and pes cavus and digital deformities such as hallux valgus, hallux limitus, and hallux flexus provide increased pain, limitation of motion, and a reduction in the ambulatory tolerance of the patient. The primary factor to consider is that osteoarthritis in the foot is usually related and secondary to repeated microtrauma and may be precipitated by inadequate and inappropriate foot care at earlier ages.

Clinically, **gouty arthritis** may provide symptoms in any joint of the foot and should always be suspected where intense pain is present without trauma or precipitated by minimal trauma.

Rheumatoid arthritis in the elderly patient usually presents as the end result of the disease with exacerbations of pain, joint swelling, stiffness, muscle wasting, and marked deformity. Residual deformities of the forefoot include but are not limited to the following:

1. Hallux rigidus
2. Arthritis of the first metatarsophalangeal joint
3. Hallux valgus
4. Cystic erosion
5. Sesamoid erosion
6. Metatarsophalangeal dislocations, deformities, and hyperkeratosis
7. Digiti flexus
8. Fused interphalangeal joints
9. Phalangeal reabsorption
10. Extensor tenosynovitis
11. Rheumatoid nodules
12. Bowstring extensor tendons with valgus displacement
13. Ganglions

Residual deformities of the rearfoot include but are not limited to the following:

1. Talonavicular arthritis
2. Rigid pronated foot
3. Ankle arthritis
4. Subtalar arthritis
5. Tarsal arthritis
6. Subachilles bursitis
7. Subcutaneous nodules
8. Plantar fasciitis
9. Spurs
10. Achilles tendon shortening

Diabetes mellitus is well known to be complicated by multiple pedal manifestations. Very often foot symptoms appearing in an individual who is not known to be diabetic will lead to the detection of the disease itself.

Neurotrophic and diabetic ulcers in the elderly patient are usually resistant to treatment and require a multifaceted approach. They can often be prevented by appropriate management of pedal lesions and a realistic approach to preventive care and health education. For example, ulceration can be precipitated by continuous pressure causing focal vascular impairment, penetration of tissue with trauma, and continued friction with thrusting and shearing of the plantar structures. Rest of the part, control of any infection present, appropriate debridement (chemical and surgical), and the use of measures to remove weightbearing are indicated. A surgical shoe, Plastizote shoe, the Darby shoe, and orthotics are included in the principles of management.

Peripheral vascular insufficiency is present in the majority of elderly patients, at some point, in varying degrees. Overt indications of decreased arterial supply in the feet are muscle fatigue, cramps, claudication, pain, coldness, pallor, paresthesias, burning, atrophy of soft tissues, trophic dermal changes such as dryness and loss of hair, onychopathy, absent pedal and related pulses, and decreased readings in vascular function studies. Calcification can be demonstrated during the course of a diagnostic radiographic study ordered for other purposes. Arch pain is often mistaken for some pathomechanical problem and blamed on so-called arch problems, when the real problem is one of local ischemia and a lack of oxygen to the part. The final result of severe arterial occlusion is gangrene, many times self-demarcating. Environmental and personal habits that place the patient at risk should be eliminated.

Edema, either related to cardiorenal disease or dependency, may be the first indication of impending arterial complications. The loss of the anatomic landmarks is a significant finding, especially when accompanied by other clinical manifestations.

The patient leaving bed following a long period of hospitalization or immobilization should have adequate supportive measures for his/her feet and ambulatory system.

Paresis of the lower extremity, often the end result of a cerebrovascular accident, may result in foot drop, trophic changes and new weight-bearing areas on the foot, for which the individual may not be able to or may have difficulty compensating for. The changes in the ambulatory status include spasticity, which produces abnormal relationships with the plane of support, especially where residual deformity is present. Associated peripheral neuropathies produce changes in the normal position sense and induce trauma to the foot and lower leg as a result of a lack of coordination. The inability to functionally adapt to gait and related system changes provides situations that can turn minor foot lesions into ulcerations. In the poststroke patient, special care needs to be provided to the foot and shoe selection deserves serious consideration.

HEALTH EDUCATION

The information provided about foot care for the elderly patient would be incomplete if some attention were not paid to health education, which is the first form of preventive medicine. Health education must include more than the basic rules for foot care. It must begin to deal with the mechanics of delivery and the quality of service, standards of care, professional qualifications, continuing education, reimbursement for services, and motivation for concern and change.

SUMMARY

Podogeriatric management has as its prime concern the total patient and the appropriate utilization of all health-related personnel in the evolution of a team approach to patient care. The key element is making comprehensive care and services readily accessible to the elderly.

SUGGESTED READINGS

Baran R, Dawber RPR: *Diseases of the Nails and Their Management.* Oxford, England, Blackwell Scientific Publications, 1984.

Beaven DW, Brooks SE: *Color Atlas of the Nail in Clinical Diagnosis.* Chicago, Year Book Inc, 1984.

Calkins E, Davis PJ, Ford, AB (eds): *The Practice of Geriatrics.* Philadelphia, WB Saunders, 1986.

Davidson, JK: *Clinical Diabetes Mellitus.* New York, Thieme-Stratton, Inc, 1986.

Eisdorfer C (ed): *Annual Review of Gerontology and Geriatrics.* New York, Springer-Verlag, 1984, vol 4.

Helfand AE (ed): *Clinical Podogeriatrics.* Baltimore, Williams & Wilkins, 1981.

Helfand AE (ed): *Public Health and Podiatric Medicine.* Baltimore, Williams & Wilkins, 1987.

Helfand AE, Bruno J (eds): Rehabilitation of the foot. *Clin Podiatry* vol 1, no 2, 1984.

Jahss MH (ed): *Diseases of the Foot.* Philadelphia, WB Saunders, 1982.

Kozak GP, Hoar CS Jr, Rowbotham JL, et al: *Management of the Diabetic Foot.* Philadelphia, WB Saunders, 1984.

Levin ME, O'Neal LW (eds): *The Diabetic Foot,* ed 3. St. Louis, CV Mosby, 1983.

Libow LB, Sherman FT (eds): *The Core of Geriatric Medicine.* St. Louis, CV Mosby, 1981.

McCarthy DJ (ed): *Podiatric Dermatology*. Baltimore, Williams & Wilkins, 1986.

Neale, D (ed): *Common Foot Disorders, Diagnosis and Management*. Edinburgh, Scotland, Churchill Livingstone, 1981.

Reichel, W (ed): *Clinical Aspects of Aging*, ed 2. Baltimore, Williams & Wilkins, 1983.

Samitz MH: *Cutaneous Disorders of the Lower Extremities*, ed 2. Philadelphia, JB Lippincott, 1981.

Samman PD, Fenton DA: *The Nails in Disease*, ed 4. London, William Heinemann Medical Books, 1986.

Steinberg FU: *Care of the Geriatric Patient*, ed 6. St. Louis, CV Mosby, 1983.

United States Department of Health and Human Services, USPHS, NIH: *Feet First*. Publ No 0-388-126. Washington, DC, US Government Printing Office, 1970.

United States Government: *Final Report of the 1981 White House Conference on Aging*. Washington, DC, US Government Printing Office, 1981, vol 3.

Williams TF (ed): *Rehabilitation in the Aging*. New York, Raven Press, 1984.

Wilson LB, Simon SP, Baxter CR (eds): *Handbook of Geriatric Emergency Care*. Rockville, MD, Aspen Systems, 1984.

Witkowski JA (ed): Diseases of the lower extremities. *Clin Dermatol* vol 1, no 1, 1983.

Yale I (ed): *Podiatric Medicine*, ed 2. Baltimore, Williams & Wilkins, 1980.

Yale I, Yale JF: *The Arthritic Foot and Related Connective Tissue Disorders*. Baltimore, Williams & Wilkins, 1984.

CHAPTER 30

Endocrinology and Aging

URIEL S. BARZEL

Age-related changes occur in the endocrine system, as in all other physiologic systems (3, 8). Some of these changes are "silent" and do not lead to any observable physiologic or pathologic change in the elderly. An example of such a silent change is the diminished secretion of *growth hormone* during sleep, as well as its decreased secretory response to stress and to dopaminergic stimuli. Other changes may be of undetermined clinical consequence, such as the substantial increase in the blood level of *norepinephrine*, which may, however, be associated with decreased sensitivity of target cells to the hormone.

In the following chapter, the discussion is limited to those hormones and endocrine organs whose age-related changes result in clinically significant variations with which the gerontologist should be acquainted. Special attention is given to presentations of endocrine pathology that deviate in the aged from those seen classically in young or middle-aged adults.

Increased sensitivity of the "osmostat" is associated with a tendency to develop the syndrome of inappropriate release of *antidiuretic hormone* (ADH) by the posterior pituitary. *Thyroid* abnormalities in the aged, both hypothyroidism and hyperthyroidism, are much less likely to be associated with clinically distinct presentations than in the young adult. Determination of blood thyroxine (or, possibly, blood thyrotropin) level is key to the recognition of thyroid disease in the aged. *Hyperparathyroidism* in all age groups is frequently recognized at first by blood calcium elevation. The problem of management of the elderly with hyperparathyroidism in whom there are no symptoms and who suffer from little or no clinical complications is addressed in detail. *Adrenal* disease in the aged is not different than in the young and is discussed because its recognition is as important in the elderly as it is in the younger

patient. Age-related *gonadal* changes are of special significance for the elderly. The women are in a hormone deficient state, but men too have progressive changes in the function of their gonads. These result in elevation of gonadotropin levels and decreased semen production. *Prolactin*-producing tumors may go unrecognized in the elderly because their clinical expression is amenorrhea in females and infertility in both males and females.

POSTERIOR PITUITARY (NEUROHYPOPHYSIS)

PHYSIOLOGIC CONSIDERATIONS

The antidiuretic hormone (ADH) (1), arginine vasopressin (AVP), is synthesized in the hypothalamus, and transferred along nerve axons into the posterior pituitary where it is stored. The stored hormone is released in response to osmolar or other stimuli. Its plasma concentration varies between 0.5 and 5.5 pg/ml, depending on the state of hydration. The half-life of AVP in plasma is 22.5 ± 4 minutes. Plasma AVP level is controlled by an "osmostat," such that, above a set osmolar point, there is a straight-line relationship between plasma AVP concentration and plasma osmolality, as determined by sodium ion concentration or manipulated experimentally with mannitol. (Increasing osmolality by glucose infusion actually decreases blood AVP.)

Nonosmolar factors that can affect AVP release include the blood volume, the arterial blood pressure, stress and nausea, humoral substances such as catecholamines, and pharmacologic agents such as ethanol, chlorpropamide, and nicotine.

The function of AVP is to inhibit renal excretion of free water. The hormone binds to vasopressin receptors in hormone responsive tubular cells. This causes a change in the permeability characteristics of these cells that, in turn, leads to free water retention.

AGING EFFECTS

There is no evidence of decreased activity of the hypothalamus in the production and axonal movement of AVP with age. There is evidence, however, that more AVP is released for any given osmotic stimulus in older subjects, suggesting that the sensitivity of the osmostat increases with age. On the other hand, the response of AVP to upright posture (which is mediated by central nervous system (CNS) dopamine and opioid receptors) may be defective in a subset of the elderly. In a study of the effect of ethanol, elderly subjects exhibited an inhibition of AVP release and subsequent escape, whereas no escape was seen in young control subjects. The secretion of AVP in response to chemical stimuli, such as chlorpropamide, may be enhanced in the aged.

Some of the age-related changes in AVP dynamics may be secondary to age-related alteration in renal anatomy and kidney function, and not due to primary hypothalamic or pituitary change.

SYNDROME OF INAPPROPRIATE ANTIDIURETIC HORMONE

The syndrome of inappropriate antidiuretic hormone (SIADH) is a state of spontaneous, euvolemic hyponatremia. It is frequently associated with pulmonary or chest wall disease, CNS disease, chlorpropamide therapy, or cancer. The elderly are prone to develop SIADH *without* underlying medical conditions. In these cases, chronic restriction of fluid intake to 500–1000 ml/day may suffice to maintain normal osmolality. Generally, patients tolerate this regime well. The elderly are also likely to develop transient hyponatremia after surgery and other insults.

DIABETES INSIPIDUS

Diabetes insipidus (DI) is manifested by persistent polyuria, thirst, and polydypsia. It is diagnosed by the demonstration of persistent hyposthenuria and elevated serum osmolality in patients with preserved renal response to vasopressin. DI is not commonly seen de novo in the elderly. It may develop as a result of head trauma, neurosurgery, or metastatic disease. Treatment, acutely, is with 5–10 U aqueous vasopressin subcutaneously every 4–6 hours. For chronic management, 2.5–5 U of vasopressin tannate in oil is given intramuscularly every 24–72 hours, or desmopressin (dDAVP), 5–20 μg, is instilled nasally every 12–24 hours. Chlorpropamide, thiazide diuretics, and clofibrate can be used as adjunctive therapy in patients with residual ADH production.

THYROID

PHYSIOLOGIC CONSIDERATIONS

The production of thyroid hormone by the thyroid gland (7) is closely modulated by the pituitary gland, which is exquisitely sensitive to the concentration of the hormone thyroxine (T_4) in the blood. Even a minor decrease in blood free thyroxine level results in increased production of thyrotropin, or thyroid stimulating hormone (TSH). Similarly, even a small elevation of blood free thyroxine suppresses TSH production. TSH production is itself under the control of the hypothalamic factor, thyrotropin stimulating hormone (TRH).

The major product of the thyroid gland is T_4. Triiodothyronine (T_3), which is metabolically much more active than T_4, is also released from the thyroid gland, but in small amounts. The major source of T_3 is peripheral conversion of T_4. In the blood, both T_4 and T_3 are bound to a carrier globulin (thyroxine binding globulin, TBG), to a prealbumin (TBPA), and to albumin. Although only small fractions of these hormones circulate free, these free fractions are the physiologically significant entities.

The blood level of the thyroid hormones, and also of TSH, have been determined with great accuracy. The normal range of T_4 is 4.5–12.0 μg/dl; its half-life is 7 days in the euthyroid person, and longer in the hypothyroid state. The range of T_3 is 70–190 ng/dl, and of TSH, it is 0.6–5.0 μU/ml. Recent advances in immunoassay technology enable the determination of blood TSH levels with such sensitivity that the lower as well as the upper limits of the normal can now be delineated, and separated from the pathologic states. A minor elevation of circulating blood free thyroxine level above the normal set point decreases TSH blood level below the normal range. A downward deviation of blood free thyroxine level from its normal set point results in an elevation of the blood level of TSH. It is important to recognize that each and every individual has a fixed normal set point of T_4, which is apparently stable throughout life.

Until the recent advent of the supersensitive TSH assay, TRH had been used as an adjunct in the diagnosis of hyper- and hypothyroidism. The intravenous injection of a bolus of TRH stimulates an immediate release of TSH into the blood. In hyperthyroidism, the TSH release is suppressed, whereas in hypothyroidism, it is markedly exaggerated.

Acute nonthyroidal illness results in immediate cessation of conversion of T_4 to T_3. This is recognized as the "low T_3 syndrome" or as the "sick euthyroid syndrome." TBG and TBPA production, as well as TSH production, may decrease or cease altogether. As a result, thyroid function tests are altered in acutely ill patients, and the establishment of the thyroid status in the sick, especially the elderly sick, is a difficult and challenging clinical problem.

AGING EFFECTS

Thyroid hormone production rate decreases with age. By age 75 years, the hormone production falls to approximately 70% that of young adults. The mechanism controlling this change is unknown, but it may be consequent to the age-related decrease in lean body mass. Blood T_4 levels are probably not affected and individual set points remain constant throughout life. There may be a 10–20% decrease in blood T_3 level.

There is some decrease of pituitary sensitivity to changes in blood T_4. In some elderly subjects, the TSH response to TRH infusion during small changes in ambient T_4 level is absent or smaller than that seen in the young. In spite of this decreased sensitivity, the inverse relationship between T_4 and TSH is maintained, and TSH blood levels do change in the elderly as thyroid gland function changes. TSH is elevated in hypothyroid patients, and is fully suppressed in hyperthyroid patients, as long as hypothalamic and pituitary functions are normal and the patient does not suffer from intercurrent disease.

The clinical manifestations of thyroid disease do change with age and will be described below.

HYPERTHYROIDISM

Although hyperthyroidism is most prevalent among young women, it is seen in all age groups and in both sexes. In one study in which women older than 60 years were screened, 1.9% were found to have hyperthyroidism, in another study, the rate was only 0.5%.

One of the most striking effects of age on hyperthyroidism is the decline in symptoms that classically have been associated with excess thyroid hormone production. The presenting symptoms of young, elderly, and very old patients with proven hyperthyroidism are presented in table 30.1. As compared with the young, the elderly with average age of 70 years had classical symptoms in only 75% of cases, while 25% had subtle clinical symptoms. In the very old, with mean age of 81.5 years, thyrotoxic symptoms averaged only two per patient, and few patients were totally asymptomatic. Major presenting symptoms in this latter group included weight

Table 30.1

Percent of Patients with Symptoms Attributable to Thyrotoxicosis[a]

Number	26	85	247
Mean age	81.5	68.6	40[b]
Range	75–95	60–82	5–73
Symptoms			
Weight loss	44	35	85
Palpitations	36	42	89
Weakness	32	28	70
Dizziness, syncope	20		
Nervousness	20	38	99
No symptoms	8		
Memory loss	8		
Tremor	8		
Local symptoms[c]	8	11	
Pruritus	4	4	
Heat intolerance	4	63	89

[a]From Tibaldi J, Barzel US, Albin J, et al: Thyrotoxicosis in the very old. Am J Med 81:619, 1986, with permission.
[b]Approximated from graph of patients' ages.
[c]Dysphagia, enlarging neck mass, and so on.

loss (44%), palpitations (36%), weakness (32%), nervousness (25%), and dizziness (25%). Clinical signs in this group (Table 30.2) included fine skin (40%), tremor (36%), tachycardia (28%), hyperreflexia (24%), and paroxysmal atrial fibrillation (20%). Although thyromegaly is found in virtually all younger patients with Graves' disease, goiter was present in only 60% of the elderly and in only 14% of the very old. Ophthalmopathy is rare in the geriatric patient.

No correlation could be established between age, clinical symptoms, signs, and hormone blood levels in studies of the very old. In view of the paucity and subtlety of symptoms and clinical findings in the geriatric patient with hyperthyroidism, it was concluded that all elderly should have periodic screening of blood thyroxine level.

Clearly, the diagnosis of hyperthyroidism rests heavily on laboratory findings. Elevated blood level of T_4 and/or T_3, as well as suppressed TSH or TSH response to TRH, are the cardinal findings in this disease. Serum cholesterol may be lowered, alkaline phosphatase may be elevated, and serum calcium may be mildly elevated in hyperthyroidism, but these laboratory tests do not contribute to the diagnosis of hyperthyroidism. The interpretation of thyroid function tests has to be done with care. For instance, increased TBG, which is present in menopausal women taking estrogen, will elevate total T_4. Free T_4 level remains normal, as is the free thyroid index, which corrects for the elevation of TBG. In

Table 30.2
Percent of Patients with Clinical Findings
Attributable to Thyrotoxicosis

Pulse > 100	28[b]	58	100
Atrial fibrillation	32	39	10
New-onset atrial fibril-			
lation	20[c]		
Lid lag	12	35	71
Exophthalmos	8	8	
Fine skin	40	81	97
Tremor	36	89	97
Myopathy	8	39	
Hyperactive reflexes	24	26	
Gynecomastia	(1 male)	1	10
None	8		
Thyroid			
Impalpable or normal	68	37	
Diffusely enlarged	12	22	100
Multinodular goiter	12	20	
Isolated nodule	8	21	

[a]From Tibaldi J, Barzel US, Albin J, et al: Thyrotoxicosis in the very old. *Am J Med* 81:619, 1986, with permission.
[b]Includes five patients with normal sinus rhythm as well as two who had atrial fibrillation.
[c]This was transient in four of five patients with conversion to normal sinus rhythm.

patients taking large doses of propranolol, there is also increased blood T_4 level. Propranolol causes a partial block in peripheral conversion of T_4 to T_3 and the resultant T_4 elevation, referred to as hyperthyroxinemia, is not associated with clinical thyroid disease. Other medications, such as danazole and amiodarone, can also influence thyroid function tests.

Radioiodine uptake has been an important diagnostic parameter in the past, but serves now only for the determination of the radioiodine dose to be used in therapy. Radioiodine thyroid scan must be used diagnostically if the patient has palpable nodules in the thyroid.

The definitive therapeutic modality is the administration of radioiodine (^{131}I). At our institution, ^{131}I is given at a dose calculated to deliver 80 μCi/g of thyroid (based on ^{131}I uptake and on an estimate of the thyroid size by physical examination). In most cases, the patient is rendered euthyroid within 8 weeks, but some cases ($\sim$10%) fail to respond to the first dose, and require retreatment, and some ($\sim$10%) develop hypothyroidism that may be permanent. Shortly after administration of the dose, transient elevation of T_4 and/or T_3 may be seen as stored hormone is released into the circulation from cells damaged by the ^{131}I.

Medical therapy of hyperthyroidism may be used as the primary modality or in the preparation of the thyrotoxic patient for ^{131}I therapy. Pretreatment is particularly important in patients with complications of hyperthyroidism, such as congestive heart failure or angina. Propylthiouracil (initial dose 100–150 mg every 8 hours) or methimazole (initial dose 10–15 mg every 6 hours, by mouth) are the major drugs for control of hyperthyroidism. Both are thioamides that interfere with organification of iodine in the thyroid gland. Their clinical effect takes 2–4 weeks to develop. A much more rapid effect can be achieved by the use of inorganic iodine, Lugol's solution, or saturated solution of potassium iodide (SSKI), which interferes with organification and with the release of hormone from the thyroid (oral dose = 5 drops tid). It may be used concurrently with a thioamide. Escape from the iodide effect occurs in 6 weeks. Propranolol (dose as low as 10 mg every 6 hours) is an adjunct in the therapy of hyperthyroidism. It will control most systemic manifestations of the disease, such as tachycardia, diaphoresis, and tremor. In severe thyrotoxicosis, glucocorticoids (hydrocortisone, 100 mg every 8 hours) can be used for a few days. Patients treated with iodide can be treated with ^{131}I within a few days after its discontinuation. ^{131}I can be given within 2 or 3 days after discontinuation of the thioamides.

Thyroid storm is a life-threatening medical emergency characterized by tachycardia and fever and must be treated in the hospital with a combination of iodide, thioamide, β-blockade, and occasionally, glucocorticoids.

HYPOTHYROIDISM

The prevalence rate of hypothyroidism in the aged is much higher than in the younger population. It has been reported to be 2.3% in men and 5.9% in women older than 60 years in the original Framingham cohort. In another study, minimally elevated TSH has been observed in 14.4% of screened "healthy" people. (Lower, but significant prevalence rates of hypothyroidism have been observed among the aged in New Zealand, West Germany, and Sweden.)

It was noted previously that the clinical array of symptoms and findings of hyperthyroidism becomes scantier with advancing age. The elderly also differ from younger patients in that they are more tolerant of symptoms and signs of hypothyroidism. They may, therefore, present with more advanced disease, especially if psychomotor retardation, depression, constipation, and cold intolerance are ascribed to old age. This and the high prevalence rate of hypothyroidism in the general population provide further justification for the routine screening of serum T_4 level in all elderly from time to time. Because of the nonspecific effect of acute illness on thyroid function tests, such screening must be limited to well individuals. Periodic screening of thyroid function is definitely indicated in people with a history of Graves' disease or Hashimoto's thyroiditis, who are at increased risk of developing hypothyroidism with age.

The finding of a falling blood T_4 in a patient with prior history of thyroid disease, or the finding of T_4 level near the lower limit of normal or below is an indication to assay of TSH blood level. If TSH is found to be elevated, it may be concluded that the pituitary gland recognizes a decrease, below the individual set point, in circulating thyroid hormone. This condition has been identified in the literature as "subclinical hypothyroidism," but had also been called "premyxedema," "preclinical hypothyroidism," and "limited thyroid reserve syndrome." For this condition of early thyroid gland failure, the supplementary administration of thyroxine in small doses is advocated so that TSH will be returned to normal. If a further fall of blood T_4 and rise of TSH is observed during follow-up, the supplementary thyroxine dose is increased until these parameters return to their baseline. This approach to maintenance of normal thyroid parameters is believed to decrease substantially the number of patients who will develop florid hypothyroidism.

Untreated hypothyroidism may be associated with psychomotor retardation, depression, constipation, and cold intolerance as well as hypothermia, hypertrophic subaortic stenosis, pericardial effusion, cerebellar dysfunction, and psychosis. The physical findings may include dryness of the skin and the hair, loss of outer third of the eyebrow hair, myxedema (nonpitting edema), slow return phase of the deep tendon reflexes, hypertension, both systolic and diastolic, and bradycardia.

The cardinal laboratory findings for thyroid failure are low blood T_4 level, low free thyroxine index, and elevated TSH blood level. This may develop not only in patients with Hashimoto's thyroiditis or Graves' disease, but also in patients receiving ^{131}I, excess thioamide drugs, or inorganic iodine, and in patients receiving lithium, aminoglutethamide, and amiodarone. Because an occasional patient may have failure of multiple endocrine glands, normal adrenal gland function must be established. This is best achieved by the demonstration of normal plasma cortisol in three samples taken every 20 minutes between 8:00 AM and 9:00 AM. Other laboratory findings that may be abnormal, but are not used diagnostically, include elevation of serum cholesterol and creatinine phosphokinase (CPK). Macrocytic anemia may be present and pernicious anemia must then be ruled out. If TSH elevation is not found in a patient with hypothyroidism, pituitary failure must be considered in the differential diagnosis. Acute illness of any kind may result in lowering of T_4 and/or T_3, and may also interfere with normal TSH secretion in patients with normal thyroid function. Abnormal thyroid function tests must therefore be interpreted with caution in the setting of acute disease.

Therapy of hypothyroidism is with thyroxine only. In a newly diagnosed case, 0.025 mg daily is the starting dose. In a patient with adrenal or pituitary failure concomitant steroid hormone therapy is mandatory. The thyroxine dose is increased by 0.025-mg/day increments every month, until TSH and T_4 had returned to normal. The average final dose of thyroxine required for full replacement in the elderly is approximately 70% of that reported for younger hypothyroid patients, about 0.115 mg/day.

CONCLUSION

Both hyperthyroidism and hypothyroidism are common in the elderly. Both can be missed easily because of the paucity of symptoms and findings in the hyperthyroid elderly, and because of the similarity of hypothyroid symptoms and findings to the effects of aging per se. For these reasons, periodic examination of blood thyroid hormone levels is recommended in all aged, and especially in those with a past history of thyroid disease. The value of the determination of blood TSH level as a primary, routine, thyroid function test is yet to be determined.

PARATHYROIDS

PHYSIOLOGIC CONSIDERATIONS

The parathyroid glands, like other endocrine glands that produce polypeptide hormones, produce hormone on a continuous basis (4). The biochemical process of hormone assembly involves the intracellular production of a preprohormone and the cleavage of the "pre-pro" moiety before secretion. Hormone not secreted into the circulation is metabolized within the gland. Thus, the amount of hormone stored in the gland is very small. The secreted hormone is an 84 amino acid chain, of which the amino-terminal (N terminal) 34 amino acid fraction is the active part. The hormone is broken down into fragments within minutes of its secretion. The inactive carboxy-terminal (C terminal) fragment is cleared relatively slowly; its blood level reflects, in people with normal renal and liver function, the integrated parathyroid hormone (PTH) secretion over time.

In the absence of the parathyroid glands, serum calcium tends to stabilize at a level of 7 mg/dl. This suggests that the normal level of serum calcium requires the continuous tonic influence of PTH.

The basic determinant of PTH secretion is feedback control by serum calcium, more specifically, by the ionized calcium level. Thus, rising calcium levels cause a decrease in the amount of hormone secreted by the gland, whereas falling calcium levels result in augmentation of hormone discharge into the circulation. There is no central nervous system or any other control over this feedback loop under normal conditions.

PTH, on the other hand, stimulates renal production of 1,25 dihydroxy-vitamin D, which is responsible for intestinal absorption of calcium. This is one way in which PTH contributes physiologically to the maintenance of normal serum calcium. (In vitamin D-deficiency states, the failure of gastrointestinal absorption of calcium, and the resulting tendency of blood calcium to fall, lead to a compensatory increase in PTH secretion.)

In vitro studies reveal that the divalent element magnesium can exert the same influence on PTH secretion as calcium. In vivo, the blood magnesium level, which is relatively low, is normally of little practical consequence. A low level of blood magnesium, however, does have a profound effect on serum calcium since it results in the inhibition of PTH secretion as well as the blocking of its peripheral effects.

Circulating calcium is partly bound to albumin, and partly complexed to phosphates and other anions. The ionized calcium level, which is the metabolically active fraction, can be estimated by reference to the albumin level (each 1.0 g/dl albumin normally binds 0.7 mg/dl calcium) or by the use of a nomogram. Methods for actual determination of ionized blood calcium levels are available, but are used primarily as research tools.

All current methods for measurement of the circulating PTH level use radioimmunoassays. As noted above, the C-terminal assay reflects the integrated secretion of the parathyroid hormone in people with normal liver and kidney function, and is therefore useful in determining over-secretion as in hyperparathyroidism. Assays of "N-terminal,"

"mid-molecule," and "whole chain" add little information in normal individuals. In people with impaired renal or liver function, blood levels cannot be interpreted without knowledge of production or metabolic rates, information that cannot be provided by a single blood level of the hormone or its fragments. The available PTH assays suffer from lack of accuracy at the lower end of the "normal" range.

AGING EFFECTS

There is no change in the feedback loop relationship between serum calcium and PTH secretion with age, nor in the sensitivity of the parathyroids to the effect of hypomagnesemia. Blood calcium in the elderly has been variously reported to be slightly higher, slightly lower, or no different than in the young. In women, the marked decrease in estrogen secretion at menopause is associated with a small increase in blood calcium. The PTH blood level seems to rise in "normal" aging, but this rise has been shown to be a reflection of reduced renal function which is encountered in some "healthy" elderly. A physiologically appropriate elevation of the PTH blood level may be found in elderly suffering from vitamin D deficiency.

HYPERPARATHYROIDISM

The prevalence of hyperparathyroidism in the elderly is estimated as 1.5%. Approximately one-half of all the patients with this condition are women older than 50 years, and 35% are older than 65. The classical presentation of this disease with kidney stones or bone disease is quite uncommon. In fact, less than one-half of the patients actually have any symptoms or complaints. The majority of cases of hyperparathyroidism are discovered today by the finding of hypercalcemia on multichannel chemistry screen. The symptoms that can be associated with this condition include bone pain, joint pain (chondrocalcinosis), polydypsia, polyuria, constipation, pruritus, and muscular weakness. In patients with dementia, hyperparathyroidism may increase the severity of the disease.

Hyperparathyroidism is by far the most common cause of hypercalcemia in outpatients. The finding of hypercalcemia and hypophosphatemia is, with rare exceptions, pathognomonic for hyperparathyroidism. Urinary excretion of nephrogenous cyclic AMP is increased. The demonstration of an elevation of PTH in this setting confirms the diagnosis. Urinary calcium excretion can be low, normal, or elevated, and therefore, does not contribute materially to the diagnosis. The hypercalciuric subject is, however, more likely to develop kidney stones, a fact to be considered in weighing the therapeutic options. The differential diagnosis of hypercalcemia includes vitamin D toxicity, metastatic disease (especially breast cancer and myeloma), sarcoidosis, hyperthyroidism (associated with minimal calcium elevation), immobilization (only in patients with increased bone turnover such as Paget's disease), and Addison's disease. In some cases of cancer, there is ectopic PTH production by neoplastic tissues, however, the hypercalcemia of malignancy is usually caused by another circulating factor that is not yet fully characterized.

The sole definitive treatment for hyperparathyroidism is surgical removal of the abnormal tissue. In 75–95% of cases, there is a single adenoma and in 1%, a carcinoma. Four-gland hyperplasia was found in less than 5% of cases in one series, but in some series, it comprised as much as 23% of the total. When the operation is performed by a surgeon skilled in parathyroid surgery, the cure rate is near 95%. In a study comparing elderly patients to young patients undergoing surgery for hyperparathyroidism, it was demonstrated that the cure rate was equal in both groups, that the length of stay in hospital was equal, but that there were a few more transient complications among the elderly.

Efforts at noninvasive localization of the abnormal glands in hyperparathyroidism have generally been disappointing, because most parathyroid lesions found today are relatively small and easily blend with surrounding tissues. Because a high cure rate is achievable without prior localization of the lesion, invasive localizing studies have been reserved primarily for surgical failures. The most accurate localizing technique depends on the catheterization of the veins draining the glands, the neck, and the mediastinum, and the sampling of venous blood specimens for PTH level. Recent improvement in ultrasound and radioisotope imaging, especially nuclear medical methods using combined pertechnetate and thalium scans, may provide reliable noninvasive localizing information, and thus make surgery shorter and, therefore, safer.

There is no effective medical treatment for hyperparathyroidism. The hypercalcemia, but not the PTH excess, has been reported to be controllable by estrogen administration. Patients taking diuretic therapy may achieve lower serum calcium levels if thiazides are replaced by furosemide. Calcitonin injections can lower blood calcium level by about 1 mg/dl and can be used as a temporary means for control. A promising diphosphonate, clodronate disodium, is no longer used because of unacceptable side effects.

There is little doubt that in symptomatic patients and in those with significantly elevated serum calcium levels, surgery is indicated. However, physicians in general, and gerontologists in particular, are faced with the difficult problem of management of the large number of asymptomatic and mild cases. In one long-term study in which patients with mild hyperparathyroidism (serum calcium no more than 1 mg/dl above the normal) were followed prospectively for 5 years, 80% still had mild and asymptomatic disease at the end of the study period. Longer observation suggests that there is a slow increase in complication rate with time, but that there are no predictive criteria to determine which patients will ultimately require surgery. While these studies suggest that over the short-term mild asymptomatic disease can be left untreated, they do not establish whether it is acceptable to not treat people with a life expectancy of 20, 15, or 10 years. Is there justification in not treating patients who can easily withstand surgery now but who may develop intercurrent disease that will preclude surgery in the future? Can the 1% probability of there being parathyroid cancer be ignored? Based on these arguments, and because of favorable experience with surgery, surgery is recommended to all patients whose life expectancy is longer than 5 years and who have no medical contraindication to the operation, regardless of symptoms or severity of disease.

HYPOPARATHYROIDISM

This rare condition may be idiopathic or can be the result of inadvertent removal of the parathyroids during thyroidectomy or other neck surgery. It is becoming less common as surgical techniques of identifying and preserving the parathyroid glands have evolved.

Symptoms may include dry skin, monilial infection of the nails, early cataract formation, and seizure disorder due to increased neuromuscular irritability. The diagnosis can be made easily with the demonstration of hypocalcemia and hyperphosphatemia in the presence of normal renal function and normal serum albumin and magnesium levels. PTH levels, which should be elevated in face of hypocalcemia, will be found to be normal or low.

Treatment of hypoparathyroidism is by the administration of calcium and pharmacologic doses

(50,000–100,000 units) of vitamin D, or by careful titration of the vitamin D metabolite, 1,25 dihydroxyvitamin D (calcitriol), against serum calcium level. As a result of therapy, serum calcium rises to normal and serum phosphorus declines, but tends to stay at the upper limit of the normal range. Metabolic alkalosis, reported to exist in hypoparathyroidism, is not affected by this therapy. Urinary calcium excretion as well as blood calcium must be monitored carefully. An increase of urinary calcium above the normal range may precede hypercalcemia as a manifestation of toxicity.

Treatment toxicity, i.e., hypercalcemia, is managed with a temporary withdrawal of the medication, steroids administration, and hydration with intravenous fluids. Recovery from hypercalcemia is said to be more rapid in patients taking calcitriol than in those taking vitamin D.

ADRENALS

Corticotrophin releasing hormone (CRH) is produced in the hypothalamus and secreted into the hypophyseal portal blood system (6). It is regulated by neural input from higher brain centers, which follows a diurnal rhythm, and by hormonal stimuli, including feedback inhibition by cortisol. CRH stimulates ACTH secretion by the pituitary, which is under feedback control by cortisol. ACTH stimulates the production and release of cortisol, as well as adrenal androgens, and aldosterone. In the circulation, cortisol is 70% bound to a specific cortisol binding globulin (CBG) and about 20% to plasma albumin. The normal plasma level of cortisol at 8:00 AM is 5–25 µg/dl, and at 4:00 PM 3–10 µg/dl.

There is no change with age in the relationships between the hypothalamus, the pituitary, and the adrenal cortex. The diurnal rhythm and the response to stress are preserved throughout life. Cortisol production rate does decrease with age, in parallel with the decrease in lean body mass and creatinine clearance, but cortisol blood levels remain unchanged as CBG concentration and affinity to cortisol do not change.

ADDISON'S DISEASE

Primary adrenal insufficiency is rare in the aged. It may, however, occur de novo as the result of septicemia and adrenal hemorrhage, among others. In the past, adrenal destruction by tuberculosis was the major cause of this disease, but presently, idiopathic atrophy is its primary cause. Acute Addisonian crisis is an emergency condition that presents with shock and fever. Chronic Addison's disease may present with hypotension, nausea, gastrointestinal pain, and muscular weakness, associated with dehydration, hyponatremia, and hyperkalemia. The diagnosis can be established by the performance of the Cortrosyn test—the injection of 0.25 mg of intravenous cosyntropin (Cortrosyn) and collection of blood for cortisol 30 minutes later. In suspected cases, cortisol therapy must be maintained until the cortrosyn test report shows this diagnosis to be incorrect. The dosage of glucocorticoids in the chronic treatment of Addison's disease in the elderly is the same as in the young—20 or 25 mg of hydrocortisone administered orally in the AM and 10 mg in the PM, and doubling or tripling of the dose during intercurrent illness. Mineralocorticoid therapy is given concurrently, 0.05–0.1 mg fludrocortisone orally once daily, and adjusted to blood pressure changes. Intravenous hydrocortisone must be used in acute Addisonian crisis, during surgery, when exposed to serious infection, and after major trauma.

CUSHING'S SYNDROME

Hyperadrenocorticism, of either pituitary or adrenal origin, is uncommon in the elderly. When it occurs, it is likely to be due to ectopic production of ACTH by neoplastic tissue, and, in rare cases, adrenal carcinoma. The diurnal variation of blood cortisol is absent in Cushing's syndrome, but this is not specific, as depression is also associated with a loss of the diurnal rhythm. An overnight dexamethasone test can serve as a screening test for Cushing's syndrome: 1.5 mg of dexamethasone is taken orally at 11:30 PM, and a blood sample for determination of cortisol is drawn between 8:00 and 9:00 AM the following morning. Cortisol suppression rules out the diagnosis. Full discussion of the diagnostic workup and treatment of this condition is beyond the scope of this chapter.

GONADS

FEMALE GONADAL FUNCTION

During the reproductive years, the ovaries secrete estrogen and progesterone in a complicated hormonal rhythm which is modulated by the pituitary hormones follicle stimulating hormone (FSH) and luteinizing hormone (LH). By the time they reach the geriatric age group, all women are in a state of gonadal insufficiency (5). As a result of the involution of the ovaries, there is a continuous and unopposed secretion of FSH and LH by the pituitary. Thus, in the normal postmenopausal female, estradiol blood level is only 13 pg/ml, and there is substantial elevation of blood FSH and LH levels, both of which are well over 50 mU/ml.

The marked deficiency of estrogen is responsible for atrophy of the female reproductive tract. Clinically, a significant result is the atrophy of the vaginal endothelium, which results in vaginitis, vaginal dryness, dyspareunia, and occasionally vaginal bleeding due to infection. These changes respond to local (or systemic) estrogen therapy. The relationship of estrogen deficiency to osteoporosis, and the place of estrogen therapy in the prevention and treatment of osteoporosis are discussed in the chapter on bone disease in the aged (Chapter 27).

MALE GONADAL FUNCTION

There is a tendency for the testes to lose Leydig cells with age (7). In spite of the change in the Leydig cell number, the blood testosterone level is probably unchanged. (The normal adult testosterone blood level is 300–1000 ng/dl.) There is concurrently a small but significant increase in LH blood level, and evidence suggests that there is some defect in the ability of the testis to respond to stimulation by gonadotropin. There is also a tendency for decreased production of sperm with age and a significant increase in FSH blood level that, in the elderly, may be three times the level of younger men.

Age is a significant correlate of both Leydig cell number and sperm production, but its predictive value for individuals is weak. Both parameters may be found in an occasional elderly person to overlap those in young controls, and it is clear that other factors, which are as yet unknown, are responsible for the large variation between individuals in the older age group.

PROLACTIN

There is no change in serum prolactin (PRL), a pituitary hormone, with age. Its normal level in the serum is less than 20 ng/ml. Thyrotropin releasing hormone (TRH) markedly stimulates PRL secretion, and aging has no effect on this response.

Prolactinoma, a PRL-producing pituitary tumor, may go undetected in the aged because its clinical manifestation is cessation of menses and infertility in the female and suppression of fertility in the male. Clinically, hyperprolactinemia is associated with suppression of gonadotropin (LH, FSH) release and secondary failure of gonadal hormone production. For this reason, PRL blood level has to be examined in postmenopausal women whose LH and FSH are in the premenopausal range, and in men with suppressed blood testosterone level. Diagnosis of prolactinoma is by the demonstration of hyperprolactinemia and examination of the sella turcica by computed tomography. Invasive tumors may require surgical removal by the transsphenoidal route. Medical treatment is with 2.5–7.5 bromocriptine given orally, the dosage being titrated against PRL blood level. Medical therapy frequently results in decreased tumor size as well. Acromegaly may coexist with prolactinoma and can be diagnosed by elevated, unsuppressed growth hormone levels, and increased somatomedin C plasma concentration. This condition is not responsive to bromocriptine therapy.

REFERENCES

1. Davis PJ, Davis FB: Water excretion in the elderly. In Sacktor B (Ed): *Endocrinology and Aging.* 1987, pp. 867–875.
2. Khoury SA, Sowers JR: Age-related changes in male sexual function. In Sowers JR, Felicetta JV (Eds): *Endocrinology of Aging.* New York, Raven Press, 1988, pp. 113–134.
3. McGinty D, Stern N, Akshoomoff N: Circadian and sleep-related modulation of hormone levels: Changes with aging. In: Sowers JR, Felicetta JV (Eds): *Endocrinology of Aging.* New York, Raven Press, 1988, pp. 75–111.
4. Peck WA (Ed): *Bone and Mineral Research.* Annual 2, New York, Elsevier, 1984.
5. Rice BF: The aging ovary. In Sowers JR, Felicetta JV (Eds): *Endocrinology of Aging.* New York, Raven Press, 1988, pp. 135–149.
6. Sapolsky, et al: Stress and glucocorticoids in aging. In Sacktor B (Ed): *Endocrinology and Aging.* Endocrinol Metabol Clin North Am, 1987, pp. 965–980.
7. Spaulding SW: Age and the thyroid. In Sacktor B (Ed): *Endocrinology and Aging,* 1987, pp. 1013–1025.
8. Urban RJ, Veldhuis JD: Hypothalamo-pituitary concomitants of aging. In Sowers JR, Felicetta JV (Eds): *Endocrinology of Aging.* New York, Raven Press, 1988, pp. 41–74.

CHAPTER 31

Diabetes Mellitus in the Elderly Patient

JAMES H. MERSEY

By any measurement diabetes mellitus is a major health concern in the elderly population. The prevalence of diabetes at age 60 years is 10%, and by age 80 years is 16–20% (1). One-half of the patients with type 2 diabetes are diagnosed after age 64 years. Blacks may have an even greater prevalence than whites in the older age groups (1).

Not only is diabetes a common disease in the elderly, but it also is an expensive one both in terms of morbidity and mortality and in health care costs. In England, two-thirds of hospitalized diabetic patients are over age 65 years (14). Excess mortality is associated with the presence of diabetes in the elderly, although the difference from normal decreases as the subjects get older. Patients without frank diabetes but with impaired glucose tolerance only may also have excess mortality (1). This is due almost entirely to cardiovascular disease. Morbidity is even further increased in elderly diabetic patients, due in particular to foot problems resulting often in amputations for gangrene (more than 50 times as common) and blindness (8).

All of these problems are not preventable by early recognition and treatment of diabetes. Mortality, due to cardiovascular disease, may be related to other risk factors that are independent of diabetes. However, a significant portion of the morbidity is clearly diabetes dependent and can be decreased through aggressive and preventive care of the elderly diabetic patient.

GLUCOSE INTOLERANCE AND AGING

It is well known that glucose tolerance declines with age even in the absence of overt diabetes. Fasting plasma glucose and hemoglobin A_{1C} values have been found to increase after age 30–40 years and glucose to rise 1–2 mg/dl per decade fasting and 8–20 mg/dl postprandially per decade (7). Recent studies have confirmed that there is an increased incidence of vascular disease associated with this declining glucose tolerance; and that hyperinsulinemia is an independent risk factor for cardiovascular disease.

What causes this age-related glucose intolerance and is it preventable? The answer to these questions is incomplete, in spite of a large volume of research. There is general agreement that insulin is still secreted in adequate amounts. Although there may be a decrease in secretion per β cell, this may be compensated for by an increase in β-cell mass (as seen in rats) and a decrease in insulin clearance (7, 12). Lipson (7) has found a loss of first phase insulin release and a decrease in total insulin response to glucose in aging rats, but such data have not been confirmed in man.

Most studies have found that peripheral responsiveness to insulin is decreased in older animals and man. Studies utilizing glucose clamp techniques to show insulin responsiveness have shown decreased insensitivity to insulin and normal or decreased maximal response (12, 13). Insulin receptors have not been found to be decreased in these patients. It has been proposed, then, that aging patients have a defective intracellular (postreceptor) response to insulin. Because intracellular responses to insulin binding at the cell membrane have not been clarified, it is not possible to be specific in describing the precise abnormality. The precise nature of the defect remains to be defined.

Whether this acquired insulin resistance is inevitable with aging is in debate. Reaven and Reaven (12) have said that the observed insulin resistance is secondary to other age-related variables like increased obesity and decreased physical activity. Other investigators have implicated decreased muscle mass and increased percent body fat. All of these factors are known to produce insulin insensitivity in peripheral tissues regardless of age. In theory, the glucose intolerance of aging could be improved or prevented by the control of obesity along with exercise to increase muscle mass and decrease body fat.

As mentioned previously, insulin levels (which are elevated in impaired glucose tolerance and type 2 diabetes and which may be elevated even in the glucose intolerance of aging) are associated with an increased risk of cardiovascular disease. Also seen and metabolically related are elevated triglycerides and low levels of high density lipoprotein (HDL) cholesterol. The correlation of triglycerides and cardiovascular disease is not well established; but the risk low HDL levels carries for coronary disease is clear; and elevated triglycerides are usually associated with low HDL levels. Therefore, if improving glucose tolerance will also improve these metabolic parameters, the risk of cardiovascular disease may also be lowered.

The glucose intolerance of aging is not classified as diabetes by current criteria (10). By earlier standards, 40% of older subjects would have been classified as diabetic. A re-examination of the data suggested that many of these subjects, although at risk for vascular disease, were not at risk for nephropathy, retinopathy, and neuropathy, and that criteria should be modified. Diabetes is defined as a fasting blood sugar greater than or equal to 140 mg/dl on two occasions or greater than or equal to 200 mg/dl at 2 hours and one other time after a standard oral glucose load of 75 g. An intermediate group, labeled as having impaired glucose tolerance, is defined as a blood sugar between 140 and 200 at 2 hours after a glucose load, plus another sugar of greater than or equal to 200 between 0 and 2 hours. From previous studies, patients with impaired glucose tolerance are at very low risk for diabetic retinopathy, neuropathy, or nephropathy. Hence, of those 40% who would previously have been classified as diabetic, one-half would now be classified as diabetic and one-half as having impaired glucose tolerance.

Of those patients over 65 years with diabetes, the vast majority (up to 95%) have type 2, noninsulin-dependent diabetes. The pathogenesis of diabetes in these patients has not been shown to be different from that of younger patients. As in the glucose intolerance of aging, the predominant problem has been shown to be peripheral insulin resistance due to a postreceptor defect. In addition, whereas insulin levels are elevated compared to nondiabetic patients, they are inappropriately low as compared to obese nondiabetic individuals. Maximal insulin secretory capacity may also be diminished because obese nondiabetic individuals who demonstrate the same peripheral resistance can further increase insulin secretion to overcome the resistance, whereas the diabetic patients cannot. The obese nondiabetic individual is still able to attain glucose tolerance by producing more insulin than the diabetic. Additional data also suggest that elevated blood glucose itself decreases β-cell function.

A small group of elderly diabetic patients have type 1, insulin-dependent diabetes. In one series in England, one-third of admissions for ketoacidosis or hyperosmolar coma occurred in patients over age 50 years. Also the mortality rate in these patients was 43% compared to 6% for patients under that age (8). As a result of these data, it must not be assumed that diabetes in the elderly is necessarily mild.

CLINICAL PRESENTATION

Elderly patients with diabetes may present in several ways. Occasionally, patients present with severely out of control glucose manifested as nonketotic hyperosmolar coma. This condition is almost entirely confined to the elderly (3). Patients usually present with central nervous system dysfunction—either with focal signs, seizures, or depressed consciousness. Patients almost always have type 2 diabetes, which can be exacerbated by infection, dehydration, or medication. The hyperosmolality results from inadequate oral replacement after urinary sodium and water loss. These patients have a high mortality rate due to severity of the condition, coexistent disease, or occasionally, inadequate management.

Other patients present with typical onset symptoms of polyuria, polydipsia, and weight loss. This presentation is often associated with infection, particularly vaginal candidal infections in women.

Probably the most common presentation is for hyperglycemia or glycosuria to be discovered incidentally during evaluation for another medical condition. Older patients often have an elevated renal threshold for glucose, and so may not have glycosuria until blood sugar exceeds 300 mg/dl. They may have hyperglycemia for an extended period without discovery unless frequent testing is performed for other reasons. In addition, often the hyperglycemia is mild and, therefore, causes no symptoms.

As a result of longstanding asymptomatic diabetes, patients may present with the complications of diabetes. Most likely to occur in this patient group is neuropathy, either a mononeuropathy or symmetrical peripheral neuropathy. Mononeuropathies include (a) unilateral leg pain or weakness; (b) cranial nerve palsy resulting in diplopia; or (c) a radiculopathy resulting in pain in a single nerve root distribution. These mononeuropathies occur in all age groups but are more prevalent in elderly patients with type 2 diabetes.

Typical symmetrical peripheral neuropathy may also be the first symptom of diabetes. These patients may present with pain, dysesthesia, tingling, numbness, or just coldness of the extremities, usually in the feet. These symptoms do not differ in the elderly, but may be difficult to differentiate because of coexistent circulatory problems or other medical conditions.

Older patients may also present with symptoms due to autonomic neuropathy, the most common of which is erectile impotence. Less common are orthostatic hypotension, gastrointestinal motility disturbances, or bladder control problems.

It is also important to mention that diabetes in the elderly may also be drug induced presenting after the institution of other medications. A list of potential medications that can induce glucose intolerance is shown in Table 31.1 (10). Most important on this list, because of frequency of use, are the thiazide diuretics and β-blockers. Thiazides induce hyperglycemia by lowering potassium which decreases insulin secretion, although direct inhibition at the β cell may also play a role. β-Blockers directly inhibit

insulin secretion to a small degree; they are unlikely to create a diabetic out of a patient with normal glucose tolerance, but could certainly convert an asymptomatic diabetic to one with symptoms.

Finally, many patients with diabetes will have acquired their disease earlier and have carried it into older age. For these patients, management may change as they age—doses of oral medications or insulin may need to be modified and diet may need to be altered. This will be discussed in the next section.

TREATMENT

The principles of management of diabetes in the elderly are not basically different from those of managing diabetes at any age but must be tailored to the older age group.

The goals of treatment for diabetes can be divided into two parts—management of acute symptoms and prevention of chronic complications. The treatment or prevention of severe hyperglycemia, hyperosmolar coma, or ketoacidosis is not different in older patients with certain cautions. Prevention of long-term complications, however, in an already elderly population may not be rational or achievable. Life expectancy may not be of long enough duration for complications to develop; and even if long enough, tight control may not be appropriate for a variety of reasons to be discussed.

Since most elderly diabetic patients have mild type 2 diabetes, dietary therapy should be successful in the majority. Again, most of these patients are obese, and weight reduction will be an important part of dietary therapy. Unfortunately, compliance with diet is difficult for most patients; for older patients this may be even more difficult. These patients have long-established eating habits that they may not be willing to change. Furthermore, they may not be capable of learning a new diet or may be dependent on institutional food, Meals on Wheels, or eating out. Major modification of diet as might be attempted with young patients may be impossible and may serve simply to confuse or alienate a patient who cannot or will not comply. The most sensible approach will be to individualize diet. For patients who are overweight, a generalized reduction in intake with avoidance of simple sugars as much as possible will be sufficient. For normal weight patients, avoidance of simple sugars and advice to eat balanced meals may be the most viable option. For a minority of inspired and biologically young patients, more aggressive diet therapy can be employed using exchange diets containing 50% carbohydrate, 15–20% protein, and 30–35% fat (unsaturated, if possi-

Table 31.1
Drugs that may Induce Glucose Intolerance

Diuretics
  Thiazides
  Furosemide
Hormones
  Glucocorticoids
  Thyroid hormone
  Oral contraceptives
  Catecholamines
Psychoactive drugs
  Major tranquilizers
  Tricyclic antidepressants
  Lithium
β-Blockers
  Propranolol
Phenytoin
Antineoplastic agents

ble). A great deal of research has been done recently on glucose response to various foods, establishing a glycemic index for many common foods, that is, a measure of glucose rise after eating different foods. This information also can be incorporated into the diet.

For patients with mild or no symptoms, a 1-month trial of diet is a reasonable period. At the end of this period, glucose should be tested. Reasonable goals for control to prevent symptomatic hyperglycemia are to keep fasting glucose less than 200 and 2 hour postprandial glucose less than 200–250. It is very important to measure postprandial glucose. Many type 2 patients can normalize fasting sugar but become severely hyperglycemic after meals; therefore, measurement of only fasting sugars can be misleading.

If diet has failed, it is then appropriate to add an oral sulfonylurea to the patient's regimen (4). The mechanism of action of these drugs is still being investigated, with differing results. Possible benefits of the drugs are stimulation of islet cell insulin secretion, increase in insulin receptor number, and potentiation of insulin action peripherally (7). In particular, these agents may inhibit hepatic glucose production to lower glucose.

There are first and second generation sulfonylureas now available. These are listed in Table 31.2, with suggested doses and half-lives (4). Second generation agents, glyburide and glipizide are more potent milligram for milligram, but are probably not more effective in glucose lowering effect. They have been more extensively studied as to mechanism of action and may have less side effects than some of the earlier agents. Glipizide has the advantage of a shorter half-life.

The major risk of using these agents is hypoglycemia. This is a particular problem in the elderly because drug metabolism and renal clearance of metabolites may be diminished and food intake is more likely to be erratic. Prolonged hypoglycemia up to several days has been described. Studies describing frequent hypoglycemia with chlorpropamide and glyburide have been published (14). Thus, hypoglycemia is a relative contraindication; dose of the chosen agent should be begun at the lowest dose and increased gradually until blood sugar control is achieved. Treating in this fashion should make the risk of hypoglycemia negligible. More than 85% of patients should be controlled by the combination of diet and oral agent (7).

If oral agent and diet therapy fail to lower blood sugar to the acceptable level, insulin therapy should be instituted. As with other therapies in the elderly, insulin should be begun at a low dose to avoid hypoglycemia. Hypoglycemia is a particular risk in the elderly because it may further impair an already impaired mental state; and because patients may have other diseases that could be worsened by low blood sugar. In particular, hypoglycemia may induce angina or infarction or induce seizures. The hormonal counterregulatory response to hypoglycemia is not impaired in the elderly, but patients are often on drugs that may mask the symptoms of hypoglycemia or block the effects of counterregulatory hormones. β-Blockers in particular may mask the symptoms and prevent recovery from hypoglycemia.

Choice of insulin is also an important consideration. Many new preparations of insulin are now available. Several manufacturers now market human insulin. This is either modified from pork insulin or synthesized through recombinant DNA technology. In addition, animal insulins have now been highly purified. Insulin preparations are also modified to be short-, intermediate-, or long-acting. The result is almost innumerable options for insulin therapy.

Because most patients have type 2 diabetes and may only need insulin intermittently and because human insulin is less likely to cause allergy and resistance, the author recommends initiating insulin therapy with human insulin. The use of human insulin is of particular importance if insulin therapy is expected to be temporary; for example, a patient is hospitalized with an illness requiring that the patient take nothing by mouth, it may be appropriate to use insulin for several days only. Use of human insulin will result in less antibody formation, so that if insulin is required a second time, insulin resistance will not occur.

One objection to the use of human insulin is cost. Recently, the cost has decreased so that human insu-

Table 31.2
Oral Hypoglycemic Agents

Name[a]	Duration of Action (hrs)	Dose (mg)
Tolbutamide (Orinase)	6– 8	500–3000
Acetohexamide (Dymelor)	8–12	500–1500
Chlorpropamide (Diabinese)	24–72	100–500
Tolazamide (Tolinase)	12–18	100–750
Glyburide (Micronase, Diabeta)	16–24	2.5–20
Glipizide (Glucotrol)	12–18	2.5–40

[a]Trade names in parentheses.

lin costs no more than purified pork, and only a few dollars more than mixed beef and pork insulin. Patients who are well controlled on beef or pork insulin do not need to be switched.

In most patients, insulin can be initiated as an outpatient. It may be necessary to have family members help in the learning process or with the administration. Home health services can facilitate the learning process or provide continuing help, such as in drawing up the insulin in patients with limited vision. Patients should be started on once a day intermediate insulin, either NPH or Lente. The appropriate dose must be individualized, but should be started at 10-15 units in patients who are overweight and 6-10 units in thin patients. Because most patients have endogenous insulin secretion, this intermediate-acting insulin will serve to raise basal levels, and hopefully, allow the patient to secrete sufficient insulin in boluses to deal with glucose rises related to meals. Further adjustment of insulin therapy is dependent on glucose response to insulin.

To determine glucose response to insulin or any therapy in a patient not hospitalized, it is necessary for the patient or family to monitor sugar levels at home. Until recent years this has consisted of urine glucose testing. In the best of circumstances, urine glucose correlates poorly with blood glucose; in older patients who may have an elevated renal threshold for glucose, the correlation can be expected to be even worse. Certainly basing adjustment of insulin dose on urine sugars in such patients will be full of errors and potentially dangerous. Because a negative urine sugar may represent hypoglycemia or a blood sugar of 300 it is very possible to overprescribe insulin.

It is now possible, with equipment and supplies readily available, to monitor blood glucose at home with automatic finger sticking devices, glucose sensitive strips, and digital glucose monitors. These strips and devices have been shown to be quite accurate (within 10%) and comparable to laboratory measurements. Ideally, blood sugar can be measured initially four times a day, before each meal, and at bedtime. Insulin dosage can then be adjusted to deal with the peaks of blood sugar. In a compliant patient, this approach removes the need for hospitalization for glucose control. In the author's experience, this home glucose testing is tolerated and appreciated by the majority of younger type 1 diabetics.

Compliance with such testing in an older age group may be more difficult. Many patients may not tolerate the discomfort of finger sticks or may not possess the dexterity or visual acuity to perform the procedure. Many patients may not be motivated to comply with such a regimen. Four times a day testing for life in such patients is not advocated; in fact, once the proper dose of insulin has been determined, testing can be done 2-3 times a week varying the time of day, to ensure that control has been maintained. If the patient is unable to perform the procedure, it may be possible for a family member or home health aide to do so.

Home blood sugar monitoring is not inexpensive, but is reimbursable by insurance for patients requiring insulin. At 1988 rates, glucose strips cost roughly $.45 apiece and monitors cost $150-190.

If home blood sugar monitoring is not possible, urine glucose monitoring is better than nothing; because this, at least, will indicate when sugar is well out of control. The author would not feel confident in making major changes in insulin therapy based on urine sugars only. Such patients may require hospitalization for control of hyperglycemia.

It is rare but not inconceivable that older patients may require twice a day insulin or a regimen of both short- and intermediate-acting insulin. Decision to proceed to such a regimen should be based on frequent blood sugar measurements as described earlier. For example, in many patients, once a day NPH or Lente will not last a full 24 hours; this will be demonstrated by morning hyperglycemia with afternoon blood sugars in a satisfactory range. A further increase in morning insulin would only risk afternoon hypoglycemia. For improved control, a small dose of intermediate-acting insulin should be added at dinner or bed time; this dose will control the morning sugar. Another alternative would be to change to Ultralente insulin, which has a longer duration of action. The author would not recommend this, because of excessive risk of nighttime hypoglycemia with insufficient action during the daytime.

Some patients will also require addition of short-acting regular insulin with one or two doses of intermediate insulin. The need for this will be demonstrated by high sugars before lunch or at bedtime. Because older patients are likely to be sensitive to regular insulin, a small dose of 3-5 units can be added to reduce these peaks in glucose. Most patients can be taught to mix insulins; for those who cannot and do not have access to family or health professionals to do this for them, premixed combinations of NPH and regular are now marketed with 70% NPH and 30% regular.

The goals for insulin therapy are the same as those for diet or oral agents—to avoid hypoglycemia and to maintain reasonable glucoses fasting and postprandially with fasting glucose 120–180 and postprandial sugar 200–250 at most.

In the care of the elderly diabetic patient receiving insulin or other oral hypoglycemic agents, it is especially important to identify the individual as diabetic in case the patient presents in an emergency setting. The use of Medic-Alert bracelets or some other type of information that the individual is diabetic and receiving insulin or other hypoglycemic agents is valuable.

COMPLICATIONS OF DIABETES

The goals of therapy in all diabetic patients are to control acute problems and prevent chronic complications. In older diabetics, the importance of prevention of chronic complications has often been discounted on the basis that older patients will not live long enough to acquire these problems. Such a short-sighted view overlooks the fact that many patients have complications at the time of diagnosis and others may have life expectancies exceeding 20 years—more than enough time to develop diabetic complications.

The complications associated with diabetes are often divided into macrovascular disease and complications specific for diabetes—retinopathy, neuropathy, and nephropathy. As described in the beginning of this chapter, older diabetic patients are at great risk for the development of large vessel disease, particularly, heart disease, cerebrovascular disease, and peripheral vascular disease with gangrene (6). Many risk factors are involved with the development of vascular disease, including smoking, abnormal lipid levels, and genetic factors (all of which are independent of diabetes) and may already have done their damage before diabetes develops. Therefore, it may be highly optimistic to assume that tight control of diabetes will prevent or decrease the frequency of these complications. Indeed, there are no data to support such an occurrence. Nonetheless, glucose control is related to levels of cholesterol and triglycerides, and improved control should decrease these levels. If physicians are willing to try to lower cholesterol levels in patients with existing vascular disease (for example, postmyocardial infarction) then it would be appropriate to try to achieve the same goal in older patients in whom lowered glucose and lipid levels might delay progression of already existing disease.

Peripheral vascular disease is much more common in diabetes, particularly in elderly patients, with 50–70% of nontraumatic amputations occurring in diabetic patients. This is often as a result of coexisting diabetic foot infections. Whereas the vascular disease cannot be reversed or prevented, the need for amputation can be prevented in many patients through careful evaluation of existing disease with bypass surgery or angioplasty being performed as needed. In addition, patient instruction in daily foot and leg examination and in the symptoms of vascular insufficiency may allow early treatment to prevent later amputation.

Diabetic individuals are at high risk to develop coronary disease. Again prevention may not be possible, but the health care provider must be sensitized to the possible presence of such problems. Diabetic patients with neuropathy often do not complain of typical anginal symptoms and may have silent infarctions. It is important to be attuned to patient complaints of shortness of breath or any vague discomfort that is exertional. If coronary disease is suspected, then appropriate evaluation and therapy may be instituted. Diabetic patients often have far advanced triple vessel disease when evaluated by angiography. Nonetheless, some may be candidates for angioplasty or bypass surgery. Most will benefit from antianginal medication.

The specific complications of diabetes—retinopathy, neuropathy, and nephropathy—occur in older diabetic patients, particularly in those who acquired diabetes at an earlier age. Numerous studies of the so-called microvascular complications of diabetes (the most notable of which is Pirart's study) have shown a direct correlation between the duration of diabetes and the presence of complications and the degree of control and the presence of complications (5). In one study, a direct correlation between the level of hemoglobin A_{1C} and the presence of retinopathy was found in elderly type 2 diabetic patients (9). Although it remains unproven that improving control in previously poorly controlled patients alters the risk for complications, most experts in diabetes would attempt to achieve good control while awaiting definitive results from studies currently underway. Few of these studies specifically involve the elderly but there is no reason to assume that this population is different.

Diabetic eye disease is of major importance in the elderly. Greater than 92% of blind diabetic patients develop their blindness over age 50 years and 40% over age 70 years. Diabetic retinopathy is as common in type 2 diabetic individuals as in type 1 diabetic individuals; but proliferative retinopathy does occur less frequently. As a result, vitreous hemorrhage and retinal detachment are less common in older patients; unfortunately macular edema, as a result of background retinopathy, is more common and may lead to visual loss. Also glaucoma, cataracts, and senile macular degeneration may be coexisting problems. The ideal approach to these problems is prevention through good blood sugar control. Because that is not always possible and patients, in fact, may present with retinopathy, it is important to treat such patients to attempt to preserve vision. Laser therapy has been clearly shown to prevent loss of vision in proliferative retinopathy. If vitreous hemorrhage and retinal detachment do occur, vitrectomy and retinal reattachment may restore vision in more than one-half of such patients. Recent results from the Early Treatment of Diabetic Retinopathy study have shown that laser therapy for macular edema may also preserve vision. Finally, surgical therapy for cataracts and appropriate management of glaucoma will also preserve vision. Management of elderly diabetic patients, then, must involve the ophthalmologist who is expert in the care of diabetic eye disease.

Nerve involvement in older diabetic individuals is at least as common an occurrence as eye disease. As described earlier, neuropathy can occur either as symmetrical peripheral neuropathy or as mononeuropathies. The presumed pathogenesis of a mononeuropathy is vascular, and as such, is reversible with revascularization and nerve regeneration. The most common mononeuropathies are oculomotor palsies and amyotrophy. These neuropathies occur more commonly in older patients and can be temporarily disabling and painful. Management is basically supportive, with pain medication if needed, eye patching to relieve diplopia, and either a cane or a walker for support, for patients with motor neuropathy.

Peripheral neuropathy occurs more frequently and is clearly related to duration of diabetes and level of glucose control (5). The pathogenesis is in debate and not suitable for discussion here; but the cause may relate to accumulation of sorbitol and depletion of myoinositol in nerve and Schwann cells. The end result is the typical stocking-glove neuropathy, with decreased sensation, dysesthesia, pain, or all of these. Not only is this uncomfortable, but it can cause related problems. Patients with neuropathy in their fingers lose manual dexterity; sometimes to the point of being unable to feed or dress themselves. Neuropathy can lead to severe muscle weakness that can result in near paralysis and loss of the ability to walk.

Most important, however, is the propensity of peripheral neuropathy to lead to diabetic foot problems. Diabetic foot ulcers and infections essentially do not occur in the absence of neuropathy (2). Because of diminished sensation, the patient's feet are more likely to suffer mechanical or thermal trauma. This often occurs with total unawareness of the damage done. For example, a patient severely burned the soles of his or her feet walking barefoot on hot sand and had no discomfort. Another patient had no idea that a nail had gone through his shoe until he saw the blood several hours later.

Also, muscle weakness in the intrinsic muscles of the foot results in protrusion of the metatarsal heads, hammer toes, and claw toes. These then become sensitive to pressure that also occurs because of foot pounding secondary to decreased sensation. The classic malperforans ulcer occurs under a protruding metatarsal head.

Therapy of peripheral neuropathy is, at present, very frustrating for the patient and the clinician. While aldose reductase inhibitors seem to help out experimentally, these are not yet available; nor are they likely to be a cure-all. Excellent control of glucose can improve some parameters of nerve function, but is unlikely to result in much clinical improvement. Treatment of painful neuropathy is just as frustrating. Attempts at controlling pain include antidepressants with or without major tranquilizers, phenytoin, carbamazepine, narcotics, and nerve stimulators. All meet with some success in some patients, but none work in all. Pain from neuropathy can severely impair the quality of life in the patients afflicted.

Prevention of foot ulcers, however, is even more important because these can often lead to foot infections, osteomyelitis, gangrene, and possible amputation. Patients must be taught basic rules of foot care as listed in Table 31.3 (6). Most of all, patients should be instructed to see their physician as soon as a problem arises.

Older patients may also develop autonomic neuropathies that are also troublesome. These include erectile impotence in men, orthostatic hypotension,

Table 31.3
Foot Care in Older Diabetics

Daily inspection of feet and toes
Daily bathing and careful drying of feet
Test for excessive hot and cold
Make sure shoes fit comfortably
Do not walk barefoot
Do not cut corns or calluses
Trim nails straight across
Physician should inspect feet at each visit
Do not smoke

diabetic gastroparesis, neurogenic bladder, and diabetic enteropathy, which can result in diarrhea and incontinence. Each of these problems are difficult to manage, but therapeutic approaches do exist, and many conditions can be improved, if not removed entirely.

Diabetic nephropathy also occurs in older patients, and with younger patients, will lead inevitably to renal failure. Progression to renal failure can be delayed with control of the hypertension that inevitably accompanies nephropathy, but it cannot be prevented altogether.

Hypertension in older diabetic patients is a major problem, involving 50% (8). Not all of these patients have renal disease. Control of blood pressure is of particular importance because of its effect on renal disease but also because of its other complications. Hypertension has been shown to be a risk factor for diabetic retinopathy, and its presence certainly predisposes one to heart disease and stroke.

An additional problem is that many commonly used antihypertensive agents conflict with the management of the patient with diabetes (11). As mentioned before, diuretics and β-blockers tend to cause glucose intolerance, and β-blockers block the awareness and recovery from hypoglycemia. Also, vasodilators and α-blockers may exaggerate orthostatic hypotension. The calcium channel blocker, verapamil, has been shown to inhibit insulin secretion but to have no net effect on glucose tolerance. Thus, the choice of antihypertensive agents is difficult. Agents shown to have little effect on glucose or lipids are converting enzyme inhibitors and centrally acting drugs, such as clonidine and methyldopa. A specific benefit of captopril has been shown in nephropathy, with reduction in proteinuria.

In addition to all of the above problems, older patients often have coexisting and equally important medical problems requiring other medications that may cause other problems for the diabetic individual. In particular, nonsteroidal-anti–inflammatory agents may affect kidney function adversely in diabetic patients and may alter metabolism of oral hypoglycemic agents.

One overriding issue for the older patient is the psychosocial aspects of the medical care needed for the management of diabetes and its complications.

Economically, purchase of the necessary medicines and supplies may be a great burden. Physician visits may be both economically and logistically difficult, particularly when podiatrist, vascular surgeon, ophthalmologist, and nephrologist all must be involved. Education of what is needed may be difficult in patients with poor memory and little family support. Modification in diet may be difficult as a result of economics, educability, and lack of family. The combination of these many social problems requires great patience and understanding on the part of the physician and health care provider team. Unreasonable demands will only serve to alienate the patient. Often, compromise must be made to allow for the best care possible and to preserve the highest and longest quality of life.

REFERENCES

1. Bennett P: Diabetes in the elderly: Diagnosis and epidemiology. *Geriatrics* 39:37, 1984.
2. Bessman A, Kasim S: Managing foot infections in the older diabetic patient. *Geriatrics* 40:54, 1985.
3. Cahill G: Hyperglycemic hyperosmolar coma: A syndrome almost unique to the elderly. *J Am Geriatr Soc* 31:103, 1983.
4. Gerich J: Sulfonylureas in the treatment of diabetes mellitus—1985. *Mayo Clin Proc* 60:439, 1985.
5. Greene D: Acute and chronic complications of diabetes mellitus in older patients. *Am J Med* 80(Suppl 5A):39, 1986.
6. Levin M: Diabetes: Geriatric complications. *Geriatrics* 38:39, 1983.
7. Lipson M: Diabetes in the elderly: Diagnosis, pathogenesis, and therapy. *Am J Med* 80(Suppl 5A):10, 1986.
8. Matz R: Diabetes mellitus in the elderly. *Hosp Pract* 21:195, 1986.
9. Nathan D, Singer D, Godine J, et al: Retinopathy in older type II diabetics—association with glucose control. *Diabetes* 35:797, 1986.
10. National Diabetes Data Group: Classification and diagnosis of diabetes mellitus and other categories of glucose intolerance. *Diabetes* 28:1039, 1979.
11. Peiris A, Gustafson A: Current therapeutic concepts in diabetic hypertension. *Diabetes Care* 9:409, 1986.
12. Reaven G, Reaven E: Age, glucose intolerance, and non-insulin-dependent diabetes mellitus. *J Am Geriatr Soc* 33:286, 1985.
13. Rowe J, Minaker K, Pallotta J, et al: Characterization of the insulin resistance of aging. *J Clin Invest* 71:1581, 1983.
14. Tattersall R: Diabetes in the elderly—a neglected area? *Diabetologica* 27:167, 1984.

CHAPTER 32

Geriatric Dermatology

BRUCE E. BEACHAM

Clinical aspects of aging skin are familiar to anyone who can picture the appearance of an elderly person. The skin becomes wrinkled on the face and is often variable in pigmentation. These changes merely reflect dehydration, and decreases in elasticity, vascularity, and subcutaneous fat in the dermis, as well as the melanocytic inability to spread out melanin granules in an orderly fashion. These most common clinical changes of the aged skin are highly variable and may be garnished with many other changes, all of which are dependent on genetic factors and the environment, especially the cumulative effects of ultraviolet radiation.

Several informative studies have characterized the most prevalent disorders of the skin of the elderly (85, 94, 95). This chapter provides a discussion of many well-known problems of aging skin and an update on therapies and diagnostic strategies when appropriate. The general categories for discussion include pruritus, common dermatoses, infections, bullous diseases, and tumors of the skin. Cutaneous manifestations of systemic diseases are beyond the scope of this chapter but are well reviewed in several texts (6, 8). The basic science of aging skin is also beyond the scope of this chapter. A variety of articles detail the great strides that have been made through biochemical, physiologic, and immunologic investigations (25, 30, 33, 43, 48, 49, 75).

PRURITUS AND XEROSIS

Pruritus is probably the most common presenting symptom in dermatology and includes both localized and generalized itching with or without an accompanying eruption. It may also be described as stinging, crawling, or burning, and is really a modified form of pain, with impulses being transmitted through slow afferent fibers. Release of biogenic amines, especially histamine, potentiates the transmission of such stimuli. Histamine release is further affected by IgE-antigen, kinins, and complement components C3a and C5a. The exact mechanism for histamine's ability to induce pruritus is unclear, but the discovery of two histamine receptors (H1 and H2) has greatly aided in our pharmacologic approach to the symptom.

In the elderly, pruritus is a common problem that has a number of causes (68). Xerosis and asteatotic eczema are regularly seen in the elderly, especially in the winter. Alkaline soaps, too frequent bathing, low humidity, rough clothing, alcohol, poor nutrition, and cholesterol-lowering drugs aggravate the above conditions and pruritus. Dry skin most commonly seen over the lower legs may fissure, appear shiny, and crack with subsequent inflammatory changes. This condition is referred to as eczema craquelé. On the back, such skin looks pale and dry, and has attached irregular small scale. Pruritus associated with xerosis is best controlled by restricting the amount of bathing, lubrication with an α-hydroxyacid lotion or ointment, and the avoidance of soap. Occasionally it may be necessary to use a mild to moderate topical corticosteroid and a systemic antihistamine to control pruritus. Antihistamines blocking H1, H2, or both types of receptors, as well as nonsedating types such as terfenadine, may be used.

Pruritus may also be associated with numerous other skin diseases besides asteatotic eczema and xerosis. These include scabies, drug sensitivity, dermatitis herpetiformis, and urticaria. If no skin disease is evident, the pruritus may be associated with an underlying systemic disorder. Pruritus may be associated with malignancy, especially myeloproliferative disorders. Other systemic diseases associated with pruritus include chronic renal failure, cholestatic liver disease, iron deficiency anemia, diabetes, thyrotoxicosis, and psychiatric and neurologic disorders.

Therapy of pruritus associated with scabies requires topical lindane therapy. A gluten-free diet or sulfone therapy is helpful for dermatitis herpetiformis. Pruritus associated with malignancy is often helped with appropriate treatment of the malignancy and a combination of H1 and H2 antihistamines.

Uremic pruritus, the etiology of which is unclear at present, occurs in 85–90% of patients with chronic renal failure who are receiving dialysis (100). Pruritus may be generalized or localized and most often occurs in the summer during and immediately following dialysis (29). Pruritus associated with uremia is often improved by parathyroidectomy (35) but in general, the most successful treatment is ultraviolet B light therapy (74). In one series, eight treatments of ultraviolet B light provided 18 months of relief from pruritus. Furthermore, it has been suggested that ultraviolet B light may have a systemic effect, but the effect of ultraviolet B light on uremic pruritus remains unknown (27).

Pruritus associated with cholestatic liver disease is relieved when serum bile concentration is lowered by external biliary drainage, oral cholestyramine, or hemodialysis. Pruritus associated with polycythemia vera has been successfully controlled with the H2 blocker cimetidine (14), and with cyproheptadine, a potent H1-blocker antihistamine and antiserotonin agent (24). Pruritus associated with iron deficiency anemia usually responds well to iron therapy (89).

COMMON DERMATOSES

CONTACT DERMATITIS

Contact dermatitis may be due to a true allergic reaction or more commonly an irritant reaction. Lesions are generally found on exposed skin in an asymmetric distribution and begin with itching and burning sensations. Erythematous macules, papules, and vesicles appear, and affected sites are often hot and swollen. Later, exudation, crusting, and secondary infection may occur. The pattern of the eruption is often diagnostic of the dermatitis, e.g., linear streaked vesicles on the extremities or swelling of the genitals in the case of poison ivy contact dermatitis. The location of the eruption will often suggest the cause and should direct questioning as to the possible allergens or irritants. Chronic allergic or irritant contact dermatitis may appear less red, scaled, dry, and fissured, but nonetheless is still secondary to repeated exposure to an irritant or allergen.

Although the elderly individual may present with typical clinical features of allergic contact dermatitis, several features of contact dermatitis in the elderly should be noted. Older individuals generally show relatively little vesiculation or inflammation and have scaling as a prominent feature of the eruption. Hyperpigmentation and lichenification are present early in the eruption, and itching is usually severe. Contact dermatitis tends to persist and is generally more resistant to therapy than in the younger age groups. These differences in clinical reactions may be related to the decreased ability to mount a delayed hypersensitivity reaction (91) and to the reduced reactions to standardized skin tests observed in the elderly (70). The exact reason for these observations is not clear at present, but decreased numbers of Langerhan cells (84) and decreased production of or responsiveness to epidermal thymocyte activating factor (ETAF) may play a role (28).

When the etiology of contact dermatitis remains obscure, patch testing can be performed to determine if the patient has a true allergy. Standardized kits for such testing are available. In cases of intractable contact dermatitis of unexplained origin, the possibility of underlying systemic disease or internal malignancy must be considered. Elderly patients with persistent eczematous dermatosis resembling contact dermatitis may in reality have a form of mycosis fungoides.

The most common causes of allergic dermatitis in the elderly are topical medications such as neomycin, nitrofurazone, paraben preservatives, vitamin E cream, lanolin, and ethylenediamine hydrochloride (2) applied to stasis ulcers. These sensitizing agents may produce widespread and even generalized eruptions and play a central role in the production of the autosensitization often associated with eruptions. Many elderly individuals have developed allergic contact dermatitis in response to medications or adhesives used in transdermal drug delivery systems (18), the most common of which include nitroglycerine, scopolamine, and clonidine. Cutaneous sensitization to these medications can result in a systemic contact dermatitis, even if the patient had previously been able to take the medication orally without problem. In the case of acrylate adhesive allergy with nitroglycerine, a silicone adhesive can be used safely. Clonidine transdermal discs are perhaps the most likely to produce sensitization: approximately

30% of all patients using this system become sensitized to it.

Several other contact dermatitis problems that appear to be more common in the elderly include hair dye dermatitis secondary to paraphenylene diamine present in older dyeing solutions, ragweed dermatitis, photodermatitis, and systemic eczematous contact dermatitis (17). Ragweed dermatitis is caused by reactions to an oleoresin and is most commonly seen in male farmers aged 40–75 years old. A chronic photodermatitis may be seen secondary to sensitization to aftershave lotion containing musk ambrette. Elderly patients often take multiple medications, and occasionally these are chemically related to topical sensitizers and result in a widespread contact dermatitis.

Therapy for contact dermatitis consists of removal of the offending agent coupled with the application of moderate- to high-potency topical corticosteroid cream or ointment. Oral antihistamines and aluminum acetate compresses may also provide some symptomatic relief. Severe or widespread contact dermatitis usually requires a 2-week course of systemic corticosteroid therapy using a tapering dosage schedule.

DERMATITIS MEDICAMENTOSA

Dermatitis medicamentosa is an acute or chronic inflammatory reaction to a drug. Almost any drug, whether ingested, injected, inhaled, or absorbed, may cause any type of skin eruption in any individual at any time. The eruption usually recurs on reexposure to the same or related drug and may be quite life-threatening, requiring emergency treatment.

Drug eruptions have been estimated to occur in 18–30% of all hospitalized patients and to account for 3–5% of hospital admissions (54). Furthermore, approximately one-third of these patients hospitalized for a drug eruption developed a second drug reaction in the hospital. The latter phenomenon reflects the so-called broadening of the base of hypersensitivity to drugs once one has developed a drug reaction. Because many elderly take multiple medications, and because of the availability of over-the-counter medications that may be added to the therapeutic regimen, and a variety of pathologic states that may predispose to certain drug eruptions, the physician must always suspect drugs as a possible etiology in cutaneous eruptions. In fact, one study found that almost 23% of cutaneous eruptions caused by drug ingestion occurred in patients over 60 years of age (41).

Drug eruptions may have a variety of clinical appearances, depending upon the type of drug, environmental factors, and pathologic state of the patient. These eruptions can be classified as erythematous, eczematoid, lichenoid, acneiform, urticarial, bullous, fixed drug, exfoliative, nodose, exanthematous, photosensitive, and purpuric. Each of these eruption patterns is associated with certain drug groups; this knowledge is often helpful in determining which drug may be responsible for certain types of eruptions. Erythematous eruptions occur often with bismuth, barbiturates, sulfonamides, antihistamines, and penicillins. Eczematoid or lichenoid eruptions may be seen with gold, quinidine, α-methyldopa, antituberculosis and antiarrhythmic drugs, and a variety of anticonvulsant medications. Acneiform eruptions are often seen with corticosteroids, bromides, and iodine. Urticarial eruptions may occur with penicillin and other antibiotics, and as reactions to sera. Bullous eruptions may be seen with iodides, penicillamine, and some anticancer drugs such as bleomycin. Fixed drug eruptions usually demonstrate one to two very intensely red, round lesions while one is taking the offending medication, and the lesions may be very hyperpigmented and less red when the drug is discontinued. These eruptions tend to occur with phenolphthalein, tetracycline, nalidixic acid, and barbiturates. Exfoliative reactions are seen more commonly with gold, and at times can appear similar to pityriasis rosea. Nodose reactions more often occur with sulfathiazole, salicylates, and birth control pills. Exanthematous eruptions may be caused by many drugs and are probably the most common pattern encountered. They are best described as erythematous maculopapular eruptions and are most difficult to differentiate from viral exanthems. Photosensitive eruptions are seen most commonly in individuals taking phenothiazines, chlorthiazides, dimeclocycline, griseofulvin, and oral hypoglycemics.

Other more clinically significant eruptions are those of Lyell's syndrome or toxic epidermal necrolysis, and extensive erythema multiforme with or without mucosal involvement. Each of these requires not only discontinuation of the offending medication but often the use of systemic corticosteroids as well as hospitalization. Less severe reactions are often best treated by antihistamines, topical menthol preparations, and steroid lotions, as well as by cessation of the offending medication.

URTICARIA

Urticaria secondary to drugs is quite common, and the offending drug may be easily identified and discontinued in straightforward cases. However, in the elderly management is often a problem in that the patient may be on many essential medications that are difficult to discontinue or replace. In these instances, the urticaria may continue beyond 6 weeks and be classified as a chronic type. Even after the suspected drugs are discontinued, the eruption may continue and its etiology becomes more and more obscure. At this juncture, not only drugs should be considered as the cause of urticaria, but also unusual sites of infection, including monilial and fungal infections, gallstones, and sinusitis. A careful history, physical examination, and judicious use of laboratory studies is essential and may be helpful. Extensive laboratory testing, however, has a very low yield and is not cost-effective (39).

Hives are characterized by edema and erythema (wheals), which last as an individual lesion from 1 to 5 hours with complete resolution to normal skin. There are often multiple lesions, which can form a variety of shapes including arcuate, circular, or serpiginous configurations. Severe pruritus usually accompanies these lesions, and rarely angioedema involving the mouth, the eyelids, or larynx may occur. A common component accompanying urticaria is dermatographism. This condition reflects histamine release with subsequent urticaria after light stroking or pressure on the skin leaving patterns conforming with the shape of the pressure.

When no obvious etiology has been uncovered to explain urticaria, it is appropriate to treat empirically with antihistamines such as hydroxyzine, an H1 receptor blocker, and cimetidine, an H2 receptor blocker, if necessary. More recently, the nonsedating antihistamine, terfenadine, has been very useful in the eldery with urticaria or pruritus. The use of doxepin, which reportedly blocks both H1 and H2 receptors, has also been quite helpful.

STASIS DERMATITIS AND ULCERATION

Stasis dermatitis is an eczematous, red, edematous, sometimes oozing eruption, with or without ulceration, on the lower legs, which invariably demonstrate venous insufficiency (Fig. 32.1). The condition may be acute, as described above, or chronic with lichenification and fibrotic and atrophic pigmented skin with scars over previously healed ulcer sites. The condition may be associated with any other medical condition that may cause edema of the lower extremities. Stasis dermatitis may be difficult to differentiate from tinea infection, and potassium hydroxide prep testing may be helpful.

Therapy is directed at removal of edema, along with lubrication and mild topical steroid prepara-

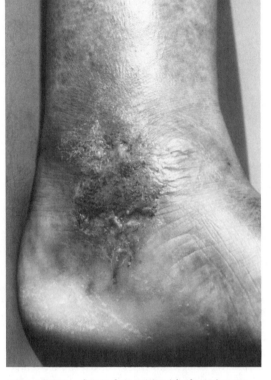

Figure 32.1. Stasis dermatitis with ulceration.

tions. Occasionally, systemic antibiotics are necessary for secondary bacterial infection, after appropriate cultures have been performed. Ulceration is best treated with aluminum acetate solution soaks, debridement using topical medications, or surgical intervention. If it is certain that no infection exists, the use of Unna paste boots or biologic dressings is quite helpful.

Finally, it is imperative that once the acute phase of this disorder has been controlled, some form of compression therapy is instituted. This will undoubtedly delay a worsening of this chronic condition, although the progress depends in great part upon the improvement of the circulation in the affected limb. This may require consultation with a vascular surgeon.

ACNE ROSACEA

Acne rosacea is a chronic inflammatory condition that occurs primarily in middle-aged and elderly individuals. Women are more frequently affected than men. It is usually localized to the central facial region, and is always associated with erythema. The erythema is often associated with small telangiectatic vessels, and there may be a varying degree of papules and pustules (Fig. 32.2). Severe nasal involvement may lead to scarring and papularity known as rhinophyma, which is often seen in males. Eye involvement, including conjunctivitis, iritis, and blepharitis, may also be seen.

The etiology of acne rosacea is still poorly understood. Dietary factors such as alcohol and caffeine, which have been reported to increase erythema, are sometimes implicated. In addition, fluorinated steroids and heat also appear to make acne rosacea worse. Increased vascular lability, increased production of sebum, and reactions to the follicular mite, *Demodex folliculorum*, have been suggested as having a role in the pathogenesis.

Acne rosacea must be differentiated from lupus erythematosus, seborrheic dermatitis, acne vulgaris, and polymorphous light eruption.

Therapy of mild acne rosacea consists of 1% hydrocortisone cream and the cessation of precipitating factors, and perhaps the use of a 1–2% precipitated sulfur preparation applied twice daily. If these measures fail or if the acne rosacea is particularly inflammatory or extensive, the use of systemic tetracycline, 250–1000 mg daily, usually controls the disease. In recalcitrant cases, the use of metronidazole both orally and topically (66) as well as oral retinoids, has been suggested to be helpful (65).

BULLOUS DISEASES

Bullous diseases of the elderly may be life-threatening. The most important encountered in this age group include bullous pemphigoid, benign mucous membrane pemphigoid, linear IgA bullous disease, epidermolysis bullosa acquisita, and pemphigus vulgaris. In the first four conditions, blisters develop at the junction between the dermis and epidermis, with some differences in each case in the exact location of the lysis.

Bullous pemphigoid is the most common blistering disorder of the elderly and occurs equally in both sexes. The mean age of onset is 72 years, and 85% of the cases begin in patients over 60 years of age (21). Bullous pemphigoid is a chronic, nonscarring, vesicular bullous disease in which nongrouped bullae occur on normal to urticarial skin. The bullae are most commonly seen over the flexural areas but may be localized. They may be pear-shaped and quite dense, and may contain clear or hemorrhagic fluid (Fig. 32.3). The oral mucosa is involved in approximately one-third of the patients, and has a negative Nikolsky's sign reflecting an inability to dislodge peripheral uninvolved epidermis. The typical course of this disease may last a year with a variable number of flares.

In bullous pemphigoid the degree of inflammation within the dermis is quite variable. It may be very sparse at times with many mononuclear cells, and quite dense at other times with numerous eosinophils. In 5–10% of the cases neutrophils may be the predominant granulocyte appearing in this inflammatory reaction. Direct immunofluorescence most often shows the deposition of IgG and C3 with or without IgA or IgM in the lamina lucida of the basement membrane zone (50, 58, 69, 81). In 70% of

Figure 32.2.   Acne rosacea.

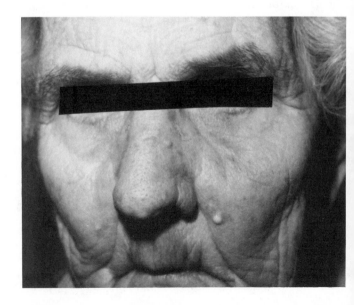

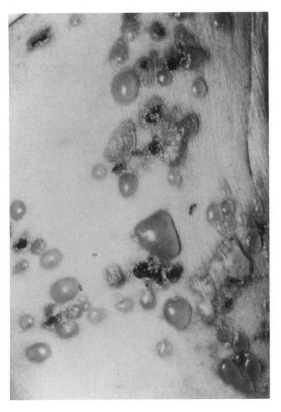

Figure 32.3. Bullous pemphigoid.

the patients, indirect immunofluorescence is also positive with IgG or C3 binding antibody found in the same location as with direct immunofluorescence (64).

Benign mucous membrane pemphigoid, epidermolysis bullosa acquisita, linear IgA bullous disease, and pemphigus vulgaris are less commonly seen in the elderly. The diagnosis and therapy of these conditions have been reviewed in detail elsewhere (22, 64, 76, 98).

Therapy for the bullous diseases outlined above depends somewhat on the type of disease that is encountered as well as the severity of that particular disease (76). In the case of bullous pemphigoid, the use of prednisone and azathioprine has often been helpful. In the neutrophil-predominant bullous pemphigoid, dapsone appears to be quite beneficial. For localized bullous pemphigoid, the treatment of choice is still topical steroids and perhaps the addition of erythromycin. Cicatricial pemphigoid is commonly managed with steroids and immunosuppressive medications. A combination of azathioprine and prednisone appears to be best at this time; however, cicatricial pemphigoid is commonly much

more difficult to control than bullous pemphigoid. Epidermolysis bullosa acquisita is typically quite difficult to control and may represent some of the misdiagnosed cases of recalcitrant pemphigoid. The best results reported so far in treating this disorder have been obtained with prednisone and azathioprine or cyclophosphamide. Linear IgA bullous disease responds relatively well to dapsone or prednisone, or a combination of both. Pemphigus vulgaris typically is best controlled with prednisone and the addition of cyclophosphamide or azathioprine, but has also been reported to respond to methotrexate, gold, high-dose prednisone (200–400 mg/day), pulsed intravenous prednisone, and plasmapheresis plus prednisone and an immunosuppressant agent (72).

INFECTIONS OF THE SKIN

SUPERFICIAL FUNGAL AND BACTERIAL INFECTIONS

Superficial and dermatophytic (tinea) fungus infections are common in the elderly person but are often not symptomatic. Several series have demonstrated incidences of tinea pedis with onychomycosis of 50% and tinea versicolor of 17% in the elderly considered in the specific studies (56). Erythrasma, a low-grade bacterial infection caused by *Corynebacterium tenuens*, involves the intertriginous and moist areas of the body, and has been reported to occur in 10% of elderly women (55). The use of Wood's light makes the diagnosis of tinea versicolor easier and is specific in the diagnosis of erythrasma, which fluoresces a coral red. Intertrigo, a mechanical frictional problem in flexural regions of the body with frequent secondary infection with monilial organisms, involves the axilla, groin, and inframammary regions, especially in diabetic individuals. More recently, tinea capitis in the elderly has been reported to be caused by *Trichophyton tonsurans*, and clinically may mimic seborrheic dermatitis or discoid lupus erythematosus (57).

Treatment of these superficial infections ranges from topical antifungal agents, such as miconazole or clotrimazole, for tinea infections, to oral griseofulvin for tinea capitis and onychomycosis. Tinea versicolor can be treated with topical selenium sulfide preparations applied to the entire integument for 10 minutes each day for 10 days and/or a short course of ketoconazole if the case has been refractory and is extensive. Erythrasma is effectively treated with Safeguard soap, topical erythromycin, or clindamycin. Intertrigo should be managed with meticulous cleaning of the involved area and proper ventilation, as well as the application of clotrimazole or miconazole topical creams.

Superficial infections present a significant problem for elderly diabetic, immunocompromised, or vascular-incompetent elderly persons. A low-grade infection often allows bacteria an excellent portal of entry. These superficial infections require treatment in such individuals to avoid more serious complications. Proper foot and leg care are essential. The use of proper orthotics to avoid the formation of large corns, and removal of any onychographytic nails by nonsurgical means such as concentrated urea ointment, are often indicated (16). Again, topical antifungals are useful in any tinea infection, but the use of griseofulvin may be indicated for the more serious type of dermatophytic infections. More serious and/or resistant yeast infections may require ketoconazole for an extended period of time, which necessitates proper monitoring of the blood count and liver profile.

DEEP BACTERIAL INFECTIONS

Cellulitis and erysipelas present as an acute problem and can be life-threatening in the elderly. Systemic antibiotics such as penicillin and erythromycin are helpful and should be used against β-hemolytic streptococcal infections for at least 10 days. In addition, the use of heat in the case of cellulitis and cool soaks in the case of erysipelas are beneficial. For recurrent attacks of cellulitis and erysipelas, it is often necessary to keep the elderly patient on continuous antibiotics at a lower dosage after adequate treatment of the initial infection has been accomplished.

VIRAL INFECTIONS

Herpes zoster and herpes simplex are viral infections that may cause significant morbidity in the elderly. Herpes zoster usually occurs in the fifth to seventh decade of life. The offending agent, varicella-zoster virus, is the same virus that causes chicken pox or varicella in children. After the primary infection, the virus remains dormant in the ganglion of the sensory nerve roots. Precipitating factors such as trauma, radiotherapy, immunosuppression, and stress have been identified as reactivating the virus and causing the clinical condition of herpes zoster. Nevertheless, the exact pathogenesis of herpes zoster remains unclear, and in most cases it seems to occur in healthy individuals, but it may also be seen in individuals with internal malignancies, especially in the lymphoma and leukemia group.

The condition usually begins with pain and burning and is followed by the appearance of grouped vesicles in a dermatomal distribution (Fig. 32.4). Occasionally there is associated headache, malaise, or

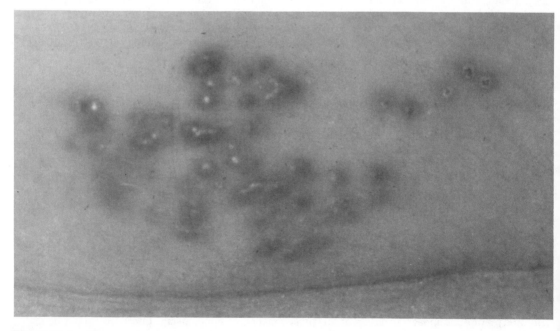

Figure 32.4. Herpes zoster.

low-grade fever. Any of the nerves can be involved, in the following order of frequency: thoracic, trigeminal, cervical, lumbar, and sacral regions. Involvement of the ophthalmic branch of the trigeminal nerve may affect the eye and result in a serious conjunctivitis, iritis, or uveitis. Involvement of the facial nerve can lead to facial palsy and ear pain known as Ramsay Hunt's syndrome.

A few vesicles outside the main distribution of the eruption are not uncommon. However, if there are more than a dozen such lesions outside the dermatomal distribution of the initial eruption, dissemination has occurred. This is more commonly seen in immunosuppressed individuals and those with lymphoreticulate disorders. A presumptive diagnosis can usually be made with the use of a Tzanck smear. Cells scraped from the base of an early vesicle with a #15 scalpel blade are smeared on a microscope slide, then stained with Wright's or Giemsa solution. Multinucleated giant cells, balloon cells, and occasionally intranuclear viral inclusion bodies are seen on microscopic examination. This test will not differentiate zoster from herpes simplex, and false positives and false negatives can occur. The use of tissue culture or monoclonal antibody identification may then be necessary for precise identification of the virus.

Therapy for the acute phase of herpes zoster is largely aimed toward symptomatic relief and control of secondary infection. Analgesia and open compresses with aluminum subacetate solution applied four times a day for 15–20 minutes are helpful. Secondary infection is best controlled with erythromycin, 250 mg orally four times daily for 10 days. The use of oral Zovirax in doses of 800–1200 mg five times a day for 10 days has also been reported to be effective (4). With the advent of newer analogues of Zovirax that provide better absorption, perhaps this treatment of the acute phase with acyclovir orally will become more feasible.

The incidence of postherpetic neuralgia increases rapidly with age. The percentage of elderly patients with postherpetic neuralgia roughly correlates with the age of the patient. For example, 60% of patients that are approximately 60 years of age will develop postherpetic neuralgia following typical herpes zoster infection. In addition, recurrence of herpes zoster infection is seen most commonly in patients more than 60 years of age. The pain experienced from postherpetic neuralgia may be so debilitating and disturbing that it rules the patient's life and can even lead to suicide. In view of the morbidity caused by postherpetic neuralgia, many therapeutic modalities have been suggested and tried to control the dis-

comfort experienced by the patient. Some of the therapeutic regimens that have been tried include antiviral agents such as acyclovir (77), and E-5-(2-bromovinyl)-2-deoxyuridine (13), which have demonstrated no effect on postherpetic neuralgia. Anti-inflammatory agents such as corticosteroids have also not been effective. Physical modalities such as regional sympathetic nerve block, posterior nerve root block, ultrasonic therapy (63), and cryocautery (82) have all been ineffective at controlling true postherpetic neuralgia. Psychoactive agents such as levodopa (42), and amitriptyline (92) have been reported to have some success in controlling the symptoms, and perhaps Triavil, which is a combination of amitriptyline and perphenazine, has provided the most significant improvement (92). Other agents that have been reported to be helpful with postherpetic neuralgia include cimetidine (63), griseofulvin (73), AMP Gel (78), and vitamin E (3). In deciding which of these therapeutic regimens are effective, it is important to evaluate critically whether the investigators are treating the acute phase of herpes zoster or the truly postherpetic neuralgia phase. It is in the postherpetic neuralgia phase that most of the modalities have little or no effect.

Herpes simplex infection of the recurrent type occurs in 20–45% of the general population in the United States. The infectious agent, herpes simplex virus, is a DNA virus that replicates in the nucleus of the cell. The epidermis, its adnexal structures, and neural tissue are selectively affected by the herpes simplex virus. Lesions of herpes simplex appear as grouped vesicles on an erythematous base. A tingling, burning sensation often precedes the clinical eruption by a few hours to days. The vesicles usually last 2–3 days before rupture, resulting in shallow erosions or crusts. Herpes simplex virus type I infection usually occurs around the mouth and in the oral cavity, but may occur at any body site where a superficial break in the stratum corneum has allowed the herpes simplex virus to enter. Herpes genitalis, usually caused by herpes simplex virus type II, is rarely seen in the elderly, but recurrent herpes simplex infection of the buttocks region, especially in elderly females, is not uncommon (67).

Diagnosis of herpes simplex virus infection can be presumptively made with a Tzanck preparation, as with herpes zoster infection. The virus may also be grown in tissue culture or identified by a micro-ELISA technique using a monoclonal antibody.

Therapy consists of drying agents such as ether, camphor, or 4% thymol in alcohol. Additionally, topical acyclovir ointment applied every 3 hours for

48–72 hours may slightly shorten the course of the infection. Intraocular lesions can be very effectively treated with idoxuridine, 0.1%, and arabinoside. The most effective systemic therapy is acyclovir, 200 mg orally five times a day for 10 days. This also may be used to prevent recurrent episodes after the initial 10 days of therapy for the acute disease, at a dose of 20 mg three times a day for 6 months or longer, if necessary. Unfortunately, recurrence after cessation of acyclovir is the rule.

Warts of all types can occur in the elderly person (1, 7, 62), but filiform and pedunculated warts of the face and neck are perhaps the most common (Fig. 32.5). Occasionally, warts may develop cutaneous horns, or become irritated, and must be differentiated by biopsy from actinic keratosis and squamous cell carcinoma.

Effective therapy for warts includes the destruction of the lesion by a variety of measures including not only physical but immunologic means. The most common form of therapy is cryosurgery, but this should not be used on eyelids or on the lower extremities. Topical caustic agents may also be used, but only with great caution.

BIOLOGIC EFFECTS OF ULTRAVIOLET IRRADIATION

Many of the changes commonly referred to as skin aging, such as fine wrinkles, irregular pigmentation, and patchy roughness, are not the result of

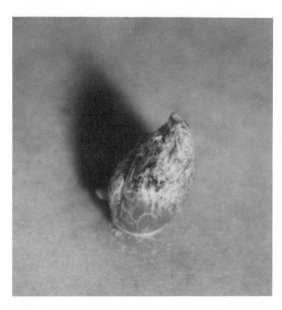

Figure 32.5. Filiform wart.

aging but the consequences of solar damage. The blue-eyed, sandy-complexioned person is more prone to develop actinic changes than dark-skinned individuals with natural pigment that provides some degrees of photoprotection. Every decade beginning at the age of 30, the number of melanocytes per unit area is reduced by approximately 10%, which increases the penetration of ultraviolet light and resultant sun damage (26).

Years of overexposure to the sun result in leathery, atrophic, pebbly, yellowish, textured, wrinkled, and sagging skin (Fig. 32.6). Despite a decreased number of melanocytes in the skin with aging, it is quite clear that the aged still get hyperpigmented or variably pigmented skin in sun-exposed areas. Experimental evidence demonstrates that indeed, any area exposed to the sun has an increased number of melanocytes (26). Chronic solar damage to the skin is caused not only by UVB but also by UVA. Chronic solar exposure appears to decrease the fibroblast's life span and reduces delayed hypersensitivity responses in the area of sun-damaged skin compared with skin protected from solar exposure. Experimental and clinical evidence have demonstrated that nonspecific immune suppression results in animal cancer formation (46, 59, 90, 96). Also, specific T-cell suppressor populations can be induced in experimental animals exposed to UVB; T cells reportedly inhibited the rejection of tumors produced by UVB radiation (20, 47). UVA exposure has been reported to induce tumors in mice and other animal models and to have a number of effects on DNA including the production of thymidine dimers, DNA protein cross-links (peak action 405 nm), single-strand breaks, and decreased synthetic repair of damaged DNA (40, 44, 86, 97).

There is a direct relationship between chronic sun exposure and the development of precancerous and cancerous growths in the skin. Early and continual solar protection can help prevent premature aging of the skin and such changes as atrophy, sebaceous hyperplasia, and life-threatening skin cancers. The best protection, perhaps, is clothing, avoidance of sunlight between the hours of 10 AM and 3 PM, and sunscreens. The daily use of tretinoin on sun-damaged skin may prevent the development of new actinic keratoses and has recently been used successfully in the treatment of photoaged skin (93).

TUMORS OF THE SKIN

The elderly frequently present with a variety of benign, premalignant, and malignant skin tumors. These skin tumors arise from one of three basic

Figure 32.6.   Actinic changes of the skin.

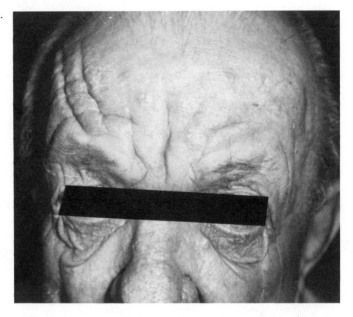

tissues in the skin: epidermal, melanocytic, or meso-dermal (Table 32.1). Epidermal tumors usually demonstrate the loss of surface lines, scaling, and hyperkeratosis, and may occasionally be pigmented. Melanocytic lesions are usually pigmented with a brown to black color. Mesodermal tumors are papulonodular in appearance and may have a red or yellow color. The various lesions may be either malignant or benign. Generally, malignant lesions have a rapid rate of growth, are irregular in contour, vary in pigment, and have a tendency to ulcerate or bleed.

Finally, skin tumors may arise from internal malignancy and may be the first sign of this occult disease.

BENIGN TUMORS OF THE EPIDERMIS

Solar lentigo, or age spots, are benign lesions seen in more than 90% of Caucasians over 70 years of age and occur in areas of highest sun exposure, especially the face and dorsal aspects of the hands (37). They are without question induced by solar radiation and are now being seen in younger populations

Table 32.1
Benign and Malignant Tumors of the Skin According to Tissue of Origin

Tissue of origin	Benign	Premalignant and malignant
Epidermal	Solar lentigo	Basal cell carcinoma
	Seborrheic keratosis	Squamous cell carcinoma
	Keratoacanthoma	
	Epidermal cyst	
	Sebaceous hyperplasia	
Melanocytic	Lentigo	Lentigo maligna
	Pigmented nevi	Lentigo maligna melanoma
	Blue nevus	Acral lentiginous melanoma
		Superficial spreading melanoma
		Nodular melanoma
Mesodermal	Dermatofibroma	Angiosarcoma
	Angioma	Kaposi's sarcoma
	Angiokeratoma	
	Fibroepithelioma	

because of our society's penchant for suntanning. Clinically, these lesions appear as macular, uniform, dark brown lesions that vary in size from pinpoint to more than 1 cm and often coalesce (9). Histologically, the rete ridges are elongated with small bud-like extensions. The number of melanocytes has been reported to be increased by approximately 10%, and they appear to have increased capacity for melanin production. Treatment of this condition with bleaching creams such as hydroquinone usually is not successful, primarily because the solar lentigo represents an epidermal proliferation. Cryotherapy or trichloracetic acid is often necessary to lighten or remove these lesions. Sunscreens undoubtedly help to decrease the rate of appearance and darkening of these lesions.

Seborrheic keratoses or seborrheic warts are also among the most common skin lesions of the elderly, and may often be confused with solar lentigo. Seborrheic keratoses, however, appear to be more variable in color, have a more hyperkeratotic and verrucous appearance, and tend to occur over the seborrheic areas. These lesions may number into the hundreds and appear primarily on the back, chest, and face, with a familial predisposition (Fig. 32.7). These lesions do not have malignant potential. Seborrheic keratoses often appear as greasy brown to black papules and look as if they are stuck on the skin. The lesion slowly enlarges over the years and may reach several centimeters in diameter. Individual lesions are variable in color, shape, and adherence and may be mistaken for a malignant melanoma, junctional nevus, or pigmented basal cell carcinoma. Occasion-

ally, the lesion may become irritated and quite tender or may develop into a cutaneous horn.

Eruptive seborrheic keratoses associated with internal malignancy are known as the sign of Leser-Trélat, first described in 1890. The lesions appear clinically as inflamed or even pigmented seborrheic keratoses. Historically, only 50% were typical seborrheic keratoses; the other half resembled acanthosis nigricans (15, 34, 88). Most commonly, the eruptive keratoses are found on the trunk, and 65% of cases occurred before or concurrent with the diagnosis of internal malignancy. Forty percent of the cases were associated with adenocarcinoma of the stomach. Lymphoma and leukemia were associated with 25% of the cases. The prognosis of this condition is extremely poor; 25% of the patients with the sign of Leser-Trélat die in 1–38 months (15, 34, 88).

Therapy is not required for seborrheic keratoses unless the lesions are cosmetically unacceptable, inflamed, or atypical in appearance. Removal may be achieved simply by curettage or with cryosurgery. In the case of a truly atypical appearing keratosis, complete excision may be necessary. In patients with numerous seborrheic keratoses, the use of topical α-hydroxyacids has been reported as an effective but slow method of removal of these lesions (87). It is particularly effective in removing early, flat seborrheic keratoses, and a more concentrated solution of glycolic acid, for example, must be used for more advanced, thicker keratoses.

Keratoacanthoma is a benign tumor occurring most commonly on sun-exposed skin in elderly individuals. The tumor most commonly is seen on the

Figure 32.7. Multiple seborrheic keratoses.

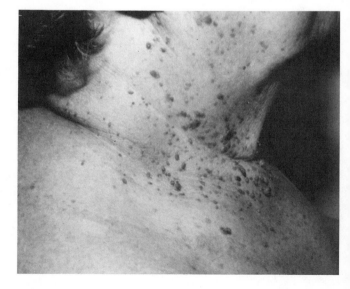

face and dorsum of the hands. It is usually solitary and dome-shaped with a central crater of keratinaceous plug (Fig. 32.8). It characteristically arises within a period of approximately 2–8 weeks, reaching a size of 1–2 cm in diameter, and may be quite destructive. It remains constant in size for another 2–8 weeks, then often involutes over several weeks becoming a depressed, hypopigmented scar. Rarely, a keratoacanthoma may transform into a squamous cell carcinoma. When this occurs, it is often controversial whether the initial lesion was not that of a squamous cell carcinoma (87).

Two variants of multiple keratoacanthomas exist and are termed multiple self-healing and eruptive (23, 79, 99).

Solitary keratoacanthoma must be differentiated from squamous cell carcinoma, which grows much more slowly, occurs in sun-exposed areas, and has an irregular shape with a tendency to ulcerate and not involute. Frequently, the diagnosis rests on histologic evaluation of the completely excised tumor, and even then differentiation from squamous cell carcinoma may be difficult (60). The patient must always be followed up carefully as if the tumor is a true carcinoma. Other disorders to rule out include

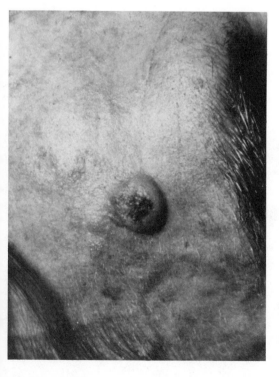

Figure 32.8. Solitary keratoacanthoma.

basal cell carcinoma, giant molluscum contagiosum, warts, irritated seborrheic keratoses, and inverted follicular keratosis, all of which warrant a biopsy to help differentiation.

Most keratoacanthomas undergo a benign self-healing course but may leave a large, unsightly scar. For cosmetic reasons and the rare case of malignant transformation, treatment is almost always preferred. Surgical excision of the solitary type is the treatment of choice for both cosmetic concerns and accurate histologic study. Curettage and electrodesiccation can also be effective in tumor removal. Others have reported the use of intralesional injection of 5-fluorouracil (5-FU) to be quite effective, especially for large mutilating types of keratoacanthoma or in lesions occurring on the nose and lips (60). Treatment for multiple keratoacanthomas is not effective, but some investigators advocate the use of systemic immunosuppressives or etretinate (11, 32).

PREMALIGNANT TUMORS OF THE EPIDERMIS

Premalignant lesions of the epidermis include actinic keratosis and Bowen's disease, both of which are predominantly seen in the elderly. Actinic keratoses appear as a keratotic papule or a red, scaling macule that may be surrounded by an erythematous halo (Fig. 32.9). They are often multiple and are more easily felt than seen since they have a rough quality. They are most prevalent in areas that receive heaviest solar exposure, such as the alopecic scalp, ears, cheeks, lower lip, nose, dorsum of the hands, and arms. Left alone, actinic keratoses gradually progress to basal cell carcinoma or squamous cell carcinoma over a period of years. At times, the scale may become quite thick, especially in lesions over the dorsal aspects of the hand, and should be viewed with suspicion. When these lesions become infiltrated or elevated, or become tender, malignant change may have occurred. Approximately 15–20% of actinic keratoses are said to evolve into squamous cell carcinomas that have an extremely low potential for metastases (61).

Solitary or multiple hypertrophic actinic keratoses may be treated with cryosurgery. For numerous poorly defined actinic keratoses on the face, scalp, and ears, topical treatment with 5-FU is preferable. The antimetabolite selectively destroys the pathologic cell leaving normal skin unharmed. The solar-damaged abnormal skin develops an inflammatory change at the site of application after 2–3 days of twice daily application. The inflammatory reaction continues to increase in intensity there-

Figure 32.9. Multiple actinic keratoses.

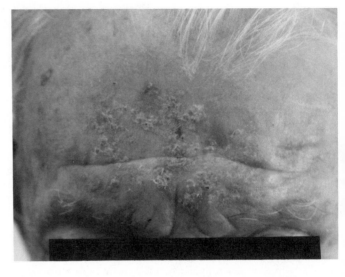

after, and treatment must be continued for 3-4 weeks. The affected area is allowed to heal spontaneously over a 2-3 week period, or a topical steroid may be applied to shorten the healing time and reduce redness. The new epidermis must be protected from the sun by a topical sunscreen. It should be noted, however, that 5-FU works poorly on lesions over the dorsal aspects of the hand and forearms, recurrent actinic keratoses, or lesions classified as cutaneous horns. Cryosurgery and surgical excision may be necessary for these resistant lesions.

Another newer method used in the treatment of multiple actinic keratoses has been the topical use of tretinoin before 5-FU or cryosurgery or as a primary

therapy (5). Actinic cheilitis of the lower lip has been treated by 5-FU, tretinoin, cryosurgery, partial lipectomy, and Moh's chemosurgery.

Bowen's disease is an intraepidermal-epidermoid cell carcinoma in situ. The lesion is usually seen as a well-circumscribed, scaly, indurated red plaque (Fig. 32.10), which may occur anywhere on the body. The lesion is often mistaken for psoriasis or eczema, which may delay biopsy. When Bowen's disease occurs on non–sun-exposed areas it may be associated with an increased prevalence of internal malignancy. The lesions may slowly enlarge over many years to nodular, invasive squamous cell carcinoma with a potential for metastasis. The lesion charac-

Figure 32.10. Bowen's disease.

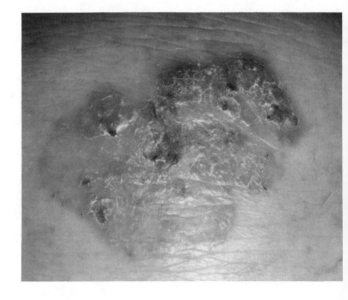

teristically resists topical steroid application, which should suggest the need for a skin biopsy. A variant of Bowen's disease, so-called erythroplasia of Queyrat, occurs on the glans penis in uncircumcised men, and may appear as a red, velvety, well-circumscribed plaque (31). In addition, Bowen's disease has been reported as a pigmented lesion resembling a melanoma or a pigmented basal cell carcinoma (19). In both these variants it is absolutely necessary to perform a biopsy in order to establish the correct diagnosis.

Treatment of Bowen's disease has included electrodesiccation and curettage, 5-FU application, cryosurgery, excision, and Moh's chemosurgery. Regardless of the type of therapy used, it is exceedingly important for these patients to have close follow-up examinations.

MALIGNANT TUMORS OF THE EPIDERMIS

In the elderly, the most common malignant tumor arising from the epidermal basal cells or cutaneous appendages is the basal cell carcinoma. This particular carcinoma is highly variable in appearance and may be flat, nodular, flesh-colored, black, scar-like, or ulcerative. They are usually found in sun-exposed areas, especially on the face and neck in light-skinned individuals. Ninety-three percent of basal cell carcinoma occur on the head and neck, 60% alone above a line drawn from the ear to the corner of the mouth, and 7% on the trunk (51). They are slow-growing and rarely metastasize.

Nodular ulcerative basal cell carcinoma, the most common form, presents as a waxy or pearly nodule with central ulceration and telangiectatic vessels threading across translucent, rolled, sloping borders (Fig. 32.11). Superficial basal cell carcinoma often presents as multiple lesions, and appears as superficial, sharply marginated plaques, with pearly, thread-like borders with a central crust. They occasionally appear like psoriasis and are often on the trunk (Fig. 32.12). Basal cell carcinoma may be deeply pigmented, looking much like a melanoma. Pigmented basal cell carcinoma does not differ in malignant potential from nonpigmented basal cell carcinoma but does seem to be more common in brown-eyed individuals. The most subtle form of basal cell carcinoma is the morpheaform or sclerosing type. It is also the most difficult to cure because of its nondistinct borders. It appears as a flatter, depressed, scarred patch that slowly enlarges to form a plaque (Fig. 32.13). Telangiectasias are present, and there is a shiny, waxy quality to the lesion.

Squamous cell carcinoma has a much greater propensity to metastasize than basal cell carcinoma but is far less frequent. It is most commonly seen on the face and the dorsal aspects of the hands but may occur on any sun-exposed surface or chronically irritated or damaged area. The clinical appearance of squamous cell carcinoma is also quite variable and may be scaled, ulcerative, nodular, and fungating. Most squamous cell carcinomas appear as solitary, keratotic nodules with an erythematous base and nondistinct borders (Fig. 32.14). These often develop into a shallow ulcer that is covered by scale and has a cribriform floor.

Figure 32.11. Nodular ulcerative basal cell carcinoma.

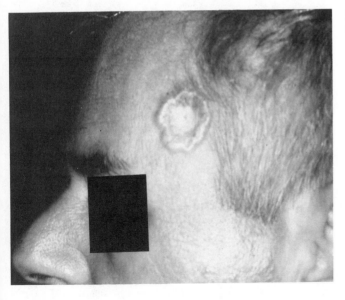

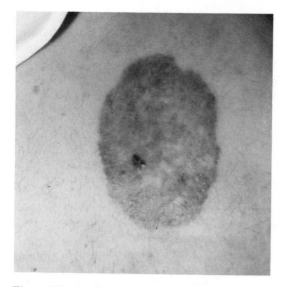

Figure 32.12. Superficial basal cell carcinoma.

Squamous cell carcinoma is usually preceded by intraepidermal carcinoma or a premalignant lesion such as an actinic keratosis, actinic cheilitis, or leukoplakia of the lower lip or buccal mucosa . Verrucous carcinoma, a special form of squamous cell carcinoma, has a warty condylomatous appearance and may be seen most commonly on the penis and foot, often misdiagnosed as a wart (83). Squamous cell carcinoma has the potential for rapid growth,

but it is unpredictable as to how long it will remain localized to the epidermis before involving the underlying dermis or metastasizing. Invasive squamous cell carcinoma arising in actinic keratoses is less likely to metastasize than carcinoma arising from Bowen's disease, previously irradiated tissue, or scars resulting from chronic infection or trauma. Squamous cell carcinoma arising in areas of no sun-exposure such as the penis, anus, or vermillion border is much more rapidly invasive than squamous cell carcinoma occurring in sun-exposed areas (71).

Therapy for either basal cell carcinoma or squamous cell carcinoma must be tailored for the individual lesion on the basis of many factors (80). These include cell type, tumor size, ease of defining margins clinically, and depth of invasion as indicated by biopsy. In addition, the age and general health of the patient, previous treatment of recurrent cancers, postoperative patient disability, length of time treatment takes, and cosmetic factors all must be taken in to account before selecting the best method of therapy for each specific skin cancer. Although the most satisfactory treatment is surgical excision with normal skin margins, it might be more appropriate to use cryosurgery, radiotherapy, or electrodesiccation and curettage. In unusually large, deep, or recurrent lesions, especially around the nose, the use of Moh's histographic chemosurgery may be necessary. Regardless of the procedure, the malignant tissue must be removed in its entirety. The area must then be observed at regular 3-month

Figure 32.13. Sclerosing basal cell carcinoma.

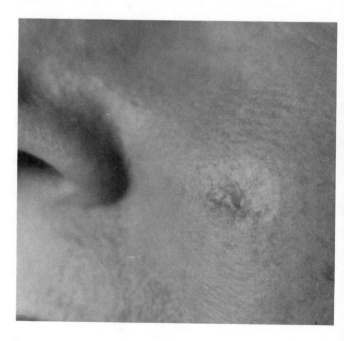

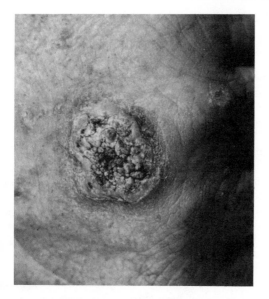

Figure 32.14. Squamous cell carcinoma.

intervals to assess whether recurrences have occurred.

MELANOCYTIC TUMORS

Many variations occur in benign, nevocellular nevi, which first appear in persons from birth to adolescence. Throughout their existence, they may change in color, shape, and size. Often these changes are normal changes associated with aging, irritation, or pregnancy. When suspicious changes occur in any type of nevocellular lesion, lesions should be removed, and histologic evaluation is mandatory.

The benign types of nevocellular tumors of the skin are junctional nevi, dermal nevi, compound nevi, halo nevi, and blue nevi. Junctional nevi are macular and have a uniform brown or black color that does not diffuse into normal skin. The margins are regular. Dermal nevi usually have little or no pigment and are elevated, skin-colored soft papules or nodules with regular margins. They grow slowly with age and may become irritated by friction and thus necessitate removal. Compound nevi combine the characteristics of dermal nevi and junctional nevi, and appear as an elevated nodule with uniform brown color and contour. The halo nevus is a junctional nevus with an area of hypopigmentation surrounding the lesion with a resulting white macule. Blue nevi are not common, and consist of small dark blue to blue-black smooth firm nodules that may occur on any surface of the body. Because of its color the blue nevus is often excised for histologic differentiation from melanoma.

The number of nevocellular nevi increases up to the fourth decade and then begins to involute. The appearance of new nevocellular nevi after the age of 40 should be viewed with suspicion and dictate close follow-up or biopsy to rule out malignancy. Those that do occur after the age of 40 are histologically junctional nevi, but 25% of those originally read as junctional nevi in this older age category were reevaluated and thought to be atypical in appearance.

Lentigines are lesions caused by a slight increase in the melanocyte number and definite increase in melanocyte pigmentation and have been discussed earlier ("Benign Tumors of the Epidermis").

Lentigo maligna is a lesion of the head and neck of the elderly that is premalignant and may develop into lentigo maligna melanoma. The lesion is irregularly pigmented and is often noted by the patient to have changed in size, shape, and contour (Fig. 32.15). The lesion histologically is essentially a melanoma in situ. There is a tendency for this tumor to extend down through hair follicles and adnexal structures into the dermis. It has been estimated that 50% of these lesions will become invasive malignant melanoma if not adequately treated, and a further 10% will metastasize (38, 45). It is also clear that lentigo malignant melanoma behaves biologi-

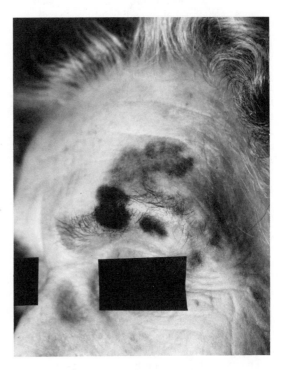

Figure 32.15. Lentigo maligna melanoma.

cally like other malignant melanomas. It is absolutely essential that lesions with these characteristics undergo biopsy in several different locations for histologic evaluation and correct diagnosis.

Therapy for lentigo maligna revolves around complete surgical excision with 0.5–1.0 cm margins and has been reported to have a 90% cure rate (52). When treating lentigo maligna or lentigo maligna melanoma, one must consider the age as well as cosmetic appearance following such a surgical procedure. Other methods that are available include cryosurgery with a double freeze-thaw cycle, which results in a full-thickness destruction of the dermis (101). It should be kept in mind that this type of procedure should be avoided in areas such as the scalp, eyelids, alae nasi, and nasolabial folds. If the patient is not a good candidate for surgical procedures, conventional radiation or ortho-voltage has also been reported to have a 90% cure rate (12).

Malignant melanoma is the most malignant of all skin cancers. Prognosis varies with the depth of invasion of the tumor. Melanoma varies from macular to nodular forms, with colors ranging from flesh-tint to pitch black. Other colors such as white, blue, purple, and red are also represented. The border tends to be irregular and growth may be rapid. In men, it tends to be seen on the upper back in the 50- to 60-year-old individuals as the nodular form, and in women, on the lower legs in the 20- to 40-year-old range, as a superficial spreading lesion.

There are four variants of melanoma. The lentigo maligna melanoma, as discussed above, occurs in the elderly individual and develops from a preexisting lentigo maligna. Superficial spreading malignant melanoma is the most common variety of melanoma. It begins as a small brown papule that later develops irregular variegated color changes ranging from various shades of brown to black, gray, and white. The borders are raised and palpable and may have pseudopods or notching. The surface may be irregular with loss of skin markings, and ulceration may occur. Satellite lesions may also be seen. These lesions expand in the horizontal plane within the dermis for years before entering the vertical growth phase. This is the case with lentigo maligna melanoma and acral lentiginous melanoma. Acral lentiginous melanoma is also a type of superficial melanoma with pigmented lesions occurring on the palms and soles, especially in blacks and elderly individuals. These lesions tend to grow slowly, and after years exhibit variations in color such as blacks, blues, and reds. They may also become papular and nodular, signaling overt melanoma.

The nodular malignant melanoma has the poorest prognosis and is often found on the upper back in middle-aged individuals. These lesions often appear as dark, blue-black to reddish brown nodules without surrounding hyperpigmented macular areas. The surface may be smooth or ulcerated. The nodular melanoma has the poorest prognosis because it has an early vertical growth phase, and often metastases are present at the time of initial presentation.

Differential diagnosis in the case of malignant melanoma may be difficult when dealing with other pigmented lesions, and almost always necessitates an excisional biopsy with histologic evaluation whenever a lesion is suspicious. Those lesions that can be confused with lentigo maligna melanoma and acral lentiginous melanoma include benign lentigos, junctional nevi, early seborrheic keratoses, and pigmented actinic keratoses. Seborrheic keratoses, nevi, pigmented basal cell carcinoma, and pigmented Bowen's disease may be mistaken for superficial spreading melanoma. Nodular melanoma may be confused with skin lesions such as blue nevi, angiokeratoma, glomus tumors, and dermatofibromas. The definitive diagnosis of suspicious pigmented lesions is best confirmed by a total excisional biopsy. When the lesion is too large to excise easily, an adequate representative incisional biopsy may be performed. This must provide enough tissue to evaluate depth of invasion for prognostic and therapeutic purposes. When the tumor thickness, measured from the stratum corneum to the deepest dermal melanoma cells, is less than 0.76 mm, metastasis to local lymph nodes is unlikely and prognosis is very favorable. If this depth is greater than 1.5 mm, prognosis is poor since the likelihood of lymph node involvement is high. When the tumor depth is 0.76–1.5 mm, prognosis and lymph node involvement are not easily predictable.

Wide excisional surgery is the preferred method of initial treatment of melanomas. On an extremity, a melanoma with a tumor depth of 0.76 mm or greater also seems best treated with wide excision plus local chemoperfusion of the limb. The value of node dissection is unclear, but when necessary, continuous node dissection is best. The treatment of disseminated malignant melanoma is chemotherapy or immunotherapy. These are experimental therapies that require well-organized surgical-oncologic-immunologic faculty working in concert.

MESODERMAL TUMORS

Mesodermal tumors of the elderly include both benign and malignant lesions. The most common benign tumors include hemangiomas, venous lakes, angiokeratomas, dermatofibromas, fibroepitheliomas, and sebaceous hyperplasia. The malignant mesodermal tumors include dermatofibroma sarcoma protuberans, Kaposi's hemorrhagic sarcoma, and angiosarcoma. These lesions are dermal or subcutaneous in position and are often papulonodular. They do not usually alter the surface texture of the epidermis and their color is usually a variation of red, blue, or yellow.

Angiomatous lesions of the skin in the elderly are quite common, easily identified by their red to blue color and the ability to force blood out of the lesion with light pressure. Cherry angiomas are bright red papular lesions seen on the trunk and are very common in the elderly. Venous lakes on the face, especially the lips, are also common in the elderly and appear as blue papular or nodular lesions. Angiokeratomas of Fordyce are small red to bluish-black papular tumors on the scrotum that begin in middleage and become quite numerous and common in the elderly. The angiomatous lesions persist indefinitely and usually require no therapy other than reassuring the patient of its benign nature.

Dermatofibromas may occur anywhere but are most common on the legs and arms. They appear as firm brown to pink papules or nodules. They dimple when palpated and have a very hard consistency. The lesions are generally asymptomatic but may become irritated from shaving, especially over the legs in women, and necessitate excision. Fibroepitheliomas or skin tags are papillomatous lesions usually occurring over the neck, axillae, groin, and inframammary regions and are thought to be familial. They begin in persons of middle age and progress in size and number. They may easily be removed by electrodesiccation and curettage, scissor excision followed by hemostasis, or cryosurgery. The occurrence of the fibroepitheliomas and their association with adenomatous colonic polyps has recently been reported, but its significance needs further study (10).

MALIGNANT MESODERMAL TUMORS

Two important malignant tumors of mesodermal origin are Kaposi's hemorrhagic sarcoma and angiosarcoma. Kaposi's sarcoma is relatively uncommon and is usually seen in elderly patients, unless immunosuppression occurs, as in the case of renal transplants or if acquired immune deficiency syndrome is present (36). Classic Kaposi's sarcoma lesions begin on the lower legs, usually as blue papules or plaques (Fig. 32.16). Elderly men are more commonly affected than women, and lesions occur much more commonly in persons of Mediterranean descent and in Africans. Cutaneous lesions may exist

alone or in conjunction with systemic lesions, particularly in the gastrointestinal and lymphoreticular systems. Therapy consists of local radiation, vinblastine, or cyclophosphamide, all with variable but generally good results, largely dependent upon the extent of disease or immunologic status of the patient.

Angiosarcoma is an aggressive tumor, usually seen in the scalp of elderly patients. The lesion may appear as reddish-purple nodules that may bleed but are generally asymptomatic (Fig. 32.17). The nodular component is often only the tip of the tumor mass, which may infiltrate deeply into the scalp and underlying tissue. Any unexplained angiomatous-appearing nodular tumor of the scalp in the elderly should alert the physician to consider the diagnosis of angiosarcoma. Treatment of this tumor requires wide excision, usually with grafting, and the prognosis is generally poor since the diagnosis is made late in the course of this malignancy.

SUMMARY

Cutaneous problems encountered when treating the elderly patient are often common to all age groups. However, changes in the skin resulting from metabolic alterations, sun exposure, occupational hazards, and underlying diseases create a milieu that allows for many disorders to occur with greater frequency and severity in the elderly than in younger individuals. The physician must be able to recognize these pathologic changes and decide on appropriate therapy. Many dermatologic problems in the elderly are benign in nature and considered largely a cosmetic problem by the practicing physician. Decision to treat or not to treat should always take into account the psychologic impact upon elderly patients who already may feel that the world has little need for them.

REFERENCES

1. Adler A, Safa B: Immunity in wart resolution. *J Am Acad Dermatol* 1:305–309, 1979.
2. Angelini G, Rantuccio F, Meneghini CL: Contact dermatitis in patients with leg ulcers. *Contact Dermatitis* 1:81, 1975.
3. Ayres S, Mikan R: Post herpes zoster neuralgia: response to vitamin E therapy. *Arch Dermatol* 108:855–856, 1973.
4. Bean B, Brava C, Balfour HH: Acyclovir therapy for acute herpes zoster. *Lancet* 2:118–121, 1982.
5. Bercovitch L: Topical chemotherapy of actinic keratosis of the upper extremity with tretinoin and 5-fluorouracil: a double blind controlled study. *Br J Dermatol* 116:549–552, 1987.
6. Braverman I: *Skin Signs of Systemic Disease.* Philadelphia, WB Saunders, 1981.

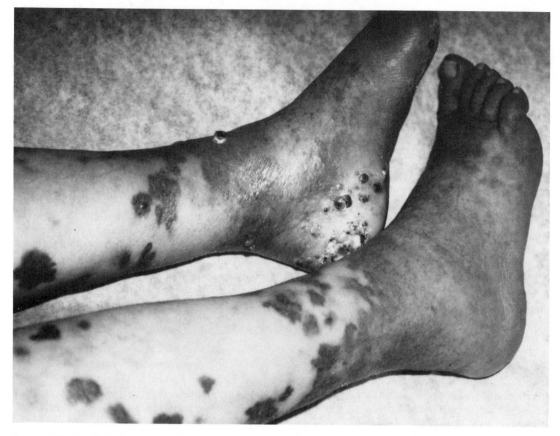

Figure 32.16. Kaposi's hemorrhagic sarcoma.

Figure 32.17. Angiosarcoma.

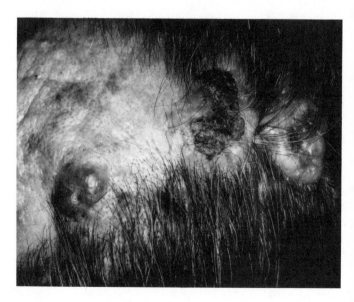

7. Briggaman RA, Wheeler JCE: Immunology of human warts. *J Am Acad Dermatol* 1:297–303, 1979.

8. Callen JP: *Cutaneous Aspects of Internal Disease.* Chicago, Year Book, 1981.

9. Cawley EP, Curtis AL: Lentigo senilis. *Arch Dermatol Syph* 62:635–641, 1950.

10. Chobanian J, et al: Skin tags as a marker for adenomatous polyps of the colon. *Ann Intern Med* 103:892, 1985.

11. Cristofolini M, Piscioli F, Zumiani G, et al: The role of etretinate in the management of keratoacanthoma. *J Am Acad Dermatol* 12:633–638, 1985.

12. Dancuart F, Harwood AR, Fitzpatrick PJ: The radiotherapy of lentigo maligna and lentigo maligna melanoma of the head and neck. *Cancer* 45:2279–2283, 1980.

13. Eaglstein WH, Katz R, Brown JA: The effects of early corticosteroid therapy on skin eruption and pain of herpes zoster. *JAMA* 211:1681–1683, 1970.

14. Easton P, Gailbraith PR: Cimetidine treatment of pruritus in polycythemia vera. *N Engl J Med* 299:1134, 1978.

15. Elewski BE, Gilgor RS: Eruptive lesions and malignancy. *Int J Dermatol* 24:617–629, 1985.

16. Farber EM, South DA: Urea ointment in the nonsurgical avulsion of nail dystrophies. *Cutis* 22:689, 1978.

17. Fisher AA: Contact dermatitis in elderly patients. In: *Contact Dermatitis.* Philadelphia, Lea & Febiger, 1986, pp 58–61.

18. Fisher AA: Dermatitis due to transdermal therapeutic systems. *Cutis* 34:526, 1984.

19. Fisher GB, Greer KE, Walker AN: Bowen's disease mimicking melanoma. *Arch Dermatol* 118:444–445, 1982.

20. Fisher MS, Kripke ML: Nature of systemic alteration induced in mice by ultraviolet irradiation and its relationship to ultraviolet carcinogenesis. *Proc Natl Acad Sci USA* 74:1688–1692, 1977.

21. Gammon WR, Chronic acquired bullous diseases in the elderly—diagnosis and treatment. Presented at the Westwood Carolina Conference on Clinical Dermatology, Oct 8–10, 1986.

22. Gammon WR, et al: epidermolysis bullosa acquisita—pemphigoid-like disease. *J Am Acad Dermatol* 11:820, 1984.

23. Ghadially FW: Keratoacanthoma. In Fitzpatrick RB, Eisen AZ, Wolfe K, Freedberg IM, Austen KF (eds): *Dermatology in General Medicine: Textbook and Atlas,* ed 2. New York, McGraw Hill, 1979, pp 383–389.

24. Gilbert HS, Warner RR, Wasserman LR: A study of histamine in myeloproliferative disease. *Blood* 28:795–805, 1966.

25. Gilchrest BA: Ageing. *Jr Am Acad Dermatol* 11:995–997, 1984.

26. Gilchrest BA, Glog FB, et al: Effects of aging and chronic sun exposure on melanocytes in human skin. *J Invest Dermatol.* 73:141–143, 1979.

27. Gilchrest BA, Rowe JW, Brown RS, et al: Ultraviolet phototherapy of uremic pruritus: long-term results and possible mechanisms of action. *Ann Intern Med* 91:17–21, 1979.

28. Gilchrest BA, Sauder DN: Autocrine growth stimulation of human keratinocytes by epidermal cell-derived thymocyte activating factor (ETAF): implications for cellular aging. *Clin Res* 32:585A, 1984.

29. Gilchrest BA, Stern R, Steinman TI, et al: Clinical features of pruritus among patients undergoing maintenance hemodialysis. *Arch Dermatol* 118:154–156, 1982.

30. Gilchrest BA, Szabo G, Flynn E, Goldwyn RM: Chronologic and actinically induced aging in human facial skin. *J Invest Dermatol* 80:815–855, 1983.

31. Goette DK: Review of erythroplasia of Queyrat and its treatment. *Urology* 8:311, 1976.

32. Goette DK, Odom RB, Arrott JW, et al: Treatment of keratoacanthoma with topical application of fluorouracil. *Arch Dermatol* 118:309–311, 1982.

33. Grove GL, Kligman AM: Age-associated changes in human epidermal cell renewal. *J Gerontol* 38:137, 1983.

34. Halery S, Feverman EJ: The sign of Leser-Trelat: a cutaneous marker for internal malignancy. *Int J Dermatol* 24:359–361, 1985.

35. Hampers CL, Katz AI, Wilson RE, et al: Disappearance of "uremic" itching after subtotal parathyroidectomy. *N Engl J Med* 279:695–697, 1968.

36. Harwood AR, Osoba D, Hofstader SL, et al: Kaposi's sarcoma in recipients of renal transplants. *Am J Med* 67:759–765, 1979.

37. Hodgson C: Lentigo senilis. *Arch Dermatol* 87:197–207, 1963.

38. Jackson R, Williamson GS, Beattie WG: Lentigo maligna and malignant melanoma. *Can Med Assoc J* 95:846–851, 1966.

39. Jacobson KW, Branch LB, Nelson HS: Laboratory tests in chronic urticaria. *JAMA* 243:1644, 1980.

40. Jarrat M, Hill M, Smiles K: Topical protection against long wave ultraviolet A. *J Amer Acad Dermatol* 9:354–360, 1983.

41. Kauppinen K: Cutaneous reactions to drugs. *Acta Derm suppl* 68:52, 1972.

42. Kernbaum S, Hauchecorne J: Administration of levodopa for relief of herpes zoster pain. *JAMA* 246:132–134, 1981.

43. Kligman AM: Perspectives and problems in cutaneous gerontology. *J Invest Dermatol* 73:39, 1979.

44. Kligman LH, Akin FJ, Kligman AM: The contribution of UVA and UVB to connective tissue damage in hairless mice. *J Invest Dermatol* 84:272–276, 1985.

45. Koh HK, et al: Lentigo maligna melanoma has no better prognosis than other types of melanoma. *J Clin Oncol* 2:994, 1984.

46. Koranda FC, Dehmel FM, Kahn G, et al: I. Cutaneous complications in immunosuppressed renal homograft recipients. *JAMA* 229:419–424, 1974.

47. Kripke ML: Immunology of UV-induced skin cancer, yearly review. *Photochem Photobiol* 32:837–839, 1980.

48. Lavker RM: Structural alterations in exposed and unexposed aged skin. *J Invest Dermatol* 73:59–66, 1979.

49. Lavker RM, Zheng PS, Dong G: Morphology of aged skin. *Dermatol Clin* 4:379–389, 1986.

50. Logan RA, Bhogal B, Das AK et. al: Localization of bullous pemphigoid antibody—an indirect immuno-

fluorescence study of 228 cases using a split-skin technique. *Br J Dermatol* 117(4):471–478, 1987.

51. Lynch PJ: Common malignant and premalignant tumors of the skin. *Ariz Med* 34:90, 1977.

52. Maize JC: Pigmented lesions in the elderly. Presented at the Westwood Carolina Conference on Clinical Dermatology, Oct 8–10, 1986.

53. Mavligit GM, Talpaz M: Cimetadine for herpes zoster. *N Engl J Med* 310:318–319, 1984.

54. Melmon KL: Preventable drug reactions—causes and cures. *N Engl J Med* 284:1361, 1971.

55. Michalowski R, Rodziewicz H: Incidence of erythrasma in elderly women. *Arch Dermatol* 92:396, 1965.

56. Michalowski R, Rodziewicz H: Pityriasis versicolor in the aged. *Br J Dermatol* 77:388, 1965.

57. Moberg S: Tinea capitis in the elderly. A report on two cases caused by *Trichophyton tonsurans. Dermatologica* 169(1):36–40, 1984.

58. Mutasim DF, Takahashi Y, Labib RS, et al: A pool of bullous pemphigoid antigen is intracellular and associated with the basal cell cytoskeleton-hemidesmosome complex. *J Invest Dermatol* 84:47, 1985.

59. Nathanson RB, Forbes PD, Urbach F: Modification by antilymphocytic serum of 6-mercaptopurine. *Proc Am Assoc Cancer Res* 14:46, 1973.

60. Odom RB, Goette DK: Treatment of keratoacanthomas with intralesional 5-fluorouracil. *Arch Dermatol* 114:1779, 1978.

61. Parler F: Skin tumors: Malignant and premalignant. *Geriatrics* 38(10):79–114, 1983.

62. Pass F: Warts: biology and current therapy. *Minn Med* 57:844–847, 1974.

63. Payne C: Ultrasound for postherpetic neuralgia. A study to investigate the results of treatment. *Physiotherapy* 70:96–97, 1984.

64. Pearson JR, Rogers RS III: Bullous and cicatricial pemphigoid. *Mayo Clin Proc* 52:54, 1977.

65. Plewig G, Wikolowski J, Wolff HH: Action of isotretinoin in acne rosacea and gram-negative folliculitis. *J Am Acad Dermatol* 6:766–785, 1982.

66. Pyer J, Burton JL: A double blind trial of metronidazole. *Lancet* 1:1211–1212, 1976.

67. Raimer SS, Pursley TV: Office management of viral skin infections in the elderly. *Geriatrics* 36:53–63, 1981.

68. Rajka G: Investigation of patients suffering from generalized pruritus, with special reference to systemic disease. *Acta Derm Venereol (Stockh)* 49:190–194, 1966.

69. Regnier M, Vaigot P, Michel S, et al: Localization of bullous pemphigoid antigen (BPA) in isolated human keratinocytes. *J Invest Dermatol* 85:187, 1985.

70. Roberts-Thompson ID, Whittingham S, Youngchaiyerd U, et al: Aging, immune response and mortality. *Lancet* 2:368, 1974.

71. Robinson JK: Skin problems of aging. *Geriatrics* 38:57–65, 1983.

72. Roujeau JC, Andre C, Fabre MJ, et al: Plasma exchange in pemphigus. *Arch Dermatol* 119:215–221, 1983.

73. Rushforth AF: Griseofulvin in herpes zoster. *Br Med J* 3:438, 1975,

74. Saltzer, EI: Relief from uremic pruritus: a therapeutic approach. *Cutis* 16:298–299, 1975.

75. Sauder DN, Carter C, Katz SI, Oppenheim JJ: Epidermal cell production of thymocyte activating factor (ETAF). *J Invest Dermatol* 79:34–39, 1982.

76. Shelley WB, Shelley ED: *Advanced Dermatologic Therapy.* Philadelphia, WB Saunders, 1987.

77. Shigeta S, Yokota T, Iwabuchi, et al: Comparative efficacy of antiherpes drugs against various strains of varicella-zoster virus. *J Infect Dis* 147:576–584, 1983.

78. Sklar SH, Blue WT, Alexander EJ, et al: The treatment and prevention of neuralgia with adenosine monophosphate. *JAMA* 253:1427–1430, 1985.

79. Sommerville J, Milne JA: Familial primary self-healing squamous epithelioma of the skin (Ferguson Smith Type). *Br J Dermatol* 62:485–490, 1950.

80. Spencer AD: Treatment of skin cancer using multiple modalities. *J Am Acad Dermatol* 7:143–171, 1982.

81. Stanley JR, Hawley-Nelson P, Yuspa SH, et al: Characterization of bullous pemphigoid antigen: a unique basement membrane protein of stratified squamous epithelia. *Cell* 24:897, 1981.

82. Suzuki H, Oaawa S, Nakagwa H, et al: Cryocautery of sensitized skin areas for the relief of pain due to postherpetic neuralgia. *Pain* 9:355–362, 1980.

83. Swanson NA, Taylor WB: Plantar verrucous carcinoma. *Arch Dermatol* 116:754, 1980.

84. Thiers BH, Maize JC, Spicer SS, Cantor AB The effect of aging and chronic sun exposure on human Langerhans cell population. *J Invest Dermatol* 82:223–226, 1984.

85. Tindall JP, Smith JG: Skin lesions of the aged and their association with internal changes. *JAMA* 186:1039, 1963.

86. Urbach F, Cole CA: Effects of light source and photosensitizer on predicted protection factors of UVA sunscreens. *Photochem Photobiol* 43:865, 1986.

87. Van Scott E: Removal of seborrheic keratoses with the topical application of alpha hydroxy acid preparations. Presented at the Westwood Carolina Conference on Clinical Dermatology, Oct 8–10, 1986.

88. Venencie PY, Perry HO: Sign of Leser–Trelat: report of two cases and review of the literature. *J Am Acad Dermatol* 10:83–88, 1984.

89. Vickers CF: Iron deficiency and the skin. *Br J Dermatol* 89(suppl 9):10, 1973.

90. Walder BR, Robertson MR, Jeremy D: Skin cancer and immunosuppression. *Lancet* 2:1282–1283, 1971.

91. Waldorf DS, Willkens RD, Decker JD: Impaired delayed hypersensitivity in an aging population: association with antinuclear activity and rheumatoid factors. *JAMA* 203:831, 1968.

92. Weis D, Sriwatana KUK, Weintraub M: Treatment of postherpetic neuralgia and acute herpetic pain with amitriptyline and perphenazine. *S Afr Med J* Aug 21:62(9), 274–275, 1982.

93. Weiss JS, Ellis CN, Headington JT, Tincoff T, Hamilton TA, Voorhees JJ: Topical tretinoin improves photoaged skin: a double-blind vehicle controlled study. *JAMA* 259:527–532, 1988.

94. Welton DG, Greenberg BG: Trends in office practice of dermatology, part I. *Arch Dermatol* 83:355, 1961.

95. Welton DG, Greenberg BG: Trends in office practice of dermatology, part III. *Arch Dermatol* 90:296, 1964.

96. Westburg SP, Stone OJ: Multiple cutaneous squamous cell carcinomas during immunosuppressive therapy. *Arch Dermatol* 107:893–895, 1973.

97. Whitman GB, Leach EE, DeLeo VA, Flein SL, Canetta B, Harber LC: Comparative study of erythema response to UVA radiation in guinea pigs and humans. *Photochem Photobiol* 42:399–403, 1985.

98. Wilson BO: Linear IgA bullous dermatosis: an immunologically defined disease. *Int J Dermatol* 24:569, 1985.

99. Winkleman RK, Brown J: Generalized eruptive keratoacanthoma: report of cases. *Arch Dermatol* 87:615–623, 1968.

100. Young AW, Sweeney EW, David DS, et al: Dermatologic evaluation of pruritus in patients on hemodialysis. *NY State J Med* 73:2670–2674, 1973.

101. Zacharian SA: Cryosurgical treatment of lentigo maligna. *Arch Dermatol* 118:89–92, 1982.

CHAPTER 33

Anemia in the Elderly

SHELDON C. KRAVITZ

Mechanisms of anemia in the elderly are no different from those in any age group—namely, blood loss, increased red cell destruction, decreased red cell production, or various combinations thereof. I would like to stress in this chapter the clinical problems prevalent in the elderly that are often associated with anemia. I make particular reference to malignancies, renal insufficiency, and anemias that may be due to the drugs often used by the elderly.

The manifestations of anemia in the elderly are apt to be referable to the cardiovascular system. Pallor and fatigue are common to all age groups. Glossitis and paresthesias are peculiar to anemia associated with vitamin B_{12} deficiency. However, increasing dyspnea and angina are often the initial manifestations of anemia in an older person, especially those with coexistent heart disease.

BLOOD LOSS

Anemia from acute hemorrhage is not usually a diagnostic problem. The anemia *per se* tends to be normochromic unless there has been considerable bleeding prior to the time the patient comes under medical care. Patients who appear with anemia secondary to long-standing bleeding have a characteristic peripheral blood picture. Hypochromia of the red cells is marked, and numerous microcytes may be seen in the peripheral smear. The serum iron levels are reduced, and the iron-binding capacity tends to be increased. Bone marrow examination shows marked reduction in stainable iron. The majority of patients who present in this manner have occult bleeding from the gastrointestinal tract. The common causes of such an anemia are carcinoma of the right side of the colon, hiatus hernia, peptic ulcer, and polyps of the small intestine. Sometimes, as in the case of hemorrhoids, the bleeding may be visible to the patient on a daily basis. Each day's blood loss

may seem insignificant. However, the total amount of blood loss may be considerable and result, in the unsuspecting patient, in a severe iron deficiency anemia. The following cases are representative of commonly encountered clinical problems.

Case 1. A 71-year-old man was noted to be pale on a chance meeting with his physician. He had been in perfect health. When his pallor was pointed out to him, he admitted to the possibility of having had recent easy fatigability. His physical examination was entirely within normal limits. His hematocrit was 23%. The hemoglobin was 6.5 g/100 ml. The white blood cell count was 6800 with 68% polymorphonuclear leukocytes (polys), 30% lymphocytes, and 2% monocytes. The platelets were normal. Examination of the peripheral blood smear revealed marked hypochromia of the red cells. A barium enema revealed a polypoid carcinoma of the cecum. The lesion was resected. The patient survived 4 years and died of metastases to the liver.

In this case, the anemia was the first sign that led to the diagnosis of his carcinoma.

Case 2. A 60-year-old man, who had been followed for chronic asthmatic bronchitis and arteriosclerotic heart disease with angina pectoris over a 10-year period, began to complain of increasing dyspnea on exertion and angina. He was admitted to the hospital *via* the emergency room because of chest pain and dyspnea. His physical examination was unrevealing. His hematocrit was found to be 23%. The hemoglobin was 7.4 g/100 ml. The white blood cell count was 7800 with a normal differential. The platelets were normal. The mean corpuscular volume (MCV) was markedly reduced to 65 μm^3 and the mean corpuscular hemoglobin (MCH) to 21 pg. The serum iron was 19 μg/ml. Three stools were positive for blood. There were ECG changes of coronary insufficiency. Upper gastrointestinal (GI) series disclosed a large hiatus hernia with marked gastroesophageal reflux. He received two units of packed red cells and was started on a bland diet, antacids, and iron. His chest pain and dyspnea disappeared. His hematocrit gradually was restored to normal, and on this regimen the patient has had no recurrence of anemia.

This case typifies the insidious appearance of a severe iron deficiency anemia associated with a large hiatus hernia, without any gastrointestinal complaints or melena. The manifestations of his anemia were those of coronary insufficiency.

Case 3. A 71-year-old man was admitted to the hospital because of progressive pallor and weakness and was found to have a severe anemia. His physical examination revealed no evidence of lymphadenopathy or hepatosplenomegaly. There was pallor of the skin and conjunctivae. He had no purpura. There were no palpable abdominal masses. His hematocrit was 25%. The hemoglobin was 7.8 g/100 ml. The white blood cell count was 25,000 with 60% mature lymphocytes in the peripheral blood. The platelets were normal. The peripheral blood smear revealed hypochromia of the red cells. The bone marrow was infiltrated with lymphocytes, indicative of chronic lymphocytic leukemia. Stools for blood were negative. Barium enema and GI series were negative.

A diagnosis of chronic lymphocytic leukemia was made. The hematology consultant pointed out, however, that the hypochromic anemia was suggestive of iron deficiency, probably due to chronic blood loss.

Since no site of bleeding could be found, the patient was transfused and followed for his lymphocytic leukemia on no therapy. He did well until 12 months later when he had a sudden drop of his hematocrit from normal levels to 28%. This time he did, indeed, have blood in his stools. Gastrointestinal x-rays were repeated and again no lesion was found. The bleeding stopped. The patient was transfused and he was again followed carefully. His leukemic status was of interest in that he had very little rise in his white cell count and did not develop any lymphadenopathy or hepatosplenomegaly. Some 18 months after the onset of his illness, the patient again became anemic, again was found to have blood in his stools, and this time was found to have a carcinoma in his cecum. It was resected and the patient did well for 3 years until he developed jaundice secondary to metastatic cancer in the liver, from which he died. A year and a half prior to his death, his white cell count began to rise progressively and reached a high of 200,000. At that time antileukemic therapy was started. The white cell count fell to below 50,000 and the patient did well until he developed liver metastases.

The interesting point in this man's case is that he was initially found to have an anemia and a coexistent chronic lymphocytic leukemia. The anemia was hypochromic, and subsequent events proved that this was undoubtedly due to occult bleeding from carcinoma of the cecum. Following resection,

the patient remained free of anemia for almost 2 years. Accurate evaluation of an anemia, despite the presence of a seemingly obvious cause such as chronic leukemia, finally resulted in uncovering an underlying carcinoma of the cecum, from which he eventually died. Currently, endoscopy provides another valuable diagnostic approach to occult gastrointestinal bleeding when results of radiologic studies are negative.

INCREASED RED CELL DESTRUCTION

Increased red cell destruction, resulting in a decrease in red cell survival, is due either to intracorpuscular defects or to extracorpuscular factors. Those hemolytic anemias that are associated with the former are usually congenital and are most often diagnosed early in life. There are, however, rare cases in which patients with hereditary spherocytosis have gone undiagnosed beyond the age of 50. I saw one such patient in her seventh decade, with previously unrecognized spherocytosis.

Hemolytic anemias are associated with varying degrees of anemia and jaundice, elevated levels of indirect bilirubin, splenomegaly, reticulocytosis, and erythroid hyperplasia of the bone marrow. The two studies that offer proof of increased red cell destruction are the demonstration of increased fecal urobilinogen excretion and decreased red cell survival. The latter studies are needed infrequently to prove the presence of hemolysis.

When a hemolytic anemia is suspected, the various causes must be considered. Table 33.1 is a simple classification that one should bear in mind when faced with the differential diagnosis of a patient with hemolytic anemia. As may be seen from this table, hemolytic anemias may occur during an acute infection. This table includes examples of organisms that may cause infection in the elderly. The hemolytic anemia that occurs in the setting of an acute infection with sepsis is usually rapidly developing with reticulocytosis and mild jaundice. The anemia tends to be self-limited and remits as the patient's infection is brought under control.

Hemolytic anemias due to autoantibodies, autoimmune hemolytic anemias (AHA), are also seen in the older age groups, particularly in patients with chronic lymphocytic leukemia, one of the commonest hematologic disorders of the elderly.

Case 4. A 66-year-old man was seen with the chief complaint of weakness and weight loss and was found to have scleral icterus and hepatosplenomegaly. His hematocrit was 23%. The white blood cell count was 132,800 with 96% mature lymphocytes. The platelets were

Infective microorganisms
  *Clostridium, Streptococcus pneumoniae, Escherichia
    coli, Salmonella, Streptococcus*
Autoantibodies (warm or cold)
  Primary or idiopathic
  Secondary to
    Lymphoproliferative disorders
    Neoplastic diseases
    Connective tissue diseases
    Infectious or granulomatous diseases
    Drugs
Hypersplenism
  Splenomegaly due to infectious or granulomatous
    disease.
  Lympho- and myeloproliferative disorders
  Reticuloendothelioses
  Congestive splenomegaly—chronic liver disease,
    splenic vein thrombosis

normal. The reticulocyte count was 12%. The direct Coombs' test was positive.

A diagnosis of chronic lymphocytic leukemia was made, complicated by AHA. The patient was started on treatment with chlorambucil and prednisone. However, his hematocrit continued to fall precipitously, reaching a low of 9.5%. Although it was difficult to cross-match his blood because of the autoantibody, the patient received five units of packed red cells, and azathioprine was added to his therapeutic regimen. Evidence of hemolysis finally disappeared, although the Coombs' test remained positive. Azathioprine was discontinued, and the patient was maintained on prednisone and chlorambucil. His white cell count returned to normal. His hematocrit also returned to normal, and the patient was still living, reasonably well, 5 years following this fulminant onset of chronic lymphocytic leukemia.

This case demonstrates a common clinical situation in which AHA is often seen. AHA also has been described in patients with malignancies arising from sites other than the lymphoid system; carcinoma of the gastrointestinal tract and lungs also have been associated on occasion with AHA. The connective tissue diseases that are most frequently seen in the elderly, such as scleroderma and periarteritis, are not as frequently complicated by AHA as is systemic lupus erythematosus, which, of course, manifests itself in the younger age groups.

Drug-induced hemolytic anemias involve drugs of varied chemical nature, many of which are commonly used in the elderly. Among these are the antibiotics, penicillin, streptomycin, and the ce-

phalosporins. The anti-inflammatory agents, indomethacin, phenylbutazone, and phenacetin, also may induce hemolytic anemias. Commonly used anticonvulsants and sedatives, diphenylhydantoin, chlorpromazine, and chlordiazepoxide, also have been associated with hemolytic anemias. Chlorpropamide, a commonly used oral hypoglycemic drug, has been associated with a hemolytic anemia and such drugs as quinidine, quinine, and α-methyldopa may be complicated by a hemolytic anemia. These drugs are capable of inducing an immunohemolytic state that may be associated with anemia of varying severity. The experience with α-methyldopa has been of great interest. This drug, commonly used in the current management of hypertension, has been found to produce an autoantibody (positive direct Coombs' test) in perhaps 30–50% of treated patients. Fortunately, only a very few develop a hemolytic anemia.

Decreased red cell survival probably exists in all patients with splenomegaly. It is possible to demonstrate trapping of tagged red cells in the spleen. This may result in transfusion requirements of great magnitude. If the patient can tolerate surgery, splenectomy may significantly reduce these transfusion requirements.

In summary, hemolytic anemias are not uncommon in the elderly. They are most frequently associated with infection, autoimmune disorders, drugs, or hypersplenism. It is important to recognize the presence of hemolytic anemia so that the management will be appropriate. The presence of an autoantibody is demonstrated by the positive/direct Coombs' test. The management of AHA consists of immunosuppressive drugs, usually prednisone. In the drug-induced anemias, withdrawal of the offending drug usually suffices.

DECREASED RED CELL PRODUCTION

Anemias due to decreased production of blood by the bone marrow have numerous causes. Table 33.2 illustrates the various mechanisms by which this type of anemia is produced.

DEFICIENCY STATES

Iron Deficiency

Iron deficiency due to blood loss and the characteristics of iron deficiency anemia were discussed earlier ("Blood Loss"). Nutritional iron deficiency anemia may be encountered in the elderly but is seen only in those who are on highly restricted diets or who are chronic alcoholics. The diagnosis of iron de-

Table 33.2
Decreased Red Blood Cell Production

Deficiency states
  Iron
  Vitamin B$_{12}$
  Folic acid
  Thyroid hormone
  Vitamin C
Marrow proliferative disorders
  Leukemias—acute and chronic
  Myelofibrosis with myeloid metaplasia
  Plasma cell dyscrasias
  Metastatic cancer
Aplastic (hypoplastic)
  Drugs
  Radiation
  Pure red cell aplasia
  Infection
Ineffective erythropoiesis
  Myelodysplastic syndromes
  Azotemia
  "Chronic illness"

ficiency is suggested by a low MCV and MCH. The total serum iron is low, and the iron-binding capacity is normal or mildly elevated. A low iron-binding capacity suggests "chronic" illness. True iron deficiency may be confirmed by a serum ferritin level that reflects the iron reserves. A bone marrow aspirate, if needed, will also reflect decreased iron stores.

Treatment consists of the administration of iron supplements. I have found the need for parenterally administered iron to be most unusual. A few people have a genuine inability to tolerate orally administered iron, and there may be a few rare examples of those who do not absorb iron. When administering iron, it is preferable to use simple preparations. Combinations of iron with multiple vitamins and other hematinics offer no additional benefit to the iron-deficient patient. Liquid preparations are available for those who may have chewing or swallowing difficulties.

Vitamin B$_{12}$ Deficiency

Vitamin B$_{12}$ deficiency is most commonly caused by a lack of intrinsic factor giving rise to the disease known as pernicious anemia. It is manifested by a slowly progressive anemia, although at times it appears that the onset of the anemia is sudden. Progressive pallor, glossitis, shortness of breath on exertion, palpitations, and, occasionally, chest pain on exertion are frequent presenting complaints. Paresthesias progressing to gross disturbance in gait

herald the neurologic complications of pernicious anemia. Changes in mental status, progressing to dementia, may be secondary to vitamin B$_{12}$ deficiency. Anorexia, weight loss, and low-grade fever also are common. The anemia tends to be severe, and it is remarkable to see how well the patient carries on despite its severity. The anemia is characterized by macrocytosis and is accompanied by depression of both the white cell count and platelets. Examination of the peripheral blood smear reveals macrocytic ovalocytes, marked variation in the size and shapes of red cells, and hypersegmentation of the polys. Changes in the blood chemistries include a mild elevation of the serum bilirubin and an extraordinary increase in lactic dehydrogenase (LDH). The bone marrow tends to be severely hyperplastic with megaloblastic erythroid hyperplasia. Nucleated red cells may constitute 50–75% of the bone marrow. If further proof of the presence of pernicious anemia is needed, estimation of vitamin B$_{12}$ absorption (the Schilling test) may be done. In pernicious anemia, the recovery of radioactivity in the urine 24 hours after the ingestion of chromium-tagged vitamin B$_{12}$ is usually less than 2% of the administered dose, although 5.5% is accepted as the lower limit of normal. That this malabsorption of vitamin B$_{12}$ is due to lack of intrinsic factor may be demonstrated by subsequently administering intrinsic factor along with the tagged vitamin B$_{12}$ and finding a rise in the urinary excretion of radioactivity to greater than 10%. Should there be no change in this so-called second stage of the Schilling test, then the vitamin B$_{12}$ malabsorption is not due to intrinsic factor deficiency and the patient does not have pernicious anemia.

Case 5. A 77-year-old man presented to a hospital emergency room complaining of ankle edema of 1 month's duration. He was found to have severe anemia with a hematocrit of 18% and an MCV of 130 µm^3. Chest x-ray revealed an enlarged heart and mild pulmonary congestion. Further history revealed the presence of mild anorexia. He was not aware of pallor. He denied pain, indigestion, change in bowel habits, or melena. He did experience very mild burning of his tongue and dyspnea on moderate exertion. He had noted tingling of his legs since the onset of the edema. He had been taking an oral multivitamin capsule daily for the past 12 years. He did not use alcohol.

On physical examination he exhibited a sallow, pallid appearance and a smooth tongue. There was no lymphadenopathy. The pulse rate was 96/minute and there was a grade III/IV systolic murmur over the precordium. The liver, spleen, and kidneys were not palpable. There were no palpable abdominal masses. Rectal examination was normal. There was 2+ edema of the ankles. Vibration sense was intact in the right lower extremity but absent at the left ankle. Position sense was intact. He exhibited no disturbance in gait.

The hematocrit was 18%. The red blood count was 1.4 million. The hemoglobin was 5.2 g/100 ml; MCV, 127 μm^3; MCH, 37.2 pg; mean corpuscular hemoglobin concentration (MCHC), 28.5%. The white blood cell count was 11,400 cells/mm^3, with 41% polys, 1% eosinophils, 4% monocytes, 53% lymphocytes, and 1% basophils. The platelets were slightly decreased. Reticulocyte count was 3.2%. The peripheral blood smear revealed occasional hypersegmented polys and a few macrocytic ovalocytes.

Bone marrow aspiration revealed a hypercellular bone marrow with severe megaloblastic erythroid hyperplasia. There was a marked increase in marrow iron, with occasional ringed sideroblasts.

A diagnosis of pernicious anemia was made at this first office visit, and the patient was started on injections of vitamin B$_{12}$, 100 μg three times a week. Within 1 week his reticulocyte count rose to 15.7% and his hematocrit to 23.5%. At the end of 2 weeks, his hematocrit was 28.5%; in 3 week, it was 30%; in 4 weeks, 34%, continuing its gradual rise until normal levels were reached. A GI series was done and found to be normal. The patient gained 12 pounds in weight over the ensuing 3 months.

This case illustrates the classic blood findings of pernicious anemia, the insidious onset of this disease, the ability to make a diagnosis in one office consultation, and the feasibility of treating the patient on an ambulatory basis. Despite the very severe anemia, the patient at no time required treatment with digitalis or diuretics for his edema, nor was he transfused.

Other causes of vitamin B$_{12}$ deficiency are most unusual. Nutritional deficiency of vitamin B$_{12}$ is rare. Since vitamin B$_{12}$ is absorbed in the terminal ileum, diseases involving this segment of the small intestine or resection of large amounts of terminal ileum may result in vitamin B$_{12}$ malabsorption and a megaloblastic anemia. These possibilities must be considered when the Schilling test demonstrates impaired vitamin B$_{12}$ absorption not corrected by intrinsic factor and in patients with a history of diarrhea, pain in the right lower quadrant, or previous intestinal surgery. Vitamin B$_{12}$ deficiency also may occur as a result of increased utilization of this vitamin by microorganisms in the gastrointestinal tract. The classic example of this is found in the megaloblastic anemia caused by fish tapeworm infestation. This disorder is rarely seen in the United States. More commonly, the "blindloop" syndrome may be created by surgical procedures that allow abnormal bacterial growth and increased utilization of vitamin B$_{12}$ within the isolated loop of intestine. This

clinical situation can be recognized by the demonstration of an abnormal Schilling test not corrected by intrinsic factor, but corrected by the administration of an intestinal flora suppressant such as tetracycline.

The management of vitamin B$_{12}$ deficiency anemia is simple and yet it is surprising to see how variably this is carried out. Vitamin B$_{12}$ is probably one of the most potent therapeutic agents known. One microgram given intramuscularly may completely eradicate the abnormal signs of pernicious anemia in the bone marrow. Doses of vitamin B$_{12}$ in excess of 100 μg are wasteful since the body is able to utilize only small amounts at a time and up to 90% of large doses of vitamin B$_{12}$ may be recovered in the urine. Therefore, the recommended treatment for a patient with pernicious anemia is 50–100 μg daily, intramuscularly, while monitoring the reticulocyte response. Reticulocytes will begin to rise in 3–5 days and will peak in 7–10 days. When the patient has had the expected rise in reticulocytes, and the hematocrit is well on its way toward normal, vitamin B$_{12}$ may be given weekly until the anemia has been corrected. At this point, vitamin B$_{12}$ injections should be given every 4–6 weeks. There are some who might reduce the frequency of maintenance doses to every 12 weeks. It must be impressed upon the patient as well as the physician that this treatment is to be continued for the rest of the patient's life. If treatment is continued, relapse of the anemia will not occur. If treatment is discontinued, it may take as long as 2 years for the anemia to reappear. Those patients who have severe neurologic complications at the onset of their disease are somewhat more difficult to treat. There is no problem with the hematologic manifestations, but the neurologic symptoms and signs may not improve completely. In some unfortunate patients, residual neurologic symptoms may be permanent and incapacitating.

All new patients with a diagnosis of pernicious anemia should have a GI series to rule out coexistent carcinoma of the stomach. Baseline gastroscopy may be done as the screening procedure. In years gone by, gastric cancer was feared as an ultimate complication of pernicious anemia. The incidence was given as four times greater than that in the normal population. Recent years have not borne out this experience. Gastric cancer is on the decline in the general population of the United States and is certainly less frequently seen in association with pernicious anemia.

Occasionally, a patient is encountered with a previous "diagnosis" of pernicious anemia, but with a history suggesting that the foundations of this diagnosis were poorly laid. The patient has been receiving vitamin B_{12} injections regularly. When there is reason to doubt that the patient has or has had pernicious anemia, the Schilling test may be of great service. Certainly the peripheral blood smear and bone marrow aspiration would not be helpful. If one could demonstrate normal vitamin B_{12} absorption, the diagnosis could be corrected and further administration of vitamin B_{12} should be discontinued.

Vitamin B_{12} levels may now be assayed in the blood and, of course, are quite low in pernicious anemia. Serum folate levels are usually normal. The serum iron in pernicious anemia is elevated, but falls precipitously as the reticulocytes rise following the administration of vitamin B_{12}. Should there be a coexisting iron deficiency, serum iron will fall to levels lower than normal and hypochromia will appear as treatment continues. In this case, the rise in hemoglobin will lag behind the hematocrit and oral iron may be required.

Folate Deficiency

Folate deficiency also results in a macrocytic anemia. Megaloblastic erythropoiesis is present in the marrow. Folate deficiency is often confirmed by low serum folate levels and normal vitamin B_{12} levels. Low red cell folate levels are more constant. Free acid is usually present in the gastric juice.

In contrast to vitamin B_{12} deficiency, folate deficiency is often brought about by nutritional deprivation. Body reserves of folic acid do not last as long as vitamin B_{12} reserves. While it may take a patient with pernicious anemia a year or two to relapse after the cessation of vitamin B_{12}, it may take only 12 weeks of folate deficiency to produce anemia. Posterior column degeneration does not occur in folate deficiency. If these patients do have neurologic complications, these tend to involve peripheral nerves and are secondary to other vitamin depletion. In the elderly, nutritional folate deficiency is seen in those who have poor access to an adequate diet and in the alcoholic. Folic acid is absorbed in the proximal portions of the small bowel, and diffuse disorders of the small bowel may be associated with folate malabsorption. Inflammatory disease of the small bowel is not a frequent clinical problem in the elderly. Infiltrative diseases in the small bowel such as lymphomas or amyloidosis or scleroderma may produce malabsorption and folic acid deficiency. Diarrhea, weight loss, and other signs of malabsorption are usually present.

Treatment of nutritional folate deficiency is also a simple matter. Restoration of a normal diet will usually be associated with a reticulocyte response and correction of the anemia. The administration of folic acid by mouth will also promptly correct the problem. The minimum daily requirement of folic acid is about 50 µg. The smallest tablet now available for commercial use contains 1 mg. One or two of these tablets daily should be more than adequate to correct the anemia. The importance of establishing the diagnosis of folic acid deficiency as the cause of megaloblastic anemia cannot be overly stressed. If folic acid is given to a patient with pernicious anemia, the hematologic manifestations will be corrected but the neurologic complications will progress.

Folate deficiency also may be caused by impaired utilization. This may be seen in patients who are taking anticonvulsive drugs such as diphenylhydantoin. In the case of diphenylhydantoin, the anemia may be corrected by the administration of folic acid while continuing the drug. In the alcoholic with folate deficiency, the simultaneous administration of folic acid and alcohol may inhibit the response to folic acid.

Other Deficiencies

Hypothyroidism is occasionally seen in the older age group and may be associated with an anemia. The anemia tends to be mild and either normocytic or macrocytic. It is not associated with megaloblastic changes in the bone marrow. Hypothyroidism and pernicious anemia may coexist, perhaps sharing an autoimmune etiology. The anemia associated with hypothyroidism is corrected by thyroid hormone.

Although it might be thought that scurvy is a disease of historic interest only, one occasionally sees vitamin C deficiency in the elderly who may have limited access to fresh food and citrus fruits. The combination of a macrocytic anemia and easy bruising should raise the suspicion of vitamin C deficiency. Megaloblastic changes may be seen in the more severe cases. These patients must be differentiated from those who have vitamin B_{12} or folate deficiency. Ascorbic acid levels in the blood may be measured. The response to vitamin C is usually dramatic.

MARROW PROLIFERATIVE DISORDERS

Leukemia

This group of diseases causes a large proportion of the anemias in the older age groups. Chronic lymphocytic leukemia may be the most common hematologic malignancy in the elderly. Anemia may be the initial manifestation of this disease or may appear as the disease progresses. These patients often present with no symptoms or signs of their disease and the disease is recognized only because they have had blood counts and examinations done for unrelated reasons. Other patients with chronic lymphocytic leukemia have generalized lymphadenopathy and splenomegaly. Some present with an intercurrent infection, often with a prolonged course. Others present with purpura due to thrombocytopenia. The white cell count may be only modestly increased, but occasional counts in excess of 100,000 are seen. The peripheral blood smear shows a preponderance of mature lymphocytes. The bone marrow also reveals a lymphocytic infiltration. The course of the anemia may be influenced by the response to antileukemic therapy. The complication of an autoimmune hemolytic anemia has already been referred to.

Chronic myelogenous leukemia also is seen in the older age group, although the peak incidence occurs between the ages of 40 and 60. These patients tend to be more symptomatic than those with chronic lymphocytic leukemia. They frequently present with a progressive anemia and/or an enlarging spleen. The diagnosis is apparent from the elevation of the white cell count and the appearance of immature granulocytes in peripheral blood. The bone marrow reveals marked granulocytic hyperplasia. The course of the anemia depends on the responsiveness of the patient to therapy. In the aggressive stage of chronic myelocytic leukemia (blastic crisis), anemia tends to be severe and is usually refractory to all treatment.

Acute leukemia, usually of the granulocytic or monocytic variety, is an all too common problem in the older age group. This disorder is usually manifested by anemia of some severity as well as thrombocytopenia and infection. Physical examination tends to be normal with the exception of pallor and purpura. Occasionally, lymph nodes or an enlarged spleen may be present. Pancytopenia is somewhat more common than cases associated with elevated white cell counts. The disease is recognized by the presence of blast cells in the peripheral blood. In some patients, these blast cells are scarce in the peripheral blood, but are readily apparent in the bone marrow. The prognosis of acute leukemia in the elderly is extremely poor. Remissions are now being achieved in a larger percentage of such patients than ever before, but they are, for the most part, quite temporary and the disease still retains a very poor prognosis. Erythroblastic leukemia or Di Gugliel mo's syndrome is a rare disorder that is seen most

often in the elderly. It is characterized by a profusion of normoblasts in the peripheral blood and bizarre, megaloblastic erythroid precursors in the bone marrow. Another peculiar form of acute leukemia, acute promyelocytic leukemia, may be complicated by severe disseminated intravascular coagulation. (The malignant promyelocyte appears to be rich in a coagulant material.)

Myelofibrosis

Myelofibrosis with myeloid metaplasia is a disorder that occurs in the older age groups. It is often an aftermath of polycythemia vera. However, it may appear as a primary illness and usually manifests with anemia and an enlarged spleen. The onset is insidious. Intercurrent infection may be the presenting manifestation or a complication during the course of the illness. Tear-drop red cells are present in the peripheral blood smear. The white cell count varies from low to normal or, on occasions, may be elevated to levels of about 40,000 or 50,000. This leukocytosis is to be differentiated from chronic myelogenous leukemia. Most often there is little difficulty in differentiating the two diseases. Attempts to aspirate the marrow in myelofibrosis usually result in a "dry tap." The diagnosis is then made by bone marrow biopsy. If, however, marrow aspiration yields cellular marrow, then one may be dealing with myelofibrosis in which there are residual islands of marrow activity. In these cases, estimation of the leukocyte alkaline phosphatase will show normal-to-increased values, in contrast to the marked decrease of this intracellular enzyme in chronic myelocytic leukemia. Also, the Philadelphia chromosome, present in 95% of patients with chronic myelogenous leukemia, is absent in myelofibrosis. The treatment of the anemia of myelofibrosis is usually unsatisfactory. The use of androgens is occasionally successful. In some patients, the spleen becomes enormous and may be associated with increasing need for transfusions. In this situation, the hypersplenism may be relieved by splenectomy. However, this should be reserved for those patients who are having great local discomfort from the enlarged spleen or for those requiring large amounts of blood.

Plasma Cell Dyscrasias

Plasma cell dyscrasias are becoming one of the most prevalent hematologic disorders in the older age group. Of the plasma cell dyscrasias, which include Waldenström's macroglobulinemia, amyloidosis, heavy and light chain disease, and multiple myeloma, the latter is by far the most common. This disease manifests itself in a variety of ways. Pain is the most common symptom of multiple myeloma and anemia is the most common sign. The combination of back pain, anemia, and azotemia should rouse the suspicion of multiple myeloma. The physical examination in such patients is often normal except for the obvious distress the patient may experience when moving about. The peripheral blood often reveals rouleau formation. The white blood cell count may be normal or low. The platelet count also may be normal or reduced. The bone marrow is characterized by an infiltration with plasma cells of varying maturity. The typical protein changes have been well described. There is a monoclonal protein spike in the γ-globulin fraction. Immunoelectrophoresis characterizes the nature of this protein abnormality. Urine electrophoresis often reveals the presence of a Bence Jones protein. X-rays of the bones reveal multiple osteolytic lesions, but in some patients only osteoporosis is present. The disease may be complicated by renal insufficiency due to protein deposits in the tubules. Hypercalcemia is a frequent problem. Criteria for staging multiple myeloma have been developed. The "tumor burden" is equated with the presence of anemia, bone lesions, renal failure, and hypercalcemia. Low tumor burden may require less aggressive therapy and be associated with longer survival. Newer approaches to therapy have prolonged the median survival of patients with this disease, although it remains ultimately fatal. Phenylalanine mustard and cyclophosphamide remain the drugs of choice, very active against myeloma. Combinations of these with vincristine, BCNU (carmustine), and steroids have been advocated early in the course of the disease, as well as for periods of relapse.

Case 6. A 64-year-old woman complained of low back pain of 6 weeks' duration. She was found to have protein in her urine and anemia, and x-rays of her spine revealed osteoporosis. Her past medical history was unremarkable. There were no abnormal physical findings.

Her initial hematocrit was 25%. The white blood cell count was 5290 cells/mm^3 with 27% polys, 4% bands, 50% lymphocytes, 16% monocytes, and 3% eosinophils. The platelets were normal. The peripheral blood smear revealed rouleau formation. Blood urea nitrogen (BUN) and calcium were normal. The serum proteins were 8.6 g/100 ml, with 3.8 g/100 ml of albumin and 4.8 g/100 ml of globulin. Protein electrophoresis of the serum revealed a monoclonal protein, IgG-λ.

Bone marrow aspiration revealed a cellular marrow with marked infiltration by plasma cells, many of which were multinucleated and bizarre in appearance.

A diagnosis of multiple myeloma was made and the patient was started on treatment with phenylalanine

mustard. Subsequently, prednisone was added. There was a rise in her hematocrit to 33%. The back pain soon disappeared and the patient did well on maintenance chemotherapy for 10 months. She subsequently had a relapse in the form of anemia and a rising BUN and creatinine. At the present time the patient has severe uremia and a profound anemia.

This case illustrates that the combination of pain and anemia frequently herald the presence of a malignancy, either metastatic cancer or multiple myeloma.

Macroglobulinemia is a far less frequent disease of the older age group and results in a severe hyperviscosity syndrome, bleeding, and anemia. The disorder is characterized by a high concentration of IgM. Treatment consists of reducing the viscosity of the blood by plasmapheresis and also by suppressing the underlying proliferative disorder with appropriate chemotherapy. Chlorambucil has achieved some success in this regard.

Metastatic Cancer

Cancer, metastatic to the bone marrow, often causes anemia. A leukoerythroblastic picture appears in the peripheral blood. In men, cancer of the prostate is the most common cause of metastases to the bone marrow; in women, breast cancer is the leading cause. Cancers of the lung and gastrointestinal tract may metastasize to the marrow as well. Cancers of the prostate and breast may, of course, be controlled for long periods even in the presence of distant metastases. Cancers from other sites, when widespread, are usually associated with an extremely poor prognosis.

APLASTIC (HYPOPLASTIC) ANEMIA

Bone marrow failure is usually characterized by pancytopenia and a hypoplastic or aplastic bone marrow. This may occur spontaneously, as an acquired hemopoietic stem-cell disorder, or may be secondary to extrinsic influences such as drugs, radiation, infection, or immunologic factors. In the elderly, acute idiopathic aplastic anemia is a rather rare occurrence. Severe aplastic anemia still carries a very unfavorable prognosis. The course is manifested by severe anemia, infection, and bleeding. Treatment is largely supportive. Bone marrow transplantation has been life-saving in the young patient with severe aplastic anemia. Beyond the age of 50, bone marrow transplantation remains a hazardous procedure. Closely matched donors are more difficult to find. Treatment with androgens and steroids meets with limited success.

In contrast to the rare idiopathic aplastic anemia, secondary myelosuppression becomes more common with increasing age. In particular, the increased exposure to drugs in the older population greatly increases the complication of bone marrow depression. The chemotherapeutic drugs and radiation used in the treatment of malignant disorders are known to cause marrow depression and, with careful monitoring, this problem can be managed while the malignancy is being treated. However, marrow suppression is an important limiting factor in the treatment of malignant disorders. An equally difficult problem may arise with the drugs that are in common use in the elderly. Chloramphenicol is now well-known for its possible effect on the bone marrow, and its use is ordinarily confined to systemic infections that are most sensitive to this drug. The sulfonamides are used extensively for urinary tract infections and may cause marrow suppression. Add to this a long list of useful drugs such as the thiazides, phenothiazines, thioureas, and antiarthritics, antiepileptics, carbamazepine, hydralazine, and antiarrhythmic drugs (particularly quinidine and the procaine derivatives) and it is apparent that those who care for the elderly often have to consider the possible role of drugs when anemia appears. In elderly patients who manifest anemia, the role of drug should be suspected immediately. The clues to drug-induced marrow suppression include pancytopenia, normochromic and normocytic red cells, and reticulocytopenia. The marrow reveals varying degrees of hypoplasia. The outcome is ordinarily successful when the diagnosis is made promptly and the offending drug is withdrawn. Some of these drugs may cause immune-mediated hematologic changes and thus a hemolytic anemia. Procainamide and quinidine are good examples of such drugs. These anemias are ordinarily associated with reticulocytosis, and drug withdrawal is also associated with a favorable outcome. The important message to those who treat the elderly is use all drugs judiciously, review frequently the drugs being taken by the patients, monitor the blood when drugs are being used that are known to cause such side effects, and maintain a high index of suspicion that drugs may be the cause of new hematologic findings.

There are other causes of aplastic anemia and red cell aplasia, but these are rare in the elderly. Paroxysmal nocturnal hemoglobinuria is such a disease and must be ruled out in cases of unexplained pancytopenia. Checking the urine for hemoglobin or hemosiderin and the sucrose hemolysis test are good screen procedures. Pure red cell aplasia is another disorder that may manifest with severe anemia. It is thought to be an autoimmune disorder and may be idiopathic or associated with other diseases such as thymoma and chronic lymphatic leukemia. The bone marrow is characterized by virtual absence of erythroid precursors. Treatment consists of immune suppressive drugs such as steroids and cyclophosphamide and transfusions as needed.

INEFFECTIVE ERYTHROPOIESIS

With increasing age and with increasing frequency, we are now seeing anemia in patients whose marrows are not aplastic but who seem to have marrow failure or decreased erythrocyte production despite normal or even increased marrow cellularity. These are the so-called refractory anemias. The anemia of chronic illness is characterized by low serum iron levels and decreased transferrin, the iron-binding protein. The anemia of chronic renal failure is due to decreased erythropoietin production. Sideroblastic anemia is a disease most common in the older population; it may occur as a primary or idiopathic disorder that is characterized by defective erythroid hyperplasia, megaloblastoid features, and numerous ringed-sideroblasts. Although these changes may be induced by certain drugs, alcohol, or lead exposure, they are most often idiopathic. Some, but very few, are responsive to pyridoxine. For the most part, these patients are chronically anemic, require transfusions at varying intervals, and eventually succumb to infection or exhibit a transition to an acute leukemia.

This leads to the general problem of "preleukemia," a concept that has been more formally categorized and better understood only over the past three decades. This is a hematologic problem of the elderly in particular, and is characterized by ineffective hematopoiesis, pancytopenia, and a hypercellular marrow. Anemia is often the initial manifestation and is frequently macrocytic. Study of the marrow reveals dysplasia of all the blood cell precursors—megaloblastic erythropoiesis, abnormal megakaryocytes, and disorderly granulopoiesis. Folic acid and vitamin B_{12} deficiency are not present, and exposure to cytotoxic therapy has not occurred. The myelodysplastic syndrome has been subclassified into five categories (Table 33.3). The progression to leukemia increases from about 10% to 60% from categories 1 to 5. The latent period ranges from 6 years to as short as 6–12 months. Treating for leukemia before it actually appears has not been successful. Once the transition to acute leukemia, usually nonlymphocytic, has occurred, the use of intensive chemotherapy regimens is quite a

Table 33.3
Myelodysplastic Syndrome

1. Refractory anemia
2. Refractory anemia with ringed sideroblasts
3. Chronic myelomonocytic leukemia
4. Refractory anemia with excess blasts
5. Refractory anemia with excess blasts in transformation

burden to the elderly, and even when remissions are achieved, they are often short-lived. I believe that it is important to recognize the myelodysplastic syndromes when they appear and to manage the patients with intelligent and physiologic support.

DISCUSSION

In this chapter I have outlined the anemias commonly encountered in the elderly, classifying them according to their pathophysiologic mechanisms. Careful history and physical examination, and characterization of the anemia by examination of the peripheral blood and bone marrow, should provide clues to the etiology of anemia. Anemia is one of the most frequent signs of illness. When the mechanism of the anemia is understood, the diagnosis of the underlying disease often becomes apparent. Treatment of anemia should not be undertaken until the underlying disorder has been diagnosed. Nothing could be more tragic than to treat a patient with a carcinoma of the colon with iron in order to correct the anemia and to assume that all is well. Valuable time lost in such a case may mean the difference between a cure and a disaster. Similarly, the use of "shot-gun" therapy for anemia is to be discouraged. The dangers of administration of folic acid to the patient with pernicious anemia have been emphasized. Although there may be a tendency in some circles to be more "conservative" in the management of an elderly person's problems, this does not preclude accurate assessment of the patient's status before deciding on the treatment to be offered.

SUGGESTED READINGS

1. Callender ST (ed): *Iron Deficiency and Iron Overload,* Clinics in Hematology, vol 2, no 2. Philadelphia, WB Saunders, 1973.
2. Carmel R: Macrocytosis, mild anemia, and delay in the diagnosis of pernicious anemia. *Arch Intern Med* 139:47, 1979.
3. Dacie JV, Worledge SM: Auto-immune hemolytic anemias. *Prog Hematol* 6:82, 1969.
4. Danielson DA, Douglas SW III, Herzog P, Jick H, Porter JB: Drug-induced blood disorders. *JAMA* 252:3257, 1984.
5. Garratty G, Petz LD: Drug-induced hemolytic anemia. *Am J Med* 58:398, 1975.
6. Girdwood RH: Drug-induced hematological abnormalities. In: *Hematological Aspects of Systemic Disease,* chapter 19. Philadelphia, WB Saunders, p 495.
7. Koeffler HP: Myelo-Dysplastic syndromes (preleukemia). *Semin Hematol* 23:284, 1986.
8. Salmon SE (ed): *Myeloma and Related Disorders,* Clinics in Hematology, vol 2, no 1. Philadelphia, WB Saunders, 1982.
9. Williams WJ: *Hematology,* ed 3. New York, McGraw-Hill, 1983.
10. Wintrole MM: *Clinical Hematology,* ed 8. Philadelphia, Lea & Febiger, 1981.

CHAPTER 34

Surgical Principles for the Aged Patient

PAUL J. MELLUZZO

A decision to recommend surgery in an elderly patient should be based on the same judgment, skills, and compassion as in all age groups.

Elderly patients have a reduced margin of reserve, because of the aging process plus, frequently, one or more chronic diseases. Nutritional status may also be marginal, as may mental and emotional status. Despite this, meticulous management will permit most older patients to benefit from needed surgery.

The sound medical and surgical principles that apply to all age groups also apply to the elderly. Advances in medical and surgical technology over the past decade enables more precise and often noninvasive diagnostic studies that can often pinpoint disease processes earlier and with less risk and discomfort.

In the past, the physician alone often made unquestionable decisions concerning health care. Today all age groups, including the elderly, expect to be informed and to participate in decisions regarding their health care. The physician, patient, and family now comprise a team working together to make decisions.

The patient should have, whenever possible, and when mental faculties are intact, a primary role in deciding the benefits of surgery. Anxiety over an impending operation, either elective or emergency, is understandable and is present in all age groups. This anxiety often can be tempered by full, complete, and candid discussions by the patient's physician and surgeon about the procedure, the risks, and the anticipated benefits. In fact, the elderly often approach these situations with more stability and maturity than those who are younger.

In addition to the patient and his or her family, it is important for the surgeon to work together with the patient's personal physician, nurses, social workers, and physical therapists to address questions concerning convalescence after the procedure, ability to carry on essential tasks by the patient without help, need for nursing care, how the patient will care for him- or herself, 1, 2, or 3 months after surgery, what sequelae will persist and what will be transient, and how "normal" will the patient be after this operation. Time spent in answering these questions and providing an outline for preoperative and postoperative care to the patient and the team involved with after care and rehabilitation will better prepare the patient psychologically and physically for the planned procedure and the recovery period.

OPERATIONS

EMERGENCY AND ELECTIVE

There is generally little controversy over the approach to an emergency procedure in the elderly. A sudden onset of a critical surgical illness, such as a perforation, gastrointestinal hemorrhage, or trauma, is usually a relatively straightforward decision for the patient, the patient's family, and the patient's physician and surgeon.

However, with elective surgical procedures, the belief that surgery is less beneficial and more risky in the elderly may interfere with sound surgical judgment. Mild, but chronic, intermittent pain from biliary calculi or the symptoms produced by chronically recurring episodes of diverticulitis often are treated at all costs with continued nonoperative therapy. If, after a judicious trial of conservative therapy, good judgment dictates that a surgical procedure is important, not only to relieve symptoms but also to prevent disastrous complications from further progression of the disease, elective surgery should be strongly advised.

Even the reluctance to have a large and symptomatic inguinal hernia repaired, because of the risk of general anesthesia, can be overcome by an explanation that the procedure can be done safely under local anesthesia. Again, these considerations need to be discussed in detail in an unhurried atmosphere of careful assessment of the risks and benefits of the elective procedure.

Once the decision to proceed with surgery has been made, a meticulous assessment of the patient's organ systems should be undertaken. This organ system review provides information important in the final decision as to whether elective surgery is or is not appropriate. In an emergency situation a rapid, but nonetheless comprehensive, review of the patient's major systems must be done before any operation. In the next section, essential evaluations by system will be reviewed.

WOUND HEALING AND NUTRITION

It is important to remember that wound healing and response to inflammation can be affected adversely by the aging process, the presence of associated disease, poor nutrition, immunologic deficiencies, and reduced function of organ systems. Coupled with these factors, diseases common in the elderly, such as diabetes mellitus, uremia, anemia, and cardiovascular abnormalities contribute to impaired healing.

It is, therefore, important to provide intelligent and meticulous care of wounds. For the surgeon this requires judicious operative techniques, careful attention to the selection of suture materials, and adherence to surgical principles that provide for the best milieu for wound healing.

Equally important is the attention given by the practitioner and surgeon, working in concert, to correct preoperatively conditions that adversely affect wound healing. Nutritional deficiencies and anemias, when recognized early in a patient who is facing elective surgery, should be corrected at home with appropriate diets and vitamin supplements supervised by family members or by dieticians.

Patients with advanced cardiac or renal disease frequently present chronic malnutrition similar to patients with cachexia from malignant disease. These patients may have accompanying defects in blood volume, serum albumin, and cardiopulmonary reserve. Vitamin deficits should be suspected if there has been marked weight loss and dietary imbalance. Attention should be given to restoring these deficits, especially vitamin C, preoperatively. In the patient with hepatic disease or jaundice, vitamin K replacement is necessary to restore clotting parameters to normal.

If the patient cannot eat because of physical or mental disorder or if severe nutritional deficiencies develop in an elderly patient who will require surgery, but in whom the prolonged time required to correct the malnutrition would increase the risk of operation, the use of parenteral hyperalimentation should be considered. Largely through the work of Dudrick et al. (1), hyperalimentation has been developed to provide practical delivery of complete nutritional needs for an extended period of time, by infusion of a hyperosmolar solution containing carbohydrates, proteins, and essential nutrients through a catheter placed in the subclavian vein. When administered properly this has proven to be highly effective in achieving a positive nitrogen balance and weight gain in a variety of clinical situations. Often it is important to resume parenteral alimentation in the postoperative period to provide a basis on which wound healing can occur.

In summary, wound healing is impaired in the elderly, but careful preoperative attention to nutrition, pre-existing disease processes, and correction of underlying deficiencies, along with adherence to meticulous surgical technique, can provide an optimum environment for wound healing during patient recovery.

FLUID AND ELECTROLYTES

Although this topic is extensively and appropriately covered in a separate chapter of this book (Chapter 22), it is worth repeating that fluid and electrolyte abnormalities, including acidosis and alkalosis should be corrected preoperatively. Older patients commonly present with cardiac insufficiency and may have a significantly expanded extracellular volume and are especially prone to hyponatremia, hypokalemia, and alkalosis. Hypokalemia is an especially common problem in patients who receive diuretics over an extended period of time. The most common form of hyponatremia in the preoperative elderly patient is a dilutional hyponatremia. This can be treated carefully with appropriate restriction of water and judicious administration of diuretics that produce a free water diuresis. Hypokalemia is frequently associated with alkalosis and accentuated by it. Common causes include either metabolic or respiratory alkalosis, potassium depletion secondary to diuretic therapy, and intestinal losses of potassium secondary to diarrhea or emesis. If the patient requires hydration preoperatively, the addition of potassium chloride to the intravenous solution is an efficacious and safe method of replacing deficient potassium (4).

PREOPERATIVE EVALUATION

Whenever possible in preparing the aged patient for surgery, five major systems should be evaluated with special care. These are the central nervous, cardiovascular, respiratory, renal, and hepatic systems. When abnormalities in these systems can be detected and corrected, or even improved, very often the operative and postoperative course of the patient is enhanced.

CENTRAL NERVOUS SYSTEM

Reduced mental status and the presence of depression seriously compromise recovery and should be assessed carefully. If possible, depression should be treated before proceeding to elective surgery. Preoperative mental status should be determined carefully so that a postoperative confusional state can be better evaluated if it occurs.

CARDIOVASCULAR SYSTEM

Careful preoperative evaluation can identify problems that can be improved or corrected and establish risk factors for morbidity and mortality that, in the case of elective surgery, would influence the decision for surgery.

Goldman and his associates have identified risk factors important in predicting cardiac complications after noncardiac operation. They developed a weighing scheme (Table 34.1) that correlates accurately with the likelihood of cardiac problems after surgery. The point total correlation seen in Table 34.2 is not only a help in eliciting risk factors but, after correction of identified problems, recalculation will graphically illustrate improvement by providing a "better score."

Marked anemia from chronic gastrointestinal blood loss or nutritional depletion must be corrected before surgery. Anemia increases cardiac output, which will be further aggravated by surgery. Judi-

cious administration of blood to correct the anemia can significantly lower the risk of heart attack during or after surgery.

In elderly patients with significant cardiovascular disease, preoperative evaluation may require more detailed cardiac studies in addition to a routine electrocardiogram. These studies may include echocardiogram, a stress test, and if significant abnormalities or symptoms are noted, coronary angio-

Table 34.1
Weighing of Cardiac Risk Factors[a]

Criteria	Points
Historical	
Age over 70 years	5
Myocardial infarction in the previous 6 months	10
Examination	
S3 gallop/jugular venous distention	11
Significant aortic valvular stenosis	3
ECG	
Premature atrial contractions or rhythm other than sinus	7
More than 5 premature ventricular contractions per minute	7
General Status	3
Abnormal blood gases	
Electrolyte abnormalities	
Abnormal renal function	
Liver disease	
Bedridden	
Operation	
Emergency	4
Intraperitoneal; thoracic; aortic	3
Total Possible	53

[a]Modified by permission from Goldman L, Caldera DL, Nussbaum SR, et al: Multifactorial index of cardiac risk in non-cardiac surgical procedures. *N Engl J Med* 297:845, 1977.

Table 34.2
Correlation of Cardiac Risk Points and Postoperative Cardiac Problems[a]

Point Total	Life-Threatening Complications (%)	Cardiac Deaths (%)
0–5	0.7	0.2
6–12	5	2
13–25	11	2
Greater than 26	22	56

[a]Modified by permission from Goldman L, Caldera DL, Nussbaum SR, et al: Multifactorial index of cardiac risk in non-cardiac surgical procedures. *N Engl J Med* 297:845, 1977.

graphy. Many elderly patients, especially those in whom major abdominal or thoracic surgery is contemplated, should be considered for invasive cardiac monitoring with a Swan-Ganz catheter. This is a balloon catheter inserted through the venous system that floats into the pulmonary artery, providing valuable information on heart performance. Preoperatively, physiologic monitoring, in addition to assessing cardiac function, can aid in safely restoring intravascular volume, and intraoperatively can be an invaluable aid to the anesthesiologist. Postoperatively, Swan-Ganz monitoring may be essential to guide the physician and nurses in maintaining appropriate fluid replacement in the early and unstable part of the postoperative course.

Thromboembolism, although a relatively rare complication, assumes a greater role with advancing age. Risk factors for blood clots are numerous and always include advancing age, obesity, orthopaedic procedures, and a history of venous disease. According to the findings of the National Institutes of Health Consensus Conference on Prevention of Venous Thrombosis and Pulmonary Embolus, the elderly population is a high risk group, justifying routine prophylaxis with low dose heparin and/or dextran (12). In addition, effective modalities in preventing deep venous thrombosis should be used. These include external pneumatic compression, gradient elastic stockings and, whenever possible, early ambulation after surgery.

RESPIRATORY SYSTEM

Elderly patients are often at risk for pulmonary complications after surgery, especially in the presence of chronic obstructive pulmonary disease. This is especially true in smokers. Many elderly people have been smokers for decades and, while it is best to encourage them to stop permanently, even abstinence from cigarettes for as little as 2 weeks before a planned operation can result in a decreased incidence of postoperative pulmonary complications. Tests of pulmonary function are helpful in determining the severity of obstructive and restrictive pulmonary dysfunction. This assessment is important in major abdominal surgery, but essential in thoracic surgery where removal of lung tissue is likely.

Arterial blood gases should be obtained in all elderly preoperative patients, to determine fitness for surgery and to provide a baseline guide for postoperative management of respiratory problems.

Attention should be directed toward control of respiratory infection with antibiotics and effective pulmonary toilet. Preoperative teaching should include breathing techniques and what to expect after surgery; assisted respiration, postural drainage, and the pulmonary toilet method. If, in the face of abnormal pulmonary studies and pulmonary insufficiency, the use of a respirator is contemplated in the initial postoperative period, a clear, concise discussion of its purpose and value can allay anxiety and prevent the panic and surprise associated with awakening postoperatively on mechanical ventilation. This information should be imparted to the patient, as well as to the family.

RENAL SYSTEM

A urinalysis, blood urea nitrogen (BUN), and serum creatinine can generally give an accurate assessment of renal function. A BUN alone may be misleading because it is affected by several extrarenal factors (gastrointestinal hemorrhage, dehydration, etc.). However, a normal BUN and creatinine, as a rule, excludes significant renal disease. Oliguria in a postoperative surgical patient almost always indicates hypovolemia, not acute renal failure.

The problem of prostatic hypertrophy with obstructive uropathy is not uncommon in elderly males. A careful history and prostate examination will alert the surgeon to the possibility of an element of obstructive uropathy. Catheterization to determine whether there is significant residual urine (greater than 1 dl) may provide useful information that would allow the physician and the patient to understand the need for postoperative urinary catheter drainage. When surgery is elective; for example, repair of a large inguinal hernia in a patient who has obstructive uropathy, preoperative evaluation by a urologist is appropriate. The obstruction may need to be corrected before the herniorrhaphy is performed. Not only will this provide a smoother postoperative course for the patient, but it may prevent a recurrence of the hernia caused by straining to void.

HEPATIC SYSTEM

The liver's importance in metabolism of protein, carbohydrate, fats, and drugs, and in the production of clotting factors, is well known. The presence of pre-existing liver dysfunction is ominous in preoperative preparation of any age group. However, it is particularly important to detect and correct liver function abnormalities whenever possible in the elderly patient with previously unsuspected liver disease. A complete history, including prior hepatitis, jaundice, alcohol abuse, a search for physical findings of liver dysfunction (i.e., palmar erythema, spider nevi, and an enlarged liver), and screening laboratory tests for liver disease, including prothrombin time, is essential.

Operating on the unrecognized liver-compromised patient often results in postoperative complications that might have been avoided. Whenever possible, correctable abnormalities of clotting factors can be treated with vitamin K, or, in the case of extensive preoperative bleeding, administration of fresh frozen plasma or fresh blood. This can reduce the risk of bleeding during or after surgery.

When metastatic liver disease is discovered preoperatively, the need for a major operative procedure may be avoided and a palliative procedure can be performed with less risk. Jaffe and associates (6) have demonstrated the effect of metastatic liver disease, as from an intestinal neoplasm, on survival. As expected, the mean survival shortens with the involvement of both lobes of the liver, presence of ascites, presence of jaundice, and abnormal function studies.

CHECKLIST FOR PREOPERATIVE PREPARATION

The preoperative preparation of the elderly patient can be a complex problem, often involving multiple disciplines. Thus, it is useful to have a preoperative checklist. Use of this list can help the surgeon avoid omission of essential steps in preparation of the elderly patient for surgery (Table 34.3).

OPERATION

It has been stressed that, in general, the elderly comprise a high risk group for surgery. Despite that fact, a second point has also been stressed: that these patients should not be denied the benefits that modern surgery provides. Careful preoperative preparation helps to anticipate and minimize this risk. This anticipation and preparation should continue immediately before and during the operative procedure itself. The elderly patient presents a challenge to the surgical team and nowhere is this more in evidence that in the close working relationship between the surgeon and the anesthesiologist. Although the anesthesiologist visits the patient preoperatively to review the record and examine the patient, it is most helpful for the surgeon to discuss in person with the anesthesiologist the specifics of the anticipated surgery of the elderly patient. The lighter the plane of anesthesia, compatible with operative requirements, the more favorable the situation for the patient.

Table 34.3
Checklist for Preoperative Preparation

I. Preoperative diagnosis
II. Explanation of planned procedure to patient and family
III. Involvement of allied health care professionals
   A. Nurses
   B. Social service
   C. Special therapists, i.e., enterostomal, respiratory, physical, occupational
IV. Operative permit
V. Mental status
VI. Cardiac
   A. ECG
   B. Stress test
   C. Invasive monitoring techniques
VII. Respiratory
   A. Chest x-ray
   B. Blood gases
   C. Pulmonary function studies
VIII. Hepatic-liver function tests, including prothrombin
IX. Renal
   A. BUN, creatinine
   B. Urinalysis
   C. Prostate examination
   D. Check residual urine if in doubt
X. Dietary
   A. Need for preoperative alimentation and hydration
   B. Liquid diet with antibiotic and mechanical preparation before lower intestinal surgery
   C. NPO before surgery
XI. Preoperative medications
XII. Pre-existing disease
XIII. Special consultations

There are many operative procedures that can be performed under local anesthesia, with the anesthesiologist in attendance to administer intravenous sedation. Obviously, this type of anesthetic provides much less risk for the patient. The choice of a local anesthetic may be more anxiety-producing than facing general anesthesia. Patients are concerned about their awareness of the environment in the operating room and the concern that they will feel pain and discomfort. Often a visit by the anesthesiologist to explain that he will be working in concert with the surgeon to provide the best possible anesthesia and sedation for the patient's surgery is enough to allay apprehension.

The anesthesiologist, in turn, may suggest types of anesthesia and agents that may be tolerated more safely by individual patients. For example, in the patient with cardiac disease, agents or techniques that would reduce the cardiac output minimally and that would allow maintenance of excellent oxygenation would be the anesthesiologist's agent of choice.

The nursing team should be aware of the planned operative procedure and the problems the elderly patient may bring to the operating room. Today, many institutions provide for preoperative surgical nursing rounds in which the nurses visit the patient preoperatively and provide specific reports to the surgical nursing team as to the particular needs and requirements of the patient upon entering the operating suite. This prevents delays and provides necessary equipment at hand, providing a more efficient and organized approach to the patient in the operating suite.

Nurses should have available venous compression devices for prevention of deep venous thrombosis and special equipment for operative positioning. They need to be alert to the need to raise the temperature in normally cold operating suites and to have available thermal blankets to provide for conservation of bodily heat in the elderly patient. Warming the skin preparation solutions before the surgical scrub is also useful toward this end.

Once the operation has started, the surgeon must adhere to sound technique and gentle handling of the tissues, the maintenance of proper hemostasis, and minimizing trauma to often fragile tissues.

In abdominal surgery it is important, when the abdomen is opened, that a thorough and complete examination be made beyond the obvious disease for which the operation is being conducted. It should be accomplished, without exception, before embarking on the specific procedure. One site particularly vulnerable to disease that is not readily detectable preoperatively is the vascular system. Frequently, this is the site of aneurysm or atherosclerotic changes that narrow the lumen of a vessel.

The findings of an aortic aneurysm may be a more important and immediate concern than the condition for which the operation was performed. For example, if a large aneurysm were encountered, a decision must be made as to whether the aneurysm should be repaired in favor of abandoning the originally planned procedure. This is a particularly difficult decision and requires mature judgment on the part of the surgeon, often in consultation with the anesthesiologist in considering possible intraoperative and postoperative complications. The handling of unexpected intraoperative findings is often a matter of the surgeon's preference and the overall condition and stability of the patient.

The limited reserve of the elderly patient calls for the establishment of certain safety measures to pro-

tect him in the postoperative period. The placement of a gastrostomy in a patient with chronic obstructive lung disease, or in a patient in whom long-term nasogastric suction would be inappropriate for any other reason, is important. Another safety measure that may be used is a temporary diverting colostomy in the case of contaminated large bowel resection, or in a patient with medical problems, including previous steroid therapy, in whom intestinal healing may not be optimum.

Nowhere is the teamwork between the surgeon and the anesthesiologist more evident than with the completion of the procedure, when a decision is made whether to remove the endotracheal tube on the operating room table, or to continue assisted breathing for a period of time in the recovery room or intensive care unit. The routine extubation of the elderly patient without attention to pulmonary, cardiac, and intraoperative complications must be avoided. If there is any question concerning the stability of the patient in the mind of the anesthesiologist or the surgeon, the patient should remain intubated.

The conclusion of the operation does not mean a less risky or uncomplicated period for the patient. Transfer to the recovery room may well require continued monitoring and a stay in the recovery room longer than that of a younger patient. Restoration of the patient's body temperature, stability of the vital signs, and adequate monitoring are all parameters used to decide when the patient can be safely transferred to his room. The surgeon and anesthesiologist should be available to decide when a patient who is not stable in the recovery room should be transferred to a monitored bed in the intensive care unit.

POSTOPERATIVE COMPLICATIONS

Complications after surgery can be divided into immediate and late complications. The immediate complications fall into two categories, respiratory and circulatory.

RESPIRATORY

Vomiting may occur on awakening from anesthesia, and the aspiration of gastric contents into the tracheal and bronchial tree can be disastrous. In almost all cases of elective intra-abdominal surgery, the patients are fasting and nasogastric tubes are placed either before or during the operation to decompress the stomach. However, in emergency surgery, or in surgery where nasogastric tubes have not completely emptied the stomach, aspiration of acidic liquid material can lead to a chemical pneumonitis. Prophylaxis is best performed by placing the patient in a lateral recumbent position with a pillow against the abdomen. The mouth and pharynx should be cleared by suction. Once an airway has been obtained, ventilation and oxygenation are provided, if needed. If aspiration occurs, treatment should consist of suction in the trachea. The use of antibiotics is controversial as is the use of steroids. Most believe that antibiotics should be withheld until there is evidence of bacterial infection.

Airway obstruction has already been mentioned, and if this is anticipated at the conclusion of the operation, the endotracheal tube should be left in place in the postanesthetic period. If the patient is already extubated, inserting an oral pharyngeal airway may be necessary. In addition, suctioning to free the airway of secretions may be helpful. Hypoventilation is a complication that may develop because of the effects of anesthetics, narcotics, and muscle relaxants. Thoracic and abdominal incisions reduce maximal breathing capacity in the postoperative period.

In the elderly there is a high prevalence of chronic pulmonary disease. Bronchial secretions are increased with anesthesia. Postoperative pain may prevent the patient from breathing deeply or coughing. These factors all contribute to the development of postoperative atelectasis.

Assisted respiration by trained personnel in the form of intermittent positive breathing and use of suction by catheters in the posterior nasopharynx and upper larynx several times a day for a few days after surgery can substantially reduce the incidence and severity of atelectasis. When atelectasis is severe, the removal of a mucous plug by bronchoscopy may be required.

CIRCULATORY

These complications can occur because of the effects of anesthesia, respiratory insufficiency, or the surgical procedure itself. Vital signs are monitored carefully with evaluation for respiratory adequacy, level of consciousness, and skin color. Marked changes in blood pressure or pulse must be detected and managed promptly. Persistent bradycardia may reduce cardiac output and cause hypotension. Tachycardia may be the result of decreased ventilation, low circulating volume, or pain. The initial management of these abnormalities should be the administration of oxygen, or, in the case of tachycardia thought to be produced by low volume, elevation of the legs to provide for an increased venous return but, at the same time, keeping the body in the horizontal position. The Trendelenburg position is no longer used because the associated diaphragmatic elevation decreases respiratory capacity.

Persistent hypotension, characterized by a fall in blood pressure, a marked increase in pulse rate, an increase in respiratory rate, pallor, cold clammy skin, and a drop in urinary output, carries a grave prognosis. Early detection is expedited by placing monitoring lines in elderly patients either before or during the operation. This can greatly facilitate differentiating hypotension caused by drugs from that of circulatory collapse. The treatment of shock is initiated by the replacement of fluids to correct hypovolemia. Where blood loss is a factor, transfusion may be necessary. The use of vasopressor drugs should be used with care and precision, in consultation with the anesthesiologist and the cardiologist.

One of the most common reasons for early postoperative shock is decreased circulation from rapid blood loss. Extensive procedures of any kind, replacement of segments of large vessels, and thoracic and pelvic procedures are especially prone to be associated with postoperative bleeding. After intrathoracic procedures, a chest tube provides an excellent means of detecting intrathoracic bleeding. The presence of shock with or without accompanying increased abdominal girth in the early postoperative period for abdominal surgery strongly suggests that bleeding is intra-abdominal. If it does not respond promptly to fluid and transfusion, the surgeon must strongly consider re-exploration.

GASTROINTESTINAL DYSFUNCTION

This may be as mild as loss of appetite brought on by the effects of the anesthetic agent or narcotics, or as severe as massive gastric and intestinal distention or ileus accompanied by nausea, vomiting, and abdominal pain. This is usually seen after extensive intra-abdominal operations, especially when intra-abdominal sepsis is a complicating factor. In the elderly, weak, or debilitated patient ileus can cause respiratory compromise by restricting diaphragmatic movement or more ominously by increasing the hazard of vomiting and aspiration of intestinal contents into the lungs.

There are several measures to prevent this complication. First, in those patients who preoperatively have abdominal distention, gastric decompression should be accomplished by use of nasogastric tube. The decompression should continue after surgery until intestinal function returns, as indicated by audible intestinal peristalsis or by passage of flatus or stool.

Recently, there has been a trend away from the routine use of nasogastric tubes postoperatively. Many patients undergoing uncomplicated, relatively brief surgical procedures may need only to remain in a fasting state with intravenous fluid replacement for the 24–48 hours before intestinal function returns. Tube decompression is not necessary in these patients; in fact, it may do more harm than good, making coughing, deep breathing, and removal of pulmonary secretions difficult.

Postoperative patients who do develop intestinal distention should have nasogastric or even "long tube" (intestinal) decompression and parenteral nutritional support until intestinal function returns. In complex surgical procedures in the elderly patient in which long-term ileus can be expected, consideration should be given to the operative insertion of an indwelling gastric tube. Not only is gastric decompression available for as long as necessary, but it can be accomplished with comfort to the patient and without compromising pulmonary function. The tube can be removed with ease at the bedside or as an outpatient when decompression is no longer required.

CONDITIONS REQUIRING SPECIAL SURGICAL CONSIDERATION

ACUTE ABDOMINAL PAIN

Unlike chronic disease processes, acute abdominal pain requires a prompt diagnostic evaluation in a brief period of time in order that treatment may be started without delay. In the case of massive intra-abdominal bleeding, the time frame may be in minutes. The most frequent conditions in the elderly associated with acute abdominal pain include appendicitis, cholecystitis, diverticulitis, perforated peptic ulcer, acute intestinal obstruction, and massive gastrointestinal bleeding.

The location of pain and tenderness is often the first clue to etiology; the right lower quadrant, appendicitis; right upper quadrant pain, acute cholecystitis; left lower quadrant, acute diverticulitis. Sudden onset of severe abdominal pain in the epigastrium and upper abdomen may be suggestive of an acute perforated ulcer. The pain associated with intestinal obstruction is usually diffuse; however, it may be centered around the umbilicus.

While detailed laboratory studies are helpful and necessary in specific acute abdominal conditions, in almost all cases it is essential to obtain a complete blood count and a flat and upright x-ray of the abdomen initially. In the case of gastrointestinal bleeding, complex studies such as angiography or scans may be required.

ACUTE APPENDICITIS

Some studies have shown that appendicitis in the elderly is not as often correctly diagnosed because of the variations in clinical presentation, resulting in a high incidence of appendiceal rupture, with excess morbidity and mortality in the elderly (5, 7, 11). However, failure to seek medical attention early may also contribute to a poor outcome.

Other studies, however, have observed that elderly patients comprise an increasing proportion of the patients with appendicitis and that they present in a manner similar to that of young patients (10). While minor variations of the prodrome can be expected, abdominal pain, localized to the right lower quadrant and with associated leukocytosis in an elderly patient whose appendix has not been removed should strongly suggest a diagnosis of acute appendicitis.

ACUTE CHOLECYSTITIS

Diseases of the biliary tract are the most common conditions requiring intra-abdominal surgery in elderly patients. Glenn (2), in 1981, revealed that 20% of patients operated on at one medical center had acute cholecystitis. In this same study, the mortality rate was 3.8% of the overall population; however, 665 patients, 65 years and older, had a mortality rate of 9.8%. Prominent contributors to this difference included: emergency operation, common duct stones, age greater than 80 years, preoperative nutritional status, and abnormal renal function.

Other studies have shown a mortality rate for emergency biliary operations in the elderly to range from 9.7–16.7%, compared to 0.8–2.3% for elective operations, (9). The most common cause of death in most series is generalized sepsis, followed by multisystem organ failure. Less common causes of postoperative mortality are myocardial failure, pneumonia, and pulmonary embolus.

Older patients commonly present with pain, jaundice, fever, and leukocytosis of greater severity than seen in younger patients. Infection becomes a major problem in this age group because of the higher incidence of common duct stones, empyema of the gallbladder, gangrene, and perforation. In the elderly patient, the presence of a normal or low total white cell count with a marked shift to the left, is a more ominous sign of impending sepsis than leukocytosis. The presence of high fever, jaundice, and right upper quadrant pain also may portend acute cholangitis, i.e. bacterial infection of the biliary tree.

The management of the elderly patient with suspected acute cholecystitis should proceed without delay, and should include intravenous fluid replacement, nasogastric tube decompression, blood cultures, and parenteral antibiotics. The diagnosis must then be established or excluded as efficiently as possible. Ultrasound examination can quickly identify the presence of a dilated gallbladder with gallstones, and even ascertain whether the extrahepatic ducts are distended or contain stones. Radioactive nucleotide scanning of the biliary tree is another rapid method to establish the presence of acute cholecystitis. Oral or intravenous cholecystograms have very little place in the diagnosis of acute biliary tract disease.

Once the diagnosis has been established and if there are no overwhelming contraindications to surgery, cholecystectomy should be performed as soon as the patient is stabilized and the appropriate resuscitative measures accomplished. Failure to operate promptly increases the risk of gangrene of the gallbladder, peritonitis, and sepsis.

Cholecystostomy, drainage of the gallbladder, can play an important role in early management of moribund or critically ill patients. Performed under local anesthesia, this procedure provides immediate drainage of the gallbladder, reducing the likelihood of sepsis or perforation.

To prevent acute cholecystitis and its attendant high morbidity and mortality in elderly patients, many now recommend that elective operation be done on symptomatic patients with biliary tract disease (3).

DIVERTICULITIS

Approximately 40% of patients over age 40 years have diverticula and almost 100% of individuals over 80 years have the condition, most frequently in the sigmoid colon. The treatment of diverticulitis, an acute inflammation of diverticuli, is initially conservative. The patient should, in most cases, be hospitalized and managed by fasting, nasogastric suction, intravenous fluids, and antibiotics. Failure to respond to initial therapy, increasing severity of symptoms, presence of free air, or the presence of acute diverticulitis in an extremely debilitated elderly patient, especially those on steroids or anti-inflammatory drugs, should prompt consideration for early surgery.

Surgery for complications of diverticulitis almost always involves the use of a colostomy. Procedure of choice for perforation or abscess is resection of the involved colon with an end sigmoid colostomy. In diverticulitis with obstruction, a proximal diverting colostomy followed later by resection of the involved intestine, is performed. Careful preoperative counseling of patient and family should emphasize that colostomy is most often temporary in diverticulitis, and is used because, with infected, inflamed, or unprepared colon, it is unsafe to reanastomose the intestine. When healing occurs and the infection subsides, the colostomy can be closed and normal bowel continuity and evacuation can be restored.

INTESTINAL OBSTRUCTION

In the elderly, acute obstruction of the intestine has a variety of causes; adhesions from previous surgery represent the most common etiology. Diverticulitis, colonic malignancy, hernias, and fecal impaction are other common causes.

The characteristic symptoms of crampy abdominal pain with distention, nausea, and vomiting in an elderly patient, with or without previous abdominal surgery, should alert the physician to consider obstruction as a diagnosis. In addition to routine blood studies, an essential diagnostic study is the flat and upright abdominal x-ray. The findings of dilated small and large intestine suggests the latter as the site of obstruction. A gentle barium enema study, often without preparation, can identify an area of diverticulitis or obstructing colonic malignancy. Dilated small intestine, alone, precludes a lower barium study, and often suggests adhesions as the cause of small bowel obstruction.

Initial therapy consists of nasogastric tube decompression and judicious replacement of fluid and electrolytes while monitoring urine output. After stabilization of associated medical conditions and restoration of circulating volume by intravenous fluids, surgical exploration should be performed promptly, to reduce the risk of major complications; strangulation, necrosis, and perforation.

PERFORATED DUODENAL ULCER

The patient presents with an acute onset of epigastric pain, a rigid upper abdomen, and, frequently, hypotension. Approximately 75% of patients will have free air under the diaphragm demonstrated on an upright chest x-ray.

Early operation to close the perforation and prevent continued peritoneal contamination is the best treatment. With early surgery, mortality rates are low. Mortality and morbidity increase sharply with delay and the development of significant peritonitis.

MASSIVE HEMORRHAGE FROM THE GASTROINTESTINAL TRACT

The most common site is the stomach and duodenum. Duodenal ulcer and gastric ulcer make up more than half the bleeding sites (13). Esophageal varices and acute erosive gastritis are other upper intestinal sites. Diverticulosis, carcinoma, and arteriovenous malformations of the colon are significant sites for lower tract hemorrhage.

The mortality from massive hemorrhage is high. Vigorous and aggressive steps must be taken to restore blood volume and stabilize the patient, while performing diagnostic studies to determine the site and etiology of the bleeding.

In the case of upper intestinal hemorrhage, fiberoptic endoscopy is essential, and is often diagnostic, precluding the need for time-consuming barium studies. Angiography may also be helpful in upper intestinal bleeding; however, it assumes a more important role in lower intestinal bleeding. Coupled with bleeding scans, angiography is important in locating the site of lower intestinal hemorrhage.

Once the site has been determined, all patients, regardless of age, should be considered for surgery promptly unless bleeding ceases promptly. This is especially important in elderly patients, who are much less able to tolerate repeated drops in hematocrit or blood pressure.

A patient should be considered for prompt surgery who (a) has a blood loss of more than 1500 ml of blood; (b) an acute fall in the hematocrit to below 25; (c) blood loss that, after initial stabilization, requires more than 1 unit of transfused blood every 8 hours to maintain a stable blood pressure and hematocrit.

CHRONIC ABDOMINAL CONDITIONS

A number of conditions within the abdomen, because of their chronicity, can be approached electively. These conditions allow adequate preoperative preparation of the patient and full and complete discussion about the operation with the patient and family. Two of these are cancer and chronic biliary tract disease. The rationale for elective surgical management of the latter was discussed in the section on Acute Cholecystitis.

The discovery of a malignancy in the gastrointestinal tract in an elderly patient requires consideration with the patient and family concerning the risks and benefits of surgery, and whether the surgery required is potentially curative or palliative. Malignancies found in the biliary system and pancreas in the elderly patient, because of their location, are often incurable. The life expectancy of such patients may be measured in months, and those involved in the patient's care should carefully weigh the need and benefit of palliative surgery to relieve biliary or upper intestinal symptoms.

In the case of colonic neoplasms, prognosis may be much better. If left in place, a colonic malignancy may eventually obstruct, bleed, or perforate. Early resection has an excellent prognosis, and although it may require an extensive operative procedure, proper patient preparation, both psychologic and physical, can keep the risks within acceptable limits.

In patients with cancer, early involvement of a medical oncologist is essential to assure optimum application of surgical, radiation and chemical management of the disease.

In summary, the surgical principles outlined in this chapter are not new or unique, nor are they for the elderly alone. They are based on sound surgical judgment, thorough medical and surgical preparation, being prepared to cope with the unexpected, and open communication of the surgeon with the patient, his or her family, physician, and all other involved health care personnel. However, the elderly do comprise a group of patients with a slim margin of reserve and, thus, the margin for error is reduced. Meticulous attention to the principles outlined herein will permit aging patients better to tolerate the risk of surgery and will help them sustain the quality of life they deserve.

REFERENCES

1. Dudrick SJ, et al: General principles and techniques of intravenous hyperalimentation in general surgery. In: Cowan G, et al. (Eds): *Intravenous Hyperalimentation.* Philadelphia, Lea & Febiger, 1972.

2. Glenn F: Surgical management of acute cholecystitis in patients sixty-five years of age and older. *Ann Surg* 193:56, 1981.

3. Harness JK, Strodel WE, Talsma SE: Symptomatic biliary tract disease in the elderly patient. *Am Surg* 52:442, 1986.

4. Hartsuck J: Fluid and electrolyte therapy. *Surgery in the Aged.* In Greenfield L (Ed): *Major Problems in Clinical Surgery*; Vol. XVII. Philadelphia, WB Saunders Company, 1975.

5. Hubbell, DS, Barton, WK, Solomon OD: Appendicitis in older people. *Surg Gynecol Obstet* 110:289, 1960.

6. Jaffe BM, et al: Factors influencing survival in patients with untreated hepatic metastasis. *Surg Gynecol Obstet* 127:1, 1968.

7. Lewis FR, Holcroft JW, Boen J, Dumphy JE: Appendicitis—A critical review of diagnosis and treatment in 1,000 cases. *Arch Surg* 110:667, 1975.

8. McSherry CK, Fentanberg H, Calhoun WF, Lahman E, Virshup M: The natural history of gallstones disease in symptomatic and asymptomatic patients. *Ann Surg* 202:59, 1985.

9. McSherry CK, Glenn F: The incidence and causes of death following surgery for non-malignant biliary tract disease. *Ann Surg* 191:271, 1980.

10. Owens BJ III, Hamit HF: Appendicitis in the elderly. *Ann Surg* 187:392, 1978.

11. Thorbjarnarson B, Loehr WJ: Acute appendicitis in patients over the age of sixty. *Surg Gynecol Obstet* 125:1277, 1967.

12. Thrombosis & Embolism Consensus Conference: *JAMA* 256:744, 1986.

13. Villar JH, Fender HR, Watson LC, et al: Emergency diagnosis of upper gastrointestinal bleeding by fiberoptic endoscopy. *Ann Surg* 185:357, 1977.

CHAPTER 35

Pressure Ulcers: Practical Considerations in Their Prevention and Treatment

JULIAN W. REED

Pressure ulcers are among the most common health risks of the elderly whether they are bedridden at home, are hospitalized in acute hospitals for other reasons, e.g., hip fractures, strokes, pneumonias, or are short or long-term residents of chronic hospitals and long-term care (LTC) facilities.

Pressure ulcers (a more exact term than decubitus ulcers) or bedsores continue to be one of the most common and most difficult problems confronting medical and nursing staffs of LTC facilities as well as acute hospitals.

The term "decubitus" is derived from a Latin word meaning "lying down." Because these ulcers can and do develop with the patient being in any position, decubitus ulcer is an inaccurate term (7).

A significant percentage of admissions from acute hospitals to LTC facilities have one or more pressure ulcers on admission, in addition to their underlying systemic illnesses and medical problems.

A pressure ulcer is an area of soft tissue breakdown, usually occurring over a bony prominence. The term pressure ulcer is preferred over decubitus ulcer because pressure is the single most important factor in their development. More than 100 years ago, Sir James Paget (8) recognized this causative factor when he described a water bed to distribute weight more evenly. Water and air beds and mattresses along with other mechanisms whose primary purpose is to distribute pressure evenly continue to be an important component in the prevention and treatment of pressure ulcers today.

Not infrequently, the presence of one or more extensive pressure ulcers is the primary reason for admission to nursing homes. Pressure ulcers inevitably impose an additional burden of frustration and despair upon the patient and his or her family. They add to the complexity of the total treatment regimen, significantly increasing the cost of care by prolonging hospitalization, and if not treated aggressively and effectively, commonly initiate a series of events that ultimately lead to increasing morbidity and death.

INCIDENCE

A Pressure Sore Study was conducted from January through December, 1977 by the Long-Term Care Audit Committee of the Baltimore City Professional Standards Review Organization (PSRO) (memorandum from Reed JW, 1978). This was a voluntary, areawide Medical Care Evaluation Study involving patients from 14 acute care facilities within Baltimore, 13 acute care facilities outside Baltimore and six extended care facilities in Baltimore. The study confirmed that 20–25% of admissions from acute hospitals to LTC facilities had one or more pressure ulcers on admission. Unfortunately, it was not determined what percentage of these patients had pressure ulcers on admission from home to the acute hospitals, although that continues to be one of the most common reasons for admissions of the high risk geriatric patient to the acute hospital.

In the last few years, many of the area acute hospitals that participated in the PSRO study have begun to utilize a protocol for the systematic prevention and treatment of pressure ulcers in the "high risk" geriatric patient. It would be highly desirable and definitely cost-effective if all acute hospitals utilized an aggressive preventive program for the high risk geriatric patient as soon as they are admitted to the acute hospital for any reason.

Unfortunately, there are still too many occasions when an elderly patient is admitted to the acute hospital with either a medical or surgical problem such as pneumonia, stroke, or hip fracture and ends up developing one or more pressure ulcers. It is as if the major treatment emphasis is placed on the primary reason for admission and their vulnerability to pressure ulcers is overlooked until an ulcer actually develops. Once developed, the treatment is usually quite satisfactory. The important issue is that the majority of these ulcers are avoidable if the preventive measures about to be described are consistently employed, especially in the high risk elderly.

PROGNOSIS

The prognosis of the patient who develops an ulcer depends on the therapeutic and preventive action taken when evidence of pressure ulcer development first presents itself. The presence of a pressure ulcer is a poor prognostic sign and its presence is often the most common event associated with the terminal phases of life. Mortality rates ranging from 50–75% have been reported (5). In the PSRO Pressure Sore Study previously described (memorandum from Reed JW, 1978), 99 patients were admitted with pressure ulcers and followed up 6 months later. Of those patients whose ulcers had healed, only four of 35 or 11% had died. However, of those patients whose ulcers had *not* healed, 41 of 64 or 64% had died.

For these reasons, it is readily apparent that a cost-effective and clinically useful method of treating pressure ulcers already present on admission to LTC facilities is needed. In addition, a method for quickly identifying those patients at highest risk for developing ulcers and preventing them needs to be implemented.

Both objectives can be accomplished with a reasonable degree of success and effectiveness by utilizing aggressive preventive measures and a predetermined protocol for treating each grade or stage of ulcer. The treatment of ulcers already present can be successfully carried out by a "team" of nurses under the supervision of a medical director and/or surgical consultant (10). The team should consist of one or more members, depending upon the number of patients to be treated in a given day. The preventive and therapeutic measures about to be described can also be carried out in the patient's home under medical or nursing supervision. These measures or similar ones should be carried out on each geriatric or chronically ill individual hospitalized in an acute hospital or residing in a LTC facility.

COST

There have been various estimates of the cost of treating patients in nursing homes with pressure ulcers. Edberg et al. (2) reported in 1973 that, depending on the number and severity of the ulcers, the estimated cost of treating a patient with pressure ulcers was $15,000–30,000, mostly because of the enormous increase in nursing time required. Medical costs have escalated significantly since then.

When the incidence of pressure ulcers is taken into consideration (10–20% of the patients in LTC facilities have one or more) along with the fact that there are now more patients in LTC facilities in the United States than in acute care hospitals, the magnitude of the problem and the astronomical costs become obvious. A 1980 survey showed that medical costs resulting from pressure ulcers can increase from $2000–10,000 per patient, with a national annual total of $3–5 billion (1). Moreover, when one considers that given adequate human and material resources, all pressure ulcers are preventable, it looms as a major health care problem of the geriatric population that is seldom appropriately addressed. The knowledge as well as the techniques and resources are available to prevent the development of these ulcers. *Most commonly, it is the lack of application of proven preventive measures to the high risk elderly*, such as high protein-calorie intake along with the avoidance of dehydration, regular turning every 2 hours, keeping the skin clean and dry especially over the pressure points, i.e., sacrum, hips, heels, and ankles, and the use of air or water mattresses either at home, in the acute hospital, or in the LTC facility that most frequently results in the development of pressure ulcers.

SITES

The most common sites of involvement of pressure ulcers are those where bony prominences underlie the skin. These most commonly include the sacral prominence in the supine position, the greater trochanter when lying on one's side, and the tuberosities of the ischium in the sitting position. Other sites involved are the posterior aspects of the heels, ankles, and knees, the iliac crests, the elbows, ribs, and occasionally, the ears and scalp.

ETIOLOGY

Pressure is the primary pathophysiologic factor in the formation of these ulcers. Prolonged pressure unrelieved by change of position leads to ischemia, then anoxia and subsequent cell death followed by necrosis. In order for pressure to cause ischemia, it must exceed the maximum capillary pressure in the skin of approximately 35 mm Hg for a prolonged period of time. Time and pressure are additive factors in the production of these wounds. Ulcers can develop after 12 hours at 100 mm Hg, but after only 2 hours at 500 mm Hg. No tissue changes are apparent at pressures of 35 mm Hg or less for prolonged periods of time, but there are microscopic changes in tissue subjected to pressures as low as 60 mm Hg (3). In the sitting position, one-half of the body's weight is supported on 8% of the sitting surface (7). Pressures in excess of 300 mm Hg occur beneath the ischial tuberosities, far exceeding capillary pressure. Although many of these figures have been drawn from animal and not human studies, the fact remains that the inevitable result of sitting or lying immobile for a prolonged period of time (i.e., more than 2 hours) will be the development of pressure ulcers over bony prominences.

The same process can occur relatively quickly, almost instantaneously, by the shearing effect, i.e., pulling a patient across wrinkled bed linen rather than lifting when transferring from bed to wheelchair. When this occurs, the skin and subcutaneous tissues are pulled taut and overstretched. This shearing force will then disrupt tissues and lead to almost immediate necrosis as a result of cellular damage produced by this maneuver. Any movement of the patient producing this shearing force should be carefully avoided. The practice of maintaining a supine patient with the head of the bed elevated to a high degree (more than 30°) also increases the likelihood of developing pressure ulcers in the usual locations, because of the combined effects of pressure and shearing force.

Although prolonged or intense pressure is the major cause of pressure ulcers, other factors may contribute to their development. The administration of sedatives (4) may exaggerate immobility related to paralysis or decreased sensation of the skin. Protein-calorie malnutrition, vitamin C deficiency, debilitated conditions with anemia, hypoproteinemia, and other metabolic disorders, low blood pressure, peripheral vascular disease, prolonged dampness from urine or feces, maceration of the skin, presence of bacterial contaminants and poor care in general have all been identified as contributing factors in the development of pressure ulcers. Finally, the advanced age of the geriatric patient leading to increased skin fragility along with edema for any reason that causes weakened skin and stasis changes are also frequently involved.

One of the most overlooked factors in the development of pressure ulcers is dehydration. In order to avoid or minimize the role of impaired fluid balance in the geriatric patient in a LTC facility, it is prudent to assume the geriatric patient is dehydrated until proven otherwise. Patients will be less likely to become dehydrated if given amounts of fluid are prescribed by the physician and recorded on an Intake and Output chart. In this way, physicians and nurses can monitor and evaluate the hydration status of their patients continuously. Dehydration often occurs rather insidiously, frequently without the patient, physician, or nurses being aware of it, especially when patient temperatures are elevated for any reason. Dehydration along with the other factors mentioned greatly increases the risk that a pressure ulcer will develop.

PREVENTION AND EARLY TREATMENT

How does one identify those geriatric patients at the highest risk of developing pressure ulcers? Perhaps even more importantly, how does one prevent ulcer development in the *high risk* patient? How does one treat the ulcer once developed to prevent its becoming more extensive and to facilitate its healing?

The Pressure Ulcer Predilection Guide (Fig. 35.1), which can be scored easily and quickly by nursing or medical personnel, is helpful in identifying promptly those patients at high risk for developing pressure ulcers, if they do not already have pressure ulcers on admission to the LTC facility. On admission, a pressure ulcer predilection score is obtained for each patient by assessment of the general

"PRESSURE ULCER PREDILECTION GUIDE"

Patient Name			Pt. #		Room #	Date Admitted
Age	Sex	Physician			Predilection Score	

General Condition	Mental State	Acitivity	Mobility In Bed	Incontinence
0 Good	0 Alert	0 Ambulatory	0 Full	0 Not
1 Fair	1 Confused	1 Walk With Help	1 Slightly Limited	1 Occasional
2 Poor	2 Apathetic	2 Chairfast	2 Very Limited	2 Usually Urine
3 Bad	3 Stuporous	3 Bedfast	3 Immobile	3 Doubly Incontinent

NOTE: A SCORE of 7 or more is considered a 'high risk" score for the development of pressure ulcers, Special attention to regular turning, protective padding over areas most vulnerable, meticulous skin care, and good intake of protien foods are especially indicated in those with a "high risk" score.

Pressure Ulcer(s) present on admission?	Yes	No

If YES, Describe briefly with length, width, and depth of each ulcer in centimeters: also, if undermined, record amount in centimeters.

LOCATION	SIZE :	LENGTH	WIDTH	DEPTH	UNDERMINED
Ex. Sacrum		6cm x	4cm x	3cm x	2cm
1.					
2.					
3.					

Referred to Pressure Ulcer Team on:

*Date of Initial Evaluation by Pressure Ulcer Team:

*All Notes by Pressure Ulcer Team Will Be In Integrated Progress Notes

Figure 35.1.   Pressure ulcers. Modified from Brandner J: Bedsores/treatment: Treating the open ischemic ulcer. *Patient Care* Aug: 231, 1974. Data from Shea JD: Pressure sores, classification and management. *Clin Orthop* 112:89 1975.

condition, mental state, activity, mobility in bed, and continence. The higher the score (on a scale of 0–15), the greater the risk of developing ulcers, if they are not already present. An alert, oriented, hydrated, ambulatory patient who is fully mobile in bed and continent with a score of 1 or 2 is much less likely to develop an ulcer than a poorly nourished, dehydrated, confused, bedfast patient who is very limited in bed mobility and doubly incontinent with a score of 14 or 15. This guide has been of practical predictive value (10) in one large nursing home for 12 years, i.e., those patients who score the highest, especially over 10, are those patients who are, in fact, at the highest risk clinically of developing ulcers, and therefore, need the most aggressive preventive program implemented promptly.

Ideally, the score should be obtained periodically (weekly or monthly) on all bedridden patients at home as well as all patients who are admitted to acute general or chronic disease hospitals. A score of 7 or more is considered a high risk score for the development of pressure ulcers. Special attention is then given to general preventive as well as therapeutic measures if one or more ulcers is already present. Regular turning of the patient, at least every 2 hours, is mandatory. Protective padding over bony prominences is utilized along with meticulous skin care. A high protein-calorie intake for the maintenance of good nutrition is immediately begun, along with careful avoidance of dehydration. Patients with scores of 10 or more are immediately placed on a foam rubber or water mattress or alternating air mattress in order to distribute the patient's weight more evenly and to reduce pressure over bony prominences. The use of floatation pads, filled with dry gel, for wheelchairs are also utilized for patients with ulcers beginning or present over the ischial tuberosities. In that regard, the Jay Cushion (Jay Medical Ltd., Boulder, CO) has been superior to the Roho (Roho, Inc., East St. Louis, IL) because it has a molded saddle that offers better support, making it easier to maintain proper sitting balance than the Roho. For patients with extensive sacral or ischial ulcers, who need to remain in the horizontal position completely, the four-wheeled self-propelling stretcher is helpful if the patient has the strength and cognitive capacity to manage it.

In the past several years, more technically advanced and expensive beds have been developed and are being more widely used for the treatment of pressure ulcers. One of these is the Clinitron bed (SSI Medical Services, Inc.) that is being used in most acute care hospitals and in many LTC facilities. The Clinitron (Charleston, SC) bed (Fig. 35.2) is basically a large tank filled with fine microspheres that utilize a constant air flow to distribute pressure evenly and eliminate maceration of the patient's skin (6). The compressed air flow causes the microspheres to act as a dense fluid. This eliminates friction and the shearing forces and the patient's skin is never exposed to pressure in excess of capillary closing pressures (35 mm Hg). This effect provides a very satisfactory environment for the healing of pressure ulcers. It allows patients to be positioned

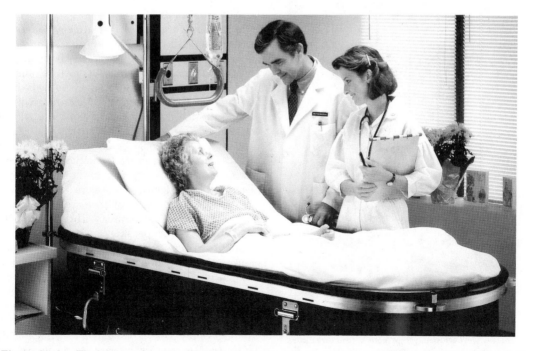

Figure 35.2. The latest model of the Clinitron Air Fluidized Support System of Clinitron Bed II is smaller and less cumbersome than the original. It is an important adjunct in the prevention and treatment of pressure ulcers in acute hospitals and LTC facilities. Courtesy of Support Systems International, Johns Island, SC.

on ulcers and operative areas (such as rotation flaps) without subsequent tissue trauma. The Clinitron also provides a cleaner support than a regular bed because the compressed air creates a laminar flow around the patient. Also, any type of fluid, excretion or drainage, tends to be dessicated by the air flow, permeating the top sheet and microspheres to a collection pan underneath. Nursing care for even large, obese patients can be accomplished quickly and easily by repositioning the patient and turning off the air flow. The patient will remain in that position for wound care or for toileting until the air flow is restarted.

A small percentage of patients react unfavorably to the sensations of lying on a Clinitron bed. Two of our patients became quite anxious and apprehensive, developed visual and auditory hallucinations after 24–36 hours on the bed. However, these quickly disappeared when the patient was taken off the bed.

Another similar type of bed which has been available for the past couple of years is the Mediscus bed (Mid-Atlantic Medical Services, Houston, TX) (Fig. 35.3). It was developed by a surgeon in England, originally for treating patients with severe burns in-

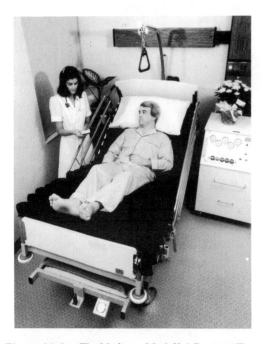

Figure 35.3. The Mediscus Mark V-A Pressure Treatment System or Mediscus bed provides another useful adjunct in the prevention and treatment of pressure ulcers. It is less expensive and more maneuverable than the Clinitron and can be leased or purchased. Courtesy of Mediscus Products, Inc., Houston, TX

volving large areas of body surface. Its use was then expanded to include the treatment of pressure ulcers. It works on a similar principle as the Clinitron bed except that the patient is supported by 21 waterproof yet vapor-permeable air sacs arranged side by side in a contiguous pattern. The patient lies on the edge of these air sacs in whatever position is most comfortable. The air pressure and temperature can be controlled in five different sections of the system by pressure control dials. Body surface pressure remains below capillary closure (35 mm Hg). Manual controls enable the patient or nursing attendant to raise the foot and head sections and to achieve a Trendelenberg or reverse Trendelenberg position. Also, the vapor-permeable surface of the air sacs eliminates moisture. A removeable headboard and adjustable footboard, and adjustable safety rails come with the bed. The Mediscus bed provides the feeling of a regular bed, seems to reduce the need for pain and sleep medication, and in the author's experience, works at least equally as well as the Clinitron in treating pressure ulcers. It is also lighter, less expensive, and more maneuverable than the Clinitron. These beds are usually reserved for those patients who are at highest risk or those who have the largest number of extensive ulcers. If these patients are in positive protein balance and the treatment protocol is followed consistently, significant healing of even large deep ulcers usually occurs.

In the prevention and early treatment of pressure ulcers, early detection followed by prompt and vigorous action are mandatory. Skin over bony prominences (sacrum, hips, ischial tuberosities, ankles, heels, etc.) should be examined daily in the bedridden high risk patient. Any patient showing redness of the skin that does not fade promptly should be treated by relieving pressure on the injured area immediately. There should be no further significant pressure on that area until all signs of inflammation disappear and until any breaks in the skin are completely healed. If significant pressure (i.e., exceeding 35 mm Hg) is not avoided on that site, it will cause further breakdown and the area will progress rapidly to a further stage. Proper skin care includes washing the area once or twice daily with a mild soap and applying a thin layer of an emollient to lubricate the skin. Cocoa butter or lanolin are effective when gently massaged in the area. The massage ostensibly stimulates vasodilation with increased blood flow to the area. It has been found empirically that Granulex Spray (Dow D. Hickman, Inc., Sugarland, TX) is useful in treating this early stage I ulcer, especially if used two or three times a day in patients who are well nourished and hydrated. Granulex contains balsam peru, a stimulant and mild bacterocidal agent that helps increase blood supply for added nourishment, castor oil, an emollient that restores tissue moisture and keeps skin soft and supple, delaying premature desiccation of epithelial tissue, and trypsin that aids in the removal of necrotic tissue. The same treatment should be given whether the patient is at home, in the acute care hospital or a resident of a LTC facility. Specific instructions should be given to the patient or family if at home, or written as orders by the physician if the patient is in the hospital or nursing home. This early, aggressive treatment may reverse the pathophysiologic process previously described and may well make the difference between a few days in bed or several weeks or months of healing an ulcer. (A more detailed treatment protocol will be presented later in this chapter.)

TREATMENT OF ULCERS

Traditionally in nursing homes, each physician prescribes his or her own protocol for the treatment of pressure ulcers. This frequently works quite well in small nursing homes, (i.e., those with less than 50 beds) since it usually involves only one or two physicians and a like number of different protocols. However, in larger nursing homes where the number of beds may reach 200 or more, this not infrequently involves a dozen or more physicians and the same number of treatment protocols. In this situation, following multiple different protocols frequently becomes somewhat inefficient and often quite time-consuming for nursing personnel who are carrying out each individual physician's orders. Therefore, in 1975, in an effort to increase efficiency and effectiveness in treating ulcers, after a literature review, a Pressure Ulcer Team was organized and a treatment protocol was developed in an effort to facilitate healing of ulcers in susceptible patients (10).

CLASSIFICATION

There are many different methods and techniques of classifying ulcers. For clarity and consistency in developing the protocol, the method chosen was the one proposed by Darrell Shea (12). In Figure 35.4, ulcers are classified according to severity in grades or stages from I-IV, where grade I is a superficial ulcer exposing the dermis and grade IV is a deep necrotic ulcer extending to bone.

The healing of pressure ulcers depends as much, if not more, on the general clinical status of the patient as on the specific treatment modality selected. More than 50 agents are mentioned in the literature,

from sugar to Maalox, that have been used in the treatment of ulcers (4). *However, it is highly unlikely that any ulcer will heal in an anemic, malnourished patient in negative protein balance, unless the clinical status is improved.* On the contrary, a properly debrided large grade II or III ulcer will usually heal in a reasonable period of time as long as the patient is not anemic or protein or calorie deficient.

NUTRITION

In this regard, it has been observed that protein-calorie malnutrition is far more prevalent in the geriatric patient, wherever he or she may happen to be, home, hospital, LTC facility, than is generally recognized. Muncie and Carbonetto (6), after studying the nutritional status of 30 randomly selected patients at an extended care facility, reported that between 47 and 66% of patients had moderate or severe protein-calorie malnutrition by anthropometric measurements and 60% had serum albumin levels of less than 3.5 g. In addition, 60% of patients were anemic and 24% were leukopenic. These findings were based on anthropometric measurements of height, weight, arm circumference, and triceps skinfold, as well as laboratory studies of hematocrit, white blood count, serum albumin, and transferrin. The authors prudently recommended that physicians generally need to increase their awareness and observation of the nutritional status of patients in LTC facilities, and become cognizant of the potential detrimental effects protein-calorie malnutrition may have on the rehabilitation process of the geriatric patient. It is noteworthy that these were randomly selected patients and not those who had pressure ulcers.

Even more significantly, for geriatric patients with pressure ulcers, Pinchofsky-Devine and Kaminski (9) studied 232 nursing home patients (mean age 72.9 + 12 years) in an effort to determine if a correlation exists between deteriorating nutritional status and the development of pressure ulcers. The nutritional status of these patients was determined using biochemical and anthropometic measurements. Overall, the incidence of some degree of malnutrition was 59%. Seventeen of the patients were found to have pressure ulcers and these patients were all malnourished. When classified as mild, moderate, or severe malnutrition, the patients with pressure ulcers were in the severely malnourished group. There was a significant correlation ($P < .001$) between the nutritional status of pressure ulcer patients and the malnourished patients. It was concluded that the development of pressure ulcers

PRESSURE ULCERS

Pressure ulcers, like burns, may be classified according to severity. J. Darrell Shea, MD, orthopedic surgeon, spinal surgery unit Orange Memorial Hospital, Orlando, Florida, has devised a system of four grades, as illustrated here. The treatment recommendations are those of Anthony Merlino, MD.

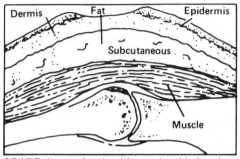

GRADE I - erythemia with associated induration, heat, and minimal abrasion-type breakdown of epidermis, exposing the dermis.
Treatment: Prompt recognition, local wound care, and removal of pressure by changing position every two hours. Ideally, erythema disappears in 2-3 days, with epithelialization in 10-14 days.

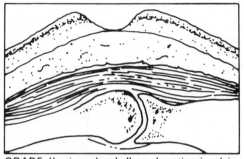

GRADE II - irregular shallow ulceration involving the subcutaneous fat with erythema, induration, and local increased temperature.
Treatment: Same as for grade I. Healing may occur in as little as three weeks but may take three months. The resulting scar is relatively unstable.

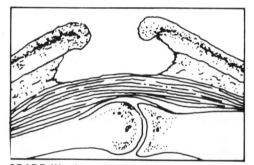

GRADE III - deep ulceration with a chronic, foul-smelling, necrotic base; thick, hyperpigmented borders; and widely undermined skin. The patient is usually toxic, anemic and hypoproteinemic.
Treatment: Same as for grades I and II, plus wet-to-dry dressings and wound debridement, possibly followed by excision of underlying body prominence and full-thickness rotation flap graft. Supportive measures include transfusions, intravenous fluids, and systemic antibiotics.

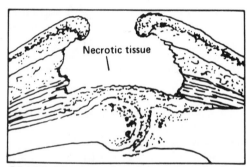

GRADE IV - deep ulceration reaching the bone, frequently with septic dislocation and/or osteomyelitis in a highly toxic patient.
Treatment: Same as for grade III plus consideration of radical measures such as amputation or joint disarticulation when the condition is life-threatening.

Figure 35.4.   Pressure Ulcers. From Shea JD: Pressure sores, classification and management. *Clin Orthop* 112:236, 1974.

correlated to a high degree with nutritional deficiencies. The authors' findings strongly suggest a need for more aggressive nutritional support in the elderly, especially those with pressure ulcers. Therefore, it is recommended that a nutritional assessment be done on all high risk patients as well as those who already have developed pressure ulcers. This can begin with weekly weighing of the patient. Patients who lose weight for 2 consecutive weeks should have a more extensive nutritional assessment. One simple method of assessment is to take a weight and height measurement on the patient and compare to a standard. If the patient's weight for height falls below the 80th percentile, he or she is considered to have malnutrition. Another anthropometric measurement is the midarm circumference of the upper arm. This value can then be compared against a specific standard and if below 80% of standard would be considered abnormal. Hematocrit, white blood cell count, white cell differential, total lymphocyte count (TLC), and serum albumin are also of value in performing nutritional assessments. For men, hematocrits less than 41% and less than 36% for women are considered abnormal. Serum albumins below 3.5 are abnormal and below 3.0 indicates significant protein loss or protein deprivation.

In the study by Muncie and Carbonetto (6), serum albumin was highly correlated to hematocrit (r=.721, P<.001). Pinchofsky-Devine and Kaminski (9) believe that adequate nutritional assessment can be performed by using only two tests, serum albumin and TLC (mm^3). When the serum albumin is below 3.3 g and the TLC is below 1220/mm^3 (the mean albumin and TLC of malnourished patients without pressure ulcers in their study), nutritional intervention should be implemented.

For patients who can take nutrition by mouth, oral supplements such as canned polymeric diets (e.g., Enrich) or standard nasogastric feedings (e.g., Ensure and Osmolite or Compleat B) are appropriate, relatively inexpensive, and should be used to supplement the patient's regular diet. (Compleat B is more bioavailable and easily digestible but is also more expensive than Ensure or Osmolite). Documentation of intake is necessary to see whether the patient is consuming the supplements. Nutritional assessments should be performed twice monthly for patient in a therapeutic phase, and especially those with pressure ulcers under active treatment.

If, in spite of the consumption of oral supplements, the patient's nutritional status has not improved, and intake is adequate, the use of nonvolitional feedings with a nasogastric or gastrostomy tube needs to be seriously considered. However, before this decision with patient, family and/or guardian is reached, many factors need to be considered including the number and extent of the ulcers, the surgical risk, level of consciousness and orientation, rehabilitation potential, life expectancy, CPR status (yes or no), and the quality of life in general. Several discussions involving patient, family, and/or guardian may be required to reach this decision. Once made, the decision is not irreversible and can be reconsidered if there is a significant change in any of the previously mentioned factors, including significant improvement or deterioration in the patient's condition. Not infrequently, providing additional nutritional support, either oral or via nasogastric tube, is the key factor that results in the healing of pressure ulcers. While the patient is nutritionally compromised (i.e., protein calorie malnourished), the ulcers remained static or even deteriorated.

Feedings must be tailored to meet the patient's calorie and protein requirements. Diet should include protein (at least 0.8 g/kg/day) and enough calories to meet the patient's basal need, (i.e., 30 cal × weight in kg plus at least 10% as a stress factor, i.e., pressure ulcers). Vitamin supplements should be provided including multi-vitamins and at least 1g of vitamin C each day. Vitamins C and E are essential for wound healing. Magnesium and zinc are also necessary for wound healing but patients usually have sufficient amounts of these trace metals for healing to occur.

PRESSURE ULCER TEAM

Ideally, Pressure Ulcer Team members should be recruited on a voluntary basis from registered nurses and licensed practical nurses on staff. The team should treat every patient referred to it by the patient's physician each day. However, if the ulcer is clean and without drainage, it could be treated every other day. New granulation tissue will not develop until all necrotic material has been removed with debridement. Manual debridement of pressure ulcers should be demonstrated to each team member by a physician. They should then be observed carrying out the procedure until judged competent to perform this independently, following a predetermined protocol. Three team members can usually treat 30–35 patients each day allowing 15–30 minutes per patient. Although the average patient has one or two ulcers, some patients have as many as 15 or 20 ulcers. This 15–30 minutes per patient includes time spent in preparing a treatment chart that is taken to the patient's bedside. Charting is done at least once or twice a week in most LTC facilities. In acute hospitals, charting should probably be done daily.

The length, width, depth, and amount of undermining (if present) of each ulcer is measured in cm and recorded when first seen and weekly thereafter. Depth and undermining, if present, must be measured accurately as these measurements are critical in determining if the ulcer is healing. Culture and antibiotic sensitivity studies are done on febrile patients and on patients whose ulcers appear to have associated cellulitis. It has been found that 75–80%

of the cultures are positive for *E. coli, Proteus mirabilis,* or *Pseudomonas* organisms and about 15–20% are positive for *Staphylococcus* or *Streptococcus* organisms. The patient's physician should be informed of the findings and usually orders a 10-day course of appropriate antibiotic. A surgical consultation should be requested when an ulcer fails to respond or deteriorates significantly. The consultant may recommend the use of skin grafts or rotation flaps carried out in an acute care hospital, if the patient's attending physician and family concur. Many factors need to be considered before this decision is reached, including whether the patient is a good surgical risk, the level of consciousness and orientation, rehabilitation potential, quality of life in general, and whether or not he or she could feasibly be cared for at home if the ulcer were surgically eliminated. Grade III or IV ulcers involving the heels or ankles may deteriorate, leading to osteomyelitis, sometimes requiring below the knee or above the knee amputations.

When the ulcer is stable or healing, patients are referred back to the nurses assigned to the general care of the patient who then continue to carry out the same protocol. Any physician who elects to treat his or her own patient can do so using any method of treatment chosen. Because the team has been in existence, more than 98% of patients with ulcers have been referred for treatment.

The therapeutic agents, debriding enzymes, dressing techniques and procedures used in the Pressure Ulcer Team Protocol (Table 35.1) have been selected based on empirical observations over the past 12 years at the Deaton Hospital and Medical Center (a 240-bed multilevel chronic hospital and extended care facility located in the Inner Harbor area of Baltimore; it opened in March 1973).

The overall objective in the treatment of superficial ulcers (grade I) involving damage to the superficial layers of the skin is conservative management directed toward cleanliness, relief of pressure, and exposure to air. The decision to use a dressing should depend, in part, upon the location of the ulcer. If the wound is in an exposed area, such as the knee or hip, it probably is best to let the ulcer dry without any dressings. In areas that are often in contact with bedclothes such as buttocks or elbows, the patient may feel more comfortable and the new granulation tissue may be protected if the ulcer is covered with a layer of gauze. A deep ulcer, grade II or III is one in which all the layers of the skin, subcutaneous tissue (fat), or superficial fascia and sometimes even muscle have been damaged by pressure or subsequent infection.

An open ulcer originates from the surface and extends downward through the various layers of tissue. A closed ulcer, partially or wholly undermined, originates in the subcutaneous tissue and proceeds toward the surface, thus allowing degenerative changes to spread in all directions, possibly even involving the bone. For clarity in identification and consistency in following the protocol, grade II and

Table 35.1
Deaton Hospital-Medical Center Pressure Ulcer Team Treatment Protocol

Grade of Ulcer	Treatment
Grade I	Good skin care, antipressure padding: maintenance of adequate nutrition and hydration levels; turning and positioning every 2 hours; Granulex spray bid or tid.
Grade II	Light cleansing with normal saline solution; topical antibiotic therapy–polysporin powder; antipressure padding or open to air.
Grade III	Cleansing with peroxide, thorough rinsing with normal saline; enzymatic debridement–Panafil or Travase (clean with normal saline solution only); Manual debridement if indicated; topical antibiotic therapy after debridement and when granulation tissue is well established–polysporin powder plus clean dressings (ABDs); sterile dressings (Telfa); antipressure padding (Reston) (much care is needed to ensure that the adhesive backing is not put on ischemic or inflamed skin, otherwise it could denude such areas); water mattress
Grade IV	Cleansing with peroxide and thorough rinsing with normal saline solution; enzymatic and/or manual debridement; packing of cavities or fistulae with 4 × 3s and/or 1–2 inches of Nugauze; sterile dressings (Telfa) with clean dressings (ABDs) clean procedure; antipressure padding (Reston); water mattress

grade III ulcers could be further broken down into those that contain necrotic material and those without any evidence of necrosis. An open deep ulcer (grade II-IV) usually involves the necrosis of a great deal of tissue. The wound must be debrided and the necrotic tissue must be removed, as this provides the substance upon which bacteria thrive. If all necrotic material cannot be removed manually, an enzymatic debriding agent should be applied to the remaining necrotic material or eschar on a daily basis. Hard eschars should be scored with a scalpel to facilitate the action of the enzyme. For enzymatic debridement, clear Panafil Ointment, a vegetable product (Rystan Co., Inc.) has been found to be effective for routine use, and Travase Ointment, a bacterial product (Flint Laboratories) activated with wet saline dressings, or Silvadene (Little Falls, NJ) (silver sulfadiazine micromized) to be effective for resistant necrotic ulcers. For a list of the enzymatic debriding agents commonly used and their composition, see Lamy(4).

Removal of the necrotic material also shortens the lag phase of wound healing, and permits the underlying normal tissue to start the proliferative phase. Granulation tissue can then develop. Once manual debridement has been performed (this may be required several times a week on large necrotic ulcers), the wound can be maintained by irrigations with cleansing agents such as hydrogen peroxide to reduce a large exudate or malodor.

After cleansing of the wound with normal saline, clear Panafil Ointment should be applied to any necrotic areas remaining. This can then be covered with Telfa (sterile 4 × 3s). ABD dressings (nonsterile) can then be applied primarily for absorptive purposes. Sufficient 1-inch thick Reston antipressure padding (cut to measure) can then be applied to cover the wound completely and act as a cushion. (Care should be taken not to create pressure by excessive padding). The entire bandage can then be covered and secured with 4-inch Conform or similar elastic tape. The edges can be secured with 1-inch Elasticon that acts as an anchor.

In certain patients with deep, undermined ulcers, daily packing with iodoform gauze, betadine compresses, or betadine viscous gauze applications will usually facilitate healing. Debrisan (Pharmacia Labs, New Brunswick, NJ), a highly hydrophilic dextrose polymer, has been found to be useful in absorbing wound exudates, reducing inflammation and edema, and preparing a wound for grafting. If used too long, however, it will damage or destroy new granulation tissue by its dehydrating action. In selected patients, when the ulcers are clean and granulating, skin grafts or rotation flaps frequently will facilitate recovery and rehabilitation.

BENEFITS OF THE TEAM

The benefits of the team approach using a standard protocol in the prevention and treatment of pressure ulcers in a LTC facility although mostly subjective, have been multiple.

First, there has been improved morale among patients, families, and staff, including the physicians and staff nurses caring for the patient. Offensive odors are reduced or eliminated, unaesthetic wounds are bandaged and protected, and morbidity generally has been lessened. The psychologic and emotional benefit to the patient of having daily efficiently organized care given, although difficult to measure, seems to be of considerable significance. Utilizing the team approach and a standard protocol technically appears to be a quicker and more efficient way of caring for large numbers of pressure ulcers, regardless of their stage or grade. Although it is difficult to quantify accurately, pressure ulcers treated in this manner seem to heal more quickly, in many cases shortening the length of stay, facilitating rehabilitation (11) and discharges to home, if feasible.

The preventive benefits from this approach, while also difficult to measure quantitatively, also seem to be significant in that fewer ulcers develop, even in susceptible or high risk patients when the preventive measures in the protocol are consistently employed. They can be modified according to the size and type of facility, if in a LTC facility or chronic hospital, as long as the operating and treatment principles and techniques are consistently utilized.

Prevention is the key factor. If the described techniques and principles are assiduously carried out, the vast majority of these ulcers can be prevented. If pressure ulcers occur, the treatment protocol presented has been found to facilitate their healing, provided that the patient remains in positive protein balance and is adequately nourished.

ACKNOWLEDGMENT. The author gratefully acknowledges the editorial assistance of Herbert L. Munci, Jr., M.D., Associate Professor of Family Practice, University of Maryland School of Medicine, in the preparation of this chapter.

REFERENCES

1. Constantian MB (Ed): *Pressure Ulcers: Principles and Techniques of Management.* New York, Little Brown Co., 1980.
2. Edberg EG, Cerney K, Stauffer ES: Prevention and treatment of pressure sores. *Phys Ther* 53:246, 1973.

3. Kosiak M: Etiology of decubitus ulcers. *Arch Phys Med Rehabil* 42:19, 1961.
4. Lamy P: Pressure sores. Chapter 25. In Lamy P: *Prescribing for the Elderly*. Littleton, MA, PSG Publishing, 1980, pp. 607–619.
5. Michochi RG, Lamy PP: The problem of pressure sores in a nursing home population: Statistical data. *J Am Geriatr Soc* 24:323, 1976.
6. Muncie HL Jr, Carbonetto C: Prevalence of protein calorie malnutrition in an extended care facility, *J Fam Pract* 14:1061, 1982.
7. Orlando JC: Pressure Ulcers: Principles of Management. In Reichel W(Ed): *Clinical Aspects of Aging*, 2nd ed. Baltimore, Williams & Wilkins, 1983, pp. 469–478.
8. Paget J: Clinical lecture on bedsores. *The Students J Hosp Gazette* (London) 1:144, 1873.
9. Pinchcofsky-Devine GH, Kiminski MV Jr: Correlation of pressure sores and nutritional status. *J Am Geriatr Soc* 34:435, 1986.
10. Reed JW: Pressure ulcers in the elderly; Prevention and treatment utilizing the team approach. *Md State Med J* 30:45, 1981.
11. Reed JW, Gessner JE: Rehabilitation in the extended care facility. *J Am Geriatr Soc* 27:325, 1979.
12. Shea JD: Pressure sores, classification and management. *Clin Orthop* 112:89, 1975.

CHAPTER 36

Eye Problems of the Aged

ROBERT L. KASPER

Perhaps it is one of the tragic ironies of life that as advanced age is approached and much of the ability to perform *physically* at previous levels is lost, people become, of necessity, visual *observers* of others' active participation. It is at this time in life that the greatest percentage of hindrances to visual acuity come to the fore. Additionally, those activities not specifically interfered with by growing older such as reading, traveling, visiting with family and friends, watching television, and attending the theater, have a greatly reduced level of enjoyment for the aged individual who cannot see well. Any measure that can be taken either to preserve or to restore vision, particularly in this age group, therefore, takes on added importance (29).

In this chapter, the most common eye disorders of the aging population, their presenting signs and symptoms, possible prevention and treatment, will be emphasized.

The eye, not unlike all other organs, is constantly undergoing change. During the early years of life, these changes are related primarily to growth and development, but as the years go by, they become degenerative signs of age. Some of these degenerative changes are so common as to be expected; yet others are considered pathologic. The line between these two groupings is a fairly narrow one.

ANATOMIC CHANGES OF AGING

The *cornea* tends to flatten with age, in the vertical meridian, leading to the onset or alteration of pre-existing astigmatism (25). Fatty invasion of the corneal margin that blurs the demarcation between cornea and sclera is called arcus senilis. Degenerative changes in the corneal endothelium are commonly seen (guttata). These may become severe enough to cause epithelial changes that can result in great discomfort and impaired vision. The *sclera* be-

comes less elastic and takes on a more yellow coloration due to fatty deposition. The *ciliary body* thickens and its processes become hyalinized. Changes in the *trabecular meshwork*, through which aqueous humor must flow as it leaves the eye, occur, such as endothelial proliferation and thickening (18), and sclerosis of the tissue (28). These changes in the trabeculation coupled with the increase in scleral rigidity might be expected to give rise to an elevation in the intraocular pressure in all aging eyes. It would appear, however, that atrophic change in the ciliary epithelium, where the aqueous is produced, brings about a gradual diminution in aqueous production yielding a fairly constant level of intraocular pressure. If the delicate balance necessary to maintain normal intraocular pressure is not continued, glaucoma can be the result.

Connective tissue in the uveal tract thickens and becomes more diffuse. Bruch's membrane of the *choroid* develops changes that lead to the development of drusen that appear as rounded, yellowish spots in the retina upon ophthalmoscopic examination. The *iris* similarly undergoes changes giving it a rigid character and resulting in a smaller pupil, probably because of the increase in connective tissue and an increase in its hyalinization, as well as sclerotic change in the iris vasculature (15).

As the *lens* ages, it undergoes a number of anatomic and metabolic changes. Because the lens is devoid of blood vessels and lies suspended in the intraocular fluid, its pathologic changes are more simple than those of other tissues. Additionally, the primary function of the lens, which is the maintenance of optical transparency, depends upon the continued operation of a fairly complicated metabolism that can respond only passively to any insult, whether traumatic, toxic, or degenerative. The result of such an insult will often be opacification and secondary optical disability (7). With increasing age, the ability to increase the thickness and curvature of the lens in order to focus upon near objects is gradually lost. This condition is called presbyopia and accounts for the need for corrective lenses for reading, and bifocal additions in people over 40 years of age.

As a result of physiologic miosis related to aging and lenticular yellowing, which to some degree is a universal occurrence, the retina of a sexagenarian receives only one-third the amount of light received by the retina of a 20-year-old (24). It follows that the intensity of the ambient light afforded the older individual has a significant effect on visual perception, particularly in view of the fact that cone sensitivity after-dark adaptation is impaired in this same group.

The *vitreous* commonly detaches from its natural connections to the retina especially in the advancing years of life and in states of high myopia. When this occurs, horseshoe-shaped retinal tears may follow, and the importance of these tears in the production of a detachment of the retina is obvious. If, in the process, a retinal blood vessel is torn, a hemorrhage into the vitreous will result.

The appearance of vitreous "floaters"—opacities that may take the form of dots, lines, or cobwebs—is most frequently a sign of "normally" occurring degenerative change. These opacities may cause considerable anxiety to a nervous patient who may fear that a visual catastrophe is imminent. When the floaters are associated with momentary flashes of light, a more significant level of suspicion must be maintained by the clinician so that a vitreous detachment or a detachment of the retina can be distinguished. The latter possibility being the only one of importance, the physician must rule out its presence (7).

Spherical or disc-shaped opacities suspended in the vitreous made up of calcium-containing lipids, are found most frequently in older males and are usually unilateral. This condition, called asteroid hyalitis, is asymptomatic and is said to be seen more frequently in diabetics and in persons with hypercholesterolemia (20).

Retinal changes in the normally aging eye are essentially limited to the vasculature. The arterioles are narrowed, pale, less brilliant, straighter in their course, and branch more acutely than the arterioles of younger individuals.

Varying degrees of venous obstruction may be seen at the arteriovenous junction. The veins, too, may be proportionately narrowed (2). These vascular changes are thought to be the result of an increase in vessel rigidity related to a generalized

fibrosis of the vessel walls (1, 16). Similar changes are seen in the vessels of the choroid that are believed to be particularly predisposed to sclerotic change. If the choriocapillaris at the posterior pole is grossly affected, there may be loss of vision resulting from senile macular disease. Degenerative changes in the outer layers of the retina also may be expressed as cystic degeneration.

The *eyelids* also undergo changes that betray advancing age, exhibiting wrinkling, relative enophthalmos, and perhaps mild ptosis. These occurrences are the result of changes in elastic tissue, loss of orbital fat, and decrease in muscle tone. These conditions can, in turn, give rise to entropion—a turning inward of the lid margin, often with trichiasis (lashes coming in contact with the conjunctiva and cornea), or ectropion—where the lid margin is turned out causing the nasolacrimal duct punctum to fall away from the globe and the palpebral conjunctiva to be exposed, producing tearing and inflammation of the eye. The loss of skin elasticity also gives rise to redundancy of the skin of the eyelids that can become severe enough to be a major cosmetic factor and even interfere with vision (blepharochalasis).

Surgery is indicated almost always with entropion, especially when trichiasis is present. The surgery usually is a minor procedure and is most often curative. Ectropion often does not require surgery if mild, but the procedure to repair the condition is not a complicated one. Treatment of blepharochalasis is limited to surgical repair, and such factors as severity, asymmetric involvement, possible visual compromise, and the possible psychosocial burden this condition might place upon certain individuals because of cosmetic effects and their relation to the patient's personality, all play a role in the surgeon's decision to operate.

Tumors of the eyelid are of special concern particularly when they are judged to be malignant. Ninety percent of eyelid tumors are of the basal cell variety, occurring with increasing frequency with age. These growths spread by direct invasion only and can be treated successfully with either surgical excision or radiation (14). Squamous cell carcinoma is much less common and more difficult to manage with a more serious prognosis. Early recognition and total excision are essential.

Altered or decreased tear secretion is commonly seen in older individuals and can be a major cause of discomfort and severe inflammatory states. This can result in secondary infection and even loss of an eye, if the cornea is not made adequately "wet" by the tear film. This condition is referred to as keratoconjunctivitis sicca, and is more commonly seen in elderly females. Treatment is generally unsatisfactory and usually centers around the instillation—often hourly—of artificial tears, appropriate antibiotics if secondary infection occurs and, reluctantly, partial surgical closure of the eyelids. This condition appears to have taken on added importance during recent years as the level of air pollution has become more of a problem; the patient with inadequate tears seems less able to cope with the ocular irritants present in the environment.

Having thus scanned in a general manner the spectrum of conditions that may affect the aging eye, it now seems in order to explore more deeply those conditions that are most common and yet can be so devastating to the visual perceptibility of the aging population.

CATARACT

A cataract can be most simply defined as any opacification of the lens. It is the most common of all those conditions that cause loss of vision not rectifiable with corrective eyeglasses. It is, therefore, a most fortunate circumstance that whereas it is so common, it is also one of the most easily and successfully remedied. Cataracts occur to some degree in over 95% of those above 65 years of age (7). However, it must be emphasized that the number of people in whom the process of lens opacification becomes advanced enough to cause significant visual disability is, nevertheless, rather small. Neither the etiology nor the mechanism of the formation of a cataract is known. It is probable that the causes of lens opacifications are many and varied, but basically loss of transparency is related to a change in the internal structure of the lens. This change is related to either accumulation of water between the lens fibers or intracellularly producing a diffractive effect, or to a coagulative opacification wherein lens protein becomes insoluble and opaque.

It is well known that the development of cataracts is definitely influenced by hereditary tendencies that appear to be transmitted by a dominant pattern.

Senile cataracts usually are either nuclear with the innermost portion of the lens involved or cortical with the portion of the lens between the nucleus and capsule involved. In nuclear cataracts, there may be deposition of yellow or brown pigment and if it becomes dark brown the term "brunescent cataract" applies. Cortical cataracts are often characterized by wedge-shaped or "spoke-shaped" opacities. The cortical cataract also can involve predominantly that portion of the cortex adjacent to the posterior lens capsule (posterior subcapsular cataract) or that part adjacent to the anterior capsule (anterior subcapsular cataract). When the lens becomes totally opaque (an intumescent cataract), degenerated lens protein may, by osmotic effects, cause the lens to swell. Continued swelling of the lens may push the adjacent iris anteriorly, narrowing the anterior chamber angle, causing angle-closure glaucoma to occur. It also is possible for continued disintegration of lens cortex to occur followed by liquification. Lens material may then escape through an intact capsule provoking a macrophage response in the anterior chamber. The lens material and macrophages may cause an obstruction to aqueous outflow by becoming concentrated in the chamber angle and the structures related to aqueous outflow located therein. When a deep anterior chamber is seen by the examining ophthalomologist, in an eye with an advanced cataract and signs of acute glaucoma, the syndrome of phacolytic glaucoma should be identified and immediate lens extraction performed.

The symptoms related to a cataract are somewhat diverse but, in addition to a decrease in visual acuity, monocular diplopia or even polyopia can be the complaint. Increasing myopia is common and, in the presbyopic or hyperopic individual, can lead to the ability to read without glasses for the first time in years, giving the mistaken impression that vision has actually improved (second sight). Light may be diffracted by the lens opacification, producing halos around lights. This symptom requires that glaucoma be ruled out.

If the lens is so opaque as to prevent direct visualization of the retina and particularly the macula and the optic nerve disc, an attempt must be made to evaluate their ability to function before deciding upon cataract surgery as a choice of treatment. The disappointment related to an individual going through the surgical procedure—which naturally is associated with some degree of general systemic stress to the elderly patient, and subsequently realizing no great visual benefit because of retinal or optic nerve disease—can be great indeed. The pupillary light reflex should be normal. The ability not only to perceive light but also to tell the direction from whence it is directed is helpful in evaluating retinal and optic nerve function in an advanced cataract. Electroretinography, ultrasonography, and glare testing can also be valuable. The decision to operate upon an elderly individual with cataracts must take into consideration a multiplicity of factors. These factors include: the best corrected visual acuity in each eye, the degree of development of the cataract, the occupational requirements of the patient, personality or intellectual considerations, concomitant ocular disease, the life expectancy of the individual, the ability of the patient to withstand the stress of surgery, problems associated with the visual correction of aphakia, the ability of the patient with unilateral cataract to manipulate or merely to tolerate a contact lens, and the physiologic state of the eye as is related to its ability to tolerate the surgery with or without an intraocular lens (IOL) implant.

The visual demands of the average individual are such that when the best corrected vision in the better eye falls below 20/60, significant discomfort is the result. If the patient has a job or vocation requiring better visual levels than 20/60 in both eyes, this situation should be considered carefully. A cataract that is nearing intumescency should be extracted under most circumstances.

The surgery can be performed under either local or general anesthesia, however, the growing popularity of outpatient surgery has further increased the logic for using local anesthesia perhaps combined with some degree of sedation. Advances in surgical techniques and instrumentation during the past 25 years has led to what has become an extremely safe procedure.

The performance of extracapsular methods of cataract surgery, the use of the operating microscope, and the advantage of having a new highly viscid material to aid in the surgery, have added greatly to making the procedure reliably reproduceable with improved results and the ability to have any complications successfully managed (17). The low rate of complication (about 2%) is divided between such possible occurrences as expulsive choroidal hemorrhage and loss of vitreous humor during surgery, intraocular infection after surgery, corneal changes, edema of the macular portion of the retina, retinal detachment, and postoperative glaucoma.

During recent years the intraocular implantation of an artificial lens at the time of cataract removal has become the overwhelmingly most popular method of the visual correction of aphakia. The IOL has developed into a device that avoids most of the optical and practical inadequacies of aphakic spectacles and contact lenses. The increased risk associated with insertion of such an implant is extremely minimal and is far outweighed by the benefits.

The use of the phacoemulsifier in recent years has gained some degree of popularity in removal of cataractous lenses, mainly because the procedure requires a smaller ocular incision and as a result affords a somewhat more rapid rehabilitation (6). Thus far, the complication rate associated with the use of this method of lens extraction, when used by the majority of ophthalmic surgeons, is slightly greater than the rate associated with more universally accepted methods.

GLAUCOMA

Glaucoma is characterized by an elevation of the intraocular pressure. This pressure elevation is determined clinically by measurement of the ocular tension usually and most accurately with the Schiötz tonometer or the Goldmann applanation tonometer.

The elevated intraocular pressure is nearly always related to changes in or around the anterior chamber angle and its structures, which decrease the normal outflow of aqueous humor from the eye. It follows that if the aqueous continues to be produced at a relatively normal rate, an elevation of the intraocular pressure must occur. The structural changes affecting the aqueous outflow may be the result of a number of pathologic conditions. Glaucoma is then comprised of a significant number of diseases depending upon the type of obstructive mechanism involved (11).

The most widely accepted general classification of the various types of glaucoma is that adopted by the International Symposium on Glaucoma in 1954.

I. Primary Glaucoma
   A. Simple (open-angle) glaucoma
   B. Closed-angle glaucoma, which may consist of four phases
      1. Preglaucoma
      2. Intermittent
      3. Acute
      4. Chronic
II. Secondary Glaucoma—due to pre-existing ocular disease; it may be of either the open- or closed-angle type
III. Congenital Glaucoma—due to obstruction resulting from congenital anomalies

In a discussion limited to those conditions primarily affecting the aging eye, there is need to discuss only the two basic types of primary glaucoma, because they are, by far, the most frequently seen in older patients. Of these, simple open-angle glaucoma is much more common. A study by Bankes et al. (3) revealed that in a sample of 5941 persons over the age of 40 years, 0.71% had simple open-angle glaucoma, and 0.17% had closed-angle glaucoma. Other studies reveal a definite increase in frequency of all types of glaucoma as age increases. There is no sex preponderance in simple glaucoma, but closed-angle glaucoma appears to affect women more commonly than men; in some studies the ratio is 2:1. Hereditary factors appear to play an important role in each type.

PRIMARY OPEN-ANGLE GLAUCOMA

The diagnosis of open-angle glaucoma depends not only upon the finding of an intraocular pressure higher than that accepted as normal (22 mm Hg), but also upon the demonstration that the eye in question is not able to withstand the elevated pressure without sustaining damage to its tissues or impairment of function.

This tissue damage or functional impairment can be demonstrated by several methods. In open-angle glaucoma, the anterior chamber angle is seen to be open upon gonioscopic examination that utilizes a contact lens and mirror combination allowing the examiner to see into the angle. The block in aqueous outflow is thought to be in the trabecular meshwork near the canal of Schlemm, but because these structures cannot be adequately seen by gross gonioscopic examination, the chamber angle looks normal.

Because open-angle glaucoma as a general rule develops slowly and insidiously and may have progressed to an advanced stage in one or both eyes before the patient is aware that something is amiss, routine measurement of intraocular pressure at intervals of 2–3 years is recommended for people over age 30 years. A family history, complaint of blurred vision not correctable with lenses, or complaint of a halo effect around lights, should raise the examiner's level of suspicion. Borderline or definitely elevated pressures must be further explored. The optic disc may be abnormally cupped and atrophic. The pressures may vary significantly at different times of day, being highest late at night or early in the morning (diurnal variation). The visual fields may show classical changes such as blind spot abnormalities, small isolated scotomata and step-like defects in the nasal field (13). Tonography can be utilized to measure the ease by which pressure applied to the eye can decrease the intraocular pressure by forcing aqueous humor through the outflow channels. The greater the degree of resistance, the more concerned the ophthalmologist must be as to the likelihood of a positive diagnosis of glaucoma. Similarly, in nearly 80% of glaucomatous eyes, an excessive elevation of the intraocular pressure may be provoked by having the patient drink a large quantity of water (1 liter) within a 5-min period. A rise in intraocular pressure of more than 8 mm Hg over the ensuing 60 min is abnormal. Eyes that have established glaucoma or are predisposed to glaucoma are known to respond to topical steroids with a rise in pressure. Steroids used topically for 1–3 weeks have been utilized by some as a diagnostic technique, but more importantly, it must be emphasized that long-term use of topical steroids in the eye for treatment of other conditions must be accompanied by periodic checks of the intraocular pressure.

Treatment should not be instituted unless visual field defects or anomalies of the optic disc can be demonstrated or, many believe, if the intraocular pressure is greater than 30 mm Hg. Treatment of open-angle glaucoma is essentially medical and surgery should be resorted to only when medical therapy has failed to control the pressure, increased cupping of the optic disc continues, or increasing visual field defects occur. Medical treatment can lower the intraocular pressure by increasing aqueous outflow with miotics (pilocarpine, Phospholine Iodide, eserine, or physostigmine) or by decreasing aqueous formation with carbonic anhydrase inhibitors (Diamox) (10), or with β-blocking agents such as timolol drops. Epinephrine (adrenalin) probably acts by increasing outflow, but may decrease formation as well. Most commonly used surgical techniques are directed at increasing aqueous drainage by creation of new drainage channels. Recently, a new, nonsurgical procedure—laser trabeculoplasty, which utilizes laser burns to the trabecular meshwork—has been found to be quite effective in reducing intraocular pressure, although the duration of effect is still to be determined (9).

PRIMARY CLOSED-ANGLE GLAUCOMA

In its initial stages, angle-closure glaucoma is usually characterized by sudden elevations of the intraocular pressure resulting from intermittent contact of the iris and the inner surface of the trabecular meshwork, obstructing the outflow of aqueous. Between such attacks, the facility of aqueous outflow is normal. Because of the pre-existent narrowness of the angle, blockage of the angle becomes possible. This effect is most likely to occur when the pupil is dilated, by darkness or artificially induced dilation. Examination of an eye with an acutely closed angle usually reveals a semidilated and fixed pupil, an edematous cornea, and decreased vision. The attack may be accompanied by varying degrees of pain, headache, nausea, and vomiting. The intraocular pressure may be markedly elevated and the severity of symptoms seems to be related not only to the pressure levels, but also to the rapidity of onset. If the iris block is not relieved within 48–72 hours, adhesions between the trabeculum and iris root develop, and chronic narrow-angle glaucoma ensues. Narrow-angle glaucoma is associated with an excellent prognosis if peripheral iridectomy is performed before adhesions (synechiae) develop. The management of this type of glaucoma is basically surgical, but medical therapy is definitely necessary preoperatively during the acute stage to lower intraocular pressure and relieve pupillary block so that surgery can be performed under the most ideal conditions. Primary angle-closure glaucoma is a bilateral disease and even if it is manifest in only one eye, it can be expected eventually to develop in the second eye. Therefore, a prophylactic peripheral iridectomy, performed surgically or via the laser, is recommended in the second eye soon after the acutely involved eye has been attended.

Provocative testing is utilized in questionable cases, consisting of artificial mydriasis or placing the patient in a darkened room for 60–90 min and checking the pressure during this period, sometimes with tonography. Many physicians are concerned about the routine use of mydriatics during a routine general physical examination, and the likelihood of inducing an unexpected attack of closed-angle glaucoma. This concern is not believed to be valid. Aside from being an uncommon happening, this procedure could be an excellent method of uncovering a hitherto unknown case under conditions where diagnosis and treatment are readily available, rather than at some future date under possibly much less desirable circumstances.

SENILE MACULAR DEGENERATION

Degeneration of the retina that affects predominantly the macular portion of the retina and that occurs not uncommonly in the aged, is most often a bilateral condition. The degree of involvement of each eye may be considerably asymmetric. The macular area is specifically concerned with central and precise vision and a lesion here usually produces a gradually increasing loss of central vision that may be severe, producing a central scotoma on visual field examination especially when the test is performed with a colored target. Because the retinal involvement remains generally limited to the macular region, peripheral vision remains essentially intact and it is possible for the physician to reassure the patient that vision will never be lost totally (21).

The condition is believed to be the result of sclerosis of the choroidal vessels, particularly the choriocapillaris, leading to a reduction of nutrition to the retinal layers of the macula and fovea that depend upon these vessels for their blood supply, as the retina in this area is avascular. Ophthalmoscopic exam-

ination most often reveals a fine stippling or even somewhat more gross clumping of pigment associated with variable degrees of depigmentation in the macular region. This appearance may be associated with cystic changes that can progress to the formation of a large macular cyst or even a hole in the retina. A macular cyst or hole is a sharply delineated round, reddish defect which ranges in size from one-sixth to one-half the diameter of the optic disc. Holes are often associated with a greater loss of vision than cysts.

Another degenerative condition involving the macular region occurs when an extravasation of blood between Bruch's membrane and the retinal pigment epithelium takes place, resulting from degenerative change in the choriocapillaris (8). A dark, rounded, elevated area is seen in the macular area. The condition, called disciform degeneration (Kuhnt-Junius disease) can appear somewhat similar to a melanoma of the choroid and requires differentiation (30). This differentiation can be aided by the use of techniques such as fluorescein angiography, radioactive phosphorus injected intravenously (19), and ultrasound examination of the ocular and orbital contents (2, 5, 16, 20).

Although no generally effective treatment for the degenerative macular conditions affecting the aging eye exists, the laser can be somewhat helpful in a small number of cases. Magnifiers, strong reading aids, and telescopic lenses may be helpful in allowing the patient to carry on a more normal existence.

RETINAL DETACHMENT

This condition, as it occurs in the elderly population, when trauma, primary retinal or choroidal infection, inflammation, and tumors are excluded as possible causes, is seen more commonly in men and is bilateral in approximately 25% of cases. As compared to the general population, an increased number of individuals who undergo cataract surgery eventually will experience a retinal detachment in that eye. This complication of cataract surgery definitely has become less common since extracapsular cataract extraction has replaced the older intracapsular method. Myopic eyes are also more susceptible to detachment.

The "detachment" is actually a separation of two retinal layers—the rod and cone layer—from the pigment epithelium, which re-establishes a potential space present during the embryonic development of the eye. Tears or holes in the retina related to degenerative retinal changes or to retinal traction from fibrous vitreous bands are literally present in all cases. Symptoms include flashes of light, floaters, distortion of images (metamorphopsia), and loss of vision.

Funduscopic examination remains the basic method of diagnosis of retinal detachment, but this should be augmented by the use of scleral depression to bring the retinal periphery into view and by the use of an indirect ophthalmoscope, which often is believed superior to the direct ophthalmoscope because of its larger field of observation, three-dimensional view, and ability to focus upon the more peripheral portions of the retina.

The treatment of retinal detachment is surgical. The basic objectives center upon the closure of the retinal hole and the approximation of the separated layers after drainage of subretinal fluid. The closure of the hole may be accomplished by diathermy, cryo-surgery, or photocoagulation. Most retinal surgeons utilize an encircling band which causes a scleral buckle that facilitates continued contact of the two retinal layers.

The only successful method of prevention of reti-nal detachment is closure of the retinal holes before the development of a detachment; this is believed to be a worthwhile procedure dependent mostly upon early discovery.

Reattachment of the retina can be accomplished in the great majority of cases, but the earlier the sur-gery is performed, the better the result. If the macu-lar area has been detached, the visual prognosis is poor.

DIABETIC RETINOPATHY

The retinopathy associated with diabetes melli-tus is so characteristic as to be virtually diagnostic of the disease, even in the absence of other clinical signs or symptoms. It is almost always bilateral, usu-ally not appearing until the patient has had diabetes for 10–15 years (12). The severity and degree of con-trol of the diabetic state is not well correlated to the degree of retinopathy. The increased frequency with which this condition is being diagnosed seems to be related to the longer survival of diabetics resulting from more effective treatment, as well as more fre-quent examinations and better recognition of early lesions. As diabetics achieve greater longevity, the retinopathy associated with the disease becomes more and more of a geriatric problem.

The retina is found to contain microaneurysms, irregular small hemorrhages, and multiple glisten-ing yellow-white exudates. New vessel formation (neovascularization) is common. As hemorrhage takes place and new vessels grow out into the vitre-ous, the proliferative phase of diabetic retinopathy occurs.

Treatment is unsatisfactory, but some legitimate benefit appears to be derived from the use of laser photocoagulation (26). This method achieves its benefit by direct destruction or closure of new or leaking blood vessels as well as by actual destruction of peripheral portions of the retina. This ablation of the peripheral retina causes a decrease in retino-pathy in the more"central" untreated areas. The ab-lation results in decreased retinal oxygen demand, thereby decreasing the tendency for abnormal, new vessel formation (23). The success of other methods of treatment has been less than satisfactory. As a re-sult, the use of photocoagulation has become gener-ally preferred, especially in the aging patient, and particularly in view of the relatively benign nature of the coagulation technique.

VASCULAR DISORDERS

Eye signs are a prominent factor in vascular dis-ease of both the extracranial and intracranial blood vessels. Those conditions that are particularly prone to develop in the aged individual have, as an etiologic basis, some relationship to arteriosclerosis.

OCCLUSION OF THE RETINAL ARTERY

Retinal artery occlusion presents a rather charac-teristic clinical picture with sudden total blindness occurring when the central artery is obstructed. An altitudinal field defect usually occurs when the supe-rior or inferior branch is involved. If the cause of the obstruction is embolic as in most cases in the elderly, movement of the embolus into more peripheral por-tions of the retinal vascular tree leads to a progres-sive decrease in the area of visual field loss. Episodes of monocular visual loss lasting several minutes and ending spontaneously are referred to as amaurosis fugax and probably are caused by emboli, although thrombotic occlusion of the retinal artery that is not complete has been implicated by some as a cause. Atheromatous involvement of the carotid artery at or near the bifurcation is most likely to be the source of emboli and, as vascular surgical techniques upon these vessels have improved during recent years, a diagnosis of repeated episodes of amaurosis fugax can lead to the discovery of otherwise unsuspected carotid disease. This knowledge, in turn, with suc-cessful vascular surgery, may be instrumental in the prevention of monocular blindness or cerebral infarction.

Ophthalmoscopic examination after retinal ar-tery occlusion reveals a diffuse, pale retinal cloudi-ness with a contrasting red area in the macula. Occasionally, stasis of blood within the arterioles can be seen to produce slowly moving segments of blood that have been compared in appearance to the "box cars" of a freight train. The pupil does not react directly to light, but the consensual reflex is present. An embolus may be seen that often appears to have a diameter greater than the vessel it obstructs. When the central retinal artery is involved, the blockage may not be visible upon funduscopic examination if it occurs behind the disc.

Treatment of the acute stage of such occlusion is probably best directed toward dilatation of the artery to allow any embolus to move along in the circulation. This effort probably must be performed within minutes of the occlusion. Ocular massage, retrobulbar injection of papaverine, or rebreathing into a paper bag to increase carbon dioxide levels are methods commonly tried. Occasionally, ocular paracentesis to lower intraocular pressure thereby increasing the pressure gradient within the retinal artery is utilized (2). Whatever method is used, the prognosis is quite poor. Only if progressive atheromatous disease is the cause of the vascular occlusion, can anticoagulant therapy be expected to help. Ophthalmodynamometry can assist in the diagnosis of atheromatous carotid occlusion, but usually only after 80 or 90% of the carotid vessel has been occluded. This examination is usually performed by two persons. One exerts an increasing pressure against the sclera and the other watches for the collapse of the retinal artery at the nerve head. Diastole corresponds to that amount of pressure which causes total collapse of the vessel. This examination is most significant when the difference between the pressures found in the two eyes is greater than 15% (22).

Auscultation over the carotids can often be helpful if a bruit is heard, indicating partial occlusion of the vessel.

TEMPORAL ARTERITIS

An additional cause of retinal and ophthalmic artery occlusion, but one that merits separate consideration, is temporal arteritis. This condition occurs almost exclusively in elderly persons and is characterized by headache and preauricular tenderness usually with a palpably enlarged temporal artery that may or may not pulsate. Pain in the jaw area upon chewing is sometimes a complaint, but generalized weakness, anorexia, and weight loss are most commonly noted. Approximately one-third to one-half of patients with temporal arteritis eventually suffer visual loss secondary to ischemic optic neuropathy related to the inflammatory arteritis. (This ischemic optic neuropathy also may be seen as a result of arteriosclerotic involvement of the small ves-

sels supplying the optic nerve.) The visual loss may occur gradually or suddenly. Biopsy of the temporal artery reveals a giant cell granulomatous reaction. The sedimentation rate is usually significantly elevated and provides a method of judging the therapy that is limited to high doses of systemic steroids initially, followed by lesser dosages over the ensuing weeks or even months (4). Steroids are definitely more helpful in preventing visual loss than in reversing an already established loss of vision.

OCCLUSION OF THE RETINAL VEIN

Retinal vein occlusion is encountered with some frequency in the elderly and again is usually related to arteriosclerotic disease with external compression of the vein by a rigid arterial wall most commonly at, or just behind, the lamina cribrosa. Loss of vision ensues, but light perception or even hand movement vision is usually retained, in contrast to the total blindness of central retinal artery occlusions. Ophthalmoscopic examination shows the fundus to be "splashed with blood," with extreme engorgement of the veins and edema of the optic disc. Unilateral absence of pulsation of the retinal vein is an occasionally helpful sign. Long-standing cases develop venous sheathing, new vessel formation and microaneurysms. This picture may be present in the distribution of a single branch vein if that is all that is involved. When the central vein is involved, 5-10% of the cases will develop new vessel formation in the iris (rubeosis iridis) which leads to "hemorrhagic glaucoma" secondary to blockage of aqueous outflow at the chamber angle. This is an extremely difficult form of glaucoma to control and often leads to eventual enucleation of the affected eye so that pain can finally be brought to an end. Anticoagulants only occasionally are helpful in the treatment of retinal vein occlusion and are probably best restricted to fresh or incomplete occlusions. Low molecular weight dextran administered intravenously has been tried with some claims of success.

OCCLUSIVE CEREBROVASCULAR DISEASE

Occlusion of the carotid, anterior, middle and posterior cerebral, and basilar arteries may all present with signs and symptoms too diverse to be described in great detail here. Yet it should be mentioned that abnormalities of vision, ocular motility, visual fields, pupillary abnormalities, nonphysiologic nystagmus, loss of binocular coordinative ability, and certain funduscopic abnormalities may be the clues leading to the diagnosis of such conditions. The use of vascular surgery as well as anticoagulant therapy and the use of aspirin to inhibit platelet aggregation are all helpful in treating occlusive cerebrovascular disease.

It might be well to remember that an evaluation of the status of the eyes may supply a rather surprising amount of information not only pertaining to the eye itself, but also to the individual's general health. Because the optic nerve and retina are actually extensions of the brain, and the retinal and choroidal vessels are important parts of the peripheral circulation often representative of the intracranial, renal, and other vessels, an examination of the optic fundus that permits a study of its blood vessels unobscured by skin, muscle, or bone, probably affords more information than any other single procedure in the entire medical field. The presence of diabetic retinopathic change, classic hypertensive findings, papilledema, and vessel changes consistent with vasculitis are but a few of the fundus changes that can greatly influence the diagnostic impression of the physician.

REFERENCES

1. Ballantyne AJ: The evolution of retinal disease. *Trans Ophthalmol Soc UK* 57:301, 1937.
2. Ballantyne AJ, Michaelson ID: *Textbook of the Fundus of the Eye*. Baltimore, Williams & Wilkins, 1970.
3. Bankes JLK, Perkins ES, Tsolakis S, Wright JE: Bedford glaucoma survey. *Br Med J* 1:791, 1968.
4. Cogen DG: *Neurology of the Visual System*. Springfield, IL, Charles C Thomas, 1970.
5. Coleman DJ: Reliability of ocular tumor diagnosis with ultrasound. *Trans Am Acad Ophthalmol Otolaryngol* 77:677, 1973.
6. Cotlier E, Rose M: Cataract extraction by the intracapsular methods and by phacoemulsification. *Trans Am Acad Ophthalmol Otolaryngol* 81:163, 1976.
7. Duke-Elder S: *A System of Ophthalmology*. Vol 11. St. Louis, CV Mosby, 1969, p. 4.
8. Gass JD: Drusen and disciform macular detachment and degeneration. *Trans Am Ophthalmol Soc* 70:409, 1972.
9. Grinich NP, Van Buskirk EM, Samples JR: Three year efficacy of argon laser trabeculoplasty. *J Am Acad Ophthalmol* 94:858, 1987.
10. Havener, WH: *Ocular Pharmacology*. St. Louis, CV Mosby, 1978.
11. Hogan MJ, Zimmerman LE: *Ophthalmic Pathology*. Philadelphia, WB Saunders, 1962, p. 688.
12. Jerneld B, Algnere P: Relationship of duration and onset of diabetes to prevalence of diabetic retinopathy. *Am J Ophthalmol* 101:431, 1986.
13. Kolker AE, Hetherington J: *Becker and Shaffer's Diagnosis and Therapy of the Glaucomas*. St. Louis, CV Mosby, 1976.
14. Kwitko ML, Weinstock FJ: *Geriatric Ophthalmology*. Orlando, Grune & Stratton, 1985.
15. Langsworthy OR, Ortega L: The iris. *Medicine* 22:287, 1943.
16. Leishman R: The eye in general vascular disease. *Br J Ophthalmol* 41:641, 1957.
17. Maumenee AE: Foreword. In: *Cataract Surgery and its Complications*. Jaffe NS (Ed): St. Louis, CV Mosby, 1981.
18. McMenamin PG, Lee WR, Aitken DA: Age-related changes in the human outflow apparatus. *J Am Acad Ophthalmol* 93:194, 1987.
19. Packer S, Lange R: Radioactive phosphorus for detection of ocular melanomas. *Arch Ophthalmol* 90:17, 1973.
20. Rodman HI, Johnson FB, Zimmerman LE: New histopathological and histochemical observations concerning asteroid hyalitis. *Arch Ophthalmol* 66:552, 1961.
21. Scheie HG, Albert DM: *Adler's Textbook of Ophthalmology*. Philadelphia, WB Saunders, 1962, p. 274.
22. Spalter H: Ophthalmodynamometry and carotid artery thrombosis. *Am J Opthalmol* 47:453, 1959.
23. Stefansson E, Hatchell DL, Fisher BL, Sutherland FS, Machemer R: Panretinal photocoagulation and retinal oxygenation in normal and diabetic cats. *Am J Ophthalmol* 101:657, 1986.
24. Weale RA: Retinal illumination and age. *Trans Illum Eng Soc* 26:95, 1961.
25. Weale RA: *The Aging Eye*. New York, Harper & Row, 1963, p. 30.
26. Wetzig PC, Worlton JT: Treatment of diabetic retinopathy by light coagulation. *Br J Ophthalmol* 47:539, 1963.
27. Wilensky JT: *Intraocular Lenses—Transactions of the University of Illinois Symposium on Intraocular Lenses*. New York, Appleton-Century-Crofts, 1977.
28. Wolter JR: Neuropathology of the trabeculum and open-angle glaucoma. *Arch Ophthalmol* 62:99, 1959.
29. Wright IS: Keeping an eye on the rest of the body. *J Am Acad Ophthalmol* 94:1196, 1987.
30. Zimmerman LE: Problems in diagnosis of malignant melanomas of the choroid and ciliary body. *Am J Ophthalmol* 75:917, 1973.

CHAPTER 37

Geriatric Ear, Nose, and Throat Problems

MILTON G. YODER

Many times otorhinolaryngologic disorders, ranging from impacted cerumen and postnasal drip to malignancies and epistaxis, are often neglected by older people. They deny their existence; and sometimes these symptoms are dismissed by older people because they assume that discomfort, loss of function, and changes in structure are obvious consequences of aging. Sometimes these problems are totally ignored for reasons associated with the stigma surrounding old age; fears of complaining too much, of beginning to fail, or of becoming senile. The same ear, nose, and throat problems that can affect the young patient also can affect the elderly patient. However, the emotional, mental, and physical needs of an elderly patient may be quite different from those of a younger person. Accordingly, the prescribed course of treatment should be developed with an understanding of the special needs for this age group (7, 20).

The sequellae of otorhinolaryngologic diseases are especially serious because they disrupt an important human function—verbal communication. The inability to hear others and/or to speak to others may be the most devastating handicap of old age. This handicap isolates a person who otherwise would have the physical and mental capacity to lead a happy and useful life. A communicatively handicapped person will withdraw from both the environment and social stimulation increasing his debilitation, depression, and lack of motivation for living (4).

EAR

Hearing impairment is classified as conductive, sensorineural, or mixed. Conductive hearing loss may be caused by anything that precludes the normal transmission of sound through the external auditory canal, tympanic membrane, or middle ear ossicles. Various conditions frequently result in conductive hearing loss including impacted cerumen, tympanic membrane perforation, otitis media, and discontinuity or fixation of the middle ear ossicles. Sensorineural hearing loss occurs when the inner ear, auditory nerve (cranial nerve eight), brain stem, or cortical auditory pathways are not functioning properly. Mixed hearing loss is a combination of a conductive hearing loss superimposed on a sensorineural hearing loss (8).

EXTERNAL AUDITORY CANAL

The aging process affects all portions of the otologic mechanism (external auditory canal, middle ear ossicles, cochlear apparatus, and vestibular system). The external auditory canal is affected by virtue of a decrease in both the number and the activity of ceruminal glands. These glands are located only in the outer one-half of the external auditory canal. Cerumen is never present in the inner half or osseous portion of the external auditory canal unless it is pushed there or accumulates as a result of pressure from the use of headphones or telephones. The cerumen can be intimately adherent to the skin of the external canal in elderly patients. The hearing loss from impacted cerumen is insidious and can result in difficulty with communication. Careful, slow, time-consuming efforts are necessary to separate the cerumen from the intact skin without causing otalgia (pain) or bloody otorrhea. These efforts include curettage, suctioning, and irrigation with room temperature water. Irrigation should not be performed if the tympanic membrane has not been examined before or if there is a history of perforation of the tympanic membrane (1).

The skin of the external auditory canal may become atrophic and dry as a result of atrophy of the epithelium and the sebaceous glands. In elderly individuals, itching of the skin can be attributed to the dryness, but pruritis sometimes is a major complaint even when no apparent clinically significant abnormality is discovered by the examining physician. This itching is a frequent but unwelcome symptom associated with senile skin. This problem can be exacerbated by vigorous efforts to remove accumulated dry cerumen with cotton-tipped applicators and other foreign instruments. This self-induced trauma further increases the problem. Bathing with hot water, especially in the winter when the air is dry, removes moisture from the skin. Drying the external canal with rubbing alcohol or alcohol-acetic acid mixture may help prevent otitis externa; however, it removes fat and increases the dryness leading to further irritation and itching of the external auditory canal. Efforts must be directed toward breaking the cycle by avoiding moisture, trauma, and defatting agents in the external auditory canal. Emollients, such as glycerine, act as an epidermal seal to slow the process of loss of moisture from the skin.

There is not an increased incidence of infections in the external auditory canal. However, there does seem to be an increased amount of otalgia and tenderness in the ear canal when there is a disease process. One aggressive external ear disease is malignant otitis externa, which is a *Pseudomonas* osteitis and osteomyelitis of the temporal bone. This life-threatening disease process is usually seen in elderly diabetic patients.

Mild dermatoses, furunculosis, and occasional infected sebaceous cysts sometimes involve the outer one-half of the external auditory canal. These infections should be treated early with topical medication in a cream vehicle. These may contain an antibiotic or steroid compound, depending upon the disease process. If necessary, adjunctive oral antibiotics may be needed (10).

Benign bony growths that narrow the external auditory canal can also predispose patients to impacted cerumen. These bony growths consist of either benign osteophytes, which may narrow the canal medially, or benign lateral osteomas. Although malignant changes occur infrequently in the external auditory canal, persistent bloody otorrhea or an increased amount of granulation-appearing tissue should arouse suspicion of a neoplastic process. It is imperative to obtain a biopsy early in order to establish the correct diagnosis. The vast majority of carcinomas of the external auditory canal are squamous cell carcinomas. Basal cell carcinomas and ceruminomas (including adenomas, pleomorphic adenomas, adenoid cystic carcinoma, and adenocarcinoma) occur. These processes should be considered in all patients who complain of chronic otalgia with or without otorrhea, hearing loss, vertigo, or facial nerve paralysis (24).

MIDDLE EAR

In 1974, Etholm and Belal (9) reported that arthritic changes of the ossicular articulations within the middle ear do occur. There is a hyalinization of the joint capsules, calcification of the articular cartilage, and calcification of the joint capsule itself. These changes are strictly age related with no sexual predilection. Surprisingly, there is almost no associated conductive hearing loss with these changes.

Atrophic or sclerotic changes of the tympanic membrane are common in the aged, but these changes do not usually cause appreciable losses of hearing. If there is marked retraction of the tympanic membrane or malfunction of the ossicular chain, there is accompanying moderate to severe conductive hearing loss. If there is a serous middle ear effusion, eustachian tube inflation with proper medication usually effectively treats this. Occasionally myringotomy with aspiration of the fluid and possible placement of a tympanostomy tube is required to restore eustachian tube function.

Perforations of the tympanic membrane can occur in various locations and are of various sizes. These may be due to direct injury from a foreign object, such as cotton-tipped applicators, pencils, or pens. These perforations also may be sustained from a blow to the ear from a fall or else a hand slap to the side of the head. The pressure changes in the middle or external ear result as a barotraumatic change. Bleeding, vertigo, and secondary infection may accompany these. Otologic examination and audiologic evaluation are necessary in these perforated tympanic membranes. When there is a small perforation in the tympanic membrane without middle ear complications, simple patching with tissue paper, temporalis fascia, or sclera (banked) may be effective in closing the perforation to restore the hearing. The larger tympanic membrane perforation may require tympanoplasty or a myringoplasty depending upon the status of the middle ear ossicles.

Otosclerosis is a bony disease causing conductive hearing loss as a result of fixation of the footplate of the stapes. Otosclerosis also may affect other parts of the labyrinth and otic capsule causing a sensorineural hearing loss. It affects approximately 10% of the population and is usually bilateral. Otosclerosis most commonly starts in early adult life; however, it may not be recognized until secondary presbycusis sets in. The aging sensorineural hearing loss added to a previously unrecognized borderline conductive hearing loss then becomes evident. The diagnosis of otosclerosis is made by the patient's medical history, otologic examination, and audiologic evaluation. There are three possible approaches to treatment. The patient may choose surgical correction, a hearing aid, or a combination of these two. The latter may be the most desirable with severe hearing loss as the surgery may improve it to the point that a hearing aid can be used to a greater advantage. In older medical literature, arguments have been made against ear surgery for the elderly patient. However, there is no age limitation as long as the general condition of the patient is good. As with younger patients, each candidate for surgery must be evaluated on an individual basis. Klotz (16) reported postoperative results of stapedectomies in elderly patients after 2½ years of observation. He found that elderly patients did just as well as younger patients. Goodhill (11) reported excellent results from stapedectomy averaging a 34.6-decibel gain for patients over 70 years of age with profound mixed type hearing loss.

In older patients with larger perforations, cotton should be worn in the ear canal during exposure to cold temperatures or cold wind to avoid vertigo. Middle ear and mastoid tumors do occur in the aged population. These malignancies must be considered when there is a chronic draining ear and an abundance of granulation tissue. However, the most common tumor in the middle ear and mastoid area has to be cholesteatoma. After thorough audiologic, otologic, and radiologic evaluation and medical therapy failure, chronic otorrhea may require mastoid and/or tympanic membrane surgery (3).

INNER EAR

Presbycusis

In the United States, hearing loss constitutes one of the most common physical disabilities. Twenty-five percent of people between 65 and 74 years of age and 50% of people 75 years of age or older experience hearing difficulties. For older adults, the major auditory dysfunction is the result of presbycusis. By taking a complete history of the patient and by having a thorough audiologic, otologic, and, if necessary, radiologic evaluation, presbycusis is a diagnosis made by exclusion. Variables associated with presbycusis include metabolism, arteriosclerosis, smoking, noise exposure, genetic factors, diet, and stress.

According to Crowe et al. (6), and Schuknecht (22), there are four categories of presbycusis: (a) sensory, (b) metabolic or strial, (c) neural, and (d) mechanical or cochlear conductive.

As a result of the imbalance in hearing for low and high frequencies, speech may be heard in a distorted or even unintelligible manner. The presbycusis patient usually will know when he is being spoken to, but the patient may not always understand what is said. The words are distorted by the patient's imperfect auditory system. When the distortion problem is compounded by a difficult listening situation, such as several people talking at once, the patient with presbycusis will have an especially difficult time. More reliance on visual cues, such as reading lips, is important. The presbycusis patient who has difficulty with vision has an even worse problem.

There is no known prevention for presbycusis. However, the amount of hearing loss in the geriatric patient is usually the end result of a combination of multiple factors. The most serious complicating factor for most male patients is that they have spent a lifetime in a noisy working environment. The effects of prolonged exposure to high intensity noise is similar to the effects of presbycusis in that the hearing for higher frequencies are usually affected first. There is no effective, after-the-fact treatment for noise-induced hearing loss. It can be prevented by avoiding excessively noisy environments and by wearing ear protective devices when exposed to high noise levels above 80 decibels.

Treatment of presbycusis with vasodilators, vitamins, diuretics, steroids, hormones, etc. has been attempted with little evidence of success. Because the possibility of improving presbycusis by medical therapy is limited, other approaches are often needed to assist the geriatric patient. The primary source of help is auditory rehabilitation. This includes the use of hearing aids, auditory training, assistive listening devices, and training in lipreading. The task of the otorhinolaryngologist and audiologist is to thoroughly examine the patient, evaluate the patient's auditory function, assess the patient's ability to benefit from amplification, and counsel the patient and his family.

Although a relatively large number of geriatric patients wear hearing aids, there are many elderly individuals who deny a hearing loss, refuse to get their hearing evaluated, and refuse to consider wearing a hearing aid. The decision to evaluate the hearing and to consider wearing a hearing aid must be made by the patient, but awareness and encouragement by family and friends should be made if there is a possibility of a hearing loss and/or lost communicative skills. If a hearing aid can help the elderly individual, the family and close friends should be counseled about the hearing aid itself, assistive listening devices, training in lipreading, and auditory training.

The hearing aid is a small, personalized, loudspeaker system consisting of a battery-operated microphone, amplifier, and speaker. The net effect of passing a sound through a hearing aid is to make the sound louder through amplification. The hearing aid cannot correct discrimination or differentiation of words as the hearing aid can only make sounds louder. Therefore, the hearing aid is most useful in face-to-face conversation as lipreading can aid in discriminating or differentiating the word. When the distance from the source of the desired sound increases, ambient noise and reverberant sound interfere more with what the individual wants to hear.

Many elderly patients purchase and wear a hearing aid for a period of time, then they have complaints concerning the hearing aids and even may stop using them. The most common complaints of hearing aid users are squealing of the aid, excessive background noise, uncomfortable loudness at certain pitches, and less effectiveness in group conversations. Adjustments to the earmold or hearing aid usually can correct these complaints.

The elderly hearing-impaired individual whose vision is also impaired is doubly handicapped because of decreased ability to lip-read. As blind individuals are more dependent on their sense of hearing, hearing-impaired individuals are more dependent on their sense of sight. Light-flashing door bells, telephones, and fire alarm systems are used by many hearing-impaired individuals.

Home assistive listening devices include special telephone devices and television and radio earpiece receivers. It is important for the hearing-impaired individual to be aware of the assistive listening devices that are available in the community. These include the infrared and loop systems that may be found in places of worship, movie theaters, or other places of public entertainment.

The patient may find that he may gain 15 decibels in hearing by the use of ear cupping, placing his hand directly behind the auricle and deflecting the sound. The patient may find that he prefers the hearing aid in the ear canal itself, or behind the ear, whatever his individual situation is. If for cosmetic reasons the patient does not want a hearing aid that can be seen, then an implantable hearing aid would be a solution to this problem. Implantable hearing aids give better sound, appear more natural and cosmetic, and require an operative procedure to implant the hearing aid within the mastoid bone.

Rules and regulations regarding the evaluation and issuance of hearing aids vary from state to state as they have resulted from certain problems and policies in those states. Most areas now require a complete audiogram by an audiologist or certified hearing aid dealer, medical evaluation by an otolaryngologist, and the opportunity for the individual to try the hearing aid before purchasing it.

Although there are many auditory function tests, the audiogram is the basic test to evaluate hearing loss. Pure-tone levels at individual frequencies can be tested as well as discrimination of words. In general, there are three types of hearing loss: neurosensory, conductive, and mixed (combination of neurosensory and conductive). Figure 37.1 shows these three types of hearing loss.

Hearing impairment presents in many different ways. The patient may be aware of a sudden, gradual, or questionable hearing loss. Sometimes the individual is not aware of a hearing loss, and he actually denies the existence of such a problem, while his family and friends are aware of the problem. When oral communication decreases between two individuals, there is a possibility of hearing loss and an audiogram should be considered. Because of the increased incidence of hearing loss in the elderly, screening of elderly people has been encouraged.

Tinnitus

Tinnitus is a major problem for the geriatric patient. Tinnitus is a buzzing, ringing, hissing, or similar type of sound that usually is related to hearing loss in the higher frequencies. This may be the result of presbycusis or prolonged noise exposure. Aspirin and other medications may cause hearing loss and tinnitus. Tinnitus is a bothersome and troubling

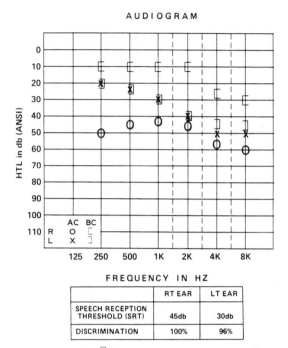

Left ear (X, ⌐) demonstrates neurosensory loss.
Right ear (O, ⌐) demonstrates conductive loss
with a mixed loss at 4K and 8K.

Figure 37.1. Audiogram of elderly individual demonstrating both neurosensory and conductive hearing losses.

symptom that may or may not be of ear origin. Sometimes there can be objective cause, and sometimes the cause cannot be found. Subjective tinnitus occurs when the patient is aware of the ringing, buzzing, humming, whistling, roaring, or clicking sound; however, the examiner cannot hear it. The objective tinnitus is a bruit that can be heard by the examining physician. There are two types; one is the ear tinnitus (tinnitus aurium) and head tinnitus (tinnitus cranii). Cochlear and retrocochlear lesions can produce unilateral tinnitus. Ménière's disease is frequently accompanied by an ipsilateral tinnitus on the side with the hearing loss and vertigo. Acoustic neuroma and cerebellar pontine angle tumors also are characterized by an ipsilateral tinnitus. Unilateral tinnitus is a bothersome symptom that requires a thorough diagnostic evaluation.

There is no specific treatment for tinnitus aurium. Tinnitus is difficult to treat, and the patient needs to understand that it may persist forever. Treatment of tinnitus may include therapy for the underlying condition, such as a psychosomatic problem. Elimination of aspirin or similar medica-

tion may reduce the tinnitus. There is hope to convert the decompensated tinnitus into a compensated state. Acoustic sedation is helpful as patients usually are most bothered at quiet times, such as when they are trying to fall asleep at night. The use of a bedside radio or tape recorder is frequently helpful in providing an artificial source of ambient noise to mask out this objective tinnitus. Some people have required the use of tinnitus maskers that give them a sound constantly throughout the day. As there is no specific medical therapy for ear tinnitus, there is no effective surgery for tinnitus per se at this time. If the tinnitus becomes a major factor and is a unilateral process, then only as a last resort would a unilateral obliterative operation be considered.

Sudden Hearing Loss

Sudden hearing loss is a topic unto its own. Vascular changes can occur involving branches of the internal auditory artery. This type of loss is due to constriction or occlusion of the blood vessels or hemorrhage within the organ of Corti. Multiple medical regimens have been tried; however, there is not one form of therapy that has been proven to be most effective.

VESTIBULAR SYSTEM

Vestibular complaints have been recorded in over 50% of elderly patients living alone. Vertigo is a specific term used to describe the symptoms of the vestibular system including the peripheral labyrinthine, retrolabyrinthine, and central nervous system vestibular components. Dizziness is a vague term that may include giddiness, imbalance, faintness, wooziness, and passing out. Dizziness may be used to describe cortical or visual disorientation, altered states of consciousness, and limb incoordinations. Balance depends on the input and proper functioning from the vestibular, visual, and propioceptive pathways. Impaired function in any one of these three components may yield symptoms of dizziness (11). In the vestibular system, the disease process is usually in the sensory epithelium, the primary afferent fibers, and the vestibular apparatus. Histopathology of the aged vestibule reveals a decrease of up to 40% in myelinated nerve fibers (with myelinated fibers of the cristae being affected most often). The otoconia of the saccule degenerate progressively from the posterior to the anterior end, and the saccular membranes have been shown to rupture more frequently in the elderly. Tissue between the endolymphatic duct and the bony vestibular aqueduct becomes fibrotic (15). Finally, postural vertigo (cupulolithiasis) is associated with dense deposits of insoluble particles in the pars superior at the ampule of the posterior semicircular canal (2). In addition to the general decrease of vestibular sensitivity, Schuknecht (23) has described four age-related conditions of dysequilibrium: (a) cupulolithiasis, (b) ampullary dysequilibrium, (c) macular dysequilibrium, and (d) vestibular ataxia.

NYSTAGMUS

Nystagmus is an objective finding that accompanies vertigo. It is characterized by a slow movement to one side with a corrective fast return movement to the other side. By convention, nystagmus is identified by the direction of the quick component. Thus, a nystagmus to the left means a nystagmus that has a slow movement to the right and a quick corrective component to the left.

The direction of the nystagmus may be horizontal, vertical, diagonal, or rotary. Manifest nystagmus can be observed with the naked eye under ordinary conditions. Occult nystagmus can be observed by using a +20 Fresnel lens to abolish fixation or by electronystagmography. Electronystagmography is a diagnostic test that allows us to differentiate central nervous disorders from peripheral disorders within the labyrinth.

Vertical nystagmus can be produced either by peripheral labyrinth or by central nervous system disorders. Peripheral vertical nystagmus can originate from the semicircular canals, utricle, and saccule of the labyrinth. The symptoms of vertigo may be accompanied by nausea, vomiting, and generalized malaise. Common causes of peripheral vertigo include labyrinthitis, Ménière's disease, and labyrinthine fistula. Central vertical nystagmus may be caused by tumor in the temporal lobe (transverse gyrus of Heschl), by cerebral arteriosclerosis, and by lesions of the midbrain, pons, cerebellum, and brain stem. Lesions of the posterior inferior cerebellar artery will involve vestibular nuclei and their connections to the medial longitudinal fasciculus. Peripheral and central pathways can interact also.

NOSE

In aging, the nose loses its internal moisture and capability as there is decreased mucous production. The mucous is of a thicker quality, and the patient may complain of a thickness in the nose. Aging also brings on an absorption of the adipose tissue and atrophy of muscle within the nose itself. The most significant nasal finding in the aged patient is the increased fragility and sclerosis of blood vessels, contributing to epistaxis.

Cartilaginous changes show that the elderly person's nasal dorsum is convex with a retracted columella and a downward rotation of the lobule. These nasal changes are accentuated by loss of muscle mass of the orbiculus oris, absorption of facial adipose tissue, loss of teeth, and absorption of the maxilla and the mandible causing a loss in the vertical dimension of the lower one-third of the face. The patient's nasal airway is decreased as the tip droops and the columella becomes retracted. There can be some fragmentation between the upper lateral cartilage and the lower lateral cartilage causing collapse in the nasal valve area. Sometimes septoplasty and a tip rhinoplasty are done for elevation of the nasal tip to improve the airway. A resection of 2–4 mm of the lower lateral cartilage rotates the tip upward to improve the nasal airway.

In the elderly, the most distressing nasal condition is epistaxis. A nosebleed can be severe enough to threaten the life of the patient; furthermore, epistaxis can be challenging to treat as elderly patients have a higher percentage of posterior nasal bleeding than other patients. Typically, posterior epistaxis occurs in the middle of the night causing the patient to wake up gagging on a mouthful of blood, which requires emergent treatment. Epistaxis can be caused by multiple factors; but certainly, the aging process with increased fragility and sclerosis of the blood vessels is the most important factor. Hypertension and sicca (dryness) condition that is accentuated by the loss of internal moisture contribute to the cause of epistaxis among the elderly. Other causes of epistaxis in the elderly are trauma, septal perforation, blood dyscrasias, use of medications (aspirin, Coumadin, etc.), benign tumors of the nose and sinuses, malignant tumors of the nose and sinus, atrophic rhinitis, Wegener's granulomatosis, and mucormycosis.

Atrophic rhinitis is a progressive chronic disease in which the nasal fossae are greatly enlarged as a result of atrophic changes in the mucosa and underlying bone. Thick, smelly, adherent crusts are formed in the nasal passages. Atrophic rhinitis is also known as ozena, derived from the Greek word meaning "stench." The infecting organisms of mucormycosis are species of *Absidia, Mucor, or Rhizopus*. It is associated with facial cellulitis, acute rhinosinusitis and gangrenous mucosal changes. It occurs in diabetic patients or in patients who have received immunosuppressive therapy for lymphomas, leukemias, or connective tissue disorders. Intranasal examination is diagnostic with the finding of a black inferior turbinate resulting from necrosis of the inferior turbinate. The disease process can progress rapidly and may cause death by extension into the intracranial area.

Acne rosacea is a pustular dermatologic condition that may affect the nose. If it becomes advanced, it develops into a rhinophyma, which is hypertrophy of the underlying sebaceous glands in the affected area giving rise to a very bulbous nasal tip. Acne rosacea can be controlled by the application of mild steroid cream to the affected areas. If the lesion advances to rhinophyma, then surgical removal should be done by dermabrasion or carbon dioxide laser resection.

Postnasal drip is one of the more frequent symptoms in the elderly patient. Postnasal drip usually is accompanied by a sinusitis and, of course, has to do with a thickening of the mucous. A key to this diagnosis is to elicit a history of the color and type of drainage, to do a thorough nasopharyngeal and nasal exam, to document with sinus x-rays, and to consider nasal and/or sinus endoscopy. Furthermore, the postnasal drip may cause a chronic cough, clearing of the throat, a catch-in-the-throat, and/or hoarseness.

Taste and smell are related chemical senses. It is possible to have malfunction of one or both of them. However, more complaints center around the loss of olfaction. An acute loss of sense of smell (anosmia) can be related to an upper respiratory infection. Because of the short-term effect, the patient is rarely seen for this condition. Chronic anosmia occurs after blockage of the air currents through the nose. This may be due to nasal polyps, benign tumors, malignant tumors, influenza-like viral infections, surgery, radiation, and high doses of aspirin or similar drugs can also cause this effect. Closed head trauma and diseases such as cancer, hyperthyroidism, hepatitis, and liver disease can also alter the sense of smell and taste (21).

ORAL CAVITY

Aging significantly alters the dentition, oral cavity mucosa, and salivary glands. The mucosa has thinner epithelium (especially tunica propria), blunted rete pegs, decreased collagen, fewer functioning capillaries, and decreased water content. Arteriosclerosis delays and reduces healing plus the tissue is more prone to injury. Salivary gland production is diminished 25% by loss of secretory parenchymal volume, acinar hyalinization, and salivary ductal adhesions. As a re-

sult, there is an increase in dental caries, mucosal atrophy, and mucosal burning with a decreased taste bud sensitivity.

Glossodynia (burning pain in the tongue) may be caused by anemia (folic acid, iron, or B_{12} deficiency), candidiasis, denture irritation, lichen planus, xerostomia, neuropathy of diabetes mellitus, postviral neuropathy, or carcinoma. Sometimes it incorporates the entire mouth to cause a burning mouth syndrome. Usually the patient does not demonstrate any lesion. If no cause can be found and psychosomatic conversion can be eliminated, then the patient may require a lemon and glycerine mouthwash and possibly a tranquilizer.

Geographic tongue is also known as migratory glossitis. This can be secondary to a minor viral infection; however, it usually is of no consequence. Some people in their normal state have geographic tongue.

Fordyce granules, which are the fourth most common oral lesion in the elderly, are ectopic sebaceous glands that are benign, raised yellow to white areas on the buccal or lip mucosa. No treatment is required.

Angular cheilitis is most evident at the oral commissures that are fissured, macerated, erythematous, and tender. Loss of connective tissue support causing redundant skin folds allows pooling of saliva and resulting candidiasis. Nystatin cream to the oral commissure usually corrects angular cheilitis; however, correction of ill-fitting dentures and management of iron or vitamin B deficiency may be required.

Candidiasis appears to be more common in the elderly than in other age groups. It occurs after prolonged and/or intensive antibiotic therapy and also in debilitated individuals. A typical clinical picture consists of white patches on the throat and hypopharynx with mild inflammatory reaction to the underlying tissue. Mycostatin mouthwash suspension is usually effective. For advanced cases, the patient may need systemic treatment with intravenous Amphotericin B.

Lichen planus is a benign chronic disease usually caused by emotional or physical stress. Nonerosive lichen planus has a roughened, asymptomatic, hyperkeratotic leukoplakia on the mucosa while the painful erosive type has vessicles and bullae. There is no definite correlation between lichen planus and oral cavity carcinoma.

Temporomandibular joint syndrome (TMJ) or Costen's syndrome is defined as a dysfunction of the temporomandibular joint with severe pain in the joint itself, the ear, or adjacent structures. Causes can be dental malocclusion, acute trauma to the mandible, clenching of the teeth with muscular contraction, arthritis, or tumors in the area. Temporomandibular joint syndrome can cause vertigo, a ringing type tinnitus, or a clicking or popping sensation when the jaw is opened. Nonsurgical treatment includes use of topical heat, soft diet, physical therapy, analgesics, steroids, dental splints, bite blocks, biofeedback, and psychotherapy. In the event that these are unsatisfactory, then exploratory surgery of the temporomandibular joint should be considered.

SPEECH ALTERATIONS

Hoarseness, difficulty swallowing, and painful swallowing increase with the patient's age. If any of these symptoms persist, they require the patient to have an indirect laryngoscopy mirror examination. If a thorough mirror examination cannot be done, then fiberoptic laryngoscopy can be carried out. Sometimes a barium swallow is also needed for aid in diagnosis. Causes range from benign vocal cord nodules and diverticulum to aggressive malignant tumors.

Vocal strain occurs more frequently in the geriatric patient. The aging process affects the voice pitch, quality, volume, and the rate of speech at varying degrees in different individuals. The voice intermittently changes with description being a tired, failing, and faltering type of voice. A wavering tone and decreased volume result in a lessened ability to communicate. Articulation also may be significantly distorted by missing teeth, dentures, or stroke. Chronic vocal strain can result from voice misuse.

The elderly voice has a change in pitch after age 50 years. According to data obtained by Honjo and Isshiki (13), men have a vocal fold atrophy causing an increase in fundamental frequency, whereas women have a vocal fold edema causing decreased fundamental frequency. The muscles of the larynx, especially the thyroarytenoid muscle, become atrophic. The voice becomes drier as the false vocal cords have a reduction in mucous glandular production and may actually show some squamous metaplasia. The cricoarytenoid joint and the cricothyroid joint may develop a relaxation of the joint capsule or partially become fixed.

As a result of some of the preceding changes, the patient may develop a spastic dysphonia type of voice. The patient develops a tight and squeezed voice sound with extreme tension and a strained, creaking, choking type of vocal attack. The patient complains of reduction in clarity and volume with no pathologic findings evident on indirect or direct laryngoscopy. Speech therapy is most helpful. For true documented spastic dysphonia, recurrent laryngeal nerve sectioning should be considered only after intensive speech therapy has been considered a failure.

Laryngeal dysfunction secondary to vocal cord paralysis entails special problems. Unilateral vocal cord paralysis can be due to many different etiologic factors ranging from laryngeal carcinoma to left chest disease to central nervous system disorders. Of patients developing unilateral vocal cord paralysis 30% never have the etiology determined. After allowing a period of about 6 months for spontaneous resolution of the paralysis, it may be desirable to eliminate aspiration of liquids and foods and to attempt to improve the voice and the effectiveness of the cough reflex by injecting Teflon (polytetrafluoroethylene) placed lateral to the paralyzed cord.

Bilateral abductive vocal cord paralysis does not affect the voice quality as much. However, it affects the inspiratory function of the larynx requiring corrective surgery. The patient would benefit from a lateralizing procedure of the vocal cord, such as arytenoidectomy, or perhaps a valved trachesostomy tube.

Dysphonia secondary to gastroesophageal reflux is usually found in obese patients who have a chronic sore throat and a globus sensation with possible pain over the thyrohyoid membrane. Physical examination reveals erythema of the arytenoid mucosa. If the problem is advanced enough, contact granuloma or hyperkeratosis of the true vocal cords can be seen. Treatment includes the use of antacids and elevation of the head of the bed.

Senile bowing of the vocal cords is secondary to muscle atrophy and loss of connective tissue. Dryness of the laryngeal mucosa (laryngitis sicca) results from atrophy of the mucous glands. Voice tremor can be associated with other tremors in the head and neck area and may be a solitary finding. The voice will quiver with sudden abrupt changes, similar to those found in spastic dysphonia.

Dysarthria also may cause inarticulation or problems in communication. Dysarthria may be found in patients suffering from cerebral vascular accidents, trauma, Parkinson's disease, Huntington's chorea, or lower or upper motor neuron disease.

TRACHEOSTOMY

If a short-term or long-term tracheostomy is necessary, the patient and the family should have proper preoperative counseling. It is necessary to explain the purpose of the procedure and that the patient will probably be without his voice until he can effectively occlude the tracheostomy tube. Humidification of the patient's immediate environment is very important. Suctioning and cleaning of the airway with saline solution is also very important in limiting crusting and thinning the secretions. Suctioning should be reduced to a minimum as soon as possible so as not to remove any more cilia from the trachea than is absolutely necessary.

FACIAL NERVE PALSY

Facial nerve palsies are usually of idiopathic origin. Bell's palsy is a diagnosis by exclusion of all other causes of the facial nerve palsy. Herpes zoster oticus (Ramsay Hunt syndrome), cholesteatoma in a chronic suppurative otitis media, carcinoma of the middle ear, and parotid tumor are a few of the causes of a facial palsy. The most important step in the initial assessment of facial palsy is exclusion of any middle ear pathology or tumors along the distribution of the facial nerve.

OTALGIA

Otalgia may originate within the ear itself or may be referred from numerous structures in the head and neck. Pain originating within the ear is usually due to an acute inflammation within the outer or middle ear. Referred pain is a common important phenomenon. A number of cranial nerve sensory components to the external and middle ear also are sensory components to the pharynx, hypopharynx, and larynx; a lesion elsewhere in the head and neck area may be manifest as otalgia. Otalgia may be a symptom of the presentation of a carcinoma on the base of the tongue, pharynx, or larynx. Furthermore, ordinary common causes of such referred pain include cervical osteoarthrosis and temporomandibular joint dysfunction. In both, pain may be centered on the ear but they usually show differing radiations with the former having a cervical root distribution and the latter having a preauricular, maxillary, and mandibular pattern to it.

HEAD AND NECK CANCERS

Head and neck cancers comprise 5% of all malignancies in the body. They occur more frequently in the elderly than in the younger population. Because of the possible pronounced functional and cosmetic deformities from ablative surgery, early diagnosis to allow the least destructive therapy is important. Poor oral hygiene, alcohol, and smoking are prime factors in the formation of these head and neck tumors.

Common geriatric complaints that should be investigated for possible malignancy include neck masses, hoarseness, dysphagia, dyspnea, hearing alterations, painful teeth, swollen face, bad breath, otalgia, and hemoptysis. Common presenting symptoms include proptosis due to tumors of the orbit or ethmoid, frontal, or maxillary sinuses; epistaxis associated with cancer of the paranasal sinuses or nose; ulceration of the mouth; hoarseness associated with laryngeal carcinoma; and dysphagia resulting from laryngeal and esophageal tumors. Facial swelling also can result from tumors of the parotid gland, floor of the mouth, maxillary sinus, palate, or mandible.

The most common malignancy in the head and neck area is epidermoid squamous cell carcinoma. If the laryngeal lesions are found early, a cure rate greater than 95% can be achieved. The early lesions are treated with radiation, carbon dioxide laser resection, or partial laryngectomy. While still providing a possible cure rate, advances in surgical techniques of partial laryngectomy can preserve the voice and deglutition in many moderately advanced cases. Total laryngectomy is still required in advanced tumors and this sometimes is done in combination with radiation.

Carcinoma of the oral cavity occurs most commonly in the older age groups. Age itself is not a contraindication to surgery as extensive head and neck surgery is generally well tolerated by the elderly patient. Johnson et al (14) reported that in 27 cases of composite resection in patients over 65 years of age, the surgical complications were equivalent to or less than those of an equally paired younger age group. There was an increase in associated medical complications for the elderly population; however, the head and neck complications were fewer. However, rehabilitation time for oral alimentation and for discharge of the patient was essentially the same in both age groups. Age also is no contraindication to partial laryngeal surgery as it seems to be tolerated relatively well in the elderly patient. Tucker (26) reviewed 27 cases of conservation laryngeal surgery in the elderly age group. He found his 11% complication rate with no deaths compared favorably wioth the rates for total laryngectomy and radiotherapy alone. McGuirt et al. (19) reported no increased incidents of surgical complications in the greater than 70-years age group. His series also had a slight increase in medical complication, however, the head and neck complications were equal.

Thyroid malignancies act more aggressively in the elderly as more anaplastic or undifferentiated carcinomas occur. Hoarseness, dysphagia, dyspnea, and enlarging neck mass are symptoms of thyroid cancer. The most useful diagnostic techniques are fine-needle aspiration and radioactive imaging. Surgical resection is the initial treatment of choice for thyroid malignancies. For follicular or papillary carcinoma, radioactive iodine ablation and thyroid supplementation are recommended after total or near-total thyroidectomy (with a modified neck dissection for positive lymphatic involvement). For medullary carcinoma, external radiation to the neck and mediastinum and thyroid supplementation should be given after total thyroidectomy and regional lymphatic resection. For anaplastic carcinoma, external radiation, possible chemotherapy, and thyroid supplementation should be given after total thyroidectomy and regional lymphatic resection (12).

The geriatric population has skin changes that are of significance to the otolaryngologist. Basal cell carcinoma, squamous cell carcinoma, malignant melanoma, and the numerous premalignant skin lesions are discussed elsewhere in this textbook.

In summary, it would appear that age alone is not a criterion for withholding curative surgery from an elderly patient. Instead, the postponement of operative procedure is unwise. Consequently, the head and neck surgeon should evaluate each patient based on preexisting medical problems, the preexisting psychologic and mental condition, the type of surgery required with possible reconstructive procedure, probable postoperative functional state, and the support facilities available where the operation will be done. Only after weighing all of these considerations should the surgeon make recommendations regarding major head and neck surgery.

There has been significant improvement in rehabilitation of the laryngectomee after total laryngectomy. In addition to an electrolarynx and esophageal speech, there are now multiple approaches to the surgical reconstruction of the speaking mechanism.

Cosmetic and reconstructive facial surgery is of growing importance to the aging population. The physician must pay careful attention to the patient's desires, needs, and physical capabilities. Reconstructive surgery is very crucial in the rehabilitation of a cancer patient. The postsurgical defect following removal of a malignancy may require both functional and cosmetic surgery. Recent developments with microsurgery, regional flaps, free flaps, and myocutaneous flaps have improved reconstructive surgery significantly (5, 17).

REFERENCES

1. Anderson RG, Meyerhoff WL: Otologic manifestations of aging. *Otolaryngol Clin North Am* 15:353, 1982.
2. Babin RW, Harker LA: The vestibule system in the elderly. *Otolaryngol Clin North Am* 15:387, 1982.
3. Ballenger JJ: *Disease of the Nose, Throat, Ear, Head and Neck*, 3rd ed. Philadelphia, Lea & Febiger, 1985.
4. Boone DR, Bayles KA: Communicative aspects of aging. *Otolaryngol Clin North Am* 15:313, 1982.
5. Chavpil M, Koopman CF: Age and other factors regulating wound healing. *Otolaryngol Clin North Am* 15:259, 1982.
6. Crowe SJ, et al: Observations on the pathology of high-tone deafness. *Johns Hopkins Hosp Bull* 54:315, 1934.
7. Cummings CW, Frederickson JM: *Otolaryngology—Head and Neck Surgery*. St. Louis, CV Mosby, 1986.
8. English GM: *Otolaryngology*. Philadelphia, Harper & Row, 1985, Revised Ed.
9. Etholm B, Belal A: Senile changes in the middle ear joints. *Ann Otol Rhinol Laryngol* 83:49, 1974.
10. Gates G: *Current Therapy in Otolaryngology—Head and Neck Surgery -3*. St. Louis, CV Mosby, 1987.
11. Goodhill V: *Ear Diseases, Deafness, and Dizziness*, New York, Harper and Row, 1979.
12. Holt GR, Mattox DE: *Decision Making in Otolaryngology*. St. Louis, CV Mosby, 1984.
13. Honjo I, Isshiki N: Laryngoscopic and voice characteristics of aged persons. *Arch Otolaryngol* 106:149, 1980.
14. Johnson JT, Rabuzzi DD, Tucker HM: Composite resection in the elderly: A well-tolerated procedure. *Laryngoscope* 87:1509, 1977.
15. Johnsson LG: Degenerative changes and anomalies of the vestibular system in man. *Laryngoscope* 81:1682, 1971.
16. Klotz RE, Kilbane M: Hearing in an aging population, preliminary report. *N Engl J Med* 266:277, 1962.
17. Koopman CF: Special considerations in managing geriatric patients, 1986. In: *Otolaryngology—Head and Neck Surgery*, St. Louis, CV Mosby, ed. 1, 1987.
18. Koopman CF Jr, Coulthard SW: The oral cavity and aging. *Otolaryngol Clin North Am* 15:293, 1982.
19. McGuirt WF, et al: The risks of major head and neck surgery in the aged population. *Laryngoscope* 87:1378, 1977.
20. Paparella MM, Shumrick DA: *Otolaryngology*, ed 2. Philadelphia, WB Saunders, 1980.
21. Patterson CN: The aging nose: characteristics and correction. *Otolaryngol Clin North Am* 13:275, 1980.
22. Schuknecht HF: Further observations on the pathology of presbycusis. *Arch Otolaryngol* 80:369, 1964.
23. Schuknecht HF: *Pathology of the Ear*. Cambridge, Harvard University Press, 1974.
24. Senturia BH, et al: *Diseases of the External Ear*. New York, Grune & Stratton, 1980.
25. Simpson WJ: Thyroid malignancy in the elderly. *Geriatrics* 37:119, 1982.
26. Tucker HM: Conservation laryngeal surgery in the elderly patient. *Laryngoscope* 87:1995, 1977.

CHAPTER 38

Geriatric Dentistry

VINCENT C. ROGERS
DOROTHY J. DUVALL

As late as the 1970s the dental profession predicted that oral and dental diseases in the elderly would be severe enough that the majority of persons 65 years and older would be edentulous and require complete or at least partial prosthetic restoration. Oral epidemiologic studies at the time supported this professional consensus and Schools of Dentistry oriented their curricula to educate future practitioners to treat the ravages of cumulative disease with clinical interventions to restore function and appearance.

Recent studies, however, do not support the earlier predictions. In fact, dental caries (decay) has declined significantly—over 50% in children under 17 years and is declining markedly in the adult population (2). Periodontal disease, the cause of most tooth loss in adults over 35 years of age, is not expected to be as prevalent to the extent predicted earlier (2, 6). The overwhelming effectiveness of public water fluoridation, advances in dental treatment technology, access to dental care through private and public programs as well as a more educated population aware of the benefits of preventive dental care, have significantly improved oral status in most western industrialized countries.

Future research will focus upon the microbiologic, immunologic, and genetic factors influencing oral and dental disease. Results of these studies should improve even further oral health for future cohorts of elderly for the year 2000 and beyond. As the present so-called "baby-boom" population approaches age 65 years, both dental caries and periodontal disease will be much less prevalent.

But what about the elderly who presently exist? It is this cohort that still has a significant distribution of disease that is traditionally associated with the aging dentition, oral tissues, and the neuromuscular system of mastication. Complications of untreated dental and periodontal disease, and oral

manifestations of systemic disease, should be relevant for the physician concerned about the total health of the elderly patient.

Physicians and nursing personnel should be able to identify common oral problems in the older patient and should consult with dental personnel on a continuing basis to assure that both normally occurring problems and those specifically associated with aging do not compromise the overall well-being of the elderly individual.

AGING DENTITION AND ORAL STRUCTURES

Gradual changes occur over time in the adult dentition. Although most tissues physiologically replace or repair themselves, enamel, the structure that covers the crown or visible part of the tooth, is not replaced by cellular repair as compared to the dentin, cementum, and pulp (Fig. 38.1). The enamel of the crown often exhibits attrition in later years—a wearing away of the occlusal and incisal surfaces of the teeth due to masticatory wear and oral habits such as bruxism or grinding. The enamel itself becomes more brittle with age. Occasionally, abrasion (a pathologic wearing away at the cementoenamel junction through some mechanical process, such as excessive tooth brushing), and erosion (a chemical dissolution in the same area) may appear. These changes, however, are not observed exclusively in the aging dentition. With the loss of enamel translucency, the aging tooth appears darker. Normally occurring insults to the dentition in the form of hot and cold liquids may result in hairline cracks and fissures in the enamel surface that may have the cumulative effect of further weakening the enamel, resulting in increased risk of fracture.

Cementum, the structure that covers root surfaces, undergoes gradual age changes also. With age,

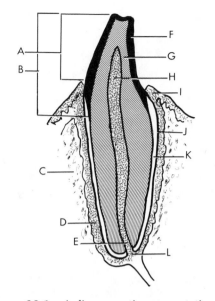

Figure 38.1. A diagrammatic representation of the dental tissue. **A**, clinical crown; **B**, anatomical crown; **C**, alveolar bone; **D**, periodontium; **E**, root canal; **F**, enamel; **G**, dentin; **H**, pulp; **I**, gum; **J**, epithelial attachment; **K**, cementum; and **L**, apical foramen. Modified from Williams PL, Warwick R: *Gray's Anatomy*, Ed. 36. Philadelphia, WB Saunders, p. 1283, 1980.

cementum gradually increases in thickness. Gingival recession, a common problem with aging, results in increased exposure of the root area. Because the exposed cementum is less dense than enamel, it is highly susceptible to decay and an increase in root caries is frequently observed in the elderly. If salivary gland function has decreased, or salivary consistency is altered, the resultant xerostomia (dry mouth) and thickened saliva also promotes enamel and root surface caries (12, 13).

Aging dentin continues to proliferate resulting in secondary dentin formation. The formation of this secondary dentin reduces the size of the pulp chamber, which contains the neural and vascular structures of the tooth. Obturation of the dentinal tubules results in decreased sensitivity in the dentition.

The oral cavity is lined with stratified squamous epithelium of three types: (a) masticatory mucosa of the gingiva and hard palate; (b) lining mucosa of the cheek, soft palate, floor of the mouth, and ventral surface of the tongue; and (c) specialized mucosa of the lips and dorsum of the tongue. With age all three mucosal types exhibit change. The lips thin at the vermillion border and become pale in appearance. The normally pink and moist mucosa and firm, pink, knife-like gingiva become thin and smooth and lose elasticity and stippling. With thinning and loss

of elasticity, the mucosa becomes less resistant to injury.

With aging, the tongue may show a loss of the papillae (which contain the taste buds), taking on a smooth appearance. The tongue may also become fissured on the dorsal surface (Fig. 38.2). Varicosities may appear more frequently on the ventral surface, which, although not pathologic, may be subject to traumatic injury with resultant hemorrhage.

Normally, copious amounts of saliva are secreted from the salivary glands. Based on several earlier clinical studies using older, often debilitated subjects, disturbed salivary gland function and associated decreased output was thought to be a consequence of aging. Later studies are not so conclusive about aging and salivary gland output and it is difficult to state definitely that in the healthy older individual salivary gland function is decreased (or impaired). Decreased salivary output may be more related to medications or systemic disease in the elderly (7).

PREVENTIVE ASPECTS

Increasingly, dentists are recognizing that the needs of the elderly dental patient of the future will be markedly different from those needs that heretofore have been identified by the dental profession. Improved preventive and restorative dental procedures have reduced the rate of edentulousness in the total United States population from 13.0% in 1957 to 11.2% in 1971. This reduction was most dramatic for persons older than 65 years, with a decrease from 67.3% in 1957 to 45.6% in 1981 (3, 5, 8).

Current national data indicate that the rate of edentulousness among persons over 65 years is de-

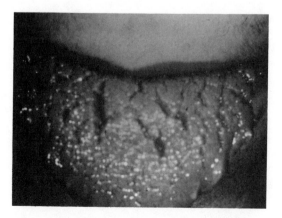

Figure 38.2. Dorsal fissuring of the tongue associated with glossitis and nutritional deficiencies frequent in elderly individuals.

clining to the extent that individuals can expect to reach old age with their teeth more or less intact. The larger numbers of elderly adults retaining all or part of their natural teeth reflect the importance that oral preventive measures have assumed in the population. Fig. 38.3 shows an elderly female, age 78 years, exhibiting the classic clinical picture of an aging dentition with associated gingival and periodontal deterioration. By contrast, Fig. 38.4 shows a female, 82 years of age, who has retained all of her teeth and who evidences excellent periodontal health through good personal oral hygiene and professional care.

The concept of oral hygiene is well-defined by Tryon (17) as "those measures necessary for the maintenance of oral health, including the cleansing of the teeth, marginal gingiva, and other tissues of the mouth, thereby contributing to a state of cleanliness of the entire oral cavity." Cleanliness of the oral cavity is of paramount importance in the prevention of inflammation, infection, pain, and subsequent loss of function.

Plaque, a colorless, mucinous, adherent film that reforms within 24 hours after removal, and attaches to the tooth surfaces, is the chief etiologic factor for gingivitis, or inflammation of the gums. The toxins produced by the bacteria resident in the plaque or teeth attack the enamel, cementum, and dentin causing carious lesions and gum disease. These same toxins, along with the mechanical irritation of the mineralized end product of plaque, or calculus, damage periodontal ligaments and bone supporting the teeth, causing mobility and eventual tooth loss. Possible saliva changes in aging may diminish the cleansing, antibacterial, and buffering functions of saliva, allowing more plaque formation upon roots

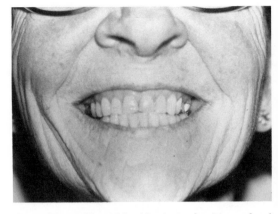

Figure 38.4. Normal, healthy, intact dentition and oral tissues in an 82-year-old female.

with subsequent root surface decay (18). Control of the plaque factor in tooth decay and periodontal problems may obviate the loss of teeth and the need for subsequent dental intervention with aggressive rehabilitation.

Oral hygiene needs are also a concern in the edentulous patient. Unclean dentures, where plaque accumulates on the tissue side of the dentures, can cause mucosal irritation in areas of constant contact. Prolonged wearing of dentures without removal can cause a decrease in the ridge size leading to poor adaptation and retention of the denture. Dentures should be removed from the mouth 6–8 hours a day. Many types of cleansers are available for dentures; but no matter what kind of cleanser is used, dentures need to be brushed daily for proper plaque removal, control of odor, and bacterial growth. Edentulous patients who do not wear dentures should also have their mouths cleansed daily of food debris and irritants. Physicians and nursing personnel need to be aware of the patient's oral status and interventions to maintain an acceptable level of health. An appropriate oral hygiene regimen, preferably individually prescribed for the patient by a dental professional, should be adhered to routinely to promote optimal cleansing of oral tissues. Modification of cleansing aids can be designed to make patients with physical limitations more self-reliant and responsible for their own care, thereby incorporating dentistry into current rehabilitation concepts about self-deficit minimalization (Fig. 38.5). Daily brushing with topical 0.4% stannous fluoride gels, such as Gel-Kam or Oral B Stop, not only prevents further dental decay but also may retard gingivitis and periodontal disease by altering the oral environment for resident microorganisms (14, 16). For daily

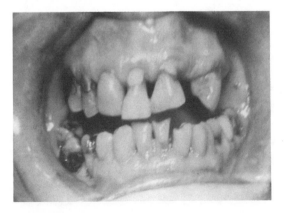

Figure 38.3. Periodontal disease associated with gingival recession, increased tooth mobility, and poor oral hygiene.

Figure 38.5. Modifications to toothbrushes to facilitate self-care by elderly with arthritis or neuromuscular deficiency observed in cerebrovascular accident, Parkinson's disease, etc.

oral hygiene, elderly patients, particularly those who are debilitated or confined to bed, may find helpful newly developed dentifrices (toothpaste) that do not foam and may be swallowed.

Preventive needs of the ambulatory elderly, those living in the community and not confined due to illness or physical limitations, are the same as the general population—periodic oral examinations to monitor oral health and facilitate early diagnosis of problems as well as regular preventive oral hygiene measures. The homebound elderly may or may not be capable of caring for themselves and because of physical limitations or illness may not be able to seek dental care routinely. The local dental society or health department may be able to recommend dentists who can accommodate this category of the elderly. Consulting or attending dentists in nursing homes should be able to accommodate the nursing home patient for dental care and oral hygiene recommendations. Nursing personnel are responsible for supervising or carrying out the daily instructions or orders of the physician and dentist, as prescribed individually for the patient, in order to obviate unnecessary problems with the oral structures.

The chief preventive measure that should be performed in all elderly patients, either ambulatory or nursing home residents, is the oral and soft tissue examination of the head and neck. The importance of a thorough oral examination cannot be overstressed. This systematic inspection should be done as part of a total physical examination in the following order so as not to overlook any area of the oral cavity:

1. Observe face and neck for any swelling, asymmetry, lesions, or unusual pigmentation.
2. Palpate lymph nodes and glands of the face and neck.
3. Observe mucosa, floor of the mouth, palate, and tongue. When observing the tongue, grasp the tip with a 4 x 4 gauze pad, gently extend and view both of the borders of the tongue bilaterally.
4. Palpate lips, mucosa, floor of the mouth, palate, and tongue.
5. Check salivary duct patency for any signs of blockage or irritation.
6. Observe the teeth for decay, mobility, and oral hygiene status.
7. Check the gingival (or gum) tissues for signs of inflammation, excess bleeding or purulence.

Any unusual findings should be recorded and a consultation requested of the attending dentist for follow-up for any necessary intervention and care. Generally any signs of erythema, edema or swelling, hemorrhage, purulence or patient complaints, or elicitation of pain should alert the physician or nurse to seek a dental consultation.

NUTRITION AND ORAL HEALTH

Although studies are showing that the oral status of the elderly has improved significantly in the past 20 years, it is estimated that of the 26 million people in the United States, aged 65 years and older, approximately one-half are edentulous (11). Overwhelmingly, the prevalence of missing teeth, ill-fitting dentures, and the associated problems relating to mastication, speech, deglutition, and digestion continue to be the major oral health problem among the elderly (4, 11). These factors not only complicate the recovery and rehabilitation of the elderly individual who is ill but also compromise the maintenance of good health of the elderly individual who is well and ambulatory.

Valid assessment of the relationships of masticatory impairment, nutritional intake, psychologic and sociologic gratification derived from eating has not been well-documented (4). Clinical observations, however, have demonstrated that diminution of masticatory function contributes to a diet that is nutritionally unbalanced and deficient in important vitamins and minerals essential to maintenance of both total and oral health. Individuals with full or partial removable dentures show a significant diminution in their ability to chew. Other factors, such as diminished sensory perception, lowered motor ability, and bone resorption (which affects retention of dentures) also compromise chewing ability in old age. Lowered biting force and a preference for a soft diet by the patient can increase the probability of inadequate nutrition (4, 11). Additionally, the presence of a maxillary denture not only reduces flavor perception but also decreases the perception of tex-tures, thus adversely affecting appetite and enjoyment of various foods.

Dietary preference of the elderly individual tends to change progressively with age as masticatory function decreases or is compromised by ill-fitting or displaced dentures. Patients may prefer more easily chewed foods, or select foods that are sweeter, saltier, or overly seasoned inasmuch as the "smell-feel" component associated with flavor is diminished (4).

Physicians, therefore, need to be aware of the potential for nutritional inadequacies not only associated with systemic disease but also those deficiencies associated with dental problems and masticatory deficiencies.

COMMON ORAL PROBLEMS IN THE ELDERLY

Because persons over 65 years see physicians more frequently than they see dentists, the recognition of oral problems by the physician plays an important role in providing total care for elderly individuals. With more frequent opportunity to evaluate the older patient, the physician is in a position to identify oral problems and make timely referrals for consultation.

Denture sore mouth or *denture stomatitis* (Fig. 38.6) is a commonly seen condition in elderly patients who wear dentures. It appears as a reddened, inflamed area most frequently seen on the palate corresponding with the outline of the denture base. Denture sore mouth most often is the result of poor oral hygiene and failure to cleanse dentures properly. Dentures must be brushed daily and removed from the mouth at least 6–8 hours each day. This daily removal and cleansing of the denture allows the under-

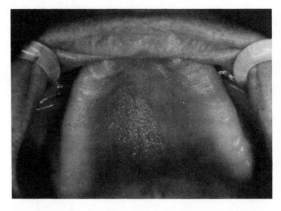

Figure 38.7. Papillary hyperplasia is a frequent observation in patients who wear dentures for long periods without removal.

lying mucosa to return to a normal state. The appearance and condition of the palatal tissues are not unlike the effect of a bandage placed firmly over the epidermis of a finger or arm for long periods of time—the skin loses its elasticity, firmness, and pigmentation with a resultant edema and hyperplasia.

Papillary hyperplasia (Fig. 38.7) is often seen in patients wearing dentures for extended periods of time without removal. This condition appears as a raised papular-like lesion in the middle of the hard palate, usually under complete dentures. Other areas of the mucosa may be involved as well. Papillary hyperplasia may also develop if the denture does not fit properly. A reline or refabrication of the denture is usually necessary at this point.

Ulcerations occasionally may appear on the lining mucosa in older adults wearing dentures if the denture is extended too far over the masticatory mucosa. The ulceration caused by an overextended denture will, on examination, be consistent with the margin of the denture or site of irritation. The condition is frequently seen in elderly patients, particularly females, who suffer a fractured hip with subsequent weight loss and debilitation. It can be said that the oral condition is indirectly related to the hip fracture. Adjustments to remove the offending area(s) is required as the condition rarely improves by itself. If left unadjusted, the area of the ulceration may hypertrophy into a larger mass of epithelial tissue known as an *epulis fissuratum* (Fig. 38.8).

Candida albicans, a normally resident organism of the oral flora in healthy persons (Fig. 38.9), may proliferate in debilitated older persons. This proliferation or imbalance may be the result of (a) malnutrition, (b) antibiotic therapy, (c) steroid therapy, (d) diabetes, or (e) oncologic chemotherapy. The clini-

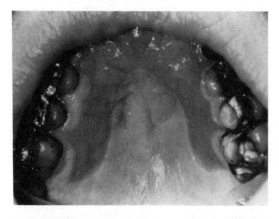

Figure 38.6. Denture sore mouth, or denture stomatitis, as a rsult of poor oral hygiene and prolonged use without removal.

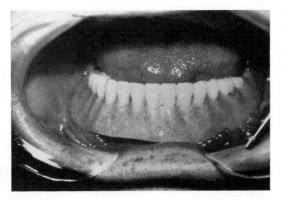

Figure 38.8. Epulis fissuratum, a hypertrophy of tissue, observed with ill-fitting dentures that irritate and ulcerate underlying tissues.

cal appearance is a creamy-colored, soft cheesy or curd-like area over erythematous epithelial tissue. This curd-like material can be wiped away with a 2 × 2 inch gauze pad revealing the erythematous tissue underneath giving the pathognomonic diagnosis of candidiasis. Antifungal oral suspensions, such as Nystatin, are the treatment of choice.

In elderly females, *postmenopausal glossodynia*, or "burning tongue" is another complaint. Pain can be mild to severe. This condition has been associated with decreased estrogen levels. In both males and females, vitamin deficiencies, especially vitamin B complex, may be implicated. Other conditions, such as anemias, Sjögren's, Mikulcz's, and Plummer-Vinson syndromes may be etiologic factors. Burning tongue may also be associated with xerostomia brought about by side effects of medications for depression, anxiety, personality and behav-

ioral disorders. Treatment may consist of (a) substitution, decrease in dosage, or discontinuance of offending medication, (b) provision of supplementary estrogen or vitamin supplements when indicated, or (c) salivary stimulants or saliva substitutes such as Xerolube or Salivart.

Angular cheilitis (Fig. 38.10) is an inflammatory fissuring and maceration at the commissures (corners) of the lips and may occur either unilaterally or bilaterally. Causes include loss of vertical dimension due to overclosure of the jaws in edentulous persons, vitamin B (especially riboflavin) deficiency, or xerostomia. Secondary infection with *C. albicans* may be present because patients have a tendency to lick the dry sore area to help keep it moist. Treatment includes fabrication or adjustment of dentures, prescription of vitamin B complex supplements or antifungal ointments, such as Nystatin, when a diagnosis of *C. albicans* is made.

Fibroepithelial polyps, or irritation "fibromas" (Fig. 38.11) are frequently observed lesions in the buccal mucosa of the tongue, the vestibular mucosa, or the lip (5). They may be either sessile or pedunculated, and are generally smooth-surfaced and firm upon palpation. Generally, they are asymptomatic, but may bleed if traumatized, or become keratotic if the source of irritation is chronic. Etiologic factors include ill-fitting dentures, fractured dental fillings or teeth, or oral habits such as cheek or lip biting. The lesion is not a true neoplasm and usually decreases in size when the cause of irritation is removed. They are remarkable only if they are a source of discomfort, or interfere with function. They may be removed with excisional biopsy as a precaution, although malignancy is rarely a factor.

Periodontal disease is the chief cause of tooth loss

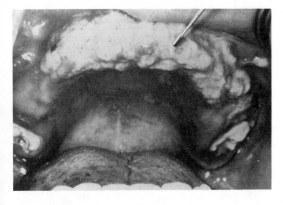

Figure 38.9. *Candida albicans*, a normally occurring organism in the oral cavity, may proliferate in debilitated elderly in the presence of poor oral hygiene or broadspectrum antibiotic therapy.

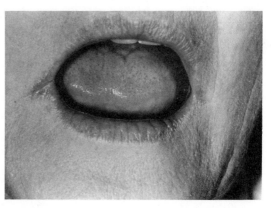

Figure 38.10. Angular cheilitis, an inflammatory fissuring at the corners of the mouth, associated here with secondary infection by *C. albicans*.

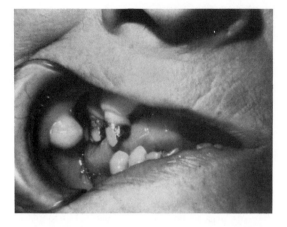

Figure 38.11. Fibroepithelial polyp, or irritation "fibroma," associated with fractured dental fillings and teeth.

in adults over 65 years of age. The incidence for periodontitis in the present cohort of elderly may range from a high of 60% to a low of 20% in the most recent studies, depending upon the epidemiologic study design and survey instrument (3, 4). The disease is caused by the formation of plaque and calculus upon the teeth and surrounding supporting tissues precipitating inflammation, tissue recession with eventual destruction of bone, and tooth loss (Fig. 38.3). In the elderly, periodontal disease is often complicated and further advanced by poor oral hygiene, diabetes, immunosuppression due to chemotherapy, osteoporosis, as well as nutrition, vitamin, and metabolic deficiencies. Individualized schedules for oral hygiene maintenance are important to assist patients with arthritis, stroke, or other physical limitations to minimize both periodontal disease and the potential for serious infections that are frequent sequelae if the condition is left unchecked.

Oral cancer has a higher incidence in older patients and is more common in males than females. Approximately 4–5% of all cancers occur in the oral cavity and adjacent tissues. Oral carcinomas are usually of the squamous cell type occurring at various sites with the following frequency (9, 15):

Lip	9%
Buccal mucosa	3%
Tongue	50%
Floor of the mouth	15%
Palate	9%
Gingiva and alveolar mucosa	12%

Carcinoma of the lip is chiefly associated with pipe smoking and exposure to sunlight, and is more common in men between the ages of 60 and 70 years. It may present initially as a crusty patch, ulcerated, elevated area or large swelling. Induration at the borders of an ulceration is highly suspicious. Carcinoma of the tongue may present as a tumor, ulceration, leukoplakia, or an erythematous patch with a leukoplakic periphery. The lateral borders and the central tip of the tongue are the most common sites. On the buccal mucosa, gingival lesions may appear as a small ulcerated, indurated mass with leukoplakia. Because of the good prognosis in early detection of oral carcinoma, periodic examination of the head, neck, and intraoral mucosa and adnexa should be conducted.

Adenocarcinomas are tumors of the minor salivary glands. They may appear as a painless, firm, or fluctuant mass, most frequently occurring at the juncture of the hard and soft palate. In these lesions, as with most cases of oral carcinoma, surgery and radiation therapy is the treatment of choice.

Any patient who receives head and neck radiation therapy should be evaluated by a dentist before treatment begins. Good oral hygiene and a daily topical fluoride regimen must be established to prevent rampant deterioration of the dentition and oral mucosa due to salivary gland damage caused by the irradiation. All necessary extractions should be performed *before* therapy whenever possible to obviate the risk of osteoradionecrosis. Extractions after irradiation should be performed in a hyperbaric O_2 chamber to reduce risk of osteoradionecrosis. Additionally, to prevent the occurrence of infection and complications in patients requiring dental extractions after radiation therapy, a separate and postoperative regimen of antibiotic therapy is recommended (15).

Elderly patients with *cardiovascular disease*, either acquired or congenital, should be evaluated for the risk of subacute bacterial endocarditis as a complication of dental treatment. There are numerous reports in the medical and dental literature of diagnoses of subacute bacterial endocarditis after cleaning of the teeth, dental restorations (fillings), and extractions. Both the physician and dentist should be knowledgeable of current recommendations for prophylactic antibiotic management of patients with cardiovascular deficits before and after treatment for dental problems.

Temporomandibular joint disorders are dysfunctions of the gliding, hinge-like movement of the articulation of the jaw located between the glenoid fossa of the skull and the condylar process of the mandible. Arthritis, gout, and degenerative changes of "normal" aging have been implicated in temporomandibular joint disorders, but studies have been sparse and inconclusive in correlating physical changes with actual symptomatology (1). Patients may experience pain, tenderness, swelling, limited movement, and clicking in the area of the joint. Degenerative joint disease, where there is a fragmenting and splintering of the articulating cartilage, predisposed possibly by age, trauma, wear and tear, malaligned teeth, ill-fitting dentures, trigeminal neuralgia, otitis, and pulpitis of the teeth, have also been cited as etiologic factors. Treatment usually is symptomatic with the use of analgesic and anti-inflammatory medications. Management of temporomandibular joint dysfunction and pain, as with other acute and chronic problems in the elderly, require the interaction of the physician and dentist for the most positive outcome for the patient.

Idiosyncratic and iatrogenic oral manifestations of *pharmacologic therapy*, particularly with psychotropic drugs, are a common cause for physician-dentist interaction and consultation in the medical management of the elderly patient. Multiple prescription and over-the-counter drug use in older persons precipitate a variety of side effects that have oral manifestations as well as systematic ramifications. Xerostomia, intraoral dermatitis, desquamation of the oral mucosa, gingival bleeding, glossodynia, and stomatodynia are among the clinical symptoms and complaints observed by the practitioner. Both physician and dentist should communicate freely to discuss possible alternatives or modifications in the prescribed medications for the most appropriate and beneficial management of the patient.

ETHICAL CONSIDERATIONS OF DENTISTRY IN LONG-TERM CARE

The growth of the elderly population in the United States is presenting unique moral and ethical decision-making dilemmas for all of the health professions. Dentists treating patients in nursing homes especially are being faced with the dilemma of whether or not to provide comprehensive dental care to individuals who are elderly, medically compromised, or debilitated. Similar to their medical colleagues, dentists have difficulty in making judgments as to what level of care is to be considered "appropriate" for a patient—not in terms of clinical indications for the care, but rather in terms of who,

when, and how much care should be provided under less than "ideal" circumstances (14).

In nursing homes, the ethical issues have a decidedly economic slant to their resolution, where decisions about the scope of dental care are often based upon the existence of resources to pay for that care by the patient, the family, or whether third-party reimbursement is available. Most of the elderly in nursing homes reached retirement age before the inclusion of dental benefits in their health insurance. Medicare, an entitlement program for persons 65 years and older, does not pay for dental care. Further, dental care is optional under Medicaid, the federal/state program passed in 1965 for medically indigent eligibles. Although Medicaid *can* provide for dental services to eligible persons of any age, states can limit the age beyond which no dental benefits are provided and the scope of those services. Fewer than 10% of the nursing homes in the United States have a visible dental care program in place! Cost is often cited by administrators as a deterrent to dental programs. These economic factors underscore the need for a multiprofessional approach to dental care, involving the dentist, physician, nurse, and the social worker who may coordinate communication with the patient and family.

In nursing homes, physicians and staff are chiefly concerned with stabilizing and maintaining the elderly resident who, more often than not, has multiple medical problems. With diminished psychologic and physiologic functions, requiring a variety of clinical interventions, concern for the dental status of the patient is often not a priority in the geriatric evaluation process. Physicians and nursing staff may be aware of oral problems, but may not know how these problems play a major role in the overall well-being of the patient. Given the more frequent contact physicians have with the elderly than does a dentist (an average of six visits to one for persons over 65 years), there is a greater opportunity for physicians to identify the dental needs of the geriatric patient (4). Thus, dental considerations for the elderly patient can be functionally integrated into the overall management of the individual.

Under ideal circumstances, where social, economic, and medical contraindications do not present barriers, physicians and dentists generally reach clinical decisions about levels of care and are reasonably confident in doing so. But under circumstances as they exist in nursing homes and extended care facilities, decisions are no longer clear-cut. Physicians in consulting with dentists find clinical-ethical decisions such as the following very difficult: Should prosthetic care be provided to patients with dementia? Should an offending tooth be extracted or aggressively treated with restoration and/or endodontic (root canal) therapy? Should dentures be provided to residents who did not have them before admission? Under what circumstances should maximum care be provided to an incompetent individual? When should no care be provided?

Often physicians are uncertain, as are dentists, regarding how much or how little care should be provided. The resolution to these dilemmas and the many others that confront physicians and dentists is determining what is an "appropriate" level of care for the patient. Appropriateness of care is that level of intervention that considers the patient's physical and mental ability to tolerate or accept treatment in the restoration and maintenance of function and yet does not unduly override the patient's own perception of need. Diverse categories of dental care are appropriate for elderly patients, especially in the nursing home setting. Although it is accepted that a team approach to treatment planning (physician, dentist, nurse, social worker, physical therapist, speech pathologist, etc.) is ideal, the dentist usually makes decisions alone. Consultations, however, should be made with other professional disciplines as available. The first decision is the determination of the extent of dental care to be provided (10).

The first category includes patients who are *unable to receive care*. *Minimal care* of patients includes the elimination of sources of infection and relief of pain through an appropriate intervention (extraction, cleaning, antibiotic therapy, etc.). The elimination of infection and restoration of teeth constitute *intermediate care* of patients. *Maximum care* is the full range of dental services that might include the construction of complete or partial dentures, fixed prosthetic devices, or combinations of these services (12). A range of preventive interventions, such as daily oral hygiene (self-care or assisted), topical fluorides and oral rinses, should be made available to minimal, intermediate, and maximum care patients to obviate or reduce the recurrence of dental problems.

The determination of the appropriate level of care, or category, is the most important aspect of treatment consideration. In addition, careful judgment and communication, whenever possible with the patient and/or the family, is necessary, so that determinations are not automatic and arbitrary.

CONCLUSION

The most significant impact of the "geriatric imperative" is the recognition by both medicine and

dentistry of the mandate to re-evaluate our perceptions and approaches to the management of the elderly patient. Dental care is a health service that should be considered part of total patient care. Related as it is to nutritional, psychologic, and physical health, dentistry needs to be accorded a position of importance in the geriatric assessment process. This incorporation into the individual's overall assessment is particularly critical in long-term care facilities, where a person's ability to benefit from medical and rehabilitative nursing care may be enhanced if he or she can masticate food properly and if the mouth is free from potentially complicating disease processes.

While dentists are clearly the logical professionals to assume a leadership role in establishing dental care services within nursing homes, physicians and nursing personnel will need to be both cooperative and responsive to the input of multiple disciplines in the health professions if the overall well-being of elderly patients is to be achieved.

REFERENCES

1. Andres R, Bierman E, Hazzard W: *Principles of Geriatric Medicine.* New York, McGraw-Hill, 1985, p. 294.
2. Beck J: The epidemiology of dental disease in the elderly. *Gerodontology* 3:5, 1984.
3. Chauncey H, Epstein S, Rose C, et al. (Eds): *Clinical Geriatric Dentistry.* Chicago, American Dental Association, 1986, p. 48.
4. Chauncey H, House J: Dental problems in the elderly. *Hosp Pract* December: 82, 1977.
5. Colby R, Kerr D, Robinson H: *Color Atlas of Oral Pathology,* ed. 3. Philadelphia, JB Lippincott, 1971, p. 94.
6. DePaola D, Cheney H (Eds): *Preventive Dentistry.* Littleton, MA, PSG Publishing Co., 1979, pp. 195–206.
7. Fox P, van der Ven P, Sonias B, et al.: Xerostomia: Evaluation of a symptom with increasing significance. *J Am Dent Assoc* 110:519, 1985.
8. Gordon S: Oral assessment of the dentulous elderly patient. *J Am Geriatr Soc* 34:276, 1986.
9. Holm-Petersen P, Löe H: *Geriatric Dentistry.* Copenhagen, Munksgaard, 1986, pp. 290–305.
10. Kerson J: Treatment planning for patients in nursing homes. *J Am Dent Assoc* 89:640, 1974.
11. Lamy P, Overholser D, Lamy M: Nutritional deficiencies. Oral Health and Aging. Chapter 7. In Tryon A (Ed): *Oral Health and Aging.* Littleton, MA, PSG Publishing Co., 1986, pp. 159–192.
12. Langer A: Oral changes in the geriatric patient. Compendium of continuing education in dentistry. 2:258, 1981.
13. Lotzkar S: Dental care for the aged. *J Public Health Dentistry* 37:205, 1977.
14. Rogers V: Ethical considerations of appropriateness of dental care for patients in nursing homes. Paper pre-

sented at the annual meeting of the American Public Health Association, Dallas, TX, 1983.

15. Shafer W, Hine M, Levy B: *A Textbook of Oral Pathology*, Ed. 4. Philadelphia, WB Saunders, 1983, pp. 119–127, 568.

16. Stallard R: *A Textbook of Preventive Dentistry.* Philadelphia, WB Saunders, 1982, pp. 189–190.

17. Tryon A (Ed): *Oral Health and Aging.* Littleton, MA, PSG Publishing Co., Inc. 1986, pp. 271–286.

18. Waldman H, Stein M: A dental plan for the chronically ill and aged. *Highland View Hospital* 2:7, 1967.

Section II

Care of the Elderly Patient: Other Considerations

CHAPTER 39

The Elderly and Their Families

JACK H. MEDALIE

The definition of elderly changes as one grows older and as the demographic distribution of the population changes. When one is 20 years old a person of 60 seems old, whereas a 60-year-old individual in good health probably thinks of someone in their 80s or 90s as old. New categories have been created in the scientific literature to reflect these changes, i.e., the *young old* (65–74 years) and the *old old* (75 and over) (8). Even these categories may change as more people pass the century mark.

The percentage of people 65 years old and older is rapidly rising in most developing countries and currently stands at 11% in the United States. This may well reach 15% before the end of the century if mortality rates continue to decline. At family gatherings such as weddings or holidays it is quite common now to have four or more generations present. By 1980, 40% of the people in their late 50s had a surviving parent and 3% of those in their 70s. This dramatic increase in the numbers of the elderly has occurred historically in a relatively short period of time so that in our society, which prides itself on individualism and self-sufficiency, it takes time before the problems and dependency needs of the aged are realized and understood. During the transition period the problem of increasing numbers of dependent elderly affects many individuals and families, despite Social Security, Medicare, pension plans, etc.

In this chapter an attempt is made, through a series of clinical family case studies, to illustrate some of the changes and problems that affect the roles and relationships of the elderly, their families, and indirectly, their health. In all cases an attempt is made to adapt the biopsychosocial model (as defined by George Engel) to clinical practice with the elderly. The understanding of the causes and ef-

fects of the behavior and diseases of the elderly and their families is based on knowledge obtained from scientific studies, as well as on clinical intuition and experience of the physicians who were closely involved with the patients and families over a long period of time.

FAMILY 1

Mr. and Mrs. A.B., both in their 70s, have two adult children (male and female) who are married and have two and three children, respectively. The eldest grandchild is 18 and until recently Mrs. A.B.'s mother lived with them until she died at age 92. Mr. A.B. was a mechanical engineer who founded his own company when he was 38 and built it into a large successful industry. His son, A.B. Jr., also an engineer, went on to get a MBA degree and now, at age 46, is running his father's business and expanding it in many new directions. Mrs. A.B. has been a housewife and mother since completing college but has always been very active in their church, parent-teacher school associations, their country club, and other charitable and social activities in their community. This elderly couple feel good about themselves and are in relatively good health. Mr. A.B. has borderline hypertension, prostatic enlargement, and occasional attacks of low back pain. Mrs. A.B. periodically is bothered by various muscular and joint pains and recently began wearing a hearing aid. They both have one or two drinks each evening, do not smoke, and exercise regularly through swimming and weekly golf outings. They have their own home in a pleasant suburban community and for the last several years have escaped the winter weather by going to Arizona or Florida. The son has his own home in the same suburban area while the daughter, a high school teacher, lives with her family on their dairy farm, run by her husband, which is 300 miles from their parents.

The son and daughter have gone through their life cycle changes from birth to marriage and children without any special crises except during adolescence. He experimented briefly with pot and speed and she became pregnant and had an abortion while at college. The family coped well with these events and their functioning by any standard is good.

The A.B. family is an example of an elderly couple living independently, in good health, and with very adequate financial resources for themselves and their family. They are active socially with an extensive network of friends and have satisfactory relationships, communication, and functioning with their children and grandchildren. They have adapted well to their various postretirement roles as spouses, parents, grandparents, and "retired folk" in the community.

There is no indication in the literature as to the percentage of families who attain this degree of economic security, healthy living, and satisfactory intra- and extra-familial relationships. It may well be higher than we think.

DISCUSSION OF FAMILY 1

Family A.B. illustrates many of the normal transitions of the life cycle. Until recently the elderly couple had looked after Mrs. A.B.'s mother, who died when Mrs. A.B. was 69 years old, as well as being parents to two adult married children and six grandchildren. More and more middle-aged and even elderly persons are finding themselves in this situation, i.e., their children become independent and leave home while at the same time their parents move from independence to a more dependent role (2). When the adult children, due to physical, mental, or economic difficulties, are still dependent on their parents who are in the 50- to 65-year age group who still have dependent parents in their 70s or older, the burden on the "sandwiched" middle-aged parents can be overwhelming.

The *developmental tasks* of the aging couple in a nuclear extended family situation include the following: (6, 12, 17)

1. *Making satisfying living arrangements.* The A.B.s have remained in their own mortgage-free home and have the financial resources to obtain the help they need for maintenance. Some elderly move to smaller apartments or mobile homes, whereas others move to retirement communities nearby or in a warmer climate. A minority move into extended care facilities or even nursing homes. Some may move in with their children or other relatives. The question often arises whether to move to a new place with better facilities, climate, and security but with no family or friends, or to remain in the same place with the network of relationships built up over the years.

2. *Adjusting to retirement.* Most people who are forced to retire because of layoffs, business closings, poor health, etc. generally have a difficult period of adjustment. Generally, most people who retire do so with a good sense of achievement and find the postretirement years very satisfying.

Mr. A.B. had built up a good engineering business and had been a good role model and mentor to his son during his professional education and training to take over the position. His son proved quite capable of running and even expanding the business so that at the age of 70, Mr. A.B. found little difficulty in retiring to concentrate on extending his and his wife's family and social interests. This behavior involving "changed activities" exemplifies one of the patterns of retirement found in a survey of retirees (6). Patterns of behaviors that are noted in retirement include:

   a. *Maintenance.* The retiree makes extraordinary efforts to continue working.
   b. *Withdrawal.* The retiree gives up former interests without adopting new ones; this often leads to withdrawal, frustration, and depression.
   c. *Satisfying a new and different set of needs.* The retiree goes off and does things he/she always wanted to do.
   d. *Changed activities,* as in the case of Mr. A.B., who satisfies his same needs by engaging in a different set of activities.

   With very few exceptions income is reduced after retirement and despite Social Security, pensions, Medicare, and often Medicaid, the retired couple has to adjust to a decreased income. In the A.B.'s case, the death of her mother relieved them of a considerable financial burden so their net available income remained almost the same as when he was working fulltime. (Later we will look at examples of people in very different circumstances.) Generally speaking, persons 65 and over constitute approximately 11% of the population but probably over 20% of those below the poverty level. Naturally this leads to dissatisfaction, depression, and further ill health.

3. *Maintaining their health and medical care insurance.* Maintaining their physical and mental health involves many factors such as nutrition, exercise, self-respect, social contacts, and medical care availability. Aging is accompanied by changes in the structure and function of many body tissues and organs. Mobility, hearing, and vision are reduced. Reduced vision often complicates the ability of the aged to use their medication in the prescribed manner and often leads to acute crises due to over- or under-use (9). Daily living becomes more difficult and everything is done at a slower pace. Bodily functions such as renal excretion, cardiac and respiratory reserves, sexual function, and general metabolic activities are all diminished.

Despite this the vast majority of the aged function well and with "training" many of the functions diminish much less than we thought. The sight of 70- and 80-year-old individuals participating in active sports such as tennis, athletics, swimming, and even long-distance running is becoming more common. Mr. and Mrs. A.B. are in very good health through regular exercise, mental stimulation of social contacts, good relationships with family and friends, eating healthy food, and maintaining satisfactory sexual intercourse. Many age-related functional deteriorations can be mitigated by mechanical devices such as bifocal lenses, hearing aids, artificial joints, and pacemakers.

While sexual capacity is reduced with age, the pleasure derived from it can be maintained into old age. It does, however, call for modifications of techniques and position in order to maintain the previous satisfaction. There are many old couples who have given up sexual intercourse but apparently maintain a satisfying relationship.

The availability of satisfactory preventive and urgent (acute) health care is a major concern of the aged. Medicare does not cover all of their needs so additional insurance is necessary and even then many aged are bewildered by all of the forms and regulations. If chronic long-term care becomes necessary (3) many elderly are doomed to second-rate care and the financial burden places them and their families in a very precarious position.

5. *Maintaining contact with the family.* Maintaining contact with the family is done fairly well and frequently in the vast majority of elderly (10). Approximately 53% of the elderly live with a family member, 37% live alone, and 10% live with nonrelated people (Table 39.1). Cutting across all types of living arrangements, socioeconomic classes, and ethnic/cultural groups is the fact that the vast majority of elderly maintain frequent contact with their family through personal meetings, telephone conversations, or periodic visits (2, 10). Even children and others living at a distance usually maintain

contact and can be relied on to visit in a crisis or emergency. This is referred by Rosenmeyr to as "intimacy at a distance" (10).

When the elderly have no spouse or children, their contact with their siblings usually becomes much more important and much closer emotionally. While contact is maintained, the quality of the relationship varies considerably. Some are disengaged and maintain only a formal type of contact, whereas others are enmeshed and consult with each other for almost every daily aspect of living. "Each family's response to later life challenges evolves from earlier family patterns developed for stability and integration" (17). Thus the parent-child, sibling, and multigenerational relationships are usually a continuation of their previous patterns, which can be exacerbated by crises and decisions surrounding the care of the elderly.

6. *Adjusting to loss.* Loss, grieving, and bereavement are accompaniments of every aging person. Parents, spouses, children, siblings, and friends are among the losses. In addition, loss of a job, income, or independence (the ability to drive or dress oneself) are other losses to which the elderly and their families have to adjust. Elderly men seem to be more prone than women to the effects of bereavement. Their mortality rates are increased as are health-compromising behaviors and various illnesses (15).

7. *Keeping active and involved in meaningful activities.* Numerous examples abound in history of outstanding personalities who continued their professional careers well into their 80s and 90s. Churchill, Adenauer, Rubinstein, Toscanini, Casals, Picasso, and Chagall continued their activities into old age with enthusiasm. There are also examples of farmers, carpenters, craftsmen, etc. who have continued working into their 80s. To do this the older person must have the interest, the physical

Table 39.1
Marital Status and Living Arrangements of Sample of Noninstitutionalized Elderly in Cleveland Area, 1982[a]

Living Arrangements	Marital Status					
	Single	Married	Widowed	Divorced/ Separated	Total	
					n	%
Alone	66	5[b]	441	75	587	36.7
With spouse alone	0	111	0	0	111	7.0
With spouse and others	1	525	0	1	527	33.0
With children (no spouse)	1	2[b]	190	11	204	12.8
With others (nonrelatives)	51	0	99	19	169	10.5
Total n	119	643	730	106	1598	
%	7.4	40.2	45.7	6.6	100.0	

[a]Modified from Zyzanski S, Medalie JH, Ford AB, et al: Living arrangements and well-being in the elderly. *Fam Med* (in press.)
[b]The spouse lives in a nursing home or other institution.

ability, and mental health necessary to carry on usual activities. Mr. and Mrs. A.B. did not have any special hobbies and did not continue their careers. But they did keep actively involved in many family, church, leisure, and social activities and, in doing so, still felt needed and received respect.

In certain lower socioeconomic groups, the grandmothers often have a vital role to play in the upbringing of the grandchildren. It is fairly common for a teenaged mother to continue her education with the help of welfare and school authorities while her mother (the grandmother) takes over the "mothering" responsibility of the infant for most of the 24 hours. In some cases the child is taken to live with the grandmother. In this sense the teenaged mothers who give their child to their own mothers might not get to bring up a child, as a mother, until they become grandmothers and take their grandchildren to raise. We have heard many times the statement, "My grandmother means more to me than my mother." In these situations the grandmothers are very actively involved and often carry on despite many health difficulties. This activity and interest lead us to the last developmental task.

8. *Satisfaction and meaning of life in old age.* "Each stage in the life cycle involves the individual in reintegrating in new, age-appropriate ways those psychosocial themes that were ascendant in earlier periods. At every stage, the individual incorporates these earlier themes in the process of bringing into balance the tension that is now focal. In old age, it is to balance the tension between a sense of *integrity*, of enduring comprehensiveness, and an opposing sense of *despair*, of dread and hopelessness" (7). It is through this last stage that the life cycle weaves back on itself in its entirety, ultimately integrating maturing forms of each of the previous stages with a comprehensive sense of *wisdom* (7).

Since the advent of the human species the elderly have enjoyed the respect and attention of the population because of their experience and wisdom. In recent times, however, the incredible speed of technological development has left the aged out of touch with recent advances so their wisdom based on experience is of historical value but little practical value for the younger generation. This gives rise to their feeling of being "out of touch" and "unneeded." How can society ensure that the expanding segment of the elderly will remain an important element in the fabric of our society? To do this will take a series of complex factors and tasks. One vital factor is what Erickson calls *involvement.* In their study of the elderly, Erickson et al. (7) found that the major involvement that made life worth living in their elderly sample was the combination of pride and gratification from their relationships with and the achievements of their children and grandchildren. Others find involvement and energies through their work, hobbies, or activities like music, carpentry, or painting. Involvement, enthusiasm, and a sense of being needed might be the key to old age happiness. Mr. and Mrs. A.B. illustrate all of the above attributes in a positive manner.

FAMILY 2

Mrs. E.F., an 82-year-old white widow, lives alone in a public housing project apartment. Her parents and siblings are all deceased. Her husband died from a myocardial infarction (after a week in the intensive care unit) eight years ago. Her only child died at the age of 10 years from leukemia. She and her husband were not well off so following his death she moved into her current apartment and lives on their Social Security and a small pension. The security in the project block is not as good as it should be, but Mrs. E.F. is fiercely independent and will not hear of any suggestion to change her life style, such as to live with a niece who is prepared to have her. She uses public transportation and is active in many church and other activities.

Her hearing has deteriorated considerably during the last few years and although she has a hearing aid, she rarely uses it. Her systolic hypertension is well controlled. During the last several years she has had numerous episodes of transient cerebral ischemic attacks (TIAs) but refused any active investigation or intervention. She gave her signed "living will" to her physician and stressed that after what her husband and child went through, she does not want to be hospitalized. All her TIAs and other illnesses have been treated at home, but once a year she comes in for her annual physical. By respecting her wishes, a good working relationship has been established with her medical caretakers. She does her physician a favor and takes aspirin daily and occasionally, other medications.

Her primary social support system consists of her church, her friends, and secondarily, contact with her physician. She is a delightfully independent person whose memory for recent events is deteriorating, but with the help of friends she still manages her affairs competently. However, she is vulnerable to a possible stroke and arrangements have been made with her friends and the project manager to check on her daily. She has a telephone system that can activate others if she needs urgent help.

DISCUSSION OF FAMILY 2

Mrs. E.F. is an example of an elderly widow who, having lost her close family, now lives alone in a public housing project apartment. Approximately 60% of noninstitutionalized widowed elderly live alone (Table 39.1, column 3), despite stories of robberies, physical attacks, and difficulties associated with daily living arrangements. All of the elderly living alone (single, widowed, divorced) can be divided into two groups (19). The first is a group of elderly, either single (never married) or widowed for a long time, who have lived alone for years and manage their affairs quite competently. They keep in contact with family, neighbors, and friends and seem satisfied with their lifestyle. The other group is those who have been recently widowed, divorced, separated, or who recently changed their living arrangement. This group often has considerable problems in adjusting, at an elderly age, to a drastic change in lifestyle. However, like Mrs. E.F., most do reasonably well as long as their health holds out and they can manage their daily activities.

As do many elderly, Mrs. E.F. has a fear of becoming dependent on others or losing her independence and ability to decide her future. Her dread of this was increased by the experience she had with hospitals where, despite intensive care, she lost her husband and only child. These experiences led her to write her living will and to emphasize, on numerous occasions, that if she has a stroke or other incapacitating condition, she does not want to be hospitalized and should be brought home to die.

Theoretically Mrs. E.F., an 82-year-old widower, living alone, in a marginal financial situation, with a precarious health situation (repeated TIAs and poor hearing), no close family but some good friends, is at high risk for a number of severe conditions. However, her fierce independence, inner strength, and enthusiasm for life have kept her functioning well for over 8 years.

FAMILY 3

Mr. C.S.T. is a 65-year-old white widower who was married twice. His first wife (M.T.) died of carcinoma of the breast and his second wife (T.A.T.) divorced him after repeatedly suffering from physical abuse while he was drunk. He has three married children from his first wife (a daughter and two sons). The latter live in Iowa and Arkansas, respectively, while his daughter and her family live in a suburb in the Cleveland area.

Until 5 years ago he had worked as a mechanic for a boss who was very tolerant of his drinking habits.

However, when he turned 60, he was forced to retire with a small pension supplementing his Social Security. Within 1 year of retirement he developed non-insulin-dependent diabetes mellitus and had two small strokes that left no motor or sensory deficits but did deteriorate his memory, cognitive ability, and emotional stability to the extent that he could not independently perform the daily living tasks. His dementia probably was due to multiple small cerebral infarcts with an overlay of alcoholic (Korsakoff's) psychosis. It was obvious that he could not continue living on his own in an apartment.

At this stage the family physician encouraged the children to meet to decide on his future. As the sons refused to take him to their homes, it was decided that he would live with his daughter and her family, with the sons contributing financially to her, rather than trying to institutionalize him.

The daughter's family consists of her husband, a truck driver whose job takes him away from home two or three nights per week, and three children aged 16, 13, and 10.

The daughter's family was generally healthy and functioning reasonably well. When the youngest boy began school, the mother went back to work as a secretary-clerk in an insurance company. As this was a full-time position it meant that R. had a few hours after school that he spent with friends or neighbors or by himself at home before his sister or his mother came home. There were no extra bedrooms in the house so an alcove off the living room was converted into a bedroom for Mr. C.S.T. During the day they employed a home-help person to watch Mr. C.S.T. and after three rapid changes they found a person who was able to deal with him satisfactorily. However, at night he would often wander and cause a commotion so the night shift became the responsibility of Mrs. K.L. with some help from daughter K.

Despite the promises of Mrs. K.L.'s brothers, they sent very little financial aid. This monetary burden further complicated the difficult adjustment of the family, with each member exhibiting the effects of the stressful

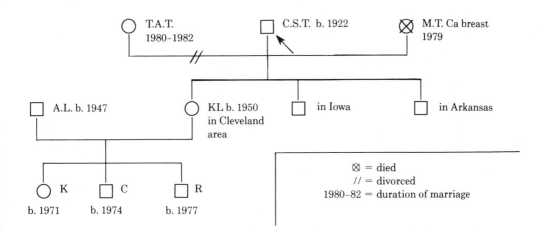

⊗ = died
// = divorced
1980–82 = duration of marriage

situation in a different way. Mr. A.L. stayed away from home more often and when at home lost his temper with his sons frequently, especially R. When he was seen for a checkup, his blood pressure had risen to the 160/100 range. Mrs. K.L. was chronically tired (understandably so) and developed epigastric discomfort that was relieved by eating. The children's schoolwork and grades deteriorated and the teachers at R.'s schools complained of his inattention during class and disruptive behavior. R. and C. had more sibling arguments/fights than before and K. began gaining weight and staying out at night much more often than her parents though appropriate. Despite utilizing the community resources, including respite care for 1 week, the stress and tension within the family increased.

Despite urgings by their physician that the family needed to find a better solution, nothing was done until Mr. C.S.T. accidentally knocked a kettle of boiling water over onto C.'s foot, necessitating hospitalization for second and third degree burns. This incident precipitated Mr. A.L.'s demand that Mr. C.S.T. be removed from the home. With the help from a social welfare agency, Mrs. K.L. agreed that her father be admitted to an institution. This relieved a great deal of stress in the family, but Mrs. K.L. did develop melena from a duodenal ulcer and the scapegoating of R. continued until some sessions with a family therapist alleviated the problem.

DISCUSSION OF FAMILY 3

The key to this family's situation was the father's chronic alcoholism, which led to physical and verbal abuse of the rest of the family as well as their economic instability. When the time came to help the disabled and dependent father, the sons who had suffered greatly from his alcoholic outbursts were not prepared to get actively involved in his care. Like many alcoholic families, the father's problem robbed his children of the capacity to be intimate (16). This carried over to their lack of close feelings for him even when he was old and disabled. The sons promised to help financially but in reality did very little so that the complete burden fell on the eldest daughter and her family. As a teenager she had helped the family a great deal by looking after her mother when she was ill with carcinoma of the breast and later trying to act as peace keeper between her father and his second wife. To escape all of this, however, she married while still in her teens and went to live with her husband. When it came to deciding who should take care of the disabled father, she reverted to her childhood role and "agreed" to take her father into her home, on condition that they would have a home helper during the day. It was difficult to find the appropriate helper at first but, as is common, eventually the right match was found. De-

spite the home helper and the appropriate use of various community resources like respite care, the presence of the demented father played havoc with the family's functioning and health.

Although one might imagine that families who have to take care of a frail elderly would work out a system whereby the duties and burdens would be fairly distributed between them, it turns out invariably that *one person is chosen to be the primary caregiver.* This primary caregiver, usually a spouse but often a daughter or daughter-in-law, takes the brunt of responsibility and the actual caregiving. If the support for the primary person is appropriate and adequate and that person is self-sufficient, then the caregiving is usually good and the person copes with the burdens. On the other hand, if these "supports" are inadequate or missing, the primary caregiver becomes the "hidden patient" and overtly or covertly develops symptoms and/or signs of a health breakdown (13). This manifests itself in various forms. In this family example, Mrs. K.L. exhibited chronic fatigue and developed epigastric symptoms that later were shown to be due to a duodenal ulcer. These were new conditions but often the caretaker who has chronic illnesses will find them aggravated or reactivated.

In this family another aspect of the hidden patient concept is seen. This is where not only the primary caretaker is affected, but the inability to deal with the stress is carried over to the entire family. Each member of the K.L. family was affected and the system as a whole began to malfunction so that in this instance the hidden patient was the entire family system. The dysfunctional family created a scapegoat in R., the youngest son, who was blamed for many disturbances or on whom the other members took out their frustrations. It is obvious that to deal with R.'s behavioral problems, the family system had to be dealt with, rather than with R. only.

It was interesting that the efforts of the family physician to help the family make changes were unsuccessful until the accidental burning of C. by his grandfather. This incident precipitated action by the family, resulting in institutional placement of the grandfather and helping the family accept family therapy on a formal basis. Another interesting medical point is the fact that it was only when Mr. C.S.T. was removed from the house, thereby relieving the acute stress, that Mrs. K.L. bled from her ulcer. This is a fairly common component of an acute breakdown, e.g., bleeding ulcer, myocardial infarction, etc., in a person after the acute, stressful period has been relieved. In essence it is a "poststress breakdown."

FAMILY 4

Mrs. G.H., a small, thin 74-year-old white widow, has a history of tuberculosis, hypertension, and asthma. She had lived by herself in a small house in Pittsburgh since her second husband's death years ago. She has three adult married children, two from her first husband and one from her second. All of her children and their families live some distance from Pittsburgh. Two years ago she had a hemiplegia and 2 months later fell and fractured the neck of her femur on her "good side." The fracture was pinned but left her as a dependent, homebound, frail woman whose mental status was normal. At this stage the children got together with their mother and after she adamantly refused to be placed in a nursing home, the children agreed that she would live with the youngest daughter (J.L.).

J.L. was 12 years younger than her stepsister, had been her father's favorite child, and had always been the child chosen to do things for her parents so the decision to let her be the caretaker was in line with the family tradition and accepted roles. After college graduation J.L. had married an accountant and moved to a Cleveland suburb. They have three sons aged 10, 8, and 4. Mrs. J.L. had not worked outside the home since her first son was born.

Mrs. G.H. proved to be a very demanding patient, parent, and grandparent so the routine of the household was quickly modified to fit in with her daily schedule. The almost continuous attention demanded by her was very trying for the rest of the family and particularly for J.L., who within a 6-month period was seen for tension headaches, nonspecific vaginitis, three episodes of low back pain, tiredness, and three episodes of depression. By contrast, in the 6 months prior to Mrs. G.H.'s arrival in the home, Mrs. J.L. had been seen once for a breast and pap checkup. The husband, aged 40, came for a visit complaining of irritability, being short-tempered with the children, and drinking more than usual, i.e., every evening after work. The 8-year-old son was brought into the practice by his mother because he had become very aggressive toward his siblings and his teacher told her he was a "disturbing influence" in class. Mrs. J.L. added that he seemed to be the cause of every argument in the home while his siblings (ages 10 and 4) were wonderful. They were quieter than usual, watched TV a great deal, played by themselves, and generally did not "trouble grandmother or us." The only other thing the mother had noticed was that the 4-year-old who had been toilet trained for almost a year now was wetting his bed once or twice per week and this upset her.

At that stage the family physician, during a home visit to Mrs. G.H., took the opportunity of discussing the family situation with her and Mrs. J.L. This led to no change and the status quo continued until 4 months later when the husband was involved in a minor car accident resulting in him being booked for driving under the influence and having his license suspended for 3 months. He subsequently signed up for an alcoholic rehabilitation program. The family physician then organized a family conference of all of the adults, including the siblings H.H. and I.K., to discuss Mrs. G.H.'s future. A heated argument ensued between Mr. J.L. and his wife's siblings. The latter refused to share the burden of their mother by taking her into their homes and also did not want her placed in a nursing home. At that point Mrs. G.H. broke up the meeting by complaining of chest pain and severe headache, both of which cleared up soon after H.H. and I.K. had gone home! Mr. J.L. was furious and told Mrs. G.H. that she was a "manipulator" and that night he went to bed on bad terms with his mother-in-law, brother-in-law, and sister-in-law, plus upsetting his wife and the household.

Two weeks later the physician was called to the home because Mrs. G.H. had suffered a stroke; she was then hospitalized. Within a week her motor paralysis cleared but she remained incontinent of urine and occasionally of feces. This was the last straw and made Mrs. J.L. agree with her husband that Mrs. G.H. should be transferred straight into a nursing home, despite her protests. At the nursing home, she became very agitated and confused and despite the efforts of the geriatrician who had taken over her care as well as the staff, she had a further stroke (or series of strokes) and died on the fifth day there.

Mrs. J.L.'s siblings refused to participate in the funeral expenses as they blamed the J.L.s for precipitating their mother's death by transferring her to the nursing home. It took some months of joint counseling by their family physician and a social worker to help Mrs. J.L. cope with her guilty feelings and to restore their family relationships and functioning to their former level. Interestingly, the youngest, aged four, ceased his bed wetting, the 8-year-old son stopped being aggressive, and the 10-year-old son began acting out somewhat, all within a few weeks after their grandmother left the house.

DISCUSSION OF FAMILY 4

The family of Mrs. G.H. illustrates some interesting points:

1. Mrs. G.H. outlived two husbands and is an example of the lower mortality rate of women as compared to men. It is evident that the proportion of women among the 65 and over group is much higher than of men (8).

2. Mrs. G.H. was a controlling, dominating, and domineering person who was used to getting her own way.

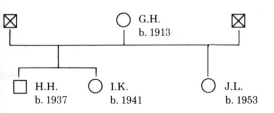

G.H.
b. 1913

H.H.
b. 1937

I.K.
b. 1941

J.L.
b. 1953

3. The choice of the primary caretaker was apparently a continuation of the traditional role in which Mrs. J.L. had always been placed as the youngest and favorite child. Apparently she had always accepted this role and accepted it yet again when her siblings and mother pressed her into it.
4. Despite her siblings pressuring her to accept the primary caregiver role, they did almost nothing to support Mrs. J.L. either materially or emotionally.
5. The support from Mrs. J.L.'s own nuclear family was forthcoming but Mrs. G.H.'s domineering and demanding personality wrecked havoc with their usual functioning. The J.L. family became considerably dysfunctional, producing health changes and increased physician contacts in each member, as well as a scapegoat. The latter phenomenon allowed the rest of the family an opportunity to maintain a type of dysfunctional homeostasis at the expense of the 8-year-old son. While the middle son became the scapegoat, the older son became quieter and more compliant, and the youngest became quieter and developed secondary enuresis. After Mrs. G.H. left the home, there was a reversal in the behavior of the children. The eldest quiet son began to act out, the scapegoat middle son settled down, and the youngest stopped wetting his bed at night.
6. During the important family conference (4) in which it looked as if some resolution of the siblings' relationships and dealings with their mother would be found, this dominating, disabled woman was still able to control them by feigning a heart attack. This prevented the family from making a decision that, in Mrs. G.H.'s mind, would have gone against her. The family meeting worsened the relationships between the siblings themselves and between them and Mr. J.L. In addition it left Mrs. G.H. both anxious and somewhat depressed, which may have contributed to her stroke. In other words, she won the battle but lost the war.
7. The decision to institutionalize an elderly person is frequently made more on the fact that the caregivers cannot continue rather than on the medical condition per se of the patient. One of the conditions that precipitates the decision that the caretaker cannot cope anymore is urinary and/or bowel incontinence, as it was in this case. In addition, two other factors that have been found to be important in influencing the decision process were very few visits by other family members and very little time for the caregivers to be by themselves. (14, 16, 18).
8. Despite the patient's own desires, she was transferred to a nursing home where she shared a room with a patient who was semicomatose and had to be turned at frequent intervals to prevent bedsores. This proved too much for Mrs. G.H., who became agitated and confused. She developed a series of strokes that led to her death within a few days of entering the hospital.
9. The guilt feelings of Mrs. J.L. were considerable and this was fueled by her siblings blaming her for their mother's death. In a way, H.H. and I.K. had never had really good feelings about their stepsister who was the favorite child and in some vicarious way took pleasure in blaming her for the death. This is an example of difficult, life-long relationships between siblings that were aggravated by their inability to cope with their dominating mother.

FAMILY 5

A cardiologist asked a family physician colleague to take over the health care of a 90-year-old man, Mr. W.M., who was in the hospital recovering from a myocardial infarction. His wife was 88 and they lived independently in an apartment. They had two children (male and female), both of whom were married and lived out of the state. Mr. W.M. had been an architect and had retired in the 1960s with a good pension for that period and some interest from stocks and bonds. Besides the recent heart attack, he had had a previous myocardial infarction 5 years earlier and a cerebral vascular accident 10 years prior to that, which had left him with a slight residual weakness of his right arm and leg, a slightly slurred speech, and some incontinence.

Mrs. W.M. had a total abdominal hysterectomy years earlier for reasons that are not clear and was still upset about it because she was not able to have more children. In addition she had mild osteoarthritis, borderline hypertension, and diminished vision and hearing. She was mentally alert and physically able to do everything in the home. She insisted on doing the housework, cooking, laundry, shopping, and looking after her husband. She was overprotective of her husband and insisted on doing everything herself yet complained that no one helped her! The W.M.s were very staunch Catholics and were devastated when their only son married out of their faith and adopted his wife's religion. They regarded this as a stab in the back and had very conflictual relationships with their son and his family.

They were a delightful couple. Her mental alertness and cooperation made the doctor-patient relationship a very satisfying and interesting experience.

DISCUSSION OF FAMILY 5

Transference has been defined as the shift of emotions from past relationships to the present doctor-patient relationship (11). The physician is imbued with characteristics, either positive or negative, and attitudes not necessarily possessed. In *counter-transference,* the physician's feelings toward persons in his/her past (such as parents) shift to the patient.

With the W.M. family, Mrs. W.M. had a very positive transference of feelings toward the physician and often made remarks like, "I wish my son would have been like you" or "I wish you would have been part of our family." In respect to the last statement, the physician inadvertently played into her feelings by replying that he felt as if he *was* part of the family!

The helplessness of Mr. W.M. and his apparent pending demise brought up many feelings (identification, empathy) in the physician in respect to his own aging—the tragedy of disability, helplessness and dependency in people who were previously active and alert; and the question of his own death. The doctor-patient relationship with the elderly can be very superficial or go to the extreme of an intense and over-involved nature. The physician has to find the appropriate balance between lack of attention and overinvolvement. If this balance can be achieved, the relationship with the elderly can be used as a very important therapeutic force (12).

Another important aspect shown by this family is the relationship between the physician, the patient, and the patient's family (5). Mrs. W.M. and her children would disagree about some aspect of her behavior or something to do with their dependent father/husband. This frequently led to long distance calls from the children to the physician, trying to get him on their side of the issue, or Mrs. W.M. would tell him about the conflict and try to get him on her side. Often the physician had to take sides when therapeutic decisions had to be made regarding active treatment of the husband and/or wife. Bowen described *triangulation* as the process whereby two family members in conflict try to ease the strain by involving a third party in the conflict (1).

During the years when the W.M.s were under the care of the family physician, he frequently found himself in this triangulated situation, which only improved when he had the opportunity of discussing it openly with Mrs. W.M. and the son and daughter when they both came to visit their parents. The children understood and the relationships improved considerably although Mrs. W.M. was not totally convinced. The physician's positive relationship with Mr. and Mrs. W.M. continued.

Another form of triangulation occurred when Mr. W.M. developed hematuria, which cleared in 2 days. The consultant urologist wanted to investigate the condition completely although the family was divided. Some members wanted him to go ahead and some did not want any active intervention. It took some skill on the family physician's part to maintain relationships with all concerned and see that the patient received the minimum of necessary investigations.

CONCLUSION

The rapid technological advances in the biomedical and bioengineering fields during the past few decades have been remarkable. These changes have affected every aspect of living, but as human adjustment never keeps pace with the technological changes, we are witness to a human society trying to adjust.

In the case of the elderly, they are living longer but their working span has not increased so the net result is an increased postwork or postretirement period. Whereas this postwork stage was once accorded great respect because of the wisdom the elderly had gained from their work experience, they are no longer given this respect. The changes have been so rapid that much of the old person's knowledge is outdated, not really needed, and not given much respect. The old person thus feels unwanted. Added to this is the fact that longer life means more chronic illness, more disability, and more of that dreaded period—dependency.

The families, which now contain fewer children, frequently have the burden of caring for their elderly parents or grandparents without sufficient resources available from the community. This sounds like a bleak picture but luckily elderly people and families have a great deal of inner strength. The vast majority of older people still keep themselves involved, receive good support from their families and friends, and remain independent.

With this background the author, in this chapter, has attempted through a series of family studies to illustrate the common problems faced by the elderly, their families, and physicians at this period in time.

REFERENCES

1. Bowen M: *Family Therapy in Clinical Practice.* New York, Jason Aronson, 1978.
2. Brody EM: Parent care as a normative family stress. *Gerontologist* 25:19, 1985.
3. Bruhn JG: Effects of chronic illness on the family. *J Fam Prac* 4:1057, 1977.
4. Clark NM, Rakowski W: Family caregivers of older adults: Improving helping skills. *Gerontologist* 3:637, 1983.
5. Doherty WJ, Baird MA: *Family Therapy and Family Medicine.* New York, Guilford Press, 1983, p. 26.
6. Duvall EM: *Marriage and Family Development,* ed 5. New York, Lippincott, 1977, pp. 385-406.
7. Erikson EH, Erikson JM, Kivnick HQ: *Vital Involvement in Old Age.* New York, WW Norton, 1986, pp. 54-56.
8. Ford AB: The aged and their physicians. In Calkins E, Davis PJ, Ford AB (Eds): *The Practice of Geriatrics.* Philadelphia, WB Saunders, 1986, pp. 7-13.
9. Fruge E, Niederehe G: Family dimensions of health care for the aged. In Henao S, Grose NP (Eds): *Principles of Family Systems in Family Medicine.* New York, Brunner/Mazel, 1985, pp. 165-192.
10. Hagestad G: The family. In Maddox GL (Ed): *Encyclopedia of Aging.* New York, Springer, 1987, pp. 247-249.

11. Kvale JN, Dayringer R: The transference phenomenon in the care of the elderly patient. *Fam Med* 19:141, 1987.

12. McDonald DE, Christie-Seely J: Working with the elderly and their families. In Christie-Seely J (Ed): *Working With the Family in Primary Care.* New York, Praeger, 1984, pp. 505–522.

13. Medalie JH: An approach to common problems in the elderly. In Calkins E, Davis PJ, Ford AB (Eds): *The Practice of Geriatrics.* Philadelphia, WB Saunders, 1986, pp. 47–59.

14. O'Quin JA, McGraw K: The burdened caregiver: an overview. In O'Quin JA, McGraw K (Eds): *Senile Dementia of the Alzheimer Type.* New York, Alan Liss Inc., 1985, pp. 65–75.

15. Osterweis M, Solomon F, Green M (Eds): *Bereavement.* Washington, Institute of Medicine, National Academy Press, 1984.

16. Tonti M: Working with the family. In Silverstone B, Burack-Weiss A (Eds): *Social Work Practice With the Frail Elderly and Their Families.* Springfield IL, Charles C Thomas, 1983.

17. Walsh F: The family in later life. In Carter EA, McGoldrick M (Eds): *The Family Life Cycle.* New York, Gardner Press, 1980, pp. 197–220.

18. Zarit SH, Reeves KE, Peterson JB: Relatives of the impaired elderly: correlates of the feelings of burden. *Gerontologist* 20:649, 1980.

19. Zyzanski S, Medalie JH, Ford AB, et al: Living arrangements and well-being in the elderly. *Family Med* (in press) 1988.

CHAPTER 40

Characteristics of the Elderly Population

DAVID L. RABIN

The major factor encouraging development of geriatrics is growth of the elderly population. Continued growth in the numbers of elderly will affect profoundly medical practice. The small proportion of the population that is now elderly (12%) are already responsible for nearly one-third of all health care expenditures. As the proportion of elderly increases, the demands for clinical services from this portion of the population will affect greatly the daily activity of primary care physicians and the concerns of the payors of health care. Much understanding of the elderly has accumulated through individual clinical experience with an aging practice population. However, it is difficult to understand the characteristics of all elderly from personal clinical experience. The number of elderly in recent years has become sufficiently large that they are able to be characterized in surveys of the nation's population and from health service data. Previously, such information was only available from local surveys that cannot reflect national needs of the elderly or permit serial studies to understand emerging needs of the elderly. Analysis of these data has shown that many elderly have complex health and social needs and that these needs are related to demographic characteristics of the elderly.

This chapter will focus on national data, on demographic, socioeconomic, health, and functional characteristics of the aged population. It also will focus on those aged most in need and the types of services they consume. Future growth of the aged population and the implications this growth may have for future health services demand will be discussed.

GROWTH IN THE SIZE OF THE ELDERLY POPULATION

Growth in the size and proportion of the elderly population has occurred continuously in this century. As shown in Table 40.1, the elderly represented 4% of the population in 1900 when they were 3 million in number. In 1980 there were 25.5 million elderly representing 11.3% of the population. Between 1950 and 1980 alone, those people 65 years and older more than doubled in number. Whereas the population as a whole has increased 200% since 1900, the proportion of the population who are elderly has grown at a rate 3½ times greater. The increase in the aged population is projected to proceed slowly, then in the 21st century, explosively, as the post-World War II baby boom ages. The proportion of the population 65 years and older may increase from 13.0% in the year 2000 to 17.37% in 2020 and 21.77% in 2040. Although the elderly will usually constitute less than one-fifth of the population, their needs loom large among the responsibilities of health care providers because of their predisposition to illness and high rates of terminal illness. Among the elderly, rates of growth have not been the same for all age groups. Thus, the "young" elderly, those 65-74 years of age, have slightly more than doubled as a proportion of the population since 1900 while those 75-84 years old, the "old" elderly have increased 3½-fold. Those 85 years and older, the old old, have increased at a fivefold rate. It is the old and the old old, together currently constituting 40% of the elderly, who have created the unexpected demand for long-term care (LTC) services. Previously, LTC had been an important but insignificant aspect of service.

Table 40.1
Actual and Projected Growth of the Older Population, 1900–2050[a]

Year	Total population all ages	55–64 Years		65–74 Years		75–84 Years		85 Years and Over		65 Years and Over	
		Number	Percent	Number	Percent	Number	Percent	Number	Percent	Number	Percent
1900	76,303	4,009	5.3	2,189	2.9	772	1.0	123	0.2	3,084	4.0
1910	91,972	5,054	5.5	2,793	3.0	989	1.1	167	0.2	3,950	4.3
1920	105,711	6,532	6.2	3,464	3.3	1,259	1.2	210	0.2	4,933	4.7
1930	122,775	8,397	6.8	4,721	3.8	1,641	1.3	272	0.2	6,634	5.4
1940	131,669	10,572	8.0	6,375	4.8	2,278	1.7	365	0.3	9,019	6.8
1950	150,967	13,295	8.8	8,415	5.6	3,278	2.2	577	0.4	12,270	8.1
1960	179,323	15,572	8.7	10,997	6.1	4,633	2.6	929	0.5	16,560	9.2
1970	203,302	18,608	9.2	12,447	6.1	6,124	3.0	1,409	0.7	19,980	9.8
1980	226,505	21,700	9.6	15,578	6.9	7,727	3.4	2,240	1.0	25,544	11.3
1990	249,657	21,051	8.4	18,035	7.2	10,349	4.1	3,313	1.3	31,697	12.7
2000	267,955	23,767	8.9	17,677	6.6	12,318	4.6	4,926	1.8	34,921	13.0
2010	283,238	34,848	12.3	20,318	7.2	12,326	4.4	6,551	2.3	39,195	13.8
2020	296,597	40,298	13.6	29,855	10.1	14,486	4.9	7,081	2.4	51,422	17.3
2030	304,807	34,025	11.2	34,535	11.3	21,434	7.0	8,612	2.8	64,581	21.2
2040	308,559	34,717	11.3	29,272	9.5	24,882	8.1	12,834	4.2	66,988	21.7
2050	309,488	37,327	12.1	30,114	9.7	21,263	6.9	16,034	5.2	67,411	21.8

[a]From: 1900–1980 U.S. Bureau of the Census, Decennial Censuses of Population. 1990–2050: U.S. Bureau of the Census, Projections of the Population of the United States, by Age, Sex, and Race. 1983 to 2080 Current Population Reports, Series P-25, No. 952, May 1984. Projections are middle series. Numbers are in thousands.

Throughout life, subgroups in the population experience different death rates. This leads to marked differences in the characteristics of the elderly population as compared to the population born. Male rates, of death from birth, are higher than female so that by age 65 years, 61% of the elderly population is female. Death rates of women continue to be lower beyond age 65 years. By age 85 years, there are only 40 men for every 100 women. Life expectancy remaining at age 65 years is, thus, far greater for women, 18.3 years as compared to 14.0 years for men. Because of the longer survivability of women, the problem of aging increasingly is becoming a women's problem. An understanding of older women's social, economic, and health characteristics is of increasing importance in considering the service needs of the elderly.

Death rates for nonwhites also are consistently higher from birth than for whites until age 65 years. Beyond age 65 years, however, differences in survival are not as great; there is even a suggestion that black death rates are lower than for whites beyond age 75 years. At age 65 years, black life expectancy is 15.4 years as compared to 16.9 years for whites. Blacks differ markedly from whites in socioeconomic characteristics, with a high proportion of black elderly in poverty. Ironically, because of poverty, their financial access to health care could be better than others because of the availability of more comprehensive payment for health care through a combination of Medicare and Medicaid eligibility.

Currently, the elderly are not equally distributed geographically with the proportion of the population who are elderly being greatest in Florida (17%) and the Northern and Central Plains states where the elderly constitute more than 13% of the population. This contrasts with the Rocky Mountain states where the elderly constitute less than 9% of the population.

HEALTH CHARACTERISTICS OF THE ELDERLY

The characteristics of the old and the frail elderly vary from those who are younger. The major reason for the recent rapid growth in the aged population has been decreases in adult death rates. Decreases in death rates of elderly adults have exceeded decreases in death rates of those younger and are responsible for the increase in the numbers of the elderly. From 1940–1980, age-adjusted death rates for the elderly decreased by 38%. The rate of decrease for the female population (48%) has been far greater than for males (26%) contributing to the increasing proportion of women with increasing age. The progressive decrease in death rates across the entire population, including children, and the marked decrease in death rates among the elderly has led to the concept of rectangularization of the survival curve as illustrated in Figure 40.1. Comparing the curve for those born in 1920, now over 65 years old, with earlier curves illustrates the effect of this phenomenon on those now becoming aged. In the 19th century, infant and child mortality rates were so high that many of those born never survived childhood. With the development of public health measures assuring a clean food and water supply, increasing agricultural production and personal income, a more adequate diet became available. Infant mortality rates dropped sharply so that by 1920, nearly all children reached adulthood. The increase in medical knowledge and in the availability of medical care for the population has more recently been associated with longer survival of the adult population, likely contributing to falling death rates among the elderly. With lower death rates across all age groups, the likelihood that a child will live to a theoretical maximum age of 100 years has increased pushing the survival curve far to the right. Of those born today, 77% are expected to live to age 65 years and 28% to age 85 years. From a medical perspective, the progressive survivability to old age of most of the population assures an increasing demand for medical care.

Of greater importance than mere survivability is the health status of the aged. Currently, the aged have multiple chronic diseases and associated impairments. If in the future, those surviving to old age will have fewer chronic diseases, the elderly will be able to maintain themselves better independently, requiring less health and social care. The evidence that this might be so is uncertain. Current indica- tions show that most people achieving age 65 years have substantial morbidity. The presence of this morbidity and the associated impairment determines the service and care needs of the population, particularly the need for LTC. LTC is needed for those so impaired that they are no longer able to care for themselves and require personal care and health services provided at home to maintain independence. Those most impaired require sheltered housing, domiciliary care, or nursing home care. It is hoped that effective health promotion for the younger adult population will move both the survivability curve and the chronic disease-free period further and further to the right. This concept of progressive changes in age-associated onset of chronic disease with associated delay in impairment and brief periods of impairment before death gives rise to the possibility of a dynamic interplay among factors determining the health status of the elderly as pointed out by Soldo and Manton. Future demand for health services will be determined by the age at which the elderly population becomes chronically ill and subsequently, as the result of chronic illness, becomes impaired. If the time between disease onset, impairment, and death is compressed, health professionals in the future will experience different, more acute, but perhaps more intense care problems in older patients than the vexing, LTC problems of today.

CAUSES OF DEATH

The causes of death in the elderly reflect those in the adult population but at a somewhat different proportion. In 1980, the leading cause of death for all elderly was heart disease. When combined with cerebral vascular disease, the third leading cause of death, vascular disease accounts for over 55% of deaths for the elderly.

The second leading cause of death for the elderly is cancer, which accounts for a proportionately smaller amount of death among the elderly than among young adults. Chronic obstructive pulmonary disease is the fourth leading cause of death, while pneumonia and influenza are the cause of more than 5% of deaths for those 85 years and older. Great progress has been made in early detection and therapy has been improved for hypertension, the major cause of cerebral vascular disease, and in the reduction of cardiovascular disease risk factors. For adults, there is a reduction in vascular disease deaths and probably a delay in the onset of chronic vascular disease. Thus, it seems likely that there will be a continued decrease in the age-specific death rates among elderly adults with more deaths occur-

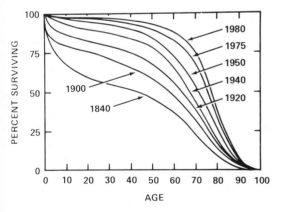

Figure 40.1. The increasingly rectangular survival curve. From the United States Bureau of Health Statistics. In Fries VF, Crapo M: *Vitality and Aging.* New York, W.H. Freeman and Co., 1981.

ring at later ages. Progress in prevention of cancer has not been as apparent although the most common causes of cancer deaths in the elderly, lung, colon, and breast cancer, all have well-defined risk factors so there is a possibility that onset could be prevented or delayed. Breast, colon, and prostate cancer, the most common cancer in older males, all can be detected early. There is suggestive evidence that early detection is associated with longer survivability. The decrease in smoking among the adult population implies that there might be a decrease in the occurrence of ischemic heart disease, lung cancer, and chronic pulmonary disease among the elderly. Possible delayed or decreased deaths from these common causes of death in the elderly raise the possibility of an even larger elderly population than expected, as current estimates are based upon past experience.

MORBIDITY

There is a difference between the causes of death and the causes of chronic illness in the elderly population. Although heart disease is the leading cause of death, rates of chronic conditions per 1000 for the elderly show that hypertensive disease (379/1000 persons 65 years and older), arthritis (465/1000), and hearing impairments (284/1000) are more prevalent than heart conditions (277/1000). Other conditions, the rates of which are at or near 100 conditions per 1000 older persons, are arteriosclerosis, orthopaedic impairments, visual impairments, and chronic sinusitis. The impact of these conditions on health service also varies from disease mortality and prevalence rates. The most significant condition affecting health care use is heart disease, which accounts for 14% of doctor visits and 21% of both hospital days and of bed days at home for the elderly. The next most significant condition is cancer, which is responsible for 7% of doctor visits and 15% of bed days. Stroke is also responsible for many hospital and bed days. These diseases, which are the major causes of death, are responsible for much health service use and costs, in part, because of the high consumption of services in the terminal phase of disease. Even if these major causes of death are delayed in onset in the elderly, they are still likely to account for a high proportion of health services needed by the elderly.

Of great significance to the elderly is their ability to function despite physical limitations. Physical limitations often come about not because of a single disease but because of the occurrence of multiple diseases in a single person, the cumulative burden of

which leads to a decrease in their ability to carry on major activities, such as walking, toileting, feeding, bathing, and dressing, or minor activities such as grooming, telephoning, managing money, shopping, doing light housework, preparing meals, and taking medication. The major activities are referred to as activities of daily living (ADL) and the minor daily activities are characterized as instrumental activities of daily living (IADL). The relationship between performance of these duties and the availability of someone in the home to assist in their being done determines the ability of the elderly population to remain independent. Although 12% of all persons 65 years and older have some ADL or IADL limitations that require the help of someone else, the rates of limitations, and the occurrence of multiple limitations per person rises rapidly with age. Thus 7% of those 65–74 years, 16% of those 75–84 years, and 44% of those 85 years and older living in the community have such limitations. Although both IADL and ADL limitations increase with age, the rate of increase is greatest for major activity limitations with 17% of those 85 years and older being mildly disabled and 10% being severely disabled. These figures are for those persons still living in the community. Those most severely disabled are removed from the community to reside in nursing homes. For those 85 years and older, over 20% are in nursing homes. There are indications that there are as many people living in the community who are as disabled as those living in nursing homes. The disabilities most likely to cause nursing home admissions are incontinence and dementia, yet many persons mildly demented or incontinent reside in the community with voluntary or paid assistance. Others, bedridden and unable to get about or to eat or dress, are maintained at home with the assistance of family and personal care providers.

In past years, many persons needing personal rather than nursing care were placed into nursing homes. This is less true now as state and federal policies are making access to both skilled and intermediate nursing home care more difficult while providing home-based alternatives. This is reflected in the slowed growth of nursing home beds and likely in reductions in the rate of turnover of nursing home beds so that the average time of residence of the older person in the nursing home is increased.

As the older population grows in size and nursing home availability is reduced, more people with substantial impairment will reside in the community. The 1982 Long-Term Care Survey indicated that there were 3.2 million elderly who needed aid with the ADL. Only 1.9 million of these people thought that they had all the help that they needed to assist them with these activities. A majority of this help (71%) was provided by relatives, usually daughters or spouses. Another 21% of persons received a combination of unpaid and paid care with several percent relying exclusively on paid care. The large number of people who need care, either unmet or met by others, indicates that there is much unmet care, the extent of which is likely to rise with time as more people reside in the community rather than in nursing homes. Because families are more dispersed, smaller in size, and have a higher proportion of members in the work force, the availability of family caregivers is limited and the availability of home health and home (personal) care is also being constrained. In the 1982 survey, before many of the effects of current restrictive policies were evident, 1.1 million people indicated that they needed additional assistance; nearly 170,000 lacked regular help with activities.

Throughout life, women tend to report more illness than men. The same continues through old age regarding activity limitations. Both for the total population and in each subgroup above the age of 65 years, women report more limitations. The differences are slighter for IADL and more marked for the more substantial impairments associated with ADL restrictions. In all, 21% of women and 16% of men 65 years and older report some degree of dependency. Another form of responding to illness or impairments is to restrict activities or to take to bed. These indicators, too, show progression with age. Those 65–74 years old report restricted activity days per person per year only 10% higher than that of the preretirement population. However, persons 75 years and older report a rate of 48 such days a year. Bed disability days per person per year are an indication of severe disability. Those 65 years and older have 14 such days whereas those 75 years and older have 18 bed days per year. Whereas advancing age is associated with increasing disability, chronic diseases, and impairments, the incidence of acute conditions falls with age. Interestingly, this too is progressive with those older having fewer acute conditions than younger adults. For those 65 years and older, the rate is 107/100 persons per year.

MENTAL HEALTH

An increasing problem for the elderly is psychiatric morbidity, particularly senile dementia. Whereas the prevalence of other psychiatric disorders decrease with age, severe cognitive impairment increases. Of those in the community, severe cognitive impairment is the most common psychiatric disorder among elderly men, followed by phobia and alcohol dependence. For older women, phobia is the most common disorder followed by severe cognitive impairment. Community surveys have indicated that Senile Dementia of the Alzheimer's Type (SDAT) is prevalent among the elderly. As many as 20% of those 65 years and older suffer from mild cognitive disability with 4% having a severe form of senile dementia. As the occurrence of senile dementia increases with age, it is predicted that 20% of those over the age of 80 years and 30% of those 85 years and older will be senile. Care of cognitive disorders is difficult in the community because of the continuous care necessary. When a continual caregiver, such as a spouse is no longer vigorous, senility may lead to institutionalization. National Nursing Home survey data indicate that prevalence rates of senility in nursing home residents by age range from 18–40% of males and 24–43% of females, and are increasing. A serious, mental health problem in the elderly is suicide, which is higher in the elderly than in other age groups, being highest in incidence for those 75–84 years old at a rate of 22/100,000 persons.

MORTALITY

The single factor most responsible for the increase in the aged population has been the unexpected and persistent decrease in death rates for the elderly population. As an example, for the largest old population group, those ages 65–74 years, the cumulative decrease in death rates between 1950 and 1983 has been 31%, resulting from progressive decreases in death rates in the decades since 1950 of 4.5, 6, and 16.4%, respectively. The death rates per 100,000 persons are much greater as age increases. In 1983, annual death rates ranged from about 3% for those 65–74 years old to 15.4% for those 85 years and older. Over time, mortality differences between men and women over 65 years have increased. At present, the ratio of deaths for those over 65 years is 1.7:1.0 (males to females), with a progressive decrease in the ratio because of the increasing numbers of females at each age from the young old to the old old. In the future, differences in mortality rates by sex are expected to narrow but substantial difference in life expectancy between men and women should persist. The common causes of mortality are more similar in men and women as they age. Delay in occurrence of cardiovascular deaths may have a bigger impact on death rates for men 65–74 years old than for women, as ischemic heart disease is more common among men than women at that age. Were a delay in cardiovascular deaths to occur, both the cause and age-specific death rates of younger old men and women would become more similar.

SOCIOECONOMIC FACTORS

A major problem for the elderly is living with a fixed and generally decreasing income. Those most elderly at present reflect a generation born at the turn of the century when the United States was still a small, dynamic rural society with many immigrants. Associated with those conditions were lower levels of education, larger numbers of foreign-born individuals, and a childhood of poverty and inadequate nutrition for many. It is this same population as adults who first paid into Social Security during their working years. Social Security subsequently became the basis for their economic security at retirement. In 1965, when those born in 1900 retired, Medicare and Medicaid were introduced. These programs were initiated at that time because the income of the elderly, combined with the rapidly increasing cost of medical care, was insufficient when chronic illness occurred, for many elderly on fixed incomes to purchase necessary medical care. When Medicare was enacted, 15% of the income of the elderly was spent on health care. Subsequent to passage of Medicare and Medicaid, this proportion dropped as government expenditures for health care increased, paying 67% of the health care costs of the elderly by the year 1984. After decreasing for a number of years, the proportion of the income of the elderly used for out-of-pocket health care expenditures has now risen to represent the same proportion reported before the passage of Medicare, despite the increase in public expenditures for health care for the elderly.

The income of the elderly decreases with increasing age with as little as $6,170 per aged unit (an aged person or couple) 80 years and older. This income contrasts with the median income of an aged unit 65–67 years old $12,380, where medical expenses are likely to be less. There remains a moderate amount of poverty among the elderly: 15% among all elderly, with a higher percentage among elderly women (18%), and even higher rates among elderly blacks (42%). With such income levels, it is easy to understand why such a high proportion of elderly once institutionalized or having a continuing need for personal care become impoverished and eligible for Medicaid. The cost of personal care provided at home can exceed $35,000 annually and, in many areas, nursing home care exceeds $30,000 per year.

Inasmuch as few elderly have LTC insurance, the burden of these costs must be borne out of pocket. Because current income can not sustain this level of expenditure, the reserves of the elderly are quickly consumed, leading to medical indigency. In 1982, Social Security was still responsible for 40% of the income of aged units 65 years and older, a percentage of their total income that has continued to fall only slowly despite the increased availability of pensions and other assets among the elderly. A factor affecting income and the financial ability to care for oneself independently is marital status. More than one-half of persons 65 years and older are married but the ratios are quite different for men and women. By age 75 years, 70% of women are widowed in contrast to the 70% of men 75 years and older who are married. The proportion of elderly living alone has increased over time. In 1950, 14% of persons 65 years and older lived alone but, by 1980, this had increased to 30%. Most of the elderly living alone are women. As a result, their independence is threatened by the onset of an illness causing impairment. The proportion of elderly living in multigenerational households with children or other relatives has also decreased in the recent past, although the proportion increases with advancing age, particularly for women. For women 75 years and older, 24% live with children or relatives. Although most elderly people live alone or with a spouse, there is substantial contact with members of the family as 80% of older people have one or more surviving children. According to a national survey, 75% of these elderly had seen one or more of their children within a week before interview. In addition to children, neighbors and relatives are important in providing support for the elderly. In the 2 days before interview in another national survey, 44% of the elderly indicated that they had been to the home of a relative or friend within the last 2 days.

FUTURE PROJECTIONS

Although it is difficult to be certain of future population trends, there may be more predictability among the aged than among other groups. Whereas death rates have fallen unexpectedly in the past and are likely to change in the future at a rate other than that predicted, major catastrophic events such as war or the effect of new diseases, such as HIV infection, will affect the elderly less than those younger. Because of the growing size and economic significance of the elderly population, many projections have been made of its likely future size. According to the Bureau of the Census (6), the median age of the

United States population will increase from age 31 in 1984 to a projected median by the year 2030 of 41 years. The largest expected proportion of aged in the population will be 22% in the year 2050. By the year 2030, when currently graduating medical students will be retiring, 21.2% of the population is expected to be over 65 years (Table 40.1). By the year 2030, 64 million people will be 65 years and older in contrast to 25.5 million aged in the 1980 census. The most meaningful aspect of the projected population increases for health care is the expected disproportionate increase in the number of persons 75–84 and 85 years and older. The proportionate increase in the population 75 years and older relative to all aged will increase steadily to the year 2040 and, for those 85 years and older until 2050, based on the aging cohort of those already born. Associated with the aging of the elderly population is a decrease in the proportion of the working population to the elderly. Currently, the ratio is 19 elderly persons per 100 working-age persons. This ratio is predicted to increase steadily to 38:100 by the year 2050. Given the high health care expenditures of the elderly, this changing ratio suggests that there will be an increasing burden on the working population to support the cost of health care services for those older and retired. This expectation alone indicates there will be continual pressure from society on health care providers to contain costs, a burden already being felt. At the same time, the increasing numbers of the elderly, their political strength, and their increasing income suggest that there will be a demand for more coverage for care, particularly LTC. If LTC insurance becomes available, the demand for both personal and health care services will increase as more of the need is met. Coordinating social and health care, which is already a problem, will become more complex but of increasing importance in order to reduce costs and provide better care.

With these uncertainties in service provision for the elderly, an even greater problem is projecting health service use based on current experience and projected growth in the elderly population. Nevertheless, combining current trends in the growth of the elderly population with current growth trends in health services use by the elderly provides a sense of the future magnitude of service demand by the elderly. Projections by the National Center for Health Statistics indicate that there will be an increase in the proportion of all physician visits made by persons over 65 years (15% in 1980) to 27% of all visits made in the the year 2040. The effect on hospital and nursing homes, however, is even more substantial. By the year 2040, 40% of all hospital days will be for those 75 years and older, twice the proportion in 1980. The greatest impact, however, will be on nursing homes. Nursing home beds, totaling 1.5 million in 1980, 80% of which are filled by those 65 years and older, will increase to 5.2 million beds by the year 2040, at which time those 75 years and older will comprise 87% of nursing home residents. These estimates are based on past patterns of service and do not reflect the recent incentives for community, as compared to institutional LTC. If more substantially impaired elderly are cared for in the community, nursing home use may not increase as much. There would be an increase in the demand for home health care and home care services, neither of which have been estimated for the future. In any case, the increased numbers of the elderly will have a profound effect on medical practice, making institutional care predominantly a service for the elderly. In the process of meeting the needs of the elderly, practice organizational forms and procedures will change, affecting the way in which health care is provided to all patients, regardless of age.

SUMMARY

The elderly constitute a large and growing proportion of the United States population. Because of their numbers, the presence of multiple chronic illnesses, and associated impairments, the elderly account for a disproportionately large portion of all health care costs and services. Mortality, morbidity, and disability rates of the elderly were reviewed and discussed regarding their possible implications. The particular social, racial, and economic characteristics associated with age were presented. The increasing demand for long-term health care is of particular significance for women, who consume most of these services, whether provided at home, in the community, or in institutions. Projections for the future indicate a doubling in the proportion of the population who are elderly as well as substantial and continuing increases in the demand for health care. This increase in demand may be particularly reflected in the need for community and institutional LTC services. Meeting these demands will force changes in the way care is provided, which will affect the medical practice of all physicians.

SUGGESTED READINGS

1. Fries VF, Crapo L: *Vitality and Aging.* New York, W.H. Freeman and Co., 1981.
2. Myers JK, Weissman M, Tischler GL et al: Six month prevalence of psychiatric disorders in three communities, 1980–1982. *Arch Gen Psychiatry* 41:959, 1984.

3. Rice D, Feldman J: Living Longer in the United States: Demographic Changes in Health Needs of the Elderly. *Milbank Fund Quarterly/Health & Society* 61:3, 1983.
4. Rabin DL, Stockton P: *Long Term Care for the Elderly: A Fact Book.* New York, Oxford University Press, 1987.
5. Soldo B, Manton K: Demographic challenges for socioeconomic planning. *J SE Planning* 19:4, 1985.
6. United States Bureau of the Census, Decennial Census of Population. 1990–2050: U.S. Bureau of Census, Projections of the Population of the United States, by Age, Sex, And Race: 1983–2080. Current Population Reports, Series P-25, No. 952, May 1984.
7. United States Senate Special Committee on Aging: *Aging America: Trends and Projections,* Washington, DC, The American Association for Retired Persons, 1984.
8. United States Senate Special Committee on Aging: *Aging America: Trends and Projections.* Washington, DC, The American Association for Retired Persons, Federal Council on Aging and the Administration on Aging, 1985 and 1986 edition.

CHAPTER 41

Retirement as Seen by the Health Professional and the Social Scientist

GORDON F. STREIB

Retirement is an event, a process, and a social institution. Widely divergent views are held by both laymen and professionals toward this multifaceted phenomenon. In this chapter, we wish to explore the way in which retirement is viewed by health professionals—those practitioners who deal with retirees on a one-to-one basis—and by social scientists, who study retirees as a category of persons and generalize about their attitudes, feelings, and behavior, They identify patterns and modalities of behavior but may never describe the retiree as an individual personality.

We refer to retirement as an event because this is the way most individual retirees experience it. On a certain day, they terminate their employment. When this takes place, a major change occurs in their roles, activities, and life rhythms. Retirement may be viewed as a process because it has continuity and goes on through time, and its true impact must be studied longitudinally. Retirement as a social institution refers to all of the body of customs, practices, behaviors, and organizations that revolve around the events and processes of stopping work late in the life cycle. As a social institution, retirement involves rites of passage, symbols, age requirements, pension plans, retirement counseling, etc.

SOCIAL SCIENCE FINDINGS

What do we know about retirement? The social scientist and health professional often regard retirement from different perspectives, based upon their training, their practice, and their purposes. The social scientist's training emphasizes the broad overview in which he is trying to generalize about the patterns and modalities that exist. He is sensitive to the heterogeneity of the aged and the variety of patterns that may be observed because of the differences arising from race, class, religion, sex, ethnicity, and the like.

The health professional, on the other hand, is concerned with the immediate case before him—usually a person who is sick or in trouble and who requires some ameliorative measures. The practitioner's focus, therefore, is upon that immediate person who has experienced difficulty and whose needs are urgent. The client or patient does not want to be told that he or she is one of a minority but wants to know what can be done to relieve his or her distress.

Many practitioners and writers in the mental health field have stressed the negative impact of retirement. These writers see retirement as a crisis situation that precipitates personal disorganization, organic illness, mental illness, and even death. In *The Encyclopedia of Mental Health* (6) there are 18 references to retirement and each time the negative or depressive effects are emphasized. One of the strongest statements was made by Kenneth Soddy (6): "Many men find their most important identity in their career, which, being relinquished, establishes a strong tendency toward early breakdown and death."[1] However, such conclusions are based upon isolated clinical observations or the uncritical use of survey research (10).

What are some of the major findings from social science research that will help the physician or other health practitioner place the individual patient in broader perspective than the single case? One result that has been confirmed by many studies is that the abrupt disruption of work patterns by retirement is not deleterious to the health of the typical retiree. In fact, for many people retirement brings relief from the stresses and strains of work and may result in increasing vitality.

The first longitudinal research on the effects of retirement was the Cornell Study of Occupational Retirement (20). The researchers initially contacted over 3000 working people 64 years of age. Follow-up questionnaires were sent at regular intervals over the next 6-year period to find out how the retirees adjusted to retirement over the years and what effect it had on their health. Contact also was maintained with those who continued to work. The data show that the proportion of those indexed in good health declines moderately through the years 65–70. This does not seem to be attributable to retirement itself because those who do not retire show the same decline. Moreover, the respondents themselves do not attribute a decline in health to retirement. More of the respondents in the Cornell study overestimated rather than underestimated the adverse effect of retirement upon their health.

These results were generally confirmed in a more recent longitudinal study, the National Longitudinal Survey, which began in 1966 with a national probability sample of 5000 men. Parnes and his associates (15) report on the 2800 remaining respondents who were 60 to 74 years old in 1981. This panel yields one of the best data sets for the study of retirement because of the quality and the size of the sample, the information gathered, the 15-year time

frame, an adequate sample of black men, and the multidisciplinary background of the investigators. A major conclusion is that retirement does not produce negative effects on the well-being of the individual. The researchers (Ref. 15, p. 169) state, "If anything, men find that retirement is better than they thought it would be. For a large proportion of retirees, the best thing about retirement, in fact, is not working."

The variation in the satisfaction of retirees can be shown to be attributable quite directly to the effects of health and income. The researchers were particularly careful in sorting out the factors responsible for a person's decision to retire. Because of the longitudinal nature of the study, it was possible to classify the reasons for retirement without relying on the retrospective reports of the respondents. The four basic categories of retirees and reasons for retirement were: (a) persons who were involuntarily retired under a mandatory plan (mandatory); (b) persons whose retirement was attributed to poor health (health); (c) individuals who retired because of labor market adversities (discouragement); (d) persons who chose retirement (voluntary). The voluntary category was divided into those who retired prior to 65 (early retirement) and those who retired at a later age (normal retirement). In this 15-year study of retirement, the important and indeed surprising finding is that only 3% retired from their jobs because of mandatory retirement plans. This is contrary to the general opinion that most older employees are "forced" from the world of work. Labor market adversities were a factor for 5% of the retirees. Health factors were of much greater importance in motivating persons to retire, for over one-third (35%) of the retirements were related to a decline in health. The majority, almost 60%, retired voluntarily. Blacks were more likely than whites to retire for health reasons.

Health reasons for retirement need to be understood in the context of the kinds of work people do and how health reasons are part of "voluntary" retirement. Parnes and associates (Ref. 15, p. 71) describe the situation this way: "Because very few disabilities or health problems entirely preclude all types of labor market activity, retirement for health reasons is almost always in some sense 'voluntary.'" The authors point out that if medical examinations were the basis for sorting out the retirees, it would still be necessary to make decisions about persons who "had to" retire because of health considerations and those who "chose to" because of the difficulties in continuing to work. The groups are distinct and

---

[1]Obviously not all professionals in the mental health field would agree with the opinions of Soddy. See, for example, Butler (4), Eisdorfer (7), or Simon (18).

they are based on answers to questions asked prior to retirement and in an interview context that did not emphasize the retirement decision.

The evidence from other large scale studies confirms that most older persons retire as soon as they consider it financially feasible (2, 3). Perhaps the most convincing illustration of this pattern is that when Social Security retirement benefits became available to men at age 62 rather than 65, the "normal" or "typical" age for retirement under the Social Security program dropped from age 65 to 63, even though this early retirement reduced benefits.

Another important source of information is the book *Retirement: Causes and Consequences* by Erdman B. Palmore and four associates at the Duke University Center for the Study of Aging and Human Development (14). The book is a summary and reanalysis of seven longitudinal researches (including the Parnes et al. study discussed above). The Duke research overcomes some of the weaknesses of earlier studies and offers a common conceptual model for analyzing the predictors and consequences of retirement. Some comparisons of the differences between men and women are provided.

There is variation in the results from the different studies but health as a variable was important in bringing about early retirement, that is, retirement before a fixed age. An important finding for health practitioners is that retirement at the normal age had little or no deleterious effects on health. Although health declines in some retirees, those persons are balanced by those retirees who enjoy an improvement in their health.

Another important longitudinal study of retirement is the Normative Aging Study conducted on a population of veterans living in Boston and environs (8). The Veterans Administration researchers found no adverse effects of retirement on health among the men who retired for non-health reasons. This study is of significance because physical examinations were used to corroborate information gathered by self-reports of health.

The study by Haynes et al. (11) of 3971 United States rubber workers provides precise epidemiological data on retirement, mortality, and health. These researchers studied death rates after early retirement (ages 62–64) and normal retirement (age 65). In the first year after early retirement, the observed mortality rates were 2 times greater than the expected rates. In contrast, the observed age-specific mortality rates for persons retired involuntarily at age 65 were lower than the expected rates in the first 2 years, about equal to the expected rates

for the third and fourth years, and lower in the fifth year. The lower-than-expected rates continued 10 years after retirement. The higher mortality rates for early retirees are related to declining health prior to retirement as evidence by an index of morbidity, by working limitations, and by uninsured absences during the 2 years before retirement.

Another area in which social science can offer perspective on the broad impact of retirement concerns mental health. The Langley Porter studies at the University of California were specifically designed to determine whether retirement was among the major precipitants of mental illness in old age. The evidence clearly shows that a breakdown of physical health often preceded the mental health problems. Spence (19) writes: "Physical problems were seen as involved in the decision-making that led to the psychiatric ward in approximately two-thirds of the cases and precipitated the psychiatric illness in 10%. . . . Even for those persons diagnosed as suffering from psychogenic disorder, studies of health history showed that physical problems often preceded the development of psychiatric symptoms. . . . Consequently, it can be said that retirement as a precipitant of mental illness in old age occurs only under rather special circumstances."

Family life and relationships also have been described in crisis terms in relation to retirement. The history behind this idea is that retirement is an emotionally charged event that damages or destroys the continuity of earlier family patterns. Research both in the United States and abroad has made quite clear the adaptability of the family in the retirement period. Data from the Cornell Study of Occupational Retirement showed continued patterns of interaction and greater closeness between the generations than expected. Adult children viewed the impact of the father's retirement as not changing family relations. Family life was not disrupted and few family crises were found in the period after retirement that could be attributed to retirement itself.

A retirement situation that is faced by an increasing number of couples is how to mesh retirement plans and activities when both husband and wife are in paid employment (9). Most men are older than their wives and the age gap may exacerbate the meshing of two lives before and during retirement. In the recent past, most married women who worked adapted their plans to their husbands (20). However, with some women having a strong commitment to their jobs or careers, they will want to continue working after the husband retires. Many women will be motivated to continue working so that they can qualify for Social Security benefits and a pension based on their own employment.

In a study of women aged 65 and over conducted by the University of Illinois at Chicago Circle (17), it was found that most retired women found satisfaction in their retirement for they enjoyed "free time" and the opportunity to be less busy. Only 25% expressed a desire to return to work, and surprisingly, these were the women who were least able physically to work. The investigators observed that these women appeared to be expressing a desire for the physical well-being enjoyed in earlier years when they were able to work, and that physical well-being and work had become synonymous.

More than half of the women retired before age 65, with the modal group retiring at age 62. The women who had worked were healthier than the women who spent their middle age as housewives. They were more self-sufficient than the housewives, less likely to complain of loneliness, less dependent on their children, and more likely to live apart from their children, even at advanced ages.

These generalizations concerning the impact of retirement do not eliminate that small percentage of persons for whom retirement is indeed a traumatic experience, nor do they mitigate the troubles and difficulties experienced by the minority of retirees. Individuals from this minority of retirees come for help to the clinicians, therapists, social workers, and psychiatrists. For this minority, there are clear and valid complaints. The work of Cottrell and Atchley (5) indicated that about one-third of the retirees in their study reported difficulty in adjusting to retirement. These results are similar to those that appeared in the earlier Cornell Study of Occupational Retirement. Atchley (1) sums up the adjustment problem by stating that the most frequently encountered difficulty is the reduction in income. Missing one's job is next in important and third is the miscellaneous collection of factors unrelated to retirement itself such as death of a spouse or illness. Atchley (1) argues that, from a positive point of view, the three things that enhance adjustment to retirement are sufficient income, good health, and the ability to gracefully give up one's job. He observes that inflexible personality often correlates with difficult adjustment to retirement.

Foner and Schwab (Ref. 9, p. 59) review the retirement literature and conclude: "There is little support in the research for the stereotypical view of retirement as a major life crisis for most people and a conspiracy against the aged." These investigators also point out that Social Security and Medicare are the bedrock foundation for the economic welfare of most retirees because of their almost universal coverage. Despite the deficiencies of these programs and those of private health and pension schemes, the government programs have created a social climate that is favorable to retirement and have legitimized retirement as an institutional arrangement.

MacBride (Ref. 13, p. 554), a Canadian researcher, reaches the same conclusion that there appear to be very little hard data to support the negative retirement stereotype. "On the whole, recent studies seem to indicate that people do quite well physically, mentally, and socially after retirement and the negative stereotype is indeed a myth."

RETIREMENT VIEWED BY THE HEALTH PROFESSIONAL

In spite of the patterns observed by social scientists that the majority of retirees have the coping mechanisms to adjust to retirement, there is a minority that finds the transition painful. The clinician will find many cases in which the persons suffer real hardship and difficulty. Among the many reasons contributing to their difficulties, we will mention four of the most significant:

Economic hardship,
The meaning of work,
Resentment at compulsory retirement,
Nonadaptive personalities.

ECONOMIC HARDSHIP

The difference in the perspective of the professional who works in a clinical setting with a troubled retiree and the social scientist who is trying to generalize about many retirees or a subgroup of them is illustrated by the way money or its absence enters into the retirement situation. Income is indeed a valid source of anxiety for many people. The Cornell Study of Occupational Retirement found that on the average, income declined about 50% from the level of the preceding working years.

The surprising finding about the marked drop in income was the attitude of retirees toward the greatly lowered income. When subjective income is considered—the way older persons evaluate their economic situation—it was found that a year after retirement two-thirds of the respondents said their income was "enough." Many of these people were living at the poverty level but had adjusted somehow.

The researchers in the Cornell longitudinal study also asked: "How often do you worry about money matters?" The results were surprising; the proportion of people who said they worried about money was essentially the same before and after retirement. The equanimity with which retirees viewed the realities of their economic position was unexpected by the researchers. There appear to be persons who are "worriers" and others who are "non-worriers." It is interesting that approximately the same proportion of those who continued to work throughout the study and those who retired reported worry about money matters.

Some of the persons who complain most bitterly about compulsory retirement and their financial situation are not those in actual need but those who frankly enjoy the acquisition of money. Watching their bank account and stock portfolios increase is to them the real goal in life—not just to have enough to live comfortably and meet their needs. Thus a decline in income represents a blow to their self-esteem and often they consider that the rest of the world similarly devalues them. For those who tend to measure their worth by their income, retirement may be an intensely threatening event.

THE MEANING OF WORK

The concept of the meaning of work is particularly significant in relation to studying retirement and the categories of "loss" that are experienced by the retiree. It is particularly important to differentiate class or occupational variables concerning the meaning of work and the transition to retirement. The intrinsic meaning of work varies by occupational level. Unskilled and semiskilled workers stress income as the primary factor that would be missed about the job, and they value routine activity and the time-filling aspects of work. Professional groups, for whom the intrinsic meaning of work involves creativity, self expression, inter-personal relations, and service to others, are less interested in retiring, even when retirement income may be sufficient.

Butler (4) has written of the difficulties of the person who is addicted to work. He says, "Without the customary defensive value of work, old emotional conflicts may re-emerge, especially if one has been a 'workaholic'—addicted to work. Without purpose, a sense of inadequacy can evolve: an apathy and inertia—and what some have called 'senile' behavior may follow unless the condition is prevented or reversed."

Still others have difficulty filling up their time. They seem to require externally imposed assignments and are unable to shift to a system of internal motivations.

The clinician involved in working with older pre-retirees and pensioners needs to understand that the emphasis upon work as an important component of life has undergone change in recent years. Popular articles on retirement often include a statement that since the United States is a "work-oriented" society, retirement poses a special problem. While this may have been true in the past, it is increasingly clear that the United States could be characterized as "income oriented" rather than "work oriented." When pensions are adequate, most workers will readily retire and take the pension (9). Although people are healthier than ever before and the length of life is increasing, a greater percentage retires before 65 than in previous years. There is an economic incentive to retire in many cases.

While there is a group who enjoy the work for its own sake, most people weigh the effort required to work against the income they would receive by not working, and increasingly decide it is to their advantage to retire. It must be pointed out that physicians, lawyers, judges, and congressmen have challenging and important work and are often reluctant to retire. However, one cannot generalize from the experience of this select minority, for the majority of workers finds it easy to leave the labor force as long as they can live comfortably on their pensions.

RESENTMENT AT COMPULSORY RETIREMENT

Health professionals will encounter in discussion with retirees who are antagonistic to retirement the notion that compulsory retirement at a fixed age is the major cause of their difficulties. This viewpoint also is held by some social scientists and laymen.

The federal law against age discrimination in employment, which became effective in 1979, raised the retirement age in private employment to 70, and there is no longer any fixed retirement age for employees of the federal government and some states. This law should reduce considerably the resentment of compulsory retirement.

Even with the new age limits, it is argued that applying a fixed age for retirement is discriminatory against the individual, who should be able to decide for himself how long he wishes to work. It also is contended that an arbitrary retirement age harms society in general by increasing unemployment, reducing the gross national product, and failing to utilize the skills and experience of an older cohort of the population.

The proponents of a more flexible retirement policy fail to recognize a number of problems and issues that will not be met by abolishing the fixed retirement age. First, almost half of the people who retire at the normal age or earlier do so because of physical or health reasons, and they and their doctors agree that they should not remain in the work force.

It is true that if employers were willing and able to alter and modify the hours and conditions of work, it might be possible to employ a substantial number of older workers at part-time jobs with reduced work requirements. This is more easily arranged in smaller and family-operated businesses than in large, bureaucratic enterprises. However, for most persons, a day will ultimately arrive when the worker, the employer, and perhaps his physician or family determine that he or she cannot continue to work. And then the problems of adjustment to retirement will have to be faced. In addition, one of the most difficult decision points in any voluntary retirement scheme will occur when the employee contends he is able to work, but the other parties involved in the work situation disagree with his self-evaluation. For example, who is to decide whether a devoted career teacher is no longer as effective in the classroom as in former years—the teacher himself, his colleagues, his superiors, his students, or their parents? If the present system seems arbitrary and cruel, one can conclude that a system of flexible retirement may demand a set of procedures and public evaluations that could be harsh and painful for some retirees. At any stage of the life cycle, many people are not always the best judges of their work performance, and the elderly are no exception.

Walker and Lazer (21) explain the difficulties in either terminating or tolerating employees whose performance is inadequate, maintaining that it is both feasible and legal to induce poorer workers to retire early. They stress that fairness should be maximized, but "the poorer performers who have an inclination to stay ... are the toughest group to confront and to help come to grips with their own aging and career patterns. Although they may represent fewer than 1 in 10 employees over the age of 60, they pose a difficult responsibility for management" (Ref. 21, p. 121). These retirees are the ones clinicians are likely to find requiring their attention and compassion and for whom "treatment" may be a difficult responsibility.

In discussions concerning the desirability of voluntary retirement standards, mention is often made of the exceptional older person who is highly capable of carrying on complex activities into the seventh and eighth decades of life. Usually these individuals are atypical human beings like Picasso, Pablo Casals, or Winston Churchill, who have an immense amount of psychic, physical, and emotional energy.

However, only a very small minority of older persons are able to invoke such resources. These persons are admirable and serve as an inspiration to all of us at any age, but clearly they are not typical of the general elderly population.

NONADAPTIVE PERSONALITIES

The work of Reichard et al. (16) shows how different personality types react in varying ways to aging and retirement. These psychologists studied 87 aging men and found a broad range of adjustment that they concluded was related to five principal personality types. These five types represent only those who were clearly successful or unsuccessful. There were some older men who had characteristics that placed them in a middle rating of adjustment, and they were excluded from the analysis (16).

Three types were classified as making a good adjustment to aging. The "mature men" moved easily into old age and were able to accept themselves realistically and to find genuine satisfaction in activities and personal relationships. They adjusted well to their new roles in retirement and found new activities and interests. The "rocking chair men" were in general those who were passive. They actually welcomed retirement because it meant freedom from responsibility and job pressures. The "armoured men" also made a good adjustment to aging because of a smoothly functioning system of defenses. These men tended to have stable work histories, to participate actively in social and civic organizations, and to make careful plans for old age. They counteracted their fear of growing old by making a special effort to remain active. This type of person might find a new job after retirement, plunge into senior citizens activities, or pursue a new hobby. They adjust well as long as their health permits them to keep up a high level of activity.

Two categories made a poor adjustment to aging and retirement. The "angry men" fought against getting old and both envied and criticized the younger generation. They often relied on counterphobic activity as a defense against anxiety and made statements about the need to keep on working or to keep busy because otherwise they would soon die. One can surmise that this type would be particularly opposed to compulsory retirement. The last category was composed of the "self-haters" who blamed themselves for their frustrations and failures. Some showed evidence of depression, and their masochism led them to flaunt their shortcomings and miseries. All of the "self-haters" made many references to death.

Reichard and her associates (16) report that the histories of the respondents suggest that their personality characteristics had changed very little throughout their lives. This study seems to show that some personality types are more vulnerable to trauma than others. Thus retirement may indeed be a crisis in the lives of the "angry men" or the "self-haters." However, the "mature men" were able to accept reality and were flexible enough to adapt to their new situation.

Reichard et al. (16) conclude that while aging may threaten the identity of some, it may allow others to consolidate their identity. They note: "Among older men not suffering from ill health or severe economic deprivation, there are some psychological gains in old age that compensate for its losses. Indeed, some men not only meet the crisis of age successfully but actually achieve greater self-acceptance than earlier in life."

Other investigators who have focused upon personality variables have reached similar conclusions in terms of the variety of responses to retirement and continuity of personality throughout the life cycle. Maas and Kuypers (12), reporting on a 40-year longitudinal study, confirm that continuity of personality continues throughout the life cycle. They suggest that pathology in old age may have roots in early adulthood.

NEW DEVELOPMENTS

A continuing interest about retirement is the degree to which it is "forced" upon people who really prefer to continue working. The National Longitudinal Survey of 5000 men found that less than 3% of retirees are mandatorily retired. Among white men, over one-half retired voluntarily and almost one-third stated they retired for health reasons.

In recent years a number of large and prominent business and industrial firms have developed various kinds of forced early retirement schemes in order to reduce costs by cutting the size of the labor force. These special kinds of negotiated retirement plans often involve executives and professionals with high skills and long service to the firm—people who are paid high salaries. Other types of "forced" retirement have been observed because of takeovers, the threat of corporative reorganization, transfer of ownership, etc. Some of the highest placed executives are often "retired" as a result of these changes, and they may find the situation traumatic. Two factors probably make such forms of retirement or lay-off difficult, namely, the suddenness with which they occur, and the harsh style or manner in which

the person is terminated. There are no systematic studies of these situations and the adjustment persons make to them. However, one can speculate, based upon knowledge from research on other critical situations, that persons who have coped with stress in the past will probably be able to do so more successfully than those who have had difficulty adjusting to past stressful events. Personality variables or types also will be involved, and the fragility of a person's self-esteem, for example, may be significant in how sudden retirement is handled. Some executives retire to the golf course, feeling bitter and unappreciated. Others mobilize their efforts and find new positions, or set up their own businesses.

When persons have difficulty adjusting to retirement, often their problems can be traced to other factors than retirement itself. For many retirees, the best thing about retirement is freedom from work. But retirees are not a homogeneous category and the quality of well-being can be traced in many cases to the effects of poor health and low income.

There are important supplementary aspects that enhance retirement and that the sensitive professional should acknowledge. It may be difficult to prescribe a specific regime but empathic insight and sensitive suggestions may be helpful. It is commonplace to suggest that retirees find a hobby or engrossing activity or become socially active. However, only about 15% of a national sample of retirees perceive themselves to be socially isolated. Almost by definition social isolation is not reported among persons with network relationships—family, friends, and kinfolks. Adult children are identified as the most important part of one's social network, and among family members, a sense of positive concern for each other has been found to be the most important bonding factor. Acquaintances in leisure groups may be important in creating social networks and breaking down isolation. For persons who refuse to break out of the shell of isolation, it is hard to prescribe what the concerned professional might offer. Many studies have found that higher levels of activity are correlated with greater satisfaction in retirement but levels of activity cannot be "prescribed." This area of life is regulated by the individual himself or herself. If people do not choose to participate in an activity, they cannot be compelled to do so.

Looking to the future, health professionals and others must recognize the importance of social networks, and future retirees may face more isolation because of small families and the lack of earlier kin networks. It may be essential to encourage persons to develop non-kin relations to reduce isolation. Whether they can be developed and whether communities will provide social opportunities for network creation may be crucial for American retirees of the future.

Preretirement programs have been a growing part of human resource management programs in the private and public sectors. The typical course provides a series of lecture discussions scheduled during the working hours for older workers who are near retirement. The topics usually include health and wellness, financial planning, work and new activities, family and friends, living arrangements, and legal matters. Most programs are rated very positively by the participants. A major drawback is that attendance is voluntary and therefore almost all of the participants are "planners"—persons who are least likely to need the curriculum. Often the persons who might need some guidance as to what lies ahead are least likely to enroll or to attend regularly. Usually persons who are hostile to retirement are the ones most likely to avoid such programs. This is an unfortunate outcome but one that is to be expected in a free society, and one in which any type of coercion into a program would probably not be effective. This is unfortunate, and it is this very small minority of older persons who will attribute the problems of retirement to other factors than their own reluctance to consider how they might adapt. Thus the physician and other health professionals who suggest that the person needs to take a preretirement course must be aware that the suggestion may be quite differentially received.

Financial planning for retirement is an area that is receiving increasing attention. There are now so many references in the mass media to the need for considering this aspect that most retirees are well aware that adjustments will need to be made. Bulletins, articles, pamphlets, tapes, and books are widely available—from Social Security, insurance companies, banks, the American Association of Retired Persons, etc. There are frequent advertisements in the newspapers for seminars on financial planning by investment firms. Continuing education courses are offered in the public schools and community colleges. In other words, there are ample resources for any retiree who wants such information. The problem for the retiree is coping with the information overload, for there is a difficulty in sorting out those items that are pertinent to the individual's situation from the plethora of information.

In general, research has shown that persons with unfavorable views of retirement are more likely to find work after retirement. Those individuals with a strong commitment to work or who have work that is very satisfying to them are also apt to have negative attitudes about retirement and will be apt to seek other employment. It is interesting to note that the National Longitudinal Study found that persons in the top income category had high rates of work participation after retirement. In other words, there were other motivating factors than financial necessity.

CONCLUSIONS

The problems the health professional faces in helping the retiree to adjust to his new situation are challenging and complex, for the retiree brings to his new role a continuity of personality and coping style that he has followed for a half of a century. Moreover, the exterior factors—the job situation, income level, and health condition—frequently cannot be modified or reversed by the therapist.

The social science findings presented in brief form in this chapter can only offer the practitioner insight and perhaps some reassurance that the troubled clients they see may not represent the typical case. As retirement has become institutionalized in American society, it has become more widely accepted, and each new cohort benefits from observing the adaptations of previous groups. It is anticipated that future retirees will experience fewer problems than the present groups. Furthermore, it is hoped that as our society matures, it will be possible for the institution of retirement to become more flexible and adaptable to the diversity of needs and personality types of older citizens of America.

REFERENCES

1. Atchley RC: *The Sociology of Retirement.* New York, Wiley-Halstead Press, 1976.
2. Barfield RE, Morgan JN, *Early Retirement: The Decision and the Experience.* Ann Arbor, Institute of Social Research, 1969.
3. Bixby LE, Retirement patterns in the United States: research and policy interaction. *Soc Secur Bull* 39(8):3, 1976.
4. Butler RN: *Why Survive? Being Old in America.* New York, Harper & Row, 1975.
5. Cottrell F, Atchley RC, *Women in Retirement.* Oxford Ohio, Scripps Foundation for Research in Population Problems, 1969.
6. Deutsch A, (Ed): *The Encyclopedia of Mental Health.* Franklin Watts, New York, 1963.
7. Eisdorfer C: Adaptation to loss of work. In Carp FM (ed): *Retirement,* New York, Behavioral Publications, 1972.
8. Ekerdt DJ, Baden I, Bossé R, Dibbs E: The effect of retirement on physical health. *Am J Public Health,* 73:779, 1983.
9. Foner A, Schwab K: *Aging and Retirement,* Monterey, CA, Brooks/Cole, 1981.

10. Friedmann EA, Orbach HL: Adjustment to retirement. In Arieti S (Ed): *The Foundation of Psychiatry,* Vol. 1 Basic Books, New York, 1974.

11. Haynes SG, McMichael AJ, Tyroler HA: Survival after early and normal retirement. *J Gerontol* 33:269, 1978.

12. Maas HS, Kuypers J: *From Thirty to Seventy.* Jossey-Bass, San Francisco, 1974.

13. MacBride A: Retirement as a life crisis: myth or reality? *Can J Psychiatry* 21:547, 1976.

14. Palmore EB, Burchett BN, Fillenbaum GG, George LK, Wallman LM: *Retirement: Causes and Consequences.* Springer Publishing Company, New York, 1985.

15. Parnes HS, Crowley JE, Haurin RJ, Less LJ, Morgan WR, Mott FL, Nestel G: *Retirement among American Men.* D.C. Heath, Lexington, MA, DC Heath, 1985.

16. Reichard S, Livson F, Petersen PG: *Aging and Personality.* Wiley Press, New York, 1962.

17. Shanas E: *Older Women, Retired Workers and Housewives.* Report to Social Security Administration on Project No. HEW SSA 10P980 20-5-01 (typescript), 1981.

18. Simon A: Mental health. In: *Physical and Mental Health,* background paper for the 1971 White House Conference on Aging. United States Government Printing Office, Washington, D.C., 1971.

19. Spence DL: Patterns of retirement in San Francisco. In: *The Retirement Process,* Carp FM, editor. United States Government Printing Office, Washington, D.C., 1968.

20. Streib GF, Schneider CJ: *Retirement in American Society: Impact and Process.* Cornell University Press, Ithaca, NY, 1971.

21. Walker JW, Lazer HL: *The End of Mandatory Retirement.* John Wiley, New York., 1978.

CHAPTER 42

Competence Issues and Adult Protective Services for the Elderly

STEVEN A. LEVENSON

Because the care of the older patient goes far beyond the treatment of the medical condition, it requires some physician understanding of many things far afield from traditional medical training. Among these are the idea of competence, and legal issues surrounding protective services and the older individual.

Pertinent laws and regulations cover five areas: those things society expects of persons permitted to live and function independently and autonomously in the community; the means of determining those who cannot meet such standards; the procedures for dealing with those who do not or cannot meet the standards; the legal and professional duties of those who deal with such individuals; and the nature and authority of the available resources and services for those who either cannot function appropriately or who can only do so with assistance.

The two goals of this chapter are to examine critically the current process of determining competence and to give an overview of the options and services available for those elderly who cannot function competently or safely.

DETERMINING THOSE WHO CANNOT MEET THE STANDARDS

Inasmuch as the label of competence is a ticket to personal freedom and autonomy, the judgment of in-competence is tantamount to confiscating that ticket. Once declared incompetent and in need of guardianship, according to the laws of most states, an individual cannot legally do a host of things, including consent to or refuse medical treatment, participate in business, make contracts or gifts, defend against suits, or marry or divorce.

Adult protective services (APS) may be provided for either the competent or the incompetent individual and may be either voluntary or involuntary. *Voluntary protective services* are those provided to an individual who (a) for physical or psychologic reasons, or both, cannot act in his or her own best interest; (b) is at risk in his or her current situation; (c) is capable of giving consent; and (d) willingly consents to receive such services. *Involuntary protective services* are provided on the order of a court to someone who (a) cannot act in his or her own best interest; (b) is at risk in his or her current situation; and (c) is either unwilling or unable to consent to use of voluntary services.

The law strives to protect individual autonomy by assuming people are able to manage their own lives and affairs until proven otherwise. As long as a person is considered able to function as a self-reliant individual, there is no legal foundation for authorizing substitute decision making or the imposition of unwanted services.

Therefore, the issue of competence is as central to the question of protective services as it is to many other areas of geriatrics.

CRITERIA FOR COMPETENCE

"Competence" may be considered to relate to one or more of the following: (a) the capacity to conduct business and financial affairs, (b) the capacity to make decisions on medical care, and (c) the capacity to function in activities of daily living.

In other words, in the broadest sense, competence means *functional capabilities:* the capacity to function adequately and appropriately in a given cultural setting to meet personal needs according to public expectations and to meet social requirements.

That competence means various things is shown by the existence of more than one definition of the term. Legal and psychologic viewpoints each employ somewhat different criteria.

The *legal* definition looks primarily at how a person conforms with a defined status; for example, age, citizenship, or defined impairments. For instance, a person is generally considered legally incompetent to consent to treatment if he or she is unconscious or suffering from the effects of drugs or alcohol, dementia, or mental illness, or if below a certain stipulated age.

Central to all legal determinations of competence is the question of whether someone can reasonably understand the condition, nature, and effect of the proposed treatments, and the risks of choosing or not choosing those treatments. Thus, the law makes a presumption that a 24-year-old person not legally insane is capable of carrying out certain legally prescribed tasks, such as writing a will. Conversely, a person who does not meet the legal definition for competence is considered incapable of legally performing the act. Thus, an 11-year-old is not considered competent to write a will, even though he or she may have more understanding of the process than someone three times the age. Regrettably, some guardianship laws still include "old age" as one of the possible defined categories for declaring incompetence.

In contrast, the *psychologic* concept of competence relates more to the specific mental or behavioral capacities needed to perform a certain task, as well as to the potential to acquire them. Thus, though a 12-year-old might be considered legally incompetent to manage his own financial affairs, he might nonetheless be perfectly capable of the most intricate mathematical computations. The Australian aborigine may not be competent to perform many of the tasks that would be required to live in Los Angeles and may or may not have the potential to learn them. An elderly individual might be legally competent, yet be unable to make decisions properly on his or her own behalf because of depression or certain thought disturbances.

The determination of competence must necessarily take both these into account. For example, deciding on the capacity of an older person to make a statement about not wanting help from outside agencies should involve a review not only of current behavior and statements, but the consistency of such wishes and reasoning with previous performance. Because many people of all ages considered competent use very poor judgment in their personal lives, poor judgment by itself is not a sufficient criterion for a label of incompetence.

From the *ethical* viewpoint, adequate consent requires not only competence, but also a capacity to make and communicate decisions that are voluntary (not made under undue coercion by others), intentional (willful, purposeful, with a particular goal in mind), and consistent with values.

CAPACITY AND THE LABEL

Competence, then, is *not* a fact, but an opinion about someone, which is frequently—though not always—based on the facts. But unlike competence itself, which can fluctuate or improve, as well as worsen, the *label* of competence is often applied irreversibly, and is invariably affected by the criteria and measuring tools.

Why, for instance, can psychiatrists sometimes be found to reach divergent, if not diametrically opposite, conclusions at a sanity trial or competence hearing? It is most likely because they have not had access to all the same information or because they are using different criteria to interpret the same information.

An older person deemed in need of protective services who agrees to those services may be less likely to have his competence challenged than if he or she fought such services. Yet, in many cases, the reason why such services are suggested in the first place is diminished competence of the individual. Therefore, there may arise the sticky position of an incompetent person labeled competent to agree to assistance, but a competent one considered *incompetent* because of refusal. Such things have been known to happen with elderly individuals.

LEVELS OF COMPETENCE

Not every task requires the same level of competence. Many determinations of competence traditionally have been blanket declarations: a person is declared either "competent" or "incompetent," period. Current thinking on the issue has begun to reflect the idea that competence determinations ought to be more *task-specific*. Assessment of both current function and potential capacities should be related to the task at hand. Thus, even an elderly person considered "senile" might have the mental functions necessary to make certain decisions on his or her own behalf, especially if either the setting or the expectations are changed somewhat.

Thus, for example, an older person acting inappropriately or inadequately in one setting may be able to function adequately if placed in a new setting. But what if that person refuses to consent to the change? Should the individual be declared temporarily incompetent, incompetent but temporarily in need of protection, or competent but temporarily in need of protection? Which option is chosen can make a difference in subsequent as well as current decision making involving that person.

Certain steps, therefore, should occur before definitive attempts are made to declare incompetence.

First, observe and gather as much data as possible over time. Though it is often done that way, competence seldom can be determined properly by a stranger in one encounter. Current behavior or thinking must be matched with past performance. Therefore, what are (or were) previous behaviors, statements, values? Can the person communicate and understand information? And, how does the person perform when asked to reason or deliberate choices about specific circumstances?

Second, rule out physical causes for mental status alterations by appropriate physical or laboratory examinations.

Third, get as much objective information as possible about actual mental status. If necessary, do more than one mental status evaluation. For instance, the person who is labeled demented but who scores high on the mental status examination, is probably not demented, and some other explanation for symptoms should be sought, or the erroneous diagnosis removed.

Fourth, information about such observations should be exchanged among those who have made some assessment because such coordination can help point out information relevant to competence that one or more individuals might have overlooked.

Finally, re-evaluate where necessary, especially when initial decision-making capabilities are unclear.

Some such multistep process should be required in all cases, even where an acute episode of apparently incompetent conduct leads to emergency institutionalization or invoking of substitute decision making. Clearly, most state laws and regulations at least nominally recognize the need for such judicious evaluation and re-evaluation. But in practice, health professionals are often not sufficiently prudent.

DEALING WITH THOSE NOT MEETING STANDARDS

APS procedures generally begin with (a) investigation of reports of possible need and evaluation of the situation; and (b) assessment of the degree of risk to the individual or others involved in the current living situation. At this point, if a need is determined, there is either (a) referral for services; or (b) arranging or petitioning for the authority (such as guardianship) necessary to implement such services. Finally, there are (a) the actual services themselves; and (b) the follow-up to ascertain the continued need for such services or additional ones.

The laws for APS usually use involuntary commitment and guardianship or conservatorship as the legal means for intervention. Other laws provide for obtaining court orders in specific situations, such as emergencies or imminent danger to a person's health or safety.

When the competence of the individual to consent or refuse consent is at issue, each state has specific procedures for competence and guardianship proceedings. The first step is invariably a required filing of a petition, usually by the person to be "protector," such as a custodian, spouse, or adult child.

Filing of the petition usually is followed by a hearing notice issued to the person presumed in need of guardianship. An examination by a court-appointed individual—typically, but not necessarily, by at least one physician—is commonly required. Sometimes, a visit to the alleged incompetent by a court-appointed person is also prescribed.

In marked contrast to most other kinds of judicial proceedings, which emphasize self-defense against possibly unfair charges, laws regarding declarations of incompetence have sometimes been lax in protecting the rights of the alleged incompetent. For example, while the standards for acceptable claims of incompetence vary among states, it is still sometimes assumed that someone petitioning for such a declaration must certainly have the other individual's best interests in mind. Many states do not *require* legal representation, although they may permit it. The alleged incompetent is usually not required to be present at the actual hearing, but may be represented by an attorney. In some cases, the petitioner may even request that the alleged incompetent not be present.

Once a court order is issued, there may be few limits imposed on the service agencies. Unless specific services are ordered by the court, the agency may have great freedom (1).

PHYSICIAN RESPONSIBILITIES

The physician's critical roles lie in *maximizing function* to minimize the need for protective services; making sure that proper *criteria* are used in the decision making and *protecting the individual* against inappropriate actions; *advocating* for the individual patient; and helping *select* the most appropriate *options*.

PHYSICIAN DETERMINATION OF DECISION-MAKING CAPACITY

The physician often has the ultimate responsibility for the conclusion about the patient's decision-making capacity, but this conclusion should not be based only on doctor-made observations. One fundamental rule of medicine is to try to gather as much information as possible in any situation, before reaching a conclusion about what to do. For non-clinical as well as clinical situations, conclusions should be reached at the proper point: at the *end,* not the *beginning,* of the process.

Other pertinent information includes results of mental status examinations, nursing staff and social service evaluations, psychiatric consultation, or other psychologic testing. It is common, but often inadequate, to rely primarily or only on a psychiatrist's consultation.

The physician should avoid the fallacy of mistakenly labeling a belligerent, uncooperative older person as incompetent simply because the patient will not accede to the physician's suggestions or those of family. It is, therefore, a good idea for competence to be assessed, where possible, *before* recommendations are made or decision-making situations arise. If nothing else, this can provide a baseline for comparing subsequent evaluations.

Another physician role is to ensure that the correct diagnosis has been made and that the treatable has not been overlooked because a relatively intact physical system is needed to be able to process, ponder, and decide upon information. Where indicated, certain physical causes of dementia and delirium, including infections, fluid and electrolyte imbal-ances, drug toxicity, endocrine dysfunctions such as thyroid disease, and other problems like anemia, heart disease, or stroke, should be ruled out.

The primary care physician is often the most important protector of a patient's rights and may well be the *only* one with the power to influence or reverse hasty judgments and erroneous assumptions on the part of transient testers. In addition, the physician should help assure the periodic re-evaluation of an individual for whom others have been granted decision-making authority, to see if there is any change in need for either that authority or those protections.

When protective services *are* truly necessary, as they often are, "health care professionals have an essential role to play, in appropriate circumstances, in encouraging their competent older patients (and almost all patients are competent for most of their lives) to accept, voluntarily, intelligently, and thoughtfully, necessary and available protective services, on either a present or a future basis. This function is generally ignored or consciously avoided by many health care professionals" (1).

SERVICES AND OPTIONS

Current laws allow a relatively limited number of legal options for the elderly unable to meet the standards for self-management: limited intervention of protective services, commitment, or guardianship. There are, however, efforts to expand the number of such options.

Protective services are those community services provided to people who are either financially, socially, physically, or psychologically unable to manage personal affairs; to protect themselves against the elements, exploitation, or physical harm; or to act safely and responsibly. The term APS refers to "a system of preventive, supportive, and surrogate services for the elderly living in the community to enable them to maintain independent living and avoid abuse and exploitation" (1). The basic roles of APS are thus: (a) to assess the needs and capacities of potential clients; (b) to coordinate or provide services to adults at risk; and (c) to actually or potentially assume decision-making authority for such persons.

One goal of APS is to prevent institutionalization where possible, or to institutionalize where necessary to protect the health, safety, or life of an elderly individual or others. Another is to provide substitute decision making, but only when truly necessary.

Examples of protective services include transportation, health services, housing and financial assistance, homemaker and home health assistance, day care, legal aid, and protective placement. They also encompass surrogate services, including guardianship, power of attorney, and emergency hospitalization. APS programs commonly refer to other resources, such as Social Service Departments, for actual provision of services.

Much of the increased need for such services may be attributable to the greater number of elderly in general—especially, those who are at high risk for health, social, economic, environmental, and legal problems—as well as to recent national trends toward deinstitutionalization of many mental patients, including some elderly confined for decades. The end result is people turned into the community who become unable, or who are ill equipped, to care for or protect themselves fully in a complex modern world.

Adult protective services have been extremely helpful to many elderly unable to manage for themselves. Most older adults voluntarily relinquish some decision-making autonomy and accept some protective services. A *transfer of authority* occurs when a still-competent person grants this power voluntarily and informally to a known and trusted individual.

A more formal arrangement of such a transfer occurs with a *power of attorney*. This is the means by which a person legally transfers some or all decision-making authority, either temporarily or permanently. It may also specify the extent and duration of the powers granted or specific individuals to execute those wishes.

The *durable* power of attorney attempts to overcome the limitation of the traditional power of attorney, which ends at a time of death or disability, either by extending the period of applicability into the time of incompetence or disability, or by allowing for it to become applicable when the principal actually becomes disabled. This has provided what some think is a better option than the "living will."

The *living will* is another way in which a person can express his or her wishes and issue directions for care before the time a state is reached where this is no longer possible. In this document, the individual may specify directions for treatment and care, or the withholding of such services, in the event of future incapacity, and may usually specify another individual to ensure that such wishes are carried out. The living will provides a certain level of legal insistence that a person's wishes about terminal care *must* be honored by the attending physician. However, health care professionals may still honor a patient's wishes even in the absence of a living will.

Several alternative protective services focus on protection of property, and thereby avoid perhaps unnecessary or difficult intrusions into the person's own affairs. These include *conservatorship* (appointment of a person to protect an individual's property and estate, but not their person or personal affairs), and *trusteeship* (appointment of a trustee to manage property specifically entrusted to him or her).

If a person requiring public assistance has not given a power of attorney to someone else, and refuses the assistance, social service agencies are frequently empowered by law to seek appointment of a substitute decision maker.

Guardianship refers to protective services imposed as a result of legal proceedings. The guardian is legally authorized to make decisions on behalf of another person. *Limited guardianship* restricts the scope and *temporary guardianship* restricts the time span, for the guardian's substitute decision making, and thereby fosters re-evaluation of the individual after a period of time, to see if such protection is still necessary.

Commitment refers to the voluntary or involuntary confinement of an individual to the protection of an agency or institution, either for a limited or indefinite time. Current laws permit involuntary commitment when a person is considered mentally ill and a danger to self or others or when a person needs treatment and is unable to make responsible decisions about choosing options for such care. Admission to a nursing home, often arranged by family over the protests of the patient, is not usually considered a commitment, but rather a placement of a person in need.

CONCLUSIONS

In summary, APS are an important public support for those elderly who are physically or psychologically incapable of functioning in their best interest or the best interest of those who live with, or depend on, them. But the consideration of such services, or *any* situation where the decision-making capacity of the older person is challenged or supplanted by others, must also examine the means by which decisions are made about who needs them, and to what extent. Therefore, a hard look must be taken at the legal and ethical issue of competence and at the criteria used for its determination, so that some more specific criteria can be devised for physicians, other professionals, lawyers, and judges alike. Legislatures should also take a hard look at the procedures, assumptions, and criteria for determining competence and incompetence at *all* ages and recognize that new understandings will necessitate new approaches.

Along these lines, some legally prescribed safeguards for the elderly should exist. Where indicated, guardianship should be used as a short-term revocable tool to help a person until matters are straightened out or until it is clear that a person's condition is not likely to change substantially. Treatment should be forced only under certain explicitly defined circumstances and the competence of the individual and the need for protective services always should be re-evaluated periodically. Substitute decision making should be used only where necessary.

Finally, alternative services must be advocated and provided so that commitment and institutionalization are less often the only real options.

REFERENCE

1. Kapp MB, Pies HE, Doudera AE: *Legal and Ethical Aspects of Health Care for the Elderly.* Ann Arbor, MI, Health Administration Press, 1985, pp. 233–235.

CHAPTER 43

Housing for the Elderly

HERBERT SHORE

Housing used in broadest terms should promote the physical and mental well-being of older people by providing opportunities for socialization and health maintenance, while permitting privacy and the continuation of one's life-style. Housing planned for the elderly is designed for greater leisure time and environmental supports. The need for good shelter remains essentially the same, but is more sensitive to the individual's health, finances, and social interests. Essentially, its purpose is to foster independent living within the framework of appropriate support services.

What is the "ideal" living arrangement for older people? When should a person enter the spectrum of housing for the elderly? What does the practitioner look for when he or she recommends such facilities? There are no simple answers, as the subject is highly complex, bridging differing needs with available resources, services and programs.

DECISION TO RELOCATE TO HOUSING FOR THE ELDERLY

Because of the large concentration of elderly in certain well-publicized retirement communities, there exists the myth that retirement usually results in migration. Although such places as St. Petersburg, Florida, and Sun City, Arizona, have attracted many older people, the majority of elderly people have been living in the same home for over 20 years. In spite of the defects of these dwellings or the deteriorating neighborhoods, the majority of these older home owners say their present housing meets their needs and they do not want to move.

Those elderly who relocate are most likely to fall into certain groups: the widowed, the disabled, the severely ill, and the well educated. Other groups who are likely to relocate are those who live with others and those who move to be near their children. Loss of income may necessitate finding less expensive housing, but it also may prevent a desired move. Newer homes in better neighborhoods are likely to be too expensive and the elderly home owner may prefer to remain in a mortgage-free house rather than face uncontrollable apartment rents.

To enable the older home owner to remain independent, certain modifications can be made to the house. Car parking should be as close to the entrance as possible. Sidewalks may need to be redesigned in order to eliminate steps. Raised vegetable gardens or flower beds make maintenance easier for the older person. Modifications should also be considered for the interior of a house. A bedroom and bath may have to be relocated on the ground floor if the elderly person has difficulty with stairs. Shower stalls with a permanent seat installed, grab bars in the shower and by the toilet, lever handles on all plumbing and doors, supplementary radiant heat sources, and nonslip floors are features that should be included if the bathroom is to be remodeled. In the kitchen, the range should have front or side controls to enable the elderly person to use them without reaching over the burners. Controls should be easy to read. Lever handles should be used so that those with arthritis can operate faucets and door handles with ease. Continuous counter space allows sliding of heavy items from sink or cooking area to the counter and, thus, eliminates burns or spills. Adequate lighting over work areas is essential.

In spite of the fact that the majority of older people do not relocate, there is a serious housing problem for the nation's elderly. They have difficulty meeting high maintenance costs, taxes, and insurance. Many neighborhoods, especially in urban areas, are deteriorating. Lack of mobility restricts access to shopping and medical services. The demand for home-delivered services, which could allow some elderly to remain in their homes, far exceeds the availability. For these and other reasons, an estimated 20% of the elderly want more suitable housing. The future need will probably be higher. Much existing housing stock, both private and public, is deteriorating and being torn down. The current federal commitment to build new housing is totally inadequate to meet present and future needs of those who cannot afford to purchase housing in the private market.

EFFECTS OF RELOCATION

Research has demonstrated positive association between housing and health and housing and social adjustment for people of all ages. One important study of the elderly carefully evaluated an original group of 352 applicants to a new elderly-designed public housing complex (2). One year later, researchers compared 190 residents who had moved into the new complex with 105 who had remained in their substandard or socially impoverished housing. For those who had moved, there was a consistent pattern in the direction of good adjustment and improved health. Those who had not been able to secure housing in the new complex consistently showed a tendency to change for the worse on items related to physical and mental well-being. Data collected over an 8-year interval continued to support these findings.

Although evidence suggests that a new environment may have positive effects on the elderly, there are those who do not adjust well to relocation. One study, which revealed that more of the new housing tenants showed an increase in health after the first year than comparison groups, also revealed that more declined (7). Certain types of relocation, especially if the elderly person is opposed to the move, are associated with an increase in illness, psychologic problems, and even death.

There are many causes for poor relocation adjustment. In "Grieving for a Lost Home," Marc Fried (4) studied forced dislocation from an urban slum. Even among families who moved to better housing and safer neighborhoods, he found intense grief responses showing most of the characteristics of grief and mourning after the death of a loved one. Feelings of loss, longing, and depression were intense and long-lasting. For the elderly, especially those whose relocation follows the death of a spouse there is a loss of identity and continuity. Loss of one's home and familiar neighborhood results in fragmentation of routines and relationships. Relocated elderly people often express a feeling of worthlessness that is especially painful for those who are forced to move from homes purchased with their own earnings into government subsidized housing. Also stressful are the tasks of adapting to strangers, an unfamiliar building, and a new neighborhood.

Perhaps the most important factor in good post-relocation adjustment is the willingness of the elderly person to make change. In addition, family, friends, and housing personnel can provide assistance to make the adjustment to new surroundings less stressful. If there is an adequate support system, the stimulation of a new environment can have a positive effect on the elderly.

KINDS OF RETIREMENT HOUSING

Retirement housing under public, profit, or non-profit sponsorship may provide some of the better possible choices among a variety of types of living arrangements. Retirement facilities offer regular housing units, except that they are especially designed and adapted for, and cater to, mature, self-directing people who wish to retain their privacy, their cherished prerogatives and their variety of interests. At the very least, sponsors try to incorporate desired features of convenience, comfort, and safety. At best, properly located, designed, programmed, and managed retirement housing offers more than a nicely laid out landscaped site, more than spacious quarters for gracious living and freedom from major worries. Some, but not all, include, either on the premises or through arrangements with community sources, essential health and social services; a carefully thought-out health program with group health insurance coverage; a doctor and nurse in residence or a medical clinic. Almost all have an intercommunication system for emergencies. Many have an activities lounge; social, cultural, and recreational programs; workshops and craft rooms; opportunities for residents to use their abilities and volunteer their services to the community. Some provide a chance for part-time employment. All offer an ever-expanding circle of social contacts through which compatible friendships can be formed.

Retirement housing is not a place of regimentation where independence is forfeited. Instead, good retirement housing can strengthen independence and generally enrich the older person's well-being.

These facilities are neither institutions nor nursing homes. They may be situated in the center of a community, in the suburbs, or on a rural site and some are part of a campus for the aged adjacent to health care facilities. Some housing facilities are for older people only. Others include or are next to housing for young families. Not all retirement housing, however, is well situated. Few have the total range of services. Some cost more than many can afford.

PUBLIC HOUSING

Those with limited incomes should look to the possibility of retirement housing sponsored by the community's Housing Authority. Such housing, garden-type or high-rise, usually blends in with the surrounding area, is especially designed for older residents, and offers some of the most conveniently located, spacious facilities available anywhere at any price. It should be noted, however, that some public housing developments are in declining neighborhoods with high crime rates.

Some housing projects have their own community centers. A few have clinics and health programs. Management makes a special effort to marshall needed services for older tenants. Emergency call systems are common features. Each local Housing Authority has its own admission requirements. Besides fixing a ceiling on maximum income per year, each locality sets its own priorities for tenant selection. Usually those older persons who are displaced by public improvements, or live in substandard housing, or have physical conditions that may be aggravated by their present living arrangements, receive first priority.

CONGREGATE HOUSING

Congregate housing can be defined as a residential environment that includes a variety of services such as housekeeping, meals, health care, personal hygiene, and transportation. These services are required to support or assist the impaired elderly tenant, but not the frankly ill. With this support or assistance, the impaired or frail elderly can maintain a semi-independent life-style as he or she grows older. These services may range from a simple package (including meals and light housekeeping) to a wide variety on a fee-for-use arrangement. The need for congregate housing exceeds the availability. Those facilities that do exist are expensive and there are rarely subsidies to assist low-income elderly.

APARTMENTS

Individual apartments with their own kitchens and bathrooms are either garden-type, motel-type, or in high-rise buildings. They may be in a single building or several adjoining buildings, but they are especially adapted or designed for the older person.

Successful types of retirement facilities offer housekeeping and optional meal service.

Usually apartments are on a pay-as-you-go *rental plan* with some charges for special services. Rental often includes utilities.

Some nonprofit sponsors, particularly church-related groups, may use other methods of financing, such as Founders Fees, and Life Lease contracts.

In *cooperative apartments,* a single mortgage covers the total facility. Each resident, however, purchases a specific number of shares in a nonprofit cooperative corporation for which he or she is entitled to an apartment or dwelling unit, and, as a member of the cooperative, has a vote and say about management. Members of the cooperative own in common the various facilities such as lounges or heating plants.

Condominiums offer another method of financing apartments or home ownership for older people. Unlike the cooperative, each resident in the condominium housing carries his or her own mortgage, owns his or her own dwelling unit, and shares in the ownership of certain common facilities.

RETIREMENT VILLAGES (GOLDEN AGE VILLAGES, RETIREMENT TOWNS)

Many retirement villages are self-contained developments offering single cottages for sale to middle-aged and older people. A few include facilities for other age groups and some include housekeeping services as well.

These villages may not be too conveniently located, nor are they related to their surrounding communities. They may have the atmosphere of country club estates with golf links, swimming pools, and natural lakes.

Those who sell cottages may provide complete maintenance of grounds and house for a fixed monthly fee. They also may offer a clubhouse, activity programs, and some form of health insurance. A few have their own diagnostic and treatment clinics available on the premises. Some have a resident doctor and, where the villages are some distance from the town, they offer their own transportation and limited shopping facilities on or near the premises.

If the village is for middle-aged and older people only, there may be some stipulation that the cottage can be sold only to those of a certain age.

MOBILE HOME PARKS

Many people like the sociability and informality of a trailer and mobile home park. In some of the trailer parks, older people comprise about 20% of the total population. In many instances, the trailers have become permanently installed. Their maintenance is comparatively easy. Some are located within a community and convenient to necessary facilities and services. Some mobile parks have a community center and lively social activity.

Usually, trailer parks have no formal health services. When located a distance from a community, there may be some problem of water supply and pressure and garbage disposal. Trailer parks may foster too much togetherness and may not be designed for people of advanced age. Resale of trailers may be difficult and depreciation is rapid.

RESIDENCE CLUB AND HOTEL TYPE

Those who do not wish to or are unable to cook meals and those who like the freedom of hotel living may find these arrangements very satisfactory. Residence club, hotel or motel-type living arrangements offer rooms or suites in high-rise buildings or in the motel-style or garden-type structures, all with central dining facilities. These accommodations usually are without kitchens although some have small pullman kitchens—for preparing snacks—with hot plates or a small range, but no ovens. Others have small lounges with community kitchens on each floor for the same purpose. Most provide at least two meals (many provide three meals) per day, and include the cost of these in the monthly charges. Maid service, towels and linens, and other special personal attentions, usually associated with good hotels, may be included in the monthly charge. A doctor or nurse may be on call. Most offer telephones and intercommunication systems. Some have a medical clinic, infirmary, or first aid room. A few residence club facilities have a full-time program director, social worker, and a range of social and cultural activities.

COMMERCIAL AND CONVERTED HOTELS

Some regular hotels are now catering to retired persons. These have converted their lobbies, convention rooms, etc., to recreation and social purposes for their older residents.

Many older hotels are conveniently located in or near the downtown area of the community, are well constructed, fireproofed, and offer gracious accommodations and settings that once served the wealthier traveler. Their facilities match some of the most modern retirement housing.

Other converted hotels have very reasonable rates; however, the elevators, doorways, and rooms are small, and walls are thin. While they may be fire retardant, some are not safe for older people.

Frequently, the hotels exist in declining areas of the central cities. These tend to be areas of high crime rates and social deviancy. The increased vulnerability of the aged make them likely targets for crime. The result is that many of the elderly become virtual prisoners in their own rooms, not venturing out for food, clothing, or recreation. This compounds declining resources and the potential for breakdown in the health and mental status of the individual is increased.

Often the low rates call for double occupancy and make it necessary to share a room with a stranger. It also may be necessary to share a bathroom with more than two persons. Maid service may be provided once a week or once a month. There may be no room service and no bellman so that the resident will have to carry his own suitcases and perform for himself other functions usually given by hotels.

In some hotels the pay plan is for: (a) first and last months' rent in advance; (b) first and last 2 months' rent in advance; (c) first month's rent in advance; or (d) yearly payment to guarantee the stay of the resident. In some instances hotels offer a "life care" plan. In effect, the plan actually provides little care except shelter and food. Hotel operators may not always have continuity and stability of sponsorship. Some do offer recreation, but one ought to check whether these are planned programs or the do-it-yourself type.

The apparent low rates may induce some to go out of state to one of these hotels even when there isn't sufficient income for emergencies, for health care, etc. In some cases, a limited budget will not permit the resident to dine out. It is suggested that before becoming committed to a year or more of residency, the prospective resident ought to stay for a trial period until he or she is fully aware of what the hotel has to offer and whether or not it is satisfactory. It cannot be stressed enough that low or very moderate income will not give one sufficient margin to risk being stranded in a strange community. Moreover, the same legal residence requirements for receiving health care from the state also apply to receiving public assistance through a public welfare agency.

DISTINGUISHING RESIDENCE CLUBS AND HOTELS FROM HOMES FOR THE AGED AND NURSING HOMES

The residence clubs and hotels with housekeeping services should not be confused with "Homes for the Aged" that provide vital services for the more infirm and ill older persons who require a protective setting and personal care. Such care includes help with bathing, dressing, walking, eating, and skilled medical, nursing, and rehabilitation services.

The confusion between a residence club, hotel-type of living arrangements and Homes for the Aged is understandable because some Homes for the Aged serve primarily ambulatory residents and offer little more than meals and housekeeping services. The modern ones, however, provide a full spectrum of services so essential to the more feeble and ill. They include both comparatively well older persons and the more infirm and ill under the same roof. Others have assigned different wings or floors for those requiring nursing care where skilled professional staff minister to their needs.

The average age of applicants to Homes for the Aged is usually 81 years. Those seeking hotel-type accommodations are a mixed age group. They include retired career women, widowers who have never cared to bother with housekeeping, couples who are usually in their late 60's, and single persons who may be of any age over 60 years and like the congeniality and friendships so easily formed in hotel living.

MULTI- OR CAMPUS-TYPE FACILITIES

One of the most interesting developments in retirement housing is the multitype facilities that include different kinds of living arrangements—independent living, congregate living, and nursing home facilities under the same roof, in adjoining buildings or spread over a broad area similar to a campus. They may contain cottages or apartments, a separate residence club building with single rooms and suites, and a central dining facility, where residents of self-contained units often have the option of taking some of their meals. In addition, there is a separate nursing home facility providing skilled medical, nursing, rehabilitative services and protective supervision.

These multipurpose housing facilities attempt to serve residents as they continue to grow older and their needs change. Thus, if one lives in an independent living unit and needs to move to the residence club, he or she can do so as soon as an opening is available, and with a minimum of uprooting. If, through some temporary illness, the resident may need nursing care or rehabilitation services, these programs are made available wherever he or she may live in the complex. In the event that the resident continues to need nursing care, he or she can reside in the nursing home.

Many people prefer the long-range security of this type of housing and retirement living. Most of the better multitype facilities try to maintain a sense of well-being by separating the living quarters

of the ill or infirm from those of the other residents.

Experience in some of the pioneering institutions for the aging around the country and the conclusions of many of the leading practitioners in the field seem to be shaping a growing movement to create a complex of specialized facilities offering the aging, wherever possible, a full spectrum of services on the same grounds. This spectrum ranges all the way from independent living to the care of the completely dependent. Such campuses may contain the following components:

Apartments—for independent living: residential, retirement hotels, villages;

Home-Operated Services—home care, Meals-on-Wheels;

Services for Nonresidents Who Come to the Campus—day care or day center, health clinic, sheltered workshops, rehabilitation services;

Homes for the Aged—personal care, helpful living in a protective environment: domiciliary, sheltered, custodial, or intermediate care;

Intermediate Care—for long-term care: medical, nursing, and rehabilitation services for the chronically ill (essentially Medicaid care);

Skilled Nursing Care Facility—usually short-term care: posthospital, convalescent, rehabilitation (Medicaid, Medicare financing);

Special Services for the Mentally Impaired.

Those who reside on such a campus most likely will escape the trauma of the moving many older people must do. The nonresidents who avail themselves of its services may find there the human resources that give them their greatest sense of security.

NONRESIDENT PROGRAMS

Sponsors may elect to develop a series of nonresident services. These can be arranged without an institutional base on an outreach and nonresident basis. When such programs are available, they are instrumental in keeping the elderly in their homes. Services may be limited, however, because of a lack of funding. In addition, a major problem is that a large number of the elderly who would benefit from these programs live in environments that limit or preclude the delivery of services.

The nonresident services may include such programs as:

Meals-on-Wheels—delivering one or more meals to the homebound thus enabling the elderly to remain in their own homes until later in their lives;

Homemaker Services—trained homemaker/housekeeper who can shop, cook, clean for, and assist older people in their own homes;

Transportation (a crying need for many older people);
Foster Homes;
Day Center—recreation and other services in a multiser-
vice center: clubs, crafts, meals, legal services, health
clinic. This program can be part of a facility or can be
free standing.
Day Care—offered for individuals who use the facility during the day on a more intensive treatment basis (meals,
recreation, physical therapy, occupational therapy, social services) and return to their own homes at the end of
the day;
Sheltered Workshops.

SPECIAL TYPES OF FINANCING

FOUNDERS FEES AND LIFE-LEASE CONTRACTS

Some nonprofit sponsors, most frequently
church-related groups, finance their retirement
housing through the help of Founders Fees. Founders Fees are sums usually ranging from $15,000–
50,000 and are paid by the initial occupants (or
"founders") of a facility. These sums entitle the residents to lifetime use of their apartments, suites, or
rooms as the case may be. In effect, they help finance
the capital investment for establishing the facility.
In this way, a resident renders himself or herself a
service and makes a contribution to the church. The
hope is that ultimately other persons who cannot afford to pay the fees may be able to come in at a reduced rate. In addition to the payment for life
tenancy, there is a monthly charge for maintenance
and other services based on operating costs.

Life Lease or Life Contract arrangements usually
call for a stipulated sum based on life expectancy actuarial tables, and guarantee to the older person lifetime occupancy of the dwelling unit. Here, too, an
additional monthly charge is made, depending upon
the additional services offered and maintenance.

Some sponsors may return a proportion of the
original investment when a resident needs to move.
The amount returned is in proportion to the length
of time that he has stayed in the facility.

It is important to understand that both Founders
Fees and Life Lease contracts guarantee an apartment, but do not in and of themselves provide for
ongoing operating services or health plans or other
programs. It is also important to understand that
the apartment reverts to the sponsor and cannot be
left as a legacy to relatives. Some sponsors have a
special fund to help those who cannot afford the full
Founders Fee. Other arrangements include escalator
clauses to increase the monthly charge in the event
that costs of services rise.

LIFE CARE

Life Care is a method of financing still used only
by some Retirement Homes for the Aged and a few
residence club living arrangements. Usually based
upon actuarial tables of life expectancy and cost of
services, an amount is paid for total life care that includes the accommodations, meals, health and personal care services. A resident usually turns over the
amount of money equal to the determined cost.
Where the individual may not have sufficient cash,
his or her assets, in the amount equal to the determined cost, become the property of the nonprofit
sponsor. Should the older person live far beyond the
expectancy set by the actuarial table, the non-profit
sponsor must still continue to care for him or her, regardless of cost.

Should the facilities fail, however, sponsors would
be hard put to live up to their agreements of Life
Care, Life Lease, or Founders Fees, and the resident
would have lost his or her lifetime savings and perhaps have no place to live. Although there have been
very few instances of failure on part of the sponsors
who guarantee life occupancy, it is still important for
one to read the fine print of the contract, get an attorney's advice, and be assured that the sponsors
can make good on their commitments.

FUTURE

The future availability of adequate housing for
the aged is difficult to predict. There is general
agreement, however, that the demand for adequate
housing at a price the elderly can afford far sur-
passes the current supply and that current programs
will not solve this problem. In recent years, federal
policy has been to limit housing assistance by target-
ing only very low income families, by reducing benefits, and by de-emphasizing new construction. At
the same time that federal programs to build housing have been reduced, new tax laws discourage private investment in housing construction and encourage owners of older housing stock to demolish
buildings in order to use land for more profitable
businesses.

Public housing programs, especially the Section 8
provision,[1] have been successful in meeting the
needs of some, but more facilities are needed. Con-

[1]Section 8 is a housing assistance payments program under
HUD, providing annual housing assistance payments or
rent subsidies to eligible older people, participating owners, developers, and public housing agencies. For example,
under this program at the present time, an elderly resident
pays no more than 30% of his income in rent.

struction and maintenance costs are very high and the problem is compounded by the necessity of diverting funds from building new units to salvaging older public housing that was poorly constructed. Furthermore, with over 60% of public housing in metropolitan areas, those in other areas are poorly served in spite of a recent trend to build housing outside central cities.

Other developments within cities have caused shortages of adequate housing for the elderly. Whereas deterioration of inner cities and the increase in crime have made some existing housing unsuitable, urban renewal projects in the last 20 years have created new problems for the older city dweller. The back-to-the-city movement of younger, more affluent families has led to the displacement of many of the elderly. As older residential hotels and boarding houses are torn down, rental apartments are converted to condominiums and, as rents and property taxes rise, the elderly find they cannot compete for housing.

Efforts are being made in the public and private sector to increase the amount of affordable housing for the elderly. More community support services are being developed to enable this group to remain in their own homes for a longer period of time. In addition to home maintenance, homemaker and home nursing services, some have suggested a reverse mortgage plan that would pay older persons to stay in their homes. Long-term care facilities are increasingly moving toward the campus concept with multilevel care: apartments for independent living, congregate housing for those who need more services, personal care facilities, and nursing homes. Many elderly are attracted by the variety of services offered by these retirement centers and by the security of knowing they will remain part of the community even when they are no longer able to live independently. HUD (United States Department of Housing and Urban Development) now has an Experimental Housing Allowance Program that has as its goal improving the quality of existing rental units as well as providing an income supplement.

The tendency of the elderly to live alone has increased housing costs and the demand for housing units. A number of demonstration projects have tried to determine if less costly shared housing would be an acceptable alternative. One project featured the conversion of single homes into shared homes consisting of a family and an elderly person. Cooperative housing or communes, some age-integrated and some age-segregated, have been tried. The success of the "granny flat" and of sheltered housing in England has been studied for its applicability to the United States. For those elderly needing more assistance, some states have had good results with careful placement in foster homes. A recurring proposal is for a family subsidy that would provide a cash allowance to enable the family to keep a resident at home and, thus, prevent unnecessary institutionalization.

In the ideal community, older people would have a number of choices of where to live and how much to spend. There would be low-cost housing built with features for the convenience and comfort of older people, including areas for recreation and services. There would be moderately priced housing for those with slightly higher incomes. There would be congregate housing for the frail elderly where group meals were served.

Older people, if they chose, could live in retirement developments where they would have the companionship of people their own age or they could continue to live in the community with neighbors of all ages.

Elderly homeowners would be able to obtain low-interest loans to keep their houses in good repair and some method would be provided for them to meet their real estate taxes.

Today, a few communities in the United States provide some of these choices but the availability of housing for older people is haphazard. Some areas have almost too much of certain types, while, in others, there is no specially designed housing at all for the elderly.

REFERENCES

1. American Institute of Architecture: *Design for Aging: An Architect's Guide*. Washington, D.C., The AIA Press, 1985.
2. Carp FM, Burnett WM (Eds): *Patterns of Living and Housing Middle Aged and Older People*. Bethesda, Maryland, United States Department of Health, Education and Welfare, 1965.
3. Chellis RD, Seagle JF Jr, Seagle BM: *Congregate Housing for Older People*. Lexington, MA, DC Heath & Co., 1982.
4. Fried M: Grieving for a lost home. In Duhl LJ (Ed): *The Urban Condition*. New York, Simon and Schuster, 1963, pp. 151-171.
5. Hoglund JD: *Housing for the Elderly*. New York, Van Nostrand Reinhold Company, 1985.
6. Lawton MP: *Social and Medical Services in Housing for the Aged*. Rockville, MD, Department of Health and Human Services, 1980.
7. Lawton MP, Nahemow L: Ecology and the aging process. In Eisdorfer C, Lawton MP (Eds): *The Psychology of Adult Development and Aging*. Washington, DC,

American Psychological Association, 1973, pp. 619-674.

8. Newman S: Housing and long-term care: The suitability of the elderly's housing to the provision of inhome services. *Gerontologist* 25:35, 1985.

9. Struyk RJ: Future housing assistance policy for the elderly. *Gerontologist* 25:41, 1985.

10. Turner MA: Building housing for the low income elderly: Cost containment in the Section 202 program. *Gerontologist* 25:271, 1985.

CHAPTER 44

New Community Options for Elderly Patients

DAVID L. RABIN
ADA ROMAINE DAVIS

A distinct characteristic of many Americans is the high value they place on independence and personal autonomy. These values are severely threatened late in life when physical frailty, combined with the high cost of health care, restrict choices available to older persons requiring long-term care. The desire of the older person to remain autonomous is frustrated by societal concerns about the cost of providing community personal and health care. As a result, older persons on fixed incomes must pay out-of-pocket for many community-based services. When impoverished, they become eligible for long-term institutional care rather than assistance from community services. Nevertheless, the increasing needs of the elderly are encouraging development of many different types of services to help in maintaining their independence. The elderly eventually needing care represent a large number of people. The number of elderly is expected to double between 1980 and 2000 (5); this large increase creates an urgency to develop a variety of community services and to increase the financial accessibility of these services.

In addition to the demographic imperative, many other factors need to be considered in developing new ways of caring for the elderly. These factors include personal preference, cost containment, the growing numbers of older persons, particularly those who are old (75+) and those who are old old (85+), changes in family structure, increasing avail-

ability of medical technology and personal wealth, and the availability of long-term care institutions.

In this chapter several causes of the increasing need for health care services and the response of both the social and health care systems to these needs will be discussed. Also described are the range of community services that are currently available and those that may become available in the future to support this population.

Causes for the rapid increase in the number of older persons, particularly those over 75, are discussed in Chapter 40. The consequences are that large numbers of older people are living in the community who have substantial physical impairment, and larger numbers are at high risk of such impairment. Nearly 80% of the care of impaired elderly is provided by family members and friends (3). Yet ability of those closest to the older person—spouses and children—to provide care is made difficult by rapidly increasing longevity and loss of a spouse, particularly for women. It also is complicated by society's recent preference for a smaller number of offspring and for grown children's tendency to move away from parents. Grown children, both sons and daughters, may be working. In cases in which parents are 85 years of age or older, children themselves may be retired and living on fixed incomes. Increasingly, parents who are in their 90s are being cared for by children in their 70s.

Each of these factors alone complicates the provision of family care for older people and increases the need to supplement this care. Family care is preferred for many reasons; it is more personal, acceptable, continuously available, adaptable, and, of perhaps greatest significance, it is less costly. Expensive institutional care is avoided, or at least postponed.

MEDICARE AND MEDICAID

With the passage of Medicare and Medicaid in 1965, institutional care became more accessible as payment became available for Skilled Nursing Facilities (SNFs) (Medicare) and Intermediate Nursing Facilities (ICFs) (Medicaid). The number of available nursing home beds increased dramatically from 1963 to the 1970s, from 563,560 to 1,537,338 (7). Studies conducted during the 1970s, however, revealed problems within long-term care institutions having to do with both quality of care and quality of life. Also, it became apparent that once frail elderly are institutionalized, i.e., to nursing homes, they remain for long periods of time, at great personal and societal cost. With nursing home costs currently at 25 to 30 thousand dollars per person per year, institutionalized elderly soon deplete their accumulated savings; impoverished, they then become eligible for Medicaid, which for some elderly means the indignity of receiving welfare after a life of independence.

Medicare and Medicaid were part of President Lyndon B. Johnson's program to declare war on poverty. Those living on social security benefits had become increasingly beset by the rising cost of acute medical care. At that time, Social Security benefits were the major source of income for most retired people. Health insurance was not affordable by many and was escalating rapidly in cost. Medicare was intended to pay the expenses of acute care—primarily hospital and, secondarily, physician care, as reflected in Medicare Part B, now an option for which older persons pay an additional annual premium. Medicaid originally was intended as a program to pay for comprehensive medical care services, including acute care, medications, preventive services, and long-term care for those on welfare and therefore unable to purchase medical care. There were several categories of welfare groups, most numerous of whom were women and children, but by 1975 nursing home costs for the elderly became the biggest single Medicaid expense, accounting for 40% of program costs when only 16.4% of Medicaid eligibles are over 65 (7). Despite attempts to contain costs, long-term care expenditures continue as the major Medicaid program cost.

While most acute care expenses for the elderly are covered by Medicare, the limited long-term care benefits of Medicare are not meeting the needs of the fastest growing segment of the elderly population. Sustaining the frail elderly in the community is one of the greatest challenges facing our society. Although personal income of older persons has increased, long-term care costs remain a challenge. Personal income for retired people includes not only Social Security benefits, but also other forms of income such as retirement pensions and personal investment income. Long-term care expenses for the elderly are funded by Medicaid, within limits, but nearly all of these funds are for nursing home care. Less than 2% of Medicaid expenditures are for home health care. Home health coverage is readily available through Medicaid in only a few states, with New York State alone accounting for 75% of all Medicaid home health expenditures as of 1983. Restricting skilled professional services to institutions rather than providing these services at home is increasingly questioned as being an appropriate policy. Many states are experimenting with providing alternatives to nursing home care by means of broader provision and better coordination of community services for those who are eligible for nursing home care but not yet institutionalized.

Although the increasing wealth of a small proportion of the elderly provides private means to purchase long-term care out of pocket—nursing home, home health care, and home care—this does not resolve the problem for the middle- and low-income elderly population who constitute most of the aged.

ALTERNATIVES TO INSTITUTIONALIZED CARE

There are many approaches to providing community rather than institutional care for the elderly across the states. Current government policies are based on accumulated experiences over the past 25 years of government-financed care. Care to those at home consists of both social and health care.

SOCIAL AND HOME HEALTH CARE

Social care relates to a broad range of services, extending from recreational, nutritional, and health promotional care provided at senior centers, transport and day care for ambulatory chronically ill elderly, personal care services in the home such as grooming, home maintenance, housekeeping, and shopping services by homemakers and chore workers, as well as home-delivered meals. Payment for and availability of these services are determined by state and local decisions regarding allocation of dollars provided under Title III of the Older Americans Act, and Title XX of the Social Security Act as coordinated through state and local Offices of Aging. Many of these services to older persons are available with few restrictions, beginning at age 60 rather than 65.

Home health services by skilled nurses or other health professionals such as physical, occupational, respiratory, and speech therapists became more readily available following the first major revision of Medicare in 1972. During the 1970s the number of home health agencies providing these skilled and professional services rose rapidly, with an associated annual increase of 25% growth rate in Medicare home health care service use.

ENCOURAGING NEW COMMUNITY CARE FOR THE ELDERLY

The cost of hospital care has been increased far in excess of the annual rate of inflation for all goods. This led to further Medicare changes in 1980 easing access to home health care in part as an alternative to hospital and skilled nursing home care. The Medicare changes permitted access to home health care even *before* hospitalization and as a result allowed proprietary agencies to provide care if acceptable to the states. During the 1970s and 1980s, we have seen a further rapid increase in access to home health care. In addition to the increase in the number of agencies, there was also a rapid change in their sponsorship, with a shift away from municipal and voluntary agencies (the predominate providers of home health care before 1980) to private nonprofit and for-profit agencies. These two types of agencies currently provide 45% of all home health care services. Another recent innovation is the growth of hospital-based home health care services, currently the most rapidly increasing sponsor of services.

Increased access to home health care was initially encouraged by the federal government in the expectation that it would reduce cost of care. Other cost-containment measures were put into effect, initially a cap on hospital expenditures and then the Diagnosis Related Group (DRG) prospective payment system. These prospective payment systems have encouraged continued decreases in hospital length of stay and use of home health care, particularly hospital-based home health care. At the same time, additional cost-containment measures were developed to constrain the use of SNFs and, more recently, home health care. Access to both these Medicare services has been made more restrictive by administrative regulatory changes denying access and limiting the length of time services that are used for eligible persons.

One result of the new regulations, despite increased availability of home care services, is a reduction in the annual rate of growth of home care agencies to the current 15% (7). The decreased availability of these long-term care services for the frail elderly is making more urgent the need for community-supported services, particularly personal care services. However, the availability of these services also has decreased as federal funds from Titles III and XX programs have diminished. Many but not all states or local governments are appropriating more for these services to compensate for the loss of federal funds. The different state and local responses to federal cutbacks create differences in service availability by area. On a local level, decreased government funding for these programs results in decreased availability of such benefits as transportation, Meals on Wheels, senior care, personal care, and personal aid services, further compromising the ability of an increasingly impaired population to receive care at home.

One of the most far-reaching Medicare changes in 1982, which has implications for long-term care, was the provision for hospice and Health Maintenance Organization (HMO) care. The hospice legislation permits payment for coordinated services, by a prospectively determined financial formula, for those who are terminally ill. Services at home by nurses, volunteers, and homemakers are encouraged, rather than similar services being given in a nursing home or hospital. The limited payment forces an integrated team approach to care and allocates dollars across multiple community and institutional providers, including the physician. This kind of allocation is similar to what occurs for closed panel HMOs providing comprehensive acute services. The 1982 legislation also encouraged enrollment in HMOs for Medicare beneficiaries providing a prospective age and area experience-specific reimbursement rate. Currently, over 140 HMOs are providing an HMO option for the elderly. An additional aspect of that legislation required HMOs to provide added services for the elderly beyond those available under Medicare. Providing additional services can have the effect of increasing discretionary income of the elderly by decreasing out-of-pocket medical care costs such as payment for medications. More important in the long run is that HMOs could provide a mechanism for providing certain services such as home health care, case assessment, case management, and even personal care to Medicare recipients who, in the absence of these services, would have to use more costly hospital or skilled nursing homes. It is presumed that paying a fixed sum may permit trade-offs among services, most of which will be community based, and that this will be more cost effective and will result in better integration of acute medical care services, with social and health-related services provided at home. To better provide home health care, HMOs have either contracted for or developed home health care agency services, allowing them to provide home care services at less cost and permitting immediate access to care for patients from hospital or community. Although these arrangements may be more easily accomplished by closed-panel HMOs than by Independent Practice Associations (IPAs) and Preferred Provider Organizations (PPOs), all HMOs have a strong incentive to decrease expensive institutional care costs.

Two other fundamental developments are occurring that should facilitate coordination of services for older persons in the community. One is the rapid growth in integration of hospitals and community care services with potential development of integrated systems of care. By 1984, 22% of hospitals had a home care service or department nearly double what it had been 2 years before, and 13% of hospitals had extended care beds (2). Many more have administrative arrangements for privileged access to long-term care and rehabilitation beds. As a result, patients leaving the hospital have easier and more ready access to home health and nursing home care. Similarly, patients in continuing care can more readily return to the hospital. Associated with hospital response to DRGs has been earlier discharge planning, particularly for Medicare patients beginning at the time they first enter the hospital. Continuing care needs at the time of discharge can thus be better predicted, coordinated, and planned with the family. Both proprietary and nonprofit hospitals are developing formal arrangements with community long-term care providers and better discharge planning. As reimbursement for care becomes more restrictive, hospitals with these alternative ways of providing care should be at an advantage in caring for elderly patients.

The other important services increasingly available are case assessment and case management services. These services assess the social and home health care needs of patients and coordinate care from among the full range of both professional and community-based services available. In a number of communities, case assessment and management services are available under Office of Aging auspices. In some states, such as the District of Columbia, Connecticut, Massachusetts, Georgia, and Minnesota, case assessment and management services are widely available through the state under public auspices. For example, private case management services by social workers to arrange for, manage, and supervise home care for the elderly also have begun to develop over the last few years to provide counsel and assistance to families and the elderly on a fee-for-service basis.

HEALTH INSURANCE

In keeping with current policies for the private sector to provide services, the federal government is encouraging the insurance industry to provide long-term care insurance. The concept is being widely studied and was recently endorsed by Department of Health and Human Services (DHHS) Secretary Otis Bowen. Some insurance is available and availability is likely to rapidly increase.

For those persons having long-term care insurance, financial ability to withstand a long period of incapacity is greatly enhanced. The increasing number of financially well-off elderly constitutes a widening market for this insurance coverage, once they understand the need for it. Part of the DHHS proposal is to educate the public about this need.

As long-term care insurance becomes more readily available and other demographic, Medicare, Medicaid, and health care institutional program changes occur, an organizational structure for providing long-term care will be established. As a result of the improved environment fostering noninstitutional care, more older persons will be served by better integrated and more accessible community systems. Because a larger and sicker population will be residing in the community, a further increased demand for services will result. Over time, these evolutionary changes should occur in the availability and use of long-term care services.

A description follows of services and housing alternatives now available and projected. The current move toward more concentrated community residential facilities will make delivery of services to older persons easier, more efficient, and therefore less costly. Older people who live in housing developed to meet their special needs are more likely to remain at home throughout life.

LINKAGE OF COMMUNITY CARE SYSTEMS

Most older Americans live at home. As people age, however, their living arrangements and ability to care for themselves change. Recent figures show that 17% of older men (65+), and 43% of older women live alone (1). Today's trend toward home care mandates that community services and agencies coordinate their efforts to provide the best care and services possible at the lowest cost. Linkages between health care agencies—hospitals, home care programs, HMOs, visiting nurse associations, and others—are vital with respect to our rapidly aging population. Below, we discuss both health care and housing for the elderly in the community.

HOSPITALS, NURSING HOMES, AND HOME CARE

HOSPITALS

The community general hospital is the primary source of health care services for older people, according to Brody and Persily (4). Their study showed that 4 million (20%) of all older people use inpatient services at least once a year, and that 27% of this number return at least twice in the ensuing year. Most of these hospital admissions are for acute episodes of chronic problems. In addition, admission rates per thousand in the over-65 population have risen 41% in just 10 years (4).

Today, in addition to providing acute care to older persons, hospitals also are the points of access to long-term care. As indicated, effective and comprehensive discharge planning assists older patients to receive coordinated, continuing care after discharge either through the home care program of the hospital or by means of referral to the appropriate facility or agency.

NURSING HOMES

Although a small number of people over 65 years of age (5% or 1.3 million) lived in institutions—primarily nursing homes—in 1980, this number increases dramatically with age, ranging from 2% for persons 65 to 74 years, to 7% for those 75 to 84 years, and jumping to 23% for people over 85 (1). The cost of care in institutions is also rising at an alarming rate, so that both federal and private organizations are mobilizing resources to provide care that will enable older people to remain in the community as long as possible. Nursing home care, then, is reserved for people whose health state is such that care in the home is no longer possible.

HOME CARE

In many cases, persons discharged from the hospital can be sent home and cared for by health care professionals and auxiliary people such as home-makers and home health aides. Until recently, people receiving home care needed only monitoring or simple nursing care such as dressing changes or parenteral medications. With the advent of DRGs and other prospective payment systems, people are being discharged from hospitals "quicker and sicker," and needing much more intensive nursing care that involves, in many cases, hyperalimentation, respirators, tracheostomy, and similar complex problems and equipment. Thus, home care costs, too, are rising because of the need for skilled nursing care over longer periods of time. Currently, though, home care is meeting the needs of many people who are not really sick enough to be hospitalized.

Home health care usually involves regular visits by a registered nurse, licensed practical nurse, home health aide, homemaker, therapist, or social worker. Services may include a combination of these providers. About 8000 home care agencies now provide multiple kinds of services to thousands of people at reasonable costs. Most professionals advocate that at least three levels of care be available in the home, based on client needs and health status, through hospital home care programs. These levels of care are delineated according to the following criteria:

1. Preventive services that include health education, outpatient care, recreation, police assistance, dental care, volunteer services, and home safety.
2. Supportive services that include legal, financial, home help, nutrition services, transportation, shopping, laundry, visitors, social, and religious supports.
3. Therapeutic services that include nursing care, family respite care, respiratory therapy, mental health therapy, laboratory services, and pharmaceutical services.

Home care is usually supervised by the physician and managed by professional nurses. Decisions regarding patients' status and needed changes are made by both. Changes are based on needs and health status, and persons may be transferred to the hospital or to a nursing home if home care is not adequate to meet the individual's needs.

Typically, home care is provided in one of three modes, depending on the initial level of care required and the age and health status of the individual. For example, one mode would be appropriate if the person were recently discharged from the hospital and needed skilled nursing care for a period of time and frequent monitoring by a physician. In this situation, the patient is quite ill at the outset, but recovers relatively quickly and can then be monitored by means of regular visits to an HMO (see below).

By contrast, another individual is one of the frail elderly who is gradually deteriorating. At first, these individuals may need only occasional visits by a nurse to see that they are managing to care for themselves adequately. Over time, additional services must be added—home health aide, homemaker, licensed practical nurse, and registered nurse. Ultimately, the individual may need to be transferred to hospital or nursing home, or to a hospice (see below). However, the person has been maintained in his or her own home for many months or even years.

A third mode may be a composite of the two preceding situations in which not only is the client recently discharged from the hospital, but he or she is also beginning to decline because of advanced age. The person experiences increasingly frequent episodes of severe illness relating to one or more health problems. Here, as before, care is based on needs as these needs change.

The most typical of these situations is that in which the person is becoming more frail and the health status is declining. Needs are met according to current status, often beginning with support services such as Meals on Wheels, and progressing through homemaker services, nursing services, intermittent skilled nursing care, special housing, continual skilled nursing care, respite care for family members, and hospice care as the person becomes terminally ill. By providing care in stages, the individual can be maintained at home, in familiar and comfortable surroundings, as long as possible.

COMMUNITY SUPPORT SERVICES

Older persons are often helped through community support services or public or private agencies that offer specialized help. Among these services are Meals on Wheels, volunteer services to help with transportation, shopping, meal preparation, laundry, and housekeeping. Within a given geographic area, centers may be available: community health center, adult or elderly day care center, social or recreational center for older persons, and other similar kinds of community support services. Many of these services are provided by volunteers such as community residents, policemen and firemen, retired people, teachers, and religious groups. These services are available through a coordinated networking system set up to monitor all older persons living in a community. Often, particularly in rural areas, not all of these services will be available; in these areas, federal and private organizations may be the primary sources of assistance to the elderly.

MANAGED CARE: HEALTH MAINTENANCE ORGANIZATIONS

Persons being cared for at home may combine home care and HMO care as their condition improves. Those who are able to travel to the HMO receive medical care, nursing care, therapy such as physical, respiratory, or speech, and social work services. HMOs provide what has recently become known as "managed" care, whereby patients' health status is regularly monitored and treatment given based on current needs. Potential or actual problems can be recognized, diagnosed, and treated before the condition worsens or complications arise. This type of managed care allows people to remain at home and their health status maintained at optimal levels for many years.

Homemaker services provide help with housekeeping, meal preparation, shopping, laundry, and personal care. Often, the homemaker may also help with correspondence and in other ways.

COMMUNITY LIFELINE

Private agencies, which provide older persons continuous telephone access to care, are springing up across the country. Access is provided either by means of a continuous telephone monitoring system or through daily (or more frequent) telephone calls from the agency to individuals living alone. In continuous monitoring, the older person wears a beeper-type of device. In the event of a fall or other emergency, the person can touch the device to summon help without having to be near a telephone.

In the near future, technology will allow patients to be monitored electronically by means of wristwatch types of computers that will transmit vital signs such as blood pressure, electrocardiogram (ECG), pulse, temperature, and other important data directly to a central location in a hospital or agency. In this way, patients can be carefully and continually assessed without the need for actual contact with health professionals, although immediate visits on an emergency basis can then be made as necessary, based on patients' status and needs. Should rehospitalization become necessary, the patient can be moved quickly from home to hospital for more intensive care and treatment.

HOUSING

Housing arrangements become increasingly important as people get older. In past years, when the family was growing and children were living at home, space was needed. Then, as children leave home and the spouse dies, older persons find that they are living alone in a house that is now too large for them. If they are on fixed incomes, the cost of repairs and maintenance is more than they can handle, and their health status may prevent their working around the house to make minor repairs, as they once had. In short, the house gradually becomes a burden.

Several alternatives are available for older persons in this situation. Below are some of the possible housing alternatives available for aging individuals.

SHARED HOUSING

People are discovering that shared housing is the answer to many of the problems that arise over the years. This plan involves either sharing the home with others, either relatives in similar circumstances or friends in the same age bracket, or renting rooms to younger people. Variations of this scheme may be to rent the house to a young couple in need of space for their family, and reserving one floor or one or two rooms for the owner. Either of these arrangements can be both socially and economically advantageous to the older person. Another variant is to have the older person exchange services for rent. In this case, the renter, depending on sex, can do housework, yard work, painting, shopping, cooking, or other similar tasks.

Another alternative for the older person living alone in a house is to make structural changes that provide greater flexibility and economic advantages. One way is to build a separate apartment within the house or attached to the house. This arrangement permits the owner either to rent the house while he/she lives in the apartment, or vice versa. Changes like this can cost a considerable sum of money. The owner needs to be wary of unknown or hidden problems that might arise in undertaking such a venture. However, it remains a viable option for those who can afford to and want to make such changes.

ECHO HOUSING OR GRANNY FLATS

Elder Cottage Housing Opportunity (ECHO) homes are small, self-contained, portable units that can be placed in the back or side yard of a single-family house (2). The idea began in Australia, where "granny flats" are manufactured to enable older parents to remain near their adult children and families. The cost of these small houses is not exorbitant and may be a reasonable way to accommodate two generations within the same geographic space, without having to pay for additional land. ECHO homes are not to be confused with mobile or prefabricated homes, which are zone restricted in many areas. ECHO homes are designed and built especially for older or disabled persons, and usually are outside zoning regulations.

SHELTERED OR SUPPORTIVE HOUSING

This general label includes a number of types of housing arrangements that provide varying degrees of care for older persons. The need for this kind of housing becomes apparent when the older person is no longer able to live alone in a house. The different categories are as follows:

- Board and Care Homes, in which the older person is able to remain almost totally independent but may need help with tasks like cooking, cleaning, laundry, or personal care. This kind of housing is not the same as a boarding house in that services are available that one would not expect to find in the old-fashioned boarding house. The amount and quality of services varies considerably, depending on costs and available personnel. Careful information gathering is essential before moving into any kind of arrangement that is new and different. Many essentially well individuals, however, find this type of living arrangement perfect for their needs.
- Congregate Housing, in which older persons live in a group situation where meals are shared. Heavy housekeeping is provided, and a staff organizes social and recreational activities. Most congregate housing facilities are sponsored by government or nonprofit organizations; they range in size from 30 to 300 units. The major difference between congregate housing and board and care homes is the number of professional staff who are available in congregate housing. Most of these facilities are rented by the unit, by the month. Other types of congregate housing are developed within existing apartment buildings or hotels in which an entire floor is leased or renovated to accommodate apartments for older persons. Having apartments together, all on one floor, allows for easier housekeeping, and health care and other services can be provided more efficiently.
- Continuing Care Retirement Communities, which enable the older person to lead an independent lifestyle in a community where a full range of services and activities is available, including 24-hour nursing care. Private investors and developers are building high-rise apartment buildings and other kinds of architectural styles as retirement communities. On entering, the person signs a contract that stipulates services, activities, and amount of nursing care provided. Older persons are urged to look at such arrangements carefully; changes in their health status may mean that that kind of arrangement is no longer possible, and a considerable amount of equity may be lost. Continuing Care Communities are generally more expensive than other similar kinds of housing such as

board and care and congregate housing, and most charge an entrance fee of from $20,000 to $100,000. Monthly charges may range from $650 to $1200 or more, depending on the quality and number of services available. The monthly charge may increase over time, making this kind of living arrangement a lifetime commitment (2).

SHELTERED HOUSING IN BRITAIN

The term "sheltered housing" refers to specially designed or converted houses, flats, or flatlets, grouped and with a resident manager. Depending on the plan and extent of renovations, there may be an alarm system, a common lounge area, laundry, and dining facilities.

Originally, sheltered housing was conceived as a house midway between an ordinary dwelling that has become too large or inconvenient for the older person to maintain and a residential home for the elderly. The British government began building sheltered housing as early as the 1960s, anticipating the need for such housing. In 1963, only about 36,000 people were living in sheltered housing. By 1978, this number had jumped to 300,000, and the most recent estimate places the figure at about 400,000. Most of this type of housing is provided by local authorities, but an increasing proportion, estimated to be about 20%, is now provided by voluntary organizations (6).

The average age of residents living in sheltered housing is 75. Many of these residents were younger at the time they began to live in this type of housing, and this population now is increasingly dependent. The inevitable problem of increasing disability among residents of elderly housing, regardless of type, is of concern to housing managers. Domiciliary services can be provided to aging residents, but as disabilities become more severe, there is greater demand for more comprehensive services, which then become expected. One alternative is to provide "staged" sheltered housing, which allows residents to move from housing with minimal services to those with more services, as health deteriorates.

This model for providing adequate and appropriate housing alternatives to aging Americans may prove to be the most economic and feasible in the future. The concept also permits flexibility both for older persons and for developers of housing, whether public or private.

CARE DURING TERMINAL ILLNESS

RESPITE CARE

A recent study conducted by the DHHS showed that women—usually spouses or relatives—provide 70% of the home care to older persons. Specifically, 1.2 million older people are cared for by 2.2 million women, either through regular visits or live-in arrangements.

Some conditions such as Alzheimer's disease or senile dementia, in which there is considerable confusion present in older persons, demands that someone be in constant attendance to prevent the person from "wandering" and thus getting lost or injured while alone outside the home, and to prevent other types of accidents or injuries. In many situations, family members are required to care for these persons over long periods of time, often years. Periodically, they need to be given time away from the continuous responsibilities of caring for the patient, and to restore the caretaker's energy level and perspective. In many situations, only one person, usually the spouse of the patient, is available to provide this ongoing care, with no other family members available to "spell" the major care provider. The older persons can thus remain in their own homes, avoiding further problems with confusion that often occur when they are taken from familiar surroundings and placed in nursing homes or other situations totally unfamiliar to them.

Ideally, care provided by family members is enhanced and supported through supervision by professional nurses who, on the basis of regular assessments of physical and mental status of patients, can ascertain current and projected health care needs. Nurses also can provide planned educational programs to teach family members about how to care for specific conditions—diabetes, chronic obstructive pulmonary disease, arthritis, and others.

HOSPICE CARE

Hospice care for terminally ill persons is provided in separate facilities or in hospitals and nursing homes where a certain number of hospice beds may be available. Hospices have an environment that is supportive and caring as death becomes imminent. Here, family pets may come to visit or even to stay, and family members may participate in caring for the dying person if they so wish. Usually, the person must be assumed to be within 6 months of dying in order to be transferred to a hospice; that is the only criterion for admission in most cases.

SUMMARY

The rapidly increasing number of elderly is creating a great need for long-term care services. The need is best satisfied in community rather than institutional settings. As the community resources and local population needs are variable, many new ways of satisfying long-term care needs are developing. Government is encouraging less reliance on institutional than community care but community services for the elderly are not well organized or adequately funded. Development of payment mechanisms for care through greater private insurance and state governments is evolving. In response, more community services for the elderly, particularly home health and home care, are available.

Closer linkings among institutional and community care provide more case management, and better integrated systems of care are also developing. These forces bring us closer to a coherent and accessible long-term care system. For those at high risk of frailty or social isolation, development of life-line services and residence in a broad range of housing alternatives promises improved ways of funding care at home efficiently and responsively.

Continued availability of community providers, better integration of services, long-term financial access to community services, and development of sufficiently assisted living-housing are only going to occur if there is a sustained and federal commitment to noninstitutional long-term care. So far, rhetoric

has far exceeded commitment. Reliance on private sector initiatives can only address a part of the need. Many of those most in need will be least able to afford sustained private expenditures even with long-term care insurance. To assure community care for the elderly by need rather than by circumstance, federal policy providing broad and universal coverage for community care and elderly housing is necessary.

REFERENCES

1. American Association of Retired Persons: *A Profile of Older Americans: 1985.* Washington DC, AARP, 1985.
2. American Association of Retired Persons: *Your Home, Your Choice.* Washington DC AARP, 1985.
3. Brody S, Poulschomb W, Masciocchi C: The family caregiving unit; a major contribution in the long-term care support system. *Gerontologist* 18:556–561, 1978.
4. Brody SJ, Persily NA: *Hospitals and the Aged: The New Old Market.* Rockville, MD, Aspen, 1984.
5. Bureau of the Census, Current Population Reports Series. *Demographic and Socioeconomic Aspects of Aging in the United States.* Washington DC: US Government Printing Office, p 23, 1, 1984.
6. Butler A, Oldman C, Greve J: *Sheltered Housing for the Elderly.* London, George Allen and Unwin, 1983.
7. Rabin DC, Stockton P: *Long-Term Care for the Elderly: A Factbook.* New York, Oxford University Press, 1978.

CHAPTER 45

Gerontologic Nursing in the Continuum of Care

ELIZABETH M. HUGHES
NORMA R. SMALL
LILLIAN M. ANDERSEN

Gerontologic nursing has evolved into a major practice discipline. Its primary goal is to improve, maintain, or rehabilitate older persons' ability to function at their optimal level; emphasis is on older persons assuming as much responsibility for their health care as possible.

The attainment of this goal is influenced, in part, by the educational preparation and work experiences of gerontologic nurses. Physicians may find themselves interacting with gerontologic nurse practitioners with master's degrees, who have a strong knowledge base in pathophysiology, pharmacology, normal processes of aging, and health promotion and maintenance measures. These nurses focus on the primary care of elderly persons and their families in meeting a myriad of complex health needs.

Some nurses have practitioner certificates in lieu of advanced academic degrees. In the mid-1970s, certificate programs mushroomed to meet the need for gerontologic nurse practitioners. However, the number of these programs is declining; emphasis is on preparation at the graduate level.

The majority of gerontologic nurses in clinical practice today have acquired their competence from a 3-year hospital diploma program, augmented by work experience, self-instruction, and continuing education. Others are graduates of a 2-year associate or a 4-year baccalaureate program; these programs offer content and clinical experience in gerontology.

Since there are various educational pathways to the practice of gerontologic nursing, physicians can expect to work with nurses who have different levels of knowledge and clinical competence. The purpose of this chapter is to highlight the major roles and functions of gerontologic nurses in clincal practice today. Professional nursing practice centers on the process of assessing, planning, implementing, and evaluating care. However, nonprofessional personnel are supervised by the professional nurse and carry out the care plan.

In caring for older people, the first step is a functional assessment to determine self-care abilities and deficits (see Chapter 3, Functional Assessment, of the Elderly Patient). In this chapter, a modified case study illustrates important nursing assessments and interventions in the areas of nutrition, life-style modification, mobility, and disease prevention.

Nurses help with their clients' self-care abilities and/or compensate for their deficits. An intervention that enhances self-care is nutritional counseling. Nurses explain the functions of basic nutrient groups and amounts necessary to maintain a healthy aging process. Attention is given to common problems of digestive changes, food intolerance, and a decreased sense of taste and smell. The accessibility of food markets and the older person's financial ability to buy and prepare food are considered. Because many older people live alone and may feel lonely or depressed, they give little attention to proper meal preparation and eating habits, resulting in malnutrition. Nursing intervenes by giving information on menu planning, meal preparation, and the use of nutritional supplements, and by obtaining assistance from a homemaker or Meals-On-Wheels.

Nurses also provide instruction on achieving a proper balance between caloric intake and energy expenditure in the form of active and passive exercise. Many elderly lead sedentary lives because of a chronic illness that limits their physical mobility; some live in unsafe neighborhoods which restrict their outside activities. Because of lack of exercise they gradually become immobile. After a medical evaluation, an exercise program is designed to fit the older person's life-style and provide enjoyment. Older people are encouraged to exercise and participate in organized group programs such as stretching and flexing exercises, aerobics, swimnastics, or walking clubs. As well as benefiting the physical and mental health of older people, these services also provide opportunities to meet new people and establish friendships. For people immobilized and confined to their homes, gerontologic nurses teach the caretakers and clients transfer skills, chair exercises, range of motion, and proper body alignment measures.

Because they no longer have work and family-raising responsibilities, many older adults believe they are free from stress. However, retirement, decreased income, and the "empty nest" create stresses in role and marital relationships. Dealing with losses which mount with increasing age—loss of roles, loss of prestige and power, loss of economic security, loss of health, loss of functional abilities, and the loss of a spouse or significant other—constitute some of the stresses older persons experience at a time when their cognitive, physical, and social resources may be diminishing. Nurses counsel and assist their clients in identifying the stresses that may inhibit their abilities for optimal functioning and to deal effectively with the stressors. If individual long-term counseling is indicated, gerontologic nurses initiate a referral to an appropriate community resource.

Life-style modifications are difficult to achieve; however, they have a great impact on the health of older adults. The attitudes that "it is too late to change" and "you can't teach an old dog new tricks" are myths about aging that many health care practitioners, as well as older people, believe. To assist them in making life-style modifications, nurses do health teaching, use peer and self-help groups, provide individual and family counseling, and employ motivational reinforcement incentives. Through personal counseling, they motivate clients to limit or cease smoking, limit alcohol consumption, modify caloric consumption, do appropriate exercises, and follow proper dietary patterns and medical regimens. They assist people in adjusting to some of the functional changes that occur with aging. Ultimately, however, each individual client establishes his or her own health goals and assumes responsibility for determining the personal costs and benefits of life-style modification. Nurses and other health care providers who ascribe to self-care concepts assist the older person in decision making and accept the older person's decision, even if it may not agree with the provider's health goals.

Disease prevention is another important nursing role. In late adulthood, prevention is focused on older persons' understanding of the strengths and weaknesses of their own body. Some disease processes cannot be avoided, either because of genetic endowment and/or more than 60 years of life-style practices that are contrary to positive health. However, nurses inform older people about personal risk factors and the normal process of aging, which assists them in monitoring their own health. Knowledge of danger signals and prompt attention to physiologic changes can avert acute illness and minimize the disability of a chronic disease. Gerontologic nurses can assist older persons in making some of the necessary accommodations to sensory and cognitive changes that occur as a person ages.

The following case of an older couple illustrates gerontologic nursing practice in various components of the long-term continuum: acute care, rehabilitation, home health care, wellness programs, the physician's office, and nursing home care.

Mr. and Mrs. George, both 74 years of age and both retired from the telephone company after over 30 years of service, live in their own home in a Washington, D.C., metropolitan suburb. They have no children but live in a supportive neighborhood. Since retirement, they have enjoyed gardening, volunteer work, and travel with the local chapter of the American Association of Retired Persons. Both consider their health to be good and neither has been to a doctor since their family physician retired 5 years ago.

One day while working in the garden, Mr. George complained of dizziness and collapsed. He was taken to the community hospital emergency room by the local fire department ambulance and was admitted to the neurology unit with a diagnosis of stroke and left side hemiplegia. Although conscious on admission, he was confused as to time, place, and person.

ACUTE CARE

Ideally, the first contact an older person has with the health care system would be when the individual is in a state of "wellness" as defined by the individual. Sixty-eight percent of older persons describe their health as good to excellent requiring little or no contact with a health care provider (7). However, the "ideal" is the exception. The first contact most older persons have with the health care system and a nurse is in the acute care hospital. Sixty-seven percent of registered nurses are employed by acute care hospitals. Sixty to seventy percent of acute care beds are occupied by persons over age 65 years. While the medical regimen is the primary focus during an acute illness, nurses provide the 24-hour care necessary for an effective medical intervention.

During an acute hospitalization, nurses perform the functions that patients would normally do for themselves if they had the necessary knowledge, ability, or skill. Nurses coordinate care, monitor vital signs, administer drugs and intravenous therapies, observe and report patient response to the medical regimen, and take the necessary measures to prevent or control complications and infections. In addition, they compensate for patients' inability to meet activities of daily living such as personal hygiene and skin care, elimination, eating or nasogastric feeding, mobility, and exercise. They reinforce the physical, occupational, and speech therapy plans for rehabilitation. Nurses provide the caring environment for the older patient who experiences a great deal of stress when his or her cognitive, physical, and social resources are compromised.

Some hospitals have established specialized geriatric units, which are staffed by nurses who have had advanced preparation in gerontologic nursing. In addition to expertise in medical–surgical nursing, the staff is skilled in principles of physical, mental, and occupational therapies. Unfortunately, some of these units lose their focus as they become backed up or serve as holding unit for hard-to-place candidates (those requiring heavy personal care or who have financial and social entanglements).

Preparation for discharge from an acute care hospital largely depends on the nurse's assessment of the patient's or caregiver's level of knowledge and ability to assume the care. Nurses serve as advocates in preventing premature discharge to inappropriate settings. By planning with the patient and family, they initiate health teaching programs that focus on the immediate "need-to-know" information in such areas as the administration of medications, proper hydration and nutrition, and dressing changes. In providing health instruction, they try to avoid overloading the patient and family with information; instead they arrange follow-up referrals to continue the health teaching plan. Hospitals reimbursed for care by federal programs (Medicare and Medicaid) are required to provide discharge planning (4).

Because of the multitude and complexity of health service needs, the ideal long-term care planning process involves a physical therapist, an occupational therapist, a nutritionist, and a social worker, in addition to the traditional physician–nurse–patient triad. Patient and family participation is essential before any plan of care can be successfully implemented.

Mr. George's condition was quickly stabilized and a comprehensive rehabilitation program was initiated. He continued to have periods of confusion which did not improve during his hospitalization; these episodes interfered with his rehabilitation program. Mrs. George stated in the health history that Mr. George had had two "spells" in the past year during which he became confused and drowsy for about 2 hours. He has not been able to manage the family finances for the past 6 months because of "memory" problems. Mr. George was transferred to a rehabilitation facility for intensive rehabilitation in order to get maximum return of functional abilities.

REHABILITATION CENTER

Nurses with special educational preparation in gerontology and rehabilitation are essential to carry out the rehabilitation plan 24 hours a day, 7 days a week. Besides implementing and reinforcing physical, occupational, and speech therapists' plans, nurses focus on providing cognitive stimulation, helping the patient deal with the loss of functional abilities, and restoring self-esteem. The discharge plan from a rehabilitation center includes teaching about life-style adjustments, nutrition, exercise, and disease prevention measures. Social services are consulted to assist in obtaining necessary community resources to implement the discharge plan.

Mr. George reached his maximum rehabilitation potential but still required assistance with all personal care except feeding. He ambulated with a walker. His cognitive function improved slightly, and he was discharged to his home. In order to monitor Mr. George's adjustment to the home environment and Mrs. George's ability to provide the necessary care, the discharge planning nurse arranged for the Visiting Nurse Association to provide the skilled nursing and rehabilitation therapy visits reimbursable under Medicare. At the suggestion of the visiting nurse, a home health aide was hired for $7.00 an hour by Mrs. George for 4 hours a day, 3 days a week, to assist with personal care and to provide respite for Mrs.

George. Mr. George also attended a medical day care center for 6 hours a day, 2 days a week where he received a nutritious meal, health monitoring, limited physical therapy, reality orientation, and an opportunity for socialization in a structured environment. This arrangement cost Mrs. George $40.00 a day and permitted her to resume some of her social contacts. The total cost per week for the care of Mr. George was $164.00. Even with two excellent retirement plans, their financial resources were being depleted.

HOME HEALTH CARE

The American Medical Association defines home health care as "the provision of nursing care, social work, therapies (such as diet, occupational, psychological, and speech), vocational and social services, and homemaker-health aide services may be included as basic components of home health care" (5). The provision of these needed services to the patient at home constitutes a logical extension of the physician's therapy. Usually at the physician's request and under his or her medical direction, personnel who provide these home health care services operate as a team in assessing and developing the home health care plan (5). Home health nurses assess complex situations and then provide skilled nursing, supervise the provision of personal care, and instruct the client and caretaker in measures which will enable them to eventually assume the care. With the trend toward home care as more cost effective than acute or long-term institutional care, the complexity of the health and disease management in the home has increased dramatically and requires highly skilled and innovative nurses. All skilled nursing care, for example, sterile dressings, intravenous fluid administration, and nasogastric feedings, must be conducted by a registered nurse or a family member trained and supervised by a registered nurse. All care is given in accordance with physician orders and is carefully documented in order to be a reimbursable expense under Medicare or other third-party payers. The criteria for allowable expense and number of visits are reviewed and revised frequently by the Health Care Finance Agency.

Families provide approximately 80% of care for their older members, thereby being the major factor determining whether an older person's final home will be a nursing home. Most caregivers are adult daughters (29%), followed by wives (23%). Husbands provide 13% of the care, with only 10% being provided by formal services, for example, home health aides (9). Caregivers encounter many conflicts in providing their services. Younger caregivers have conflicts in fulfilling employment and family responsibilities, which results in 29% terminating their jobs, working fewer hours, or rearranging schedules around caregiving obligations. Younger children frequently compete for the attention of their mothers; when the older person lives in the home, there may be intergenerational conflicts due to changing values. The caregiving obligation may extend over long periods of time. Approximately 50% of caregivers provide care for 1 to 4 years, and 20% for 5 or more years—with little respite. Frequently, the care of the caregiver is overlooked until there is an acute crisis, such as illness or mental health problems.

The home health nurse is frequently in a position to assess the strain of caregiving on the caregiver and the family. She recommends community resources, such as adult day care, Meals-On-Wheels, respite care, and Legal Counsel for the Elderly. The local Area Office on Aging, created by the Older Americans Act (3), serves as a clearinghouse for services and programs provided by community groups, churches and synagogues, public agencies, and private companies. Often families are reluctant to use public services because of the "means" test that determines their financial status or private services, which deplete the older person's financial assets.

Mrs. George was encouraged by the home health nurse to resume participating in the local senior center activities as a respite while Mr. George was at the medical day care center. The center's services include a nutritious lunch, a wellness program, and educational and recreational activities.

WELLNESS PROGRAMS

The increasing number of older persons has brought a concomitant increase in the availability of wellness programs in senior centers, congregate housing arrangements, and senior social groups and organizations. The success of these programs depends on the group, the content, and the teaching-learning process. The homogeneity of the group's interests, socioeconomic status, and education are important in selecting content for a successful program. The relevance of the content to the individual's perceived risk of acquiring health problems, and the benefit to be achieved from participation in a program, are key motivators in promoting self-care practices. The nurse's knowledge and application of adult learning theory and teaching strategies, along with knowledge of the sensory and cognitive changes in aging, are essential in planning and implementing an effective "wellness" program.

As part of the program, the nurse conducted blood glucose screenings. Mrs. George had an elevated glucose level and was referred to a local physician who works collaboratively with a gerontologic nurse practitioner (GNP). On Mrs. George's first visit, the GNP took a complete health history, did a complete physical examination, and ordered x-rays and laboratory tests. The physician and the GNP met with Mrs. George to discuss the laboratory findings and to recommend a treatment plan. Mrs. George was diagnosed as having diabetes mellitus, which could be controlled by diet. The GNP explained the diet and saw Mrs. George on subsequent visits, making modifications according to protocol and discussing the client's status with the physician after each visit. Prior to leaving the physician's office, the office nurse reinforced the GNP's health teaching.

THE PHYSICIAN'S OFFICE

Most older persons age 65 or older report one or more chronic conditions, with 71.8% of these older persons reporting that their usual source of care is a physician's office (6). In the physician's office, the registered nurse obtains information useful in designing and implementing a treatment plan. She or he provides patients with written health instructions, clarifies written orders, does health teaching, and reinforces the need for follow-up visits, frequently making "reminder" and reassurance telephone calls.

Physicians who provide care to large numbers of older persons find that GNPs are assets to their practice. Gerontologic nurse practitioners are "educationally prepared to assume expanded roles in providing primary health care to older persons and their families. They possess in-depth knowledge of physical assessment, and can manage stable, chronic, and most acute illnesses or conditions afflicting older adults" (1). With the GNP managing the time-consuming routine care, the physician has more time to manage the complex diagnostic and acutely ill patients. This collaboration provides optimal care to the older patient. Currently there are 466 GNPs certified by the American Nurses' Association (ANA) (1).

Mr. George's dementia became progressively worse. His two days a week at the medical day care program, where he participated in exercises, reality orientation, and a group reminiscing program had to be discontinued because of urinary incontinence. Mrs. George continued to meet all his personal care needs with the help of the personal care aide. There was no longer justification to have skilled nursing visits. Mr. George became increasingly unsteady on his feet even with a walker and began trying to get out of bed at night to walk. He became very belligerent when Mrs. George tried to stop him. Mrs.

George was providing 24-hour care, and not watching her diet or getting sufficient rest. At the suggestion of the GNP, she began attending an Alzheimer's and Related Disorders support group. The group was led by a gerontological nurse who provided information on how to control disruptive behaviors.

The GNP from the physician's office made house calls to assess how Mrs. George was coping with the situation since it was evident that her blood glucose was not in sufficient control with diet management. On one such visit, it was noted that Mrs. George's leg was edematous with an ulcer. After collaborating with the physician and Mrs. George, the decision was made to place Mr. George in a nursing home in order that Mrs. George could be admitted to the hospital for treatment of her leg ulcer and stabilization of her diabetes with insulin.

NURSING HOMES

While less than 5% of the older population is found in nursing homes or long-term care facilities at any point in time, 20% of people reaching the age of 65 can expect to spend some time in a long-term care facility. Most residents of long-term care facilities are the very frail elderly who have become medically indigent and, therefore, eligible for Medicaid. They have multiple chronic mental and/or physical disabilities that require 24-hour care, which many families are unable to provide. Daughters, who traditionally care for an elderly parent, are part of the labor force; many are single parents meeting their own children's educational and living expenses. Children may live considerable distances from their parents. In order for parents to join them, they would have to relinquish their roots and familiar surroundings. The only answer for many families facing competing personal and work demands is to find an adequate nursing home for their elderly parent.

Nursing homes provide essentially three levels of nursing care. While the terminology may be different based on the reimbursement structure, the three levels are skilled, intermediate, and custodial nursing. Medicare reimburses for a limited number of days per year in a skilled nursing facility, usually following an acute hospitalization. Skilled nursing requires the clinical decision-making skills of a professional nurse. Medicaid, a joint program between the federal government and the states for the medically indigent, finances the majority of nursing home care. The program reimburses skilled and intermediate levels of care that require registered nurse supervision. Very few third parties reimburse for custodial care, which does not require registered nurse supervision. Nursing homes are licensed by the state (minimal standards to operate) and are certified to receive federal funds for Medicare as well as federal and state funds for Medicaid residents.

To deal with the funding constraints, nursing homes carefully monitor their case mix of private pay, Medicare, and Medicaid residents. Currently, federal Medicaid regulations do not require a specific number of nursing care hours per resident per day. States are permitted to determine an "adequate" level, usually 2.0 hours per day for intermediate care and 2.4 hours/day for skilled nursing care. These hours include all the contact time the staff has with the resident: health and safety assessment and monitoring, care planning and collaboration with physician and other health team members, bathing, feeding, medication administration, toileting, transfer and ambulation, cognitive stimulation, counseling of resident and family, and evaluation and documentation in compliance with federal and state regulations. Nursing home administrators prefer to accept intermediate Medicaid residents requiring less costly "light care." This in turn creates a backup of "heavy care" Medicaid recipients in expensive acute care beds in areas where there is a nursing home bed shortage.

Licensed practical nurses and nursing assistants provide most of the care in nursing homes. Seventy-one percent of the personnel in skilled nursing facilities are aides, 14% are licensed practical nurses, and 15% are registered nurses (8). Figures published by the ANA in 1984-1985 showed one full-time registered nurse for 33 nursing home residents, and this person usually holds an administrative position (2).

The low financial compensation and low status contribute to the dearth of professional nurses choosing long-term care positions. Rewards are found in caring for the residents rather than from monetary incentives and status. Nurses are paid less than their acute care counterparts and work with a limited number of unskilled staff. They plan and care for the personal, rehabilitative, and emotional needs of many residents and are often the sole advocate or surrogate family member for residents who have no family or friends.

For older persons, moving to a nursing home is one of the most stressful events in their life since it is usually preceded by another catastrophic event such as the death of a spouse or an acute illness. The person is required to give up a life-style of independence or semi-independence, as well as possessions and social contacts. He or she must make new relationships, adapt to a new role, and adjust to new living arrangements and institutional rules. All these stressors confront an already physically, emotionally, and/or cognitively impaired individual. Nurses assist the residents in coping with the adjustment to a new life-style and to the demands of their new and final home.

The nursing staff facilitates the transition by creating a nurturing home-like environment, which promotes the self-care abilities and preserves the dignity of a nursing home resident. Some homes encourage their residents to bring a small piece of furniture from home and other personal belongings, such as pictures or lamps. Resident councils, which give residents an opportunity for input into their environment, are mandated for nursing homes receiving Medicare/Medicaid reimbursement.

Selecting roommates who are compatible with each other is vitally important and often difficult to achieve. With a limited supply of nursing home beds, and the requirement to designate beds as skilled or intermediate care for reimbursement purposes, an oriented person may be placed with an individual who is disoriented. A prospective resident and his or her family, feeling fortunate to find a vacancy, may be forced to compromise by taking the available bed. Nurses collaborate with the administrator to rearrange roommate assignments when possible; the quality of a resident's life can be improved if a roommate shares mutual interests and develops a supportive relationship.

Responsive physicians can make a significant difference in the resident's adjustment to a nursing home and the care he receives. However, some physicians are reluctant to make nursing home calls to individuals who have been their patients for years. This can be devastating to the residents, who may want to hold on to the few remaining and important contacts in their life. Nurses expend time and energy in maintaining telephone contact with physicians to report changes in health status, obtain medication orders, and maintain compliance with federal and state regulations. Physicians' attentiveness to such regulatory requirements and acknowledgment of nurses' observations and assessments can have a positive influence on the nursing staff and ultimately patient care.

Mrs. George's diabetes was stabilized, but she was found to also be suffering from chronic congestive heart failure and hypertension, probably stress induced. She returned to her home to worry about how the nursing home bills would be paid. She accepted the fact that she could no longer give Mr. George the care he needed. In less than a year, their savings were depleted and Mr. George became eligible for Medicaid. It became evident that Mrs. George could no longer maintain their home; it would have to be sold. Mrs. George, left with only her pension and social security, was forced to move to a subsidized apartment building, which necessitated her relinquishing many cherished family possessions. With her limited income, she frequently had to choose between eating and filling her prescriptions, further complicating her health problems. The county health department operated a nursing clinic, staffed by a GNP, in the apartment building to monitor the health status of the residents and to conduct a health promotion program. The GNP communicated her concerns about Mrs. George's status to her private physician and arranged a social service referral. The GNP in the nursing clinic met regularly with Mrs. George to help her through the numerous adjustments she was having to make. Eventually, Mrs. George became very active in the activities of the building and became increasingly conscientious about her health care practices and the management of her chronic health problems.

QUALITY OF GERONTOLOGIC NURSING

The level and quality of gerontologic nursing services vary throughout the health delivery system. Services are influenced by the nurses' educational preparation, their clinical expertise, and the numbers which can be employed under the reimbursement system. To address the quality issue, the ANA offers two certifying examinations. For one, nurses who have completed a master's degree program or a 9- to 12- month GNP certificate program recognized by the ANA are eligible to take the Gerontological Nurse Practitioner Certification Examination. This examination tests knowledge in history taking, physical examination, and assessments in mental, psychosocial, biochemical, and environmental factors. Also included are the areas of planning treatment; management plans; health maintenance; use of research in practice; legal, ethical, and advocacy issues; and quality assurance.

Registered nurses, regardless of educational preparation, who have had 2 years of experience in gerontologic nursing are eligible to take the Gerontological Nurse Certification Examination. The examination covers the nursing process of assessing, planning, implementing, and evaluating care; nursing practice and policy issues; federal regulation compliance; protection of patients and staff; management; patient advocacy; and patient education.

Currently, 2,462 nurses are certified as gerontologic nurses or as nurse practitioners (7). In addition to certification, the ANA has also established a set of standards of care that provide the guidelines for the practice of gerontologic nursing.

CONCLUSION

Gerontologic nurses provide care to a vulnerable segment of the population having complex health, psychosocial, and nursing problems. In the 20 years since gerontologic nursing was recognized by the ANA as a specialty, it has developed its own body of knowledge and skills through advanced nursing education, practice, and research. As our older population continues to increase in number and in age, the need for gerontologic nurses is evident. Currently, approximately 20% of individuals over age 65 have some limitations in performing their activities of daily living.

Recruiting nurses to work with the elderly is difficult. Gerontologic nursing suffers from issues common to the field of gerontology, that is, lower status, lower pay, and a negative image in comparison to other specialities. The challenge confronting our legislative bodies, the health care industry, and the nursing profession is to attract, educate, and retain gerontologic nurses to meet the demand for quality care of our aging population.

REFERENCES

1. American Nurses Association: *The Measure of Distinction Among Professional Certification.* Kansas City, MO, American Nurses' Association, 1986.
2. American Nurses' Foundation and Foundation of American College of Health Care Administrators: *Professional Practice for Nurse Administrators in Long-Term Care Facilities: Annual Report of Project.* Kansas City, MO, American Nurses' Foundation and Foundation of American College of Health Care Administrators:, 1984.
3. *Compilation of the Older Americans Act of 1965 and Related Provisions of Law as Amended Through December 19, 1981* (May 1982, Sec. 305(b)(1), p 15). Washington, DC, U.S. Government Printing Office.
4. *Federal Register.* (June 17, 1986). Vol. 51, No. 16, pp 24042–24052.
5. Friedman J: *Home Health Care.* New York, WW Norton, 1986.
6. Walden D, Wilensky G: *National Health Expenditure Study* Data Preview 12. National Center for Health Services Research, Hyattsville, MD, 1982.
7. Palmore E: *Handbook on the Aged in the United States.* Westport, CT, Greenwood Press, 1984.
8. US Department of Health & Human Services: *Report on Nursing: Fifth Report to the President and Congress with Status of Health Personnel in the United States.* Rockville, MD, Bureau of Health Professions, 1986.
9. Stone R, Cafferata GL, Sangl J: *Caregivers of the Frail Elderly: A National Profile.* National Center for Health Services Research and Health Care Technology Assessment, Rockville, MD, 1986.

CHAPTER 46

Medical Care in the Nursing Home

STEVEN LIPSON
JAMES J. PATTEE

Medical care of the elderly is changing as a result of the rapid growth of the frail elderly population, our increasing knowledge of the aging process, and the demands to limit the rapid increase in expenditures for care of the elderly. In order to be effective in providing medical care for this population, the physician must have some understanding of the various organizations and institutions involved in providing care for the elderly, and how they affect his or her practice. Nowhere is this need better expressed than in the nursing home.

The "nursing home" today is a composite of a social care institution for the frail elderly with an overlay of a medical care institution. Although many see the nursing home as a poor relation of the acute care hospital, the nursing home differs in philosophy, organizational structure and staffing, and service population. Since nursing homes are licensed as health care facilities, they are subject to many of the same regulatory requirements as hospitals, but are simultaneously required to meet more of the human needs of the resident population. Thus, the activities program may be more in evidence than the medical care program and, at times, is more important to the patient.

One of the roots of the modern nursing home, like the acute care general hospital, is the almshouse or poorhouse. In many cities and rural areas at the beginning of this century, local governments, church groups, and other voluntary organizations established homes for the elderly and chronically ill who had no families able or willing to care for them. The 1935 advent of Social Security gave rise to further development of private boarding and nursing homes. Although some of these institutions included physician involvement and sick care early in their history, many more added or expanded this component during the 1960's, supported by the passage of Medicare and Medicaid legislation. Reimbursement for care of Medicare and Medicaid patients initially provided much of the financial support for explosive growth of the nursing home industry. This expansion is now fueled by the continued growth of the frail elderly population.

Despite the rapid increase in the number of nursing home beds, now estimated at more than 1.6 million (of which 1.3 million were occupied by residents age 65 years or older) and less than 125,000 were unoccupied (7), these facilities constitute only a part of the continuum of services that make up the long-term care system for the elderly. Home health services, sheltered housing, life-care communities, geriatric day care programs, Meals-On-Wheels, and other community-based programs and services for the aged are increasingly available throughout the country (see Chapters 43 and 44 for discussions of some of these areas). At any one time, approximately 5% of all those 65 years of age and older are in nursing homes. The proportion of the elderly population who are in nursing homes increase from less than 1.5% of those 65–74 years to 22% of those 85 years and older (7). For most of the elderly, even those 85 years and over, families and friends provide much of the help they need to stay at home, with relatively few needing the 24-hour care of the nursing home.

Frequently, the frail older person must be institutionalized when this social support system breaks down. The factors which produce this breakdown are thus disproportionately represented in the nursing home population. They include lack of any living children (approximately 37% of elderly nursing home residents), incontinence (approximately 47%), immobility (approximately 63%), and dementia or other cognitive impairment (approximately 63%) (7). Thus the nursing home population represents the "tail end" of a spectrum of problems that make it difficult to care for the elderly person at home.

It is apparent that this population is also difficult to care for in the nursing home, and so it should not be surprising that many have felt that these facilities do a poor job. The recent Institute of Medicine project, "Improving the Quality of Care in Nursing Homes," cited 22 separate reports over a period of 15 years which "identified both grossly inadequate care and abuse of residents" (5). The report comments that although they could not find specific data to show improvement, "informed observers" feel that the worst practices now occur less often than 15 years ago. Medicine and nursing are cited for their own share of deficiencies in the Institute of Medicine report which focuses on regulatory changes which may improve the system.

WHAT IS A NURSING HOME?

The spectrum of long-term care facilities for the elderly includes chronic hospitals, nursing homes, and a variety of congregate living facilities for the elderly which do not provide ongoing professional nursing services and vary in the range of other services they provide. Congregate living facilities include homes for the aged and well elderly, group homes, senior housing, sheltered housing, and assisted living. It should not be surprising to find that these institutions care for populations similar to those in nursing homes, except for those with severe physical and/or cognitive impairment, who are usually cared for by family at home or are placed in a nursing home.

There are a variety of facilities which may be included in the common label of "nursing home." They share the characteristic of being primarily organized to provide personal nursing services, including bathing, dressing, and feeding. They differ in the level of professional nursing care provided, that is, the intensity of specialized nursing services. The definitions are arbitrary and relate to licensing and reimbursement requirements, rather than any medical rationale. Nursing and related care homes were defined in the 1985 National Nursing Home Survey as those "that had three or more beds set up and staffed for use by residents and that routinely pro-

vided nursing and personal care services" (6). Of the 19,100 facilities estimated by the survey, three quarters were certified to provide skilled nursing care (by Medicare, Medicaid, or both programs) or intermediate nursing care (by Medicaid) (6). Certification by Medicare allows the nursing home to receive reimbursement for care to Medicare beneficiaries, which is limited to those who require 24-hour skilled care by licensed nursing staff, such as injections every 4 hours, or those who are being rehabilitated from an acute illness or injury. Certification by Medicaid allows for reimbursement for skilled or the lesser level of intermediate nursing services, when medically necessary for the care of Medicaid beneficiaries.

Though there are differing state and federal requirements for physician services, depending on the level of the facility and the level of nursing care the individual patient requires, these are less significant to the practicing physician than the differences between the hospital and the nursing home in general. The hospital may admit patients even though it may later decide to transfer them to another facility for definitive care, while the nursing home may not admit or keep patients if it cannot provide them with appropriate care. Thus, if a patient in a nursing home develops a decubitus ulcer which requires skilled nursing care, the patient must be moved to a bed or facility licensed and staffed to provide that level of care. In general, nursing homes may not admit or keep patients with infectious diseases, such as active tuberculosis, without receiving specific permission from licensing authorities.

In acute care hospitals the average patient receives 6 or more hours of care a day, provided by licensed nurses, whereas nursing homes provide 2–4 hours of care, provided primarily by nursing assistants or aides, while licensed nurses function as supervisors or charge nurses. Diagnostic studies including x-ray, electrocardiogram, and laboratory services can be obtained in the nursing home, but are usually provided by outside contractors. Stat blood work may take 4–6 hours or longer for results to be available, and diagnostic studies other than portable x-rays are done on an outpatient basis at nearby facilities. Although nasogastric or gastrostomy feeding and short-term intravenous therapy or total parenteral nutrition are available at increasing numbers of facilities in urban areas, they are far from universal at this time. Physical, occupational, and speech therapy and social work services vary in level of availability depending on the size and sophistication of the individual long-term care facility.

The nursing home may be thought of as a congregate living facility where professional nursing and medical and related services are provided. Similarly, an inpatient component of a hospice program looks like a nursing home devoted to the care of the terminally ill in terms of the emphasis on meeting their nursing and personal care needs.

NURSING HOME ORGANIZATION

Three quarters of the 19,100 nursing homes in the country are proprietary, organized and run for the purpose of producing profits for the owners (6). For the physician, this is less important than the size of the nursing home, with the average facility housing 85 beds and only 6.3% having 200 or more beds. As in the case of clinical resources, the nursing home commonly has less depth and variety in administrative resources than does the hospital. The licensed administrator of the facility, with a secretary, usually make up the full-time administrative staff. The director of nursing may be responsible for hiring, firing, and supervising nursing staff, but may also have to give medications when the facility is short staffed. The assistant director of nursing may also be responsible for in-service training, while the consulting dietitian serves as a food service manager. In general, department or program heads will be hands-on or working managers, reporting directly to the administrator.

Although in theory the physicians caring for patients in a nursing home are responsible to the administrator and governing body of the institution through a medical director or principal physician, routine interactions are with the nursing staff and director of nursing. Most primary care physicians will rarely if ever have contact with the administrator. This is particularly true in the most common organizational structure for the medical staff of a nursing home, the open medical staff.

MEDICAL STAFF ORGANIZATION

Most hospitals have a highly structured medical staff, with departments, committees, and specific policies and procedures. Most nursing homes have an open medical staff where any licensed physician in the community may admit and care for patients in the facility. Credentialing is frequently limited to documentation of a state medical license, professional liability insurance, and an agreement to abide by the policies and procedures of the facility. Utilization review and quality assurance functions are performed by outside physicians under contract to the

nursing home, and the medical director is responsible for emergency medical care if the attending physician is not available.

Larger nursing homes may establish a formally organized medical staff similar to that of a hospital, with committees responsible for credentialing, utilization review, and infection control. The medical staff usually elects a chief of staff, who may also serve as medical director.

Under a closed medical staff structure, a limited number of physicians provide care to nursing home residents under contract to the facility. They may be paid directly by the facility which then seeks reimbursement from Medicare and other third parties, or more commonly the physicians will bill the patients and their insurers directly for their services. Mechanisms for performing functions such as utilization review vary widely, though usually they are provided by outside organizations.

Although most nursing homes follow the open staff model, an increasing number have a mixed structure, part open and part closed. In these facilities, any physician in the community may admit and care for patients, but there are a small number of physicians who have agreed to take responsibility for medical care of any resident in the facility when requested. This most frequently occurs when the attending physician is unable or unwilling to meet the medical needs of the resident by timely visits to the nursing home. We are unaware of any recent statistical data on this, but our personal experience suggests that this pattern is becoming quite common, and that where such physicians are available to provide care, they become the physicians for most (75–90% or more) of the residents in a nursing home.

THE PATIENT POPULATION

In 1985, 88% of the residents in nursing homes in the United States were 65 years of age or older. Forty-five percent of this 1.3 million were 85 years or older. Predominately female (75%) and white (93%), about 92% needed assistance in one or more activities of daily living (7). This demographic description is oversimplified. In reality there are several different populations of patients who enter nursing homes. The first group are those who after an acute illness need care for a period before they can return to the community. Included are frail elderly after repair of hip fractures, cardiac bypass surgery, strokes, or other significant medical or surgical events. This group account for an estimated 30% of nursing home admissions and generally are discharged within 3-6 months. A second population is made up of individuals whose functioning is deteriorating relatively rapidly, though this may not be evident at first. They comprise approximately 30% of nursing home admissions, with stays of less than 6 months before death. The average length of stay for the combined short stay population is about 1.8 months. The remaining 40% of elderly admitted to nursing homes will generally stay until they die or are transferred to another facility, but this occurs at a slow rate over a period of years. The average length of stay for these admissions is between 2 and 3 years, though some residents stay much longer (3, 4).

PAYMENT FOR NURSING HOME CARE

Currently 1-2% of nursing home revenues come from Medicare, largely for those short stay residents recovering from acute illnesses or receiving terminal care. Medicaid funding provides about half of all funds for care in nursing homes, with great variability from state to state. The remainder comes from patients and families, since there is virtually no commercial insurance which covers long-term nursing home care. Such insurance is becoming more available, and at present, several proposals are being discussed regarding changes in the financing of nursing home care.

The Medicare prospective payment system for hospitals, based on diagnostic related groups (DRGs) was implemented in 1983, to restrain the rapid growth of Medicare expenditures. Many feel that this has created a "revolving door" effect for the frail elderly, and is changing the case mix in nursing homes toward more acutely ill patients. Data from the 1985 National Nursing Home Survey show that 1985 nursing home residents were older, more dependent in activities of daily living, and more likely to have been in a hospital before the nursing home admission than those surveyed in 1977 (7). It seems rational that pressures to limit hospital admission and to shorten the stay for those admitted will force sicker patients into the long-term care facility, and will encourage the provision of more sophisticated types of care in that environment.

CARE IN THE NURSING HOME

With almost half the nursing home residents over the age of 85, and requiring assistance in areas such as bathing, dressing, and toileting, it is clear that these institutions contain the oldest and frailest of the elderly. Most of the care provided in the institution is, by necessity, nursing care to meet the personal needs of the patients. While the physician plays a critical role in identifying the medical treatment required by the patient, this accounts for a relatively small portion of the care effort. The facility exists to provide *nursing care,* with medicine, social work, and other modalities being necessary but adjunctive to this core requirement.

The nursing home is a medical facility, but most of the residents will live there until they die, and so the facility becomes their home. Who would want to live for 2 years or more in a home with the atmosphere of a hospital? The nursing home staff frequently become a second family for residents, share their joys, and grieve over their death. This is perhaps the only way to explain why some individuals would take jobs for little more than the minimum wage to bathe, feed, dress, and care for individuals who may be incontinent, confused, abusive, or dying. Even those with minimum skills can find less demanding employment in today's marketplace.

THE PHYSICIAN'S ROLE

Since the nursing home is a licensed health care facility, patients can only be admitted under the care of a physician who must specify the resident's diet, medications, care plan, and treatment goals. With variations depending on the specific patient, the institution, and state requirements, the physician must visit the resident on a regular basis, at least every 30 days for the first 90 days of stay, and then every 60 or 90 days. In addition, the physician must visit in a timely fashion when required by the resident's condition. In order to provide appropriate and effective care for the nursing home resident, especially the one who recently was a patient in an acute care hospital where the physician visited daily and nursing care was provided by registered nurses, the physician must learn to utilize the resources of the nursing home.

In general, physicians are well prepared to diagnose and treat acute, episodic illness. They have less training in and are psychologically less comfortable in dealing with incurable chronic disease. The average nursing home resident has three or four chronic conditions and is taking six drugs. It is not surprising to note that a recent study found 161 adverse drug reactions or interactions in a 72-bed nursing home over a 24-month period (2). A fall or drug reaction may result in lengthy hospitalization or death. The nursing home population includes the frailest of the frail elderly, and the physician must modify his or her approach and behavior to minimize any further losses. Once the patient enters the nursing home, the most common contacts by the physician are routine visits and telephone calls.

PHYSICIAN VISITS AND TELEPHONE CALLS

Routine visits to the nursing home patient are not just for checking physical status and signing orders. Regular assessment of elderly residents is essential to maintain their status and minimize any further losses due to disease or treatment. Cognitive and functional status must be carefully assessed and regularly documented. The use of standardized assessment instruments such as the Folstein Mini-Mental Status and the Katz Activities of Daily Living (ADL) scale should be encouraged so that observer variability is minimized. Nursing, physical therapy, or activities staff should be questioned for clues for causes of change in emotional state or confusion. The consulting pharmacist, social worker, or dietitian may have left notes which are more informative than laboratory reports. Since the physician's visits are limited, it is important to utilize all sources of information.

Periodic monitoring and careful documentation of changes in mental functioning, mobility, or neurologic findings may be vital to the explanation of later changes in status. To accomplish these objectives, the physician must visit at a time when the staff who care for the patient on a daily basis are available and have time to discuss findings with the physician. Visits made at mealtimes, at night, or on weekends may be convenient for the physician, and may meet the letter of regulatory requirements for physician documentation, but they do not allow for the provision of effective medical care. The community-based physician must appreciate that nursing home visits are as important as office and hospital visits, and these visits must fit into the mainstream of medical practice.

The demonstrated concern of the physician as an advocate for his or her patients in the nursing home is a powerful tool. A disinterested, nonsupportive practitioner can have a devastating effect on nursing home staff and the care given the residents. Working daily in an environment which is emotionally dominated by terminal illness, dementia, and behavior problems is highly demanding. Every visit by the physician should be seen as an opportunity to share knowledge and skills with the staff; to learn from the resident, family, and caregivers what values the resident prizes; and to enhance those values in the care process. This becomes even more important with the severely impaired and dying patient, as discussed below.

Telephone calls do more than relay laboratory reports. Since the nursing staff are the ones who see the patient daily, they must be kept informed of the patient's status and of what special parameters are to be monitored. This will allow them to be more effective in relating to concerned family members and in notifying the physician when changes occur. An effective working relationship with nursing staff is the best way to avoid frequent "nuisance" phone calls or, perhaps worse, the failure to notify the physician when a significant change does occur. With the cognitively impaired or aphasic patient, the skills of the nurse are even more important, since symptoms may not be expressed and atypical presentation of acute illness is common in the frail elderly. The physician has a right to expect that phone calls from the nursing staff will be concise, clear, and comprehensive in the information transmitted. In return, the physician has an obligation to respond promptly and professionally to telephone calls and to give precise, clear telephone orders which are appropriate to the facility's resources. Just as the nursing home is unlikely to have respirators or renal dialysis equipment available, the staff may be unable to monitor vital signs every 15 minutes around the clock without reducing care to other residents. When in doubt, it is appropriate to ask the nursing staff as to the intensity of care which can be reasonably provided.

SUPPORTIVE CARE

The majority of patients admitted to the nursing home will live there until they die. Thus they may all be seen as suffering from a terminal disease. While many die suddenly, for some a decision must be made regarding how far aggressive treatment should be taken, and at what point the emphasis should shift to providing comfort instead of prolonging the dying process. This has been labeled "comfort care" or "supportive care" by some facilities. Section III of this book, Ethical Issues in the Elderly Patient, provides guidance for such decision making.

Because of the involvement of the nursing home staff with the patient, special concerns arise when such decisions are made for a nursing home resident. The physician should share the reasoning for the decision with the staff involved in the patient's care. If aggressive treatment is being discontinued, or the patient is not being transferred to the hospital despite acute illness, the staff must be assured that the decision is not to abandon the patient, but rather to continue care which provides comfort and relieves pain and suffering. Nursing staff may well have become a second family to the resident and deserve the opportunity to participate in and understand the basis for such decisions. Terminal care equivalent to that given in the best hospice programs is frequently seen when staff are so involved.

The physician must continue visiting the patient, communicating with family members and staff, and demonstrating that care of the dying is as important as that of those who are expected to continue living. This psychologic support function of the physician may be the greatest value of the physician's visiting. In addition to showing the staff that they are not left "holding the bag," the presence of the physician serves to assure the family that loving and appropriate medical and nursing care is being administered to their relative. With the current concern to limit unnecessary medical expenditures, the obligation to see that any individual patient receives all appropriate and effective care uniquely devolves on to the physician. Cost containment is a reality. Our challenge is to provide care effectively, efficiently, and humanely.

THE ROLE OF THE MEDICAL DIRECTOR

The requirement by the Medicare program that each "skilled nursing facility" have a physician designated as medical director was a direct result of a public perception that physicians had abandoned their elderly patients to nursing homes (8). The establishment of a medical director and specific requirements for physician involvement have solidified the concept of the nursing home as a medical care facility (1). Current federal regulations require that a medical director be retained by the facility with responsibility for "the over-all coordination of the medical care in the facility to ensure the adequacy and appropriateness of the medical services provided to patients and to maintain surveillance of the health status of employees" (42 CFR 405.1122).

Federal guidelines delineate specific areas of responsibility for the medical director. In general, the medical director must see that there are rules regarding physician services and that they are adhered to. This would include educating physicians as to the requirements, and communicating with those who do not comply in order to gain their cooperation. The medical director must advise the facility administrator as to staffing and services necessary to provide appropriate medical care for the residents, and must monitor the health of the employees, especially where it may have impact on the residents. In practice, the medical director reviews the patient care policies annually, sits on the infection control and pharmacy services committee, and assures that staff are checked to prevent the introduction of communicable disease. The medical director may also advise on the medical appropriateness of admission of any patient, may be requested to participate in the staff in-service program, and may serve as a consultant to all of the services in the nursing home.

Where, as in the majority of nursing homes today, there is an open medical staff, the medical director is likely to be the only physician with a substantive commitment to the facility. Thus he or she may be involved in improving relationships with the outside medical community to attract more patients to the facility or in correcting deficiencies identified by federal or state inspectors. The development of provisions for medical utilization review and quality assurance generally is dependent on the medical director, though most often groups outside the nursing home are retained to perform these functions.

A conscientious medical director will take the federal requirements as a minimum in meeting his or her obligations. Advising the administration of the nursing home of situations which jeopardize the well-being of the staff or patients should not be based on or limited to reviewing patient care policy statements. The medical director should be visible and observant. Though some are precluded by their contract from having their own patients in the facility, they should closely monitor the patient care and be instrumental in identifying problems and solutions. Both the nursing home staff and the medical staff should see the medical director as available to resolve conflict and provide consultation in difficult situations.

Though the medical director has little if any administrative authority in most nursing homes, it is clear that the role allows for significant influence and molding of the character of the facility. This is probably most evident in the area of the protection of patient's rights and the development of policies and procedures which address these rights. Though the field is still full of conflict, the care of the dying patient and the patient's right to refuse treatment are vital areas for the medical director's involvement. Nursing homes are starting to establish institutional ethics or patient care advisory committees to address these issues. Unfortunately, in some instances the most reluctant participants have been the medical director and the medical staff. We must not be afraid to get involved in these areas.

CURRENT MEDICAL ISSUES IN THE NURSING HOME

Although, as we have mentioned, there is increasing pressure to make the nursing home more of a medical facility, there is considerable feeling that this would be detrimental to its character. This "medicalization" would move the nursing home closer to the hospital and further from the "home for the aged." The movement seems inevitable, given the social and political forces involved, but it also appears that the medical community can add weight to the argument that there should be limits to the change and finesse exercised in its application. Given the limited resources of the nursing home and the recognition that many residents live there for years before they die, it seems that a "home with nursing and medical care" is more appropriate than a modification of the hospital.

A variety of social pressures also seek to minimize the use of the nursing home for long-term care of the elderly by expanding the availability and range of home health services. It is argued that home care is preferred by most elderly, that home care is cheaper (at least to third parties), and that it is more humane. While we agree in large part with these arguments, it seems clear that until we develop cures for Alzheimer's disease and the other debilitating chronic diseases of the elderly, nursing homes continue to be needed for those frail elderly who cannot be maintained in the community. Where the balance will be between home care and institutional care remains to be seen, though the preliminary 1985 National Nursing Home Survey data suggest that there are few currently in institutions who could easily be cared for at home (7).

Society has begun to recognize that people do not lose the right to make their own decisions regarding medical care by reason of age or illness, but our health care institutions are still digesting this truth (see Chapter 51, A Framework for Geriatric Ethics). Hospitals and nursing homes will need to carefully examine their procedures and policies in this area. Can a patient refuse physical therapy? A bath? A tranquilizer? What are the limits on patient autonomy due to residence in an institution? Who will be the guardian for the resident's autonomy? At what point may a family place an infirm parent in a nursing home against the parent's will?

The most immediate issue facing nursing homes is the growing number of Acquired Immune Deficiency Syndrome patients. When these individuals become so debilitated that they cannot be cared for at home, they are generally admitted to hospitals. Several states have begun to request that nursing homes accept these patients, so as to minimize the enormous costs to state Medicaid funds. Though the care can be provided, the impact on the nursing home and its other residents has not been assessed. We find that many elderly nursing home residents have little understanding of what this disease is, and are terrified of having such patients live with them. Do we have the right to inflict this imposition on the frailest of the elderly?

SUMMARY

The nursing home is not simply a poor relation of the hospital. As an amalgam of a social care institution for the frail elderly and a health care facility, it has a unique set of strengths and characteristics. Within the limitations of such an institution, it can provide humane and effective medical and personal care. The physician caring for a patient in the nursing home must recognize the limitations of the setting and modify his or her pattern of practice. The staff of the facility must be enlisted as partners in care, and must also be treated as a second family of the patient. Because of the frailty of the residents, their prolonged length of stay, and the social and political pressures on the long-term care facility, the physician must act as an advocate for the patient even more than in the hospital. The physician provides the channel to bridge the gap between the hospital and nursing home, and by his or her effective presence in the nursing home lends professional credibility to that institution and its staff. In ways, the nursing home is the most difficult setting in which to practice geriatrics, but the patients are also the most in need of the physician's skills and efforts. If geriatrics represents the "fruition" of the clinician, perhaps medical care in the nursing home presents the fruition of the geriatrician (9).

REFERENCES

1. American Medical Association: *The Medical Director in the Long-Term Care Facility.* Chicago, American Medical Association, 1977.
2. Cooper J: Drug-related problems in a geriatric long term care facility. *J Geriatr Drug Ther* 1:47, 1986.
3. Kane R, Bell R, Riegler S, et al: Predicting the course of nursing home patients. *Gerontologist* 23:200, 1983.
4. Keeler E, Kane R, Solomon D: Short and long term residents of nursing homes. *Med Care* 19:363, 1981.
5. National Academy of Sciences, Institute of Medicine: *Improving the Quality of Care in Nursing Homes.* Washington, DC, National Academy Press, 1986, p 3.
6. National Center for Health Statistics: G. Strahan: Nursing home characteristics, preliminary data from

the 1985 National Nursing Home Survey. *Advance Data From Vital and Health Statistics.* No. 131. DHHS Pub. No. (PHS) 87-1250. Public Health Service. Hyattsville, Md., Mar. 27, 1987.

7. National Center for Health Statistics, E. Hing: Use of nursing homes by the elderly, Preliminary data from the 1985 National Nursing Home Survey. *Advance Data From Vital and Health Statistics.* No. 135. DHHS Pub.

No. (PHS) 87-1250. Public Health Service. Hyattsville, Md., May 14, 1987.

8. Reichel W: Role of the medical director in the skilled nursing facility: historical perspectives. In Reichel W (ed.): *Clinical Aspects of Aging,* ed 2. Baltimore, Williams & Wilkins, 1983, pp 570-579.

9. Williams TF: Geriatrics: the fruition of the clinician reconsidered. *The Gerontologist* 26:345-349, 1986.

CHAPTER 47

Sexuality, Intimacy, and Touch in Older Adults

CATHERINE E. O'CONNOR
EDNA M. STILWELL

An holistic view of sexuality and the older person connotes the capacity for involvement in all of life. The components embrace three major areas: physiologic release of sexual tensions; psychologic expression of emotions and commitment to others; and social identification of gender and roles in life. Therefore, it is more than the physical act of sexual union. Within the broad definition of sexuality, intimacy and closeness coupled with skin contact or touching, are considered essential for survival. Yet, they are not necessarily substitutes for, nor limited to, a heterosexual relationship. Moreover, these needs do not disappear with old age. These factors of sexuality, intimacy, and touch enhance communication, personality, and the quality of life for older adults (5, 23).

MYTHS, ATTITUDES, AND STEREOTYPES

One of the most important considerations that older adults and health care providers need is an awareness of stereotypes, negative attitudes, and myths that are prevalent in our society surrounding sexuality and the older person.

However, it is well documented and cited by experts (14–16, 19) that:

Older people remain interested in sex;
Sexual activity is possible well into the last years of one's life;
Older adults find each other physically attractive and sexually desirable;
Older men are not likely to be child molesters any more than younger men;

Sexuality contributes to overall well-being, rather than posing a danger to health;
Healthy sexual expression in old age is a sign of a healthy mental status.

PHYSICAL CHANGES

FEMALE

Cessation of fertility is the major occurrence in this period. Postmenopausal women, because of sex steroid insufficiency, have varying degrees of atrophy of the reproductive and urinary tract organs. Thinning and drying of vaginal walls occur, as well as decreased skin elasticity and diminished glandular tissue and tone. These changes increase the susceptibility to bleeding, infections, and irritations. In addition to stressful life-styles, genetic factors, exercise, and diet, insufficient sex steroid hormones also have been implicated as factors in coronary heart disease and osteoporosis (14).

MALE

Although reproduction is possible into old age, it is less likely because of the decreased number and viability of sperm. Testosterone production continues into old age, but the concentration may decrease, affecting genital tissue. This reduction of hormone is accompanied by a gradual decline in sexual energy and muscle strength. The testes become less firm and smaller in size; production of the volume and viscosity of seminal fluid is diminished. Hypertrophic changes in the prostate gland make contractions weaker. These changes increase the susceptibility to hesitancy, decrease in urine flow, frequency of urination, and nocturia. Starting in approximately the third decade of life, prostatic enlargement takes place as an unrelenting process, although the rate varies (14).

The above-mentioned findings are indicative of general statements on the subject, i.e., that there is a decrease of sexual interest and activity in older men, and that studies have shown a decrease in mean serum testosterone with age (18, 26, 27) with a wide variation so that many subjects in their eighth decade still have testosterone levels well within the normal range for young men, whereas a few have very low values. However, new studies contradict previous findings. Harman and Tsitouras (7), Sparrow et al. (23), and Tsitouras et al. (27) have demonstrated in their studies that serum testosterone does not decline with age. Some authors (25, 28) found in their group of subjects that sexual activity does decrease in a highly predictable fashion. Their data suggest that, although serum testosterone levels may affect sexual activity in older men to some degree, age itself is probably the most influential variable.

MAJOR CHANGES IN SEXUAL RESPONSE CYCLE

The sexual response cycle consists of four stages as identified by Masters and Johnson (14–16): (a) excitement; (b) plateau; (c) orgasmic; and (d) resolution. However, some changes take place in these stages in older adulthood.

EXCITEMENT

In the male, erection builds slowly and takes longer to attain. In females, lubrication time is delayed from 15–30 seconds to 5 min. and the expansion capacity of the vagina is reduced.

PLATEAU

Erection tends to last longer in males, although there is less vascular engorgement of the penis, whereas in females, uterine elevation is reduced. However, clitoral response remains similar to younger years.

ORGASMIC

The number of contractions for males and females is decreased and of shorter duration. Female contractions may be spastic rather than rhythmic in nature.

RESOLUTION

Recovery may take 12–48 hours in the male. Loss of erection and return to the flaccid state may occur more rapidly. Females remain multiorgasmic.

SEXUAL/INTIMATE BEHAVIOR HISTORY

In obtaining a sexual history, the interviewer needs to be certain that a climate is established before history-taking that legitimizes the discussion of sexuality surrounding the older person's concerns. Thus, the person is not criticized for a lack of knowledge. Acceptance of the patient, as a person, allows the interviewer to explore present or potential problems (9).

It is important to address general questions before specific ones are asked. In addition, a nonjudgmental attitude of the interviewer increases the level of comfort of the informant. Such areas as the onset of menopause, frequency of Pap smears, or frequency of prostatic examinations offer a transition to questions about opportunity, satisfaction, fear of failure, and anxieties surrounding intimate sexual relationships.

Thus, psychosocial as well as specific physical aspects of sexual functioning need to be included in data gathering. A variety of approaches in terms of when and how the information is obtained may be used based on the expertise of the caregiver and the setting. The procurement of this information often requires more than one interview. When the standard history and physical examination format is used, the inclusion of information may be placed appropriately at the review of the genitourinary system.

Cues or clues that the older person may be hesitant to express in more direct words may alert the health care professional to areas of concern. These may be implied through body language, humor, or indirect questions or remarks.

Professional language regarding sexual expression and intimate behavior may be inappropriate and deter understanding. Lay terms based on cultural, ethnic, or client usage may be necessary (6).

CONTENT OF HISTORY

The following areas represent the most important content to be assessed but do not cover an exhaustive treatment of the topic:

How are persons defining their own gender? What kinds of behaviors are attributed to being male or female?

What are the person's past and current close relationships with others? Describe the state of sexual patterns: marriages, divorce, widow(er)hood, and sexual partnerships.

What types of intimate relationshhips are most pleasurable, such as, but not limited to: touching, physical closeness, stroking, petting, sexual intercourse, masturbation, and oral-genital sex?

Have there been any changes in life-style that have decreased the opportunities for close relationships such as: a temporary or permanent loss of a spouse or partner, moving to a more restrictive environment—that is, living with other family members or in a nursing home.

The degree of adaptation to age-related changes in sexual functioning such as: decreased vaginal lubrication, pain (dyspareunia), and benign prostatic hypertrophy.

The presence of disease or abnormalities that may interfere with normal sexual functioning such as: diabetes, bleeding, infections, Peyronie's disease, prostatitis, obesity, and venereal disease.

A history of surgical procedures that may interfere with functioning or self-image such as: mastectomy, hysterectomy, and prostatectomy.

The use of drugs and medications with special emphasis on various classifications that may suppress libido, such as: anticholinergics, antispasmodics, antihypertensives, antianxiety agents, antidepressants, tranquilizers, sedatives, narcotics, stimulants, and alcohol.

Other concerns—what personal, moral, and religious values influence sexuality? What myths are subscribed to? What knowledge base is possessed regarding sexual health?

PLAN OF CARE

Listen to the older person's concerns related to sexuality. Assurance that sexual feelings are normal is necessary, thus dispelling any myths related to sexuality.

Educate the person to the physiologic changes related to aging so that adaptation to these changes is promoted. Through increased understanding, an older person's sexual capacity can be maintained into old age.

Promote sexual health through history, physical examination, and tests such as: Pap smears, self-breast examination, regular prostatic and testicular examinations.

Share the known facts and involve the older adult in decision-making related to the use of drugs or surgical procedures that affect sexual function.

Recognize alternate life-styles or different modes of sexual expression, such as: homosexuality, bisexuality, and oral-genital sex (9, 10).

Accept that a successful sexual response is not limited to orgasm or penetration but involves contentment, closeness, satisfaction, and a feeling of warmth.

Include the need for privacy as an essential part of the older person's environment including living space as well as during health care procedures.

Assess the need for touch (8). Do not assume that all older persons need or want to be touched (11).

Professionals' behavior that is perceived to be seductive may invite sexual response in patients, and therapeutic limits may need to be defined.

Modify procedures such as the pelvic examination by using a smaller size speculum in adults with a decreased vaginal introitus.

Consult other health care providers such as: sexual counselors, urologists, gynecologists, nurses, social workers, and pharmacists as the need indicates.

Encourage romance and creativity in lovemaking to counteract the results of boredom, fatigue, and tension (9).

Encourage continuance of the style of dress, grooming, and manners that the person has identified as enhancing his or her sexual identity.

Alert the older person that sexual potency is maintained through continued use, which includes masturbation, touching, sensuality, and fantasizing.

Include the attitudes and behaviors of family and staff or others involved in working with the older adult when developing the plan of care.

Consider the use of such therapies as estrogen replacement or penile prosthesis for some older patients.

AIDS

Few diseases have provoked as much anxiety as AIDS (the Acquired Immune Deficiency Syndrome) (1, 12). Currently, the spread of AIDS is seen in certain at-risk groups (2). Persons with sexual partners who have confirmed HIV antibody tests are at risk to develop the disease (3), as well as drug users who share needles (3), males who have sex with other males (often a covert group in the elderly [20, 21]), and hemophiliacs (3). Moss and Miles (17) suggest that 10% of AIDS cases are in persons over 50 years of age, with 25% of those over 60 years, and 4% in persons over 70 years. They project that if the present age distribution holds, there will be 27,000 AIDS cases in persons over 50 years old by 1991. Sabin (22) called AIDS the new "great imitator," and points out that HIV dementia can represent a serious pitfall for the diagnosis of Alzheimer's disease in those over 50 years of age.

Older persons need to be educated to safe sexual practices. These include limiting sexual contact to one person who only has sex with that person and avoiding exposure to the partner's body fluids and wastes (4). Safety remains uncertain regarding the practices of using condoms or protected intercourse with spermicidal jelly containing nonoxynol-9 (4). There is little evidence to suggest AIDS could be spread by air, water, food, insects, or casual non-sexual interpersonal contact (12). Health professionals need to recognize and plan to teach the risks that accompany sexual practices and also provide resources for elderly persons (13).

DEALING WITH SEXUAL AGGRESSION

Health professionals may need help in dealing with sexual aggression or acting-out of older persons (10). The most frequent ways of acting-out are: (a) using sex talk or foul language; (b) sexual acts, such as touching or grabbing at intimate zones; and (c) implied sexual behavior, such as reading pornographic magazines (24). Often, arousing the ire of the staff through covert or overt sexual acting-out is a way of validating oneself as a person or gaining negative attention. When attention is craved, sometimes it is better to incite an angry response than to be ignored. When health care workers recognize the older person's need for intimate touch and affection, then more acceptable behavior with the professional may be demonstrated by hugging, kissing on the cheek, and providing privacy (9). Thus, sexual education is necessary for all health care professionals and will prepare them to handle a variety of situations and problems.

HEALTH CARE PROVIDERS' ATTITUDES AND HUMAN SEXUALITY

Sexual health is an important component of over-all well-being and should be incorporated routinely into the health history and examination of older adults. The exploration of attitudes and feelings about the health care provider's own sexuality is necessary to experience a certain level of comfort when dealing with older adults' sexual concerns. Professionals may now find that sexually active, healthy, married, unmarried, and remarried older adults are seeking more information than ever before.

Many unanswered research questions arise. Travis (26) suggested a few:

Does institutionalization diminish sexual attractiveness?
What is the effect of lack of privacy in nursing homes?

How is the spouse of a disabled mate supported or counseled?
What staff attitudes are imposed on older residents' sexuality?
What family dynamics affect newlywed older adults?

There is much work to be done regarding human sexuality and health care providers' attitudes; new information needs to be generated to provide genuinely adequate care and increase the quality of life of older adults through maximizing their sexual health and potential for a full, rich life.

CONCLUSION

As time passes, sexuality in old age will receive greater attention from all concerned. Professionals will be better able to diagnose and treat problems regarding an older person's sexuality. And older persons themselves, through heightened awareness, will become their own advocates. Therefore, their desire and capacity for an active, satisfying sexual experience will be enhanced.

REFERENCES

1. Amchin J, Polan H: A longitudinal account of staff adaptation to AIDS patients on a psychiatric unit. *Hosp Commun Psychiatry* 37:1235, 1986.
2. Anderson D: AIDS: An update on what we know now. *RN* March:49, 1986.
3. Castro K, Hardy A, Curran J: The acquired immuno-deficiency syndrome: Epidemiology and risk factors for transmission. *Med Clin North Am* 70:635, 1986.
4. Chamberland M, Castro K, Haverkos H, et al: Acquired immunodeficiency syndrome in the United States. *Ann Intern Med* 101:617, 1984.
5. Ebersole P, Hess P: *Toward Healthy Aging*, ed 2. St. Louis, CV Mosby, 1985.
6. Friedman J: Development of sexual knowledge inventory for elderly persons. *Nurs Res* 28:374, 1979.
7. Harman SM, Tsitouras PD: Reproductive hormones in aging men. I. Measurement of sex steroids, basal LH and Leydig cell response to hCG. *J Clin Endocrinol Metabol* 51:35, 1980.
8. Hartman S: Hug a patient, p.r.n. *Nurs 86* August:88, 1986.
9. Higgins L, Hawkins J: *Human Sexuality Across the Life Span*. Belmont, California, Wadsworth Health Sciences Division, 1984.
10. Hogan R: *Human Sexuality: A Nursing Perspective*, ed 2. New York, Appleton-Century-Crofts, 1985.
11. Hollinger LM: Perception of touch in the elderly. *J Gerontol Nurs* 6:741, 1980.
12. Krim M: AIDS: The challenge to science and medicine. *QRB* August:278, 1986.
13. List of AIDS support or organizations. *JAMA* 254:2522, 1985.
14. Masters WH, Johnson VE: Sexual inadequacy in the aging male. Sexual inadequacy in the aging female. In

Masters WH, Johnson VE (Eds): *Human Sexual Inadequacy.* Boston, Little, Brown, 1970.

15. Masters W, Johnson V: *Human Sexual Response,* ed 2. Boston, Little, Brown, 1984.
16. Masters W, Johnson V: *Masters and Johnson on Sex and Human Loving.* Boston, Little, Brown, 1986.
17. Moss RJ, Miles SH: AIDS and the geriatrician. *J Am Geriatr Soc* 35:460, 1987.
18. Pirke KM, Doerr P: Age-related changes and interrelationships with plasma testosterone, estradiol, and testosterone-binding globulin in normal adult males. *Acta Endocrinol* 74:792, 1973.
19. Purdy L, Colby T, Yousem S, Battifora H: Pulmonary Kaposi's sarcoma. *Am J Surg Pathol* 10:301, 1986.
20. Renshaw D: Sex, age and values. *J Am Geriatr Soc* 33:635, 1985.
21. Ross M: Social and behavioral aspects of male homosexuality. *Med Clin North Am* 70:537, 1986.
22. Sabin TD: AIDS: The new "great imitator." *J Am Geriatr Soc* 35:467, 1987.
23. Sparrow D, Bosse R, Rowe JW: The influence of age, alcohol consumption and body build on gonadal function in men. *J Clin Endocrinol Metabol* 51:508, 1980.
24. Steinke E, Bergen M: Sexuality and aging. *J Gerontol Nursing* 12:6–10, 1986.
25. Szasz G: Sexual incidents in an extended care unit for aged men. *J Am Geriatr Soc* 31:407, 1983.
26. Travis S: Older adults' sexuality and remarriage. *J Gerontol Nursing* 13:9, 1987.
27. Tsitouras PD, Martin CE, Harman SM: Relationship of serum testosterone to sexual activity in healthy elderly men. *J Gerontol* 37:288, 1982.
28. U.S. Department of Health and Human Services: Healthy old men show no change in sex hormone output. In: *Special Report on Aging 1980.* Washington, DC, US Government Printing Office, 1980.

CHAPTER 48

Accidents in the Elderly Population

HAROLD KALLMAN
SHEILA KALLMAN

Accidents are a common cause of morbidity and mortality in the elderly population. Despite a decline of 30% in accident-related mortality in the last 30 years, accidental death remains the sixth most common cause of death in individuals 65 years of age and older and the death rate per hundred thousand dramatically rises with each decade after age 65. In 1982, the death rate per 100,000 as a result of accidents for individuals between the ages of 65 and 74 years was 51; between the ages of 75 and 84 it was 104; and for 85 years or older it was 256 (64). Only heart disease, malignancy, cerebrovascular disease, and diabetes mellitus supersede accidents as a cause of death in the elderly. In individuals aged 85 and older, accidents were the fifth most common cause of death, surpassing diabetes mellitus. These statistics are not peculiar to 1982; similar statistics are recorded since 1960. Considering that in 1982 life expectancy at age 75 was 10.8 years, the impact of accidents on potential longevity becomes apparent.

Analysis of accidental death by etiology revealed that in 1980, approximately 48,300 Americans died in vehicular-related accidents, 12% of whom were 65 years of age or older. Only vehicular-related pedestrian deaths far exceeded population norms (22.1% in a population of 11.3% elderly) (2). In 1981, 48,200 Americans died of nontransport accidental deaths. Of these, 16,100 (33.4%) were 65 years of age or older (1). Moreover, approximately one-half of such deaths in the elderly occurred from falls, and the incidence of accidental deaths in the elderly related to falls, fires, and suffocation (64), dramatically increased with increasing age. Falls continue to play a major role in accidental death despite a decline in

mortality rate of over 50% since 1930, 24% alone since 1971.

Disability from injury, bed days, and fractures also increases with age and as individuals age they increasingly incur accidental injury and death in the house environment. In individuals 75–84 years of age, 10% of all accidental deaths occur in hospitals and other long-term care institutions (23, 57).

Not only does injury and disability in the elderly affect the quantity of life, but it also affects its quality. Many elderly restrict their activity and socialization through fear of falling despite the fact that most falls cause only minor injury or no injury at all. Families, too, are stressed. Fear of injury to a parent or spouse is a common underlying factor in decisions to institutionalize loved ones. Fear of accidents leads to relocation of children or parents, loss of employment for caregivers, or depletion of financial resources to hire caregivers. Increased dependency and financial stress have been noted as a risk factor in elderly abuse and neglect (1).

Accidental injury in the elderly is accompanied by increased complications, prolonged healing, loss of functional ability, dependency, and immobility. These consequences, initiated by trauma, may result in a gradual but persistent decline, eventually resulting in the elderly individual becoming bed or chair bound. The resulting immobility eventually contributes to morbidity and mortality. Such deaths are usually not listed as accident related, but are undoubtedly a consequence of trauma or fear of trauma.

Considering these impressive statistics, physicians caring for elderly patients must confront a number of important questions:

- Why are so many elderly individuals so vulnerable to injury?
- What risk factors associated with aging lead to this increased incidence of injury in nonvehicular and pedestrian accidents?
- Which of these risk factors are age related, disease or treatment related?
- What preventive measures can be utilized to decrease the risk and exposure to injury?

This chapter will examine these questions. Future research will seek answers to many of these problems. These answers offer promise to prevent accidental injury and death, not only in the elderly but also in other age groups.

PHYSIOLOGIC CHANGES WITH AGE

As individuals age, specific changes generally occur in the structure and function of many organs. Many of the functional declines, while they are not specific markers (41, 56) of age and may be preventable, are so consistently associated with the aging process as to reflect aging per se in our present culture.

Homeostasis, the speed and accuracy of restoration of the internal environment, is slowed and the appreciation of external change is often delayed. Awareness of hunger, thirst, ambient temperature change, bodily position, and joint movement is less accurate. Response to insulin and antidiuretic hormone is less acute. Acidosis, body sway, and alteration of body posture in the erect position take longer to correct. These changes result in an increased vulnerability to external environmental stress.

With age, hyaline cartilage dehydrates and frequently is converted to fibrous cartilage. Calcium may accumulate. Weight-bearing areas become thinner and less elastic. Skin loses elasticity and becomes thinner and more vulnerable to injury. Joints become less flexible, the cushion effect of intervertical disks and menisci decline. The heart chambers, valves, and blood vessels become less compliant, and the lung loses its elastic recoil. Cardiac conduction defects and rhythm disturbances are more common, although these changes may reflect disease, not aging (56). Baroreceptor and β-adrenergic receptor regulation also decline (38) and probably play a role in the increased incidence of orthostasis with increased age.

Bone increasingly loses mineral content, particularly in Caucasian women. Muscle mass declines 30–35% between ages 20 and 80. This loss of bone and muscle mass increases the risk of injury and fracture.

The brain shows a gradual decline in weight. By age 80, 7% of brain mass (100 g) is lost (38). This change is most apparent in the frontal area of the cortex. A similar loss of matter occurs in the cerebellum, but this process starts 10 years later. Conduction velocity declines in peripheral nerves associated with a decline in large nerve fibers. This change is particularly apparent in the dorsal roots. Motor response to stimuli and stretch reflexes are delayed. Reaction time is prolonged mainly due to slowed integrative function in the central nervous system. Proprioception declines and a greater angle of movement around a joint is required to appreciate position change. This difference is especially true of the lower extremity.

Many changes occur in the eye. The lens becomes more rigid, yellow, and less transparent due to an increase in insoluble protein content as well as liquefaction of some protein molecules. The pupil diameter decreases.

The net effect of these changes is that 3 times the illumination is required at age 80 as compared to age 20 to yield equal light passage to the retina. Flicker fusion and peripheral vision decline. Objects sidewise to the head are less well perceived. Glare is less well tolerated. Dark and light adaptation are slower. Upward gaze beyond 15° is lost without head movement. Near vision deteriorates and the colors green and blue are not well differentiated (34).

Considering the importance of vision in balance, ambulation, and performance of daily activity, these changes profoundly affect the elderly individual's ability to move about, drive an automobile, climb stairs, take medication, cook and obtain objects from shelves above and below eye level.

Equally dramatic changes occur in both hearing and vestibular function. Hearing declines especially over 2000 Hz, and decreased hearing occurs even in the 1000- to 2000-Hz range. Hearing on average declines 40–50 dB levels by age 75. Considering that background noise occurs mainly at 500–1200 Hz, its effect represents a considerable functional decline. Auditory reaction time and sound orientation decrease. These changes may influence pedestrian injury.

The number of taste papillae decline. Taste and smell also decrease. The smell of heating gas as well as other odors requires higher concentration for perception. Men tend to appreciate gas odor less well than women. These declines may play a role in poisoning as well as in fire and gas asphyxiation.

MEDICAL ILLNESS, MEDICATION, ACCIDENTS, AND PREMONITORY FALLS

Considering the functional complexity required in ambulation, driving, stair use, and instrumental activities of daily living, it is not surprising that unresolved illness with subsequent decrease in function results in a propensity to falls and other accidents. Acute illness presenting as premonitory falls is also associated with accidental injury, and 25% of all falls in the elderly are related to acute illness.

Aches, pains, musculoskeletal complaints related to joint motion limitation, visual loss, and hearing decline are frequent concerns of elderly patients. Such complaints limit mobility and are related to chronic disease states. These complaints are not related to the major causes of mortality (heart disease and cancer), yet by their nature they increase dependence and influence accident occurrence.

Medication use and the altered physiologic states resulting from illness and age decline also change pharmacokinetics and lead to an increased incidence of drug-related iatrogenic injury.

Individuals hospitalized as a result of injury from falls have a high incidence of mortality. Mortality within 1 year of such hospitalization approaches 50% (60). These statistics are imposing. Mortality from hip fracture is approximately 20% (31) in the first 6 months. Moreover, 25% of all falls serve as premonitory signs for acute illness or acute deterioration of chronic illness. Falls associated with syncope are often reported as a frequent manifestation of myocardial infarction (10, 58) or arrhythmia (21, 23).

GAIT DISTURBANCE

Gait disturbances affect 15% of the elderly (48). Critchey (18) described the gradual appearance of a broad-based gait, small shuffling steps, decreased foot elevation, diminished arm swing, stooped posture, flexion of the hips and knees, and uncertainty and stiffness on turning in elderly individuals. This gait is more commonly observed in elderly men. Elderly women will often show a waddle gait, more erect posture, and closer foot placement. This may be associated with genu varus. For women, stepping down from stools or benches is especially difficult.

Many individuals who fall do so because they do not have sufficient muscle strength or neurological reaction to compensate for loss of balance in time to prevent a fall. Weakness of the foot dorsiflexors has been implicated as a causative factor in falls (68). Stumbling or sideways loss of balance often progresses, despite attempts at regaining balance, until a fall occurs. Falls also occur due to poor foot placement, or failure to advance the foot sufficiently quickly to support forward trunk placement necessary for ambulation. Other causes of abnormal gait include spinal stenosis, stroke, peripheral neuropathy, pseudoclaudication (63), osteoarthritis, Parkinson's disease, and hip pathology.

DROP ATTACK

Elderly patients may suddenly discover themselves on the floor after extending their heads to look upward or upon turning their heads. These individuals are unable to stand or move their lower extremities while retaining consciousness. Upon being lifted and put on their feet or when pressure is applied to their soles, function is restored. The exact etiology of these attacks is unknown, but usually such attacks are attributed to ischemic changes especially in the reticular substance of the brain stem. Frequently, dizziness, diplopia, dysarthria, or dysphagia may occur episodically, as well as transient bilateral visual field defects (43) and ataxia (76).

Investigation requires a careful search for possible contributing factors such as anemia, polycythemia, congestive heart failure, hypoxemia, cardiac arrhythmia, postural hypotension, and carotid sinus hypersensitivity. The use of a cervical collar applied backwards to limit head extension and placement of articles on lower shelves may be helpful.

DIZZINESS

Dizziness is a common complaint in the elderly occurring in approximately 20% (46) of patients. Evaluation of this complaint often requires inquiry into the exact meaning of the word "dizzy" and categorizing the complaint into one of seven specific entities: true vertigo, postural orthostasis, weakness, combined weakness and orthostasis, syncope, fear of falling, or manipulation.

Faintness, giddiness, or dizziness as a result of positional change may be drug related, associated with cardiac bradytachyarrhythmias (33), especially atrial fibrillation (20) or anemia. Malaise or weakness called "dizziness" is frequent in chronic infection, carcinomatosis, and malnutrition. Combined faintness and weakness are seen in hypothyroid states and prolonged bed rest. Syncope is common in transient ischemic attack (TIA), seizure disorder, aortic valvular disease, straining at micturition or defecation, paroxsymal tachycardia, or bradycardia. Patients may use the word "dizziness" to describe unsteadiness and fear of falling. Often this is related to gait instability, prolonged bed rest, or generalized weakness.

DEMENTIA AND DEPRESSION

The prevalence of dementia (37) increases steadily after age 65 and particularly after age 75. These elderly individuals demonstrate poor judgment, hyperkinesis, a general decline in balance, apraxia, and in advanced disease become generally immobile. Frequently narcoleptics or benzodiazepines are prescribed. For these multiple reasons, individuals with dementia experience a higher incidence of falls and accidents.

Depression, too, is common in the elderly population. A prevalence of 10% is cited in the elderly (33). An increased incidence of accidents and falls in these patients has been attributed to the lack of attention to environmental factors, a desire for self-injury, and to general health decline.

DEFICITS IN SPECIAL SENSES

Cataracts, glaucoma, macular degeneration, visual loss due to stroke, and diabetic retinopathy all increase with age (34). Entropion, or ectropion, or tearing related to epiphora may affect vision and cause accidents.

Proprioceptive loss related to stroke or peripheral vascular disease, hearing loss with otosclerosis, and other sensory deficits may be involved in falls, pedestrian accidents, or accidental drug ingestion.

CARDIOVASCULAR DISEASE

The incidence of congestive heart failure and myocardial infarction increases with age. Hypertension, cardiac arrhythmia, and valvular disease are common in the elderly.

Electrocardiograms registered by telemetry indicating coronary insufficiency have been reported under normal automobile driving conditions (26). Falls in the nursing home (58) have been found to be associated with acute cardiac abnormalities.

Holter monitor studies of the elderly incurring falls often reveal cardiac arrhythmia as an underlying etiology. These studies are indicated in view of the fact that resting cardiograms in these individuals revealed only a 25% incidence of abnormality (21).

ORTHOSTASIS

The Framingham study (36) and the Hypertension Detection and Follow-up program (26) have shown that morbidity and mortality are significantly related to hypertension. Elderly patients receiving antihypertensive medication are at distinct risk of suffering positional orthostasis and experiencing falls. Homeostatic control of blood pressure declines with age. Approximately 20% of individuals aged 65 and older suffer a fall in systolic blood pressure of 20 mm Hg or more, and at least a 10 mm Hg decline in diastolic blood pressure on standing from a supine position, with the prevalence increasing to 30–50% in individuals 75 and older (55). Approximately 5% of normal elderly suffer a decline of over 40 mm Hg in their systolic blood pressure. Some studies have attributed up to 20% of all falls to this phenomenon alone (34).

On standing, a failure of the heart rate to increase by 10 or more beats may indicate autonomic nervous system functional decline. Postural orthostasis may be exaggerated by hypokalemia, volume depletion, polypharmacy, electrolyte imbalance, prolonged bed rest (67), and dilatation of splachnic blood vessels postprandially. Such blood pressure declines were formerly thought to cause strokes and TIAs. At present, localized functional loss is thought less commonly to occur, and dizziness or syncope is considered a more common occurrence (34).

DRUGS

Not only are the elderly more vulnerable to injury due to disease but drug use, drug toxicity, and drug interaction are more frequent with each decade after age 65 (5). Alteration in pharmacokinetics due to physiological decline, disease, and marked variability in elderly patients' drug levels despite similar dosing regimes result in many iatrogenic accidents and hospital admissions. Antihypertensives, Dilantin, diuretics, narcoleptics, aminophylline, quinidine (29), digitalis, anti-inflammatory drugs, hypnotics, sedatives, analgesics, tricyclics, benzodiazepines, and antihistamines are responsible for hospital admission, orthostasis, confusion, cardiac arrhythmia, and undoubtedly falls and other accidents (54, 66). Over-the-counter medications, medication swapping, and alcohol consumption all contribute to this problem. The elderly also make errors in drug use. This is understandable when one notes that 87% of individuals over age 75 are responsible for their own medication dispensing (5). Errors have been shown to increase when three or more medications are prescribed (5).MacDonald et al. (45) noted that compliance can be improved when physicians spent as little as 15 minutes with patients discussing medications and medication use prior to hospital discharge. Care should be taken in writing instructions. Some elderly are illiterate, others are legally blind and have difficulty reading drug labels. Simulated medication charts with pictures of medication, use of different colored labels, use of egg crates or other dispensing aids, larger prescription print, careful explanation of drug effects and precautions are worthwhile preventative measures.

FALLS

In a landmark study Sheldon (61) highlighted the frequency and importance of falls in individuals over age 65, with a dramatic increase over the age of 75. Although the majority of falls suffered by the elderly result in only minor injury (2, 35), the propensity of premonitory falls and the prevalence of osteoporosis are major contributing factors both to fracture and fatal outcome. Women over age 75 are at particular risk of falling and sustaining a serious injury. In women between the ages of 75 and 79 the incidence of hip fracture is 6 of 1000, for those 85–89 the incidence is 48.6 of 1000 (35). It has been estimated that for every 210,000 people in the general population, 16 hospital beds will be continually occupied by individuals who have sustained a hip fracture (51). The importance of age in survival from falls is illustrated by the fact that the death rate in females is increased almost 5 times between ages 65 and 74 and 75 and 84, but the injury rate is less than doubled (9).

One-third to one-half (49) of elderly persons residing in the community (53) and almost one-half of elderly persons residing in long-term care institutions fall each year (49). One-fifth of all fatal falls occur in the nursing home setting. Two-thirds of those who fall will experience recurrent falls. Only 35% of all falls are reported to physicians and many of these only after injury or physician inquiry. In the United States, 200,000 elderly suffer hip fractures each year. Of these individuals 15 to 20% die from complications associated with this injury, while many more die from immobility and its complications. Sheldon (61) has noted that when elderly individuals start to fall, they continue to fall, unable to correct the loss of balance. Forty-three percent of elderly women and 21% of elderly men answered affirmatively to the question, "Are you likely to fall?" (61).

Stairs (7) have been frequently identified as the greatest hazard in fall occurrence. In 1982 stairs accounted for 1,203,041 falls and were considered the most hazardous consumer product (7). Bicycle-associated falls, the next accident-associated consumer product, accounted for 573,662 falls. One individual in seven will suffer a stair-related accident in his lifetime. Most serious accidents occur in falls down steps. Eighty-five percent of all stair-associated deaths involve individuals over 65 years of age.

Investigation of stair ascent and descent (7) has revealed that coordinated visual and kinesthetic function is required to successfully traverse stairs. Individuals visually assess stairs as they approach them; then they kinesthetically test their observation by foot wriggling on the first two or three steps. Regular foot placement occurs until the last two or three steps, when the process is reversed and kinesthetic placement precedes visual testing in gait control. In traversing middle steps unseen or or unsuspected hazards are especially dangerous. Ability to identify tread edge is especially important, and rug patterns that distract the eye increase the possibility of stair accident. The need for accurate visual interpretation of tread edge allows visual distraction (stripes parallel to the tread or strong designs) to be dangerous. Many accidents occur because individuals miss the last step during descent. Handrails are particularly used by older individuals not only for support but to allow their upper extremities to help pull themselves up stairs and to control descent rate.

Other household hazards, such as throw rugs, waxed floors, spilled liquid or urine, poor lighting, and pets, also contribute to home accidents. Other risk factors associated with falls include female sex, chronic illness, acute illness, alcohol use, cardiac arrhythmia, and isolation. Wild et al. (72) noted that 62% of fallers, but only 32% of nonfallers, had cognition disorders and 26% of the fallers, but only 10% of the nonfallers, had incontinence. General good health correlated negatively and depression positively with fall incidence.

Owen (52) states that falls are the result of either deficient perception or coordination or both or are associated with physiologic change due to illness or medication. After age 75, the proportion of falls secondary to tripping, inappropriate activity, imprudent judgment, perceptual error, or improper footwear or associated with environmental hazards decline while those related to medication use, loss of balance, cardiac and neurological illness, visual impairment, functional disability, dizziness, syncope, and orthostasis become more common.

Wild (73, 74) has studied 125 fallers who reported falls occurring in a community place of residence and its environs (front and back steps, garden, porch). Falls occurred while walking on a level surface, with turning, on stairs, during position change, getting into or out of bed, or on or off chairs or the toilet. Two-thirds of these individuals sustained some injury and 18 (14.6%) had fractures, 3 of the hip. Explanation of the falls included dizziness, giddiness, blackout, light-headed feeling, "the body just gave way," and trip, slip, or miss. Fallers had difficulty rising from a chair and had a greater prevalence of arthritis and stroke. Perry (53) studied fallers in a house setting, institutional setting, and those seeking treatment in a hospital emergency department. Fallers were noted to increase with age. Fractures occurred in 10.5%. In the over-80-year-old group, 31% of men and 47% of women had suffered prior falls. In women over 75, 40% of all falls resulted in fracture, and 38% reported a fall the previous year. Disability or illness was reported in 75% of these falls. Thirteen percent reported prior ingestion of alcohol. Orthostasis was a commonly noted physical finding.

Isaacs (27) grouped individuals into three categories in predicting falls. A high risk group displayed the following characteristics: low gait speed, high sway, low mobility, age of 75 or older, acute illness, previous history of a fall, multiple medication use, and multiple chronic illness. Individuals with chronic or acute illness involving neurological deficits, cardiac disease, congestive heart failure, arthritis, muscle wasting, or incontinence were at particular risk. Such individuals were commonly housebound.

A low risk group was indicated by elderly individuals who demonstrated high-speed gait, minimal sway, and high mobility. These individuals were usually younger than 75 years and frequently left their home 20 or more days per month.

The intermediate group was characterized as generally well, fairly functional, but with a specific risk factor. These individuals were moderately immobile and left their home between 5 and 20 days per month.

HIP FRACTURE

For each fall leading to death there are 20 that lead to hip fracture, 84% of which occur in individuals 65 years or older (8). Only 10 other diagnostic-related groups cause greater hospitalization. In women, most hip fractures result from falls from standing height onto a hard surface.

Hip fracture was studied by Crane and Kernek (17) in 159 patients. Of these individuals one-third survived at least 10 years. Fifty-five percent of the

10-year survivors still resided at home. There was a 15% fracture-associated mortality.

Jensen et al. (30) noted that prefracture function and socialization were as important in predicting outcome as was age. Mortality in hip fracture was higher in men (90%) than in women (64.7%) 10 years after fracture. Postoperative ambulation was decreased. Only 45% were returned to full ambulation, 32% ambulated in a limited capacity, and 23% were nonambulaters. In the immediate postoperative period the statistics were even worse with only 9% fully ambulatory, 14% partially ambulatory, and 77% nonambulatory. This highlights the importance of rehabilitation in functional return. At 1 year, Ceder (13) reported a 15% mortality rate in individuals residing in the community and a 45% mortality rate in individuals residing in an institutional setting prior to their hip fracture.

OTHER INJURIES

Although many authors indicate hip fracture as a cause of death, in an analysis of 1981–1983 total accidents in Dade County, Copeland (16) observed that craniocerebral trauma was the leading cause of death, and that complications of pneumonia and pulmonary emboli frequently led to fatal outcomes. The majority of these deaths occurred within 2 weeks of the fall. Stairs, street curbs, bathroom, and bedroom areas were associated with a greater proportion of fatal falls.

In Sweden, Benger and Johnell (11) studied forearm fractures occurring from falls in comparable age groups of women in two separate time spans, 1953–1957 and 1980–1981. In the latter period, he noted a 6-fold increase in forearm fractures in individuals over the age of 70. Although the reason for this significant increase was unknown, the known association of forearm fracture and osteoporosis in the elderly raises concern and requires further evaluation.

FALLS IN THE NURSING HOME AND HOSPITAL

Despite protection from many environmental risk factors (stairs, kitchens, icy sidewalks), 25–50% of residents in nursing homes fall yearly. Analysis of risk factors in such fallers usually indicates confusion, weakness, dementia, acute illness, chronic disability (71), and the use of multiple drugs. Eighty percent of individuals falling were of age 75 or older. Twenty percent of falls were associated with acute illness. Transfer to bed, chair, wheelchair, or toilet were common factors. Most of these individuals were receiving narcoleptics or more than three drugs. Cardiac disease and cardiac arrhythmia were common. Most of the falls occurred during hours of daytime activity. In 20% of falls reported in a long-term care facility, the interviewed nursing staff admitted prior apprehension in relation to the patient's status. Tinetti et al. (70) examined nine factors related to falls and noted a multifactorial etiology. Almost all recurrent fallers had multiple problems including poor back flexibility, decreased lower extremity strength, poor distant vision and symptoms when turning or extending the neck, poor endurance, decreased mental status, hearing problems, or orthostasis.

Coincidentally, the design of modern nursing homes and hospitals, by stressing privacy, makes patient observation difficult. Falls tend to increase as the opportunity for direct observation decreases. Only 25% (34) of all falls in institutions are witnessed. Most falls occur in the patient's room or in the adjacent bathroom. Hallway falls occur with self-ambulation. Wheelchair use for seating, rather than for mobility, continues to be hazardous (12). Postprandial hypotension has been identified in one-third of nursing home residents and is often associated with falls (44).

In the hospital setting most falls occur between 10 AM and 4 PM and more frequently during the first week of hospitalization when patients are most likely to be more ill and more confused.

In evaluating in-hospital accidents occurring in bed, Rubenstein et al. (59) noted that 88% of the beds were in the low position, side rails in place and elevated. Most frequently the accident occurred while the patient was climbing over the side rail for toilet use. Falls seemed specifically related to side rail use. Such side rail use was mandated by nursing protocols. Protection from medicolegal exposure was considered equally important as patient protection. Side rails increase the height of a fall and the extent of injury. Closer supervision, open wards, or use of half rails may be a better alternative.

EVALUATION AND PREVENTION OF FALLS

In evaluating an elderly individual who falls, a detailed history of the event, including frequency of falling, medication, medical history and alcohol use, is helpful. Unfortunately, many patients are not able to give a detailed history. For this reason, questioning family and caregivers may yield valuable information. Questions should be directed toward elucidating acute illness, possibility of arrhythmia,

cerebrovascular insufficiency, seizure, "silent" myocardial infarction, anemia, electrolyte disturbance, and infection. Footwear and ambulatory aids should be checked. The use of a home hazard checklist (24, 69) may be helpful both in fall evaluation and prevention.

Physical examination should be directed toward acute injury, cognition decline, and acute medical illness. When the patient is capable of standing and walking, evaluation for postural hypotension and gait disorder is helpful. Attention to vision, carotid bruit, symptoms with head movement, general muscular strength, nervous system function, and cardiac state are necessary.

No specific laboratory evaluation is indicated. Suggested are complete blood count (CBC), electrolytes, blood sugar, and electrocardiogram (ECG) to rule out myocardial infarction and arrhythmia. Other testing should be individualized by the history and physical exam.

Historical evaluation should indicate the type of movement and activity resulting in the fall (27). Such movement has been classified as basic (daily activity with minimal body displacement), extended (unusual activity), and extreme (high risk, rapid, with great body displacement).

Risk factors often reflect the force of the injury and the ability of bone to withstand the force without fracture.

Preventive Home Measures: Stairs, Bathroom, and Kitchen

Stairwells should have two-sided rails and have a contour indicating the top and bottom of the stairwell and the tread edge. Rails should allow adequate hand grasp by being at least 2 inches from the wall. The length of the rail should be sufficient to allow use to ground and landing level. Slippery or uneven treads, steep stairwells, and winding treads may be hazardous. Stairwells should be well illuminated.

Showers used by the elderly should be 6 feet long, equipped with a seat and detachable shower hose, and externally temperature controlled. Showers should be step-in with minimal lip and have appropriate grab bars capable of supporting 250 or more pounds. Water temperature should be controlled not to exceed 108 degrees.

Toilet seats should be 18 inches in height with grab bars.

Stove controls should be front or side mounted so as not to require a person's hand or forearm to extend over heat elements. Electricity is preferable to gas. Shelved items should not be placed higher than eye level. Lamps should be pull-down to allow bulb change without climbing. Light switches should be accessible from doorways, and adequate light should be available from bed to bathroom. Bed and chair height should allow seating with feet resting on the floor with knees flexed to 90 degrees, usually 17-18 inches from the floor.

Linoleum should not be slippery; throw rugs may be dangerous, and carpeting should not be worn. A small nonskid rug placed by the sink may help avert the hazard of water spill. Thresholds between rooms should be minimized or removed. Factors related to the environment can often be altered but patient compliance to effect change is often poor.

Special care is necessary during periods of medication change or when unexpected weight loss occurs. Exercise programs may increase bone mineral content, strength, and endurance and elevate mood. Balance is more difficult to improve but may be helped by heel-to-toe exercise, gait training, and use of assistive devices. Endurance training, by improving impaired function and strengthening normal function, may help in fall prevention. Care is required in prescribing assistive devices for patients with dementia because inappropriate use may result in the device being a hazard. Assistive devices also may require repair. Appropriate footwear, often a good jogging shoe with a wide heel and toe box, will lessen fall potential. Caregiver education is helpful. During ambulation, the caregiver should be instructed to support the patient while allowing the patient to set the pace. Gait training will require special attention to technique as well as correcting for path deviation when walking gait is initiated or stopped. Observation for impulsivity and reaching balance is necessary, since falls can occur with normal gait.

BURNS

Patients aged 65 constitute about 20% (62) of all burn victims admitted to hospitals. These individuals represent a particular challenge to physicians during their acute care management and rehabilitation care. Chronic disease and especially preexisting cardiopulmonary and renal disease involve special care in intravenous fluid therapy. Preexisting pulmonary disease increases the victim's vulnerability to inhalation injury. Poor healing of donor sites and graft loss due to inadequate vascular supply are complications of stasis and perfusion decline with heart failure. Prolonged hospital stay, injury due to protein loss with hypermetabolic states, and nosocomial infection increase morbidity and mortality.

The use of cimetidene and antacids to decrease the incidence of gastric bleeding (62) also have been recommended.

Prior to 1940 there were no published reports of survival in individuals over age 60 suffering second degree burns involving greater than 10% of body surface area (6). Today, survival still varies considerably with age. Collective data from 34,731 burn cases indicates a 56.5% survival rate in elderly patients (25). Those who had burns involving 20% or less of surface area had a more favorable prognosis. Those who had burns involving 70% or more of surface area did not survive. Baux's formula suggesting that mortality rate is equal to percentage of second and third degree burn plus age of the patient still remains fairly predictive (6).

Anous and Heimbach (6) divided geriatric burn patients into four groups. Patients in group A ranged from ages 61 to 87 years with an average burn percentage of 84%. Because survival would be unprecedented, only morphine and minimal fluids were prescribed. Mean survival time was 3 hours and cardiovascular collapse occurred. Group B averaged 77 years of age with a mean burn percentage of 56%. Despite aggressive attempts at resuscitation the mean survival was 3 days. The cause of death was cardiovascular collapse or inhalation injury. Group C had a mean age of 73 years, a mean survival time of 18 days, and burns of 31%. These patients required substantially more intravenous fluids than anticipated using Baxter's formula. Sepsis due to *Staphylococcus aureus* or *Pseudomonas* was the direct cause of death in 75% of these individuals, and pneumonia was invariably fatal. Group D, the survivors, had a mean age of 69 years and a mean burn of 23%. These patients usually did not exceed Baxter's calculation of intravenous fluid requirement. Early mobilization and a more conservative nonoperative approach was considered advantageous to survival (25). Although surgery is usually performed to decrease healing time, the associated use of general anesthesia, blood loss, and donor harvesting were poorly tolerated. Wounds that can heal by primary intention, despite cosmetic and functional impairment, should be allowed to do so.

Other factors suggestive of poor prognosis include preexisting mental, cardiovascular, and gastrointestinal disease, decreased arterial oxygen saturation below age-predictive norms, serum osmolality variance from norm, and lower extremity burns.

Many of the elderly who sustained severe burns either lived alone or were known to ingest alcohol

(15). Flame fires were the most common type of fire leading to severe burns. These occurred most often in the victims' homes, and cigarette smoking and electrical shorts were major contributing causes. In a 5-year study in metropolitan Dade County, 50% of the victims had blood alcohol levels equal to or exceeding 0.1%. Elderly patients have a decreased metabolism and volume of distribution for alcohol, and this may account for elevated blood levels with alcohol ingestion.

Other causes for burns include scalds both from tap water and bath/shower exposure (40). A full thickness burn can occur at exposure to 120° F for 10 minutes, 127° F for 1 minute, and at 130° F for 30 seconds. Lowering the hot water heater temperature to 112–120° F would help prevent 3000 hospital admissions for scald that occur yearly.

Fatal fires occurring in buildings invariably involve the building contents rather than the structure (14). The most common source responsible for the fire is cigarettes. The fire usually starts as a smoldering fire and subsequently becomes a flame fire. With the advent of synthetic material use in home furnishings, flaming fires have increased.

The hazards of smoldering and flaming fires are different. Smoldering fires are slower. Natural fibers such as those used in cotton mattresses usually cause smoldering fires while synthetics, such as those used in polyurethane mattresses, cause flame fires. Often a smoldering fire will continue until the article is consumed without involving other room contents. Inhalation of toxic gasses, carbon monoxide, and smoke may kill an incapacitated or sleeping victim (asphyxiation). Flaming fires, by involving more of the room contents and by causing a great deal of smoke, carbon monoxide, and carbon dioxide production as well as toxic heavy gasses, allow less time for escape. The elderly are particularly vulnerable to such fires.

All mattresses sold in the United States after 1971 are required by law to be resistant to a dropped cigarette (50). More recently the upholstered furniture industry has adopted a voluntary labeling program to indicate which furniture is cigarette resistant.

The use of fire and smoke detectors, inspection of home wiring, and lowering of water heater temperatures could help limit the number of burn victims. Fire drills, emphasizing escape routes and assemblage points, also have saved lives and prevented family members from reentering buildings looking for victims who had already succeeded in escaping but had not been located.

POISONING

Patients 65 years of age or older represent 13% (50) of all reported poisoning deaths, and individuals over age 80 constitute the highest cohort group suffering death from poisoning. The incidence of death from poisoning in individuals over age 80 exceeds by 3 times the incidence of death from poisoning of children under age 5. The majority of these poisonings are unintentional and less than 20% of deaths are attributed to suicide (50). Unintentional drug-related deaths include falls and driving accidents.

At a poison control center in Maryland, a study investigated 276 agents that were involved in elderly deaths (39). Of these drugs accounted for 148, household products 42, personal care products 34, plants 7, and miscellaneous 57. The drugs most commonly involved were topical agents, sedatives, hypnotics, minor tranquilizers, analgesics, and antidepressants. Exposure was mainly in the victim's home (64%).

Improved storage, using locked cabinets limiting accessibility to poisons, clear separation of cleaning material from medication, and specially designed labels using larger type and drawings to indicate appropriate use of contents could help prevent poisoning. Medications should be regularly inspected, and outdated and inappropriate medications should be discarded.

VEHICULAR ACCIDENTS

Deaths occurring from vehicular accidents and vehicular/pedestrian accidents are a frequent cause of mortality in individuals aged 65 and older.

PEDESTRIAN TRAFFIC ACCIDENTS

Elderly pedestrians were the victims of 25% of all motor vehicular injuries and 34% of all motor vehicular deaths in 1981 (65). These numbers were more pronounced in the 75-year-old and older group. The death and injury rate increased with age after age 65. Potential factors responsible for these statistics are decreased velocity of ambulation, peripheral vision and hearing, increased reaction time, incidence of falls, and susceptibility to serious injury with falling.

The majority of these vehicular/pedestrian deaths occurred at intersections. Only 5% of individuals over age 70 can ambulate 83 m/minute (32). Traffic lights at some intersections are regulated to require this rate of walking velocity to successfully achieve intersection crossing. Curb height also presents a problem and compounds the difficulty of traffic observation while successfully stepping over the curb.

Allard (4) has investigated the relationship of the location of an older city dweller's place of residence to the risk of fatal vehicular/pedestrian injury. Risk increased with the proximity of residents to the downtown area where there was increased business and commercial vehicular traffic.

DRIVER-RELATED ACCIDENTS

Davidson (19) studied the relationship between drivers' abilities and their accident records. A poor accident record was associated with poor binocular acuity. Poor right eye acuity and hyperphoria of one diopter or greater were also considered risk factors. This study was done in England where driving is performed on the left side of the road. No conclusion was reached by the author as to whether left eye visual acuity would be of greater significance in the United States or whether this represented ocular or cortical dominance. Graca (22) noted that dynamic visual acuity has a greater association with driving performance than static visual acuity. Other visual changes that decline with aging include flicker fusion, peripheral vision, stereoscopic acuity, angular visual threshold, and accommodation. Night vision also declines with a decreased ability to adapt to the dark and tolerate glare, and a decreased translucency of the eye. Dynamic perception tasks (detecting presence, rate, and direction of angular motion) decline similarly.

Individuals 25 years of age or younger have the highest incidence rate of driver-related accidents. Accident rates then decline until drivers reach the age of 60. After that age rates again rise, especially after age 75. Accident rates per 100,000 miles of driving occur twice as frequently at age 70 as in drivers aged 40–55 (22). Fatalities increase by 45%. Traffic violations in elderly individuals for illegal passing, failing to yield the right of way, illegal turning, and failing to obey signs all increase after age 60. Failure to obey signs show the most dramatic rise. Violations for equipment failure decline. Many of these traffic violations may be related to visual loss. In one study of elderly volunteers, 57% were unaware of any visual problems (22).

Auditory changes occurring with aging may restrict traffic cueing. The risk of driving with specific diseases or deficits, such as hearing loss, have not been evaluated. However, a 10-year age-adjusted accident rate for drivers with chronic medical conditions was approximately twice that of healthy drivers (22).

Nine states require an increased frequency of testing for drivers license renewal after age 65. Forty-one states have no age-specific regulation. In only two states, California and Oregon, is the physician responsible to report a potentially unsafe driver.

Individuals over age 70 drive fewer miles, consume less alcohol when driving, and have lower accident rates and less traffic violations than individuals under age 25. However, accidents, deaths, and traffic violations per 100,000 miles do increase after age 65. Research to determine specific driving risk factors would be helpful to prevent individuals who have these factors from driving altogether or from driving without specific restrictions regardless of their age. Education directed toward problems faced by elderly drivers and more specific testing, especially of visual parameters and performance abilities as indicated through research, should be incorporated in the relicensing process. Such research and subsequent testing would require an allotment of personnel and fiscal resources and would represent a societal decision toward increased road safety.

REFERENCES

1. Accident Facts, 1982 Edition. National Safety Council. Chicago, IL.
2. *Accident Mortality*, vol 2, section 5. National Safety Council. Chicago, IL, 1980.
3. American Academy of Family Physicians: The Aging Process—Some Specific Problems. Home Study Self Assessment, 21:33, 1980.
4. Allard R: Excess mortality from traffic accidents among elderly pedestrians living in the inner city. *Am J Public Health* 72:853, 1982.
5. American Academy of Family Physicians: The Aging Process I. *Home Study Self Assessment*. Monograph #10, American Academy of Family Physicians, 1979.
6. Anous MH, Heimbach DM: Causes of health and predictors in burned patients more than 60 years of age. *J Trauma* 26:135, 1986.
7. Archea JC: Environmental factors associated with stair accidents in the elderly. *Clin Geriatr Med* 1:555, 1985.
8. Baker SP, Harvey AH: Fall injuries in the elderly. *Clin Geriatr Med* 1:501, 1985.
9. Barker S, O'Neill B, Karpf R: *The Injury Fact Book.* Lexington, MA, Lexington Books, 1984.
10. Bayer AJ, Joginder SC, Raafat RF, Pathy MSJ: Changing presentation of myocardial infarction with increasing old age. *J Am Geriatr Soc* 34:263, 1986.
11. Bengner V, Johnell O: Increasing incidence of forearm fractures—comparison of epidemiologic patterns 25 years apart. *Acta Orthop Scand* 56:158, 1985.
12. Berry G, Fisher R, Lang S: Detrimental incidents including falls in an elderly institutional population. *J Am Geriatr Soc* 29:322, 1981.
13. Ceder L, Ekelund L, Inerot S: Rehabilitation after hip

fracture in the elderly. *Acta Orthop Scand* 50:681, 1979.

14. Clarke, FB, Birky MM: Fire safety in dwellings and public buildings. *Bull NY Acad Med* 57:1047, 1981.

15. Copeland AR: Accidental fire deaths—the five year metropolitan Dade County experience from 1978 until 1983. *Z Rechtsmed* 94:71, 1985.

16. Copeland, AR: Fatal accidental falls among the elderly—the metropolitan Dade County experience. 1981-83. *Med Sci Law* 25:172, 1985.

17. Crane JC, Kernek CB: Mortality associated with hip fractures in a single geriatric hospital and residential health facility—a ten year review. *J Am Geriatr Soc* 31:472, 1983.

18. Critchey M: Senile disorders of gait. *Geriatrics* 3:364, 1948.

19. Davidson PA: Interrelationship between British drivers' abilities, age and road accident histories. *Ophthalmol Physiol* 5:195, 1985.

20. Goldberg A, Rafferty E, Cashma P, et al.: Ambulatory cardiographic records in transient cerebral attacks or palpitations. *Br Med J* 4:569, 1975.

21. Gordon MR: Occult cardiac arrhythmias associated with falls and dizziness in the elderly, detection by holter monitoring. *J Am Geriatr Soc* 24:418, 1976.

22. Graca JL: Driving and aging. *Clin Geriatr Med* 2 (3):577, 1986.

23. Gryfe CI, Amies A, Ashley MJ: A longitudinal study of falls in an elderly population I. Incidence and morbidity. *Age Ageing* 6:201-10, 1977.

24. Home Safety Checklist for Older Consumers. US Department of Health and Human Services. US Government Printing Office:1985-475–981: 32202.

25. Housinger T, Suffle F, Ward S, et al.: Conservative approach to the elderly patient with burns. *Am J Surg* 148:817, 1984.

26. Hypertension detection and follow-up program cooperative group—five year findings of the hypertension detection and follow-up program. *JAMA* 242:2562, 1979.

27. Isaacs B: Clinical and laboratory studies of falls in old people—prospects of prevention. *Clin Geriatr Med* 1:513, 1985.

28. Iskrant AP, Jolief VP: *Accidents and Homicide, Vital and Health Statistics*. Monographs American Public Health Association. London, Harvard University Press, 1968.

29. Jahnigen D, Hannon C, Laxson L, et al.: Iatrogenic disease in hospitalized elderly veterans. *J Am Geriatr Soc* 30:387, 1982.

30. Jensen JS, Tondevold E, Sorensen PH: Social rehabilitation following hip fractures. *Acta Orthop Scand* 50:777, 1979.

31. Jensen S, Tondevold E: Mortality after hip fractures. *Orthop Scand* 50:161, 1979.

32. Kallman H (Moderator): Care of the aging woman, part 1. *Female Patient* 11:26, 1986.

33. Kallman H: Depression in the Elderly: Desyrel—a compendium of three years of clinical use—Symposium. Chicago, IL, Mead Johnson, 1984, 31-38.

34. Kallman H, Vernon MS: The aging eye. *Postgrad Med* 81:108, 1987.

35. Kane RL, Kane RA, Arnold SB: Prevention and elderly risk factors. *Health Serv Res* 19:945, 1985.

36. Kannel WB: Some lessons in cardiovascular epidemiology from Framingham. *Am J Cardiol* 37:269, 1976.

37. Kay DWK. The epidemiology of brain deficit in the aged: problems in patient identification. In Eisdorfer C, Friedel RO (Eds): *The Cognitively and Emotionally Impaired Elderly*. Chicago, Year Book Medical Publications, 1977.

38. Kenney RA: *Physiology of Aging: A Synopsis*. Chicago, Year Book Medical Publishers, Inc., 1982.

39. Klein-Schwartz W, Oderda GM, Booze L: Poisoning in the elderly. *J Am Geriatr Soc* 31:195, 1983.

40. Lewis JM: Prevent burn injury to older adults. *J Gerontol Nurs* 11:8, 1985.

41. Lindeman RD, Tobin J, Shock N: Longitudinal studies on rate of decline in renal function with age. *J Am Geriatr Soc* 33:278, 1985.

42. Lipsitz LA: Abnormalities in blood pressure homeostasis that contribute to falls in the elderly. *Clin Geriatr Med* 1:637, 1985.

43. Lipsitz LA: The drop attack—a common geriatric symptom. *J Am Geriatr Soc* 31:617, 1983.

44. Lipsitz LA, Nyquist RP, Wei JY, Rowe JW: Postprandial reduction in blood pressure in the elderly. *N Engl J Med* 309:81, 1983.

45. MacDonald ET, et al.: Improving drug compliance after hospital discharge. *Br Med J* 2:618, 1977.

46. Moriamatsu M: Vertigo and dizziness in the elderly. *Jpn J Geriatr* 12:405, 1975.

47. Morris EV, Isaacs B: The prevention of falls in a geriatric hospital. *Age Ageing* 9:181, 1980.

48. Newman G, Dovenmuehle R, Basse E: Alteration of neurological status with age. *J Am Geriatr Soc* 8:915, 1960.

49. Nickens H: Intrinsic factors in falling among the elderly. *Arch Intern Med* 145:1089, 1985.

50. Oderda GM, Klein-Schwartz W: Poison prevention in the elderly. *Drug Intell Clin Pharm* 18:183, 1984.

51. Overstall PN: Prevention of falls in the elderly. *J Am Geriatr Soc* 28:481, 1980.

52. Owen DH: Maintaining posture and avoiding tripping—optical information for defecting and controlling orientation and locomotion. *Clin Geriatr Med* 1:581, 1985.

53. Perry BC: Falls among the elderly—a review of the methods and conclusions of epidemiologic studies. *J Am Geriatr Soc* 30:367, 1982.

54. Reichel W: Complications in the care of 500 hospitalized patients. *J Am Geriatr Soc* 13:973, 1965.

55. Robbins AS, Rubenstein LZ: Postural hypotension in the elderly. *J Am Geriatr Soc* 32:769, 1984.

56. Rodeheffer RJ, Gerstenblith G, Becker LC, Fleg JL, Weisfelt ML, Lakatta EG: Exercise cardiac output is maintained with advancing age in healthy human subjects: cardiac compensation and increased stroke volume compensate for a diminished heart rate. *Circulation* 69:203, 1984.

57. Rodstein M: Accidents among the aged: incidence, causes, prevention. *J Chron Dis* 17:515, 1964.

58. Rodstein M, Camus AS: Interrelations of heart disease and accidents. *Geriatrics* 28:87, 1973.

59. Rubenstein HS, Muller FH, Postree S, et al.: Standards of medical care based on consensus rather than evidence, the case of routine bed rail use for the elderly. *Law Med Health Care* 11:271, 1983.

60. Rubenstein LZ: Falls in the elderly—a clinical approach. *West J Med* 138:273, 1983.

61. Sheldon JH: *The Social Medicare of Old Age*. London, Oxford University Press, 1948.

62. Slater H, Garsford JC: Burns in older patients. *J Am Geriatr Soc* 29:74, 1981.

63. Smigiel M, Davis DH: Pseudoclaudication review of etiology. Diagnosis and treatment. *Clin Geriatr Med* 1:373, 1985.

64. *Statistical Abstract of the United States*, 106 ed.. US Department of Commerce, 1986.

65. Statistics Bulletin. Met Life Insurance Company. July–Sept 1982, p. 10.

66. Steel K, Gertman PM, Crescenz C, et al.: Iatrogenic illness on a general medical service at a university hospital. *N Engl J Med* 304:638, 1981.

67. Thomas JE, Schinger A, Fealey RD: Orthostatic hypotension. *Mayo Clin Proc* 56:117, 1981.

68. Tideiksaar R: Gerontological Society of America. Meeting, Chicago, IL, Nov 19–23, 1986.

69. Tideiksaar R: Preventing falls: home hazard checklists to help older patients protect themselves. *Geriatrics* 41:26, 1986.

70. Tinetti ME, Williams TF, Mayewski R: Fall risk index for elderly patients based on number of chronic disabilities. *Am J Med* 80:429, 1986.

71. Wells BG, Middleton B, Lawrence G, et al.: Factors associated with the elderly falling in intermediate care facilities. *Geriatr Gerontol* 19:142, 1985.

72. Wild D, Nayak USL, Isaacs B: Characteristics of old people who fell at home. *J Exp Gerontol* 2:271, 1980.

73. Wild D, Nayak USL, Isaacs B: Description classification and prevention of falls in old people. *Rheumat Rehabil* 20:153, 1981.

74. Wild D, Nayak USL, Isaacs B: How dangerous are falls in old people? *Br Med J* 282:266, 1981.

75. Wild D, Nayak USL, Isaacs B: Prognosis of falls in old people at home. *J Epidemiol Commun Health* 35:200, 1981.

76. Williams D, Wilson TG: The diagnosis of major and minor symptoms of basilar insufficiency. *Brain* 85:741, 1982.

77. Williamson J, Chopen N: Adverse reactions to prescribed drugs in the elderly, a multicenter investigation. *Age Ageing* 9:73, 1980.

CHAPTER 49

Iatrogenic Disease in the Elderly

FRANK C. SNOPE

The need for a chapter on iatrogenic disease in the elderly is, in some ways, a testimony to the failure of our educational programs in medical education. The potential for iatrogenesis in the use of drugs and diagnostic and therapeutic procedures is adequately stressed in educational courses for health professionals, from anatomy and physiology through clinical medicine. In spite of that emphasis, health professionals often seem to neglect fundamentals when dealing with elderly patients and their problems. Altered physiologic states, side effects of pharmacotherapeutic agents, and other basics are frequently overlooked in our treatment of the elderly patient.

The reasons for this seemingly contradictory behavior and for the need to devote considerable time and energy to the subject of iatrogenesis are not entirely clear. It is rare, for instance, for a conference on geriatric medicine to be presented without one discussion being devoted to iatrogenesis. The medical literature contains many references to iatrogenic disease, many in readily accessible journals. A review of the English language medical literature since 1982 revealed 62 articles dealing with iatrogenesis. In addition, the subject of iatrogenesis has attracted a wide audience as evidenced by articles on the subject by nurses (1–3, 16, 17), pharmacists (13), podiatrists (8), and lawyers(6, 15).

A frequently offered explanation for the continued presence of iatrogenic disease is that of our increased technologic capabilities. We are able to do more things to more people and we have increasing numbers of older people who become ill and require diagnostic and therapeutic intervention. As a consequence, we may have *unavoidable* side effects. This

aspect of the problem was presented in an innovative and detailed article by Moser (14) in 1956.

On the other hand, as Steel has pointed out (24), iatrogenesis may be the result of increased reliance on data collection methods which have greater potential for problems than others. He states that "history taking, the most highly regarded and effective means of data collection by almost any criteria . . . carries with it little or no risk, [but] is performed with less skill than it might be." He points out that in a survey of 11 textbooks of general history taking and physician diagnosis, none dealt with an example of a person over 70 years of age. None of the texts discussed the possibility of dealing with a patient who is hard of hearing or how to collect information from a patient in a nursing home. He further comments on the lack of emphasis on functional status, the inadequacy of emphasizing a single chief complaint, the neglect of recording "over-the-counter" drug use and the inadequacy of the traditional review of systems when dealing with elderly patients. So it appears that while we are taking greater and greater risks with invasive procedures, we are becoming less and less adept at the most informative and least harmful method of data collection: the medical history.

FREQUENCY OF IATROGENIC DISEASE IN THE ELDERLY

That iatrogenic illness is more frequent in the elderly population has been accepted as fact by most individuals who provide medical care for the elderly. A number of past studies point in that direction. Reichel (18) in 1965 reported on a prospective study of 500 elderly indigent patients admitted to a teaching service. Of this group of patients, followed over an 8-month period, 146 patients suffered 193 "adverse effects." Schimmel (20) in 1964 reported on 1,014 patients admitted to the medical service of a teaching hospital during an 8-month period. Patients of all ages were included in the study. Two hundred forty untoward episodes were reported as occurring in 198 different patients. This represented 20% of the patients at risk who "suffered one or more episodes of medical complications in the hospital." In a study conducted by Steel (23) in 1981, 290 of 815 patients seen on a medical service during the period of study suffered iatrogenic illnesses. Steel reviewed all admissions without regard to age. None of these studies provided a comparison population.

In a recent study at a Veterans Administration Hospital Jahnigen et al (10) reviewed 222 consecutive admissions in March and April 1981. Of these, 174 patients were 65 years of age or older and 48 patients were less than 65 years old. The study team divided the patients into three categories, depending on their perception of the seriousness of the patients' problems on admission. Approximately 90% of the 222 patients fell into the category with the least critical illnesses. The overall complication rates cited by this study were 29% for patients under age 65 and 45% for those over age 65. Of considerable interest was the fact that "psychiatric deterioration was observed in 10.7% of patients over 65 but in none of the younger subjects." This study, while dealing with a select population, provides a clearer indication that iatrogenic disease is, in fact, more common in hospitalized elderly patients than it is in a younger control population.

CHARACTERISTICS OF THE ELDERLY POPULATION

If one accepts that elderly patients are at greater risk for iatrogenic illness, one must next consider the characteristics of the elderly population which tend to make them more "susceptible" to iatrogenesis. Since the population of individuals over the age of 65 is no more homogeneous than that of a younger age group, assessing group characteristics is not easy. However, a few salient features of the population over the age of 65 need to be borne in mind. Among these are the increasing numbers of people over the age of 65, the behavioral characteristics of the elderly population, and the altered physiologic states which occur as a result of the aging process.

The demographic changes affecting the population of the United States have been dealt with in great detail by many authors. The aging of the population is an accepted demographic forecast and should come as no surprise to anyone. What does require emphasis is the fact that the greatest increase will occur in the percentage of "very old" (age 85 and older). This group, with their increasing number of illnesses, their greater need for hospitalization, and their gradual loss of functional capability, are highly vulnerable for the untoward effects of medical treatment.

Behavioral characteristics of the elderly population are discussed in greater detail in Chapter 40, "Characteristics of the Elderly Population." One characteristic which bears noting here is the underreporting of medical problems by the elderly population. This characteristic was noted by Williamson et al. (26) in a study in Scotland in 1964. He found that elderly people living at home frequently did not report major medical problems such as incontinence, visual and hearing disturbances, and gait problems. When one considers the tendency for elderly individuals to have more illnesses and to use more drugs, then the underreporting of illness becomes a major concern for physicians in preventing iatrogenic problems.

Finally, it must be borne in mind that aging alters physiology. In particular, the ability of the kidneys and liver to detoxify therapeutic agents declines with age. The increased ratio of fat to muscle mass in the elderly patient has consequences in the use of fat-soluble drugs. Brain reserve is decreased, and as a result psychoactive drugs are tolerated less well in the elderly population. These and many other changes in the aging organism place the elderly patient at increased risk. Those who provide health care to the elderly population simply cannot ignore these facts when they are planning diagnostic or therapeutic regimens for their patients.

WHERE IATROGENESIS OCCURS

With the elderly population at higher risk for iatrogenic disease, one must now look at those situations in which iatrogenesis is most likely to occur. For all practical purposes these include hospitalization, the use of drugs, and the performance of procedures (diagnostic or therapeutic). While iatrogenesis may occur in any situation in which an elderly patient is treated by a health practitioner (i.e., in a nursing home or at home) the three areas mentioned have been most intensively studied.

Hospital

The hospital is a particularly risky area for elderly patients. The previously cited studies of Reichel (18), Schimmel (20), and Steel (23) all point to significant percentages of untoward events in the hospital setting. Reichel's detailed analysis of untoward reactions reveals that even "innocuous" procedures may create significant problems. He notes syncope and barium aspiration occurring with gastrointestinal series and avulsion of skin secondary to tape removal as examples of this type of problem. In Schimmel's series, those who suffered fatal episodes secondary to agents or procedures were, with one exception, 50 years and older. All three authors note the frequent occurrence of falling with its resultant trauma as a complication of hospitalization.

One of the problems with a great potential for loss of functional ability in an elderly person is psychiatric deterioration. Jahnigen et al. (10) noted, "Major psychiatric deterioration was observed in 10.7% of patients over 65" in his study of 174 patients over the age of 65 hospitalized at a Veteran's Administration hospital. Reichel (18) noted 19 episodes of "hospital induced major psychologic decompensation." Most of the episodes described seem to be unrelated to drug therapy. If so, they probably represent episodes of confusion and delirium in individuals with diminished brain reserve in whom the hospital represents a major stress factor.

Further evidence of the hospital as a factor in iatrogenesis is provided in studies by Gillick et al. (9) and Warshaw et al. (25). Gillick pointed out that of 502 general medical patients, 15% reported confusion, falling, not eating or incontinence unrelated to acute illness. When they considered the elderly population alone, these symptoms occurred in 41%. Of even greater significance was the fact that over 50% of the time, the symptoms produced an intervention (e.g., drug administration, catheter insertion, restraint). Warshaw in his study of 279 hospitalized patients found "considerable" age-correlated disability. He also found that more than half of the patients, 75 years or older, needed assistance with activities of daily living. While the study did not evaluate the course of the patients' functional levels, Warshaw commented, "Hospitalization may have a negative impact on functional recovery at the same time that medical and surgical interventions are successful."

Hospitalization, when necessary, can mean the difference between life and death. However, it is a course of action which carries potentially grave risks for the elderly population. With its confusing array of people and things, its unfamiliar surroundings, and its emphasis on aggressive high-technology activities, hospitalization for an elderly person requires careful consideration of the pros and cons by the doctor, the patient, and the family.

Drug Therapy

Medical literature contains many references to the hazards of drug therapy for the elderly. Of 62 articles dealing with iatrogenesis in the elderly since 1982, one-sixth dealt directly with drug therapy as a major cause. This is not surprising in view of the elderly person's decreased ability to clear toxic substances through the liver and kidneys, the greater likelihood of being on multiple drugs due to multiple illnesses and the altered parameters of body mass, body muscle, and body fat. Lamy (12), in an excellent review article on adverse drug reactions in the elderly, cites U.S. data indicating that "12 to 17% of all hospital admissions of elderly people are due to adverse drug effects." He further points out poor prescribing habits on the part of physicians, disturbed nutritional status, and increased traveling on the part of the elderly as additional risk factors.

In the previously mentioned studies of hospitalized patients (18, 20, 23) complications of drug therapy were among the leading causes of iatrogenesis. In Reichel's study, 54 of the 193 untoward reactions were caused by medications. In Schimmel's series, one half of all the episodes were related to drugs being used in treatment. Of these, 14 were classified as major and there were 4 deaths. Steel's study of 497 complications attributed 208 to the use of drugs. Certainly the hospitalized elderly patient runs a significant risk of problems with drug therapy.

In view of the increased number of drugs taken by people over the age of 65, a study by Smith et al. (22) in 1965 has particular relevance. Smith and his group studied all patients on a 33-bed semi-private medical ward between January 1, 1965 and December 31, 1965. Of the total 900 patients studied during the year, 151 drug reactions in 119 persons were noted. Although age did not affect the rate of adverse reactions in this group, it was noted that untoward reactions were "increasingly more common when the number of drugs given was increased." They also noted a relationship between the number of drugs administered and the mortality rate and average hospital stay. These results are noted in Figure 49.1. Clearly then, the mere fact that elderly individuals tend to use more drugs increases their risk for adverse reactions.

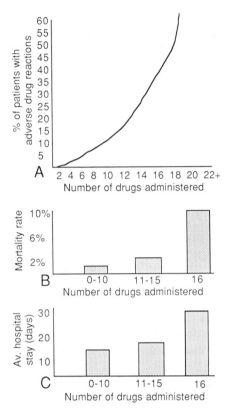

Figure 49.1. The relationship of adverse drug reactions to (1) number of drugs administered, (2) mortality rate, and (3) duration of hospitalization. Reproduced with permission from: Smith JW, Seidl LG, Cluff LE: Studies of the epidemiology of adverse drug reactions— V. clinical factors influencing susceptibility. *Ann Intern Med* 65:631., 1966.

Most of the data on adverse reactions to drugs come from hospital studies. Little is known about the occurrence of untoward reactions to drugs in the physician's office or patient's home setting. Lamy (12) estimates that adverse effects in "community-living" elderly may be as high as 40%. Some indirect evidence may be obtained by studies of admissions to hospitals caused by adverse reactions to drugs.

Caranasos et al. (5) in 1974 studied all admissions to the medical service of a teaching hospital for a 3-year period. Drug-induced illness accounted for 2.9% of these admissions. Of these, nearly 50% were in individuals aged 61 and older. In 18% of the cases of drug-induced illness, an over-the-counter drug was implicated. In a study of hospital admissions caused by iatrogenic disease, Lakshmann (11) noted that 5.4% of 834 admissions were due to Iatrogenic problems, 35 of these cases caused by medications.

Lakshmann stated, "These types of adverse effects are probably more closely related to physician and patient characteristics than age, number of drugs or underlying illnesses." In any case, both studies emphasized the fact that a considerable proportion of the admissions to a hospital from a community are drug related.

Finally, a word about compliance. Much has been written over the years about the problem of compliance in adhering to drug regimens and the consequent difficulty in deciding when symptoms represent true adverse reactions. It has been my experience that elderly people, to the extent that they are physically capable of complying, will adhere to drug regimens if they feel that they are getting better or at least their symptoms are no worse. When elderly patients do not comply with drug regimens, it may be appropriate to ask whether they are beginning to experience undesirable side effects.

Procedures

The advances of technology, particularly in the ability to do invasive procedures, has brought with it a marked increase in procedure-related adverse effects. In the English-language medical literature on iatrogenic diseases in the elderly, 27 of 62 articles dealt with complications of diagnostic, therapeutic, and surgical procedures. Here again the elderly are at increased risk in view of the increased occurrence of multiple illnesses in the elderly population coupled with altered physiologic states. What is often not appreciated is that procedures which are considered "benign" often carry increased risk for the elderly. A barium enema, if not properly evacuated, may cause serious bowel obstruction. Barium material may extravasate into an aged and "flabby" bowel. Intravenous contrast material for an intravenous pyelogram (IVP) may cause fluid retention and congestive heart failure because of its high sodium content. Even a simple venipuncture, in a frail elderly individual with atrophic skin and subcutaneous tissue, may result in hemorrhage and consequent immobility.

Complication rates on the newer and more invasive procedures such as cardiac catheterization are well known. Schroeder et al. (21) reported that cardiac catheterization had a 15% complication rate. The same publication found a significant complication rate for thoracentesis and bronchoscopy. In Reichel's (18) study, procedures "caused" the untoward reaction in 31 of 193 reactions studied. Steel (23) reported that 175 of 497 complications were due to diagnostic and therapeutic procedures, and of these, 45 were due to cardiac catheterization.

As previously noted, some of the studies were done on patients of all ages and the studies lacked comparison groups. As a consequence, no conclusions may be drawn as to age per se as a factor in increased complications secondary to procedures. But as Steel (24) so eloquently points out, "Since exposure is the major determinant of risk, the more drugs a person receives and the more procedures an individual undergoes, the greater the risk." As individuals age, they gradually increase their exposure.

PREVENTION

In spite of considerable attention to the subject of iatrogenesis and the wealth of material in the medical literature, iatrogenic disease continues to be a frequent cause of morbidity and mortality in the elderly. Studies on hospitalized patients since the early 1960s have found no appreciable downward trend in the complication rate. The mere fact that there will be more elderly people, particularly more frail elderly people, as we enter the next century, will increase the number of iatrogenic problems. The cost in terms of patient suffering, physician and hospital utilization, and dollars has yet to be calculated, but its immense proportions are beginning to be seen.

What then is to be done about the continuing problem of iatrogenic disease in the elderly? The answer, of course, if the obvious one: prevention. The risks for iatrogenic disease will become greater as time goes by and our technology improves. Our goal then must be to reduce to a minimum the "price we pay" for our medical advances. The responsibility for this will fall on the physician, most especially the primary care physician. Steel (24), Friedman (7), and Barry (4) have all underscored the central role of the physician in the prevention of iatrogenic disease.

The major preventive role of the primary physician starts with the prevention of morbidity secondary to "life-style illnesses." If people eat less, exercise more, cease smoking, and reduce stress, much of the morbidity seen in the later years can be reduced, if not eliminated. With less morbidity there is less exposure to risk and less possibility for iatrogenesis.

Beyond the obvious, what are the techniques that can assure a minimum risk for iatrogenic problems? As Steel (24) had advised, we need to go back to basics. We need to perform data collection in the least harmful and most productive way possible. All patients over the age of 65 should have a comprehensive data base clearly recorded in their office medical record. This data base should include the following elements:

1. A current list of all problems for which a patient is being treated or has been treated in the past. This should include fully diagnosed illnesses as well as symptom complexes for which there seems no explanation.
2. A drug list which includes dosages and problems with previous medications. The list should also include all over-the-counter medications used by the patient.
3. An estimation of the patient's functional status. This does not have to be an extensive formal statement of functional status, but should include the patient's ability to use the telephone, to cook, to bathe and dress, to manage stairs, and to open bottles of medication properly. A visit to the patient's home will often reveal much of this information clearly and succinctly.
4. An estimation of the patient's ability to see and hear adequately. Patient compliance can be improved considerably by simple visual and auditory screening and appropriate adjustments made to the demonstrated deficiencies.
5. Formal mental status testing should begin at age 65 and should be recorded periodically in the ensuing years. The Folstein Mini-Mental Status Examination, or other similar formal brief mental status screening serves adequately for this purpose. With knowledge of baseline intellectual function, a physician is better equipped to combat psychiatric deterioration under the stress of illness or hospitalization.

This list is not all inclusive. It assumes the presence of a comprehensive history and physical examination recorded on the chart. The items mentioned are those that have a particular significance in dealing with the older adult.

The hazards of drug therapy have been extensively discussed here and in the medical literature. Drug therapy in the elderly individual should never be instituted without an adequate knowledge of the physiology, the action of the drug, its side effects, and the appropriate dosage for the individual. Barry (4) has proposed a set of questions to be asked prior to the institution of drug therapy which will help to reduce the risk of iatrogenesis:

1. Is the treatment necessary?
2. Is it the safest available?
3. Is it being administered appropriately?
4. Is it effective?
5. Is it acceptable to the patient?
6. Do the benefits outweigh the risks?

Once the decision has been made to institute drug therapy in an elderly individual, the following guidelines should be considered:

1. Except for emergency situations, start with a low dosage and work up slowly to the desired therapeutic effect. For

the most part elderly patients need less medication for the desired effect than younger adults.

2. Acquaint the patient with the possible side effects of the medication used and ask him or her to report evidence of side effects early. In view of elderly patients' tendency to underreport illness, an aggressive approach to the patient in reviewing side effects is indicated.

3. Continually review patients' drug lists with the aim to reduce the amount of drugs given to a minimum. The question of whether this drug is necessary for this patient at this time is one that bears constant repetition.

Placing an elderly patient in the hospital is a move that should be taken only after careful consideration of the risks involved. Once the decision to place an elderly patient in the hospital has been made, a few guidelines will be helpful in maintaining optimal functional status and avoiding iatrogenic illness:

1. Ambulate the patient as soon as feasible. Loss of function is rapid in elderly patients, and consequently time in bed should be reduced to a minimum. Whenever possible, use a chair rather than a bed for resting.

2. Maintain reality orientation as much as possible. This can be done by the use of calendars, clocks, radios, and television and by allowing relatives and friends to visit freely. Resist the use of psychoactive drugs and restraints to treat nocturnal confusion. Rather, make an attempt to discover the cause of the acute confusional state and treat appropriately. Drug therapy, infection, and metabolic alterations should be high on the list of possible causes of acute confusion.

3. Begin discharge planning immediately so that total time in the hospital is kept down. At no time is the team approach to the care of the patient more necessary than at the time of discharge planning.

The work of Rubenstein et al. (19) and others points to the usefulness of providing a special unit within the hospital for certain categories of elderly patients. Many hospitals are beginning to adopt this approach, but the benefits in terms of patient outcomes, particularly in regard to maintenance of functional status, have yet to be fully determined.

Finally, the risk of "procedural medicine" for elderly patients is well known. Here again, Barry (4) has provided an extremely useful list of guidelines in approaching the decision as to whether a procedure is warranted. The following questions should be asked when one is entertaining a procedural intervention in an elderly adult (4):

1. Is the test necessary to make the diagnosis?
2. Is it the least invasive test available?
3. Will the result change the treatment of the patient?
4. Do I know how to interpret the result?

As Barry points out, the answer to the last question is often the most difficult. It involves knowledge of specificity and sensitivity of testing procedures and disease prevalence, terms which are often unfamiliar to the practicing primary care physician. Barry's article provides an excellent review of this topic.

SUMMARY

Iatrogenic disease is a widespread problem in the elderly. Its incidence in the hospitalized patient has varied little over the last 25 years. Hospitalization, drug therapy, and the performance of procedures all carry increased risks in the elderly population. Increasing exposure to risk is anticipated as medical technology becomes increasingly more complex and invasive and the elderly population grows. The role of the primary care physician is a critical one. It involves a thorough understanding of the unique characteristics of the elderly population, an emphasis on low-risk data collection, and utilization of certain techniques to reduce risks to the minimum possible level.

REFERENCES

1. Barrowclough F: Clinical forum 11. Iatrogenic disorders in the elderly. Do they really need all those drugs? *Nurs Mirror* 155:22, 1982.
2. Barrowclough F, Pegg M: Clinical forum 11. Iatrogenic disorders in the elderly. Drugs in the later years of life. *Nurs Mirror* 155:25, 1982.
3. Barrowclough F, Pegg M: Clinical forum 11. Iatrogenic disorders in the elderly. Why don't they comply? *Nurs Mirror* 155:32, 1982.
4. Barry PP: Iatrogenic disorders in the elderly: Preventive techniques. *Geriatrics* 41:42, 1986.
5. Caranasos GJ, Stewart RB, Cluff LE: Drug-induced illness leading to hospitalization. *JAMA* 228:713, 1974.
6. Ficarra BJ, Corso FM: Iatrogenic surgical liability. *Leg Med:* 236–257, 1985.
7. Friedman M: Iatrogenic disease—addressing a growing epidemic. *Postgraduate Med* 71:123, 1982.
8. Friend G: Correction of iatrogenic floating toe following resection of the base of the proximal phalanx. *Clin Podiatr Med Surg* 7:115, 1986.
9. Gillick MR, Serrell NA, Gillick LS: Adverse consequences of hospitalization in the elderly. *Soc Sci Med* 16:1033, 1982.
10. Jahnigen D, Hannon C, Laxson L, et al: Iatrogenic disease in hsopitalized elderly veterans. *J Am Geriatr Soc* 30:387, 1985.
11. Lakshmann MC, Hershey CO, Breslau D: Hospital admissions caused by iatrogenic disease. *Ann Intern Med* 146:1931, 1986.
12. Lamy PP: Adverse drug reactions in the elderly: an update. In Ham RJ (Ed): *Geriatric Medicine Annual—1986*. Oradell, NJ, Medical Economics Books, 1986, p 128.

13. Lamy PP: The elderly and drug interactions. *J Am Geriatr Soc* 38:589, 1986.
14. Moser RH: Diseases of medical progress. *N Engl J Med* 255:606, 1956.
15. Parsons MS: Five common legal risks—could these stories have happened to you? *Nursing Life* 6:26, 1986.
16. Patel KP: Clinical forum 11. Iatrogenic disorders in the elderly. A prescribing dilemma. *Nurs Mirror* 155:26, 30, 1982.
17. Pegg M: Clinical forum 11. Iatrogenic disorders in the elderly. Drug interactions. *Nurs Mirror* 155:31, 1982.
18. Reichel W: Complications in the care of five hundred elderly hospitalized patients. *J Am Geriatr Soc* 13:973, 1965.
19. Rubenstein LZ, Abrass IB, Kane RL: Improved care for patients on a new geriatric unit. *J Am Geriatr Soc* 29:531, 1981.
20. Schimmel EM: The hazards of hospitalization. *Ann Intern Med* 60:100, 1964.
21. Schroeder SA, Marton KI, Strom BL: Frequency and morbidity of invasive procedures: Report of a pilot study from two teaching hospitals. *Arch Intern Med* 138:1809, 1978.
22. Smith JW, Seidl LG, Cluff LE: Studies on the epidemiology of adverse drug reactions. V. Clinical factors influencing susceptibility. *Ann Intern Med* 65:629, 1966.
23. Steel K: Iatrogenic illness on a general medical service at a university hospital. *N Engl J Med* 304:638, 1981.
24. Steel K: Iatrogenic disease on a medical service. *J Am Geriatr Soc* 32:455, 1984.
25. Warshaw GA, Moore JT, Friedman SW, et al: Functional disability in the hospitalized elderly. *JAMA* 248:847, 1982.
26. Williamson J, Stokoe JH, Gray S, et al: Old people at home: Their unreported needs. *Lancet* 1:1117, 1964.

CHAPTER 50

The Dying Patient

JOHN R. MARSHALL
JOEL E. STREIM

Geriatric care includes that period of life that ends an ongoing process. At what moment the geriatric patient becomes the dying patient is not clear. While one phase of life typically blends almost imperceptibly into the next, an awareness of fatal illness must begin at some point. The patient's response usually begins when formally told of the prognosis, though it often precedes this moment by anticipation or by "reading" clues from nearby persons. Some even suggest that the aged individual experiences psychologic disruption as part of the actual dying process rather than as a reaction to the realization of its inevitability.

In recent years much effort has gone into describing the "normal course," or the stages through which the dying patient passes. Delineation of these stages expedites recognition of different coping styles and psychosocial variables and, in general, alerts professionals to the dying patient's situation.

The drawbacks in describing these stages of dying are important to keep in mind. One might assume that the general trends are more important than individual differences and that there is a single pathway, deviations from it being abnormal. The consequence of this assumption is that the inexperienced professional might view these stages as far more invariable than are intended.

STAGES OF DYING

A leading contributor to our understanding of the process of human dying is Dr. Elizabeth Kubler-Ross, who has described five stages (8). These stages are actually stages of bereavement, for the patients are grieving about themselves—their pains, their losses, their past beings, and their lost futures. During this process, which may be experienced by families as well as patients, a series of defensive measures are utilized to allow slower and less painful giving up of old ties, to make the losses more bearable, and to accommodate the altered situation. In dying, of course, the patient does not pass through this process as in bereavement in which there may be an eventual return to normal functioning.

The first stage is denial and is characterized by patients' attempts to avoid the painful awareness of their terminal illnesses. In effect, a patient says, "I won't believe this is happening to me." This is usually a brief period in which the denial ebbs and flows and is gradually replaced by awareness of the reality of the situation. In a very few patients this psychologic defense is persistently used, even until death.

During the second stage the patient may become angry. "Why me?" is often the verbalization of this rage. The anger may be expressed openly but is more often seen in increasing irritability and covertly angry behaviors. It is the source of the seemingly inappropriate hostility toward nursing staff and others, viewed as less powerful and therefore "safer" objects of displaced anger than the patient's own physician.

Another less well-known and less visible stage described by Kubler-Ross is that of bargaining. It is a psychologic attempt to postpone the inevitable: "If I do not do, or think, certain things, I will be spared."

Depression, the fourth stage, occurs when denial is no longer tenable and when the rage has at least partially subsided. It is the reaction most pervasive to the impending loss, not only of life but of status, personal goals, and friends and other loved ones. Affect may be flat, somber, tearful, or sometimes irritable. Symptoms of this phase include insomnia, morbid dreams, restlessness or anergy, anorexia, withdrawal, and apathy. In some respects this is the most easily understood phase for it is easy to empathize with: "I too would be depressed if I were dying."

Finally, if the process continues "successfully" and if there is enough time, some patients reach a degree of acceptance. This is a frequently misunderstood phase. It is not a period of resignation or hopelessness, nor is it a happy time. Rather, as implied, the patient appears to accept his or her "fate." Generally it is devoid of extremes of feeling, often includes notable decreases in anxiety and depression, and embodies a degree of quiet expectation.

These stages vary with most patients. Some persons may experience only a few of them, may pass through in different sequences, or may demonstrate all stages during the same interview. For the older person, characteristics of his or her developmental stage in the normal life cycle can influence these stages of dying substantially. Such characteristics may include an extensive life history with its longitudinal view and sense of accomplishment (and failures), a physical well-being (or progressive deterioration), and a position of esteem or respect among loved ones (or isolation). Given these distinctive developmental factors, geriatric patients may approach death from a much different perspective than younger persons.

PATIENT ATTITUDES TOWARD DYING

Many older persons seem to be less fearful of death than expected (5, 6). Though they may not talk readily of it, when they do, their attitudes are more likely to be accepting and favorable, often reflecting an attitude of expectant waiting. This greater acceptance appears to be more prevalent among patients who live in hospitals or homes for the aged and are generally less active and independent than those living in their own home environment. Religious beliefs may modify a person's view of death, so that some may look forward to death as a pleasant occurrence or relief. This is particularly important for it contradicts a common presumption in our society that no one really wants to die unless one is suicidal, psychotic, or a religious or political fanatic. In fact, contrary to what one might expect, the elderly as a group in a developmental stage closest to death are not more apprehensive about death. Conversely, some evidence suggests that those who are developmentally furthest from death show the most preoccupation with it.

As a result of these age-related changes and developmental characteristics, the "classic" stages of dying may be modified, significantly modulated, or absent. When an elderly person has been aware of progressive physical deterioration and its implications, the realization of having a terminal illness does not require an extensive use of initial denial. The threat of impending death may be blunted when one is aged and ill, and often these patients report a sense of relief as an initial response to a serious prognosis. Anger, too, may be less visible, though irritability, subdued resentment, and occasional outbursts of "temper" may be seen. When bargaining occurs it seems to have a different quality and often comes in the context of the process of a life review. The bargains are less apt to reflect yearnings to extend life, and more likely to represent wishes to fulfill life schemes, for example, "I wish I could live until I knew I'd have grandchildren," or "If only my son would take over the farm, I would die a happy man."

The stage of depression poses a special problem in the elderly, for the incidence of major depression is increased substantially in this age group and it is very difficult to separate an affective disorder from this common stage in the process of dying. This is an important distinction because the treatment and outcome of each is different. Some geriatric patients may not be able to help because they (and many professionals) believe that feeling bad is a normal part of the aging process and must be endured. These elderly patients may tolerate unhappiness, lethargy, loss of appetite, sleep disturbance, and other suffering with philosophic resignation—"It's part of growing old." Apathy, as a symptom of depression, may leave such patients further entrenched in this resignation.

Clinical recognition of major depression is based on patient and caregiver reports and close scrutiny for classic signs and symptoms of an affective disorder. Of course, many of the signs and symptoms of major depression are identical to those of the depressive stage of dying; however, the diagnosis of major depression should especially be considered (a) if the patient has had signs or symptoms of affective disorder in the past, (b) if there is a family history of affective disorder, or (c) if the presentation includes symptoms which seem incongruous with or out of proportion to what might be expected in the patient's situation. A patient with major depression is likely to be responsive to appropriate psychotropic drugs. Untreated, the depression may add needlessly to suffering and may hasten the patient's death. The depressive phase of dying is less likely to be responsive to drugs. However, specific symptoms such as insomnia, restlessness, and anxiety may be ameliorated with the use of psychotropic medication, even if a clear diagnosis of affective disorder cannot be made. Given the frequent difficulty in distinguishing an affective disorder from the depressive stage of dying, medication trials may be needed to maximize symptomatic relief.

Finally, it appears that elderly patients more often achieve a stage of acceptance of their ultimate fate. It is not clear whether they progress to this phase more easily than younger patients or are just more accepting. It is important that resignation not be misconstrued as acceptance. Many older patients give up their wish to live because of physical deterioration or a lack of quality in their contacts with people or surroundings. Despair is not acceptance.

Perhaps it is during the stage of acceptance that some patients experience the most spiritual awareness and growth. In facing and accepting death, patients may experience a shift in their values and may see time, accomplishments, and relationships from a new perspective. Life review is often part of an endeavor to complete unfinished business, to resolve conflicts within relationships, and to understand the meaning or purpose of life. Clergy or other spiritual caregivers may have an important role in facilitating growth through these tasks and meeting the patient's spiritual needs.

PROFESSIONAL BEHAVIORS AND ATTITUDES

Medical professionals do not always handle dying patients well. Attitudes towards dying patients are sometimes based on unexamined beliefs, dogmatic misconceptions, and unexplored uncomfortable feelings (7). Personal interactions with the patient become filled with perfunctory rituals, awkward reassurances, and intellectualized jargon when the fact of approaching death becomes obvious to all. The result of these maneuvers may be an increasing emotional distancing between staff and patient at a time when closeness is most needed. Sociologic field studies have demonstrated striking changes in hospital staff behaviors: Doctors make rounds less often or with more haste, nursing staff terminate their procedures and enter the patient's room less frequently, or the patient may be moved to a single room further from the nursing station (3). Effectively, the still living patient is treated as if he or she were a "nonperson," that is, already dead.

This failure to render appropriate, effective, and sustained care to the dying patient has multiple causes. By training and tradition, medical professionals are dedicated to the maintenance of life. They see themselves as implacable foes of the many causes of death and experience its arrival as a defeat. Beyond this very narrow conceptualization of their role, they have had little or no formal training or ethic to guide them in administering to the dying and in seeing that the patient and his or her family approach death only on the most favorable human terms. Practical time limitations for both nurses and physicians (though overrationalized) also cause them to place a lower priority on those whose days are clearly numbered. Perhaps most importantly, medical staff, as representative of our society, share in the general denial of the reality of dying, even to an exaggerated degree. It has been shown that physicians (and perhaps nurses) have an above average fear of death when compared with their patients and the general public. The more anxiety produced in the health care professional by the dying, the more apt the professional is to shun or relate poorly to terminal patients. More formal training is needed to help health professionals deal effectively with dying patients.

Death of younger patients may be regarded as premature or wrong, and may arouse marked anxiety in medical personnel. By contrast, such anxiety may be mitigated or absent when dealing with the elderly patient. It can be comforting to view the death of an aged person as natural, the reasonable last stage in the longitudinal process of living. It is as things should be. At a more personal level, the death of an elderly patient may even be reassuring for it implies that we can depend on death to ignore us until later in our lives.

There are problems with the presumption that all elderly patients are appropriately ready for death. It may lead the medical team member to join society in viewing the older patient's death as relatively less important. As opposed to a child with prospects of a full future, a young married adult with small children, or a middle-aged person actively working and contributing to society, these older persons may come to be viewed as having less value: "They have had a full life and there is not much more to live for." In a complex care setting, this attitude can be an important factor, subtly or covertly influencing what is done or not done in the patient's behalf. This belief, often barely conscious, may allow the physicians and other health professionals easy rationale for abandonment of these patients, avoidance of personal contacts, nonconfrontation of their own ambivalent feelings, or acceptance of deaths which could have been postponed or made easier.

At a more personal level, aged patients can re-evoke feelings surrounding the fact or the manner of death of the health professional's own parents or other significant persons. This may be particularly true if the disease process is similar. If a health professional is older, identification may occur more easily, with anxiety about his or her own death.

MANAGEMENT

Ideally, management of the dying patient begins well before death is imminent. Since it is often difficult for many health professionals to deal with the patient who is obviously near death, it is also unlikely that these practitioners will address issues about dying in advance.

Persons inexperienced in attending dying patients may be troubled by the fear that initiating such discussions will horrify families and cause unnecessary distress, aggravating the patient's condition. There is no evidence to support the notion that talking about death hastens its arrival or makes dying more painful; in fact, there is much to the contrary. It is a rare patient or family member who has not entertained private thoughts and harbored concerns about dying. The best approach is to be compassionately truthful. Human communication is complex enough without unwarranted deceptions. In the stage of denial, information should be presented gently but clearly and consistently. By openly and directly acknowledging these issues, the health professional can validate the concerns of patient and family and provide tremendous relief. The ability to listen and understand, accept the feelings expressed, and give clear, honest answers to questions are major assets for this encounter. Most patients do not ask for more than this and greatly appreciate what we have to offer when this is managed well.

Health care practitioners have an important responsibility to educate and advise patients and families, and help them plan in the present for the kind of treatment they want while they remain alive, as well as the type of care they want when death is near. In the process of such planning, patients, families, and health professionals discuss and clarify their concerns and opinions regarding health care delivery for the dying patient. Of necessity the practitioner's role in such discussion entails explicit communication about the patient's illness, prognosis, treatment options, and possible outcomes, especially death. "We are having this discussion so that you have an element of control in what happens to you as you are dying, even if you become unable to participate in decisions regarding your care. Talking about this helps us to know what your concerns and wishes are." Discussion is specifically helpful in delineating the patient's attitudes, opinions, and wishes concerning available options for emergency and nonemergent medical care (e.g., cardiopulmo-

nary resuscitation and advanced life support with potential use of assisted ventilation, pacemaker, and pressors; or other therapeutic measures such as dialysis, blood transfusions, intravenous fluids, parenteral nutrition, tube feedings, antibiotics, or surgery) as well as the place where care can be given (e.g., hospital, nursing home, home care, or other arrangement).

Too often, such discussion and planning do not occur because of professional attitudes toward dying and elderly patients described above. Families may avoid or discourage communication about dying because of denial, anger, or fear. A common and usually inappropriate presumption is that the geriatric patient is not competent to participate in this process. On the contrary, most elderly patients are competent to make decisions regarding how and where they live out their lives as they are dying. From both a legal and clinical perspective, competence to make such decisions requires only that the patient understand that he or she is ill and dying, the basic nature of the available options for care, and the possible consequences of the decisions. In the situation in which the dying patient is incompetent or unable to plan, it is important to determine if an advanced directive, substituted judgment, or proxy decision maker is available.

Even if the planning process is not limited by the patient's competence, it should be recognized that health care professionals, patients, and families cannot anticipate every possible situation. Therefore, such planning often does not represent a fixed or final decision which is made at the present time, regarding the nature and location of care to be given to the dying patient as time goes on. Rather, this process begins a discussion which provides guidelines for further care that are especially crucial if the patient later becomes unable to participate in treatment decisions.

Planning for the care of the dying patient has become a more formalized, even codified part of the professional–patient relationship in recent years. Many clinicians, especially in geriatric practice, discuss a "critical care plan" with all their patients as a routine part of the clinical interview. Some state legislatures have approved statutes which permit a patient to execute a "living will." This is a legal declaration by the patient to the physician regarding the extent and nature of care to be given if the patient becomes terminally ill. Although there has been disagreement and debate about the wisdom and efficacy of such legal directives, many practitioners feel that these measures afford them additional legal protection and increase the likelihood that their patient's wishes will be respected and followed. In addition to giving patients an added measure of control over what happens to them as they are dying, living wills and critical care plans may promote communication among health professional, patient, and family. This in turn may help to reduce the likelihood that the fears of the elderly dying patient will remain unaddressed and to limit the chances of the patient's being isolated and abandoned.

Though experience is necessary to prepare one for terminal care, there are principles which are helpful and which should be integrated into professional training. To render effective care as the patient is dying, it is not necessary to be a psychiatrist; nor does it follow that psychiatrists are more proficient. One must try to understand the patient in terms of what has been. By helping a patient who is attempting to put his or her life into perspective, one can more easily empathize. One can comprehend the pain of immobilization for a man who describes himself as a life-long doer or the sense of loss experienced by a person who has lived as a part of three generations in the same house and is now moved to a nursing home. It is empathy, not sympathy, which is the critical attitude for this process.

When it is understood that the feelings a person experiences in the process of dying are aspects of their grief for themselves, therapeutic measures become clearer. For many patients, outward expression of feelings and thoughts may facilitate the work of grieving. By an attitude of noncritical acceptance, the health professional often helps the patient objectify his or her turmoil and, with time, move toward some level of acceptance of the situation.

Geriatric patients often have fears more frightening than the fact of death itself (10). These have to do with the process of dying and include loss of autonomy and control over decision making as well as pain, distortion of bodily structure and deterioration of bodily functions, unresolved financial matters, isolation and abandonment. Unfortunately, glib reassurances too often are used in these moments instead of listening for the precise nature of the fear. "Don't worry about that, things will turn out all right." An appropriate intervention can be made after a concrete honest exploration of the patient's fears is pursued. For example, in a discussion of pain control, health professionals can convey their confidence in the recent and extensive advances in this area. When the patient and family understand that their complaints will be taken seriously, that the staff regard most pain as needless, and that reassessment will be continuous, much anxiety may be alleviated.

Pain management for the dying patient might be expected to be easier in some respects, for staff may feel free of the usual apprehensions about addition. However, in practice, many physicians and nurses behave as if it is bad or immoral even for dying patients to take narcotics. Use of doses and schedules which are inadequate for satisfactory analgesia, or even withholding medications, is a common problem in terminal care. Another task for medical educators is to teach the importance of aggressive symptom control in dying patients (2). Multiple narcotic and nonnarcotic drugs and different routes of administration including oral or rectal suppositories, and subcutaneous or intravenous infusions provide an impressive armamentarium of pain relief choices. Pain control can be titrated in almost all situations to allow patients to function with the balance of pain control and sedation that they choose. Other pain control modalities such as nerve blocks, electrical nerve stimulation, and relaxation techniques may be useful, and help to avoid unwanted sedation.

As the goal of reversal of the disease process is deemed impossible, there comes a shift to patient comfort through skilled, intensive symptom control. Symptoms other than pain may become major foci of discomfort and need continual attention (9). Common symptoms include anorexia, dysphagia, nausea, vomiting, dry mouth and eyes, hiccoughs, dyspnea, cough, sleep disturbances, constipation, diarrhea, urinary symptoms, fever, pruritus, weakness, lethargy, and confusion. Suffering from these symptoms can and should be alleviated with good medical care.

Psychiatric disorders prevalent in the elderly may also be found while the patient is dying. Psychotropic drugs may be needed. Usually smaller doses than usual are effective in elderly patients. Control of specific symptoms should guide decisions about drug treatment, for it is often difficult to distinguish some psychologic responses from disorders that are likely to respond to medication. General sedation is no favor to the patient, and care must be taken that "tranquilizing" medications are not given because medical personnel are anxious or need to "do something." Oversedation may only increase a patient's distress, especially if it is associated with mental clouding or confusion. This may intensify a sense of loss of control or aggravate some patients' fears of dying in their sleep.

Perhaps the greatest fear that dying patients have is the dread of being left alone. This is a very real fear and one likely to occur in the hospital, particularly when the medical staff runs out of procedures for the terminally ill patient. These moments can be anticipated and the patient reassured that when certain procedures are no longer appropriate, they will not be deprived of human contact—either professional or familial.

Work with the family of the dying patient offers the medical staff an opportunity not only to benefit the patient but to practice important crisis intervention and preventive medicine. Most patients and families have anxieties about the unknown course of the illness and the actual events which might occur near or at the time of death. Prior discussion of possible respiratory distress, bleeding, agitation, seizures, inability to eat or drink, and other disturbing changes helps to prepare patients and families for death. For example, family members may attempt to nurture or may try to delay death by forcing food and fluids on anorexic patients. If this is not interrupted, the patient may become despondent or frustrated; if it continues after the patient is obtunded, the patient may aspirate and stop breathing. In either case, the family member who is doing the feeding may be left with guilt. Understanding the family's concerns about nutrition, counseling them, and tailoring management strategies to address these concerns can decrease tension surrounding eating and promote comfort for both patient and family. When staff are able to empathize effectively with families and appreciate their anguish, much of the maladaptive behavior exhibited by relatives diminishes (12).

Enhancing the process of bereavement will have positive long-term effects for the survivors (11). Particularly if the patient has been ill for an extended period, the family will begin the process of mourning in expectation of the eventual death. This may lead to a tendency to withdraw prematurely from the patient, increasing the isolation and heightening the sense of abandonment. It also adds to the burden of guilt when family members realize that their sense of loss at the time of death is not acute. For the family, this is the last opportunity to affirm old relationships and even heal old wounds by direct communication with the dying member. That the bereaved are at high risk for practically the whole range of medical and psychiatric illness is well documented. Those with unresolved feelings of guilt and anger are particularly susceptible.

Thus health care professionals must conceive of their roles more broadly. They must avoid conspiring unwittingly with the family and perpetrating myths, for example, that the patient does not know he or she is dying and it is better not to talk about it. Medical staff may facilitate communication and re-

duce fear and isolation by saying something like, "Sometimes families are reluctant to talk about the fact that one of them is seriously ill—this is usually a mistake. Even though it is painful, it is usually better to discuss issues now than regret later that it was not done." When possible, health care team members should not hesitate to maintain contact with the bereaved after the death. This should be an accepted, even formalized aspect of the health care provider's function. Though this is done with some frequency now, particularly by experienced nursing staff, it is too often clandestine or regarded as "outside" of the professional relationship.

HOSPICE

As noted above, part of the health professional's role is to inform and advise patients and their families about the available options for care of the dying in their community. Perhaps the best opportunity for highly specialized treatment of the dying patient occurs in the hospice (1). A variety of models of terminal care have evolved since the first American hospice was established in 1974 (4). Most existing programs, though differing in their organization and the type of facility in which patients are located, reflect the philosophy of hospice care. The term *hospice* is derived from the medieval French word for a way station or shelter where pilgrims found rest and comfort on their arduous journey to the Holy Land, during the Crusades. Hospice is now defined as a program of palliative and supportive services which provides medical, psychologic, social, and spiritual care for dying patients and their families, either directly or on a consulting basis with the patient's primary care physician. This is an alternative to conventional hospital care, which is traditionally intended to be curative.

Hospice services are provided by an interdisciplinary team which includes physicians who are skilled at symptom control, as well as nurses, social workers, spiritual counselors, bereavement workers, other health care professionals, family members, and often volunteers. Care may be given at home, in an inpatient setting, or through combinations of these arrangements. Some hospitals have teams which specialize in palliative and terminal care and provide consultation to primary care providers in the hospital. Other hospitals have terminal care areas, with part of an acute care unit designated for palliative care, or separate terminal care units, affiliated with or physically part of a hospital but autonomous in their philosophy, organization, and operating policies. There are free-standing hospices which provide terminal care in edifices separate from hospital or home, many of which attempt to create a home-like environment and offer home care services.

Home care is based on the availability and willingness of a dedicated caregiver, usually family member or friend, with a sufficient network of support to provide adequate care at home. The primary caregiver and family are educated, directed, counseled, and supported in their patient care efforts by members of the interdisciplinary health care team. This team may be hospital based, free-standing hospice-based, community based, or independently structured (using the existing resources of hospitals and community agencies). Interdisciplinary team members provide care through scheduled home visits and telephone calls and are available on an on-call basis around the clock (12).

Several specific issues need to be discussed as patients and families are counseled about the hospice option. The patient's fears about separation from or the limited availability of his or her physician can best be addressed by directly describing the physician's role and extent of involvement in relation to other health professionals who may become involved in the patient's care. Explicit descriptions of the roles of other members of an interdisciplinary team can allay anxiety about systems of care unfamiliar to patients and families. Patients need to know whom they can count on, and how care will actually be delivered. Also, most patients fear being a burden and disrupting the lives of family members. This concern should be discussed with the whole family. Another frequent worry is the cost of nontraditional care. Patients and families need to be informed about cost and how insurance and other resources will meet expenses. Health insurers in the United States are more likely to provide coverage for hospice care since studies have demonstrated that the costs of terminal care in this setting are comparable to or less than cost of care using more traditional models. For terminally ill patients 65 years of age or older, Medicare hospital insurance currently will pay for most of the care provided by Medicare-certified hospice programs, but the extent of this coverage is being reevaluated.

Despite the diversity of organization or location of care, several features are characteristic of hospice care. First, there is a commitment to respect and foster patient control and decision making, which preserves a sense of self-esteem and integrity. It also permits flexibility, since some patients fluctuate in their wishes for caring (palliative) or curing (life-prolonging) approaches. Second, the whole family is considered as the unit of care. Family education and

support are provided before death and bereavement services extend through the mourning process. An advantage of hospice care is that patients "live until they die," without being separated from friends and family. Third, emphasis is on skilled, effective symptom control. Palliative care is not passive care, but rather requires specialized training and expertise, and a commitment of time and intensity of effort which are no different from that necessary in the quality practice of acute care medicine. Because the staff in these settings can focus on the dying patient and on improving the quality of life that remains, these patients are less likely to be seen as treatment failures, cases in which the only result is death. Management efforts are regarded as successful and gratifying by patient, family, and medical staff.

PROFESSIONAL TRAINING

Particular attention must be paid to the needs of physicians, nurses, social workers, ministers, and any others who work with the patient. Specific training is needed for these persons since, at present, almost no formal instruction in the care of dying patients is offered as part of their professional studies. (This is slowly changing.) Though necessary, didactic material alone is insufficient to equip persons to work effectively in this area. The task is great; geriatric staff must come to terms with their feelings about both death and old people. Small group training sessions with an experienced supervisor appear to offer the support to explore these feelings without unnecessary anxiety or defensiveness and are ideally suited to the team approach.

Beyond the training period, it is important to have a vehicle which permits (and forces) periodic reexamination of medical staff practices and attitudes. Weekly team meetings to discuss currently dying patients are used in some settings. Others have found it useful to do psychologic "autopsies"—careful review of the events, attitudes, and staff procedures which accompanied a patient's death. These meetings can provide an outlet for health care team members' feelings of guilt, loss, and failure concerning a patient who died and can enhance the possibility for more effective care of future dying patients.

Both the geriatric and the dying patient's care has suffered from a very limited range of professional roles and lack of formal training. It is usually misleading and inappropriate to say "There is not much more that can be done." The "natural" attitude toward patients in these stages of life must be continually examined and feelings of defeat, hopelessness, and despair replaced with positive and specific measures to combat needless suffering, emotional isolation, and loss of dignity. The addition of this positive dimension of care is a rewarding experience for staff as well as the patients and families who are served.

REFERENCES

1. Carlson JP, Murray CL, Martinson P: The hospice concept: comfort care for dying patients. *Postgrad Med* 77:55, 1985.
2. Foley KM: The treatment of cancer pain. *N Engl J Med* 313:84, 1985.
3. Glaser BA, Strauss AL: The social loss of dying patients. *Am J Nurs* 64:119, 1964.
4. Gotay CC: Models of terminal care: A review of the research literature. *Clin Invest Med* 6:131, 1983.
5. Hinton JM: Facing death. *J Psychosom Res* 10:22, 1966.
6. Kastenbaum R: The mental life of dying geriatric patients. *Gerontologist* 7:97, 1967.
7. Kastenbaum R: Should we have mixed feelings about our ambivalence toward the aged? *J Geriatr Psychiatry* 7:94, 1974.
8. Kubler-Ross E: *On Death and Dying.* New York, Macmillan, 1969.
9. Levy MH, Catalano RB: Control of common physical symptoms other than pain in patients with terminal disease. *Semin Oncol* 12:411, 1985.
10. Marshall JR: Geriatric patients' fears about death. *Postgrad Med* 57:144, 1975.
11. Marshall JR, Abroms GM, Miller NH: The doctor, the dying patient and the bereaved. *Ann Intern Med* 70:615, 1969.
12. Sergi-Swinehart P: Hospice home care: How to get patients home and help them stay there. *Semin Oncol* 12:461, 1985.

Section III

Ethical Issues in the Elderly Patient

CHAPTER 51

A Framework for Geriatric Ethics[1]

LAURENCE B. McCULLOUGH
STEVEN LIPSON

"Geriatric ethics" quickly calls to mind cases involving the seriously or terminally ill and the refusal of treatment by the elderly or their proxies. In part, this response reflects the dominance in the medical literature of discussions of ethical issues raised by such cases. In a recent selected, although representative, bibliography of ethics and geriatrics Cassell et al. devote most of their discussion to such topics as foregoing life-sustaining therapy, decisions about resuscitation, nutritional support, and advance directives (7). Thus, there is a natural tendency to equate geriatric ethics with the ethics of death and dying. This tendency is reinforced by the increasing attention of courts, legislatures, and even the federal government to ethical issues in death and dying (1, 17, 18, 20, 23, 24, 26).

It must be emphasized that we do not equate geriatric ethics with the ethics of death and dying. Doing so may blind the clinician to significant ethical issues that arise in the day-to-day care of the elderly patient. Thus, only two of the chapters in this section are directed to ethical issues in death and dying. Truthtelling, confidentiality, informed consent, and long-term care decision making all involve substantive ethical issues of direct concern for all physicians who care for elderly patients. These are addressed in the chapters that follow, along with termination of treatment and termination of food and water.

The goal for all of these chapters is to provide a practical guide for the clinician for dealing with ethi-

cal issues that may arise in managing the care of elderly patients. To this end, each chapter provides an analysis of ethical issues and identifies clinically oriented strategies for applying these ethical analyses in clinical practice. In adopting this approach, the authors of each chapter understand ethics to be more than a purely theoretical matter. Ethics should bear directly on clinical practice and assist the physician, the elderly patient, and the elderly patient's family in dealing with ethical issues in a reliable, effective manner.

SPECIAL FEATURES OF THE ELDERLY

The changes that accompany aging have been described many times and are discussed in detail elsewhere in this book. These include biochemical and physiologic changes, as well as changes in social relationships, financial resources, and patterns of illness. In this section we are concerned with those special features of the elderly that mandate ethical concerns.

Increasing age frequently brings with it a progressive set of *personal and environmental losses.* These include the loss of a spouse, friend, or other relative; decrease in income; decrements in physical and cognitive functioning; and the loss of social status. Although these losses are not inevitable or universal, most elderly persons experience some degree of loss in one or more of these areas (11).

The inherent *ageism* of American society has been clearly described in recent years (5). This bias may be seen as inevitable in a society that places great emphasis on individual self-reliance, independence, and the "frontier spirit." Although there have

[1]Research for this chapter was supported by the Retirement Research Foundation, the Atlantic Richfield Foundation, an anonymous Dutch foundation, and the Bureau of Health Professions, U.S. Public Health Service.

been increasingly successful efforts to change mandatory retirement and other overt expressions of ageism, more subtle forms persist and pervade institutions and services. In addition, the current cohort of elderly have spent much of their lives confronting the image of older persons as dependent, disabled, and without value. It is hoped that this will not be true of future cohorts.

Aging is also frequently accompanied by a *burden of illness and disability.* The demonstration in recent studies that disability and loss of function are not inevitable does little to change the reality that most of the elderly carry a significant burden of chronic disease and progressive disability. The frequent sensory loss and dementia can making getting old a kind of hell.

As a consequence of the losses and burdens associated with aging, the elderly frequently experience *dependency* on family, friends, and paid caretakers in meeting their daily needs. Because the elderly constitute a population of survivors, this dependency can be quite foreign to prior patterns of independent living.

Although all of us are intellectually aware of our own mortality, the elderly are unique in that they universally are faced with death in the relatively near future. Most have thought about the end of their lives and discussed it with family and friends, although they may still wish to fight to remain alive when they become seriously ill. The elderly tend to recognize the *inevitability and imminence of death* (16).

These five special features of the elderly play a major role in the framework for geriatric ethics that we develop in this chapter. Before doing so, however, it is necessary to define some key terms and concepts that will be employed in this and the next five chapters.

DEFINITIONS AND CONCEPTS

Ethics is an intellectual and practical discipline that studies morality. *Morality,* in turn, has two main concerns. The first is with right and wrong conduct. "What ought or should I do or not do?" is a basic question in morality. In medicine, the focus is on what is in the best interests of the patient, what Pellegrino calls a right and good decision for this patient here and now (21, 22). The second, often overlooked, concern of morality involves expectations of character or the virtues. That is, we are interested in more than right and wrong conduct. We are also interested in whether someone is a good or bad person, someone we should look up to and emulate as a role model or not. In medicine, the focus is on such matters as compassion, sensitivity, and honesty in one's dealings with patients. This chapter addresses both conduct and character.

Morality has many sources in our society. The most prominent of these include the law, our political heritage as a free people, religions, ethnic and cultural traditions, families, the traditions and practices of medicine itself, and personal experience.

Law and Morality. The United States is founded on the principle of the rule of law. It should come as no surprise, therefore, that the law looms large in our thinking about right and wrong conduct. However, the law is of only limited help in this endeavor. Before showing why this is so, it is important to keep in mind some fundamental distinctions. Common law is written by our courts and is based on precedent, statutes, and the constitutions of our state and federal governments. Statutory law is written by our legislatures and requires only a majority vote to pass. Regulatory and administrative law is written by the bureaucracy, under the authority granted to it by the legislative branch of government. As such, it is necessarily limited to the intent of the legislature when it enacted the authorizing legislation.

In all three of its forms, the law is limited. It is bound by precedent and written constitutions, which are result of a particular history and therefore could, in principle, be different than what they happen to be. A legislative majority does not always imply careful and systematic reflection on the ramifications of statutes in the lives of citizens. Regulatory and administrative law inherits these problems. In addition, the law is incomplete, because it tends to be reactive. Thus, there is little legal guidance on many ethical issues that arise in the care of geriatric patients, for example, whether to respect the desire of the frail elderly to continue to live at home even when doing so may involve some level of risk.

Political Traditions and Morality. Our political traditions certainly emphasize individual freedom and self-determination (14). But surely these are not the whole of morality, for they concern only our government and its conduct.

Religions and Morality. Religions play a powerful role in shaping morality for faith communities and, to some extent, the society at large. Ultimately, however, the source of religious morality is found in revelation. The authority for revelation lies in acts of faith and the experience of faith communities, which not everyone shares. Because of this defining feature of religions, they are limited in that not everyone shares in a particular faith tradition. We are a religiously pluralistic society.

Ethnic, Cultural, and Family Traditions and Morality. Ethnic and cultural traditions—of race, national heritage, and the like—are also important sources of morality. However, they tend to be highly culture bound and often are the source of excluding others from the scope of moral concern. The same is true of families as sources of morality.

Medicine and Morality. The traditions and practices of medicine are obviously an important source of morality for physicians. They are reinforced by personal experience. While the traditions and practices of medicine provide the beginning point of geriatric ethics, they are not sufficient alone to provide a complete account of right and wrong medical conduct and good and bad medical character.

Ethics and Morality. Because there are many and diverse sources of morality, because each is limited, and because each can and does come into conflict with others, the intellectual and practical discipline of ethics is required to bring order to our thinking about and evaluation of conduct and character in the care of elderly patients. Ethics does so by insisting on clarity, consistency, coherence, and universality.

Clarity requires us to avoid vagueness, ambiguity, and confusion in our thinking. Thus, we need to identify with precision the meaning of such basic ethical terms and concepts as beneficence, respect for autonomy, and paternalism. The authors undertake the task of clarifying key terms and concepts in the chapters that follow. *Consistency* simply means that we must avoid contradiction. For example, to assert that the elderly should have final decision-making authority about the termination of treatment and that the physician is the one to decide whether life-sustaining intervention is in the best interests of the patient (15) involves a contradiction. *Coherence* requires that our thinking about morality display a high degree of unity, mainly by being based in a clearly defined foundation that is then consistently developed in concrete, applicable detail. Finally, *universality* means that any claims that we make about right and wrong conduct and about good and bad character must appeal to justifications that any reasonable person could accept. Law, religions, our political traditions, ethnic and cultural traditions, families, and personal experience do not pass this test.

THE STARTING POINT FOR GERIATRIC ETHICS

The traditions and practices of medicine provide us with a starting point for geriatric ethics that, when interpreted in terms of ethical principles and virtues, meets the test of universality: the commitment to act primarily in a way that protects and promotes the best interests of the patient and only secondarily promotes one's own self-interest and the interests of others. Ethical principles are general guides to right and wrong conduct. Virtues are those traits of character that blunt self-interest and direct our moral concern to others. The virtues are in this way constitutive of good character. We shall discuss four principles of geriatric ethics as well as the special virtues required in the medical care of the elderly. These principles and virtues make concrete and clinically applicable the commitment to protect and promote the best interests of the patient. Together they provide a framework for geriatric ethics that will permit the physician to (a) identify and analyze ethical issues and conflicts that arise in the care of elderly patients and (b) develop clinical strategies for managing those issues and conflicts in an effective, fair, and reasonable fashion. For a summary of the four principles, see Table 51.1.

FOUR PRINCIPLES OF GERIATRIC ETHICS

The four ethical principles in the framework for geriatric ethics are beneficence, respect for autonomy, justice, and family responsibility. Each is discussed below with a view toward providing an analysis that results in concrete, clinically applicable formulations.

PRINCIPLE OF BENEFICENCE

The oldest principle of geriatric ethics has its roots in the perspective that medicine takes on the best interests of the patient. By "medicine" is meant a social institution or practice that is based in scientific knowledge and clinical experience that form the basis for justifying diagnostic, therapeutic, and prognostic decisions and judgments of physicians. Thus, the term "medicine" is not used to mean organized medicine, for example, the American Medical Association. The implication is that clinical judgment about the best interests of the patient should be objective in character. Clinical judgment should depend minimally on the individual, personal experience, and outlook of a particular physician, but rather should follow rigorous patterns of scientific and clinical analysis and judgment. This objective character of clinical judgment is essential to the legitimacy of the perspective that medicine

Table 51.1
Four Ethical Principles

Beneficence: Act toward others in a way that results in the greater balance of good over harm:

Goods and harms are defined from medicine's objective perspective on the best interests of the patient.

The goods are prevention of premature or unnecessary death and the prevention, cure, or at least amelioration of disease, injury, handicap, and unnecessary pain and suffering.

Unnecessary pain and suffering do not result in an increase of one or more of the other goods of beneficence in medicine.

Respect for autonomy: Act in a way that respects the values and beliefs of the patient:

Recognize and acknowledge the validity of the values and beliefs of the older person.

Do not interfere in the autonomous decisions and actions of the older person.

Implement decisions that are based on the values and beliefs of the older person.

Justice: Render to each person his or her due:

Distribute a fair portion of benefits and burdens of health care for the geriatric patient to the older person and to family and society.

Family responsibility: Identify the obligations of family members (spouse, siblings, and adult children) and negotiate differences in understandings of these obligations in a fair (just) manner.

---

takes on the best interests of the patient. Therefore, ad hoc or purely intuitive perspectives on the patient's best interests are to be employed only when it is impossible to form a more objective perspective on them.

There are two levels at which the concrete content of that perspective needs to be specified. The first is general in that it applies to any patient. The second is specific to the geriatric patient.

Beauchamp and McCullough have identified the more general content of medicine's perspective on the best interests of the patient in terms of the specific goods that medicine, on the basis of clinical science and experience, is competent to seek on behalf of the patient (2). The first and most basic of these is to prevent premature death, which is not identical with "prolonging life at all costs." "Premature" is not age specific. Rather, it refers to the fullness of a life. Thus, it is reasonable to think of the death of an elderly patient as premature when he or she has major life projects still to complete and thus has not brought his or her life to a sort of completeness of closure (6).

The good of preventing premature death is basic in that if premature death occurs the other goods of medicine cannot be sought on behalf of the patient. These are the prevention, cure, or at least amelioration of disease, injury, handicap, and unnecessary pain and suffering. The latter are pain and suffering that do not result in an increase in one or more of the other goods. The harms that medicine seeks to avoid

or prevent are premature death, disease, injury, handicap, and unnecessary pain and suffering.

Given the nature of these goods and the vicissitudes of the human condition, the goods and harms that make up medicine's perspective on a patient's best interests can come into conflict. The task of clinical judgment is to determine the course that maximizes goods and minimizes harms in diagnostic and therapeutic interventions. Thus, clinical judgment already is shaped by the ethical principle of beneficence, which directs us to act to others in a way that results in the greater balance of good over harm for them. The principle of beneficence generates ethical obligations for the physician to act in a way that results in a greater balance of medical goods over medical harms.

Rowe has made a number of recommendations regarding the health care of the elderly (25). These can be restated in the language of the principle of beneficence, thus providing specific content for this principle in geriatric ethics. This more specific content is the following:

1. The physician is obligated to make an extra effort to elicit information from the elderly patient, because of the underreporting of illness by the elderly. Such information is essential for developing an objective perspective on the patient's best interests.
2. The physician has an ethical obligation to maintain the functional capability of the elderly patient, by ameliorating the losses for which the elderly are at risk, including pain, suffering, and handicaps.

3. Clinical judgment should be shaped by an awareness that the losses or dependency caused by *diagnostic* and *therapeutic* interventions may be as serious, far reaching, and irreversible as those of chronic disease or illness. Medical interventions in the care of the elderly are not in every case beneficent; they must be shown to be so by careful clinical judgment and assessment.

4. The physician is obligated to attempt to increase the longevity of the elderly patient, with an eye to reducing the risks of possible prolonged dependence. The goal should not be prolonging life at all cost.

In addition to these four based on Rowe, we add a fifth:

5. In situations where the death of the elderly patient cannot be prevented, the obligation to attempt to do so diminishes. In the face of the imminence of death, the goods of preventing or at least ameliorating unnecessary pain and suffering should become primary considerations.

PRINCIPLE OF RESPECT FOR AUTONOMY

Medicine's is not the only legitimate perspective on the patient's best interests. As Beauchamp and McCullough have shown, a second perspective on the best interests of the patient must also be considered—that of the patient him- or herself (2). Each of us has values and beliefs by which we give meaning to the world and our experience of it, including (a) the experience of illness, disease, injury, pain, and suffering and (b) the reality and eventual imminence of our death. These values and beliefs are shaped by personal experience, families, religions, and the other sources of morality mentioned earlier. Thus, the values and beliefs of an elderly patient about what is good and harmful in medical care will range far beyond the goods and harms that shape the principle of beneficence, to include the elderly person's values and beliefs about personal and environmental loss, ageism, the burdens of illness and disability, dependency, and the recognition of the inevitability and imminence of death. Thus, the ethical principle of beneficence must be balanced by an ethical principle that focuses the physician's concern on the values and beliefs of the patient.

The ethical principle of respect for autonomy directs us to act in a way that respects the values and beliefs of another, even if and especially when we may think that the consequences of acting on those values and beliefs may be harmful to the other person. This principle is grounded by the recognition that the values and beliefs of another person are constitutive of his or her very identity as a unique, individual human person, who is capable of deciding for him- or herself about how he or she wants to live and die. Given the settled nature of the values and

beliefs of elderly persons and of the meaning of values and beliefs that have shaped and given meaning to a life for seven decades or more, respect for autonomy is a compelling principle in geriatric ethics.

Because of the diversity of values and beliefs among the elderly, it is not possible to specify the content of this principle. That will change with each individual patient. In addition, the physician should expect an elderly person's values and beliefs to cover a much larger terrain than the medically oriented goods of beneficence. These will include personal values, such as dignity, independence, and the relative weights to be given to length versus quality of life; family values such as not being a burden on one's children and being remembered well after one is dead; and social values such as maintaining one's identity and place in the community. The scope of concern of the principle of beneficence is clearly a subset of the scope of concern of the principle of respect for autonomy.

Before turning to more specific comments about respect for autonomy, it is necessary to address the relationship between competence and autonomy. The authors understand competence to be the ability to perform a specific task (2). We understand autonomy to be the capacity to make decisions that express or reflect one's values and beliefs. Autonomous decisions must "(1) be based on adequate knowledge, (2) exhibit understanding and related intentionality, (3) not be internally constrained, and (4) not be externally constrained" (2). One can thus be competent and nonautonomous, for example, when one is coerced to do something that one does competently. One can also be incompetent to do something, yet autonomously attempt it. "Whereas autonomy is self-governance and reduced autonomy is reduced self-governance, competence is the ability to perform a task and diminished competence is a diminished or lesser ability to perform it" (2).

Autonomy and competence are thus similar in some respects. Both come in degrees and are task specific. Judgments of overall competence or overall autonomy make little sense. Instead, clinical judgment should focus on the level of competence or autonomy for the task or decision at hand. Both concepts involve thresholds, above which everyone is to be regarded as competent (when they can perform the task in question) or autonomous (when they fulfill the four conditions just above). Autonomy and competence are also distinct. Reduced autonomy can often cause diminished competence in the elderly, but diminished competence is not directly correlated with reduced autonomy. Older patients may not be judged competent in some respects, (e.g., managing his or her financial affairs or not being oriented as to place or time), but may be able to make autonomous decisions about medical care, which express or reflect their values and beliefs (2). This aspect of autonomy and respect for autonomy are especially important in the care of the frail elderly, who may be able to make decisions, even if they are unable to carry them out unassisted. Because competence and autonomy are not identical, the results of examinations of mental competence must be reinterpreted in terms of the four conditions for autonomous decisions.

The first obligation, generated by the principle of respect for autonomy for the physician caring for the geriatric patient, is to recognize and acknowledge the validity of the values and beliefs of the older person. In this, its most fundamental sense, the ethical principle of respect for autonomy is a powerful antidote to ageism, by obligating the physician to take the time to elicit and understand his patients values and beliefs. Butler has identified "tendencies frequently observed in older persons": changes in the sense of time, a sense of the life cycle, an interest in life review, reparation and resolution, attachment to the familiar, conservation of continuity, the desire to leave a legacy, transmission of power, a sense of consummation or fulfillment in life, and capacity for growth (5). The values and beliefs of the older person may cluster around these concerns in ways that are significant for the older person. Identifying the older person's values and beliefs is the first step of obtaining a "value history" (Pellegrino, personal communication, 1980; 19).

Discussion with the patient of these general concerns provides the context for more specific, health-related concerns. These include the patient's attitudes about death, illness, disease, injury, pain and suffering—especially how the patient balances these off against each other. In addition, the value history should include the patient's attitudes about personal and environmental losses, the burdens of chronic illness and disability on him- or herself as well as on his or her family, and dependency and its impact on the older person and the older person's family. The physician should be especially alert to ageist attitudes about these and other matters in the elderly patient and seek to correct them. The chapters on truth telling (Chapter 55) and on informed consent (Chapter 52) provide additional details about what might usefully be included in a value history and its role in effective clinical care of the elderly patient. The value history is summarized on pages 615–616.

The second obligation of the principle of respect for autonomy is to not interfere in the autonomous decisions and actions of the elderly patient. Such interference, when it is undertaken for the good of the elderly patient, constitutes medical paternalism. "Paternalism is (1) the intentional limitation of autonomy of one person by another (2) where the person who limits autonomy appeals exclusively to grounds of beneficence for the person whose autonomy is limited" (2). Paternalism would be justified only if the principle of beneficence were the sole ethical principle of geriatric ethics. But it is not.

The antipaternalistic implications of the principle of respect for autonomy in geriatric ethics are worth underscoring. There is a tendency to think that the elderly who are chronically ill or who are dependent on others are not autonomous. This is not so. To be autonomous means that one has the capacity to make decisions that express or reflect one's values or beliefs. It is a form of ageism to believe that chronic illness or dependency necessarily reduces or eliminates that capacity. These conditions may reduce or eliminate physical autonomy, the ability to effect what one has decided. But they do not necessarily reduce or eliminate moral autonomy, the capacity to make decisions that express or reflect the older person's values and beliefs. As Butler points out, the elderly in most cases are quite able to make their own decisions about medical care, as well as other matters (5).

The third obligation generated by the ethical principle of respect for autonomy is that the physician should implement decisions that are based on the values and beliefs of the elderly patient. Obviously this meaning of the principle applies to the full range of medical care. It is important to include because many of the frail elderly are not able, physically, to carry out decisions that they have made autonomously. The physician is a major "gatekeeper" in the system and thus can act in place of the elderly person's diminished physical autonomy.

Together these three obligations provide the content for a basic principle of geriatric ethics proposed by Christiansen: Do not compound the losses of the elderly unnecessarily (8, 9). One of the most ethically significant losses that the elderly can experience is the loss of dignity in the form of the failure of the physician to acknowledge the values and beliefs of the older person, to not interfere with autonomous decisions, and to implement autonomous decisions. Those elderly who are more accepting of the authority of physicians (13) are especially vulnerable to the compounding of losses of autonomy.

Rowe has proposed a clinical principle of health care for the elderly that is directly supportive of the ethical principle of respect for autonomy (25). He emphasizes the importance of the physician's evaluating what the patient can do versus what the patient wishes to do. His main focus of concern is the identification and potential reversibility of functional deficits, physical as well as cognitive. In particular, Rowe underscores the point that dementia is not part of the normal aging process. Evaluating what the patient can do versus what the patient is willing to do can help prevent unnecessary acceptance by the patient of reductions of his or her autonomy.

PRINCIPLE OF JUSTICE

The ethical principles of beneficence and respect for autonomy would be sufficient for a framework for geriatric ethics if the physician–patient relationship occurred in isolation. However, third parties are directly affected by decisions and actions undertaken on behalf of the patient's best interests. The most important third parties in the care of geriatric patients are (a) health care institutions, including the physician's private practice, managed health care delivery systems, hospitals, home health agencies, hospices, and nursing homes; (b) private insurers and employers who manage pension and insurance plans; (c) society, especially the institutions of government that pay for the health care of the elderly, Medicare and Medicaid, and (d) the family of the older person.

With respect to all of these third parties, the physician faces a common, perplexing problem: Acting on the best interests of the patient may harm the best interests of one or more third parties. It is tempting here simply to state that the physician's ethical obligations are only to his or her patient and to no one else. However, the realities of clinical practice and its effects on others force an ethical issue: How should the physician balance the best interests of the geriatric patient against the best interests of third parties when the two are in conflict? The task here is to find a fair balance. Ethical issues of fairness involve the principle of justice.

In its most formal and admittedly abstract terms the principle of justice requires us to render to each person his or her due. Substantive justice concerns the outcome that is due to each person. Procedural justice concerns the process that is due to each person. Both are relevant to any adequate framework for geriatric ethics.

The central consideration in substantive justice is how to distribute benefits and burdens. This is called distributive justice. Applying concepts of distributive justice to health care for the elderly involves decisions about how to distribute a benefit, health care for the elderly, and two burdens: (a) the cost of care, which is to be distributed among all parties, and (b) risks of increased morbidity and mortality, which are to be borne by the elderly.

The basic goal of distributive justice is that like cases are to be treated alike. There are a number of criteria by which cases are thought to be like each other. One criterion is equality, the intuitive appeal of which is obvious in a society like ours. The benefits and burdens of health care for the elderly should be equal to those of younger age groups. This approach poses an immediate problem, however, because the elderly consume a disproportionate share of the health care budget. The burden of paying for medical care falls unequally on the elderly and nonelderly. How can we justify this unequal distribution of benefits and burdens? Is it fair?

One way to show that it is fair is to argue in terms of merit—that the elderly have earned this unequal distribution of health care benefits. One can correctly argue that the elderly have raised children and contributed to the growth of wealth and social institutions. In addition, they accept loss of income and social status when they retire. In short, the elderly have made and continue to make an unequal share of sacrifices that benefit following generations. Out of reciprocal distributive justice, based on merit, the elderly should receive, or are in justice entitled to, unequal benefits. But, how much benefits?

Reciprocal distributive justice toward the elderly would quickly exhaust the resources of any society. Some reasonable limit must be found. One major criterion for limiting the distribution of health care benefits to the elderly is based on need. The problem, however, is in defining need. One way to deal with this problem is to claim that only the most basic health care needs of the elderly should be met. This ultimately involves establishing a hierarchy among the goods that define beneficence, because those goods are based on the health care needs of the elderly. Preventing premature death is surely a basic need of the elderly, as it is of people of all ages. Alternatively, one could emphasize the other goods of beneficence, out of a recognition of the imminence of death.

On either account, we confront a central ethical problem in distributive justice and health care for the elderly: how to allocate scarce medical resources. It concerns how to define, in a way consistent with the demands of distributive justice based on need and merit, a fair level of health care services for the elderly, while at the same time distributing to the elderly the burdens of limited health care, that is, economic costs as well as the costs of possibly increased morbidity and mortality relative to a distribution scheme with more services.

Because of the difficulties associated with determining substantive distributive justice, some have advocated a reliance on procedural notions of justice (12). The basic idea here is that we owe in justice to others what we can agree on through processes that respect the autonomy of all parties involved. No specific outcome is identified ahead of time; this is left up to the free exchanges and negotiations among the parties concerned. This approach to justice and health care may have only limited applicability in a system like ours that is based on legally guaranteed entitlements. However, it does have considerable applicability in finding a fair balance between the best interests of the older person and those of his or her family, to which we now turn.

PRINCIPLE OF FAMILY RESPONSIBILITY

The involvement of families in the care of the elderly, especially the frail elderly, has been well documented (3). It is important to recognize that the burden of caring for the frail elderly falls primarily on relatives, especially wives, daughters, and daughters-in-law (3). In acting on the best interests of the older person the physician may place unreasonable demands on such caregivers. In short, there may be an unequal distribution of benefits and burdens between the elderly patient and his or her family. This situation raises questions of distributive justice as families seek a fair resolution of that unequal distribution.

Part of the problem is the uncertain nature of family responsibility. Spouses have ethical obligations to each other based on what they understood their marriage promises to be and how they have treated each other over the years. This, however, is a highly variable phenomenon. Adult children have similarly uncertain ethical obligations of reciprocal justice to parents, stepparents, and parents-in-law. As a consequence, substantive distributive justice has little applicability. Instead, procedural distributive justice moves to the foreground. The task for the parties involved is to identify what they take their responsibilities to be and negotiate their differences in a fair and reasonable fashion. The physician has a key role to play in this process, particularly regarding long-term care, which is considered in Chapter 56.

SPECIAL VIRTUES IN CARING FOR GERIATRIC PATIENTS

Earlier we pointed out that morality, the subject matter of ethics, concerns decisions and actions, as well as habits and expectations of character. Ethical principles apply to decisions and actions. The virtues apply to character. Elderly patients, like all patients, expect their physician to be compassionate and honest and to display integrity in all that he or she does. Because of the special features of the elderly discussed above, the care of the elderly also calls for special virtues. Any adequate framework for geriatric ethics must therefore identify and discuss these special virtues.

ACCEPTANCE OF MORTALITY

The most important virtue for the physician to develop and sustain is the intellectual and emotional acceptance of the relatively imminent and inevitable death of the geriatric patient. Physicians cannot be effective in caring for the elderly until they have dealt with and accepted their own mortality (10). Nothing in the training or experience of physicians prepares them for this necessity (4), and it conflicts with the basic emphasis of the beneficence model on the preservation of life. Thus, the physician tends to see efforts with the elderly fail, while the geriatric patient frequently has accepted the inevitable end of life.

ACCEPTANCE OF DIFFERENT VALUES

The acceptance of mortality involves perhaps the most extreme divergence of values that occurs between the physician and the elderly patient. Other differences are worth noting. In addition to differences in gender, race, religion, socioeconomic class and levels of education, the older person has spent much of his or her life in a world without the knowledge and technology that has become part of routine medical care. Thus, it should not be surprising that the elderly patient has different attitudes regarding the benefits or burdens of medical procedures that the physician accepts as routine. The refusal of intravenous feeding or basic diagnostic or therapeutic procedures may express or reflect different values, rather than a lack of rationality or understanding. To provide care effectively for the elderly, the physician must seek to understand the basis of such decisions and the values upon which they are based. Just as we recognize the great biologic variability within the elderly, so we must recognize differences in their value systems. It is inappropriate for the physician to assume that he or she knows what an elderly individual takes to be important in his or her life, no matter how much experience the practitioner has with older patients.

APPRECIATING THE VALUE TO THE PATIENT OF SMALL GAINS

Because the elderly recognize the nearness of death, and because many carry a major burden of chronic disease and disability, it is easy for the physician to assume that nothing effective can be done for the patient. Instead of seeking to cure or remove disability, the physician must recognize the importance and value to the patient of what appear to the physician to be small gains (27). It is common to hear from disabled men, for example, that they see no value in continuing to live if they cannot stand and walk, even though they may be mobility independent in a wheelchair. The difference may appear small or even irrational to the physician, but it clearly has great value to some patients. In the same vein, it is important to appreciate that the elderly patient is very likely to value treatment that results in slowing the progression of disability, another type of significant gain for the physician to seek.

WORKING EFFECTIVELY WITH OTHER PROFESSIONALS

Achievement of these small gains frequently involves the efforts of care providers other than the physician. The special skills of the physical or occupational therapist, speech pathologist, social worker, or nurse may be more vital to the management of a given problem than those of the physician, who must assume the role of case manager or coordinator. The physician must recognize that other professionals may be just as knowledgeable in their field as the physician is in medicine, and learn to work with these professionals. At the same time, the physician must continue to maintain his or her relationship with the patient and family, lest they feel abandoned. The elderly patient must know who is "in charge" of his or her care. Two-way communication between the patient and physician must continue, particularly with respect to such matters as truthtelling (Chapter 55) and informed consent (Chapter 52).

CONCERN FOR FAMILY

The patient's family is also a major part of the care team. Research has confirmed that most of the personal care needs of the elderly are met by family and friends, rather than health care professionals (3). Balancing the patient's autonomy and confidentiality with a beneficent concern for family and friends is a taxing exercise, but is an important virtue to cultivate in the care of the elderly. This is discussed in greater detail in Chapter 55.

COMPASSION AND SENSITIVITY

It is easy to label many elderly patients as "difficult" in terms of their medical care, personality, and social relationships. Despite the complexity of their physical problems and treatments, the burdens of chronic disability and imminent death mean that the physician has a special obligation to provide compassionate care and to maintain sensitivity to the human needs of the elderly. Although these virtues pertain to all of medical care, they become difficult at times to maintain with the elderly. However, they are central virtues of the physician who cares for elderly patients.

ETHICAL CONFLICT

The present framework for geriatric ethics, described in terms of ethical principles and special virtues, is designed to aid the physician in identifying, preventing, and managing ethical conflict. Ethical conflict occurs because of conflicting values and beliefs. This is distinct from psychologic conflict and is not to be construed as a battle of wills.

Incorporating ethics into clinical judgment and decision making enhances the ability of the physician to think carefully through ethical conflicts in terms of the ethical principles and the special virtues discussed above. This clinical ethical skill involves (a) identifying the elements of an ethical conflict in terms of the four principles and (b) utilizing the ethical principles virtues discussed above to reason one's way through to a conclusion about how that conflict should be addressed. In short, incorporating ethics to clinical practice involves accepting the intellectual discipline that the proposed framework imposes on clinical judgment and decision making. Doing so equips the physician to manage ethical conflict in a reliable way when it occurs and, importantly, to anticipate and prevent unnecessary ethical conflicts in the care of elderly patients. To these ends, the physician and elderly patient must share in decision making about the ethically significant aspects of the patient's care. The alternative is to fail to respect the dignity and worth of the geriatric patient, thus inviting the charge of ageism.

The next five chapters provide the physician with concrete applications of this framework to specific aspects of clinical care that potentially involve ethical conflict. These chapters emphasize management as well as prevention of ethical conflict in the care of geriatric patients. Indeed, these chapters together with the present chapter culminate in the concept of a value history, which is essential for preventive geriatric ethics.

REFERENCES

1. Ball JR: Withholding treatment—a legal perspective. *J Am Geriatr Soc* 32:528, 1984.
2. Beauchamp TL, McCullough LB: *Medical Ethics: The Moral Responsibilities of Physicians.* Englewood Cliffs, NJ, Prentice-Hall, 1984.
3. Brody E: *Long-Term Care of Older People: A Practical Guide.* New York, Human Services Press, 1977.
4. Bunkin IA: When does a surgeon retire? *JAMA* 250:757, 1983.
5. Butler RN: *Why Survive? Being Old in America.* New York, Harper and Row, 1975.
6. Callahan D: What do children owe elderly parents? *Hastings Cent Rep* 15:31, 1987.
7. Cassell CK, Meier DE, Traines ML: Selected bibliography of recent articles in ethics and geriatrics. *J Am Geriatr Soc* 34:399, 1986.
8 Christiansen D: Dignity in aging. *Hastings Cent Rep* 4:6-8, 1974.
9. Christiansen D: Dignity in aging: Notes on geriatric ethics. *J Humanistic Psychology* 18:41, 1978.
10. Deckert G: Psychology of aging. Presentation at Family Medicine and the Aging Patient, Asheville, NC, 1982.
11. Edel L: The artist in old age. *Hastings Cent Rep* 15:38, 1985.
12. Engelhardt HT: *The Foundations of Bioethics.* New York, Oxford University Press, 1986.
13. Haug M: Doctor–patient relationships and the older patient. *J Gerontol* 34:852, 1979.
14. Katz J: Informed consent—a fairy tale? Law's vision. *University of Pittsburgh Law Review* 39:137, 1977.
15. Levinsky NG: Fighting for life. *J Am Geriatr Soc* 34:666, 1986.
16. Lipson S, McCullough LB: Toward a framework for geriatric ethics. In Tilquin C (Ed): *System Science in Health–Social Services for the Elderly and Disabled.* Montreal, Canada, Charles Tilquin, 1985.
17. Lo B: The Bartling case: protecting patients from harm while respecting their wishes. *J Am Geriatr Soc* 34:44, 1986.
18. Lynn J: Brief and appendix for *amicus curiae*; the American Geriatrics Society—in the matter of Claire C. Conroy. *J Am Geriatr Soc* 32:915, 1984.
19. McCullough LB: Medical care for elderly patients with diminished competence: an ethical analysis. *J Am Geriatr Soc* 32:150, 1984.
20. Nevins MA: Analysis of the supreme court of New Jersey's decision in the Claire Conroy case. *J Am Geriatr Soc* 34:140, 1986.
21. Pellegrino ED, Thomasma DC: *A Philosophical Basis of Medical Practice.* New York, Oxford University Press, 1981.
22. Pellegrino ED: The anatomy of clinical judgments. In Engelhardt HT, Spicker SF, Towers B (Eds): *Clinical Judgment: A Critical Appraisal.* Dordrecht, Holland, D. Reidel Publishing Company, 1979, pp. 169-194.
23. President's Commission for the Study of Ethical Problems in Biomedical and Behavioral Research: *Deciding to Forego Life-Sustaining Treatment.* Washington, DC, U.S. Government Printing Office, 1983.
24. President's Commission for the Study of Ethical Problems in Biomedical and Behavioral Research: *Making Health Care Decisions.* Washington, DC, U.S. Government Printing Office, 1983.
25. Rowe JW: Health care of the elderly. *N Engl J Med* 312:827, 1985.
26. Saber DG, Tabor WJ: Withholding of life-sustaining treatment from the terminally ill, incompetent patient: Who decides? *JAMA* 248:2250, 2431, 1982.
27. Williams TF: Rehabilitation in the aging: Philosophy and approaches. In Williams TF (Ed): *Rehabilitation in the Aging.* New York, Raven Press, 1984, pp. 13-16.

CHAPTER 52

Informed Consent[1]

LAURENCE B. McCULLOUGH
STEVEN LIPSON

ETHICAL BASIS OF INFORMED CONSENT

Informed consent is one of the foundations upon which the physician builds an effective and lasting relationship with the elderly patient. Practicing the clinical skills of informed consent that are described in this chapter produces positive benefits for the geriatric patient, because a patient who understands and participates with the physician in decisions about diagnostic and therapeutic interventions will be more likely to cooperate in their implementation. Thus, the ethical principle of beneficence supports an obligation to obtain informed consent, a dimension of consent that is often overlooked in much of the literature on the subject. Practicing the clinical skills of informed consent also provides the opportunity to make diagnostic and therapeutic decisions that directly reflect or express the values and beliefs of the older patient. Thus, the ethical principle of respect for autonomy supports an obligation to obtain informed consent. In the literature, respect for autonomy is acknowledged as the main ethical foundation of obligations regarding informed consent in patient care (1, 6). The principle of beneficence can be understood as a buttressing consideration and plays a key role in the definition of standards of disclosure.

Only in this century did the concept and practice of informed consent become a part of the practice of medicine (6). Informed consent, as it shall be described in this chapter and as it should be practiced, cannot be found in the writings of medical ethics before the beginning of this century. Faden and Beauchamp have recently shown that prior to the 20th

century, matters of disclosure or truthtelling—which are now seen as elements of informed consent—were handled in two alternative ways (6). The first view was that the physician should be guided by a beneficence-based discretion. Patients should be told little or nothing about their condition and what could be done for it. Obviously, this approach would lead to minimal disclosure and minimal participation in decision making by patients. It is clearly paternalistic. Patients were expected simply to accept what the physician offered to them, with little or no discussion of alternatives, risks, and benefits. The second view was that the physician should be forthcoming with patients, including dying patients. The justification for this approach was twofold. First, it was thought that this approach would benefit the patient by alleviating fears based on ignorance or uncertainty. Second, this approach would respect the dignity of the patient (1, 6, 10).

The major historical force for change in the thinking and practice of physicians regarding informed consent has been the common law. Beginning in the early decades of the 20th century, a body of court opinion developed that asserted certain legal rights of patients to make decisions regarding their medical care. These rights were based in the legal principle of self-determination. Justice Cardozo's statement in the landmark 1914 case that begins this legal history is succinct: "Every human being of adult years and sound mind has the right to determine what shall be done with his own body; and a surgeon who performs an operation without his patient's consent commits an assault" (12). The ethical principle of respect for autonomy is the direct analogue of the legal principle of self-determination.

The principle of respect for autonomy along with the principle of beneficence form the ethical basis of informed consent in clinical care, including the care

[1]Research for this chapter was supported by the Retirement Research Foundation, the Atlantic Richfield Foundation, an anonymous Dutch foundation, and the Bureau of Health Professions, U.S. Public Health Service.

of the geriatric patient. The requirements of informed consent are based on these two principles and apply in the care of all autonomous patients, in which category most elderly patients are found. Special considerations arise regarding informed consent for elderly patients who experience reduced autonomy. These will be discussed after analysis of (a) the three requirements of informed consent, which include the different standards of disclosure that shape the informed consent process, and (b) barriers to informed consent by the elderly patient.

REQUIREMENTS OF INFORMED CONSENT

There is a clear consensus in the literature on informed consent that it is a *process* involving both the patient and the physician (1, 6, 10). It is not the patient's signature on a hospital form or in the patient's chart. These are only indications that the process of informed consent has taken place and therefore should not be equated with that process. At the end of Chapter 51 it was pointed out that to make ethics a living part of clinical practice rather than some dead abstraction, the physician and the elderly patient must share in decision making about ethically significant aspects of the patient's care. Along with truthtelling (see Chapter 55), informed consent is one of the principal means by which this clinical ethical strategy is put into effect. Thus, the importance of informed consent for the ethical practice of medicine in the care of the geriatric patient cannot be overstated.

The process of informed consent has three requirements: (a) adequate disclosure of information by the physician to the elderly patient, (b) understanding of that information by the elderly patient, and (c) a voluntary decision by the elderly patient regarding medical interventions and procedures.

ADEQUATE DISCLOSURE OF INFORMATION

The first requirement of informed consent, like the others, involves two-way communication between the physician and the patient. The physician must disclose to and discuss with the patient an adequate amount of information about the patient's condition and about alternative ways in which that condition can be managed. Each of these requires further explanation.

Discussing an elderly patient's condition, when it involves chronic disease or disability, is a sensitive matter. The central fact of progressive loss of physical or cognitive function must be presented in a way that fulfills the demands of the special virtues discussed in Chapter 51. Care should be taken not to compound losses unnecessarily in the discussion of them and their meaning with the patient. The advantage of chronic conditions is that they provide many opportunities to discuss them over time with the elderly patient. As the patient identifies and applies his or her values and beliefs about such conditions, this information should be recorded in the chart as part of the patient's value history. As we shall see below and in the next two chapters this information plays a key role in the management of the care of patients who become irreversibly nonautonomous.

The full range of alternatives for managing the patient's condition should also be discussed with the patient. This must include information about both diagnostic and therapeutic interventions, as well as the risks and benefits of each. In addition, the alternative of no diagnostic or therapeutic intervention should also be discussed, along with the risks and benefits of this approach to managing the patient's condition. Finally, the prognosis for each alternative approach should be identified and discussed with the patient. Again, the main focus of the discussion with the patient should be the patient's values and beliefs regarding these alternatives. These should also be recorded as part of the value history.

Standards of Adequate Disclosure

The key term in the first requirement of informed consent is "adequate." What is an adequate level of disclosure? In the recent history of informed consent three standards have emerged: the professional community or professional practice standards, the reasonable person standard, and the subjective standard (1, 6). Each plays an important role in informed consent with elderly patients.

The Professional Community Standard. On this standard adequate disclosure is defined in terms of the customary rules or traditional practices of the professional community of physicians. The relevant community may be local or regional. It may also be national, especially since geriatric medicine is increasingly recognized as a distinctive branch of biomedical science and clinical practice. This standard is physician centered and is based on the principle of beneficence: From medicine's perspective the physician determines the amount of information the disclosure of which maximizes benefit and minimizes risk.

This standard tends toward limited disclosure, in part because of the traditional belief among physicians that disclosure of a great deal of information is harmful to the patient, on the assumption that a patient may out of fear reject a medical intervention that is beneficial. However, no scientific evidence has ever been adduced in support of this claim (10). Indeed, it may well be that disclosing information to patients reduces fear born of anxiety, uncertainty, and ignorance.

While this standard is the dominant *legal* standard of informed consent in the states, it is a questionable *ethical* standard. This is because the professional community standard takes its authority from the values and beliefs that undergird and justify customary and usual clinical practice. There is no guarantee that these values and beliefs will be consistent with those of the elderly patient. Indeed, given the analysis of the special virtues of the physician in Chapter 51, there may be divergence between the values of the physician and the values of the patient. Thus, under a professional community standard there can be a paternalistic approach to disclosure that is inconsistent with what the patient needs to know. This is especially the case with chronic disease and disability, the meaning and impact of which for elderly persons and their families are not defined solely or even at all in terms of medical diagnosis. For these reasons, more patient-centered standards are ethically required.

The Reasonable Person Standard. This is the first of two patient-centered standards for disclosure in informed consent that have emerged in recent years. On this standard the physician is to disclose and discuss with the patient what a hypothetical "reasonable person" would need and want to know. "Reasonable person" means that the physician is to think in terms of the information needs of a patient who is competent to make his or her own decisions; who is free of unreasoning fears or anxiety; who therefore is capable of thinking things through clearly, consistently, and coherently; and who is capable of participating in decisions about his or her medical care. A helpful rule of thumb for disclosure under this standard is that the physician should share with the elderly patient any information that has been part of the physician's clinical judgment about the patient's diagnosis, alternative diagnostic and therapeutic interventions, and the prognoses associated with alternative ways of managing the patient's condition (Wear S, personal communication, 1981). This is more information than tends to be disclosed under the professional community standard but less than all of the information that could possibly be shared with the patient. Physicians often object that patient-centered disclosure requirements mean that the patient needs to be pro-

vided an instant medical education. This objection is an unfair distortion of patient-centered standards of disclosure.

The advantage of the reasonable person standard is that it requires a level of disclosure designed to bring the patient's thinking, to the extent possible, into close parallel with the physician's clinical judgment. This standard promotes trust and facilitates mutual decision making, by treating the elderly patient as an adult. The reasonable person standard is therefore a powerful antidote to ageism, especially inadvertent ageism on the part of the physician, because it directs the physician's attention to the patient's autonomy and his or her concerns and needs. For these reasons the authors recommend the reasonable person standard, on ethical grounds, as the guiding standard of disclosure for informed consent in the care of the geriatric patient. This is a good example of how medical ethics differs from the law.

The Subjective Standard. There are times, however, when the reasonable person standard needs to be suppplemented by a third standard of disclosure of information, that is, when that information pertains to seriously debilitating or life-threatening conditions. In Chapter 51, the authors called attention to the variability of values and beliefs among the elderly. Nowhere is that variability more important than in how the elderly will give meaning to seriously debilitating or life-threatening conditions. Such values cannot be predicted, because they are a highly individual, personal matter. In situations of serious illness information must be conveyed to the patient in an amount and way that meets the personal needs of the individual elderly patient. While the reasonable person standard is patient centered, it is not finely enough tuned to the needs of individual, elderly patients when they must confront serious and far-reaching changes in their health status. Hence, a subjective standard of disclosure is pertinent to the ethics of informed consent.

This standard requires that the physician aim for the ideal of providing the elderly patient with all of the information that he or she, in his or her particular circumstances and with his or her particular values and beliefs, needs to know. The decisions, for example, that a patient with chronic obstructive pulmonary disease or unstable angina must make about seriously debilitating and life-threatening conditions reach into the heart of human experience. These include decisions by each individual patient about the quality of his or her life in a seriously debilitated condition, about how aggressively to prolong his or her dying process, about how he or she will die, and about how he or she will be remembered by loved ones, friends, and caregivers. The somewhat abstract nature of the reasonable person standard makes it an inappropriate guide for the physician's disclosure of information pertaining to matters such as those just listed.

The subjective standard of disclosure is a demanding one. It takes time. However, there is usually time over the course of caring for the elderly patient to disclose the information at a pace that the patient can deal with effectively. Thus, the subjective standard does not require that information be disclosed all at once. Indeed, doing so may disable the expression of autonomy and thus undercut the very purpose of informed consent. Timing of disclosure, guided by the special virtues identified in Chapter 51, is an important clinical skill in implementing the subjective standard. It is wise in some cases to start slowly and proceed toward fuller disclosure as the patient comes to grips with his or her condition.

Adopting this standard when it is appropriate to do so leaves the physician vulnerable to second guessing. However, this is the necessary price to pay for avoiding the compounding of loss for the elderly by withholding information that he or she needs to know. No matter which of these three standards is appropriate in a particular case, disclosure of information to the patient should be undertaken in a way that takes into account the patient's education level. In the authors' experience this means the use of simplified explanations that (a) are free of technical jargon; (b) use a level of language that the patient can understand (usually 10th grade); (c) proceed stepwise, moving on to the next step only when the patient comprehends the present step; (d) utilize repetition as needed; and (e) include teaching the patient that questions are welcome and encouraged.

UNDERSTANDING OF INFORMATION BY THE PATIENT

The second requirement of the informed consent process is that the elderly patient must understand the information that has been disclosed. For each alternative approach for managing the patient's condition, including nontreatment, the patient must, as it were, project him- or herself into the alternative futures that each approach makes possible and assess the risks, benefits, and prognoses of each in terms of his or her values and beliefs. The outcome of this process should be the articulation of a value-based preference for the alternative(s) that the patient believes to be appropriate or the best. While individuals are sometimes capable of making such

assessments intuitively, this process usually involves time for careful reflection. Because most of the medical conditions of the elderly are chronic in nature there usually is time for reflection, if the process of disclosure and discussion is started early in the course of chronic condition. The physician should play a supportive role in this process. The physician can help the patient to reach realistic assessments, based on what the patient can do rather than what the patient may erroneously think he or she can do (11). Guided by the values that shape the principle of beneficence in medicine and the values identified by Butler (3), as discussed in Chapter 51, the physician can help the elderly patient to identify which of his or her values are relevant and which the patient assigns the greater weight or importance. These values will pertain to such matters as length versus quality of life, maintaining independence, the extent to which the patient is willing to be or not be a burden on others, especially family, the extent to which the patient wants to make his or her own decisions, and how aggressively the patient wants his or her condition managed. In all these respects, the physician should be especially alert to and seek to correct ageist attitudes of elderly patients toward themselves, especially regarding their ability to make their own decisions.

Discussion with the patient of his or her value-based preferences should be directed to the specific interventions that are involved in each alternative approach to the clinical management of the patient's condition. Both diagnostic and therapeutic interventions should be identified and discussed. Ideally, these discussions should occur before a crisis ensues and acute care interventions are considered. To this end, the patient's value-based preferences should be elicited and made part of the patient's value history, as discussed in Chapter 55. Obtaining this kind of detailed value history is essential in the care of elderly patients who later become incompetent to make their own decisions, as discussed below.

VOLUNTARY DECISION BY THE PATIENT

The final requirement of the informed consent process is that the patient make a voluntary decision about medical intervention for his or her condition. It is important to be clear about the meaning of "voluntary" in analyzing this requirement. "Voluntary" does not mean that the patient is under no influences of any kind in making his or her decision. This would be an absurd notion of an autonomous decision, because no one could ever fulfill it. Rather, autonomous decisions—the making of which is an important goal of informed consent—are an individual's own decisions in the sense that they do not result from controlling influences (1, 6).

Controlling influences can be either internal or external in origin. Internal controlling influences include physical and psychologic phenomena that can override an elderly patient's value-based preferences, such as severe pain or depression. In addition, ageist attitudes toward oneself can be a controlling internal influence on decision making by elderly patients, because such attitudes can lead the elderly to unrealistic or even irrational conclusions about the lack of the value of their lives to themselves and others. The role of the physician is to detect such controlling influences and seek to remove them. Reduced autonomy that is due to such influences should not be regarded as a normal part of the aging process.

External influences are those individuals, groups, and institutions that override the patient's value-based preferences. These include the patient's family and friends, hospitals and nursing homes, and the health care bureaucracy. The task of the physician is to shield the elderly patient from such influences. This can lead to awkward situations, especially regarding maintenance of confidentiality, as discussed in Chapter 55. Because the elderly are more inclined than other age groups to accept the physician's authority (7), the physician him- or herself can become a controlling external influence. Thus, the physician must be careful in making recommendations to the elderly patient too soon in the informed consent process. They should ideally be made after the patient has arrived at a value-based preference and is thus in the best position to consider the physician's judgment in a critical light.

BARRIERS TO INFORMED CONSENT

Having set out the three requirements for informed consent, we turn next to a consideration of barriers to informed consent that can be encountered by the physician in the medical care of the elderly patient. Factors that are mistakenly taken to be barriers to informed consent are discussed, followed by consideration of genuine barriers and how they should be addressed by the physician.

FALSE BARRIERS TO INFORMED CONSENT

The most prominent false barrier to informed consent is the inability of the physically impaired but cognitively intact elderly patient to effect his or her decisions. The distinction between physical and moral autonomy, as discussed in Chapter 51, is relevant here. Physical autonomy is the ability to carry

out or to effect one's decisions. Moral autonomy is the capacity to make one's own decisions, to arrive at value-based preferences about how one wants one's medical condition managed. The latter is independent of the former. Thus, the absence of physical autonomy does not imply the absence of moral autonomy. Informed consent is about the exercise of moral autonomy by the elderly patient, and so reduced or even absent physical autonomy is not a true barrier to informed consent by the physically impaired, cognitively intact elderly patient. This false barrier to consent can be compounded by the institutional setting in which the consent process is attempted (8).

Another false barrier to informed consent is ageism (4). This can be manifested in seeking consent from family members for "old old" patients (those over age 85) on the assumption that they are not capable of participating in the informed consent process. Ageism can also be manifested in treating sensory deficits as barriers to informed consent. That an elderly patient is unable to read an informed consent form because of visual impairment does not mean that he or she is incapable of hearing the information and discussing it with the physician. Similarly, hearing-impaired patients may be quite capable of dealing with written materials. In short, sensory deficits must be carefully assessed in each individual patient and not be assumed to disqualify the older person automatically from participating in the consent process.

GENUINE BARRIERS TO INFORMED CONSENT

There are, however, genuine barriers to participation in the informed consent process by the elderly. These mainly include cognitive impairments that disrupt the exercise of autonomy that is pertinent to fulfilling the three requirements of informed consent discussed above. To the extent that cognitive impairments interfere with fulfilling these requirements, the elderly patient experiences reduced autonomy.

Note that we have not used the language of diminished competence here. As pointed out in Chapter 51, autonomy and competence are not identical concepts or phenomena. Competence is the simple ability to perform a task, in this case, to express a decision (1). Autonomy is the ability to make a decision that expresses or is based in one's values and beliefs (1). Mental status examinations are designed to detect diminished mental competence, but not necessarily reduced autonomy. These examinations focus on elements of mental competence that are relevant to the ability to absorb and retain information and the ability to make a voluntary decision. Thus, they are helpful for detecting cognitive impairments that can reduce autonomy and thus constitute barriers to informed consent among the elderly, but do not define reduced autonomy for a specific decision. These impairments include memory loss, the aphasias, and depression.

ADDRESSING BARRIERS TO CONSENT

It is now well established that such impairments are not to be regarded as part of the normal process of aging but as abnormal conditions that should be prevented, ameliorated, and, when possible, cured (2, 5). Thus, it is a mistake to accept barriers to informed consent as either inevitable or untreatable. We therefore turn to a consideration of three strategies for dealing with barriers to informed consent that reduce the capacity for autonomous decision making by the elderly. These strategies will play a major role in the next two chapters, which address termination of treatment and termination of food and water.

REVERSE REDUCED AUTONOMY

The first clinical strategy for dealing with barriers to informed consent among the elderly should be to prevent or remove them (9). For example, when it is otherwise safe to do so, medications that are reducing autonomy can be discontinued. Depression can be treated, with the goal of reversing the reduced state of the patient's autonomy. The goal should be to avoid the loss of or to restore the elderly patient's capacity to complete the requirements of informed consent. In this way, the patient can make his or her own decisions about medical interventions, which is the major goal of the informed consent process. In most cases this strategy will be successful in restoring the elderly patient to full participation with the physician in the decision-making process.

CONSTRUCT DECISIONS BASED ON THE VALUE HISTORY

In some cases, however, it will not be possible to restore the elderly patient's capacity for autonomous decision making. In these cases a decision should be constructed on the basis of the patient's value history. If the patient has already made a decision about the specific medical intervention that is being considered and there is no reason to think that the patient changed his or her mind, that decision should be taken into account. Even if the patient has not made a decision about specific intervention, it may well be

possible to construct such a decision by identifying what follows from relevant values and beliefs that were elicited in the value history or that may be identified with the help of others, especially family members. In the latter circumstance the family should be asked, "What was important to the patient?" and "What would the patient have decided on the basis of those values?" and not "What is important to you?" and "What is your decision?" In this way the family can focus on the patient's values and beliefs and not their own, which may not be identical.

Both of these strategies—identifying a previously made specific decision or constructing a decision based on the patient's values and beliefs—project the patient's past autonomy into the present. Respect for the projection of one's autonomy into the future is the basis of advance directives, which are discussed in detail in the next two chapters. Note that the strategies discussed above are not forms of "substituted judgment." Neither the physician nor the family is substituting their values and beliefs for those of the patient. Instead, the goal of these strategies for dealing with barriers to informed consent is to be faithful to the patient's values and beliefs and avoid decisions made on the basis of other, potentially conflicting values and beliefs.

SUBSTITUTED JUDGMENT

There are some barriers to informed consent that are appropriately addressed by substituted judgment. These barriers occur when it is not possible to construct a decision on the basis of the patient's values and beliefs. In these circumstances, the principle of beneficence becomes the main source for defining the patient's best interests. Veatch has recently suggested that the family should also be allowed to substitute its judgment, based on its values and beliefs, provided that such substituted judgment is reasonable (13). That is, the family's decision should not require the physician to act in a way fundamentally at odds with reasonable applications of the principle of beneficence in defining the patient's best interests.

It is important to note that substituted judgment should parallel the informed consent process. A reasonable person standard should govern disclosure. The person performing the substituted judgment needs to address the following items. First, is there some good to be gained for the patient? Second, at what price in disease, injury, handicap, pain and suffering to the patient is that good going to be achieved? Third, what is a reasonable balancing between benefits and risks? Fourth, what is the rationale, the reasons that the person making the substituted judgment has for the balancing that is made? That is, substituted judgment should not be intuitive, a "gut" reaction. Instead, reasons should be given that others, including the physician, can test for reasonableness. In this way, substituted judgment approximates a more objective standard of decision making than is possible with "seat of the pants" decisions. The principle of beneficence will guide substituted judgment, but allows for variability in reasoned applications to a clinical situation. Thus, substituted judgment allows for reasonable disagreement between the person performing such judgment and the patient's physician.

PREVENTIVE ETHICS

It should be apparent that the least attractive of the above three clinical strategies for dealing with informed consent is substituted judgment, because it holds the greatest potential for decision making that does not respect the patient's past autonomy and for increasing stress and anxiety for all who are involved in the care of elderly patients for whom substituted judgment is being attempted. Because they are based on respect for the elderly person's autonomy and thus reduce stress and anxiety regarding the preferences of the elderly patient, the strategies of identifying a previously made specific decision or constructing a decision based on the patient's values and beliefs are to be preferred.

To increase the likelihood that these two strategies can be employed and reduce the need for substituted judgment, informed consent should be practiced in a preventive mode in the form of the development and recording in the chart of the elderly patient's value history. It is the ethical obligation of the elderly patient's primary physician to obtain the value history and to ensure that it is available when constructed decisions are necessary. A key part of this process will be periodic discussions, with the consent of the elderly patient, of the contents of the value history with the elderly patient's family members. In this way, they can be confident that the constructed decision is faithful to the patient's values and beliefs.

Thus informed consent has both an acute care mode and a preventive care mode. The latter is infrequently acknowledged and is thus underutilized. Instead, informed consent tends to be seen as just one more legal and bureaucratic burden. As Faden and Beauchamp have shown, however, fulfilling bureaucratic rules is not genuine informed consent (6). Rather, informed consent is an ongoing clinical practice in which respect for autonomy becomes a living ethical principle that can serve as a guide for the many decisions that must be made in caring for the elderly patient. The most ethically conflictual of these concern termination of treatment, termination of food and water, and long-term care, which are addressed in the chapters that follow.

IMPLEMENTING THE INFORMED CONSENT PROCESS

The informed consent process can be effectively implemented by completing the following steps.

1. The physician should prepare by reviewing the patient's history, present condition, alternatives available, their prognoses, and the patient's values and beliefs.
2. Describe to the patient his or her condition, alternatives available, and their prognoses.
3. Assist the patient to identify relevant values and beliefs, beginning with a discussion of the patient's values and beliefs regarding the prevention, cure, and amelioration of disease, injury, handicap, pain and suffering, and regarding the prevention of premature death. Specifics of the alternatives should then be discussed.
4. The patient should be assisted in assessing the alternatives in terms of his or her values and beliefs.
5. The patient should be encouraged to express a value-based preference among the available alternatives, including nontreatment.
6. The physician should make his or her own recommendation.
7. The physician and the patient should discuss differences, if they occur, between the patient's preference and the physician's recommendation. The discussion should focus on the values and beliefs that lead to these, with a view toward negotiation.
8. A shared decision is achieved. If not, the patient's preference should serve as the guide for managing the patient's condition. The physician should be open to changes in the patient's thinking as management proceeds.

REFERENCES

1. Beauchamp TL, McCullough LB: *Medical Ethics: The Moral Responsibilities of Physicians.* Englewood Cliffs, NJ, Prentice-Hall, 1984.
2. Blass JP: Pragmatic pointers on managing the demented patient. *J Am Geriatr Soc* 34:548, 1986.
3. Butler RN: *Why Survive? Being Old in America.* New York, Harper and Row, 1975.
4. Cassell CK: Ethical issues in mental health care of the elderly. In Abrahams JP, Crooks V (Eds): *Geriatric Mental Health.* New York, Grune & Stratton, 1984, pp. 229–241.
5. Cassell CK, Jameton AL: Dementia in the elderly: an analysis of medical responsibility. *Ann Intern Med* 94:802, 1981.
6. Faden RR, Beauchamp TL: *A History and Theory of Informed Consent.* New York, Oxford University Press, 1986.

7. Haug M: Doctor–patient relationships and the older patient. *J Gerontol* 34:852, 1979.

8. Lidz CW, Meisel A, Osterweis M, et al: Barriers to informed consent. *Ann Intern Med* 99:539, 1983.

9. McCullough LB: Medical care for elderly patients with diminished competence: an ethical analysis. *J Am Geriatr Soc* 32:150, 1984.

10. President's Commission for the Study of Ethical Problems in Medicine and Biomedical and Behavioral Research: *Making Health Care Decisions.* Washington, DC, U.S. Government Printing Office, 1982.

11. Rowe JW: Health care of the elderly. *N Engl J Med* 312:827, 1985.

12. *Schloendorff v. Society of New York Hospitals,* 211 N.Y. 125, p. 127; 105 N.E. 92 (1914).

13. Veatch RM: *A Theory of Medical Ethics.* New York Basic Books, 1981.

CHAPTER 53

Termination of Treatment[1]

LAURENCE B. McCULLOUGH
STEVEN LIPSON

The majority of deaths among the elderly in our country now take place in institutional settings, principally the hospital, but also the nursing home and hospice. As a consequence, life-prolonging interventions are readily available in the medical care of most seriously ill elderly, directly in the hospital and by means of transfer from the nursing home to the hospital. The hospice has been established as an institutional setting from which most life-prolonging medical interventions have been barred. Thus, the main focus in the present chapter is on hospitalized and nursing home patients.

An additional consequence of this important change in how the elderly die is that health care professionals, including the physician, are directly involved in decisions about the use of life-prolonging interventions. Family members, hospitals, nursing homes, and hospices are involved as well. As one might expect, not all of the parties who are intimately involved in the care of seriously ill elderly patients share a common view about what medical interventions will protect and promote the best interests of the patient. As one might also expect, the parties other than the patient may give considerable weight to their own interests in decisions about the use of life-prolonging medical interventions. In short, the care of seriously ill and dying elderly patients is rife with the potential for ethical conflict. This conflict has entered the public arena, in a plethora of court cases involving the seriously ill and dying elderly and in the form of statutes regarding advance directives such as living wills. Cassell et al. and McCarrick provide excellent reviews of these

legal developments (1, 7). There has also been a Presidential commission (11) and the creation of similar commissions by a number of the states, including New Jersey and New York (7). Professional groups, including the American Medical Association, have also addressed the topic (7).

This chapter addresses ethical issues in the termination of such treatment. Legal and public policy developments are addressed only insofar as they create ethical issues for the physician. Readers are urged to keep informed about legal and public policy developments in their state, as well as at the federal level, and to be alert to the ethical issues that they are attempting to resolve as well as the ethical issues they raise. Because so much ethical controversy surrounds the termination of food and water, the ethical issues involved in such decisions are addressed separately, in Chapter 54.

In addressing ethical issues in the termination of treatment we first identify the basic ethical issue involved in such decisions. We then argue for the primacy of the ethical principle of respect for autonomy and for autonomy-based rights of the elderly to decide their own fate through the process of informed consent. Because there are cases where this clinical ethical strategy does not apply, the range of cases in which the principle of beneficence properly guides clinical judgment and decision making are addressed. The chapter closes with a consideration of ethical obligations that are owed to the dying elderly patient and to his or her family—a set of issues that has been neglected in much of the ethics literature and totally overlooked by the law.

In addition to autonomy-based and beneficence-based considerations, justice-based considerations can be expected to become increasingly important, especially if the allocation of scarce medical resources is invoked as a reason to terminate treat-

[1]Research for this chapter was supported by the Retirement Research Foundation, the Atlantic Richfield Foundation, an anonymous Dutch foundation, and the Bureau of Health Professions, U.S. Public Health Service.

ment of the seriously ill elderly patient. We share the view of others that, for the present at least, the physician's primary ethical obligations are owed to the patient (5, 9, 12, 13). Thus, the patient's best interests—determined by the patient or by the physician, as described in what follows—should be the basis for such obligations. It would be reasonable to change this view if and only if our democratic processes produced a public policy that made it plain to all that resource allocation should take primacy over the physician's ethical obligation to protect and promote the best interests of the patient, a remote prospect in our view.

BASIC ETHICAL ISSUE

The basic ethical issue raised by the medical care of the seriously ill or dying elderly patient is the proper limit that should be placed on the beneficence-based and autonomy-based ethical obligations of the physician to employ or authorize life-prolonging medical and other interventions, including both diagnostic and therapeutic procedures.

In terms of the principle of beneficence, there are two directly related ethical issues that must be addressed: (a) whether less weight than is usually the case should be assigned to the good of preventing the death of the elderly patient, and (b) whether greater weight than is usually the case should be assigned to the goods of preventing and ameliorating disease, injury, handicap, and unnecessary pain and suffering, especially those that are iatrogenic in origin. As the weight assigned to the former decreases and the weight assigned to the latter increases, the ethical obligation to intervene with life-prolonging measures diminishes. This applies to decisions about whether to discontinue such measures, as well as to decisions to withhold such measures, because the justification for *starting* such measures may no longer justify *continuing* as the relative weight of the above two sets of factors changes over the course of time.

In terms of the principle of respect for autonomy, the ethical issue to be addressed concerns informed consent: implementing the autonomous decisions of the elderly patient, either as directly expressed by the patient or as they can be reliably constructed on the basis of a value history.

Substituted judgment by the family appeals for its justification to respect for the reasonable and reasoned decisions by the family or others with such responsibility, tempered by beneficence-based considerations that set the boundaries on reasonable substituted judgment, as described in Chapter 52.

PRIMACY OF RESPECT FOR AUTONOMY

In the law and in much of the bioethics literature, decisions about termination of treatment have been addressed in terms of the patient's right to noninterference in decisions about medical care, including life-prolonging medical care (2, 6, 10). The dominant concept has been the legal principle of self-determination, which generates a right to refuse such medical care. We wish to go beyond this analysis, to address the more substantive ethical issues that are involved, with a view toward distancing ethics from legal considerations. As we shall see shortly, there are ethical traps awaiting the physician who approaches decisions about termination of treatment solely in the terms of the law.

Decisions about how aggressively to treat the seriously ill elderly patient, especially decisions about whether to terminate life-prolonging treatment, call the physician's attention to values and beliefs that are central in the life of any elderly person. These include whether and to what extent one will resist death, how one will die, how one will be remembered by survivors, and individual interpretations of religious traditions. Such values are at the core of the values by which the elderly patient has lived and given meaning to his or her life. Indeed, it is difficult to imagine more basic values in an individual's life. Neither medicine nor the individual physician possesses sufficient wisdom to know what such values should be or how they should be weighted for an individual whose life has spanned seven decades or more. For these reasons, the ethical principle of respect for autonomy should be given primacy in clinical judgment and decision making regarding termination of treatment.

INFORMED CONSENT AND ADVANCE DIRECTIVES

This principle is implemented by fulfilling the three requirements for informed consent, which are described in Chapter 52. The goals of this process should be the expression of the patient's autonomy in a value-based preference regarding the termination of treatment and the implementation of that preference by the physician (Table 53.1).

Perhaps the worst time in the course of the history of serious or life-threatening illness to fulfill these requirements is in the midst of crisis, especially that of the intensive care unit. It is far better that decisions about termination of treatment be anticipated in advance of crisis. This is the purpose of so-called "advance directives" (4). The reader should familiarize him- or herself with his or her state's law—both common and statutory—regarding the use of such advance directives. The two main legal forms of advance directives are the "living will" and the "durable power of attorney." Each raises ethical issues that require the serious attention of the physician.

LIVING WILL

The living will legally permits the patient to project his or her autonomy into the future, exercising the prerogatives of informed consent, to refuse life-prolonging medical interventions in advance. These instruments were pioneered by the California legislature after the Karen Quinlan case and have been adopted by many states (7). They are, however, limited in at least three important ways. First, the living will is not valid unless the patient is suffering from a terminal disease, with "terminal" sometimes left undefined in authorizing legislation. Yet, there are many life-threatening conditions of the elderly that are not, strictly speaking, terminal, for example, pneumonia. The living will does not apply to such individuals. Second, many of the states prescribe the wording of the living will. It is the physician's ethical obligation to determine if this is the case and to ensure that the patient's living will conforms to the legally prescribed wording, as well as the signature of witnesses. Third, and ethically most worrisome, the living will legislation typically applies only to (a) the termination of "mechanical and other artificial means" that (b) are being used to combat the terminal pathology. The phrase "other artificial means" is often left undefined. This is bad enough, but it seems to be the legislative intent in many states that the living will does not legally authorize the termination of life-prolonging interventions for nonterminal conditions. Thus, if the patient is suffering a life-threatening, but treatable, potentially reversible condition secondary to the terminal pathology, the living will does not legally authorize the withholding of such treatment, for example, antibiotics for pneumonia secondary to terminal cancer. A clinical judgment based in beneficence that death by pneumonia may be less painful than death by cancer may not be a legally mitigating factor. Nor is an express value-based preference that such treatment be withheld or discontinued, unless a durable power of attorney has been executed. Finally, living wills usually do not cover the right to refuse in advance the provision of nutrition and hydration. However, a small number of state courts struck down this restriction on the patient's exercise of the legal right to refuse treatment (7).

In short, the living will is a useful and powerful means for the patient to project his or her autonomy into the future, to authorize the termination of treatment, but only some kinds of treatment and perhaps only treatment for terminal pathologies. The ethical obligation of the physician, as part of the informed consent process relating to the execution of living wills, is to inform the patient about these limitations. This is yet another example where the law is out of step with reasonable ethical analysis and clinical judgment based on such analysis.

DURABLE POWER OF ATTORNEY

There is a legally available alternative in all states to the living will, the durable power of attorney. This procedure allows any legally competent adult to execute instructions in advance of situations wherein he or she will have become incompetent. These instructions typically take the form of authorizing another individual to make treatment decisions when the author of the durable power of attorney is no longer legally competent or able to make his or her own decisions. These instructions are not limited as to type, for example, "mechanical and other artificial means," or situation, that is, they apparently apply to nonterminal situations as well. Thus, they overcome the most important shortcomings of the living will. Again, the physician bears the ethical obligation to learn about whether durable power of attorney is a legally available option in his or her state for advance directives regarding termination of treatment. Peculiar limitations that may have been imposed by statute or court ruling should be disclosed to the patient as part of the informed consent process, so that the patient understands the legal applicability of the durable power of attorney.

ETHICAL PITFALLS REGARDING DURABLE POWER OF ATTORNEY

There is no doubt that decisions regarding the termination of life-prolonging medical interventions are among the most stressful encountered by physicians caring for elderly patients. Indeed, as courts and legislatures become more involved in such decisions, the level of stress seems only to increase, not decrease. However, this may not be an appropriate reaction to durable power of attorney, because of the many advantages that this legal advance directive offers over living wills. Indeed, one result of the widespread use of durable power of attorney is that it may reduce the number of cases going to court and thus reduce stress on the part of the physician who worries about being hauled into court.

Despite its many advantages, there are two ethical pitfalls regarding durable power of attorney that are worth noting. In the previous chapters, a case has been made for the importance of the value history in the care of elderly patients. Obtaining such a history over time permits the physician and the elderly patient to arrive at shared decisions about the management of the patient's care when the patient is no longer able to participate autonomously in shared decision making. Developing the value history requires that the physician and the elderly patient engage in sustained conversation over time to carefully explore the patient's value-based preferences. The goal should be to develop specific decisions in advance or at least to have sufficient information to construct reliable decisions on the basis of a detailed value history.

The ethical pitfall of the durable power of attorney is that it may be thought of and utilized in simply legal terms, as the means to provide authority to someone else to whom the physician can talk about termination of treatment when the patient becomes legally incompetent. Our concern is that solving the legal worries of the physician and the patient may undercut the need for the sustained dialogue with the patient required to develop a value history. After all, it is just such a value history that should be the basis for decision making by the person bearing the elderly patient's durable power of attorney. For this person to be as uncertain as the physician or the patient's family about what the patient really would want only worsens matters. Thus, the legal instrument of durable power of attorney should not be taken as a substitute for the value history. Indeed, ethically speaking, the execution of such an advance directive by the elderly patient makes the development of a value history essential for the faithful execution of the power of attorney by whomever bears it.

The second pitfall concerns the impetus given to the physician's self-interest by legal solutions to ethically and legally stressful situations. The temptation of many physicians will be to view the durable power of attorney or the living will as a means to reduce liability for malpractice actions, for example, for wrongful death. Acting on this temptation is understandable in the face of a perceived malpractice "crisis" in this country. However, acting on this temptation places the self-interests of the physician ahead of the best interests of the patient. This totally undermines the ethical foundations of the physician–patient relationship.

Both of these pitfalls underscore the importance of recognition by the physician that law and ethics are not equivalent, as pointed out in Chapter 51. Moreover, legally attractive solutions to difficult issues such as the termination of treatment create ethical issues that are not even addressed by the law.

PATIENTS WITH NEITHER LEGAL INSTRUMENTS NOR A VALUE HISTORY

It sometimes happens that the physician confronts nontreatment decisions regarding the irreversibly nonautonomous or irreversibly incompetent elderly patient who has not executed any legal advance directive(s) and who is also in a situation where his or her value history cannot be determined. The latter can occur when the patient has no primary physician and is a stranger to the physicians charged with his or her care. This can also occur when neither family nor other individuals knew the patient well enough to provide the value history and when there is no family or other such individuals available or known to the patient's physician. In these cases, the main guide to decisions about termination of treatment is necessarily the ethical principle of beneficence, in some cases tempered by the family's autonomy.

We propose the relevance of a four-part classification of such patients. This classification marks out sectors along a continuum of prognoses from irreversibly dying to positive prognosis.

PATIENTS WHO ARE IRREVERSIBLY DYING

At one end of this continuum of cases are found those elderly patients who are irreversibly dying and whose death is imminent. The clinical reality in such cases is that there is no known medical intervention by which the patient's death can be prevented. No ethical theory obligates anyone to attempt the impossible. Thus, in these cases it is ethically permissible to terminate life-prolonging treatment. In such cases, the physician is correct to recommend such termination of treatment to the patient's family. In those rare cases in which continuing life-prolonging treatment results in positive, serious harm to the patient in terms of iatrogenic disease, injury, or handicap or in unnecessary pain and suffering, then there is a positive ethical obligation, not simply a permission, to terminate such treatment. In these cases the physician correctly advocates the termination of life-prolonging treatment to the patient's family.

SERIOUSLY ILL PATIENTS WHO ARE EXPECTED TO BECOME IRREVERSIBLY DYING

The next sector along this continuum is marked by patients who are not irreversibly dying but whose condition is so serious that they are reliably expected to soon enter the clinical–ethical class of cases just described. In these situations, life-prolonging treatment was at first reasonably administered in the hope that the patient would recover. Thus, consideration of termination of treatment well into a patient's course does not imply that the original decision to intervene with life-prolonging measures was a mistake. Thus, it is inconsistent in such cases to claim that one should never have initiated such treatment if one was only going to consider its termination later.

The main ethical point here is that, as the clinical picture changes, the ethical picture changes because beneficence-based determinations of the patient's interest in continuing life change. The physician's task is to assess whether the cost of a higher degree of medical certainty about a probably eventually grim prognosis is worth the accumulating iatrogenic disease, injury, handicap, and unnecessary pain and suffering. As pointed out in Chapter 51, following the logic of the principle of beneficence, as the ability to prevent premature death decreases, these other beneficence-based considerations should move to the fore in the physician's clinical judgment.

The physician necessarily confronts quality-of-life judgments in such cases. The goods and harms of the principle of beneficence should govern such assessments, and these assessments should be made on as objective a basis as possible. Intuition and instinct in such cases are not an adequate substitute for a thorough review of the literature and reasonable consultation with colleagues. An ethics committee or a patient care review committee can be a very useful forum for developing clinically based, empirically sound and well-reasoned quality-of-life judgments. The family's judgments in such matters should also be taken into account by the physician. The physician should share with the family his or her objective basis for the assessment of the patient's expected quality of life and why that quality of life may no longer be in the patient's best interests.

SERIOUSLY ILL PATIENTS WHO ARE EXPECTED TO IMPROVE

The next sector along the continuum of patients with neither legal instruments nor a value history is marked by those patients for whom life-prolonging treatment is being continued in the expectation that they will improve and most likely eventually recover to some reasonable level of quality of life. Again, quality of life assessments should be made on a rigorous, clinically sound basis, as described just above. In these cases, because continuing life-prolonging treatment is in the patient's best interest on the basis of beneficence, the physician should recommend continuation of treatment. The physician should resist requests by the family for termination of treatment. Because families often make such requests out of confusion or even despair, the physician should carefully and compassionately explain his or her reasoning to the family.

PATIENTS WHO ARE EXPECTED TO RECOVER

The final sector of the continuum is marked by those patients who are reasonably expected to recover. Here the beneficence-based calculus is straightforward: Life-prolonging treatment should be continued, because it is reasonably and compellingly in the patient's best interests to do so. In these cases, the physician has an ethical obligation to continue treatment and to recommend its continuation of the family. Family refusal of treatment in such cases should be resisted vigorously, including seeking court-ordered treatment if necessary.

OBLIGATIONS TO DYING PATIENTS AND THEIR FAMILIES

The impression left by the legal and ethical literature on the subject of death and dying is that once decisions about termination of treatment have been made, the matter ends. We believe strongly that this is an error, because it blinds the physician to important ethical issues that remain. These include (a) considerations about what medical interventions are to be terminated; (b) considerations about how the patient will die; (c) special virtues in the care of the dying elderly patient, especially with respect to language use; and (d) obligations to the family of the dying patient.

WHAT INTERVENTIONS ARE TO BE TERMINATED

Decisions about termination of treatment tend to focus on "Do Not Resuscitate" orders (10, 11). However, the logic of the ethics of informed consent is that the patient has the right to refuse any and all life-prolonging medical interventions, including both diagnostic and therapeutic interventions, as

Table 53.1
Advance Directives and Substituted Judgment

Advance directives: Expression in advance of the patient's autonomy in a value-based preference regarding the termination of treatment or the termination of food and water. This is an autonomy-based method of decision making.

Living wills are express written or (where legally permitted) oral instructions about treatment that is to be withheld when the patient is terminally ill and no longer autonomous.

Durable power of attorney allows any competent patient to authorize another person to make decisions regarding the termination of treatment or termination of food and water when the patient is no longer competent to do so. Ideally, the person assigned durable power of attorney should be acting as an advocate for the value-based preferences of the patient.

Substituted judgment is required when the value-based preferences of the previous competent, but now incompetent, patient are not known.

In these cases the principle of beneficence serves as the main basis for determining what course of care is in the best interests of the patient.

Decisions by surrogates in these cases should parallel the informed consent process.

Surrogate, beneficence-based decisions should be reasonable.

---

well as food and water. The logic of the ethical principle of beneficence is that for the first two classifications of patients—those who are irreversibly dying and those who are expected to become irreversibly dying—only those interventions that reduce unnecessary pain and suffering should be continued. The special ethical considerations surrounding food and water are addressed in Chapter 54. It is pointed out here that on the basis of either informed consent or the principle of beneficence, it is permissible and even obligatory to terminate all life-prolonging treatment, including treatment for secondary, reversible conditions. The ethical obligation to do so is even stronger when the patient has made an explicit decision about the intervention, for example, the use of antibiotics or hemodialysis, as part of the value history or in an advance directive. Unneeded diagnostic measures should also be terminated, for example, obtaining arterial blood gases.

HOW THE PATIENT WILL DIE

In short, after an ethically sound decision about termination of treatment has been reached, the physician confronts ethical issues about how the patient will die. Ideally, these should be taken up with the patient in advance, so that informed consent can guide the physician and the patient's family. In addressing these issues, it is important to remember that only some interventions are to be terminated, not all. That is, the obligation to care for the dying patient remains, even while some forms of medical intervention are to be terminated.

A central ethical consideration here is the effective management of the patient's pain and suffering. Palliation may, for example, require the use of addictive analgesic medications. The normal objection to using such drugs over a period of time, namely, avoiding the handicap of addiction, becomes moot in cases where life-prolonging treatment is being terminated. Palliation may also require medication that obtunds consciousness. This should be discussed with the patient in advance. Otherwise, beneficence-based judgments should guide the physician's clinical judgment. Sometimes palliation involves the use of medications that themselves can be marginally life threatening, for example, by suppressing respiratory function as a side-effect of pain relief. If the patient has consented to such medication in advance, there is an ethical obligation to use it if no other reasonable alternative will produce the same analgesic effect. Beneficence-based judgments would also be consistent with the use of such medications, because at worst they hasten but do not directly cause the patient's death, which is imminent or is expected to become so. This sort of reasoning should be explained to the patient's family, to obviate guilt.

VIRTUES AND THE USE OF LANGUAGE

Chapter 51 describes the number of special virtues that should characterize the physician who cares for elderly patients. Taken together, these virtues create an obligation not to abandon the elderly patient—either out of a sense of failure or fear of mortality. This has important implications for the language that should be used to discuss termination of treatment, with the patient in advance and also with the patient's family. Phrases such as "There is nothing more that we can do" or "We are considering stopping all measures" can send the signal that *all* forms of caring will stop, which should never be the case. The dying elderly patient remains a member of the moral community notwithstanding the fact that he or she is dying. Physicians, like the rest of us, are not ethically free to abandon the dying. Their care should not be left to nurses or house staff. Thus, the physician should visit the dying patient regularly and monitor the care that is to continue until the patient's death. As pointed out in Chapter 51, the physician should "remain in charge."

OBLIGATIONS TO THE FAMILY OF THE DYING PATIENT

Family members and other survivors who have been important to the dying elderly patient have an inescapable ethical claim on the physician: to know that they authorized all that should have been done and that the patient will not be abandoned as he or she dies (3). This does not mean that families have the prerogative to insist that life-prolonging treatment continue irrationally beyond the bounds of informed consent by the patient or beneficence-based judgments in the absence of consent. Rather, family members have an ethical claim on the physician to be able to live out their own lives with confidence that they were a good spouse, child, sibling, or friend. To fulfill the ethical obligation generated by this claim the physician should take pains to explain the basis of decisions to terminate treatment and to explain what will continue to be done for the patient. In addition, the physician should make him- or herself available to the family, because the physician's presence—especially in the room of those who die in institutional settings—has the powerful symbolic significance to many families that their loved one is not being abandoned.

OBLIGATIONS TO THE CARE TEAM

Whenever a physician reaches a justifiable decision to allow a patient to die, the reasoning behind that decision should be thoroughly explained to the other health care professionals who will be caring for the patient. Their views should be elicited and compassionately discussed. In our experience, this is most effectively accomplished in a group meeting, in which individuals can express their views and arrive at an appreciation for those of others. The goal of such a meeting should be acceptance by all concerned of the decision to allow the patient to die.

INSTITUTIONAL SETTINGS

The management of ethical issues regarding termination of treatment inevitably involves institutional settings. The hospice is perhaps the most hospitable institution in these matters, for it has been established principally to avoid some of the problems that arise in hospitals. In hospitals the main problem is fragmentation of responsibility for the care of the dying patient. It is the ethical responsibility of the elderly dying patient's primary physician to be an advocate for the patient's autonomous decisions. A major role of the physician in this respect is to ensure the "portability" of the value history. If the primary physician does not have direct responsibility for the patient's care, he or she is ethically obligated to transmit the value history to the physician who is in charge, for example, the intensive care unit physician (8).

If there is no primary physician for the patient, the physician in charge of the hospital unit or department is ethically responsible for seeing to it that an individual physician is placed in charge of the patient's care. The physician in either case is responsible for assuring that the patient's chart states clearly and unequivocally what is and is not to be done for the patient. This information should be placed at the beginning of the patient's chart, so that it is readily accessible.

In the nursing home setting, it is important that the staff understand that the rescue squad is not to be summoned. The patient's primary physician should see to it that the emergency room is avoided, because he or she will then lose control of the plan that has been agreed on with the patient or the substitute decision maker. Again, discussion with staff should take place, so that they understand the rationale of the decision. The patient's chart should contain notice that the rescue squad is not to be summoned.

REFERENCES

1. Cassell CK, Meier DE, Traines ML: Selected bibliography of recent articles in ethics and geriatrics. *J Am Geriatr Soc* 34:399, 1986.
2. Hammerman D, Dubler NN, Kennedy GJ, et al: Decision making in response to an elderly woman with dementia who refused surgical repair of her fractured hip. *J Am Geriatr Soc* 34:234, 1986.
3. Hauerwas S: *Truthfulness and Tragedy.* Notre Dame, IN, University of Notre Dame Press, 1981.
4. Lazaroff AE, Orr WF: Living wills and other advance directives. *Clin Geriatr Med* 2:521, 1986.

5. Levinsky NG: Fighting for life. *J Am Geriatr Soc* 34:666, 1986.
6. Marsh FH: Refusal of treatment. *Clin Geriatr Med* 2:511, 1986.
7. McCarrick PM: *Withholding or Withdrawing Nutrition and Hydration.* Washington, DC, National Reference Center for Bioethics Literature, Kennedy Institute of Ethics, Georgetown University, 1986.
8. Miles SH: Advance directives to limit treatment: the need for portability. *J Am Geriatr Soc* 35:74, 1987.
9. Pellegrino ED: The autonomy of clinical ethical judgements. In Engelhardt HT, Spiker SF, Towers B (Eds): *Clinical Judgement: A Critical Appraisal.* Dordrecht,
Holland, D. Reidel Publishing, 1979, pp. 169–194.
10. Petty TL: Resuscitation decisions. *Clin Geriatr Med* 2:535, 1986.
11. President's Commission for the Study of Ethical Problems in Medicine and Biomedical and Behavioral Research: *Decision to Forego Life-Sustaining Treatment.* Washington, DC, U.S. Government Printing Office, 1983.
12. Siegler M: Decision-making strategy for clinical ethical problems in medicine. *Arch Intern Med* 142:2178, 1982.
13. Yarborough MA, Kramer AM: The physician and resource allocation. *Clin Geriatr Med* 2:465, 1986.

CHAPTER 54

Termination of Food and Water[1]

LAURENCE B. McCULLOUGH
STEVEN LIPSON

Chapter 53 noted that the great majority of deaths among the elderly in the United States occur in institutional settings. It addressed the termination of treatment, excluding termination of food and water, with primary reference to the institutional setting of the hospital. The ethical issues addressed in this chapter occur in the nursing home and hospice, as well as in the hospital. The termination of food and water are addressed separately, in part because of the increasing legal attention to the subject and in part because of the special nature of the ethical issues that the physician confronts when the termination of food and water is seriously considered. Cassell et al. and McCarrick provide very useful reviews of the legal and ethical literature on this complicated subject (1, 3).

The first step in the ethical analysis offered in this chapter is the clarification of key terms and concepts. The second step is an analysis of the basic ethical issue involved in the termination of food and water. Following this are a consideration of the ethical issues that arise if food and water are regarded as forms of the medical treatment and a consideration of the ethical issues if food and water are considered as forms of medical or human (personal) care. The chapter closes with ethical obligations to patients for whom the provision of food and water has been justifiably terminated.

[1]Research for this chapter was supported by the Retirement Research Foundation, the Atlantic Richfield Foundation, an anonymous Dutch foundation, and the Bureau of Health Professions, U.S. Public Health Service.

KEY TERMS AND CONCEPTS

Obviously, the key terms and concepts in any ethical analysis of the termination of food and water are "food" and "water" and, as a consequence, the "provision" of food and water.

"Water" is the easiest of these three to clarify: it is the chemical substance whose formula is H_2O, but with a saline content compatible with the needs of our species. Its provision occurs by means of drinking, by means of a nasogastric tube, or by means of an intravenous line. Drinking water poses no special burdens, unless the patient has difficulty swallowing or there is some obstruction of the gastrointestinal tract. In these circumstances, the other two means of provision of water are considered. Both of these means of providing water involve varying levels of risks of morbidity, injury, pain, suffering, and (remotely) mortality. The fact that the skills involved in the provision of water by these two means are not great does not diminish or remove the fact that they can and do involve risks to the patient, risks that increase with the frailty of the patient, the severity of his or her condition, the impact of possibly excessive hydration on the patient's condition, and the length of time the method is employed. Thus, "provision" in the case of water involves special, though not high-level, clinical skills and a burden of risk as the price for benefits of maintaining desired levels of hydration. These risks can include restraining the patient in a way that assaults the patient's dignity and the memories of survivors. They can also include transfer from the nursing home to the hospital, with all the risks attendant upon such a change in care setting.

"Food" is more difficult to define, because its nature changes as the means of provision changes. "Food" connotes what we usually eat and where we eat it. Thus, its provision involves not only nutrition but communal rituals that have great significance in our lives, for example, sharing a meal with family, friends, or colleagues. Strictly speaking, this double meaning of food is restricted to taking food by mouth. "Food" is transformed into "foodstuffs" or "nutritional substances" or "nutrition" when its provision is by means of a nasogastric tube, gastrostomy tube, or by total parenteral nutrition. With these means of provision "food" no longer has the connotation of something that binds us together in communal rituals; it is simply the provision of substances that the patient needs. These three forms of provision of nutrition also involve varying levels of risk of morbidity, injury, pain, suffering, and (less remotely) mortality as the price for the benefit of meeting a patient's nutritional needs. Their provision also involves increasingly more complex and higher level clinical skills and more attentive monitoring than in the case of intravenous provision of water. Again the risks of such interventions as restraint or institutionalization must also be considered and evaluated. In addition, some forms of administering nutrition, for example, the nasogastric tube, involve the loss of the sensory aspects of eating, thus diminishing the sense in which they constitute "feeding."

BASIC ETHICAL ISSUE

The ethical issue that the physician, the elderly patient, the patient's family, and the institution in which the patient is located confront in the termination of food and water is whether such termination can be justified, especially in cases where pathologic processes resulting from such termination may contribute to the cause of the elderly patient's death. The basic issue underlying this ethical issue is whether the provision of food and water is a form of medical treatment or a form of medical or human care. Some courts in recent cases have taken the view that the provision of food and water is a form of medical treatment (3). This view has been called into question by those who view this provision as a form of care (2).

Whether the provision of food and water is a form of treatment or a form of care is impossible to answer, if one does not attend to the variation of meaning of the key terms that have been described in the previous section. Surely, the provision of food that can be successfully eaten by mouth and the provision of water that can successfully be drunk are not medical treatment, but a form of caring for someone. This provision fosters important moral bonds among human beings and requires no special skill. By the same token, however, the provision of total parenteral nutrition by means of a central line is a form of medical treatment, just as is the provision of air by means of mechanical ventilation.

The problem, of course, lies with the center of the continuum, especially nasogastric tube feeding and, to a lesser extent, feeding with a gastrostomy tube. The former may be a form of care; it may also be medical treatment. The latter may be medical treatment, but can also be thought of as a form of care.

This last set of concerns constitutes a Gordian knot, and the best way to deal with such a knot is not by untying it but by simply cutting it. We do so by not trying to argue conclusively one way or another, because we believe that no conclusive argument is or will be available. Instead, the ethical issues of regarding the provision of food and water as medical treatment shall be explored, followed by exploration of the ethical issues of regarding that provision as a form of medical care. On either account, there are ethically sound justifications for the termination of food and water.

FOOD AND WATER AS MEDICAL TREATMENT

The ethical issues involved in terminating food and water, when the provision of the latter is regarded as medical treatment, are the same as those addressed in Chapter 53, Termination of Treatment. The primacy of the ethical principle of respect for autonomy in the termination of treatment here means that the autonomous elderly patient has the ethical right to refuse the provision of food and water, either at the moment that provision is required or in advance, provided that the three requirements of informed consent are satisfied. This ethical right extends to the provision of food and water by mouth, as well as all other means. That an elderly patient refuses that provision of food and water, in whatever form, should not be taken as conclusive clinical evidence that the patient is not autonomous. To do so would be to erect a false barrier to informed consent and act contrary to the special virtue of accepting the mortality of the patient and divergence between the patient's values and beliefs about his or her best interests and the physician's perspective on those interests which is shaped by the principle of beneficence. Obviously, the patient's values and value-based preferences in these matters should be elicited and included in the value history. It is important to note that in most states with living wills, the living will does not cover the termination of food and water, although this restriction has been struck down by a number of state courts.

For patients without advance directives or a value history, the four-part classification of cases presented in Chapter 53 applies. These patients should be managed in terms of the principle of beneficence and respect for the family's autonomy, as explained in that chapter. The main item of concern is the careful balancing of the benefits and burdens of the provision of food and water and the need to recognize that there are circumstances when the burdens outweigh the benefits, for example, providing intravenous fluids to an irreversibly nonautonomous patient with serious problems of fluid retention.

In short, when the provision of food and water is regarded as a medical treatment, there are ethical justifications for the termination of that provision. This implies that both the withholding and withdrawal of that provision are justifiable. As pointed out in Chapter 53, it is a mistake to hold that treatment that is to be withheld should never have been initiated, because the patient's condition and prognosis can and do change over time. Palliation should be managed along the lines discussed in the previous chapter; that is, it should be administered when it protects the patient's prior or present expressions of autonomy or beneficence-based interest in avoiding unnecessary pain and suffering in cases of irreversibly nonautonomous patients.

FOOD AND WATER AS FORMS OF MEDICAL CARE

The provision of food and water can also be reasonably regarded as forms of care. By "care" it is meant those basic forms of regard that human beings show to each other in the course of their lives together. These forms of basic regard usually do not involve complex or high-level skills, but sometimes can. The provision of food and water takes on a powerful symbolic significance in medical practice, because of the association between "food" and "water," on the one hand, and the rituals that bond human beings together in communities and families. The provision of food and water, by whatever means, is thus seen as a powerful bond between the patient and the physician, as well as others who are caring for the seriously ill elderly patient. As a consequence, it seems ethically almost unnatural to terminate that provision, because that is seen as

terminating the moral bond with the patient, that is, as terminating the physician–patient or the nurse–patient relationship. This hesitancy about terminating food and water as forms of caring is reinforced by worries that such termination may be uncomfortable or stressful for the patient or the patient's family and by worries that such termination may contribute to the cause of the patient's death. People who care for another individual do not contribute to his or her death, so this line of reasoning concludes.

There is a flaw in this line of ethical reasoning, however, because it involves two questionable implicit assumptions. The first is that the termination of food and water as forms of caring means that caring per se is to be terminated. This assumption is questionable because, in our experience, the powerful symbolic significance of providing food and water tends to blind the physician and other members of the team to the fact that many other forms of care are being provided, including keeping the patient comfortable, warm, and clean; visiting the patient's room; and psychologically supporting the patient and the patient's family. The provision of these forms of care has great value to the patient, the patient's family, health care professionals, and institutions. That value is not dependent on the provision of food and water. Thus it is reasonable to regard the provision of food and water as *a* form of medical care and caring, not *the* form of medical care and caring.

The second implicit, questionable assumption in the above line of reasoning is that termination of forms of care is never justified. In other words, the provision of forms of care is always justified on the basis of the principle of beneficence and such justification properly and always overrides objections that might be based on the principle of respect for autonomy. In short, paternalism is being assumed in the above line of reasoning as always being justified when it comes to medical care. As pointed out in Chapter 51, however, paternalism requires justification; that justification cannot simply be assumed if one takes seriously a framework for geriatric ethics that includes both the principle of beneficence and the principle of respect for autonomy. Is the implicit paternalism of the view that medical care must always be provided justified?

It is not justified for two main reasons. First, it is simply not the case that all forms of medical care are always justified by the principle of beneficence. To say they are must assume, contrary to clinical facts and experience, that the provision of forms of care always results in a greater balance of good over harm for the patient. Yet, there are many clinical circumstances when the opposite is the case: The harms of iatrogenic disease, injury, handicap, unnecessary pain and suffering, and even death outweigh the benefits of meeting the patient's needs for adequate hydration and nutrition. Indeed, there are instances when termination of nutrition and hydration may improve the quality of the patient's care, for example, terminating hydration for a patient with end-stage renal failure who is not receiving dialysis.

As pointed out in Chapter 51, the justification of paternalism must appeal to beneficence-based judgments that the patient's best interests will be protected and promoted by the intervention in question. The provision of food and water as forms of medical care can sometimes fail this crucial test.

The second fault in the line of reasoning that forms of medical care can never be terminated is that no place at all is given to the ethical import of the principle of respect for autonomy. Ironically, in the name of caring for someone, no respect is shown for his or her dignity, values, and beliefs about the burdensome nature of providing food and water, values that may well be different from those of the caregiver. Almost all of the special virtues in caring for the elderly that are identified in Chapter 51 are undercut by this posture. McCormick has also shown that this sort of vitalism is inconsistent with the basic tenets of the Judeo-Christian tradition (4).

On the basis of these two objections, a line of argument can be developed that justifies the termination of food and water when they are regarded as forms of caring. In circumstances in which the burdens of such provision outweigh the benefits, their justification diminishes. In accordance with the arguments about the primacy of respect for autonomy presented in Chapter 53, we conclude that the patient's perspective on the weighing of such benefits and burdens should be the physician's primary guide. For patients who are irreversibly nonautonomous and who have no advance directives or value history, the beneficence-based approach described in the previous section should guide the physician.

INTERESTS OF INSTITUTIONS

In the present environment, in which cases involving the termination of food and water are receiving court review (3), institutions may be reluctant to permit the termination of food and water for any patient in the institution, including the hospital, nursing home, or hospice. The physician's ethical obligation to the patient in this respect is, first, to become familiar with the institution's policies and practices.

This information should then be conveyed to the patient in advance, because the patient may want to choose an institution on the basis of such policy, both because it may be against and because it may permit the termination of food and water. In cases where there is a conflict between the physician's ethical obligation to the patient and the institution's policy and when transfer is not available, the physician should act as the patient's advocate. Institutional timidity can often be successfully challenged and countered by ethical arguments that show that termination of food and water is consistent with sound medical ethical judgment about the best interests of the patient. Simply to acquiesce to institutional policy, especially when it has resulted from an ad hoc, unreflective process, will not well serve the seriously ill or dying elderly patient and thus can seriously impair the physician–patient relationship. Yet, again, this is an area where law and ethics diverge: An institution's self-interest in avoiding litigation is not self-justifying ethically.

OBLIGATIONS TO DYING PATIENTS AND THEIR FAMILIES

It is important to recall that when the provision of food and water is to be terminated on reliable ethical grounds, not all medical treatment and forms of caring are going to be terminated. Thus, it is important to assure the patient and the patient's family that the patient is not going to be abandoned. The physician must assure them that he or she will remain in charge and see to it that appropriate treatment and care continue right up to the patient's death.

Of special concern in the termination of food and water is palliative care for the patient. Here the ethical analysis in Chapter 53 applies and provides adequate guidance. The main ethical concerns are the best interests of the patient as well as the family's ethical claim on the physician to be able to remember their loved one well. These obligate the physician to be thorough in explanations given to the patient and the patient's family and in the support that is owed to them as the dying process completes its course. They also obligate the physician to be present to the dying elderly patient and to the family. This presence may, perhaps, be the most symbolically significant and powerful of all forms of medical care and caring.

OBLIGATIONS TO THE CARE TEAM

Because of the special ethical sensitivity and often strong emotional response that are part of decisions to terminate food and water, the physician should be especially diligent in fulfilling his or her ethical obligation to explain the decision and the ethical reasoning that supports it to all of the members of the health care team. There should be an opportunity to sit together as a group, to air everyone's views, and to discuss them respectfully and sympathetically. Those who have strong moral objections to the decision should be allowed to withdraw from the case, if they choose to do so. The physician should take the lead in ensuring that members of the team provide support for each other, so that they are in a better position to provide support for the dying patient and the patient's family and loved ones.

REFERENCES

1. Cassell CK, Meier DE, Traines ML: Selected bibliography of recent articles in ethics and geriatrics. *J Am Geriatr Soc* 34:399, 1986.
2. Lynn J (Ed): *By No Extraordinary Means*. Bloomington, IN, Indiana University Press, 1986.
3. McCarrick PM: *Withholding or Withdrawing Nutrition or Hydration*. Washington, DC, National Reference Center for Bioethics Literature, Kennedy Institute of Ethics, Georgetown University, 1986.
4. McCormick RM: To save or let die—the dilemma of modern medicine. *JAMA* 229:172, 1974.

CHAPTER 55

Truthtelling and Confidentiality[1]

DAVID DOUKAS
LAURENCE B. McCULLOUGH

Whereas Chapter 51 emphasizes decision making between the physician and the elderly patient and Chapter 52 provides an analysis of informed consent, this chapter analyzes the ethical dimensions of truthtelling and confidentiality, two of the most basic building blocks of the physician–patient relationship and of informed consent.

The ethical obligations of the physician regarding truthtelling and confidentiality are, for the most part, the same as those owed to other patients. However, special considerations arise for those elderly patients with progressively debilitating chronic conditions, for patients with various forms of cognitive impairment, and for patients with terminal processes. For both truthtelling and confidentiality, the analysis will proceed in terms of the ethical principles of beneficence and respect for autonomy, which are explained in chapter 51.

TRUTHTELLING

The focus of truthtelling in the clinical setting is on the two-way communication with the elderly patient about (a) his or her condition(s), (b) available medical interventions, (c) the risks of these interventions as well as the risks of nonintervention, (d) the meaning of loss for which the elderly are at risk (as described in Chapter 51), and (e) the possible impact of the patient's condition and care on the patient's family. Because the focus of truthtelling is on

two-way communication and discussion, it is important to distinguish truthtelling from informed consent, of which truthtelling is but a part, as described in Chapter 52.

GENERAL CONSIDERATIONS

The physician's ethical obligation to disclose and discuss information with a patient is based on both respect for the patient's autonomy and beneficence. Certainly, any meaningful exercise of autonomy by the patient regarding decisions about medical care requires that the patient be provided with an accurate and adequate informational base. An autonomy-based ethical analysis of truthtelling helps to explain why, when patients are treated by physicians, they rightly expect that matters pertinent to their care, as well as those options which may be entertained for their care, will be disclosed to and discussed with them.

There is also a beneficence-based justification for the ethical obligation of truthtelling. In addition to autonomy-based rights of the elderly to information, the physician should recognize the need of the patient to be provided information that will help to reduce anxiety and fear and that will therefore promote the mutual trust that is essential to an effective and lasting physician–patient relationship (4). This elemental trust allows both parties to openly discuss and actively plan for the future of the patient's condition and care.

The need for information and the opportunity to discuss its implications in a patient's life are especially important to recognize in the elderly patient, because, as described in Chapter 51, he or she expe-

[1]Research for this chapter was supported by the Retirement Research Foundation, the Atlantic Richfield Foundation, an anonymous Dutch foundation, and the Bureau of Health Professions, U.S. Public Health Service.

riences social and environmental loss, an increasing burden of chronic illness and disability, dependency, and the imminence of death. Thus, truthtelling is a strong antidote to ageist assumptions that the elderly cannot cope with such information and therefore should, on paternalistic grounds, be protected from it for their own good. The physician should especially recognize the need for the seriously ill elderly patient to confront the probability of and to eventually work through the psychologic process of dying. To prevent a patient from experiencing this process deprives him or her of the opportunity to reflect on his or her own death.

The primary opposing ethical consideration to truthtelling is beneficence based. The physician has an obligation to create or maintain the greatest amount of good, while avoiding harm, with the aim of producing a net health benefit for the patient. This obligation sometimes is consistent with incomplete disclosure, but never with false disclosure. The justification for this is based on the distinction between (a) truthfulness in the sense of total disclosure of all medical information relevant to the patient's care and (b) honesty in the sense of incomplete but true disclosure of medical information (11). False disclosure is never justified. It violates both beneficence, because it undermines trust, and respect for autonomy, because it undermines the patient's right to information relevant to his or her care. When a physician asserts a beneficence-based discretion to protect a patient through incomplete disclosure with no intention eventually to provide full disclosure on the grounds of preventing patient harm of "lost hope," that physician is violating the patient's autonomy. The patient thereby suffers a loss of dignity. Thus, incomplete disclosure can only be employed as a temporary clinical strategy.

FORMS OF DISCLOSURE

Disclosure has many forms (5, 14). The direct form of disclosure is the truthful release of information to the patient in a form that he or she can understand. It is justified by both respect for autonomy and beneficence and is therefore most clinically appropriate. The direct form allows the patient to fully understand his or her health status and treatment options. This increased patient understanding can thereby lead to increased patient satisfaction in the doctor–patient relationship.

The indirect methods of patient disclosure involve the use of nonverbal cues and circumferential language to convey information. However, as Bedell notes (3), when physicians use nonverbal and indirect patient cues from the patient as the basis for deducing a patient's desire to withhold resuscitation, most judgments are in conflict with the patient's beliefs and preferences. Blunt disclosure, utilizing technical jargon, without using language a patient can understand, is a disservice to the patient, for although the physician feels his duties to explain to the patient have been fulfilled, the patient may have no comprehension of the terms being used. The end result is nondisclosure by obscuring the truth through the use of technical or scientific terms. The concept of gradual disclosure (10) has an inherent flaw if used within the context of a rapidly deteriorating patient, for full disclosure may not be complete prior to the onset of incompetence. The physician needs to appreciate that the patient must possess all data prior to the loss of competence in order to make an autonomous health care decision.

NONDISCLOSURE

Nondisclosure is often founded upon the physician's discretionary usage of "therapeutic privilege" to withhold information from the patient, on a beneficence-based concern to avoid imminent and serious harm to the patient. The ethical problem of nondisclosure lies in the possible erroneous assessment the physician may make in ascertaining the potential harms in telling the truth, for example, loss of hope. Further, nondisclosure negates the autonomy claims of the patient to have such information revealed prior to a health care decision. As a result, autonomy-based obligations place the burden of proof on the physician if less than full disclosure is contemplated. Otherwise, therapeutic privilege can quickly collapse into an excuse for invoking a beneficence-based paternalistic justification to withhold information from the patient for his or her "own good." As Veatch maintains, the only justifiable nondisclosure is when the competent patient directly requests that information not be disclosed. (14). However, Veatch's viewpoint rules out *all* discretionary withholding of information, which may not be reasonable. Discretion in disclosure and nondisclosure can be easily abused. Physician excuses such as "You can't tell the patient everything" and "We'll never know [the diagnosis or prognosis] for sure" paternalistically obscure the patient's understanding of his or her health by incompletely informing the patient of all reasonable aspects of his or her disease and its treatment. Therefore, the goal of facilitating the maintenance of the patient's autonomy, rather than the physician's beneficence-based paternalism, should be to delineate the type, timing, and amount of information that is be disclosed to the patient.

CONSIDERATIONS SPECIFIC TO THE GERIATRIC PATIENT

The physician has a duty to inform the elderly patient of chronic physical and mental diseases that have been diagnosed. This duty is often interpreted differently from the duty to inform the elderly patient of acute changes, for there are perceived differences of prognostic significance between an acute and treatable disease which is not life threatening and a chronic, debilitating disease which will most likely lead to the patient's demise. The physician will often find it easier to tell the patient of the former than of the latter. However, disclosure is of paramount importance in both circumstances, if the patient is to understand the nature of the available diagnostic and therapeutic options and the prospects for the future. Thus, when the elderly patient is adequately informed about his or her disease process, he or she will be better prepared to respond to functional losses, increased dependence, and the imminence of death.

Talking with the elderly patient about serious, potentially life-threatening disease involves a perspective different from that used when talking with younger patients. While Rakel and Belgum (10) argue in favor of physician discretion through the gradual disclosure of prognoses over time to the "dying patient," older patients may not have enough time for this process compared with younger patients. The difference lies in the fact that the aged patient is more likely to have decreasing abilities in memory and cognitive skills, although his or her reasoning skills or judgment might be preserved (12). As a result, if disclosure is postponed for too long a period of time, the patient will be placed at risk of never being able to share in decision making about the management of his or her care. Ultimately, if the physician waits long enough, the patient's reasoning ability could be reduced to nil, thus rendering the patient incompetent and nonautonomous. Therefore, the elderly patient must be adequately informed early in the course of a serious illness, prior to the onset of processes that can diminish the patient's mentation and autonomous decision-making capabilities. As a result, a prolonged titration of medical information over time (to allow the patient time to accept the facts) may impinge upon the patient's autonomy if the process is overly protracted. Ironically, in these circumstances beneficence-based discretion on the part of the physician would be counterproductive to benefiting the patient.

Once a diagnosis of chronic disease has been made, it is important that the patient realistically acknowledge his or her eventual deterioration. That acknowledgment should not be purchased at the cost of lost hope of amelioration or palliation, however. The physician who discloses this information must not become resigned to the terminal or chronic prognosis to the point that other options and treatment regimens could be overlooked in discussions with the patient. Maintaining a realistic hope for the patient enables him or her to plan for the future and develop individual coping mechanisms to comprehend the impending decline with some personal perspective.

Because it is difficult sometimes for the physician to accept the mortality of elderly patients and to acknowledge differences of values between him- or herself and the patient, it can be a difficult task for the physician to plan ahead for the medical demise of an elderly patient. However, it is surely better in the long run for patients and for their families for the physician to face this deterioration prospectively rather than on a spontaneous basis. It is therefore important not to confuse speaking with the patient with informed consent itself. If a physician narrowly interprets speaking to a patient as simply a legal burden, then an important ethical dimension of disclosure is lost (8). The elderly patient may thus lose an important opportunity to begin to plan for and cope with diseases and disabilities that can accompany aging.

The disclosure process is complicated when the patient has a deteriorating course that may eventually result in reduced autonomy. The elderly patient is unique in medicine, because of the diminution and wavering of competence that can occur over time. Veatch has elucidated four different types of patients as they are treated toward life's end, illustrating the heterogeneity with which diminished competence and reduced autonomy present in the elderly patient (15).

The first, the *competent patient*, is able to voice his or her own health care decisions. This patient autonomously decides his or her own medical destiny from among the options offered by the physician. The second type of patient is the *incompetent patient who has expressed prior wishes* as to how medical decisions should be effected if future incompetence precludes consent. In this circumstance, the patient has given a directive prior to the onset of incompetence and has expressly requested certain types of treatment or nontreatment. The physician can thereby treat this patient even when incompetence overtakes the patient in the course of disease. The third type of patient is the *never competent patient* (e.g., the severely or profoundly mentally retarded adult) or the *incompetent patient without either expressed treatment wishes or a family member to act as a proxy consenting agent*. This type of patient is usually treated using substituted judgment, in the form of a court-appointed guardian or by court judgment. However, substituted judgment is really a beneficence-based decision, as explained in Chapter 52. The fourth type of patient is the incompetent, nonexpressive patient, or the *never competent patient, with a family*. In this circumstance Veatch argues that the family possesses "limited familial autonomy" to make decisions for the patient, based on the premise that the family possesses a societal claim to act as caretaker of and decision maker for the incompetent family member (within certain limits). Thus, the physician has a mode with which an incompetent patient, either formerly competent or incompetent, may be treated, particularly in the event that no prior wishes were ever voiced (13).

ADVANCE PLANNING: THE VALUE HISTORY

It should be stressed that had a patient received adequate disclosure prior to incompetence, the necessity for limited familial autonomy would probably be needed only in acute care situations, rather than chronic health care. As a result, in the context of chronic disease, adequate disclosure of the disease process would likely limit the necessity of the above categories to the first three, negating the need for the fourth.

In Chapter 52 the two major legal instruments for advance planning, the living will and the durable power of attorney, are discussed. However, in circumstances of vague or inflexible wording, the living will may not accurately reflect the patient's values (7). Likewise, the person holding durable power of attorney may not always know or anticipate the values of the patient in the process of making a substituted judgement (3). At the heart of both of these legal advance directives is the ethical concept of a value history. The value history is a response to the need to ascertain the values of the patient prior to the patient's inability to speak for him- or herself. The term "value history" was originally coined by Pellegrino (personal communication, 1980) and preliminarily described (9) as an eliciting of the patient's values and preferences as they are directed toward specific aspects of health care. This clinical tool can be valuable when speaking to patients about the future quality of life. Further, it can help to clarify medical options available to patients. When possible, this crucial aspect of medical planning should ideally be discussed longitudinally in the patient's primary physician's office, rather than in the hospital setting. Also, if the patient is irreversibly incompetent, the family can have an important role in the construction of a value history if one was not previously elicited. In this circumstance, the physician is obliged to render a full and direct disclosure to the family. The autonomy-based obligations originally directed toward the patient are thereby redirected toward the family, as they attempt to formulate treatment decisions on the basis of the patient's values and beliefs. However, there is an inherent risk in eliciting the value history from the patient's family since their own values may become mixed unconsciously with those of the patient's.

There are many variables that should be discussed with the elderly patient in the course of developing and recording the patient's value history. The variables should be those most likely to be necessitated by the patient's present condition and its prognosis. Thus, not all variables need to be discussed at once and those that are relevant should be discussed over time as long as encroaching incompetence is not foreseen.

Acute Care Interventions

Cardiopulmonary Resuscitation. The first and most important variable is the allowing or withholding of cardiopulmonary resuscitation (CPR) during coronary or pulmonary arrest. The autonomous decision to withhold CPR is necessary for No-Code status. An early and direct approach, especially in light of Bedell and Delbanco's study of No-Code orders (3), on this question will decrease physician uncertainty and ambiguity about the patient's values and preferences.

Respirator. The use or withholding of a respirator in the event of pulmonary arrest is important to discuss with pulmonary patients (e.g., those with chronic obstructive pulmonary disease), as well as all other patients.

Intubation. This should be discussed both as an integral invasive therapeutic measure necessary for CPR and the use of a respirator and in its use independently of these.

Chronic Care Interventions

Total Parenteral Nutrition. It is necessary to discuss peripheral or central intravenous total parenteral nutrition for patients who may have a prolonged period of recuperation.

Intravenous Fluids. Intravenous (IV) hydration and medication administration should be discussed as a basic medical therapeutic tool. The use of IVs for the purposes of comfort or pain medications should also be discussed.

Feeding Tubes. The allowing or withholding of any or all nasogastric, gastrostomy, and small bowel feeding tubes for long-term feeding should be discussed in the context of long-term recuperative or vegetative medical care.

Dialysis. The indications, risks, and benefits of dialysis should be discussed, including its use to attempt to treat cognitive impairments that can result from toxins in the blood.

Medications. If deteriorating health is evident, the usage or withholding of antibiotics (e.g., for acute urinary or pulmonary infection in a terminal patient) and other medications should be discussed. Pain-controlling medications should still be offered to the patient as allowable.

Other Advance Designations

Proxy Consent. There should be clarification of inclusion or exclusion of family members for proxy consent if incompetence of the patient and ambiguity about medical treatment occurs. The proxy directive should be repeated in the company of those chosen in order to receive their consent to act as such. Further, the patient may prefer that no proxy be assigned and that only the patient's advance directives be followed, such that the family could not intervene in the patient's prior health care decisions.

Organ Donation. This sensitive issue should be brought up with the patient, rather than obtaining proxy consent through a family member after the patient's death. However, local jurisdiction may have legal restraints giving the family decision priority over the patient's advance directive.

Autopsy. The patient's preferences should be elicited. These can be a valuable guide for the family after the patient's death, when they legally assume the authority for authorizing autopsy.

If a patient decides to give an advance directive in any of the above variables, this value history should be duly noted in the medical record. Further, if any aspect of these variables is answered in a noncommittal fashion, a beneficence-based presumption in favor of treatment, if medically indicated, is defensible. In addition, treatment can be justified as an effort to return autonomy to the patient. The patient should be informed of this manner of managing incompleteness and ambiguity by the physician. The patient in all cases should be offered regular opportunities to review and change his or her value history in the future.

CONFIDENTIALITY

Like truthtelling, the ethical obligation of confidentiality is grounded in respect for the patient's autonomy. The patient possesses an autonomy-based right to control the disclosure of information about him- or herself to others. Any such disclosure, without the patient's express permission, constitutes a violation of the autonomy-based right to privacy.

Confidentiality is also justified on the basis of beneficence, because patients are more likely to be forthcoming with their physicians if they can be confident that information they reveal will be kept private. As pointed out in Chapter 51, extra effort is sometimes necessary to elicit information from elderly patients. An assurance of confidentiality can be an important aid in this process.

Confidentiality can be justifiably overridden if there is a risk of serious, far-reaching, and irreversible harm to a third party (2). Requests of confidentiality by the elderly patient to withhold the diagnosis and prognosis from spouse and family are not unusual. Difficulties can easily arise when the patient is unable to decide the best treatment choice, but will not allow discussion with the family to decide on future health care. Therefore, the nondisclosure between the patient and the family member, who may well be a possible future proxy, can precipitate a crisis in which no family member can decide for the patient what is to be done or not done medically.

The question of disclosure to family members of the patient is quite important since physicians formerly thought that it was far easier to disclose the illness and its prognosis to the family without informing the patient, who would be "spared" the knowledge. However, true proxy consent for the elderly patient does not entail informing the family first and the patient not all or afterward. Though based on the beneficence claims of protecting the patient from harmful information, the obligation of confidentiality to the patient is violated by not disclosing medical information to him or her while telling others.

The patient's ability to choose his or her own treatment is predicted on truthful disclosure by the physician. Therefore, based on stricter adherence to individual autonomy claims, the physician's first duty is to inform the patient and then, only after the patient consents, to inform the family members of the diagnosis and prognosis of the disease. As a result, it is the autonomous right of the patient to not have medical information disclosed to family members without prior consent.

Respect for individual autonomy transcends the necessity to inform the family, even though they eventually become the proxy consenter for him or her. Therefore, if a patient has designated that no disclosure may occur while he or she is alive until death and explicit medical instructions have been made by the patient, then no form of disclosure to the family is justified. This notion of autonomy is supported by Annas's contention that there is a loss of patient privacy when disclosure is made to the family rather than to the patient (1).

Other areas of medical care for the elderly have less well defined borders between disclosure and confidentiality. One such problem arises when family members request that the physician not tell the patient of dire diagnoses or prognoses, prior to when the physician has actually made a diagnosis. This action would violate the patient's autonomy claim to disclosure, as well as the confidentiality that should exist if such information had been already conveyed.

This problem parallels the difficulty of a physician who, for example, tells the family that the prognosis is poor immediately after the patient has had surgery and the patient has not yet been informed. Again, even if such a judgment error has occurred, the patient has the ultimate claim of autonomy and confidentiality to this health information, despite any beneficence claim by the family to not reveal this information. Lastly, an elderly patient may surrender his or her autonomy in regard to disclosure and confidentiality to another family member because of feelings of depression and dependency. Here, the physician can attempt to correct this "nonautonomous" surrender of autonomy by counseling the patient about his or her ability to successfully determine the best future health care course.

The patient has the autonomous right to refuse treatment despite family opinion, once they have been told. As a result, a difficult situation can arise if a patient has declined all therapy, yet allows for family disclosure. A conflict between the family and the physician can then ensue, based on the family's desire to treat the patient despite the terminal prognosis. Similarly, if disclosure is forbidden by the patient, the family may desire treatment founded not on the basis of disagreement about the treatment plan, but due to the lack of information about the patient's prognosis. To prevent the occurrence of such ethically conflicting situations, the physician will persuade the patient of the necessity for family disclosure, if situations of proxy consent are foreseen, due to the physician's responsibility to render benefit to the patient without resorting to paternalism which would violate the patient's autonomy. Once the family can be informed, treatment options can be openly discussed in a family conference involving the patient, family, and physician in order to reach conclusion about the choice of treatment. This option is a beneficence-based attempt by the physician to facilitate a definitive health care decision, while also respecting the autonomy of the patient.

Alternatively, the physician can attempt to further counsel the patient in order to allow for an autonomous decision to be made so that some form of advanced planning option can be designated. Finally, the patient may want the proxy family member to know only a limited amount of information in order to make a decision for the patient. However, this attempt to respect the patient's autonomy is inadequate as a result of incomplete disclosure to the family member which would thereby preclude the possibility of an autonomous decision by that individual. This lack of disclosure may become moot if the patient falls ill enough, such that it is obvious to the proxy that death is imminent.

Another method to deal with intrafamily disclosure has been elucidated by one of the authors (6). Doukas has coined the phrase, "family covenant," to describe the relationship that can exist among the family, patient, and physician. The family covenant is a mutually consented to health care agreement between autonomous family members and their family physician. All consenting parties recognize (a) the family as the unit of care and (b) the moral equality of autonomy and beneficence claims when the health care of one family member has impact on the health and welfare of another family member. The family covenant allows for the consent of family members to recognize the claims of the individual, as well as the claims of other family members, and attempts to resolve conflicting claims between them.

Such dilemmas would be resolved on the basis of whether health information belonging to one family member has impact on the health and welfare of other family members. If a patient's medical decision affects no other family members, then his or her right of privacy binds the physician to an obligation of confidentiality. However, should an individual's decision affect the health and welfare of other family members within the covenant, then autonomy claims of the that patient can sometimes justifiably be overridden on the basis of beneficence-based obligations to the affected family members. The family physician must then weigh the conflicting obligations in the context of the particular case. While it can be expected that the family physician can harm one family member while helping another, the family covenant helps all consenting parties to understand more clearly that such conflicts can arise.

The family covenant is a flexible agreement allowing for the mutual consent by the family and physician regarding specific dimensions of health care, such as disclosure and confidentiality. For example, sometimes an elderly family member wishes that all decisions regarding health care be made by his or her spouse. Typically, physicians are comfortable in abiding by such requests. The family covenant is clinically applicable here, because it enables the physician to identify two pitfalls in acceding to such requests. First, the elderly patient who makes such a request needs to appreciate that the physician is no longer under an obligation of confidentiality when it comes to the disclosure of medically relevant information to the patient's spouse. The patient should explicitly consent to full disclosure to the spouse and to the risk that the patient may be psychologically stressed by such disclosure. Second, the patient should be informed that he or she is free to reverse his or her prior decision. At the same time, the patient needs to appreciate the implications of a change of mind in these matters. Mainly, the patient needs to authorize any further disclosure of information to his or her spouse. This is because confidentiality now must be maintained. The patient needs to be aware that this change may cause psychologic stress for his or her spouse. Such stress, however, does not constitute a harm to the health and welfare of the spouse. In these circumstances, therefore, the family covenant does not justify further disclosure of medical information to the spouse, without the patient's explicit consent to do so.

CONCLUSION

In this chapter, we have attempted to delineate the moral responsibilities of the physician regarding truthtelling and confidentiality when dealing with elderly patients, with special reference to those patients who may eventually become incompetent secondary to their health. The resurgence of the autonomy model in the patient care literature over the last two decades has strengthened the autonomy claims of full and direct disclosure of medical information necessary for an informed patient health decision. These autonomy claims also illustrate the necessity for complete confidentiality of all medical information between the physician and the elderly patient, unless specifically consented to by the patient or the existence of some harm to a third party is evident. Further, the family covenant illustrates that truthtelling and confidentiality should be upheld within the family unless the covenant formulated between them and their physician specifies a distinct alternative plan of action.

REFERENCES

1. Annas G: Rights of the terminally ill patient. *J Nurs Adm* March-April:40–44, 1974.
2. Beauchamp TL, McCullough LB: *Medical Ethics: The Moral Responsibilities of Physicians*. Englewood Cliffs, NJ, Prentice-Hall, 1984.
3. Bedell S, Delbanco T: Choices about cardiopulmonary resuscitation in the hospital. *N Engl J Med* 310:1089–1093, 1984.
4. Cassell E: Telling the truth to the dying patient. In Tache J, Selye H, Day SB (eds): *Cancer, Stress, and Death*. New York, Plenum Press, 1979. p 121.
5. Dervin J, Dervin P, Jonsen A: Ethical considerations in eldercare. In O'Hara-Devereaux M, Andrus L, Scott C, et al (eds): *Eldercare: A Practical Guide to Clinical Geriatrics*. New York, Grune and Stratton, 1981, p 15.
6. Doukas D: The family covenant—beyond the traditional medical contract. Presented at the National Convention of the Society of Teachers of Family Medicine, Nashville, TN, 1985.
7. Eisendrath S, Jonsen A: The living will—help or hindrance? *JAMA* 249:2054–2058, 1983.
8. Faden R, Beauchamp T: *A History and Theory of Informed Consent*. New York, Oxford University Press, 1986.
9. McCullough L: Medical care for elderly patients with diminished competence—an ethical analysis. *J Am Geriatr Soc* 32:150–153, 1984.
10. Rakel R, Belgum D: Care of the dying patient. In Rakel R (ed): *Textbook of Family Medicine*, ed 3. Philadelphia, W.B. Saunders, 1984, p 118.

11. Salzman L: Truth, honesty and the therapeutic process. *Am J Psychiatry* 130:1281–1282, 1973.
12. Standley B, Guido J, Stanley M, et al: The elderly and informed consent. *JAMA* 252:1302–1306, 1984.
13. Steinbrook R, Lo B: Decision making for incompetent patients by designated proxy. *N Engl J Med* 310:1598–1601, 1984.
14. Veatch RM: When should the patient know? *Barrister* 8:15–20, 1981.
15. Veatch RM: An ethical framework for terminal care decision. *J Am Geriatr Soc* 32:665–669, 1984.

Value History

DAVID DOUKAS
STEVEN LIPSON
LAURENCE B. McCULLOUGH

The goal of taking and recording a value history on every elderly patient is to provide, as much as possible and in advance, a set of decisions about critical care that are based on the patient's values and beliefs. These advance decisions and the values and beliefs that underlie them can serve as reliable guides for medical and nursing interventions when the patient becomes irreversibly incompetent to participate in the process of informed consent (see chapter 52) regarding his or her care. The value history can be obtained over time, particularly as a patient's chronic conditions deteriorate and hospitalization can be expected. The value history should be portable. Indeed, it is the ethical obligation of the physician who obtains and records the patient's value history to see to it that the previously obtained and recorded value history becomes part of the chart of the patient in the hospital (especially in the critical care unit) and in the nursing home.

The value history begins with a consideration of values related to decisions about medical interventions. It then proceeds to specific advance decisions and the patient's reasoning about them in terms of his or her values and beliefs. The patient should not be limited to the values he or she identifies in the first part in reasoning about decisions in the second part of the value history. The third part of the value history should contain directives that are executed in accordance with the law of the relevant jurisdiction. Ideally, after the value history is completed, the physician should arrange for a family conference, so that the patient's decisions can be explained to the family.

PART I: IDENTIFICATION OF VALUES

A. *Basic Life Values.* The patient should first be asked to choose which of the two value statements is most in accord with his or her basic views about medical care:

1. I want to live as long as possible, regardless of the quality of life that I may experience as a result of medical interventions intended to prolong my life.
2. I want to preserve a good quality of life, even if this means that some medical interventions will not be administered and that I may therefore not live as long as I might if they were administered.

B. *Values Relevant to the Patient's Views on Quality of Life.* There are many values that help each of us to define the quality of life that we would like to live when we are in a hospital or nursing home. The following list contains some of the most common of these. The patient should be asked to review the following list, add any value statements to it that he or she finds relevant, and select the three that are most important to him or her.

1. I want to maintain my capacity to think clearly.
2. I want to feel safe and secure.
3. I want to avoid unnecessary pain and suffering.
4. I want to be treated with respect.
5. I want to be treated with dignity when I can no longer speak for myself.
6. I do not want to be an unnecessary burden on my family.
7. I want to maintain a good relationship with my family.
8. I want to be able to be with my loved ones before I die.
9. I want to be able to make my own decisions.
10. I want to experience a comfortable dying process.
11. I want to leave good memories of myself to my loved ones.
12. I want to be treated in accord with my religious beliefs and traditions.
13. I want respect shown for my body after I die.
14. I want to help others by making a contribution to medical education and research.
15. Other values important to me are:

C. *Ranking of Values.* The patient should be asked to identify and rank his or her three most important values.

PART II: ADVANCE DIRECTIVES

The patient should be asked to make whatever advance directives he or she chooses and to explain them to you in terms of the values identified in the previous section. The patient is not to be limited to the values ranked in Part I Section C. The reader should explain to the patient that for those directives not decided, the following strategy will be implemented. First, the patient will be asked to make the relevant decision when the time comes. Second, the patient can designate someone to decide for him or her, an important consideration if he or she is not able to participate in the informed consent process later. Third, the patient can execute a living will. Fourth, in the absence of these the physician and the patient's family will do their best to determine what the patient would want done. The outcome of this process, it should be explain to the patient, is difficult to predict and may not respect the patient's wishes.

A. *Acute Care Interventions*
1. The patient should be asked whether he or she wishes to receive cardiopulmonary resuscitation if he or she experiences cardiac or pulmonary arrest. The procedures involved should be described. The patient's reasoning should be elicited in terms of the values in Part I.
2. The patient should be asked whether he or she wishes to be placed on a respirator in the event of respiratory arrest or failure. The procedures involved should be described. The patient's reasoning should be elicited in terms of the values in Part I.
3. The patient should be asked whether he or she wishes to have an endotracheal tube employed, to utilize either of the first two interventions. The patient should be informed that refusal of an endotracheal tube implies that the first two interventions will not be undertaken. The procedures involved should be described. The patient's reasoning should be elicited in terms of the values in Part I.
4. The patient who is a resident in a nursing home should be asked whether he or she wants the rescue squad (911) called in the event of cardiac or pulmonary arrest. The patient should be informed that refusal of the rescue squad means that he or she will almost certainly die.

B. *Chronic Care Interventions*
5. The patient should be asked whether he or she wants to have total parenteral nutrition administered to meet nutritional needs. The procedures involved should be described. The patient's reasoning should be elicited in terms of the values in Part I.

6. The patient should be asked whether he or she wants intravenous hydration administered. The patient should understand that this is a separate question from the intravenous administration of pain medications. The latter will be supplied as needed. The procedures involved should be described. The patient's reasoning should be elicited in terms of the values in Part I.
7. The patient should be asked whether he or she wants medications *used to treat the patient's disease process(es)* administered. These should be distinguished from pain medications, which will be administered, and from hydration. The procedures involved should be described. The patient's reasoning should be elicited in terms of the values in Part I.
8. The patient should be asked whether he or she wants nutrition to be administered by feeding tubes, including nasogastric tubes or any other enteral feeding tubes. The procedures involved should be described. The patient's reasoning should be elicited in terms of the values in Part I.
9. The patient form whom renal failure is a possibility should be asked whether he or she wants to receive dialysis. The procedures involved should be described. The patient's reasoning should be elicited in terms of the values in Part I.

PART III: OTHER ADVANCE DESIGNATIONS

The patient should be informed, if the relevant jurisdiction provides for them, that a living will and/or durable power of attorney may be executed. The physician should acquire the proper forms for the execution of these documents, as provided for in relevant statutory law. The patient should also be informed about organ donation and provided with the appropriate, legally authorized documents to execute, should he or she decide to donate organs or tissue. Finally, the patient should be asked about his or her views about autopsy. The value of autopsy should be explained. The patient should be made aware that legally his or her heirs may have to make this decision. The patient's value-based decision should be communicated to the family during the family conference convened to discuss the patient's value history.

CHAPTER 56

Long-Term Care Decision Making[1]

EMILY M. AGREE
STEVEN LIPSON
LAURENCE B. McCULLOUGH
BETH J. SOLDO

Enduring physical dependency is the hallmark of long-term care. Deficits in the patient's capacity for self-care are the results of underlying, and often multiple, chronic conditions. Regardless of the pathology involved, long-term care patients present with a complex array of both medical and personal care problems. Inadequate nutrition, substandard housing, and social isolation only serve to exacerbate the problems of functional dependency in many cases.

Caring for the elderly patient with long-term care needs poses distinctive ethical challenges for the clinician. These challenges and the ethical issues that shape them can be accommodated within the general ethical framework presented in Chapter 51. However, the nature of long-term care is such that significant ethical issues are not always as crisply defined as those involved in other clinical situations, such as decisions to withhold treatment in terminal care (Chapter 53). This chapter provides an analysis of the basic ethical issues in long-term care decision making by elderly patients and their families.

We begin by reviewing the distinctive features of long-term care that give rise to a unique subset of ethical issues in geriatric medicine. This is followed by a discussion of the role of values in defining the patient's long-term care needs and identifying appropriate options, and the presentation of a clinical

strategy for incorporating the ethical analysis of this chapter into the clinical care of elderly patients confronting long-term care decisions.

LONG-TERM CARE AND LONG-TERM CARE DECISION MAKING

REDEFINING HEALTH CARE GOALS

The first feature of long-term care decision making is that this process requires an implicit redefining of health care goals. In most acute care episodes, the primary objective is to fully cure the patient and thereby return him or her to prior normal health and function. While recent evidence suggests that recovery of some degree of lost function is possible for many frail elderly (7), amelioration is the overriding concern in long-term care. Amelioration includes the less tangible goals of palliation, management, comfort, and preservation of personal dignity and independence (1, 2). How the physician ought to reconcile these diverse, and sometimes competing, goals is a theme that underlies many of the ethical issues in long-term care.

Balancing these concerns is an essential part of long-term care decision making, that is, the process by which various care options are identified and evaluated based, in part, on a thorough assessment of the patient's physical and cognitive capacities (5). As a result of this process, a change may be made in either the care plan or the living arrangement of the patient. The outcome of a long-term care decision, for example, may be the relocation of a frail older pa-

[1]Research for this chapter was supported by the Retirement Research Foundation, the Atlantic Richfield Foundation, an anonymous Dutch foundation, and the Bureau of Health Professions, U.S. Public Health Service.

tient to a daughter's home or to a nursing home or the introduction of additional, more intensive services into the home.

Long-term care decision making is therefore not concerned only with decisions of whether or not to institutionalize an older patient. Rather, the process of long-term care decision making is really a sequence of decisions over time, concerning increasing or decreasing levels of care (8). Medical and nonmedical events may precipitate specific decisions. Unanticipated medical crises, such as a cerebrovascular accident or a fractured hip, often require an assessment of chronic care options in the context of hospital discharge planning. Nonmedical events may trigger the decision as well. The death of a caregiving spouse, physical deterioration of the home, or loss of a neighbor who helped with grocery shopping, for example, may force a reassessment of options. The physician, particularly one with a longstanding relationship to the patient, may be consulted and involved even in those decisions that result from nonmedical factors.

THE LABOR-INTENSIVE, NONTECHNICAL NATURE OF PERSONAL CARE

The second feature of long-term care decision making relevant to its ethical aspects is the labor-intensive, nontechnical nature of personal care. Personal care is an important part of long-term care and involves assistance that compensates for chronic limitations in basic self-care activities. Because both the "formal," or professional, and "informal," or family- and community-based, care systems correctly claim competency in rendering this type of care, there is no natural division, or ready definition, of labor between the two systems.

The vast majority of noninstitutionalized frail elderly depend on family and friends for providing direct, hands-on care. Most often it is the spouse or adult children who provide daily assistance with eating, bathing, dressing, toileting, and mobility (7, 9). Even at the extremes of disability, where the demands on the caregiver are unrelenting and require 40 or more hours of services each week, kin bear primary responsibility for personal care (6). Thus, a care plan for sustaining a frail older patient in the community usually requires the involvement and approval of nonprofessionals, whose lack of expertise is offset by commitment, flexibility, and concern for idiosyncratic needs that generally characterize family relations.

The family also may be a legitimate party to the decision to institutionalize the elderly patient. The caregiving capacities and resources of even the most committed families are not without limits. Those who reach their limits—usually as a result of behavioral problems or incontinence in the patient—may initiate a search for institutional alternatives in response to their own needs, as well as the needs of the elderly patient. It has been estimated that family members are the primary decision maker in over half of all nursing home placements (10, 12). In a very real sense, then, relatives often "earn" the right to be party to a range of long-term care decisions.

RELIANCE ON THIRD-PARTY PAYERS

The third factor that shapes long-term care decision making is reliance on third-party payers, which in turn affects the cost and availability of alternative care arrangements (3, 4, 12). The present reimbursement system favors institutional care over home care. In many areas of the country the demand for formal home care providers greatly exceeds the supply. Even when services are available, the number of contact hours often falls short of what is required to sustain many frail elderly in the community.

At the other end of the spectrum, Medicare and Medicaid regulations governing reimbursable nursing home care limit the options of long-term care patients. Medicare pays for short-stay, rehabilitation-oriented nursing home care only under very limited conditions, while Medicaid essentially requires beneficiaries to spend themselves into poverty to qualify for nursing home reimbursement.

Additional constraints on long-term care decision making also have been created as a consequence of the prospective payment system utilized by Medicare. Hospitals are reimbursed for the care of older patients based on anticipated average length-of-stay within diagnostic-related groups (DRGs), adjusted by hospital type and region. However, reimbursements linked to average lengths of stay are not adjusted by severity. The very frail elderly, suffering from multiple chronic conditions, may be especially vulnerable to early discharge under DRGs. The pressure for early discharge seems to have increased the use of "step down" facilities, including temporary nursing home placements, and has curtailed the range of options available at discharge.

Thus, a wide range of factors make the decision-making process surrounding long-term care extremely complex and difficult. In the next section, we present a model for understanding and organizing this process from a clinical perspective.

ETHICAL MODEL FOR LONG-TERM CARE DECISION MAKING

In the gerontologic literature, the notion of "need" is used interchangeably to mean both an actual physiologic deficit, and a care requirement. The assumption that deficits in health and functioning constitute a warrant for action is commonplace in both the medical and social caregiving fields.

In acute care, at least, there has been little reason to distinguish between these aspects in patient assessment because the protocols for treating acute conditions and injuries are so well established, and the standards of action and criteria of success are usually straightforward. The preservation of life and restoration of functional health are the guiding values. The near identity of "deficit" with "need" in defining an appropriate care option is so complete and automatic that the value-based criteria by which alternative actions are evaluated are often hidden. In the context of acute care medicine, the physician assumes, and expects the patient to equate, "I have a broken leg" with "I need to have my leg repaired," which then identifies appropriate treatment—setting the leg in a cast and planning rehabilitative care.

The extension of this logic to chronic illness and disability, especially long-term care decision making, is problematic. Findings from laboratory, clinical, and functional batteries indicate status, the type and extent of deficit, but not need. In translating diagnosed deficits into care needs, the physician and patient implicitly call on their fundamental values. In acute care the values of the patient and the physician are almost always congruent and unambiguous. This is not always the case in long-term care. Preservation of life and restoration of maximum functional status cannot simply be assumed to be the primary values in defining long-term care needs and identifying appropriate care options.

As shown in Figure 56.1, an initial ethical model for long-term care decision making indicates that values enter into clinical decision making in two places: the definition of need and in the identification of appropriate care options.

The following case study nicely illustrates this initial framework: Mrs. S, a 67-year-old woman with an enlarged heart, was placed on a diuretic and told that she would no longer be able to work or to travel as extensively as she had previously, because the strain on her heart would be too great. She agreed to take the medication and alter her diet, but continued to travel, to work, and generally to continue with her previous life, accommodating to her heart condition by monitoring her own pulse and resting more frequently. Apparently, she values such activities more than the preservation of her life.

The principle of beneficence directs the physician to attain the greater balance of good over harm for the patient (Chapter 51). In long-term care decision making the physician applies beneficence to define care needs in terms of reducing the risk of the harms that might occur if the patient's deficits were not addressed, for example, in the case of Mrs. S, the risk of a coronary from an enlarged heart. Mrs. S, however, valued her active life more than a reduction in her risk of a heart attack and therefore interpreted her need and appropriate care options rather differently: She accepted those portions of the physician's recommended treatment that did not impair her ability to uphold her values of activity and independence.

This initial framework is not adequate to all long-term care decision making. Consider the case of Mr. B, an 89-year-old man with severe degenerative arthritis. An initial assessment of the patient's condition indicates that he has deficits in motion at his joints, particularly the knees and ankles, and decreased muscle strength resulting from years of reduced activity. He has been living with his younger (81-year-old) sister since his wife died 5 years ago,

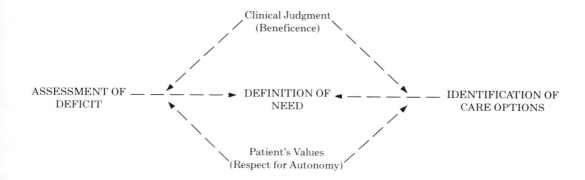

Figure 56.1. An initial ethical model of long-term care decision making.

and his sister has been responsible for all caregiving. When his sister suffered a stroke and was placed in an area nursing home, Mr. B's daughter approached his physician about nursing home placement for her father.

From the physician's point of view, employing the principle of beneficence, Mr. B's condition indicates that he should continue to receive assistance with walking and several instrumental activities of daily living, such as shopping, housework, and meal preparation. The patient, however, insists that he requires no assistance with walking, as he "gets around the house just fine" holding onto one piece of furniture then another. He states that his shopping could be done by his daughter, that he can hire a maid to do housework, and that he can get Meals-On-Wheels to provide hot food. Thus, an autonomy-based assessment of the patient's deficits leads to the identification of appropriate care options.

The patient's daughter, Mrs. R, states that she feels that her father must have supervision and that without his sister, he is not safe living in such a large house by himself. She feels that his restricted mobility is likely to lead to a fall and that he will be unable to get help. These are beneficence-based judgments.

She is also concerned about providing services to her father on a regular basis, because she is preparing to retire and would like to devote time to her husband. She is also not sure if she would be physically capable of meeting her father's needs in addition to her responsibilities at home. These judgments are based on the principles of family responsibility and justice.

Thus, two additional influences must be accounted for in the long-term care decision-making process: family involvement and the availability and affordability of services in the community. The initial ethical model of long-term care decision making must therefore be expanded to take account of how all four ethical principles shape that decision making process. This complete ethical model is depicted in Figure 56.2.

Family members are often involved in a long-term care decision, both as caregiving resources and advisors. They therefore influence the choice of care options through both their cooperation and their values. In cases where the patient is extremely impaired they may be called on to make substituted judgments (see Chapter 52).

Availability and cost of services (including the supply of informal caregivers and the limitations on what they can reasonably be expected to provide) also influence the identification of appropriate care options and, in some cases, the definition of need. The relative weighting of harms and benefits is in

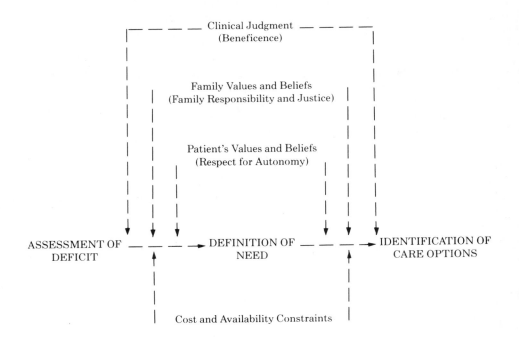

Figure 56.2.   An ethical model of long-term care decision making.

part dependent on whether a particular care option is available to the patient, as well as on the perceived costs involved in implementing it.

ROLE OF ETHICAL PRINCIPLES IN THE DEFINITION OF LONG-TERM CARE NEEDS AND IDENTIFICATION OF APPROPRIATE CARE OPTIONS

As described in Chapter 51, the dominant ethos of moral responsibility in medicine is the principle of beneficence, which directs the physician to promote the best interests of the patient by seeking the greater balance of good over harm in treatment and care. To apply this principle, the physician must identify and weigh the goods and harms that define a patient's best interests.

As we have seen above, often in acute care medicine the definition of these is so obvious as to mask their value underpinnings, for example, health as a paramount good, and disease, pain, injury, and premature death as harms. Even when multiple needs are present, such as in the emergency treatment of the victims of an automobile accident who have injuries to multiple organ systems, the principle of beneficence is implicitly and regularly employed to establish priorities for treatment. The guiding value for both patient and physician is assumed to be the preservation of life: Treat first those conditions that are immediately life-threatening. The successful application of beneficence in clinical decision, however, depends on a correspondence between the physician's values and those of the patient.

The distinctive feature of long-term care decision making is that there is no single criterion, such as the preservation of life, against which to evaluate the patient's condition. The principle of beneficence cannot unambiguously assign priority to competing long-term care goods such as maintaining independence versus preventing the risk of injury, as illustrated in the case of Mrs. S. When beneficence-based clinical judgment is caught between competing goods, as it always is in the long-term care decision-making process, respect for the older person's autonomy becomes an essential element in the decision-making process: The older person's preferences should be taken into account in the definition of need and in the identification of appropriate care options.

In Mr. B's case, Mr. B, his physician, and his daughter agree on the definition of his care needs: assistance with walking, shopping, meal preparation, and housework. Mr. B's physician applies the principle of beneficence to define the patient's need. Mr. B uses his own values and beliefs and arrives at the same definition, as well as the identification of what he takes to be the appropriate care option. When she balances the demands of family responsibility and justice, however, Mr. B's daughter identifies a different care option. This analysis requires further explanation.

In long-term care decision making the principle of respect for autonomy properly moves to the fore as an essential ethical component of the decision-making process. Because the principle of beneficence cannot by itself adequately account for the best interests of the patient, the patient's own values and beliefs also should serve as the basis for defining long-term care needs and identifying care options. The patient must evaluate alternative interventions in terms of his or her own definition of best interests. In Mr. B's case, he values his independence and privacy and therefore would prefer to respond to his care needs with the assistance of family and paid help in his own home.

In addition, involved family members must balance obligations regarding the care of the older person against other obligations and interests, through the principles of justice and family responsibility. Mr. B's daughter, for example, found that she had to balance obligations to her husband and her own retirement plans with her obligation to care for her father and her desire to know that he is safe and secure. Spouses, siblings, and adult children all have legitimate interests that they may wish reasonably to protect and obligations to others (such as Mr. B's daughter to her spouse) that they are not free to abandon without sufficient justification.

All of these principles—beneficence, respect for autonomy, justice, and family responsibility—operate simultaneously in long-term care decision making and therefore must be balanced against each other in the decision-making process. Our current health care system is biased toward reliance on beneficence as applied by the physician, and in many cases, by family members. The wishes of the older patient are often ignored, discounted, or overridden. Mrs. R went directly to her father's physician to discuss care arrangements, without first asking her father what was important to him.

In cases where the individual is cognitively intact, there is no ethical justification for excluding the older person from the decision-making process. Yet, the assumption is often made that the physically impaired elderly are not capable of making their own decisions. We are prone to confuse the inability to implement a decision without help with the inability to make or to influence that decision.

No single principle, therefore, can be regarded as alone adequate to long-term care decision making and thus capable of overriding the ethical considerations introduced by the other principles. In the language of bridge players, no single principle can play the role of "trump," that is, automatically override the demands of other principles. This is especially the case for beneficence. Paternalism (as defined in Chapter 51) on the part of the physician or involved family members is one of the most serious ethical issues in long-term care decision making (13). Paternalism here is a form of ageism that should conscientiously be prevented by the clinician caring for geriatric patients confronted with long-term care decisions.

The means for incorporating the ethical principle of respect for autonomy into the long-term care decision-making process are described in the following section. These techniques are similar to those suggested for informed consent, as described in Chapter 52.

INCORPORATING ETHICAL PRINCIPLES INTO LONG-TERM CARE DECISION MAKING

Alternative ways of providing long-term care are frequently equivalent in terms of medical outcome. A patient's recovery following a stroke may be identical if he or she recuperates at home or in a nursing home, provided appropriate care is given in each setting. Even in the absence of constraints imposed by the availability and cost of services, the long-term care choice among suitable and feasible alternatives should be based on which one best supports or enhances those aspects of life the patient and family hold important, their value systems. Too often we have observed caring physicians or family members acting in a paternalistic fashion, unilaterally making the decision as to how the elderly patient is to live out his or her life. Incorporating the ethical principles of beneficence, respect for autonomy, family responsibility, and justice into long-term care decision making is a complex process. Because of this complexity, many elderly and their families will need the assistance of a neutral negotiator to arrive at a decision with which they can live. The physician or other professional working with the patient must be able to fill this role as well as ensuring that the patient's decision is fully informed.

To assist the reader in understanding this process, we have divided it into four steps: information collection and sharing; values identification; definition of need and identification of care options; and negotiation. In practice, several of these steps may occur simultaneously.

INFORMATION COLLECTION AND SHARING

Just as medical decision making in acute care requires a careful assessment of history, physical findings, laboratory and ancillary test results, the physician involved in long-term care decision making must evaluate this data base as well as several other factors. Determination of cognitive and activities-of-daily-living functioning, emotional state and social support system (both formal and informal) must be added to the assessment of physical health to produce a picture of what the patient is capable of doing today, as well as a prognosis in terms of physical and mental health and functioning in the future. Information from caretakers, therapists, and nursing staff, if available, can assist in identifying the patient's current functional status and potential for improvement. In this integrative process, the recognition of lifelong values and beliefs may be more important than specific disease processes. For example, a man who has always been cared for by his family is less likely to struggle with disability so as to maximize his independence than one who has functioned independently all of his life.

In addition to this expanded patient assessment, the physician must be generally knowledgeable regarding the range of long-term care alternatives available in the community, their admission criteria, and costs (1, 2). Depending on the locality, these may include not only nursing homes and home care, but hospices, senior centers, adult day care of various types, shared housing, sheltered or assisted living, retirement communities, respite care, and others. It is impractical for physicians other than those practicing in rural areas to be thoroughly knowledgeable of the characteristics of all of the community's resources. Thus we strongly encourage ongoing liaison and good working relationships with case assessment and case management resources such as hospital discharge planners, community programs for the elderly (e.g., those sponsored by the Areawide Agencies on Aging), and home health agencies that provide such services (e.g., local Visiting Nurse Associations). Social workers and nurses working in these agencies and programs should be part of the team approach to caring for the elderly (see Chapter 51).

The obligation of the physician to ensure that decisions made by a patient (or by families on the patient's behalf) are fully informed holds even though long-term care decisions are qualitatively different. The decision maker(s) must have the necessary information regarding the patient's status and care alternatives. The extent, timing, and method of sharing this "data base" must be individualized, and generally begins at the "reasonable person" standard of disclosure, that is, what information a "reasonable person" would need and want to know to make a decision. As discussion with the patient and family progresses, the standard of information sharing shifts to the subjective one, what this individual needs to know (see Chapter 52).

VALUES IDENTIFICATION

As described in Chapter 51 the physician caring for the elderly patient has an obligation to discuss and document the patient's value system, that is, those values and beliefs that the patient holds to be important. Ideally these discussions should occur over a period of time, and, with the patient's consent or by his or her own action, should be shared with involved family members. Frequently, however, physicians must care for elderly patients they have never met before and assist them in a long-term care decision. Patients who have seemingly never expressed their values and families who have never talked about them also seem to be prevalent. To assist the physician in helping patients and families to identify those values most pertinent to long-term care decision making, we suggest the physician probe the following areas. We have found them to be the most frequently invoked by patients and families.

Length Versus Quality of Life. Many individuals have very strong feelings regarding this distinction. To some, life has a sacred character, and the preservation of life is a highly prized value. If quality of life is more important, the physician is obliged to question what this means to the individual, particularly how it differs from maintaining independence or other particular interests of the patient.

Maximizing the Independence of the Older Person. The current trend among professionals in aging is to give this value the highest ranking. It is important to find out how the patient and family rank it in comparison to other values. Is it more important than safety, prolongation of life, etc? We cannot assume the patient shares our value system. The statement "I'm old and tired and want someone else to take care of me" may represent a valid value of the patient or may be an acceptance of society's ageism, assuming that the elderly cannot be independent.

Values Regarding the Interests of the Patient. This set of values includes interests such as privacy, being treated with dignity, physical and emotional comfort, safety, security, and the availability of needed personal and medical care. The question is which of these are important to the individual and how does he or she rank them in comparison to other values?

Interpersonal Concerns. These include concerns such as the avoidance of "unfair" physical, emotional, or financial impact on one or more parties. Will caring for the patient at home mean that a family member will have to quit a job or give up a college tuition fund? How are these concerns ranked in the value systems of the family?

If this values identification has not been performed until there is an immediate need for a decision, we strongly suggest that the discussion be held in private, between patient and physician. The physician or other case manager can then repeat the process with the involved family member(s). The disabled or ill elderly person frequently feels helpless and powerless, and may be unwilling to express his or her own values in the presence of family members. Sensitive issues may be involved. The physician must always be careful to maintain the confidential character of the discussion, unless given permission to share the content with others.

DEFINITION OF NEED AND IDENTIFICATION OF APPROPRIATE CARE OPTIONS

Integration of the patient's physical, emotional, and social functioning with his or her values system leads to a definition of long-term care needs. Although this sounds like a difficult task, clinical experience suggests that it is one that many elderly perform naturally. They are quite comfortable determining which of their deficits or disabilities don't matter and should just be "lived with." If the patient is informed as to his or her status and prognosis, and has a clear sense of his or her values, he or she generally finds it easy to define needs and identify appropriate care options. That is, needs that relate to the values the patient ranks most highly come first. It is not uncommon for patients to rank independence or maintenance of good family relationships higher than purely medical needs.

Once the patient's needs have been identified, the patient should be asked to rank the care options, in terms of which are most supportive of his or her values. In this process the physician and other caretakers may gain insight that will help them accept decisions that appear less than optimal or seem to ignore the medical needs of the patient. For example, the frail cardiac patient may refuse to enter a nursing home despite the recognition that her status is so marginal that 24-hour professional nursing supervision is needed to maintain her status. Recognition that privacy and independence are far more important in her values than any possible prolongation of life forces the physician, home health nurse, and family to address the need to respect her autonomy and her values. If an informed patient may refuse a surgical procedure, she may refuse a nursing home or other long-term care alternative as well (see Chapter 52).

With the patient's consent, the physician should share the information regarding status and prognosis with other involved family members after they have identified their own values which are pertinent to the care of the patient. These individuals should then be guided through a definition of need and ranking of care options. Although this process may be performed with the patient present, we find many families are more open and comfortable doing it apart.

NEGOTIATION

After going through the identification of values, definition of need, and identification of appropriate care options separately, the patient and involved family members should share with each other their values and the preferences based on them. Similarities and differences in values and rankings of values should be pointed out and explored. To one person, valuing independence may mean living alone, while to another it is living in a situation where all care needs are met by professional staff. Only after all the parties in a long-term care decision share the information about the patient's status and each other's values should the discussion move to consideration of care options.

The reversal of the usual practice of immediate discussion of whether the patient should go to a nursing home or not has the potential advantage of creating a common ground of shared values for decision making. If possible, the patient should be asked which care option meets his or her value preferences, and why. Family members should then be provided with the same opportunity. In the discussion, the physician must not take sides, but should attempt to correct any factual misunderstanding. The goal of the process is not to force everyone to accept and implement the patient's wishes. The process of negotiation may help to bring to light a legitimate basis for a refusal to do so, based on other interests and obligations. Respect for autonomy requires each party to recognize that he or she has no absolute right or "trump" to override another. We believe that this open decision making reduces guilt, hostility, and stress among the involved parties.

Agreement by patient and family on a decision will not always be the outcome of this process. At a minimum, each party's values and preferences will have been solicited and taken seriously. If no agreement occurs, then attention should be called to common values, where they exist. Reasons for disagreement should be clearly identified and a compromise sought.

We believe that long-term care decision making by family members on behalf of elderly who are too disabled to participate on their own should follow the approach to overcoming the barriers to informed consent given in Chapter 52. That is, an attempt should be made to identify the patient's value system from advance directives, other direct communications, or a values history. Only if none of these can be performed should the family be asked for "substituted judgment."

BARRIERS TO THE DECISION MAKING PROCESS

The barriers to long-term care decision making can include the false barriers of physical impairment and ageism, and the genuine barrier of cognitive impairment, as discussed in Chapter 52. In addition, we wish to call attention to barriers that seem to be specific to the long-term care decision-making process.

The system constraints imposed by the current long-term care reimbursement system and the DRG hospital reimbursement have been discussed earlier in this chapter. Their main impact is to compress and fragment the long-term care decision-making process. The physician has a key role to play in discharge planning, by preventing or at least mitigating these potentially adverse influences on long-term care decision making by the elderly and their families.

Additional barriers to the decision-making process can arise from emotional factors that affect family members' ability to participate. Guilt, anger, or hostility can emerge in response to the emotionally laden long-term care decision. The physician should recognize these and help family members work through them. Some family members may attempt to use their own values as "trumps" in the decision-making process, as a way to manage their own emotional response or to try to control the process so as to favor their own interest. Others may adopt the role of a dictatorial parent, reversing the prior parent–child relationship. The physician must remind all those involved that serious weight must be given to each participant's values and beliefs.

Other factors can affect the patient's ability to participate. Two in particular deserve careful consideration. The first is subclinical brain damage that diminishes the capacity of the elderly patient to engage in the decision-making process and that is not recognized or accepted by the patient or family members. This can pose a very delicate situation for the physician, as he or she seeks to help the patient or family to accept the possibility of such an impairment in a way that is sensitive and compassionate.

A second, less subtle factor is the surrender of autonomy on the part of the older person. Sometimes this surrender to the health care professional or family member is itself autonomous. The patient has decided that he or she does not want to deal with the burden of long-term care decision making, and trusts another to act as his or her advocate. In our experience, one should not accept every such surrender at face value. We have encountered a number of patients who, when challenged on their request to have someone else make the decision, demonstrate that they are quite capable of making their own decisions. Some may be testing whether the "system" is really going to allow them to make decisions, while others may have reasons that are not clear even to themselves.

The surrender of autonomy may also be nonautonomous, and should be addressed by the physician, as a way to respect and restore autonomy. Sometimes the patient is simply tired and needs time to regain the strength to confront decisions about changes in care. This factor can be compounded by the pressure for early discharge of the hospitalized patient. In such cases, the physician may have to resist such pressure or find other ways of protecting the patient's opportunity for autonomous decision making.

Other nonautonomous surrenders of decision-making authority to a physician or family member may represent a longstanding pattern to accept the authority of a spouse or the paternalism of the medical profession. It may also be due to an attempt by the physician or other caretaker to dominate and control the decision-making process. The physician must be alert to his or her own and others' paternalism and point out any failure to acknowledge and take seriously the patient's values and preference.

PHYSICIAN'S ROLE IN LONG-TERM CARE DECISION MAKING

The role that we have described for the physician is markedly different from the traditional, paternal-

istic one. There is no place in the approach described in this chapter for the physician to simply give his or her opinion on what the decision should be and expect compliance of all involved. This is appropriate, since long-term care decisions are frequently neutral in terms of medical outcomes. Even if the competent patient refuses to accept necessary medical care the physician has no right to compel acceptance.

The physician has an obligation to objectively present factual information and experience-based opinions. This includes the assessment of the physical and functional status of the patient and his or her prognosis. Though patients and families should be encouraged to do their own data collection and visit long-term care sites and agencies, the physician can contribute observations regarding care alternatives which are within the realm of his or her special competence and experience (e.g., which nursing homes seem to provide the most consistent nursing care; which home health agencies maintain close contact and work well with the physician in monitoring an unstable patient, etc). We believe it inappropriate for the physician to present his or her own value-based recommendation. "Where would you place your mother?" has only one answer: "That depends on what is important to her and to me."

We have found that this entire process of identifying values, defining need and identifying care options, and negotiating takes approximately 90 minutes when done in a research setting. As is the case with any clinical intervention, the experienced practitioner will modify and abbreviate the process to fit the individual situation. If done over a period of months, before the situation becomes critical, it should not be an onerous process for the physician, patient, or family. The great advantage of the long-term care decision-making process discussed in this chapter is that it returns control to the patient, and may well reduce the demands for physician involvement in long-term care decisions, particularly by practicing "preventive ethics" to avoid crisis decisions.

Finally, the physician should recognize that long-term care decision making is an ongoing, repetitive process. If the patient's physical or mental condition changes, or if there is a change in the patient's social support system, a new decision may have to be made. The physician must be as sensitive to changes such as "burnout" in a caretaker as he or she is to the development of another stroke or further cognitive decline in the patient. Monitoring must include being alert for changes in status as well as changes in the social context of the patient's life. Even though physicians can rarely cure the elderly patient's disease, they must constantly look for opportunities to address those deficits which the patient perceives to be important.

SUMMARY

Long-term care decision making poses special challenges to the physician who cares for elderly patients. Long-term care is not synonymous with nursing home placement. Long-term care decision making involves a wide range of decisions about support services and living arrangements. Long-term care decisions also involve the participation of many parties: the physician, whose role is to evaluate the medical acceptability of various options and to guide patients and their family members through the decision-making process; the older patient, whose values must be taken into account in the decision-making process; and involved family members or other potential caregivers, whose legitimate obligations to others must be carefully balanced against their moral obligations to the patient.

Unlike acute care situations, where the principle of beneficence provides a reliable basis for defining the patient's needs, long-term care decision making is more complex and requires reliance on the principles of respect for autonomy, justice, and family responsibility, as well as beneficence, for guidance in making an appropriate decision.

These decisions also are made within a health care system that creates financial constraints restricting the number of available options, as well as pressure for quick decisions, in order to discharge patients from hospitals as soon as they are medically stable. All possible alternatives are not universally available therefore to individual patients in different areas and with differing resources.

Finally, long-term care decision making extends the perspective and ethical obligations of the physician beyond those typically involved in acute care situations. The challenge for the physician is to complement medical perspectives on the care of the elderly patient by managing the patient's care so that such values of patients and families as comfort, dignity, and independence are taken into account as important objectives of long-term care. In this way, the physician will be in a strong position to respond effectively and sensitively to the long-term care needs of geriatric patients.

REFERENCES

1. American Association of Retired Persons: *Making Wise Decisions for Long Term Care.* Washington, DC, American Association of Retired Persons, Health Advisory Services, 1986.
2. American Association of Retired Persons: *The Right Place at the Right Time: A Guide to Long-Term Care Choices.* Washington, DC, American Association of Retired Persons, 1985.
3. Avorn J: Benefit and cost analysis in geriatric care: turning age discrimination into health policy. *N Engl J Med* 310:1294, 1984.
4. Bayer R: Coping with cost containment. *Generations* 10:39, 1985.
5. Brody EM: *Long-Term Care of Older People: A Practical Guide.* New York, Human Services Press, 1977.
6. Brody EM: Parent care as normative family stress. *Gerontologist* 25:19, 1985.
7. Manton KG, Soldo BJ: Dynamics of health changes in the oldest old: new perspectives and evidence. *Milbank Memorial Fund Quarterly: Health and Society* 63:206, 1985.
8. Kane RL, Kane RA: Alternatives to institutional care of the elderly: beyond the dichotomy. *Gerontologist* 20:249, 1980.
9. Soldo BJ, Agree EM, Wolf DA: The balance between formal and informal care. In Ory MG, Bond K (Eds): *Aging and Health Care: Social Science and Policy Perspectives.* Boston, Tavistock, in press.
10. Soldo BJ, DeVita CJ, Myllyluoma J: Characteristics of the decision-making process resulting in institutional placements (Working Paper MDU-1979-002). Washington, DC, Center for Population Research, Georgetown University, 1979.
11. Soldo BJ: In-home services for the dependent elderly: determinants of current use and implications for future demand. *Research in Aging* 7:281, 1985.
12. Townsend AL, Poulshock SW: Intergenerational perspectives on impaired elders' support networks. *J Gerontol* 41:101, 1986.
13. Wetle T: Long term care. *Generations* 10:30, 1985.

Index

Page numbers followed by *t* or *f* denote tables or footnotes respectively.

Myocellular mitochondrial enzyme activities, 65
Myopathies, 168–170
Myopia, 450
Myosclerosis, senile, 312
Myringoplasty, 456
Myxedema, 144
Myxomatous degeneration of cardiac valves, 69

Narcotics abuse, 134–135
Nasal dorsum, 459
Nasogastric tubes
 decompression, 430
 postsurgical use of, 427, 429
Nasotracheal suctioning, 99
National Ambulatory Medical Care Survey (NAMCS),
 41–2
National Disease and Therapeutic Index (NDTI)
 survey, 41
National Nursing Home survey, 491, 535, 540
Naughton protocol for activity testing, 71
Neck
 cancer of, 462–463
 infections of, 200
Neologisms, 164
Neoplasias, 170–171
Nephrocalcinosis, 259
Nephrolithiasis, 259
Nephropathy. See Diabetic nephropathy
Nephrosclerosis, 326
 arteriolar, 239–240
Nephrotoxins, 243
Nervous system. See also Central nervous system
 in aging and disease, 179–180
 infections of, 171
Neuralgia
 postherpetic, 397
 trigeminal, 171
Neuritic plaques, 149
Neuritis, interdigital, 368
Neurofibrillary tangles, 164
Neurogenic bladder, 389
Neurohypophysis, 373–374
Neuroleptics, 57–58
 side effects of, 57–58, 167
Neurologic disease, 163–174. See also specific diseases
 therapy for, 173
Neuroma, 368–369
Neuromuscular disorders, 168–170
 impaired swallowing with, 189
Neuromuscular junction disorders, 304–305
Neuropathic bladder, 24
Neuropathies, 169
 with diabetes, 384, 387, 388
Neuropsychiatric disorders
 causes of, 7
 importance of differentiating, 142
Neuropsychiatric drugs, 55
Neurosyphilis, 166
Neurotransmitters, 149–150
Neurotrophic ulcers, 109

Nevi, 405–406
Nevocellular tumors, 405
Niacin, 107
 deficiency of, 209
Nitrates, 76
Nitrofurantoin, 206
Nitroglycerin, 76
Nitroprusside, 73–74, 120
No-Code orders, 611
Nocturia, 24
Nodular melanoma, 406
Nodular ulcerative basal cell carcinoma, 403f
Nonadaptive personalities, 500–501
Nondisclosure, 609–610
Noninvasive studies, 109–110
Nonresident services, 514–515
Nonsteroidal anti-inflammatory drugs, 42
 for rheumatoid arthritis, 321
Norepinephrine deficit, 150
Normative Aging Study, 497
Nose, changes in with aging, 459–460
Nurse
 gerontologic, 527–533
 in rehabilitation process, 184–185
 in surgery, 427
Nursing assistants, 532
Nursing homes, 522
 care in, 537
 definition of, 535–536
 dental care in, 471
 falls in, 552–553
 growing need for, 493
 medical care in, 534–540
 medical director in, 539
 medical issues in, 540
 moving to, 532
 nurse in, 531–533
 organization of, 536
 patient population of, 536–537
 payment for, 537
 physician's role in, 537–539
 special units in for Alzheimer's patients,
  148
 termination of treatment in, 601
Nutrient drug interactions, 223–224
Nutrition, 207. See also Diet; Food
 aging and, 208
 decubitus ulcers and, 439–441
 deficiency of, 169
 in institutional milieu, 220–223
 longevity and, 207–208
 oral health and, 467–468
 termination of, 603–607
 toenails and, 365
 wound healing and, 423
Nutritional status
 assessment of, 32, 208–211
 indices of, 210
Nutrition counseling, 528
Nutrition deficiency disease, 209–210

clinical course of, 338
differential diagnosis of, 338, 339t
lesions of, 285
manifestations of, 340–341f
pathophysiology of, 337–338
treatment for, 341–342
Pain, 62
in dying patient, 570
management of, 62
Pancreas
cancer of, 193
diseases of, 192–193
Pancreatic ducts, dilation of, 189
Pancreatitis, 192–193
Papauarine-Phentolamine injections, 278
Papillary hyperplasia, 468
Papillary necrosis, 237
Papillotomy, 192
Pap smear, 288, 289
Paraphimosis, 274, 275f
Parathyroid hormone
bone resorption and, 331
ectopic production of, 379
excess, 379
secretion of, 378
Parathyroids
aging effects on, 378
hyperparathyroidism and, 378–379
hypoparathyroidism and, 379–380
physiologic considerations in, 377–378
Parenteral nutrition, total, 219, 612
Paresis, 371
Parkinson's disease, 167–168
bradykinesias with, 302
dementia with, 144
incontinence with, 286
management of, 302
Partial thromboplastin time, activated, 96
Pasteurella multocida infection, 200
Patellar fractures, 359
Patellectomy, 318
Paternalism, 582, 609
in long-term care decision making, 622
Patient
creating partnership with, 7
keeping informed, 51
knowledge of, 6–7
risk factors of in drug perscriptions, 51
total understanding of, 8
Patient-doctor communication, 5–6
Patient-doctor relationship, 6–7
Peak expiratory flow, 103
Pederson narrow bivalve speculum, 284
Pedestrian accidents, 555–556
Pelvic fractures, 354. See also Hip, fractures of
complications of, 355
Pemphigoid, bullous, 394–395
Pemphigus vulgaris, 395
Pendulum exercises, 348–349
Penicillamine, 193
d-Penicillamine (Cuprimine), 322

Penicillin, 204–205
Penile prosthesis, 278
Penis
carcinoma of, 274
diseases of, 274
revascularization of, 278
Percutaneous translumenal angioplasty, 112–113, 239
coronary (PTCA), 78–79
Performance activities of daily living, 32
Pericardial tamponade, 69
Pericarditis, 69
Periodontal disease, 466, 469–470
Peripheral arteriolar resistance, 67
Peripheral neuropathy, 300–301
with diabetes, 388. See also Diabetic neuropathy
Peripheral vascular disease
arteriography for, 111
associated disease of, 106–107
in diabetes, 387
diagnosis of, 108–111
digital subtraction angiography for, 110–111
history of, 108–109
noninvasive studies for, 109–110
pathophysiology of, 108
physical examination for, 109
risk factors and prevention of, 106–107
theory of, 106
types of, 111–121
Peripheral vascular insufficiency, 297, 371
Peritoneal dialysis, 246
Peritonitis, 430
Pernicious anemia, 144
Peroxidases, 229
Pes cavus, 370
Pes planus, 370
Peyronie's disease, 274, 277
Pfeiffer, Jules, 6
pH
balance of, 259–260
kidney stones and, 242
renal stones and, 241
Phalangeal fractures, 354
Pharmacodynamics in elderly, 48–49
Pharmacokinetics in elderly, 44–48
Phenacetin, 234
Phenylalanine mustard, 419
Phenytoin, 52
Philadelphia chromosome, 418
Phimosis, 274
Phosphates
depletion of, 259
in urine, 229–230
Phosphate therapy, intravenous, 259
Phosphaturia, 331
Phosphorus, RDAs for, 214–216
Phosphorylase deficiency, 297
Photocoagulation, 451
Photosensitivity, 392
Physical activity, 89–90. See also Exercise
Physical function, 29
Physical modalities, 181–183

Stomach
carcinoma of, 192
diseases of, 191–192
Stomatodynia, 471
Stoves, 553
Streptomycin, 104
Streptococcus
of CNS, 171
dermal infection of, 204
group D, 201–202
viridans, 68
endocarditis, 202
Streptokinase, 96
Stress, 25
Stroke
causes of, 172–173
death from, 171
disabilities from, 172
dysphagia with, 190
protection from, 240
risk factors for, 172
therapy for, 173
ST wave change, 75
Subacromial bursitis, 346
Subarachnoid hemorrhage, 144, 174
Subcapital fractures, 357
Subdural hematoma, 299–300
with head trauma, 165
Substantive justice, 583–584
Substituted judgment, 592–593
termination of treatment and, 596, 600t
Subtrochanteric fractures, 358
Subungual heloma, 364
Subungual hematoma, 363–364
Subungual keratosis, 364–365
Sucralafate, 191–192
Suicide, 127
hypochondriasis and, 130
Sulfa crystals, 230
Sulfonylurease, 385
Sun, overexposure to, 398
Sundown syndrome, 183
Sunscreens, 398
Support services. *See also* Community support
services
for dementia patient families, 147–148
need for, 37
Support systems, 16
strategies to strengthen, 24–25
Supracondylar fractures, 352, 359
Surgery
cardiac risk factors in, 424
conditions requiring special consideration in, 429–431
emergency and elective, 422–423
iatrogenic disease with, 562–563
postoperative complications of, 427–429
preoperative evaluation for, 424–426
preoperative preparation checklist for, 426–427
principles of in elderly, 422–431
risks of, 564

Surgical bladder neck suspension, 282
Surgical team, 426–427
Swallowing, difficult and painful, 461
Swan-Ganz catheter, 74, 100, 102
monitoring with, 425
Sympathetic inhibitors, 83–84
Sympatholytic antihypertensive therapy, 56
Syncope, 75
Syndrome of inappropariate antidiuretic hormone. *See* SIADH
Syphilis, 169
dementia with, 166
lesions of, 286
Syphilitic aortic insufficiency, 68
Systemic lupus erythematosus, 238
Systemic sclerosis, progressive, 310
Systolic Hypertension in the Elderly Program (SHEP), 82
Systolic pressures, 109

Tabes dorsalis, 280
Tachycardia, 66, 428
Tardive akathisia, 303
Tardive dyskinesia, 303
Task Force on the Periodic Health Examination, U.S., 13
Taste, changes in with age, 460
Tear secretion, 446–447
Technological developments, 11
Teeth
in elderly, 464–472
ethical considerations in long-term care of, 471–472
loss of, 465–466, 469–470
preventive care of, 465–467
Temporal arteritis, 310, 452
Temporomandibular joint disorders, 470–471
Temporomandibular joint syndrome, 460–461
Tendinitis
of biceps, 347
calcific, 326
Tenesmus, 287
Terminal illness care, 525
Terminal reservoir syndrome, 196
Testis, cancer of, 276
Testosterone
for impotence, 278
reduced production of, 542
Tetanus antibodies, 206
Tetracyclines, 197, 205
Tetrahydroaminoacridine, 150
Theophylline, 103
Therapeutic equipment, 181–183
Therapeutic milieu, 154–155
basic concepts in design of, 155–156
custodial care in contrast to, 156–159
evaluation and revision of, 162
physical setting in, 159
program in, 156–157
implementation of, 161–162
residents in, 158
response of to, 159–161